Weiss Ratings' Guide to Banks

Weiss Ratings'
Guide to Banks

A Quarterly Compilation of Financial
Institutions Ratings and Analyses

Spring 2017

GREY HOUSE PUBLISHING

Weiss Ratings
4400 Northcorp Parkway
Palm Beach Gardens, FL 33410
561-627-3300

Independent. Unbiased. Accurate. Trusted.

Published by Grey House Publishing, Inc., located at 4919 Route 22, Amenia, NY 12501; telephone 518-789-8700. Grey House Publishing neither guarantees the accuracy of the data contained herein nor assumes any responsibility for errors, omissions or discrepancies. Grey House Publishing accepts no payment for listing; inclusion in the publication of any organization, agency, institution, publication, service or individual does not imply endorsement of the publisher.

Grey House
Publishing

4919 Route 22
PO Box 56
Amenia, NY 12501-0056

Edition No. 105, Spring 2017

ISBN: 978-1-68217-407-4
ISSN: 2158-5962

Contents

Terms and Conditions

Date of Data Analyzed: September 30, 2016
Data Source: Call Report data provided by SNL Financial.

Welcome to Weiss Ratings
Guide to Banks

Most people automatically assume their bank will survive, year after year. However, prudent consumers and professionals realize that in this world of shifting risks, the solvency of financial institutions can't be taken for granted. After all, your bank's failure could have a heavy impact on you in terms of lost time, lost money (in cases of deposits exceeding the federal insurance limit), tied-up deposits, lost credit lines, and the possibility of being shifted to another institution under not-so-friendly terms.

If you are looking for accurate, unbiased ratings and data to help you choose a commercial bank, savings bank, or savings and loan for yourself, your family, your company or your clients, Weiss Ratings' Guide to Banks gives you precisely what you need.

Weiss Ratings' Mission Statement

Weiss Ratings' mission is to empower consumers, professionals, and institutions with high quality advisory information for selecting or monitoring a financial services company or financial investment.

In doing so, Weiss Ratings will adhere to the highest ethical standards by maintaining our independent, unbiased outlook and approach to advising our customers.

Why rely on Weiss Ratings?

Weiss Ratings provides fair, objective ratings to help professionals and consumers alike make educated financial decisions.

At Weiss Ratings, integrity is number one. Weiss Ratings never takes a penny from rated companies for issuing its ratings. And, we publish Weiss Safety Ratings without regard for institutions' preferences. Our analysts review and update Weiss ratings each and every quarter, so you can be sure that the information you receive is accurate and current – providing you with advance warning of financial vulnerability early enough to do something about it.

Other rating agencies focus primarily on a company's current financial solvency and consider only mild economic adversity. Weiss Ratings also considers these issues, but in addition, our analysis covers a company's ability to deal with severe economic adversity in terms of a sharp decline in the value of its investments and a drop in the collectibility of its loans.

Our use of more rigorous standards stems from the viewpoint that a financial institution's obligations to its customers should not depend on favorable business conditions. A bank must be able to honor its loan and deposit commitments in bad times as well as good.

Weiss's rating scale, from A to F, is easy to understand. Only a few outstanding companies receive an A (Excellent) rating, although there are many to choose from within the B (Good) category. A large group falls into the broad average range which receives C (Fair) ratings. Companies that demonstrate marked vulnerabilities receive either D (Weak) or E (Very Weak) ratings. So, there's no numbering system, star counting, or color-coding to keep track of.

How to Use This Guide

The purpose of the *Guide to Banks* is to provide consumers, businesses, financial institutions, and municipalities with a reliable source of banking industry ratings and analysis on a timely basis. We realize that the financial safety of a bank is an important factor to consider when establishing a relationship. The ratings and analysis in this Guide can make that evaluation easier when you are considering:

- A checking, merchant banking, or other transaction account
- An investment in a certificate of deposit or savings account
- A line of credit or commercial loan
- Counterparty risk

The rating for a particular company indicates our opinion regarding that company's ability to meet its obligations – not only under current economic conditions, but also during a declining economy or in an environment of increased liquidity demands.

To use this Guide most effectively, we recommend you follow the steps outlined below:

Step 1 To ensure you evaluate the correct company, verify the company's exact name as it was given to you. It is also helpful to ascertain the city and state of the company's main office or headquarters since no two banks with the same name can be headquartered in the same city. Many companies have similar names but are not related to one another, so you will want to make sure the company you look up is really the one you are interested in evaluating.

Step 2 Turn to Section I, the Index of Banks, and locate the company you are evaluating. This section contains all federally-insured commercial banks and savings banks. It is sorted alphabetically by the name of the company and shows the main office city and state following the name for additional verification.
If you have trouble finding a particular institution or determining which is the right one, consider these possible reasons:

- You may have an incorrect or incomplete institution name. There are often several institutions with the same or very similar names. So, make sure you have the exact name and proper spelling, as well as the city in which it is headquartered.
- You may be looking for a *bank holding company*. If so, try to find the exact name of the main bank in the group and look it up under that name.

Step 3 Once you have located your specific company, the first column after the state shows its current Weiss Safety Rating. Turn to *About Weiss Safety Ratings* for information about what this rating means. If the rating has changed since the last edition of this Guide, a downgrade will be indicated with a down triangle ▼ to the left of the company name; an upgrade will be indicated with an up triangle ▲.

Step 4 Following the current Weiss Safety Rating are two prior ratings for the company based on year-end data from the two previous years. Use this to discern the longer-term direction of the company's overall financial condition.

Step 5   The remainder of Section I; provides insight into the areas our analysts reviewed as the basis for assigning the company's rating. These areas include size, capital adequacy, asset quality, profitability, liquidity, and stability. An index within each of these categories represents a composite evaluation of that particular facet of the company's financial condition. Refer to the Critical Ranges In Our Indexes table for an interpretation of which index values are considered strong, good, fair, or weak. In most cases, lower-rated companies will have a low index value in one or more of the indexes shown. Bear in mind, however, that Weiss Safety Rating is the result of a complex qualitative and quantitative analysis which cannot be reproduced using only the data provided here.

Step 6   If the company you are evaluating is not highly rated and you want to find a bank with a higher rating, turn to the page in Section II that has your state's name at the top. This section contains Weiss Recommended Banks by State (rating of A+, A, A- or B+) that have a branch office in your state. If the main office telephone number provided is not a local telephone call or to determine if a branch of the bank is near you, consult your local telephone Yellow Pages Directory under "Banks," "Savings Banks," or "Savings and Loan Associations." Here you will find a complete list of the institution's branch locations along with their telephone numbers.

Step 7   Once you've identified a Weiss Recommended Company in your local area, you can then refer back to Section I to analyze it.

Step 8   In order to use Weiss Safety Ratings most effectively, we strongly recommend you consult the *Important Warnings and Cautions* listed. These are more than just "standard disclaimers." They are very important factors you should be aware of before using this Guide. If you have any questions regarding the precise meaning of specific terms used in the Guide, refer to the Glossary.

Step 9   Make sure you stay up to date with the latest information available since the publication of this Guide. For information on how to set up a rating change notification service, acquire follow-up reports, check ratings online or receive a more in-depth analysis of an individual company, call 1-877-934-7778 or visit www.weissratings.com.

About Weiss Safety Ratings

The Weiss Ratings are calculated based on a complex analysis of hundreds of factors that are synthesized into five indexes: capitalization, asset quality, profitability, liquidity and stability. Each index is then used to arrive at a letter grade rating. A weak score on any one index can result in a low rating, as financial problems can be caused by any one of a number of factors, such as inadequate capital, non-performing loans and poor asset quality, operating losses, poor liquidity, or the failure of an affiliated company.

Our **Capitalization Index** gauges the institution's capital adequacy in terms of its cushion to absorb future operating losses under adverse business and economic scenarios that may impact the company's net interest margin, securities' values, and the collectability of its loans.

Our **Asset Quality Index** measures the quality of the company's past underwriting and investment practices based on the estimated liquidation value of the company's loan and securities portfolios.

Our **Profitability Index** measures the soundness of the company's operations and the contribution of profits to the company's financial strength. The index is a composite of five sub-factors: 1) gain or loss on operations; 2) rates of return on assets and equity; 3) management of net interest margin; 4) generation of noninterest-based revenues; and 5) overhead expense management.

Our **Liquidity Index** evaluates a company's ability to raise the necessary cash to satisfy creditors and honor depositor withdrawals.

Finally, our **Stability Index** integrates a number of sub-factors that affect consistency (or lack thereof) in maintaining financial strength over time. These include 1) risk diversification in terms of company size and loan diversification; 2) deterioration of operations as reported in critical asset, liability, income and expense items, such as an increase in loan delinquency rates or a sharp increase in loan originations; 3) years in operation; 4) former problem areas where, despite recent improvement, the company has yet to establish a record of stable performance over a suitable period of time; and 5) relationships with holding companies and affiliates.

In order to help guarantee our objectivity, we reserve the right to publish ratings expressing our opinion of a company's financial stability based exclusively on publicly available data and our own proprietary standards for safety.

Each of these indexes is measured according to the following range of values.

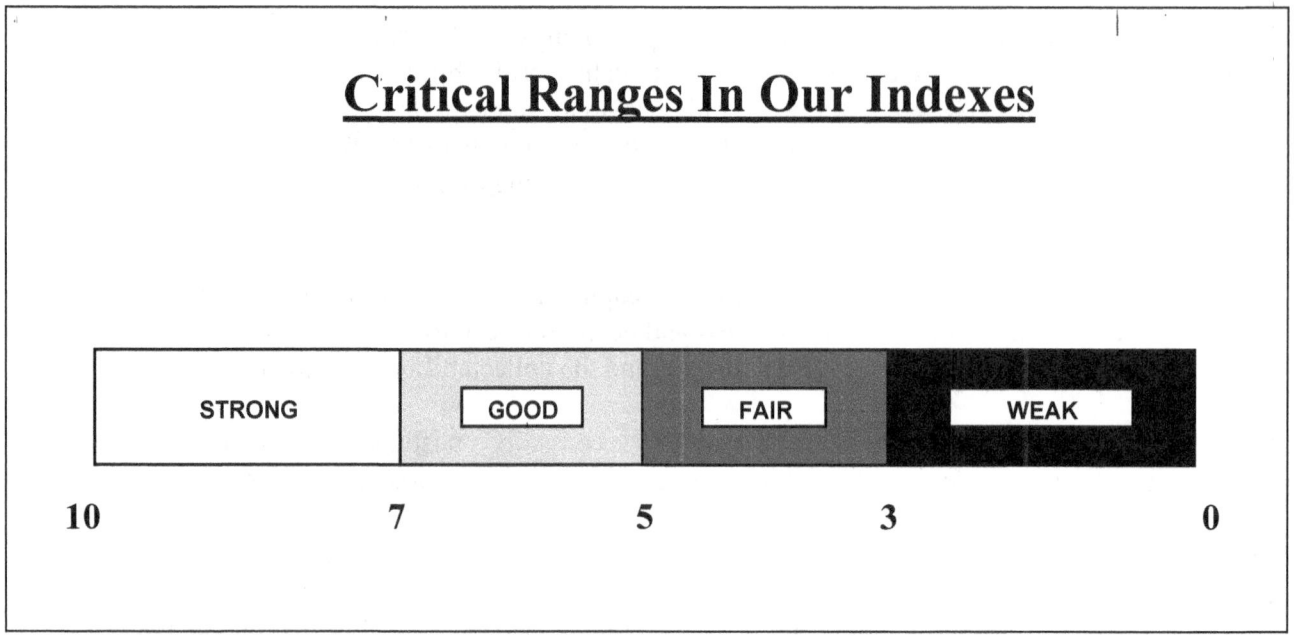

Finally, the indexes are combined to form a composite company rating which is then verified by one of our analysts. The resulting distribution of ratings assigned to all banks looks like this:

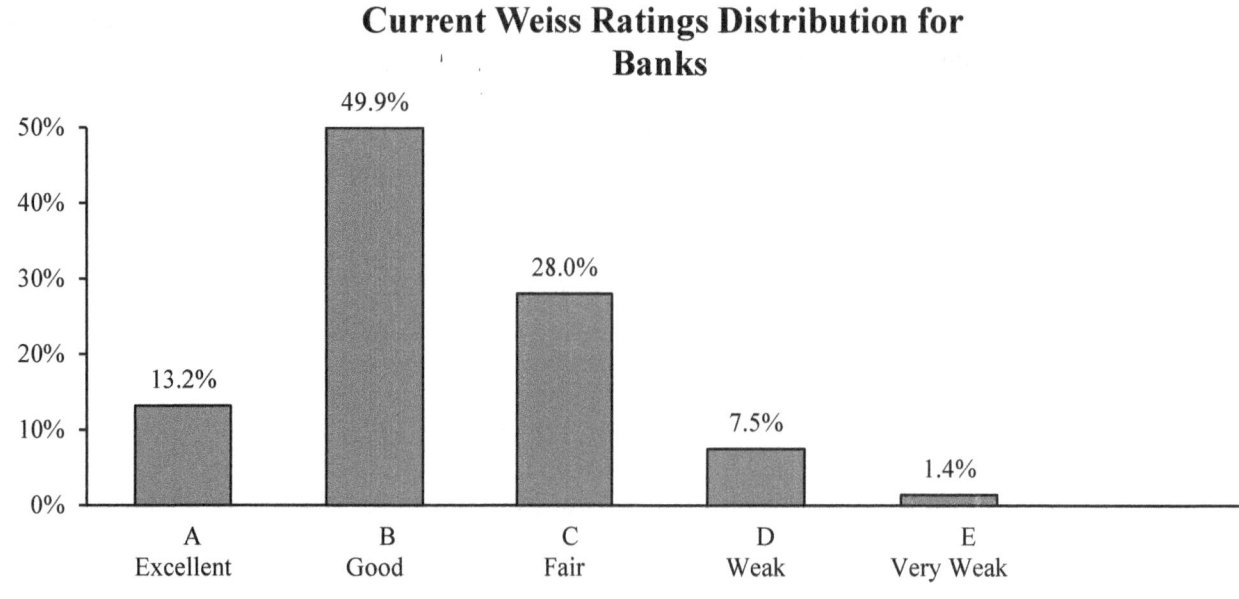

What Our Ratings Mean

A   **Excellent.** The institution offers excellent financial security. It has maintained a conservative stance in its business operations and underwriting practices as evidenced by its strong equity base, high asset quality, steady earnings, and high liquidity. While the financial position of any company is subject to change, we believe that this institution has the resources necessary to deal with severe economic conditions.

B   **Good.** The institution offers good financial security and has the resources to deal with a variety of adverse economic conditions. It comfortably exceeds the minimum levels for all of our rating criteria, and is likely to remain healthy for the near future. Nevertheless, in the event of a severe recession or major financial crisis, we feel that this assessment should be reviewed to make sure that the company is still maintaining adequate financial strength.

C   **Fair.** The institution offers fair financial security, is currently stable, and will likely remain relatively healthy as long as the economic environment remains relatively stable. In the event of a severe recession or major financial crisis, however, we feel this company may encounter difficulties in maintaining its financial stability.

D   **Weak.** The institution currently demonstrates what, in our opinion, we consider to be significant weaknesses which could negatively impact depositors or creditors. In the event of a severe recession or major financial crisis, these weaknesses could be magnified.

E   **Very Weak.** The institution currently demonstrates what we consider to be significant weaknesses and has also failed some of the basic tests that we use to identify fiscal stability. Therefore, even in a favorable economic environment, it is our opinion that depositors or creditors could incur significant risks.

F   **Failed.** The institution has been placed under the custodianship of regulatory authorities. This implies that it will be either liquidated or taken over by another financial institution.

+   The **plus sign** is an indication that the institution is in the upper third of the letter grade.

-   The **minus sign** is an indication that the institution is in the lower third of the letter grade.

U   **Unrated.** The institution is unrated due to the absence of sufficient data for our ratings.

Peer Comparison of Bank Safety Ratings

Weiss Ratings	Veribanc	Bauer Financial	IDC Financial	Bankrate.com	Lace Financial
A+, A, A-	Green, Three Stars w/ Blue Ribbon recognition	5 stars, 4 stars	201-300	1, Five stars	A+, A
B+, B, B-	Green, Three Stars w/out Blue Ribbon recognition	3 ½ stars	166-200	2, Four stars	B+
C+, C, C-	Green Two Stars, Yellow Two Stars	3 stars	126-165	3, Three stars	B, C+
D+, D, D-	Green one star, Yellow one star, Green no stars	2 stars	76-125	4, Two stars	C, D
E+, E, E-	Yellow no stars, Red no stars	1 star	1-75	5, One star	E

Important Warnings and Cautions

1. **A rating alone cannot tell the whole story.** Please read the explanatory information contained here, in the section introductions and in the appendix. It is provided in order to give you an understanding of our rating philosophy as well as to paint a more complete picture of how we arrive at our opinion of a company's strengths and weaknesses. In addition, please remember that our safety rating is not an end-all measure of an institution's safety. Rather, it should be used as a "flag" of possible troubles, suggesting a need for further research.

2. **Safety ratings shown in this directory were current as of the publication date.** In the meantime, the rating may have been updated based on more recent data. Weiss Ratings offers a notification service for ratings changes on companies that you specifiy. For more information call 1-877-934-7778 or visit www.weissratings.com.

3. **When deciding to do business with a financial institution, your decision should be based on a wide variety of factors in addition to Weiss Safety Rating.** These include the institution's pricing of its deposit instruments and loans, the fees you will be charged, the degree to which it can help you meet your long-term planning needs, how these costs/benefits may change over the years, and what other choices are available to you given your current location and financial circumstances.

4. **Weiss Safety Ratings represent our opinion of a company's insolvency risk.** As such, a high rating means we feel that the company has less chance of running into financial difficulties. A high rating is not a guarantee of solvency nor is a low rating a prediction of insolvency. Weiss Safety Ratings are not deemed to be a recommendation concerning the purchase or sale of the securities of any bank that is publicly owned.

5. **All firms that have the same Weiss Safety Rating should be considered to be essentially equal in safety.** This is true regardless of any differences in the underlying numbers which might appear to indicate greater strengths. Weiss Safety Rating already takes into account a number of lesser factors which, due to space limitations, cannot be included in this publication.

6. **A good rating requires consistency.** If a company is excellent on four indicators and fair on one, the company may receive a fair rating. This requirement is necessary due to the fact that fiscal problems can arise from any *one* of several causes including poor underwriting, inadequate capital resources, or operating losses.

7. **Our rating standards are more conservative than those used by other agencies.** We believe that no one can predict with certainty the economic environment of the near or long-term future. Rather, we assume that various scenarios – from the extremes of double-digit inflation to a severe recession – are within the range of reasonable possibilities over the next one or two decades. To achieve a top rating according to our standards, a company must be adequately prepared for the worst-case reasonable scenario, without impairing its current operations.

8. **We are an independent rating agency and do not depend on the cooperation of the companies we rate**. Our data are derived, for the most part, from quarterly financial statements filed with federal regulators. Although we seek to maintain an open line of communication with the companies being rated, we do not grant them the right to influence the ratings or stop their publication. This policy stems from the fact that this Guide is designed for the protection of our customers.

9. **Inaccuracies in the data issued by the federal regulators could negatively impact the quality of a company's Safety Rating.** While we attempt to find and correct as many data errors as possible, some data errors inevitably slip through. We have no method of intercepting fraudulent or falsified data and must take for granted that all information is reported honestly to the federal regulatory agencies.

10. **Institutions that operate exclusively or primarily as a trust company may have skewed financial information.** Due to the nature of their business, these companies often record high profit levels compared to other more "traditional" banks. Trust companies can usually be recognized by the initials "TC" or "& TC" in their names.

11. **This Guide does not cover nonbank affiliates of banking companies.** Although some nonbank companies may be affiliated with the banks cited in this Guide, the firms are separate corporations whose financial strength is only partially dependent on the strength of their affiliates.

12. **There are many companies with the same or similar sounding names, despite no affiliation whatsoever.** Therefore, it is important that you have the exact name, city, and state of the institution's headquarters before you begin to research the company in this Guide.

13. **Affiliated companies do not automatically receive the same rating.** We recognize that a troubled institution may expect financial support from its parent or affiliates. Weiss Safety Ratings reflect our opinion of the measure of support that may become available to a subsidiary bank, if the subsidiary were to experience serious financial difficulties. In the case of a strong parent and a weaker subsidiary, the affiliate relationship will generally result in a higher rating for the subsidiary than it would have on a stand-alone basis. Seldom, however, would the rating be brought up to the level of the parent.

    This treatment is appropriate because we do not assume the parent would have either the resources or the will to "bail out" a troubled subsidiary during a severe economic crisis. Even when there is a binding legal obligation for a parent corporation to honor the obligations of its subsidiary banks, the possibility exists that the subsidiary could be sold and lose its parental support. Therefore, it is quite common for one affiliate to have a higher rating than another. This is another reason why it is especially important that you have the precise name of the company you are evaluating.

14. **This publication does not include foreign banking companies, or their U.S. branches.** Therefore, our evaluation of foreign banking companies is limited to those U.S. chartered domestic banks owned by foreign banking companies. In most cases, the U.S. operations of a foreign banking company are relatively small in relation to the overall size of the company, so you may want to consult other sources as well. In any case, do not be confused by a domestic bank with a name which is the same as – or similar to – that of a foreign banking company. Even if there is an affiliation between the two, we have evaluated the U.S. institution based on its own merits.

Section I

Index of Banks

An analysis of all rated

U.S. Commercial Banks and Savings Banks

Institutions are listed in alphabetical order.

Section I Contents

This section contains Weiss Safety Ratings, key rating factors, and summary financial data for all U.S. federally-insured commercial banks and savings banks. Companies are sorted in alphabetical order, first by company name, then by city and state.

Left Pages

1. Institution Name

The name under which the institution was chartered. If you cannot find the institution you are interested in, or if you have any doubts regarding the precise name, verify the information with the bank itself before proceeding. Also, determine the city and state in which the institution is headquartered for confirmation. (See columns 2 and 3.)

2. City

The city in which the institution's headquarters or main office is located. With the adoption of intrastate and interstate branching laws, many institutions operating in your area may actually be headquartered elsewhere. So, don't be surprised if the location cited is not in your particular city.

Also use this column to confirm that you have located the correct institution. It is possible for two unrelated companies to have the same name if they are headquartered in different cities.

3. State

The state in which the institution's headquarters or main office is located. With the adoption of interstate branching laws, some institutions operating in your area may actually be headquartered in another state.

4. Safety Rating

Weiss rating assigned to the institution at the time of publication. Our ratings are designed to distinguish levels of insolvency risk and are measured on a scale from A to F based upon a wide range of factors. See *About Weiss Safety Ratings* for specific descriptions of each letter grade.

Highly rated companies are, in our opinion, less likely to experience financial difficulties than lower rated firms. See *About Weiss Safety Ratings* for more information. Also, please be sure to consider the warnings regarding the ratings' limitations and the underlying assumptions.

5. Prior Year Safety Rating

Weiss rating assigned to the institution based on data from December 31 of the previous year. Compare this rating to the company's current rating to identify any recent changes.

6. Safety Rating Two Years Prior

Weiss rating assigned to the institution based on data from December 31 two years ago. Compare this rating to the ratings in the prior columns to identify longer term trends in the company's financial condition.

7. Total Assets

The total of all assets listed on the institution's balance sheet, in millions of dollars. This figure primarily consists of loans, investments (such as municipal and treasury bonds), and fixed assets (such as buildings and other real estate).

Overall size is an important factor which affects the company's ability to diversify risk and avoid vulnerability to a single borrower, industry, or geographic area. Larger institutions are usually, although not always, more diversified and thus less susceptible to a downturn in a particular area. Nevertheless, do not be misled by the general public perception that "bigger is better." Larger institutions are known for their inability to quickly adapt to changes in the marketplace and typically underperform their smaller brethren.

8. One Year Asset Growth

The percentage change in total assets over the previous 12 months. Moderate growth is generally a positive since it can reflect the maintenance or expansion of the company's market share, leading to the generation of additional revenues. Excessive growth, however, is generally a sign of trouble as it can indicate a loosening of underwriting practices in order to attract new business.

9. Commercial Loans/ Total Assets

The percentage of the institution's asset base invested in loans to businesses. Commercial loans are the traditional bread and butter of commercial banks, although many have increased their business lending in recent years.

10. Consumer Loans/ Total Assets

The percentage of the institution's asset base invested in loans to consumers, primarily credit cards. Consumer lending has grown rapidly in recent years due to the high interest rates and fees institutions are able to charge. On the down side, consumer loans usually experience higher delinquency and default rates than other loans, negatively impacting earnings down the road.

11. Home Mortgage Loans/ Total Assets

The percentage of the institution's asset base invested in residential mortgage loans to consumers, excluding home equity loans. Savings banks have traditionally dominated mortgage lending.

This type of loan typically experiences lower default rates. However, the length of the loan's term can be a subject for concern during periods of rising interest rates.

12. Securities/ Total Assets

The percentage of the institution's asset base invested in securities, including U.S. Treasury securities, mortgage-backed securities, and municipal bonds. This does not include securities the institution may be holding on behalf of individual customers.

Although securities are similar to loans in that they represent obligations to pay a debt at some point in the future, they are a more liquid investment than loans and usually present less risk of default. In addition, mortgage-backed securities can present less credit risk than holding mortgage loans themselves due to the diversification of the underlying mortgages.

13. Capitalization Index

An index that measures the adequacy of the institution's capital resources to deal with potentially adverse business and economic situations that could arise. It is based on an evaluation of the company's degree of leverage compared to total assets as well as risk-adjusted assets. See the Critical Ranges In Our Indexes for a description of the different critical levels presented in this index.

14. Leverage Ratio

A regulatory ratio defined by the federal banking regulators as core (tier 1) capital divided by tangible assets. This ratio answers the question: How much does the institution have in stockholders' equity for every dollar of assets? Thus, the Leverage Ratio represents the amount of actual "capital cushion" the institution has to fall back on in times of trouble. We feel that this is the single most important ratio in determining financial strength because it provides the best measure of an institution's ability to withstand losses.

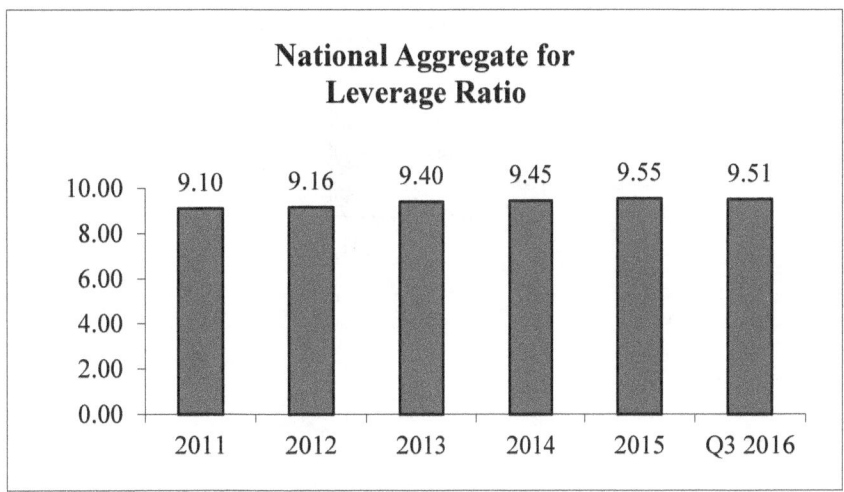

15. Risk-Based Capital Ratio

A regulatory ratio defined by the federal banking regulators as total (tier 1 + tier 2) capital divided by risk-weighted assets. This ratio addresses the issue that not all assets present the same level of credit risk to an institution. As such, all assets and certain off-balance sheet commitments are assigned to risk categories based on the level of credit risk they pose and then weighted accordingly to arrive at risk-weighted assets.

For instance, assets with virtually no risk, such as cash and U.S. Treasury securities, are risk-weighted at 0% and therefore, not included in the calculation. Assets with low risk, for example, high quality mortgage-backed securities and state and municipal bonds, are partially weighted at 20%.

Those assets possessing moderate risk, such as residential mortgages and state and local revenue bonds are partially weighted at 50%. And finally, assets considered to possess "normal" or "high" risk, including certain off-balance sheet commitments such as unfunded loans, are risk-weighted at 100%. The summation of these categories of risk-weighted assets results in the figure used in the denominator of this ratio.

Please be aware that not all banks and savings banks are required to report risk-weighted assets as defined by the federal regulators. Consequently, we have estimated this figure when necessary based on estimates used by the regulators themselves.

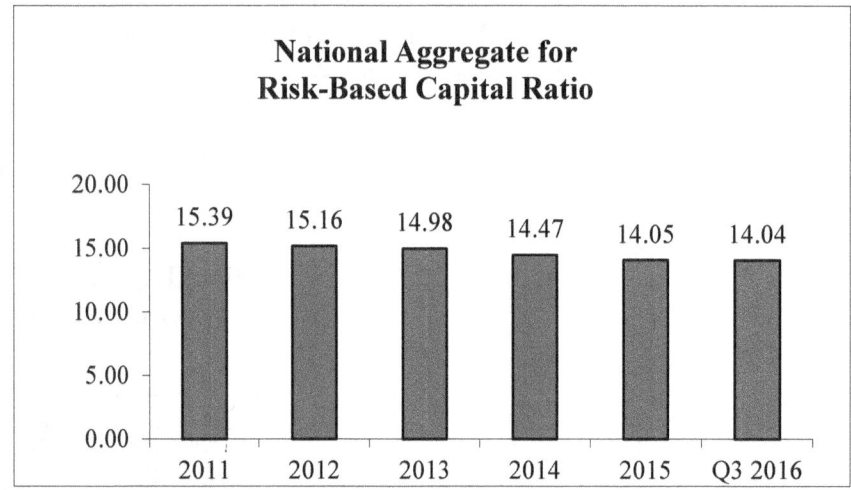

National Aggregate for Risk-Based Capital Ratio

Year	Value
2011	15.39
2012	15.16
2013	14.98
2014	14.47
2015	14.05
Q3 2016	14.04

Right Pages

1. **Asset Quality Index**

An index that measures the quality of the institution's past underwriting and investment practices, as well as its loss reserve coverage. See the Critical Ranges In Our Indexes for a description of the different critical levels presented in this index.

2. **Adjusted Nonperforming Loans/ Total Loans**

The percentage of the institution's loan portfolio which is either past due on its payments by 90 days or more, or no longer accruing interest due to doubtful collectability plus a portion of all restructured loans, less government guaranteed GNMA loans and those loans protected by the FDIC. This ratio is affected primarily by the quality of the institution's underwriting practices and the prosperity of the local economies where it is doing business. While only a portion of these loans will actually end up in default, a high ratio here will have several negative consequences including increased loan loss provisions, increased loan collection expenses, and decreased interest revenues.

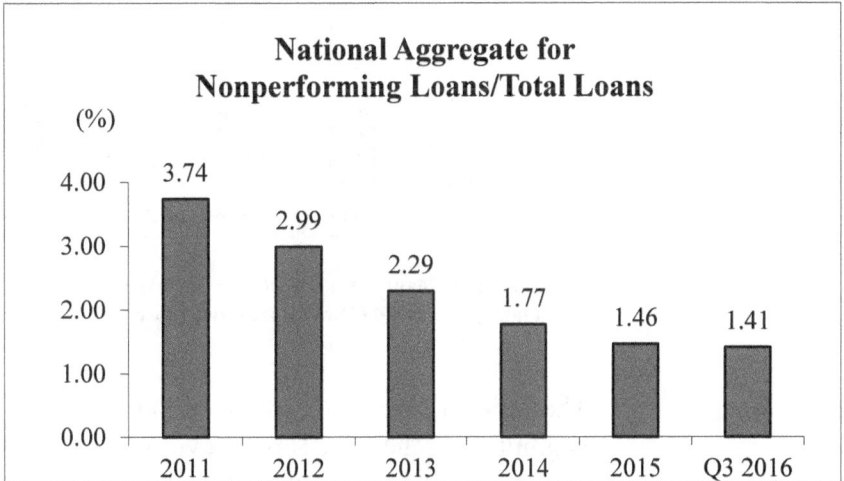

[1]Nonperforming loans were adjusted in 2011 to include a portion of all restructured loans, less government guaranteed GNMA loans and those loans protected by the FDIC.

3. Adjusted Nonperforming Loans/ Capital

The percentage of past due 90 days and nonaccruing loans plus a portion of all restructured loans, less government guaranteed GNMA loans and those loans protected by the FDIC to the company's core (tier 1) capital plus reserve for loan losses. This ratio answers the question: If all of the bank's significantly past due and nonaccruing loans were to go into default, how much would that eat into capital? A large percentage of nonperforming loans signal imprudent lending practices which are a direct threat to the equity of the institution.

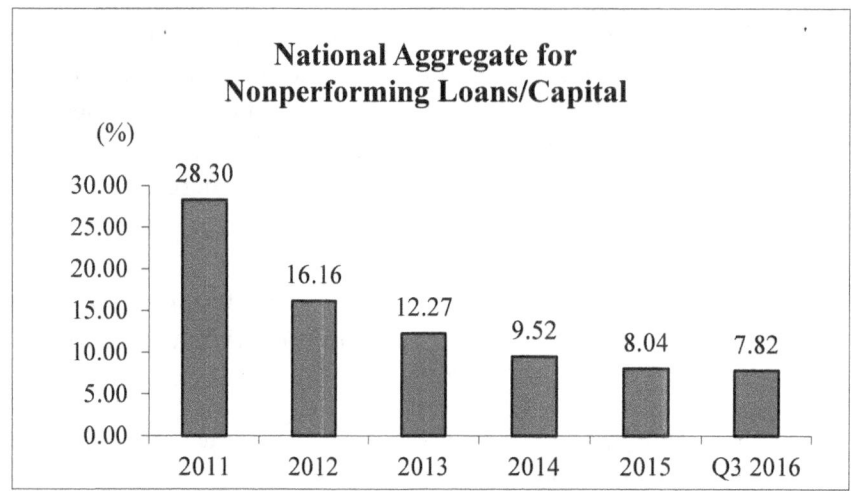

[1] Nonperforming loans were adjusted in 2011 to include a portion of all restructured loans, less government guaranteed GNMA loans and those loans protected by the FDIC.

4. Net Charge- offs/ Average Loans

The ratio of foreclosed loans written off the institution's books since the beginning of the year (less previous write-offs that were recovered) as a percentage of average loans for the year. This ratio answers the question: What percentage of the bank's past loans have actually become uncollectible? Past loan charge-off experience is often a very good indication of what can be expected in the future, and high loan charge-off levels are usually an indication of poor underwriting practices.

5. Profitability Index

An index that measures the soundness of the institution's operations and the contribution of profits to the company's financial strength. It is based on five sub-factors: 1) gain or loss on operations; 2) rates of return on assets and equity; 3) management of net interest margin; 4) generation of noninterest-based revenues; and 5) overhead expense management. See the Critical Ranges In Our Indexes for a description of the different critical levels presented in this index.

6. Net Income

The year-to-date net profit or loss recorded by the institution, in millions of dollars. This figure includes the company's operating profit (income from lending, investing, and fees less interest and overhead expenses) as well as nonoperating items such as capital gains on the sale of securities, income taxes, and extraordinary items.

7. Return on Assets The ratio of net income for the year (year-to-date quarterly figures are converted to a 12-month equivalent) as a percentage of average assets for the year. This ratio, known as ROA, is the most commonly used benchmark for bank profitability since it measures the company's return on investment in a format that is easily comparable with other companies.

Historically speaking, a ratio of 1.0% or greater has been considered good performance. However, this ratio will fluctuate with the prevailing economic times. Also, larger banks tend to have a lower ratio.

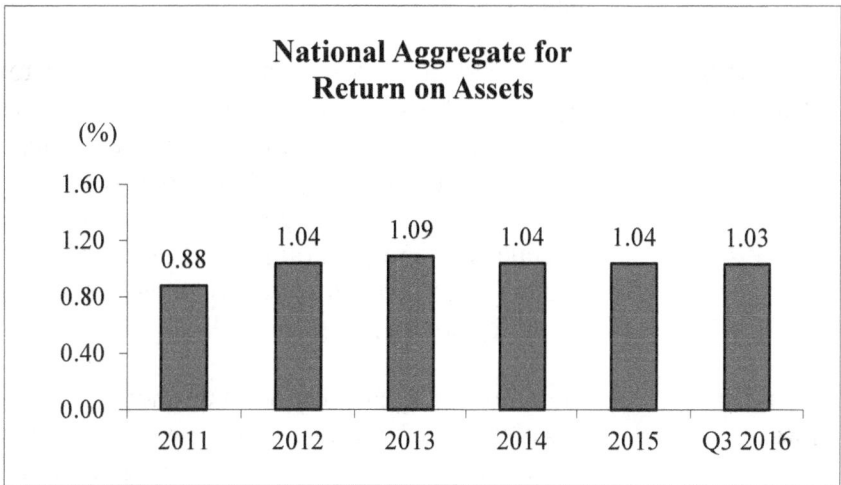

8. Return on Equity The ratio of net income for the year (year-to-date quarterly figures are converted to a 12-month equivalent) as a percentage of average equity for the year. This ratio, known as ROE, is commonly used by a company's shareholders as a measure of their return on investment. It is not always a good measure of profitability, however, because inadequate equity levels at some institutions can result in unjustly high ROE's.

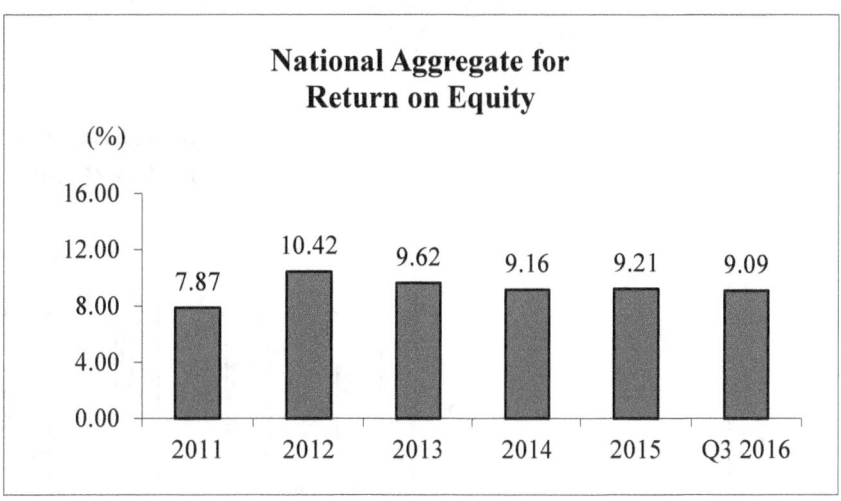

9. Net Interest Spread

The difference between the institution's interest income and interest expense for the year (year-to-date quarterly figures are converted to a 12-month equivalent) as a percentage of its average revenue-generating assets. Since the margin between interest earned and interest paid is generally where the company generates the majority of its income, this figure provides insight into the company's ability to effectively manage interest spreads.

A low Net Interest Spread can be the result of poor loan and deposit pricing, high levels of non-accruing loans, or poor asset/liability management.

10. Overhead Efficiency Ratio

Total overhead expenses as a percentage of total revenues net of interest expense. This is a common measure for evaluating an institution's ability to operate efficiently while keeping a handle on overhead expenses like salaries, rent, and other office expenses. A high ratio suggests that the company's overhead expenses are too high in relation to the amount of revenue they are generating and/or supporting. Conversely, a low ratio means good management of overhead expenses which usually results in a strong Return on Assets as well.

11. Liquidity Index

An index that measures the institution's ability to raise the necessary cash to satisfy creditors and honor depositor withdrawals. It is based on an evaluation of the company's short-term liquidity position, including its existing reliance on less stable deposit sources. See the Critical Ranges In Our Indexes for a description of the different critical levels presented in this index.

12. Liquidity Ratio

The ratio of short-term liquid assets to deposits and short-term borrowings. This ratio answers the question: How many cents can the institution easily raise in cash to cover each dollar on deposit plus pay off its short-term debts? Due to the nature of the business, it is rare (and not expected) for an established bank to achieve 100% on this ratio. Nevertheless, it serves as a good measure of an institution's liquidity in relation to the rest of the banking industry.

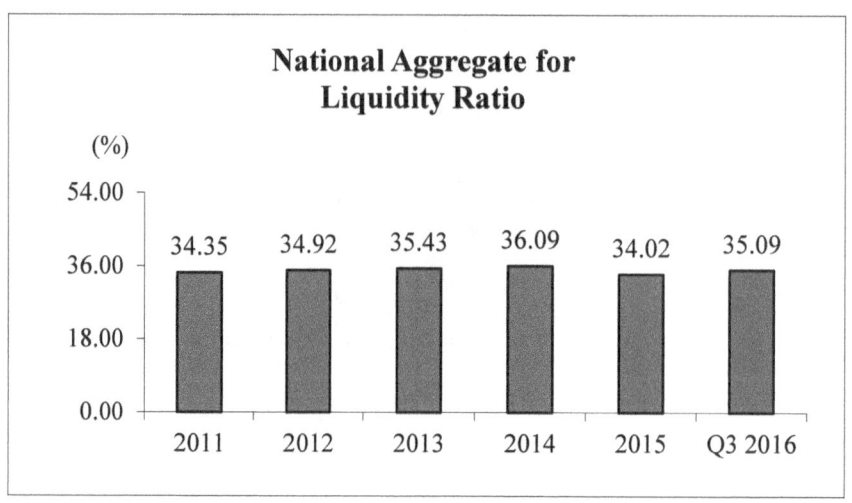

13. Hot Money Ratio

The percentage of the institution's deposit base that is being funded by jumbo CDs and brokered deposits. Jumbo CDs (high-yield certificates of deposit with principal amounts of at least $100,000) and brokered deposits (pooled funds sold by brokers seeking the highest interest rate available) are generally considered less stable (and more costly) and thus less desirable as a source of funds.

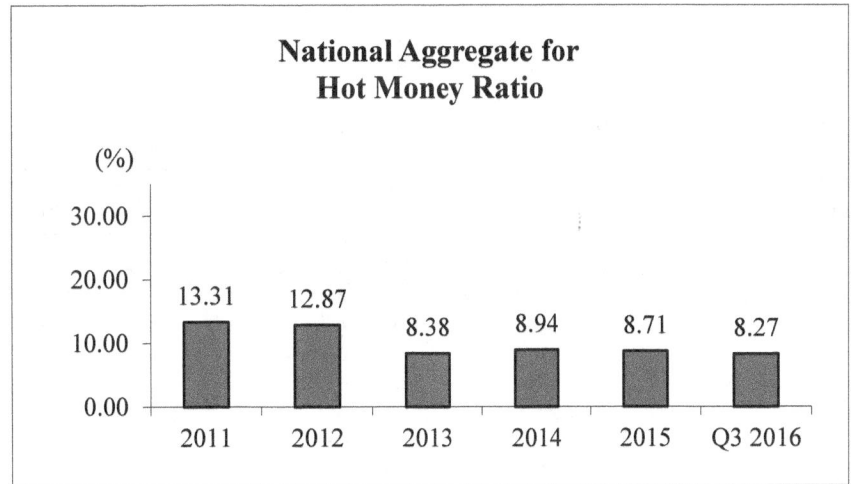

14. Stability Index

An index that integrates a number of factors such as 1) risk diversification in terms of company size and loan diversification; 2) deterioration of operations as reported in critical asset, liability, income and expense items, such as an increase in loan delinquency rates or a sharp increase in loan originations; 3) years in operation; 4) former problem areas where, despite recent improvement, the company has yet to establish a record of stable performance over a suitable period of time; and 5) relationships with holding companies and affiliates. See the Critical Ranges In Our Indexes for a description of the different critical levels presented in this index.

Name	City	State	Rating	2015 Rating	2014 Rating	Total Assets ($Mil)	One Year Asset Growth	Comm-ercial Loans	Cons-umer Loans	Mort-gage Loans	Secur-ities	Capital-ization Index	Lever-age Ratio	Risk-Based Capital Ratio
▲ 1880 Bank	Cambridge	MD	C+	C	C-	314.7	-1.17	5.3	0.8	27.8	12.5	10.0	12.9	17.3
▲ 1st Advantage Bank	Saint Peters	MO	D-	E-	D-	92.1	11.87	10.6	0.2	9.3	4.4	4.4	8.9	10.7
1st Bank	Broadus	MT	A-	A-	B+	47.7	-0.59	9.0	1.7	1.0	0.0	10.0	12.0	24.4
1st Bank & Trust	Broken Bow	OK	A-	A	A+	135.7	3.76	3.2	16.6	18.8	27.5	7.2	9.2	16.0
1st Bank of Sea Isle City	Sea Isle City	NJ	C+	C+	C+	241.9	1.93	0.3	0.2	45.2	6.1	8.5	10.0	17.9
▲ 1st Bank Yuma	Yuma	AZ	C+	C-	B-	276.1	10.23	7.2	0.5	3.2	9.2	7.8	10.0	13.2
1st Cameron State Bank	Cameron	MO	C-	C-	C-	57.5	9.42	0.7	1.8	34.0	20.8	6.5	8.5	22.3
1st Capital Bank	Monterey	CA	C+	B-	B-	523.7	4.26	9.1	0.1	24.3	16.1	6.9	8.9	14.2
1st Colonial Community Bank	Cherry Hill	NJ	C	C-	C-	481.8	7.80	4.8	1.0	34.3	23.8	4.8	6.8	11.9
1st Community Bank	Sherrard	IL	C	C-	C-	62.4	-10.19	9.3	2.5	20.1	13.9	8.4	9.9	15.3
1st Constitution Bank	Cranbury	NJ	B	B-	C	1055.3	7.64	30.4	0.1	6.2	21.7	6.9	10.3	12.4
1st Equity Bank	Skokie	IL	B	C+	C+	93.7	-6.56	15.7	0.1	22.6	0.4	10.0	15.2	20.3
▲ 1st Equity Bank Northwest	Buffalo Grove	IL	C-	D+	D	36.7	-1.45	6.2	0.4	19.6	0.0	10.0	22.1	33.5
1st Financial Bank USA	Dakota Dunes	SD	C	C	C+	677.6	-5.37	0.2	76.5	0.0	4.6	10.0	20.2	24.3
1st Manatee Bank	Bradenton	FL	B-	B	B+	154.9	13.53	18.6	0.3	17.5	11.0	10.0	14.2	19.2
▲ 1st National Bank	Lebanon	OH	B-	B-	B	150.8	13.52	2.7	0.6	33.7	13.4	8.1	9.8	16.2
1st Security Bank of Washington	Mountlake Terrace	WA	A-	A-	B+	827.0	29.79	12.0	20.6	23.7	9.8	8.2	10.3	13.5
1st Source Bank	South Bend	IN	A-	A-	A-	5439.2	6.73	43.2	2.4	6.9	15.1	8.7	11.2	13.9
1st State Bank	Saginaw	MI	B-	B-	B-	219.8	6.44	29.6	0.8	7.4	6.3	6.0	9.0	11.7
1st State Bank of Mason City	Mason City	IL	B	B-	B	28.1	-8.70	1.5	11.6	16.9	39.6	10.0	13.3	29.0
1st Summit Bank	Johnstown	PA	B	B	B	977.2	5.17	7.1	3.0	22.2	46.3	7.0	9.0	17.5
1st Trust Bank, Inc.	Hazard	KY	D+	D-	C-	253.4	28.00	42.1	1.6	10.0	2.9	4.7	8.8	10.8
1st United Bank	Faribault	MN	B+	B+	B	153.7	12.46	8.7	1.6	6.9	35.0	6.0	8.0	13.2
21st Century Bank	Loretto	MN	B+	B	B-	374.7	5.46	16.2	0.1	8.4	13.8	10.0	13.2	19.5
5Star Bank	Colorado Springs	CO	B-	B-	B	154.3	3.30	7.9	0.5	14.3	2.7	7.6	10.4	13.0
A J Smith Federal Savings Bank	Midlothian	IL	C	C-	C+	204.3	-2.02	0.0	0.1	48.5	21.8	10.0	13.9	34.3
▲ AB&T National Bank	Albany	GA	C+	C	C	143.0	8.71	17.3	3.1	17.9	2.6	5.8	9.3	11.6
▲ Abacus Federal Savings Bank	New York	NY	B-	B-	D	255.7	9.70	0.0	0.1	33.9	1.5	10.0	15.9	29.3
Abbeville Building & Loan	Abbeville	LA	B-	C+	B-	66.4	1.63	0.0	0.1	34.2	3.5	10.0	20.3	39.3
Abbeville First Bank	Abbeville	SC	B-	C+	C+	73.0	8.05	1.5	0.9	45.2	31.8	9.6	10.7	23.2
AbbyBank	Abbotsford	WI	B	B	B-	430.8	28.20	3.7	0.6	18.2	13.0	7.7	10.8	13.0
ABC Bank	Chicago	IL	C-	D+	D	339.7	-1.27	1.5	0.5	10.6	23.6	10.0	11.9	16.4
▲ Abington Bank	Abington	MA	C+	C	C+	135.6	3.54	1.4	0.1	44.3	11.4	6.8	8.8	13.7
Academy Bank, N.A.	Colorado Springs	CO	A	A	A-	1044.9	17.72	17.1	1.2	7.8	20.0	10.0	16.8	26.3
Acadia Trust, N.A.	Portland	ME	U	U	U	11.9	10.33	0.0	0.0	0.0	0.0	10.0	88.2	108.0
ACB Bank	Cherokee	OK	B	B	B-	115.4	5.61	7.7	2.5	8.6	13.4	4.9	8.7	11.0
Access Bank	Omaha	NE	B-	B	B-	316.6	14.85	27.2	1.8	8.8	15.4	9.2	11.1	14.3
Access National Bank	Reston	VA	B+	A-	A-	1362.2	21.88	19.4	0.5	16.9	14.5	5.2	8.1	11.2
AccessBank Texas	Denton	TX	B-	B-	C+	293.6	49.28	15.4	1.5	15.3	9.9	9.3	10.5	15.3
ACNB Bank	Gettysburg	PA	B	B	B	1197.0	6.91	4.7	1.2	28.7	16.9	6.9	8.9	14.5
Adams Bank & Trust	Ogallala	NE	A-	A-	B	705.7	5.75	10.5	1.9	12.2	5.9	7.5	10.8	12.9
Adams Community Bank	Adams	MA	C	D	C+	477.0	17.68	2.1	1.9	62.5	8.2	7.4	9.3	15.3
Adams County Bank	Kenesaw	NE	B-	B-	B-	170.1	-2.43	5.0	1.0	4.6	30.7	6.3	8.3	12.0
▲ Adams County Building and Loan Co.	West Union	OH	C	C	C-	24.2	0.83	0.0	0.2	38.1	24.2	10.0	17.8	26.9
Adams Dairy Bank	Blue Springs	MO	B-	B-	B-	109.1	5.98	4.4	0.7	31.5	12.3	6.8	8.8	15.0
Adams State Bank	Adams	NE	A-	A-	B+	48.8	-1.77	5.4	4.0	15.7	19.4	10.0	19.1	22.8
Adirondack Bank	Utica	NY	C-	C	C	809.6	11.53	14.2	1.3	19.6	34.6	5.1	7.1	14.6
Adirondack Trust Co.	Saratoga Springs	NY	C+	C+	C+	1156.2	6.78	5.9	10.5	12.8	24.0	7.3	9.2	14.1
Admirals Bank	Boston	MA	D	D+	D+	482.0	9.45	1.4	11.1	4.8	0.0	9.9	10.9	15.1
Adrian Bank	Adrian	MO	C	C+	B	140.0	1.79	7.5	5.0	10.7	26.9	8.7	10.1	15.7
Adrian State Bank	Adrian	MN	C+	C	C	43.0	-0.08	6.6	2.7	3.2	16.2	7.4	9.6	12.8
Advantage Bank	Loveland	CO	D	D	E-	274.5	3.21	11.2	0.2	20.5	7.8	7.4	9.3	12.8
Advantage Bank	Oklahoma City	OK	B	B	B	63.2	6.20	4.3	3.0	21.7	15.7	7.2	11.9	12.7
Advantage Community Bank	Dorchester	WI	B+	B+	B+	136.6	2.69	10.2	2.0	16.6	13.5	10.0	11.7	16.6
▼ Affiliated Bank	Arlington	TX	B-	B-	B-	616.5	14.03	4.8	1.4	32.8	0.0	6.3	10.1	12.0
Affinity Bank	Atlanta	GA	E-	E-	E-	251.9	-3.29	35.0	0.3	0.9	4.7	0.3	4.9	6.5
AIG Federal Savings Bank	Wilmington	DE	U	U	U	33.5	68.88	0.0	0.0	0.0	71.8	10.0	95.0	444.9
AimBank	Littlefield	TX	B	B	B	831.1	4.21	19.9	1.2	13.7	13.2	6.8	9.0	12.3
Alamerica Bank	Birmingham	AL	D+	D	D	36.3	0.65	9.0	0.7	9.5	3.4	10.0	15.9	19.6
Alamosa State Bank	Alamosa	CO	A-	A-	A-	236.0	5.78	6.9	3.5	9.2	25.3	7.0	9.0	17.6

Asset Quality Index	Adjusted Non-Performing Loans as a % of Total Loans	Adjusted Non-Performing Loans as a % of Capital	Net Charge-Offs Avg Loans	Profitability Index	Net Income ($Mil)	Return on Assets (R.O.A.)	Return on Equity (R.O.E.)	Net Interest Spread	Overhead Efficiency Ratio	Liquidity Index	Liquidity Ratio	Hot Money Ratio	Stability Index
2.9	3.61	20.9	0.02	5.7	7.4	3.18	23.96	4.01	68.2	2.8	7.4	14.2	4.8
3.4	0.71	6.3	0.22	3.0	0.4	0.57	6.52	3.88	84.3	0.6	8.8	43.9	2.3
5.2	2.15	8.7	0.00	6.9	0.6	1.47	13.07	3.19	59.5	5.7	45.8	6.7	8.1
7.5	0.14	0.9	0.36	9.7	2.4	2.32	25.94	4.38	48.8	4.6	28.2	7.5	7.8
4.0	2.91	18.8	0.00	2.9	0.6	0.32	3.09	3.63	79.9	4.2	23.4	8.7	5.4
3.4	0.99	6.7	-0.01	5.3	2.0	0.95	9.67	4.53	71.1	3.7	19.9	10.8	6.4
9.5	0.25	1.4	0.00	1.9	0.1	0.15	1.75	2.63	91.9	4.6	41.1	12.1	4.0
6.6	0.41	3.2	-0.01	3.5	2.0	0.51	5.93	3.12	70.5	5.0	16.2	2.3	6.0
5.8	0.69	6.4	0.18	4.1	2.9	0.78	12.09	3.14	62.0	3.3	3.0	10.5	3.0
7.6	0.03	0.2	0.03	2.5	0.2	0.41	4.26	2.97	87.2	1.0	19.6	34.0	4.1
5.9	0.76	5.1	-0.04	5.2	7.4	1.00	8.57	3.95	66.0	3.6	12.2	10.9	8.5
4.3	1.20	6.3	0.26	5.3	0.9	1.29	8.46	3.62	62.0	1.3	16.2	27.9	7.1
3.9	0.97	3.2	0.55	1.4	0.0	0.10	0.44	2.83	96.5	1.2	29.6	45.3	5.8
1.7	4.10	13.6	3.73	8.3	5.7	1.10	5.63	18.13	74.3	0.4	16.6	15.5	7.7
5.0	1.44	8.0	0.02	3.6	0.7	0.60	6.14	4.04	81.8	1.0	16.1	32.4	6.6
4.5	1.56	10.9	0.13	4.1	1.0	0.91	8.83	3.31	84.9	1.6	14.3	23.2	5.1
6.8	0.09	0.7	0.00	8.4	8.3	1.41	13.46	4.29	65.4	1.7	12.9	14.6	7.2
7.2	0.46	2.8	0.14	6.9	43.3	1.09	8.59	3.54	63.0	2.8	14.3	15.2	10.0
4.3	1.55	11.1	-0.04	4.3	1.3	0.75	8.57	3.69	67.2	4.1	14.2	7.5	5.8
7.7	0.37	1.1	0.34	4.9	0.3	1.30	10.22	2.84	57.6	5.5	66.1	11.9	6.3
7.7	0.67	3.5	0.09	4.8	7.8	1.09	12.01	3.11	59.8	3.6	34.7	15.4	6.1
1.8	2.15	19.6	0.15	3.8	0.8	0.49	5.65	3.65	71.6	0.9	23.2	41.1	3.4
6.4	0.35	2.2	0.56	3.8	0.4	1.18	13.21	3.90	64.4	6.4	49.2	4.0	6.3
5.1	1.06	5.9	0.13	5.4	2.5	0.91	6.87	3.75	57.6	3.1	16.1	0.1	6.3
4.3	0.53	4.0	0.04	5.8	1.1	0.98	9.03	4.67	59.0	1.8	18.4	20.4	7.9
7.0	2.36	9.3	0.01	2.3	0.5	0.32	2.18	2.35	86.9	4.6	41.9	12.6	6.2
6.1	0.38	3.3	-0.01	3.6	0.5	0.49	3.90	3.98	82.5	3.3	4.2	11.6	6.4
8.4	0.61	2.7	0.00	3.4	0.4	0.21	1.26	3.25	91.4	1.3	23.1	5.2	7.3
3.4	5.47	15.4	0.00	2.5	0.0	0.00	0.01	2.71	100.0	3.4	35.6	16.7	8.1
5.3	3.04	15.1	-0.03	3.8	0.6	1.09	9.85	3.65	78.2	2.6	38.7	24.1	4.8
4.9	1.23	9.0	0.01	6.8	3.6	1.37	13.77	3.61	55.4	2.1	19.5	18.7	5.4
1.3	5.32	27.7	0.37	3.9	2.1	0.86	7.29	4.01	73.8	1.0	22.1	34.5	6.0
3.3	2.12	17.1	0.00	3.7	0.5	0.52	6.00	3.62	78.1	4.1	19.8	9.0	5.3
7.4	1.51	5.2	1.01	5.2	4.8	0.62	3.50	3.14	82.6	2.3	28.4	28.2	8.2
6.5	na	0.0	na	9.5	0.4	4.19	4.42	0.66	85.9	4.0	na	0.0	6.3
4.7	0.90	7.1	-0.15	9.7	1.9	2.27	26.14	4.86	45.0	0.6	4.7	39.6	7.0
8.4	0.01	0.0	0.03	3.7	1.3	0.59	5.02	3.73	74.4	1.9	23.8	20.9	6.1
6.2	0.59	5.0	-0.04	9.3	14.3	1.51	18.12	3.60	60.0	1.7	8.9	15.9	8.8
7.3	0.03	0.2	-0.03	4.4	1.5	0.79	6.87	3.70	65.7	1.3	17.5	26.7	6.9
6.2	1.01	7.4	0.04	4.7	7.9	0.92	10.66	3.48	67.8	3.9	10.7	9.2	7.5
6.4	0.58	4.4	-0.05	6.7	5.9	1.17	10.86	4.51	65.0	2.4	6.8	16.3	7.7
4.4	1.46	12.3	0.05	2.9	2.0	0.56	5.32	3.37	80.5	3.1	12.0	13.0	5.8
6.5	0.50	3.5	0.00	5.3	1.7	1.38	18.02	3.05	49.9	1.2	11.3	27.4	4.4
4.7	5.63	17.2	0.00	3.4	0.2	0.96	5.24	3.74	84.6	2.5	49.5	27.2	7.4
5.1	1.31	9.4	0.00	4.9	0.7	0.83	9.26	3.52	66.4	0.9	10.5	32.4	5.5
8.4	0.00	0.0	-0.06	6.7	0.6	1.64	8.72	3.71	54.6	2.4	16.7	17.1	8.6
3.2	2.19	17.5	0.09	3.2	3.4	0.58	7.79	3.22	77.8	2.2	9.4	17.5	3.8
6.3	0.57	3.7	0.02	3.6	5.5	0.66	6.55	2.84	76.6	4.6	21.9	7.6	8.1
1.6	2.25	14.4	0.15	0.0	-3.4	-1.01	-8.55	4.37	125.0	1.3	30.1	23.2	4.4
3.2	2.39	14.1	0.61	6.3	1.5	1.44	14.16	3.83	53.6	3.5	27.9	13.2	7.0
7.2	0.08	0.6	-0.04	6.8	0.5	1.67	17.45	4.10	55.9	3.3	8.4	11.9	5.4
4.9	0.30	2.4	0.03	5.1	2.4	1.19	12.85	4.76	63.9	0.8	16.1	39.6	0.9
6.1	0.67	4.2	0.16	5.6	0.6	1.32	10.76	5.69	77.4	4.8	20.3	4.1	6.5
7.8	0.67	3.7	0.04	5.1	1.0	0.95	8.14	3.36	60.2	4.5	29.9	8.7	7.0
3.6	1.18	10.1	0.04	9.1	5.8	1.36	13.71	5.17	64.9	0.5	9.0	60.7	7.6
5.1	0.25	3.3	-0.04	0.0	-1.8	-0.91	-13.19	2.93	229.5	1.1	10.8	29.0	1.6
10.0	na	0.0	na	9.9	1.4	5.55	5.87	0.69	42.4	4.0	na	100.0	8.0
4.6	1.19	9.2	0.58	4.8	6.5	1.04	10.86	3.82	64.9	1.1	7.8	25.5	7.1
0.8	6.65	28.8	0.24	2.6	0.1	0.55	3.40	4.70	89.0	0.6	15.1	60.5	4.3
8.7	0.08	0.4	-0.03	6.9	3.0	1.73	19.25	3.37	48.1	3.4	28.9	14.5	6.8

Name	City	State	2015 Rating	2014 Rating	Total Assets ($Mil)	One Year Asset Growth	Asset Mix (As a % of Total Assets)				Capital- ization Index	Lever- age Ratio	Risk- Based Capital Ratio
			Rating				Comm- ercial Loans	Cons- umer Loans	Mort- gage Loans	Secur- ities			
▲ Albany Bank and Trust Co., N.A.	Chicago	IL	B	B-	C+	545.1	-3.22	8.8	0.3	4.7	24.3	10.0	15.6	21.4
▲ Albina Community Bank	Portland	OR	C+	C+	D-	173.7	7.52	15.3	0.5	2.3	18.7	8.9	10.2	14.9
Alden State Bank	Sterling	KS	C	C-	D+	18.6	-10.08	10.6	6.8	21.9	21.9	10.0	12.0	25.7
Alden State Bank	Alden	MI	B	B	B	200.9	5.29	5.3	2.9	24.7	10.0	10.0	12.2	17.9
Alden State Bank	Alden	NY	B	B	B	294.7	7.10	5.2	1.6	49.9	18.4	10.0	12.4	19.3
Alerus Financial, N.A.	Grand Forks	ND	B+	A	A	1933.7	23.24	22.5	4.5	15.0	13.9	6.1	9.4	11.8
Algonquin State Bank, N.A.	Algonquin	IL	D-	D-	D	137.4	5.93	0.1	0.5	13.7	52.4	9.5	10.6	28.6
All America Bank	Oklahoma City	OK	B	B	B-	376.8	10.02	5.4	2.2	12.3	20.4	6.5	10.3	12.1
Allegheny Valley Bank of Pittsburgh	Pittsburgh	PA	B-	B-	B-	442.6	8.19	6.7	0.3	28.2	23.4	7.3	9.2	13.3
Allegiance Bank	Houston	TX	B	B	B	2460.0	22.19	15.0	0.5	8.9	12.6	6.0	9.4	11.7
Alliance Bank	Francesville	IN	B+	B+	B+	294.6	-0.13	8.2	0.5	5.7	36.3	9.9	11.0	17.0
Alliance Bank	Topeka	KS	B-	C+	C+	100.8	5.52	15.6	2.6	16.9	11.8	9.5	10.6	16.1
Alliance Bank	Saint Paul	MN	C-	D+	C+	576.2	-3.89	15.0	1.1	5.3	12.2	8.0	11.2	13.4
Alliance Bank	Cape Girardeau	MO	A-	A-	B+	196.0	17.77	4.2	2.4	17.3	6.6	10.0	15.6	19.0
Alliance Bank	Sulphur Springs	TX	B-	B-	B-	705.6	6.38	6.0	1.4	9.0	41.5	7.6	9.4	16.2
Alliance Bank	Mondovi	WI	B-	B-	B-	164.6	3.37	4.0	3.6	17.6	17.4	7.7	9.4	14.3
Alliance Bank & Trust Co.	Gastonia	NC	E-	E-	E-	147.1	-3.00	9.3	0.3	15.8	9.7	3.5	7.0	10.3
▲ Alliance Bank Central Texas	Waco	TX	C+	C-	D+	201.8	2.63	6.6	2.1	34.2	21.5	7.6	9.4	16.1
Alliant Bank	Madison	MO	B	B	C+	152.9	1.70	5.1	1.3	24.2	5.9	8.1	9.7	13.7
▲ Allied First Bank,sb	Oswego	IL	D	E-	E-	92.8	-21.11	8.4	1.6	30.7	7.8	6.2	8.2	12.9
▼ AllNations Bank	Calumet	OK	D-	D-	C+	46.5	-5.55	9.2	7.1	7.9	40.2	6.1	8.2	17.9
Ally Bank	Midvale	UT	A-	A-	A-	114517.8	6.83	34.8	28.4	8.3	11.2	10.0	15.5	17.7
▼ Alma Bank	Astoria	NY	D	C+	B+	1034.5	-1.32	15.7	0.1	2.3	4.4	9.5	11.9	14.6
Almena State Bank	Almena	KS	C+	C+	C	81.6	36.47	17.1	5.1	9.8	4.8	4.1	9.0	10.6
AloStar Bank of Commerce	Birmingham	AL	B-	B-	C	1028.3	11.89	25.5	0.0	0.1	8.6	10.0	17.2	22.4
Alpine Bank	Glenwood Springs	CO	B+	B+	B+	2964.9	9.35	2.8	1.0	19.2	22.7	7.3	9.3	12.7
Alpine Bank & Trust Co.	Rockford	IL	B	B	B	1256.1	4.52	10.4	6.4	9.1	27.9	6.4	8.4	12.5
Alpine Capital Bank	New York	NY	B+	B+	B+	250.3	-10.83	4.6	6.7	6.3	12.6	10.0	16.1	26.5
Altamaha Bank and Trust Co.	Vidalia	GA	B	B	B-	158.7	2.60	7.9	5.2	17.7	21.0	9.8	10.9	17.0
AltaPacific Bank	Santa Rosa	CA	A	A-	B+	380.5	11.60	4.9	0.7	4.6	19.7	10.0	15.0	19.6
Alterra Bank	Leawood	KS	C	B-	C+	289.7	-1.22	32.2	0.0	4.1	2.3	5.8	9.6	11.6
▲ Alton Bank	Alton	MO	B+	B	B-	64.4	-0.14	4.3	8.5	16.6	34.6	10.0	12.6	15.5
Altoona First Savings Bank	Altoona	PA	B-	B-	B-	210.6	4.87	3.8	3.9	32.5	1.1	10.0	13.5	22.4
Alva State Bank & Trust Co.	Alva	OK	B+	A-	A-	313.2	4.31	10.5	2.2	3.1	13.4	10.0	13.5	15.8
Amalgamated Bank	New York	NY	D+	D+	D-	4061.3	7.10	15.5	0.1	15.0	31.4	6.6	8.6	13.2
Amalgamated Bank of Chicago	Chicago	IL	C+	C	D+	829.1	6.68	3.6	5.4	2.5	21.5	8.8	10.2	21.1
Amarillo National Bank	Amarillo	TX	B	A-	A-	3828.5	1.02	24.8	16.9	5.7	6.8	9.6	12.4	14.7
Ambler Savings Bank	Ambler	PA	B	B	B-	341.5	5.08	1.0	0.0	48.0	26.8	10.0	11.5	23.4
Amboy Bank	Old Bridge	NJ	B	B	B	2382.0	7.13	2.1	0.0	17.3	15.3	8.3	14.0	13.6
Amerasia Bank	Flushing	NY	B+	B+	B+	512.8	8.58	3.2	0.1	15.9	0.5	8.6	10.9	13.9
▼ America's Community Bank	Blue Springs	MO	B-	B	B	30.6	7.49	17.9	0.5	16.3	0.9	10.0	11.6	19.3
American B&T of the Cumberlands	Livingston	TN	B	B-	B-	218.8	8.77	11.3	6.6	29.4	4.2	6.4	8.4	13.2
▲ American Bank	Bozeman	MT	B	C	C-	362.4	7.76	13.4	0.4	15.4	6.9	9.1	11.0	14.3
American Bank	Wagoner	OK	C	C	C+	30.8	-0.79	1.1	5.3	3.6	26.7	10.0	20.1	91.5
American Bank	Allentown	PA	B	B+	B+	555.8	0.45	9.2	0.1	11.5	11.9	6.7	10.0	12.3
▼ American Bank & Trust	Wessington Springs	SD	A-	A-	A-	623.6	5.30	10.7	2.6	1.2	17.7	8.3	10.9	13.6
▲ American Bank & Trust Co.	Opelousas	LA	B+	B+	B+	180.3	5.13	9.4	4.5	23.0	29.7	9.7	10.8	17.1
American Bank & Trust Co., Inc.	Bowling Green	KY	B+	B+	B+	285.3	4.66	6.0	2.2	34.7	8.2	7.5	9.3	13.0
American Bank & Trust Co., Inc.	Covington	LA	C	C-	C	116.1	0.63	5.8	2.5	16.1	8.8	8.3	9.9	16.8
▼ American Bank & Trust Wisconsin	Cuba City	WI	B-	B	C+	148.2	4.02	10.9	3.3	8.2	9.5	10.0	11.1	15.8
American Bank and Trust Co.	Tulsa	OK	B	B	C	187.6	-14.71	23.0	0.6	3.1	33.5	10.0	11.7	17.2
▼ American Bank and Trust Co., N.A.	Davenport	IA	D	D+	C-	332.9	-3.44	7.7	0.7	22.3	21.6	9.2	10.4	15.6
American Bank Center	Dickinson	ND	B+	B+	B+	1328.1	-0.26	6.2	10.2	4.3	31.6	6.4	8.4	12.6
▲ American Bank of Baxter Springs	Baxter Springs	KS	C+	D+	D-	91.5	2.48	4.2	1.4	7.7	33.0	10.0	11.3	27.9
American Bank of Commerce	Wolfforth	TX	B-	B-	B-	807.6	7.72	9.6	0.6	8.0	26.2	7.5	9.4	13.1
American Bank of Commerce	Provo	UT	B	B	B	78.0	3.87	3.4	1.2	5.9	0.0	10.0	14.4	20.0
American Bank of Missouri	Wellsville	MO	B-	B-	B-	194.9	21.39	4.0	0.3	30.4	5.5	6.4	9.5	12.0
American Bank of Oklahoma	Collinsville	OK	C+	C	C-	250.1	9.84	18.0	14.3	17.8	0.3	7.4	9.9	12.8
American Bank of Sidney, Nebraska	Sidney	NE	B-	C+	C	83.3	0.95	6.6	14.5	4.7	30.2	10.0	11.7	23.2
American Bank of the North	Nashwauk	MN	D	D	E+	571.0	-1.38	11.6	1.9	20.6	13.5	5.3	8.2	11.2

Asset Quality Index	Adjusted Non-Performing Loans as a % of Total Loans	as a % of Capital	Net Charge-Offs Avg Loans	Profitability Index	Net Income ($Mil)	Return on Assets (R.O.A.)	Return on Equity (R.O.E.)	Net Interest Spread	Overhead Efficiency Ratio	Liquidity Index	Liquidity Ratio	Hot Money Ratio	Stability Index
6.4	0.91	3.9	0.01	4.2	3.0	0.71	4.70	3.19	60.3	2.1	28.1	21.0	7.5
7.6	0.10	0.6	-0.03	3.7	0.3	0.26	2.58	3.57	90.2	4.3	29.3	9.5	5.6
8.5	0.00	0.0	-0.17	2.2	0.0	0.20	1.68	3.53	92.6	2.7	35.4	17.8	5.0
5.0	2.53	13.6	0.02	8.0	1.9	1.43	11.83	4.60	57.2	4.9	29.7	6.1	6.3
4.4	3.23	17.8	0.40	6.1	2.3	1.06	8.57	3.99	54.8	3.6	16.9	11.2	7.1
5.7	0.62	4.6	0.14	5.4	11.7	0.81	7.07	3.84	84.0	4.1	8.5	7.6	9.6
6.4	3.34	7.5	-0.37	0.6	0.6	0.54	4.60	2.86	114.4	6.9	60.6	4.2	4.2
5.9	0.99	6.7	0.04	4.9	3.2	1.15	9.99	4.27	69.4	2.3	17.3	13.0	6.6
3.6	2.05	14.5	0.06	4.1	2.2	0.67	5.90	3.53	74.5	4.3	22.5	7.7	6.5
5.5	1.02	7.7	0.04	5.4	17.7	1.03	9.01	4.40	58.6	1.7	24.2	29.2	7.9
6.0	0.67	3.2	0.00	5.6	2.9	1.31	11.16	3.63	67.4	4.9	37.6	9.3	8.4
5.7	0.57	3.4	0.02	4.5	0.5	0.73	6.91	3.62	68.2	3.1	28.4	15.5	6.0
2.2	2.81	17.6	-0.16	6.8	6.2	1.44	12.08	4.10	67.7	3.2	15.3	12.6	8.1
8.3	0.41	2.0	0.09	5.7	1.3	1.00	6.22	4.10	63.3	1.3	12.0	26.6	7.8
7.9	0.38	1.9	0.07	4.0	4.8	0.93	9.49	3.06	78.7	5.0	36.6	8.2	5.8
3.6	2.24	15.5	-0.02	3.7	1.0	0.85	8.55	3.49	76.6	3.7	21.7	11.2	5.9
1.6	4.71	42.2	0.26	1.4	0.3	0.32	4.61	3.76	90.8	2.1	23.8	19.2	0.3
6.6	0.40	2.7	0.05	3.5	1.1	0.69	6.75	3.56	80.9	1.4	26.8	30.7	5.1
6.7	0.18	1.3	0.02	5.0	1.4	1.26	13.13	4.08	74.1	1.0	13.5	31.6	6.8
2.6	3.42	24.7	0.28	4.5	0.7	0.86	11.07	3.06	97.1	2.0	25.8	20.5	1.5
3.4	2.22	9.7	1.16	0.3	-0.3	-0.73	-7.14	3.30	105.5	5.3	34.9	5.5	2.9
6.7	0.44	2.1	0.30	6.3	931.7	1.11	7.29	2.63	57.0	1.2	15.2	15.2	10.0
0.7	5.08	33.6	0.21	4.0	4.1	0.53	4.53	3.75	71.3	1.0	10.5	31.5	8.8
6.0	0.34	3.3	0.03	9.6	1.3	2.55	28.22	5.19	60.5	0.6	6.7	37.9	6.2
5.5	1.59	6.0	0.39	3.9	5.1	0.66	3.68	3.39	65.5	2.0	31.3	38.5	6.9
7.2	0.64	4.4	-0.12	6.7	26.7	1.25	12.74	4.47	65.2	4.9	16.3	3.7	7.8
8.1	0.28	2.0	0.04	4.7	10.9	1.18	13.10	3.19	77.2	4.3	22.0	6.9	7.6
8.5	0.61	1.6	0.00	4.8	2.3	1.10	7.54	2.83	51.3	3.8	61.6	22.2	7.6
3.8	2.44	14.3	0.17	6.1	1.7	1.44	13.35	4.86	71.6	2.4	24.3	17.9	6.1
7.3	0.10	0.4	0.00	8.8	3.5	1.30	8.22	5.86	60.6	4.6	27.3	6.9	8.1
0.0	5.44	39.9	1.71	2.7	-0.8	-0.33	-2.51	4.25	66.1	0.8	12.7	34.7	6.7
5.5	1.30	5.7	-0.01	7.5	1.0	1.93	16.72	4.23	57.8	2.9	25.1	15.6	6.9
7.9	0.63	3.0	0.05	3.5	0.8	0.48	3.60	3.38	75.7	2.4	33.7	22.4	6.6
3.4	2.32	12.9	-0.07	8.9	5.6	2.25	18.52	3.96	38.6	1.5	18.1	24.4	8.4
4.7	2.07	13.7	0.14	1.7	8.9	0.31	3.45	2.72	90.2	4.1	15.9	8.0	5.5
4.1	3.38	13.6	0.13	4.6	2.2	0.38	3.81	3.04	86.9	6.1	39.2	2.5	3.7
4.7	1.03	6.1	1.14	6.0	35.3	1.27	10.35	3.54	50.1	2.7	17.1	15.4	10.0
9.3	0.55	2.8	0.08	3.8	2.1	0.81	7.04	3.13	67.2	2.1	26.9	20.3	6.4
4.2	2.29	11.8	-0.04	7.3	29.8	1.71	13.08	3.53	53.9	2.0	8.4	15.4	8.6
5.9	0.21	1.7	0.01	10.0	5.6	1.55	14.07	4.62	40.5	0.6	10.4	48.1	7.7
8.7	0.30	1.5	0.00	3.1	0.1	0.32	2.66	3.38	91.6	1.6	34.6	42.1	6.1
6.5	0.50	4.2	-0.01	6.1	2.2	1.37	16.89	3.91	66.6	0.9	20.4	38.2	5.7
6.6	0.00	0.0	0.00	8.1	7.2	2.70	26.89	4.11	52.3	4.5	18.5	5.4	5.8
9.8	1.93	1.4	-0.19	1.7	0.0	0.08	0.37	2.77	97.3	6.7	95.9	9.7	5.6
7.3	0.12	0.9	0.00	4.7	3.8	0.90	8.83	2.84	51.2	3.0	9.8	13.5	7.6
7.8	0.14	0.9	0.91	4.7	3.8	0.82	6.77	3.72	69.3	3.3	6.4	11.8	9.0
8.7	0.18	1.0	0.00	5.6	1.9	1.39	12.23	4.01	64.3	4.2	23.2	8.4	6.8
5.1	0.98	7.8	0.21	4.4	1.5	0.66	7.25	3.74	69.3	2.1	15.2	18.3	7.6
4.0	2.29	12.6	0.17	2.8	0.3	0.29	2.92	3.72	89.8	4.7	41.3	12.1	4.7
3.5	2.23	14.7	0.00	4.4	0.8	0.76	5.92	3.81	68.2	3.7	16.6	10.8	7.3
8.8	0.10	0.5	-0.04	4.5	1.3	0.85	7.46	3.58	72.5	3.2	36.4	17.9	5.5
3.5	3.08	18.4	-0.23	0.6	-0.6	-0.25	-2.28	3.30	105.8	4.2	19.9	7.9	4.1
3.9	2.07	13.9	0.40	5.6	9.6	0.96	10.69	3.81	64.1	4.4	7.1	4.9	7.6
6.8	2.90	9.1	0.82	5.4	1.3	1.89	18.15	2.34	106.8	3.1	29.2	15.7	4.8
7.7	0.20	1.3	0.01	4.1	3.8	0.64	6.71	3.67	73.8	2.8	25.4	16.4	6.3
4.0	1.77	8.9	0.79	5.2	0.4	0.76	5.09	5.12	77.3	4.2	25.6	8.7	7.1
4.6	0.77	6.7	-0.08	5.1	1.2	0.88	7.81	3.80	69.7	0.9	5.1	29.3	6.4
4.8	0.43	3.3	0.03	4.4	1.6	0.83	8.57	4.29	73.9	0.8	17.9	42.8	4.9
8.0	0.43	1.6	0.00	3.9	0.6	0.92	8.02	3.21	68.7	4.8	28.4	6.3	6.1
0.3	6.30	52.0	-0.03	3.9	2.6	0.62	6.96	3.70	75.0	4.2	7.6	6.3	3.6

Name	City	State	2016 Rating	2015 Rating	2014 Rating	Total Assets ($Mil)	One Year Asset Growth	Commercial Loans	Consumer Loans	Mortgage Loans	Securities	Capitalization Index	Leverage Ratio	Risk-Based Capital Ratio
American Bank, N.A.	Le Mars	IA	B-	B	B	270.4	-1.54	7.3	1.6	5.6	2.2	9.3	11.3	14.4
American Bank, N.A.	Corpus Christi	TX	B	B	B	1276.1	-1.50	18.9	0.5	7.4	27.6	6.7	8.7	14.0
American Bank, N.A.	Dallas	TX	C+	C	D+	56.0	-3.59	0.2	44.4	0.9	31.8	8.4	10.0	18.9
American Bank, N.A.	Waco	TX	B	B-	C+	429.0	2.77	12.2	2.0	24.3	24.1	7.8	9.6	15.5
American Business Bank	Los Angeles	CA	B-	B-	B-	1816.8	12.69	9.7	0.2	0.5	51.6	5.6	7.6	16.9
American City Bank	Tullahoma	TN	B	B	C+	292.9	11.43	26.4	3.5	20.1	5.2	10.0	18.0	18.5
▼ American Commerce Bank, N.A.	Bremen	GA	C+	B-	B-	225.9	24.31	3.7	1.3	12.3	5.7	9.8	11.5	14.8
American Community Bank	Glen Cove	NY	B+	B-	C	180.5	5.69	3.3	0.0	5.0	15.5	10.0	14.0	19.1
American Community Bank & Trust	Woodstock	IL	B	B	B	549.0	14.21	11.1	0.1	9.7	12.5	10.0	13.1	20.2
American Community Bank of Indiana	Munster	IN	B	B	B-	200.2	4.78	6.8	0.5	33.1	2.3	8.0	9.6	13.6
▲ American Continental Bank	City of Industry	CA	A-	B+	B	206.2	-0.07	4.8	0.0	11.0	7.0	10.0	13.8	19.5
▲ American Eagle Bank	South Elgin	IL	C+	C+	D	194.1	4.28	1.8	50.4	7.8	0.0	4.1	9.1	10.5
American Eagle Bank of Chicago	Chicago	IL	C+	C+	D	83.3	8.92	3.3	33.7	8.9	0.0	8.6	10.9	13.9
American Enterprise Bank	Buffalo Grove	IL	D-	D-	D-	208.5	-1.89	14.7	0.0	2.3	4.5	9.6	10.7	14.8
American Exchange Bank	Elmwood	NE	B-	B	B-	45.1	-1.30	13.0	1.9	9.0	24.3	9.0	12.1	14.2
▼ American Exchange Bank	Henryetta	OK	B-	B	B	59.6	-1.61	6.3	11.1	33.4	9.7	10.0	12.3	19.1
American Exchange Bank	Lindsay	OK	B-	B-	B+	60.3	0.57	5.7	2.8	9.8	55.9	9.9	11.0	21.4
American Express Bank, FSB	Salt Lake City	UT	B+	B+	B+	45999.4	-9.59	45.1	26.0	0.0	0.8	10.0	13.6	18.7
American Express Centurion Bank	Salt Lake City	UT	B+	B+	B+	39039.1	29.54	0.4	63.4	0.0	1.6	10.0	15.9	18.3
American Federal Bank	Fargo	ND	B+	B+	B-	554.9	6.56	4.5	1.5	15.3	9.9	7.6	9.4	14.4
American First National Bank	Houston	TX	A-	B+	B	1300.0	14.96	7.9	0.3	3.7	6.1	10.0	12.6	15.4
American Founders Bank, Inc.	Louisville	KY	D	D-	E-	99.9	-62.76	11.0	0.1	24.0	10.8	10.0	12.9	19.3
American Heritage Bank	Clovis	NM	B-	B-	C	87.8	-0.21	11.7	0.7	7.5	31.2	8.9	10.3	15.2
American Heritage Bank	Sapulpa	OK	B-	B-	B-	1064.1	0.85	4.8	3.8	13.3	57.7	7.3	9.2	21.8
American Heritage National Bank	Long Prairie	MN	A	A-	A-	257.9	9.56	10.9	0.5	7.5	1.8	10.0	12.2	16.4
American Interstate Bank	Elkhorn	NE	A	A	A	108.1	2.39	7.3	0.9	22.4	10.5	10.0	14.4	19.6
▲ American Investors Bank and Mortgage	Eden Prairie	MN	C-	C	C	89.5	-7.47	0.0	0.4	20.4	19.8	6.9	9.0	12.8
▲ American Metro Bank	Chicago	IL	D+	D-	E+	65.6	2.33	3.8	0.0	20.1	0.0	10.0	11.9	17.3
American Momentum Bank	College Station	TX	A-	B+	C+	1130.5	2.63	4.9	0.1	13.9	6.9	10.0	17.1	19.0
American Nation Bank	Ardmore	OK	A-	A-	A-	377.5	3.23	6.3	6.3	18.3	35.1	8.8	10.2	16.6
▲ American National Bank	Oakland Park	FL	A-	B	B-	277.6	0.80	8.3	0.1	2.5	2.8	10.0	13.7	16.3
American National Bank	Omaha	NE	B	B+	B+	3026.5	6.01	14.4	20.9	6.5	17.2	5.4	9.4	11.3
American National Bank & Trust	Wichita Falls	TX	A-	A-	B	543.9	14.31	6.8	4.5	10.3	21.8	10.0	12.8	17.7
American National Bank and Trust Co.	Danville	VA	A-	A-	A	1611.6	6.71	10.6	0.3	13.9	21.6	10.0	11.3	15.1
▲ American National Bank of Beaver Dam	Beaver Dam	WI	C+	C	C	118.0	1.74	5.5	1.5	25.2	11.6	8.6	10.1	15.2
American National Bank of Minnesota	Brainerd	MN	B-	C	D+	239.6	-4.59	3.4	2.1	30.6	7.6	10.0	12.7	17.9
American National Bank of Mount Pleasant	Mount Pleasant	TX	A-	A-	B+	91.8	1.49	9.1	10.3	19.9	31.0	10.0	13.3	23.4
American National Bank of Texas	Terrell	TX	B	B	B	2728.4	4.00	6.2	1.4	13.6	20.4	6.3	8.3	12.1
American National Bank-Fox Cities	Appleton	WI	B	B	B	243.2	-3.35	21.0	0.4	4.1	21.0	10.0	13.3	17.1
American Patriot Bank	Greeneville	TN	E-	E-	E-	58.0	-11.98	8.5	1.7	25.5	4.0	0.0	2.0	4.2
American Plus Bank, N.A.	Arcadia	CA	A-	A	A	456.1	23.64	10.7	0.0	15.5	2.0	9.3	12.0	14.4
American Pride Bank	Macon	GA	A-	A-	B+	147.9	19.13	2.8	0.2	5.4	12.9	10.0	18.7	23.3
American River Bank	Rancho Cordova	CA	B	B	B	654.0	4.62	3.7	0.1	2.4	38.8	9.4	10.6	19.4
▲ American Riviera Bank	Santa Barbara	CA	B+	B+	B+	463.6	104.18	11.0	0.3	13.9	1.4	7.4	9.8	12.9
American Savings Bank	Tripoli	IA	A-	A	A	51.8	-5.10	10.5	1.8	9.7	47.5	10.0	18.7	28.0
American Savings Bank	Middletown	OH	B-	B-	B-	39.3	1.12	6.6	1.6	52.4	2.6	10.0	19.9	31.1
American Savings Bank, F.S.B.	Honolulu	HI	B+	B+	B	6336.7	8.22	10.7	2.5	35.3	15.7	6.6	8.6	13.3
▲ American Savings Bank, FSB	Portsmouth	OH	B	B-	C	272.9	7.93	4.5	1.1	48.8	9.6	8.9	10.2	15.0
American State Bank	Osceola	IA	B+	B+	B	188.1	6.52	15.2	4.6	12.3	17.7	7.4	9.3	12.9
▼ American State Bank	Sioux Center	IA	B-	B-	B-	817.7	7.08	14.1	1.9	3.7	1.2	9.0	11.8	14.2
▲ American State Bank	Arp	TX	C+	C+	B-	290.0	4.31	11.1	3.0	20.8	9.0	6.3	8.7	12.0
American State Bank & Trust Co	Williston	ND	A-	A-	A-	592.6	-9.81	4.7	3.2	6.4	51.3	8.4	9.9	20.0
American State Bank & Trust Co.	Great Bend	KS	B-	B-	C+	401.7	20.42	8.9	1.2	2.6	26.3	7.0	10.4	12.5
American State Bank of Grygla	Grygla	MN	B	B	B-	49.4	2.04	5.6	7.1	14.7	15.9	9.8	10.8	18.3
American Trust & Savings Bank	Dubuque	IA	B-	B-	C+	1077.2	7.21	14.8	2.3	6.5	8.6	6.9	10.9	12.5
▼ American Trust and Savings Bank	Lowden	IA	B-	B	B	34.9	-1.63	1.9	2.0	1.6	40.7	10.0	17.8	42.7
American Trust Bank	Kirksville	MO	B-	B-	C+	59.2	-5.29	2.9	0.9	32.6	6.8	10.0	11.2	19.2
American Trust Bank of East Tennessee	Knoxville	TN	B	B-	B-	142.0	3.21	9.9	1.1	14.1	10.6	10.0	13.1	20.0
Americana Community Bank	Sleepy Eye	MN	E-	D-	E-	122.9	3.42	8.7	0.6	7.3	16.2	3.1	5.5	10.1
▼ Americas United Bank	Glendale	CA	B	B+	B-	227.3	3.81	6.4	0.0	0.3	4.0	8.8	11.3	14.0

Asset Quality Index	Adjusted Non-Performing Loans as a % of Total Loans	as a % of Capital	Net Charge-Offs Avg Loans	Profitability Index	Net Income ($Mil)	Return on Assets (R.O.A.)	Return on Equity (R.O.E.)	Net Interest Spread	Overhead Efficiency Ratio	Liquidity Index	Liquidity Ratio	Hot Money Ratio	Stability Index
3.4	1.61	10.6	0.00	5.6	2.7	1.30	11.60	3.34	54.2	3.0	13.4	14.0	7.7
6.3	1.47	9.2	0.01	5.0	11.6	1.22	12.98	3.79	69.6	6.5	36.9	2.4	8.8
6.2	0.51	2.1	3.80	6.4	0.5	1.17	11.92	7.90	48.9	3.0	54.4	27.1	3.9
7.6	0.35	2.3	0.02	4.7	3.6	1.13	11.52	3.65	69.5	1.5	15.2	24.4	6.4
9.1	0.26	1.3	-0.02	3.9	9.8	0.76	9.38	3.05	69.3	7.1	50.4	2.7	6.5
4.5	1.44	7.2	0.30	10.0	5.2	2.50	12.51	4.87	39.7	0.8	6.8	27.9	8.3
3.0	1.44	9.8	-0.15	4.4	1.5	0.97	8.18	4.07	74.1	0.6	13.3	53.0	5.4
7.0	0.60	2.8	-0.02	4.9	1.3	0.98	6.95	4.27	77.2	3.0	24.6	14.9	7.7
6.8	1.01	4.4	0.15	4.7	3.2	0.82	6.08	3.05	62.4	4.4	38.3	12.1	7.3
5.2	1.21	9.3	0.02	5.0	1.3	0.87	8.94	3.93	65.4	2.4	12.0	16.8	5.4
7.6	0.07	0.4	-0.02	6.2	1.6	1.07	7.82	3.36	54.7	1.4	31.8	37.9	7.4
4.8	0.29	2.7	0.30	6.9	1.5	1.04	11.86	4.59	57.4	0.6	9.6	41.9	4.9
6.8	0.06	0.4	0.18	3.8	0.3	0.52	4.72	3.67	73.0	0.6	14.9	50.6	5.1
0.3	5.35	29.8	-0.11	0.0	-4.2	-2.55	-24.49	3.23	177.2	1.7	21.2	23.3	4.1
8.4	0.01	0.1	-0.06	4.3	0.3	1.02	8.88	3.88	67.1	2.9	18.0	14.6	5.6
2.9	3.59	20.6	-0.07	7.5	0.9	2.06	17.09	5.40	62.5	4.2	20.1	8.3	6.4
9.3	0.00	0.0	0.01	4.3	0.5	1.03	9.66	3.35	70.4	5.5	67.1	11.8	6.3
5.5	0.72	3.8	1.32	10.0	2468.0	6.42	46.21	5.45	52.0	3.9	21.1	0.6	9.1
4.4	0.99	3.7	2.28	10.0	1323.6	4.83	28.05	5.49	52.4	2.2	39.6	0.0	8.8
8.0	0.09	0.7	0.00	5.2	5.4	1.32	14.40	4.14	65.9	2.3	9.6	5.0	7.2
5.8	0.94	5.6	0.10	7.4	11.9	1.30	10.19	4.21	52.2	1.0	21.0	41.5	10.0
0.3	9.91	54.2	0.88	2.3	-0.6	-0.77	-6.09	3.44	123.2	2.7	19.5	13.4	1.8
4.7	2.43	12.1	-0.01	5.3	0.7	1.12	10.55	4.36	65.9	3.0	40.8	20.8	6.4
8.8	0.47	1.8	-0.07	4.0	7.9	0.98	10.30	3.19	71.5	4.2	28.6	13.2	8.1
7.4	0.18	1.0	-0.01	7.2	2.1	1.12	9.12	3.75	55.1	4.3	20.3	4.3	7.6
8.6	0.00	0.0	-0.20	8.6	1.6	2.04	14.00	3.71	46.6	3.6	11.6	10.4	9.3
8.1	0.23	1.9	0.27	3.1	0.2	0.34	4.07	3.31	66.1	1.8	17.3	20.3	2.6
0.8	4.74	28.2	0.68	4.1	0.7	1.44	12.81	4.22	73.7	0.8	20.9	56.3	2.4
5.4	1.40	6.7	0.07	6.0	8.3	0.98	5.61	4.13	64.4	4.3	9.8	6.5	9.5
5.6	1.94	10.0	0.06	6.4	4.4	1.57	14.95	3.88	60.6	1.6	33.8	38.0	7.4
6.3	0.00	0.0	0.05	5.9	2.1	1.01	7.79	3.91	56.7	4.1	16.8	8.0	7.1
4.4	0.89	6.9	0.09	5.4	26.9	1.21	12.82	3.68	66.7	4.3	8.3	5.4	9.3
7.4	0.64	3.1	0.03	6.0	4.5	1.17	8.63	3.80	71.1	3.6	15.4	11.0	8.1
7.3	0.43	2.5	0.01	5.8	13.0	1.10	7.82	3.60	61.3	2.0	15.5	19.3	10.0
4.0	1.33	9.3	0.54	3.8	0.6	0.72	7.33	3.78	78.6	4.6	19.3	5.4	5.5
5.3	2.06	11.1	-0.03	4.3	2.0	1.12	8.97	4.68	74.8	1.3	15.3	22.0	6.5
5.3	3.37	14.0	0.07	6.9	1.2	1.68	12.48	4.32	61.9	2.5	26.1	18.0	7.9
8.1	0.23	1.7	0.04	4.8	19.9	1.01	10.57	3.70	70.0	4.2	9.4	6.7	8.2
4.9	1.27	6.2	-0.02	7.1	3.0	1.63	12.27	3.42	53.6	0.9	25.0	24.0	9.2
0.3	4.93	99.1	0.07	0.5	-0.1	-0.31	-14.84	3.97	106.7	1.5	8.7	22.0	0.0
6.9	0.27	1.8	0.00	7.9	3.8	1.18	9.79	3.48	40.4	0.7	11.4	41.7	7.9
7.0	0.68	2.6	-0.01	7.7	2.0	1.95	10.31	4.33	61.9	0.9	20.0	36.0	7.3
4.7	1.50	6.8	-0.30	5.4	4.8	1.01	7.44	3.64	61.6	4.8	44.1	11.8	8.1
7.4	0.02	0.2	-0.05	5.9	3.0	0.94	9.02	4.92	66.1	4.7	22.7	5.1	6.7
8.9	0.00	0.0	0.05	7.7	0.7	1.71	9.09	3.70	44.6	4.5	64.2	16.7	9.2
8.2	0.83	3.3	0.00	3.0	0.1	0.34	1.72	4.45	95.1	3.9	10.7	8.5	5.9
5.0	1.38	11.0	0.19	5.3	41.1	0.89	9.53	3.59	62.0	4.5	13.1	5.7	8.5
5.7	0.51	4.0	0.09	4.8	1.8	0.89	8.08	4.11	75.1	1.9	12.4	19.1	5.5
7.8	0.19	1.4	0.05	7.3	2.3	1.67	17.52	4.11	61.5	1.0	8.5	29.9	7.0
2.7	1.84	12.2	-0.10	8.5	10.9	1.79	14.94	3.66	47.4	1.9	11.1	19.1	8.8
4.6	1.45	11.6	0.05	3.5	1.7	0.79	7.35	3.55	75.4	0.9	9.0	31.9	7.5
5.8	1.93	7.8	0.11	7.8	8.1	1.75	16.86	3.41	49.9	5.7	39.9	5.0	7.8
7.6	0.05	0.3	-0.01	5.7	3.0	1.09	9.76	4.17	64.6	3.7	10.5	10.2	6.7
8.1	0.00	0.0	0.01	5.4	0.5	1.32	11.93	3.94	68.5	4.2	30.7	11.0	6.4
6.9	0.49	3.3	0.01	4.1	6.0	0.77	6.99	3.34	78.3	4.3	12.6	6.5	7.5
8.8	0.23	0.3	-0.42	3.1	0.1	0.31	1.71	3.19	81.2	5.6	71.8	12.4	7.3
6.4	1.33	8.3	0.03	4.5	0.4	0.79	7.61	3.29	63.4	1.8	24.4	22.7	4.9
4.8	1.41	6.7	-1.66	7.4	1.4	1.31	10.10	3.86	75.2	1.5	26.6	28.6	6.4
2.3	3.44	31.2	-0.11	1.5	0.1	0.07	1.22	3.58	100.2	5.4	37.5	5.9	0.7
6.7	0.20	1.4	-0.01	3.5	0.8	0.48	4.02	3.33	76.8	1.2	16.9	28.7	7.9

Name	City	State	2015 Rating	2014 Rating	Rating	Total Assets ($Mil)	One Year Asset Growth	Comm-ercial Loans	Cons-umer Loans	Mort-gage Loans	Secur-ities	Capital-ization Index	Lever-age Ratio	Risk-Based Capital Ratio
AmeriFirst Bank	Union Springs	AL	C-	D+	D	151.1	7.76	11.2	2.8	19.7	23.5	9.0	10.3	14.8
Ameriprise National Trust Bank	Minneapolis	MN	U	U	U	28.2	-30.83	0.0	0.0	0.0	25.8	10.0	102.	361.9
Ameris Bank	Moultrie	GA	B	B	B-	6488.0	24.40	4.6	1.2	23.8	13.0	5.5	9.3	11.4
AmeriServ Financial Bank	Johnstown	PA	C-	C+	C+	1127.3	4.41	13.7	1.7	16.3	12.3	5.6	8.6	11.4
AmeriState Bank	Atoka	OK	B+	B+	B+	224.5	2.86	9.6	8.9	19.8	4.6	7.5	9.3	13.6
AmFirst Bank	McCook	NE	C+	B-	B-	255.3	-1.50	7.6	5.8	4.9	14.7	7.3	10.0	12.7
AMG National Trust Bank	Greenwood Village	CO	A-	A-	A-	374.1	30.11	1.8	3.9	3.6	45.2	6.0	8.0	13.3
▲ Amistad Bank	Del Rio	TX	B	B-	B-	28.2	-1.84	2.2	1.1	4.8	0.0	10.0	13.8	18.7
▲ Amory Federal S&L Assn.	Amory	MS	C+	C	D+	88.5	-3.21	0.0	0.7	71.1	6.4	10.0	11.9	26.1
Anahuac National Bank	Anahuac	TX	A-	A-	B	112.9	-1.30	5.4	8.3	17.9	29.0	10.0	11.1	18.8
ANB Bank	Denver	CO	B-	B-	C+	2585.6	4.96	6.3	0.3	11.2	34.8	5.6	7.6	13.0
Anchor Bank	Aberdeen	WA	C+	C+	C+	436.1	14.51	8.4	1.2	16.0	6.6	10.0	13.3	15.3
Anchor Bank, N.A.	Saint Paul	MN	B+	B+	B+	2012.9	3.18	25.1	0.7	5.7	18.1	6.9	9.4	12.4
▲ Anchor Commercial Bank	Juno Beach	FL	C	D	E	110.0	4.29	9.7	2.6	12.8	12.0	9.7	10.8	16.8
Anchor D Bank	Texhoma	OK	C	B	B+	176.5	2.16	8.8	6.9	5.9	22.8	9.8	10.8	15.0
Anchor State Bank	Anchor	IL	C+	C-	D	14.1	-6.78	6.4	1.5	2.3	14.1	10.0	12.3	20.0
▲ Andalusia Community Bank	Andalusia	IL	C+	C-	D	39.9	1.42	4.6	6.3	44.2	14.4	10.0	14.6	27.3
Anderson Brothers Bank	Mullins	SC	C-	D	D-	584.7	14.68	6.2	29.5	17.6	5.0	6.6	9.4	12.2
Anderson State Bank	Oneida	IL	C+	C+	C+	85.1	5.20	2.6	2.5	5.4	40.6	10.0	14.1	30.4
Andes State Bank	Lake Andes	SD	C-	C	C-	26.6	5.77	4.6	7.0	6.5	15.7	7.9	9.6	18.0
Andover Bank	Andover	OH	B	B+	B+	401.2	13.41	1.4	0.9	31.1	38.9	7.8	9.5	21.7
Andover State Bank	Andover	KS	C+	C+	C	81.4	0.58	10.5	1.2	26.3	6.8	6.6	8.6	12.4
Andrew Johnson Bank	Greeneville	TN	B+	B+	B	344.2	6.65	5.9	1.6	33.1	10.8	8.3	9.9	14.4
Androscoggin Savings Bank	Lewiston	ME	C+	C+	B-	921.8	7.46	11.2	0.1	24.7	9.1	9.1	10.9	14.2
Angelina Savings Bank, SSB	Lufkin	TX	C+	B-	B-	65.0	-0.21	5.9	15.3	19.7	0.6	6.3	8.3	21.7
Ann Arbor State Bank	Ann Arbor	MI	A-	A-	A-	270.5	7.95	19.7	0.8	7.7	24.7	9.2	11.2	14.4
Anna State Bank	Anna	IL	B+	B+	B+	74.1	-1.98	1.6	2.6	24.0	40.4	10.0	16.8	36.1
Anna-Jonesboro National Bank	Anna	IL	B	B	B-	236.2	2.26	3.7	5.3	26.4	42.4	10.0	13.3	25.6
Annandale State Bank	Annandale	MN	B-	B-	B-	143.2	6.28	6.2	0.8	17.8	36.0	6.0	12.0	11.8
Anstaff Bank	Green Forest	AR	B	B+	B+	444.0	2.69	7.1	2.4	11.8	22.0	7.3	9.2	13.2
Anthem Bank & Trust	Plaquemine	LA	D+	D	D	135.2	1.73	11.5	1.4	27.3	21.9	8.4	9.9	17.0
Antwerp Exchange Bank Co.	Antwerp	OH	B-	B-	B-	99.5	2.71	5.6	3.5	23.8	12.9	8.6	10.1	14.1
ANZ Guam, Inc.	Hagatna	GU	C-	C	C	369.2	7.57	14.8	0.5	9.7	0.0	10.0	14.0	53.4
Apex Bank	Camden	TN	B-	B-	C+	435.1	14.81	3.9	2.9	43.0	2.3	10.0	17.1	23.2
Apollo Bank	Miami	FL	C+	C	C-	556.2	8.85	5.2	4.3	19.5	11.5	7.3	9.8	12.7
Apollo Trust Co.	Apollo	PA	B-	B	B	159.8	0.35	5.3	0.8	25.6	45.1	9.0	10.4	20.3
Apple Bank for Savings	New York	NY	C+	C+	C+	12874.6	4.07	44.9	0.1	1.6	5.5	4.3	6.4	12.4
Apple Creek Banking Co.	Apple Creek	OH	C+	C+	C+	140.8	6.43	4.7	0.3	22.8	14.9	5.1	7.1	11.5
Apple River State Bank	Apple River	IL	B	B-	B-	313.4	6.24	12.4	3.6	12.0	31.2	8.1	9.7	15.6
▲ Applied Bank	Wilmington	DE	A-	B+	A	170.2	-15.15	0.6	0.0	2.9	0.0	10.0	15.4	55.9
Aquesta Bank	Cornelius	NC	B-	B-	C+	342.9	26.52	9.7	0.3	7.7	20.6	5.5	8.1	11.4
Arbor Bank	Nebraska City	NE	C+	C+	C+	280.4	5.76	11.0	1.7	14.1	11.6	4.7	8.2	10.9
Arcola First Bank	Arcola	IL	B	B+	B+	116.0	-0.73	0.6	0.2	3.3	78.5	10.0	12.0	36.0
Argentine Federal Savings	Kansas City	KS	C	D+	C	50.8	2.64	0.0	0.4	70.5	13.5	10.0	14.0	29.4
Arizona Bank & Trust	Phoenix	AZ	B	B	B	574.6	-4.22	15.5	1.6	18.5	22.8	8.0	9.7	14.3
Arkansas County Bank	De Witt	AR	C+	B-	B	173.2	-5.98	5.0	2.8	15.7	29.5	9.9	10.9	17.9
Arlington Bank	Upper Arlington	OH	A-	A-	B+	305.4	7.40	4.0	0.5	37.6	8.3	10.0	11.7	17.8
Arlington State Bank	Arlington	MN	B-	B	B-	56.2	-2.26	2.8	1.5	3.4	40.9	8.4	9.9	22.1
Armed Forces Bank, N.A.	Fort Leavenworth	KS	A	A	B	1087.6	1.06	19.7	0.6	11.2	26.9	10.0	20.6	29.9
Armstrong Bank	Muskogee	OK	C	C+	B+	887.4	6.48	5.9	7.2	23.3	12.4	8.6	10.1	14.2
Armstrong County Building and Loan Assn.	Ford City	PA	C	C-	C+	86.3	-1.22	0.0	1.0	57.0	31.5	10.0	14.4	32.1
Aroostook County Federal S&L Assn.	Caribou	ME	B-	B-	B-	113.7	7.18	7.9	3.7	60.5	10.1	10.0	11.2	19.1
Arrowhead Bank	Llano	TX	C+	C+	C+	162.0	-2.11	4.9	4.7	17.5	17.4	7.7	9.5	16.5
▲ Arthur State Bank	Union	SC	C	D+	E-	465.6	-5.91	5.8	1.7	27.4	15.4	6.6	8.6	13.1
▲ Artisans' Bank	Wilmington	DE	C-	E-	E-	507.8	7.52	4.9	0.2	17.9	20.1	5.7	8.0	11.5
Arundel Federal Savings Bank	Glen Burnie	MD	C+	C+	C+	450.8	-3.40	0.0	0.0	58.6	30.6	10.0	13.8	32.8
Arvest Bank	Fayetteville	AR	C+	C+	C	17047.2	9.35	8.7	5.9	15.1	27.8	5.6	7.6	13.1
Asheville Savings Bank, SSB	Asheville	NC	B-	C+	C	796.2	0.15	2.9	3.3	24.0	13.9	10.0	11.4	16.2
Ashton State Bank	Ashton	IA	B+	B	B+	49.6	1.32	4.9	2.3	10.2	31.8	10.0	11.5	15.9
Ashton State Bank	Ashton	NE	D-	D	D	22.7	-1.55	1.9	2.5	0.3	4.0	7.8	10.0	13.1

Asset Quality Index	Adjusted Non-Performing Loans as a % of Total Loans	as a % of Capital	Net Charge-Offs Avg Loans	Profitability Index	Net Income ($Mil)	Return on Assets (R.O.A.)	Return on Equity (R.O.E.)	Net Interest Spread	Overhead Efficiency Ratio	Liquidity Index	Liquidity Ratio	Hot Money Ratio	Stability Index
5.8	0.59	3.7	-0.20	2.5	0.4	0.39	3.63	3.93	90.8	2.9	11.2	14.1	5.0
10.0	na	0.0	na	9.2	2.9	12.26	14.20	1.30	82.8	4.0	na	0.0	7.7
4.9	1.08	9.0	0.06	7.0	58.1	1.25	10.68	4.27	64.0	3.9	11.1	9.2	7.6
7.1	0.20	1.7	0.58	2.2	2.1	0.24	2.70	3.44	79.1	3.4	6.3	11.1	7.2
7.1	0.10	0.7	0.10	7.9	3.1	1.84	20.13	4.69	66.9	1.5	14.6	23.9	6.3
4.3	1.14	8.0	0.35	4.0	1.5	0.79	7.78	4.18	75.8	1.8	11.0	19.8	6.2
8.9	0.00	0.0	0.00	8.3	3.2	1.23	14.79	1.96	78.8	6.3	37.4	0.2	5.9
7.7	0.00	0.0	0.29	4.4	0.2	0.76	5.59	4.43	80.8	3.9	25.6	10.5	6.4
6.9	1.31	7.7	0.29	2.7	0.3	0.41	3.48	3.18	77.3	1.2	29.0	49.5	5.6
7.7	0.73	3.6	0.05	6.4	1.3	1.51	13.52	4.58	68.8	2.4	21.6	17.8	7.4
9.0	0.20	1.4	-0.05	4.4	22.3	1.18	14.01	3.33	67.7	4.8	19.9	4.5	7.0
4.0	1.69	10.0	0.15	3.0	1.3	0.41	2.93	4.22	86.1	1.6	7.8	20.1	5.7
7.4	0.37	2.7	0.03	5.9	14.3	0.98	9.81	3.67	61.0	4.8	10.8	3.0	7.9
3.4	1.57	9.2	-0.04	3.0	0.4	0.44	4.11	3.72	89.7	1.7	34.8	33.0	3.6
7.9	0.06	0.4	1.16	3.3	0.6	0.49	4.71	4.23	62.7	0.6	2.9	33.9	8.0
8.1	0.11	0.4	-1.20	6.4	0.2	2.13	18.33	3.43	74.1	4.6	44.5	10.7	4.5
5.9	1.93	8.2	0.07	3.3	0.3	0.86	5.82	4.15	81.0	5.1	29.4	5.0	5.6
2.2	1.12	8.7	1.08	7.5	4.8	1.17	12.34	7.88	62.9	1.1	10.2	28.4	5.1
9.1	0.29	0.7	-0.01	2.9	0.4	0.59	4.09	2.14	72.4	5.4	68.1	12.9	6.8
7.8	0.32	1.4	0.05	3.6	0.1	0.66	6.82	3.05	68.3	2.3	42.7	31.3	4.2
6.2	0.98	4.8	0.02	4.6	3.1	1.02	9.80	3.79	71.4	5.2	41.6	9.0	6.0
6.4	0.63	5.4	0.00	3.4	0.3	0.46	5.46	4.06	83.1	3.7	11.9	10.1	5.0
5.7	0.66	4.9	0.09	6.5	2.5	1.00	10.14	4.60	64.3	4.1	17.0	8.1	6.1
4.5	0.81	5.8	0.11	3.8	4.3	0.67	5.90	3.53	75.4	2.8	13.7	11.6	7.0
5.9	0.78	4.3	0.08	3.4	0.2	0.46	5.36	3.46	83.2	5.7	55.6	9.1	4.2
6.5	0.51	3.0	0.03	6.9	2.6	1.37	12.06	3.75	58.2	2.1	28.1	20.5	7.1
9.0	0.26	0.7	0.09	4.8	0.5	0.95	5.82	3.60	63.1	3.7	45.0	17.5	7.8
3.7	5.48	20.8	0.03	5.6	1.8	1.03	7.55	3.87	59.9	2.4	33.0	21.7	6.9
5.1	2.73	11.4	0.00	4.2	1.0	0.94	7.70	3.60	76.3	5.4	34.9	4.8	6.6
7.0	0.15	1.0	-0.01	5.3	4.3	1.33	14.53	3.63	65.0	2.5	19.8	16.6	6.9
4.7	1.22	7.3	0.04	1.6	0.1	0.12	1.20	3.62	98.1	1.7	19.3	22.8	5.0
4.1	1.62	11.7	0.06	4.3	0.6	0.76	7.44	3.81	72.1	4.0	12.3	8.2	5.8
5.6	3.00	7.8	0.03	1.5	0.0	0.01	0.05	2.57	99.0	6.8	71.6	6.3	5.8
2.6	4.22	21.2	0.24	10.0	12.0	4.13	22.61	8.00	29.9	0.6	10.6	52.4	8.0
4.9	0.59	4.4	0.01	4.0	3.0	0.74	7.31	4.06	71.2	3.6	20.1	11.6	5.9
9.5	0.00	0.0	0.02	4.0	0.9	0.79	7.29	3.92	79.5	5.6	43.8	7.0	6.8
7.4	0.05	0.6	0.01	3.5	44.1	0.46	5.72	1.81	55.3	1.6	14.6	23.4	6.1
6.5	0.37	3.2	0.04	3.8	0.6	0.61	8.35	4.00	76.5	5.4	31.1	3.3	4.2
5.0	0.97	5.7	0.06	5.2	3.0	1.31	13.29	3.51	62.3	2.7	20.7	16.1	5.1
9.3	0.00	0.0	0.09	5.9	3.0	1.49	9.52	2.11	56.7	8.0	80.1	0.3	8.3
8.7	0.07	0.5	0.12	4.4	1.8	0.74	9.96	3.67	73.0	3.5	17.9	12.0	3.6
4.0	1.56	14.4	0.02	4.2	1.8	0.90	10.94	3.77	78.2	2.4	6.7	16.1	3.9
10.0	0.00	0.0	0.00	3.9	0.7	0.77	5.83	2.58	69.6	6.7	83.2	8.9	8.1
9.3	0.53	2.7	0.00	2.0	0.1	0.27	1.90	3.60	87.8	1.9	17.9	19.7	6.3
6.5	0.38	2.6	-0.27	6.8	6.0	1.40	13.25	4.35	64.2	4.4	24.9	6.4	6.1
3.6	2.01	10.8	0.45	5.0	1.6	1.24	11.45	4.21	65.4	2.5	18.0	16.7	6.4
6.5	1.06	6.8	0.01	8.0	3.1	1.40	12.36	3.80	60.5	1.9	22.0	20.9	7.2
8.5	0.64	2.3	0.15	4.4	0.5	1.09	11.23	3.13	65.7	5.6	57.0	9.8	6.1
6.0	3.79	9.9	-0.78	6.4	6.9	0.88	3.91	3.08	82.6	4.8	20.7	5.1	9.3
2.9	1.71	12.2	0.29	9.6	14.8	2.27	18.80	5.55	59.5	1.7	17.7	22.7	8.2
7.5	2.16	9.5	0.00	1.8	0.0	0.06	0.44	1.45	85.2	2.0	39.0	34.7	6.9
5.7	1.69	11.4	0.12	3.5	0.5	0.55	4.81	3.50	75.0	2.4	23.9	17.7	6.0
7.1	0.85	5.0	-0.01	3.4	0.7	0.57	6.13	3.16	74.0	5.5	37.9	5.9	5.4
3.9	1.87	13.7	0.03	3.7	2.2	0.62	7.05	3.90	77.3	4.3	18.1	7.2	2.6
2.7	2.46	19.3	-0.12	3.2	2.0	0.53	5.68	3.41	81.1	3.0	24.8	14.9	4.4
7.2	2.07	9.4	0.03	2.5	1.0	0.30	2.17	2.47	79.8	2.6	39.7	25.1	6.9
4.1	1.40	9.8	0.17	3.7	70.4	0.57	5.69	3.04	82.5	6.1	33.6	3.8	6.9
7.3	0.56	3.5	0.05	3.9	4.8	0.81	7.33	3.29	72.4	3.9	20.3	6.1	6.8
8.6	0.18	0.9	-0.01	7.4	0.7	1.81	15.55	3.64	45.6	3.6	31.7	14.4	7.5
0.0	12.73	78.6	-0.11	4.0	0.2	0.87	8.97	4.09	71.0	1.6	22.7	24.0	4.6

Name	City	State	2015 Rating	2014 Rating	Rating	Total Assets ($Mil)	One Year Asset Growth	Comm-ercial Loans	Cons-umer Loans	Mort-gage Loans	Secur-ities	Capital-ization Index	Lever-age Ratio	Risk-Based Capital Ratio
Asian Bank	Philadelphia	PA	C	C-	D	161.8	24.54	0.4	0.0	11.8	5.1	5.7	7.7	11.7
Asian Pacific National Bank	San Gabriel	CA	C+	B-	B	57.4	0.50	0.7	0.0	3.7	39.7	10.0	16.4	30.4
Associated Bank, N.A.	Green Bay	WI	B-	B-	B-	29058.9	6.31	17.4	1.4	21.8	21.0	6.4	8.4	12.3
Associated Trust Co., N.A.	Milwaukee	WI	U	U	U	52.2	63.69	0.0	0.0	0.0	1.9	10.0	93.4	169.6
Astoria Bank	Lake Success	NY	B-	B-	C+	14718.9	-1.74	0.7	0.1	37.6	20.6	10.0	11.8	22.1
▼ Astra Bank	Belleville	KS	B-	B	B	256.2	-6.52	8.7	1.9	10.0	23.5	6.7	9.3	12.3
Atascosa National Bank	Pleasanton	TX	C-	C-	C-	92.6	-0.60	3.7	1.1	2.8	31.3	5.9	7.9	26.4
Athens Federal Community Bank, N.A.	Athens	TN	A-	A-	B	426.1	35.61	5.5	3.7	24.5	13.1	10.0	11.2	18.5
Athens State Bank	Athens	IL	B	B-	B-	136.9	2.30	3.9	7.2	24.5	28.0	8.9	10.3	18.8
Athol Savings Bank	Athol	MA	C+	B-	B-	381.7	7.25	1.1	5.3	46.0	28.1	10.0	13.3	24.1
Atkins Savings Bank & Trust	Atkins	IA	A-	A-	B+	82.1	4.63	8.1	3.6	13.1	32.9	10.0	12.8	18.8
Atlanta National Bank	Atlanta	IL	B-	C+	C+	57.2	-0.37	2.9	3.6	10.7	61.8	10.0	12.9	30.5
▲ Atlantic Capital Bank, N.A.	Chattanooga	TN	C	C	D+	2760.0	141.63	19.3	1.1	3.6	12.9	6.3	10.3	12.0
▲ Atlantic Coast Bank	Jacksonville	FL	C	D	E	936.3	14.68	3.7	4.5	31.8	5.2	7.1	9.1	13.4
Atlantic Community Bank	Bluffton	SC	C+	C+	D+	81.9	2.00	2.2	0.6	29.0	0.9	8.1	9.7	14.0
Atlantic Community Bankers Bank	Camp Hill	PA	B	B	B	578.2	-3.82	1.6	0.0	0.5	16.5	10.0	12.8	24.0
Atlantic National Bank	Brunswick	GA	B-	B-	B-	166.1	4.58	4.0	1.2	35.2	9.0	9.4	10.6	21.8
Atlantic Stewardship Bank	Midland Park	NJ	B-	C+	C	755.3	6.97	5.0	0.0	14.5	20.7	7.5	9.4	13.1
Atlantic Trust Co., N.A.	Atlanta	GA	U	U	U	201.2	8.95	0.0	0.0	0.0	0.0	10.0	72.7	155.2
Auburn Banking Co.	Auburn	KY	B-	B-	B-	76.0	6.01	6.5	6.3	27.3	17.1	6.8	8.8	13.8
▲ Auburn Savings Bank, FSB	Auburn	ME	C-	D-	D	70.9	-1.09	4.2	0.3	61.3	5.9	7.3	9.2	15.8
Auburn State Bank	Auburn	NE	A-	A	A-	172.3	78.84	3.9	1.6	10.4	41.2	10.0	16.2	27.7
AuburnBank	Auburn	AL	B+	B	B	852.4	4.11	5.5	1.1	12.6	29.3	8.9	10.3	17.7
▼ Audubon Savings Bank	Audubon	NJ	D-	D	D-	165.0	-10.30	1.1	0.0	31.9	22.7	4.8	6.8	12.7
Audubon State Bank	Audubon	IA	B	B	B	106.8	-1.15	7.7	3.6	10.7	10.4	8.1	9.7	14.1
▼ Austin Bank, Texas N.A.	Jacksonville	TX	B+	A-	A	1576.2	0.49	8.7	6.3	25.8	10.3	10.0	12.6	17.6
Austin Capital Bank SSB	Austin	TX	B+	B+	B	102.1	22.99	2.3	1.7	37.1	1.8	9.9	10.9	19.8
Austin County State Bank	Bellville	TX	B+	B+	B	141.7	10.33	16.1	2.4	25.1	14.0	8.0	9.7	14.9
Auto Club Trust, FSB	Dearborn	MI	D	D	D	401.2	111.26	0.0	8.7	25.7	41.2	10.0	15.8	30.7
AVB Bank	Broken Arrow	OK	B-	B-	C+	308.9	11.57	15.6	0.6	12.6	14.0	10.0	12.2	16.1
Avidbank	Palo Alto	CA	B	B-	B-	679.3	17.77	21.0	0.9	1.4	14.8	5.4	9.7	11.3
Avidia Bank	Hudson	MA	C+	C+	C+	1342.6	9.08	20.7	0.7	26.1	13.8	4.8	8.0	10.9
Avon Co-operative Bank	Avon	MA	D+	C-	C-	89.6	-3.40	0.2	0.5	68.0	15.8	9.1	10.4	21.8
Avon State Bank	Avon	MN	B+	A-	B-	108.8	3.81	2.7	3.8	22.4	37.2	10.0	11.8	33.2
Axiom Bank, N.A.	Maitland	FL	B	B	B	634.2	-9.83	0.6	0.0	52.3	6.0	10.0	15.0	26.5
▲ BAC Community Bank	Stockton	CA	B-	C+	C	587.0	11.88	4.8	1.2	6.2	28.3	7.8	9.5	14.7
BAC Florida Bank	Coral Gables	FL	C+	C+	C	1926.1	12.64	7.1	0.3	54.4	3.7	6.2	8.2	14.9
Badger Bank	Fort Atkinson	WI	B+	A-	B+	133.3	6.80	2.5	2.7	33.0	18.1	10.0	11.0	19.8
Baker-Boyer National Bank	Walla Walla	WA	B	B	B	583.2	4.20	9.3	0.8	11.9	34.1	6.7	8.7	15.5
Balboa Thrift and Loan Assn.	Chula Vista	CA	B+	B	B-	235.7	9.71	0.1	76.7	1.4	0.0	10.0	15.6	17.8
Baldwin State Bank	Baldwin City	KS	C+	C	C	69.6	5.06	4.8	4.5	18.4	43.7	9.4	10.6	26.7
Ballinger National Bank	Ballinger	TX	C	C	C	46.1	-1.94	5.3	3.5	10.4	52.7	8.1	9.7	22.4
Ballston Spa National Bank	Ballston Spa	NY	C+	C+	C+	439.8	2.22	5.3	4.9	31.6	18.8	7.1	9.1	13.6
Bally Savings Bank	Bally	PA	C-	C-	C-	53.4	-4.10	0.0	0.0	49.6	15.5	7.0	9.0	24.1
Baltic State Bank	Baltic	OH	B	B	C	49.0	6.77	5.0	4.0	39.1	10.6	10.0	11.2	15.3
Banamex USA	Los Angeles	CA	B-	B-	C+	168.7	-65.44	1.5	8.9	0.2	0.0	10.0	53.0	313.6
Banc of California, N.A.	Irvine	CA	B+	B+	B-	11183.0	54.43	6.1	0.2	30.6	26.3	7.5	9.3	14.4
▼ BancCentral, N.A.	Alva	OK	C	C+	C+	443.8	-6.06	12.0	1.1	3.2	37.8	7.1	9.1	13.9
BancFirst	Oklahoma City	OK	B+	B	B	6769.8	5.92	12.4	4.1	11.7	6.9	6.9	8.9	13.7
▼ Banco Do Brasil Americas	Miami	FL	C	B-	C-	466.3	48.01	3.3	0.8	41.4	15.3	8.5	10.0	19.4
Banco Popular de Puerto Rico	San Juan	PR	C-	C-	D+	30240.0	9.38	5.8	10.6	21.9	19.2	10.0	12.0	19.7
Banco Popular North America	New York	NY	C+	C+	D+	8450.8	13.06	3.4	2.8	10.3	21.9	10.0	13.2	18.4
▲ Banco Santander Puerto Rico	San Juan	PR	C	D+	D+	5256.5	-3.45	14.3	8.8	23.9	4.6	10.0	16.5	26.6
Bancorp Bank	Wilmington	DE	D-	D+	C-	4202.3	-10.85	5.4	14.8	2.5	34.0	5.4	7.4	14.8
BancorpSouth Bank	Tupelo	MS	B+	B+	B	14603.8	6.02	10.1	1.6	19.3	16.7	6.6	9.6	12.2
Bancroft State Bank	Bancroft	WI	C+	C	D+	72.0	-0.08	6.1	3.1	21.9	14.1	10.0	11.3	18.0
Bandera Bank	Bandera	TX	B	B	B	58.9	0.24	5.1	4.9	33.9	8.6	10.0	11.1	26.3
▲ Banesco USA	Coral Gables	FL	C+	C	C	969.9	3.75	14.9	0.0	9.0	16.8	8.1	9.8	13.4
Bangor Savings Bank	Bangor	ME	B-	B-	B-	3585.4	11.65	6.5	0.5	22.4	25.7	8.7	10.1	15.0
Bank & Trust Co.	Litchfield	IL	B-	B-	B-	284.7	4.77	5.9	6.9	16.4	24.8	9.3	10.6	15.6

Asset Quality Index	Adjusted Non-Performing Loans as a % of Total Loans	as a % of Capital	Net Charge-Offs / Avg Loans	Profitability Index	Net Income ($Mil)	Return on Assets (R.O.A.)	Return on Equity (R.O.E.)	Net Interest Spread	Overhead Efficiency Ratio	Liquidity Index	Liquidity Ratio	Hot Money Ratio	Stability Index
2.9	1.61	14.0	0.01	4.0	0.9	0.76	9.11	3.48	64.4	0.9	25.0	43.4	4.2
9.4	0.57	1.2	0.00	2.7	0.2	0.45	2.72	3.16	84.4	1.0	27.9	59.2	7.7
4.2	1.64	12.5	0.38	4.2	162.0	0.76	7.04	2.87	65.9	2.1	15.9	2.2	9.8
10.0	na	0.0	na	9.5	6.5	21.17	23.17	0.83	74.7	4.0	478.3	0.0	5.7
5.2	1.77	10.4	0.04	3.7	64.1	0.57	4.66	2.49	68.5	4.6	13.5	5.0	8.5
3.5	2.38	15.6	0.05	5.1	2.5	1.26	12.22	4.14	73.7	4.3	10.5	5.9	6.7
10.0	0.00	0.0	0.02	2.5	0.3	0.37	4.84	1.82	74.9	6.9	90.9	7.2	3.5
6.0	0.84	4.7	0.06	5.5	2.6	0.89	7.71	4.26	72.4	2.2	21.3	18.7	7.0
4.8	1.60	8.4	-0.01	4.9	1.3	1.29	12.00	3.48	68.1	4.6	40.7	12.4	6.3
9.3	0.37	1.7	0.15	2.9	1.5	0.52	3.74	2.97	83.5	3.6	37.7	16.1	7.2
8.5	0.09	0.4	0.05	7.4	1.0	1.56	12.51	3.66	40.1	3.0	42.7	20.9	7.3
8.8	1.41	3.4	0.19	3.1	0.3	0.77	5.97	3.22	78.2	5.6	56.7	9.9	6.6
7.5	0.40	2.8	0.14	3.6	13.4	0.66	5.34	3.41	70.5	3.7	15.9	4.1	4.5
2.8	2.23	19.3	0.03	3.0	4.6	0.69	7.60	3.09	74.0	1.2	11.1	16.2	3.3
6.7	0.39	3.1	0.43	3.5	0.3	0.52	4.30	4.17	73.2	2.2	17.4	17.8	5.0
8.0	0.90	2.5	0.10	4.3	3.2	0.81	6.29	1.99	73.0	3.3	52.9	24.6	7.3
6.7	0.79	4.2	0.14	4.4	1.3	1.02	9.79	2.85	67.7	4.1	34.3	12.7	6.1
7.0	0.17	1.2	-0.09	4.1	4.3	0.77	8.15	3.41	72.7	2.8	21.4	14.4	5.6
6.5	na	0.0	na	10.0	10.4	7.89	9.39	1.06	79.6	4.4	161.4	100.0	7.0
5.2	0.96	7.2	-0.03	7.9	1.0	1.81	21.27	4.25	62.2	2.5	16.7	16.8	6.4
2.7	2.73	23.9	0.29	3.0	0.2	0.44	4.90	3.96	79.4	1.5	9.3	22.3	4.1
9.0	0.28	0.9	0.06	5.3	1.4	1.07	6.69	3.34	54.6	3.5	27.8	13.4	8.0
7.2	0.45	2.1	-0.27	5.2	6.3	1.01	9.37	3.11	61.0	3.0	31.8	16.1	6.4
6.4	0.44	3.7	0.00	0.1	-0.5	-0.34	-5.13	2.56	115.3	4.1	18.6	8.5	1.6
4.9	0.84	5.8	0.01	7.6	1.4	1.65	17.11	3.65	61.1	1.8	16.9	20.5	6.7
4.3	2.08	12.0	0.24	6.8	13.3	1.13	8.83	4.33	61.2	3.8	11.0	10.1	10.0
9.0	0.11	0.7	0.00	5.5	0.7	0.98	8.71	3.83	62.2	1.6	26.8	27.6	6.8
5.7	1.52	9.8	0.14	5.6	1.3	1.31	13.51	4.25	63.1	0.9	23.4	37.9	6.8
8.8	0.59	2.1	0.09	0.0	-1.5	-0.59	-3.51	1.91	135.9	1.7	36.8	36.7	6.0
6.1	1.21	6.5	-0.04	3.4	1.1	0.47	3.83	3.74	84.3	1.5	13.6	23.4	6.8
7.5	0.14	0.9	-0.01	7.0	6.8	1.44	14.84	4.12	53.2	4.6	33.9	9.7	5.9
5.5	0.70	6.6	0.23	4.0	6.4	0.66	7.38	3.72	74.2	1.6	9.6	12.7	6.8
6.1	1.11	8.0	0.00	1.8	0.1	0.21	2.05	2.37	99.2	1.0	23.4	34.3	5.4
9.4	0.54	1.7	0.01	4.1	0.7	0.92	7.28	2.52	64.7	6.5	68.4	7.8	7.3
5.6	2.72	12.4	0.40	3.4	2.3	0.46	3.21	3.21	82.6	1.0	25.5	40.9	7.5
4.7	1.72	9.8	0.00	4.2	3.8	0.93	9.44	3.69	75.9	5.6	37.1	4.5	5.5
3.7	2.65	23.1	0.07	4.3	10.2	0.73	9.01	2.76	58.7	0.8	17.7	44.0	6.1
6.0	1.41	7.6	0.02	5.8	0.9	0.92	8.10	3.83	67.1	4.5	30.7	9.5	6.2
6.1	0.78	4.0	0.21	4.8	3.9	0.91	10.23	3.45	74.9	6.1	42.3	3.3	6.6
4.9	0.54	3.0	1.39	5.3	0.9	0.53	3.35	7.53	65.6	0.5	9.6	58.6	7.8
7.0	0.71	2.7	-0.04	3.6	0.4	0.78	7.34	2.71	75.1	6.1	46.4	4.3	5.4
4.9	2.39	8.5	0.21	3.3	0.2	0.70	7.12	3.40	83.3	5.1	62.2	13.2	5.7
4.6	0.84	6.5	0.15	3.5	1.7	0.53	6.31	3.56	80.3	4.8	6.2	2.5	4.7
3.1	4.60	27.9	0.00	4.2	0.3	0.76	8.58	2.43	53.4	2.8	45.6	26.1	4.4
8.7	0.03	0.2	-0.10	6.0	0.6	1.50	13.30	5.09	70.9	3.4	16.3	12.1	6.4
8.9	4.64	1.4	0.00	0.9	0.0	0.00	0.00	0.00	0.0	9.8	186.0	0.0	6.7
5.5	1.28	9.1	0.00	6.0	86.3	1.16	12.25	3.50	69.6	3.1	30.1	6.8	7.3
3.7	2.56	13.4	0.07	2.7	3.3	0.97	9.31	3.65	87.7	1.7	26.3	26.5	6.2
6.4	0.63	4.2	0.11	5.5	51.8	1.03	10.87	3.29	60.5	5.6	28.6	5.4	8.1
8.4	0.00	0.0	0.02	2.4	-0.1	-0.03	-0.24	3.00	97.0	1.8	19.7	21.0	5.6
1.0	6.49	29.1	0.79	5.1	203.0	0.94	7.23	4.74	66.2	3.5	20.4	12.3	7.8
3.8	2.19	11.4	0.08	3.2	29.1	0.48	2.11	3.70	69.6	1.9	24.0	25.8	7.4
1.1	7.69	30.6	1.41	3.7	21.0	0.53	3.21	4.45	61.9	3.9	24.7	12.9	7.1
3.5	2.84	18.8	0.01	0.0	-67.7	-0.93	-13.36	2.41	142.4	1.8	29.7	0.0	3.8
5.7	0.67	5.0	0.04	5.4	98.7	0.94	8.25	3.55	72.5	3.9	8.0	8.4	9.0
5.6	1.18	6.7	0.04	4.3	0.6	1.15	9.85	3.73	67.8	4.9	37.2	9.8	4.9
7.9	1.06	5.3	0.06	4.6	0.5	1.06	9.71	3.66	72.8	4.6	42.6	12.4	6.9
4.9	1.13	8.2	0.00	3.5	4.2	0.57	6.07	3.71	85.5	1.8	25.4	21.6	5.5
7.5	0.54	3.4	0.07	3.9	17.7	0.69	6.42	3.08	75.3	3.9	11.2	6.6	8.1
5.8	0.73	4.3	0.01	4.4	1.5	0.72	6.73	3.53	73.4	2.4	23.8	17.7	6.2

Name	City	State	2015 Rating	2014 Rating	Total Assets ($Mil)	One Year Asset Growth	Asset Mix (As a % of Total Assets) Commercial Loans	Consumer Loans	Mortgage Loans	Securities	Capitalization Index	Leverage Ratio	Risk-Based Capital Ratio
Bank @LANTEC	Virginia Beach	VA	D+	C-	C-	112.7	1.88	0.7	0.6	52.3	5.1	9.2	10.5	17.0
▲ Bank 1st	West Union	IA	B+	B	B	121.1	-2.22	5.1	2.7	15.3	20.1	10.0	12.0	17.6
Bank 21	Carrollton	MO	B-	B-	C+	99.8	9.85	16.6	1.9	39.1	6.2	6.3	8.4	12.1
BANK 34	Alamogordo	NM	C	C	C-	328.8	22.34	3.1	0.1	22.1	9.7	8.4	9.9	14.4
Bank 7	Oklahoma City	OK	B	B	B+	618.9	23.58	34.2	0.6	4.9	0.0	5.8	9.5	11.6
Bank and Trust of Bryan/College Station	Bryan	TX	A-	A-	B	518.7	10.43	4.7	0.6	18.4	19.2	8.5	10.0	15.1
Bank and Trust, SSB	Del Rio	TX	B+	B+	B+	434.2	2.04	4.6	2.4	31.8	36.6	6.7	8.8	21.3
Bank First National	Manitowoc	WI	B+	B+	B+	1344.6	12.20	15.9	2.1	18.3	11.4	5.4	8.7	11.3
Bank Forward	Hannaford	ND	B	B-	C+	526.4	6.32	6.3	2.6	11.9	5.8	6.3	9.2	12.0
Bank Independent	Sheffield	AL	B	B+	B+	1284.9	6.81	16.8	1.9	17.2	4.1	4.4	9.6	10.7
Bank Iowa	West Des Moines	IA	B-	B-	B-	1138.3	1.43	6.5	1.2	10.5	22.2	7.8	9.5	13.8
Bank Leumi USA	New York	NY	C+	B-	C-	7128.2	22.24	24.3	0.0	0.4	19.0	7.0	9.0	14.0
Bank Midwest	Spirit Lake	IA	B	B	B	792.9	9.43	20.0	0.9	7.4	5.0	7.1	10.1	12.6
Bank Mutual	Brown Deer	WI	B-	B-	B-	2651.8	7.55	8.3	0.7	21.5	18.3	8.5	10.0	13.9
Bank Northwest	Hamilton	MO	B	B	B	114.9	4.34	4.8	2.4	12.3	13.4	7.2	9.1	13.0
▼ Bank of Abbeville & Trust Co.	Abbeville	LA	C+	B-	B-	183.0	2.72	6.2	2.2	9.4	57.7	10.0	15.5	37.6
Bank of Advance	Advance	MO	A-	A	A	305.1	-0.56	5.9	6.4	30.4	18.2	10.0	15.0	22.9
▼ Bank of Akron	Akron	NY	D+	C	B	292.7	6.80	11.6	0.7	17.1	14.5	7.2	9.4	12.7
Bank of Alapaha	Alapaha	GA	B	B	B	144.5	5.92	20.3	7.5	18.3	14.6	8.1	11.3	13.4
Bank of Alma	Alma	WI	A	A	A-	229.4	5.46	3.1	1.4	8.9	37.2	10.0	41.8	65.1
Bank of America California, N.A.	San Francisco	CA	B	B-	C	22770.0	-2.37	0.0	0.0	57.9	0.0	10.0	13.9	39.9
Bank of America, N.A.	Charlotte	NC	B-	C+	C	1659793.0	2.68	15.0	10.6	11.0	24.8	7.9	9.6	14.3
Bank of Anguilla	Anguilla	MS	B-	B-	B-	140.8	10.26	5.7	5.6	7.7	22.1	8.9	10.3	14.1
Bank of Ann Arbor	Ann Arbor	MI	B+	B+	B	1288.6	5.61	13.8	0.6	6.5	10.6	6.2	8.2	12.2
▼ Bank of Baker	Baker	MT	C+	A-	A-	150.8	-4.56	13.3	1.6	4.1	25.2	8.4	9.9	14.6
Bank of Bartlett	Bartlett	TN	D-	D-	D-	358.7	6.39	4.5	2.5	14.0	26.2	4.4	6.4	12.1
Bank of Bearden	Bearden	AR	B	B	B	42.8	7.52	11.9	12.1	13.2	19.4	10.0	14.2	37.8
▼ Bank of Beaver City	Beaver	OK	B-	B	B-	134.7	-4.15	13.6	3.0	13.3	29.1	8.6	10.1	15.6
Bank of Belle Glade	Belle Glade	FL	C	C	C	97.6	9.71	5.2	0.8	11.5	38.5	6.1	8.1	26.6
Bank of Belleville	Belleville	IL	C+	B-	B-	172.8	24.70	14.5	0.6	12.8	11.0	6.2	8.3	11.9
▲ Bank of Bennington	Bennington	NE	B	B	C	111.7	29.41	19.9	5.2	13.7	13.3	6.0	10.8	11.8
▲ Bank of Bennington	Bennington	VT	B-	C+	C+	409.8	6.56	1.8	0.2	58.4	12.5	7.9	9.6	17.4
Bank of Benoit	Benoit	MS	C-	C-	D+	17.2	-3.13	6.0	9.8	2.0	35.6	10.0	11.8	27.0
Bank of Billings	Billings	MO	C+	C-	C	52.4	2.25	10.6	3.4	32.3	1.7	10.0	11.1	15.3
▲ Bank of Bird-in-Hand	Bird in Hand	PA	C-	D	D	162.5	47.64	7.8	0.1	31.4	0.0	6.8	9.5	12.3
Bank of Birmingham	Birmingham	MI	C	C-	C	301.4	28.03	11.1	1.2	10.1	0.9	4.0	8.5	10.5
Bank of Blue Valley	Overland Park	KS	C	C	C	688.9	7.76	18.6	1.5	5.5	15.8	7.1	10.5	12.6
Bank of Bluffs	Bluffs	IL	B-	B-	B-	57.9	-0.11	4.7	5.8	16.1	29.7	10.0	15.1	23.7
Bank of Bolivar	Bolivar	MO	C+	C+	C+	246.1	6.97	5.1	3.0	25.8	11.4	7.5	9.4	12.9
Bank of Botetourt	Buchanan	VA	C+	C	C+	353.0	10.35	5.8	4.7	25.4	4.6	7.6	9.7	13.0
Bank of Bourbonnais	Bourbonnais	IL	B+	B	B	72.1	-15.97	3.6	4.3	14.0	21.1	10.0	11.0	19.9
Bank of Bozeman	Bozeman	MT	C	C+	D+	65.7	3.06	8.8	1.0	17.1	5.1	8.2	10.8	13.5
Bank of Brenham, N.A.	Brenham	TX	B+	B+	B+	271.2	59.32	2.5	1.1	8.1	73.7	6.1	8.1	23.0
Bank of Brewton	Brewton	AL	C	D+	C	53.7	7.53	7.1	8.6	3.6	40.4	10.0	18.1	32.3
Bank of Bridger, N.A.	Bridger	MT	B	B	B	398.8	1.46	6.0	3.3	9.2	46.1	7.7	9.5	18.8
Bank of Brodhead	Brodhead	WI	A-	B+	B+	141.8	0.79	5.8	1.7	9.2	40.5	10.0	14.7	24.9
▲ Bank of Brookfield-Purdin, N.A.	Brookfield	MO	B-	C+	B-	91.3	-0.24	1.2	1.4	6.0	47.9	10.0	11.3	29.7
Bank of Brookhaven	Brookhaven	MS	B	B+	B+	158.9	5.65	8.6	2.7	12.5	39.7	10.0	11.5	18.6
Bank of Buffalo	Buffalo	KY	B-	B+	B+	77.2	3.85	1.7	7.2	25.8	38.3	9.5	10.7	17.7
Bank of Burlington	Burlington	CO	B	C+	C+	53.7	-27.95	13.7	0.7	0.1	17.8	10.0	14.0	20.3
Bank of Cadiz and Trust Co.	Cadiz	KY	C+	C+	B-	112.2	2.88	2.7	3.8	26.3	30.9	6.2	8.2	16.1
Bank of Cairo and Moberly	Moberly	MO	B+	A-	A	99.3	6.71	8.0	2.8	21.7	25.1	10.0	18.5	26.2
Bank of Calhoun County	Hardin	IL	C	C-	C-	67.1	-3.24	0.8	2.7	28.7	27.3	6.7	8.8	17.0
Bank of Camilla	Camilla	GA	B+	B	C	100.2	3.69	6.3	1.5	10.5	35.6	10.0	15.2	24.4
Bank of Canton	Canton	MA	C+	C+	C	665.6	2.75	3.7	0.3	39.4	10.5	8.3	9.8	14.9
Bank of Carbondale	Carbondale	IL	A-	B+	B-	251.0	15.37	7.2	2.7	13.5	23.9	10.0	11.6	18.6
▲ Bank of Cashton	Cashton	WI	B	B	C+	82.6	6.87	17.4	1.9	11.5	21.4	9.0	10.3	14.4
Bank of Castile	Castile	NY	B	B	B	1366.7	10.13	12.9	0.7	15.8	23.0	4.4	7.7	10.7
Bank of Cattaraugus	Cattaraugus	NY	D+	D+	D+	21.3	7.23	3.9	7.3	16.6	33.6	6.4	8.4	22.3
Bank of Cave City	Cave City	AR	B-	B-	B-	106.0	8.16	4.1	4.3	22.8	10.1	6.5	8.5	14.6

Asset Quality Index	Adjusted Non-Performing Loans as a % of Total Loans	as a % of Capital	Net Charge-Offs Avg Loans	Profitability Index	Net Income ($Mil)	Return on Assets (R.O.A.)	Return on Equity (R.O.E.)	Net Interest Spread	Overhead Efficiency Ratio	Liquidity Index	Liquidity Ratio	Hot Money Ratio	Stability Index
7.1	0.42	3.2	0.03	1.9	0.1	0.10	0.84	3.15	95.5	3.6	13.7	11.0	6.2
8.5	0.03	0.2	0.03	5.5	1.2	1.33	11.26	3.79	61.8	4.3	28.8	9.4	7.4
6.5	0.26	2.4	0.01	5.7	1.0	1.38	15.71	4.14	66.7	2.6	7.7	15.5	4.8
5.2	0.48	3.7	0.00	3.0	1.1	0.50	4.71	4.37	91.5	2.9	16.9	14.6	4.3
4.5	0.70	5.8	0.10	10.0	12.2	2.80	29.97	5.51	41.2	1.6	16.2	22.7	7.8
8.8	0.04	0.2	-0.01	8.0	5.5	1.47	14.91	4.11	47.9	4.6	23.1	5.7	7.7
8.9	0.04	0.2	0.01	4.7	3.8	1.17	11.97	3.44	71.4	3.4	22.9	12.8	7.3
8.2	0.11	0.9	-0.06	6.7	11.7	1.19	12.92	3.23	50.1	4.2	16.6	8.4	8.2
4.2	1.22	10.0	0.00	6.2	5.9	1.52	14.45	4.15	74.7	3.3	7.8	10.3	7.2
4.7	1.06	8.7	0.27	5.5	8.6	0.93	8.88	5.49	73.7	2.8	7.3	14.1	8.6
7.1	0.56	3.7	0.04	4.4	9.5	1.12	11.70	3.42	67.0	4.1	24.8	11.9	7.5
4.6	2.10	14.3	0.17	3.4	17.8	0.36	3.71	2.80	76.5	1.2	21.9	39.0	6.6
5.2	0.61	4.7	0.05	5.9	7.8	1.33	12.14	4.30	70.2	2.1	9.5	18.0	8.3
7.1	0.54	3.8	0.03	4.0	13.3	0.69	6.88	2.99	68.9	4.1	18.6	9.0	6.7
4.3	1.63	12.3	0.08	8.5	1.8	2.03	23.14	4.43	51.8	3.0	13.6	13.7	7.0
8.1	1.32	2.6	0.06	2.4	0.5	0.33	2.10	2.85	87.8	4.0	63.8	20.7	7.5
5.6	1.68	7.7	0.21	10.0	5.5	2.37	16.57	4.74	52.9	2.4	10.6	16.4	9.5
1.6	3.46	25.6	0.54	4.3	1.4	0.67	6.81	4.15	72.2	3.2	8.7	12.3	6.3
6.3	0.60	3.6	0.14	5.2	0.9	0.88	7.75	4.18	60.5	1.5	16.9	24.8	6.3
7.0	2.67	3.8	-0.03	10.0	4.0	2.36	5.77	4.24	17.6	7.0	62.2	3.9	9.0
5.6	3.74	15.2	0.10	9.1	246.0	1.45	10.49	2.82	17.9	7.3	47.7	0.0	8.1
4.0	1.59	8.7	0.44	6.4	14747.0	1.20	9.44	2.87	53.4	6.5	40.4	3.0	9.7
3.9	2.17	12.1	0.74	4.2	0.8	0.74	7.45	4.60	76.2	0.8	8.0	33.1	3.6
8.5	0.31	2.3	0.09	7.3	12.6	1.37	17.12	3.83	52.7	4.7	24.4	8.1	7.0
2.9	5.01	27.9	-0.03	9.0	2.3	2.04	20.38	4.08	46.3	4.9	20.6	3.6	7.8
2.6	3.59	28.8	0.20	1.9	0.6	0.23	2.95	3.27	91.9	4.7	28.7	6.8	1.7
8.0	0.09	0.4	0.00	5.4	0.5	1.39	10.15	4.01	60.9	3.4	22.9	13.0	7.8
3.7	2.37	13.7	0.32	4.8	1.2	1.17	11.52	4.12	72.6	1.7	20.3	23.6	7.0
6.7	1.79	5.9	0.00	2.8	0.3	0.35	4.24	2.25	77.6	6.7	59.6	3.0	4.0
5.9	0.41	3.4	0.05	3.4	0.7	0.58	7.12	3.31	71.8	1.4	25.1	20.2	4.3
5.0	0.67	4.2	0.21	6.6	0.9	1.20	9.86	4.38	65.1	4.8	20.7	4.1	7.0
7.0	0.56	4.3	-0.04	4.1	2.4	0.79	8.35	3.02	65.4	1.8	15.4	13.2	5.7
6.4	2.91	7.1	0.25	2.6	0.0	0.25	2.20	4.32	91.3	3.0	74.6	32.6	3.9
6.3	0.41	2.9	0.08	4.0	0.2	0.55	3.50	4.61	79.2	4.4	13.6	6.1	5.7
8.8	0.00	0.0	0.00	2.1	0.5	0.48	4.50	2.48	67.3	1.5	16.5	24.6	2.9
5.4	0.32	3.0	0.48	5.2	1.8	0.86	10.45	3.94	58.8	1.5	17.8	13.8	5.1
6.2	0.32	2.1	0.30	2.9	2.1	0.44	3.86	3.53	82.0	4.1	21.0	8.4	5.7
6.3	1.17	4.9	0.13	3.5	0.3	0.66	4.67	3.93	82.1	2.0	25.1	15.3	6.8
7.3	0.21	1.7	0.13	3.6	1.1	0.63	6.58	3.81	77.4	2.3	10.5	16.9	5.2
3.5	1.92	15.3	0.29	4.5	1.8	0.70	7.22	3.98	71.8	1.7	13.7	21.7	4.6
8.7	0.00	0.0	0.13	3.1	0.3	0.45	4.32	2.42	73.4	1.3	24.6	30.9	6.3
8.7	0.00	0.0	-0.01	2.6	0.2	0.35	3.24	4.44	91.6	1.3	19.9	29.2	4.5
7.2	0.97	2.0	0.08	3.6	1.4	0.77	5.93	3.16	64.2	2.5	50.7	42.9	7.7
4.3	7.46	15.1	0.05	2.7	0.3	0.72	4.10	4.19	81.5	5.3	37.6	7.3	6.5
7.6	0.50	2.4	0.14	4.7	2.8	0.92	9.12	3.47	60.8	3.0	32.2	17.4	5.9
8.2	0.85	3.1	0.00	5.2	1.0	0.93	6.28	3.70	62.3	2.9	45.6	26.5	8.2
9.5	0.21	0.5	-0.09	3.5	0.6	0.84	7.37	2.69	71.9	6.0	61.4	7.8	6.7
8.9	0.07	0.3	0.05	4.9	1.2	1.05	9.17	3.90	66.8	5.0	38.0	9.4	6.8
3.8	3.28	16.0	0.01	9.3	1.2	2.16	19.82	3.81	41.9	2.1	45.7	22.1	7.7
8.8	0.00	0.0	0.00	4.6	0.5	1.12	8.38	3.67	67.0	4.6	47.5	13.3	5.3
8.2	0.24	1.6	0.00	3.1	0.6	0.69	8.07	3.44	81.8	3.1	30.6	16.6	3.9
4.9	4.01	12.0	0.22	6.6	1.0	1.38	7.66	3.59	59.8	6.1	43.0	3.6	9.0
4.9	2.11	12.6	0.00	3.7	0.4	0.80	8.30	2.76	72.4	3.8	28.4	12.3	4.4
5.8	3.45	9.3	-0.62	5.3	0.9	1.21	7.90	3.95	72.7	2.9	48.3	27.6	7.2
5.2	0.89	6.7	-0.03	3.8	2.9	0.57	6.36	3.56	80.6	4.2	12.3	6.8	5.5
5.8	1.71	8.3	0.37	6.0	1.7	1.06	8.77	3.52	59.2	5.1	32.4	6.1	7.1
5.8	0.73	4.4	0.09	6.4	0.9	1.55	14.03	3.72	59.3	4.2	34.0	11.8	7.6
8.5	0.21	1.9	0.02	7.0	12.0	1.21	16.09	3.50	50.7	1.9	2.9	14.2	6.7
8.9	0.53	2.3	0.23	2.9	0.1	0.37	4.71	4.26	90.1	5.2	28.8	2.0	3.2
4.3	1.34	10.9	0.28	5.6	1.1	1.42	15.60	4.52	65.4	1.6	9.1	21.5	5.5

Name	City	State	2015 Rating	Rating	2014 Rating	Total Assets ($Mil)	One Year Asset Growth	Asset Mix (As a % of Total Assets) Comm-ercial Loans	Cons-umer Loans	Mort-gage Loans	Secur-ities	Capital-ization Index	Lever-age Ratio	Risk-Based Capital Ratio
Bank of Central Florida	Lakeland	FL	B	B-	B-	425.0	-0.27	16.3	2.1	15.0	24.3	6.2	8.3	11.9
Bank of Charles Town	Charles Town	WV	C+	C	C-	374.3	12.12	3.5	2.3	38.2	6.7	6.7	9.1	12.3
Bank of Charlotte County	Phenix	VA	A-	A-	A-	131.5	0.69	6.5	3.9	39.3	16.0	10.0	14.3	21.4
Bank of Cherokee County	Hulbert	OK	C+	B-	C+	101.6	-3.56	4.6	7.8	24.3	5.0	6.8	8.8	15.6
Bank of Chestnut	Chestnut	IL	D+	D+	D+	17.4	2.33	4.0	10.2	29.1	16.1	9.5	10.7	15.4
Bank of Clarendon	Manning	SC	A-	A-	A-	247.8	8.26	5.8	2.8	12.8	21.5	10.0	14.0	24.3
Bank of Clarke County	Berryville	VA	B+	B+	B+	660.7	4.05	4.6	2.0	29.6	16.0	10.0	11.4	15.2
Bank of Clarks	Clarks	NE	D+	D-	D	35.4	2.39	6.2	11.4	4.8	9.7	7.6	11.3	13.0
Bank of Clarkson	Clarkson	KY	A-	A-	A-	121.1	4.32	4.4	4.5	26.3	35.9	10.0	12.5	22.3
Bank of Cleveland	Cleveland	TN	B	B	B	242.4	9.59	3.0	0.8	18.6	2.4	10.0	16.5	20.4
Bank of Clovis	Clovis	NM	B-	B-	B	209.5	-4.81	9.6	3.3	7.7	46.6	9.8	10.9	27.5
Bank of Colorado	Fort Collins	CO	A-	A-	B+	3203.4	9.88	3.7	1.0	13.7	23.4	6.8	8.8	13.3
Bank of Columbia	Columbia	KY	C-	D+	D	133.5	4.34	8.7	5.9	20.6	18.4	8.5	10.0	14.4
Bank of Commerce	Sarasota	FL	E-	E-	E-	195.7	-7.23	5.8	0.3	6.0	14.3	0.2	3.3	7.9
Bank of Commerce	Ammon	ID	A	A	A-	1064.4	6.38	12.2	1.2	3.1	17.0	10.0	15.5	21.5
Bank of Commerce	Chanute	KS	B-	B-	B-	176.3	-0.76	8.6	3.2	15.1	40.0	6.5	8.5	17.5
▲ Bank of Commerce	White Castle	LA	B	B-	C+	59.2	5.67	14.7	3.1	8.8	23.1	10.0	12.4	18.1
Bank of Commerce	Greenwood	MS	B+	B+	B	362.7	4.76	7.6	3.7	21.8	20.6	7.5	9.3	13.4
Bank of Commerce	Chelsea	OK	B+	A-	B	141.4	-9.46	10.9	6.2	12.4	22.0	10.0	12.3	17.3
Bank of Commerce	Chouteau	OK	C	C	C+	38.6	1.72	4.8	4.8	16.9	26.7	6.7	8.7	18.0
▼ Bank of Commerce	Duncan	OK	D+	C+	B	282.4	-2.46	18.1	2.9	6.9	5.1	8.0	11.3	13.3
Bank of Commerce	Stilwell	OK	A-	A-	B+	82.5	-5.13	21.2	4.9	8.2	24.6	10.0	12.3	19.3
Bank of Commerce	McLean	TX	B+	B+	B+	38.3	7.10	26.7	0.2	5.4	13.3	10.0	13.9	27.4
Bank of Commerce	Rawlins	WY	B+	B	B	123.8	-4.26	7.7	2.2	15.4	38.6	10.0	12.3	23.9
Bank of Commerce & Trust Co.	Crowley	LA	B-	B-	C+	333.8	1.32	3.7	2.3	6.2	67.1	10.0	12.1	27.8
▼ Bank of Commerce and Trust Co.	Wellington	KS	B-	B	B-	59.7	6.18	6.5	4.9	16.5	46.6	7.5	9.3	20.7
Bank of Cordell	Cordell	OK	C+	C+	C	44.4	2.97	13.4	1.3	41.8	0.7	6.2	8.2	12.6
Bank of Coushatta	Coushatta	LA	B-	B-	C+	205.0	3.54	2.6	2.9	12.4	63.7	8.0	9.7	18.8
▲ Bank of Crocker	Waynesville	MO	C-	D+	D+	125.7	0.97	2.9	3.1	19.5	26.4	9.1	10.4	20.8
▲ Bank of Crockett	Bells	TN	A-	B+	B	146.8	4.93	4.7	2.0	3.2	60.9	10.0	11.6	23.6
Bank of Cushing	Cushing	OK	A-	A-	B+	115.3	-3.20	10.6	4.5	2.3	58.6	10.0	12.8	19.0
Bank of Dade	Trenton	GA	B+	B+	A-	96.9	4.61	0.8	4.7	19.9	51.9	10.0	12.0	28.5
Bank of Dawson	Dawson	GA	A-	A-	B+	108.5	-1.67	6.4	3.9	19.4	15.9	10.0	19.0	27.3
Bank of Deerfield	Deerfield	WI	A	A	A-	136.0	5.47	6.7	1.1	35.1	4.7	10.0	13.0	15.5
Bank of Delight	Delight	AR	A-	A-	A-	100.0	7.43	5.8	3.5	15.0	13.5	10.0	18.3	24.1
Bank of Delmarva	Salisbury	MD	C-	D+	D	508.9	5.29	7.2	0.5	18.7	10.0	7.4	9.3	12.9
Bank of Denton	Denton	KS	C+	C+	C+	16.7	-5.84	2.0	10.1	21.9	37.9	10.0	18.9	36.4
Bank of Denver	Denver	CO	D	C	B-	187.2	-17.90	0.4	7.3	9.0	15.1	10.0	11.0	15.8
Bank of DeSoto, N.A.	Desoto	TX	B+	B-	C+	191.7	-0.67	6.0	16.3	13.4	1.7	8.3	9.9	17.7
Bank of Dickson	Dickson	TN	B	B+	B+	226.6	-0.13	4.0	2.0	36.0	33.5	10.0	12.6	24.6
Bank of Dixon County	Ponca	NE	B	B	B-	92.8	11.68	6.3	5.5	11.6	22.3	8.7	10.1	19.0
Bank of Doniphan	Doniphan	NE	B-	B-	B-	105.7	3.87	11.5	5.5	16.0	18.5	5.4	9.0	11.3
Bank of Dudley	Dublin	GA	B	B	B-	210.6	7.11	7.4	4.5	17.9	15.0	10.0	11.2	17.9
Bank of Early	Blakely	GA	C	C+	B-	132.1	18.32	9.5	3.8	13.6	2.7	6.3	9.2	11.9
Bank of Eastern Oregon	Heppner	OR	D+	C-	C-	376.1	10.37	9.2	1.0	5.0	5.0	7.7	10.1	13.1
▲ Bank of Eastman	Eastman	GA	D	D-	E	172.4	-5.36	6.6	5.3	22.6	7.4	6.2	8.3	13.0
Bank of Easton	North Easton	MA	B-	B-	B-	133.1	5.31	0.0	0.4	43.7	21.0	10.0	11.3	24.8
Bank of Edison	Edison	GA	C	C	C+	45.5	7.91	4.3	5.9	9.1	39.8	8.7	10.2	17.9
Bank of Edmonson County	Brownsville	KY	B+	A-	A-	214.9	8.51	3.0	3.3	28.1	21.1	10.0	11.7	19.3
Bank of Edwardsville	Edwardsville	IL	B-	B-	B-	1787.4	2.81	4.1	1.4	9.7	44.9	8.7	10.1	18.9
Bank of Elgin	Elgin	NE	B+	B+	B-	56.5	-0.84	1.8	1.5	1.1	6.5	10.0	11.7	16.9
Bank of Elk River	Elk River	MN	C+	C-	D+	395.6	9.02	15.6	2.1	9.3	25.4	7.5	9.3	15.0
Bank of England	England	AR	A-	B+	B	348.0	-1.67	7.2	1.1	56.3	4.9	10.0	12.7	26.7
Bank of Erath	Erath	LA	B	B+	B+	101.8	3.16	27.7	3.9	15.6	17.4	10.0	12.8	19.6
▲ Bank of Estes Park	Estes Park	CO	B-	C	C	126.5	-2.79	2.7	0.2	11.6	29.5	7.9	9.6	18.4
Bank of Eufaula	Eufaula	OK	B	C-	C+	100.9	7.96	4.5	7.2	16.8	47.0	10.0	13.6	33.7
▲ Bank of Evergreen	Evergreen	AL	C+	D+	C+	61.2	3.94	11.4	4.4	23.8	23.8	10.0	11.1	19.2
Bank of Fairport	Maysville	MO	E-	E+	E	23.2	2.18	5.7	2.5	13.5	43.9	5.4	7.4	16.8
Bank of Farmington	Farmington	IL	A-	A-	A-	157.6	11.38	5.9	5.2	15.9	24.3	10.0	11.5	16.1
Bank of Fayette County	Piperton	TN	C	C	C-	457.6	23.15	3.9	7.9	30.7	10.7	6.3	8.4	12.1

Asset Quality Index	Adjusted Non-Performing Loans		Net Charge-Offs Avg Loans	Profitability Index	Net Income ($Mil)	Return on Assets (R.O.A.)	Return on Equity (R.O.E.)	Net Interest Spread	Overhead Efficiency Ratio	Liquidity Index	Liquidity Ratio	Hot Money Ratio	Stability Index
	as a % of Total Loans	as a % of Capital											
8.2	0.25	1.9	0.01	4.9	2.7	0.86	10.09	3.49	59.6	5.3	31.8	4.2	4.8
4.6	1.31	11.4	0.08	4.0	1.7	0.62	7.15	3.63	75.7	2.7	6.4	14.0	4.1
7.2	0.81	3.9	-0.10	6.0	1.1	1.07	7.49	4.55	64.6	2.8	16.2	15.3	7.8
6.1	0.62	4.2	0.18	3.1	0.3	0.39	4.54	3.87	88.3	2.2	31.5	23.1	4.9
2.9	1.21	8.4	0.03	3.4	0.1	0.48	4.41	4.18	85.2	1.6	13.9	21.3	4.3
8.7	0.51	2.0	0.00	5.8	2.0	1.07	7.82	3.66	63.2	2.8	25.3	15.9	8.2
5.0	2.14	13.8	0.07	5.1	4.6	0.94	8.08	4.06	73.0	4.2	20.8	8.0	7.7
2.0	1.23	8.5	0.71	4.5	0.2	0.72	6.54	4.80	72.9	4.7	12.6	3.4	5.7
8.3	0.24	1.1	0.05	6.9	1.1	1.26	9.76	3.94	59.5	4.7	45.4	13.1	7.9
3.3	2.79	14.0	0.21	9.6	2.6	1.50	9.26	4.64	56.3	4.5	7.3	4.4	9.0
7.4	1.12	4.3	1.04	4.5	1.3	0.80	7.45	3.87	63.5	3.8	35.3	14.4	6.5
6.5	0.83	5.8	0.05	6.6	37.2	1.63	16.20	3.45	58.6	4.2	16.0	8.1	8.8
2.5	2.61	16.6	0.19	6.6	1.7	1.69	16.14	4.25	60.4	2.9	23.3	15.1	5.8
0.0	4.40	64.9	-0.81	2.3	0.9	0.59	19.95	2.80	113.7	1.7	24.4	23.6	0.1
8.5	0.32	1.2	0.39	7.3	10.3	1.32	8.55	3.91	47.8	5.0	43.8	13.5	9.5
7.8	0.32	1.8	0.01	3.4	1.1	0.78	9.17	2.71	74.4	3.8	15.7	10.0	5.2
8.5	0.00	0.0	0.15	4.2	0.4	0.94	7.71	3.88	75.4	3.2	6.9	12.1	6.5
5.8	0.69	4.7	0.16	7.5	3.7	1.43	14.70	4.10	44.1	0.8	10.1	33.2	6.4
3.7	4.32	21.7	1.56	3.9	0.7	0.58	4.77	4.14	74.1	1.6	11.5	21.6	7.2
7.9	0.09	0.5	0.07	4.4	0.3	1.00	11.87	4.28	77.7	4.5	30.6	9.3	5.0
1.5	5.16	32.1	0.09	7.0	3.2	1.48	12.26	5.22	53.9	1.6	13.1	22.9	8.1
6.5	0.68	3.5	0.06	7.8	1.2	1.82	14.14	5.03	56.9	3.1	15.1	13.7	7.0
8.8	0.67	1.9	0.01	8.0	0.6	2.05	14.11	3.23	53.5	3.5	54.7	19.0	8.0
8.5	0.75	3.0	0.04	5.2	1.0	1.03	8.28	3.96	64.5	1.5	18.0	25.1	7.5
9.5	0.67	1.5	0.14	3.6	1.6	0.62	5.43	2.41	66.4	4.4	46.6	14.6	5.9
6.4	1.37	5.9	0.00	4.0	0.4	0.79	8.10	3.20	75.5	3.4	35.3	16.7	6.0
8.6	0.00	0.0	-0.05	9.0	0.7	2.23	27.68	4.51	50.9	0.6	3.0	27.0	5.7
5.5	4.26	12.7	-0.25	4.9	2.0	1.32	12.39	3.28	62.0	3.1	44.5	21.5	5.2
4.5	2.35	10.4	0.13	2.1	0.4	0.40	3.78	3.29	86.6	2.2	28.7	21.3	5.0
9.2	0.39	1.0	0.01	6.0	1.3	1.24	10.01	3.69	53.9	3.3	50.0	22.8	7.1
6.3	2.60	7.0	-0.07	6.2	1.1	1.28	9.79	4.76	71.6	4.4	70.8	19.6	8.5
7.0	1.48	5.1	-0.71	5.3	1.0	1.39	11.51	3.83	68.8	5.5	48.6	8.7	6.6
5.6	2.61	9.9	0.11	7.5	1.2	1.36	7.45	5.00	53.0	1.6	14.0	22.7	7.4
7.6	0.53	3.4	0.01	9.5	2.1	2.25	16.93	4.17	55.1	0.6	10.3	50.4	9.5
7.1	0.16	0.6	0.07	6.3	1.1	1.51	8.19	3.73	56.4	1.3	20.5	28.9	8.8
2.2	2.19	16.9	0.39	4.8	3.0	0.81	8.67	3.80	65.1	2.0	15.4	13.5	5.3
7.0	1.80	4.7	0.17	4.1	0.1	0.93	5.11	3.40	66.9	5.5	43.1	4.2	6.0
0.9	3.40	20.0	0.08	4.2	1.0	0.74	6.63	4.05	74.3	4.1	15.1	7.8	5.6
5.5	0.70	3.7	0.43	7.4	2.3	1.57	16.02	7.47	64.0	2.7	45.0	28.6	7.5
5.9	2.47	11.7	0.07	3.9	1.2	0.73	5.50	3.41	72.1	3.4	32.6	15.7	7.2
5.6	0.82	4.4	0.06	4.7	0.7	0.96	9.50	3.40	59.9	3.5	28.3	13.8	5.3
7.6	0.02	0.2	0.00	3.6	0.5	0.60	5.69	4.03	81.4	4.0	13.7	8.4	6.5
4.8	1.71	9.8	0.09	4.8	1.3	0.81	7.26	4.07	71.6	3.5	18.7	11.7	6.3
3.2	1.99	17.3	0.04	3.6	0.4	0.50	5.09	4.75	85.6	1.1	12.1	29.8	4.9
2.3	2.67	18.8	-0.20	5.8	2.6	0.95	9.16	5.26	70.7	4.3	15.3	6.4	5.8
1.3	5.34	39.9	-0.41	3.5	0.7	0.53	6.51	4.38	88.3	1.8	17.2	20.1	1.3
10.0	0.25	1.2	0.00	3.5	0.6	0.60	5.24	2.60	69.7	3.9	43.4	16.2	6.5
6.1	0.67	3.7	0.13	3.8	0.3	0.88	8.87	3.81	79.4	3.2	33.5	16.9	4.7
4.7	2.86	16.3	0.05	6.5	2.4	1.52	12.92	3.88	62.6	0.9	19.7	35.8	7.9
8.2	0.83	3.2	0.10	3.8	9.2	0.71	6.61	2.52	75.0	4.3	27.1	11.8	8.0
6.9	0.00	0.0	0.00	7.6	0.7	1.79	14.92	3.62	52.8	4.7	24.7	5.0	7.2
3.5	1.96	12.3	-0.01	6.9	3.3	1.16	11.75	3.88	67.3	4.6	35.4	10.6	4.8
5.1	2.02	12.0	-0.04	10.0	7.1	2.83	23.06	3.69	86.7	0.6	5.9	36.1	8.9
5.2	3.39	17.1	0.91	3.8	0.5	0.59	4.44	4.21	79.0	2.3	22.3	18.3	7.6
9.3	0.00	0.0	0.00	4.1	0.9	1.01	10.08	3.20	72.6	6.9	53.5	1.9	6.1
6.4	2.44	6.0	1.89	4.8	1.0	1.26	8.97	3.58	65.1	3.5	46.5	19.3	6.6
3.4	3.09	16.9	0.40	6.5	0.5	1.10	9.80	4.65	58.1	1.7	30.3	28.4	5.4
4.9	2.38	11.8	-0.04	0.0	-0.2	-0.91	-11.64	3.75	128.9	4.7	27.8	4.8	1.3
8.4	0.08	0.5	0.23	5.3	1.0	0.90	7.56	3.61	60.4	1.6	24.7	25.7	6.8
2.8	1.94	17.3	0.08	6.2	3.5	1.13	13.02	4.47	60.9	0.9	5.5	29.9	4.3

Name	City	State	2015 Rating	2014 Rating	Rating	Total Assets ($Mil)	One Year Asset Growth	Comm-ercial Loans	Cons-umer Loans	Mort-gage Loans	Secur-ities	Capital-ization Index	Lever-age Ratio	Risk-Based Capital Ratio
Bank of Feather River	Yuba City	CA	A-	A-	B	91.1	24.84	11.9	0.2	6.4	0.0	10.0	12.2	15.6
▼ Bank of Fincastle	Fincastle	VA	D-	D-	C	224.6	2.02	5.9	1.3	14.1	21.0	7.7	9.5	13.4
Bank of Forest	Forest	MS	B	B	B	161.0	7.08	4.4	4.7	8.3	35.4	10.0	13.7	23.5
▲ Bank of Frankewing	Frankewing	TN	B+	B-	C-	221.6	3.86	9.8	4.5	19.1	3.9	10.0	11.8	17.1
Bank of Franklin	Meadville	MS	B	B	B-	135.3	3.05	10.3	4.6	19.8	30.1	7.3	9.2	14.8
Bank of Franklin County	Washington	MO	C-	C	C-	212.1	2.25	9.9	1.5	25.0	12.2	6.3	9.8	12.0
Bank of Galesville	Galesville	WI	A-	B	B	95.0	-0.50	6.1	3.0	18.9	13.9	10.0	18.0	23.5
Bank of Geneva	Geneva	IN	A	A	A-	231.0	5.24	6.2	1.5	26.6	2.8	10.0	12.1	16.9
Bank of George	Las Vegas	NV	A-	B-	C-	159.5	19.33	12.9	0.5	2.3	3.9	10.0	14.4	17.6
Bank of Gibson City	Gibson City	IL	C+	C+	C+	79.4	2.28	5.4	3.6	10.1	23.5	6.6	8.6	15.3
Bank of Gleason	Gleason	TN	A-	A-	B+	120.0	-0.72	1.9	6.4	10.0	63.4	10.0	19.9	43.9
Bank of Glen Burnie	Glen Burnie	MD	C-	C-	C	390.4	-0.91	1.0	19.5	25.2	25.2	6.6	8.6	14.7
▼ Bank of Glen Ullin	Glen Ullin	ND	D-	C+	B-	57.6	-2.48	3.6	1.5	2.3	0.9	6.7	9.5	12.3
Bank of Grain Valley	Kansas City	MO	A-	A-	A-	87.6	5.59	12.6	1.0	7.2	24.6	10.0	21.6	39.9
Bank of Grandin	Grandin	MO	B	B	B	153.5	-0.52	10.3	5.9	12.4	37.0	10.0	15.4	23.3
▲ Bank of Gravett	Gravette	AR	B-	D+	B	113.5	-6.51	4.5	4.8	22.6	19.4	10.0	13.4	22.0
Bank of Greeley	Greeley	KS	B+	B+	B+	36.4	-0.02	5.1	4.7	15.4	13.4	10.0	12.9	23.3
▲ Bank of Greeleyville	Greeleyville	SC	C	C-	D+	83.3	-2.10	12.8	11.9	12.7	13.7	9.1	10.4	16.5
Bank of Greene County	Catskill	NY	B+	B+	B+	891.2	16.23	4.4	0.5	34.9	34.5	6.5	8.5	16.1
Bank of Grove	Grove	OK	B-	C+	C	148.6	2.02	4.4	2.0	33.8	13.4	5.9	7.9	12.2
Bank of Guam	Hagatna	GU	C+	C+	C+	1832.8	16.38	9.4	11.5	9.0	24.3	5.0	7.0	12.3
Bank of Gueydan	Gueydan	LA	C+	C+	C+	78.5	-2.69	3.5	6.7	1.9	62.2	10.0	19.7	49.9
▲ Bank of Halls	Halls	TN	B+	B	B-	75.2	0.49	13.9	2.1	6.9	43.5	10.0	11.1	18.2
▲ Bank of Hamilton	Hamilton	ND	C+	D+	C+	18.9	3.11	6.1	4.2	0.5	20.1	10.0	13.7	45.2
Bank of Hancock County	Sparta	GA	B+	B+	B+	85.0	-0.75	4.1	5.8	17.4	60.1	10.0	23.4	46.2
▲ Bank of Harlan	Harlan	KY	C	C	B-	128.1	-1.24	10.1	1.7	20.2	42.0	10.0	11.7	22.2
Bank of Hartington	Hartington	NE	B-	B-	C+	86.1	7.59	12.0	2.0	6.6	18.3	6.1	8.1	11.8
Bank of Hawaii	Honolulu	HI	B	B	B	16037.0	5.49	5.0	4.7	21.8	38.1	4.9	6.9	14.0
Bank of Hays	Hays	KS	B	B	B-	264.2	3.05	14.8	1.8	9.2	31.3	6.7	8.8	14.9
Bank of Hazelton	Hazelton	ND	C+	B-	C+	47.5	-0.85	0.8	0.8	0.5	25.8	6.7	8.7	18.3
▲ Bank of Hazlehurst	Hazlehurst	GA	C+	D+	D	128.8	7.61	24.3	4.9	5.1	16.6	10.0	11.6	18.1
Bank of Hemet	Riverside	CA	A	A	A	651.3	2.83	1.8	0.1	0.7	6.3	7.5	9.3	13.7
Bank of Herrin	Herrin	IL	B-	B-	B-	253.5	2.37	6.5	2.7	16.1	30.6	7.6	9.4	15.1
Bank of Hillsboro	Hillsboro	MO	B	B-	B	66.2	1.46	6.6	1.1	7.2	24.6	10.0	11.2	16.1
Bank of Hindman	Hindman	KY	C+	B-	B	197.3	6.85	4.0	1.3	11.3	55.5	8.5	10.0	17.9
Bank of Holland	Holland	NY	B-	C+	C+	112.6	18.64	0.9	2.9	39.7	21.0	6.9	8.9	14.8
Bank of Holly Springs	Holly Springs	MS	B	B-	C+	215.2	1.23	6.9	10.6	24.1	15.7	10.0	14.6	23.7
Bank of Holyrood	Holyrood	KS	B+	B+	B+	62.6	0.12	16.3	10.3	24.3	15.9	10.0	12.9	20.8
▲ Bank of Hope	Los Angeles	CA	B-	C+	C+	13504.4	78.21	12.5	0.3	2.9	11.6	8.0	12.8	13.3
Bank of Houston	Houston	MO	D-	D-	D-	41.9	0.70	3.4	1.3	5.9	28.0	6.9	8.9	16.3
Bank of Hydro	Hydro	OK	A-	A-	B+	125.9	-1.00	5.0	3.0	31.9	0.6	8.2	9.8	13.5
▲ Bank of Iberia	Iberia	MO	D+	D+	D	59.2	4.93	2.9	7.7	30.0	17.7	6.2	8.2	15.1
▲ Bank of Idaho	Idaho Falls	ID	B+	B-	C+	286.7	6.30	13.2	3.3	8.2	17.4	9.0	10.4	14.4
Bank of Jackson	Jackson	TN	B-	B-	B-	165.0	7.96	6.5	1.2	11.5	58.8	8.5	10.0	21.0
Bank of Jackson Hole	Jackson	WY	A-	B	C+	654.0	8.68	4.8	0.4	15.3	14.2	10.0	11.3	15.6
Bank of Jamestown	Jamestown	KY	B-	B-	B-	180.7	4.67	2.0	2.0	9.5	44.3	10.0	11.1	16.2
Bank of Kampsville	Kampsville	IL	B	B+	B+	106.0	-0.32	3.6	7.1	17.4	34.1	10.0	16.3	24.9
▼ Bank of Kaukauna	Kaukauna	WI	D+	D+	D	90.5	1.03	20.0	1.7	16.6	7.3	8.1	9.8	13.9
Bank of Kilmichael	Kilmichael	MS	B	B	B	158.8	10.57	15.5	5.3	12.5	29.7	6.8	8.8	14.6
Bank of Kirksville	Kirksville	MO	B	B	C+	435.7	-4.88	4.0	0.7	17.6	45.9	8.5	10.0	25.7
▼ Bank of Kremlin	Kremlin	OK	C	A-	B-	266.2	4.25	5.0	4.4	7.1	6.7	9.3	10.5	14.7
Bank of Labor	Kansas City	KS	C-	D+	D+	572.2	7.30	17.3	0.3	3.8	41.1	7.9	9.6	16.1
Bank of LaFayette, Georgia	Lafayette	GA	B	B	B	230.4	0.34	0.9	5.4	22.6	55.6	10.0	14.3	35.7
▲ Bank of Lake Mills	Lake Mills	WI	B-	B-	C+	210.3	-2.05	3.2	8.6	35.6	9.3	10.0	11.4	16.2
Bank of Lake Village	Lake Village	AR	A-	A-	A-	65.3	1.59	2.8	2.0	3.6	31.9	9.8	10.9	21.4
Bank of Lancaster	Kilmarnock	VA	C+	C	C	463.9	9.79	6.2	0.8	41.4	11.3	6.9	8.9	13.6
Bank of Landisburg	Landisburg	PA	B+	A-	B+	267.0	4.60	1.2	1.6	46.3	22.1	10.0	18.5	32.4
Bank of Laverne	Laverne	OK	B+	B+	B+	59.2	-5.55	6.8	9.6	1.1	24.6	10.0	16.9	26.2
Bank of Lee's Summit	Lee's Summit	MO	B	B	B-	314.6	4.83	5.4	0.3	5.5	26.6	10.0	12.1	22.9
Bank of Lewellen	Lewellen	NE	B-	B-	B	23.5	-3.76	3.2	1.6	0.1	26.8	10.0	25.2	50.8

Asset Quality Index	Adjusted Non-Performing Loans as a % of Total Loans	as a % of Capital	Net Charge-Offs Avg Loans	Profitability Index	Net Income ($Mil)	Return on Assets (R.O.A.)	Return on Equity (R.O.E.)	Net Interest Spread	Overhead Efficiency Ratio	Liquidity Index	Liquidity Ratio	Hot Money Ratio	Stability Index
8.4	0.00	0.0	0.00	7.5	0.7	1.10	8.86	5.05	61.3	1.7	21.2	22.5	7.8
0.3	8.92	54.1	3.14	0.1	-1.4	-0.88	-8.97	3.22	89.7	4.1	28.3	10.6	3.7
6.3	1.62	5.8	0.02	4.4	1.2	1.02	7.35	3.90	75.1	3.1	39.0	19.4	7.6
5.1	1.66	9.1	-0.08	5.1	1.3	0.79	6.68	4.14	71.7	1.6	24.2	26.4	7.0
5.5	1.44	8.5	0.38	4.0	0.6	0.59	6.05	4.40	81.8	2.9	26.4	15.9	5.4
2.3	3.20	23.1	0.42	3.3	0.8	0.52	5.07	3.48	74.4	3.9	13.6	9.4	4.8
5.5	1.78	7.5	0.02	9.4	1.7	2.35	13.09	4.67	58.2	3.6	11.1	7.5	9.5
7.5	0.26	1.8	0.01	9.8	4.0	2.34	19.90	4.74	50.4	3.2	6.3	12.1	8.9
7.2	0.00	0.0	-0.04	7.8	2.0	1.85	12.39	4.25	55.2	5.0	16.3	2.0	6.5
3.5	1.40	9.1	0.10	4.6	0.5	0.85	6.92	3.00	59.3	3.8	22.4	10.9	5.8
9.0	0.63	0.9	0.49	6.1	1.3	1.43	6.65	4.06	58.6	4.5	82.7	20.7	7.4
3.9	1.02	7.3	0.56	2.0	0.8	0.25	2.89	3.11	88.9	3.6	32.3	14.5	4.2
0.0	6.69	62.7	-0.01	10.0	1.2	2.73	26.69	5.07	41.5	0.6	1.4	32.9	8.1
8.9	0.00	0.0	0.05	5.8	0.9	1.38	6.36	3.48	60.5	5.5	54.0	9.8	9.1
3.5	6.26	21.3	0.46	7.2	1.9	1.67	11.09	4.28	53.7	2.3	37.4	27.4	9.0
6.4	1.33	5.8	0.06	3.4	0.7	0.79	5.90	4.16	82.3	2.3	24.5	18.6	6.0
8.6	0.01	0.0	0.02	4.8	0.3	1.19	9.45	3.26	65.0	5.0	38.3	9.1	7.4
2.8	2.45	14.6	0.38	4.8	0.7	1.15	10.60	4.83	71.8	3.0	30.0	16.6	5.5
6.7	0.84	5.6	0.03	5.3	6.5	1.03	12.35	3.58	59.5	4.8	4.3	1.8	6.4
8.3	0.07	0.7	0.15	5.0	1.3	1.22	15.56	4.03	65.2	0.9	20.1	11.0	4.5
4.1	1.49	12.3	0.18	4.6	10.4	0.83	11.80	4.59	79.0	1.9	18.7	20.5	4.7
7.6	4.09	4.9	0.70	2.9	0.3	0.51	2.66	2.43	77.4	4.0	83.5	25.2	6.2
4.4	4.34	17.0	0.00	6.3	0.7	1.24	10.68	4.00	55.0	1.9	31.6	27.8	7.2
9.3	0.00	0.0	-0.03	2.7	0.1	0.44	3.16	1.94	74.4	6.7	87.8	6.9	5.5
8.2	2.30	3.2	-0.01	4.7	0.7	1.10	4.65	4.40	73.4	4.8	51.2	12.8	7.4
5.6	3.36	11.8	0.72	2.5	0.3	0.28	2.45	3.58	90.0	2.9	36.2	19.0	5.7
8.2	0.00	0.0	0.00	5.1	0.8	1.22	14.79	4.25	68.9	4.2	8.1	6.2	5.4
7.6	0.54	3.9	0.01	5.9	138.0	1.17	17.13	2.90	57.9	5.2	29.2	7.8	6.7
6.7	0.57	3.8	0.00	5.3	2.1	1.08	12.38	3.44	53.1	2.5	27.1	18.4	5.4
9.0	0.05	0.2	0.00	3.8	0.3	0.86	9.66	3.01	67.7	4.1	58.6	17.6	4.8
2.9	3.67	19.5	0.99	7.8	1.9	1.94	15.06	3.86	55.3	3.2	22.0	13.6	7.0
7.6	0.13	0.8	0.01	9.6	10.1	2.10	22.35	3.67	46.0	5.1	27.1	3.8	8.7
4.2	2.47	14.3	0.08	4.9	2.2	1.19	12.46	3.84	64.4	4.7	24.4	5.3	5.4
7.2	0.37	2.1	0.00	4.4	0.5	1.03	8.98	4.05	73.0	4.1	23.6	9.1	7.0
4.0	3.31	11.7	0.06	3.5	1.0	0.69	5.30	2.91	67.9	2.6	50.8	34.5	7.1
4.2	2.24	15.3	0.11	3.7	0.5	0.69	7.48	4.08	81.0	4.8	34.4	8.5	4.6
4.1	2.90	13.2	0.31	7.5	2.8	1.79	12.10	5.19	66.3	1.1	17.8	30.7	9.4
7.8	0.43	2.2	0.78	7.8	0.9	1.89	14.80	4.03	37.4	1.7	17.6	22.1	7.0
4.0	0.79	5.5	0.08	8.1	79.8	1.15	9.25	3.83	50.0	1.0	14.1	28.8	9.6
1.7	8.63	35.8	0.43	0.0	-0.2	-0.52	-5.70	3.19	115.3	5.4	45.0	8.7	2.8
8.3	0.00	0.0	0.00	9.8	2.5	2.62	28.16	4.43	43.0	1.5	9.4	23.4	7.5
4.7	1.06	7.2	0.29	1.9	0.1	0.20	2.51	4.57	85.5	2.7	34.8	20.0	3.0
6.1	0.32	2.1	-0.19	6.7	3.4	1.63	15.87	4.87	74.9	4.9	18.2	3.2	5.4
6.4	2.30	7.8	-0.02	3.7	0.9	0.74	6.76	3.25	67.3	3.7	55.7	21.2	5.4
5.3	1.70	10.0	0.06	6.1	5.2	1.09	9.85	3.67	57.7	4.4	28.6	8.7	6.7
7.3	0.91	4.0	0.50	3.6	1.0	0.75	6.97	3.48	71.1	2.4	27.3	19.0	5.5
8.6	0.49	1.5	-0.04	4.1	0.6	0.79	4.88	3.15	67.0	3.9	44.4	16.5	8.1
1.1	4.69	31.7	0.06	3.5	0.5	0.80	7.88	3.38	79.8	2.5	16.3	6.9	4.7
7.3	0.24	1.4	0.20	5.9	1.6	1.35	14.23	4.30	65.6	2.2	30.8	23.4	6.2
7.5	1.07	4.5	0.15	5.1	4.4	1.31	12.90	2.39	49.2	3.8	20.5	10.5	6.6
2.6	3.08	20.4	0.04	6.7	3.1	1.49	13.79	3.80	58.6	1.3	13.4	26.5	7.7
5.6	1.80	7.4	0.00	1.8	1.0	0.26	2.70	3.39	96.2	6.0	45.3	5.2	5.4
6.4	2.49	6.6	-0.07	4.1	1.3	0.72	5.33	3.31	70.7	3.8	31.0	13.1	7.0
4.3	1.85	11.9	0.14	4.4	0.5	0.34	2.93	4.56	88.0	2.4	13.8	12.1	6.7
4.0	2.24	11.4	0.13	4.3	0.4	0.75	6.75	3.88	73.5	3.1	21.0	14.1	6.4
4.6	1.40	11.4	0.33	3.5	2.0	0.58	6.36	3.54	78.6	2.5	12.1	16.4	4.6
5.5	3.64	13.3	0.14	4.8	1.6	0.84	4.50	3.41	64.0	2.6	18.8	16.6	8.7
8.0	0.01	0.0	0.14	6.2	0.6	1.27	7.74	4.68	60.1	2.3	28.5	19.5	6.9
6.7	0.88	2.9	0.18	4.0	1.6	0.71	3.84	3.08	66.1	6.6	57.4	4.8	8.1
7.3	2.19	3.9	0.00	4.7	0.2	0.96	3.90	3.53	61.5	4.5	55.6	13.3	6.7

Name	City	State	Rating	2015 Rating	2014 Rating	Total Assets ($Mil)	One Year Asset Growth	Comm-ercial Loans	Cons-umer Loans	Mort-gage Loans	Secur-ities	Capital-ization Index	Lever-age Ratio	Risk-Based Capital Ratio
Bank of Lexington, Inc.	Lexington	KY	B	B	B	262.2	8.16	1.5	0.2	43.9	5.7	8.7	10.1	16.4
Bank of Lincoln County	Fayetteville	TN	A-	B	C+	134.3	2.47	6.3	2.2	13.9	9.8	10.0	13.9	17.5
Bank of Lindsay	Lindsay	NE	C	C	C-	67.2	24.71	18.5	2.2	0.2	1.1	5.7	10.7	11.5
▼ Bank of Little Rock	Little Rock	AR	C+	B-	C+	210.3	5.90	17.7	2.1	15.6	32.1	9.3	10.5	17.5
Bank of Locust Grove	Locust Grove	OK	B	C+	C	31.2	-1.87	18.0	35.6	5.2	11.7	10.0	12.1	17.2
Bank of Louisiana	New Orleans	LA	D-	D	D	75.7	-2.55	1.5	7.6	37.6	1.3	9.0	10.3	16.0
Bank of Louisiana	Louisiana	MO	C	C	C-	48.8	-4.29	5.4	1.6	15.4	29.5	10.0	11.0	16.2
Bank of Lumber City	Lumber City	GA	C	C-	C-	24.3	14.59	6.1	10.1	17.9	25.8	10.0	15.2	25.0
Bank of Luxemburg	Luxemburg	WI	C+	C+	C+	301.4	11.12	14.7	2.0	16.4	14.8	6.5	9.8	12.1
Bank of Macks Creek	Macks Creek	MO	D+	D	E-	23.6	20.03	1.5	1.7	29.6	8.5	9.3	10.5	18.2
Bank of Madison	Madison	GA	B	B	B	213.5	3.79	3.8	0.7	14.1	30.4	10.0	14.0	22.0
Bank of Magnolia Co.	Magnolia	OH	C+	C+	C+	83.9	6.40	5.2	3.1	20.4	41.6	9.6	10.7	21.0
Bank of Maple Plain	Maple Plain	MN	B+	B+	B	89.3	7.69	5.7	1.6	15.5	38.6	10.0	12.0	27.0
▲ Bank of Marin	Novato	CA	B+	B	B-	2054.8	9.16	6.8	1.3	4.8	20.8	8.7	10.9	13.9
Bank of Marion	Marion	VA	B	B	B	362.3	1.72	1.7	3.6	27.6	26.4	10.0	11.6	22.1
Bank of Mauston	Mauston	WI	B	C+	C+	284.3	0.85	3.9	2.6	12.0	31.9	10.0	11.4	17.8
Bank of Maysville	Maysville	KY	B	B	B	122.7	2.80	0.2	1.2	32.8	33.5	10.0	16.6	31.8
Bank of McCrory	McCrory	AR	C+	C+	C+	79.9	-4.63	3.7	2.1	3.7	48.3	9.3	10.5	22.3
Bank of McKenney	McKenney	VA	B	B	B	221.7	2.23	6.7	0.9	22.7	12.6	10.0	12.0	16.6
Bank of Mead	Mead	NE	B-	B-	B-	27.7	3.02	10.9	5.2	14.8	34.8	9.0	10.3	21.3
Bank of Milan	Milan	TN	B	B	B-	64.9	3.41	9.9	2.2	24.0	34.6	8.6	10.1	16.8
Bank of Millbrook	Millbrook	NY	B-	B-	C+	229.1	9.94	1.7	2.3	22.9	32.4	9.8	10.8	23.4
Bank of Milton	Milton	WI	B	B	C+	110.1	7.19	7.0	2.2	20.2	20.8	5.7	8.7	11.5
Bank of Minden	Mindenmines	MO	B	B	B-	29.2	-1.47	12.2	2.0	15.1	4.5	10.0	14.4	25.1
Bank of Mingo	Williamson	WV	D-	E+	C-	74.3	-10.73	7.6	6.2	22.5	38.0	4.2	6.2	13.6
Bank of Missouri	Perryville	MO	B+	B+	A-	1330.0	18.72	8.9	2.8	20.6	16.0	8.2	11.0	13.5
Bank of Modesto	Modesto	IL	C+	C+	C+	48.6	0.78	5.3	3.1	6.7	22.7	9.4	10.6	15.6
Bank of Monroe	Union	WV	B+	B+	B+	131.4	5.01	2.7	3.4	22.8	30.3	10.0	15.2	29.5
Bank of Montana	Missoula	MT	A-	A-	A-	63.0	21.40	16.8	3.7	12.8	0.0	9.9	11.0	16.1
Bank of Montgomery	Montgomery	IL	C-	C-	D+	42.8	4.95	9.7	1.4	15.9	43.3	6.3	8.3	17.8
Bank of Monticello	Monticello	GA	C-	D+	E-	101.3	1.88	5.8	7.8	28.3	13.0	5.7	7.7	15.5
Bank of Monticello	Monticello	MO	B-	C+	C	108.4	1.59	4.8	3.4	14.7	18.3	9.5	11.2	14.6
Bank of Morton	Morton	MS	A-	B+	B+	65.6	3.23	2.1	9.6	39.5	16.5	10.0	13.9	20.5
Bank of Moundville	Moundville	AL	C-	C-	D+	92.0	0.42	10.9	2.7	3.4	62.0	8.6	10.1	24.6
Bank of Mount Hope, Inc.	Mount Hope	WV	B	B+	B+	124.0	-9.65	13.0	8.3	17.4	45.2	10.0	12.5	30.0
Bank of Napa, N.A.	Napa	CA	B	B	B	242.3	18.05	4.9	0.1	2.3	36.8	10.0	11.0	18.1
▼ Bank of Nebraska	La Vista	NE	C-	B	B	144.5	1.36	11.8	0.6	21.4	0.2	5.7	9.2	11.5
Bank of New Cambria	New Cambria	MO	B-	C+	C+	32.0	-1.78	2.5	1.5	5.6	30.8	10.0	11.6	19.9
Bank of New Castle	New Castle	DE	C	C	C	17.4	0.18	0.0	0.0	0.0	3.2	10.0	97.1	483.2
Bank of New England	Salem	NH	C+	C+	C+	777.4	16.27	5.4	0.1	0.5	0.1	9.2	13.3	14.3
Bank of New Glarus	New Glarus	WI	B-	B-	B-	253.0	5.76	10.4	2.3	15.2	13.1	8.6	10.3	13.8
Bank of New Hampshire	Laconia	NH	C+	C+	C+	1423.8	14.69	5.1	2.3	28.0	21.2	6.9	8.9	13.5
Bank of New Jersey	Fort Lee	NJ	C+	C+	C+	835.1	3.07	3.8	0.2	10.4	8.0	6.7	9.2	12.3
Bank of New Madrid	New Madrid	MO	B+	B+	B-	91.2	1.58	3.3	3.2	16.2	40.6	8.8	11.5	14.0
Bank of New Mexico	Grants	NM	C+	B-	B-	157.3	-2.19	5.2	2.2	5.5	49.6	6.3	8.4	13.3
▲ Bank of New York Mellon	New York	NY	B-	C+	C+	299651.0	-0.84	1.1	0.0	0.6	38.1	4.9	6.9	13.3
Bank of New York Mellon Trust Co., N.A.	Los Angeles	CA	U	U	U	2073.8	3.44	0.0	0.0	0.0	31.2	10.0	79.8	910.6
▲ Bank of Newington	Newington	GA	C	C-	D-	111.3	28.15	8.7	2.3	22.2	0.5	5.4	8.1	11.3
Bank of Newman Grove	Newman Grove	NE	C	C-	C	33.3	-2.44	1.4	2.0	0.0	25.8	7.8	9.5	14.2
Bank of North Carolina	High Point	NC	B-	B-	B-	6799.4	30.87	5.9	0.3	13.0	12.5	5.9	9.8	11.7
Bank of O'Fallon	O'Fallon	IL	B+	B+	B+	303.1	5.69	5.2	2.7	40.6	25.6	10.0	13.0	28.1
▼ Bank of Oak Ridge	Oak Ridge	LA	C-	C	C+	51.3	-2.36	22.8	3.2	0.3	45.4	9.9	10.9	20.5
Bank of Oak Ridge	Oak Ridge	NC	B-	B-	C	378.4	8.52	11.3	0.6	22.1	12.5	8.5	10.2	13.7
Bank of Oakfield	Oakfield	WI	B	B	B	87.5	0.74	7.3	1.4	20.5	16.9	10.0	12.1	18.2
Bank of Ocean City	Ocean City	MD	B+	B+	A-	328.9	8.90	2.9	0.6	11.4	22.1	7.2	9.1	16.3
Bank of Odessa	Odessa	MO	B+	B+	B	229.8	-1.47	5.7	3.3	35.0	22.7	10.0	21.4	38.3
▲ Bank of Okolona	Okolona	MS	B	B-	B-	169.3	6.83	20.8	6.9	16.4	15.7	9.7	10.8	14.9
Bank of Old Monroe	Old Monroe	MO	A	A	A	316.9	2.51	4.5	0.6	10.7	25.7	10.0	15.1	20.7
Bank of Ontario	Ontario	WI	B-	B-	C+	38.4	3.54	4.4	4.6	29.3	5.8	10.0	12.7	21.9
▲ Bank of Orchard	Orchard	NE	B	B+	B	24.4	-2.09	8.6	5.3	0.5	11.4	10.0	14.6	28.3

Asset Quality Index	Adjusted Non-Performing Loans as a % of Total Loans	as a % of Capital	Net Charge-Offs Avg Loans	Profitability Index	Net Income ($Mil)	Return on Assets (R.O.A.)	Return on Equity (R.O.E.)	Net Interest Spread	Overhead Efficiency Ratio	Liquidity Index	Liquidity Ratio	Hot Money Ratio	Stability Index
7.9	0.48	3.6	0.00	4.9	1.7	0.88	8.79	3.65	65.1	0.8	18.7	34.7	6.1
7.4	0.75	3.8	-0.05	6.7	1.1	1.09	7.98	5.08	66.2	1.5	23.0	26.6	6.7
6.7	0.00	0.0	0.00	5.4	0.4	0.93	8.77	3.64	66.0	0.6	5.2	39.6	4.3
4.6	1.94	9.5	1.86	3.0	0.6	0.38	3.52	3.80	86.9	5.2	33.9	4.2	5.8
5.2	1.12	5.5	0.08	9.7	0.4	1.51	12.86	6.08	61.1	4.6	16.3	5.1	7.0
0.3	10.70	53.9	0.10	0.0	-0.6	-0.99	-8.33	6.77	122.8	5.1	20.1	2.3	5.9
3.9	3.93	19.5	0.00	3.8	0.3	0.66	5.88	4.00	84.5	2.9	17.7	14.8	5.8
7.6	0.45	1.5	0.89	3.9	0.2	0.99	6.24	5.82	81.0	2.9	50.3	21.1	4.1
4.3	1.01	7.5	0.26	4.5	1.7	0.80	7.95	4.28	73.4	3.6	18.2	11.5	5.4
6.2	0.90	5.3	0.00	3.0	0.2	0.88	8.56	4.16	79.6	3.7	30.5	11.7	1.7
4.9	3.36	13.7	0.02	5.9	1.8	1.14	7.93	4.04	64.4	3.8	27.3	12.0	6.9
6.1	1.61	5.8	-0.14	3.5	0.5	0.78	6.91	3.43	75.1	6.2	46.5	3.4	6.2
8.1	0.99	2.7	-0.64	5.0	0.9	1.29	10.70	2.96	56.9	5.8	57.1	8.8	7.3
5.6	0.69	4.3	-0.21	7.2	18.1	1.21	10.73	4.01	56.9	4.9	24.7	6.7	9.0
5.5	2.43	11.3	0.20	4.4	2.2	0.81	6.85	3.76	71.2	3.8	25.5	11.4	6.3
4.6	2.37	11.5	0.23	9.3	5.2	2.40	21.38	3.87	40.9	1.7	17.4	21.5	8.1
7.8	1.12	3.5	0.06	4.4	0.8	0.82	4.45	3.61	69.7	3.7	27.6	12.3	8.1
6.9	2.01	7.2	0.47	3.3	0.4	0.61	5.73	2.88	66.8	5.5	51.8	9.7	5.4
4.6	2.92	15.8	0.02	4.3	1.1	0.67	5.76	4.24	79.2	3.4	26.0	13.3	6.4
8.7	0.10	0.5	0.13	4.4	0.2	0.87	8.57	3.42	64.1	4.3	38.0	12.6	5.9
8.7	0.00	0.0	0.25	4.5	0.5	1.09	10.54	4.01	77.1	5.4	41.4	8.0	6.1
5.2	3.20	12.6	0.24	3.5	1.2	0.73	6.70	2.84	76.7	6.1	41.1	3.1	6.4
6.8	0.11	0.8	0.12	6.2	1.2	1.47	16.33	3.99	64.2	2.8	29.7	17.6	6.6
8.7	0.00	0.0	-0.05	4.6	0.2	0.75	5.28	4.24	68.4	2.9	39.0	20.5	7.4
3.2	2.96	19.2	0.46	0.0	-0.6	-1.08	-16.84	3.92	124.3	3.0	44.8	22.3	2.1
6.8	0.94	6.2	0.09	4.7	8.7	0.91	7.84	4.03	70.2	1.5	6.1	22.1	8.9
8.2	0.29	1.7	0.00	3.6	0.2	0.59	5.83	3.23	71.4	3.8	24.2	10.8	5.1
8.1	1.02	3.1	-0.01	5.3	1.0	1.01	6.98	3.77	67.0	4.0	43.6	16.0	7.9
8.3	0.00	0.0	0.00	9.6	2.1	4.75	42.64	4.04	37.2	1.5	19.9	21.2	8.0
6.0	1.63	6.7	-0.27	3.0	0.3	0.85	8.79	3.25	80.4	5.2	55.2	11.6	3.6
3.2	2.16	14.3	-0.54	4.7	0.8	1.07	14.05	3.72	74.0	2.9	28.7	16.6	2.8
4.3	1.77	10.8	0.07	5.3	1.1	1.35	12.65	3.72	62.1	2.2	12.4	17.7	6.2
6.1	0.67	3.5	0.27	10.0	1.3	2.74	19.95	5.70	54.4	1.5	14.8	24.0	8.9
7.9	1.88	4.5	0.05	2.0	0.3	0.48	4.72	2.93	89.5	3.2	66.9	30.0	4.5
8.6	0.04	0.2	0.01	3.6	0.7	0.70	5.65	3.08	76.6	4.2	41.1	14.3	6.8
8.9	0.13	0.6	0.00	4.4	1.3	0.74	6.56	3.54	68.4	5.4	48.9	10.3	6.9
2.0	2.47	20.5	0.02	6.2	1.7	1.53	16.47	4.01	72.2	2.2	13.4	17.9	6.6
9.0	0.28	1.1	-0.02	3.3	0.1	0.50	4.28	3.58	79.5	5.7	45.7	6.3	5.3
7.5	0.00	0.0	0.00	2.0	0.0	0.18	0.18	0.44	33.9	4.5	171.0	100.0	7.3
3.6	0.77	5.1	0.00	8.4	6.8	1.22	9.70	4.08	43.5	0.6	4.7	40.4	8.9
4.5	1.05	7.0	0.16	5.5	1.9	1.05	9.47	4.14	65.8	3.8	17.5	10.2	6.7
6.4	0.61	4.4	0.25	3.0	4.5	0.44	4.07	3.57	86.1	4.4	19.0	6.7	7.9
3.5	1.42	11.1	0.26	3.5	3.0	0.49	5.35	3.05	67.2	0.8	14.5	36.5	6.0
9.0	0.17	0.7	0.05	6.3	1.1	1.56	13.32	4.69	65.3	2.4	11.5	16.8	6.8
7.5	0.79	3.5	-0.06	3.7	0.9	0.79	7.49	3.90	77.7	5.2	43.3	10.0	6.3
9.0	0.36	0.7	-0.06	4.1	1688.0	0.79	9.92	1.01	68.8	3.7	53.7	25.0	5.1
6.5	na	0.0	na	10.0	66.2	4.30	4.98	0.84	65.7	10.0	355.2	0.0	7.0
3.2	1.79	16.4	0.10	7.3	1.4	1.93	22.85	5.18	55.3	1.3	12.8	26.6	3.1
7.2	0.00	0.0	0.19	2.4	0.1	0.27	2.74	2.91	91.0	3.7	26.0	11.8	4.9
5.7	0.41	3.2	-0.04	5.9	50.7	1.12	9.02	4.01	58.0	1.5	13.5	22.1	7.9
6.4	1.89	8.8	0.02	4.6	2.7	1.17	8.85	2.53	51.0	2.2	8.2	17.5	7.9
9.2	0.01	0.0	0.23	2.0	0.1	0.31	2.84	2.46	76.3	3.3	69.7	30.0	5.2
4.9	1.23	8.9	0.02	4.3	2.2	0.80	7.63	3.90	77.6	0.8	17.5	28.2	5.2
5.1	2.29	12.0	0.05	4.9	0.6	0.91	7.55	3.98	66.3	2.3	29.4	19.6	6.3
8.4	0.15	0.9	-0.02	5.1	2.1	0.92	9.45	3.20	55.9	5.5	45.5	8.2	5.6
6.1	2.71	8.4	0.09	6.2	2.1	1.16	5.58	3.48	46.8	3.6	18.1	11.5	7.1
5.9	0.00	0.0	0.64	8.0	2.5	2.00	17.72	5.54	56.5	0.7	12.2	36.0	8.2
8.8	0.49	1.9	-0.01	9.0	4.1	1.72	11.69	4.16	49.0	3.3	25.0	8.5	8.7
4.3	2.37	14.0	0.75	5.4	0.4	1.28	10.15	4.88	67.5	1.6	17.7	24.3	6.7
8.6	0.00	0.0	-0.13	5.2	0.2	1.16	8.31	3.02	57.4	3.7	73.6	21.9	7.0

Name	City	State	2015 Rating	2014 Rating	Rating	Total Assets ($Mil)	One Year Asset Growth	Commercial Loans	Consumer Loans	Mortgage Loans	Securities	Capitalization Index	Leverage Ratio	Risk-Based Capital Ratio
Bank of Orrick	Orrick	MO	C-	C-	D-	33.0	0.69	3.4	2.6	16.9	32.2	6.8	8.8	17.2
▲ Bank of Palmer	Palmer	KS	C	C	C	42.8	2.18	1.9	3.8	9.8	36.5	8.2	9.8	17.2
Bank of Pensacola	Pensacola	FL	D+	C-	D+	84.2	17.82	1.6	2.4	8.6	55.5	10.0	14.1	44.8
▲ Bank of Perry County	Lobelville	TN	B-	C+	C	153.1	2.89	8.6	14.4	40.4	4.3	8.5	10.0	14.8
▼ Bank of Pine Hill	Pine Hill	AL	D	D+	D+	23.4	-3.73	0.0	2.3	9.2	65.0	10.0	12.6	35.7
Bank of Pontiac	Pontiac	IL	A-	A-	A-	511.4	5.15	8.9	4.1	24.2	19.2	10.0	12.9	21.6
Bank of Prague	Prague	NE	B	B	B	24.0	1.15	12.7	9.2	2.4	14.5	10.0	16.5	21.6
Bank of Prairie Du Sac	Prairie Du Sac	WI	A+	A+	A	381.4	2.27	10.9	1.0	5.6	35.0	10.0	15.7	22.2
Bank of Prairie Village	Prairie Village	KS	B	B	B	105.8	0.09	16.0	2.7	27.6	28.0	7.7	9.5	15.8
▼ Bank of Prescott	Prescott	AR	B	B+	A-	86.2	5.17	20.3	4.7	13.5	39.3	10.0	13.6	19.4
Bank of Princeton	Princeton	NJ	B-	C+	C+	1008.7	-1.30	5.1	0.1	8.4	11.5	6.1	10.0	11.8
Bank of Protection	Protection	KS	B	B	B	60.4	-2.49	3.2	4.2	7.0	15.9	10.0	13.4	19.7
Bank of Putnam County	Cookeville	TN	B-	B-	B-	744.6	78.95	4.0	3.5	22.7	34.8	5.8	7.8	18.0
Bank of Rantoul	Rantoul	IL	A-	A	A-	226.2	-2.05	14.9	0.5	2.6	43.7	9.0	10.3	16.8
Bank of Richmondville	Cobleskill	NY	B-	B-	B-	149.1	7.87	3.8	1.8	37.6	23.9	10.0	11.9	25.1
Bank of Rio Vista	Rio Vista	CA	B-	B-	C+	219.2	8.89	3.9	0.6	0.2	53.1	10.0	11.6	22.8
Bank of Ripley	Ripley	TN	C+	C+	C+	206.2	3.70	0.4	7.3	10.2	50.8	10.0	14.4	26.7
Bank of River Oaks	Houston	TX	B	B+	B	441.2	-2.70	24.7	2.1	10.3	12.6	8.4	10.7	13.6
Bank of Romney	Romney	WV	C+	C+	C+	266.3	3.34	2.6	5.6	45.4	24.8	10.0	11.7	20.6
Bank of Ruston	Ruston	LA	B	B	B	231.8	27.38	7.3	2.1	36.4	0.8	7.5	9.9	12.9
Bank of Salem	Salem	AR	B-	B-	B	129.4	1.33	12.9	5.2	25.8	2.1	9.1	10.4	14.4
Bank of Salem	Salem	MO	C+	C+	C+	98.2	6.35	1.9	3.5	27.1	37.3	7.7	9.4	20.1
Bank of San Antonio	San Antonio	TX	B	B	B	622.9	18.65	24.6	0.9	9.5	9.6	4.8	9.1	10.9
Bank of San Francisco	San Francisco	CA	B	B	B	226.0	13.71	31.4	0.1	24.3	0.0	8.7	10.1	14.4
Bank of San Jacinto County	Coldspring	TX	B	B	B	37.4	1.01	4.6	3.5	32.4	10.0	10.0	13.5	40.8
▲ Bank of Santa Clarita	Santa Clarita	CA	C+	C	C	316.9	13.65	3.5	6.9	5.3	7.0	6.4	8.4	12.7
Bank of Soperton	Soperton	GA	C-	C-	C-	49.7	20.89	17.4	6.2	25.0	7.9	7.4	9.3	13.3
Bank of South Carolina	Charleston	SC	B+	B+	B+	409.7	6.57	11.8	1.4	16.5	28.1	7.9	9.6	15.1
Bank of South Texas	Pharr	TX	B-	C+	C-	121.2	15.53	8.8	1.5	26.5	7.2	6.3	8.3	12.3
Bank of Southern California, N.A.	San Diego	CA	B-	C+	C+	418.5	22.08	11.9	0.4	20.9	1.2	6.5	8.9	12.1
Bank of Southside Virginia	Carson	VA	A	A	A	551.2	0.15	2.5	15.6	8.0	22.2	10.0	16.6	30.8
Bank of Springfield	Springfield	IL	C	C	C	898.7	7.14	17.4	1.3	10.0	5.8	4.3	8.8	10.6
Bank of St. Croix	Christiansted	VI	C-	D+	D+	135.5	8.06	1.5	0.2	22.7	33.3	8.6	10.0	32.7
Bank of St. Elizabeth	Saint Elizabeth	MO	A-	A-	A-	119.1	1.33	0.8	5.1	50.8	0.0	8.9	10.3	17.2
Bank of St. Francisville	Saint Francisville	LA	B	B	B	111.1	1.27	4.3	4.3	24.6	16.2	9.5	10.7	15.9
Bank of Star City	Star City	AR	B+	B+	B+	90.9	-2.28	10.8	2.1	17.0	21.2	10.0	16.0	23.2
Bank of Star Valley	Afton	WY	B+	B+	B	160.5	10.34	11.0	5.0	12.0	26.3	9.8	10.9	17.5
▲ Bank of Steinauer	Steinauer	NE	C	D+	D	11.5	-1.55	7.2	10.5	33.0	4.5	8.8	10.2	14.1
Bank of Stockton	Stockton	CA	A-	A-	B+	2747.4	8.80	6.8	14.6	5.7	31.1	8.5	10.7	13.8
Bank of Stronghurst	Stronghurst	IL	C+	C+	C+	75.3	-3.36	1.3	1.2	6.4	68.4	10.0	15.9	45.1
Bank of Sullivan	Sullivan	MO	C+	C+	C	428.5	10.91	10.0	2.4	32.9	6.7	6.9	9.0	12.4
Bank of Sun Prairie	Sun Prairie	WI	A-	B+	B	338.8	7.91	8.3	1.0	10.2	5.4	10.0	14.1	18.2
Bank of Sunset and Trust Co.	Sunset	LA	B	B+	B+	122.1	1.84	15.1	1.0	17.7	23.0	8.4	9.9	15.5
▲ Bank of Tampa	Tampa	FL	B	B-	C+	1515.9	6.57	18.5	2.2	4.2	26.8	6.5	8.5	12.4
Bank of Tennessee	Kingsport	TN	B	B	B	1027.2	10.13	7.6	1.3	23.6	17.3	6.6	8.9	12.2
Bank of Terrell	Dawson	GA	C+	C+	C+	152.8	6.67	6.1	2.8	34.1	7.5	9.1	10.4	15.5
Bank of Tescott	Tescott	KS	A	A	A	364.6	10.08	3.5	2.5	25.7	12.1	10.0	12.5	15.2
Bank of Texas	Midland	TX	A-	A-	A-	281.1	10.31	27.0	0.2	3.3	1.0	10.0	12.0	15.2
Bank of the Bluegrass & Trust Co.	Lexington	KY	A-	A-	B	236.7	4.94	2.6	2.0	23.6	19.3	10.0	12.6	18.9
Bank of the Cascades	Bend	OR	B-	B-	C-	3167.5	28.62	11.3	1.4	13.3	21.2	5.4	8.3	11.3
Bank of the Federated States of Micronesi	Pohnpei	FM	B+	B+	B+	153.9	4.72	7.3	10.5	1.4	18.1	10.0	14.0	27.6
Bank of the Flint Hills	Wamego	KS	B	B	B	183.2	6.73	12.6	1.0	18.1	11.4	8.2	10.5	13.5
Bank of the James	Lynchburg	VA	B-	B-	B-	560.3	10.33	11.2	1.3	21.9	7.7	5.9	9.1	11.7
Bank of the Mountains, Inc.	West Liberty	KY	B-	B-	B-	67.0	-0.21	6.6	17.1	28.0	8.3	9.6	10.7	16.2
Bank of the Orient	San Francisco	CA	C-	C-	D+	559.1	13.46	8.4	0.0	8.7	4.7	10.0	11.3	15.2
Bank of the Ozarks	Little Rock	AR	B+	B+	B	18430.0	97.63	2.6	5.4	5.9	7.3	6.5	14.6	12.1
Bank of the Pacific	Aberdeen	WA	B-	B-	B-	895.7	10.00	11.4	6.9	8.8	11.2	7.1	9.5	12.6
Bank of the Panhandle	Guymon	OK	A	A	A	134.2	-7.79	11.6	1.5	9.0	30.7	10.0	12.4	18.3
▲ Bank of the Prairie	Olathe	KS	B	B-	C	109.6	18.34	17.8	0.8	21.8	10.2	7.6	9.4	13.9
Bank of the Rockies, N.A.	White Sulphur Spring	MT	C-	C	D+	138.9	3.69	8.7	1.5	12.9	15.5	8.7	10.1	14.6

Asset Quality Index	Adjusted Non-Performing Loans as a % of Total Loans	as a % of Capital	Net Charge-Offs Avg Loans	Profitability Index	Net Income ($Mil)	Return on Assets (R.O.A.)	Return on Equity (R.O.E.)	Net Interest Spread	Overhead Efficiency Ratio	Liquidity Index	Liquidity Ratio	Hot Money Ratio	Stability Index
7.4	0.36	2.0	0.34	1.7	0.0	0.13	1.31	3.67	96.4	5.1	32.9	6.5	4.0
4.5	1.42	7.5	0.26	3.2	0.2	0.66	6.73	3.20	79.9	5.2	46.2	9.9	5.1
9.5	0.00	0.0	0.02	0.2	-0.1	-0.15	-0.96	2.17	106.6	6.4	76.9	8.7	4.8
4.0	0.81	6.3	0.24	8.7	2.1	1.83	18.47	4.90	56.4	1.3	9.4	20.2	7.7
7.1	7.01	10.3	-0.06	0.0	-0.1	-0.59	-4.47	2.42	122.8	3.8	76.1	20.4	4.5
5.9	1.27	6.2	0.66	6.0	3.8	1.03	7.95	3.78	54.2	3.8	22.8	10.4	7.0
6.6	0.00	0.0	0.18	8.9	0.4	2.11	12.68	4.38	60.7	3.7	26.2	11.3	6.3
8.7	0.12	0.5	-0.01	9.4	4.7	1.64	10.37	3.96	42.0	5.5	43.1	7.9	9.4
9.2	0.00	0.0	-0.01	4.8	0.9	1.04	11.26	3.70	63.2	2.0	29.2	24.1	5.7
3.7	5.33	20.6	0.00	5.1	0.8	1.25	9.37	4.04	69.3	2.4	26.1	18.5	7.2
4.2	0.99	7.5	0.00	5.9	8.8	1.17	12.17	4.01	60.3	2.4	10.7	16.9	7.9
7.2	0.46	2.1	0.04	5.4	0.6	1.22	9.48	4.39	63.7	1.4	13.4	24.8	7.2
9.1	0.06	0.4	0.20	4.4	5.0	1.06	14.88	3.23	71.0	4.7	45.9	13.2	5.1
5.9	1.64	7.7	0.48	9.7	4.0	2.39	20.12	4.50	39.4	2.1	3.1	17.4	8.4
6.0	2.04	10.0	0.17	3.4	0.6	0.57	4.84	3.96	76.7	4.1	22.3	8.7	6.6
9.4	0.07	0.2	-1.41	3.8	1.1	0.68	5.28	3.35	82.1	5.9	49.7	7.0	6.7
5.8	3.94	10.0	0.15	3.1	1.0	0.66	4.29	4.10	86.7	3.5	45.0	18.9	6.6
5.8	0.39	2.6	0.31	4.8	3.3	0.99	9.59	3.78	69.6	4.3	22.9	7.7	5.3
3.1	4.14	22.0	0.12	3.9	1.3	0.64	6.15	3.79	77.1	1.5	20.1	23.0	5.5
6.3	0.38	3.1	0.02	6.0	1.8	1.11	11.35	4.32	60.8	0.8	11.6	18.3	5.7
3.6	1.80	11.9	0.06	7.9	1.2	1.23	11.64	4.93	59.4	1.3	11.1	27.0	6.5
6.2	0.99	4.7	0.09	3.1	0.4	0.53	5.64	3.19	77.9	3.1	27.7	15.2	5.5
8.0	0.00	0.0	0.17	5.0	3.7	0.85	8.64	3.54	67.6	4.3	15.1	6.6	6.3
8.4	0.02	0.2	-0.01	4.6	1.2	0.72	7.33	4.06	69.7	3.1	19.1	13.5	6.0
9.1	0.00	0.0	-0.01	3.8	0.2	0.84	6.46	4.19	82.8	5.9	62.3	8.8	6.4
7.1	0.00	0.0	0.00	3.3	1.1	0.47	5.55	2.79	69.5	1.6	23.7	14.0	4.6
4.6	0.93	7.3	0.02	6.3	0.5	1.51	16.24	5.35	73.1	1.6	16.1	23.3	2.2
5.8	0.87	5.4	0.03	7.1	4.1	1.34	13.42	4.16	59.3	4.2	24.2	8.5	7.1
5.4	0.32	2.7	-0.02	4.0	0.6	0.65	5.79	5.71	84.2	0.9	22.7	36.3	7.1
5.6	0.35	3.0	0.02	4.8	2.1	0.75	7.54	4.24	68.6	2.4	17.0	17.1	5.3
7.1	0.90	2.1	0.27	6.3	5.2	1.26	7.51	3.61	61.0	6.5	60.7	6.9	9.4
3.4	1.55	13.7	0.03	4.1	4.2	0.63	7.23	3.65	72.7	4.2	9.3	6.4	5.1
5.9	4.13	12.8	-0.01	2.6	0.6	0.60	5.65	2.64	85.2	6.7	64.9	6.1	6.0
8.0	0.11	0.9	0.26	8.8	1.8	2.05	17.22	4.62	59.1	4.0	15.2	8.9	8.8
4.1	2.41	14.6	0.51	5.0	0.9	1.13	10.48	4.96	76.7	2.4	10.8	16.3	6.6
6.8	0.60	2.4	0.26	5.8	1.0	1.44	9.47	4.73	70.4	3.2	26.4	14.3	7.2
4.9	1.60	8.5	0.02	7.1	1.9	1.61	15.29	3.97	58.9	2.9	27.1	15.9	7.3
7.9	0.00	0.0	0.00	4.5	0.1	0.97	9.97	4.54	78.6	4.3	11.1	5.9	3.3
7.2	0.44	2.2	0.10	6.4	27.6	1.46	9.67	3.82	57.6	5.7	37.3	7.8	9.7
9.7	0.00	0.0	0.04	2.2	0.2	0.32	1.99	2.35	86.2	5.4	73.0	13.6	7.0
3.6	1.42	12.0	0.28	5.9	3.2	1.03	11.14	3.92	65.1	1.9	3.3	18.0	5.2
6.6	0.47	2.4	-0.46	5.9	2.6	1.04	7.40	3.71	67.8	3.0	17.8	14.3	7.6
8.7	0.00	0.0	-0.04	4.7	1.0	1.00	10.12	3.83	68.7	1.4	5.1	22.8	6.4
5.8	1.02	7.0	0.07	4.9	10.4	0.95	11.44	3.43	67.8	6.5	36.0	1.9	6.9
6.3	0.93	7.3	0.07	5.3	9.7	1.31	13.96	4.05	71.7	4.5	9.6	5.2	7.7
4.7	1.18	8.7	0.63	4.9	1.5	1.33	13.07	4.49	62.8	0.7	12.6	42.1	5.1
8.2	0.38	2.3	0.02	9.0	5.2	1.97	15.65	4.13	46.4	1.3	3.0	21.9	9.0
8.2	0.25	1.5	0.00	5.8	2.9	1.39	11.89	2.82	40.9	0.7	23.7	64.3	7.9
5.7	1.84	10.2	0.11	6.3	2.0	1.13	8.35	3.94	65.5	3.6	27.9	13.0	7.7
6.5	0.61	4.6	-0.06	3.8	12.8	0.59	5.05	3.56	77.0	5.1	22.1	3.8	7.2
4.8	4.52	10.6	0.28	5.4	1.4	1.32	8.98	4.42	67.4	6.2	75.5	10.7	8.1
5.1	0.87	5.9	0.11	4.8	1.4	1.06	9.81	3.94	70.3	1.8	14.3	16.7	7.3
5.5	0.57	4.8	0.10	4.6	3.1	0.78	8.47	3.78	72.7	2.1	11.1	17.9	5.2
3.9	1.57	9.9	0.32	4.5	0.4	0.73	6.92	5.89	80.1	1.7	18.5	22.0	5.7
5.6	0.64	4.2	-0.03	1.9	1.3	0.34	2.98	3.85	93.0	1.9	15.1	19.7	6.6
5.7	0.47	2.8	0.06	10.0	194.1	2.01	13.42	4.92	33.9	1.2	8.5	21.3	10.0
6.7	0.24	1.8	0.03	4.6	5.6	0.88	8.07	4.28	73.7	3.3	13.5	6.1	7.6
8.6	0.05	0.2	0.02	7.1	1.9	1.80	14.33	4.18	61.7	3.0	21.4	12.7	8.7
7.5	0.01	0.1	-0.09	6.5	1.0	1.23	12.89	4.13	61.5	0.8	15.5	41.7	5.7
2.0	4.23	27.6	0.00	6.0	1.5	1.46	12.93	4.96	76.8	4.2	22.7	8.4	6.1

Name	City	State	2015 Rating	Rating	2014 Rating	Total Assets ($Mil)	One Year Asset Growth	Comm-ercial Loans	Cons-umer Loans	Mort-gage Loans	Secur-ities	Capital-ization Index	Lever-age Ratio	Risk-Based Capital Ratio
Bank of the Sierra	Porterville	CA	A-	A-	B-	1971.6	14.96	6.4	0.7	7.0	27.1	10.0	11.8	16.9
Bank of the South	Pensacola	FL	D+	D+	D+	83.6	13.65	0.1	0.5	1.5	57.9	10.0	18.3	78.1
Bank of the Southwest	Roswell	NM	B-	B-	B-	142.8	-3.95	34.3	5.6	13.1	0.1	8.6	10.1	14.6
Bank of the Valley	Bellwood	NE	C+	B-	B	218.4	29.10	5.7	1.7	3.8	14.1	5.3	9.0	11.2
Bank of the West	San Francisco	CA	B	B	B	82566.8	11.54	13.8	19.0	8.7	14.7	8.0	10.8	13.4
▼ Bank of the West	Thomas	OK	B+	A-	A	140.4	4.31	10.3	0.4	11.0	0.0	8.7	12.0	13.9
▲ Bank of the West	Grapevine	TX	B-	B-	B-	452.2	9.05	9.1	0.7	7.1	9.1	7.9	9.6	13.6
Bank of Tioga	Tioga	ND	B	C	B-	330.9	7.18	2.4	0.9	3.0	71.1	6.9	8.9	20.0
Bank of Travelers Rest	Travelers Rest	SC	B	B	B-	631.3	11.13	5.9	4.3	13.1	25.3	7.5	9.4	15.3
Bank of Turtle Lake	Turtle Lake	ND	B	B	B	50.9	-5.08	8.4	2.7	1.2	12.1	7.9	10.4	13.3
Bank of Utah	Ogden	UT	A	A	A	1062.7	10.92	6.3	0.3	3.4	11.9	10.0	13.1	17.2
Bank of Utica	Utica	NY	B+	A-	A	1035.9	1.68	3.0	0.4	0.2	91.7	10.0	16.5	18.4
▲ Bank of Vernon	Vernon	AL	B+	B-	C-	143.2	-0.34	16.8	2.5	15.9	17.3	10.0	16.5	24.1
Bank of Versailles	Versailles	MO	B+	B	C	239.1	4.44	1.0	0.7	58.8	2.3	10.0	11.8	20.7
Bank of Vici	Vici	OK	C	C	C	39.6	-2.43	16.0	13.2	3.3	24.6	9.8	10.9	20.0
Bank of Walker County	Jasper	AL	B-	B	B	64.7	-10.88	12.4	5.3	20.2	18.3	10.0	13.4	20.5
Bank of Walnut Grove	Walnut Grove	MS	B+	B+	B+	59.1	4.06	1.8	11.7	20.2	7.7	10.0	14.7	30.5
Bank of Walterboro	Walterboro	SC	C+	C+	C+	186.9	-3.47	6.1	1.6	12.8	26.9	9.7	10.8	20.7
Bank of Washington	Washington	MO	D-	D	D-	584.7	-2.86	22.2	0.7	11.3	9.1	9.7	12.8	14.7
▲ Bank of Washington	Lynnwood	WA	C+	C	C	176.2	9.77	4.8	1.1	21.0	9.8	10.0	11.1	15.3
Bank of Waynesboro	Waynesboro	TN	A-	B+	B	150.2	1.43	7.2	6.6	26.7	12.0	10.0	14.0	20.1
▲ Bank of Wedowee	Wedowee	AL	B-	C	D+	130.8	9.22	5.3	4.2	20.1	39.0	9.4	10.6	18.9
Bank of Western Oklahoma	Elk City	OK	B-	B-	C+	239.7	5.12	6.7	1.1	18.9	4.2	4.1	8.1	10.5
Bank of Weston	Weston	MO	C+	C+	C+	130.1	5.57	8.5	0.7	18.1	17.8	6.0	8.3	11.8
Bank of Whitewater	Whitewater	KS	C-	D+	D+	20.8	-7.76	7.9	12.3	13.4	20.9	7.5	9.3	17.3
▲ Bank of Whittier, N.A.	Whittier	CA	C+	B	B-	62.4	4.63	0.8	0.4	22.1	0.0	10.0	15.9	18.0
Bank of Wiggins	Wiggins	MS	B+	B+	B+	181.7	-2.11	14.9	7.3	18.0	28.2	10.0	15.5	28.9
Bank of Winnfield & Trust Co.	Winnfield	LA	B	B	B	143.9	2.35	9.1	3.9	14.7	32.8	10.0	12.0	25.2
Bank of Winona	Winona	MS	B	B-	B-	114.8	2.37	0.7	4.3	17.9	42.0	9.5	10.6	21.3
Bank of Wisconsin Dells	Wisconsin Dells	WI	B-	B-	C+	481.7	8.01	6.9	0.4	8.6	9.1	8.7	11.7	13.9
Bank of Wolcott	Wolcott	IN	C+	C+	B-	150.7	-2.13	7.3	1.1	16.0	19.7	8.8	10.2	15.6
▲ Bank of Wrightsville	Wrightsville	GA	C-	D+	D	51.8	-0.99	6.5	4.1	17.2	34.0	7.4	9.3	16.7
Bank of Wyandotte	Wyandotte	OK	D+	C-	D+	13.2	0.27	6.9	7.5	10.2	34.1	6.5	8.5	13.3
Bank of Yates City	Yates City	IL	D+	C	C	68.0	9.79	6.4	13.0	22.6	26.4	8.1	9.7	15.8
Bank of Yazoo City	Yazoo City	MS	B-	B-	B-	249.4	3.44	4.8	1.8	17.1	43.3	9.5	10.6	19.8
▲ Bank of York	York	AL	B	C+	C+	96.5	-6.94	3.1	1.8	6.2	49.2	10.0	11.2	26.0
Bank of York	York	SC	B	B	B	222.1	7.21	5.6	3.6	10.4	19.8	10.0	12.1	26.8
Bank of Zachary	Zachary	LA	B-	B	B	233.4	13.03	3.0	1.8	28.4	32.8	7.2	9.2	18.8
▲ Bank of Zumbrota	Zumbrota	MN	B-	C+	C+	156.6	1.95	10.8	3.9	14.9	19.5	9.8	11.9	14.9
Bank Plus	Estherville	IA	D-	D	C-	124.5	-3.00	4.2	2.1	8.8	11.8	5.8	8.7	11.6
Bank Rhode Island	Providence	RI	B-	B-	B-	2125.8	3.46	18.6	0.1	10.5	12.4	6.2	8.9	11.9
Bank SNB	Stillwater	OK	B	B+	B	2460.6	19.95	22.0	0.8	7.4	17.4	9.2	12.3	14.4
Bank Star	Pacific	MO	B	B	B-	67.8	1.26	5.1	2.3	23.8	4.1	9.5	10.7	17.0
Bank Star One	Fulton	MO	B	B	B	87.3	4.44	2.4	1.3	34.1	5.6	10.0	12.1	20.5
BANK VI	Salina	KS	B+	B-	C+	82.6	8.73	17.4	0.9	29.6	4.1	9.3	10.6	15.0
▲ Bank, N.A.	McAlester	OK	B+	B	B	350.9	-7.10	5.2	3.0	16.6	32.8	10.0	11.2	19.2
Bank2	Oklahoma City	OK	A-	A-	A-	131.1	5.03	7.4	1.5	25.6	17.8	10.0	12.0	17.7
Bank3	Memphis	TN	D	D	D+	37.7	251.73	15.2	0.9	0.4	0.0	10.0	61.1	105.4
bankcda	Coeur d'Alene	ID	D+	D+	C-	106.0	7.51	17.0	0.5	8.8	15.1	7.1	9.1	12.7
BankChampaign, N.A.	Champaign	IL	B-	B-	B-	212.5	3.95	11.9	0.2	22.4	15.6	7.3	9.2	14.0
BankCherokee	Saint Paul	MN	C-	D+	D	266.4	2.32	19.1	0.7	8.5	26.0	5.8	7.8	13.8
Bankers Trust Co.	Des Moines	IA	B-	B	B	4115.1	21.80	18.6	0.3	9.6	10.4	4.4	8.6	10.7
Bankers' Bank	Madison	WI	B	B+	A-	503.1	21.15	1.3	0.6	1.0	19.6	10.0	12.5	26.4
Bankers' Bank Northeast	Glastonbury	CT	C-	C-	C+	158.9	-4.69	0.0	0.5	1.2	39.8	9.2	10.5	33.9
▲ Bankers' Bank of Kansas	Wichita	KS	B-	B-	C+	172.6	-0.04	10.6	11.7	1.3	4.8	10.0	13.5	18.3
Bankers' Bank of Kentucky, Inc.	Frankfort	KY	B-	B	B	102.4	23.46	2.1	0.0	1.7	0.0	10.0	13.3	41.6
Bankers' Bank of the West	Denver	CO	B+	B	B+	320.2	-8.41	7.3	0.1	0.8	10.9	10.0	13.1	17.9
BankFinancial, F.S.B.	Olympia Fields	IL	B-	B-	C-	1537.9	7.58	26.7	0.1	7.0	1.5	9.3	10.5	15.2
BankFirst	Norfolk	NE	A-	A	A	393.0	16.41	10.8	0.6	6.2	28.3	9.8	12.3	14.8
▲ BankFirst Financial Services	Columbus	MS	C+	C	C+	923.5	0.44	10.1	1.7	16.9	12.5	6.2	8.9	11.9

Asset Quality Index	Adjusted Non-Performing Loans as a % of Total Loans	as a % of Capital	Net Charge-Offs Avg Loans	Profitability Index	Net Income ($Mil)	Return on Assets (R.O.A.)	Return on Equity (R.O.E.)	Net Interest Spread	Overhead Efficiency Ratio	Liquidity Index	Liquidity Ratio	Hot Money Ratio	Stability Index
6.2	1.03	5.5	0.06	5.6	12.9	0.96	7.79	3.95	68.6	3.0	23.0	16.1	8.6
10.0	0.00	0.0	0.06	0.4	-0.1	-0.24	-1.25	1.85	117.4	7.6	94.3	3.5	5.1
4.8	0.60	4.6	0.22	4.2	0.9	0.83	8.35	6.14	83.9	4.6	12.3	4.1	5.1
4.5	0.78	6.3	0.01	3.8	0.9	0.67	7.32	3.74	71.8	0.9	13.2	22.7	6.0
5.0	0.70	4.6	0.21	4.2	438.3	0.76	4.74	3.12	64.3	2.8	19.5	11.2	8.8
4.3	1.04	7.1	0.00	9.9	2.4	2.25	19.02	4.98	53.6	1.0	9.6	29.9	9.0
4.9	0.32	2.2	0.38	4.7	3.4	1.07	11.29	4.50	70.9	4.5	21.4	6.0	6.5
9.2	0.00	0.0	0.09	6.0	6.1	2.64	24.79	4.63	60.4	3.0	43.9	21.6	5.6
5.9	0.68	4.0	0.11	4.9	5.0	1.09	11.10	3.65	70.9	3.2	34.0	16.9	6.4
1.0	4.73	32.4	0.45	7.2	0.5	1.24	12.27	4.09	51.9	1.6	16.5	23.6	5.3
7.2	0.20	1.1	-0.01	9.4	12.4	1.67	12.19	4.10	58.0	4.8	21.3	5.3	9.8
9.8	1.18	0.5	1.51	5.0	7.8	1.05	5.42	2.02	32.0	5.5	90.5	17.8	9.6
5.5	1.69	6.9	0.33	5.1	0.9	0.84	5.15	4.34	63.4	2.0	19.5	19.4	6.6
5.9	1.53	9.7	-0.03	3.0	0.3	0.16	1.29	3.43	94.4	2.4	11.5	16.4	5.8
4.0	2.33	8.8	0.64	4.0	0.3	0.89	8.03	3.93	79.5	3.2	53.8	24.5	5.3
6.6	1.13	5.3	0.10	3.7	0.2	0.41	3.05	4.09	82.3	1.3	27.5	32.6	6.3
8.3	0.05	0.1	0.18	4.5	0.5	1.04	7.20	4.18	70.7	3.1	53.8	25.2	7.8
5.1	2.29	9.0	0.32	3.5	1.0	0.68	6.44	3.07	71.4	2.7	42.6	26.6	5.6
0.3	9.02	46.6	0.05	3.4	3.1	0.70	5.53	3.66	81.5	3.9	11.7	8.8	5.9
5.1	1.02	6.5	-0.07	3.5	0.7	0.55	5.01	3.25	91.7	1.7	16.4	21.3	6.7
6.2	0.97	4.7	0.04	7.8	1.4	1.27	9.37	4.55	59.3	3.1	20.6	14.0	7.8
4.5	2.94	13.1	0.16	4.1	0.8	0.79	6.79	3.71	67.3	3.8	33.4	13.6	5.9
4.0	0.92	9.5	0.08	6.9	2.8	1.57	17.88	4.79	65.2	1.1	3.3	25.9	6.2
4.6	1.42	11.3	-0.04	4.1	0.9	0.88	10.88	4.07	77.6	3.3	11.3	12.1	4.6
5.8	0.87	4.4	0.01	5.9	0.2	1.40	15.43	4.15	65.0	4.7	34.4	6.9	3.6
8.5	0.00	0.0	-0.13	3.3	0.2	0.46	2.85	2.13	82.1	2.6	60.5	39.6	7.8
6.1	1.40	5.0	0.30	5.0	1.3	0.91	5.98	4.02	67.3	2.7	36.7	21.8	7.6
5.5	3.42	11.2	0.01	3.9	1.0	0.90	8.44	3.38	75.7	4.4	42.2	13.7	7.2
7.1	0.44	1.6	0.72	5.0	1.1	1.23	10.98	4.08	66.7	4.1	46.7	16.0	6.2
4.0	1.38	8.3	0.12	8.5	4.9	1.42	12.02	4.12	47.1	1.6	13.0	14.9	7.1
3.8	2.47	15.1	0.19	5.9	1.6	1.37	13.58	3.76	60.1	2.0	30.8	22.5	7.1
5.5	1.18	6.4	-0.10	3.1	0.3	0.66	7.52	3.59	85.3	4.4	37.8	12.5	2.6
8.5	0.19	0.9	0.60	4.3	0.1	0.56	5.96	5.45	82.9	4.6	35.1	7.7	3.7
3.7	1.87	11.8	0.44	1.7	0.0	0.04	0.37	3.83	89.7	4.1	36.3	13.3	4.6
9.2	0.06	0.3	0.08	4.3	1.7	0.90	8.96	3.44	68.7	3.0	34.4	17.9	5.8
9.3	0.31	1.1	-0.04	4.1	0.8	1.09	9.56	3.11	73.8	2.5	40.2	27.1	6.4
7.7	1.34	4.3	0.04	3.3	0.8	0.51	4.17	2.66	79.7	5.0	51.4	12.9	7.0
5.8	0.88	5.2	0.16	4.1	1.2	0.70	7.34	3.84	73.9	3.9	28.1	11.5	5.2
3.8	1.89	10.9	0.00	5.3	1.5	1.26	10.50	3.71	68.8	1.7	16.0	20.3	7.1
0.0	3.46	29.8	0.27	4.6	0.9	0.95	9.04	4.02	72.4	1.6	7.4	18.0	6.2
3.6	1.21	10.2	0.37	3.8	9.0	0.57	4.46	3.21	68.8	3.4	5.4	8.6	7.7
5.2	1.31	7.6	0.28	5.0	12.9	0.72	5.55	3.60	64.8	1.4	14.0	18.1	8.1
8.4	0.14	1.0	0.09	4.5	0.3	0.61	5.74	4.38	75.0	5.0	19.1	2.4	5.3
8.1	0.63	3.4	0.60	4.1	0.3	0.50	4.16	4.49	80.9	4.5	25.2	6.9	5.9
8.7	0.16	1.1	0.00	6.0	0.8	1.26	12.14	3.54	69.8	3.9	16.2	9.3	7.1
5.3	2.10	10.3	-0.47	7.8	5.3	1.98	18.38	3.95	61.0	4.7	42.6	12.1	6.8
5.4	1.20	6.5	-0.25	7.1	1.1	1.20	9.39	3.99	77.0	0.7	13.0	38.6	7.5
9.0	0.00	0.0	0.00	0.0	-0.9	-10.82	-30.80	1.23	1006.0	4.3	131.7	39.6	3.8
4.6	1.46	9.7	-0.02	2.0	0.2	0.23	2.42	3.87	92.7	4.6	21.8	5.7	5.0
6.2	0.67	4.9	0.24	5.1	1.9	1.17	12.93	3.78	72.4	1.1	16.7	17.5	6.3
5.3	0.76	5.4	0.00	3.2	0.8	0.38	4.93	3.40	78.7	5.5	35.6	4.9	2.4
7.7	0.44	3.5	0.12	5.2	28.1	0.94	11.12	3.21	62.4	3.8	11.7	9.7	7.1
8.0	1.21	2.4	0.72	3.8	2.7	0.71	5.58	1.36	80.6	6.9	58.7	3.4	6.4
9.6	0.00	0.0	0.01	2.1	0.2	0.20	1.88	1.88	95.8	6.0	38.5	1.1	6.5
5.5	1.24	5.3	0.34	4.8	1.2	0.89	6.82	3.32	80.7	1.6	34.2	12.0	6.8
9.6	0.00	0.0	-0.01	3.8	0.4	0.55	3.82	3.51	84.4	8.0	79.7	0.0	6.0
5.7	1.43	6.4	-0.06	5.3	2.3	0.93	7.14	3.01	75.9	1.6	36.4	31.2	6.3
6.8	0.32	2.4	0.18	3.4	5.9	0.52	4.38	3.32	75.4	2.9	14.3	7.6	7.0
5.2	1.12	5.9	0.04	7.0	3.5	1.26	9.42	3.62	49.7	3.4	30.5	14.4	8.1
3.3	1.80	14.8	0.08	4.7	5.5	0.79	8.67	3.65	68.4	2.7	10.2	14.8	6.0

Name	City	State	2015 Rating	2014 Rating	Rating	Total Assets ($Mil)	One Year Asset Growth	Comm-ercial Loans	Cons-umer Loans	Mort-gage Loans	Secur-ities	Capital-ization Index	Lever-age Ratio	Risk-Based Capital Ratio
BankGloucester	Gloucester	MA	C-	C-	D+	230.2	9.28	4.3	0.4	35.0	9.3	6.3	8.3	12.2
BankIowa of Cedar Rapids	Cedar Rapids	IA	B+	B+	B+	595.8	9.30	9.8	2.3	18.8	14.6	7.8	10.5	13.2
BankLiberty	Kansas City	MO	A-	A-	B+	431.1	-1.94	15.6	0.5	15.2	5.0	7.8	11.0	13.2
BankNewport	Middletown	RI	B-	B-	C+	1428.2	6.66	5.5	2.4	33.1	15.0	8.3	9.9	13.8
BankORION	Orion	IL	B-	B-	B-	434.8	3.69	6.9	2.7	9.5	38.2	8.1	9.7	16.1
BankPacific, Ltd	Hagatna	GU	C+	C	C+	141.6	11.73	10.1	11.9	40.1	1.6	10.0	11.3	19.8
BankPlus	Belzoni	MS	B	B	B	2675.2	4.17	10.1	2.2	16.5	22.5	6.9	9.5	12.5
▲ BankSouth	Dothan	AL	A-	A-	A-	170.7	0.53	10.5	1.1	36.6	16.2	10.0	20.9	32.5
BankSouth	Greensboro	GA	A-	B+	B	531.4	21.08	2.1	0.8	40.8	3.9	9.3	10.5	15.4
BankStar Financial	Elkton	SD	B	B	B-	148.5	13.80	6.8	3.3	20.3	10.1	7.1	9.1	12.7
BankTennessee	Collierville	TN	B-	B-	C+	287.6	5.07	15.3	2.1	19.1	5.5	6.9	9.3	12.4
BankUnited, N.A.	Miami Lakes	FL	A-	B+	A-	27180.9	21.12	12.0	0.1	14.7	21.7	7.5	9.3	13.6
BankVista	Sartell	MN	C	C	C-	194.8	22.24	16.8	1.6	17.1	0.3	6.5	9.0	12.1
Bankwell Bank	New Canaan	CT	B	B	B-	1560.6	19.44	12.7	0.1	13.0	6.4	7.5	10.5	12.9
BANKWEST	Rockford	MN	B-	B-	C+	130.2	6.06	12.2	1.9	13.7	15.1	7.0	9.0	14.2
Bankwest of Kansas	Goodland	KS	B	B+	B+	91.6	-1.41	5.0	1.5	2.4	16.8	10.0	12.4	16.9
BankWest, Inc.	Pierre	SD	C	C+	C+	982.5	10.09	9.0	8.7	4.2	12.4	6.1	9.5	11.8
Banner Bank	Walla Walla	WA	A-	A-	A-	9557.8	89.21	11.1	1.3	9.0	13.0	7.0	10.7	12.5
Banner Banks	Birnamwood	WI	B-	B-	B-	94.1	-0.90	1.7	0.5	7.5	33.1	10.0	13.7	30.9
▼ Banner Capital Bank	Harrisburg	NE	C+	B+	A-	130.8	15.66	11.5	2.3	2.7	7.8	5.2	9.8	11.1
Banterra Bank	Eldorado	IL	B-	B-	B-	1422.5	7.85	16.2	19.3	7.2	23.2	6.4	9.1	12.0
Bar Harbor Bank & Trust	Bar Harbor	ME	B+	B+	B+	1717.0	9.56	4.1	0.4	32.4	31.3	7.4	9.3	17.2
Bar Harbor S&L Assn.	Bar Harbor	ME	B-	C+	C+	99.9	7.70	0.0	0.1	68.5	4.9	7.3	9.2	18.8
▲ Baraboo National Bank	Baraboo	WI	B-	C-	D+	412.1	-5.56	4.3	2.2	11.1	11.7	10.0	13.6	20.8
Barclays Bank Delaware	Wilmington	DE	C+	C+	C	31244.4	17.40	0.6	78.3	0.0	0.2	10.0	11.1	15.3
Barrington Bank & Trust Co., N.A.	Barrington	IL	B-	B-	B-	2077.6	13.55	26.7	16.8	30.4	5.1	5.5	9.6	11.4
Barwick Banking Co.	Barwick	GA	D-	D-	D-	11.5	0.78	3.0	1.5	1.6	45.2	6.7	8.8	53.2
▼ Basile State Bank	Basile	LA	C-	C-	C+	54.3	-2.76	5.4	10.3	43.3	4.0	8.8	11.0	14.0
Bath Savings Institution	Bath	ME	B	B	B-	820.1	4.98	4.5	0.8	31.4	23.0	10.0	11.7	19.0
Bath State Bank	Bath	IN	B+	B	C	150.4	5.78	2.8	1.0	16.5	21.1	9.2	10.4	17.2
Battle Creek State Bank	Battle Creek	NE	B-	B-	C+	32.8	-0.67	51.7	1.3	2.6	7.9	10.0	13.1	17.4
Baxter State Bank	Baxter Springs	KS	B	B	B	28.6	1.79	2.8	11.6	26.9	17.1	10.0	20.6	46.8
▲ Bay Bank	Green Bay	WI	C+	C-	D	82.4	0.74	9.2	4.5	17.0	14.2	10.0	13.8	21.0
▼ Bay Bank, FSB	Columbia	MD	C	B-	B-	605.6	27.73	9.9	0.3	27.1	8.7	8.3	10.8	13.6
Bay Commercial Bank	Walnut Creek	CA	A-	A-	B+	652.7	3.60	9.4	0.2	3.9	2.3	8.7	11.2	13.9
Bay Port State Bank	Bay Port	MI	D	C-	D+	92.9	-1.48	12.4	2.7	22.8	0.1	4.3	7.4	10.6
Bay State Savings Bank	Worcester	MA	C	C	C	384.9	8.10	2.8	1.3	48.8	7.7	6.4	8.4	13.0
Bay-Vanguard FSB	Sparrows Point	MD	C-	C+	D+	167.3	1.16	1.6	7.5	45.7	10.7	10.0	11.6	21.0
▲ Baybank	Gladstone	MI	C	C	B	88.4	2.38	16.8	5.5	17.7	34.1	7.2	9.1	13.2
▲ BayCoast Bank	Swansea	MA	C	C-	C-	1252.6	14.12	9.1	3.8	30.6	14.1	7.2	9.4	12.7
BCB Community Bank	Bayonne	NJ	D+	C-	D+	1676.1	7.90	1.1	0.0	25.8	3.2	5.8	7.8	11.6
▲ BCBank, Inc.	Philippi	WV	C	D	C+	117.6	3.00	7.4	6.0	16.2	17.4	10.0	11.2	17.2
Beach Community Bank	Fort Walton Beach	FL	E-	E-	E-	531.0	-1.95	5.1	0.2	17.4	6.6	0.0	3.6	5.1
▲ Beal Bank USA	Las Vegas	NV	C-	D+	C+	5424.2	3.48	48.5	0.0	6.8	23.5	10.0	30.1	33.6
Beal Bank, SSB	Plano	TX	C+	C	C-	2424.9	21.97	21.9	0.7	42.9	2.4	10.0	35.6	62.4
Bear State Bank	Little Rock	AR	B	B	B	2003.8	36.53	13.1	1.8	17.9	9.9	7.8	10.4	13.2
▼ Beardstown Savings s.b.	Beardstown	IL	C	C+	C+	48.7	6.97	1.1	6.6	48.9	26.2	9.6	10.7	22.2
Beartooth Bank	Billings	MT	B-	C+	B-	43.3	11.35	11.4	1.2	14.5	0.1	10.0	14.6	18.5
Beauregard Federal Savings Bank	DeRidder	LA	A-	A-	A-	60.5	2.66	2.9	8.2	41.2	15.6	10.0	18.5	33.2
Bedford Federal Savings Bank	Bedford	IN	B-	B-	C	123.0	-3.87	3.0	2.5	59.6	0.0	9.1	10.4	17.1
Bedford Loan & Deposit Bank	Bedford	KY	B-	B-	B-	92.9	7.90	1.3	5.1	31.1	37.8	10.0	13.2	26.3
Belgrade State Bank	Belgrade	MO	C-	D	C+	241.6	5.60	10.1	4.5	31.2	9.2	8.0	9.6	14.6
Bell Bank	Fargo	ND	B+	B+	B+	3993.4	13.62	13.2	2.8	15.2	1.9	5.2	9.3	11.1
Bellevue State Bank	Bellevue	IA	B-	B-	B-	98.3	7.94	11.4	5.2	19.8	6.8	4.5	13.9	10.8
Belmont Bank & Trust Co.	Chicago	IL	B-	C+	C	365.5	15.28	13.4	0.2	11.7	21.9	8.3	9.9	13.9
Belmont Federal S&L Assn.	Belmont	NC	B-	B-	B-	95.5	-0.39	0.0	0.1	58.1	6.4	10.0	18.5	40.6
Belmont Savings Bank	Belmont	MA	C+	C	C	2073.8	22.54	0.2	3.5	47.3	7.7	5.6	7.6	11.5
Belmont Savings Bank	Bellaire	OH	B	B-	C+	465.7	-17.11	0.0	2.6	12.7	81.3	10.0	13.1	57.0
Belpre Savings Bank	Belpre	OH	D	D	C+	47.7	-5.65	0.0	14.1	47.0	5.3	10.0	15.0	30.2
Belt Valley Bank	Belt	MT	B	B	B-	58.4	-2.58	5.0	4.5	28.1	12.2	10.0	14.3	20.8

Asset Quality Index	Adjusted Non-Performing Loans as a % of Total Loans	as a % of Capital	Net Charge-Offs Avg Loans	Profitability Index	Net Income ($Mil)	Return on Assets (R.O.A.)	Return on Equity (R.O.E.)	Net Interest Spread	Overhead Efficiency Ratio	Liquidity Index	Liquidity Ratio	Hot Money Ratio	Stability Index
2.5	2.38	22.3	0.07	3.4	0.7	0.44	5.26	3.58	80.0	1.6	15.4	22.8	4.7
6.5	0.35	2.5	-0.03	5.6	5.7	1.31	11.77	3.51	66.2	3.5	5.4	9.9	8.0
5.8	0.46	3.0	-0.05	7.0	4.0	1.23	10.71	5.11	61.8	3.2	11.1	12.4	7.7
6.2	0.88	6.5	0.03	4.3	8.9	0.85	8.29	3.23	66.0	3.9	19.0	8.4	8.2
4.8	1.56	8.3	-0.03	4.5	2.9	0.92	8.20	3.44	64.7	3.0	17.8	14.2	6.2
3.0	3.11	19.8	0.11	3.5	0.4	0.44	3.77	5.05	89.7	4.6	22.8	5.5	6.1
5.7	1.58	10.4	0.43	4.7	16.4	0.82	8.80	3.74	72.9	3.9	11.0	9.2	7.3
8.9	0.04	0.2	-0.03	5.4	1.6	1.22	5.96	3.54	63.9	3.4	22.3	12.5	8.4
5.3	1.01	7.7	-0.12	10.0	10.8	3.12	29.10	4.79	79.7	4.0	12.1	8.4	7.1
5.1	0.63	5.4	0.00	5.4	1.3	1.18	10.84	4.05	67.7	1.7	10.5	20.2	6.6
5.0	0.55	4.1	0.02	5.9	3.0	1.40	13.69	4.43	64.7	3.1	12.8	13.3	6.7
7.1	0.75	5.5	0.10	5.6	175.4	0.92	9.27	3.83	59.1	1.6	17.0	20.7	9.1
2.6	1.44	12.3	0.35	7.4	1.4	1.06	11.75	3.90	61.9	0.7	12.8	31.3	5.3
5.8	0.43	3.3	0.01	5.8	11.6	1.09	10.19	3.63	48.6	0.8	13.5	40.6	8.1
4.7	1.45	10.2	-0.08	7.3	1.7	1.78	19.08	4.61	65.4	5.2	27.6	2.9	5.5
7.5	0.00	0.0	0.00	4.4	0.6	0.82	6.41	4.54	77.7	4.6	24.2	5.7	7.2
3.4	1.62	12.5	0.05	8.6	13.2	1.90	18.24	4.62	68.7	1.6	12.0	8.4	8.4
6.1	0.45	3.1	-0.04	5.5	65.2	0.91	6.66	4.24	69.9	4.3	13.8	6.8	8.9
8.3	0.40	1.1	-0.03	3.1	0.5	0.64	4.62	2.74	76.7	5.9	61.6	8.7	7.5
5.7	0.36	2.9	0.00	5.9	1.3	1.40	13.17	4.29	63.9	0.6	6.2	36.2	5.0
3.7	1.39	10.0	0.11	5.9	14.5	1.41	14.12	3.74	62.2	2.9	18.2	15.3	9.6
7.2	0.69	4.5	0.01	5.2	13.7	1.10	11.10	3.00	59.1	0.7	8.2	11.0	8.6
6.3	0.62	5.2	0.00	5.2	0.7	1.00	10.93	2.87	46.4	0.8	16.1	37.1	5.6
4.0	2.01	8.5	0.11	5.0	3.9	1.27	9.54	3.19	77.7	4.4	31.9	9.8	4.7
2.5	1.65	9.6	3.21	9.0	334.3	1.51	11.94	9.27	44.4	1.1	21.3	5.7	9.5
6.1	0.34	3.1	0.08	8.8	21.2	1.45	14.01	3.08	74.6	3.4	3.9	8.1	7.8
10.0	0.00	0.0	0.08	0.1	-0.1	-0.64	-7.42	1.60	134.6	6.3	87.6	9.5	1.8
2.1	3.26	21.6	0.34	8.4	0.8	1.83	17.07	5.46	65.7	1.6	14.8	23.5	7.6
8.9	0.31	1.7	0.00	4.4	5.3	0.89	7.24	3.48	69.3	2.2	16.7	17.9	7.8
5.4	1.06	6.3	0.01	5.5	1.5	1.33	12.27	3.94	67.5	2.8	28.1	16.9	6.8
8.0	0.02	0.1	0.00	3.2	0.1	0.52	3.92	3.30	78.8	0.8	15.7	36.5	6.4
4.2	4.33	11.5	0.50	4.3	0.2	0.80	3.54	5.38	84.2	6.2	41.0	2.1	7.5
3.0	4.54	18.4	0.53	6.7	0.8	1.26	8.92	4.71	69.7	1.7	20.7	22.9	6.2
2.4	3.31	23.4	0.11	2.6	1.2	0.30	2.31	4.19	89.6	3.1	16.3	13.4	6.6
6.7	0.29	2.0	0.06	5.7	4.0	0.84	7.23	4.28	62.8	1.8	19.8	21.7	8.7
2.1	2.15	23.3	0.04	3.1	0.3	0.35	4.89	3.94	84.3	1.6	7.0	20.7	3.8
3.9	1.12	10.3	0.16	2.7	0.9	0.33	3.74	3.24	82.3	2.7	10.2	14.8	4.7
2.7	4.57	26.7	0.99	1.2	-0.4	-0.28	-2.37	4.04	84.0	2.9	19.7	14.8	6.3
3.1	2.74	15.9	0.87	4.0	0.6	0.80	8.60	3.88	78.1	4.1	40.7	14.7	5.7
6.2	0.63	5.1	0.00	2.8	4.1	0.47	5.66	3.36	86.3	3.2	15.2	13.2	6.6
2.8	2.03	19.3	0.03	3.3	5.7	0.44	5.63	3.30	79.5	1.1	9.7	29.0	6.7
4.0	3.12	17.5	0.00	2.3	0.3	0.38	3.74	4.00	92.1	4.0	17.3	8.8	4.8
0.3	22.06	338.0	0.07	0.2	-1.4	-0.35	-9.19	2.58	110.9	0.7	12.7	35.6	1.1
0.4	17.62	35.0	0.39	7.5	155.0	4.03	11.66	7.17	27.9	1.5	28.8	34.6	7.4
3.4	7.80	15.1	0.06	10.0	74.4	4.21	10.26	5.54	42.9	1.0	23.5	15.9	7.3
4.4	1.24	8.8	0.10	5.0	14.2	0.97	8.03	3.97	66.5	2.3	9.7	17.1	9.6
4.1	2.83	15.7	0.10	2.7	0.1	0.36	3.24	3.84	86.2	3.8	36.4	14.9	4.8
7.4	0.19	0.9	-0.11	4.6	0.3	1.02	7.02	4.71	72.9	1.2	13.7	28.6	6.5
6.3	1.64	5.8	0.15	9.7	1.0	2.29	13.05	4.95	54.6	3.0	19.9	14.6	9.5
5.7	0.48	3.4	0.07	4.0	0.6	0.63	6.40	3.98	73.8	2.3	15.3	17.4	5.7
5.9	2.20	8.2	-0.09	3.0	0.3	0.47	3.34	3.97	86.9	3.3	38.9	18.3	6.8
2.0	2.78	22.0	0.18	5.5	1.9	1.06	11.20	4.29	69.0	1.6	16.4	23.8	4.6
7.9	0.18	1.7	0.00	6.7	32.9	1.13	12.21	4.10	68.8	4.1	4.3	4.4	8.5
4.7	1.04	5.8	0.01	9.3	1.6	2.21	16.31	3.96	45.1	4.1	16.9	8.2	9.3
3.7	1.36	9.4	0.17	8.5	3.7	1.42	14.42	4.11	42.1	0.9	18.6	37.1	5.6
9.0	0.91	3.2	0.00	2.8	0.3	0.40	2.16	3.19	83.6	1.7	36.2	40.5	7.8
7.5	0.29	3.1	0.00	3.8	8.7	0.60	7.93	2.49	57.2	1.8	7.7	9.1	6.2
9.5	2.68	3.1	0.42	5.4	3.4	0.93	6.95	2.83	49.8	2.9	54.4	31.8	4.4
4.4	2.92	11.8	0.50	0.0	-0.6	-1.61	-10.59	2.61	183.3	2.6	34.6	20.4	4.9
4.2	3.22	16.2	0.04	6.1	0.5	1.03	7.41	4.38	63.6	3.6	18.1	11.2	6.9

Name	City	State	2015 Rating	2014 Rating	Rating	Total Assets ($Mil)	One Year Asset Growth	Asset Mix (As a % of Total Assets) Commercial Loans	Consumer Loans	Mortgage Loans	Securities	Capitalization Index	Leverage Ratio	Risk-Based Capital Ratio
Ben Franklin Bank of Illinois	Arlington Heights	IL	D-	D-	D-	79.9	-6.20	1.5	0.6	34.8	9.4	8.1	9.7	16.8
▲ Benchmark Bank	Gahanna	OH	C+	C-	D-	137.2	7.27	2.3	0.0	44.2	1.6	9.0	10.3	14.7
▲ Benchmark Bank	Plano	TX	B-	C+	B-	527.5	4.07	7.9	3.0	18.6	0.5	5.9	9.4	11.7
Benchmark Community Bank	Kenbridge	VA	A	A	A	542.7	6.83	5.9	3.4	43.4	6.6	10.0	11.8	18.3
Bendena State Bank	Bendena	KS	C+	C+	C+	61.9	8.97	5.2	4.0	13.6	19.0	5.3	8.2	11.2
Beneficial Bank	Philadelphia	PA	C+	C+	C	5580.0	17.91	6.0	7.4	18.8	20.2	10.0	15.0	21.5
Beneficial State Bank	Oakland	CA	C+	C+	C-	641.1	52.66	15.6	13.4	4.6	4.4	9.0	10.3	14.2
Bennington State Bank	Salina	KS	B+	A-	A-	717.5	8.67	10.5	1.8	14.2	27.8	7.2	9.2	14.0
Benton County State Bank	Blairstown	IA	B+	B+	B+	42.4	4.36	7.9	0.1	8.5	15.3	10.0	14.4	16.7
Benton State Bank	Benton	WI	D+	D+	D+	63.5	2.33	4.7	7.4	36.0	5.0	6.2	8.2	12.3
Berkshire Bank	Pittsfield	MA	C+	C+	C+	7893.9	1.39	12.6	5.7	24.7	13.5	4.9	7.6	10.9
Berkshire Bank	New York	NY	B-	B-	B	710.1	-5.18	0.9	0.1	9.0	31.1	10.0	14.7	27.4
Bessemer Trust Co.	Woodbridge	NJ	B+	A-	B+	871.3	44.33	5.8	17.8	0.0	47.8	5.1	7.1	18.8
Bessemer Trust Co. of California, N.A.	San Francisco	CA	U	U	U	8.0	12.80	0.0	0.0	0.0	62.0	10.0	100.	447.1
Bessemer Trust Co. of Delaware, N.A.	Wilmington	DE	U	U	U	16.5	6.99	0.0	0.0	0.0	65.6	10.0	94.2	252.9
Bessemer Trust Co., N.A.	New York	NY	B+	B+	B+	2117.1	19.62	7.2	12.7	0.0	19.0	4.6	6.6	23.1
Best Hometown Bank	Collinsville	IL	D	D-	D+	109.6	6.64	0.7	0.3	51.1	22.9	10.0	12.3	24.3
Better Banks	Peoria	IL	C+	C+	C	285.4	11.45	4.5	22.2	21.2	25.4	5.9	7.9	13.4
Beverly Bank	Beverly	MA	C+	B-	C+	401.6	6.92	6.6	0.1	37.7	5.5	7.3	9.2	12.9
Beverly Bank & Trust Co., N.A.	Chicago	IL	B-	B-	B-	1136.4	30.63	33.1	12.0	3.6	11.8	5.2	9.9	11.2
Biddeford Savings Bank	Biddeford	ME	B-	C	C	433.9	6.08	6.2	0.5	45.6	8.2	7.7	9.8	13.1
Big Bend Banks, N.A.	Marfa	TX	A-	A-	B	124.0	-4.77	1.7	4.7	4.5	73.0	10.0	12.6	39.4
Big Horn Federal Savings Bank	Greybull	WY	C+	C+	C+	235.1	0.52	7.7	3.4	11.8	25.0	7.9	9.6	20.9
Bippus State Bank	Huntington	IN	B	B	B-	146.0	6.55	14.4	3.7	10.8	12.7	8.0	10.6	13.3
Biscayne Bank	Coconut Grove	FL	B+	B	C+	747.2	25.10	2.5	0.8	46.1	0.5	6.4	8.4	13.9
Bison State Bank	Bison	KS	D	D	D+	8.3	-9.00	6.5	8.8	6.0	48.7	9.2	10.4	24.6
Black Hills Community Bank, N.A.	Rapid City	SD	B-	B	B	215.2	25.58	12.7	0.8	10.4	4.3	9.1	11.0	14.3
Black Mountain Savings Bank, SSB	Black Mountain	NC	C+	B-	B-	36.6	0.04	0.0	0.5	63.9	0.0	10.0	13.0	34.0
Black River Country Bank	Black River Falls	WI	B	B	B-	74.2	1.92	5.3	4.2	36.2	7.3	10.0	13.5	20.6
Blackhawk Bank	Beloit	WI	C+	C	C-	658.8	7.35	21.4	0.8	11.4	29.2	6.7	8.7	13.3
Blackhawk Bank & Trust	Milan	IL	B+	A-	A-	1254.3	7.97	9.6	1.0	8.6	52.5	8.9	10.2	18.2
BlackRidgeBANK	Fargo	ND	C-	D+	D	430.1	7.59	11.7	2.4	23.2	8.2	6.1	8.5	11.8
Blackrock Institutional Trust Co., N.A.	San Francisco	CA	U	U	U	4428.8	-3.58	0.0	0.0	0.0	7.5	10.0	68.3	92.9
Blanco National Bank	Blanco	TX	B	B	B-	183.2	2.44	3.7	3.3	15.1	38.6	8.1	9.8	18.7
BLC Community Bank	Little Chute	WI	A-	A	B-	192.6	11.05	6.6	0.6	15.6	17.2	10.0	15.5	21.7
Blissfield State Bank	Blissfield	MI	B-	B-	B-	96.3	2.41	5.0	2.6	18.8	31.4	9.9	10.9	19.6
BloomBank	Bloomfield	IN	B	B-	C	387.2	0.51	5.3	1.0	18.6	23.1	9.8	10.9	16.5
Bloomsdale Bank	Bloomsdale	MO	A-	A-	A-	225.9	5.32	4.8	1.8	20.1	30.0	7.4	9.2	15.0
Blue Grass Federal S&L Assn.	Paris	KY	D	D	C-	34.0	-12.34	0.9	3.2	56.3	15.4	10.0	24.4	48.0
Blue Grass Savings Bank	Blue Grass	IA	B	B	B-	192.3	3.42	8.3	0.9	14.1	45.6	10.0	15.1	28.1
Blue Grass Valley Bank	Blue Grass	VA	C-	C-	C	39.1	0.42	5.8	5.9	34.1	6.3	10.0	12.1	19.1
Blue Hills Bank	Hyde Park	MA	C+	C	C-	2310.8	19.64	6.9	1.4	33.8	18.0	10.0	12.9	17.0
Blue Ridge Bank	Walhalla	SC	B	B	B	112.6	5.38	1.2	3.1	42.0	34.7	9.0	10.4	20.9
Blue Ridge Bank	Luray	VA	B+	B+	B	296.4	15.25	6.2	4.9	33.4	11.2	9.3	10.6	15.5
Blue Ridge Bank and Trust Co.	Independence	MO	C+	C	C-	515.5	6.09	10.5	11.0	8.0	17.2	6.9	8.9	12.7
Blue Sky Bank	Pawhuska	OK	B	B	B+	204.1	-8.65	31.5	1.0	9.0	2.2	9.4	12.2	14.5
▼ Bluegrass Community Bank	Danville	KY	D	C+	B-	72.5	0.08	5.6	3.0	31.8	13.3	7.0	9.0	15.2
BlueHarbor Bank	Mooresville	NC	B	B	B	169.2	11.20	10.5	0.4	13.6	10.0	10.0	14.2	16.9
BMO Harris Bank, N.A.	Chicago	IL	C+	B-	B-	106682.9	0.94	23.8	6.1	7.3	16.0	8.9	11.0	14.1
BMO Harris Central N.A.	Roselle	IL	U	U	U	7.8	1.25	0.0	0.0	0.0	0.0	10.0	86.1	440.6
BMW Bank of North America	Salt Lake City	UT	A-	B+	B+	9928.6	-0.42	0.0	75.6	0.0	23.7	10.0	14.1	15.8
BNA Bank	New Albany	MS	A-	A-	A-	463.7	5.89	2.2	4.0	22.2	33.0	10.0	12.7	21.6
BNC National Bank	Glendale	AZ	B+	A-	B+	941.8	7.97	6.7	2.7	9.3	43.5	8.1	9.8	18.2
BNY Mellon Trust of Delaware	Wilmington	DE	B-	B-	B-	137.7	-42.44	0.0	0.0	25.6	0.0	10.0	46.4	97.9
▲ BNY Mellon, N.A.	Pittsburgh	PA	B-	C+	B	23365.9	7.63	1.1	8.7	30.0	11.3	5.3	7.8	11.2
Bodcaw Bank	Stamps	AR	B+	B+	B+	78.8	3.35	3.7	4.5	2.6	60.5	10.0	11.5	29.6
Boelus State Bank	Boelus	NE	C+	C+	C+	15.4	2.13	1.7	6.7	1.3	4.7	10.0	13.6	26.4
Bofl Federal Bank	San Diego	CA	A-	A-	A-	7848.0	25.57	5.3	1.2	54.9	5.7	7.3	9.2	14.8
Bogota Savings Bank	Bogota	NJ	B	B+	B+	611.7	10.20	0.0	0.1	55.5	10.3	9.3	10.5	17.8
Boiling Springs Savings Bank	Rutherford	NJ	C+	C+	B-	1591.1	5.82	0.0	0.0	51.4	9.8	10.0	12.8	21.2

Asset Quality Index	Adjusted Non-Performing Loans as a % of Total Loans	Adjusted Non-Performing Loans as a % of Capital	Net Charge-Offs Avg Loans	Profitability Index	Net Income ($Mil)	Return on Assets (R.O.A.)	Return on Equity (R.O.E.)	Net Interest Spread	Overhead Efficiency Ratio	Liquidity Index	Liquidity Ratio	Hot Money Ratio	Stability Index
2.7	4.05	26.1	-0.23	0.0	-0.8	-1.30	-12.95	3.26	147.7	3.0	26.6	15.4	3.0
3.7	1.79	14.1	0.04	4.8	4.9	5.21	50.73	4.45	90.0	0.9	12.6	32.8	3.5
6.1	0.33	2.7	0.13	5.9	5.6	1.42	15.39	4.60	80.2	3.5	8.1	6.7	7.5
7.5	0.68	4.4	0.04	7.3	5.1	1.26	10.87	4.55	65.8	3.9	15.1	9.4	8.2
5.5	1.05	8.9	0.02	5.6	0.6	1.32	15.51	3.97	60.9	3.7	5.3	9.6	4.3
7.5	0.44	2.0	0.04	3.1	17.0	0.43	2.45	3.05	80.1	4.5	26.1	4.8	7.9
3.9	1.36	9.1	0.00	3.1	1.3	0.32	2.75	4.43	79.3	0.9	19.6	34.8	6.5
4.7	1.48	9.3	0.65	7.1	8.7	1.63	17.47	3.08	41.5	3.3	17.5	12.8	8.0
7.5	0.00	0.0	0.00	7.0	0.4	1.29	8.93	4.24	57.6	1.7	23.7	24.4	6.3
2.1	1.94	18.6	0.20	4.1	0.4	0.78	9.72	4.62	78.8	0.9	8.5	31.3	4.4
5.2	0.53	5.2	0.21	4.2	49.2	0.84	7.30	3.29	62.1	1.2	6.9	26.7	8.0
7.7	1.44	4.3	0.01	3.6	3.8	0.71	4.71	2.97	72.5	3.4	55.7	26.2	9.3
7.5	0.00	0.0	0.00	8.7	10.9	1.70	24.29	1.13	78.5	5.9	31.4	0.0	6.4
10.0	na	0.0	na	10.0	0.6	10.51	10.63	0.72	69.9	4.0	na	0.0	6.3
10.0	na	0.0	na	10.0	4.1	34.54	38.69	0.80	73.6	4.0	na	0.0	6.3
7.7	0.00	0.0	0.00	9.1	30.4	1.87	19.70	0.69	89.9	7.8	60.1	0.0	7.6
9.6	0.12	0.7	0.05	0.1	-0.4	-0.55	-6.19	2.31	123.2	1.6	30.8	32.0	3.9
4.3	0.55	4.3	0.02	3.8	1.8	0.89	9.87	3.28	73.2	5.1	31.6	5.6	5.4
6.8	0.31	2.7	0.01	3.7	1.7	0.59	6.45	3.42	73.7	2.7	10.0	13.6	5.3
6.6	0.21	1.5	0.08	2.9	2.2	0.27	2.73	3.20	84.4	3.0	14.7	13.5	6.8
6.0	0.51	4.3	-0.05	3.5	2.1	0.65	6.71	3.48	73.9	2.2	11.4	11.1	5.7
9.4	0.02	0.0	0.02	5.3	1.2	1.26	8.69	3.91	65.7	6.3	67.8	9.4	8.7
6.8	0.83	3.4	0.03	2.9	0.6	0.31	3.13	3.08	84.3	5.3	43.7	9.1	5.5
5.3	0.83	5.7	0.03	6.5	1.7	1.58	15.32	3.99	64.6	2.3	13.2	12.5	7.2
8.7	0.19	1.8	0.02	8.2	6.6	1.29	15.45	3.74	44.2	1.4	14.9	22.6	5.4
5.4	1.70	5.4	1.15	0.6	0.0	-0.25	-2.37	3.14	107.6	5.5	43.4	4.3	4.5
7.3	0.12	0.8	0.00	4.3	1.5	1.01	8.95	3.65	71.1	0.8	15.3	38.8	7.8
9.9	0.00	0.0	0.00	2.6	0.1	0.35	2.70	3.10	84.3	1.5	34.2	46.1	6.2
4.9	2.30	12.9	0.00	5.9	0.8	1.43	10.83	3.95	61.6	3.2	15.1	13.0	8.2
3.6	2.01	12.9	0.28	5.5	5.3	1.06	10.82	3.57	64.9	4.1	17.6	8.3	5.6
6.7	1.79	7.1	1.44	4.5	7.9	0.86	7.53	3.01	54.7	4.1	21.2	10.3	8.7
2.1	1.93	16.9	0.13	4.9	2.4	0.76	6.26	4.24	73.3	2.5	14.2	11.1	6.6
6.5	na	0.0	na	9.5	248.1	7.46	9.75	1.51	66.9	4.0	46.8	0.0	7.0
6.8	0.94	4.8	0.14	5.0	1.6	1.17	11.66	4.81	74.0	4.8	39.6	11.0	6.5
7.6	0.04	0.2	0.00	8.3	2.4	1.73	11.02	3.51	53.3	1.8	27.3	19.7	8.9
5.4	1.20	5.4	0.02	3.9	0.6	0.88	7.85	3.58	77.6	4.9	52.7	12.6	6.7
5.4	0.92	5.1	0.27	4.2	2.3	0.80	6.46	4.20	77.3	2.9	30.7	17.5	5.9
7.0	0.22	1.4	0.18	8.9	3.7	2.23	21.45	4.14	50.6	1.5	25.8	27.9	8.1
4.4	6.70	17.2	0.24	0.0	-1.9	-6.84	-27.06	3.69	292.0	2.1	36.6	29.8	4.1
7.5	1.43	4.3	-0.11	4.9	1.4	1.02	6.69	2.69	40.0	3.3	50.0	22.7	7.4
1.5	6.65	35.1	0.09	3.7	0.2	0.53	4.36	4.18	79.4	3.7	28.2	12.8	6.3
7.9	0.45	2.6	0.27	2.7	5.7	0.34	2.56	2.59	75.3	1.9	20.7	11.0	8.7
4.6	3.28	17.0	0.01	4.7	0.7	0.82	8.12	4.05	69.9	3.6	41.4	17.2	5.5
8.2	0.16	1.2	0.52	5.3	1.9	0.93	8.67	3.70	59.8	1.1	11.0	29.0	6.0
3.8	1.32	8.6	-0.29	4.2	2.8	0.74	8.02	3.47	70.9	4.0	19.6	9.2	5.4
4.8	1.50	9.4	0.03	7.9	3.0	1.90	16.80	4.54	54.8	0.8	13.4	33.9	7.3
6.0	0.62	4.4	0.07	0.9	-0.1	-0.21	-2.23	3.62	98.3	1.4	26.4	30.8	3.7
8.6	0.33	1.9	-0.04	4.4	0.8	0.70	4.88	3.95	70.6	2.7	13.9	15.3	7.0
4.3	1.57	8.7	0.16	3.4	488.1	0.62	4.14	2.76	71.9	4.1	29.9	8.9	8.4
10.0	na	0.0	na	4.7	0.1	0.77	0.90	3.77	-1400.0	4.0	na	0.0	6.4
5.6	0.16	0.8	0.28	9.0	114.4	1.46	10.69	2.76	26.2	1.5	29.5	0.4	10.0
6.4	1.24	5.2	0.11	6.3	4.3	1.26	9.96	3.54	56.4	2.8	28.2	17.0	7.7
7.6	0.60	2.9	0.22	5.3	6.7	0.98	9.52	3.31	75.3	3.5	35.0	12.1	7.5
3.2	14.15	11.8	0.07	9.5	2.3	2.14	3.93	2.22	56.1	8.1	83.2	0.0	8.2
6.8	0.04	0.3	0.00	5.7	161.2	0.93	6.48	1.52	65.9	0.8	19.7	64.9	8.2
6.7	2.53	6.2	1.07	4.2	0.5	0.86	7.12	3.14	65.7	3.7	74.9	26.4	6.7
8.3	0.43	1.3	0.00	4.0	0.1	0.75	5.55	2.58	55.4	5.0	58.7	11.3	6.5
7.1	0.63	5.8	0.07	9.8	102.0	1.82	21.21	3.88	31.8	2.3	14.3	7.0	8.3
7.5	0.44	3.3	0.00	4.2	2.8	0.62	5.96	2.30	56.2	0.7	12.9	41.3	6.7
5.1	1.79	11.3	0.05	2.9	4.4	0.38	2.94	2.95	77.8	1.3	9.1	26.8	8.4

Name	City	State	2015 Rating	2014 Rating	Rating	Total Assets ($Mil)	One Year Asset Growth	Commercial Loans	Consumer Loans	Mortgage Loans	Securities	Capitalization Index	Leverage Ratio	Risk-Based Capital Ratio
BOKF, N.A.	Tulsa	OK	B	B+	B+	32669.4	7.62	19.5	1.2	6.4	28.8	5.9	8.0	11.7
BOM	Montgomery	LA	B+	B+	A-	310.0	37.56	10.2	4.7	25.3	5.6	10.0	11.0	15.0
Bonanza Valley State Bank	Brooten	MN	C	C	C	60.2	-1.76	13.6	2.7	28.2	12.1	6.6	9.1	12.2
Bonduel State Bank	Bonduel	WI	B+	A-	A-	55.4	6.09	8.3	2.9	6.3	46.7	10.0	22.2	57.1
Boone Bank & Trust Co.	Boone	IA	A-	A-	A-	147.5	-0.04	5.1	0.5	5.5	45.7	9.2	10.5	17.0
Boonville Federal Savings Bank	Boonville	IN	C-	C-	C-	46.3	-1.42	3.1	6.6	49.4	8.5	9.0	10.4	20.7
▼ Border State Bank	Greenbush	MN	C+	B-	C+	407.1	4.53	11.9	7.3	13.2	14.4	9.8	10.9	14.9
Boston Private Bank & Trust Co.	Boston	MA	B	B+	B+	7512.5	7.23	6.3	2.3	32.4	17.7	6.8	8.8	13.0
Boston Trust & Investment Mgmt Co.	Boston	MA	A-	A-	A-	48.7	-3.70	0.1	0.0	0.0	4.4	10.0	52.1	90.0
Boundary Waters Bank	Ely	MN	D	D	E-	125.8	8.86	2.4	0.9	16.8	10.5	6.9	8.9	12.7
Bradford National Bank of Greenville	Greenville	IL	B	B	B	278.9	0.45	3.5	1.7	15.9	42.4	9.0	10.3	18.3
Brady National Bank	Brady	TX	B-	B-	B-	115.5	5.79	12.0	2.6	11.8	44.6	7.1	9.1	17.4
▲ Brainerd S&L Assn., A Federal Assn.	Brainerd	MN	D	D	D	64.7	1.91	0.2	1.3	53.1	14.0	6.8	8.8	15.5
Braintree Co-operative Bank	Braintree	MA	D+	D+	C-	259.3	3.32	3.0	0.4	39.6	25.6	5.9	7.9	12.4
Branch Banking and Trust Co.	Winston-Salem	NC	B	B	B-	217378.1	6.61	11.8	7.6	15.8	21.8	7.7	9.5	13.4
Brand Banking Co.	Lawrenceville	GA	D	D	D	2400.7	8.66	29.6	6.5	11.5	5.8	5.6	9.5	11.5
Brannen Bank	Inverness	FL	C+	C+	C+	471.5	9.08	0.5	1.2	38.6	27.3	5.0	7.0	18.9
Branson Bank	Branson	MO	B-	C-	D+	189.8	5.43	4.0	2.3	25.4	4.7	8.8	10.2	14.4
Brantley Bank and Trust Co.	Brantley	AL	B+	B+	B+	73.8	4.92	8.2	5.5	4.1	56.9	10.0	13.8	27.0
Brattleboro S&L Assn.	Brattleboro	VT	C-	C-	C-	177.2	8.78	4.0	1.0	44.6	0.4	7.2	9.2	13.6
Brazos National Bank	Richwood	TX	B+	B+	B	29.7	9.55	0.9	2.8	76.6	0.0	10.0	19.3	40.6
Breda Savings Bank	Breda	IA	A	A	A-	54.8	2.88	4.8	1.6	12.3	48.5	10.0	13.9	24.9
Bremer Bank, N.A.	Saint Paul	MN	B+	B+	B	11413.6	11.32	10.4	2.6	6.4	23.7	6.5	8.6	12.1
Bremer Trust, N.A.	Saint Cloud	MN	U	U	U	10.6	10.07	0.0	0.0	0.0	2.9	10.0	85.4	157.9
Brenham National Bank	Brenham	TX	B	B-	C+	312.9	5.67	5.7	1.0	7.3	46.4	8.1	9.7	15.6
Brentwood Bank	Bethel Park	PA	B-	B-	B-	562.9	4.83	3.9	0.0	34.7	20.0	8.7	10.1	14.5
Brickell Bank	Miami	FL	E+	E+	C-	503.5	-1.13	19.7	0.8	41.3	8.0	3.7	5.7	13.1
Brickyard Bank	Lincolnwood	IL	D-	D-	D-	116.8	2.66	9.3	1.1	13.1	7.6	6.1	8.1	13.7
Bridge City State Bank	Bridge City	TX	B	B-	B-	188.2	2.32	4.7	1.0	8.8	55.9	7.3	9.2	21.0
Bridge Community Bank	Mount Vernon	IA	B+	B+	B	84.9	5.37	12.0	5.8	19.1	18.4	9.9	10.9	16.2
Bridgehampton National Bank	Bridgehampton	NY	B+	B-	B-	3833.3	9.30	11.7	0.4	10.2	23.5	7.9	9.6	13.2
Bridgeview Bank Group	Bridgeview	IL	B-	C-	D-	1181.1	12.16	9.6	0.1	23.9	9.8	7.9	9.6	13.4
▲ Bridgewater Bank	Bloomington	MN	B+	B	C+	1181.5	41.40	10.6	0.4	11.8	15.9	6.9	9.2	12.4
Bridgewater Savings Bank	Raynham	MA	C	C	C	533.8	4.68	9.4	3.4	27.6	19.5	7.6	9.4	15.3
Brighton Bank	Brighton	TN	E-	E-	E-	53.5	1.48	5.8	1.4	44.1	8.2	2.5	5.1	9.6
Brighton Bank	Salt Lake City	UT	A-	A-	A-	198.8	4.89	3.9	0.2	5.1	25.9	10.0	11.7	20.6
Bristol County Savings Bank	Taunton	MA	C+	B-	B-	1842.0	8.60	5.5	13.9	30.2	16.5	8.9	12.3	14.1
▲ Broadway Federal Bank, F.S.B.	Los Angeles	CA	B-	C+	D	413.3	2.33	0.1	0.0	26.8	3.5	10.0	11.7	19.2
Broadway National Bank	San Antonio	TX	B	B	B	3409.6	5.64	5.0	3.1	8.2	47.1	8.6	10.1	16.2
▼ Brookline Bank	Brookline	MA	B	B+	B	3868.9	10.46	23.9	0.5	10.4	7.1	7.4	10.0	12.8
Brookville Building and Savings Assn.	Brookville	OH	C+	C+	C+	44.2	1.95	2.4	0.7	49.8	21.2	10.0	17.3	37.7
Brown Brothers Harriman Trust Co.	Wilmington	DE	U	U	U	8.3	2.48	0.0	0.0	0.0	74.2	10.0	81.8	254.0
Brown Brothers Harriman Trust Co., N.A.	New York	NY	U	U	U	12.9	-0.54	0.0	0.0	0.0	62.7	10.0	71.2	182.2
Bruning State Bank	Bruning	NE	B-	B-	B	347.2	6.55	8.1	0.8	1.5	26.6	7.9	10.6	13.3
▲ Brunswick Bank and Trust Co.	New Brunswick	NJ	C+	C	C	169.5	23.22	2.0	0.1	14.1	9.4	10.0	15.0	23.5
Brunswick State Bank	Brunswick	NE	B+	B+	B	97.2	-2.60	14.9	6.1	0.2	5.7	6.3	10.5	12.0
▲ Brush Country Bank	Freer	TX	C	C+	C+	40.2	-8.21	15.9	16.7	5.7	10.4	7.3	9.2	17.4
Bryant Bank	Tuscaloosa	AL	B	B	B-	1458.7	6.13	11.3	0.9	8.5	27.4	7.3	9.2	14.0
Bryant State Bank	Bryant	SD	B	B	B	32.4	8.61	6.5	4.1	0.6	16.7	10.0	13.0	21.5
Bryn Mawr Trust Co.	Bryn Mawr	PA	B+	B+	B+	3156.8	7.59	8.9	0.8	19.2	11.7	5.9	9.2	11.7
▼ BTC Bank	Bethany	MO	B+	B+	B	440.7	15.78	6.6	1.7	12.1	21.4	10.0	12.3	16.5
▲ BTH Bank, N.A.	Quitman	TX	B	B-	C+	1120.0	32.76	24.7	1.2	23.6	19.0	10.0	11.7	16.5
▲ Buckeye Community Bank	Lorain	OH	B+	B-	C+	158.3	-0.54	28.9	0.3	9.6	15.5	10.0	11.6	15.9
Buckeye State Bank	De Graff	OH	E+	E-	D	97.9	83.71	1.9	66.1	4.4	4.8	2.0	7.6	9.0
Buckholts State Bank	Buckholts	TX	A-	A-	A-	69.9	-6.96	9.5	3.5	10.9	44.0	10.0	16.1	37.4
Buckley State Bank	Buckley	IL	B	B-	B-	43.6	-4.08	9.0	1.1	0.7	35.4	10.0	12.0	20.2
Bucks County Bank	Doylestown	PA	C	C-	C-	203.0	5.85	13.0	0.0	10.2	2.4	7.6	10.7	13.0
Buena Vista National Bank	Chester	IL	B+	B	B	206.8	-1.12	3.5	6.8	20.3	36.4	9.9	10.9	18.6
Buffalo Federal Bank	Buffalo	WY	B-	B-	C-	108.7	-0.79	10.0	4.8	16.0	21.2	9.8	10.9	15.8
Builders Bank	Chicago	IL	D+	D	D+	74.3	-55.20	0.0	0.0	5.2	0.0	10.0	20.2	44.6

Asset Quality Index	Adjusted Non-Performing Loans as a % of Total Loans	as a % of Capital	Net Charge-Offs Avg Loans	Profitability Index	Net Income ($Mil)	Return on Assets (R.O.A.)	Return on Equity (R.O.E.)	Net Interest Spread	Overhead Efficiency Ratio	Liquidity Index	Liquidity Ratio	Hot Money Ratio	Stability Index
5.5	1.42	8.5	0.29	4.4	178.0	0.75	8.19	2.59	68.7	4.2	18.0	6.5	8.6
5.7	0.31	2.2	0.17	8.4	4.4	2.04	18.65	4.97	66.8	1.7	10.0	20.7	7.1
5.5	0.76	6.3	0.15	4.8	0.6	1.22	13.24	3.78	65.3	1.4	9.2	23.6	4.3
8.6	2.77	3.5	0.08	4.8	0.5	1.05	4.84	3.29	56.6	6.6	84.0	8.2	8.0
9.2	0.00	0.0	0.00	6.9	1.4	1.36	12.44	3.58	52.8	3.9	42.2	15.8	8.1
5.1	1.30	7.5	0.01	1.8	0.1	0.15	1.49	3.17	94.7	2.4	35.5	24.2	5.3
2.8	2.29	15.2	-0.01	5.9	4.2	1.43	12.86	3.94	66.2	1.4	14.1	21.6	6.8
6.7	0.50	4.1	-0.12	4.6	44.9	0.82	8.63	3.01	69.8	4.0	17.9	6.5	8.0
6.5	0.00	0.0	0.00	10.0	12.4	36.96	43.90	4.68	56.9	3.3	102.4	100.0	10.0
3.7	0.87	7.1	0.16	2.8	1.4	1.51	16.34	4.27	104.5	0.9	20.4	36.9	0.9
5.0	1.90	8.9	0.03	5.2	2.8	1.36	11.09	3.65	64.3	4.8	38.0	10.5	7.6
7.9	0.30	1.4	-0.01	3.6	0.7	0.77	8.65	2.92	75.9	3.6	30.9	14.0	5.7
4.2	1.99	14.8	-0.01	0.7	0.1	0.11	1.33	3.13	108.5	1.9	24.2	13.0	3.7
4.8	1.60	12.1	0.06	1.8	0.4	0.20	2.44	3.13	91.7	4.7	34.7	9.7	3.8
4.8	0.84	5.7	0.19	5.7	1758.9	1.11	8.67	3.24	63.6	4.8	18.9	4.6	9.6
1.1	3.51	29.1	0.40	4.4	13.5	0.78	7.99	3.76	76.5	0.9	7.5	28.1	5.5
3.9	2.63	18.5	0.09	4.7	4.5	1.31	16.83	3.25	63.0	4.9	48.1	12.3	4.7
4.8	0.88	6.3	0.30	5.4	1.3	0.95	9.07	4.10	69.0	1.4	11.8	21.5	6.2
5.8	5.41	13.0	0.17	5.3	0.6	1.14	8.05	4.79	60.6	5.0	65.8	14.3	6.5
5.3	0.73	6.4	-0.02	2.5	0.5	0.36	3.89	3.27	87.7	3.6	8.2	10.4	4.6
8.0	0.04	0.2	0.02	9.9	1.0	4.34	20.46	5.28	83.8	1.0	10.6	30.3	9.1
9.0	0.02	0.1	-0.31	7.6	0.7	1.65	11.75	4.35	52.2	5.1	60.3	13.1	8.9
5.6	0.85	6.3	-0.03	6.6	92.0	1.12	11.50	3.70	60.4	4.0	20.9	7.9	8.0
10.0	na	0.0	na	9.5	2.6	36.02	44.69	0.27	72.8	4.0	280.8	0.0	6.3
7.7	0.48	2.2	0.00	5.2	2.9	1.28	12.42	3.73	65.7	5.7	50.9	8.9	6.3
8.4	0.23	1.7	0.02	3.8	2.5	0.61	5.55	2.97	69.0	3.3	5.2	11.4	7.0
1.7	3.88	40.4	0.01	0.0	-4.9	-1.30	-20.32	2.81	137.7	1.3	31.2	46.8	2.8
1.6	7.37	47.9	0.12	0.2	-0.3	-0.29	-3.61	3.02	107.7	1.5	30.6	32.7	3.1
6.5	2.46	8.5	0.75	4.5	1.4	1.00	10.72	3.23	60.9	6.6	68.3	7.1	5.7
8.2	0.11	0.7	0.05	5.4	0.7	1.07	9.92	3.96	65.6	3.2	15.9	10.2	6.4
7.8	0.13	0.9	0.03	5.5	29.4	1.02	8.96	3.65	54.5	4.4	10.4	3.9	7.3
5.5	1.42	11.1	1.03	4.9	7.2	0.88	7.71	4.18	84.1	2.1	5.9	17.5	5.4
5.7	0.53	4.3	0.08	8.6	10.2	1.29	13.84	4.08	45.2	1.1	14.6	18.6	8.1
7.7	0.24	1.8	0.00	2.7	1.5	0.38	3.79	3.38	85.0	4.1	22.0	8.9	6.5
0.3	3.93	52.0	0.79	3.2	0.4	0.90	18.92	4.89	83.4	1.8	7.6	19.1	0.0
5.6	2.12	9.4	-0.05	8.7	3.2	2.19	18.00	4.62	57.3	6.5	40.5	0.1	8.2
5.0	1.09	6.9	0.04	3.7	10.7	0.86	6.53	3.09	76.1	3.4	19.3	11.1	9.7
3.5	2.16	14.5	-0.13	3.5	1.9	0.64	5.03	2.98	85.7	0.6	14.4	54.7	6.3
7.7	0.65	3.0	0.09	4.4	26.4	1.07	9.54	3.49	71.1	6.8	42.7	2.2	9.4
5.9	0.71	5.7	0.02	7.3	32.4	1.23	12.13	3.66	47.4	2.1	4.5	10.7	7.9
9.8	0.09	0.3	0.00	2.9	0.1	0.43	2.52	3.44	82.5	4.2	41.1	14.1	6.9
10.0	na	0.0	na	10.0	0.7	11.51	14.58	0.84	82.1	4.0	401.7	0.0	5.8
10.0	na	0.0	na	9.5	1.4	14.70	22.48	0.84	82.7	4.0	221.1	0.0	6.7
8.6	0.00	0.0	0.00	4.1	2.2	0.85	8.17	3.26	68.8	3.5	9.2	10.8	6.6
4.4	1.89	8.2	0.07	2.8	0.5	0.35	2.43	3.92	87.8	1.1	22.6	33.2	5.5
5.5	0.39	3.0	0.20	9.7	1.9	2.52	24.51	4.49	46.1	0.6	7.5	36.3	7.9
5.6	0.21	1.1	1.20	3.4	0.1	0.25	2.52	3.72	81.6	3.2	48.9	21.6	5.3
8.6	0.26	1.5	0.09	4.9	13.5	1.25	13.85	3.28	64.2	2.2	21.9	19.8	7.8
8.2	0.00	0.0	0.00	4.9	0.3	1.24	10.04	3.26	62.4	4.8	34.4	9.2	7.3
5.8	0.52	4.4	0.08	6.3	25.2	1.10	9.18	3.87	63.6	3.6	10.5	6.9	7.9
4.7	1.25	7.2	0.20	7.6	4.1	1.31	10.27	4.18	49.4	1.0	5.9	28.6	7.5
8.5	0.08	0.5	0.02	4.1	6.8	0.89	7.38	3.14	56.5	1.1	20.2	33.7	8.4
6.3	0.56	3.6	0.13	5.3	1.2	0.98	8.70	4.06	63.7	1.8	11.4	8.5	6.1
4.5	0.29	3.0	0.06	0.0	-0.2	-0.31	-3.27	3.33	105.2	0.5	8.6	63.2	3.3
9.4	0.20	0.5	0.03	7.4	1.0	1.83	11.75	3.60	54.1	4.3	55.6	16.3	8.2
8.4	0.13	0.6	-0.11	4.3	0.3	0.85	7.18	2.98	57.9	5.5	43.7	7.4	6.1
2.8	1.82	13.9	0.28	2.9	0.5	0.33	3.04	3.64	82.5	1.2	9.1	27.9	5.4
5.3	1.30	5.3	0.03	5.8	1.7	1.08	8.79	4.16	64.4	4.7	32.4	8.7	7.1
5.3	1.52	8.6	-0.12	4.0	0.5	0.67	6.09	4.44	82.2	3.5	22.2	12.4	6.2
9.3	0.00	0.0	-0.13	1.0	-0.3	-0.39	-2.58	2.67	97.2	2.6	68.9	81.6	4.2

Name	City	State	2016 Rating	2015 Rating	2014 Rating	Total Assets ($Mil)	One Year Asset Growth	Commercial Loans	Consumer Loans	Mortgage Loans	Securities	Capitalization Index	Leverage Ratio	Risk-Based Capital Ratio
Burke & Herbert Bank & Trust Co.	Alexandria	VA	A-	A	A	2922.5	9.25	1.5	0.1	10.9	36.6	10.0	11.6	16.2
▲ Burling Bank	Chicago	IL	C+	C-	D+	130.9	7.40	7.5	0.2	25.1	26.4	8.9	10.3	19.3
▲ Burton State Bank	Burton	TX	B-	B-	B-	55.8	-5.64	1.3	4.9	14.1	15.8	10.0	11.6	33.8
Busey Bank	Champaign	IL	B+	B	B	3914.7	2.87	9.7	0.3	12.8	19.7	8.8	10.2	14.2
Business Bank of Saint Louis	Clayton	MO	B+	B+	B-	584.9	5.14	13.0	9.1	7.5	9.4	9.9	12.7	15.0
▼ Business Bank of Texas, N.A.	Austin	TX	D-	D+	C	108.8	-10.03	17.7	0.0	5.3	27.5	8.3	9.9	15.4
Business First Bank	Baton Rouge	LA	B-	B-	C+	1107.8	3.85	20.1	0.7	7.9	18.9	5.9	9.7	11.7
Butte State Bank	Butte	NE	B	B-	B-	37.3	-7.59	12.7	3.8	1.6	27.2	10.0	13.1	21.5
▲ Byline Bank	Chicago	IL	D+	D-	E	2747.9	8.27	7.3	0.1	13.4	28.3	6.1	8.3	11.8
Byron Bank	Byron	IL	B	B	B-	244.6	5.90	4.8	2.2	13.4	40.4	8.4	10.0	17.8
▲ Byron State Bank	Byron	NE	B	B-	C+	43.9	-5.73	14.5	5.3	3.9	0.6	10.0	12.9	15.1
Cache Bank & Trust	Greeley	CO	C-	D+	D	121.2	-16.97	8.9	2.1	9.4	45.8	9.9	11.0	21.7
Cache Valley Bank	Logan	UT	B-	C+	B-	973.0	12.35	11.5	0.8	7.6	1.4	8.2	10.6	13.5
Cadence Bank, N.A.	Houston	TX	C	B-	B-	9425.3	14.27	44.0	0.7	13.3	11.0	7.6	11.1	13.0
Caldwell Bank & Trust Co.	Columbia	LA	D+	C-	C+	192.4	8.57	7.4	7.9	27.1	8.3	8.4	9.9	14.4
Calhoun County Bank, Inc.	Grantsville	WV	B-	B-	B-	131.4	-2.34	7.5	7.1	46.8	9.6	9.1	10.4	18.5
California Bank of Commerce	Lafayette	CA	B-	B-	B	768.7	47.83	33.9	0.3	1.1	2.2	4.3	9.2	10.7
California Business Bank	Irvine	CA	D	D	E+	82.1	5.04	8.4	1.7	1.1	0.0	10.0	14.0	24.6
California First National Bank	Irvine	CA	A-	A	A	840.8	18.72	50.1	0.0	0.0	11.0	10.0	14.0	16.7
California International Bank, N.A.	Rosemead	CA	D	D	D	53.1	6.77	5.0	0.0	6.1	2.6	10.0	26.2	37.4
▲ California Pacific Bank	San Francisco	CA	A	A-	A-	95.5	0.14	3.8	0.0	2.8	0.0	10.0	30.2	50.5
California United Bank	Los Angeles	CA	B	B	B-	2893.7	11.09	17.3	0.4	2.4	14.4	5.3	9.5	11.3
Callaway Bank	Fulton	MO	B-	C+	C+	345.8	2.92	6.7	1.5	20.3	18.9	7.3	9.2	13.4
Calumet Bank	LaGrange	GA	C+	C+	C+	156.5	2.23	9.7	0.6	13.7	16.6	9.0	10.3	14.9
Calvin B. Taylor Banking Co.	Berlin	MD	A-	A-	A-	509.8	5.53	3.0	0.3	18.4	22.7	10.0	15.5	31.2
Cambridge Appleton Trust, N.A.	Boston	MA	U	U	U	7.2	36.69	0.0	0.0	0.0	0.0	10.0	54.3	221.6
Cambridge Savings Bank	Cambridge	MA	C+	C+	C+	3454.9	19.20	5.4	0.1	18.2	13.2	6.3	9.1	12.0
Cambridge State Bank	Cambridge	MN	B	B	C	71.0	6.96	14.5	0.7	16.2	18.5	10.0	12.9	21.3
Cambridge Trust Co.	Cambridge	MA	B+	B+	B+	1801.1	6.75	2.9	1.9	31.8	22.9	5.7	7.7	12.1
Camden National Bank	Camden	ME	B	B+	B+	3871.8	36.12	8.1	0.5	24.2	22.9	6.1	8.1	12.3
Camp Grove State Bank	Camp Grove	IL	D+	C-	C-	18.8	-2.76	1.3	5.0	3.6	15.7	10.0	13.8	31.1
Campbell & Fetter Bank	Kendallville	IN	B-	B-	B-	335.2	5.97	4.9	5.7	34.0	43.0	7.0	9.0	21.2
Campbell County Bank, Inc.	Herreid	SD	A	A	A	101.9	-3.58	4.6	0.4	0.0	25.4	10.0	16.7	23.2
Campus State Bank	Campus	IL	C-	D+	D+	22.7	-1.23	0.0	12.1	19.7	15.5	8.3	9.9	17.4
Canandaigua National Bank and Trust Co.	Canandaigua	NY	B	B	B-	2401.3	8.83	10.5	17.7	18.9	13.8	5.8	8.6	11.6
Canandaigua National Trust Co. of Florida	Sarasota	FL	U	U	U	3.7	1.08	0.0	0.0	0.0	13.8	10.0	97.6	467.7
Canton Co-operative Bank	Canton	MA	C+	C+	B-	111.8	2.99	0.1	0.1	28.5	22.5	10.0	16.1	23.0
Canton State Bank	Canton	MO	C	C-	D	30.8	-3.22	6.4	3.2	18.1	24.1	9.3	10.5	18.3
Canyon Community Bank, N.A.	Tucson	AZ	D	D	E+	77.6	15.31	3.2	0.1	0.8	27.4	10.0	16.6	35.2
Capaha Bank SB	Tamms	IL	B-	B-	B-	194.0	0.98	4.4	1.3	16.7	5.3	6.0	10.6	11.7
Cape Ann Savings Bank	Gloucester	MA	B-	B-	B-	592.4	10.02	1.6	0.3	41.5	22.5	10.0	19.4	35.4
Cape Cod Five Cents Savings Bank	Orleans	MA	B-	C+	C+	3044.5	6.76	4.7	0.3	54.8	9.6	7.2	9.1	15.1
▲ Capital Bank	Little Rock	AR	C	D+	D+	150.7	3.42	6.2	2.7	5.2	54.7	8.3	9.8	17.9
Capital Bank	San Juan Capistrano	CA	B+	B+	B+	292.5	4.34	11.2	0.1	12.5	1.0	5.9	9.1	11.7
Capital Bank	Fort Oglethorpe	GA	B	B-	C+	114.2	3.38	4.4	0.7	23.2	13.1	8.9	10.2	15.0
Capital Bank	Houston	TX	B-	B-	B	367.9	6.75	8.4	2.1	8.1	5.2	5.2	9.1	11.2
Capital Bank and Trust Co.	Irvine	CA	U	U	U	136.3	89.59	0.0	0.0	0.0	59.2	10.0	65.5	164.6
Capital Bank Corp.	Raleigh	NC	B	B	C	7790.0	7.30	18.7	4.5	15.3	14.5	7.2	10.5	12.7
Capital Bank of New Jersey	Vineland	NJ	A-	B+	B+	448.1	21.47	15.1	0.2	6.8	25.2	7.2	9.1	12.7
Capital Bank of Texas	Carrizo Springs	TX	B	B	B-	64.9	1.28	4.5	1.0	11.4	21.8	10.0	12.7	38.3
▲ Capital Bank, N.A.	Rockville	MD	B	C+	C	910.8	30.38	8.5	2.2	27.8	5.6	6.7	9.2	12.3
Capital Bank, SSB	El Paso	TX	C-	D+	D+	365.5	5.17	20.1	1.2	4.3	0.3	7.4	9.5	12.8
Capital City Bank	Tallahassee	FL	C	C	C-	2731.5	5.21	5.5	9.5	10.2	25.0	8.8	10.2	16.4
Capital City Bank	Topeka	KS	C+	C+	C+	427.5	7.05	14.1	1.6	13.7	27.6	6.5	8.5	12.7
Capital Community Bank	Provo	UT	B	B	C+	263.5	34.87	16.9	12.4	2.6	0.0	5.8	10.0	11.6
Capital One Bank (USA), N.A.	Glen Allen	VA	C+	C+	C	105930.3	9.55	6.4	72.8	0.0	16.1	9.7	10.8	15.4
Capital One, N.A.	McLean	VA	C+	C+	C	279255.3	9.75	7.9	22.1	7.8	18.0	5.8	7.8	12.1
Capitol Bank	Madison	WI	C+	B-	B+	332.9	10.02	8.1	0.4	7.8	24.3	7.7	10.9	13.1
Capitol Federal Savings Bank	Topeka	KS	B	B	B	9284.2	-5.85	0.0	0.0	71.8	17.8	9.9	10.9	28.7
Capitol National Bank	Lansing	MI	D	D-	D-	120.1	4.94	11.2	0.4	6.8	1.8	7.1	9.1	15.2

Asset Quality Index	Adjusted Non-Performing Loans as a % of Total Loans	as a % of Capital	Net Charge-Offs Avg Loans	Profitability Index	Net Income ($Mil)	Return on Assets (R.O.A.)	Return on Equity (R.O.E.)	Net Interest Spread	Overhead Efficiency Ratio	Liquidity Index	Liquidity Ratio	Hot Money Ratio	Stability Index
6.7	1.17	5.4	0.00	5.5	22.8	1.11	8.96	3.71	68.5	4.8	26.4	8.5	10.0
8.9	0.00	0.0	0.00	3.5	0.7	0.78	8.20	3.40	73.0	4.5	40.0	12.5	4.8
9.4	0.20	0.5	-0.02	3.8	0.4	0.92	7.23	2.36	60.0	4.9	68.8	15.1	6.4
6.9	0.77	4.8	0.24	5.7	30.3	1.04	10.08	3.19	60.0	4.8	13.8	3.6	8.6
5.6	0.01	0.0	0.11	5.3	4.4	1.03	8.24	3.44	64.3	1.3	15.3	11.0	7.8
5.7	0.00	0.0	5.69	0.0	-1.9	-2.12	-22.87	3.47	67.8	1.7	21.4	22.5	5.6
5.9	0.77	5.4	0.07	3.5	4.4	0.51	4.99	3.71	79.9	1.3	18.5	29.0	7.3
8.1	0.77	3.1	-0.13	4.9	0.3	1.12	8.78	3.98	81.7	2.6	37.2	22.5	6.9
1.9	3.42	26.2	0.56	1.3	4.4	0.22	2.34	3.57	91.7	4.2	21.5	9.9	4.2
5.2	1.78	8.8	0.09	5.0	2.4	1.32	11.90	3.32	66.7	1.5	17.5	25.6	5.8
6.6	0.17	1.1	-0.02	8.8	0.6	1.76	14.58	3.77	31.7	1.1	11.7	29.1	5.8
9.3	0.00	0.0	0.00	1.6	0.3	0.34	3.05	3.00	99.5	3.3	36.3	17.2	4.4
3.6	1.07	7.1	0.00	9.4	10.6	1.53	14.88	4.50	52.8	3.0	21.9	14.7	8.5
3.0	2.62	17.3	0.81	4.1	45.1	0.66	4.51	3.52	57.1	1.6	12.7	11.0	8.0
2.4	2.73	20.6	0.35	6.2	1.8	1.31	13.48	4.91	61.0	0.5	11.8	59.8	6.0
4.6	1.17	7.8	0.07	4.5	0.7	0.70	7.25	4.73	74.3	1.8	17.6	20.2	5.3
6.7	0.21	1.8	-0.06	4.5	3.4	0.67	5.96	4.26	70.6	3.2	16.9	12.6	5.9
7.3	0.06	0.3	0.33	0.0	-2.0	-3.17	-24.14	2.38	260.8	1.6	35.0	45.2	4.9
8.4	0.00	0.0	0.01	5.8	6.4	1.03	7.37	2.93	44.8	0.5	12.6	66.6	8.5
6.6	0.80	1.9	-0.23	0.0	-1.0	-2.46	-10.39	3.42	170.2	1.4	32.4	50.4	5.0
8.9	0.00	0.0	-0.43	8.6	1.0	1.35	4.61	4.05	55.3	3.4	62.4	25.2	7.7
6.7	0.04	0.3	-0.02	5.6	20.7	0.99	8.57	3.81	56.9	5.5	22.0	1.3	8.6
4.5	1.39	9.9	0.10	4.1	1.8	0.69	7.43	3.71	80.6	3.6	9.7	10.3	5.0
4.7	1.58	9.6	0.00	3.8	0.7	0.64	6.12	3.71	77.6	1.8	18.5	20.6	5.9
7.2	1.60	5.1	0.11	5.8	3.7	1.02	6.31	3.31	52.3	6.2	48.9	5.0	8.0
10.0	na	0.0	na	9.5	0.1	1.55	2.76	3.64	95.6	4.0	202.0	0.0	5.0
7.2	0.30	2.4	0.00	3.4	14.9	0.61	6.65	3.04	69.8	3.3	14.4	10.8	7.1
6.0	2.38	10.2	-0.03	3.9	0.5	0.88	6.56	3.77	74.4	6.5	41.9	0.3	6.1
9.0	0.12	1.0	0.00	5.1	12.5	0.94	13.19	3.20	69.4	4.8	25.6	5.0	7.1
5.7	0.87	6.9	0.15	5.7	30.9	1.08	10.04	3.33	56.3	3.8	11.1	9.6	7.7
1.8	8.45	25.6	1.29	0.7	0.0	-0.11	-0.81	3.19	96.3	3.0	51.5	20.0	6.3
8.9	0.21	1.1	0.00	3.5	1.4	0.57	6.19	2.78	74.5	4.9	43.8	11.5	5.4
7.2	0.00	0.0	0.00	9.0	1.6	2.05	12.15	4.15	49.0	1.2	12.5	15.0	10.0
5.7	0.97	5.9	0.00	3.3	0.1	0.66	6.84	2.95	79.8	4.0	30.2	10.1	4.3
4.7	0.74	6.4	0.17	6.1	17.6	1.02	11.53	3.58	63.6	4.3	8.2	5.9	8.2
10.0	na	0.0	na	0.0	-0.1	-5.15	-5.23	0.35	133.9	4.0	na	0.0	7.0
7.0	2.42	8.2	0.00	2.4	0.4	0.43	2.69	2.99	88.8	5.2	48.8	11.0	7.6
4.2	2.76	15.4	0.14	2.9	0.1	0.42	3.90	3.64	86.8	4.0	28.8	11.1	4.7
6.4	2.35	4.8	0.00	0.0	-0.3	-0.57	-3.37	2.85	117.4	6.9	61.9	2.3	4.4
4.6	1.44	10.2	-0.03	4.6	1.1	0.71	6.94	3.90	73.8	1.6	8.0	5.8	6.1
6.4	2.44	8.1	0.00	3.5	2.2	0.56	2.29	2.79	73.8	2.8	44.3	25.8	8.1
7.1	0.62	5.5	-0.01	4.0	14.8	0.67	7.31	3.04	72.0	3.4	10.9	11.8	7.3
6.1	1.11	4.1	-0.01	2.9	0.7	0.70	6.11	2.73	72.4	1.3	33.2	71.0	4.5
7.5	0.02	0.2	0.00	8.0	2.2	1.06	10.65	4.62	59.1	1.8	22.6	22.1	5.4
5.9	1.12	7.3	0.00	5.3	1.1	1.28	12.66	4.57	76.1	4.8	21.3	4.5	5.8
4.7	0.28	2.4	0.14	6.2	2.7	1.03	11.28	4.53	64.8	1.6	11.5	22.0	5.9
10.0	na	0.0	na	9.5	16.1	15.56	26.66	2.08	83.0	9.8	184.8	0.0	9.5
6.9	0.46	3.3	0.10	5.3	51.3	0.91	7.06	3.69	61.7	2.5	13.5	12.9	9.2
8.1	0.25	1.6	0.24	5.8	3.2	1.05	10.81	3.65	58.6	4.4	34.3	11.0	5.4
8.9	0.00	0.0	0.00	3.4	0.3	0.61	4.68	2.77	77.5	5.8	43.4	5.2	7.0
5.0	0.61	5.7	0.38	7.9	7.0	1.17	12.76	5.44	70.0	1.3	9.8	25.8	6.5
8.1	0.08	0.6	-0.01	2.0	1.1	0.40	4.23	3.40	85.1	2.1	26.8	20.9	5.7
4.3	1.66	9.3	0.05	2.9	8.1	0.39	3.29	3.27	86.7	6.1	28.4	1.9	7.6
7.7	0.14	1.0	-0.11	3.8	2.2	0.69	8.24	3.35	75.0	2.1	9.9	17.9	4.3
4.8	0.65	5.4	-0.02	8.3	2.3	1.34	13.33	5.16	58.3	0.6	14.1	53.4	6.1
2.2	1.95	10.7	4.17	10.0	1979.2	2.58	23.44	11.79	43.7	0.7	19.7	61.5	7.8
3.4	1.70	11.6	0.94	3.7	1069.4	0.53	4.03	3.76	70.8	6.3	35.9	1.2	7.2
2.9	2.29	13.8	0.09	5.5	2.3	0.98	8.81	3.25	57.8	1.8	26.9	17.8	6.3
9.6	0.50	2.8	0.00	4.2	62.7	0.74	6.64	1.76	43.5	1.6	15.9	24.0	9.1
1.1	3.52	21.7	-1.23	2.6	0.5	0.50	5.50	3.75	89.0	5.0	32.5	6.3	4.1

Name	City	State	2015 Rating	2014 Rating	Total Assets ($Mil)	One Year Asset Growth	Comm-ercial Loans	Cons-umer Loans	Mort-gage Loans	Secur-ities	Capital-ization Index	Lever-age Ratio	Risk-Based Capital Ratio
Capon Valley Bank	Wardensville	WV	B-	B-	C+	151.3	2.18	3.2	10.1	38.6	10.2	10.0	11.0	17.0
CapStar Bank	Nashville	TN	B-	B-	C+	1318.1	16.05	29.6	0.5	5.9	16.5	3.9	8.7	10.5
Capstone Bank	Tuscaloosa	AL	B-	B-	B-	474.6	6.65	19.9	1.7	11.3	8.6	8.2	10.8	13.5
Cardinal Bank	McLean	VA	B+	B+	B+	4182.9	8.86	4.3	0.1	22.6	9.3	6.3	10.1	12.0
Carlsbad National Bank	Carlsbad	NM	B+	A-	A-	328.0	2.07	5.5	3.6	17.5	51.5	7.4	9.3	21.8
Carmine State Bank	Carmine	TX	B	B+	B+	72.8	1.02	2.7	8.8	10.1	29.4	10.0	12.7	43.6
Carolina Alliance Bank	Spartanburg	SC	B-	B-	B+	626.3	41.03	9.7	0.6	9.2	15.6	7.3	10.4	12.8
Carolina Bank	Greensboro	NC	B-	C+	C-	708.8	2.94	8.0	0.3	13.3	7.9	8.7	10.1	14.0
Carolina Bank & Trust Co.	Darlington	SC	B	B	B-	446.3	11.11	8.2	1.6	18.2	7.9	10.0	11.3	17.2
Carolina Premier Bank	Charlotte	NC	C-	D-	C	243.6	0.56	11.6	0.3	18.1	13.7	6.9	9.0	12.6
Carolina Trust Bank	Lincolnton	NC	C-	D+	C-	372.2	11.98	11.9	1.1	12.9	7.2	4.4	8.0	10.7
Carroll Bank and Trust	Huntingdon	TN	B-	B-	B-	266.0	-0.39	4.3	7.3	29.9	11.8	7.6	9.4	13.4
Carroll Community Bank	Sykesville	MD	C	C	C-	165.1	21.24	2.1	0.2	31.1	4.3	8.4	9.9	15.0
Carroll County S&L Assn.	Carrollton	MO	C+	C+	C+	19.8	-5.31	0.0	0.4	38.7	34.1	10.0	17.1	55.7
Carroll County State Bank	Carroll	IA	A-	A-	B+	553.4	5.34	8.6	0.8	10.1	26.4	10.0	11.5	15.5
Carroll County Trust Co.	Carrollton	MO	B	B-	B-	154.5	-1.32	4.0	1.9	5.8	45.9	10.0	11.0	20.2
Carrollton Bank	Carrollton	IL	B-	B	B	1398.8	15.29	26.7	0.5	12.0	9.5	3.7	7.8	10.3
Carrollton Federal Bank	Carrollton	KY	B-	B-	B-	33.2	-3.63	0.0	3.6	50.4	8.5	10.0	14.6	26.4
Carson Bank	Mulvane	KS	C	C-	C-	112.4	6.11	7.8	2.3	18.6	25.6	6.0	8.0	16.1
Carter Bank & Trust	Martinsville	VA	D+	D+	C+	4743.9	-3.35	7.4	0.4	3.0	19.8	6.1	8.1	13.3
Carthage Federal S&L Assn.	Carthage	NY	B	B	B	199.1	3.93	0.0	2.3	64.5	4.5	10.0	11.4	25.6
Carver Federal Savings Bank	New York	NY	D	D+	D	702.9	-4.09	9.5	0.0	18.8	9.7	7.7	9.5	14.8
Carver State Bank	Savannah	GA	D	D+	D+	39.7	-6.27	9.7	3.8	26.0	8.3	7.3	9.2	14.7
Casey County Bank	Liberty	KY	B-	B-	C+	176.1	2.13	6.9	6.3	23.9	19.3	10.0	12.6	18.6
Casey State Bank	Casey	IL	B+	B+	C+	263.2	7.84	22.0	3.6	13.7	20.3	10.0	11.4	15.2
Cashmere Valley Bank	Cashmere	WA	A-	B+	B+	1461.8	7.71	4.4	12.2	8.0	32.0	9.9	10.9	18.2
Cass Commercial Bank	Saint Louis	MO	A	A	A	742.9	4.17	24.6	0.0	0.7	0.0	10.0	13.5	16.5
Cass County Bank, Inc.	Plattsmouth	NE	B-	B	B-	66.8	0.89	13.4	2.1	24.5	4.8	9.0	10.7	14.2
Castle Rock Bank	Castle Rock	CO	B+	A-	B+	147.9	8.59	2.7	0.5	12.6	27.5	9.0	10.3	19.2
Castle Rock Bank	Castle Rock	MN	A-	A-	A-	201.3	12.87	11.2	3.4	10.2	51.0	10.0	13.3	26.5
Castroville State Bank	Castroville	TX	B-	B-	B-	141.5	5.56	4.1	4.3	22.2	40.2	7.4	9.3	24.6
▲ Catahoula-LaSalle Bank	Jonesville	LA	C	B-	B-	183.8	-1.35	12.2	6.5	8.1	29.1	9.4	10.6	15.3
Cathay Bank	Los Angeles	CA	B+	B	B	14054.0	10.57	15.8	0.0	20.1	9.1	9.2	11.5	14.3
▲ Catskill Hudson Bank	Kingston	NY	C-	D	D+	489.8	7.27	8.8	1.2	3.2	34.0	5.4	7.4	13.0
Cattaraugus County Bank	Little Valley	NY	C+	C+	C+	221.5	11.05	13.2	0.9	18.3	11.9	6.1	8.4	11.8
Cattle National Bank & Trust Co.	Seward	NE	A-	A-	A-	250.9	5.88	2.7	0.5	20.2	16.8	10.0	12.2	17.0
Cayuga Lake National Bank	Union Springs	NY	B	B+	B+	150.9	1.72	2.1	2.7	32.9	33.1	6.8	8.8	19.2
CB&S Bank, Inc.	Russellville	AL	C+	C+	C+	1546.1	4.21	5.8	1.7	10.2	48.5	9.4	10.6	18.8
▲ CBank	Cincinnati	OH	B	B-	B	141.5	18.06	18.1	0.7	9.6	6.8	10.0	12.1	15.2
CBBC Bank	Maryville	TN	B	B	C	341.9	4.05	1.2	0.7	6.3	39.3	10.0	14.9	26.4
CBC Bank	Bowling Green	MO	D+	D	D	33.2	1.76	5.1	1.1	16.3	49.5	7.1	9.1	20.5
CBC National Bank	Fernandina Beach	FL	B+	A-	B-	612.7	39.72	5.1	0.9	43.2	3.3	9.6	10.7	20.9
CBI Bank & Trust	Muscatine	IA	B+	B+	B+	536.5	6.85	9.2	2.0	19.0	17.3	9.4	10.6	14.9
CBT Bank	Clearfield	PA	B	B	B-	466.9	7.55	10.8	3.1	15.8	12.8	9.7	10.8	15.1
CBW Bank	Weir	KS	A-	A-	B+	22.7	31.47	1.8	0.6	4.0	8.5	10.0	18.4	104.9
CCB Community Bank	Andalusia	AL	B	B	B	464.4	4.58	8.6	2.0	18.7	5.2	8.5	10.7	13.8
Cecil Bank	Elkton	MD	E-	E-	E-	219.4	-22.47	0.5	0.2	21.6	7.6	0.0	2.7	5.3
Cecilian Bank	Cecilia	KY	B-	B	B-	859.4	41.09	4.2	2.9	17.6	26.0	8.4	9.9	15.1
Cedar Hill National Bank	Charlotte	NC	U	U	U	11.5	-2.26	0.0	0.0	0.0	71.7	10.0	78.8	156.1
Cedar Rapids Bank and Trust Co.	Cedar Rapids	IA	B+	B-	B-	890.4	2.20	25.0	0.8	6.5	20.1	7.8	10.4	13.1
Cedar Rapids State Bank	Cedar Rapids	NE	C-	C-	D	41.8	4.01	18.7	3.1	0.4	13.0	6.3	8.7	12.0
Cedar Security Bank	Fordyce	NE	D-	E+	C	54.0	5.19	13.3	3.9	11.6	5.3	7.3	11.5	12.7
Cedar Valley Bank & Trust	La Porte City	IA	C+	C+	C+	59.3	4.61	7.9	3.7	15.6	46.0	6.4	8.4	15.7
CedarStone Bank	Lebanon	TN	B-	B	C	177.4	4.02	7.7	3.3	23.6	23.7	9.2	10.4	16.4
Celtic Bank	Salt Lake City	UT	B	B	C+	517.4	20.46	37.8	5.5	0.9	1.3	10.0	16.2	19.2
CenBank	Buffalo Lake	MN	B	B	B	58.8	1.99	5.8	5.8	3.2	33.9	6.4	8.4	13.1
Cendera Bank, N.A.	Bells	TX	C-	C+	C+	78.1	10.53	5.7	1.4	44.9	7.9	9.7	10.8	19.6
Cenlar FSB	Ewing	NJ	A-	A-	B+	1049.4	22.93	0.0	0.1	29.9	62.0	6.7	8.7	26.7
Centennial Bank	Conway	AR	B-	B-	B-	9751.6	15.12	12.6	0.4	11.7	15.5	5.9	9.6	11.7
Centennial Bank	Trezevant	TN	B-	B-	B-	370.4	16.69	12.9	6.8	20.6	4.2	6.1	9.6	11.9

Asset Quality Index	Adjusted Non-Performing Loans as a % of Total Loans	as a % of Capital	Net Charge-Offs Avg Loans	Profitability Index	Net Income ($Mil)	Return on Assets (R.O.A.)	Return on Equity (R.O.E.)	Net Interest Spread	Overhead Efficiency Ratio	Liquidity Index	Liquidity Ratio	Hot Money Ratio	Stability Index
3.9	2.16	14.2	0.22	4.1	0.8	0.73	6.70	4.50	78.7	2.0	15.1	19.0	5.8
7.7	0.42	3.4	0.20	3.8	6.4	0.69	7.60	3.21	66.5	2.9	12.8	14.3	6.6
4.7	0.73	5.4	0.33	4.7	2.7	0.77	6.60	3.83	66.9	1.5	7.5	19.7	6.5
7.5	0.00	0.0	-0.01	7.6	42.8	1.41	13.37	3.39	56.6	0.9	3.1	17.6	9.6
7.2	1.09	4.5	0.03	5.9	3.7	1.54	16.84	3.04	60.0	6.1	48.5	5.6	6.4
9.1	0.13	0.3	0.14	3.9	0.6	1.03	7.97	3.21	71.8	3.2	79.9	40.5	7.0
4.0	0.80	5.4	-0.02	4.8	3.1	0.67	5.95	3.77	76.8	1.7	16.1	14.6	6.8
4.7	1.66	11.7	0.03	4.6	4.7	0.89	8.95	3.64	75.8	3.5	17.2	10.0	5.8
4.6	2.47	13.9	0.24	4.5	2.3	0.71	6.19	4.02	67.4	4.0	23.8	9.7	6.2
4.0	1.07	8.3	0.25	2.6	0.7	0.39	4.09	3.88	88.3	1.8	19.9	9.7	4.8
4.0	1.59	14.3	0.07	3.4	1.0	0.37	4.33	3.87	83.3	0.7	16.6	38.3	3.9
7.8	0.10	0.7	0.12	4.1	1.2	0.58	6.12	4.56	78.1	1.5	7.5	22.9	5.6
8.9	0.12	1.0	-0.02	2.1	0.2	0.14	1.35	3.31	93.2	0.9	19.1	22.9	3.9
7.6	2.96	7.1	0.30	2.8	0.1	0.45	2.71	2.04	72.1	3.6	68.6	20.7	7.2
7.7	0.87	4.6	-0.10	5.9	4.8	1.20	10.10	4.15	61.6	2.5	33.3	17.6	7.4
5.0	2.74	10.9	0.09	4.6	1.6	1.37	12.57	3.38	66.5	2.0	30.6	15.7	6.8
8.3	0.08	0.7	0.00	4.4	10.1	1.03	12.94	3.05	65.5	2.6	13.5	15.9	7.6
8.0	0.83	4.0	0.03	3.5	0.1	0.57	3.92	4.15	82.5	2.0	15.5	19.0	6.6
7.0	0.35	2.2	0.01	3.0	0.5	0.64	7.74	3.27	84.0	3.0	18.9	14.2	4.2
1.6	5.32	34.5	0.06	3.3	19.8	0.54	6.10	2.38	63.1	2.9	36.5	26.6	7.6
9.7	0.12	0.8	0.05	4.3	1.0	0.71	6.59	3.19	64.5	1.2	14.2	28.1	6.5
1.8	2.30	17.4	0.04	1.1	-0.1	-0.01	-0.15	3.49	102.0	0.9	16.7	33.2	4.3
1.4	6.23	37.1	-0.01	0.3	-0.2	-0.75	-7.98	4.98	122.4	0.8	21.6	41.5	3.0
3.4	3.03	16.1	0.68	4.5	1.1	0.82	6.69	4.14	65.4	3.0	11.5	13.8	7.0
5.4	1.14	7.0	0.18	4.9	2.2	1.14	9.77	3.88	64.1	2.2	8.6	17.4	6.6
6.6	0.69	3.7	0.12	6.2	13.8	1.33	11.30	3.37	53.7	4.8	27.5	9.5	9.0
6.9	0.02	0.1	-0.01	8.3	7.7	1.40	10.84	3.40	44.0	4.1	18.9	8.3	8.6
5.6	0.93	6.6	-0.01	3.1	0.2	0.33	2.86	4.90	75.3	2.6	6.1	15.0	5.9
5.0	2.41	10.3	-0.19	6.9	1.7	1.57	14.54	3.60	56.1	3.3	46.8	20.2	8.2
5.8	2.60	7.9	-0.03	5.3	1.9	1.29	9.51	3.03	48.1	4.0	57.4	19.6	7.4
9.0	0.00	0.0	0.11	4.5	1.0	0.90	9.60	3.37	61.2	1.6	24.8	25.9	5.5
2.7	4.03	20.1	0.17	4.9	1.6	1.18	11.21	3.60	69.4	3.6	30.0	13.6	5.9
5.5	0.84	5.8	0.07	7.4	131.8	1.34	9.65	3.44	50.4	0.8	14.4	31.5	9.9
3.9	2.06	13.2	0.14	2.4	1.5	0.44	5.94	3.20	79.0	3.4	19.0	12.2	2.6
5.3	0.60	5.1	-0.12	3.7	1.1	0.66	7.53	4.15	76.9	4.9	5.6	1.3	4.8
7.5	0.47	2.8	0.00	6.9	3.2	1.71	14.13	3.94	56.2	1.7	5.0	18.1	7.8
9.8	0.20	1.0	0.02	4.4	1.0	0.86	10.58	3.33	67.2	3.5	35.2	15.7	5.1
4.5	3.84	14.9	0.00	3.9	8.8	0.77	6.26	3.63	76.8	5.7	43.3	9.8	8.4
8.0	0.05	0.3	0.03	4.2	1.0	0.88	6.82	3.58	75.9	1.0	20.3	34.0	7.5
8.8	0.48	1.5	0.05	4.1	2.4	0.94	5.95	3.18	69.5	3.3	50.0	22.4	6.3
8.5	0.00	0.0	-0.06	1.7	0.1	0.33	3.44	2.81	96.9	6.0	40.7	3.8	4.2
5.0	1.21	9.7	0.22	8.5	5.7	1.43	13.39	4.00	86.1	0.8	3.7	27.8	6.3
5.8	0.77	5.1	-0.03	5.5	3.9	1.04	9.02	3.64	64.8	2.9	22.5	15.4	6.5
4.6	0.81	5.7	0.08	4.4	2.7	0.79	6.44	3.63	72.9	2.9	11.6	10.9	7.0
10.0	3.02	1.4	0.12	9.5	0.8	4.38	23.76	1.41	61.5	7.9	109.9	2.6	8.0
4.6	1.25	9.3	0.22	8.5	5.9	1.72	16.15	4.60	60.5	1.2	11.3	23.4	7.7
0.3	13.52	186.3	0.99	0.2	0.0	0.00	0.07	2.73	129.7	2.8	26.4	16.7	0.3
3.7	2.88	16.2	0.15	4.1	4.7	0.80	8.39	3.43	70.5	2.5	21.9	17.0	6.5
10.0	na	0.0	na	9.5	0.3	3.50	4.50	1.00	80.3	10.0	423.3	0.0	8.0
8.0	0.20	1.2	-0.02	6.7	9.7	1.44	12.87	3.82	54.6	1.4	17.2	19.8	6.3
5.7	0.44	3.7	-0.01	5.5	0.4	1.19	14.18	4.02	64.1	0.9	10.8	31.1	4.3
0.0	5.36	29.5	0.21	2.7	0.1	0.26	2.27	4.66	55.7	1.8	15.0	20.0	5.3
6.9	1.01	5.5	0.01	4.1	0.4	0.83	9.90	3.68	75.6	4.7	27.9	6.4	4.1
8.8	0.01	0.1	-0.02	4.0	0.8	0.63	6.06	4.00	75.1	1.5	26.7	29.8	5.4
4.3	1.76	7.9	0.62	10.0	17.2	4.70	30.23	6.07	48.1	0.5	11.4	7.8	8.0
7.9	0.11	0.7	0.03	4.5	0.5	1.16	13.39	3.40	64.5	3.8	17.8	10.5	5.0
7.9	0.00	0.0	0.01	2.3	0.1	0.16	1.45	4.14	95.6	1.2	21.6	23.0	6.7
9.7	0.40	1.3	0.03	9.5	19.8	2.56	30.49	2.04	91.3	7.9	68.6	0.0	7.2
4.7	0.98	7.3	0.19	10.0	134.3	1.89	14.59	4.81	37.0	1.8	6.0	12.2	10.0
3.8	1.54	11.8	0.08	6.6	2.7	1.00	10.39	5.34	61.2	1.0	10.3	22.2	5.6

Name	City	State	Rating	2015 Rating	2014 Rating	Total Assets ($Mil)	One Year Asset Growth	Comm- ercial Loans	Cons- umer Loans	Mort- gage Loans	Secur- ities	Capital- ization Index	Lever- age Ratio	Risk- Based Capital Ratio
Centennial Bank	Lubbock	TX	B+	B+	B-	697.9	-1.78	12.1	1.5	10.0	21.7	9.5	10.7	14.6
Centennial Bank & Trust	Denver	CO	B-	B-	B-	892.7	475.53	9.8	0.7	19.0	17.2	6.9	9.2	12.4
Center National Bank	Litchfield	MN	B+	B+	B+	198.1	7.92	8.2	5.7	7.1	51.5	9.6	10.7	16.9
Center Point Bank and Trust Co.	Center Point	IA	B-	B-	B-	33.4	0.35	6.1	2.4	28.8	23.7	5.4	7.4	11.3
Centera Bank	Sublette	KS	B	B	B	260.2	1.13	5.1	1.3	6.6	38.5	6.6	8.6	14.6
CenterBank	Milford	OH	C+	C+	C	152.8	10.47	14.6	0.8	18.0	4.5	5.9	9.4	11.7
CenterPointe Community Bank	Hood River	OR	B-	B-	C+	133.3	6.90	10.3	0.0	5.0	19.8	7.8	9.6	14.1
CenterState Bank of Florida, N.A.	Winter Haven	FL	B-	B	C+	5005.5	27.56	5.4	1.7	13.3	20.6	5.8	8.4	11.6
Centier Bank	Merrillville	IN	B+	B	B	3455.2	18.38	5.0	0.4	18.5	8.4	8.0	10.1	13.3
Centinel Bank of Taos	Taos	NM	A-	B+	B	217.9	10.18	2.0	0.9	19.2	36.8	6.9	8.9	24.1
Central Bank	Little Rock	AR	B+	B+	B+	117.9	10.86	7.1	0.4	15.4	33.1	10.0	14.5	24.2
▲ Central Bank	Tampa	FL	B-	C	C-	125.9	14.56	10.0	0.4	11.7	9.9	8.8	10.2	14.4
▲ Central Bank	Storm Lake	IA	C+	B-	B-	729.1	6.50	20.0	1.7	14.1	6.2	4.3	8.7	10.7
▲ Central Bank	Savannah	TN	D+	D	E+	96.3	-3.41	1.9	4.0	41.1	19.9	6.3	8.3	16.2
Central Bank	Houston	TX	B+	B+	B	606.5	6.95	8.1	0.2	31.4	15.3	6.7	8.9	12.3
▲ Central Bank	Provo	UT	A-	B+	A-	989.4	13.80	4.3	1.0	3.1	36.2	10.0	15.4	24.0
Central Bank & Trust Co.	Lexington	KY	B-	C+	C	2098.1	5.99	9.3	3.9	16.8	13.2	8.6	10.4	13.8
Central Bank and Trust	Lander	WY	B	B	B	154.5	-4.41	11.3	2.4	14.4	29.9	7.3	9.2	15.7
Central Bank and Trust Co.	Hutchinson	KS	A-	B+	B	281.8	1.01	14.5	0.8	13.4	15.6	7.3	9.9	12.7
Central Bank Illinois	Geneseo	IL	A-	A-	B	574.0	11.38	5.3	0.8	8.1	33.5	10.0	11.2	15.4
Central Bank of Audrain County	Mexico	MO	B	B	B	165.2	2.96	3.3	3.6	15.1	27.8	5.4	7.4	13.4
▲ Central Bank of Boone County	Columbia	MO	B	B-	B	1708.3	11.40	6.3	6.0	12.7	29.6	5.2	7.9	11.2
Central Bank of Branson	Branson	MO	B-	B-	B-	327.3	8.53	10.6	5.1	14.2	15.6	6.9	10.1	12.5
Central Bank of Jefferson County	Lexington	KY	B-	C+	C-	172.8	-6.21	7.5	1.0	26.4	7.9	10.0	11.3	15.1
▲ Central Bank of Kansas City	Kansas City	MO	B	B-	C+	153.5	16.72	15.7	0.1	3.4	0.5	10.0	16.3	27.4
Central Bank of Lake of the Ozarks	Osage Beach	MO	B	B	B	661.5	7.66	3.8	4.7	15.0	34.7	6.7	8.7	14.4
Central Bank of Moberly	Moberly	MO	B-	B-	B-	154.6	0.50	7.8	13.6	4.3	39.1	6.7	8.7	12.8
Central Bank of Oklahoma	Tulsa	OK	C+	C+	C+	732.9	11.12	15.1	0.2	10.1	1.5	7.7	12.2	13.1
Central Bank of Sedalia	Sedalia	MO	B	B	B	411.4	4.75	7.2	20.6	10.8	22.4	6.0	8.4	11.8
Central Bank of St. Louis	Clayton	MO	B-	B-	B-	1812.7	13.82	13.5	0.9	12.0	11.8	5.5	9.2	11.4
Central Bank of the Midwest	Lee's Summit	MO	B-	B-	C+	1698.3	7.99	10.7	7.6	4.4	14.5	5.6	8.8	11.4
Central Bank of the Ozarks	Springfield	MO	B-	B	B-	1293.6	11.59	9.3	14.8	8.5	15.0	4.8	8.8	10.9
Central Bank of Warrensburg	Warrensburg	MO	B	B	B	221.8	4.46	8.7	2.0	11.2	23.2	10.0	11.1	16.1
Central Federal S&L Assn.	Cicero	IL	D+	D	D+	173.7	4.05	0.0	0.1	44.4	19.1	7.9	9.6	19.5
Central Federal S&L Assn. of Chicago	Chicago	IL	B-	C+	C+	112.8	2.35	0.0	0.0	34.2	5.6	10.0	21.7	29.9
Central Federal S&L Assn. of Rolla	Rolla	MO	C-	C+	C+	74.3	20.24	2.0	0.8	41.6	9.6	10.0	27.5	50.3
Central National B&T Co. of Enid	Enid	OK	D+	C-	C	591.9	-0.97	19.5	3.8	7.5	14.3	6.1	9.1	11.8
Central National Bank	Junction City	KS	B-	B	B	910.2	4.13	5.2	2.0	8.6	38.5	7.7	9.4	20.5
Central National Bank	Waco	TX	B+	B+	B+	804.6	2.26	17.0	1.4	30.8	11.1	6.8	8.8	12.8
Central National Bank of Poteau	Poteau	OK	A-	A-	A-	229.3	-1.68	9.2	4.1	15.5	29.7	9.5	10.7	18.7
Central Pacific Bank	Honolulu	HI	A-	A-	B+	5309.9	6.28	9.1	8.4	22.1	28.1	9.4	10.6	15.3
▲ Central Savings Bank	Sault Sainte Marie	MI	C+	C-	C-	260.1	0.53	7.1	3.4	17.7	28.5	10.0	12.1	19.7
Central State Bank	Calera	AL	A-	A-	A-	238.7	12.54	6.1	2.7	19.1	18.7	10.0	12.0	17.4
▲ Central State Bank	Elkader	IA	B+	B+	B+	228.6	4.99	9.2	1.8	14.7	9.8	9.4	10.7	14.5
Central State Bank	State Center	IA	B	A-	A-	246.3	10.10	18.8	0.5	2.9	30.2	10.0	13.0	15.8
Central State Bank	Pleasant Hill	IL	B-	B	B-	130.4	6.37	10.6	10.2	27.8	1.4	10.0	14.3	18.6
Central State Bank	Beulah	MI	C-	C-	C+	74.6	3.55	6.1	0.7	23.8	16.2	10.0	13.3	25.5
Central Trust Bank	Jefferson City	MO	B-	B-	B-	2705.6	0.35	5.3	6.3	7.5	48.0	5.2	7.2	15.1
▲ Central Valley Community Bank	Fresno	CA	B+	B-	B-	1297.9	5.22	6.8	1.8	1.0	42.5	6.4	8.4	14.1
CentreBank	Veedersburg	IN	C	B-	C+	73.8	9.32	13.3	3.3	22.4	2.0	8.8	10.2	17.6
Centreville Bank	West Warwick	RI	C+	C+	C+	1136.4	10.56	0.3	0.4	35.6	38.3	10.0	21.2	36.9
Centric Bank	Harrisburg	PA	C+	C+	C	463.3	32.66	22.4	0.1	11.1	3.8	5.3	9.8	11.3
▲ Centrue Bank	Streator	IL	B-	C	D	992.2	5.37	6.5	0.3	5.5	18.5	10.0	11.8	15.7
CenTrust Bank, N.A.	Northbrook	IL	D-	E-	D-	89.6	30.40	20.5	0.9	9.1	5.6	8.0	10.2	13.3
Century Bank	Shenandoah	IA	B+	B+	B	89.2	3.64	5.1	1.4	3.9	33.7	8.1	9.8	14.6
Century Bank	Lucedale	MS	B+	B+	B	277.2	6.79	9.0	10.3	14.5	20.1	10.0	11.2	15.7
Century Bank	Santa Fe	NM	B-	C+	C+	798.2	9.06	16.6	3.8	5.1	36.5	6.3	8.3	12.4
Century Bank and Trust	Milledgeville	GA	B-	B-	C+	240.2	5.51	4.9	1.3	17.0	30.8	9.8	10.9	16.7
Century Bank and Trust	Coldwater	MI	B	B	B	294.4	2.50	10.2	2.4	15.2	21.6	10.0	12.3	17.7
Century Bank and Trust Co.	Medford	MA	C+	C+	C+	4287.6	11.45	4.1	0.1	5.9	49.3	4.2	6.2	12.8

Asset Quality Index	Adjusted Non-Performing Loans as a % of Total Loans	as a % of Capital	Net Charge-Offs Avg Loans	Profitability Index	Net Income ($Mil)	Return on Assets (R.O.A.)	Return on Equity (R.O.E.)	Net Interest Spread	Overhead Efficiency Ratio	Liquidity Index	Liquidity Ratio	Hot Money Ratio	Stability Index
6.5	0.55	3.3	0.03	5.8	7.4	1.40	12.43	4.39	68.2	2.9	15.2	14.8	7.5
4.9	0.88	6.9	0.29	2.3	2.0	0.33	2.71	4.32	82.5	3.0	11.4	11.1	5.9
8.8	0.02	0.1	0.11	5.2	1.9	1.27	11.83	3.49	62.1	4.4	24.6	7.1	7.1
6.0	0.39	3.0	0.16	4.3	0.2	0.86	10.74	3.94	66.3	2.2	23.7	19.0	3.6
6.6	0.51	3.0	-0.06	5.3	2.6	1.28	13.65	3.55	62.0	3.8	23.0	11.0	6.1
5.6	0.18	1.5	0.13	5.8	1.1	1.02	10.73	4.33	64.3	1.3	10.8	26.5	5.6
8.6	0.00	0.0	0.00	4.3	0.7	0.73	7.95	4.15	73.2	5.0	22.9	3.0	5.2
5.3	0.95	7.3	-0.02	4.6	28.3	0.79	7.26	4.25	74.3	4.4	21.2	8.3	8.0
5.6	0.55	4.3	0.03	6.8	26.4	1.09	10.74	3.54	60.4	4.0	13.2	9.0	8.3
9.7	0.00	0.0	0.00	5.7	2.4	1.46	15.70	3.14	62.8	5.7	52.7	9.5	6.1
5.9	2.16	8.1	0.00	3.8	0.7	0.77	5.12	3.27	70.6	1.1	28.9	51.3	7.5
4.9	0.35	2.3	-0.97	6.9	1.5	1.69	16.17	3.27	56.1	0.9	24.7	44.7	6.5
4.4	0.66	5.9	0.14	6.0	4.7	0.88	9.74	4.08	71.5	1.6	5.8	20.7	6.1
2.3	5.12	31.5	0.56	3.5	0.5	0.71	8.92	4.13	83.6	2.0	26.8	22.3	2.3
8.8	0.01	0.1	-0.02	5.6	5.2	1.18	13.46	4.61	72.6	1.7	10.2	20.2	7.2
6.5	0.98	3.2	0.80	9.7	10.6	1.53	9.74	4.63	52.0	4.8	38.6	10.6	8.8
4.1	2.04	13.8	0.14	4.4	13.5	0.87	8.25	3.72	77.5	3.8	14.4	10.3	7.7
7.1	0.72	4.5	0.06	7.3	2.1	1.81	19.63	3.80	57.3	4.0	11.0	8.1	6.3
8.5	0.09	0.6	0.01	9.4	4.3	2.01	20.68	3.87	56.2	2.1	12.6	16.5	7.5
6.4	1.12	5.8	-0.04	8.1	7.1	1.71	14.04	4.39	50.8	3.5	26.7	10.8	8.2
5.0	1.29	8.3	0.03	6.2	1.4	1.09	13.54	3.35	58.4	4.7	24.0	5.2	6.5
7.8	0.30	2.2	0.05	7.0	15.3	1.24	14.84	3.16	57.4	5.6	26.3	3.5	7.3
4.0	1.63	10.9	0.45	5.1	2.1	0.93	9.56	4.02	66.1	4.2	16.7	7.3	6.6
4.4	1.51	10.1	0.01	3.4	0.7	0.54	3.89	3.58	80.4	1.6	12.7	22.0	6.7
4.9	1.81	6.6	0.03	9.6	3.3	3.03	16.63	4.13	61.2	1.7	36.5	18.7	7.8
5.4	1.02	5.7	0.20	7.8	5.8	1.22	14.07	3.65	60.0	3.7	31.9	13.8	6.5
7.8	0.10	0.6	0.04	4.1	0.8	0.70	8.33	2.83	68.6	4.8	12.4	2.7	6.3
2.6	0.64	4.3	0.25	6.6	5.5	1.07	5.53	4.16	52.9	1.6	10.8	20.9	7.4
4.2	0.92	7.1	0.04	7.9	4.0	1.31	14.27	3.64	55.0	4.3	10.4	6.4	7.0
5.0	0.93	7.2	0.09	7.4	16.8	1.28	12.39	3.55	56.8	4.1	8.5	7.0	8.1
4.2	0.91	6.7	0.27	5.4	11.0	0.91	6.45	4.18	66.4	4.9	15.2	3.4	8.1
5.2	0.61	4.8	0.20	5.8	9.2	1.03	11.45	3.62	64.6	4.4	13.5	6.1	7.0
5.8	0.77	4.2	0.02	5.7	1.6	0.97	5.94	3.75	63.1	4.0	23.9	9.9	7.9
3.4	5.12	26.3	-0.16	1.7	0.3	0.19	1.98	2.80	98.5	3.2	47.0	21.9	4.3
7.4	0.00	0.0	-0.03	3.7	0.5	0.53	2.35	4.18	78.8	0.7	11.6	39.0	6.7
8.4	0.72	1.7	0.00	1.9	0.1	0.19	0.71	3.01	93.7	4.4	43.9	13.4	5.9
1.5	3.10	25.1	0.21	5.0	5.6	1.22	13.88	4.34	72.9	3.5	9.7	7.1	6.0
7.3	0.79	3.2	0.09	3.9	6.3	0.77	7.74	2.89	80.0	4.3	15.8	6.7	8.0
8.4	0.17	1.4	0.02	7.5	10.6	1.83	20.85	3.70	48.5	2.1	18.7	17.5	7.5
7.2	0.50	2.9	0.01	8.2	3.6	2.04	19.78	4.36	57.6	2.2	13.7	17.9	7.2
7.1	0.59	3.4	0.04	5.6	37.1	0.96	8.69	3.35	63.6	1.8	10.4	19.8	10.0
2.7	5.19	22.5	0.12	4.3	1.6	0.84	6.76	3.75	72.6	3.0	39.5	19.9	6.3
8.7	0.24	1.3	0.13	6.1	2.3	1.35	11.24	4.52	66.0	1.4	10.1	25.0	7.5
7.7	0.13	0.9	0.05	5.5	2.2	1.33	11.65	3.70	61.6	3.1	22.2	14.3	8.2
4.8	3.96	18.5	-0.22	7.2	3.5	2.01	15.43	3.40	41.2	2.0	40.8	43.5	8.3
3.3	2.94	17.6	0.11	9.8	2.3	2.36	16.29	4.85	49.6	1.2	6.5	26.9	8.9
5.3	2.38	9.5	-0.04	2.8	0.2	0.44	3.25	3.33	85.6	5.7	47.2	6.8	4.9
6.6	1.14	5.4	0.12	4.7	18.1	0.92	10.79	2.26	67.9	5.2	23.6	4.2	6.8
7.3	0.45	2.5	-1.20	6.2	13.0	1.36	11.49	4.06	71.2	6.0	42.3	7.6	8.7
4.0	2.02	12.0	0.67	2.8	0.1	0.15	1.49	4.09	79.1	3.9	32.4	12.6	4.9
10.0	0.63	1.4	-0.07	2.3	2.9	0.39	1.50	2.62	90.9	5.1	66.4	16.5	8.8
5.5	0.47	4.1	0.10	4.0	2.3	0.74	7.25	3.77	68.1	1.3	8.0	24.1	4.4
6.6	0.35	1.9	-0.03	3.5	4.6	0.62	4.51	3.44	75.4	1.8	14.1	10.2	5.8
3.1	1.37	9.5	0.69	0.0	-0.8	-1.28	-12.64	4.04	105.2	0.5	11.5	59.8	2.7
8.5	0.19	1.1	0.07	5.2	0.6	1.00	10.12	3.45	57.9	4.9	34.2	8.0	5.8
6.1	1.10	6.1	0.20	5.0	1.8	0.88	7.87	4.97	74.5	3.4	22.0	12.7	6.5
6.4	0.52	3.2	0.12	5.0	7.0	1.23	13.29	4.36	71.4	4.8	31.3	7.7	5.8
4.4	2.59	13.5	0.09	5.4	1.7	0.97	9.40	3.90	68.9	3.9	24.9	10.6	6.1
5.0	2.47	11.3	0.02	4.8	2.0	0.91	7.86	3.59	72.5	5.6	35.2	4.1	6.2
9.2	0.15	0.9	0.00	3.1	18.6	0.59	10.05	2.16	70.8	3.8	14.3	9.9	4.2

Name	City	State	2015 Rating	2014 Rating	Rating	Total Assets ($Mil)	One Year Asset Growth	Asset Mix (As a % of Total Assets)				Capital-ization Index	Lever-age Ratio	Risk-Based Capital Ratio
								Comm-ercial Loans	Cons-umer Loans	Mort-gage Loans	Secur-ities			
Century Bank of Florida	Tampa	FL	D	D	D-	75.9	7.59	12.9	0.9	19.9	7.2	6.6	8.6	13.0
▲ Century Bank of Georgia	Cartersville	GA	B+	B	B	177.1	9.02	6.4	1.0	10.7	13.5	9.6	10.7	22.8
▲ Century Bank of Kentucky, Inc.	Lawrenceburg	KY	C	C-	C-	118.1	3.62	2.9	1.5	35.5	13.9	10.0	11.0	16.5
Century Bank of the Ozarks	Gainesville	MO	B+	B+	B+	168.7	-1.63	7.1	3.7	22.6	5.1	6.6	9.1	12.2
Century S&L Assn.	Trinidad	CO	C	C	C	100.1	0.19	0.4	0.8	15.5	62.9	10.0	13.2	46.9
Century Savings Bank	Vineland	NJ	C+	C+	C+	460.4	2.31	1.3	0.0	16.4	53.6	10.0	13.4	29.7
CerescoBank	Ceresco	NE	B+	B+	B+	44.6	-3.29	9.2	5.8	18.7	25.6	10.0	16.7	20.8
▲ CFBank	Worthington	OH	C+	C	D	405.7	23.13	15.9	0.1	13.0	2.3	7.7	10.3	13.1
▼ CFG Community Bank	Baltimore	MD	C-	B+	B-	676.3	1.49	28.6	0.3	4.0	1.3	6.1	9.7	11.8
cfsbank	Charleroi	PA	C+	C+	C+	515.7	-2.83	2.1	1.5	41.1	30.4	10.0	13.9	31.6
Chain Bridge Bank, N.A.	McLean	VA	C+	C+	C+	618.6	40.55	3.4	0.9	19.3	34.3	4.2	6.2	14.9
Chambers Bank	Danville	AR	B-	C	C-	703.6	3.74	8.1	0.8	14.1	5.7	9.8	13.1	14.8
Chambers State Bank	Chambers	NE	B+	B+	B+	59.8	41.61	7.3	3.5	0.5	0.0	10.0	35.6	38.7
Champion Bank	Parker	CO	D	D	D-	50.4	-6.18	1.1	0.2	18.6	0.0	10.0	15.6	20.2
Champlain National Bank	Willsboro	NY	C+	C+	B-	306.7	9.63	8.0	1.2	18.6	30.6	6.2	8.3	14.2
▲ Chappell Hill Bank	Chappell Hill	TX	C-	D-	D-	25.0	1.25	4.7	3.0	23.0	0.7	8.6	10.1	23.9
Charles River Bank	Medway	MA	C-	C-	C-	230.5	3.81	3.2	1.3	39.4	17.6	6.2	8.2	14.1
Charles Schwab Bank	Reno	NV	B+	B	B	165183.0	28.39	0.0	2.2	5.5	85.7	5.0	7.0	18.9
Charlevoix State Bank	Charlevoix	MI	C+	C	C	206.4	9.65	4.8	2.0	14.6	20.9	6.2	8.2	14.5
▲ Charlotte State Bank & Trust	Port Charlotte	FL	B-	C	C-	332.8	10.33	0.1	0.2	17.1	34.0	7.0	9.0	16.8
Charter Bank	Johnston	IA	B+	B+	B+	148.2	7.01	4.6	2.3	16.1	31.1	9.8	10.9	16.8
Charter Bank	Biloxi	MS	C	C	C	124.2	0.58	11.1	1.5	20.6	13.1	10.0	11.3	17.3
Charter Bank	Corpus Christi	TX	B	B	B	245.0	-10.98	10.9	0.5	4.9	47.1	6.6	8.6	17.1
Charter Bank	Eau Claire	WI	A	A	A-	837.5	37.59	13.6	0.5	15.8	23.0	10.0	12.2	16.1
Charter West Bank	West Point	NE	B	B	B	222.0	4.89	11.2	3.1	10.2	13.1	7.1	9.5	12.6
CharterBank	West Point	GA	A-	B+	B	1440.8	40.41	4.5	1.5	16.5	14.3	10.0	11.5	15.3
Chase Bank USA, N.A.	New York	NY	B-	C+	C-	130692.7	-10.19	4.7	72.1	0.0	0.0	5.7	13.7	11.5
Chasewood Bank	Houston	TX	D	D	D+	103.4	0.83	7.6	0.8	7.8	36.7	6.5	8.5	16.4
Chattahoochee Bank of Georgia	Gainesville	GA	B-	B-	C+	187.4	25.05	10.2	0.6	6.2	9.3	9.0	11.8	14.2
Cheaha Bank	Oxford	AL	A	A	A-	201.4	3.79	6.3	5.2	19.7	36.5	10.0	12.0	20.5
Chelsea Groton Bank	Norwich	CT	B-	C+	C+	1032.7	5.72	5.2	0.5	46.4	19.3	10.0	14.4	19.4
Chelsea Savings Bank	Belle Plaine	IA	A	A	A-	124.7	3.08	8.6	2.1	10.5	52.6	10.0	17.3	33.6
Chelsea State Bank	Chelsea	MI	B+	B+	B-	265.4	-0.21	11.8	0.4	6.7	22.4	10.0	11.2	17.9
▼ Chelten Hills Savings Bank	Abington	PA	D+	C	D	27.6	-8.87	0.0	0.0	72.9	1.9	10.0	12.2	26.0
Chemical Bank	Midland	MI	C+	C+	C+	9717.6	21.55	13.5	12.0	21.2	10.5	4.5	8.1	10.8
Chemung Canal Trust Co.	Elmira	NY	C+	C+	C+	1726.7	5.90	9.8	9.3	15.4	17.8	5.5	7.5	11.5
Cherokee State Bank	Cherokee	IA	A	A	A	208.9	3.04	2.9	1.0	4.7	37.4	10.0	11.7	17.4
Chesapeake Bank	Kilmarnock	VA	B-	B-	C+	715.1	8.17	10.9	1.1	12.1	25.4	9.4	10.6	14.6
▲ Chesapeake Bank & Trust Co.	Chestertown	MD	B-	B-	C+	114.8	9.54	5.1	0.8	21.5	29.2	7.7	9.4	15.1
Chesapeake Bank of Maryland	Baltimore	MD	C+	C+	D+	175.4	2.65	0.8	0.3	37.6	6.3	10.0	11.7	18.0
Chester County Bank	Henderson	TN	B	B-	B-	70.7	-0.18	3.1	6.4	14.7	32.8	9.0	10.3	24.3
Chester National Bank	Chester	IL	C+	C+	B-	97.5	3.84	1.4	1.3	29.9	28.5	7.1	9.1	23.7
▼ Chesterfield State Bank	Chesterfield	IL	D-	D	D-	19.5	-15.28	9.8	10.9	36.3	1.3	8.6	10.1	16.3
Chetopa State Bank & Trust Co.	Chetopa	KS	B-	B	B	31.2	5.68	6.6	4.3	16.9	21.1	8.1	9.7	15.6
Cheyenne State Bank	Cheyenne	WY	B-	B-	B	46.0	-0.91	5.8	2.3	21.4	3.2	10.0	14.0	20.8
Chicago Trust Co., N.A.	Lake Forest	IL	U	U	U	17.0	14.88	0.0	0.0	0.0	0.6	10.0	93.7	273.0
Chillicothe State Bank	Chillicothe	MO	B	B	B	132.7	5.72	3.2	3.6	24.1	35.3	6.2	8.2	18.5
Chinatown Federal Savings Bank	New York	NY	B+	B	C+	132.6	-4.79	0.0	0.2	15.0	2.9	10.0	22.1	37.7
Chino Commercial Bank, N.A.	Chino	CA	B+	B+	B+	182.2	10.98	1.8	0.3	9.2	12.2	7.1	9.0	15.2
Chippewa Valley Bank	Winter	WI	B	B-	C	351.6	15.21	9.4	0.6	22.9	9.9	7.1	9.1	14.9
Chisholm Trail State Bank	Park City	KS	C	C	C	71.5	-2.95	1.1	2.8	20.0	33.6	7.5	9.3	19.5
Choice Bank	Oshkosh	WI	B	B	B	319.1	23.23	14.5	0.2	26.1	8.7	7.0	9.1	12.5
Choice Financial Group	Fargo	ND	B+	B+	B+	1151.7	23.80	11.8	1.3	7.7	6.0	6.1	9.8	11.8
ChoiceOne Bank	Sparta	MI	B-	B-	B-	595.1	7.63	16.0	3.6	14.2	29.2	7.5	9.3	13.5
▲ CIBM Bank	Champaign	IL	C	D+	C	631.3	19.06	8.0	0.2	23.9	16.5	8.6	10.0	14.2
▼ Ciera Bank	Graham	TX	B+	B+	B	522.4	3.87	13.8	1.5	15.4	9.1	9.8	11.9	14.9
▲ Cincinnati Federal	Cincinnati	OH	C	C	C	156.8	8.03	0.4	0.0	53.9	1.2	10.0	11.7	17.9
Cincinnatus S&L Co.	Cincinnati	OH	B	B-	C	82.0	0.05	1.3	0.9	57.0	0.0	10.0	25.1	40.3
Cissna Park State Bank	Cissna Park	IL	B-	C+	C+	61.6	2.69	6.6	0.9	2.9	35.0	6.5	8.5	15.4
CIT Bank, N.A.	Pasadena	CA	B+	B+	A-	42949.9	-1.46	23.8	0.0	13.9	6.2	9.3	10.9	14.4

Arrows denote recent upgrades ▲ or downgrades ▼

www.weissratings.com

Asset Quality Index	Adjusted Non-Performing Loans		Net Charge-Offs Avg Loans	Profitability Index	Net Income ($Mil)	Return on Assets (R.O.A.)	Return on Equity (R.O.E.)	Net Interest Spread	Overhead Efficiency Ratio	Liquidity Index	Liquidity Ratio	Hot Money Ratio	Stability Index
	as a % of Total Loans	as a % of Capital											
1.9	4.93	34.0	0.27	2.8	0.3	0.46	5.42	4.16	88.6	3.4	29.1	14.5	3.4
6.2	1.07	4.6	-0.13	6.9	1.8	1.37	13.05	3.46	67.2	4.5	42.9	13.1	6.3
2.9	4.02	24.9	-0.02	6.3	1.3	1.46	13.49	3.87	67.3	2.1	12.7	18.3	6.9
4.3	1.23	9.6	0.14	8.9	2.7	2.10	22.66	4.90	57.8	3.5	7.3	10.5	7.9
6.9	4.93	9.2	0.26	2.2	0.2	0.26	2.00	2.36	85.2	3.0	65.2	48.4	6.5
7.4	2.00	5.0	0.25	2.7	1.5	0.43	3.25	2.73	79.4	6.2	59.7	8.8	6.6
8.4	0.03	0.1	0.16	6.9	0.5	1.39	8.51	3.82	53.3	3.8	26.8	11.9	7.2
5.0	0.71	5.2	-0.02	3.4	1.6	0.58	5.47	3.23	72.6	0.8	15.2	33.1	4.2
1.8	2.22	18.3	0.20	8.6	8.6	1.79	14.56	5.33	60.9	0.5	5.5	42.2	9.5
9.8	0.20	0.8	0.00	2.4	1.1	0.27	1.92	2.23	84.2	2.9	44.5	25.5	7.6
9.8	0.00	0.0	0.00	3.4	2.4	0.62	8.26	2.66	67.7	7.1	66.7	4.0	5.2
3.4	1.60	9.4	0.55	5.6	7.1	1.41	10.57	4.28	64.0	1.0	7.9	30.2	7.1
7.1	0.46	1.1	0.00	8.6	0.7	2.14	7.93	4.94	42.6	4.2	46.9	15.2	7.2
0.1	10.35	44.5	-0.07	7.2	1.0	2.70	18.57	3.86	93.2	0.8	17.6	38.0	5.1
7.6	0.68	4.4	0.01	3.7	1.3	0.60	7.86	3.90	79.3	3.0	10.6	13.5	4.6
8.9	0.33	1.4	-0.04	2.9	0.2	0.92	9.19	2.86	75.8	5.2	50.6	10.9	5.2
6.8	0.41	3.3	0.00	2.3	0.5	0.31	3.72	3.02	87.4	2.6	24.4	17.0	4.8
10.0	0.23	0.3	0.00	5.4	1068.0	0.95	13.94	1.74	17.3	8.4	95.9	0.0	5.7
4.0	1.69	10.7	-0.01	6.1	2.0	1.50	17.60	3.70	67.4	6.5	49.0	3.3	5.3
4.3	1.81	10.0	0.00	7.3	4.6	1.92	21.60	3.48	61.8	6.5	46.4	2.0	6.3
8.9	0.13	0.7	0.00	5.4	1.1	0.99	8.84	3.46	58.5	4.5	44.2	13.6	7.0
4.3	1.75	10.4	0.20	2.4	0.2	0.16	1.33	4.73	91.4	0.9	21.2	38.6	5.9
4.6	2.58	12.4	0.34	10.0	6.1	3.05	31.31	6.78	50.5	6.0	57.4	8.9	6.9
7.5	0.67	3.8	-0.01	9.6	14.1	2.28	17.33	4.18	43.6	1.7	20.3	16.4	9.5
6.5	0.28	2.0	0.21	6.1	2.4	1.43	15.11	4.18	73.7	1.7	5.5	19.4	8.0
7.0	0.75	4.4	-0.14	5.2	8.5	0.88	6.15	3.86	73.2	2.5	20.8	15.5	8.9
3.2	1.16	6.0	2.60	7.3	1036.4	0.97	4.77	7.56	56.9	0.3	12.6	99.0	8.4
5.1	1.33	7.0	0.00	1.1	0.1	0.08	0.92	2.87	101.6	2.8	57.3	48.6	3.7
7.3	0.00	0.0	0.00	4.1	0.9	0.70	5.69	3.68	64.7	1.2	19.3	30.0	7.2
8.8	0.21	0.9	0.14	9.3	2.4	1.60	12.98	5.12	55.0	1.2	24.2	32.2	7.8
6.1	1.52	7.5	0.06	3.3	4.9	0.66	4.43	3.35	78.4	4.5	25.1	9.8	8.9
9.1	0.76	1.7	0.03	7.0	1.7	1.85	10.29	3.70	49.9	6.7	70.2	7.3	9.4
6.3	1.60	7.9	-0.12	5.5	2.6	1.26	11.12	3.79	66.3	5.5	36.8	5.0	7.9
6.5	0.29	1.7	3.22	1.0	-0.1	-0.50	-4.18	4.09	72.1	0.8	20.2	42.1	5.2
3.4	1.06	10.1	0.14	6.6	88.1	1.25	11.31	3.62	56.5	3.6	9.7	8.7	8.3
4.0	1.21	10.6	0.11	3.3	7.0	0.56	6.79	3.37	78.8	4.9	12.5	3.0	6.6
8.7	0.20	0.9	0.00	8.2	2.3	1.51	12.54	3.91	49.7	3.3	36.6	6.6	8.4
4.5	1.63	9.7	0.29	5.9	6.2	1.20	10.44	4.63	74.4	1.8	15.6	14.2	7.6
5.7	0.86	5.1	0.11	5.0	0.9	1.10	12.09	3.15	67.5	2.9	17.1	14.9	6.1
8.5	0.24	1.4	0.07	2.7	0.4	0.33	2.69	3.46	85.6	1.9	26.0	22.2	5.9
7.5	0.42	1.5	-0.01	4.4	0.5	0.84	8.07	3.85	72.1	3.1	58.5	28.0	5.4
10.0	0.09	0.4	0.00	3.3	0.5	0.71	7.67	2.64	73.6	5.4	57.4	11.1	5.3
0.3	4.87	35.8	0.11	5.2	0.2	1.13	11.75	3.88	69.3	3.0	14.1	13.5	4.4
8.4	0.00	0.0	0.09	5.3	0.3	1.29	12.94	3.43	65.0	1.0	7.2	29.3	6.1
8.7	0.31	1.3	0.02	3.0	0.1	0.34	2.42	4.30	86.7	2.3	32.6	22.3	5.7
6.6	na	0.0	na	9.5	1.7	13.30	14.34	0.60	71.8	4.0	na	0.0	5.7
5.2	1.52	8.5	0.03	4.4	1.0	0.97	11.40	2.95	67.3	5.5	34.8	4.5	5.7
4.3	4.30	11.6	0.05	4.7	0.4	0.40	1.84	4.77	80.1	5.5	46.7	8.8	8.2
5.0	1.19	7.2	0.04	6.1	1.2	0.97	10.61	3.84	60.4	4.9	26.9	5.0	5.5
5.4	1.04	7.7	0.07	7.3	4.6	1.85	20.01	4.70	57.2	4.2	18.6	7.6	5.2
9.3	0.18	0.8	-0.01	2.6	0.3	0.47	4.94	3.13	87.1	6.1	47.4	4.6	4.7
4.9	0.94	7.7	0.13	6.3	2.4	1.06	11.46	3.25	48.7	0.6	11.5	35.7	6.0
6.2	0.89	7.5	-0.07	10.0	19.4	2.32	21.38	4.51	56.6	1.3	7.5	9.4	9.9
4.4	0.94	5.9	-0.03	5.4	4.4	1.02	8.66	3.80	71.1	4.6	33.6	9.5	7.4
4.9	1.31	8.8	-0.07	3.1	3.1	0.68	6.75	3.05	83.6	1.8	15.5	15.1	6.0
4.5	1.51	8.9	-0.02	8.8	7.9	2.06	15.55	4.72	55.0	2.3	12.0	17.4	9.4
7.7	0.74	5.1	0.02	2.6	0.5	0.44	3.80	2.83	84.8	0.8	10.3	33.1	6.0
6.3	2.63	9.0	0.12	4.9	0.6	0.99	4.02	4.22	78.5	2.3	10.6	16.0	6.2
8.9	0.00	0.0	0.02	4.0	0.4	0.91	10.08	2.69	68.3	4.9	44.4	11.4	5.0
5.9	0.87	5.0	0.49	4.9	102.2	0.88	6.98	3.48	59.8	1.1	22.1	31.2	9.7

Name	City	State	2015 Rating	2014 Rating	Total Assets ($Mil)	One Year Asset Growth	Comm- ercial Loans	Cons- umer Loans	Mort- gage Loans	Secur- ities	Capital- ization Index	Lever- age Ratio	Risk- Based Capital Ratio
							Asset Mix (As a % of Total Assets)						
Citibank, N.A.	Sioux Falls	SD	B	B	B-	1356393.0	1.39	11.0	12.0	6.5	24.2	7.9	9.6	14.2
Citicorp Trust Delaware, N.A.	Greenville	DE	U	U	U	25.3	-57.97	0.0	0.0	0.0	0.9	10.0	79.7	410.2
Citizens & Northern Bank	Wellsboro	PA	A-	A-	A-	1230.5	0.94	7.1	1.0	28.4	32.2	10.0	12.7	21.0
Citizens 1st Bank	Tyler	TX	A+	A+	A+	723.6	-1.17	2.7	1.1	10.6	57.6	10.0	20.4	50.8
Citizens Alliance Bank	Clara City	MN	B	B	B-	688.5	9.86	15.7	1.8	8.0	17.4	6.0	8.5	11.7
Citizens and Farmers Bank	West Point	VA	B+	B+	B	1418.4	3.70	3.5	22.2	21.0	14.5	8.7	10.3	13.9
Citizens B&T Co. of Grainger County	Rutledge	TN	B+	B+	B+	205.4	3.30	1.3	2.1	9.2	59.7	10.0	16.5	36.1
Citizens Bank	Enterprise	AL	C	C	C+	131.9	15.71	10.2	1.2	14.5	20.6	8.3	9.8	16.1
▼ Citizens Bank	Greensboro	AL	B+	A-	A-	101.6	1.70	6.8	5.8	7.8	47.2	10.0	12.3	24.4
Citizens Bank	Batesville	AR	C+	B-	B-	786.6	36.33	7.5	2.6	20.2	18.9	5.7	7.7	11.7
Citizens Bank	Nashville	GA	B-	B-	C	253.0	0.71	6.0	3.8	28.1	13.8	10.0	12.5	21.9
▼ Citizens Bank	Sac City	IA	C	C+	C+	52.0	-4.73	6.3	2.3	8.9	38.4	6.4	8.4	15.7
Citizens Bank	Mooresville	IN	B-	C+	C	438.4	-0.03	3.3	40.0	6.1	21.6	8.0	9.7	13.5
Citizens Bank	Hartford	KY	D+	B-	C-	54.9	81.89	2.4	8.7	26.1	26.1	8.7	10.2	16.5
Citizens Bank	Hickman	KY	B+	A-	A-	119.0	2.63	4.2	3.5	14.1	19.3	10.0	13.3	17.3
Citizens Bank	Morehead	KY	B-	B-	B-	130.8	2.95	2.1	6.0	41.7	14.0	6.3	8.3	14.0
Citizens Bank	Mount Vernon	KY	C+	B-	C+	142.4	-2.61	2.2	5.1	41.4	10.5	8.5	10.0	16.1
▲ Citizens Bank	Amsterdam	MO	C+	C-	C	60.8	3.60	15.0	4.4	33.3	0.0	5.1	8.1	11.1
▲ Citizens Bank	New Haven	MO	B	C+	C+	174.9	1.96	5.7	1.6	22.2	14.1	10.0	13.4	15.9
Citizens Bank	Byhalia	MS	B-	B-	B-	73.6	1.00	2.4	8.9	20.4	28.2	10.0	11.5	23.2
Citizens Bank	Columbia	MS	B-	B-	B	400.1	0.86	7.1	6.9	23.5	12.0	9.8	10.9	16.3
Citizens Bank	Farmington	NM	A-	A-	A-	702.7	-4.31	6.5	1.1	11.2	63.6	8.0	9.7	24.7
Citizens Bank	Corvallis	OR	B	B+	B+	703.2	12.89	7.8	0.7	5.2	30.6	8.7	10.1	17.0
Citizens Bank	Olanta	SC	B-	B-	B-	422.7	7.55	7.0	5.4	21.0	15.7	8.2	9.8	17.1
Citizens Bank	Carthage	TN	A+	A+	A+	568.2	4.70	3.7	3.5	11.4	61.5	10.0	17.4	29.9
Citizens Bank	Elizabethton	TN	A-	A-	B+	766.5	13.35	28.3	2.1	6.1	30.3	10.0	11.8	22.4
Citizens Bank	Hartsville	TN	B	B	B	205.1	11.42	6.3	3.6	23.7	12.3	7.8	9.9	13.2
▲ Citizens Bank	New Tazewell	TN	C	C	C-	171.3	5.12	11.4	2.6	34.3	5.8	6.6	8.8	12.2
Citizens Bank	Amarillo	TX	B	B	B+	151.5	4.99	3.7	0.1	3.6	6.0	4.5	9.8	10.8
Citizens Bank	Kilgore	TX	B	B-	B-	383.7	-0.87	19.7	0.8	6.1	12.6	10.0	11.1	18.2
Citizens Bank	Mukwonago	WI	C	C	B-	704.4	6.02	7.4	0.4	10.7	20.1	10.0	12.4	20.8
Citizens Bank & Trust	Guntersville	AL	B-	B-	B-	395.2	7.68	10.9	2.7	11.8	22.0	7.8	9.5	13.4
Citizens Bank & Trust	Rock Port	MO	B	B	B	90.2	6.65	11.3	3.5	8.0	39.4	10.0	11.4	22.1
Citizens Bank & Trust Co.	Van Buren	AR	A-	A-	A-	383.7	3.58	5.5	5.9	18.6	33.5	10.0	12.4	20.5
Citizens Bank & Trust Co.	Eastman	GA	D+	D	D-	125.4	-2.18	6.2	2.4	22.1	24.9	5.2	7.2	13.2
Citizens Bank & Trust Co.	Campbellsville	KY	B	B-	B-	208.4	-3.28	3.7	2.5	16.4	47.8	10.0	15.7	30.2
Citizens Bank & Trust Co.	Covington	LA	C+	C+	C	119.1	3.57	3.5	0.7	18.2	10.7	7.5	9.3	15.8
Citizens Bank & Trust Co.	Plaquemine	LA	B	B	B	265.7	10.46	4.9	1.2	18.8	10.5	10.0	12.0	16.4
Citizens Bank & Trust Co.	Vivian	LA	B-	B-	C-	136.9	-3.98	7.5	6.7	31.8	27.8	10.0	12.2	20.5
Citizens Bank & Trust Co.	Hutchinson	MN	B	B	C+	213.7	2.26	14.0	1.4	19.1	32.5	6.6	8.6	14.5
▼ Citizens Bank & Trust Co.	Marks	MS	D+	C	C	143.3	3.32	14.5	3.2	13.6	14.6	3.5	8.2	10.3
Citizens Bank & Trust Co.	Big Timber	MT	B-	C+	C-	109.7	4.17	4.9	2.1	4.4	24.7	8.4	10.0	16.6
Citizens Bank & Trust Co.	Saint Paul	NE	B+	B+	B+	174.4	8.90	8.8	3.2	4.7	15.2	6.0	10.8	11.8
Citizens Bank & Trust Co.	Atwood	TN	C-	D+	D+	25.2	1.94	1.4	12.3	19.0	44.2	7.7	9.4	23.4
Citizens Bank & Trust Co. of Ardmore	Ardmore	OK	B	B-	B-	201.7	0.78	7.7	3.0	24.2	31.7	8.6	10.1	16.3
Citizens Bank & Trust Co. of Jackson	Jackson	KY	D+	C	C	152.5	0.15	11.0	6.9	25.0	5.7	5.8	8.6	11.6
▲ Citizens Bank & Trust, Inc.	Trenton	GA	B+	B	B-	100.0	4.83	0.7	15.7	36.7	25.3	10.0	11.3	20.0
Citizens Bank and Trust	Lake Wales	FL	C+	C+	C	518.1	7.87	4.8	4.0	15.4	26.7	6.2	8.3	13.9
Citizens Bank and Trust Co.	Kansas City	MO	C+	C+	C	920.5	2.89	14.1	0.4	19.1	20.2	6.2	8.7	11.9
Citizens Bank and Trust Co.	Blackstone	VA	A-	A-	A-	354.5	2.11	3.4	2.6	23.4	24.2	10.0	13.2	24.6
Citizens Bank Co.	Beverly	OH	A	A	A-	188.8	1.04	6.4	1.9	23.5	24.6	10.0	13.2	21.4
Citizens Bank Minnesota	New Ulm	MN	B	B	B+	363.4	1.52	5.6	1.3	21.0	22.3	6.8	10.4	12.3
Citizens Bank of Ada	Ada	OK	B-	B-	C+	216.0	-1.12	18.9	2.6	20.6	20.0	7.3	9.2	13.7
Citizens Bank of Americus	Americus	GA	B	B	C+	272.3	8.98	8.7	2.0	9.9	16.3	7.7	9.5	16.3
Citizens Bank of Cape Vincent	Cape Vincent	NY	C+	C+	C+	64.7	4.94	0.6	2.9	40.1	35.5	8.0	9.6	24.4
Citizens Bank of Charleston	Charleston	MO	A-	A-	A-	127.3	5.34	9.9	5.2	7.1	10.5	10.0	16.7	22.1
Citizens Bank of Chatsworth	Chatsworth	IL	E-	E-	E-	33.6	-3.95	10.0	2.3	6.5	22.3	2.2	6.3	9.3
▲ Citizens Bank of Clovis	Clovis	NM	B	B-	B-	364.8	8.12	4.5	0.7	4.5	36.1	8.7	10.1	16.5
Citizens Bank of Cochran	Cochran	GA	B-	C	C-	75.0	5.12	15.2	7.2	16.8	24.1	10.0	13.3	20.5
Citizens Bank of Cumberland County	Burkesville	KY	B	B	B	72.5	3.24	7.9	12.4	23.8	13.1	10.0	12.3	18.3

Asset Quality Index	Adjusted Non-Performing Loans as a % of Total Loans	as a % of Capital	Net Charge-Offs Avg Loans	Profitability Index	Net Income ($Mil)	Return on Assets (R.O.A.)	Return on Equity (R.O.E.)	Net Interest Spread	Overhead Efficiency Ratio	Liquidity Index	Liquidity Ratio	Hot Money Ratio	Stability Index
5.8	1.55	6.7	0.96	5.1	9427.0	0.94	8.60	3.23	55.7	5.1	39.9	8.0	8.7
10.0	na	0.0	na	8.0	0.4	1.67	2.14	0.62	82.8	4.0	497.6	0.0	7.0
5.2	2.66	12.3	0.13	6.4	11.1	1.22	8.68	3.76	62.0	4.3	13.0	7.1	10.0
8.9	1.72	3.2	0.21	8.6	11.1	2.05	9.40	3.64	32.1	2.8	44.5	26.0	10.0
5.6	0.47	3.5	0.02	7.3	8.2	1.66	17.78	3.71	52.8	2.5	18.2	16.8	7.8
5.2	0.76	4.4	1.57	6.0	11.3	1.08	9.61	6.38	64.3	2.9	16.5	14.9	9.1
4.9	10.29	18.3	0.07	4.4	1.3	0.89	5.20	3.63	71.5	5.0	60.7	15.1	8.0
7.3	0.58	3.3	0.00	3.2	0.5	0.51	4.73	3.50	82.7	3.5	31.8	14.5	4.8
6.2	1.65	5.3	0.53	4.5	0.5	0.61	4.69	3.46	45.5	2.9	50.4	29.6	7.7
4.7	0.75	6.2	0.11	4.1	4.7	0.84	9.06	3.92	68.9	1.6	10.3	21.6	5.5
4.0	4.03	18.6	0.35	4.3	1.9	1.00	8.20	3.73	70.6	1.3	26.7	31.6	5.8
7.1	1.04	5.9	0.00	3.8	0.3	0.81	9.16	3.12	78.0	2.5	29.9	19.1	5.1
4.1	0.51	3.5	0.06	3.9	2.3	0.73	7.38	3.36	70.4	4.1	9.5	7.1	5.6
4.7	1.38	7.9	-0.05	1.3	-0.1	-0.14	-1.08	3.58	99.7	5.1	31.8	5.9	6.3
5.7	1.90	9.3	0.09	5.1	1.0	1.17	8.45	4.33	65.3	1.0	8.1	30.2	7.5
4.6	0.89	7.8	0.08	3.7	0.7	0.73	7.58	4.10	81.7	4.1	9.5	7.4	5.7
3.2	2.49	17.2	0.10	4.1	0.9	0.86	8.27	4.21	77.5	1.3	13.7	27.3	5.7
7.9	0.20	2.0	0.04	6.7	0.7	1.63	21.52	5.44	69.8	4.2	8.3	6.3	4.1
8.0	0.29	1.5	-0.40	4.1	1.0	0.73	5.55	3.91	75.6	4.5	14.7	5.2	6.6
7.8	1.02	4.1	0.23	3.4	0.3	0.50	4.27	3.67	82.4	4.0	47.9	16.1	5.7
4.3	1.50	9.4	0.11	7.4	5.2	1.73	17.71	4.60	65.0	2.1	9.1	18.0	7.3
9.8	0.37	1.1	0.14	5.9	7.7	1.42	14.43	3.07	58.8	4.1	60.0	19.7	7.6
5.4	1.35	6.8	0.19	4.4	3.6	0.72	6.97	3.50	65.9	6.2	41.6	2.8	5.8
5.7	0.62	3.5	0.00	4.3	2.2	0.72	6.88	3.83	74.8	4.6	33.7	9.9	5.9
10.0	0.98	1.8	0.09	10.0	9.6	2.31	13.59	4.76	32.1	3.6	74.3	31.5	9.6
7.3	0.35	1.9	0.21	6.6	7.9	1.53	11.71	4.02	62.0	3.9	19.1	9.8	8.5
5.8	0.67	4.7	0.03	7.6	1.8	1.19	12.07	4.60	56.8	0.9	11.6	33.2	5.6
4.0	1.17	10.4	0.13	4.0	1.1	0.89	10.36	4.41	79.1	2.8	10.8	14.6	4.5
7.1	0.00	0.0	-0.04	8.8	2.4	2.16	22.39	4.52	52.1	2.3	9.6	16.9	7.0
6.4	1.82	8.1	0.05	4.0	1.6	0.57	5.07	3.57	70.0	4.9	36.2	9.3	5.7
2.4	5.49	23.9	0.09	4.7	5.1	0.99	8.06	3.24	62.1	3.5	23.1	12.3	7.1
5.1	1.01	6.6	0.60	3.9	2.3	0.80	8.25	4.15	72.0	2.0	11.5	18.9	5.3
8.3	0.59	2.2	0.13	4.8	0.8	1.14	9.69	3.14	67.2	3.1	25.1	14.5	7.5
6.3	1.36	6.0	0.05	9.1	4.3	1.50	12.05	4.11	50.5	1.6	19.1	24.4	8.3
7.0	0.50	3.5	-0.02	2.8	0.5	0.47	6.94	4.13	89.7	3.6	24.7	12.0	1.6
7.3	1.48	4.3	0.04	4.7	1.5	0.92	5.91	3.60	70.5	4.6	32.1	8.9	7.4
5.1	1.40	8.6	0.05	3.3	0.4	0.46	4.57	4.01	85.1	4.6	31.0	8.6	5.2
4.9	2.32	12.0	0.02	4.5	1.4	0.71	6.47	3.95	72.5	3.9	19.3	10.1	6.2
3.7	4.02	19.9	0.25	3.9	0.8	0.74	5.64	4.79	88.0	3.5	28.8	13.6	7.7
4.8	1.79	11.7	0.00	7.0	2.7	1.71	19.13	3.81	52.3	5.3	23.0	1.4	6.2
2.8	2.08	17.3	0.08	3.9	0.8	0.80	8.50	4.23	74.2	2.5	10.9	16.3	4.6
4.2	2.07	10.6	-0.12	5.3	0.7	0.90	7.82	3.90	62.1	4.0	36.4	13.8	6.6
5.7	0.59	4.2	0.01	7.8	1.8	1.44	13.77	4.47	49.1	1.5	6.3	21.1	7.4
5.8	1.43	5.4	0.00	2.6	0.1	0.39	4.29	2.81	85.6	1.4	28.4	32.7	3.6
8.9	0.10	0.5	0.00	5.0	2.0	1.29	13.18	3.41	68.8	3.2	25.5	14.4	6.4
1.2	5.21	44.9	0.33	3.9	0.9	0.78	8.00	3.97	75.1	0.7	9.2	34.9	4.7
5.5	1.04	5.3	0.27	5.8	0.8	1.05	9.54	5.19	65.5	3.1	22.9	14.1	6.3
4.5	1.44	10.8	0.04	4.0	3.6	0.94	10.83	3.55	80.2	4.9	23.0	3.4	5.4
8.4	0.13	1.0	0.02	3.4	4.3	0.62	6.30	3.28	77.9	2.3	8.4	11.5	5.5
6.8	1.55	6.0	-0.01	5.9	2.9	1.09	8.38	3.63	63.4	4.8	37.5	10.0	7.7
9.0	0.04	0.2	0.05	7.2	2.2	1.52	11.49	4.47	54.8	4.4	23.5	7.2	7.7
5.9	0.83	5.4	0.14	4.2	2.0	0.74	6.84	3.27	67.2	3.9	16.0	9.4	6.8
6.3	0.68	4.5	0.05	4.3	1.6	0.97	11.06	4.23	78.5	3.9	15.1	9.6	4.9
5.8	0.86	4.8	-0.93	7.7	2.8	1.39	14.88	3.50	58.2	3.7	27.8	12.3	5.1
4.9	2.44	12.0	0.20	3.4	0.3	0.54	5.65	3.61	78.7	4.7	18.2	4.7	5.4
6.0	0.82	3.4	-0.02	7.8	1.3	1.31	8.18	4.28	47.1	2.1	18.3	18.9	8.8
1.8	2.70	25.9	1.00	0.0	-0.1	-0.46	-7.44	3.34	115.9	4.5	15.0	5.6	1.1
8.9	0.01	0.1	0.01	4.8	3.4	1.26	12.44	2.97	55.3	1.2	22.9	27.0	6.6
5.7	0.79	3.5	-4.27	6.7	1.6	2.94	22.28	4.69	87.7	1.7	27.7	26.6	5.6
4.6	1.77	9.2	0.55	7.6	0.9	1.66	13.81	4.72	59.0	3.0	23.2	14.8	7.7

Name	City	State	2015 Rating	2014 Rating	Rating	Total Assets ($Mil)	One Year Asset Growth	Comm-ercial Loans	Cons-umer Loans	Mort-gage Loans	Secur-ities	Capital-ization Index	Lever-age Ratio	Risk-Based Capital Ratio
▲ Citizens Bank of Edina	Edina	MO	A-	A-	A-	69.8	5.80	6.8	3.1	5.7	7.6	10.0	11.2	15.0
Citizens Bank of Edinburg	Edinburg	IL	C	C	C	24.1	6.32	5.7	3.6	13.4	24.8	7.5	9.3	15.8
Citizens Bank of Edmond	Edmond	OK	B+	B	C	242.6	-3.11	3.7	0.6	16.0	15.4	10.0	11.4	15.5
Citizens Bank of Eldon	Eldon	MO	B	B	B	145.8	9.62	5.0	8.2	20.6	19.5	10.0	13.8	18.4
Citizens Bank of Fayette	Fayette	AL	B	B	B	190.5	-0.61	9.7	4.4	4.2	63.0	10.0	19.5	39.0
▲ Citizens Bank of Florida	Oviedo	FL	C+	C-	C-	257.0	8.87	6.2	0.5	9.5	12.0	7.6	9.4	13.1
Citizens Bank of Forsyth County	Cumming	GA	B-	B-	C+	293.5	13.53	5.5	1.7	11.2	33.0	7.3	9.2	14.7
Citizens Bank of Kansas	Kingman	KS	B-	B-	B-	224.1	-4.14	12.0	1.0	13.7	35.8	8.7	10.1	14.1
▲ Citizens Bank of Kentucky	Paintsville	KY	B-	C+	B-	593.3	4.62	5.8	4.4	21.0	25.9	10.0	11.1	17.5
Citizens Bank of Lafayette	Lafayette	TN	B	B	B-	862.5	4.63	4.4	7.2	16.3	37.3	8.3	9.9	18.3
Citizens Bank of Las Cruces	Las Cruces	NM	A-	A-	A-	503.4	5.08	7.1	0.9	8.7	34.9	7.5	9.4	14.8
Citizens Bank of Logan	Logan	OH	C+	C-	D	178.7	-5.91	5.1	8.1	33.4	5.1	7.1	9.1	13.5
Citizens Bank of Morgantown, Inc.	Morgantown	WV	B	B	B	36.5	-0.50	3.1	2.4	45.0	30.7	10.0	18.1	34.9
Citizens Bank of Newburg	Rolla	MO	C-	C-	C	157.6	-0.22	7.2	2.8	23.8	14.7	7.9	11.2	13.2
Citizens Bank of Northern Kentucky, Inc.	Newport	KY	C+	C+	C+	228.9	-4.24	3.6	1.1	15.9	21.1	9.2	10.4	16.4
Citizens Bank of Pagosa Springs	Pagosa Springs	CO	B-	B-	C+	78.9	10.39	3.0	0.5	14.0	34.4	6.8	8.8	14.8
Citizens Bank of Pennsylvania	Philadelphia	PA	C+	C	C+	35754.1	5.38	16.3	9.9	9.6	28.9	6.9	8.9	13.9
Citizens Bank of Philadelphia, Mississippi	Philadelphia	MS	B-	B-	B-	1024.8	6.68	3.9	1.9	8.1	44.6	6.9	8.9	17.7
▲ Citizens Bank of Rogersville	Rogersville	MO	B-	B-	C	77.9	3.03	11.0	5.3	22.6	17.4	7.9	9.6	13.6
▲ Citizens Bank of Swainsboro	Swainsboro	GA	B-	C+	C+	170.8	11.33	9.3	7.9	26.1	11.2	9.3	10.6	15.7
Citizens Bank of The South	Sandersville	GA	B	B	C+	222.6	5.56	10.1	4.9	28.2	16.6	10.0	11.1	18.9
Citizens Bank of Valley Head	Valley Head	AL	C+	C	C-	26.6	2.72	11.0	8.5	32.0	8.4	10.0	11.7	22.3
Citizens Bank of West Virginia, Inc.	Elkins	WV	B	B-	B-	235.7	6.15	4.6	14.1	39.7	11.2	9.7	10.8	17.4
Citizens Bank of Weston, Inc.	Weston	WV	B	B+	B+	193.1	-0.71	17.3	3.3	20.5	21.9	9.2	10.4	17.2
Citizens Bank of Winfield	Winfield	AL	A	A	A	216.6	3.68	2.8	7.7	4.1	70.5	10.0	22.8	46.3
Citizens Bank, N.A.	Providence	RI	C+	C	C	114604.5	9.23	21.9	16.1	12.1	12.7	8.3	10.5	13.6
Citizens Bank, N.A.	Abilene	TX	B+	B+	B	105.2	-2.56	11.4	7.8	18.5	11.8	8.0	9.7	13.3
Citizens Bank, Ville Platte, Louisiana	Ville Platte	LA	B	B	B	245.4	-2.69	5.3	4.5	27.0	30.3	10.0	14.2	32.7
Citizens Building and Loan, SSB	Greer	SC	B+	B+	B	126.5	5.48	0.1	0.2	45.5	17.9	10.0	21.5	40.9
Citizens Business Bank	Ontario	CA	A	A	A-	8038.7	5.50	5.1	0.3	4.2	38.8	9.9	10.9	18.1
▲ Citizens Commerce National Bank	Versailles	KY	E	E-	E-	220.8	1.18	3.7	1.2	20.6	24.3	3.8	5.8	10.5
Citizens Community Bank	Hahira	GA	A-	B+	B+	135.9	5.48	6.2	4.9	25.7	20.6	10.0	11.2	17.7
Citizens Community Bank	Mascoutah	IL	A-	A-	B	349.6	10.73	6.1	1.4	13.9	35.6	9.5	10.6	17.7
▲ Citizens Community Bank	Pilot Grove	MO	B	B-	B-	107.4	-3.37	4.8	2.8	15.8	16.8	10.0	11.1	16.7
Citizens Community Bank	Winchester	TN	B	B	B	209.9	5.58	12.3	3.8	19.3	17.1	10.0	12.0	17.2
Citizens Community Bank	South Hill	VA	C+	C+	C	207.0	18.78	8.3	2.0	27.0	7.6	8.2	9.9	13.5
Citizens Community Federal N.A.	Altoona	WI	C+	C	C	696.1	19.99	3.7	27.4	29.9	12.5	7.4	9.3	14.0
Citizens Deposit Bank & Trust	Vanceburg	KY	B	B	B-	403.1	4.95	2.2	2.7	21.6	25.0	7.2	9.1	14.7
Citizens Deposit Bank of Arlington, Inc.	Arlington	KY	A	A	A	202.6	9.84	11.6	4.9	16.9	34.1	10.0	14.4	22.4
▲ Citizens Federal S&L Assn.	Covington	KY	B+	C+	B-	37.6	8.86	0.0	0.0	45.0	25.3	10.0	27.7	64.2
Citizens Federal S&L Assn.	Bellefontaine	OH	C	C	C	137.6	-3.13	0.0	0.1	59.3	19.4	10.0	11.5	24.7
Citizens First Bank	The Villages	FL	B+	B+	B	1994.7	9.05	1.7	0.0	3.5	78.9	6.7	8.7	21.3
Citizens First Bank	Clinton	IA	C+	C+	C+	179.6	0.24	28.5	3.2	14.8	5.3	7.3	9.8	12.8
Citizens First Bank	Wartburg	TN	B-	B-	C+	162.8	3.53	6.9	6.3	30.3	12.4	7.2	9.1	14.0
Citizens First Bank	Viroqua	WI	D+	D	C+	185.6	6.60	5.6	3.6	10.6	16.4	9.8	11.0	14.8
Citizens First Bank, Inc.	Bowling Green	KY	B	B-	B-	441.6	4.03	9.9	0.9	13.1	12.6	7.6	9.8	13.0
Citizens First National Bank	Storm Lake	IA	A-	A	A-	217.4	4.11	12.7	5.4	3.7	41.0	8.4	10.0	17.2
▲ Citizens First State Bank of Walnut	Walnut	IL	D-	E-	E-	49.9	-4.54	4.6	7.2	24.7	35.6	4.5	6.5	15.0
Citizens Guaranty Bank	Irvine	KY	C-	C-	C	155.6	2.78	6.3	6.8	38.1	8.9	5.9	7.9	11.7
Citizens Independent Bank	Saint Louis Park	MN	C-	C-	D	293.4	-0.45	11.0	6.9	13.3	23.9	9.9	10.9	19.3
Citizens National Bank	Greenleaf	KS	B-	B-	B-	170.6	-0.07	2.6	2.4	11.4	58.7	8.1	9.8	22.7
Citizens National Bank	Sevierville	TN	B-	C	C	927.6	5.67	4.8	0.5	15.7	15.1	9.2	10.5	14.4
Citizens National Bank	Cameron	TX	C+	B-	B-	405.4	-1.57	4.5	0.7	5.7	50.4	9.6	10.7	20.6
Citizens National Bank	Crockett	TX	C	C-	C-	94.0	-3.32	6.9	7.9	6.7	22.5	7.9	9.6	23.6
Citizens National Bank	Henderson	TX	B-	C+	B	1653.3	0.70	7.6	4.1	17.3	39.4	5.8	7.8	13.9
Citizens National Bank	Windsor	VA	C+	C+	C+	52.0	-5.22	10.7	1.3	16.2	10.1	10.0	13.4	17.9
Citizens National Bank at Brownwood	Brownwood	TX	B+	B+	B+	206.1	-0.16	11.7	6.7	13.6	34.6	10.0	12.3	20.4
Citizens National Bank of Albion	Albion	IL	A-	A-	A-	321.4	1.26	14.2	3.9	15.4	22.9	10.0	15.3	21.2
Citizens National Bank of Bluffton	Bluffton	OH	B	B	B+	760.7	5.95	8.1	0.4	7.8	16.7	7.2	9.1	13.9
Citizens National Bank of Cheboygan	Cheboygan	MI	C+	C+	C+	290.7	4.76	3.0	2.1	19.7	31.9	7.4	9.2	18.3

Asset Quality Index	Adjusted Non-Performing Loans as a % of Total Loans	as a % of Capital	Net Charge-Offs Avg Loans	Profitability Index	Net Income ($Mil)	Return on Assets (R.O.A.)	Return on Equity (R.O.E.)	Net Interest Spread	Overhead Efficiency Ratio	Liquidity Index	Liquidity Ratio	Hot Money Ratio	Stability Index
5.9	0.03	0.2	0.14	9.8	0.8	1.60	14.50	4.57	39.9	2.1	6.2	17.6	7.4
9.0	0.04	0.2	0.00	4.2	0.2	0.87	8.90	3.48	64.7	3.4	26.1	12.5	4.1
5.8	1.19	7.0	0.09	4.0	1.7	0.89	8.77	3.97	81.8	4.3	18.2	6.9	6.6
5.8	1.26	6.5	0.24	5.0	1.0	0.94	6.89	3.82	64.7	4.2	22.1	8.2	7.7
5.7	6.00	7.8	-0.17	4.7	1.8	1.24	6.32	2.93	55.9	3.7	64.6	26.6	7.0
4.1	0.85	5.8	0.00	3.6	0.9	0.49	5.17	3.88	80.3	2.3	21.4	17.7	4.2
4.8	1.54	9.5	-0.59	5.6	2.0	0.94	10.13	3.64	60.1	3.4	37.6	17.1	4.8
6.1	0.96	5.0	0.04	3.8	1.4	0.82	6.27	3.98	78.1	4.0	15.6	8.8	7.7
4.3	2.35	12.2	-0.06	5.0	4.8	1.07	7.70	3.57	74.3	2.8	24.6	15.4	8.0
4.5	1.92	10.1	0.16	5.8	6.9	1.08	9.99	3.87	58.9	2.3	34.0	24.2	6.7
8.8	0.09	0.5	0.05	8.6	7.4	1.96	19.61	3.88	57.8	4.5	27.3	7.9	8.0
3.7	1.87	15.8	0.11	3.8	0.8	0.61	6.13	4.42	82.3	2.3	10.6	16.9	3.6
9.2	0.43	1.4	0.03	4.8	0.3	0.97	5.44	5.02	74.1	3.1	31.3	16.4	7.2
1.8	5.93	31.6	0.13	3.9	0.7	0.56	5.05	3.50	71.8	3.3	16.4	12.3	6.1
4.6	2.43	13.0	0.07	2.9	1.1	0.58	5.40	3.55	94.9	5.6	32.7	2.9	6.4
7.2	0.59	2.8	0.12	3.8	0.4	0.74	7.92	3.62	79.9	6.2	46.6	3.7	4.9
4.7	1.27	8.2	0.40	3.4	149.7	0.56	5.16	2.54	65.0	5.4	34.7	6.1	7.3
5.1	2.64	11.6	0.79	3.7	5.3	0.71	7.96	3.16	74.6	3.7	25.0	14.0	7.4
4.4	0.81	5.6	0.03	4.3	0.6	0.95	8.75	4.36	73.5	3.9	13.3	9.1	6.1
4.4	1.01	6.3	0.37	5.5	1.1	0.89	8.37	4.73	66.5	2.1	12.0	18.4	5.7
5.3	1.31	7.3	0.35	4.4	1.1	0.69	6.19	4.40	71.2	1.5	17.6	25.3	5.5
3.5	2.76	14.5	0.42	3.3	0.1	0.66	5.74	5.18	92.2	5.2	35.4	6.8	4.5
4.6	0.97	6.4	0.11	4.6	1.4	0.79	7.88	4.13	72.5	1.7	8.7	20.0	5.1
4.7	1.75	10.1	0.34	4.8	1.2	0.86	8.39	3.36	57.4	4.7	26.8	6.2	6.5
8.6	2.78	2.7	0.75	9.3	2.7	1.70	7.06	4.67	38.7	3.2	58.2	30.5	8.3
3.7	1.29	9.1	0.27	4.3	635.9	0.77	5.17	2.94	63.7	4.2	15.3	5.0	7.7
6.6	0.01	0.1	-0.01	8.1	1.6	2.00	15.19	4.37	57.0	1.2	7.2	26.7	9.6
8.4	0.93	3.3	0.01	4.9	1.7	0.91	6.54	3.11	59.5	2.2	36.8	29.4	8.0
7.0	1.32	4.2	-0.27	4.7	0.7	0.76	3.52	3.71	66.6	0.8	21.3	54.0	7.2
7.6	0.51	2.3	-0.12	8.3	76.4	1.28	10.28	3.53	45.1	4.6	17.0	5.7	10.0
1.6	5.26	46.6	0.31	2.1	0.5	0.33	5.72	3.19	94.1	1.5	19.9	26.0	1.0
6.4	1.11	6.5	0.22	6.9	1.6	1.61	14.57	4.57	69.3	2.4	28.5	19.4	7.1
3.9	3.07	15.5	0.11	5.9	2.7	1.08	9.94	3.35	45.6	1.5	15.3	24.3	6.2
4.4	3.45	19.3	0.07	4.1	0.6	0.72	6.64	3.27	71.0	3.3	21.8	13.3	6.0
4.4	3.03	15.0	-0.31	10.0	2.6	1.68	14.23	5.63	46.7	2.0	20.4	19.7	7.5
6.2	0.53	4.1	0.02	3.5	0.8	0.52	5.04	3.85	75.9	1.4	9.8	23.8	4.8
2.9	1.24	9.9	0.09	3.3	2.5	0.49	4.95	3.25	79.9	1.4	10.8	24.4	5.7
6.2	0.45	3.1	0.06	6.3	3.3	1.10	10.45	3.73	57.2	2.3	6.8	16.6	7.0
8.4	0.64	2.5	0.07	6.9	2.4	1.62	10.79	3.80	55.7	1.2	29.2	41.0	9.7
10.0	0.00	0.0	0.00	7.0	0.5	1.86	6.67	3.19	29.0	3.6	56.4	20.0	7.8
7.4	0.91	5.6	0.02	2.1	0.3	0.24	2.33	2.71	92.1	1.3	28.1	33.5	5.3
7.9	2.22	4.5	-0.05	5.5	15.6	1.05	11.89	2.49	45.4	7.4	73.2	4.6	7.4
5.7	0.51	4.0	0.24	3.7	1.0	0.73	7.64	3.52	73.4	1.5	12.8	23.2	5.5
4.4	1.46	10.8	0.22	4.4	0.7	0.59	6.57	4.64	78.2	2.8	20.6	15.3	4.5
1.6	3.23	19.9	-0.05	5.6	1.9	1.37	11.42	4.36	70.0	3.1	20.0	14.1	7.8
6.2	0.39	2.8	-0.05	5.3	3.4	1.04	9.75	3.95	66.3	1.6	8.2	20.9	6.3
8.3	0.14	0.7	0.19	6.6	2.6	1.57	15.47	3.30	50.6	5.4	45.4	8.9	8.4
4.2	1.27	7.9	0.32	1.4	0.0	0.01	0.23	3.08	99.5	5.5	48.3	8.3	1.4
2.6	2.27	20.7	0.04	3.1	0.6	0.49	6.14	4.14	87.6	1.0	6.6	30.1	4.8
3.3	2.97	15.2	-0.01	2.2	0.6	0.28	2.55	3.05	91.9	6.3	37.6	0.1	5.5
9.3	0.10	0.4	-0.01	3.9	1.0	0.77	7.86	3.15	74.8	5.9	49.0	7.2	5.8
4.6	0.55	3.5	0.06	5.8	9.8	1.43	13.20	3.93	63.0	1.6	12.4	18.8	7.7
9.2	0.00	0.0	0.00	3.6	2.9	0.90	8.76	2.95	70.7	4.4	39.9	12.9	6.9
7.4	1.00	3.7	-0.02	2.9	0.3	0.42	4.24	3.66	87.0	5.1	49.3	11.1	5.0
6.2	0.86	5.3	0.10	4.3	9.2	0.74	7.77	3.52	75.4	5.4	29.1	6.8	7.6
7.4	0.44	2.4	-0.04	2.6	0.1	0.35	2.68	4.44	94.0	0.8	18.2	42.8	5.9
4.5	3.60	15.7	0.35	6.4	2.3	1.48	12.08	3.87	54.8	4.0	30.7	11.9	7.9
7.4	0.79	3.7	0.00	5.6	2.5	1.06	6.87	3.50	53.6	2.6	20.6	16.7	8.3
5.4	0.51	4.0	0.04	7.8	10.6	1.90	20.17	3.99	55.5	2.2	6.2	8.9	8.4
5.1	1.59	8.0	-0.08	3.5	1.2	0.60	6.78	3.39	80.1	6.1	52.0	6.4	4.3

Name	City	State	Rating	2015 Rating	2014 Rating	Total Assets ($Mil)	One Year Asset Growth	Comm-ercial Loans	Cons-umer Loans	Mort-gage Loans	Secur-ities	Capital-ization Index	Lever-age Ratio	Risk-Based Capital Ratio
Citizens National Bank of Crosbyton	Crosbyton	TX	B-	B-	B-	45.2	4.45	3.0	4.9	5.4	5.5	10.0	16.2	40.9
Citizens National Bank of Greater St. Louis	Maplewood	MO	C+	C+	C	439.8	3.10	15.3	2.2	12.8	23.2	10.0	12.1	16.3
Citizens National Bank of Hammond	Hammond	NY	D	D+	D	23.2	8.59	3.9	7.2	38.8	30.3	6.6	8.6	22.6
Citizens National Bank of Hillsboro	Hillsboro	TX	B-	B-	B	208.5	-2.75	4.7	2.7	4.1	75.6	9.3	10.6	27.5
Citizens National Bank of Lebanon	Lebanon	KY	B	B-	B-	119.7	3.53	2.2	3.4	11.8	53.7	9.2	10.4	21.1
Citizens National Bank of McConnelsville	McConnelsville	OH	B-	B-	B-	87.5	2.51	6.5	4.9	38.5	21.6	10.0	12.1	25.2
Citizens National Bank of Meridian	Meridian	MS	B+	B+	B	1293.1	13.64	8.9	2.3	15.7	27.2	7.5	10.3	13.0
Citizens National Bank of Park Rapids	Park Rapids	MN	B+	A-	A-	242.2	-0.82	5.5	14.6	26.7	13.1	8.9	10.3	15.5
Citizens National Bank of Quitman	Quitman	GA	B-	C+	C	95.2	0.76	2.5	13.6	17.3	12.9	10.0	12.6	17.9
Citizens National Bank of Somerset	Somerset	KY	B+	B+	A-	383.7	5.76	3.2	6.6	22.2	31.3	9.6	10.7	19.5
Citizens National Bank of Texas	Waxahachie	TX	C+	C	C	834.4	18.08	9.2	0.9	8.9	2.9	6.7	9.9	12.3
Citizens National Bank of Woodsfield	Woodsfield	OH	C-	C-	C-	106.6	-1.56	3.4	1.7	27.5	46.4	5.1	7.1	18.9
Citizens National Bank, N.A.	Bossier City	LA	A-	A-	A-	872.7	3.49	11.1	1.2	14.0	21.1	10.0	11.6	16.4
Citizens Progressive Bank	Winnsboro	LA	D	D+	C-	168.9	32.78	11.5	5.4	15.6	6.8	5.5	8.3	11.4
Citizens S&L Assn., FSB	Leavenworth	KS	C-	D+	C-	197.8	-3.21	0.0	0.6	36.0	50.1	10.0	19.3	52.8
▲ Citizens Savings Bank	Anamosa	IA	B+	B	B	124.2	-2.77	5.4	0.9	10.0	42.2	7.2	9.2	15.0
Citizens Savings Bank	Hawkeye	IA	B+	B+	B+	29.7	2.65	0.8	1.2	7.5	48.3	10.0	12.7	28.0
Citizens Savings Bank	Marshalltown	IA	C+	C+	C+	56.9	1.09	4.6	1.9	24.8	0.5	6.1	8.2	12.8
Citizens Savings Bank	Spillville	IA	A	A	A-	104.4	1.32	2.9	0.5	3.6	46.1	10.0	13.9	18.3
Citizens Savings Bank	Bogalusa	LA	C	D	C	212.3	3.13	2.1	5.9	40.6	10.4	10.0	13.9	22.4
Citizens Savings Bank	Martins Ferry	OH	B+	B+	B	424.0	4.23	17.3	3.4	18.9	7.5	6.5	9.3	12.1
Citizens Savings Bank	Clarks Summit	PA	B-	B-	B-	330.9	0.48	0.0	0.1	75.8	11.1	10.0	13.7	28.0
Citizens Savings Bank and Trust Co.	Nashville	TN	D-	D	D-	109.9	4.50	2.9	1.8	6.4	3.2	7.3	9.2	13.1
Citizens State Bank	Vernon	AL	C	B-	C-	77.6	-5.11	3.2	2.7	10.6	60.9	10.0	13.3	38.7
▼ Citizens State Bank	Perry	FL	C-	C-	D	267.3	-5.10	5.2	50.5	3.1	7.0	5.9	8.7	11.6
Citizens State Bank	Monticello	IA	B+	B+	B+	368.2	1.36	5.8	0.7	4.2	31.9	9.3	10.5	14.6
Citizens State Bank	Sheldon	IA	A-	A-	A-	116.5	0.19	7.7	7.4	15.7	17.0	10.0	12.2	17.5
Citizens State Bank	Wyoming	IA	A	A	A	92.2	-3.54	7.7	3.2	4.4	37.3	10.0	22.6	36.8
Citizens State Bank	Lena	IL	B	B	B-	239.5	4.22	9.2	4.6	12.7	19.4	10.0	11.7	16.6
Citizens State Bank	Gridley	KS	B-	B-	B-	179.6	2.34	12.9	3.9	17.8	14.8	5.8	7.8	11.9
Citizens State Bank	Hugoton	KS	A-	A-	B+	115.7	-1.18	5.3	1.5	4.9	19.9	10.0	13.8	18.6
Citizens State Bank	Marysville	KS	A-	A-	A-	323.3	6.63	12.0	1.2	8.1	15.2	6.2	9.5	11.9
Citizens State Bank	Morland	KS	D+	C-	C-	35.8	-9.65	7.4	4.0	11.9	15.6	6.7	8.7	13.6
Citizens State Bank	Moundridge	KS	B	B	B-	436.5	3.00	5.2	1.4	6.5	33.3	9.5	10.8	14.6
Citizens State Bank	Paola	KS	B	B	B-	81.9	-2.31	3.1	0.5	6.7	62.4	10.0	15.3	36.3
Citizens State Bank	Carleton	NE	D+	D+	D+	18.7	-0.68	9.4	5.5	4.4	0.7	7.4	9.3	15.2
Citizens State Bank	Wisner	NE	B-	B	B-	330.5	1.93	8.2	1.7	5.4	8.7	5.9	9.6	11.7
▼ Citizens State Bank	Okemah	OK	B+	A-	B+	346.1	-0.69	3.9	0.5	26.3	3.1	7.3	10.5	12.8
Citizens State Bank	Anton	TX	D+	C-	D+	37.5	19.21	7.5	2.9	0.0	9.3	4.8	7.9	10.9
Citizens State Bank	Buffalo	TX	A-	A-	A-	855.0	11.66	2.7	1.6	2.8	80.1	9.2	10.5	29.8
Citizens State Bank	Corrigan	TX	A-	A-	A-	130.8	2.52	11.1	10.7	10.9	37.3	9.2	10.4	19.8
▼ Citizens State Bank	Ganado	TX	D-	D	D+	61.5	-3.08	3.2	1.4	5.9	59.4	5.8	7.8	24.7
Citizens State Bank	Miles	TX	A-	A-	A-	123.5	9.67	9.3	3.1	31.7	0.7	6.7	8.7	12.5
Citizens State Bank	Roma	TX	B	B	B	83.2	-1.52	3.6	15.3	18.4	37.7	8.7	10.1	20.1
Citizens State Bank	Sealy	TX	A-	A-	A-	246.8	3.12	2.6	2.1	17.7	55.8	9.8	10.9	24.9
▲ Citizens State Bank	Somerville	TX	B+	B	B	444.7	-1.25	9.5	4.4	21.0	21.2	10.0	11.1	17.5
Citizens State Bank	Tyler	TX	C+	B+	A-	325.4	-0.28	6.0	2.7	14.8	1.4	9.2	11.4	14.3
Citizens State Bank	Waco	TX	B-	B-	C+	177.2	20.11	4.8	3.4	51.4	20.5	6.5	8.5	13.9
Citizens State Bank	Cadott	WI	B-	B-	B	119.8	4.18	9.2	3.2	17.5	20.4	8.5	10.0	14.4
Citizens State Bank	Hudson	WI	C+	C	D-	159.2	1.95	8.9	1.1	25.0	15.7	6.4	8.4	12.8
Citizens State Bank and Trust Co.	Ellsworth	KS	B	B	B	171.9	0.94	3.6	2.8	18.7	34.0	7.4	9.2	16.8
▲ Citizens State Bank and Trust Co.	Hiawatha	KS	B	C+	C+	84.4	-1.57	5.7	2.9	13.5	31.0	10.0	15.9	22.0
Citizens State Bank and Trust Co.	Woodbine	KS	D+	D	D-	21.5	27.45	7.7	1.7	6.5	12.0	8.7	11.6	13.9
Citizens State Bank at Mohall	Mohall	ND	C+	B-	B	66.4	-0.18	8.8	3.5	14.3	20.0	7.0	9.0	13.0
Citizens State Bank Midwest	Cavalier	ND	B-	B-	C-	121.2	1.91	12.4	3.3	6.8	14.2	9.8	11.7	14.8
Citizens State Bank Norwood Young Ameri	Norwood Young Ame	MN	B	B-	C	78.6	1.81	14.9	1.7	5.1	0.0	10.0	11.0	15.6
Citizens State Bank of Arlington	Arlington	SD	B	B	C+	99.7	-4.77	3.2	2.1	4.2	20.8	10.0	13.8	19.6
Citizens State Bank of Cheney, Kansas	Cheney	KS	B+	B+	A-	57.6	-4.15	10.3	14.8	10.4	20.3	9.2	10.5	15.1
Citizens State Bank of Finley	Finley	ND	C+	C+	C+	136.7	0.48	9.2	1.6	0.6	25.1	8.5	10.0	14.1
Citizens State Bank of Glenville	Glenville	MN	C+	C+	C+	40.3	6.73	5.1	5.5	8.3	30.9	10.0	11.6	29.7

Asset Quality Index	Adjusted Non-Performing Loans as a % of Total Loans	as a % of Capital	Net Charge-Offs Avg Loans	Profitability Index	Net Income ($Mil)	Return on Assets (R.O.A.)	Return on Equity (R.O.E.)	Net Interest Spread	Overhead Efficiency Ratio	Liquidity Index	Liquidity Ratio	Hot Money Ratio	Stability Index
8.7	0.11	0.3	-0.02	3.5	0.3	0.77	4.80	2.17	67.1	3.3	65.4	27.7	7.3
3.8	3.53	18.5	-0.02	2.9	-0.4	-0.12	-0.96	3.59	85.6	3.2	18.1	13.1	6.9
5.0	1.41	8.5	0.13	2.9	0.1	0.38	4.21	3.72	86.6	5.2	22.4	1.0	2.3
10.0	0.19	0.4	0.00	4.0	1.4	0.90	7.73	2.45	64.7	5.8	55.5	10.0	7.4
5.9	2.19	6.8	-0.07	4.7	1.2	1.30	12.36	3.19	69.6	4.9	40.1	10.7	6.6
5.4	2.29	11.7	0.06	3.5	0.4	0.60	4.86	3.46	75.3	3.6	14.7	11.0	6.2
5.6	1.24	7.4	0.01	6.0	13.7	1.46	12.98	3.51	65.6	3.0	17.3	14.5	8.9
5.0	0.91	6.3	0.44	5.6	2.2	1.22	11.62	3.99	63.2	2.6	9.8	15.5	7.9
3.8	2.18	12.0	0.55	4.3	0.6	0.78	6.06	3.89	68.1	1.5	14.5	23.6	6.5
4.9	1.10	6.0	0.51	5.4	3.8	1.32	12.66	3.72	67.1	3.1	14.0	13.3	7.8
3.8	0.72	5.6	0.00	8.6	11.0	1.91	18.17	4.78	63.1	4.7	17.4	4.1	8.0
8.9	0.00	0.0	0.03	2.6	0.3	0.38	5.25	2.51	80.3	6.9	53.7	1.8	3.5
6.8	0.73	4.2	0.10	5.4	6.7	1.05	8.73	4.32	67.9	3.6	16.5	11.1	7.6
0.9	2.95	25.0	0.22	5.1	1.2	1.02	9.12	4.55	72.4	0.7	19.8	54.6	5.6
8.9	0.94	1.8	-0.23	1.9	0.8	0.54	2.84	2.16	99.3	3.9	59.2	20.6	7.2
7.3	0.57	3.0	0.00	6.9	1.5	1.60	15.45	4.12	56.3	4.5	31.3	9.2	7.2
10.0	0.00	0.0	0.00	3.5	0.2	0.76	6.15	2.98	69.3	6.4	72.6	7.7	6.2
6.1	0.17	1.4	0.00	5.6	0.6	1.35	16.76	3.57	62.1	5.2	27.5	3.4	4.5
9.0	0.45	1.6	-0.02	8.3	1.3	1.69	11.32	4.10	42.4	3.8	55.8	10.4	8.7
2.2	4.94	24.5	0.02	4.4	1.1	0.68	4.91	4.90	78.2	1.8	21.0	21.1	7.7
6.2	0.42	3.5	0.11	6.0	3.5	1.13	11.87	3.85	62.2	4.5	4.2	4.1	5.6
7.6	1.12	6.3	0.01	3.4	1.3	0.51	3.71	3.21	77.9	3.0	6.6	13.1	7.2
0.0	7.34	52.9	0.00	2.8	0.1	0.17	1.83	4.87	91.2	0.7	21.5	60.4	4.7
4.9	7.34	14.9	-0.21	2.7	0.2	0.38	2.87	2.17	59.3	2.6	60.0	44.1	5.9
2.2	0.84	6.8	0.88	3.9	1.7	0.81	9.47	4.40	66.3	0.8	17.4	39.0	3.4
5.7	0.69	3.8	-0.03	8.2	5.5	1.96	15.43	3.69	48.8	2.8	27.8	16.7	9.3
7.8	0.00	0.0	0.00	5.8	1.2	1.31	10.07	3.53	60.0	5.0	28.2	4.5	8.5
8.3	0.12	0.3	0.03	7.6	1.3	1.75	7.51	3.99	54.8	4.5	49.7	14.2	9.7
4.4	1.75	10.3	0.05	7.0	3.0	1.69	13.21	3.86	59.8	2.9	13.3	14.3	8.0
5.8	0.38	3.2	0.00	4.9	1.2	0.90	11.41	4.05	66.4	3.9	9.7	8.9	5.1
7.5	0.00	0.0	-0.06	6.2	1.0	1.12	8.45	4.42	62.7	0.8	8.8	32.6	8.2
6.9	0.27	2.1	-0.01	9.2	5.2	2.20	20.93	3.72	37.0	1.7	8.6	20.2	8.5
5.4	0.26	2.1	0.73	1.8	0.1	0.21	2.54	3.46	82.4	3.5	14.0	11.3	4.0
5.7	1.34	6.1	-0.05	4.9	3.1	0.94	7.86	3.61	66.6	4.6	33.9	9.8	6.7
6.2	0.71	1.3	0.46	3.9	0.6	0.92	4.37	3.42	68.8	3.3	52.1	20.8	7.8
6.7	0.04	0.4	-0.01	4.3	0.1	0.70	7.72	4.56	78.3	1.4	9.1	23.6	3.0
4.4	0.41	3.2	-0.01	5.9	3.3	1.37	13.15	3.99	60.8	1.5	6.7	21.9	7.1
5.6	0.94	8.2	-0.01	8.6	4.4	1.84	17.35	5.16	82.8	0.4	3.6	5.4	7.5
7.1	0.00	0.0	0.14	4.0	0.2	0.73	9.16	3.39	65.2	0.8	19.8	41.8	2.8
8.8	1.44	1.9	0.03	5.9	8.2	1.37	11.13	3.47	50.0	3.2	67.3	34.7	7.9
6.4	0.73	3.3	0.25	8.3	2.0	1.99	18.82	4.38	54.2	1.8	20.6	22.2	7.8
10.0	0.00	0.0	0.00	0.2	-0.1	-0.21	-2.99	1.97	117.4	4.1	76.8	21.3	1.9
7.0	0.45	4.0	0.01	10.0	2.7	2.92	34.62	5.37	41.4	0.6	7.9	42.9	7.7
5.4	1.04	5.0	0.44	4.2	0.5	0.87	8.53	5.43	83.2	2.0	41.7	44.1	6.6
9.5	0.01	0.1	0.00	5.9	2.4	1.33	12.00	3.56	55.0	5.4	64.3	13.8	7.6
5.3	1.53	8.3	0.35	6.8	4.1	1.21	11.36	4.65	62.2	4.3	22.8	7.9	6.2
2.8	1.28	9.2	0.04	8.9	3.8	1.56	14.03	4.12	51.2	2.7	7.7	14.9	7.8
5.7	0.72	6.3	0.02	5.2	1.2	1.00	12.44	4.62	71.0	3.8	2.9	8.6	3.9
3.8	2.51	15.9	0.00	4.0	0.6	0.64	6.39	3.96	76.0	4.1	21.7	8.6	6.1
8.7	0.09	0.7	-0.05	3.6	0.8	0.64	7.59	3.75	80.4	2.8	14.3	14.8	4.2
6.7	0.36	2.2	0.08	5.3	1.7	1.32	13.02	3.58	65.5	3.5	22.0	9.1	6.2
8.7	0.00	0.0	0.00	4.4	0.7	1.14	7.48	3.24	69.0	5.3	26.6	2.2	7.5
7.2	0.00	0.0	-0.03	3.3	0.1	0.95	7.80	4.99	87.9	1.4	3.5	22.8	3.9
3.1	1.58	12.1	0.35	4.7	0.5	0.99	10.67	3.64	58.8	2.3	6.6	16.6	5.0
4.7	0.94	5.8	-0.07	5.2	0.8	0.96	7.85	3.99	65.1	3.0	7.9	13.3	6.2
4.6	1.09	6.5	0.06	6.1	0.6	0.98	6.75	5.12	63.3	4.4	25.8	8.0	6.3
4.5	1.74	8.5	0.44	4.4	0.6	0.82	5.83	3.66	62.0	3.3	15.4	12.6	6.8
4.9	1.28	6.7	0.69	5.8	0.6	1.26	11.43	3.92	63.3	2.1	21.8	19.1	8.3
3.2	1.99	12.0	0.01	4.9	1.2	1.16	11.49	4.00	72.8	2.9	11.7	14.3	5.8
7.2	1.58	4.7	0.00	3.3	0.2	0.72	6.31	2.94	74.5	6.9	69.7	3.9	5.5

Name	City	State	2015 Rating	2014 Rating	Total Assets ($Mil)	One Year Asset Growth	Commercial Loans	Consumer Loans	Mortgage Loans	Securities	Capitalization Index	Leverage Ratio	Risk-Based Capital Ratio
▼ Citizens State Bank of Hayfield	Hayfield	MN	D	C-	C-	90.0	8.35	12.4	3.4	10.3	7.5	3.8	7.0	10.4
Citizens State Bank of La Crosse	La Crosse	WI	B+	B+	B+	209.1	13.25	12.2	1.1	24.8	2.4	5.8	8.7	11.6
Citizens State Bank of Lankin	Lankin	ND	C-	C+	C	40.3	-10.56	4.6	3.8	3.2	21.6	8.8	10.2	15.0
Citizens State Bank of Loyal	Loyal	WI	B+	B+	B+	201.3	4.38	5.1	0.4	10.4	26.3	10.0	11.8	16.7
Citizens State Bank of Luling	Luling	TX	B	B	B	68.4	2.94	7.4	1.2	7.6	6.9	10.0	11.8	17.0
Citizens State Bank of Milford	Milford	IL	C-	C-	C-	43.9	-14.13	12.3	1.4	0.8	27.1	7.4	9.3	14.3
Citizens State Bank of New Castle, Indiana	New Castle	IN	B-	B-	B-	488.2	3.97	5.8	15.2	22.4	23.8	7.3	9.2	17.8
Citizens State Bank of Ontonagon	Ontonagon	MI	C	C-	D+	56.4	5.30	3.2	6.1	11.8	36.1	10.0	12.4	38.1
▼ Citizens State Bank of Ouray	Ouray	CO	D+	B-	B	99.5	6.41	1.2	0.6	6.2	48.4	7.9	9.6	24.7
Citizens State Bank of Roseau	Roseau	MN	A-	A-	A	206.0	-1.22	6.8	6.8	6.2	43.2	10.0	12.3	16.0
Citizens State Bank of Taylor County	Reynolds	GA	C+	C+	C+	63.1	33.24	6.7	4.1	11.6	24.5	8.1	9.8	18.9
▲ Citizens State Bank of Tyler, Inc.	Tyler	MN	D+	D	D+	21.5	9.73	7.2	4.0	4.8	35.4	7.3	9.2	31.5
Citizens State Bank of Waverly	Waverly	MN	B-	B	B	66.3	-2.46	3.3	1.2	18.8	13.8	7.7	9.5	14.4
Citizens Tri-County Bank	Dunlap	TN	C+	C+	C	792.3	20.77	2.0	8.6	18.8	32.0	7.5	9.3	20.3
Citizens Trust Bank	Atlanta	GA	B-	C+	C	405.9	6.69	9.6	1.8	7.2	30.5	10.0	11.9	20.1
Citizens Union Bank of Shelbyville	Shelbyville	KY	C+	C+	C	574.1	8.80	4.2	0.9	14.7	9.4	8.6	12.0	13.8
Citizens' Bank, Inc.	Robertsdale	AL	C	C-	C	106.7	5.59	5.0	1.9	18.2	20.0	9.9	11.0	18.0
Citizens-Farmers Bank of Cole Camp	Cole Camp	MO	A	A	A	123.6	9.15	4.2	6.2	27.2	21.6	10.0	15.9	27.0
City Bank	Lubbock	TX	B	B	B-	2554.1	7.27	9.7	5.3	12.9	13.2	7.6	9.4	14.5
City Bank & Trust Co.	Natchitoches	LA	B-	B-	B-	231.0	3.70	2.9	3.3	13.3	59.5	9.1	10.4	18.9
City Bank & Trust Co.	Lincoln	NE	B-	B-	B-	148.0	-5.31	10.2	1.9	12.5	17.2	10.0	13.8	21.4
City Bank and Trust Co.	Guymon	OK	B+	B+	B+	168.0	-8.77	5.2	5.3	19.9	45.1	9.4	10.6	22.0
▲ City First Bank of D.C., N.A.	Washington	DC	C-	D-	C+	256.9	2.91	7.5	0.0	3.0	25.4	10.0	13.8	22.7
▼ City National B&T Co. of Lawton, Oklahom	Lawton	OK	B+	A	A	440.5	34.42	4.2	1.8	20.8	13.1	9.0	10.3	22.9
City National Bank	Los Angeles	CA	B-	B-	B	45519.6	28.90	17.8	2.3	14.7	31.2	4.5	6.5	12.4
City National Bank	Corsicana	TX	C	C	C	46.3	-0.10	12.4	4.4	33.9	7.0	9.1	10.4	19.1
City National Bank of Colorado City	Colorado City	TX	B+	B+	B+	123.4	-2.52	6.4	7.5	9.1	49.0	8.0	9.6	18.9
City National Bank of Florida	Miami	FL	B	B-	B-	7755.8	24.69	13.5	0.7	10.6	23.0	10.0	12.1	15.7
City National Bank of Metropolis	Metropolis	IL	B	B+	B+	399.6	-0.87	3.2	3.5	17.6	54.8	10.0	12.1	28.3
City National Bank of New Jersey	Newark	NJ	E-	E	E-	223.0	-9.84	6.3	0.4	5.4	22.6	3.6	5.6	11.3
City National Bank of San Saba	San Saba	TX	C+	C+	C+	56.6	1.08	2.4	3.4	0.3	63.7	10.0	15.0	34.1
City National Bank of Sulphur Springs	Sulphur Springs	TX	B	B	B	495.7	7.28	6.0	6.7	27.5	12.9	7.3	9.2	13.6
City National Bank of Taylor	Taylor	TX	C+	C+	C+	198.1	1.43	3.7	1.0	35.8	33.7	10.0	11.0	23.6
City National Bank of West Virginia	Charleston	WV	B+	B+	B	3848.8	10.25	4.5	0.8	36.2	13.1	6.5	8.6	12.5
▼ City Savings Bank & Trust Co.	DeRidder	LA	B+	A-	A-	324.0	5.09	10.5	5.5	26.7	11.9	7.7	9.4	14.5
City State Bank	Norwalk	IA	B	B	B	343.8	10.76	5.3	1.0	14.3	11.4	6.5	8.5	12.1
City State Bank	Fort Scott	KS	C+	C+	C+	41.1	7.76	2.6	3.1	20.6	20.4	6.5	8.5	16.7
Citywide Banks	Aurora	CO	B	B-	B	1368.3	4.40	13.2	0.4	9.0	17.9	7.3	10.2	12.8
▲ Civic Bank & Trust	Nashville	TN	B-	C-	B+	164.1	16.30	11.6	2.9	16.5	19.5	10.0	14.2	17.8
Civis Bank	Rogersville	TN	E-	E-	E-	106.4	-5.82	3.5	1.7	24.8	8.7	0.5	3.8	6.9
Civista Bank	Sandusky	OH	B	B-	C+	1370.9	4.58	8.6	1.2	12.5	14.6	7.7	9.6	13.1
▲ Clackamas County Bank	Sandy	OR	A	A-	B+	206.9	8.73	0.7	0.6	10.4	30.6	10.0	11.8	23.3
▼ Clare Bank, N.A.	Platteville	WI	B+	A-	A-	277.1	0.50	3.3	1.7	25.6	31.9	9.8	10.9	27.3
Claremont Savings Bank	Claremont	NH	C+	C	C+	384.8	5.12	4.1	1.8	53.5	19.0	10.0	13.6	19.6
Clarence State Bank	Clarence	MO	B-	B-	B-	18.4	-3.10	5.4	2.4	5.3	34.6	10.0	23.0	46.7
Clarion County Community Bank	Clarion	PA	B-	B-	B	140.0	6.86	10.2	1.8	36.1	9.1	7.5	10.9	12.9
Clarke County State Bank	Osceola	IA	B	B	B-	104.7	-1.77	5.7	1.2	14.7	24.0	10.0	11.4	16.5
Clarkson Bank	Clarkson	NE	B+	A-	A-	55.1	-1.62	2.7	1.3	0.1	49.4	10.0	12.8	20.0
Clarkston State Bank	Waterford	MI	C+	C+	C	175.5	12.82	8.0	3.7	4.7	6.0	4.1	8.8	10.6
Classic Bank, N.A.	Cameron	TX	B-	C+	C	304.7	5.17	5.4	2.3	18.5	27.7	7.3	9.2	15.0
Clatsop Community Bank	Seaside	OR	B	B	C+	87.6	8.64	7.0	1.6	7.4	25.9	10.0	11.4	16.1
Claxton Bank	Claxton	GA	C	C-	C	114.7	3.57	3.6	1.6	14.8	20.4	8.0	9.7	15.1
▼ Clay City Banking Co.	Clay City	IL	D+	C	C+	134.9	5.05	10.3	2.9	22.5	8.3	6.1	8.8	11.8
Clay County Bank, Inc.	Clay	WV	A-	A-	A-	86.3	4.81	1.0	13.9	41.0	17.1	10.0	13.8	32.9
▲ Clay County Savings Bank	Liberty	MO	C	C-	C-	93.3	5.60	2.2	0.2	35.5	4.0	10.0	11.1	18.1
Clay County State Bank	Louisville	IL	B	B	B	83.9	-1.46	7.6	6.7	13.8	39.8	10.0	13.2	25.3
Clayton Bank and Trust	Knoxville	TN	B	B-	C+	908.2	22.39	18.9	11.7	8.5	6.2	10.0	18.7	19.2
Clear Lake Bank and Trust Co.	Clear Lake	IA	B+	B+	B+	369.5	4.46	14.2	5.3	18.8	10.9	6.2	8.4	11.9
Clear Mountain Bank	Bruceton Mills	WV	B+	B	B	548.5	6.76	6.2	7.3	35.5	12.7	10.0	11.0	15.7
ClearPoint Federal Bank & Trust	Batesville	IN	U	U	U	104.4	1.07	0.0	0.0	0.0	95.7	10.0	16.0	45.5

Asset Quality Index	Adjusted Non-Performing Loans as a % of Total Loans	as a % of Capital	Net Charge-Offs Avg Loans	Profitability Index	Net Income ($Mil)	Return on Assets (R.O.A.)	Return on Equity (R.O.E.)	Net Interest Spread	Overhead Efficiency Ratio	Liquidity Index	Liquidity Ratio	Hot Money Ratio	Stability Index
1.2	3.22	31.2	0.05	2.9	0.3	0.39	5.28	4.12	84.9	4.5	15.5	5.7	3.7
6.0	0.28	2.7	0.11	9.8	4.2	2.82	32.83	4.13	46.7	0.7	10.7	19.6	7.1
4.6	3.27	18.1	0.11	2.4	0.0	-0.10	-0.99	4.78	84.8	4.4	18.1	6.3	5.4
5.7	1.57	7.9	0.02	5.7	1.7	1.14	9.49	3.93	63.1	4.3	22.1	7.9	6.9
7.4	0.00	0.0	0.06	3.7	0.3	0.51	4.34	4.32	81.2	3.6	25.7	12.4	6.5
8.6	0.18	1.0	-0.01	2.6	0.1	0.28	2.93	3.81	92.6	5.1	33.6	6.2	3.0
6.4	0.32	2.1	0.27	5.2	3.8	1.03	11.70	3.68	66.9	5.1	33.6	6.7	4.2
5.8	6.27	12.9	1.12	2.6	0.2	0.50	3.91	3.23	84.2	7.1	79.5	4.2	5.3
6.7	1.84	5.4	-0.08	1.2	-0.1	-0.07	-0.72	2.81	106.9	6.2	62.7	7.3	5.0
6.3	1.88	7.7	0.00	5.4	2.2	1.39	11.08	3.35	61.8	1.4	16.7	27.1	8.9
4.5	3.00	13.5	-0.05	2.6	0.1	0.33	3.07	3.82	90.4	4.8	37.7	10.2	4.6
5.1	5.32	12.4	0.08	2.7	0.1	0.48	5.53	2.38	80.6	6.7	71.1	3.1	3.5
3.9	1.05	7.2	-0.03	6.2	0.7	1.44	10.50	4.28	62.3	5.0	18.8	2.7	4.9
3.7	1.83	9.7	0.29	6.6	7.8	1.40	13.78	4.55	63.9	2.6	34.1	20.6	6.6
5.5	2.31	9.2	0.12	3.2	1.9	0.62	4.90	3.28	81.6	1.7	25.9	25.6	5.7
3.1	1.98	12.3	-0.05	5.0	4.0	0.96	7.24	4.01	73.9	2.2	9.9	17.7	6.5
5.4	1.21	6.7	0.16	3.1	0.5	0.64	5.83	4.00	86.1	4.2	25.1	8.7	5.5
6.6	1.38	5.4	0.09	6.5	1.0	1.12	7.10	3.71	55.0	2.3	20.6	18.2	8.4
6.0	1.04	6.7	0.19	4.7	22.9	1.09	11.59	3.67	78.8	2.9	21.3	11.9	8.0
9.0	0.43	1.3	0.08	4.3	2.0	1.16	11.18	2.99	71.5	6.3	63.2	8.7	6.0
5.3	1.84	8.4	0.19	3.0	0.5	0.41	2.95	3.13	80.5	4.4	22.4	6.8	6.5
9.2	0.05	0.2	0.17	4.9	1.6	1.19	11.62	3.37	69.0	2.8	29.6	17.7	6.3
1.8	6.67	23.6	0.28	4.2	0.7	0.65	4.63	3.67	81.8	1.2	28.5	35.7	7.0
4.8	2.83	11.9	1.38	4.6	3.4	1.07	10.93	3.26	79.5	6.5	50.0	3.7	7.0
8.1	0.28	2.4	-0.02	3.7	166.4	0.55	7.04	2.87	70.4	5.9	37.6	1.3	6.5
8.7	0.00	0.0	0.04	3.1	0.2	0.56	5.49	3.82	85.5	1.9	21.6	20.6	5.3
7.5	0.01	0.0	0.43	5.8	1.4	1.47	15.48	3.45	58.4	3.1	45.7	23.2	6.3
7.9	0.56	3.1	-0.01	4.6	46.4	0.88	6.37	3.16	52.5	2.5	12.6	7.3	9.1
8.7	1.01	3.2	0.24	3.6	2.9	0.95	7.95	2.43	63.0	2.7	46.6	29.0	6.2
1.6	5.11	34.2	5.78	0.0	-3.8	-2.01	-37.04	2.68	139.0	3.3	25.0	13.6	1.1
9.7	0.00	0.0	0.01	2.5	0.2	0.39	2.68	3.08	85.2	6.3	72.3	8.4	7.1
5.2	0.67	4.8	0.01	7.7	6.2	1.77	16.91	4.55	68.4	2.9	26.3	16.1	7.0
5.5	1.81	9.3	-0.11	3.6	1.2	0.83	7.64	3.55	80.6	4.8	37.8	2.4	6.2
5.4	0.92	8.0	0.13	8.2	38.5	1.33	13.94	3.46	56.0	3.1	8.2	13.0	8.8
5.4	0.74	5.4	0.17	8.8	4.5	1.86	17.53	4.71	62.5	2.1	12.2	18.4	7.9
6.4	0.38	3.1	0.00	4.9	3.0	1.20	13.88	3.21	68.5	3.0	20.4	14.3	5.8
9.0	0.00	0.0	0.00	4.4	0.3	0.97	11.23	3.79	74.2	3.6	42.7	17.4	4.7
6.5	0.38	2.6	-0.01	4.8	8.4	0.84	8.37	4.07	73.7	4.4	19.8	7.1	8.2
7.8	0.79	4.2	-0.01	3.3	0.6	0.56	3.76	3.71	82.6	0.8	21.3	46.6	6.4
0.3	5.87	81.4	0.37	0.1	-0.6	-0.74	-18.35	4.33	113.0	1.7	15.6	22.3	0.2
5.0	1.04	7.7	-0.05	6.8	14.7	1.33	13.70	3.94	62.7	3.7	6.7	4.6	8.4
9.1	0.00	0.0	-0.01	7.6	2.9	1.92	15.40	3.87	60.3	5.1	37.3	8.4	7.3
7.8	0.78	3.6	0.00	5.1	2.5	1.16	10.20	2.47	52.8	5.4	38.2	6.6	8.1
6.4	1.43	7.5	-0.02	2.5	1.6	0.56	4.02	3.42	85.9	2.7	19.9	15.8	7.2
9.0	0.05	0.1	0.17	3.4	0.1	0.85	3.86	3.01	74.8	5.7	61.4	7.6	6.8
7.1	0.39	2.8	0.09	3.5	0.6	0.54	4.95	3.85	79.4	0.7	11.3	35.0	6.2
6.1	1.63	9.0	0.25	4.2	0.6	0.77	6.75	3.64	71.2	3.7	17.3	10.8	7.0
6.0	2.16	7.2	-0.02	5.1	0.5	1.19	9.51	3.06	60.8	3.0	40.9	20.5	8.1
6.2	0.20	1.8	-0.03	4.8	1.0	0.78	7.41	4.18	69.5	4.0	4.6	7.1	5.7
4.5	1.53	9.8	0.14	4.3	2.4	1.06	10.88	4.03	76.5	2.7	14.6	15.6	6.2
8.6	0.00	0.0	0.02	3.9	0.4	0.64	5.24	4.01	78.8	5.0	31.3	5.9	6.3
3.3	2.40	14.7	0.57	2.8	0.3	0.31	3.34	4.67	82.2	2.8	18.5	15.4	5.4
1.7	4.32	35.3	0.07	3.6	0.5	0.53	5.94	3.81	81.0	2.1	8.9	17.7	5.2
6.5	1.53	6.0	-0.03	6.1	0.7	1.03	7.33	4.20	65.8	3.0	34.8	18.2	8.4
8.4	0.74	4.2	0.06	2.2	0.2	0.34	3.07	3.65	91.7	4.2	21.5	7.9	6.0
4.3	4.39	16.3	0.13	4.3	0.7	1.05	7.81	2.93	62.9	4.0	21.3	9.5	7.6
4.4	1.95	8.2	0.13	10.0	22.0	3.64	19.97	5.46	34.4	1.3	14.7	24.2	8.7
6.1	0.26	2.3	0.10	8.3	5.0	1.81	20.03	4.13	56.3	3.6	10.9	10.4	7.6
5.3	1.21	7.9	0.09	4.9	3.2	0.80	7.36	4.05	72.5	1.7	17.6	21.7	7.3
10.0	na	0.0	na	4.5	0.7	0.90	5.22	2.31	77.1	8.6	115.8	0.9	8.2

Data as of September 30, 2016

Name	City	State	2015 Rating	2014 Rating	Rating	Total Assets ($Mil)	One Year Asset Growth	Asset Mix (As a % of Total Assets) Comm- ercial Loans	Cons- umer Loans	Mort- gage Loans	Secur- ities	Capital- ization Index	Lever- age Ratio	Risk- Based Capital Ratio
Cleo State Bank	Cleo Springs	OK	A	A	A	94.2	-5.31	15.7	6.3	0.3	56.0	10.0	17.7	18.2
Cleveland State Bank	Cleveland	MS	B-	B-	B-	231.3	9.60	8.6	5.0	13.6	32.1	8.3	9.8	18.1
▲ Cleveland State Bank	Cleveland	WI	B	B-	B-	106.6	3.25	5.5	4.2	24.4	31.1	10.0	11.0	17.9
Clifton Savings Bank	Clifton	NJ	B-	B	B	1306.8	14.45	0.1	0.0	48.5	24.6	10.0	18.9	35.2
Clinton Bank	Clinton	KY	B	B+	B+	60.0	0.64	5.7	2.1	6.1	35.1	10.0	18.7	26.7
Clinton National Bank	Clinton	IA	B-	B-	B-	399.8	4.22	8.3	1.5	8.9	39.4	10.0	12.6	21.8
Clinton Savings Bank	Clinton	MA	C+	C+	C	522.1	6.81	5.0	2.0	35.1	16.6	8.4	9.9	14.5
Clover Community Bank	Clover	SC	B+	B+	B	132.8	5.16	6.2	2.9	9.0	29.9	8.8	10.2	16.5
CNB Bank	Clearfield	PA	B	B	B-	2519.7	12.53	11.9	2.3	21.9	20.0	7.2	9.1	13.2
CNB Bank & Trust, N.A.	Carlinville	IL	B-	B-	B-	901.6	7.10	13.6	1.3	8.4	16.7	6.3	8.4	12.0
CNB Bank, Inc.	Berkeley Springs	WV	C+	C+	C+	335.5	8.55	2.8	2.4	40.5	24.5	8.7	10.2	17.6
Coastal Bank & Trust	Jacksonville	NC	C	C-	D	96.9	25.80	4.6	0.7	15.2	8.4	6.2	8.2	12.1
Coastal Carolina National Bank	Myrtle Beach	SC	C	C	D+	193.3	15.87	5.7	3.2	26.6	10.2	6.2	8.2	12.4
Coastal Commerce Bank	Houma	LA	A-	A-	B+	430.9	0.71	36.3	2.9	12.5	12.3	7.6	9.4	13.0
Coastal Community Bank	Everett	WA	B-	C+	C+	698.6	15.66	10.0	0.2	9.8	6.7	8.2	10.5	13.5
Coastal Heritage Bank	Weymouth	MA	C-	D+	C-	487.5	64.37	6.2	0.4	52.4	11.6	6.9	8.9	13.3
▲ CoastalStates Bank	Hilton Head Island	SC	D+	E+	E+	426.7	6.65	18.2	8.8	29.1	9.5	3.8	6.7	10.4
▲ Coastway Community Bank	Warwick	RI	C+	C-	D	632.5	22.09	4.3	0.2	45.9	0.0	7.4	9.3	13.0
Coatesville Savings Bank	Coatesville	PA	C	C-	C-	208.0	5.01	4.0	0.1	43.7	10.6	6.7	8.8	13.6
CoBiz Bank	Denver	CO	B+	A-	A-	3419.4	4.45	21.4	0.8	7.9	13.1	7.5	10.4	12.9
▲ Coconut Grove Bank	Miami	FL	B	B-	B-	661.5	3.17	2.0	0.4	3.5	42.9	10.0	15.8	34.0
Coffee County Bank	Manchester	TN	B	B-	C+	156.5	12.57	5.1	11.8	35.0	6.9	10.0	12.3	17.3
Colchester State Bank	Colchester	IL	B	B	B+	61.2	1.08	3.8	4.5	9.3	48.8	10.0	14.4	30.5
▼ Coleman County State Bank	Coleman	TX	B	A	A-	105.3	-2.23	9.2	3.4	16.6	6.3	8.6	10.4	13.9
Colfax Banking Co.	Colfax	LA	B	B	B	103.4	3.56	2.9	2.9	24.0	46.5	7.9	9.6	20.7
Collegiate Peaks Bank	Buena Vista	CO	A-	B+	B	429.1	2.70	11.2	0.3	9.7	10.9	9.7	10.8	15.4
Collins State Bank	Collins	WI	C+	C+	C+	69.0	8.00	7.2	3.7	24.3	25.5	7.6	9.4	14.5
Collinsville Building and Loan Assn.	Collinsville	IL	B-	B-	B-	123.9	2.50	0.0	0.0	67.9	22.8	10.0	27.1	75.7
Collinsville Savings Society	Collinsville	CT	C-	D+	D+	155.8	4.57	6.8	2.1	44.0	8.0	6.8	8.8	12.6
Colombo Bank	Rockville	MD	D	D	E-	202.6	2.86	3.9	0.3	35.9	9.4	8.3	9.9	16.9
Colonial Co-operative Bank	Gardner	MA	E-	E-	E-	72.8	4.49	0.1	0.6	73.2	0.0	4.5	6.5	12.9
Colonial Federal Savings Bank	Quincy	MA	B	B	B-	287.1	2.09	0.0	0.6	42.6	39.0	10.0	14.0	30.7
Colonial Savings, F.A.	Fort Worth	TX	C-	C+	B+	1204.5	7.75	0.6	0.3	46.5	10.8	9.6	10.8	30.6
Colony Bank	Fitzgerald	GA	B-	B-	C+	1151.0	2.27	4.0	1.8	16.6	24.9	9.3	10.5	16.5
Colorado Bank and Trust Co. of La Junta	La Junta	CO	B-	B-	C+	133.8	15.23	10.4	3.0	11.1	25.1	6.0	8.0	16.0
Colorado Federal Savings Bank	Greenwood Village	CO	C+	B-	B	1884.5	29.51	1.2	0.0	19.6	47.9	7.3	9.2	24.1
Colorado National Bank	Palisade	CO	D-	D-	D-	61.7	-10.78	5.8	0.2	1.0	5.0	6.7	8.7	18.2
Columbia Bank	Lake City	FL	C-	C	D-	199.4	12.37	5.0	0.8	16.1	16.7	10.0	11.1	17.8
Columbia Bank	Columbia	MD	B	B-	B-	2285.3	9.57	7.7	1.4	14.5	19.4	6.6	8.7	12.2
Columbia Bank	Fair Lawn	NJ	B-	C+	C	5045.1	5.61	3.5	0.0	38.4	15.2	9.3	10.6	15.7
Columbia National Bank	Columbia	IL	B	C+	C	48.3	2.40	18.7	3.2	24.8	18.3	10.0	12.0	22.8
▼ Columbia S&L Assn.	Milwaukee	WI	E-	D-	D-	24.4	2.18	1.6	0.8	53.9	0.1	6.7	8.7	13.5
Columbia State Bank	Tacoma	WA	B+	B+	B	9578.9	9.47	15.0	0.5	2.9	24.6	6.7	9.4	12.2
Columbus Bank and Trust Co.	Columbus	NE	B-	B-	C+	119.5	5.08	19.3	2.1	5.9	17.1	5.2	9.3	11.1
Columbus First Bank	Worthington	OH	B	B	B	310.3	1.70	11.5	0.0	24.9	0.0	6.7	8.7	12.8
Columbus State Bank	Columbus	TX	B-	B-	B	106.6	8.63	0.3	0.3	0.3	67.7	10.0	12.7	27.5
Comanche National Bank	Comanche	TX	B+	B+	B+	320.1	-0.31	2.5	3.3	10.3	53.3	10.0	11.7	25.2
Comenity Bank	Wilmington	DE	C-	C-	C-	10938.5	17.53	0.0	90.7	0.0	1.5	10.0	14.5	16.4
Comenity Capital Bank	Salt Lake City	UT	C-	C-	C	5621.2	64.94	0.4	89.3	0.0	0.7	9.6	12.8	14.7
Comerica Bank	Dallas	TX	B-	B	B	74277.6	4.47	35.7	0.9	2.8	16.8	6.7	9.9	12.3
Comerica Bank & Trust, N.A.	Ann Arbor	MI	U	U	U	57.8	3.36	0.0	0.0	0.0	0.0	10.0	98.9	287.8
▼ Commencement Bank	Tacoma	WA	B-	B-	B	206.6	8.25	19.0	0.9	4.9	1.5	9.3	11.6	14.5
Commerce Bank	Evansville	IN	C+	C	C	142.8	21.70	18.3	0.5	13.0	1.3	10.0	14.1	20.3
Commerce Bank	Edina	MN	B	B	C	177.6	-1.01	10.6	0.1	8.3	1.1	10.0	14.8	18.2
Commerce Bank	Kansas City	MO	A-	A-	A-	24613.3	3.22	12.2	9.9	9.2	38.1	6.5	8.7	12.2
Commerce Bank	Corinth	MS	A	A	A	107.7	10.95	12.5	7.2	29.1	19.1	10.0	11.5	20.8
Commerce Bank	Laredo	TX	A	A	A-	536.8	-4.27	4.1	1.1	10.8	63.8	10.0	13.2	34.7
Commerce Bank & Trust Co.	Worcester	MA	B-	B-	B-	1911.9	8.15	27.2	4.6	4.0	4.3	6.1	8.9	11.8
Commerce Bank of Arizona, Inc.	Tucson	AZ	E-	E-	E+	171.2	-3.37	11.9	0.1	8.9	2.1	1.6	6.4	8.6
▲ Commerce Bank of Temecula Valley	Murrieta	CA	B	C+	C	71.1	-0.78	23.7	0.1	1.2	0.0	10.0	14.7	19.6

Asset Quality Index	Adjusted Non-Performing Loans as a % of Total Loans	as a % of Capital	Net Charge-Offs Avg Loans	Profitability Index	Net Income ($Mil)	Return on Assets (R.O.A.)	Return on Equity (R.O.E.)	Net Interest Spread	Overhead Efficiency Ratio	Liquidity Index	Liquidity Ratio	Hot Money Ratio	Stability Index
5.5	5.39	10.3	0.01	9.0	1.7	2.39	13.12	4.14	44.3	5.3	65.8	13.0	8.5
7.3	0.52	2.5	0.07	4.1	1.2	0.73	7.55	4.05	74.0	4.7	38.7	11.2	5.9
4.7	2.50	12.4	-0.07	4.6	0.7	0.88	7.99	3.97	74.1	4.6	39.3	7.7	6.1
10.0	0.38	1.4	0.05	2.8	3.1	0.33	1.71	2.33	71.5	1.8	25.0	29.9	9.0
6.8	1.08	3.2	-0.01	5.3	0.5	1.06	5.66	3.79	64.5	2.3	20.1	18.1	7.4
8.6	0.31	1.2	-0.02	2.8	1.2	0.43	3.03	3.13	86.6	5.3	40.9	8.2	7.3
4.5	1.70	12.2	-0.03	3.3	2.3	0.59	5.82	3.41	81.4	2.2	19.1	18.2	6.7
4.8	2.31	10.8	-0.01	5.2	1.0	0.99	9.36	4.21	73.2	5.5	40.2	6.9	6.1
5.3	1.04	7.8	0.08	4.8	16.0	0.90	9.97	3.57	69.5	4.4	7.3	5.2	7.5
4.1	1.31	11.1	0.03	5.6	6.5	0.98	11.27	3.91	58.5	1.7	8.8	20.2	5.4
5.1	1.56	9.7	0.14	3.7	1.5	0.63	6.89	3.58	82.0	1.8	22.6	22.2	4.8
7.5	0.14	1.1	0.21	3.2	0.3	0.44	5.05	3.83	89.6	1.8	24.7	22.2	3.3
5.2	0.97	7.9	0.00	2.7	0.4	0.29	3.14	3.57	86.9	1.1	17.0	30.4	5.3
6.0	0.83	6.2	0.49	9.2	6.9	2.14	21.50	4.70	52.0	1.3	16.6	28.4	8.3
4.0	0.77	5.6	0.08	4.3	3.6	0.74	7.72	4.22	71.1	4.2	17.6	8.0	5.4
7.6	0.34	3.0	0.03	2.7	1.4	0.39	4.33	3.31	81.2	2.3	13.5	17.6	3.8
3.1	1.64	17.3	0.41	3.5	1.9	0.60	7.11	4.54	85.5	4.0	13.5	8.5	3.5
4.7	1.52	14.4	0.02	3.6	2.8	0.64	6.75	3.37	74.8	3.1	4.3	12.2	4.3
3.1	2.20	18.9	0.01	3.5	0.9	0.60	6.72	3.36	72.9	1.3	11.2	26.2	4.6
6.4	0.48	3.5	0.23	6.3	29.7	1.18	11.03	3.98	61.1	4.5	9.3	4.7	9.2
9.6	0.91	1.9	-0.11	4.0	4.2	0.85	5.43	2.35	65.8	6.0	63.4	10.7	7.1
4.2	1.91	11.8	0.38	10.0	3.2	2.82	22.81	4.86	47.4	1.2	14.8	28.3	8.2
5.0	4.01	10.9	-0.17	4.6	0.4	0.96	6.52	3.34	58.9	3.3	42.6	19.0	6.3
3.1	2.82	20.3	0.14	9.2	1.7	2.16	21.26	4.96	58.0	2.9	10.6	14.1	8.3
8.8	0.17	0.8	0.02	4.4	0.8	1.01	9.94	3.93	77.3	1.8	28.6	27.0	7.1
7.8	0.27	1.7	0.04	6.7	3.7	1.17	10.23	4.48	54.9	4.0	19.4	9.4	6.8
5.4	0.37	2.5	0.29	3.9	0.4	0.83	8.62	3.89	75.5	4.3	34.1	11.4	5.3
9.9	0.13	0.3	0.29	3.5	0.5	0.52	1.91	2.37	67.3	3.2	39.0	18.6	7.8
2.1	3.16	27.8	0.02	2.1	0.4	0.30	3.20	3.14	88.2	1.4	10.7	18.7	4.9
3.7	1.81	12.2	-0.12	1.1	0.2	0.12	1.23	3.37	103.4	0.7	15.2	49.1	4.1
0.3	4.70	56.2	-0.01	2.1	0.1	0.18	2.32	3.82	92.8	1.2	13.4	29.1	2.0
10.0	0.19	0.7	0.00	3.9	1.7	0.78	5.62	3.02	65.8	4.0	44.1	16.2	7.5
1.7	4.73	20.3	0.17	5.2	8.2	0.89	4.58	4.97	90.0	6.3	34.1	3.0	10.0
4.5	2.53	15.1	0.08	4.6	7.1	0.82	7.88	3.57	69.0	2.1	19.4	19.2	7.6
4.5	2.13	10.9	0.28	5.5	1.0	1.04	12.95	3.92	70.2	5.0	37.5	9.0	4.1
8.4	1.00	2.7	0.10	3.1	5.4	0.39	3.73	1.87	62.2	4.9	48.9	13.3	7.0
6.9	0.00	0.0	0.01	0.0	-0.7	-1.58	-15.88	3.90	119.0	4.4	25.7	7.8	4.2
2.3	5.27	28.7	-0.54	1.3	0.0	-0.03	-0.27	3.46	101.0	2.1	26.4	20.5	4.1
4.5	0.84	6.8	0.05	4.5	15.4	0.95	6.80	3.25	69.1	3.4	17.2	12.7	7.7
7.7	0.53	3.7	0.17	4.1	27.6	0.75	7.61	2.81	62.3	3.2	12.0	12.9	7.5
8.6	0.00	0.0	0.13	5.5	0.6	1.56	12.78	3.18	62.8	5.7	44.9	6.6	5.3
0.3	11.72	94.3	0.08	0.9	-0.1	-0.28	-3.00	4.57	106.8	0.6	9.1	43.5	2.6
6.3	0.48	3.2	0.19	6.2	74.8	1.09	7.97	4.16	62.3	5.7	25.6	2.3	9.2
3.6	1.28	9.8	-0.04	4.9	1.1	1.17	10.23	4.07	65.5	4.0	6.5	7.5	6.8
7.1	0.23	1.9	0.11	4.6	1.8	0.76	8.89	3.18	66.0	0.9	19.1	34.5	5.4
10.0	0.00	0.0	0.00	3.1	0.5	0.66	5.17	2.53	72.4	6.8	103.2	11.4	7.4
8.7	0.44	1.3	-0.04	4.5	2.2	0.91	7.10	3.55	70.6	2.0	34.2	29.2	8.0
1.4	3.69	17.3	5.40	10.0	356.3	4.49	31.29	25.82	46.6	0.5	10.2	71.0	9.3
1.6	3.04	15.6	4.73	10.0	128.1	3.33	25.33	16.53	42.4	0.4	9.6	0.8	9.3
5.2	1.51	9.5	0.30	3.9	345.6	0.65	6.09	2.71	68.1	6.0	29.2	2.8	9.0
8.1	na	0.0	na	10.0	11.3	27.91	29.34	0.63	59.6	4.0	na	0.0	5.7
7.3	0.00	0.0	-0.03	3.8	0.7	0.51	4.18	4.04	79.7	1.3	19.3	24.2	7.4
8.6	0.05	0.3	0.00	3.0	0.4	0.38	2.91	3.16	78.2	2.0	29.7	16.6	6.0
5.4	1.20	6.3	0.03	4.3	1.0	0.78	5.23	3.72	71.5	0.8	17.6	12.6	6.3
7.6	0.42	2.5	0.24	6.2	206.7	1.14	12.18	3.08	61.9	5.5	29.8	6.3	8.6
8.0	0.44	2.3	0.17	7.7	1.5	1.84	15.25	4.00	55.6	3.6	35.2	15.6	8.7
6.9	2.09	4.3	1.78	5.5	3.2	0.75	5.02	2.73	44.8	3.6	77.7	33.1	9.1
4.3	1.23	9.5	0.11	4.2	9.5	0.67	7.30	3.04	56.0	4.7	23.3	7.8	6.4
0.2	4.77	48.3	0.05	1.2	0.1	0.08	1.27	4.39	98.1	3.3	12.8	12.1	1.9
6.4	0.45	2.2	-0.02	5.0	2.9	5.47	32.48	4.55	82.8	4.1	18.8	8.2	6.3

Name	City	State	Rating	2015 Rating	2014 Rating	Total Assets ($Mil)	One Year Asset Growth	Asset Mix (As a % of Total Assets)				Capital-ization Index	Lever-age Ratio	Risk-Based Capital Ratio
								Comm-ercial Loans	Cons-umer Loans	Mort-gage Loans	Secur-ities			
Commerce Bank Texas	Stockdale	TX	B	B	B-	51.3	0.02	13.0	0.5	22.2	19.7	10.0	12.8	19.5
Commerce Community Bank	Oak Grove	LA	B-	B	B-	60.6	10.66	14.5	2.6	7.0	31.0	8.1	10.3	13.4
Commerce National Bank & Trust	Winter Park	FL	B	B-	D+	90.5	7.44	5.4	0.5	20.1	9.9	10.0	13.0	17.7
Commerce State Bank	West Bend	WI	C+	C	C	471.2	17.25	20.2	0.2	18.5	5.0	5.3	9.3	11.3
CommerceWest Bank	Irvine	CA	A-	A-	A-	489.4	3.74	24.5	0.1	1.4	9.3	10.0	12.0	15.9
Commercial & Savings Bank of Millersburg	Millersburg	OH	B	B-	B-	654.3	3.48	15.0	2.0	16.8	20.8	7.1	9.1	13.3
▲ Commercial Bank	Crawford	GA	B+	B-	B-	132.9	9.00	3.5	2.1	29.2	21.6	10.0	11.3	18.4
Commercial Bank	Parsons	KS	B+	B+	B	332.2	6.94	8.9	4.9	10.9	58.5	6.3	8.3	17.6
Commercial Bank	West Liberty	KY	A-	B+	A-	142.5	4.62	21.9	6.1	18.8	31.8	10.0	12.1	20.1
Commercial Bank	Alma	MI	C+	C+	C+	398.8	4.90	4.9	1.9	35.1	5.4	6.5	8.5	14.2
Commercial Bank	Saint Louis	MO	C-	C-	C-	185.0	0.47	19.6	1.8	12.9	31.7	6.3	8.3	13.1
Commercial Bank	De Kalb	MS	B	B-	C	135.2	6.91	6.5	13.4	12.9	26.2	9.2	10.4	15.9
Commercial Bank	Honea Path	SC	B+	B+	A-	179.5	4.03	2.2	3.0	14.0	49.2	10.0	13.7	36.9
Commercial Bank	Harrogate	TN	B	B-	C	942.6	17.16	8.3	1.6	24.6	11.4	8.2	9.8	15.5
Commercial Bank	Mason	TX	C+	C+	C+	41.0	5.99	5.0	3.0	20.8	36.4	6.6	8.6	14.9
Commercial Bank	Whitewater	WI	D+	D+	D+	95.4	-4.12	0.3	0.4	15.4	31.2	9.3	10.5	33.1
Commercial Bank & Trust Co.	Monticello	AR	B	B	B	192.5	2.21	10.6	7.2	13.8	37.7	8.9	10.3	17.1
Commercial Bank & Trust Co.	Paris	TN	A-	B+	B	734.9	9.23	12.8	3.6	17.6	21.0	9.0	10.3	16.0
Commercial Bank & Trust of PA	Latrobe	PA	B+	A	A	372.5	-5.34	4.0	0.5	18.6	36.4	10.0	14.9	23.8
Commercial Bank of California	Irvine	CA	C+	C	C-	790.6	140.87	10.4	0.3	2.4	7.7	8.0	9.6	14.1
Commercial Bank of Grayson	Grayson	KY	B-	B-	B-	176.5	1.97	4.2	8.8	16.1	51.6	10.0	15.0	28.1
Commercial Bank of Mott	Mott	ND	A	A	A-	95.6	-6.29	6.2	2.0	2.9	14.4	10.0	12.6	16.8
Commercial Bank of Nelson	Nelson	NE	B	B	B	46.1	17.53	23.7	2.6	0.2	37.5	10.0	12.2	15.9
Commercial Bank of Oak Grove	Oak Grove	MO	B+	B+	B	70.3	-2.15	0.9	1.2	28.2	20.2	10.0	15.1	29.8
▲ Commercial Bank of Ozark	Ozark	AL	C-	C-	C-	87.3	1.45	4.2	5.9	18.3	38.6	6.0	8.0	17.2
Commercial Bank of Texas, N.A.	Nacogdoches	TX	B+	B+	B+	664.4	20.62	8.4	5.9	14.9	28.5	8.6	10.1	15.1
Commercial Banking Co.	Valdosta	GA	B	B	B	232.1	2.11	7.1	1.7	28.6	11.2	10.0	13.1	21.1
Commercial Capital Bank	Delhi	LA	B+	A-	A-	109.4	38.64	10.5	2.7	13.4	6.4	10.0	11.5	15.2
Commercial National Bank of Brady	Brady	TX	A+	A+	A+	158.5	0.59	3.7	2.9	17.3	38.4	10.0	11.6	21.8
Commercial National Bank of Texarkana	Texarkana	TX	B	B	C+	209.6	0.68	12.7	2.6	13.5	42.0	6.3	8.3	15.4
Commercial Savings Bank	Carroll	IA	B	B	B	159.9	5.15	9.6	2.7	24.5	10.4	6.3	8.3	18.5
Commercial Savings Bank	Upper Sandusky	OH	B	B	C+	346.6	4.45	7.6	3.5	17.1	2.6	8.5	10.9	13.7
Commercial State Bank	Donalsonville	GA	C+	B-	B-	88.1	-7.37	18.2	4.8	7.4	23.9	10.0	15.2	24.4
▲ Commercial State Bank	Cedar Bluffs	NE	E	E-	E	21.2	-6.75	4.6	1.9	1.1	33.2	6.3	8.3	12.9
Commercial State Bank	Republican City	NE	A	A	A	59.6	-7.54	3.5	0.5	0.0	58.1	10.0	27.0	35.8
Commercial State Bank	Wausa	NE	B-	B-	B	98.1	4.34	19.5	4.7	6.0	3.5	7.1	10.7	12.6
Commercial State Bank	Andrews	TX	B+	B-	C+	518.8	-3.39	25.2	1.2	3.7	8.1	10.0	11.3	15.3
Commercial State Bank	Kingwood	TX	A-	B+	B	343.7	4.40	14.2	1.6	8.5	15.0	10.0	11.7	16.4
Commercial State Bank	Palmer	TX	C+	C	C+	70.9	-3.36	13.5	4.7	9.6	25.7	6.9	8.9	16.4
Commercial State Bank of Wagner	Wagner	SD	B+	A-	A-	155.6	5.75	5.1	3.4	5.6	29.0	9.9	10.9	16.6
Commercial Trust Co. of Fayette	Fayette	MO	B-	B-	C+	127.2	0.65	1.9	4.5	39.4	12.0	8.6	10.1	20.4
Commodore Bank	Somerset	OH	C-	C-	C-	83.0	1.84	6.3	6.8	31.1	29.6	6.8	8.8	16.3
▲ Commonwealth Bank and Trust Co.	Louisville	KY	B-	C+	C	951.0	11.11	7.6	3.2	18.1	25.8	7.5	9.3	13.5
Commonwealth Business Bank	Los Angeles	CA	B-	C+	C+	892.8	14.63	10.5	0.3	0.9	4.5	9.4	11.7	14.5
Commonwealth Co-operative Bank	Hyde Park	MA	B	B	B	183.4	5.18	2.0	0.2	53.9	14.7	10.0	13.7	26.9
Commonwealth Community Bank, Inc.	Hartford	KY	A-	B+	A-	152.1	2.91	0.4	3.0	18.9	59.7	10.0	14.8	38.2
▲ Commonwealth National Bank	Mobile	AL	E+	E-	E+	55.9	-2.94	6.8	2.0	8.1	33.1	5.6	7.6	21.5
Community 1st Bank	Auburn	CA	C+	C+	C-	350.6	44.02	3.8	0.6	4.5	28.8	7.2	9.1	14.9
Community 1st Bank	Post Falls	ID	B-	B-	C+	106.0	8.08	15.9	1.2	3.5	16.4	10.0	11.1	17.9
Community 1st Bank Las Vegas	Las Vegas	NM	E-	D-	D-	119.6	-3.34	3.9	1.7	16.8	22.9	3.5	5.5	10.8
Community Bank	Pasadena	CA	B-	B-	B-	3537.4	2.91	16.0	0.1	1.6	25.1	6.5	9.2	12.1
Community Bank	Dunlap	IA	C	C-	C	85.9	-10.16	3.0	4.2	15.8	11.7	10.0	12.3	15.3
Community Bank	Indianola	IA	C+	C+	C+	161.4	0.91	7.4	1.1	12.2	31.1	6.7	8.7	15.1
Community Bank	Nevada	IA	A-	A-	B+	195.5	2.32	4.7	0.6	5.3	1.0	8.4	10.6	13.6
▼ Community Bank	Winslow	IL	B	B+	A-	199.4	4.35	5.4	1.5	19.5	39.3	10.0	12.8	24.2
Community Bank	Liberal	KS	B-	B-	B-	112.0	5.49	9.8	13.3	0.6	31.9	9.2	10.4	15.5
Community Bank	Topeka	KS	B-	B-	B-	88.4	4.81	9.9	1.5	22.5	8.8	3.9	9.5	10.4
Community Bank	Ellisville	MS	B	B	B	720.7	5.83	6.7	5.0	24.6	14.8	6.3	8.3	14.5
Community Bank	Zanesville	OH	C-	C+	C+	418.1	3.89	7.2	4.5	31.9	15.3	6.4	8.4	13.6
Community Bank	Alva	OK	B+	B+	B	107.2	1.00	10.5	2.4	5.2	60.0	8.2	9.8	16.7

Asset Quality Index	Adjusted Non-Performing Loans as a % of Total Loans	as a % of Capital	Net Charge-Offs Avg Loans	Profitability Index	Net Income ($Mil)	Return on Assets (R.O.A.)	Return on Equity (R.O.E.)	Net Interest Spread	Overhead Efficiency Ratio	Liquidity Index	Liquidity Ratio	Hot Money Ratio	Stability Index
7.3	0.00	0.0	0.00	4.9	0.3	0.81	4.79	4.72	72.3	3.4	19.6	12.6	7.4
8.3	0.22	1.2	0.00	5.6	0.5	1.07	10.56	4.00	64.9	1.9	30.6	27.3	5.5
4.2	1.74	9.4	-0.66	7.8	1.8	2.80	23.24	3.99	79.6	2.0	22.4	19.6	5.5
6.1	0.41	3.4	-0.03	5.4	3.2	0.95	10.11	3.64	62.3	0.7	11.4	33.9	4.3
7.2	0.00	0.0	-0.03	5.7	3.5	1.01	7.68	4.14	60.9	3.0	13.2	5.8	8.2
4.7	1.28	9.3	0.05	5.7	5.0	1.03	10.59	3.61	60.7	4.0	12.1	8.0	6.4
5.2	1.90	10.3	0.05	8.9	2.1	2.18	19.44	4.35	53.6	4.0	17.7	9.0	7.1
8.3	0.42	1.7	0.02	4.7	2.8	1.15	11.48	3.24	67.6	4.9	48.2	12.6	6.9
7.4	0.89	3.5	0.05	4.5	1.0	0.96	6.48	4.34	82.1	2.3	29.8	20.1	8.1
4.4	1.68	13.9	-0.10	4.2	2.4	0.79	9.35	3.10	66.2	1.1	18.8	7.7	4.6
4.8	1.19	7.7	-0.87	1.7	0.2	0.14	1.60	3.44	99.2	4.0	32.2	12.3	3.7
6.5	0.34	1.8	0.03	5.2	0.8	0.77	7.41	4.53	72.2	3.5	24.1	12.3	5.1
7.9	2.91	7.0	0.27	4.8	1.5	1.16	7.99	3.23	63.1	5.5	71.7	14.0	8.5
4.2	2.19	14.8	0.24	4.6	5.3	0.78	7.68	3.63	66.8	1.4	14.6	20.7	5.5
9.0	0.00	0.0	0.00	5.2	0.3	1.05	12.17	3.95	62.2	4.5	38.5	12.2	5.0
8.7	0.17	0.6	0.00	1.4	0.1	0.08	0.77	2.38	95.0	5.5	67.7	11.9	5.5
5.2	0.93	4.8	0.39	6.6	2.2	1.55	15.11	4.23	63.7	1.3	19.8	28.4	7.1
6.5	0.48	2.8	0.06	7.0	8.4	1.57	14.00	3.83	63.9	4.2	25.4	8.7	8.3
9.3	0.32	1.2	0.00	4.7	3.3	1.18	7.66	4.43	78.2	5.5	42.1	7.3	9.4
5.8	0.12	0.7	-0.15	3.1	2.0	0.42	4.72	4.30	88.9	5.2	33.1	5.1	6.5
8.7	0.69	1.8	0.08	3.8	0.9	0.71	4.71	3.84	79.8	6.7	58.4	4.6	7.7
6.0	0.83	5.0	0.01	9.0	1.5	2.14	15.77	4.15	47.1	1.8	3.4	18.6	8.6
8.3	0.00	0.0	0.00	5.9	0.4	1.29	10.32	4.43	61.3	2.7	3.3	14.3	7.1
4.8	5.21	17.9	0.28	2.7	0.2	0.42	2.60	3.27	81.8	5.0	30.2	5.4	5.9
5.1	1.59	8.1	0.19	2.2	0.2	0.26	3.07	3.60	94.6	5.0	41.4	10.5	4.1
6.6	0.35	2.3	0.15	6.1	4.9	1.15	10.75	3.91	66.3	3.9	18.2	9.8	6.3
6.4	1.07	5.3	0.44	3.7	1.1	0.65	5.01	3.35	75.2	1.3	25.8	29.4	7.4
4.9	2.53	17.5	0.93	9.2	1.3	1.82	15.69	5.12	56.7	0.8	8.2	33.1	8.2
9.0	0.03	0.1	0.01	7.4	2.1	1.74	14.64	3.97	57.8	4.6	30.6	8.7	9.1
7.9	0.19	1.1	0.01	5.9	2.1	1.39	16.46	3.54	67.7	4.3	34.1	11.7	6.0
7.2	0.27	2.3	-0.04	5.7	1.7	1.41	17.40	3.26	55.2	4.8	25.6	5.0	5.5
4.9	0.83	6.0	0.02	7.1	3.6	1.39	12.89	4.40	61.5	1.8	7.8	17.7	6.8
2.5	6.57	22.9	1.92	2.2	0.1	0.09	0.55	4.27	74.2	2.3	19.4	18.0	6.1
5.1	0.85	5.0	-0.01	2.3	0.1	0.33	4.25	2.70	83.3	1.7	35.6	28.8	0.8
9.1	0.00	0.0	-0.01	9.5	0.8	1.63	6.02	4.04	37.2	4.0	82.9	24.7	8.0
3.4	1.66	12.4	0.14	5.4	0.9	1.23	11.69	4.21	67.8	1.3	6.8	25.6	6.8
5.2	1.64	9.6	0.36	7.0	5.9	1.57	14.03	4.90	56.9	1.2	21.4	31.5	7.5
7.7	0.10	0.6	0.02	5.8	2.8	1.14	9.79	4.59	65.2	4.0	28.8	11.0	6.3
4.6	1.77	10.5	0.15	6.8	0.9	1.58	17.82	4.68	63.5	3.9	22.0	10.2	4.7
4.7	1.52	8.5	0.34	10.0	2.8	2.45	21.22	4.86	41.2	1.1	5.9	27.4	8.1
8.4	0.29	1.7	0.00	4.5	1.1	1.17	12.03	3.01	64.4	4.6	33.5	9.9	6.1
3.5	2.77	16.7	0.25	1.7	0.1	0.12	1.34	3.89	95.7	4.5	30.1	8.6	4.5
5.0	0.83	5.7	0.07	4.3	7.8	1.13	11.80	3.20	84.5	3.6	17.8	11.0	5.2
3.6	1.24	8.0	0.00	9.0	8.0	1.32	11.22	4.23	48.9	0.7	15.9	37.6	8.4
6.4	1.96	10.0	0.00	3.4	0.7	0.57	3.97	3.36	80.0	1.2	27.4	28.7	7.5
9.8	0.38	0.7	-0.08	5.4	1.4	1.29	8.71	3.73	65.9	4.4	72.8	19.5	8.0
1.7	7.33	35.4	0.28	2.0	0.2	0.45	5.84	4.66	92.2	2.1	23.4	19.1	2.2
7.8	0.50	2.8	-0.01	3.3	1.1	0.48	5.13	3.11	74.9	3.6	22.3	10.1	3.9
8.5	0.46	2.4	0.72	3.8	0.5	0.59	5.38	3.83	76.4	3.6	35.4	15.5	6.8
0.3	12.93	88.5	-0.17	0.3	-0.3	-0.27	-4.85	3.58	107.6	4.8	34.0	8.8	2.0
6.7	0.21	1.4	0.21	4.9	22.6	0.83	9.14	3.36	59.1	2.1	21.4	17.6	7.8
1.7	3.41	21.0	0.38	4.1	0.6	0.89	6.62	4.48	72.1	3.6	10.1	10.3	6.0
7.8	0.00	0.0	0.07	3.5	0.8	0.62	6.86	3.37	75.9	1.9	21.5	20.8	5.2
7.1	0.04	0.3	0.00	9.0	2.1	1.44	14.14	3.64	36.3	0.5	6.5	46.5	7.7
6.3	2.12	8.5	0.41	3.4	0.9	0.63	4.68	3.00	63.0	3.3	38.8	18.3	7.6
4.8	0.82	4.5	0.03	3.9	0.6	0.69	6.50	3.62	77.2	1.7	22.5	24.1	6.6
8.8	0.00	0.0	-0.08	5.3	0.6	0.94	10.02	3.93	69.3	4.2	24.5	8.1	5.8
5.0	0.76	6.3	0.11	6.9	5.8	1.09	13.22	3.73	58.0	2.1	16.2	18.6	6.1
2.6	2.30	17.6	0.82	3.2	1.4	0.45	5.20	4.11	75.8	3.1	11.6	13.3	4.1
9.0	0.02	0.1	-0.05	6.3	1.3	1.61	15.25	3.94	51.6	3.0	60.0	35.9	7.2

Name	City	State	2015 Rating	2014 Rating	Rating	Total Assets ($Mil)	One Year Asset Growth	Comm-ercial Loans	Cons-umer Loans	Mort-gage Loans	Secur-ities	Capital-ization Index	Lever-age Ratio	Risk-Based Capital Ratio
Community Bank	Bristow	OK	B+	B+	B+	82.3	0.33	5.6	4.6	28.3	25.2	6.6	8.6	15.4
Community Bank	Joseph	OR	C+	C+	C+	375.6	4.05	6.6	0.6	4.0	25.9	7.4	9.3	14.9
Community Bank	Carmichaels	PA	B-	B-	B-	832.5	1.09	7.7	13.6	30.7	11.5	8.3	9.9	14.5
Community Bank	Avon	SD	B	B	B	52.7	-1.58	7.0	5.6	6.2	45.5	10.0	15.1	28.7
Community Bank	Lexington	TN	B	B-	B-	133.6	7.67	7.3	3.8	31.9	11.6	7.5	9.3	13.3
Community Bank	Bridgeport	TX	C	C	C	71.0	-4.24	11.0	1.6	16.0	10.6	6.8	8.8	14.5
Community Bank	Longview	TX	A-	A-	A-	214.9	-2.06	14.4	2.6	38.5	0.0	8.3	9.8	15.6
Community Bank & Trust	Ashland City	TN	C-	C-	D+	210.5	3.62	4.7	1.7	11.9	42.8	9.0	10.3	20.4
Community Bank & Trust	Waco	TX	B+	B+	B+	425.1	5.77	27.6	2.8	22.0	23.7	10.0	13.9	21.1
Community Bank & Trust - Alabama	Union Springs	AL	E	E	E	50.4	-0.86	5.0	4.8	11.7	47.5	5.3	7.3	18.2
Community Bank & Trust - West Georgia	LaGrange	GA	E-	E-	E-	84.8	-3.18	6.8	1.9	20.6	12.3	0.7	4.4	7.4
Community Bank and Trust	Neosho	MO	B-	B-	B-	306.4	2.80	2.6	1.7	20.1	21.1	5.7	7.7	14.4
Community Bank and Trust Co.	Muscatine	IA	C+	B-	C+	254.6	-3.00	13.1	4.7	13.7	19.4	8.1	9.7	14.5
Community Bank and Trust of Florida	Ocala	FL	B-	B-	B	679.9	9.34	4.0	0.8	6.8	48.9	6.2	8.2	16.4
Community Bank Delaware	Lewes	DE	B	B	B	168.4	3.13	3.9	0.4	35.0	6.4	10.0	11.1	15.5
▲ Community Bank Mankato	Vernon Center	MN	C-	D+	C-	259.0	5.47	8.9	1.9	16.0	3.5	5.2	7.9	11.2
▲ Community Bank of Bergen County, NJ	Maywood	NJ	C+	C-	D+	337.4	2.49	0.9	0.6	41.3	20.2	6.6	8.6	15.5
Community Bank of Cameron	Cameron	WI	B	B	B	110.3	5.67	4.4	2.7	36.2	4.9	7.2	9.2	15.1
Community Bank of Easton	Easton	IL	A-	A-	A-	33.8	10.01	14.7	8.3	5.2	1.5	10.0	16.3	28.0
Community Bank of El Dorado Springs	El Dorado Springs	MO	A	A	A	102.2	-4.24	2.1	2.8	8.1	47.1	10.0	15.5	30.0
Community Bank of Elmhurst	Elmhurst	IL	D+	D	D	159.2	0.03	5.8	0.2	7.4	47.0	5.4	7.4	13.1
Community Bank of Georgia	Baxley	GA	B-	C+	C-	70.4	-3.72	9.4	2.7	10.4	10.3	10.0	14.3	20.3
Community Bank of Louisiana	Mansfield	LA	B	B	B+	434.7	7.32	4.2	2.6	12.2	49.7	6.7	8.7	17.7
Community Bank of Marshall	Marshall	MO	B-	B-	B-	143.3	3.85	2.9	2.6	11.2	42.0	10.0	11.1	21.4
Community Bank of Memphis	Memphis	MO	C+	C+	C+	44.7	-2.15	2.1	3.5	18.6	22.7	8.3	9.8	18.9
▼ Community Bank of Mississippi	Forest	MS	B-	B	B	788.4	10.99	7.1	2.9	17.1	18.1	6.1	8.1	14.1
Community Bank of Missouri	Richmond	MO	B	B	B-	49.7	-0.53	7.8	1.1	17.7	9.5	10.0	13.0	18.1
Community Bank of Oak Park River Forest	Oak Park	IL	B-	C+	D+	301.1	6.53	11.2	0.2	13.5	14.6	6.8	9.6	12.3
Community Bank of Oelwein	Oelwein	IA	B	B	B	114.0	3.74	3.8	2.9	8.8	53.3	8.4	9.9	22.6
▲ Community Bank of Oklahoma	Verden	OK	B-	B-	B-	39.4	2.17	16.7	8.1	6.8	14.2	10.0	13.1	15.9
▲ Community Bank of Parkersburg	Parkersburg	WV	A-	B+	B+	244.4	6.32	3.8	7.0	52.8	13.3	9.9	10.9	18.2
Community Bank of Pickens County	Jasper	GA	D	D-	E+	329.2	2.33	4.3	2.3	19.0	9.5	7.2	9.2	13.5
Community Bank of Pleasant Hill	Pleasant Hill	MO	B-	B-	D+	60.1	13.97	5.1	1.1	1.5	32.5	7.7	9.4	14.2
Community Bank of Raymore	Raymore	MO	B-	B-	D+	207.0	12.80	13.6	0.4	1.6	24.5	5.6	8.0	11.4
Community Bank of Santa Maria	Santa Maria	CA	C+	C+	C+	238.8	8.40	10.6	0.4	1.0	36.0	7.3	9.2	14.0
Community Bank of Snyder	Snyder	TX	D+	D+	C+	112.4	-13.81	2.4	1.9	5.6	46.4	8.4	9.9	16.7
Community Bank of the Bay	Oakland	CA	C+	C+	C+	259.8	1.48	15.8	0.1	2.5	1.0	6.9	9.5	12.4
Community Bank of the Chesapeake	Waldorf	MD	B-	B-	B-	1279.8	15.38	8.0	0.0	19.8	11.6	8.2	10.7	13.5
Community Bank of the Midwest	Great Bend	KS	B-	B-	B	168.3	-5.25	12.3	3.3	8.7	10.6	6.2	8.2	12.6
▲ Community Bank of the South	Merritt Island	FL	C	C-	C+	135.5	-0.40	3.6	0.3	3.1	15.8	8.5	10.0	24.4
Community Bank of Trenton	Trenton	IL	C-	C+	B-	80.2	6.26	8.1	3.4	27.7	19.4	10.0	11.6	18.1
Community Bank of Wichita, Inc.	Wichita	KS	C+	C+	C+	75.8	2.75	27.6	5.8	13.3	13.8	7.0	9.4	12.5
Community Bank Owatonna	Owatonna	MN	C+	C+	C+	53.2	0.36	13.7	1.2	14.7	17.1	9.1	10.4	14.3
Community Bank, Coast	Biloxi	MS	C+	C+	C+	754.8	2.12	5.2	3.4	26.3	8.9	6.4	8.4	12.6
Community Bank, N.A.	De Witt	NY	B+	B+	B+	8666.6	8.74	5.1	14.2	22.7	32.8	6.4	8.4	15.5
Community Bank, North Mississippi	Amory	MS	C+	B-	B-	532.9	5.70	4.4	2.4	24.9	23.8	7.2	9.2	16.8
Community Bankers' Bank	Midlothian	VA	C	C+	C	126.6	-13.16	8.4	0.6	2.9	20.1	10.0	13.2	20.4
Community Banking Co. of Fitzgerald	Fitzgerald	GA	A-	A-	B+	128.0	2.31	8.7	7.9	23.4	12.5	10.0	11.9	18.6
Community Banks of Shelby County	Cowden	IL	C-	C-	C-	47.0	-3.25	8.0	4.0	10.7	13.5	10.0	11.3	22.2
Community Business Bank	West Sacramento	CA	A-	A-	A-	284.5	17.61	14.9	0.1	2.9	19.1	8.3	10.6	13.6
Community Capital Bank of Virginia	Christiansburg	VA	B	C+	B	126.4	31.20	12.2	0.0	8.6	11.1	10.0	11.3	19.5
Community Commerce Bank	Claremont	CA	B-	C+	C	189.3	5.92	0.0	8.4	5.0	0.3	10.0	27.2	35.3
Community Development Bank, FSB	Ogema	MN	B-	C+	C+	77.3	5.26	9.0	5.3	11.8	12.2	9.3	10.8	14.4
Community Federal Savings Bank	New York	NY	D-	D-	D	132.8	-14.74	3.8	0.0	15.3	6.3	7.7	9.5	19.9
Community Financial Bank	Prentice	WI	D	D+	D+	29.1	9.21	4.2	2.4	29.2	0.0	10.0	14.5	22.3
Community Financial Services Bank	Benton	KY	B-	B-	B-	927.5	18.45	11.6	13.3	20.8	7.7	5.6	9.5	11.4
Community First Bank	Kansas City	KS	B-	B-	C+	138.6	10.69	23.5	1.2	10.7	3.3	5.7	9.5	11.5
Community First Bank	New Iberia	LA	A-	B+	B+	325.2	0.06	11.5	4.1	26.3	14.9	8.8	10.2	15.5
▲ Community First Bank	Butler	MO	B-	B	B-	166.9	2.35	10.6	3.4	22.2	7.3	6.3	8.4	12.2
▼ Community First Bank	Maywood	NE	D+	C+	C	131.3	1.16	9.6	2.6	4.5	18.4	7.2	10.0	12.7

Asset Quality Index	Adjusted Non-Performing Loans as a % of Total Loans	as a % of Capital	Net Charge-Offs Avg Loans	Profitability Index	Net Income ($Mil)	Return on Assets (R.O.A.)	Return on Equity (R.O.E.)	Net Interest Spread	Overhead Efficiency Ratio	Liquidity Index	Liquidity Ratio	Hot Money Ratio	Stability Index
8.3	0.26	1.8	0.06	8.7	0.9	1.48	18.81	4.42	57.8	4.1	37.2	13.8	5.9
5.3	0.98	6.1	0.00	3.6	2.0	0.74	7.59	4.27	83.4	5.6	36.8	4.7	5.8
3.8	0.80	6.1	0.12	5.1	5.5	0.88	8.42	3.76	66.5	3.6	2.5	9.6	6.3
8.6	0.45	1.3	0.20	4.1	0.3	0.74	4.74	3.70	66.9	3.3	55.7	23.7	7.0
5.8	0.76	6.0	0.10	6.5	1.2	1.19	12.50	4.64	62.2	0.8	11.7	33.9	5.7
8.6	0.21	1.4	-0.03	2.7	0.2	0.41	4.65	3.75	82.5	4.2	39.5	13.9	4.2
7.3	0.60	4.4	0.02	9.0	3.5	2.14	22.35	3.65	42.0	2.8	19.3	15.2	7.2
5.3	2.15	8.9	0.19	2.5	0.7	0.41	4.07	3.26	88.0	2.9	40.5	21.6	4.7
8.2	0.70	3.2	0.20	4.7	3.0	0.97	7.08	3.80	69.7	2.5	33.9	21.6	6.7
2.4	5.47	21.3	0.12	2.1	0.3	0.68	10.14	3.48	90.9	2.5	43.7	30.1	0.6
1.7	3.20	38.2	0.10	0.5	-0.2	-0.30	-6.60	4.23	109.9	3.6	22.5	11.7	0.6
7.4	0.33	1.9	0.20	3.8	1.8	0.80	9.70	3.05	82.0	5.7	34.6	3.2	5.4
3.3	2.01	12.5	0.14	4.0	1.7	0.88	7.86	3.46	70.6	3.4	31.7	15.1	6.5
6.7	1.02	4.6	-0.08	4.1	3.8	0.77	8.69	3.23	71.1	5.7	59.3	11.2	5.5
8.3	0.32	2.3	-0.01	4.5	0.9	0.75	6.52	3.61	67.8	0.7	10.4	35.7	7.7
2.8	1.33	13.1	-0.02	6.9	3.4	1.75	22.76	4.27	57.7	2.2	9.3	17.7	4.8
3.3	2.29	17.0	0.28	3.6	1.3	0.55	6.19	3.50	76.7	3.6	23.2	11.5	4.2
4.3	1.79	13.6	0.07	6.1	1.2	1.45	15.85	3.81	61.6	1.9	18.4	15.1	6.5
7.9	0.00	0.0	0.00	9.8	0.5	1.87	11.65	3.49	22.8	4.8	44.5	11.8	8.0
6.7	1.97	5.4	0.00	8.5	1.7	2.15	13.50	3.30	35.2	4.9	54.1	13.9	9.7
6.6	1.21	6.9	0.00	1.7	0.4	0.34	4.40	3.14	87.3	6.1	53.0	7.3	2.7
4.1	3.67	16.2	0.21	5.5	0.5	0.97	7.20	4.41	63.2	1.7	25.1	24.5	5.9
8.3	0.53	2.6	0.13	4.3	3.4	1.06	11.97	3.21	64.1	2.2	19.7	18.4	5.4
9.1	0.19	0.8	-0.02	3.7	0.7	0.65	5.88	2.62	69.5	5.3	40.2	8.3	6.0
8.2	0.02	0.1	0.08	4.0	0.2	0.65	5.63	2.92	60.1	4.1	40.4	14.6	6.1
4.7	1.35	10.3	0.03	6.2	5.8	1.02	12.45	4.81	66.4	2.1	26.5	20.1	5.8
6.8	0.94	5.2	0.21	5.4	0.4	1.10	8.56	5.27	71.5	2.7	10.9	14.8	6.1
3.8	2.03	13.8	-0.49	5.4	2.1	0.96	9.85	4.39	74.1	4.2	15.3	7.5	4.6
9.2	0.16	0.6	-0.24	4.4	0.9	1.07	10.53	2.52	57.6	3.1	68.2	51.9	6.2
3.8	2.55	13.9	0.00	7.2	0.6	1.82	14.24	5.54	68.0	2.8	12.9	14.9	6.9
6.1	0.48	3.4	0.00	6.6	3.0	1.70	15.19	4.11	64.9	3.7	12.4	10.3	7.4
0.5	3.95	29.2	0.88	3.8	1.3	0.53	5.70	4.08	64.7	0.7	15.3	43.8	3.1
6.2	0.91	5.2	0.00	3.8	0.4	0.96	9.83	3.02	80.0	6.3	39.9	1.3	4.9
7.5	0.08	0.6	-0.19	6.3	2.3	1.53	18.57	3.24	73.9	4.4	14.5	6.1	5.6
7.8	0.54	3.0	-0.03	3.3	0.6	0.36	3.95	3.88	85.2	5.4	43.4	8.6	5.4
8.9	0.00	0.0	0.00	1.8	0.1	0.15	1.55	2.92	90.7	4.5	49.0	15.0	3.6
3.0	1.50	10.8	0.21	4.8	1.4	0.77	8.06	4.03	72.2	1.9	24.1	21.2	4.7
4.0	1.31	9.6	0.08	4.7	7.2	0.79	7.19	3.61	61.2	0.8	11.0	26.5	7.7
7.9	0.26	1.8	0.36	5.0	1.6	1.26	15.56	3.43	61.3	4.3	30.9	10.7	4.6
6.0	2.05	6.5	-0.14	2.8	0.4	0.35	3.60	2.55	82.0	4.6	50.7	14.7	5.1
1.2	8.87	46.4	0.22	3.4	0.4	0.62	5.19	3.29	75.8	3.4	24.5	13.0	5.2
6.2	0.33	2.5	0.09	4.7	0.5	0.82	8.69	4.65	72.2	2.3	16.8	17.5	5.2
6.3	0.64	4.0	0.00	3.6	0.2	0.55	5.42	3.89	77.8	4.0	28.7	11.0	4.5
3.3	1.76	14.8	0.26	4.2	3.9	0.68	6.83	3.80	69.9	1.4	17.2	26.5	5.9
5.9	0.48	3.3	0.14	6.5	73.3	1.15	8.55	3.75	57.7	5.0	15.4	2.5	10.0
6.5	0.48	3.0	0.02	3.0	1.7	0.42	4.30	3.12	79.0	1.5	22.6	26.5	6.0
5.9	2.28	8.9	-0.05	1.7	0.2	0.15	1.19	2.61	97.9	1.1	26.6	17.2	5.5
6.3	0.73	3.8	0.21	5.4	0.9	0.91	7.13	3.92	65.6	1.8	15.9	20.1	7.4
8.9	0.25	1.0	0.00	1.8	0.0	0.12	1.09	2.53	94.8	5.6	52.7	8.8	5.4
8.5	0.00	0.0	0.00	7.2	2.3	1.17	10.17	4.29	54.2	1.3	29.1	25.0	7.5
2.7	3.22	20.7	0.00	3.4	0.5	0.54	3.75	3.23	65.6	1.1	11.7	28.3	6.8
3.5	3.89	9.4	-0.02	8.5	1.6	1.17	4.22	5.06	69.5	1.0	26.9	53.8	8.4
5.1	0.85	5.2	-0.01	5.3	0.5	0.90	7.83	4.08	61.5	1.5	14.8	22.9	6.1
3.7	3.46	18.7	0.02	0.0	-4.4	-4.20	-40.65	3.03	177.3	3.1	49.2	26.1	4.7
6.5	0.69	3.5	0.00	0.5	-0.4	-2.03	-13.28	3.82	104.3	3.5	23.3	12.6	5.5
4.3	0.67	5.6	-0.06	6.4	7.5	1.14	12.12	3.90	60.9	0.6	5.6	22.3	6.4
8.3	0.07	0.6	0.02	7.4	1.3	1.26	13.52	5.09	60.4	0.6	2.5	34.4	5.2
5.4	1.30	8.4	0.02	7.0	3.8	1.54	15.26	4.46	64.5	1.7	14.2	20.5	8.3
4.3	1.11	10.2	0.07	7.8	2.3	1.82	21.42	4.00	51.4	1.4	5.6	23.4	7.0
1.4	2.88	19.2	-0.03	4.3	0.8	0.83	7.20	4.56	77.6	1.9	5.7	18.5	5.9

Name	City	State	2016 Rating	2015 Rating	2014 Rating	Total Assets ($Mil)	One Year Asset Growth	Comm-ercial Loans	Cons-umer Loans	Mort-gage Loans	Secur-ities	Capital-ization Index	Lever-age Ratio	Risk-Based Capital Ratio
Community First Bank	Reynoldsville	PA	C+	C	C	121.1	9.70	9.2	2.9	43.7	4.3	7.6	9.4	13.1
Community First Bank	Walhalla	SC	C-	C-	D	324.4	-4.59	2.7	5.7	12.4	26.8	8.1	9.7	16.7
Community First Bank	Kennewick	WA	B	B+	B+	282.1	5.73	7.6	0.8	6.4	22.3	7.3	9.2	15.0
Community First Bank	Boscobel	WI	B-	B-	B-	243.3	3.51	5.6	1.5	22.2	28.1	8.6	10.0	17.4
Community First Bank	Rosholt	WI	C+	B-	B-	76.0	1.57	2.8	1.5	13.0	36.2	8.6	10.0	16.0
Community First Bank & Trust	Columbia	TN	B-	C+	D+	472.3	3.06	4.3	1.4	19.7	17.8	7.4	9.3	14.4
Community First Bank of Indiana	Kokomo	IN	B-	B-	B-	223.1	3.44	17.5	0.9	10.1	3.5	7.6	10.9	13.0
Community First Bank of the Heartland	Mount Vernon	IL	B+	B+	B+	168.8	1.39	12.4	0.5	13.7	9.0	6.2	8.5	11.9
Community First Bank, N.A.	Forest	OH	C-	C-	C-	54.5	2.47	3.6	1.3	30.3	24.4	8.1	9.7	19.2
Community First Banking Co.	West Plains	MO	A	A	A-	165.1	7.64	8.1	3.8	24.8	15.7	10.0	13.0	17.9
Community First National Bank	Manhattan	KS	B-	B	B	245.7	20.54	11.2	2.0	23.5	0.0	7.4	9.3	13.0
Community National B&T of Texas	Corsicana	TX	B+	B+	A-	649.4	24.04	6.5	1.7	15.0	17.4	7.6	9.4	13.0
Community National Bank	Seneca	KS	A-	A-	A-	398.3	13.14	2.5	0.6	6.4	61.6	6.9	8.9	19.0
Community National Bank	Monett	MO	B+	B+	B+	107.1	10.84	8.3	3.4	16.8	7.9	7.7	9.5	15.5
Community National Bank	Dayton	TN	B	B	C+	217.2	3.80	6.4	2.0	12.6	23.9	10.0	11.6	19.9
Community National Bank	Hondo	TX	B	C+	C+	197.5	1.66	8.6	2.8	9.7	25.3	7.7	9.4	15.7
▼ Community National Bank	Midland	TX	C-	B	B	996.4	-7.60	27.0	1.5	5.8	10.3	6.8	9.9	12.4
Community National Bank	Newport	VT	B-	B-	B-	605.2	2.86	10.8	1.2	27.7	13.8	7.1	9.0	13.5
Community National Bank & Trust	Chanute	KS	B-	B-	B-	970.7	4.90	10.2	2.4	16.8	16.7	6.1	8.5	11.8
Community National Bank in Monmouth	Monmouth	IL	B-	C+	C+	42.0	-3.55	11.8	9.0	15.6	23.6	10.0	16.1	25.9
Community National Bank of Okarche	Okarche	OK	A	A	A	86.5	3.15	5.6	3.6	7.5	40.6	10.0	14.3	25.3
Community Neighbor Bank	Camden	AL	A-	B+	B+	107.6	1.52	12.0	7.1	19.0	15.7	10.0	14.7	23.5
Community Point Bank	Russellville	MO	C+	C+	C+	113.1	15.34	4.1	4.4	24.9	14.3	8.7	10.1	14.0
▲ Community Pride Bank	Isanti	MN	B+	B+	B-	107.0	6.79	17.7	1.1	11.2	13.6	10.0	11.5	16.2
Community Resource Bank	Northfield	MN	B-	B-	B-	273.9	8.15	8.7	1.5	13.1	13.4	8.3	10.2	13.6
Community Savings	Caldwell	OH	C-	C	D	53.6	-4.18	0.0	8.4	41.4	19.8	10.0	12.3	27.6
Community Savings Bank	Edgewood	IA	B-	B	B-	421.4	28.54	15.0	2.0	9.2	15.9	7.9	10.0	13.2
Community Savings Bank	Chicago	IL	C-	D+	D+	402.0	-1.20	0.0	0.0	30.8	34.2	10.0	15.2	38.6
Community Savings Bank	Bethel	OH	B+	B+	B-	77.7	1.28	4.4	0.8	40.7	15.1	10.0	15.0	26.0
Community Shores Bank	Muskegon	MI	D	E-	E	180.9	-4.76	21.2	1.0	11.2	10.6	5.9	8.0	11.7
Community Spirit Bank	Red Bay	AL	B-	B-	C	143.7	4.99	12.5	4.9	21.9	19.0	9.1	10.4	16.6
▼ Community State Bank	Bradley	AR	C-	B-	B-	15.6	-10.82	10.0	6.6	17.1	25.8	10.0	12.7	27.9
Community State Bank	Lamar	CO	A-	A-	A-	88.7	5.64	15.0	3.9	8.7	14.7	10.0	14.7	21.2
Community State Bank	Starke	FL	C+	C+	C-	90.9	33.83	5.6	2.9	14.6	26.4	8.1	9.8	21.5
Community State Bank	Ankeny	IA	B+	B+	B	580.9	-0.83	14.0	0.2	12.1	15.5	8.9	11.7	14.1
Community State Bank	Paton	IA	B+	B+	B+	41.7	-0.59	2.5	3.6	2.9	55.0	10.0	18.0	35.8
Community State Bank	Spencer	IA	A-	B+	B	149.8	1.15	14.4	1.8	6.6	34.5	8.6	10.1	18.5
Community State Bank	Tipton	IA	B	B	B	116.4	3.51	7.0	1.7	8.8	36.5	8.5	10.0	17.0
▼ Community State Bank	Galva	IL	C	B+	B+	198.4	-1.13	8.8	2.5	14.9	20.4	9.9	10.9	15.0
Community State Bank	Avilla	IN	B+	B+	B+	230.1	10.51	11.7	2.0	35.1	9.5	8.7	10.2	15.5
▲ Community State Bank	Brook	IN	D+	E+	B	60.6	-2.89	8.1	2.1	25.6	14.7	10.0	12.5	19.0
Community State Bank	Royal Center	IN	D+	B	B	122.3	5.50	7.0	4.0	15.7	10.5	7.3	9.3	12.8
▲ Community State Bank	Coffeyville	KS	B+	B	B	160.3	-8.16	7.5	1.7	7.6	49.5	9.1	10.4	20.2
Community State Bank	Saint Charles	MI	C	C-	D+	193.2	2.37	9.0	2.1	15.8	38.7	8.3	9.9	21.1
Community State Bank	Shelbina	MO	B-	B	B-	60.8	8.75	5.9	7.4	22.8	38.1	7.0	9.0	23.3
Community State Bank	Hennessey	OK	D+	D+	D	50.9	2.95	11.7	7.5	4.8	16.4	6.1	8.1	15.8
Community State Bank	Poteau	OK	B	B	B	232.6	2.43	8.6	3.4	22.4	14.8	7.6	9.4	13.8
Community State Bank	Union Grove	WI	C-	C-	D+	327.7	4.58	16.6	0.9	9.6	34.5	7.7	9.5	15.4
Community State Bank of Canton	Canton	OK	C+	C+	C	40.4	-1.06	12.3	10.5	6.0	19.1	10.0	11.2	18.1
Community State Bank of Missouri	Bowling Green	MO	B+	B+	B+	231.5	4.06	8.1	0.7	14.8	35.8	9.0	12.7	14.2
Community State Bank of Orbisonia	Orbisonia	PA	B-	B	B	325.3	3.25	1.6	5.4	63.0	5.2	9.2	10.4	18.3
▲ Community State Bank of Rock Falls	Rock Falls	IL	D+	C	C-	246.6	-0.66	12.1	2.7	29.1	15.4	8.0	9.7	15.3
▲ Community State Bank Of Southwestern In	Poseyville	IN	B-	C+	C+	77.7	2.09	7.7	1.5	31.1	4.9	7.0	9.0	14.5
Community Trust Bank	Irvington	IL	B-	C+	B+	80.5	-7.65	5.4	1.0	13.9	24.4	10.0	13.9	24.2
Community Trust Bank, Inc.	Pikeville	KY	B-	B-	B-	3907.2	3.24	6.7	15.6	22.0	15.8	10.0	12.1	17.5
Community Valley Bank	El Centro	CA	B+	B	C+	147.9	9.36	13.7	0.1	3.9	1.7	9.9	11.0	17.9
Community West Bank, N.A.	Goleta	CA	C	C-	C-	664.2	10.55	6.9	28.9	4.7	4.8	7.7	10.5	13.1
CommunityBank of Texas, N.A.	Beaumont	TX	B	B	B	2936.4	3.40	17.6	1.3	7.9	6.1	8.2	10.6	13.5
Compass Bank	Birmingham	AL	C	C+	C+	84983.5	0.36	21.3	5.8	16.8	14.3	6.9	8.9	13.5
Compass Savings Bank	Wilmerding	PA	C	C	C+	63.5	24.20	0.0	0.3	75.4	11.8	5.8	7.8	16.5

Asset Quality Index	Adjusted Non-Performing Loans as a % of Total Loans	as a % of Capital	Net Charge-Offs Avg Loans	Profitability Index	Net Income ($Mil)	Return on Assets (R.O.A.)	Return on Equity (R.O.E.)	Net Interest Spread	Overhead Efficiency Ratio	Liquidity Index	Liquidity Ratio	Hot Money Ratio	Stability Index
4.2	1.45	12.8	0.05	3.6	0.5	0.56	5.90	3.86	79.5	1.4	4.8	22.5	5.7
3.9	1.78	9.2	0.07	2.1	0.8	0.31	3.32	3.27	94.4	4.6	40.3	12.3	2.9
7.2	0.65	3.8	0.00	5.3	2.7	1.32	13.03	3.33	64.2	6.1	40.1	3.0	6.5
6.3	0.60	3.4	0.04	3.8	1.6	0.87	8.53	3.47	80.5	4.5	28.7	6.0	5.8
8.9	0.00	0.0	0.00	3.3	0.4	0.64	5.87	4.17	85.8	5.9	45.1	4.9	5.9
4.9	1.66	10.7	-0.04	4.6	2.7	0.78	7.50	3.57	75.8	2.0	21.0	19.3	5.1
4.6	1.24	8.0	-0.15	7.6	1.9	1.21	10.72	4.63	60.3	2.9	14.6	14.6	6.4
5.9	0.47	4.0	0.03	8.3	2.3	1.81	18.89	4.59	62.6	3.3	10.1	11.8	7.6
9.4	0.01	0.1	0.02	2.3	0.1	0.31	3.18	2.87	87.2	5.9	44.9	4.8	4.8
7.8	0.50	2.6	0.10	6.8	2.0	1.63	12.45	4.09	64.1	3.9	8.5	8.6	9.1
5.1	1.20	10.0	0.32	6.0	1.8	1.12	12.15	3.80	78.8	1.5	17.6	23.9	5.0
5.1	0.87	5.9	0.02	7.2	6.0	1.33	12.94	5.19	62.9	3.6	17.7	11.4	8.0
9.0	0.38	1.3	-0.01	9.3	6.5	2.15	23.84	3.17	46.2	6.6	57.2	4.8	7.0
6.6	0.52	3.3	0.04	4.9	1.0	1.23	13.28	3.42	68.4	4.6	30.7	8.3	6.8
4.3	3.79	17.9	-0.03	4.2	1.4	0.87	7.38	4.18	77.8	4.2	23.1	8.2	6.1
6.1	0.50	2.9	0.10	4.9	1.4	0.95	8.96	3.98	70.9	4.1	37.4	13.5	5.9
3.3	2.15	13.9	2.69	1.9	-3.3	-0.42	-3.84	3.71	57.3	4.4	13.9	5.8	6.3
4.4	0.73	5.8	0.07	5.1	4.4	0.97	8.95	4.06	68.3	3.5	13.4	11.1	7.3
5.8	0.53	3.9	0.02	4.5	6.1	0.84	9.11	3.70	71.8	3.0	10.1	13.6	6.3
5.0	4.32	16.5	0.03	3.7	0.2	0.61	3.94	3.75	73.0	5.1	38.5	8.5	6.1
8.7	0.00	0.0	-0.01	7.9	1.3	1.90	13.07	3.74	49.1	1.2	22.2	30.8	9.6
5.9	1.78	6.9	0.24	5.6	0.8	0.95	6.67	4.58	69.4	2.8	32.1	18.2	7.9
7.8	0.30	2.3	-0.01	3.5	0.6	0.78	7.64	3.09	71.0	1.1	15.0	24.9	5.9
8.0	0.11	0.7	-0.19	5.6	1.0	1.28	10.00	4.25	63.0	3.7	15.0	10.3	6.4
3.7	1.93	13.7	0.18	5.6	1.9	0.98	8.47	4.12	64.1	2.0	12.7	18.2	6.2
7.1	1.19	5.7	0.06	1.3	0.0	0.02	0.20	3.39	97.9	5.3	33.7	5.3	4.7
3.9	1.78	13.0	0.46	4.0	2.4	0.78	7.22	3.96	69.0	1.5	15.0	24.2	6.0
6.1	3.29	11.1	-0.05	1.6	0.6	0.19	1.22	2.55	100.8	3.8	51.5	18.8	6.6
7.0	0.89	4.4	0.11	4.4	0.3	0.57	3.84	3.77	79.8	2.3	22.6	18.3	6.7
2.1	3.05	24.4	0.05	2.0	0.2	0.16	1.74	3.56	94.0	4.3	13.1	6.3	2.0
5.8	0.55	3.3	0.27	3.7	0.8	0.71	6.83	4.48	77.0	1.8	23.4	22.4	5.4
3.7	6.08	20.9	0.92	1.3	-0.3	-1.98	-11.40	3.66	83.3	3.0	46.2	19.0	5.7
8.1	0.00	0.0	0.05	7.8	1.2	1.90	13.13	4.34	51.0	0.8	17.4	43.9	8.7
4.9	2.56	11.3	0.47	2.9	0.3	0.53	5.18	3.95	89.4	5.9	40.7	4.0	4.5
5.2	0.45	2.8	na	2.4	0.2	0.00	0.00	na	80.7	4.8	23.2	4.3	6.6
8.8	0.00	0.0	0.00	5.6	0.4	1.20	6.60	3.41	50.7	5.6	64.3	11.2	7.6
7.1	0.89	4.9	0.03	6.3	1.8	1.56	14.03	3.63	60.9	1.8	23.5	12.2	7.5
9.1	0.08	0.4	0.01	4.5	0.8	0.93	9.30	3.22	63.6	5.9	42.3	5.1	6.5
2.6	2.96	19.2	0.61	6.2	2.1	1.43	12.56	4.80	62.4	1.2	10.8	18.5	6.4
7.6	0.44	3.3	-0.01	7.3	2.1	1.24	12.29	4.18	57.1	3.0	12.7	13.8	6.0
1.4	7.29	37.9	5.79	6.9	1.3	2.96	28.66	3.85	26.6	0.9	19.2	34.9	4.7
1.5	3.60	28.3	0.04	3.1	0.4	0.43	4.45	4.13	71.4	3.5	14.0	8.5	6.2
6.2	1.28	4.8	0.00	5.7	1.4	1.12	10.42	3.56	57.2	4.7	23.8	5.0	6.1
2.6	4.82	21.6	-0.11	3.1	0.8	0.54	4.80	3.46	79.4	6.5	50.3	3.3	5.6
5.4	1.26	6.6	0.18	6.7	0.6	1.26	13.94	3.17	45.8	4.7	23.2	5.2	5.7
2.1	4.13	23.9	0.36	4.7	0.5	1.17	14.97	4.47	74.8	6.3	49.0	3.5	3.3
5.0	1.00	7.5	0.02	5.4	2.3	1.34	13.93	4.88	74.7	1.3	18.4	28.0	6.1
2.3	5.11	24.6	0.00	4.1	2.6	1.05	10.78	3.84	76.2	5.4	46.3	9.6	5.3
4.5	1.91	9.0	1.07	4.3	0.2	0.72	6.56	4.48	79.3	3.5	23.5	12.1	5.1
8.9	0.28	1.2	0.01	5.4	2.3	1.30	10.25	3.28	63.0	2.4	19.4	17.2	8.1
5.0	1.31	9.7	0.13	4.3	1.7	0.69	6.73	3.92	70.7	1.3	8.9	26.4	6.0
2.0	3.02	22.3	0.60	4.7	1.5	0.79	7.92	3.76	64.3	3.0	15.8	14.2	5.6
8.9	0.00	0.0	0.00	4.2	0.6	0.98	10.91	3.40	74.0	3.5	24.4	12.2	5.7
6.0	1.24	4.9	0.65	4.0	0.6	0.92	6.78	4.10	74.9	4.2	23.2	5.7	5.5
3.8	1.76	10.3	0.28	6.5	34.3	1.18	8.79	3.76	58.2	1.6	6.9	21.3	9.9
7.4	0.10	0.6	-0.01	5.6	1.0	0.95	8.43	4.72	66.1	1.2	24.1	32.3	6.2
3.1	1.06	8.5	-0.10	6.4	4.2	0.89	8.51	4.59	70.1	0.5	3.0	32.2	6.5
5.1	1.07	7.2	0.13	5.3	20.6	0.96	7.25	4.06	62.1	3.9	19.8	7.2	9.0
3.0	1.94	14.5	0.36	3.0	274.6	0.42	3.03	2.73	71.6	2.8	22.7	11.1	8.7
6.2	0.80	7.6	0.34	3.3	0.3	0.72	9.16	2.78	62.5	0.7	16.6	49.5	3.8

Name	City	State	2016 Rating	2015 Rating	2014 Rating	Total Assets ($Mil)	One Year Asset Growth	Asset Mix (As a % of Total Assets)				Capital- ization Index	Lever- age Ratio	Risk- Based Capital Ratio
								Comm- ercial Loans	Cons- umer Loans	Mort- gage Loans	Secur- ities			
Computershare Trust Co., N.A.	Canton	MA	U	U	U	28.5	11.50	0.0	0.0	0.0	0.0	10.0	89.0	229.5
Concorde Bank	Blomkest	MN	C+	C	C-	54.3	1.00	5.3	3.4	22.0	9.4	8.3	9.9	14.8
Concordia Bank	Concordia	MO	B+	A-	B+	63.5	2.68	4.0	1.7	23.4	8.7	8.9	10.3	14.1
Concordia Bank & Trust Co.	Vidalia	LA	B	B	B-	511.1	-1.52	3.1	2.8	13.6	47.3	10.0	12.1	21.7
▼ Congressional Bank	Bethesda	MD	C	C+	C+	836.7	79.63	26.1	5.9	20.2	6.5	9.9	11.0	15.2
Conneaut Savings Bank	Conneaut	OH	C	C-	C-	77.2	-4.15	0.1	0.5	56.8	18.1	10.0	11.2	25.5
Connecticut Community Bank, N.A.	Norwalk	CT	D-	D-	D-	453.9	-5.06	20.9	0.1	5.9	7.8	7.6	9.4	13.4
▲ Connection Bank	Fort Madison	IA	B-	C+	C+	267.2	73.38	7.3	1.7	23.7	21.8	6.1	8.7	11.8
ConnectOne Bank	Englewood Cliffs	NJ	C-	C	B	4326.8	12.78	10.4	0.0	6.6	7.8	5.8	9.6	11.6
Consumers National Bank	Minerva	OH	C+	B-	B-	431.7	4.47	9.1	1.3	8.9	30.4	7.7	9.4	14.7
▲ Continental Bank	Salt Lake City	UT	A-	A-	A	161.3	-1.03	49.2	0.0	0.0	7.0	10.0	16.7	20.4
Continental National Bank	Miami	FL	C+	B-	C+	485.1	16.71	2.1	4.7	12.5	21.7	6.0	8.0	16.1
Converse County Bank	Douglas	WY	B	B+	B+	489.5	-4.71	7.7	5.3	5.9	60.8	7.4	9.3	21.8
▲ Conway Bank, N.A.	Conway Springs	KS	D+	D	D-	62.4	7.17	7.6	0.7	15.3	7.5	8.2	9.8	15.4
Conway National Bank	Conway	SC	B-	C+	C+	1111.2	4.56	4.8	4.6	13.0	48.2	8.0	9.7	19.0
▲ Cooperative Bank	Roslindale	MA	B-	C	C	357.1	9.63	1.0	0.0	44.2	11.1	9.0	10.4	16.9
Cooperative Bank of Cape Cod	Hyannis	MA	C+	C+	C+	875.6	6.78	4.0	0.1	54.4	6.1	7.4	9.2	14.7
Copiah Bank	Hazlehurst	MS	B-	B-	C	206.2	22.95	6.9	3.4	15.3	15.6	7.5	10.3	12.9
Corder Bank	Corder	MO	D+	D+	D	19.7	2.72	8.7	4.7	17.9	11.7	7.7	9.5	18.8
Core Bank	Omaha	NE	C+	C	D+	430.7	6.16	23.8	0.5	13.4	0.7	5.1	9.1	11.1
CoreFirst Bank & Trust	Topeka	KS	D+	D	D	897.5	1.70	9.5	5.1	4.9	29.5	8.2	9.8	13.7
Corn City State Bank	Deshler	OH	B+	B+	B+	63.8	-0.37	0.5	3.3	30.5	47.9	10.0	15.7	38.1
▲ Corn Growers State Bank	Murdock	NE	E+	D-	D-	27.4	5.01	2.7	6.2	10.8	19.4	4.8	6.8	14.9
▼ Corner Stone Bank	South West City	MO	C+	B-	C	144.6	4.15	11.4	9.8	27.7	14.4	10.0	12.5	18.7
Cornerstone Bank	Eureka Springs	AR	C+	C+	B	205.5	12.12	2.9	2.7	16.1	17.2	9.7	10.8	15.3
Cornerstone Bank	Atlanta	GA	E-	E-	E-	241.9	-0.89	9.0	0.6	18.5	14.0	0.7	3.9	8.0
Cornerstone Bank	Clarinda	IA	C+	C+	C	38.8	1.21	2.5	5.7	36.2	6.2	10.0	14.2	30.6
▲ Cornerstone Bank	Overland Park	KS	B-	C	D+	165.4	-1.02	22.8	0.3	16.4	12.0	7.5	10.5	12.9
Cornerstone Bank	Wilson	NC	C-	D	E+	109.1	1.87	12.2	2.0	14.4	14.1	8.4	10.0	16.4
Cornerstone Bank	Fargo	ND	D+	C-	D+	791.6	-0.23	10.0	3.1	12.2	20.0	5.9	8.8	11.7
▼ Cornerstone Bank	York	NE	B-	B+	B+	1471.7	3.63	13.6	1.9	3.4	17.2	5.9	8.6	11.7
▲ Cornerstone Bank	Mount Laurel	NJ	D-	E-	E-	246.5	7.74	8.2	0.1	12.5	22.1	4.1	6.1	10.6
Cornerstone Bank	Watonga	OK	C+	C	C+	169.8	8.07	5.6	5.0	4.8	48.3	6.1	8.1	16.4
Cornerstone Bank, Inc.	West Union	WV	B-	B-	B-	177.3	0.61	2.7	1.2	8.5	55.3	9.0	10.3	29.8
CornerStone Bank, N.A.	Lexington	VA	C	A-	B+	129.3	6.99	5.4	2.4	24.9	7.2	10.0	11.0	15.0
Cornerstone Community Bank	Red Bluff	CA	B	B	B-	195.5	13.46	12.6	1.6	5.8	7.2	7.7	10.5	13.1
Cornerstone Community Bank	Grafton	WI	C+	C+	C	160.6	9.30	10.9	0.0	11.8	0.5	5.2	8.7	11.1
Cornerstone National Bank	Easley	SC	C+	C+	C+	146.3	2.50	2.7	0.8	4.9	30.9	10.0	13.1	22.5
▲ Cornerstone National Bank & Trust Co.	Palatine	IL	A-	B	B-	512.1	1.26	14.5	0.4	7.6	27.3	10.0	11.1	15.5
CornerStone State Bank	Montgomery	MN	B	B	B-	166.6	21.96	10.1	3.3	18.9	26.5	9.1	10.4	14.9
Cornhusker Bank	Lincoln	NE	B	B	B	492.5	6.90	8.8	1.6	15.3	17.1	6.3	8.5	12.0
Cortland Savings and Banking Co.	Cortland	OH	B-	B-	B-	617.6	9.02	9.8	0.5	8.2	26.2	7.3	9.2	14.5
CorTrust Bank N.A.	Mitchell	SD	B	B	B	756.8	7.55	14.3	4.5	5.2	13.7	8.7	11.4	13.9
Corydon State Bank	Corydon	IA	A	A	A	108.3	6.42	10.3	4.1	12.8	13.9	10.0	18.3	24.1
▲ Cottonport Bank	Cottonport	LA	B	B-	B-	329.8	0.94	6.9	3.5	19.1	19.1	10.0	11.7	18.7
Cottonwood Valley Bank	Cedar Point	KS	B-	C-	B-	33.0	-3.80	6.9	1.6	1.5	17.7	10.0	14.0	29.3
Coulee Bank	La Crosse	WI	B	B	B	337.2	4.08	17.4	1.6	10.9	23.2	6.9	8.9	12.7
Country Bank	New York	NY	B-	C+	D+	604.3	11.45	2.1	0.0	13.1	23.9	7.5	9.4	12.9
▲ Country Bank for Savings	Ware	MA	B	C+	C+	1473.6	6.66	2.1	0.4	31.5	24.1	10.0	14.3	20.2
▲ Country Club Bank	Kansas City	MO	B+	B	B-	1346.4	2.27	15.9	0.9	9.6	29.5	6.5	8.5	12.8
Country Club Trust Co., N.A.	Kansas City	MO	U	U	U	17.5	5.29	0.0	0.0	0.0	88.6	10.0	101.	404.7
COUNTRY Trust Bank	Bloomington	IL	U	U	U	28.8	-0.23	0.0	0.0	0.0	80.3	10.0	97.1	172.9
Countryside Bank	Countryside	IL	C	D+	C-	573.2	0.29	5.9	0.1	6.0	19.3	7.3	9.2	13.0
Countryside Bank	Unadilla	NE	B	B	B	76.9	0.76	4.8	4.6	17.0	28.2	10.0	15.7	25.8
▲ County Bank	Rehoboth Beach	DE	D+	D	D+	345.0	-0.57	5.7	2.0	13.1	9.7	9.4	10.7	14.5
▲ County Bank	Sigourney	IA	B	B-	B	125.9	8.45	13.6	2.3	9.6	2.1	8.4	11.1	13.7
County Bank	Brunswick	MO	B-	B-	B-	83.1	5.37	6.6	4.1	25.5	9.1	5.9	8.0	11.7
County First Bank	La Plata	MD	C-	C-	C-	227.0	1.91	4.1	0.2	10.8	20.8	10.0	11.0	16.4
County Savings Bank	Essington	PA	D+	C-	C-	73.2	16.30	0.0	0.4	41.7	6.3	4.8	6.8	20.5
Countybank	Greenwood	SC	B-	B-	C+	379.0	8.35	4.6	2.0	29.3	27.9	6.0	8.0	12.2

Asset Quality Index	Adjusted Non-Performing Loans as a % of Total Loans	as a % of Capital	Net Charge-Offs Avg Loans	Profitability Index	Net Income ($Mil)	Return on Assets (R.O.A.)	Return on Equity (R.O.E.)	Net Interest Spread	Overhead Efficiency Ratio	Liquidity Index	Liquidity Ratio	Hot Money Ratio	Stability Index
6.5	na	0.0	na	10.0	3.0	15.03	16.45	0.77	73.8	4.0	na	0.0	6.6
4.3	2.01	13.1	0.01	5.2	0.5	1.32	13.66	4.08	67.8	3.8	26.1	11.2	5.1
7.2	0.22	1.5	0.75	3.8	0.3	0.62	6.14	4.32	76.3	4.8	21.1	4.2	5.5
7.6	1.46	5.3	0.01	4.6	4.7	1.22	10.05	3.23	67.3	2.4	35.6	24.0	7.9
2.6	2.68	18.6	0.13	7.3	7.5	1.26	12.72	4.95	71.1	2.1	20.0	17.8	5.8
8.1	1.24	6.8	0.03	2.7	0.2	0.39	3.58	3.18	81.7	5.1	35.5	7.0	4.5
1.3	3.01	21.1	0.04	0.2	-1.4	-0.40	-4.22	3.51	107.4	3.7	21.2	11.2	3.3
5.7	0.67	4.6	0.02	6.3	2.1	1.52	17.87	4.91	74.4	5.0	29.8	5.8	5.6
2.3	2.00	15.8	0.10	5.6	35.5	1.13	8.93	3.47	41.9	1.3	12.4	18.2	9.2
5.1	1.05	6.2	0.12	3.4	1.8	0.55	5.63	3.76	75.4	4.4	25.3	7.7	5.6
5.4	2.16	9.9	0.74	10.0	4.8	3.91	22.73	8.52	44.4	0.3	15.4	9.1	8.2
6.5	0.47	2.9	0.06	3.1	1.8	0.52	6.27	3.40	79.6	6.1	47.6	5.4	4.3
9.0	0.02	0.1	0.10	4.3	3.9	1.02	11.29	2.13	58.5	2.3	37.3	28.4	5.8
3.9	2.07	14.0	-0.10	1.4	0.1	0.16	1.20	3.60	97.5	4.4	23.4	7.2	5.2
6.5	1.32	5.5	0.18	4.3	6.4	0.81	8.32	3.08	66.3	4.4	43.6	16.4	6.9
5.3	1.11	7.9	0.00	5.1	3.1	1.22	11.79	3.24	62.9	2.9	21.2	14.9	6.0
4.5	1.76	15.0	0.03	3.1	2.9	0.46	4.87	3.08	78.1	4.1	11.6	7.3	5.9
4.7	1.54	10.1	0.45	4.5	0.9	0.68	6.52	4.59	79.6	3.2	23.5	13.9	5.2
1.2	4.75	27.8	0.02	4.1	0.1	0.70	7.15	3.62	61.2	3.6	34.7	13.2	5.5
3.7	0.78	7.0	0.18	5.8	3.6	1.10	12.98	3.95	73.1	4.7	3.5	2.4	4.1
1.6	4.43	24.4	0.14	2.8	3.9	0.57	5.87	3.14	88.7	5.0	17.1	2.2	4.4
9.6	0.00	0.0	0.00	4.6	0.5	1.15	7.37	2.83	57.4	3.9	41.2	15.8	8.5
4.8	1.54	10.6	1.99	0.3	-0.1	-0.54	-8.01	3.12	85.1	6.0	42.7	3.8	1.6
2.2	4.15	23.4	0.15	8.0	2.0	1.91	15.52	5.49	64.4	1.0	15.5	31.7	7.8
3.0	2.51	15.1	0.14	7.2	2.3	1.54	14.57	4.71	67.6	1.2	7.9	22.8	7.2
1.7	3.09	40.3	-0.67	2.3	0.9	0.52	14.36	3.45	95.6	1.6	27.1	28.3	0.3
6.1	2.12	8.4	-0.11	2.3	0.1	0.29	2.07	3.37	90.5	2.8	42.6	23.8	5.6
5.6	1.65	10.6	-0.11	4.3	1.2	1.02	9.95	3.66	72.2	4.9	14.1	2.8	4.9
4.7	1.34	8.3	0.30	4.4	2.4	2.99	28.84	3.38	82.9	2.1	27.2	21.1	2.4
1.1	3.72	27.1	0.00	3.4	2.7	0.45	4.80	3.90	73.2	3.2	6.4	12.1	5.4
3.4	2.21	17.4	-0.03	7.1	17.6	1.65	18.11	3.97	61.2	2.4	7.2	16.5	9.0
3.1	2.09	17.8	-0.06	0.3	-0.3	-0.14	-2.36	3.11	104.4	2.7	36.8	20.8	0.0
6.4	0.59	2.6	-0.06	3.3	0.8	0.60	8.12	3.67	83.3	5.0	47.9	11.9	3.4
8.9	1.43	2.8	0.00	3.6	0.9	0.72	7.13	2.71	66.9	4.2	79.9	24.0	5.7
3.0	2.68	18.0	-0.11	4.7	0.5	0.54	4.92	4.21	77.6	1.3	15.5	28.3	6.1
7.3	0.07	0.5	0.00	4.8	1.1	0.81	7.34	3.97	67.4	1.6	21.6	21.5	6.3
4.1	0.63	5.5	0.02	5.5	1.1	0.95	10.99	4.25	58.5	1.3	8.2	10.8	4.8
7.9	0.04	0.2	0.00	3.1	0.5	0.49	3.73	3.29	81.5	4.7	44.4	12.5	6.6
5.6	1.46	7.6	-0.02	5.3	3.3	0.88	7.81	3.20	66.5	5.3	35.6	5.8	7.2
4.8	1.83	9.5	-0.10	4.9	1.3	1.07	10.23	3.67	69.5	4.3	27.2	9.1	6.0
6.1	0.41	3.2	0.01	5.1	4.1	1.13	12.98	3.64	71.9	2.9	13.7	14.4	6.4
4.9	1.04	6.9	0.11	4.3	3.8	0.85	9.27	3.66	74.8	2.7	12.9	13.1	5.5
7.6	0.21	1.4	0.37	4.7	4.1	0.74	6.28	4.62	74.0	2.7	4.3	14.6	7.0
4.7	2.04	8.8	0.60	10.0	2.3	2.87	15.25	4.76	20.5	0.9	19.3	35.1	8.7
5.8	1.20	6.6	0.20	4.1	1.9	0.77	6.63	4.10	74.8	3.1	23.4	14.4	5.2
9.1	0.94	1.8	-0.09	3.8	0.2	0.93	6.50	3.35	71.9	5.5	65.6	11.8	5.9
5.7	0.72	5.5	0.00	5.0	2.8	1.13	12.15	3.56	67.5	4.7	19.4	4.3	6.7
4.2	1.26	9.2	-0.04	5.3	4.4	0.97	10.88	4.19	60.7	0.8	15.8	28.0	4.7
5.7	1.83	9.0	0.06	4.0	7.0	0.66	4.39	3.24	67.6	2.4	28.1	26.2	8.7
7.7	0.47	3.2	0.05	5.3	13.2	1.30	14.90	3.61	76.9	5.2	24.8	5.2	7.9
10.0	na	0.0	na	9.5	0.7	5.70	5.68	0.75	90.3	4.0	na	0.0	7.0
10.0	na	0.0	na	10.0	2.5	12.51	12.90	2.44	87.0	4.0	na	0.0	8.0
2.9	1.72	10.5	0.67	6.8	6.9	1.59	15.98	4.65	62.3	4.4	26.0	7.5	5.2
8.6	0.01	0.1	-0.01	4.3	0.6	1.05	6.90	3.19	68.8	5.3	39.9	8.2	7.7
2.2	3.65	21.8	1.51	4.0	1.6	0.63	5.62	4.19	67.9	4.7	26.6	5.8	5.4
5.0	0.71	4.8	0.30	6.3	0.9	0.99	8.93	4.88	64.4	3.4	11.2	11.8	6.9
8.3	0.01	0.1	-0.03	4.6	0.7	1.10	13.71	4.07	74.6	2.7	5.4	13.8	5.3
2.5	3.60	20.0	-0.21	3.3	0.7	0.40	3.66	3.55	80.9	4.5	30.8	9.0	6.3
7.2	0.66	4.7	0.00	2.3	0.1	0.19	2.69	3.05	90.9	5.5	46.1	8.1	2.8
5.7	0.56	4.0	0.00	4.9	3.4	1.25	15.83	3.44	81.6	5.1	23.0	2.7	4.8

Name	City	State	2015 Rating	2014 Rating	Total Assets ($Mil)	One Year Asset Growth	Commercial Loans	Consumer Loans	Mortgage Loans	Securities	Capitalization Index	Leverage Ratio	Risk-Based Capital Ratio
Covenant Bank	Leeds	AL	E-	E-	D-	64.5	-13.45	10.0	2.0	18.5	21.6	4.2	6.2	11.3
▲ Covenant Bank	Doylestown	PA	D+	D+	C+	316.9	25.63	20.6	0.1	9.3	9.3	7.9	11.0	13.2
Covington County Bank	Collins	MS	C+	C+	B-	71.3	6.70	5.7	3.7	7.4	32.8	6.4	9.4	12.1
Covington S&L Assn.	Covington	OH	C	C-	C	66.9	2.34	0.1	0.5	36.7	36.7	10.0	15.0	39.4
Cowboy Bank of Texas	Maypearl	TX	B+	B+	B+	78.4	16.76	0.8	6.4	34.8	13.8	8.0	9.7	14.9
Cowboy State Bank	Ranchester	WY	C	C-	D	46.2	11.36	10.5	3.9	12.0	20.4	7.7	9.5	13.2
Crawford County Trust and Savings Bank	Denison	IA	B	B	B-	133.8	-0.66	4.0	4.4	12.6	5.4	5.9	8.7	11.7
Credit First N.A.	Brook Park	OH	U	U	U	52.2	9.42	0.0	0.0	0.0	0.0	10.0	98.0	474.8
Credit One Bank, N.A.	Las Vegas	NV	U	U	U	194.3	14.70	0.0	0.0	0.0	1.6	10.0	52.9	122.8
Crescent Bank & Trust	New Orleans	LA	D+	D+	D	1065.6	4.97	1.3	85.1	1.5	8.6	8.4	11.4	13.7
CresCom Bank	Charleston	SC	A-	A-	B+	1652.8	24.42	8.0	0.4	26.4	20.5	8.7	10.1	14.8
Crest Savings Bank	Wildwood	NJ	C+	C+	C+	457.9	3.27	0.8	1.7	56.8	4.9	5.8	7.8	13.7
Crestmark Bank	Troy	MI	B-	B	B-	876.1	14.69	57.3	4.4	0.2	2.3	5.7	10.1	11.5
Crockett National Bank	San Antonio	TX	A-	A-	A-	619.7	9.85	2.0	0.1	38.4	4.2	8.6	10.1	14.5
Croghan Colonial Bank	Fremont	OH	B-	C+	C+	806.7	4.08	7.1	6.3	13.4	21.9	8.2	9.8	13.6
Crookston National Bank	Crookston	MN	B-	B-	C+	62.9	5.34	6.3	2.8	12.8	20.1	7.3	9.2	16.0
Cross County Bank	Wynne	AR	A-	A-	A-	236.7	0.83	4.8	1.2	10.9	4.8	10.0	11.8	15.6
Cross County Savings Bank	Middle Village	NY	B	B	B-	381.9	-1.03	0.0	0.0	46.4	9.9	10.0	11.8	21.2
Cross Keys Bank	Saint Joseph	LA	B+	A-	A-	342.1	7.04	10.4	0.9	12.2	29.6	10.0	11.9	17.0
Cross River Bank	Teaneck	NJ	A	A-	A-	543.3	27.13	5.8	33.2	9.4	2.0	10.0	11.9	15.0
CrossFirst Bank	Leawood	KS	C+	C+	C+	1921.3	28.67	26.0	0.6	3.6	29.0	5.0	8.7	11.0
Crossroads Bank	Effingham	IL	A-	A-	A-	159.4	6.61	15.0	2.0	12.7	13.3	10.0	13.4	16.5
Crossroads Bank	Wabash	IN	C+	C+	C-	345.4	3.95	8.3	3.9	26.7	22.0	8.3	9.9	14.4
Crowell State Bank	Crowell	TX	B-	B-	C+	35.0	0.08	12.7	6.7	7.8	21.8	9.1	10.4	16.9
Crown Bank	Edina	MN	C+	C	D+	217.4	2.14	45.3	2.5	8.3	0.2	7.0	9.9	12.5
Crown Bank	Elizabeth	NJ	D	D	D	500.0	-2.67	4.9	0.0	4.1	7.3	10.0	14.6	19.3
Crystal Lake Bank & Trust Co., N.A.	Crystal Lake	IL	B-	C+	C+	946.3	5.14	27.1	17.4	2.9	18.0	5.8	9.3	11.6
CSB Bank	Capac	MI	C+	C+	C	254.2	4.14	3.8	1.7	23.0	36.7	6.9	8.9	16.4
CTBC Bank Corp. (USA)	Los Angeles	CA	B-	B-	B-	2914.0	13.40	8.0	0.0	25.1	8.6	10.0	12.8	18.5
▲ Culbertson Bank	Culbertson	NE	C+	C-	C-	15.4	-1.34	4.2	1.0	0.3	46.2	10.0	14.1	30.6
Cullman Savings Bank	Cullman	AL	A-	A-	A-	273.4	13.01	3.6	1.2	42.3	7.9	10.0	15.7	22.3
Cumberland Bank & Trust	Clarksville	TN	B	B	C+	179.0	4.10	10.2	1.1	14.1	9.4	8.8	11.1	14.0
Cumberland Federal Bank, FSB	Cumberland	WI	B	B	B	125.3	12.62	1.8	1.7	26.2	47.1	9.9	10.9	21.4
Cumberland Security Bank, Inc.	Somerset	KY	A	A-	A-	185.3	10.02	6.5	3.4	29.4	12.7	10.0	13.0	18.5
Cumberland Valley National B&T Co.	London	KY	C	C	C-	440.4	0.08	7.5	2.3	13.5	19.9	9.0	10.4	15.0
▼ Currie State Bank	Currie	MN	C-	C	C-	70.4	3.25	7.0	1.8	8.3	1.9	5.1	8.8	11.1
▼ CUSB Bank	Cresco	IA	B	B+	B+	476.0	2.19	9.5	4.1	10.2	21.3	6.7	11.7	12.3
Custer Federal State Bank	Broken Bow	NE	B-	B-	C+	121.5	0.80	8.4	5.6	18.2	6.8	5.5	8.7	11.4
Customers Bank	Phoenixville	PA	B-	B-	C+	9574.3	26.37	7.0	0.8	3.8	5.4	6.2	8.2	11.9
Cypress Bank, SSB	Pittsburg	TX	B-	B-	C+	175.3	-0.82	5.0	8.9	36.8	22.1	8.6	10.1	18.5
D.A. Davidson Trust Co.	Great Falls	MT	U	U	U	6.6	2.02	0.0	0.0	0.0	83.5	10.0	78.0	186.4
D.L. Evans Bank	Burley	ID	B+	B+	B	1271.8	7.38	9.2	2.2	4.8	22.9	7.3	9.2	14.0
Dacotah Bank	Aberdeen	SD	B	B	B	2271.8	4.53	11.4	2.7	4.7	11.5	8.0	10.7	13.3
Dairy State Bank	Rice Lake	WI	B-	C+	C+	488.9	-3.23	9.3	1.1	9.6	54.4	10.0	11.7	26.0
Dairyland State Bank	Bruce	WI	B-	B-	B-	82.2	-1.43	5.7	2.3	23.4	8.7	7.6	9.4	14.0
Dakota Community Bank & Trust, N.A.	Hebron	ND	B+	B+	B+	752.2	-1.86	10.0	1.6	5.1	23.4	6.5	8.5	13.3
Dakota Heritage Bank of North Dakota	Hunter	ND	B+	B+	B+	203.7	2.37	7.7	3.2	2.9	15.8	6.6	9.4	12.2
Dakota Prairie Bank	Fort Pierre	SD	B+	B+	B	79.2	0.63	12.9	3.4	1.9	10.0	10.0	11.1	15.3
▼ Dakota Western Bank	Bowman	ND	A-	A	A	251.3	-2.78	9.7	2.5	2.0	25.9	10.0	11.8	15.5
Dalhart Federal S&L Assn., SSB	Dalhart	TX	C+	C+	C+	110.5	3.68	0.5	2.1	49.2	30.9	9.6	10.8	25.1
Dallas Capital Bank, N.A.	Dallas	TX	C-	D+	D	751.3	31.45	4.4	0.0	6.1	28.7	7.6	9.4	14.0
Damariscotta Bank & Trust Co.	Damariscotta	ME	C	C	C-	187.7	5.80	3.4	1.3	31.8	16.5	7.2	9.1	16.5
Damascus Community Bank	Damascus	MD	D+	D+	D	314.4	8.61	11.0	18.9	17.0	15.1	5.6	8.0	11.5
▲ Danville State Savings Bank	Danville	IA	B+	B+	B+	153.6	2.75	2.8	3.1	17.0	63.3	10.0	11.4	25.3
Darien Rowayton Bank	Darien	CT	C-	D+	C-	599.1	-14.45	0.4	40.8	18.1	1.6	6.2	8.8	11.9
Dart Bank	Mason	MI	B-	C+	C-	351.4	14.75	5.6	1.0	25.4	17.4	7.7	9.9	13.1
Davis Trust Co.	Elkins	WV	B-	B-	B-	146.7	2.56	4.8	2.8	14.0	16.3	10.0	12.2	18.8
De Witt Bank & Trust Co.	De Witt	IA	B+	B+	B+	159.4	6.76	10.7	2.3	8.2	24.4	8.9	10.4	14.1
Dean Co-operative Bank	Franklin	MA	C+	C	C	282.6	8.10	2.6	0.7	46.7	18.7	6.9	8.9	14.9
Dearborn Federal Savings Bank	Dearborn	MI	B	B	B-	261.3	-2.16	0.0	0.1	66.7	3.9	10.0	27.0	54.7

Asset Quality Index	Adjusted Non-Performing Loans as a % of Total Loans	as a % of Capital	Net Charge-Offs Avg Loans	Profitability Index	Net Income ($Mil)	Return on Assets (R.O.A.)	Return on Equity (R.O.E.)	Net Interest Spread	Overhead Efficiency Ratio	Liquidity Index	Liquidity Ratio	Hot Money Ratio	Stability Index
1.7	3.50	30.0	1.06	0.0	-0.5	-0.84	-14.00	3.03	123.3	1.6	12.0	21.4	0.8
2.2	2.09	15.2	0.14	1.6	0.4	0.20	1.94	4.08	87.6	2.6	10.3	15.4	5.5
6.5	0.89	4.4	0.11	3.9	0.4	0.65	6.56	3.84	77.4	2.4	37.7	26.5	4.8
10.0	0.70	2.0	-0.01	2.1	0.2	0.30	2.00	2.55	87.9	6.3	54.7	4.3	6.8
7.1	0.34	2.5	0.00	9.8	1.3	2.36	24.37	4.36	56.4	1.0	13.9	31.6	6.3
4.5	2.04	12.3	-0.54	4.5	0.4	1.09	11.49	5.12	79.5	3.7	26.4	12.2	4.3
7.0	0.04	0.3	0.06	6.8	1.6	1.62	18.87	3.64	58.2	3.9	15.5	9.4	6.3
10.0	na	0.0	na	9.5	8.6	22.70	23.60	0.00	59.1	4.0	na	100.0	6.5
8.0	na	0.0	na	10.0	75.8	60.57	102.07	0.47	77.7	4.1	137.9	100.0	9.5
1.1	3.42	20.6	5.25	7.2	12.8	1.61	13.91	12.37	47.9	0.6	12.7	54.8	9.5
8.0	0.37	2.5	-0.03	6.1	13.1	1.16	11.25	3.72	69.3	1.9	22.4	17.2	7.8
6.8	0.36	3.6	-0.01	3.0	1.4	0.42	5.21	3.09	80.2	3.5	12.7	11.4	4.4
3.6	1.53	10.8	0.43	10.0	10.7	2.26	21.62	9.43	77.0	0.2	9.2	96.3	9.1
7.2	0.27	2.3	0.03	9.8	11.7	3.36	34.07	3.75	74.1	0.8	5.5	32.9	8.6
4.2	0.94	6.4	0.06	5.8	6.9	1.15	8.93	4.27	65.0	4.3	9.3	6.0	7.5
8.7	0.00	0.0	0.00	4.3	0.5	1.10	12.13	3.11	66.0	4.8	33.8	8.9	4.8
6.1	0.79	4.9	0.06	7.0	1.9	1.08	8.95	4.68	60.3	1.6	10.1	21.9	7.1
6.6	1.62	9.2	-0.04	3.8	1.3	0.45	3.80	4.05	79.9	4.6	25.8	6.6	6.2
8.8	0.16	0.8	0.17	4.8	2.7	1.10	8.49	4.16	72.3	2.0	31.3	26.3	7.2
6.8	0.13	0.8	0.52	10.0	9.3	2.76	25.19	6.36	46.6	2.7	17.4	15.7	7.6
8.3	0.19	1.3	0.10	3.2	8.4	0.64	6.72	3.35	66.2	2.7	34.8	25.0	7.4
7.3	0.00	0.0	0.00	6.0	1.3	1.05	8.04	3.22	51.2	3.8	22.0	10.7	8.0
3.8	2.32	14.7	0.23	6.0	3.0	1.17	11.20	3.88	64.8	2.7	21.4	15.9	5.8
7.4	0.28	1.5	0.05	7.9	0.6	2.02	20.96	4.16	57.9	1.3	14.3	28.0	5.8
5.0	0.27	2.1	0.06	4.7	1.9	1.16	12.27	4.37	74.6	2.1	13.3	18.4	3.9
0.0	8.02	32.3	-0.40	6.7	6.6	1.70	11.40	3.97	64.0	1.0	25.5	38.0	8.8
3.6	0.72	5.6	0.24	4.6	5.9	0.82	9.13	2.77	51.7	1.5	10.4	19.5	6.2
6.7	0.84	4.8	0.31	3.5	1.2	0.63	6.73	3.22	78.7	6.2	45.4	4.0	5.0
8.7	0.03	0.2	-0.03	3.9	13.8	0.65	4.40	3.05	65.6	2.4	13.2	17.1	10.0
8.9	0.00	0.0	-0.07	2.8	0.1	0.58	4.14	3.90	84.4	5.3	60.3	10.1	4.7
6.1	1.75	8.9	0.05	6.0	2.0	1.07	6.83	4.17	59.4	0.8	12.1	29.5	8.0
4.7	1.90	11.9	0.01	6.2	1.4	1.03	9.29	4.20	61.1	1.5	18.8	19.3	6.9
6.1	1.26	5.5	0.00	4.9	0.8	0.92	8.26	3.17	58.6	2.1	40.5	33.4	6.9
8.5	0.33	1.7	0.01	9.5	3.1	2.25	17.38	4.37	56.3	3.7	21.5	11.0	8.6
5.2	1.05	6.1	-0.02	2.6	1.3	0.40	3.82	3.38	86.4	2.4	21.9	17.7	6.2
2.1	1.74	16.4	0.05	9.6	0.8	1.46	17.14	5.03	49.3	0.4	3.4	21.4	6.0
4.1	3.45	19.5	0.12	6.2	5.1	1.43	11.45	3.55	49.9	1.9	21.0	20.5	8.5
3.3	1.17	10.6	-0.03	5.5	0.7	0.78	8.90	3.84	58.3	0.5	2.4	43.1	5.2
6.1	0.28	2.9	0.02	5.3	63.7	0.94	12.66	2.91	54.1	0.6	6.2	27.2	6.1
5.6	0.79	5.2	0.07	4.1	0.9	0.64	6.44	3.86	74.6	1.3	26.9	33.1	5.6
10.0	na	0.0	na	10.0	0.1	2.62	3.35	2.23	94.8	10.0	356.7	0.0	7.0
7.5	0.59	3.8	0.02	5.9	9.9	1.08	11.37	4.28	65.8	4.3	21.2	8.7	8.8
4.6	1.76	12.1	0.18	5.8	16.3	0.97	8.92	4.00	63.1	3.4	8.6	11.4	8.9
6.2	2.74	8.5	0.05	3.6	2.3	0.64	5.20	2.99	71.7	4.9	48.0	12.5	6.5
6.2	0.71	5.1	-0.03	3.8	0.5	0.77	7.58	4.08	81.0	4.2	24.2	8.7	6.0
6.2	0.70	5.0	0.00	7.5	9.8	1.74	19.90	3.81	58.8	3.7	25.8	11.4	7.3
6.7	0.10	0.7	0.02	6.8	2.4	1.59	15.37	4.31	56.6	3.4	11.1	11.7	7.2
6.8	0.17	1.1	0.20	6.5	0.9	1.50	14.29	4.18	62.2	1.4	15.7	25.6	7.2
4.9	1.72	9.2	0.44	7.2	2.9	1.58	12.89	4.27	53.5	3.1	4.7	12.3	8.7
9.1	0.38	2.0	0.06	3.4	0.5	0.58	5.26	4.08	81.0	1.9	39.3	44.2	6.0
8.2	0.15	0.9	0.00	1.7	1.3	0.26	2.24	2.23	83.8	1.8	39.1	22.7	4.6
3.6	2.89	18.9	0.06	2.8	0.5	0.38	3.98	3.30	82.5	3.9	30.4	12.2	4.8
3.2	1.12	9.6	-0.22	2.0	0.4	0.19	2.24	3.27	94.3	1.7	17.3	22.0	3.8
5.0	5.21	14.7	0.05	6.4	1.8	1.60	13.59	3.20	51.8	5.3	72.7	15.2	7.3
6.7	0.02	0.1	0.05	2.5	1.7	0.39	4.15	2.61	86.1	1.0	25.2	42.2	3.4
3.9	2.41	16.1	0.17	4.3	2.0	0.80	7.95	4.21	84.9	3.9	15.0	9.2	5.2
5.0	2.32	9.6	0.08	3.5	0.7	0.62	5.97	4.10	81.1	4.9	35.2	8.2	4.8
6.9	0.64	4.0	0.07	5.5	1.8	1.47	13.45	3.38	70.2	4.2	27.1	9.9	7.2
4.5	1.85	14.0	0.06	3.4	1.1	0.55	6.16	3.61	81.6	4.2	21.2	8.2	5.0
8.4	1.33	3.4	0.04	4.8	1.6	0.80	3.00	3.23	72.1	4.2	32.6	11.7	7.2

Name	City	State	2015 Rating	2014 Rating	Rating	Total Assets ($Mil)	One Year Asset Growth	Comm-ercial Loans	Cons-umer Loans	Mort-gage Loans	Secur-ities	Capital-ization Index	Lever-age Ratio	Risk-Based Capital Ratio
Dearborn Savings Bank	Lawrenceburg	IN	B	B	B	125.1	6.62	0.9	0.2	48.0	4.0	10.0	13.6	24.3
▲ Decatur County Bank	Decaturville	TN	C	C-	C-	90.2	1.55	6.0	14.8	12.7	29.8	6.8	8.8	13.5
Decorah Bank & Trust Co.	Decorah	IA	A	A	A	403.1	2.37	13.5	2.9	10.8	20.2	10.0	11.5	16.4
Dedham Institution for Savings	Dedham	MA	C+	C+	C+	1377.1	5.05	1.1	0.1	46.2	20.6	9.8	10.9	15.9
Dedicated Community Bank	Darlington	SC	C	C+	C+	59.6	20.40	11.0	3.4	19.7	17.4	8.4	9.9	16.9
Deerwood Bank	Deerwood	MN	C+	C	C	505.3	-4.20	13.7	1.0	8.4	5.1	9.1	11.0	14.3
Defiance State Bank	Defiance	IA	D+	E-	C-	33.4	3.37	6.8	6.1	7.7	4.4	5.7	8.5	11.6
Del Norte Bank	Del Norte	CO	C+	C+	C+	71.1	21.32	3.9	1.0	29.2	10.1	7.1	9.0	13.4
Delanco Federal Savings Bank	Delanco	NJ	D	D-	D-	128.9	0.95	1.6	0.5	52.5	16.2	6.9	8.9	17.5
Delaware County Bank and Trust Co.	Powell	OH	D+	C	D+	566.2	4.35	5.9	1.3	29.1	16.9	6.8	8.8	13.4
Delaware National Bank of Delhi	Delhi	NY	C+	C+	C+	309.3	9.96	5.0	1.1	15.8	35.4	6.9	8.9	25.3
Delaware Place Bank	Chicago	IL	D	D-	D	233.1	-10.22	43.3	0.2	2.3	17.8	5.9	8.3	11.7
Delta Bank	Vidalia	LA	B	B	B	265.9	4.51	7.1	2.5	16.6	19.4	6.1	8.1	12.1
Delta Bank, N.A.	Manteca	CA	D-	D-	D-	112.2	7.64	3.6	0.0	0.8	38.4	5.1	7.1	17.7
Delta National Bank and Trust Co.	New York	NY	C	C	C	432.2	-5.74	12.5	0.6	0.0	35.6	10.0	12.5	26.8
DeMotte State Bank	Demotte	IN	B	B	B-	388.5	4.99	11.2	1.0	16.1	35.4	10.0	12.6	20.7
Denali State Bank	Fairbanks	AK	B-	B-	B-	275.5	-0.28	6.9	5.0	8.0	34.5	9.1	10.4	18.3
Denison State Bank	Holton	KS	A-	B	B	319.8	6.12	7.3	2.3	14.7	34.4	10.0	12.5	19.1
Denmark State Bank	Denmark	WI	B+	B+	B-	432.2	4.72	12.2	2.4	11.0	14.8	10.0	11.3	15.8
Denver Savings Bank	Denver	IA	B-	B-	B-	155.7	10.17	7.0	1.6	18.9	31.8	7.5	9.3	13.3
Department Stores National Bank	Sioux Falls	SD	B+	B+	B	424.7	-9.51	0.0	15.5	0.0	0.0	10.0	15.2	40.0
Depository Trust Co.	New York	NY	U	U	U	4370.7	44.26	0.0	0.0	0.0	0.0	10.0	15.4	53.0
Desjardins Bank, N.A.	Hallandale	FL	C+	C+	C+	214.6	0.83	0.9	3.8	60.4	10.7	10.0	13.2	27.7
Deutsche Bank National Trust Co.	Los Angeles	CA	U	U	U	226.0	17.55	0.0	0.0	0.0	43.3	10.0	77.9	298.5
Deutsche Bank Trust Co. Americas	New York	NY	B	B	B+	54669.0	2.35	4.0	0.2	5.9	0.0	10.0	16.3	63.0
Deutsche Bank Trust Co. Delaware	Wilmington	DE	B+	B+	A-	328.9	-2.38	10.7	0.2	0.0	1.2	10.0	95.8	125.1
Deutsche Bank Trust Co., N.A.	New York	NY	U	U	U	135.0	1.76	0.0	0.0	0.0	75.0	10.0	91.0	649.5
Devon Bank	Chicago	IL	D+	D+	D	256.6	2.00	13.0	2.3	16.9	11.6	5.8	8.4	11.6
Dewey Bank	Dewey	IL	D+	C-	C-	23.3	-6.76	1.7	0.7	7.7	37.7	7.2	9.1	16.7
DeWitt Bank and Trust Co.	De Witt	AR	B+	A-	A-	106.2	-17.05	6.4	0.4	2.3	37.7	10.0	20.5	34.1
DeWitt Savings Bank	Clinton	IL	C	C+	C+	106.9	6.58	0.0	13.1	31.9	35.6	10.0	11.9	25.6
Diamond Bank	Murfreesboro	AR	B+	B+	B+	514.1	6.59	4.1	2.6	20.0	25.0	8.4	9.9	15.0
Dickinson County Bank	Enterprise	KS	C	C-	D+	10.3	-5.99	8.5	8.3	39.1	7.6	10.0	12.2	22.2
Dieterich Bank, N.A.	Dieterich	IL	B	B	B	599.7	1.61	9.1	1.8	11.6	25.3	8.3	10.0	13.6
Dilley State Bank	Dilley	TX	B+	B+	A-	124.6	-4.23	1.2	1.0	0.2	78.4	10.0	16.6	58.5
Dime Bank	Norwich	CT	C-	C-	C	810.5	2.69	4.5	0.1	33.2	19.8	7.4	10.9	12.8
Dime Bank	Honesdale	PA	C	D+	D	637.5	4.26	11.8	1.3	14.2	15.9	8.4	10.7	13.7
Dime Community Bank	Brooklyn	NY	B+	A-	B	5806.7	20.59	0.0	0.0	1.2	0.2	5.9	9.0	11.7
Discover Bank	Greenwood	DE	C	C	C	89341.4	6.00	0.2	81.8	0.2	2.9	10.0	11.7	16.1
Dixon Bank	Dixon	KY	B	B	B	86.1	-2.35	3.8	5.3	6.1	62.9	10.0	21.3	48.5
DMB Community Bank	De Forest	WI	A-	B+	B-	429.2	11.94	1.6	0.7	17.9	11.0	9.7	11.0	14.7
DNB First, N.A.	Downingtown	PA	B-	C+	C+	763.5	2.90	5.0	0.8	10.1	25.8	7.1	9.1	13.2
DNB National Bank	Clear Lake	SD	C+	C+	C+	70.8	7.84	5.5	1.1	7.6	42.1	7.5	9.3	18.9
Dollar Bank, Federal Savings Bank	Pittsburgh	PA	B-	B	B	7508.4	4.16	7.1	1.8	58.5	12.8	10.0	11.6	19.0
Dolores State Bank	Dolores	CO	A-	B+	A-	237.2	0.25	4.8	4.1	26.7	35.3	10.0	12.6	23.4
Donley County State Bank	Clarendon	TX	C	C+	C+	38.7	-3.92	4.3	2.5	0.1	30.1	10.0	19.5	58.2
Doolin Security Savings Bank, FSB	New Martinsville	WV	D-	D-	D	46.6	-5.93	0.0	4.6	12.4	37.8	9.2	10.5	36.7
Douglas National Bank	Douglas	GA	A	A	A-	172.5	7.45	8.1	2.9	20.2	8.4	10.0	12.2	15.8
Drake Bank	Saint Paul	MN	B+	B+	B	99.7	13.24	29.8	1.6	16.1	4.8	9.3	10.5	16.4
Drummond Community Bank	Chiefland	FL	A-	A-	A-	443.5	19.55	3.8	2.5	16.7	41.9	10.0	12.9	23.2
DSRM National Bank	Albuquerque	NM	U	U	U	3.7	-0.13	0.0	0.0	0.0	60.5	10.0	85.1	266.0
Du Quoin State Bank	Du Quoin	IL	B+	A-	B+	108.9	4.10	4.5	1.5	15.3	58.3	6.2	8.3	21.0
Dublin National Bank	Dublin	TX	C-	C	D	31.9	-7.64	2.8	3.5	2.4	72.6	10.0	12.0	54.2
Dubuque Bank and Trust Co.	Dubuque	IA	B+	B+	B	1448.8	0.19	12.9	0.8	12.5	17.4	7.0	9.5	12.5
Durand State Bank	Durand	IL	B	B-	C+	95.1	1.62	5.2	4.8	18.6	32.0	10.0	11.4	18.6
Durden Banking Co., Inc.	Twin City	GA	A-	B+	B+	161.9	3.22	6.6	5.1	28.3	24.6	10.0	15.1	25.9
▲ Dutton State Bank	Dutton	MT	C+	B	B-	57.3	-2.66	16.6	4.4	11.7	0.5	8.1	11.5	13.4
Dysart State Bank	Dysart	IA	E	D-	D-	14.5	-7.86	2.0	2.7	20.4	3.0	5.9	7.9	14.1
▲ E*TRADE Bank	Arlington	VA	B	C	C	35648.3	21.00	0.0	0.8	6.8	84.6	6.5	8.5	38.0
E*TRADE Savings Bank	Arlington	VA	B	B-	C+	1883.8	59.93	0.0	0.0	3.8	79.7	10.0	11.9	69.2

Asset Quality Index	Adjusted Non-Performing Loans as a % of Total Loans	as a % of Capital	Net Charge-Offs Avg Loans	Profitability Index	Net Income ($Mil)	Return on Assets (R.O.A.)	Return on Equity (R.O.E.)	Net Interest Spread	Overhead Efficiency Ratio	Liquidity Index	Liquidity Ratio	Hot Money Ratio	Stability Index
7.7	0.75	3.9	0.00	4.0	0.6	0.62	4.48	3.08	71.3	1.3	23.0	30.4	8.0
3.6	2.32	14.4	0.46	3.5	0.6	0.94	10.94	4.87	85.0	3.0	30.4	16.2	3.2
7.1	0.72	4.0	-0.04	8.0	5.3	1.76	13.21	3.95	57.1	3.7	22.0	11.3	9.3
7.6	0.75	4.9	-0.07	3.6	6.2	0.61	5.79	3.10	74.6	3.4	24.4	15.2	8.1
5.0	1.56	9.5	0.01	2.5	0.1	0.24	2.31	4.08	93.2	3.3	35.9	16.9	4.3
4.0	0.80	5.3	0.02	7.0	5.7	1.49	13.48	4.74	71.6	4.8	22.8	4.3	7.8
5.1	1.15	7.5	0.00	3.5	0.2	0.76	9.35	3.08	75.8	3.3	41.7	18.7	3.5
5.3	0.44	3.6	0.01	5.5	0.4	0.86	9.68	4.90	71.2	1.8	10.9	19.5	4.5
2.1	4.52	31.1	0.00	0.9	0.0	0.04	0.45	3.11	101.6	3.7	21.7	11.3	4.0
5.0	1.68	12.5	-0.09	1.2	0.1	0.01	0.11	3.37	101.0	4.0	7.7	7.4	5.5
6.4	1.12	5.9	0.08	3.1	0.9	0.43	4.57	2.60	78.2	4.6	38.4	11.3	4.8
4.1	1.49	10.2	0.04	0.7	0.1	0.03	0.27	3.03	114.3	2.2	20.6	16.0	4.0
5.9	0.58	4.7	0.01	6.9	3.2	1.61	19.15	4.59	65.8	1.5	9.8	22.7	6.5
9.3	0.00	0.0	-0.90	0.0	-1.2	-1.48	-18.94	3.21	159.4	6.1	58.1	8.6	2.8
9.9	0.00	0.0	0.00	1.9	0.3	0.10	0.84	1.23	95.3	4.1	76.1	11.7	6.3
4.2	4.54	18.6	0.03	4.6	2.5	0.87	6.99	3.58	68.7	4.5	35.2	10.8	6.9
5.7	0.78	3.8	0.08	4.4	1.9	0.96	8.86	4.69	81.1	5.3	37.7	6.9	6.2
5.2	2.45	10.6	-0.03	7.1	4.1	1.71	13.21	3.67	56.1	3.4	18.3	12.2	8.0
7.3	0.55	3.5	0.26	4.8	2.6	0.84	7.33	3.75	67.1	3.4	16.7	12.1	6.6
8.6	0.06	0.4	-0.02	3.5	0.8	0.71	6.68	3.13	71.0	1.5	33.7	39.9	5.3
7.5	2.16	2.4	1.18	5.1	2.1	0.74	4.77	3.21	56.2	3.3	90.6	99.9	8.0
10.0	na	0.0	na	8.5	30.0	1.30	8.11	-0.23	83.0	4.0	108.3	0.0	7.0
9.4	0.07	0.4	-0.01	2.7	0.5	0.29	2.19	3.60	89.7	5.3	24.7	1.0	6.6
10.0	na	0.0	na	10.0	10.2	6.63	8.28	0.84	84.6	4.0	312.3	0.0	7.0
9.5	0.84	1.3	0.15	3.9	229.0	0.61	3.43	1.04	63.3	8.4	85.7	0.2	9.6
7.9	0.00	0.0	0.00	9.5	7.5	3.08	3.24	1.62	40.2	5.1	457.0	88.0	7.0
10.0	na	0.0	na	9.0	1.5	1.46	1.66	0.80	94.8	4.0	na	0.0	7.0
1.6	3.70	29.4	0.01	2.7	0.7	0.37	4.40	4.20	90.6	3.1	18.9	13.9	3.4
6.5	0.00	0.0	0.05	1.5	0.0	0.09	0.68	4.22	97.5	5.8	53.7	5.7	4.1
8.5	1.23	2.1	-0.02	4.1	0.5	0.54	2.61	3.31	81.2	3.9	59.1	18.9	8.5
7.1	1.06	4.4	0.15	2.1	0.2	0.24	1.98	3.45	93.0	4.0	42.3	15.7	6.5
5.9	0.81	5.1	0.11	6.1	5.8	1.55	14.31	4.03	63.1	1.1	16.3	30.3	7.4
4.7	1.81	10.1	-0.04	5.1	0.1	1.32	11.39	4.92	74.5	3.4	21.0	12.2	4.3
4.6	1.11	6.9	0.34	4.2	3.4	0.77	7.46	3.34	67.9	3.9	17.4	9.9	6.9
10.0	1.00	0.7	-0.37	4.4	0.6	0.66	4.00	2.25	59.3	7.2	92.2	7.4	8.3
3.2	2.94	18.0	0.18	1.9	1.5	0.25	2.33	2.89	92.5	2.5	19.9	16.3	6.1
2.2	2.41	15.5	0.23	4.9	4.6	0.98	9.03	4.04	66.1	1.5	2.9	19.9	6.3
6.7	0.19	2.0	0.00	8.8	73.9	1.81	18.48	2.78	29.3	2.7	1.7	14.1	8.2
2.2	1.68	10.0	2.10	10.0	1750.2	2.68	23.06	8.75	37.8	0.9	18.7	11.5	10.0
8.5	3.07	3.1	-0.41	4.4	0.7	1.01	4.78	3.09	60.2	3.9	85.0	27.0	7.1
7.5	0.01	0.1	-0.01	6.7	3.4	1.11	10.09	3.59	53.0	0.6	13.4	18.7	6.4
5.1	1.37	9.4	0.07	3.3	3.2	0.57	5.72	3.25	79.7	3.6	16.5	8.6	5.7
7.2	0.00	0.0	0.00	4.2	0.5	0.88	9.27	3.51	78.5	4.5	44.8	12.3	5.2
8.2	0.53	3.7	0.06	3.5	32.5	0.59	5.32	2.84	72.2	4.2	11.5	4.7	8.2
7.5	0.91	3.8	-0.01	5.8	2.0	1.16	8.86	4.16	57.5	4.7	37.6	10.5	7.5
9.5	0.00	0.0	0.40	2.4	0.1	0.34	1.81	2.57	88.9	3.4	72.5	30.0	6.9
9.2	1.04	1.7	0.00	0.0	-0.2	-0.52	-4.66	2.57	132.0	7.5	85.8	2.9	4.8
7.5	0.36	2.3	0.04	10.0	3.2	2.48	20.32	4.64	51.9	0.7	7.9	22.7	8.6
7.1	0.22	1.5	0.13	6.7	1.1	1.48	13.66	5.18	67.7	1.5	18.7	26.0	6.2
7.8	0.94	3.3	0.30	5.8	3.9	1.23	8.83	4.87	72.5	4.9	38.5	10.0	7.9
10.0	na	0.0	na	5.9	0.0	0.90	1.07	0.94	91.7	4.0	na	100.0	4.8
9.0	0.36	1.3	0.03	5.1	0.9	1.09	9.25	4.37	70.5	3.8	54.6	19.5	8.3
9.6	0.00	0.0	-0.45	1.2	0.0	0.18	1.50	2.19	108.2	6.9	77.6	5.3	5.6
5.4	1.22	7.7	0.02	7.2	15.7	1.40	14.28	3.35	66.6	4.6	24.8	8.3	7.7
7.1	0.66	3.2	0.63	4.1	0.6	0.81	7.03	3.77	68.9	1.6	22.7	24.7	5.7
6.7	1.20	4.6	0.00	8.9	2.5	2.07	14.20	4.69	61.0	1.9	25.9	22.7	9.4
3.3	1.20	8.7	0.02	8.3	0.6	1.32	11.14	5.48	61.0	2.9	2.9	13.5	6.6
3.1	5.05	33.9	0.00	2.0	0.0	0.25	3.49	2.71	88.5	5.8	36.3	0.0	1.0
6.1	12.10	14.9	-0.36	5.8	332.2	1.25	13.90	2.63	44.8	3.9	92.1	0.0	6.7
8.9	1.75	2.9	-0.10	4.2	11.1	0.79	7.06	1.97	45.8	6.7	90.5	0.0	7.5

Name	City	State	2015 Rating	Rating	2014 Rating	Total Assets ($Mil)	One Year Asset Growth	Asset Mix (As a % of Total Assets)				Capitalization Index	Leverage Ratio	Risk-Based Capital Ratio
								Commercial Loans	Consumer Loans	Mortgage Loans	Securities			
Eagle Bank	Everett	MA	D+	D+	D	433.2	2.03	3.6	0.0	24.0	24.6	10.0	11.5	15.3
Eagle Bank	Glenwood	MN	B+	A-	A-	143.0	4.94	7.3	3.7	14.3	9.6	10.0	13.1	21.9
Eagle Bank	Polson	MT	C	C-	C-	57.6	-0.19	10.3	5.4	7.9	26.7	6.7	8.7	16.3
Eagle Bank and Trust Co.	Little Rock	AR	B	B	B	392.5	3.57	3.5	1.1	14.3	45.2	10.0	11.8	21.1
Eagle Bank and Trust Co. of Missouri	Hillsboro	MO	C+	C	C	932.5	3.67	6.5	0.9	12.8	17.2	8.6	10.5	13.9
Eagle Community Bank	Maple Grove	MN	E-	E-	E-	23.0	7.54	17.3	0.9	19.1	0.6	2.4	5.5	9.4
Eagle Savings Bank	Cincinnati	OH	B+	B	B	114.9	8.80	1.6	0.0	46.2	0.0	9.1	11.7	14.3
▲ Eagle State Bank	Eagle	NE	C	D+	D-	27.7	16.52	6.4	2.2	9.3	6.3	5.7	8.7	11.6
Eagle Valley Bank, N.A.	Saint Croix Falls	WI	C-	D	E-	132.7	-0.71	11.5	0.7	22.3	8.5	8.0	9.7	14.0
▲ EagleBank	Bethesda	MD	A-	B+	B	6749.0	15.10	17.4	0.1	5.4	6.4	8.2	13.0	13.5
Eaglemark Savings Bank	Carson City	NV	A-	A-	A-	33.0	-12.20	0.0	35.2	0.0	0.0	10.0	21.8	47.0
Earlham Savings Bank	West Des Moines	IA	C+	C+	C+	275.6	1.64	15.5	2.7	13.9	31.7	6.9	8.9	15.5
East Boston Savings Bank	East Boston	MA	B-	C+	C	4082.1	26.33	3.1	0.2	12.9	2.1	6.2	11.1	11.9
East Cambridge Savings Bank	Cambridge	MA	C	C	C	1007.1	3.50	2.5	1.1	43.4	13.3	8.7	10.1	16.3
East West Bank	Pasadena	CA	B+	B+	B+	33219.9	6.80	22.7	0.3	10.9	10.2	6.8	9.2	12.3
East Wisconsin Savings Bank, S.A.	Kaukauna	WI	D+	D+	D+	232.8	0.93	0.6	7.5	43.8	30.7	7.5	9.4	20.0
Eastbank, N.A.	New York	NY	B+	B+	B+	190.1	-2.93	0.8	0.0	7.6	31.9	10.0	16.7	23.7
Eastern Bank	Boston	MA	B-	B-	B-	9966.0	3.83	13.5	6.3	14.4	9.1	5.8	9.7	11.6
Eastern Colorado Bank	Cheyenne Wells	CO	B+	B+	B	370.6	5.34	6.3	0.4	8.4	21.5	8.2	9.8	13.6
Eastern International Bank	Los Angeles	CA	B-	B	B	113.7	-4.97	0.0	0.0	0.2	0.0	10.0	16.1	22.6
Eastern Michigan Bank	Croswell	MI	B-	C+	C+	323.5	14.07	8.4	1.7	10.5	34.5	7.7	9.5	17.8
Eastern National Bank	Miami	FL	C	C	C-	404.8	-1.33	15.6	0.8	24.1	2.5	7.2	9.7	12.6
Eastern Savings Bank	Norwich	CT	D	D+	D+	197.7	6.50	5.0	4.4	38.8	0.4	5.6	7.6	11.6
Eastern Savings Bank, FSB	Hunt Valley	MD	D	D	E	346.3	-6.16	0.0	0.1	52.2	0.5	10.0	18.3	34.0
Easthampton Savings Bank	Easthampton	MA	B-	B-	B	1492.9	4.92	6.6	0.7	40.2	19.4	7.4	9.3	15.0
Eastman National Bank of Newkirk	Newkirk	OK	A-	A-	A-	254.7	2.20	14.0	2.4	16.1	24.0	10.0	11.1	16.8
Eaton Federal Savings Bank	Charlotte	MI	B-	B-	B-	289.2	-0.37	0.1	0.0	43.8	31.5	10.0	18.0	38.9
▲ Eclipse Bank, Inc.	Louisville	KY	C+	B-	B-	138.1	-1.05	13.8	0.5	8.0	7.8	10.0	12.4	15.2
Edgar County Bank and Trust Co.	Paris	IL	B	B	B-	429.8	4.23	14.4	0.5	7.6	32.8	8.0	9.6	14.4
Edgartown National Bank	Edgartown	MA	B-	B-	B-	194.3	2.66	2.9	0.1	42.8	8.4	6.3	8.4	14.6
Edgewater Bank	Saint Joseph	MI	D+	D+	D-	154.1	16.88	5.7	0.8	31.5	6.5	7.0	9.0	14.0
Edison National Bank	Fort Myers	FL	C	C	C	278.7	1.09	1.3	2.0	29.8	7.3	6.0	8.0	18.8
Edmonton State Bank	Edmonton	KY	A	A	A-	462.5	0.91	6.3	6.5	20.7	13.3	10.0	14.5	19.9
Edon State Bank Co. of Edon, Ohio	Edon	OH	B	B	B	63.1	-2.21	1.6	0.3	7.4	52.4	10.0	18.4	48.7
Edward Jones Trust Co.	Saint Louis	MO	U	U	U	67.1	9.53	0.0	0.0	0.0	61.2	10.0	96.2	350.0
EH National Bank	Beverly Hills	CA	D-	D	D	259.7	13.77	6.4	0.0	0.3	8.0	9.3	10.8	14.5
Eitzen State Bank	Caledonia	MN	B+	B+	B+	96.6	6.16	8.9	2.7	5.6	19.0	7.6	9.4	14.5
El Dorado Savings Bank, F.S.B.	Placerville	CA	B-	C+	C+	2103.5	6.28	0.0	0.0	20.6	63.4	8.1	9.7	33.3
Elberfeld State Bank	Elberfeld	IN	B-	B-	B-	81.4	9.49	6.7	0.9	7.4	22.6	8.5	10.0	19.7
Elberton Federal S&L Assn.	Elberton	GA	C	C-	D+	22.8	8.09	0.0	0.3	69.4	19.2	10.0	22.0	40.9
Elderton State Bank	Elderton	PA	B+	B+	B	249.1	4.64	10.2	1.5	13.2	4.6	10.0	11.5	15.5
Elgin State Bank	Elgin	IA	D	D-	D-	21.9	-4.52	3.9	2.0	8.7	45.9	5.8	7.8	20.3
Elizabethton Federal Savings Bank	Elizabethton	TN	A-	B+	B+	313.0	-2.28	0.0	0.7	31.6	50.7	10.0	35.4	108.2
Elk State Bank	Clyde	KS	C	C-	C-	95.2	81.99	6.3	2.0	10.4	39.3	8.2	9.8	19.3
Elkhorn Valley Bank & Trust	Norfolk	NE	B+	B+	A-	762.9	5.00	10.0	3.2	4.6	46.0	9.3	10.5	16.3
Elkton Bank & Trust Co.	Elkton	KY	B	B+	B+	136.2	4.80	5.8	5.3	13.6	40.0	10.0	13.8	29.4
Elmira Savings Bank	Elmira	NY	C+	C+	C+	567.6	0.23	3.8	6.4	55.4	7.8	6.1	8.2	13.8
Elsa State Bank and Trust Co.	Elsa	TX	B	B	B-	192.5	4.73	7.5	4.8	13.6	27.4	8.5	10.0	18.3
Elysian Bank	Elysian	MN	C+	C+	C-	41.6	4.80	7.5	8.3	18.7	4.2	10.0	11.2	19.5
Embassy Bank for the Lehigh Valley	Bethlehem	PA	B	B	B	890.0	11.28	4.1	0.1	49.9	10.1	6.1	8.2	12.5
Embassy National Bank	Lawrenceville	GA	B+	B+	C+	110.8	34.86	1.0	0.0	2.0	0.0	10.0	11.0	17.2
Emerald Bank	Burden	KS	D+	C-	D+	17.8	10.72	6.1	9.6	30.8	7.7	8.7	10.1	18.4
Emigrant Bank	New York	NY	C+	C	C-	6685.4	1.11	29.2	0.3	19.2	22.9	10.0	15.9	19.4
Emigrant Mercantile Bank	New York	NY	U	U	U	3.5	-1.42	0.0	0.0	0.0	0.0	10.0	84.9	429.3
Empire National Bank	Islandia	NY	B-	B-	C+	767.9	33.31	10.7	0.0	7.3	34.5	9.0	10.3	17.9
▲ Empire State Bank	Newburgh	NY	C-	C-	C-	247.0	31.68	15.3	0.1	16.3	5.0	6.6	8.6	12.2
Emprise Bank	Wichita	KS	B+	B+	B+	1571.7	3.09	12.7	2.8	18.5	17.5	5.5	8.0	11.4
▲ Encore Bank	Naples	FL	C	D+	D-	382.0	11.90	2.3	1.5	24.7	16.8	6.7	8.7	13.0
EnerBank USA	Salt Lake City	UT	B+	B+	B+	1340.4	15.17	0.0	93.2	0.0	1.0	7.3	11.9	12.8
Englewood Bank & Trust	Englewood	FL	B-	C+	C-	259.1	13.48	2.5	0.6	22.0	29.4	6.8	8.8	15.7

Asset Quality Index	Adjusted Non-Performing Loans as a % of Total Loans	as a % of Capital	Net Charge-Offs Avg Loans	Profitability Index	Net Income ($Mil)	Return on Assets (R.O.A.)	Return on Equity (R.O.E.)	Net Interest Spread	Overhead Efficiency Ratio	Liquidity Index	Liquidity Ratio	Hot Money Ratio	Stability Index
9.3	0.13	0.6	0.00	1.4	0.9	0.29	2.48	2.77	93.3	3.1	37.1	18.6	6.3
8.5	0.05	0.2	0.00	4.9	1.2	1.15	8.64	3.37	71.3	5.2	29.5	4.4	9.0
6.7	0.46	2.6	0.00	3.5	0.3	0.78	8.49	3.67	76.7	1.7	19.8	22.9	4.2
7.5	1.49	5.4	0.00	3.6	1.9	0.63	5.29	3.25	77.8	4.1	43.0	9.8	6.1
3.2	1.85	12.1	0.03	4.8	5.9	0.85	7.66	3.53	66.7	3.8	11.2	9.6	7.0
1.8	2.24	28.5	1.11	2.0	0.1	0.26	4.68	4.99	88.2	1.8	15.3	20.0	0.0
7.4	0.64	3.9	-0.03	5.8	1.2	1.46	12.75	3.13	71.5	2.0	17.2	19.3	6.1
8.2	0.00	0.0	0.01	4.0	0.2	0.97	10.50	3.43	68.2	4.7	24.4	5.0	3.7
7.2	0.18	1.4	0.01	2.5	0.5	0.54	5.65	3.43	84.8	1.7	13.3	20.5	2.2
6.5	0.43	2.7	0.13	9.4	75.7	1.62	12.83	4.36	39.3	3.0	9.6	8.0	9.7
7.1	0.00	0.0	0.00	10.0	2.5	9.86	50.69	12.31	75.7	4.6	81.5	18.3	8.9
5.3	1.06	6.4	0.39	3.5	1.2	0.58	6.59	3.30	72.0	5.4	41.0	7.6	5.0
4.9	0.58	4.5	0.02	4.2	22.7	0.81	6.88	3.44	59.5	1.4	7.2	18.7	8.0
8.8	0.14	1.0	0.00	2.7	3.2	0.43	4.37	3.07	82.3	1.7	19.9	24.1	6.9
6.0	0.67	5.1	0.16	6.8	319.7	1.31	12.84	3.31	49.7	2.4	19.9	14.0	10.0
5.9	1.08	6.6	0.00	1.8	0.5	0.26	2.69	2.90	96.7	4.1	40.1	14.4	4.9
8.0	0.00	0.0	0.00	4.3	0.8	0.57	3.43	3.60	71.6	3.0	49.5	27.1	8.0
5.7	0.59	4.5	0.01	3.8	46.9	0.63	5.10	3.30	79.4	5.2	18.1	1.4	9.2
6.7	0.41	2.8	-0.07	6.7	4.6	1.69	15.80	4.40	60.1	1.9	15.6	18.3	7.1
7.5	0.00	0.0	0.00	3.3	0.3	0.39	2.49	3.13	77.2	1.5	29.9	32.7	7.9
7.2	0.41	2.0	0.06	3.8	1.5	0.66	7.03	3.20	72.6	6.4	49.9	4.1	4.7
5.9	0.58	4.5	0.07	3.0	1.1	0.34	3.32	3.71	85.7	0.8	11.5	34.6	5.1
1.9	2.75	28.7	0.05	0.7	-0.1	-0.09	-1.14	3.24	103.9	0.9	7.5	31.2	4.2
0.3	25.79	87.4	0.27	4.9	3.6	1.38	7.87	6.72	83.3	3.7	30.2	13.4	4.2
6.4	0.71	5.2	0.02	4.0	8.4	0.76	7.63	3.34	65.3	1.5	18.8	24.7	7.4
6.3	0.91	5.5	0.00	9.9	3.2	1.69	15.53	4.37	49.0	4.1	8.4	6.5	7.6
7.6	1.80	5.6	-0.03	3.8	1.7	0.76	4.33	3.18	74.5	3.8	44.0	16.7	6.9
3.5	1.39	8.8	-0.01	3.0	0.3	0.28	2.18	3.85	86.8	1.0	15.7	31.1	6.5
5.0	1.21	7.4	0.00	6.1	4.7	1.49	13.93	3.58	67.0	2.2	15.4	13.2	6.6
9.3	0.00	0.0	0.00	3.7	0.8	0.56	6.03	3.16	73.2	4.5	11.1	4.8	5.7
4.6	1.02	8.8	0.00	1.9	0.3	0.32	3.42	3.39	88.4	4.1	19.4	8.8	3.2
8.6	0.34	2.0	-0.05	3.0	1.3	0.59	7.31	2.68	80.6	5.9	43.3	4.9	4.3
7.5	0.77	3.7	0.00	6.6	5.5	1.59	11.16	4.14	63.2	3.7	17.6	11.0	9.2
9.7	0.00	0.0	0.00	3.9	0.4	0.86	4.81	2.68	68.8	6.8	75.7	5.7	7.7
10.0	na	0.0	na	10.0	5.5	11.92	12.81	1.79	73.1	4.0	na	0.0	9.0
0.8	3.81	23.1	1.00	0.6	-0.3	-0.16	-1.43	3.78	88.8	0.7	18.8	51.8	4.7
4.8	1.94	13.2	-0.06	5.8	1.0	1.36	13.18	3.16	59.0	3.4	20.0	12.5	7.2
8.7	1.55	3.6	0.06	3.9	9.3	0.60	6.10	2.20	63.7	6.6	81.8	10.9	7.5
7.0	0.79	3.9	0.00	3.9	0.4	0.63	6.25	3.57	74.4	4.6	45.2	13.1	6.6
9.9	0.21	0.8	0.00	2.7	0.1	0.49	2.17	3.95	86.9	2.3	28.9	18.4	6.9
3.3	3.11	21.3	0.04	6.2	2.0	1.06	9.43	3.81	51.4	1.9	9.2	19.2	7.2
9.2	0.12	0.6	0.02	1.5	0.0	0.10	1.35	3.40	97.0	6.1	56.7	4.2	1.3
9.9	1.15	1.4	-0.18	5.5	2.2	0.93	2.66	2.81	51.6	4.3	81.7	23.8	8.1
5.9	1.85	10.0	-0.02	2.4	0.2	0.26	2.97	3.06	82.4	1.8	28.4	24.9	4.0
7.7	0.51	2.0	-0.01	5.1	6.0	1.06	10.21	2.81	53.1	5.9	52.3	8.3	7.3
8.8	0.65	1.9	0.66	4.2	0.9	0.88	6.33	3.94	68.6	3.9	46.8	17.4	7.1
4.0	1.09	10.1	0.04	4.1	3.3	0.78	7.96	3.27	70.2	1.4	10.4	23.9	6.8
6.2	0.64	3.7	0.16	5.5	1.9	1.32	13.20	5.35	75.0	2.4	19.2	17.6	5.5
4.6	2.62	12.5	-0.03	5.0	0.4	1.22	10.93	4.36	66.7	6.2	39.8	2.0	4.9
6.5	0.47	4.6	0.05	4.5	5.4	0.86	10.28	3.30	64.2	3.5	5.3	10.3	5.8
6.7	0.00	0.0	-0.04	8.0	1.5	2.05	19.08	5.65	70.2	2.0	27.2	20.2	7.4
4.6	2.11	11.8	0.35	2.5	0.0	0.27	2.67	4.10	92.3	2.8	32.3	16.6	3.9
2.9	5.41	22.3	0.21	4.8	28.4	0.58	3.44	3.77	75.2	6.2	30.0	2.0	10.0
10.0	na	0.0	na	0.0	0.0	-0.88	-1.03	0.12	1366.7	4.0	na	0.0	6.2
7.7	0.30	1.7	0.03	3.3	2.5	0.48	4.41	3.22	77.0	4.7	15.4	4.3	6.0
2.3	1.46	13.4	0.07	2.8	0.5	0.30	3.35	3.55	82.2	1.8	12.9	17.5	3.7
6.7	0.43	3.6	0.10	5.9	17.9	1.54	16.28	3.74	69.2	4.8	19.6	4.7	8.9
8.4	0.00	0.0	-0.01	2.7	1.2	0.43	4.37	3.32	77.1	2.5	16.8	16.7	5.1
5.5	0.27	2.0	0.91	10.0	22.9	2.38	21.07	8.11	38.1	0.2	6.5	20.2	9.2
4.8	2.24	13.7	0.05	6.3	3.1	1.63	18.80	3.57	62.2	6.3	39.6	0.8	5.9

Name	City	State	2015 Rating	2014 Rating	Total Assets ($Mil)	One Year Asset Growth	Comm-ercial Loans	Cons-umer Loans	Mort-gage Loans	Secur-ities	Capital-ization Index	Lever-age Ratio	Risk-Based Capital Ratio
Enloe State Bank	Cooper	TX	B	B+	B	31.7	4.90	10.9	3.4	20.2	6.3	9.5	10.8	14.6
Ennis State Bank	Ennis	TX	C+	B-	B-	182.9	4.14	14.7	1.1	11.5	7.6	7.1	9.3	12.6
Entegra Bank	Franklin	NC	B-	B	D+	1217.8	23.78	2.4	0.4	22.4	26.5	10.0	11.5	17.9
Enterprise Bank	Omaha	NE	B-	B-	B-	257.9	8.57	13.8	1.6	7.9	1.7	6.2	9.0	11.9
Enterprise Bank	Allison Park	PA	D-	D	D	269.7	7.30	13.3	0.0	6.5	0.0	6.0	8.8	11.7
Enterprise Bank & Trust	Saint Louis	MO	B+	B+	B+	3896.5	11.45	41.1	0.7	5.1	13.4	5.4	9.9	11.3
Enterprise Bank and Trust Co.	Lowell	MA	B-	B-	C+	2470.8	12.55	17.3	0.4	11.5	14.1	5.9	9.0	11.7
Enterprise Bank N.J.	Kenilworth	NJ	A-	A-	A-	207.3	12.72	3.6	0.2	7.7	2.0	10.0	13.3	15.9
Enterprise Bank of South Carolina	Ehrhardt	SC	E-	E-	E+	312.7	1.74	3.8	2.0	17.4	14.8	0.9	4.1	9.0
Ephrata National Bank	Ephrata	PA	C+	C+	B-	969.7	12.28	4.1	0.5	16.4	30.7	8.8	10.2	15.1
▲ Equitable Bank	East Weymouth	MA	C	C	C	323.6	45.00	4.2	5.4	40.6	17.8	7.7	9.4	16.8
Equitable Bank	Grand Island	NE	B-	B-	C	227.3	7.63	7.8	1.6	19.9	0.6	9.1	11.8	14.3
▼ Equitable Bank, S.S.B.	Wauwatosa	WI	E-	E-	E+	304.9	2.68	0.5	0.3	47.9	7.7	2.1	5.3	9.2
Equitable S&L Assn.	Sterling	CO	B	B	B	176.1	-2.78	0.0	0.7	84.4	5.4	10.0	14.5	29.4
▼ Equitable S&L Co.	Cadiz	OH	D+	C-	C	13.4	-0.99	0.0	0.5	52.3	20.0	10.0	20.9	48.2
Equity Bank	Wichita	KS	B	B	B-	1557.0	9.95	14.6	1.1	18.3	29.6	6.4	8.4	13.5
Equity Bank	Minnetonka	MN	C-	D+	C+	50.9	0.88	20.9	0.2	14.5	1.2	10.0	12.0	16.2
Ericson State Bank	Ericson	NE	B-	B-	C+	77.1	-6.12	9.1	8.8	2.3	5.3	8.1	10.0	13.4
▲ ESB Financial	Emporia	KS	B	B-	B-	215.2	5.44	10.4	8.8	17.4	22.0	8.1	10.0	13.4
Escambia County Bank	Flomaton	AL	C+	C+	B-	76.0	-5.34	3.8	5.4	9.0	66.9	10.0	14.8	38.2
Esquire Bank, N.A.	Garden City	NY	B	C+	D+	406.8	23.72	24.9	2.4	12.0	23.7	10.0	11.2	16.0
ESSA Bank & Trust	Stroudsburg	PA	C+	C+	C+	1763.5	10.02	2.6	10.7	37.4	22.1	6.8	8.8	13.7
▲ Essex Bank	Richmond	VA	C+	D	C+	1204.1	4.82	9.7	0.4	15.3	20.0	8.0	9.9	13.4
▲ Essex Savings Bank	Essex	CT	C+	C+	C	373.9	6.37	3.6	1.0	51.4	0.3	7.0	9.0	14.8
Eureka Homestead	Metairie	LA	C-	C-	C-	92.0	-2.94	0.0	0.2	74.8	9.1	10.0	13.3	27.2
Eureka Savings Bank	La Salle	IL	B-	C+	C	350.2	-0.66	0.3	0.5	34.8	58.5	10.0	20.8	60.1
EvaBank	Cullman	AL	B	B	C+	392.3	13.83	4.4	6.9	38.2	17.6	10.0	16.9	26.9
Evangeline Bank and Trust Co.	Ville Platte	LA	B	B	B	575.4	0.25	5.7	3.9	24.0	29.8	10.0	18.8	35.1
▲ Evans Bank, N.A.	Hamburg	NY	C+	C+	C+	1075.2	17.46	15.7	0.1	11.6	9.8	6.1	9.3	11.8
EVB	Glen Allen	VA	B-	C+	C	1315.2	5.80	7.9	2.5	16.6	20.0	8.4	9.9	14.1
EverBank	Jacksonville	FL	B-	B-	B-	28693.2	13.82	2.7	0.0	47.9	2.1	5.9	7.9	12.5
Evercore Trust Co., N.A.	New York	NY	U	U	U	24.5	-0.94	0.0	0.0	0.0	20.3	10.0	77.0	225.4
Everence Trust Co.	Goshen	IN	U	U	U	6.9	4.34	0.0	0.0	0.0	68.5	10.0	98.8	317.9
Everett Co-operative Bank	Everett	MA	B+	A-	A-	437.2	7.00	0.9	0.1	45.1	7.3	10.0	12.8	19.7
Evergreen Bank Group	Oak Brook	IL	B	B	B-	762.4	14.63	3.6	47.1	3.9	10.9	7.3	10.2	12.7
Evergreen Federal S&L Assn.	Grants Pass	OR	B	B-	B-	434.1	5.73	1.7	0.2	23.4	11.4	10.0	11.0	17.0
Evergreen National Bank	Evergreen	CO	D+	D	D-	110.2	5.44	3.9	1.4	18.1	30.1	6.6	8.6	19.1
EverTrust Bank	Pasadena	CA	B+	B+	B+	831.4	10.35	5.5	0.0	0.5	12.8	10.0	14.7	20.7
Evolve Bank & Trust	Memphis	TN	C+	B-	B-	412.0	13.85	17.7	1.1	34.1	4.5	5.5	8.0	11.4
Exchange Bank	Santa Rosa	CA	B+	B	B-	2139.0	7.41	8.6	0.4	11.3	27.9	7.4	9.2	13.0
Exchange Bank	Milledgeville	GA	A-	A-	B-	236.8	3.59	3.6	0.9	17.8	31.7	10.0	12.6	20.3
Exchange Bank	Gibbon	NE	B+	B+	B+	801.2	9.13	5.9	0.8	10.7	24.7	8.9	10.3	14.3
Exchange Bank	Skiatook	OK	B-	C	C+	97.3	7.84	4.7	2.9	17.6	27.7	8.3	9.9	16.2
Exchange Bank and Trust Co.	Natchitoches	LA	A-	A-	A-	127.6	-1.18	3.1	1.6	22.0	53.9	10.0	11.1	25.4
▲ Exchange Bank and Trust Co.	Perry	OK	B-	B-	B-	273.4	-1.31	6.5	5.5	20.8	27.9	9.1	10.4	16.7
Exchange Bank of Alabama	Altoona	AL	B+	B+	A-	280.9	7.18	3.5	2.5	12.6	22.7	10.0	12.1	20.3
▼ Exchange Bank of Missouri	Fayette	MO	B	A-	B+	175.7	6.53	6.8	1.7	11.6	9.1	6.9	9.4	12.4
Exchange Bank of Northeast Missouri	Kahoka	MO	C+	C+	C	141.1	-1.68	3.2	1.6	10.9	28.6	8.8	10.2	14.3
Exchange National Bank & Trust Co.	Atchison	KS	B+	B	B	396.0	3.75	5.2	16.6	17.3	21.8	8.0	9.7	16.0
Exchange State Bank	Adair	IA	B	B	B-	36.6	3.26	4.0	1.8	10.3	25.9	10.0	12.3	19.4
Exchange State Bank	Collins	IA	B	B-	B-	109.0	3.34	9.1	0.8	13.7	10.6	7.6	9.9	13.0
Exchange State Bank	Springville	IA	B-	B-	B-	45.7	-0.30	4.5	1.0	14.7	35.7	6.0	8.0	11.9
Exchange State Bank	Lanark	IL	B-	B-	B-	95.6	3.41	6.5	1.0	6.0	51.4	8.2	9.8	20.5
Exchange State Bank	Carsonville	MI	B+	B+	B	161.0	6.15	6.6	1.8	12.6	26.6	10.0	11.1	22.0
Exchange State Bank	Luverne	MN	B	B	B	153.0	-1.62	4.0	1.8	4.0	12.7	8.8	10.5	14.0
Exchange State Bank of St. Paul, Kansas	Saint Paul	KS	B-	C+	C+	65.6	-4.09	12.8	2.7	15.3	24.5	8.3	9.8	18.7
Executive National Bank	Miami	FL	B-	C+	C+	391.0	15.26	5.2	0.1	18.1	11.0	8.7	10.1	16.6
Extraco Banks, N.A.	Temple	TX	B-	C+	C+	1365.2	-2.50	2.9	4.8	18.1	23.8	8.3	9.9	16.9
F & C Bank	Holden	MO	B+	B+	B	179.9	7.18	3.7	2.6	26.5	6.9	8.1	10.1	13.4
F & M Bank and Trust Co.	Manchester	GA	E-	E-	E-	82.6	0.11	4.2	2.5	20.1	8.9	1.2	5.1	8.2

Asset Quality Index	Adjusted Non-Performing Loans as a % of Total Loans	as a % of Capital	Net Charge-Offs Avg Loans	Profitability Index	Net Income ($Mil)	Return on Assets (R.O.A.)	Return on Equity (R.O.E.)	Net Interest Spread	Overhead Efficiency Ratio	Liquidity Index	Liquidity Ratio	Hot Money Ratio	Stability Index
5.7	0.77	5.6	-0.01	9.2	0.4	1.69	16.50	5.19	52.5	1.6	12.0	21.5	6.5
3.3	0.96	7.6	-0.03	6.2	2.0	1.53	16.16	4.98	67.0	4.2	11.6	7.0	5.9
6.0	1.57	8.0	0.09	3.4	4.4	0.52	4.20	3.32	78.9	2.3	23.5	18.8	6.8
6.6	0.17	1.3	0.00	4.6	1.5	0.77	8.56	3.11	64.1	0.8	18.3	33.0	5.3
0.3	3.82	35.8	0.13	4.0	1.3	0.68	7.86	3.99	80.1	0.5	8.5	4.8	4.5
6.6	0.60	4.5	0.12	7.5	37.0	1.33	12.57	3.89	49.8	1.7	9.1	8.9	8.5
5.5	0.96	7.7	-0.01	4.6	14.4	0.82	9.04	4.00	68.9	4.0	3.4	4.2	8.0
7.2	0.13	0.9	0.00	5.8	1.4	0.91	7.10	3.98	57.8	0.6	7.2	36.4	7.6
1.7	4.98	40.4	0.20	2.4	1.0	0.41	10.17	3.03	88.3	4.7	33.5	9.3	0.3
8.9	0.26	1.4	-0.04	3.4	5.8	0.83	7.94	3.05	80.2	4.8	31.7	6.6	6.8
4.9	1.27	8.8	0.00	2.6	0.6	0.31	3.85	3.72	89.1	2.8	28.9	16.4	4.0
4.1	1.32	9.3	0.02	3.4	0.9	0.53	4.49	3.40	77.2	3.8	4.5	8.7	7.0
1.7	3.39	44.4	0.20	0.0	-1.7	-0.75	-14.67	3.89	97.3	1.6	6.9	21.0	0.3
9.9	0.00	0.0	0.00	3.8	0.8	0.59	4.12	3.14	74.1	1.8	15.0	19.9	7.9
7.0	3.45	9.7	0.00	0.7	0.0	-0.29	-1.39	3.34	107.4	5.0	33.8	4.4	5.9
6.4	0.75	4.9	0.11	4.4	10.0	0.81	8.70	3.27	65.6	1.6	13.1	22.9	7.3
4.2	2.40	15.6	0.00	1.4	0.0	-0.07	-0.56	4.19	101.9	3.1	10.9	13.1	6.6
5.0	0.38	3.1	0.95	8.1	1.2	1.92	20.78	4.55	44.5	0.5	7.1	47.3	4.4
5.9	0.48	2.9	0.11	4.6	1.7	1.08	11.12	3.50	69.2	4.0	17.2	9.2	6.2
6.5	2.65	4.8	0.12	2.1	0.2	0.32	2.07	3.18	95.1	3.4	68.7	28.1	7.3
8.4	0.00	0.0	-0.01	4.8	2.3	0.86	7.31	4.22	70.5	5.3	35.0	5.5	5.8
3.9	1.87	14.2	0.23	2.9	5.9	0.45	4.65	2.97	78.9	1.3	14.2	12.5	6.9
5.0	1.70	11.5	0.08	3.8	7.6	0.86	8.70	3.88	70.5	1.2	17.9	31.3	6.5
5.3	0.43	3.7	0.00	3.8	1.6	0.58	4.96	3.48	89.0	4.3	13.1	6.5	6.9
7.7	0.92	5.3	0.00	1.6	0.1	0.18	1.32	2.42	92.2	0.3	4.3	68.5	6.6
6.4	5.81	10.2	0.47	3.0	1.3	0.50	2.42	2.42	70.0	6.1	75.0	11.6	6.2
4.6	2.81	11.6	0.44	10.0	7.1	2.62	14.41	6.67	38.8	0.9	27.2	47.3	8.2
5.7	3.06	9.8	0.07	3.9	2.6	0.63	3.40	3.64	75.8	2.5	35.3	22.1	8.3
3.6	1.42	11.6	0.00	3.8	5.2	0.69	7.25	3.70	75.5	4.2	3.7	6.3	7.6
4.8	1.56	10.7	0.13	4.3	7.7	0.79	7.04	3.85	73.1	3.1	20.7	12.1	7.6
4.9	0.75	8.5	0.08	3.7	96.8	0.48	6.09	2.88	71.7	0.8	3.9	13.1	6.0
6.5	na	0.0	na	9.5	2.2	12.07	13.79	2.08	78.9	4.0	262.6	0.0	6.9
10.0	na	0.0	na	0.0	-0.4	-9.04	-8.88	1.56	105.7	4.0	na	100.0	6.5
6.7	0.92	5.9	0.10	4.7	2.3	0.72	5.62	3.11	61.1	0.9	13.0	33.1	7.9
4.4	0.34	2.5	0.45	6.3	5.9	1.09	11.21	4.21	51.9	0.8	17.1	30.3	6.3
8.4	0.45	2.6	0.00	4.2	2.3	0.74	6.72	3.77	71.5	5.1	28.2	4.2	5.9
5.6	1.22	6.9	0.11	1.7	0.2	0.29	3.13	3.43	93.7	6.8	45.9	0.2	4.3
5.1	0.10	0.4	-0.21	6.7	6.5	1.06	5.72	3.54	49.1	0.8	19.7	47.5	8.4
3.7	0.83	8.1	0.32	4.7	2.1	0.76	7.86	4.33	90.0	0.5	4.2	40.8	4.3
5.9	1.31	7.9	-0.10	6.5	16.1	1.04	11.84	3.84	63.9	5.3	27.6	6.4	8.2
5.8	1.91	8.4	0.02	6.1	1.9	1.08	8.26	4.23	65.8	3.1	27.4	15.0	6.8
6.3	0.50	3.1	0.01	7.5	10.5	1.80	16.52	3.45	43.1	1.2	24.7	32.0	8.4
5.8	0.82	4.6	0.19	5.1	0.9	1.29	12.52	4.49	73.6	3.0	22.7	14.3	4.9
9.4	0.51	1.8	0.24	6.1	1.5	1.56	12.86	3.39	58.7	4.5	21.4	6.2	9.0
4.2	2.17	12.5	0.03	7.6	3.5	1.71	15.79	4.30	61.8	0.6	6.9	36.1	8.0
8.6	0.52	2.4	0.03	4.8	1.7	0.83	6.89	3.33	67.9	3.1	21.6	14.4	6.5
6.1	0.21	1.6	0.03	1.9	-1.3	-0.93	-9.58	4.02	127.9	2.3	8.1	17.1	6.7
4.0	2.09	12.0	0.00	4.6	1.1	1.03	8.82	3.78	72.7	3.7	22.3	11.2	6.4
6.7	0.27	1.7	0.07	6.4	3.5	1.19	12.51	3.46	54.2	4.2	18.3	7.6	5.6
7.8	0.04	0.2	-0.05	5.0	0.3	1.19	8.04	3.65	67.1	4.6	35.1	9.9	7.0
8.2	0.00	0.0	-0.04	4.6	0.9	1.12	11.64	3.46	63.5	1.6	10.5	22.1	6.3
9.0	0.00	0.0	0.03	5.6	0.4	1.08	12.14	3.65	58.2	5.2	44.2	9.7	4.3
8.3	0.49	1.8	-0.07	3.9	0.8	1.02	9.27	2.95	69.9	2.3	33.6	21.5	7.0
6.4	1.29	7.1	-0.01	5.3	1.3	1.07	9.61	3.87	61.6	5.1	34.4	7.1	6.7
7.2	0.02	0.1	-0.03	4.7	1.2	1.03	9.89	3.69	66.2	1.6	16.4	23.4	6.1
8.5	0.00	0.0	0.00	4.5	0.5	0.90	9.54	3.63	67.8	3.0	35.5	18.6	4.8
3.9	1.56	10.7	-0.03	3.9	1.4	0.51	5.34	3.62	79.6	4.3	24.1	7.7	6.1
8.6	0.41	2.2	0.09	4.2	10.5	1.03	10.49	3.63	77.7	5.9	29.0	2.7	9.0
5.8	0.68	4.9	0.08	6.9	2.2	1.65	16.07	5.08	65.2	4.0	8.2	7.8	7.7
0.3	7.78	80.9	0.65	3.1	0.6	1.03	20.32	4.22	80.7	0.7	14.8	44.5	0.0

Name	City	State	2015 Rating	2014 Rating	Rating	Total Assets ($Mil)	One Year Asset Growth	Commercial Loans	Consumer Loans	Mortgage Loans	Securities	Capitalization Index	Leverage Ratio	Risk-Based Capital Ratio
▲ F & M Bank Minnesota	Olivia	MN	B-	B-	B-	117.2	0.76	3.0	1.4	1.3	18.6	7.9	9.8	13.3
F & M Community Bank, N.A.	Preston	MN	C	B+	A-	118.0	7.07	9.3	2.1	13.9	17.2	7.5	11.3	13.0
F&M Bank	Washington	GA	B+	B	B	250.3	0.81	4.1	3.2	20.9	33.8	10.0	15.9	26.4
F&M Bank	Falls City	NE	B-	B-	B-	122.3	-0.65	1.6	1.9	6.9	51.5	7.4	9.3	16.6
F&M Bank	West Point	NE	B	B-	C+	263.4	-0.83	7.3	1.0	5.0	10.9	8.1	10.5	13.4
F&M Bank	Edmond	OK	B	B-	C+	394.8	11.73	6.1	2.9	16.5	22.3	7.1	9.1	13.6
F&M Bank	Clarksville	TN	C+	C+	C	947.1	10.00	5.1	2.0	20.2	6.6	5.3	9.5	11.2
▼ F&M Bank and Trust Co.	Hannibal	MO	D-	D+	D-	119.9	4.94	5.9	5.3	37.1	9.5	6.4	8.4	12.8
Fahey Banking Co.	Marion	OH	B	B-	B-	216.1	2.65	2.2	0.5	6.0	34.1	10.0	25.1	32.9
Fairfax State Savings Bank	Fairfax	IA	B	B-	C	137.6	-1.06	5.1	2.7	11.3	40.4	10.0	12.9	19.1
Fairfield County Bank	Ridgefield	CT	B-	B-	C+	1546.5	1.30	8.0	0.2	24.2	9.6	9.4	11.5	14.5
Fairfield Federal S&L Assn. of Lancaster	Lancaster	OH	C	C-	C-	270.1	3.80	0.0	0.4	75.7	3.0	8.3	9.9	21.4
Fairfield National Bank	Fairfield	IL	B+	B+	B+	496.1	3.23	25.3	2.8	9.9	35.3	9.3	10.5	23.7
Fairmount State Bank	Fairmount	IN	C	C	C	43.0	1.67	2.0	6.2	11.8	22.2	10.0	14.4	27.1
Fairport Savings Bank	Fairport	NY	C-	C-	D+	256.9	2.65	0.8	0.0	72.1	9.4	9.5	10.7	18.9
Fairview S&L Assn.	Fairview	OK	B+	B+	B+	41.8	0.20	3.3	2.3	35.0	3.8	10.0	17.8	28.1
▲ Fairview State Banking Co.	Fairview	IL	C+	C-	C-	28.7	18.93	5.0	8.3	25.9	19.7	10.0	12.1	18.4
Falcon International Bank	Laredo	TX	A-	A-	B	1036.6	5.37	9.2	1.6	10.7	8.2	10.0	11.7	18.4
Falcon National Bank	Foley	MN	B+	B+	B	227.7	22.57	21.0	0.7	12.3	6.8	6.2	8.3	12.0
Fall River Five Cents Savings Bank	Fall River	MA	C	C	C-	845.0	3.75	9.2	1.1	25.5	14.5	7.7	9.5	13.4
Falls City National Bank	Falls City	TX	B-	B-	C+	340.1	0.73	2.6	3.6	12.1	38.0	7.5	9.3	22.2
Family Bank	Pelham	GA	C+	C	C-	93.5	3.93	5.9	7.7	45.6	11.8	9.8	10.9	15.1
Family Federal Savings, F.A.	Fitchburg	MA	C-	C	C	93.0	2.36	0.0	0.3	63.1	24.2	10.0	12.6	27.6
Fannin Bank	Bonham	TX	B-	B	B-	91.5	5.04	7.0	4.2	14.7	31.8	7.0	9.0	15.8
Far East National Bank	Los Angeles	CA	B	B+	B	1317.1	2.78	8.6	0.0	2.3	7.9	10.0	19.0	24.6
Farm Bureau Bank, FSB	Sparks	NV	C-	C-	C	833.3	14.48	6.5	80.0	0.2	0.5	3.9	9.6	10.4
Farmers & Mechanics Bank	Galesburg	IL	B+	A-	B+	355.9	22.37	9.7	3.2	16.9	29.4	7.6	9.4	15.5
Farmers & Merchants Bank	Piedmont	AL	B	B	B	195.3	4.92	8.2	2.4	19.0	31.4	10.0	14.0	22.3
Farmers & Merchants Bank	Waterloo	AL	A	A	A-	79.7	3.06	3.0	2.3	0.4	81.7	10.0	21.9	44.6
Farmers & Merchants Bank	Stuttgart	AR	B	A-	A	979.2	37.27	8.3	2.2	10.2	16.4	9.1	10.9	14.3
Farmers & Merchants Bank	Lodi	CA	A-	A-	A	2727.4	9.10	7.4	0.2	9.8	15.5	7.4	10.6	12.8
Farmers & Merchants Bank	Monticello	FL	B-	B-	C	463.0	5.53	11.5	1.0	13.0	23.5	7.4	9.3	13.9
▲ Farmers & Merchants Bank	Eatonton	GA	B-	C-	D+	170.2	-4.50	2.4	2.7	12.5	43.9	10.0	13.1	23.1
Farmers & Merchants Bank	Lakeland	GA	E-	E-	E-	547.5	1.10	6.3	5.4	20.4	10.0	0.6	4.4	7.2
Farmers & Merchants Bank	Statesboro	GA	C	D	E	179.7	3.24	7.4	1.6	14.2	18.0	6.4	8.4	14.7
Farmers & Merchants Bank	Salisbury	NC	C+	C-	C-	575.0	5.14	4.9	0.5	18.5	2.8	9.8	10.9	16.1
▼ Farmers & Merchants Bank	Tolna	ND	D+	C	B-	97.5	-5.61	12.9	2.8	1.5	11.8	4.9	9.1	11.0
Farmers & Merchants Bank	Miamisburg	OH	B	B	B	128.8	8.56	9.4	1.9	26.2	19.4	8.6	10.1	16.6
Farmers & Merchants Bank	Duke	OK	C+	C+	C+	18.2	4.32	7.2	1.8	0.3	21.1	10.0	11.2	24.6
Farmers & Merchants Bank	Dyer	TN	D+	D+	C-	110.6	19.65	7.6	2.9	7.6	56.0	8.0	9.7	20.1
Farmers & Merchants Bank	New Castle	VA	A-	A-	B+	56.8	2.94	2.0	3.7	34.2	32.8	10.0	19.0	43.9
Farmers & Merchants Bank	Timberville	VA	B-	B	B-	745.5	13.55	2.6	9.8	25.0	3.3	9.2	11.3	14.4
Farmers & Merchants Bank	Berlin	WI	B-	B	B	253.0	10.05	8.2	5.6	24.9	14.3	9.6	10.8	14.9
Farmers & Merchants Bank	Tomah	WI	B-	C	D+	198.2	1.37	11.0	0.8	11.1	27.1	10.0	11.2	16.6
Farmers & Merchants Bank & Trust	Burlington	IA	C+	C	C	204.7	7.20	7.4	2.1	27.4	24.7	7.0	9.0	15.5
Farmers & Merchants Bank & Trust	Marinette	WI	C-	C-	D+	140.7	-2.20	7.4	2.0	24.8	25.8	9.1	10.4	16.5
Farmers & Merchants Bank of Colby	Colby	KS	A	A	A	188.8	10.84	8.1	0.5	1.7	27.7	9.7	12.9	14.7
Farmers & Merchants Bank of Hutsonville	Hutsonville	IL	B	B	B-	41.2	1.64	7.9	9.1	23.7	4.6	10.0	18.2	32.7
Farmers & Merchants Bank of Long Beach	Long Beach	CA	A	A	A	6627.9	10.86	1.3	0.4	8.3	42.5	10.0	13.8	21.1
Farmers & Merchants Bank of Orfordville	Orfordville	WI	B	B	B	49.0	1.04	4.7	6.1	30.5	24.6	10.0	13.2	23.4
Farmers & Merchants Savings Bank	Lone Tree	IA	B-	B-	C+	87.4	-9.67	6.1	1.8	18.4	30.2	10.0	12.0	16.1
Farmers & Merchants Savings Bank	Manchester	IA	B	B	B	558.7	6.80	32.2	0.7	7.4	5.9	5.8	10.3	11.6
Farmers & Merchants Savings Bank	Waukon	IA	A	A	A-	152.2	2.68	4.4	3.6	11.4	24.9	10.0	12.5	17.5
Farmers & Merchants State Bank	Neola	IA	C	C-	C	61.3	2.05	4.4	3.6	11.8	29.0	7.9	9.6	22.7
Farmers & Merchants State Bank	Winterset	IA	A-	A-	A-	191.8	8.35	3.1	2.5	7.3	33.5	10.0	11.9	17.6
Farmers & Merchants State Bank	New York Mills	MN	B	B	B-	60.6	-3.19	9.9	2.6	6.4	29.7	10.0	14.4	26.1
Farmers & Merchants State Bank	Archbold	OH	B+	B+	B+	1024.2	9.07	10.4	3.0	5.3	20.2	6.9	9.9	12.4
Farmers & Merchants State Bank	Waterloo	WI	B-	C+	C+	162.2	1.94	2.3	1.0	15.9	9.5	9.4	11.7	14.5
Farmers & Merchants Union Bank	Columbus	WI	B	B	B	351.1	14.47	8.9	0.8	10.2	4.5	6.1	10.2	11.8
Farmers & Stockmens Bank	Clayton	NM	B+	B+	B	202.2	8.20	8.7	0.8	12.3	9.1	6.8	9.5	12.4

Arrows denote recent upgrades ▲ or downgrades ▼

www.weissratings.com

Asset Quality Index	Adjusted Non-Performing Loans as a % of Total Loans	as a % of Capital	Net Charge-Offs Avg Loans	Profitability Index	Net Income ($Mil)	Return on Assets (R.O.A.)	Return on Equity (R.O.E.)	Net Interest Spread	Overhead Efficiency Ratio	Liquidity Index	Liquidity Ratio	Hot Money Ratio	Stability Index
5.1	0.03	0.2	0.01	5.8	1.3	1.50	14.24	4.11	58.0	4.7	24.0	5.5	6.1
2.3	3.52	21.3	0.10	5.1	0.9	1.07	9.32	4.31	75.8	2.5	5.3	13.3	8.0
6.4	1.80	5.8	0.15	5.2	2.0	1.05	6.41	4.27	68.0	1.9	29.1	24.9	7.1
9.2	0.00	0.0	0.00	4.0	0.9	1.01	10.67	3.02	57.9	5.9	49.9	7.6	6.1
7.0	0.16	1.1	0.00	5.4	2.6	1.30	12.97	3.82	67.6	3.5	16.1	11.8	6.5
8.5	0.10	0.7	-1.17	7.2	5.3	1.88	20.97	3.97	70.3	2.9	13.0	14.4	5.3
3.9	1.13	9.8	0.06	4.0	4.5	0.66	5.34	3.93	78.4	1.0	9.0	30.2	5.8
3.6	1.36	12.0	1.96	0.0	-0.9	-0.97	-8.69	2.86	91.8	3.1	8.2	12.9	4.6
4.8	2.48	6.0	-0.17	6.5	1.8	1.10	4.42	3.98	66.4	2.4	32.2	15.4	8.1
7.7	0.51	2.0	0.18	3.7	0.9	0.89	6.95	3.01	71.9	5.9	51.5	7.9	5.9
4.4	2.31	15.2	0.12	4.1	7.9	0.68	5.75	3.85	76.6	4.2	10.9	6.8	8.1
5.6	1.30	10.8	0.01	2.6	0.7	0.36	3.67	3.25	82.8	1.8	13.8	20.2	4.8
7.6	0.41	2.2	0.05	6.0	4.7	1.27	11.47	3.00	46.0	1.2	28.6	31.7	7.3
5.2	2.81	9.2	0.17	2.3	0.1	0.27	1.88	3.89	88.1	5.0	34.7	7.7	5.9
9.8	0.01	0.1	0.00	2.1	0.5	0.26	3.07	3.08	91.0	1.6	11.4	21.8	4.1
8.9	0.00	0.0	0.04	6.8	0.4	1.27	7.28	4.19	56.9	2.0	25.7	20.8	7.9
5.2	2.12	10.9	0.17	4.6	0.3	1.24	10.09	4.05	64.8	1.6	20.2	25.2	4.8
5.8	1.18	6.2	0.02	6.4	8.9	1.17	10.28	3.67	61.5	1.8	25.0	30.1	9.2
6.9	0.10	0.9	0.17	7.3	2.4	1.56	18.11	4.57	63.9	3.1	12.2	9.7	6.0
4.9	1.08	7.6	0.22	2.4	1.8	0.29	2.95	3.20	85.1	2.1	18.9	17.2	5.8
4.9	2.68	9.9	0.46	8.4	3.9	1.51	17.25	3.90	26.5	4.6	45.2	13.2	4.6
3.2	2.47	17.0	0.09	3.8	0.4	0.56	5.28	4.37	83.1	2.1	8.1	18.0	5.7
6.6	1.90	9.6	0.08	1.5	0.2	0.21	1.68	2.59	98.8	2.3	32.3	22.6	6.4
4.6	1.52	8.9	0.00	5.2	0.8	1.16	13.14	4.54	74.2	4.5	30.7	9.0	5.6
6.9	0.07	0.2	-0.42	4.4	10.7	1.07	5.13	3.06	69.3	1.6	24.9	32.1	7.8
3.3	0.39	3.7	0.66	3.1	2.1	0.35	3.58	3.76	71.0	0.3	3.1	35.8	4.4
4.0	1.53	9.4	0.34	6.1	2.6	1.09	9.12	3.58	64.2	4.7	27.1	6.5	7.4
7.9	1.47	5.4	0.06	3.9	1.1	0.77	5.43	4.28	81.3	3.7	35.9	15.2	7.2
9.8	2.12	1.0	0.12	7.6	1.2	2.00	8.83	3.60	35.2	4.1	91.6	26.7	7.8
5.3	1.01	6.2	0.09	5.6	6.3	0.86	6.78	4.19	62.7	2.9	10.5	14.2	8.1
8.5	0.26	1.7	0.00	7.4	23.2	1.19	11.35	3.91	54.9	2.3	13.5	17.8	9.9
3.7	2.45	16.0	0.04	4.7	3.8	1.14	11.92	3.75	71.6	3.5	26.3	13.0	4.7
1.8	10.91	34.1	0.26	1.2	0.4	0.32	2.39	3.08	89.6	2.8	40.6	24.1	5.6
0.3	6.65	87.4	0.47	3.8	11.6	2.84	82.53	3.97	77.8	0.7	11.1	42.7	1.3
6.7	0.48	3.0	0.03	2.9	0.6	0.42	3.84	3.55	86.5	4.6	34.7	10.3	3.3
3.0	3.04	17.8	0.12	4.0	2.8	0.67	6.17	3.77	76.8	4.5	28.4	8.2	6.5
1.6	1.85	15.4	-0.04	4.8	0.9	1.26	11.57	4.09	66.3	2.9	16.2	14.5	6.0
5.2	1.14	7.5	0.07	5.6	1.1	1.13	10.92	4.46	63.9	4.8	13.9	3.1	5.9
9.0	0.00	0.0	0.00	4.2	0.1	1.04	9.60	3.05	62.4	3.9	65.3	18.0	5.1
5.9	1.80	6.0	-0.01	1.8	0.4	0.47	4.53	3.12	91.2	4.9	34.1	8.1	4.2
9.1	0.28	0.8	0.00	6.1	0.5	1.13	5.99	4.01	57.4	4.3	38.6	12.8	7.6
3.6	1.37	10.1	0.26	7.1	6.8	1.34	11.22	4.28	60.6	3.7	5.3	9.6	7.1
3.9	1.73	11.9	0.51	5.7	1.9	1.04	9.61	5.14	61.7	0.9	7.8	30.3	6.1
3.5	3.96	19.8	0.18	3.6	1.1	0.74	6.41	3.39	73.8	2.1	17.6	5.2	6.4
4.1	2.23	14.7	0.00	3.5	1.0	0.64	7.27	3.48	80.1	5.0	22.6	2.7	4.3
4.4	2.07	11.0	0.03	2.2	0.3	0.27	2.54	3.52	92.3	4.4	41.6	13.6	4.7
8.5	0.01	0.1	0.00	9.7	2.5	1.84	13.56	4.11	32.7	0.7	13.4	38.7	8.6
8.4	0.00	0.0	0.00	6.2	0.5	1.68	9.49	2.83	41.0	2.3	37.7	28.7	7.6
9.5	0.11	0.4	-0.01	6.4	53.8	1.14	8.17	3.53	54.6	4.5	32.4	13.2	10.0
6.4	1.03	4.6	-0.18	5.6	0.4	1.01	7.83	3.64	58.7	3.4	34.2	15.8	7.0
6.9	0.09	0.4	-0.25	4.0	0.5	0.78	5.99	3.39	65.9	2.6	23.9	16.9	5.1
5.1	0.91	6.7	0.26	6.9	6.3	1.58	15.04	4.09	56.7	2.0	12.5	18.6	8.2
6.2	1.51	7.5	-0.06	8.1	2.0	1.76	14.23	3.77	50.7	3.7	31.1	5.2	8.8
6.6	1.28	4.6	0.00	2.6	0.2	0.45	4.67	2.45	83.0	6.3	70.0	7.9	4.9
8.7	0.13	0.6	0.00	5.6	1.5	1.05	8.71	3.43	58.9	4.3	38.0	13.1	7.7
8.4	0.93	3.0	0.01	3.8	0.4	0.89	6.20	3.14	73.6	4.0	41.2	15.5	7.4
7.9	0.18	1.3	0.07	5.7	7.9	1.06	10.20	3.61	63.3	2.9	4.8	13.2	8.6
4.0	1.02	6.7	0.00	5.4	1.3	1.01	8.98	3.38	60.1	3.6	8.8	10.5	6.4
4.6	1.76	12.7	-0.01	8.1	3.0	1.24	11.62	4.18	40.4	0.6	3.9	37.9	6.0
4.6	1.17	8.8	0.02	6.9	2.5	1.68	14.88	3.95	75.1	1.3	21.9	29.5	7.2

Name	City	State	2016 Rating	2015 Rating	2014 Rating	Total Assets ($Mil)	One Year Asset Growth	Asset Mix (As a % of Total Assets) Commercial Loans	Consumer Loans	Mortgage Loans	Securities	Capitalization Index	Leverage Ratio	Risk-Based Capital Ratio
Farmers & Traders Bank of Campton	Campton	KY	B-	B-	B-	50.3	8.07	3.6	4.6	20.9	47.8	7.6	9.4	18.6
▲ Farmers & Traders Savings Bank	Bancroft	IA	B-	B-	B-	55.8	1.27	4.0	1.8	4.8	30.3	9.0	10.3	15.4
Farmers and Drovers Bank	Council Grove	KS	A-	A	A	188.6	8.72	2.6	7.6	15.3	42.0	10.0	26.0	45.6
Farmers and Mechanics Federal S&L Assn	Bloomfield	IN	C-	C-	C-	70.2	0.29	0.0	0.1	41.7	38.5	10.0	17.7	47.0
Farmers and Merchants Bank	LaFayette	AL	B+	B+	B+	138.9	4.26	8.7	5.2	5.2	48.0	10.0	14.4	24.4
Farmers and Merchants Bank	Sylvania	GA	C+	C+	C	114.2	1.45	2.8	4.2	7.4	44.9	10.0	14.1	28.5
Farmers and Merchants Bank	Boswell	IN	B-	C+	C	126.5	5.34	5.2	0.8	17.9	26.4	9.8	10.9	16.9
Farmers and Merchants Bank	Laotto	IN	B	B	B	136.5	10.73	7.0	2.7	26.2	27.5	8.6	10.1	16.5
Farmers and Merchants Bank	Mound City	KS	D	D	D+	39.9	1.17	11.6	8.1	35.3	13.8	4.6	6.6	11.1
▼ Farmers and Merchants Bank	Upperco	MD	B	B+	B+	370.0	10.49	6.2	0.2	9.1	13.8	8.0	10.6	13.4
Farmers and Merchants Bank	Baldwyn	MS	A-	A-	A-	304.5	3.17	3.3	8.0	11.7	33.9	10.0	13.5	22.1
▲ Farmers and Merchants Bank	Axtell	NE	D	D	D-	8.6	0.40	7.4	4.0	0.5	47.1	8.0	9.7	23.4
Farmers and Merchants Bank	Milford	NE	B	B	B	596.4	-2.21	4.1	7.5	5.9	48.6	8.4	9.9	17.3
Farmers and Merchants Bank	Milligan	NE	B-	B	B-	73.6	12.17	3.9	1.2	5.0	0.0	6.3	10.9	12.0
Farmers and Merchants Bank	Caldwell	OH	B	B	B	109.8	2.10	8.3	10.9	40.9	20.2	10.0	13.2	21.7
Farmers and Merchants Bank	Arnett	OK	B-	B-	B-	53.9	-3.13	3.8	6.6	1.9	36.6	10.0	13.0	30.3
Farmers and Merchants Bank	Maysville	OK	B-	B-	B-	20.9	-0.93	28.6	13.0	1.3	24.5	5.7	7.7	13.4
▼ Farmers and Merchants Bank	Holly Hill	SC	B-	B+	B+	277.3	5.15	3.4	4.3	12.5	28.0	10.0	15.9	36.9
Farmers and Merchants Bank	Adamsville	TN	B	B-	B-	35.7	5.65	2.8	6.2	21.5	20.5	10.0	12.2	25.4
Farmers and Merchants Bank	De Leon	TX	D+	D+	D+	81.0	1.65	3.9	5.2	25.0	10.7	8.3	9.8	17.3
Farmers and Merchants Bank	Rudolph	WI	B	B-	B-	29.6	2.25	15.0	1.5	29.1	9.9	10.0	11.8	19.2
Farmers and Merchants Bank of Ashland	Ashland	NE	B-	B	B	75.3	6.59	5.9	1.3	15.3	15.6	9.6	10.7	16.0
Farmers and Merchants Bank of Kendall	Kendall	WI	A-	A-	B	73.5	1.23	2.8	2.1	8.4	0.0	10.0	13.9	16.8
Farmers and Merchants Bank of St. Clair	Saint Clair	MO	B	B	B	189.2	7.19	6.1	2.6	27.2	9.8	10.0	11.5	18.3
Farmers and Merchants National Bank	Nashville	IL	B	B	B	170.7	-1.09	3.3	1.4	17.7	29.4	10.0	13.0	21.0
Farmers and Merchants National Bank	Hatton	ND	C-	C	D+	28.5	11.47	19.0	2.3	2.9	5.0	8.8	10.2	14.7
Farmers and Merchants National Bank	Fairview	OK	A	A	A	104.3	1.39	3.6	3.4	9.5	52.4	10.0	12.5	25.9
Farmers and Merchants State Bank	Bushnell	IL	C+	C+	C+	65.9	5.23	3.4	7.4	12.5	26.2	7.0	9.0	17.0
Farmers and Merchants State Bank	Argonia	KS	D	C-	C-	34.8	-2.40	9.1	2.7	20.6	6.1	6.3	8.4	12.5
Farmers and Merchants State Bank	Alpha	MN	C	C+	C-	37.1	3.17	6.5	4.3	9.7	7.1	10.0	11.3	17.8
Farmers and Merchants State Bank	Appleton	MN	B+	B	B	48.7	6.70	3.5	2.0	2.6	17.5	10.0	13.7	18.3
▼ Farmers and Merchants State Bank	Blooming Prairie	MN	D	C-	D+	83.1	6.63	10.0	2.1	13.3	0.0	2.7	6.2	9.7
Farmers and Merchants State Bank	Pierz	MN	B	B	B-	184.7	4.59	9.0	2.1	13.1	15.4	9.4	10.6	14.6
Farmers and Merchants State Bank	Sacred Heart	MN	D	D	D	24.8	4.78	6.4	1.0	2.1	29.4	9.3	10.5	18.7
Farmers and Merchants State Bank	Springfield	MN	B-	B-	C	121.2	3.22	5.0	1.8	2.9	16.8	6.1	8.1	13.6
▼ Farmers and Merchants State Bank	Langdon	ND	B+	A-	A-	94.5	9.24	4.3	2.8	1.4	25.8	10.0	13.0	19.0
Farmers and Merchants State Bank	Bloomfield	NE	B	B	B-	121.4	-3.00	4.7	3.8	0.2	19.4	7.8	10.9	13.1
Farmers and Merchants State Bank	Plankinton	SD	B+	B+	B	105.5	2.64	10.7	5.4	7.2	2.8	6.9	10.0	12.4
Farmers and Merchants State Bank	Scotland	SD	C+	B-	C+	27.5	3.16	9.2	14.2	1.0	21.3	9.0	10.3	15.1
Farmers and Merchants Trust Co.	Chambersburg	PA	B	C+	C-	1108.4	6.89	9.8	0.4	15.8	14.0	8.6	10.0	15.8
Farmers and Miners Bank	Pennington Gap	VA	B+	B+	B+	138.6	1.10	2.5	7.5	20.9	20.4	10.0	13.0	30.0
Farmers and Traders Savings Bank	Douds	IA	C-	C-	C-	19.7	1.80	5.5	11.8	40.6	0.0	9.1	10.4	17.5
Farmers Bank	Greenwood	AR	B	B-	B-	198.2	0.41	3.5	5.5	25.6	38.9	10.0	19.1	35.0
Farmers Bank	Hamburg	AR	D+	D+	D+	41.2	-1.20	3.6	2.1	11.2	31.0	10.0	11.4	27.9
Farmers Bank	Ault	CO	A	A-	B+	221.6	1.15	7.2	0.7	6.7	0.4	10.0	13.5	17.4
▲ Farmers Bank	Greensboro	GA	B	C	C-	88.9	-9.09	10.2	0.8	5.0	42.8	10.0	14.3	26.8
Farmers Bank	Buhl	ID	B+	B+	B	438.5	-0.48	10.3	2.0	3.0	51.1	10.0	14.3	25.8
▲ Farmers Bank	Nicholasville	KY	B	B-	B-	118.4	2.12	3.1	1.0	35.8	14.6	10.0	11.7	18.9
Farmers Bank	Carnegie	OK	C-	C	C-	36.8	1.51	8.7	6.0	21.1	8.9	10.0	12.3	16.3
Farmers Bank	Parsons	TN	C+	C+	C+	33.9	0.20	4.8	6.6	18.9	8.2	10.0	13.8	29.8
▲ Farmers Bank	Portland	TN	A-	B	C	591.1	7.37	4.4	1.5	16.2	26.3	10.0	11.1	15.5
Farmers Bank	Windsor	VA	B	B-	C	405.7	0.29	9.4	0.4	10.8	31.0	10.0	11.5	17.9
Farmers Bank & Capital Trust Co.	Frankfort	KY	B-	B-	B-	649.1	-6.41	4.1	0.5	16.8	39.5	7.8	9.5	17.8
Farmers Bank & Trust	Atwood	KS	C+	C+	C+	87.7	-5.40	6.0	1.1	2.9	46.8	8.4	10.0	19.3
Farmers Bank & Trust	Great Bend	KS	A	A	A-	770.7	2.87	2.9	0.4	5.7	54.6	10.0	15.8	24.1
Farmers Bank & Trust Co.	Magnolia	AR	C+	C+	C+	1302.4	3.49	11.2	2.9	23.9	12.0	6.2	9.1	11.9
Farmers Bank and Savings Co.	Pomeroy	OH	B	B	B-	274.3	3.92	2.1	4.7	40.6	16.1	9.5	10.6	17.8
▼ Farmers Bank and Trust Co.	Blytheville	AR	B-	B	B-	491.3	7.93	22.9	1.6	13.0	3.4	6.2	9.1	11.9
Farmers Bank and Trust Co.	Marion	KY	A	A	A	168.8	20.00	6.2	3.8	32.8	10.8	10.0	13.1	18.8
Farmers Bank and Trust Co.	Princeton	KY	A	A	A	121.2	1.79	3.8	2.4	15.5	17.6	10.0	15.8	23.1

Asset Quality Index	Adjusted Non-Performing Loans as a % of Total Loans	as a % of Capital	Net Charge-Offs Avg Loans	Profitability Index	Net Income ($Mil)	Return on Assets (R.O.A.)	Return on Equity (R.O.E.)	Net Interest Spread	Overhead Efficiency Ratio	Liquidity Index	Liquidity Ratio	Hot Money Ratio	Stability Index
4.7	2.40	10.3	0.67	3.5	0.3	0.75	6.79	3.75	80.2	2.7	36.4	21.1	5.3
6.9	0.28	1.6	0.07	4.0	0.4	0.90	8.70	3.29	68.5	3.5	35.6	16.1	6.0
8.5	0.91	1.5	0.17	5.7	1.3	0.99	3.63	3.26	53.3	2.6	36.3	22.0	8.6
10.0	0.08	0.2	0.00	1.5	0.1	0.17	0.92	2.66	97.6	4.2	63.9	18.0	7.3
7.8	1.55	3.6	0.37	4.5	1.0	0.98	6.64	4.05	71.9	3.4	50.3	21.5	8.1
3.7	6.98	19.7	0.89	2.9	0.6	0.69	4.97	3.56	86.4	3.1	46.4	23.1	6.0
6.4	0.59	3.2	-0.08	3.8	0.7	0.79	7.17	3.44	70.7	1.9	20.4	20.1	6.6
9.0	0.09	0.5	0.03	5.3	1.3	1.31	12.62	3.82	67.0	6.3	40.8	1.8	6.2
2.1	1.85	20.2	0.03	5.6	0.4	1.33	19.78	4.03	66.1	1.5	3.1	20.6	4.2
4.4	0.74	5.3	0.02	6.8	2.9	1.08	10.23	4.20	61.1	2.0	4.4	15.1	6.4
5.3	2.01	7.5	0.19	6.4	2.8	1.24	8.95	4.91	69.9	2.0	32.4	26.9	7.8
9.0	0.44	1.4	0.00	1.8	0.0	0.12	1.36	2.99	95.8	5.3	36.9	3.8	3.0
7.9	0.21	0.9	0.21	4.5	5.3	1.15	11.53	2.61	57.4	4.2	45.1	2.9	7.2
6.6	0.00	0.0	0.00	6.7	0.5	2.01	16.72	4.57	51.3	0.6	3.4	6.4	5.7
3.8	3.50	18.5	0.57	8.7	1.1	1.38	10.64	5.22	56.8	3.4	16.3	12.1	8.3
8.7	0.07	0.2	0.23	3.6	0.3	0.83	6.61	2.33	66.6	6.0	58.0	7.2	6.3
7.7	0.01	0.1	0.10	7.2	0.3	1.73	23.06	4.01	62.2	5.3	47.6	7.4	5.0
6.3	2.90	7.1	0.89	3.1	0.9	0.40	2.79	3.10	72.9	5.1	44.1	10.6	6.9
7.7	1.07	4.2	0.07	4.9	0.2	0.90	7.37	4.37	69.3	3.2	37.0	17.8	5.4
7.5	0.68	3.8	-0.02	1.8	0.1	0.15	1.54	3.70	90.6	5.0	32.4	6.6	5.1
8.4	0.59	3.1	0.03	3.6	0.1	0.52	4.39	3.77	79.9	2.3	31.7	21.4	6.4
8.8	0.00	0.0	0.07	3.9	0.4	0.69	6.25	3.97	76.8	4.4	23.6	6.9	6.5
5.5	1.10	6.8	-0.01	10.0	1.6	2.98	21.55	4.89	47.0	1.5	7.5	22.1	8.2
6.8	0.70	4.2	0.28	4.0	1.0	0.70	6.09	4.09	76.1	3.1	21.3	14.2	6.3
8.4	0.74	3.5	0.14	4.4	1.4	1.13	8.58	3.45	71.9	4.4	13.3	5.9	7.7
7.8	0.00	0.0	-0.02	3.0	0.1	0.61	5.23	3.33	82.6	2.2	28.7	20.2	5.3
9.0	0.75	2.1	0.06	8.3	1.6	2.03	15.16	3.84	50.4	3.2	42.4	19.5	9.4
8.6	0.11	0.6	0.08	3.4	0.3	0.52	5.92	3.13	81.5	5.6	38.5	5.6	4.3
3.0	1.93	16.1	0.25	3.9	0.2	0.65	8.16	4.94	86.5	0.6	4.9	38.2	3.9
4.6	2.88	15.9	0.14	3.6	0.2	0.55	5.92	3.32	68.5	2.0	37.7	22.9	4.8
6.7	0.65	3.0	-0.05	6.2	0.5	1.53	11.19	3.77	56.6	4.8	38.1	10.3	7.8
1.9	2.91	32.5	0.21	2.6	-1.1	-1.80	-21.72	4.46	137.3	4.4	18.3	6.8	4.4
4.2	2.06	13.8	0.07	9.5	3.0	2.24	20.95	4.51	52.2	2.6	16.6	12.2	8.2
7.9	0.34	1.4	0.02	1.3	0.0	0.12	1.08	2.96	95.5	4.1	53.6	15.1	3.9
4.4	0.54	3.8	0.13	4.0	0.6	0.69	8.32	3.54	69.9	4.6	18.0	5.1	4.8
4.9	1.92	9.6	-0.36	8.1	1.4	2.02	15.72	3.83	45.7	3.4	22.0	12.8	8.9
6.5	0.23	1.5	0.02	5.8	0.9	1.02	9.76	3.96	60.2	3.7	8.8	9.3	6.4
5.5	0.31	2.3	0.16	9.6	1.7	2.11	21.84	4.50	38.9	1.3	13.1	24.6	7.9
7.6	0.01	0.1	0.00	3.9	0.2	0.74	7.08	3.94	76.4	3.1	16.8	13.7	5.3
5.1	1.30	9.2	0.44	4.6	6.9	0.85	8.01	3.77	67.0	4.9	11.1	2.2	8.3
6.3	2.40	7.6	-0.16	4.5	0.8	0.76	5.89	4.36	77.9	3.7	53.1	19.7	7.4
4.9	0.96	6.8	-0.04	2.9	0.1	0.42	3.97	3.65	84.9	2.2	22.4	18.6	4.6
7.7	2.02	4.8	0.09	3.9	1.1	0.72	3.74	4.23	82.6	3.6	23.7	11.8	7.1
9.7	1.10	2.2	-0.01	0.7	-0.1	-0.23	-2.30	2.18	114.4	3.8	64.1	20.3	4.2
7.5	0.24	1.3	0.07	9.6	3.6	2.23	16.79	4.60	48.4	1.6	19.0	24.5	8.5
9.0	0.00	0.0	-3.92	5.7	1.2	1.50	10.96	3.27	72.1	3.1	22.5	14.2	5.6
7.8	1.20	3.4	-0.04	5.0	3.3	1.00	7.03	3.10	64.5	5.9	62.0	10.9	8.4
7.9	0.92	5.4	0.00	4.1	0.6	0.69	5.98	4.18	72.8	2.8	16.4	15.2	6.4
3.7	2.76	15.9	0.07	2.4	0.1	0.29	2.44	4.86	94.7	1.0	12.1	31.7	5.0
4.7	3.69	12.0	0.03	4.3	0.2	0.70	5.10	4.10	77.4	4.0	51.7	17.1	6.1
6.8	0.72	4.1	0.06	7.1	5.7	1.31	11.59	4.60	62.1	1.5	17.3	25.5	6.7
5.8	1.57	7.6	-0.20	5.0	3.3	1.05	8.70	3.82	67.8	3.5	25.0	12.6	6.8
5.6	1.52	7.1	0.08	4.4	5.2	1.00	10.14	3.17	75.1	5.2	35.1	6.6	6.2
5.7	1.91	6.6	0.02	3.3	0.5	0.72	6.65	3.17	77.6	5.9	39.1	3.7	5.4
7.6	1.93	4.7	0.05	8.1	9.6	1.72	10.04	3.68	48.7	2.4	47.3	34.5	10.0
3.6	2.05	16.3	0.27	7.2	16.4	1.71	16.22	4.32	59.3	0.8	5.3	32.0	9.7
4.9	1.16	7.6	0.28	4.8	1.8	0.87	7.97	4.24	71.5	2.2	12.2	17.7	6.6
3.3	2.09	16.5	-0.09	9.3	7.3	2.08	22.35	4.12	51.1	1.3	13.1	26.7	6.7
6.8	0.90	5.0	0.35	8.1	2.3	1.92	14.07	4.96	62.7	1.8	10.9	19.7	8.6
8.5	0.25	1.0	0.00	7.0	1.6	1.67	10.76	4.20	62.3	4.1	17.2	8.1	9.4

Name	City	State	Rating	2015 Rating	2014 Rating	Total Assets ($Mil)	One Year Asset Growth	Commercial Loans	Consumer Loans	Mortgage Loans	Securities	Capitalization Index	Leverage Ratio	Risk-Based Capital Ratio
▲ Farmers Bank of Appomattox	Appomattox	VA	A-	B+	B+	234.7	5.08	3.3	12.4	21.2	34.2	10.0	12.6	19.8
Farmers Bank of Cook	Cook	NE	B	B	B	91.4	1.56	4.5	2.3	10.4	36.2	9.2	10.5	17.7
Farmers Bank of Green City	Green City	MO	C+	C+	C	43.6	7.05	9.7	4.8	11.4	28.7	8.1	9.7	14.8
Farmers Bank of Liberty	Liberty	IL	D+	D	C	91.3	0.25	5.3	6.0	18.6	22.4	9.8	10.9	15.7
Farmers Bank of Lincoln	Lincoln	MO	A-	A-	B+	112.1	6.40	3.8	2.6	39.7	8.5	9.8	10.9	18.0
Farmers Bank of Lohman	Lohman	MO	B-	B-	B-	68.4	2.71	3.4	2.9	9.0	65.5	10.0	13.9	32.3
Farmers Bank of Milton	Milton	KY	B	B	B	230.6	3.89	3.2	3.0	29.7	36.3	10.0	14.5	24.5
Farmers Bank of Mt. Pulaski	Mount Pulaski	IL	C+	C+	B-	49.0	11.68	3.7	5.4	23.9	31.5	10.0	13.9	28.8
▲ Farmers Bank of Northern Missouri	Unionville	MO	A-	A-	B+	360.2	8.08	3.4	1.4	9.7	29.9	10.0	11.2	17.8
Farmers Bank of Osborne, Kansas	Osborne	KS	B+	B+	B+	59.6	0.13	5.4	2.2	3.2	22.4	10.0	11.2	15.2
▲ Farmers Bank of Willards	Willards	MD	C+	C-	D+	328.6	4.67	6.7	2.4	36.4	2.9	10.0	11.4	15.5
Farmers Bank, Frankfort, Indiana	Frankfort	IN	B	B	B-	506.1	4.55	9.0	2.1	7.2	23.6	7.4	10.0	12.8
Farmers Building and Savings Bank	Rochester	PA	B+	B+	B	93.3	-0.31	0.1	0.0	45.6	26.2	10.0	19.6	50.7
Farmers Deposit Bank	Cynthiana	KY	B-	B-	C	127.3	-3.15	5.1	0.9	17.0	52.7	10.0	20.1	40.1
Farmers Deposit Bank	Liberty	KY	D+	C	C	47.4	-0.40	11.5	9.0	19.2	3.7	8.9	10.2	15.5
Farmers Exchange Bank	Cherokee	OK	B	B	B-	336.2	19.14	35.4	5.6	10.1	18.5	4.4	8.1	10.7
Farmers National Bank	Prophetstown	IL	A	A	A-	579.0	6.84	3.1	0.7	4.6	41.2	10.0	13.9	21.2
Farmers National Bank	Phillipsburg	KS	A	A	A	127.9	2.60	17.7	3.4	6.8	29.9	10.0	16.2	22.5
Farmers National Bank of Canfield	Canfield	OH	B-	B-	B-	1942.3	14.77	8.7	10.8	16.8	18.7	6.1	8.8	11.8
Farmers National Bank of Danville	Danville	KY	B+	B+	B	474.2	7.34	3.7	1.2	27.2	28.3	10.0	11.0	17.5
Farmers National Bank of Emlenton	Emlenton	PA	C+	C+	C+	691.8	19.21	6.4	1.0	37.3	14.5	5.7	7.7	12.7
Farmers National Bank of Griggsville	Griggsville	IL	B-	C+	B-	86.1	9.50	3.1	5.9	11.4	9.9	7.7	9.6	13.1
Farmers National Bank of Lebanon	Lebanon	KY	C-	C	C+	102.7	0.57	4.2	2.9	8.3	42.0	9.0	10.3	18.5
Farmers National Bank of Scottsville	Scottsville	KY	B+	B+	B+	243.4	-2.17	4.9	2.1	19.4	27.3	10.0	14.8	21.3
Farmers Savings Bank	Colesburg	IA	A-	A-	A-	172.6	3.33	7.6	3.4	6.2	23.9	10.0	13.0	17.4
▼ Farmers Savings Bank	Fostoria	IA	B+	A-	A-	107.8	3.69	6.5	2.4	20.2	18.9	10.0	15.1	17.3
Farmers Savings Bank	Frederika	IA	B	B	B	45.4	0.43	5.7	2.4	13.3	19.5	10.0	17.1	27.2
Farmers Savings Bank	Marshalltown	IA	B	B-	B-	97.2	-1.15	7.3	1.2	11.1	29.3	10.0	14.2	23.0
Farmers Savings Bank	Victor	IA	B+	B+	B+	42.2	8.90	7.9	5.0	17.6	7.3	10.0	17.1	20.7
Farmers Savings Bank	Wever	IA	B-	B-	B-	135.3	3.74	11.4	4.5	34.9	4.3	9.6	10.7	15.8
Farmers Savings Bank	Spencer	OH	A-	A-	A-	283.7	2.82	0.8	0.6	15.4	66.4	10.0	24.6	68.5
Farmers Savings Bank	Mineral Point	WI	B	B	B	275.1	2.72	7.8	11.1	12.4	34.3	6.4	8.4	14.9
Farmers Savings Bank & Trust	Traer	IA	B	B-	B-	170.5	-1.32	3.2	1.2	13.3	33.4	6.7	8.7	14.5
Farmers Security Bank	Washburn	ND	B	B	B	51.4	-0.20	7.7	3.7	2.7	16.8	9.9	11.1	15.0
Farmers State Bank	Dublin	GA	B+	B+	B+	120.6	3.21	5.4	6.7	15.9	21.6	10.0	14.2	20.6
Farmers State Bank	Lincolnton	GA	B+	B+	A-	127.6	-0.62	5.9	7.0	23.0	31.3	10.0	14.1	25.2
Farmers State Bank	Algona	IA	B	B	B-	104.0	-1.68	8.3	1.4	13.9	19.0	9.4	10.6	15.1
Farmers State Bank	Lake View	IA	B-	C+	C+	32.8	3.57	10.5	5.5	14.1	33.7	10.0	11.9	29.8
Farmers State Bank	Marcus	IA	A-	A-	A-	69.4	-4.83	7.7	2.3	4.7	37.5	10.0	12.9	21.7
Farmers State Bank	Marion	IA	A	A	A	715.0	7.41	9.5	1.4	10.4	15.8	10.0	13.8	18.3
▲ Farmers State Bank	Mason City	IA	B+	B	B	179.2	4.96	3.7	2.3	15.7	42.9	10.0	11.2	21.2
Farmers State Bank	Waterloo	IA	B	B	B-	819.6	19.91	12.1	4.8	19.9	11.7	4.5	8.0	10.8
Farmers State Bank	Yale	IA	C+	C+	C+	45.7	-3.76	3.4	2.3	11.3	36.7	8.6	10.1	14.8
▲ Farmers State Bank	Elmwood	IL	D	D	C-	50.3	-1.64	1.7	0.9	16.7	48.0	7.3	9.2	20.0
Farmers State Bank	Pittsfield	IL	B-	B-	B-	242.6	0.46	4.0	1.2	6.0	14.4	9.5	11.7	14.6
Farmers State Bank	Brookston	IN	D	D	D+	72.8	6.91	4.1	3.0	37.9	12.5	5.9	7.9	13.2
Farmers State Bank	Lagrange	IN	B	B	B	595.6	4.20	4.3	1.5	31.8	15.4	7.8	9.5	15.5
▲ Farmers State Bank	Dwight	KS	C+	C-	C-	16.0	-4.46	4.4	1.8	3.3	20.4	10.0	12.0	24.2
Farmers State Bank	Fairview	KS	E+	D-	D	22.5	-7.77	0.8	3.2	12.5	12.4	6.4	8.4	13.3
Farmers State Bank	Holton	KS	B-	C+	C	60.0	5.95	4.3	1.2	24.1	26.0	8.2	9.8	17.5
Farmers State Bank	McPherson	KS	A-	A-	B+	105.7	3.72	7.0	4.3	19.3	38.7	7.5	9.3	15.1
Farmers State Bank	Phillipsburg	KS	D	C	C-	36.6	5.02	9.9	9.0	11.9	24.6	7.0	9.0	13.9
Farmers State Bank	Wathena	KS	B	B	B	62.3	1.45	12.5	4.5	14.5	46.9	10.0	16.5	31.2
Farmers State Bank	Westmoreland	KS	A-	A-	B+	163.6	2.03	8.3	2.5	15.7	16.8	10.0	14.6	15.5
Farmers State Bank	Booneville	KY	B-	C+	C+	50.7	0.33	4.0	5.5	22.2	42.8	9.6	10.8	22.9
Farmers State Bank	Cameron	MO	B-	B-	B-	214.0	1.30	2.1	2.6	45.2	5.3	6.8	9.9	12.4
Farmers State Bank	Victor	MT	B-	B-	C+	368.9	6.42	5.4	3.0	10.8	38.3	9.7	10.8	19.1
Farmers State Bank	Carroll	NE	C+	C	C	27.9	-0.37	1.9	1.5	0.1	54.6	8.0	9.7	21.3
Farmers State Bank	Dodge	NE	C+	C+	C	138.4	17.76	11.9	1.0	4.3	3.0	3.7	8.0	10.4
Farmers State Bank	New Madison	OH	B	B	B	153.8	6.05	3.6	4.5	26.5	18.9	10.0	12.5	19.2

Arrows denote recent upgrades ▲ or downgrades ▼

www.weissratings.com

Asset Quality Index	Adjusted Non-Performing Loans as a % of Total Loans	Adjusted Non-Performing Loans as a % of Capital	Net Charge-Offs / Avg Loans	Profitability Index	Net Income ($Mil)	Return on Assets (R.O.A.)	Return on Equity (R.O.E.)	Net Interest Spread	Overhead Efficiency Ratio	Liquidity Index	Liquidity Ratio	Hot Money Ratio	Stability Index
7.7	0.85	3.7	0.14	5.6	2.2	1.30	10.37	3.89	63.2	3.2	39.6	18.7	7.2
9.1	0.00	0.0	-0.05	4.3	0.6	0.84	7.89	4.64	79.5	2.7	29.3	17.9	6.1
6.9	0.32	2.0	0.00	3.8	0.2	0.61	6.37	3.79	74.0	1.3	11.1	26.4	5.0
1.7	3.91	23.9	0.06	5.7	0.7	1.03	9.59	3.97	59.9	3.2	22.9	13.9	6.0
8.8	0.19	1.3	0.04	6.6	1.3	1.66	15.74	3.91	58.2	2.5	16.8	16.5	7.5
9.7	0.01	0.0	0.11	3.7	0.4	0.75	5.24	2.69	65.1	6.3	88.4	10.8	7.2
4.6	4.52	17.0	0.12	4.4	1.6	0.93	6.25	3.79	67.3	1.8	26.3	24.6	7.5
5.8	2.94	9.5	-0.26	3.0	0.2	0.46	3.18	3.35	83.0	4.1	51.7	16.3	5.9
5.6	2.42	12.4	0.04	6.6	3.4	1.24	10.59	3.72	55.7	4.1	26.7	10.1	7.7
4.4	3.03	16.6	0.01	5.6	0.6	1.23	10.74	4.04	67.3	2.7	21.8	15.9	7.6
2.8	3.18	21.5	0.31	5.0	2.1	0.86	7.60	4.47	66.0	2.0	10.8	18.8	5.6
4.6	1.53	9.6	-0.03	5.3	3.4	0.92	9.34	3.90	68.7	4.2	26.7	9.7	7.4
6.9	3.58	8.5	0.09	5.3	0.9	1.23	6.49	3.18	50.6	7.2	60.6	0.0	8.2
7.7	1.88	3.5	3.14	2.9	0.4	0.44	2.21	3.43	90.3	6.1	58.0	8.5	6.6
1.2	3.72	24.2	0.19	4.5	0.3	0.94	7.54	4.51	79.2	2.7	24.1	16.3	4.5
4.8	1.49	12.1	-0.05	9.3	4.7	1.91	21.32	4.58	39.2	2.9	4.0	13.3	7.5
8.1	0.84	2.8	-0.04	6.8	6.7	1.60	10.60	3.54	44.1	1.6	33.2	33.8	9.5
7.7	0.90	3.6	0.01	6.8	1.0	1.08	6.70	3.47	51.9	2.9	20.5	15.1	8.7
5.2	0.64	5.0	0.13	5.5	15.3	1.08	10.51	3.98	61.6	4.2	9.9	7.1	7.1
5.7	1.70	9.5	0.10	5.8	4.0	1.15	10.02	3.80	70.5	3.6	11.8	10.5	6.9
5.3	0.66	5.8	0.04	3.6	3.1	0.61	7.24	3.26	73.9	2.6	6.3	15.2	5.6
3.5	1.02	7.8	0.04	7.6	1.1	1.82	19.16	4.35	57.6	1.4	14.3	25.2	7.0
8.9	0.05	0.2	4.08	2.6	0.4	0.51	4.98	3.54	87.3	3.7	40.3	16.5	5.2
8.7	0.44	1.8	0.02	5.1	1.9	1.04	6.96	4.01	68.5	3.1	29.5	16.1	8.3
7.8	0.76	3.8	0.01	5.4	1.6	1.29	9.18	4.17	62.5	1.3	12.1	13.9	8.6
7.1	1.09	5.4	0.12	4.9	0.7	0.84	5.60	3.56	63.7	2.9	21.4	15.0	8.3
6.5	2.35	7.2	-0.03	3.9	0.2	0.65	3.82	2.47	61.6	5.4	51.2	9.6	7.2
6.2	1.64	6.2	-0.15	4.2	0.6	0.75	5.38	3.59	75.0	4.4	42.1	13.2	6.3
8.3	0.00	0.0	0.00	7.0	0.5	1.65	9.75	3.70	53.3	4.7	35.5	10.0	7.0
3.9	1.56	11.4	0.67	6.5	1.2	1.15	10.97	4.23	46.7	3.1	13.1	13.2	7.9
5.9	9.29	10.3	-0.82	7.5	3.8	1.84	7.18	3.53	45.3	4.2	79.9	24.5	9.4
8.0	0.12	0.7	-0.01	5.1	2.6	1.29	14.71	3.09	61.2	5.2	34.4	5.9	6.6
9.0	0.00	0.0	0.00	5.5	1.7	1.37	16.20	3.24	62.7	5.4	38.7	6.5	4.9
2.7	4.63	28.7	0.03	6.8	0.5	1.22	11.46	4.26	57.1	4.2	14.3	7.1	5.9
4.8	2.46	10.8	0.00	5.4	1.2	1.32	9.33	4.26	68.2	3.0	29.7	16.4	7.7
5.1	3.06	10.9	0.35	5.1	1.2	1.26	8.58	4.43	73.6	2.0	33.0	27.9	8.2
7.8	0.39	2.3	0.02	5.1	1.0	1.25	11.70	3.57	64.6	5.1	32.9	6.0	6.7
8.8	0.00	0.0	-0.02	3.7	0.2	0.75	6.54	3.03	67.0	6.7	65.6	4.1	5.7
8.6	0.30	1.1	0.24	5.7	0.8	1.41	11.04	3.05	50.2	5.9	53.0	6.6	7.8
8.4	0.30	1.6	0.09	6.8	8.2	1.55	11.18	3.69	59.7	3.5	17.8	11.6	9.7
8.3	0.37	1.6	0.02	5.4	1.5	1.10	9.25	3.91	59.6	2.9	42.4	23.2	6.9
7.7	0.18	1.7	0.04	6.6	8.6	1.52	18.87	3.85	55.1	1.0	6.1	18.4	7.0
4.9	3.68	19.2	0.20	3.4	0.2	0.52	4.98	3.86	64.0	3.4	43.2	18.5	5.6
4.6	1.88	8.1	0.04	1.2	0.1	0.15	1.64	3.28	95.6	3.2	41.0	19.0	3.6
4.3	0.79	4.9	0.00	4.3	1.6	0.89	7.44	3.53	77.7	3.9	13.6	9.0	7.7
4.4	0.81	7.0	0.64	1.7	0.1	0.11	1.28	3.77	91.9	3.2	21.3	13.6	2.4
5.4	0.87	6.3	0.07	5.8	5.0	1.11	11.29	4.09	64.8	4.5	22.3	6.5	7.0
8.7	0.00	0.0	0.00	2.8	0.1	0.57	4.80	3.10	81.3	5.3	46.3	6.5	5.1
4.7	1.38	9.1	0.96	2.0	0.0	0.17	2.10	3.33	77.3	5.1	36.7	4.7	1.7
7.3	0.64	3.6	0.02	4.9	0.4	0.87	8.85	3.76	69.6	2.7	29.4	17.8	4.6
8.8	0.00	0.0	0.02	5.9	1.1	1.45	14.67	4.04	67.3	5.2	44.0	9.9	7.3
2.1	3.57	24.8	1.48	1.9	-0.1	-0.18	-1.92	3.80	78.4	1.5	25.0	28.1	5.1
8.0	1.17	3.1	-0.17	4.4	0.5	1.00	5.74	4.02	76.6	5.6	49.5	8.0	7.1
7.3	1.25	5.5	0.15	5.8	1.4	1.12	7.70	3.64	58.4	1.7	15.7	21.8	7.2
5.1	2.40	8.6	0.68	3.9	0.3	0.87	7.35	4.03	81.7	2.9	40.9	22.6	5.8
5.1	0.75	5.9	0.12	4.6	1.3	0.77	7.19	4.21	71.8	3.8	10.9	9.8	6.3
5.6	1.21	5.4	-0.27	4.4	2.2	0.86	7.54	4.15	77.1	5.0	46.4	11.6	5.9
8.9	0.00	0.0	0.00	4.1	0.2	0.70	7.58	2.55	70.4	3.7	67.2	22.9	4.9
6.3	0.15	1.4	0.60	3.5	0.6	0.56	5.88	4.11	65.4	0.9	11.3	32.5	5.0
7.6	0.18	1.0	0.18	4.5	1.0	0.87	7.33	3.86	71.2	1.7	11.9	20.1	7.0

Name	City	State	Rating	2015 Rating	2014 Rating	Total Assets ($Mil)	One Year Asset Growth	Commercial Loans	Consumer Loans	Mortgage Loans	Securities	Capitalization Index	Leverage Ratio	Risk-Based Capital Ratio
Farmers State Bank	West Salem	OH	C+	C+	C+	105.0	6.30	3.0	1.4	33.2	15.3	7.9	9.6	15.6
Farmers State Bank	Quinton	OK	C+	B-	B-	93.7	0.49	4.8	6.3	14.7	40.4	6.8	8.8	16.5
Farmers State Bank	Hosmer	SD	B	B-	B	20.7	4.40	34.2	2.8	0.0	2.7	10.0	15.4	15.8
▲ Farmers State Bank	Marion	SD	C+	C+	C-	88.3	3.03	4.7	3.2	7.9	1.2	7.0	9.9	12.5
Farmers State Bank	Parkston	SD	B	B+	B+	201.5	-0.01	6.9	2.6	0.0	41.0	8.2	9.8	16.8
Farmers State Bank	Stickney	SD	B+	B+	B-	113.7	-2.62	4.1	1.3	0.5	13.0	7.6	11.2	13.0
Farmers State Bank	Mountain City	TN	C+	B-	C	136.9	0.57	4.1	6.2	28.2	26.8	10.0	15.0	25.1
▲ Farmers State Bank	Center	TX	C	D	A-	344.3	-3.37	13.4	2.7	7.2	31.7	10.0	11.5	18.1
Farmers State Bank	Groesbeck	TX	B+	B+	B+	133.8	-1.99	2.4	4.6	17.7	25.4	6.9	8.9	18.9
Farmers State Bank	Winthrop	WA	C+	C	C	32.2	8.47	4.8	1.7	1.5	44.0	10.0	11.4	49.6
Farmers State Bank	Markesan	WI	C+	B	B	79.9	5.86	10.6	1.9	12.5	32.1	10.0	12.9	20.4
Farmers State Bank	Pine Bluffs	WY	D+	D-	E+	26.6	11.37	6.6	2.1	5.2	15.4	7.9	9.6	18.8
Farmers State Bank & Trust Co.	Mount Sterling	IL	C+	C+	C+	85.1	0.57	15.0	2.9	12.3	17.0	6.5	8.5	12.5
Farmers State Bank & Trust Co.	Church Point	LA	B+	B	B	105.2	1.49	11.3	2.6	11.0	23.6	8.7	10.1	15.1
Farmers State Bank and Trust Co.	Jacksonville	IL	B-	C+	C+	194.6	1.28	9.0	7.5	13.2	30.9	10.0	12.0	17.5
Farmers State Bank Hillsboro	Hillsboro	WI	A-	A-	A-	151.1	3.42	6.4	1.6	10.2	47.1	10.0	15.9	29.5
Farmers State Bank of Aliceville, Kansas	Westphalia	KS	A	A	A-	136.5	0.96	3.4	10.6	17.3	5.4	10.0	12.9	19.1
Farmers State Bank of Alto Pass, Ill.	Harrisburg	IL	D+	C-	C-	200.7	-3.89	13.7	3.0	19.5	15.2	7.3	9.4	12.8
Farmers State Bank of Blue Mound	Blue Mound	KS	B-	C+	D+	43.1	-1.21	7.0	3.6	4.0	8.5	10.0	16.6	23.7
Farmers State Bank of Brush	Brush	CO	A-	B+	B+	100.4	-1.55	3.6	1.9	5.0	26.8	10.0	18.0	27.2
Farmers State Bank of Bucklin, Kansas	Bucklin	KS	C	C+	C	43.6	-0.30	5.5	1.6	2.7	29.5	6.7	8.7	17.8
Farmers State Bank of Calhan	Calhan	CO	B	B+	B+	237.9	5.46	4.7	2.6	17.0	42.9	9.5	10.7	19.2
Farmers State Bank of Camp Point	Camp Point	IL	C-	C	C-	48.1	1.67	4.5	2.4	4.9	50.0	10.0	11.6	22.9
▲ Farmers State Bank of Canton	Canton	SD	C	C	C	47.5	-1.13	5.0	3.9	24.1	15.5	10.0	11.3	16.6
Farmers State Bank of Danforth	Danforth	IL	B	B-	B-	61.9	-3.17	5.2	0.9	7.2	48.6	10.0	11.5	21.4
Farmers State Bank of Emden	Emden	IL	B-	B-	B-	36.9	-3.15	3.6	1.3	4.1	56.0	10.0	25.4	47.3
Farmers State Bank of Hamel	Hamel	MN	B-	B-	C+	122.0	3.75	3.0	0.4	11.0	50.1	9.0	10.3	27.4
Farmers State Bank of Hartland	Hartland	MN	B-	C+	B-	126.8	8.39	12.4	1.3	3.2	10.7	7.8	10.1	13.2
Farmers State Bank of Hoffman	Hoffman	IL	B	B	B	145.4	2.83	3.7	1.4	13.2	45.6	10.0	14.4	27.2
Farmers State Bank of Hoffman	Hoffman	MN	B+	B+	B+	29.6	5.21	7.6	3.5	5.6	33.1	10.0	12.9	22.5
Farmers State Bank of Medora	Medora	IL	C+	B-	B-	20.1	2.91	6.2	8.4	3.8	54.0	10.0	16.4	30.6
Farmers State Bank of Munith	Munith	MI	B-	B-	C	68.3	7.72	1.3	3.9	34.9	23.3	8.2	9.8	18.9
Farmers State Bank of Newcastle	Newcastle	TX	C+	C	C	42.1	-5.14	7.4	3.7	8.0	35.9	7.4	9.3	18.4
Farmers State Bank of Oakley, Kansas	Oakley	KS	A-	A-	A-	132.7	9.99	7.3	0.7	2.1	23.9	10.0	13.5	18.1
Farmers State Bank of Trimont	Trimont	MN	C+	B	B+	60.7	-2.37	11.5	2.0	3.2	36.6	10.0	15.1	23.6
Farmers State Bank of Turton	Turton	SD	B	B	B	28.0	-1.64	3.2	3.8	0.0	12.2	10.0	11.5	19.9
Farmers State Bank of Underwood	Underwood	MN	C+	B-	B	65.1	7.44	9.0	5.1	17.6	5.8	6.7	8.7	12.4
Farmers State Bank of Watkins	Watkins	MN	B+	B+	B+	44.8	8.36	5.7	5.1	14.3	35.4	10.0	12.2	21.6
Farmers State Bank of Waupaca	Waupaca	WI	A	A-	A-	176.9	-2.56	7.2	3.9	23.0	33.2	10.0	15.2	20.9
Farmers State Bank of West Concord	West Concord	MN	C+	C+	C+	49.8	4.04	7.4	6.2	29.3	21.1	9.1	10.4	18.0
Farmers State Bank of Western Illinois	Alpha	IL	B	B	B	127.7	1.82	4.0	2.8	8.3	28.5	10.0	12.4	19.4
▼ Farmers State Bank, Allen, Oklahoma	Allen	OK	C-	B	B	44.7	4.56	16.7	15.5	15.0	5.8	10.0	12.1	24.0
Farmers State Bank, S/B	Bolivar	MO	C+	C+	D+	66.9	0.92	0.7	3.1	24.7	15.5	10.0	15.5	25.3
Farmers State Bank, Spencer	Spencer	NE	D+	D+	D	47.0	21.04	13.0	0.4	0.8	3.3	6.5	9.8	12.1
Farmers Trust & Savings Bank	Earling	IA	B	B	B-	86.1	-5.35	10.4	1.5	8.0	2.9	8.2	10.2	13.5
Farmers Trust & Savings Bank	Williamsburg	IA	A+	A+	A+	138.1	-0.72	7.6	4.0	17.0	34.6	10.0	23.0	33.7
Farmers Trust and Savings Bank	Buffalo Center	IA	A-	A-	B+	247.4	-0.83	11.8	1.1	6.2	2.4	8.6	10.5	13.8
Farmers Trust and Savings Bank	Spencer	IA	B-	B-	B-	369.0	2.56	12.0	1.1	7.6	18.7	6.5	9.2	12.1
Farmers-Merchants Bank & Trust Co.	Breaux Bridge	LA	D+	B-	B-	281.8	-5.08	8.5	4.9	16.0	15.4	9.8	13.3	14.8
Farmers-Merchants National Bank of Paxto	Paxton	IL	B	B	B	117.1	0.79	3.6	1.2	10.5	63.7	10.0	11.7	29.5
Farmington Bank	Farmington	CT	C	C	C	2831.3	4.62	15.9	0.1	31.0	5.0	5.1	8.2	11.1
Farmington State Bank	Farmington	WA	C	C+	C+	8.9	-12.15	3.5	0.7	0.7	1.5	10.0	18.1	28.0
Fauquier Bank	Warrenton	VA	C+	D+	B-	622.5	5.07	4.0	2.6	26.2	7.4	7.2	9.2	13.2
Fayette County Bank	Saint Elmo	IL	E-	E-	D-	36.1	-12.47	15.1	5.5	39.8	13.2	0.3	4.0	6.7
Fayette County National Bank of Fayettevill	Fayetteville	WV	B	B	B	94.0	-3.13	1.0	3.5	47.4	30.0	10.0	11.3	23.8
Fayette Savings Bank, SSB	La Grange	TX	B	B	B-	119.6	12.16	0.7	2.0	47.3	17.6	6.9	8.9	15.1
Fayetteville Bank	Fayetteville	TX	A-	A-	A-	448.0	10.84	3.2	1.2	4.3	81.0	8.7	10.1	29.0
FBT Bank & Mortgage	Fordyce	AR	A-	B+	B+	155.1	5.62	8.0	8.8	22.2	27.3	10.0	11.4	19.4
▲ FCN Bank, N.A.	Brookville	IN	B	B-	C+	430.8	3.55	5.7	1.3	18.4	35.8	8.2	9.8	18.5
FDS Bank	Mason	OH	A+	A+	A+	178.7	-2.05	1.1	0.9	0.0	63.7	10.0	39.6	43.9

Asset Quality Index	Adjusted Non-Performing Loans		Net Charge-Offs Avg Loans	Profitability Index	Net Income ($Mil)	Return on Assets (R.O.A.)	Return on Equity (R.O.E.)	Net Interest Spread	Overhead Efficiency Ratio	Liquidity Index	Liquidity Ratio	Hot Money Ratio	Stability Index
	as a % of Total Loans	as a % of Capital											
5.6	1.17	7.7	0.03	3.6	0.5	0.61	6.37	4.04	84.8	5.0	24.2	3.3	5.5
5.7	1.14	5.7	0.20	3.5	0.5	0.70	8.16	4.28	83.9	5.4	43.6	8.4	4.4
7.1	0.84	3.7	0.00	8.7	0.3	1.87	12.62	4.72	62.4	0.9	28.6	49.5	5.7
4.6	0.34	2.7	0.00	5.9	0.9	1.46	12.83	4.29	66.6	4.5	11.7	5.0	6.9
8.3	0.00	0.0	-0.12	4.2	1.3	0.84	8.54	3.32	65.5	5.0	40.7	10.0	6.1
7.1	0.00	0.0	-0.02	9.0	1.3	1.50	13.89	3.91	40.9	3.7	9.0	10.0	7.4
3.2	4.70	18.1	0.06	4.1	0.7	0.63	4.14	4.39	79.1	2.6	18.0	16.4	6.6
3.4	5.47	21.7	1.80	3.9	3.1	1.12	9.66	3.56	69.0	2.3	31.4	22.5	5.7
8.6	0.27	1.4	0.06	4.8	1.1	1.08	11.13	4.02	75.2	5.1	35.6	7.5	6.5
9.8	1.31	2.1	0.09	2.9	0.1	0.46	3.95	2.73	73.2	7.9	86.9	0.0	5.4
2.4	6.15	26.4	0.63	3.0	0.3	0.45	3.16	4.16	86.2	3.9	42.7	16.2	7.2
7.1	0.36	1.9	0.02	2.9	0.1	0.68	6.78	3.62	78.9	5.8	48.7	6.4	2.7
6.7	0.31	2.4	0.03	4.8	0.5	0.84	9.57	3.97	68.8	1.5	14.2	24.3	4.6
3.9	2.36	13.4	0.06	6.6	1.2	1.51	14.83	4.96	69.1	3.7	30.6	13.4	7.4
5.6	1.20	5.3	0.08	3.2	0.8	0.53	4.50	3.21	82.7	5.1	32.2	5.8	6.4
6.5	2.46	7.5	0.01	7.7	1.9	1.64	10.76	3.58	40.6	4.8	55.0	14.5	8.0
5.9	1.11	6.2	-0.02	8.1	1.3	1.29	9.99	3.52	36.7	1.6	18.7	23.6	7.9
1.2	3.55	27.5	0.12	3.8	1.3	0.83	8.96	4.37	81.1	2.9	14.6	14.3	5.4
7.2	0.51	2.0	0.97	4.8	0.3	1.06	6.37	4.68	77.2	2.7	23.2	16.5	7.8
7.4	0.00	0.0	0.02	6.0	0.8	1.11	6.02	4.05	62.7	1.9	16.8	19.7	7.9
8.6	0.00	0.0	0.01	3.1	0.2	0.48	4.43	4.11	84.9	4.7	39.3	11.3	5.7
4.7	2.50	11.2	0.03	4.5	1.7	1.01	8.84	3.83	76.1	4.2	39.2	13.8	6.4
5.3	3.89	12.2	-0.03	4.0	0.3	0.80	5.39	2.95	69.7	5.7	40.8	5.4	3.7
7.0	1.24	6.9	0.11	2.1	0.15	1.35	3.52	97.1	4.1	14.6	8.1	5.6
8.5	0.74	2.8	0.01	4.5	0.4	0.89	7.82	3.31	67.2	6.0	55.9	6.8	5.6
7.1	7.56	9.6	0.00	3.3	0.1	0.47	1.89	2.54	73.8	3.4	58.1	23.3	7.2
9.9	0.00	0.0	-0.01	3.7	0.8	0.87	7.95	2.79	73.5	5.9	62.1	10.6	6.7
4.4	1.23	8.7	0.35	6.6	1.4	1.52	12.93	4.63	59.9	4.0	19.3	5.0	7.8
9.3	0.29	0.8	0.04	4.3	1.0	0.92	6.23	3.39	66.9	5.6	45.4	7.5	7.9
8.7	0.41	1.6	0.00	6.0	0.3	1.45	10.72	3.66	59.7	3.7	50.6	18.5	7.6
5.9	6.47	12.3	0.04	4.2	0.1	0.81	4.67	3.56	69.0	5.6	80.8	12.0	6.7
4.8	1.80	10.6	-0.11	3.9	0.3	0.58	5.86	4.02	82.8	5.5	37.5	5.9	4.9
6.4	0.70	2.8	0.59	6.4	0.5	1.39	15.44	3.83	56.5	7.1	57.0	0.0	3.8
5.4	0.00	0.0	-0.02	6.6	1.1	1.11	8.10	3.52	47.3	1.3	15.4	26.6	8.5
4.2	5.60	16.7	0.99	3.6	0.3	0.61	4.08	3.23	54.8	3.8	41.4	16.2	6.6
7.1	0.09	0.5	0.05	5.8	0.2	1.11	9.79	4.44	60.2	2.0	16.9	19.1	7.0
6.4	0.19	1.5	0.18	7.3	0.8	1.60	18.40	4.55	63.9	1.4	20.3	27.1	5.7
6.9	1.41	5.5	-0.01	5.9	0.4	1.33	10.39	4.28	66.3	5.4	44.6	8.6	8.0
7.9	0.72	2.5	0.66	6.5	1.9	1.43	9.59	4.28	65.9	4.2	37.2	13.1	7.6
5.6	0.97	6.1	0.02	4.1	0.3	0.91	8.65	4.50	76.9	5.1	24.2	2.6	4.9
7.0	1.28	5.5	0.00	3.8	0.7	0.75	5.89	3.88	73.9	4.2	29.0	10.4	7.2
1.1	5.33	35.1	0.23	9.0	0.7	2.03	17.15	5.36	60.9	0.9	7.5	31.1	7.9
5.4	4.58	19.3	0.06	2.3	0.1	0.27	1.82	3.94	89.2	2.4	18.4	17.4	6.5
6.9	0.00	0.0	0.67	2.2	0.1	0.40	3.74	3.56	68.0	0.6	10.7	45.2	4.1
7.1	0.07	0.5	-0.09	6.2	1.0	1.39	13.97	4.13	62.0	3.7	12.3	10.2	6.7
7.9	1.10	2.9	-0.01	9.1	2.4	2.34	10.07	3.99	45.9	5.9	45.0	5.7	9.8
6.1	0.33	2.5	0.02	8.0	3.4	1.80	16.83	3.78	51.4	4.0	10.9	7.8	8.3
4.7	1.03	8.0	0.08	6.0	4.1	1.50	16.24	3.34	52.7	2.8	5.3	8.6	6.1
1.4	5.75	29.3	0.21	4.8	2.2	0.99	7.73	4.40	73.1	3.4	24.6	13.1	7.7
7.8	2.35	5.5	0.49	4.2	0.8	0.94	7.42	3.16	69.5	4.2	50.2	16.7	6.6
5.4	0.94	9.3	0.04	3.4	12.0	0.59	7.42	2.74	70.7	2.9	4.4	11.6	6.1
7.6	0.00	0.0	0.00	3.5	0.1	0.62	3.69	4.59	81.3	6.5	49.7	0.0	6.2
6.0	0.70	5.2	-0.22	3.6	3.2	0.70	7.62	3.54	81.5	4.4	14.2	6.2	4.0
0.0	19.74	233.3	5.03	0.0	-0.8	-2.84	-60.31	2.76	136.0	0.5	10.3	65.2	0.6
5.3	2.51	13.3	0.07	4.3	0.5	0.67	5.84	4.05	76.6	4.2	9.4	6.7	6.8
7.5	0.74	6.2	0.00	4.7	0.6	0.74	8.40	3.64	74.7	1.6	26.2	26.6	5.3
9.6	0.00	0.0	0.01	5.4	4.2	1.30	11.28	3.32	50.0	3.2	69.8	42.3	7.5
7.8	0.73	3.5	0.39	5.2	1.4	1.26	11.51	4.26	74.7	2.6	37.6	22.9	6.5
5.4	1.37	6.9	-0.02	4.6	3.0	0.94	8.90	3.38	59.7	5.0	44.0	11.0	6.3
10.0	0.00	0.0	7.09	9.5	334.8	221.15	488.87	0.70	22.2	8.8	117.5	0.0	9.7

Name	City	State	Rating	2015 Rating	2014 Rating	Total Assets ($Mil)	One Year Asset Growth	Asset Mix (As a % of Total Assets)				Capital-ization Index	Lever-age Ratio	Risk-Based Capital Ratio
								Comm-ercial Loans	Cons-umer Loans	Mort-gage Loans	Secur-ities			
Federal Savings Bank	Chicago	IL	A	B+	B+	458.6	57.31	0.7	0.0	85.2	0.4	10.0	15.4	25.5
Federal Savings Bank	Dover	NH	C-	C+	C+	315.6	3.53	5.2	0.4	52.2	7.8	8.2	9.8	16.0
Federated Bank	Onarga	IL	C	C-	C-	82.2	-0.53	3.1	2.6	12.2	42.4	7.1	9.1	20.2
Federation Bank	Washington	IA	B-	B-	B-	116.2	1.77	6.8	4.5	14.5	27.9	6.3	8.8	12.0
Feliciana Bank & Trust Co.	Clinton	LA	B+	B+	C+	114.4	1.17	8.9	2.9	32.3	15.8	10.0	11.5	18.4
Fidelity Bank	Atlanta	GA	C+	C	C-	4389.8	25.54	4.0	40.7	15.7	3.9	6.0	8.1	11.8
▲ Fidelity Bank	West Des Moines	IA	B	B	B-	84.6	6.70	3.0	0.2	43.9	1.5	7.1	9.3	12.6
Fidelity Bank	Wichita	KS	B-	B-	B	1958.7	11.12	4.9	7.6	15.7	11.3	6.6	8.6	13.3
▲ Fidelity Bank	New Orleans	LA	B	B-	C	780.0	-3.36	0.5	0.3	34.6	13.2	10.0	16.5	24.1
Fidelity Bank	Edina	MN	A	A	A	554.4	13.08	19.2	0.5	31.1	11.3	10.0	11.4	16.0
Fidelity Bank	Fuquay-Varina	NC	C+	C	C	1808.3	7.85	3.6	0.6	3.2	24.4	7.9	9.6	15.8
Fidelity Bank	Wichita Falls	TX	B+	B+	B	454.2	15.56	15.5	2.7	14.5	2.8	8.3	10.4	13.6
Fidelity Bank & Trust	Dubuque	IA	B	B	B-	777.7	22.16	11.7	1.3	10.8	11.9	8.3	11.1	13.6
▼ Fidelity Bank of Florida, N.A.	Merritt Island	FL	D-	C	D+	177.8	-22.52	3.6	0.0	9.0	15.7	8.1	9.7	15.4
Fidelity Bank of Texas	Waco	TX	B+	B	B	94.1	1.32	6.2	3.6	37.5	2.1	10.0	14.3	28.7
Fidelity Co-operative Bank	Leominster	MA	C+	C+	C+	777.8	24.60	13.7	0.3	30.8	11.3	6.3	8.3	12.3
Fidelity Deposit and Discount Bank	Dunmore	PA	B-	B-	B	771.1	5.77	9.1	5.9	25.7	16.6	8.9	10.3	15.3
Fidelity Federal S&L Assn. of Delaware	Delaware	OH	C+	C+	B-	102.9	0.28	0.0	0.5	32.5	37.3	10.0	21.2	57.5
Fidelity National Bank	West Memphis	AR	B	B	B	395.8	0.55	3.9	1.3	8.4	47.9	9.7	10.8	19.4
Fidelity Personal Trust Co., FSB	Boston	MA	U	U	U	92.6	3.27	0.0	0.0	0.0	72.2	10.0	88.4	88.9
Fidelity S&L Assn. of Bucks County	Bristol	PA	D+	C	C+	96.2	-5.37	0.0	0.1	50.8	7.9	10.0	13.1	28.6
Fidelity State Bank and Trust Co.	Dodge City	KS	B	B+	B+	175.6	-1.58	3.1	0.4	1.9	32.2	10.0	16.6	60.7
Fidelity State Bank and Trust Co.	Topeka	KS	C+	C+	C+	116.1	12.35	11.2	15.6	9.1	25.9	6.6	8.6	15.2
▼ Field & Main Bank	Henderson	KY	B-	B+	B+	403.5	1.57	14.0	1.7	24.7	6.7	6.0	9.3	11.7
Fieldpoint Private Bank & Trust	Greenwich	CT	C-	C-	D+	884.2	12.56	4.5	5.1	37.4	19.2	8.4	9.9	16.1
Fifth District Savings Bank	New Orleans	LA	B-	B	B	402.0	2.87	0.0	0.3	65.3	20.7	10.0	17.2	37.0
Fifth Third Bank	Cincinnati	OH	B-	B-	C+	140771.4	0.94	26.1	9.5	11.1	21.4	8.6	10.5	13.8
Finance Factors, Ltd.	Honolulu	HI	B	B	B-	560.9	9.13	0.0	1.0	36.4	19.0	10.0	11.5	18.2
Financial Federal Bank	Memphis	TN	A	A	A	478.2	13.14	8.3	2.3	28.1	0.0	10.0	14.1	17.6
Financial Security Bank	Kerkhoven	MN	C+	C+	C+	79.6	8.29	15.0	1.1	11.2	3.8	4.8	8.7	10.9
FineMark National Bank & Trust	Fort Myers	FL	C+	C+	C	1310.0	27.98	3.5	3.7	39.1	23.8	7.2	9.1	16.0
Finwise Bank	Sandy	UT	B-	B-	C+	47.3	38.26	6.6	7.8	14.2	1.1	10.0	12.0	16.5
First & Farmers National Bank, Inc.	Somerset	KY	B	B-	C+	503.4	2.62	4.0	3.8	23.3	39.1	9.9	10.9	17.1
First & Peoples Bank and Trust Co.	Russell	KY	C	C	C	199.7	1.27	5.8	10.7	12.9	51.9	10.0	18.6	41.7
First Advantage Bank	Clarksville	TN	B-	B-	B-	526.2	7.33	9.1	9.0	13.2	9.3	9.8	12.0	14.9
First Alliance Bank	Cordova	TN	D	E+	D+	122.0	1.75	23.8	2.1	11.5	5.4	6.8	10.4	12.4
First American Bank	Fort Dodge	IA	C	C	C-	1075.4	-0.82	4.8	0.1	15.8	28.4	7.7	9.5	17.7
First American Bank	Elk Grove Village	IL	B	B-	B-	3557.6	2.68	11.0	0.4	5.7	57.7	7.2	9.1	19.3
▲ First American Bank	Artesia	NM	A-	B+	B+	1076.7	-0.66	12.2	0.4	7.8	36.7	7.7	9.5	17.4
▲ First American Bank	Stonewall	OK	B-	C+	B-	30.9	2.68	10.3	12.2	24.7	7.2	10.0	11.1	17.0
First American Bank and Trust	Vacherie	LA	A-	A-	A-	840.2	0.78	2.0	1.4	22.4	30.9	10.0	12.9	23.6
▲ First American Bank and Trust Co.	Athens	GA	B-	C+	C+	487.3	4.71	2.4	0.6	15.7	23.3	8.6	10.0	16.9
First American Bank, N.A.	Hudson	WI	C+	C+	B-	184.9	5.81	8.6	1.3	17.0	7.1	7.4	9.6	12.8
First American International Bank	Brooklyn	NY	C+	B-	B-	792.9	32.18	0.0	0.1	46.6	7.7	8.6	10.1	15.6
▲ First American National Bank	Iuka	MS	C	C+	C+	258.1	-1.79	2.4	6.4	24.1	35.5	10.0	11.1	20.4
First American State Bank	Greenwood Village	CO	C	C-	C-	266.6	-2.49	4.1	1.0	31.1	18.4	5.6	7.6	13.8
First American State Bank	Oldham	SD	B-	C+	C+	70.7	2.49	11.4	22.3	10.0	17.3	10.0	13.5	21.0
First American Trust, F.S.B.	Santa Ana	CA	U	U	U	3620.3	24.25	0.0	0.0	0.0	77.0	6.0	8.0	32.5
First and Farmers Bank	Portland	ND	C	C-	D+	53.8	0.40	9.4	4.0	2.9	26.4	5.6	7.6	11.6
First Arkansas Bank and Trust	Jacksonville	AR	C	C+	C+	728.1	7.26	8.5	16.8	8.2	26.1	10.0	15.1	20.6
▲ First Bank	Ketchikan	AK	B-	C+	C+	534.9	3.43	3.7	1.4	6.1	45.0	8.1	9.7	18.0
First Bank	Wadley	AL	B+	B	B	78.7	7.50	3.9	1.9	4.9	46.7	8.1	9.7	17.6
First Bank	Clewiston	FL	B-	C+	C+	309.5	10.71	2.8	2.5	18.5	9.5	6.8	8.8	12.9
First Bank	Dalton	GA	B-	C	C	263.5	22.23	12.1	1.8	15.4	17.5	6.4	8.4	12.2
First Bank	Sterling	KS	B+	A-	A-	134.1	1.59	3.0	0.5	9.8	32.9	10.0	13.1	20.2
▲ First Bank	Creve Coeur	MO	B-	C	C+	6128.9	4.15	11.2	0.3	11.6	32.3	8.3	9.9	15.7
First Bank	McComb	MS	B	B	B-	461.9	10.94	8.9	1.7	19.1	16.7	7.7	9.5	14.7
First Bank	Southern Pines	NC	B-	B-	B-	3536.3	8.07	4.2	1.5	21.9	9.6	8.1	10.2	13.4
First Bank	Hamilton	NJ	C+	C+	C+	1007.7	24.71	10.2	0.5	4.5	8.2	6.9	8.9	12.7
First Bank	Erick	OK	B+	B	C+	75.7	-4.35	18.3	5.3	11.9	14.0	9.0	10.3	15.8

Asset Quality Index	Adjusted Non-Performing Loans as a % of Total Loans	as a % of Capital	Net Charge-Offs Avg Loans	Profitability Index	Net Income ($Mil)	Return on Assets (R.O.A.)	Return on Equity (R.O.E.)	Net Interest Spread	Overhead Efficiency Ratio	Liquidity Index	Liquidity Ratio	Hot Money Ratio	Stability Index
8.4	0.40	2.7	-0.03	10.0	17.3	7.25	46.12	3.48	79.9	0.3	6.7	25.9	8.8
9.1	0.09	0.8	0.04	2.6	0.7	0.30	2.99	3.42	89.7	3.5	7.1	10.6	5.8
8.0	0.08	0.3	-0.76	3.1	0.4	0.67	5.26	3.22	89.2	6.0	50.5	5.9	5.2
3.9	1.43	9.3	0.00	5.9	1.2	1.44	14.47	4.03	65.3	4.4	23.6	6.8	6.0
7.3	0.41	2.5	0.12	5.6	1.2	1.39	12.19	4.54	69.4	0.7	12.7	46.6	6.5
3.5	0.87	8.8	0.07	5.1	24.4	0.78	9.16	3.37	76.8	1.8	4.6	15.6	6.9
6.9	0.24	2.2	0.00	8.6	1.3	2.13	19.97	4.26	77.3	0.5	3.3	41.4	6.3
3.8	1.26	8.5	0.05	4.2	11.8	0.69	7.60	3.17	70.4	2.9	3.5	13.1	8.3
7.2	1.04	4.3	0.01	4.0	4.6	0.77	4.59	4.38	88.0	3.7	17.1	9.2	7.9
7.1	0.00	0.0	0.00	8.1	7.5	2.02	12.31	3.72	45.8	5.0	4.2	0.3	10.0
8.4	0.37	1.9	0.08	3.4	7.0	0.53	5.11	2.99	75.4	6.4	43.2	5.4	7.9
5.1	1.01	7.6	0.05	9.4	5.1	1.59	14.83	4.89	48.5	4.1	11.8	7.7	7.1
5.1	0.73	4.7	0.13	5.4	5.6	0.97	7.17	3.66	56.4	2.7	15.5	15.7	7.3
0.0	9.25	52.0	0.73	0.5	-1.2	-0.72	-4.98	1.56	197.2	1.3	26.6	32.6	5.5
4.9	2.96	13.0	0.15	6.0	0.7	0.98	7.03	4.10	65.4	5.1	38.5	9.0	7.4
4.9	1.04	9.2	0.04	2.7	2.6	0.47	5.66	3.48	87.8	2.5	7.0	8.5	4.6
4.4	1.25	8.2	0.23	5.5	6.1	1.08	10.32	3.78	63.1	4.0	5.2	7.2	7.1
9.9	0.00	0.0	0.03	2.2	0.2	0.29	1.36	3.60	96.2	6.8	67.3	6.0	7.2
7.0	0.70	3.0	-0.01	4.9	3.7	1.27	11.59	3.01	60.2	1.8	17.4	21.2	7.1
10.0	na	0.0	na	9.5	44.8	63.83	75.90	2.69	41.6	4.0	na	100.0	9.0
5.9	2.62	11.5	0.45	0.4	-0.2	-0.26	-2.15	2.71	113.7	3.4	42.7	18.5	6.0
9.7	1.33	1.7	-0.02	4.3	1.2	0.94	5.40	2.85	61.5	7.1	74.0	4.8	8.3
7.6	0.04	0.3	0.00	3.3	0.7	0.71	8.01	2.80	76.2	5.0	27.1	4.4	5.7
3.3	1.61	13.3	0.16	5.3	3.0	0.99	8.92	4.38	71.6	1.4	8.5	23.3	6.9
8.5	0.00	0.0	0.00	2.7	2.3	0.37	3.57	2.59	84.0	0.6	10.5	46.1	5.8
9.6	0.44	1.8	0.00	3.6	1.8	0.59	3.41	3.26	70.6	3.0	30.0	16.7	7.9
4.4	1.45	8.8	0.40	6.8	1207.2	1.16	9.17	3.04	57.4	5.1	22.0	2.6	10.0
7.5	0.90	4.7	-0.29	3.9	2.5	0.61	4.95	3.98	79.4	1.5	22.5	26.4	7.7
7.3	0.10	0.6	-0.02	9.4	8.4	2.41	17.14	3.43	45.1	0.4	5.3	67.0	9.2
8.2	0.07	0.6	0.01	4.6	0.6	1.07	12.31	4.23	73.6	1.6	6.9	20.3	5.5
7.5	0.61	4.4	-0.02	3.8	6.5	0.70	7.84	2.93	69.7	3.1	14.1	13.6	6.4
4.5	1.00	6.6	-0.46	8.3	0.5	1.44	10.62	4.75	75.9	0.8	14.5	35.6	4.7
4.9	0.98	4.6	0.15	5.2	3.9	1.04	7.55	3.97	67.8	3.2	36.8	18.0	8.2
7.5	1.60	3.3	0.27	1.8	0.2	0.13	0.76	3.18	95.4	5.3	42.6	9.1	6.5
3.7	1.66	10.0	0.06	3.7	2.0	0.53	4.22	4.16	79.2	1.1	16.0	30.9	7.7
1.0	6.43	48.0	1.13	2.8	0.2	0.22	1.96	4.55	89.8	1.5	11.1	23.7	5.4
6.1	1.59	8.0	0.12	2.8	4.0	0.50	5.07	2.61	87.7	5.8	30.2	4.9	6.0
6.0	2.81	11.0	-0.34	5.4	35.0	1.38	13.97	2.98	67.0	5.3	30.7	7.0	7.3
8.3	0.45	2.4	0.06	6.1	12.3	1.50	15.31	4.03	64.1	4.8	23.8	7.2	8.9
4.8	0.90	5.5	0.05	7.3	0.4	1.62	15.09	4.86	64.8	1.1	22.0	32.9	7.6
6.5	1.71	7.2	0.32	7.3	8.9	1.37	10.66	4.05	58.6	4.4	28.6	9.2	8.7
4.5	1.21	6.7	-0.03	4.0	3.1	0.86	8.77	3.22	74.0	4.3	23.3	7.6	5.4
5.6	0.59	4.4	0.06	3.5	0.9	0.72	7.51	3.84	82.6	3.5	21.2	11.9	5.2
6.2	0.53	4.0	-0.03	3.6	3.2	0.59	5.68	3.48	77.8	1.2	16.3	26.6	5.1
5.9	2.17	9.3	0.17	2.6	0.5	0.26	2.38	3.66	91.5	5.1	40.5	9.4	5.8
9.0	0.02	0.2	0.20	2.8	0.7	0.34	4.77	3.10	74.2	2.9	23.6	15.2	3.0
5.2	0.96	3.9	4.53	3.8	0.3	0.52	3.99	9.09	56.8	2.3	9.9	17.1	5.5
10.0	na	0.0	na	5.0	20.9	0.89	10.78	1.37	35.4	8.7	106.9	0.1	5.4
5.3	1.33	10.3	-0.18	3.8	0.3	0.61	7.78	3.69	76.3	3.9	9.3	8.6	3.8
2.1	5.36	20.3	0.15	4.8	5.6	1.07	5.54	4.47	80.9	4.6	21.6	5.5	8.6
6.5	0.83	3.6	-0.01	4.3	3.6	0.95	9.51	3.51	79.0	5.0	43.9	10.9	6.4
7.7	0.55	2.0	0.17	5.8	0.8	1.36	11.67	4.41	64.9	5.9	61.7	8.5	6.3
4.7	1.69	12.2	0.08	4.3	1.8	0.78	9.12	4.16	74.2	3.6	20.3	11.4	4.3
4.2	1.19	9.4	0.24	7.7	2.4	1.29	15.51	4.21	60.4	2.3	15.7	17.8	4.4
8.9	0.11	0.4	0.00	5.2	1.0	1.02	7.52	3.74	65.7	3.9	26.3	11.1	8.7
6.7	0.74	4.0	0.17	4.0	30.9	0.68	5.45	3.14	70.6	5.8	32.1	5.4	8.2
8.7	0.03	0.2	0.05	4.5	3.6	1.05	11.18	3.18	69.0	3.7	8.9	6.6	5.2
4.1	1.73	12.5	0.15	5.0	20.7	0.81	6.93	4.07	70.8	2.8	14.3	10.6	8.6
5.5	0.46	3.9	0.07	4.1	4.6	0.65	7.86	3.12	61.4	1.0	11.8	32.0	5.5
8.1	0.07	0.4	0.04	7.8	1.2	1.98	19.58	5.01	56.1	3.8	21.5	10.7	5.9

Name	City	State	Rating	2015 Rating	2014 Rating	Total Assets ($Mil)	One Year Asset Growth	Asset Mix (As a % of Total Assets) Commercial Loans	Consumer Loans	Mortgage Loans	Securities	Capitalization Index	Leverage Ratio	Risk-Based Capital Ratio
First Bank	Burkburnett	TX	B+	B+	A-	377.7	10.26	18.6	1.6	34.8	0.0	8.6	10.0	13.9
First Bank	Strasburg	VA	B-	B	B-	711.9	3.46	3.5	0.6	23.2	20.3	6.5	8.5	13.9
First Bank & Trust	Evanston	IL	C+	C+	C+	1226.7	27.13	23.3	0.9	4.0	11.2	5.7	7.9	11.5
First Bank & Trust	Brookings	SD	A-	B+	B+	1337.9	1.60	9.0	1.9	7.1	16.4	8.9	10.9	14.1
First Bank & Trust	Sioux Falls	SD	A-	A-	B+	808.7	11.33	20.9	1.3	6.8	6.3	6.7	10.1	12.2
First Bank & Trust	Lubbock	TX	B+	B	B-	863.1	9.46	16.8	2.0	16.7	14.4	8.7	10.1	14.6
First Bank & Trust	Seymour	TX	C+	C+	C	170.6	-5.53	3.3	1.1	0.5	73.2	10.0	11.9	32.2
First Bank & Trust Co.	Duncan	OK	A-	A-	A-	586.7	0.08	5.3	3.5	28.0	16.0	10.0	13.5	21.8
First Bank & Trust Co.	Perry	OK	A	A	A-	146.6	-2.36	5.0	8.3	15.2	37.3	10.0	12.0	19.8
First Bank & Trust Co.	Wagoner	OK	A-	A-	B	287.9	7.53	19.1	4.9	26.4	2.0	10.0	11.3	15.0
First Bank & Trust East Texas	Diboll	TX	B+	B+	B+	1017.6	9.17	9.1	5.7	18.7	25.1	7.4	9.3	13.9
First Bank & Trust, IL	Paris	IL	B	B	B	448.9	1.24	9.4	8.9	17.9	12.9	8.7	10.3	13.9
First Bank and Trust	New Orleans	LA	C	C+	C	818.6	6.47	12.4	3.9	21.3	1.2	6.3	9.1	12.0
▲ First Bank and Trust Co.	Cozad	NE	B+	B-	B-	248.9	-1.95	11.3	1.7	1.9	22.9	10.0	11.9	15.1
First Bank and Trust Co.	Minden	NE	C+	C+	C+	67.4	-8.91	3.8	1.5	11.7	46.1	9.7	10.8	18.4
First Bank and Trust Co.	Clinton	OK	B	B	B-	52.4	-0.18	2.6	13.0	22.8	35.5	10.0	12.4	30.2
First Bank and Trust Co.	Lebanon	VA	A	A	A-	1563.5	9.43	7.7	2.6	15.5	3.6	10.0	11.5	16.2
▲ First Bank and Trust Co. of Illinois	Palatine	IL	C+	C-	D-	203.7	-10.73	12.0	0.0	0.4	1.0	9.1	11.3	14.3
First Bank and Trust Co. of Murphysboro	Murphysboro	IL	C-	C-	C-	72.8	0.50	8.3	3.7	20.2	29.8	7.2	9.1	17.5
▲ First Bank and Trust of Childress	Childress	TX	C-	C-	C	92.2	3.84	10.0	4.5	13.2	37.0	9.8	10.8	20.4
First Bank and Trust of Fullerton	Fullerton	NE	B	B	B	81.0	-0.54	3.5	1.8	0.9	11.0	10.0	15.4	18.1
First Bank and Trust of Memphis	Memphis	TX	B-	B-	B-	61.3	-1.24	16.1	1.5	10.0	3.1	9.6	11.8	14.7
First Bank Blue Earth	Blue Earth	MN	A-	A-	A-	205.2	4.66	8.5	1.8	4.6	25.0	8.9	10.2	15.0
First Bank Financial Centre	Oconomowoc	WI	B-	C+	C+	1031.2	13.43	8.1	1.0	18.3	20.2	6.8	8.8	13.7
First Bank Hampton	Hampton	IA	A	A	A	147.0	1.58	14.4	3.1	8.1	28.9	10.0	12.3	16.9
▲ First Bank Kansas	Salina	KS	B-	C+	C+	416.2	1.51	4.2	4.0	14.9	43.7	5.8	7.8	15.9
First Bank of Alabama	Talladega	AL	A-	A-	B+	383.6	-5.67	6.6	1.6	10.4	43.7	10.0	15.2	26.1
First Bank of Baldwin	Baldwin	WI	B-	C+	C-	158.1	1.12	8.9	1.9	12.4	27.9	8.7	10.2	15.9
First Bank of Bancroft	Bancroft	NE	B-	B-	B-	22.0	0.44	4.4	1.8	7.0	21.7	10.0	16.1	26.3
First Bank of Berne	Berne	IN	B	B+	A-	632.3	12.28	2.5	0.9	22.1	16.7	7.7	9.5	14.6
First Bank of Boaz	Boaz	AL	A+	A+	A+	208.8	3.78	3.4	2.4	6.4	67.9	10.0	16.6	33.0
First Bank of Celeste	Celeste	TX	C+	C+	C+	43.5	3.09	7.4	8.7	5.0	14.3	6.8	8.8	17.9
First Bank of Chandler	Chandler	OK	A-	A-	A-	90.7	2.14	18.9	5.6	20.9	1.0	9.3	11.6	14.4
First Bank of Charleston, Inc.	Charleston	WV	B-	C+	C-	195.7	-3.67	13.7	0.8	20.8	20.8	10.0	11.0	15.7
First Bank of Coastal Georgia	Pembroke	GA	B	C	C-	118.6	3.35	0.4	0.9	11.8	62.1	10.0	13.5	35.8
First Bank of Greenwich	Cos Cob	CT	C-	C	C	255.8	19.06	7.5	0.5	36.6	8.1	6.9	8.9	13.0
▲ First Bank of Highland Park	Highland Park	IL	C	C-	B-	1449.7	2.68	39.4	0.2	4.2	9.3	5.1	9.8	11.0
First Bank of Linden	Linden	AL	B+	B+	B+	79.4	0.90	8.7	6.9	6.3	39.6	10.0	13.5	22.9
First Bank of Manhattan	Manhattan	IL	C+	C	C-	157.9	2.77	1.4	1.3	17.4	29.4	8.5	10.0	20.8
First Bank of Missouri	Gladstone	MO	B+	B+	B	473.2	2.65	10.2	0.5	3.6	21.9	10.0	16.4	23.0
First Bank of Muleshoe	Muleshoe	TX	C+	C+	B-	106.4	5.78	3.7	1.3	0.5	76.5	10.0	13.1	61.7
First Bank of Newton	Newton	KS	B-	B-	B-	190.0	3.32	11.3	12.4	38.2	11.5	6.5	8.9	12.2
First Bank of Ohio	Tiffin	OH	A-	A	A	175.3	2.37	0.0	51.4	0.1	37.5	10.0	37.2	55.8
First Bank of Okarche	Okarche	OK	A	A	A	84.2	1.34	11.8	2.5	0.7	24.3	10.0	12.9	21.9
First Bank of Owasso	Owasso	OK	A	A	B	264.1	1.35	6.9	0.6	8.9	8.9	10.0	13.1	15.2
▼ First Bank of Pike	Molena	GA	D	C	C+	43.9	2.47	2.7	9.9	27.0	24.3	6.7	8.7	16.8
First Bank of Tennessee	Spring City	TN	D+	D	D+	299.2	6.83	9.3	2.4	23.9	5.9	8.4	10.3	13.7
▲ First Bank of the Lake	Osage Beach	MO	C-	D	C-	57.6	1.12	2.4	0.8	6.4	1.7	8.3	9.8	21.9
First Bank of the Palm Beaches	West Palm Beach	FL	C	C+	D+	148.0	19.99	5.3	0.4	23.4	0.4	8.5	10.0	15.8
▲ First Bank of Utica	Utica	NE	C	D+	D+	74.7	11.03	8.5	3.8	11.9	6.1	7.8	10.2	13.2
▲ First Bank Richmond, N.A.	Richmond	IN	C+	C-	C-	552.2	4.70	6.9	0.8	17.7	27.2	9.6	10.7	15.5
First Bank Texas, SSB	Baird	TX	B-	B-	B-	420.3	-1.12	19.1	2.9	12.2	0.7	7.1	9.7	12.5
▼ First Bank, Upper Michigan	Gladstone	MI	D+	B	B-	195.0	6.76	11.8	10.9	23.0	13.6	6.6	8.6	12.5
First Bankers Trust Co., N.A.	Quincy	IL	B-	B-	B-	942.6	7.39	3.6	4.9	8.4	36.4	6.5	8.5	13.8
First Bethany Bank & Trust	Bethany	OK	B-	B-	B-	196.9	1.94	4.1	0.6	9.2	46.8	7.5	9.3	14.6
First Business Bank	Madison	WI	C+	B	B-	1273.1	4.76	25.0	0.1	2.6	12.4	5.6	10.3	11.4
First Business Bank-Milwaukee	Brookfield	WI	C	B-	B-	241.6	-0.51	19.7	0.1	2.7	17.2	5.2	7.6	11.1
First Cahawba Bank	Selma	AL	B	B	B-	100.0	4.85	15.2	4.8	21.2	13.5	10.0	13.2	20.2
First Capital Bank	Laurinburg	NC	C-	C-	C-	53.6	2.14	2.4	6.4	30.7	0.0	10.0	14.8	22.0
First Capital Bank	Germantown	TN	C+	B-	C+	279.2	15.02	13.2	0.5	10.6	0.7	4.5	9.3	10.8

Asset Quality Index	Adjusted Non-Performing Loans as a % of Total Loans	as a % of Capital	Net Charge-Offs Avg Loans	Profitability Index	Net Income ($Mil)	Return on Assets (R.O.A.)	Return on Equity (R.O.E.)	Net Interest Spread	Overhead Efficiency Ratio	Liquidity Index	Liquidity Ratio	Hot Money Ratio	Stability Index
5.3	0.61	4.7	0.13	9.8	7.9	2.95	29.77	4.99	64.2	3.2	13.3	12.9	7.7
5.7	0.77	5.5	-0.03	5.5	4.8	0.90	10.87	3.71	73.0	4.5	26.4	7.0	5.0
6.0	0.81	6.5	0.03	3.9	4.9	0.62	7.66	3.03	68.5	4.0	28.2	14.2	5.5
5.8	1.16	7.4	0.00	7.4	11.8	1.19	10.45	3.96	62.1	3.7	7.2	7.9	9.1
6.9	0.25	1.9	0.32	8.4	7.2	1.29	10.88	5.16	61.5	3.6	10.1	8.3	8.3
5.3	1.21	7.9	0.06	7.8	11.6	1.90	18.81	4.18	67.9	1.2	11.0	26.1	7.0
5.1	11.70	18.1	0.11	2.8	0.7	0.55	3.88	2.15	84.8	6.5	74.4	9.3	5.6
5.6	2.13	9.8	0.39	8.0	7.8	1.76	13.23	3.76	60.5	3.5	26.7	13.0	9.5
8.3	0.26	1.2	-0.07	7.4	2.1	1.89	14.84	4.41	59.3	4.6	33.4	9.8	8.3
6.5	0.57	4.1	0.05	10.0	5.8	2.74	22.67	4.88	45.0	0.6	9.9	43.1	8.9
5.6	1.17	7.7	0.17	7.2	9.3	1.27	12.73	3.97	59.3	4.6	23.1	8.3	8.0
5.1	0.56	4.0	0.07	4.7	2.7	0.79	7.68	3.64	67.8	1.4	14.4	25.5	6.1
3.5	1.06	9.5	-0.02	5.6	8.4	1.39	15.32	4.40	73.6	1.3	5.6	25.2	5.4
5.4	1.25	6.3	-0.09	8.1	3.7	1.93	15.35	4.17	50.0	4.4	22.1	6.9	9.1
9.0	0.00	0.0	0.00	3.2	0.3	0.54	5.09	3.24	81.4	4.8	27.7	6.2	4.8
6.9	1.42	5.2	0.09	3.7	0.3	0.71	5.70	3.65	80.6	2.3	21.1	17.9	6.3
7.3	0.53	3.6	-0.06	8.1	14.9	1.31	11.23	3.90	55.8	2.3	11.1	17.4	9.5
5.6	0.51	2.8	-0.54	4.6	1.9	1.23	11.65	4.77	81.5	1.1	15.4	29.9	4.2
4.0	2.50	14.6	0.13	1.9	0.2	0.28	3.02	3.79	91.0	3.3	11.7	12.2	4.3
2.4	3.93	20.0	-0.01	4.1	0.7	0.98	10.48	3.32	68.7	0.7	16.8	52.1	4.2
7.2	0.00	0.0	0.00	4.5	0.6	0.91	6.01	3.35	59.1	2.1	13.4	18.5	8.0
8.2	0.00	0.0	0.00	5.1	0.6	1.29	11.22	3.18	59.2	0.7	12.2	32.9	6.2
5.6	0.70	4.4	-0.03	7.2	2.8	1.84	17.19	3.42	51.3	2.7	19.6	15.9	8.6
6.3	0.91	7.2	0.07	4.1	6.0	0.81	8.78	3.55	78.5	2.1	11.3	14.1	6.2
6.2	1.87	8.8	-0.02	6.7	1.7	1.53	12.33	3.65	53.3	4.3	31.2	10.3	8.6
8.8	0.15	0.9	0.08	4.9	4.0	1.29	14.96	3.16	70.7	4.6	39.4	11.9	5.6
9.1	0.54	1.6	0.19	6.7	4.8	1.63	10.57	4.06	56.8	1.6	23.3	25.6	7.0
3.5	2.22	12.8	-0.02	6.0	2.0	1.70	15.54	3.85	74.8	4.5	20.9	6.1	4.4
7.7	0.16	0.5	-0.02	5.5	0.2	1.05	6.68	3.91	58.6	4.8	48.1	10.6	6.4
5.3	0.79	5.7	0.23	8.3	8.6	1.85	19.38	3.80	54.9	4.5	18.6	5.9	8.1
9.5	0.02	0.0	0.04	7.3	2.3	1.46	7.97	3.28	44.1	5.6	71.2	13.2	9.1
8.3	0.00	0.0	0.01	4.0	0.3	0.84	9.48	3.79	79.9	4.6	49.4	13.7	4.6
6.2	0.40	2.7	0.01	10.0	2.2	3.38	29.79	5.28	38.1	1.3	13.7	27.8	8.5
3.7	2.18	13.5	1.11	4.8	1.2	0.80	7.13	3.56	57.4	0.9	24.1	29.0	5.4
8.1	2.01	3.7	-5.18	7.2	1.7	1.85	14.10	3.40	67.2	4.5	35.5	11.1	5.9
1.9	2.94	26.8	0.16	3.7	1.1	0.61	6.29	3.43	63.5	0.6	6.6	37.1	5.3
2.9	2.46	19.3	-0.17	4.2	10.4	0.97	9.83	2.41	61.0	0.7	10.7	24.2	8.1
8.5	0.00	0.0	-0.03	4.9	0.6	0.98	6.90	4.65	68.7	2.3	49.7	35.0	7.8
5.8	1.29	6.5	0.04	3.7	0.9	0.82	7.94	3.61	78.1	3.1	28.4	15.6	5.8
5.9	2.00	7.1	0.16	5.3	3.5	0.99	5.85	3.53	56.1	4.6	33.0	9.5	7.8
9.7	0.09	0.1	0.05	2.8	0.3	0.41	3.10	2.46	82.5	6.0	76.6	11.8	6.9
4.3	0.84	6.9	0.16	4.8	1.6	1.14	13.23	3.86	67.5	3.9	8.7	8.6	5.5
5.7	0.52	0.7	1.42	7.2	1.7	1.33	3.57	4.99	46.3	2.9	64.0	52.5	7.6
8.7	0.00	0.0	0.05	9.0	1.3	2.14	17.48	3.80	43.3	3.4	54.3	20.6	9.0
7.3	0.02	0.1	-0.02	9.7	5.0	2.44	19.20	4.55	48.6	4.8	3.5	1.7	9.5
3.9	1.15	6.8	2.23	0.5	-0.9	-2.85	-26.54	5.03	148.7	3.7	41.3	16.6	3.5
1.4	4.59	34.0	0.65	6.6	2.8	1.28	12.38	4.55	64.0	2.3	10.2	17.0	7.6
2.5	1.92	12.3	-0.05	3.4	0.3	0.75	6.81	3.18	77.1	1.5	34.4	45.4	5.9
6.4	0.77	4.9	-0.01	2.7	0.4	0.36	3.54	4.37	83.1	4.7	35.3	9.7	4.4
2.8	1.51	12.1	0.00	4.2	0.4	0.70	7.54	3.95	70.2	1.7	2.1	19.4	4.4
4.0	1.74	10.1	0.27	3.4	2.2	0.53	4.84	3.56	76.0	1.6	18.1	10.8	5.4
3.6	1.34	10.6	0.14	6.2	3.3	1.07	13.03	4.91	69.9	1.7	13.2	21.4	4.7
2.2	2.61	20.7	0.36	8.9	2.7	1.96	17.00	4.52	60.0	1.6	21.1	24.0	5.7
5.7	0.69	4.1	0.13	4.7	6.3	0.95	9.96	3.12	61.6	3.3	7.2	11.8	6.3
7.6	0.68	3.1	0.00	4.1	1.4	0.98	9.94	3.16	70.5	4.6	29.8	8.4	6.2
3.9	1.13	8.1	-0.01	7.5	13.3	1.39	13.41	3.89	61.9	0.9	15.5	1.0	7.9
4.4	0.60	4.6	-0.01	2.4	0.6	0.28	3.84	2.49	81.6	3.7	26.1	9.9	4.8
8.2	0.55	2.7	0.45	4.3	0.5	0.68	5.11	4.09	71.0	3.9	20.0	9.9	6.5
1.6	5.17	26.8	1.32	4.7	0.3	0.62	4.12	5.54	81.4	0.8	19.0	30.4	7.3
4.0	0.68	6.1	-0.01	5.5	1.8	0.91	9.60	3.51	54.8	0.5	9.9	60.1	4.6

Name	City	State	2015 Rating	2014 Rating	Rating	Total Assets ($Mil)	One Year Asset Growth	Asset Mix (As a % of Total Assets)				Capital-ization Index	Lever-age Ratio	Risk-Based Capital Ratio
								Comm-ercial Loans	Cons-umer Loans	Mort-gage Loans	Secur-ities			
First Capital Bank	Quanah	TX	C	C	C	48.4	3.88	15.4	7.4	14.2	0.6	8.9	10.7	14.1
First Capital Bank of Kentucky	Louisville	KY	C+	C+	C+	522.8	4.77	2.6	0.3	19.4	9.9	5.7	9.3	11.5
First Carolina Bank	Rocky Mount	NC	C-	C-	D-	180.2	21.13	5.9	1.1	27.1	14.1	10.0	11.1	17.4
First Central Bank	Cambridge	NE	B-	B+	B	100.7	6.77	15.2	3.4	2.7	13.0	8.9	10.3	28.8
First Central Bank McCook	McCook	NE	C-	B-	B-	104.6	4.91	15.7	2.2	2.6	11.4	7.8	11.4	13.2
First Central National Bank of Saint Paris	Saint Paris	OH	B	B	B	88.8	1.71	3.1	2.1	12.8	26.6	10.0	17.4	27.1
First Central Savings Bank	Glen Cove	NY	D+	D+	D+	536.8	1.94	12.5	0.0	11.2	11.5	7.6	9.4	13.6
First Central State Bank	De Witt	IA	B	B	B	350.2	5.67	11.4	3.1	12.7	19.1	8.9	10.9	14.1
First Century Bank	Tazewell	TN	C	D+	C-	297.4	12.15	5.6	2.1	25.3	6.3	7.9	9.6	14.0
First Century Bank, Inc.	Bluefield	WV	B-	C+	C+	412.6	0.70	5.6	3.7	25.2	24.0	10.0	11.0	19.2
First Century Bank, N.A.	Gainesville	GA	B-	C	D	117.3	17.00	0.3	0.0	8.4	13.5	6.3	8.3	37.4
▼ First Chatham Bank	Savannah	GA	E-	E-	E-	369.6	2.71	7.8	0.8	9.2	10.0	1.8	6.0	8.8
▲ First Choice Bank	Cerritos	CA	B+	B	B-	833.1	5.56	11.2	0.0	12.6	4.1	10.0	12.1	15.6
First Choice Bank	Pontotoc	MS	B	B	B	269.1	1.76	5.1	7.0	19.3	35.4	10.0	13.6	24.0
First Choice Bank	Mercerville	NJ	C	C	C+	1105.5	-4.50	2.4	0.8	21.0	41.8	8.3	9.9	19.2
First Citizens Bank	Luverne	AL	A-	B+	B	235.3	4.02	6.8	5.3	11.9	40.4	10.0	12.2	20.6
First Citizens Bank	Mason City	IA	A-	A-	A-	1248.0	6.73	14.1	0.9	8.2	29.2	10.0	11.4	15.5
First Citizens Bank	Elizabethtown	KY	B	B	B-	293.9	-4.45	1.7	0.6	19.7	25.3	8.6	10.1	15.3
First Citizens Bank of Butte	Butte	MT	B-	C+	C+	63.5	0.93	14.5	3.5	16.8	20.1	9.8	10.8	19.4
First Citizens Bank of Polson, N.A.	Polson	MT	E-	E-	E	21.1	-1.06	31.2	5.7	16.3	8.7	4.2	6.2	11.8
First Citizens Community Bank	Mansfield	PA	B+	B+	B	1195.0	25.50	5.2	1.0	21.7	29.0	7.2	9.1	15.1
First Citizens National Bank	Dyersburg	TN	B+	A-	A-	1623.1	28.81	5.2	1.5	10.0	35.1	8.3	9.9	16.4
First Citizens National Bank of Upper Sand	Upper Sandusky	OH	B-	C+	B-	241.3	4.88	6.2	1.0	22.7	26.1	10.0	16.8	26.6
First Citizens State Bank	Whitewater	WI	A-	A-	A-	292.6	17.98	5.2	0.9	17.8	30.2	10.0	18.5	29.1
▼ First Citrus Bank	Tampa	FL	D+	C	D+	305.8	16.02	7.5	0.2	7.9	0.3	4.2	8.9	10.6
First City Bank	Columbus	OH	C+	B	B	54.6	2.14	5.0	2.4	22.2	6.8	10.0	13.2	19.0
First City Bank of Florida	Fort Walton Beach	FL	E-	E-	E-	205.6	-2.30	6.1	0.5	16.5	10.0	0.0	2.6	4.7
First Clover Leaf Bank, N.A.	Edwardsville	IL	B-	B	B-	668.1	8.81	9.8	0.6	17.4	15.7	10.0	12.0	15.0
First Collinsville Bank	Collinsville	IL	B-	B-	B-	850.3	11.16	3.2	4.0	43.0	14.4	6.6	8.6	14.8
First Colony Bank of Florida	Maitland	FL	A-	A-	B	202.5	13.26	11.3	0.4	0.6	15.7	8.8	10.2	15.3
First Colorado National Bank	Paonia	CO	C+	C+	C	58.9	7.66	9.3	0.6	5.8	0.1	10.0	17.6	19.7
First Columbia Bank & Trust Co.	Bloomsburg	PA	A-	A-	B+	676.7	4.18	4.1	0.8	30.9	25.5	10.0	11.2	19.6
First Command Bank	Fort Worth	TX	B	B+	B+	719.0	0.15	10.9	25.0	0.0	52.9	6.1	8.2	13.8
First Commerce Bank	Marysville	KS	B+	A-	B+	66.1	5.38	9.4	4.5	31.6	0.9	9.8	10.9	15.8
First Commerce Bank	Lakewood	NJ	B-	B-	B-	826.0	29.98	12.4	0.0	27.5	2.1	10.0	12.7	15.0
First Commerce Bank	Lewisburg	TN	A-	A-	B+	328.9	10.02	9.7	3.2	14.2	16.8	8.6	10.0	14.3
▼ First Commercial Bank	Dexter	MO	C-	B-	C	231.6	4.70	16.5	0.8	4.4	17.6	9.2	10.7	14.4
▲ First Commercial Bank	Jackson	MS	B	B-	B+	359.4	-1.96	20.4	1.7	11.3	5.5	10.0	12.2	15.2
First Commercial Bank (USA)	Alhambra	CA	B	B	C+	498.7	-0.17	8.9	0.0	2.8	2.3	10.0	22.8	27.0
First Commercial Bank, N.A.	Seguin	TX	B-	B-	B-	326.4	108.05	5.4	1.1	9.2	30.4	8.2	9.8	18.1
▲ First Commons Bank, N.A.	Newton Centre	MA	B-	C+	C+	347.4	18.52	4.8	0.1	37.2	6.5	8.0	9.7	15.0
First Commonwealth Bank	Indiana	PA	B	B	B-	6623.5	4.04	16.0	8.4	11.0	18.0	5.6	9.0	11.5
First Commonwealth Bank of Prestonsburg	Prestonsburg	KY	B+	B+	A-	298.7	-1.03	4.3	1.5	27.4	44.5	9.9	10.9	22.3
First Community Bank	Mobile	AL	C	C	C+	369.1	8.78	10.8	3.5	14.3	19.8	8.4	10.0	14.3
First Community Bank	Batesville	AR	B-	B-	B-	1140.3	11.13	9.7	4.5	22.0	14.8	5.4	8.6	11.3
First Community Bank	Santa Rosa	CA	B-	C+	C-	1057.2	9.72	7.1	0.0	9.1	3.9	9.9	11.4	15.0
▲ First Community Bank	Newell	IA	C-	C+	B+	94.8	0.77	1.0	2.1	4.5	18.4	7.9	9.6	15.1
First Community Bank	Elgin	IL	B+	B+	B-	171.5	-1.17	4.7	0.1	4.0	20.2	10.0	12.7	22.7
First Community Bank	Harbor Springs	MI	B-	B+	B+	265.2	-2.10	10.6	0.7	14.4	8.3	8.9	10.5	14.1
First Community Bank	Lester Prairie	MN	C+	C+	C+	58.8	3.94	5.6	2.0	11.0	30.2	7.9	9.6	17.0
First Community Bank	Glasgow	MT	C	C-	C-	275.9	0.84	3.6	1.4	7.7	40.0	9.5	10.6	17.9
First Community Bank	Beemer	NE	B-	C+	C+	137.7	0.21	9.6	2.3	0.7	11.2	8.4	10.0	13.6
First Community Bank	Lexington	SC	B-	B-	B-	913.3	7.46	4.2	0.9	11.3	31.3	8.1	9.7	15.3
▼ First Community Bank	Corpus Christi	TX	B	B+	B+	402.8	3.17	11.9	6.5	16.4	12.4	9.2	10.5	15.3
First Community Bank	Bluefield	VA	B	B	B	2425.2	-1.17	3.7	3.2	26.8	11.8	7.4	9.2	13.6
▲ First Community Bank	Milton	WI	B+	B	B	97.7	4.88	5.7	1.0	15.3	27.0	6.6	9.9	12.2
▲ First Community Bank and Trust	Beecher	IL	D+	D+	D+	149.4	4.23	10.4	0.7	13.4	21.0	9.6	10.7	18.9
First Community Bank of Central Alabama	Wetumpka	AL	B+	B+	B+	346.8	5.44	7.8	4.6	17.7	31.2	6.2	8.2	13.6
First Community Bank of Cullman	Cullman	AL	C+	B-	B-	79.3	-2.43	4.9	3.6	38.8	11.5	10.0	11.9	19.6
First Community Bank of East Tennessee	Rogersville	TN	C+	C	D	172.2	-1.13	6.6	2.9	15.1	14.3	10.0	11.7	17.1

Arrows denote recent upgrades ▲ or downgrades ▼

www.weissratings.com

Asset Quality Index	Adjusted Non-Performing Loans		Net Charge-Offs Avg Loans	Profitability Index	Net Income ($Mil)	Return on Assets (R.O.A.)	Return on Equity (R.O.E.)	Net Interest Spread	Overhead Efficiency Ratio	Liquidity Index	Liquidity Ratio	Hot Money Ratio	Stability Index
	as a % of Total Loans	as a % of Capital											
5.3	0.86	6.4	0.05	3.7	0.2	0.52	4.91	5.48	84.4	3.4	9.9	11.7	4.4
4.4	0.70	6.0	-0.01	3.7	2.5	0.65	7.07	3.30	75.8	1.7	10.2	17.5	5.6
7.5	0.71	4.6	-0.01	2.1	0.3	0.28	2.34	3.21	84.1	1.2	27.9	37.5	4.5
6.1	0.36	2.6	0.00	7.5	0.9	1.19	11.92	4.44	57.6	0.6	5.1	34.5	6.3
2.3	2.37	15.3	0.00	9.2	1.2	1.59	14.54	4.69	48.4	0.7	15.0	47.0	6.4
8.8	0.15	0.5	0.00	3.8	0.5	0.70	4.05	3.38	72.3	3.8	37.8	15.4	7.6
1.5	3.22	22.7	-0.15	1.4	0.3	0.06	0.58	2.91	101.1	0.9	18.5	36.7	5.1
4.4	1.18	7.4	0.01	6.3	3.0	1.14	10.43	3.43	53.8	3.3	19.6	12.7	7.7
5.3	0.74	5.6	0.13	3.4	1.3	0.63	6.02	4.09	78.4	2.8	10.3	14.5	4.9
4.5	2.63	13.2	0.15	3.9	2.1	0.69	6.29	3.34	75.0	3.8	30.8	12.8	5.8
9.9	0.00	0.0	0.00	4.1	1.0	1.13	13.98	2.09	81.5	7.8	74.4	0.2	4.0
1.6	3.47	34.2	1.21	2.7	1.0	0.38	6.14	3.62	80.9	3.5	18.2	11.9	0.3
6.6	0.37	2.3	0.31	6.2	6.1	0.99	8.46	3.95	55.8	1.8	21.0	13.1	7.0
8.5	0.57	2.1	0.15	4.6	1.8	0.89	6.69	3.88	68.9	1.8	22.8	21.7	7.2
2.5	5.51	26.1	-0.04	4.5	9.0	1.08	11.25	2.61	83.3	3.1	38.2	20.7	5.4
7.7	0.87	3.3	0.07	6.3	2.3	1.32	10.45	4.12	63.8	2.3	30.7	21.6	7.2
8.6	0.36	1.9	0.04	6.1	13.4	1.50	12.49	3.20	55.4	3.5	21.5	13.2	10.0
5.6	1.29	7.5	0.01	9.8	4.0	1.80	18.18	3.53	59.3	4.3	12.6	6.1	7.5
6.9	0.65	3.1	0.00	4.3	0.5	1.00	9.37	3.61	74.5	5.3	28.6	3.1	5.5
1.3	4.54	41.2	1.63	0.0	-0.1	-0.78	-8.09	4.04	107.3	3.8	22.2	10.3	2.0
5.1	1.55	10.2	-0.06	5.8	9.7	1.10	10.43	3.68	62.4	3.4	13.6	12.0	9.7
7.5	0.66	3.5	0.10	5.6	12.2	1.19	11.01	4.25	66.5	3.1	26.9	17.7	9.0
8.9	0.04	0.2	0.11	4.1	1.4	0.76	4.49	3.53	76.5	4.9	23.8	4.0	7.6
9.1	0.00	0.0	0.16	5.2	2.1	0.94	5.33	3.12	63.8	3.3	41.6	18.8	7.8
1.7	2.19	18.3	0.06	3.3	1.0	0.47	5.25	3.91	78.1	1.8	19.2	13.1	4.1
7.5	0.00	0.0	-0.03	2.5	0.1	0.21	1.53	4.10	93.4	4.0	16.7	8.6	6.5
0.3	11.84	182.9	0.41	0.7	-0.4	-0.22	-8.62	3.17	106.8	1.6	17.0	23.1	1.1
4.5	1.61	9.2	na	2.3	0.7	0.00	0.00	na	37.7	3.1	13.1	13.0	7.2
4.4	1.34	11.4	0.07	5.4	6.1	0.97	10.99	2.94	56.7	2.6	12.5	15.8	5.7
5.5	0.51	3.1	0.00	7.1	2.5	1.74	16.70	3.87	54.8	4.5	37.8	11.5	8.0
3.0	1.50	6.8	0.57	9.2	1.7	3.75	19.84	5.30	64.4	3.3	8.1	11.7	7.5
7.0	0.77	4.2	0.01	5.3	5.3	1.08	8.84	3.32	63.1	3.0	9.2	13.5	8.3
5.9	0.58	2.7	0.24	6.3	8.6	1.60	20.59	2.79	63.4	7.1	58.6	2.1	6.0
6.1	0.47	3.6	0.00	6.9	0.8	1.57	14.45	3.60	57.6	3.2	10.9	12.7	8.1
3.8	2.31	15.6	0.00	9.1	8.9	1.60	17.47	4.37	37.8	0.7	8.8	34.0	7.8
8.4	0.14	0.9	0.02	7.2	3.3	1.39	13.92	4.13	54.8	1.2	16.3	28.6	6.4
1.9	3.91	25.3	0.00	6.8	2.1	1.21	10.81	3.74	51.9	2.6	7.3	15.1	6.7
7.3	0.59	3.5	0.08	4.1	2.5	0.86	7.01	3.49	71.8	0.9	9.6	17.8	7.6
6.7	0.55	2.2	0.27	4.3	1.8	0.51	2.25	2.88	63.3	0.5	5.0	44.0	7.6
8.8	0.03	0.2	-0.05	4.0	1.7	0.83	9.56	3.98	78.6	6.2	46.1	4.0	5.6
9.0	0.00	0.0	0.00	4.2	1.6	0.64	6.57	3.23	66.5	0.9	23.9	42.8	4.7
4.7	1.01	7.8	0.45	4.6	45.1	0.90	8.44	3.29	56.9	4.7	8.2	3.1	8.4
8.1	0.44	1.8	0.22	5.7	3.6	1.62	13.52	3.52	66.4	3.7	44.9	17.9	7.8
3.0	2.38	16.6	0.06	4.4	2.7	1.02	9.82	3.99	75.6	2.1	13.8	18.2	5.5
5.1	1.28	10.8	0.12	5.4	8.4	1.03	11.95	3.91	60.5	0.8	11.0	33.9	7.0
4.4	1.05	7.0	-0.18	9.8	19.8	2.63	23.25	4.06	37.2	2.0	15.9	19.3	8.9
1.9	3.00	16.2	0.69	4.2	0.6	0.88	7.11	3.07	61.0	5.8	43.1	5.7	6.7
6.0	2.64	9.3	-0.05	4.1	0.9	0.68	5.21	3.11	74.7	4.4	35.4	11.5	6.8
3.6	1.26	9.1	-0.07	6.7	3.2	1.59	15.08	4.69	67.8	4.0	13.3	8.7	7.3
5.8	0.96	4.8	0.03	3.5	0.3	0.75	7.69	3.63	78.7	3.0	30.8	16.9	4.2
2.5	4.82	20.8	0.14	5.9	2.2	1.09	9.82	3.71	69.5	5.7	40.5	5.7	6.1
6.9	0.14	0.9	0.00	4.0	0.8	0.75	7.38	3.92	70.9	0.9	22.0	38.7	6.3
5.6	0.87	5.0	0.02	4.1	5.4	0.82	7.72	3.42	72.7	3.7	27.3	12.2	6.5
4.6	0.91	6.1	0.39	7.4	4.8	1.57	15.65	5.70	72.3	1.8	17.4	20.8	7.6
4.1	1.37	10.7	0.10	6.6	20.0	1.09	8.25	4.05	59.7	3.5	6.4	10.7	9.6
6.1	0.49	2.9	0.00	7.2	1.3	1.74	17.31	3.53	59.4	4.6	37.0	10.9	7.3
2.2	6.03	25.9	0.59	3.1	0.5	0.45	3.80	4.30	83.2	5.1	30.5	5.0	5.3
5.9	0.62	4.1	0.18	8.5	5.1	1.96	23.34	3.97	50.7	2.2	22.2	18.8	6.7
9.3	0.04	0.2	-0.01	3.3	0.3	0.51	4.42	3.10	76.0	1.2	21.3	30.5	5.9
8.4	0.50	2.6	-0.37	3.1	0.8	0.58	4.93	3.61	84.5	3.7	12.5	10.0	5.0

Name	City	State	Rating	2015 Rating	2014 Rating	Total Assets ($Mil)	One Year Asset Growth	Asset Mix (As a % of Total Assets)				Capital-ization Index	Lever-age Ratio	Risk-Based Capital Ratio
								Comm-ercial Loans	Cons-umer Loans	Mort-gage Loans	Secur-ities			
First Community Bank of Eastern Arkansas	Marion	AR	B+	A-	A-	151.0	1.31	6.1	1.9	16.9	13.1	10.0	12.4	17.5
First Community Bank of Hillsboro	Hillsboro	IL	B-	B-	C+	92.3	27.28	10.9	4.0	17.2	33.7	7.0	9.0	17.3
First Community Bank of Mercersburg	Mercersburg	PA	B-	B-	C+	176.4	5.90	3.3	2.0	45.4	5.1	10.0	11.4	16.9
First Community Bank of Tennessee	Shelbyville	TN	A	A	A	479.7	18.89	6.3	1.0	39.2	13.7	9.7	10.8	15.6
▼ First Community Bank of the Heartland, Inc	Clinton	KY	B	B+	B+	187.7	2.19	3.8	3.5	9.5	21.2	7.4	9.3	14.9
First Community Bank of the Ozarks	Branson	MO	B	C+	C-	96.4	-1.01	4.2	2.1	17.2	30.3	9.4	10.6	15.7
First Community Bank, N.A.	San Benito	TX	B	B	B-	351.8	5.34	9.9	1.6	10.5	19.3	6.4	8.5	14.3
First Community Bank, Xenia-Flora	Xenia	IL	B+	B+	B-	39.5	-1.79	5.2	6.9	23.0	23.9	10.0	12.8	20.9
First Community Financial Bank	Plainfield	IL	B+	A-	C	1243.0	22.03	22.1	0.4	10.2	15.1	8.4	10.5	13.7
First Community National Bank	Cuba	MO	D-	E+	B-	200.7	-9.59	3.0	3.0	30.0	13.7	6.0	8.0	14.1
First Community Trust, N.A.	Dubuque	IA	U	U	U	6.9	2.81	0.0	0.0	0.0	69.9	10.0	96.9	247.6
First County Bank	Stamford	CT	C-	C	C	1519.3	5.95	4.6	0.6	45.2	17.8	7.6	9.4	14.7
▼ First County Bank	New Baden	IL	C+	C+	C+	488.7	12.43	2.2	5.7	46.3	8.8	6.6	8.7	14.7
First Covenant Bank	Commerce	GA	C+	C	D+	189.8	8.56	1.2	0.4	2.6	12.9	5.4	7.4	20.1
First Credit Bank	Los Angeles	CA	C+	B+	A-	489.1	21.33	0.6	0.0	13.8	6.0	10.0	36.8	39.7
First Dakota National Bank	Yankton	SD	B	B+	B+	1430.9	14.35	10.1	1.3	6.8	11.3	6.7	10.2	12.3
First Delta Bank	Marked Tree	AR	B-	B-	B-	59.1	-9.51	3.1	1.3	4.2	44.7	9.9	10.9	20.1
First Eagle Bank	Chicago	IL	A	A	A	528.3	9.59	0.9	0.0	17.3	20.0	10.0	13.5	19.7
▲ First Electronic Bank	Salt Lake City	UT	B	B	C+	18.8	34.82	0.0	19.2	0.0	1.8	10.0	54.2	148.8
First Enterprise Bank	Oklahoma City	OK	D+	D+	D+	172.3	5.51	16.6	1.2	19.8	0.0	8.9	11.0	14.1
First Exchange Bank	Mannington	WV	C	C-	D+	228.1	5.51	5.3	4.5	45.8	8.8	8.4	9.9	14.9
First Exchange Bank of Alabama	Louisville	AL	C+	C+	C-	140.8	8.11	7.7	2.4	18.0	26.2	8.3	9.8	16.3
First FarmBank	Greeley	CO	C+	B	B	157.2	10.99	6.9	0.6	11.4	11.6	7.7	9.9	13.1
First Farmers & Merchants Bank	Cannon Falls	MN	B+	B+	A-	277.6	3.14	9.7	3.0	9.4	12.5	10.0	12.8	16.2
First Farmers & Merchants National Bank	Fairmont	MN	B+	B+	A-	105.9	3.56	23.0	5.5	13.3	11.0	10.0	12.9	15.5
▼ First Farmers & Merchants National Bank	Luverne	MN	B	B+	A-	162.4	-0.02	13.9	3.3	2.5	4.6	10.0	15.3	17.3
First Farmers & Merchants State Bank	Brownsdale	MN	B+	B+	A-	82.8	-1.99	8.9	1.9	4.4	26.0	10.0	14.4	20.4
First Farmers & Merchants State Bank	Grand Meadow	MN	B+	B+	A-	57.8	2.21	8.4	0.4	7.3	11.7	9.4	11.2	14.5
First Farmers and Commercial Bank	Pikeville	TN	B-	B	B-	110.9	-0.88	6.6	4.8	13.0	25.4	10.0	11.3	21.3
First Farmers and Merchants Bank	Columbia	TN	B-	B-	B-	1340.5	9.30	10.6	1.4	17.0	28.0	6.2	8.2	12.8
First Farmers Bank & Trust	Converse	IN	B-	C+	B+	1547.3	4.97	13.9	0.7	5.3	18.5	8.1	9.9	13.4
First Farmers Bank and Trust Co.	Owenton	KY	C+	C+	C+	119.3	4.41	3.5	2.1	28.5	10.9	10.0	12.9	15.4
First Farmers National Bank of Waurika	Waurika	OK	B+	B+	B+	44.5	-2.73	1.6	4.5	3.0	57.8	10.0	20.7	54.8
First Farmers State Bank	Minier	IL	B+	B-	B-	171.1	4.04	6.0	0.3	7.7	30.7	9.7	10.8	18.4
First Federal Bank	Dunn	NC	C	C-	C	169.4	4.38	3.2	1.0	40.4	20.9	10.0	12.1	22.5
First Federal Bank	Dickson	TN	A-	A-	B+	507.0	5.43	2.9	3.4	19.1	42.2	9.2	10.4	24.5
First Federal Bank & Trust	Sheridan	WY	C	C	C+	256.7	5.07	7.5	0.9	21.2	30.0	10.0	16.7	26.1
▲ First Federal Bank Littlefield, Texas	Littlefield	TX	B-	C+	C+	48.2	-1.53	11.3	9.7	20.6	0.0	10.0	18.1	21.7
First Federal Bank of Florida	Lake City	FL	B	B	B	1223.6	7.10	13.3	5.8	22.9	28.7	10.0	11.8	18.0
First Federal Bank Of Kansas City	Kansas City	MO	B-	B-	C	689.9	44.35	0.0	0.2	59.5	18.0	10.0	18.0	36.9
First Federal Bank of Louisiana	Lake Charles	LA	C	C-	C-	829.4	4.06	2.5	1.7	27.5	25.6	10.0	12.4	22.7
First Federal Bank of Ohio	Galion	OH	D+	D+	D	238.5	3.14	0.1	0.7	28.9	29.6	10.0	15.0	34.5
First Federal Bank of the Midwest	Defiance	OH	B	B-	C+	2433.3	10.01	16.9	0.6	9.4	9.6	6.7	10.4	12.3
▼ First Federal Bank of Wisconsin	Waukesha	WI	C	B-	C	244.5	1.90	3.4	0.1	35.7	18.9	10.0	13.9	22.0
▲ First Federal Bank, A FSB	Tuscaloosa	AL	C+	D	C+	123.6	9.99	0.0	0.8	63.9	0.9	9.9	10.9	17.9
▲ First Federal Community Bank of Bucyrus	Bucyrus	OH	C-	C-	C-	143.2	4.68	4.5	4.5	56.8	10.9	6.6	8.6	14.3
First Federal Community Bank, N.A.	Dover	OH	B	B	B-	296.1	9.47	9.9	3.1	26.4	4.0	7.8	9.5	13.2
▼ First Federal Community Bank, SSB	Paris	TX	B-	B-	B-	386.9	8.76	10.9	2.7	40.6	6.0	9.9	10.9	16.5
▼ First Federal of Northern Michigan	Alpena	MI	C	C+	C	329.2	-2.76	5.9	0.4	23.7	37.4	6.6	8.6	16.3
▲ First Federal of South Carolina, FSB	Walterboro	SC	D+	D	E-	76.9	6.27	0.4	1.5	50.1	16.3	6.0	8.0	16.1
First Federal S&L Assn.	Hazard	KY	C+	B-	B-	71.4	-6.20	0.0	2.1	58.9	1.3	10.0	25.2	51.9
First Federal S&L Assn.	Morehead	KY	C	C	C	33.1	-0.09	0.4	1.4	64.8	0.0	10.0	28.4	49.7
First Federal S&L Assn.	Aberdeen	MS	C+	B-	B	32.4	4.45	0.0	2.0	58.7	11.6	10.0	21.0	51.5
First Federal S&L Assn. of Bath	Bath	ME	B-	B-	C+	132.8	10.56	0.8	1.0	65.1	2.6	10.0	15.8	28.1
First Federal S&L Assn. of Centerburg	Centerburg	OH	C+	C+	C+	23.4	-3.90	0.0	0.5	50.3	16.3	10.0	18.5	40.2
First Federal S&L Assn. of Central Illinois	Shelbyville	IL	B-	B-	B-	107.2	4.58	6.6	6.3	32.5	14.3	10.0	11.2	18.3
First Federal S&L Assn. of Delta	Delta	OH	C-	C-	C-	161.2	2.55	0.4	0.8	51.7	6.4	10.0	12.2	33.4
First Federal S&L Assn. of Greene County	Waynesburg	PA	C+	C+	C+	892.2	-0.22	0.0	0.9	66.0	21.2	10.0	13.7	30.2
First Federal S&L Assn. of Greensburg	Greensburg	IN	C	C-	D+	147.3	2.86	1.2	2.1	39.9	15.5	8.8	10.2	21.2
First Federal S&L Assn. of Lakewood	Lakewood	OH	C+	C+	C	1617.8	0.50	0.7	2.5	63.3	4.3	9.5	10.7	17.0

Asset Quality Index	Adjusted Non-Performing Loans as a % of Total Loans	as a % of Capital	Net Charge-Offs Avg Loans	Profitability Index	Net Income ($Mil)	Return on Assets (R.O.A.)	Return on Equity (R.O.E.)	Net Interest Spread	Overhead Efficiency Ratio	Liquidity Index	Liquidity Ratio	Hot Money Ratio	Stability Index
4.5	2.79	15.6	0.01	5.7	1.1	0.99	7.67	3.88	62.1	1.7	21.9	22.7	7.5
4.9	1.64	9.4	0.06	3.9	0.6	0.94	9.22	3.08	71.9	4.2	18.9	7.6	4.8
6.8	0.61	4.3	0.29	3.4	0.6	0.50	4.28	4.17	78.4	3.2	4.9	11.9	6.3
7.5	0.18	1.1	0.06	8.9	6.2	1.84	15.50	3.25	77.6	1.6	11.9	22.2	8.2
5.3	0.94	6.4	0.18	4.2	1.4	1.04	8.81	4.18	75.8	1.9	15.8	19.4	7.3
6.3	0.79	4.2	-0.08	4.3	0.8	1.12	10.20	3.94	74.4	2.5	22.6	17.4	4.8
7.4	0.44	3.0	0.02	5.7	2.8	1.09	12.34	4.80	70.2	3.0	13.1	13.6	5.0
8.3	0.14	0.7	-0.07	5.8	0.4	1.31	9.99	3.79	65.2	3.6	27.6	13.1	7.8
6.3	1.06	7.2	0.05	6.0	9.6	1.15	9.91	3.66	57.5	1.7	13.2	22.0	9.3
0.3	9.45	68.0	1.28	0.4	-1.4	-0.95	-11.44	3.92	96.0	2.4	16.1	17.0	3.0
10.0	na	0.0	na	9.5	0.9	19.11	19.13	3.14	67.3	4.0	na	0.0	5.7
5.4	1.48	11.1	0.39	2.2	2.3	0.21	2.39	3.09	83.6	2.3	5.7	16.1	6.1
2.5	2.41	21.7	0.25	4.6	2.9	0.81	9.27	3.05	62.5	2.6	9.3	15.5	5.6
8.3	0.55	1.6	0.05	2.8	1.0	0.64	8.54	3.18	88.4	7.5	60.5	0.2	4.0
2.4	6.71	14.7	0.06	10.0	15.9	4.77	11.75	6.51	12.5	0.6	19.6	50.6	9.5
5.2	1.15	8.5	0.02	7.2	12.5	1.22	12.12	4.37	62.0	3.7	8.4	9.9	8.6
8.8	0.16	0.7	0.30	4.3	0.3	0.69	6.33	3.35	70.8	3.8	34.2	13.9	5.1
8.9	0.23	1.1	-0.02	9.3	8.3	2.32	16.40	4.31	41.3	1.8	25.9	16.4	9.8
7.8	0.00	0.0	0.00	10.0	1.2	9.36	17.77	5.38	79.7	4.1	135.9	66.2	6.3
1.9	2.91	21.0	0.03	9.1	2.6	2.09	19.13	5.23	62.3	1.3	13.0	27.2	8.8
2.5	2.57	20.2	0.00	6.2	2.6	1.57	15.78	4.03	62.6	3.3	12.4	12.0	5.6
4.1	2.22	13.7	1.19	3.4	0.7	0.68	6.69	3.90	85.9	1.0	26.3	48.9	3.3
3.9	1.06	7.8	0.08	4.0	0.6	0.56	5.99	4.15	73.2	0.6	9.6	41.7	5.7
5.3	1.18	6.7	0.06	6.7	3.2	1.54	11.19	4.18	67.2	4.2	16.3	7.5	8.2
3.3	3.10	19.7	0.24	5.1	0.9	1.16	8.88	4.02	67.9	0.9	6.5	30.7	7.7
3.2	1.92	10.1	0.01	8.4	2.6	2.03	13.89	4.45	67.7	4.0	9.2	7.8	8.5
7.6	0.55	2.4	0.34	4.8	0.7	1.11	7.50	4.02	68.4	3.9	25.6	10.9	7.6
3.2	1.37	9.2	0.02	4.7	0.5	1.11	9.85	4.13	73.6	1.9	6.3	18.7	6.9
5.4	2.14	9.3	0.13	3.4	0.4	0.50	4.47	3.74	83.0	1.6	29.3	29.9	5.8
8.3	0.41	2.9	0.02	4.2	8.0	0.82	8.91	3.22	69.0	4.0	14.3	8.8	7.7
3.7	2.44	17.0	0.32	6.0	12.2	1.07	10.51	3.88	62.2	3.4	15.7	8.2	8.9
3.9	2.62	15.1	0.00	7.3	1.1	1.28	8.55	4.37	61.7	2.8	16.8	15.1	7.1
8.3	1.85	2.9	-0.05	5.1	0.4	1.32	6.26	3.62	67.8	2.9	50.3	26.1	8.1
8.6	0.06	0.3	0.01	5.4	1.7	1.36	12.08	3.49	63.6	3.2	25.3	13.9	6.3
7.0	1.11	5.9	0.00	2.2	0.5	0.40	3.27	3.58	95.1	1.8	27.3	23.7	6.3
5.9	2.43	8.8	0.22	6.5	5.5	1.50	12.47	3.64	58.8	3.5	35.8	16.0	7.3
5.2	3.12	11.3	0.09	2.0	0.4	0.19	1.21	3.22	89.0	3.5	18.5	11.9	6.5
7.8	0.29	1.4	0.00	3.5	0.2	0.66	3.59	4.05	79.3	0.7	10.3	35.3	6.8
4.8	1.30	6.1	0.07	6.5	11.3	1.23	9.82	3.72	68.6	4.1	26.0	7.8	9.4
9.2	0.56	2.1	0.01	3.0	1.9	0.42	2.86	2.15	85.4	1.8	26.0	24.1	7.9
7.3	0.84	4.1	0.07	2.4	2.8	0.46	3.64	2.97	86.7	3.9	19.7	10.1	7.1
7.7	1.62	4.4	0.37	1.3	0.1	0.07	0.47	2.63	96.0	6.0	59.6	9.7	6.4
4.8	1.12	8.0	-0.01	6.2	20.2	1.14	9.15	3.72	61.8	3.9	8.7	8.4	9.3
5.3	2.70	12.9	0.22	1.9	0.4	0.24	1.68	3.33	87.8	2.1	26.5	20.5	6.5
4.8	1.81	12.5	0.32	3.2	0.8	0.88	7.63	2.76	92.2	0.6	11.6	51.1	4.6
2.5	2.67	22.2	0.56	3.8	0.6	0.59	6.82	4.08	83.5	4.1	12.2	7.8	4.6
4.7	0.97	8.0	-0.03	6.3	2.5	1.17	12.41	3.71	62.1	3.2	11.8	12.3	6.1
5.4	0.83	5.8	0.18	3.7	1.3	0.46	4.11	3.84	80.1	1.3	15.5	28.2	6.1
6.0	1.33	7.8	-0.03	2.5	0.6	0.23	2.31	3.06	89.2	4.8	33.8	8.9	5.4
6.0	0.44	3.5	0.20	2.4	0.2	0.37	5.79	3.78	86.4	3.9	23.7	10.5	1.3
4.2	6.22	17.8	0.12	2.8	0.2	0.30	1.22	3.13	86.2	2.3	28.5	19.5	5.7
5.7	3.35	9.8	0.53	2.1	0.0	0.15	0.51	3.69	91.6	2.6	12.4	15.9	6.1
9.7	0.31	0.9	0.00	2.9	0.1	0.42	1.99	2.73	74.4	2.1	44.3	41.2	6.8
4.6	3.70	18.9	0.04	3.9	0.5	0.58	3.64	4.57	77.6	4.2	21.1	8.4	7.0
9.9	0.00	0.0	0.00	2.6	0.1	0.42	2.29	3.09	83.1	2.8	41.8	19.2	6.1
6.2	0.90	5.4	0.10	4.1	0.6	0.72	6.56	3.84	74.2	2.1	20.3	19.0	6.4
10.0	0.18	0.8	0.00	1.8	0.3	0.22	1.78	2.93	91.7	6.2	43.7	3.3	6.0
9.5	0.48	2.4	0.02	2.9	2.3	0.34	2.50	2.60	78.4	2.1	30.4	23.3	7.7
2.6	4.36	24.1	0.04	2.9	0.4	0.38	3.77	3.08	80.7	5.2	24.1	2.1	5.3
6.6	0.65	4.9	0.01	3.3	6.6	0.55	5.29	2.69	76.0	2.8	7.6	14.7	7.7

Name	City	State	2015 Rating	2015 Rating	2014 Rating	Total Assets ($Mil)	One Year Asset Growth	Commercial Loans	Consumer Loans	Mortgage Loans	Securities	Capitalization Index	Leverage Ratio	Risk-Based Capital Ratio
▲ First Federal S&L Assn. of Lorain	Lorain	OH	C	C-	C-	425.2	0.75	0.0	0.3	54.1	24.0	10.0	15.4	32.0
First Federal S&L Assn. of McMinnville	McMinnville	OR	B-	C+	C	396.0	6.89	0.3	0.1	38.5	31.7	10.0	14.7	28.3
First Federal S&L Assn. of Newark	Newark	OH	D+	C	C	187.6	4.84	0.0	0.2	52.8	6.9	10.0	18.0	28.9
▲ First Federal S&L Assn. of Pascagoula-Mo	Pascagoula	MS	C+	C	C	291.9	2.46	0.0	0.5	78.4	10.2	6.9	8.9	18.8
First Federal S&L Assn. of Port Angeles	Port Angeles	WA	C+	C+	C-	1011.3	9.99	1.5	1.1	33.8	27.3	10.0	13.8	21.2
First Federal S&L Assn. of Ravenswood	Ravenswood	WV	C-	C-	C-	17.8	6.77	0.0	0.1	65.3	0.2	6.0	8.1	17.2
First Federal S&L Assn. of San Rafael	San Rafael	CA	B-	B-	B-	186.0	-0.60	0.0	0.0	2.5	0.0	10.0	20.7	27.9
First Federal S&L Assn. of Valdosta	Valdosta	GA	C	C-	D+	168.0	2.58	0.2	1.5	68.7	1.6	10.0	16.8	27.1
First Federal S&L Assn. of Van Wert	Van Wert	OH	C+	B-	B-	107.4	-2.29	0.0	0.2	38.4	42.2	10.0	19.7	51.7
First Federal S&L Assn. of Wakeeney	WaKeeney	KS	D+	D	D+	27.5	-9.40	0.1	1.4	24.9	35.3	10.0	12.2	37.8
First Federal S&L Bank	Olathe	KS	C+	C+	B-	79.8	2.69	0.0	0.0	83.4	0.0	9.3	10.6	20.4
First Federal Savings Bank	Ottawa	IL	C	C	C-	359.8	-1.11	0.0	0.1	61.4	9.6	9.2	10.5	21.3
First Federal Savings Bank	Evansville	IN	C	C	C	400.0	-0.75	11.9	1.4	17.9	23.6	6.9	9.0	14.7
First Federal Savings Bank	Huntington	IN	B	B	C	296.1	7.87	13.8	3.4	15.6	22.1	10.0	11.2	16.7
First Federal Savings Bank	Rochester	IN	B-	C+	C	351.2	-2.11	0.0	0.2	67.7	0.0	10.0	12.1	21.0
First Federal Savings Bank of Angola	Angola	IN	B	B	B	136.5	-1.49	0.5	4.2	62.8	0.0	10.0	17.2	42.6
First Federal Savings Bank of Kentucky	Frankfort	KY	B-	B-	B-	232.9	0.80	0.9	0.4	62.4	1.1	10.0	14.3	23.4
First Federal Savings of Middletown	Middletown	NY	C-	D+	C-	155.3	0.74	0.0	0.0	1.0	35.0	10.0	35.4	120.4
First Fidelity Bank	Fort Payne	AL	C	C	C	92.4	1.04	8.1	2.1	26.4	33.8	7.1	9.1	21.7
First Fidelity Bank	Burke	SD	A-	A-	B+	350.0	0.20	3.8	2.3	1.7	37.8	8.3	9.9	15.6
First Fidelity Bank, N.A.	Oklahoma City	OK	B-	C+	C-	1502.7	4.57	5.8	16.2	7.3	29.2	7.2	9.2	14.9
▲ First Financial Bank	Bessemer	AL	C-	D+	D+	170.5	3.05	2.6	1.9	12.7	33.2	7.5	9.3	16.6
First Financial Bank	El Dorado	AR	B+	B	C+	901.5	4.87	5.5	2.4	5.2	2.0	10.0	12.5	20.9
▼ First Financial Bank	Aneta	ND	B-	B	B	41.3	-11.58	11.8	1.9	1.4	27.0	7.7	9.4	14.5
First Financial Bank in Winnebago	Winnebago	MN	B	B	B+	43.6	1.96	10.6	3.2	6.4	24.2	10.0	15.2	21.2
First Financial Bank, N.A.	Terre Haute	IN	A-	A-	B	2925.9	2.88	16.0	8.3	10.6	29.5	10.0	12.7	17.5
First Financial Bank, N.A.	Cincinnati	OH	B	B	B	8352.7	6.26	20.2	0.5	8.5	21.1	6.2	9.0	11.9
First Financial Bank, N.A.	Abilene	TX	A-	A-	A-	6660.7	3.33	7.5	6.0	14.8	40.7	7.2	9.2	15.9
First Financial Northwest Bank	Renton	WA	A-	A-	A-	1071.6	9.52	0.7	0.0	23.5	12.5	9.3	11.4	14.4
First Financial Trust & Asset Mgmt Co.	Abilene	TX	U	U	U	13.8	19.98	0.0	0.0	0.0	53.1	10.0	106.	334.7
First Financial Trust, N.A.	Wellesley	MA	U	U	U	8.7	5.83	0.0	0.0	0.0	38.3	10.0	92.1	241.8
First Florida Bank	Destin	FL	A-	B+	B	381.0	23.57	3.9	0.6	12.8	25.7	9.5	10.7	22.4
First Florida Integrity Bank	Naples	FL	C+	C	C-	1226.9	6.69	3.7	0.4	22.0	18.7	5.7	7.9	11.5
▼ First Foundation Bank	Irvine	CA	B	B+	B	3589.6	59.88	5.1	0.8	16.1	15.1	6.4	8.4	12.9
First Freedom Bank	Lebanon	TN	B-	B	B	434.8	38.45	12.1	7.5	12.1	0.0	6.2	9.2	11.9
First FSB of Champaign-Urbana	Champaign	IL	C+	C+	B-	181.8	5.74	4.6	1.3	28.3	0.1	7.1	9.1	20.5
First FSB of Lincolnton	Lincolnton	NC	B	B	B-	369.3	5.85	0.7	0.6	57.6	9.5	10.0	14.6	26.6
First FSB of Mascoutah	Mascoutah	IL	C-	C	C	99.1	7.14	0.6	0.6	31.5	50.4	10.0	13.7	33.7
▲ First FSB of Twin Falls	Twin Falls	ID	B-	C+	C+	586.6	3.40	4.9	4.2	37.3	2.7	9.9	10.9	17.4
First FSB of Washington	Washington	IN	C-	C	C+	70.0	3.90	2.5	3.1	46.3	3.4	10.0	13.4	29.1
▲ First General Bank	Rowland Heights	CA	B-	C	C	815.5	14.64	10.0	0.0	14.2	0.7	10.0	11.4	15.4
First Green Bank	Orlando	FL	B-	B	B-	491.4	31.46	6.9	1.2	7.4	3.6	8.4	11.7	13.7
First Guaranty Bank	Martin	KY	C+	B-	B	47.7	-7.86	4.0	6.2	15.8	23.6	9.7	10.8	28.1
First Guaranty Bank	Hammond	LA	B	B-	B-	1437.3	0.84	14.4	1.1	9.3	33.2	8.3	9.9	13.7
First Harrison Bank	Corydon	IN	B+	B+	B-	739.3	59.83	3.1	5.9	15.8	33.4	7.4	9.3	15.3
First Hawaiian Bank	Honolulu	HI	B+	A-	A-	19842.2	5.24	16.1	6.9	13.7	27.0	6.3	8.3	13.4
First Heritage Bank	Shenandoah	IA	B	B-	C+	41.4	0.37	11.1	2.8	19.7	24.0	9.8	10.9	15.6
First Heritage Bank	Centralia	KS	B	B+	B+	134.8	3.70	16.7	1.3	7.8	40.5	10.0	11.2	17.9
First Home Bank	Seminole	FL	C	D+	E+	132.8	32.37	39.7	0.5	12.2	0.1	8.3	9.8	15.5
First Home Bank	Mountain Grove	MO	C	C+	D+	219.9	7.02	2.6	1.1	24.4	27.0	6.1	8.1	14.5
First Hope Bank, A National Banking Assn.	Hope	NJ	C	C	C	488.7	5.72	4.0	0.2	13.5	25.2	6.6	8.6	12.6
First Illinois Bank	East Saint Louis	IL	A	A	A	47.3	8.71	6.5	1.9	1.1	80.6	9.9	11.0	63.2
First Independence Bank	Detroit	MI	C+	C+	C+	236.1	-3.54	15.3	0.1	20.3	3.3	7.7	9.4	13.6
First Independent Bank	Russell	MN	B	B	B-	275.7	-3.09	6.4	4.1	8.5	18.4	9.1	10.7	14.3
First Independent Bank	Aurora	MO	C+	C+	C+	97.0	-0.84	7.1	5.2	22.2	31.3	8.7	10.2	19.8
First Intercontinental Bank	Doraville	GA	A	A-	C	330.9	4.28	30.7	0.1	0.0	7.7	10.0	16.1	21.5
▼ First International Bank & Trust	Watford City	ND	B	B+	B+	2228.2	5.99	13.7	6.0	13.7	15.0	7.2	9.5	12.7
First Internet Bank of Indiana	Fishers	IN	B-	B-	C+	1821.0	56.41	5.0	9.1	11.8	26.2	6.6	8.6	12.2
First Interstate Bank	Billings	MT	B-	B-	C+	8944.7	4.25	8.3	10.5	11.3	23.3	7.8	9.6	13.9
First Iowa State Bank	Albia	IA	A	A	A-	149.2	2.72	6.7	1.6	11.1	28.3	10.0	14.4	21.9

Arrows denote recent upgrades ▲ or downgrades ▼
102
www.weissratings.com

Asset Quality Index	Adjusted Non-Performing Loans		Net Charge-Offs Avg Loans	Profitability Index	Net Income ($Mil)	Return on Assets (R.O.A.)	Return on Equity (R.O.E.)	Net Interest Spread	Overhead Efficiency Ratio	Liquidity Index	Liquidity Ratio	Hot Money Ratio	Stability Index
	as a % of Total Loans	as a % of Capital											
3.7	5.41	21.5	0.13	2.4	1.0	0.31	2.03	3.35	89.5	3.0	32.8	17.7	6.7
8.0	0.97	3.7	-0.02	3.4	1.6	0.55	3.73	3.44	77.0	5.5	45.7	8.1	6.6
6.7	2.00	8.7	0.01	0.6	-0.4	-0.31	-1.72	3.18	114.4	1.3	13.8	26.9	7.0
6.7	0.77	6.8	0.07	3.3	1.2	0.57	6.52	3.22	75.8	0.7	13.8	49.4	4.2
8.0	0.83	3.9	-0.03	2.5	2.5	0.35	2.48	3.13	86.0	4.0	27.2	13.7	7.4
9.8	0.00	0.0	0.00	3.6	0.1	0.57	5.82	3.57	77.4	2.7	23.3	16.1	5.7
7.1	0.00	0.0	0.00	3.0	0.4	0.31	1.51	3.59	85.0	0.6	8.6	41.7	7.7
5.9	2.37	11.6	0.08	2.3	0.3	0.28	1.62	3.99	88.8	2.1	11.2	18.1	6.8
10.0	0.00	0.0	0.12	2.6	0.3	0.40	2.30	2.61	84.2	5.4	55.4	12.0	7.9
10.0	0.21	0.6	0.00	0.7	0.0	-0.12	-1.00	2.44	103.8	5.8	53.3	7.5	5.0
3.2	2.68	20.0	0.03	10.0	1.9	3.13	29.18	4.91	34.1	0.5	8.3	47.6	9.4
4.2	2.56	16.1	-0.03	2.9	1.6	0.56	5.33	2.61	86.7	2.1	24.9	19.4	4.8
5.4	0.62	4.0	0.06	2.9	1.5	0.50	4.77	3.19	85.9	4.0	19.4	6.1	6.0
4.6	2.38	12.8	0.03	7.1	2.8	1.29	11.46	3.65	57.8	1.7	21.6	23.0	6.7
4.0	3.18	19.3	0.32	3.6	1.6	0.59	4.77	3.78	87.8	2.4	10.7	16.7	6.3
9.5	0.01	0.0	0.01	4.2	0.7	0.69	4.00	2.73	64.1	3.6	33.9	15.0	7.8
2.6	2.92	17.4	0.04	3.6	0.9	0.51	2.61	3.75	78.5	1.5	7.9	21.9	7.1
10.0	2.50	0.7	0.00	1.2	0.2	0.13	0.37	1.60	99.7	6.9	136.4	13.2	6.6
5.7	1.71	7.7	-0.09	2.9	0.3	0.45	5.04	3.04	79.8	3.4	53.8	21.6	4.4
7.5	0.34	1.8	0.04	6.9	4.5	1.68	17.41	3.55	55.6	5.2	36.1	6.7	6.3
4.2	1.34	8.0	0.06	5.5	14.0	1.27	12.13	3.37	69.1	5.4	26.7	5.0	9.7
4.0	4.53	18.0	0.15	2.5	0.6	0.46	4.68	3.05	90.0	5.7	41.3	5.8	3.9
4.7	1.32	8.7	0.17	10.0	24.8	3.77	30.30	4.91	49.0	0.6	6.1	28.0	9.5
7.2	0.05	0.3	0.00	5.0	0.3	0.95	9.85	4.05	63.7	3.9	11.3	8.6	4.9
4.1	3.26	13.4	0.92	5.3	0.4	1.19	7.65	3.94	64.6	4.7	27.5	6.6	8.8
5.6	1.20	5.6	0.15	5.4	21.9	1.02	7.67	3.81	66.9	4.8	19.7	4.5	9.7
6.0	0.60	4.4	0.08	6.5	71.7	1.16	10.91	3.75	55.8	3.5	12.5	8.2	8.0
5.9	1.01	5.4	0.19	8.4	75.2	1.56	13.29	4.16	52.0	4.7	20.3	5.8	9.7
7.5	0.40	2.7	-0.03	5.6	6.7	0.90	7.71	3.53	58.9	0.8	14.9	35.6	9.3
10.0	na	0.0	na	9.5	5.3	54.71	55.34	2.80	45.2	4.0	na	0.0	7.0
6.5	na	0.0	na	10.0	0.2	3.59	3.74	1.64	84.9	4.0	na	0.0	5.0
7.7	0.85	3.5	0.03	4.8	2.4	0.94	8.68	3.45	66.5	3.7	55.1	20.4	6.7
8.2	0.25	2.1	0.04	3.2	4.4	0.49	5.65	2.99	72.5	2.8	6.2	13.1	6.6
5.6	0.54	5.1	-0.01	5.2	17.5	0.84	9.80	3.19	58.6	2.9	31.2	11.8	6.4
4.4	1.19	8.5	0.10	5.1	2.0	0.70	7.08	3.91	67.3	1.3	22.0	29.7	5.2
5.7	1.04	6.2	-0.01	3.3	0.6	0.45	4.87	2.81	83.2	5.8	42.5	5.3	5.5
6.4	1.86	9.7	0.02	4.4	2.2	0.84	5.73	3.45	64.9	1.1	21.1	32.3	7.9
7.9	1.29	3.9	0.17	1.5	0.1	0.13	0.94	2.19	96.0	4.0	52.5	17.0	6.2
7.0	0.41	2.6	-0.02	4.0	2.7	0.62	5.66	3.76	81.8	4.3	22.5	7.8	7.1
6.5	1.79	7.3	0.02	1.0	-0.1	-0.12	-0.92	3.38	105.2	2.7	45.4	26.9	6.0
4.0	0.99	7.2	0.02	10.0	10.2	1.78	15.82	4.01	29.0	0.7	13.0	39.2	8.5
6.3	0.10	0.7	0.05	3.7	1.5	0.47	3.88	4.24	79.9	1.4	18.1	27.6	6.7
4.2	4.77	17.9	0.10	2.8	0.2	0.43	3.60	3.02	86.3	5.2	44.2	9.6	6.5
4.6	2.35	14.1	0.32	5.0	12.2	1.11	11.18	3.47	57.3	1.1	10.5	29.8	7.3
4.7	1.34	7.1	0.19	5.2	4.7	0.86	8.42	3.54	68.4	6.1	43.6	3.8	6.4
7.0	0.33	2.3	0.06	7.0	180.2	1.25	9.55	2.83	47.1	2.3	22.1	19.5	8.3
7.0	0.00	0.0	0.12	7.5	0.6	1.98	17.49	4.34	58.8	3.2	22.2	13.6	6.3
8.7	0.00	0.0	0.00	4.0	1.0	0.98	7.93	3.47	76.2	1.2	10.2	20.4	8.1
5.2	0.55	3.6	-0.14	9.6	3.3	3.48	36.11	4.56	47.4	1.3	8.8	25.7	2.7
9.1	0.05	0.4	0.02	2.5	0.5	0.33	3.77	2.97	84.8	3.5	30.7	14.3	4.5
4.8	1.69	12.0	0.37	2.8	1.4	0.39	4.40	3.37	84.4	4.7	16.6	4.1	4.8
7.8	3.47	4.0	0.15	3.3	0.2	0.61	5.13	2.93	75.7	2.6	38.3	24.7	6.6
5.6	0.85	5.9	0.23	3.8	0.5	0.69	8.23	4.19	91.6	1.9	18.7	19.7	3.9
4.7	1.06	6.7	0.09	8.2	3.4	1.65	15.61	4.43	49.7	4.0	19.9	9.6	6.3
5.6	1.06	5.3	0.11	3.8	0.5	0.62	6.10	3.53	73.2	4.0	45.6	15.7	5.4
7.9	0.58	2.5	0.12	10.0	5.6	2.37	14.69	4.19	45.4	1.7	26.7	26.5	7.7
4.4	1.67	12.3	0.23	7.5	25.4	1.56	16.39	4.62	61.4	3.4	6.3	11.0	8.4
7.9	0.13	1.1	0.22	4.7	9.7	0.83	10.26	2.64	54.2	0.6	11.8	56.1	6.6
4.2	1.56	9.6	0.11	7.2	79.5	1.23	10.84	3.58	56.5	4.4	19.0	7.4	8.8
5.6	2.37	9.6	0.06	8.0	2.0	1.74	11.56	4.25	52.5	3.9	36.6	14.5	8.7

Name	City	State	2015 Rating	2014 Rating	Total Assets ($Mil)	One Year Asset Growth	Commercial Loans	Consumer Loans	Mortgage Loans	Securities	Capitalization Index	Leverage Ratio	Risk-Based Capital Ratio
First Iowa State Bank	Keosauqua	IA	A	A	A-	142.7	2.66	15.4	2.6	11.5	28.3	10.0	11.9	17.6
First Ipswich Bank	Ipswich	MA	B	B	B-	366.8	5.61	10.2	0.1	17.4	17.7	7.2	9.2	14.3
First Jackson Bank, Inc.	Stevenson	AL	B	B-	B-	241.9	4.39	6.4	4.9	15.0	29.5	9.3	10.6	17.1
First Kansas Bank	Hoisington	KS	C+	C+	C+	178.0	-0.72	2.3	0.7	6.2	71.9	5.7	7.7	23.6
First Kentucky Bank, Inc.	Mayfield	KY	B	B	B	399.3	2.96	5.4	6.2	27.9	23.7	7.6	9.4	14.5
First Keystone Community Bank	Berwick	PA	B	B	B+	965.2	-0.40	5.6	0.7	20.0	37.1	6.7	8.7	14.5
First Landmark Bank	Marietta	GA	C+	C+	B-	524.6	17.56	14.5	0.3	1.8	16.0	5.5	9.5	11.4
First Liberty Bank	Oklahoma City	OK	B+	B+	B+	298.1	19.97	27.3	0.2	14.4	10.1	6.2	10.6	11.9
▼ First Liberty National Bank	Liberty	TX	B-	B	B	293.8	-5.45	9.8	18.0	10.1	32.1	10.0	12.1	23.5
First Madison Bank & Trust	Athens	GA	A	A	B+	193.2	7.51	8.6	2.5	16.4	0.3	10.0	12.5	18.7
First Madison Valley Bank	Ennis	MT	B-	B-	B-	157.8	8.15	5.6	4.1	14.5	30.1	7.1	9.0	16.1
First Mariner Bank	Baltimore	MD	D	D-	E	929.9	4.18	8.4	3.1	26.4	16.7	7.6	9.4	14.0
First Merchants Bank	Muncie	IN	B+	B+	B	7006.5	13.47	16.4	1.1	11.0	18.8	7.9	10.7	13.2
First Metro Bank	Muscle Shoals	AL	A	A	A	566.6	2.77	8.1	3.0	20.4	24.0	10.0	11.8	21.2
▼ First Mid-Illinois Bank & Trust, N.A.	Mattoon	IL	B+	A-	A-	2110.2	1.25	14.5	1.7	8.6	26.3	6.7	8.7	12.9
First Midwest Bank	Itasca	IL	B	B	B	11445.2	16.49	20.9	2.0	6.0	17.1	4.3	8.7	10.7
First Midwest Bank of Dexter	Dexter	MO	B	B-	B-	317.9	2.57	17.1	2.2	12.7	7.5	7.3	9.5	12.7
First Midwest Bank of Poplar Bluff	Poplar Bluff	MO	B-	B-	B-	383.8	7.52	21.3	2.9	20.2	7.1	4.8	8.4	10.9
First Midwest Bank of the Ozarks	Piedmont	MO	B	B	B	119.6	2.44	14.8	5.3	14.9	16.3	7.9	9.7	13.3
First Minnesota Bank	Minnetonka	MN	B+	B+	B	405.6	-2.25	3.2	0.8	7.9	56.4	10.0	13.0	23.9
First Minnetonka City Bank	Minnetonka	MN	B+	A-	B	215.9	10.88	8.9	1.9	12.5	36.1	9.0	10.3	18.4
First Missouri Bank	Brookfield	MO	B	B+	B+	173.0	-4.32	11.4	2.1	21.2	8.9	9.5	10.6	15.2
First Missouri Bank of SEMO	Kennett	MO	B-	B	B	190.6	11.12	12.4	1.6	22.5	3.3	7.2	9.4	12.6
First Missouri State Bank	Poplar Bluff	MO	B-	B-	C+	163.0	-1.27	7.1	5.0	34.7	3.2	10.0	12.1	16.6
First Missouri State Bank of Cape County	Cape Girardeau	MO	C+	C+	C+	138.7	8.09	8.2	2.3	24.2	5.6	4.3	8.6	10.7
First Montana Bank, Inc.	Missoula	MT	B-	B-	B-	300.4	3.47	12.0	8.4	10.5	17.1	8.4	10.2	13.6
First National B&T Co. of Ardmore	Ardmore	OK	B	B	B	490.7	-1.05	9.4	3.4	9.8	38.3	7.4	9.3	15.5
First National B&T Co. of Bottineau	Bottineau	ND	C-	D+	C-	150.8	1.15	3.2	3.0	6.9	31.4	9.7	10.8	17.1
First National B&T Co. of Broken Arrow	Broken Arrow	OK	C	C	D+	187.3	-4.46	12.0	0.6	24.0	14.6	7.6	9.4	14.8
First National B&T Co. of Iron Mountain	Iron Mountain	MI	C+	C+	C+	325.0	0.71	10.0	2.3	12.9	36.4	6.7	8.7	14.1
First National B&T Co. of McAlester	McAlester	OK	C+	B-	C+	449.4	-0.47	4.1	2.2	9.4	37.5	10.0	11.7	19.9
First National B&T Co. of Miami	Miami	OK	C+	C	C	144.8	8.10	5.8	4.7	16.1	20.7	6.3	8.3	15.7
First National B&T Co. of Newtown	Newtown	PA	C+	C+	C+	922.0	7.93	0.7	1.2	10.8	50.4	7.1	9.1	21.9
First National B&T Co. of Okmulgee	Okmulgee	OK	B+	B-	B-	249.8	-7.16	13.7	3.5	16.0	35.3	10.0	11.9	17.3
First National B&T Co. of Rochelle	Rochelle	IL	B-	C+	C+	281.5	2.88	2.0	2.0	8.7	45.9	6.8	8.8	19.9
First National B&T Co. of Vinita	Vinita	OK	B-	B-	B-	367.8	5.56	16.7	4.1	8.0	39.3	6.9	8.9	15.2
First National B&T Co. of Weatherford	Weatherford	OK	C+	B	B	224.0	1.79	12.9	2.4	9.2	8.6	9.8	11.4	14.9
First National B&T Co. of Williston	Williston	ND	B+	A-	A-	444.0	-8.81	4.3	1.1	4.7	54.9	8.5	10.0	20.0
First National Bank	Hamilton	AL	A	A	A	288.8	3.69	2.9	10.7	12.4	46.1	10.0	15.7	30.2
First National Bank	Paragould	AR	A-	A	A	1136.0	12.61	6.5	2.8	25.9	9.3	8.4	10.4	13.7
First National Bank	Waverly	IA	B	B	B-	348.8	3.39	16.7	1.5	14.8	7.4	10.0	12.7	16.3
First National Bank	Mattoon	IL	C-	C	C	86.6	16.40	11.2	3.7	12.3	25.0	7.2	9.1	13.8
First National Bank	Vandalia	IL	B+	B-	B-	318.4	2.94	5.4	1.1	16.0	32.9	10.0	11.5	18.3
First National Bank	Cloverdale	IN	C+	C	C+	280.2	7.90	3.3	1.2	20.5	15.4	7.7	9.4	19.4
First National Bank	Goodland	KS	B	B	C+	179.3	-1.28	2.5	1.3	1.5	37.5	10.0	13.3	21.2
First National Bank	Arcadia	LA	B-	B+	B+	240.1	7.83	7.9	1.5	23.3	3.0	4.3	8.0	10.7
First National Bank	Damariscotta	ME	B	B	B-	1600.4	6.28	6.8	1.6	25.3	29.7	6.9	8.9	16.2
First National Bank	Slayton	MN	B-	B-	C+	203.3	2.26	4.4	9.5	3.5	20.2	9.6	10.7	14.9
▲ First National Bank	Camdenton	MO	C	D	D	212.5	0.40	0.3	0.4	10.2	53.4	10.0	16.5	54.1
First National Bank	Milnor	ND	B	B+	B+	68.0	-4.58	7.8	3.4	2.0	38.4	10.0	16.0	25.7
First National Bank	Alamogordo	NM	A	A	A	331.2	3.01	3.0	1.3	5.4	43.7	10.0	11.8	22.6
First National Bank	Heavener	OK	B+	B+	B+	78.2	1.94	3.1	4.0	15.5	6.0	8.3	9.9	17.5
First National Bank	Fort Pierre	SD	A	A	A	886.8	10.48	7.6	18.6	6.3	15.1	10.0	23.8	30.7
First National Bank	Rotan	TX	B+	B+	B	71.7	-3.74	6.2	3.8	0.7	44.2	10.0	11.9	22.7
First National Bank	Spearman	TX	B+	B	B+	202.8	3.15	8.0	2.0	7.2	27.4	10.0	11.5	17.9
First National Bank	Wichita Falls	TX	B+	B+	B+	448.7	7.95	6.2	1.5	23.9	6.0	6.8	9.6	12.3
First National Bank	Altavista	VA	B-	C+	C+	421.1	12.56	12.8	15.8	17.3	5.7	6.0	9.2	11.7
First National Bank	Waupaca	WI	D	D+	D	492.4	-12.06	6.2	1.6	20.0	11.7	10.0	14.9	19.7
▼ First National Bank & Trust of Elk City	Elk City	OK	B+	A	A-	323.4	2.71	9.8	1.1	15.4	30.1	8.9	10.3	17.9
First National Bank - Fox Valley	Neenah	WI	B	B	B-	475.3	11.03	18.7	1.3	16.8	7.5	9.9	11.1	14.9

Asset Quality Index	Adjusted Non-Performing Loans as a % of Total Loans	as a % of Capital	Net Charge-Offs Avg Loans	Profitability Index	Net Income ($Mil)	Return on Assets (R.O.A.)	Return on Equity (R.O.E.)	Net Interest Spread	Overhead Efficiency Ratio	Liquidity Index	Liquidity Ratio	Hot Money Ratio	Stability Index
7.8	0.73	3.6	-0.01	6.3	1.5	1.44	10.48	5.26	66.7	4.9	28.0	5.1	8.3
3.2	2.24	16.7	0.00	2.2	0.5	0.17	1.61	3.21	82.7	3.6	6.2	6.0	7.0
5.4	0.89	4.6	0.47	4.9	2.1	1.17	11.06	3.67	60.1	1.5	27.5	30.2	5.5
9.9	0.00	0.0	0.00	3.5	1.1	0.84	8.88	2.60	70.4	5.7	45.8	7.0	5.7
6.8	0.27	1.8	0.08	4.7	3.2	1.08	11.13	3.72	74.8	1.9	25.3	15.2	6.7
4.8	1.61	9.2	0.37	4.1	6.8	0.93	8.51	3.21	62.5	3.8	6.5	8.8	7.7
3.7	0.78	5.4	0.01	5.8	3.7	1.01	8.77	3.99	61.8	1.6	22.4	25.6	6.6
7.9	0.24	1.8	-0.04	5.3	1.8	0.92	8.38	4.48	74.6	1.4	14.6	26.0	6.2
5.7	1.36	6.1	0.41	3.0	1.3	0.56	4.68	3.11	73.1	3.6	27.5	12.6	6.8
7.3	0.00	0.0	0.12	9.6	2.4	1.70	13.95	4.50	43.9	2.1	21.3	19.4	7.9
5.3	1.20	6.8	0.07	5.4	1.6	1.41	15.10	4.01	67.2	5.5	45.5	8.5	5.1
3.9	1.71	12.0	0.18	1.2	2.3	0.32	2.93	3.41	91.6	0.7	8.5	34.4	2.0
5.8	0.74	4.7	0.06	6.3	63.9	1.25	8.92	3.97	59.9	3.5	13.9	5.4	9.3
8.8	0.31	1.6	0.05	8.7	5.6	1.32	11.64	3.69	47.4	2.4	15.7	17.0	8.3
7.6	0.41	2.9	0.04	5.5	15.2	0.96	9.21	3.40	62.5	4.5	14.2	5.8	8.3
5.8	0.62	4.9	0.24	6.1	86.3	1.08	9.39	3.77	59.4	4.5	11.3	4.9	8.6
6.9	0.29	2.4	0.00	5.2	2.1	0.86	9.39	3.64	66.2	1.0	6.0	29.7	5.7
4.8	0.65	6.0	0.25	5.7	3.8	1.33	15.89	3.85	64.7	1.1	2.1	27.3	6.5
4.6	0.95	6.8	0.05	5.7	0.8	0.95	9.73	4.01	67.5	1.2	15.7	29.7	5.9
8.4	1.80	4.3	0.07	4.3	2.3	0.77	5.66	3.16	67.5	3.0	41.9	16.1	6.9
6.6	0.83	4.1	0.08	6.1	2.3	1.47	13.54	3.65	59.8	5.5	46.9	9.2	6.4
5.4	0.63	4.2	-0.04	5.3	1.7	1.30	12.30	4.06	66.6	1.1	14.1	30.8	6.9
3.9	1.59	13.8	0.07	6.2	2.1	1.52	15.75	4.12	59.0	2.2	4.0	17.1	5.6
4.6	1.52	10.2	0.04	8.8	2.4	1.97	16.61	4.03	50.6	1.3	4.8	23.9	7.5
3.6	1.70	15.4	0.09	4.7	1.2	1.10	13.08	3.61	68.3	1.1	4.7	27.5	5.7
4.3	1.12	7.4	-0.02	4.9	1.9	0.85	7.87	4.23	71.8	4.4	14.6	5.7	5.8
8.5	0.18	1.0	0.04	4.7	4.0	1.08	11.56	3.58	72.2	2.5	27.9	18.4	6.1
1.6	3.30	17.2	1.18	3.6	0.7	0.63	6.00	2.94	54.2	3.8	16.6	10.3	7.0
4.6	1.82	11.8	0.00	3.3	0.8	0.55	5.88	3.82	80.8	5.1	26.6	3.6	5.0
3.2	3.45	19.7	0.32	3.5	1.4	0.58	6.20	3.57	78.0	3.4	42.4	18.1	4.4
2.2	6.33	27.0	0.05	6.5	5.2	1.54	12.52	3.40	55.8	3.7	30.2	13.3	8.9
7.6	0.29	1.9	0.03	3.5	0.5	0.50	6.23	3.62	79.2	4.3	15.5	6.7	4.5
4.7	3.90	15.1	0.25	3.8	5.1	0.76	8.32	2.78	72.3	6.6	51.7	3.5	6.1
5.3	2.68	11.4	0.02	6.3	2.8	1.39	10.94	3.90	66.4	2.2	30.3	21.2	8.3
6.3	1.07	3.4	0.01	4.9	3.5	1.71	16.90	2.82	73.6	4.9	40.0	10.2	5.0
3.4	2.56	14.6	0.20	5.5	3.9	1.38	14.95	3.57	63.5	1.2	14.7	18.5	5.7
4.5	1.16	7.7	1.45	5.3	1.8	1.06	9.00	4.75	58.7	2.8	9.6	14.3	7.7
3.4	7.49	27.3	-0.02	6.1	4.9	1.42	13.64	3.00	46.4	6.3	49.3	4.7	6.2
8.4	0.28	0.7	-0.08	6.9	3.4	1.59	9.74	4.13	59.2	4.2	48.7	16.3	8.9
8.0	0.21	1.5	0.52	6.8	9.7	1.22	11.58	3.86	51.6	0.6	4.9	35.5	9.6
4.6	1.42	8.7	0.60	5.6	2.6	1.03	7.98	4.19	52.1	3.5	14.8	11.6	7.6
6.8	0.43	2.5	0.12	2.2	0.3	0.43	4.44	3.39	90.5	2.6	28.9	18.4	4.3
6.8	1.10	5.3	0.01	5.1	2.5	1.05	8.35	3.80	65.6	4.1	27.4	10.5	7.2
5.9	0.95	4.8	-0.20	3.0	0.8	0.40	4.13	3.02	83.2	5.8	45.3	6.5	5.5
5.0	2.84	11.3	-0.04	4.6	1.5	1.15	7.98	3.65	76.3	3.8	13.1	9.8	7.8
5.2	0.61	5.6	0.01	8.1	3.2	1.83	22.47	5.21	66.8	3.0	10.1	13.1	6.9
6.9	0.80	5.5	0.10	5.6	14.0	1.19	13.05	3.31	52.5	1.5	17.7	19.7	7.4
6.2	0.29	1.4	2.27	4.2	0.9	0.61	5.54	6.08	60.9	4.5	21.8	6.0	6.1
7.8	4.00	5.3	-0.14	2.7	1.1	0.71	4.26	2.58	99.6	5.8	68.0	11.8	5.7
6.6	0.04	0.1	0.00	5.0	0.6	1.16	7.02	4.28	72.0	4.2	26.0	9.2	7.8
7.9	1.50	5.3	0.01	6.8	4.2	1.69	13.49	4.16	63.4	5.4	34.9	5.0	8.6
6.4	0.56	4.0	0.24	7.5	0.7	1.16	12.24	5.19	68.6	3.2	16.5	13.0	6.8
6.3	1.00	2.8	4.07	10.0	16.0	2.44	10.10	9.39	39.4	3.5	15.2	11.4	8.8
3.1	5.43	22.0	1.49	4.2	0.5	0.99	8.12	3.90	71.6	3.2	21.8	13.6	6.9
6.0	1.24	6.3	-0.01	6.8	2.5	1.65	13.52	4.33	59.4	1.1	19.9	32.3	7.5
6.4	0.28	2.3	-0.03	8.0	5.6	1.74	17.53	4.59	70.6	1.1	5.3	25.8	7.8
4.8	0.42	3.5	0.05	4.5	2.4	0.82	8.79	3.75	73.1	4.1	13.2	8.1	4.2
0.7	11.60	48.8	0.99	0.4	-2.9	-0.75	-4.94	3.98	85.4	1.3	20.8	28.5	6.5
4.8	1.72	9.4	-0.03	8.9	5.0	2.09	18.82	3.74	45.6	1.7	27.3	25.6	8.7
5.7	0.77	5.2	-0.03	5.0	2.7	0.79	6.95	3.82	65.9	2.4	17.9	14.3	5.9

Name	City	State	2015 Rating	2014 Rating	Rating	Total Assets ($Mil)	One Year Asset Growth	Comm-ercial Loans	Cons-umer Loans	Mort-gage Loans	Secur-ities	Capital-ization Index	Lever-age Ratio	Risk-Based Capital Ratio
▲ First National Bank Alaska	Anchorage	AK	A	A-	A	3665.8	0.77	7.9	0.5	2.9	50.1	10.0	13.7	20.8
First National Bank and Trust	Atmore	AL	B-	B-	C-	131.2	3.44	5.1	4.4	12.9	31.9	10.0	12.7	19.6
First National Bank and Trust	Phillipsburg	KS	A-	B+	B+	201.1	1.35	6.3	4.9	11.5	28.8	10.0	14.9	21.6
▲ First National Bank and Trust	London	KY	C+	C	C	203.7	-3.24	5.5	4.0	15.3	44.7	10.0	11.2	20.3
First National Bank and Trust Co.	Clinton	IL	C	C+	C+	124.2	2.86	1.9	0.5	11.7	24.7	9.7	10.8	20.8
First National Bank and Trust Co.	Chickasha	OK	B	B+	B-	523.8	0.88	19.1	2.7	8.1	28.3	10.0	11.6	18.5
First National Bank and Trust Co.	Shawnee	OK	C	C	C+	240.8	-5.72	9.0	0.9	6.2	51.4	10.0	12.3	25.5
First National Bank and Trust Co.	Beloit	WI	B-	B	B-	1140.5	35.59	6.8	1.3	17.3	24.7	6.6	8.6	13.6
First National Bank at Darlington	Darlington	WI	B+	A-	A-	141.4	40.12	4.1	3.8	7.5	21.1	10.0	13.3	19.5
First National Bank at Paris	Paris	AR	A-	A-	A-	139.3	5.78	3.5	8.4	23.4	8.8	10.0	11.6	17.4
First National Bank at Saint James	Saint James	MN	C-	D+	C-	29.7	-2.05	4.8	5.1	25.1	17.1	6.6	8.6	15.7
First National Bank in Amboy	Amboy	IL	C+	B-	C+	200.5	17.05	5.1	2.1	9.2	45.1	8.4	9.9	18.9
▼ First National Bank in Carlyle	Carlyle	IL	B-	B+	B+	191.3	28.27	2.3	1.5	8.2	41.1	9.5	10.7	18.9
First National Bank in Cimarron	Cimarron	KS	B-	B-	B-	87.0	-3.23	11.2	2.8	8.8	43.5	6.1	8.2	14.4
First National Bank in Cooper	Cooper	TX	B-	B-	C+	47.1	-3.59	2.2	7.2	18.0	25.5	10.0	12.7	38.7
▲ First National Bank in Creston	Creston	IA	B+	B	B	228.3	-3.60	9.2	4.2	17.2	9.6	7.7	9.4	13.1
First National Bank in DeRidder	DeRidder	LA	B+	B+	A-	238.4	2.26	3.5	2.8	31.1	26.1	10.0	11.1	18.3
First National Bank in Fairfield	Fairfield	IA	B	B	B-	166.3	13.79	14.3	1.6	14.0	7.6	3.7	8.2	10.3
First National Bank in Falfurrias	Falfurrias	TX	C+	C	C	67.4	1.33	9.0	9.3	1.0	41.7	10.0	12.1	48.9
First National Bank in Frankfort	Frankfort	KS	B	B	B-	41.3	1.63	4.2	4.0	10.4	39.7	8.2	9.8	17.1
First National Bank in Fredonia	Fredonia	KS	A-	A-	A	92.7	-4.00	4.5	7.1	9.3	65.5	10.0	16.0	38.2
First National Bank in Georgetown	Georgetown	IL	C+	C+	C+	55.4	10.65	8.1	0.4	5.6	11.7	6.7	8.7	12.3
First National Bank in Hominy	Hominy	OK	D	D+	C	42.4	3.81	12.6	8.9	10.2	34.8	5.9	7.9	19.1
First National Bank in Howell	Howell	MI	B-	C	D	383.1	8.06	3.9	3.0	8.7	38.7	8.9	10.3	17.0
First National Bank in Marlow	Marlow	OK	B-	B-	B-	63.7	-0.21	10.9	7.4	15.9	22.8	6.7	8.8	14.0
First National Bank in New Bremen	New Bremen	OH	B	B	B	272.9	3.17	7.2	2.7	12.8	25.7	7.9	9.6	22.3
First National Bank in Okeene	Okeene	OK	B+	A-	A-	70.7	10.03	3.7	0.3	0.1	14.0	10.0	19.3	27.3
First National Bank in Olney	Olney	IL	B	B	B	336.7	5.88	5.0	3.3	16.1	28.1	8.6	10.1	15.9
First National Bank in Ord	Ord	NE	C	C	C	130.9	-1.45	4.4	2.3	11.8	37.8	6.1	8.1	15.2
First National Bank in Paxton	Paxton	IL	B-	C+	C+	79.7	2.86	6.2	1.7	9.3	37.7	8.2	9.8	20.4
First National Bank in Philip	Philip	SD	A	A	A-	236.0	-3.33	7.3	0.8	0.3	15.7	10.0	12.2	16.5
First National Bank in Pinckneyville	Pinckneyville	IL	A-	A-	A-	86.7	7.91	0.9	6.4	26.7	47.0	10.0	15.9	34.6
▲ First National Bank in Port Lavaca	Port Lavaca	TX	B	B-	B-	280.8	5.72	3.2	2.3	27.3	41.7	9.7	10.8	25.2
▲ First National Bank in Pratt	Pratt	KS	C-	C	C	97.1	-8.38	9.4	1.1	6.1	32.1	10.0	11.2	17.6
First National Bank in Sioux Falls	Sioux Falls	SD	B+	A-	B	1105.4	2.99	13.5	0.7	19.6	22.9	10.0	12.9	17.2
First National Bank in Staunton	Staunton	IL	A-	A-	B+	497.1	2.38	4.4	4.3	27.0	24.4	10.0	12.1	18.1
First National Bank in Taylorville	Taylorville	IL	A+	A	A	199.9	0.49	5.4	3.8	10.2	50.5	10.0	15.2	31.1
First National Bank in Tigerton	Tigerton	WI	B-	B-	B-	21.4	-0.23	0.2	2.5	33.2	15.8	10.0	15.5	43.3
First National Bank in Tremont	Tremont	IL	B-	B-	C+	119.0	-1.74	6.5	2.4	24.9	29.7	10.0	11.4	19.9
First National Bank in Trinidad	Trinidad	CO	C	C	C+	215.2	6.50	0.8	1.0	29.2	19.0	10.0	11.1	28.0
▲ First National Bank in Wadena	Wadena	MN	C	C	C+	56.4	0.92	4.9	2.0	23.1	38.6	7.5	9.4	18.0
▲ First National Bank Mahnomen Twin Valley	Mahnomen	MN	B-	C+	B-	96.8	2.77	13.5	7.2	8.2	7.8	8.1	9.7	13.7
▲ First National Bank Minnesota	Saint Peter	MN	B	B-	C+	198.9	0.39	13.4	2.6	6.9	15.4	10.0	11.1	16.3
First National Bank North	Walker	MN	B+	B+	B	518.3	4.07	5.4	5.2	22.7	17.6	8.1	9.8	17.5
First National Bank Northeast	Lyons	NE	B	B	B+	281.9	4.22	6.5	1.0	1.7	36.9	6.0	11.7	11.8
First National Bank Northwest Florida	Panama City	FL	C+	C	C	122.0	5.13	1.6	0.1	11.5	10.2	10.0	12.8	30.9
First National Bank of Absecon	Absecon	NJ	C-	C-	C-	153.4	4.22	0.7	0.1	19.5	48.3	8.6	10.1	29.5
First National Bank of Albany	Albany	TX	A	A	A-	488.6	3.60	14.2	5.0	10.2	44.4	8.2	9.8	18.8
First National Bank of Allendale	Allendale	IL	B+	A-	B+	209.4	13.20	8.9	7.9	22.1	20.8	8.9	10.3	16.4
First National Bank of Alvin	Alvin	TX	B+	B+	A-	124.8	4.65	1.7	1.0	2.1	70.0	10.0	13.6	38.4
▲ First National Bank of America	East Lansing	MI	C-	D+	C-	1048.4	31.85	0.5	1.3	70.6	5.3	8.7	10.1	15.3
First National Bank of Anderson	Anderson	TX	B	B	B	161.4	-4.89	8.1	5.6	13.0	21.0	10.0	11.0	18.6
First National Bank of Anson	Anson	TX	C	C	C	59.9	1.69	9.0	10.3	21.2	25.7	7.4	9.3	17.5
▲ First National Bank of Arenzville	Arenzville	IL	B-	C+	C+	82.0	-4.81	10.2	5.0	15.6	16.0	8.4	9.9	14.0
First National Bank of Aspermont	Aspermont	TX	B+	A-	A-	58.6	-3.34	6.1	2.2	2.1	77.4	10.0	17.3	58.9
First National Bank of Assumption	Assumption	IL	C-	C-	C	23.1	0.30	2.2	4.4	12.0	31.7	7.1	9.1	24.2
First National Bank of Ava	Ava	IL	A-	A-	A-	62.2	1.96	7.9	3.7	21.6	34.5	10.0	13.5	20.7
First National Bank of Bagley	Bagley	MN	C+	C+	C+	85.7	4.30	9.2	8.6	19.0	21.7	5.8	7.8	12.7
First National Bank of Ballinger	Ballinger	TX	B-	B-	B-	145.2	-3.51	12.4	2.2	16.3	14.0	8.7	10.1	16.2
First National Bank of Bangor	Bangor	WI	A-	B+	B+	230.8	3.43	2.3	1.5	17.7	31.7	10.0	24.2	35.9

Asset Quality Index	Adjusted Non-Performing Loans as a % of Total Loans	as a % of Capital	Net Charge-Offs Avg Loans	Profitability Index	Net Income ($Mil)	Return on Assets (R.O.A.)	Return on Equity (R.O.E.)	Net Interest Spread	Overhead Efficiency Ratio	Liquidity Index	Liquidity Ratio	Hot Money Ratio	Stability Index
8.9	0.75	2.4	0.03	6.6	32.0	1.19	8.40	3.56	56.3	5.9	29.4	3.6	10.0
8.7	0.21	0.8	0.05	3.5	0.8	0.81	6.26	3.71	83.1	3.8	34.6	14.3	6.6
7.9	0.82	3.2	0.01	5.2	1.9	1.24	8.09	4.06	68.9	2.8	20.4	15.6	8.4
5.9	2.93	11.0	0.07	2.9	0.7	0.45	3.82	3.60	89.0	3.5	27.9	13.4	6.2
8.0	1.01	2.5	0.00	2.5	0.3	0.32	2.89	2.12	84.9	6.7	54.6	3.3	5.6
4.5	2.54	12.4	-0.05	8.7	6.1	1.52	12.08	4.76	54.4	3.9	28.0	10.1	8.7
6.6	2.76	7.7	0.57	2.0	0.4	0.21	1.63	3.04	93.4	5.4	46.0	9.7	6.3
7.9	0.34	2.4	0.06	3.7	5.7	0.68	6.52	3.59	80.4	4.8	27.0	8.5	8.3
8.3	0.32	1.4	0.05	4.5	0.8	0.78	5.71	3.49	65.4	4.1	37.9	13.7	7.6
5.5	0.73	4.4	0.09	7.5	1.7	1.63	11.38	4.63	67.6	1.4	13.4	25.9	8.7
4.1	2.29	14.7	0.00	3.3	0.1	0.49	5.80	4.34	86.2	2.5	32.3	20.3	3.9
5.6	1.78	7.4	0.12	4.1	1.3	0.88	8.23	3.50	76.6	5.8	44.7	6.3	5.6
8.0	0.00	0.0	-0.01	3.2	0.7	0.54	4.40	3.02	79.3	5.4	34.9	4.9	7.1
8.7	0.03	0.2	0.00	4.6	0.7	1.05	12.15	3.77	71.6	4.0	18.4	9.1	5.4
8.9	0.41	1.1	0.01	3.2	0.2	0.52	4.02	2.72	74.5	3.7	62.3	21.0	5.7
7.5	0.13	1.1	0.05	6.2	2.5	1.44	15.53	3.75	69.4	2.7	9.4	14.9	7.5
7.1	1.25	7.0	0.02	4.8	1.6	0.89	8.49	4.07	70.9	3.4	12.6	11.6	7.4
5.0	0.52	5.1	-0.03	5.3	1.1	0.94	11.43	3.83	61.6	2.0	4.1	18.1	5.5
5.9	4.01	7.7	0.84	2.4	0.2	0.33	2.81	2.50	86.9	6.1	49.2	5.1	5.0
7.5	0.92	4.2	0.07	5.0	0.4	1.18	11.03	3.62	65.6	4.6	46.4	12.8	7.1
7.9	2.08	3.8	0.55	5.9	1.0	1.40	8.66	3.30	55.1	4.4	56.5	15.7	7.9
1.8	1.77	14.7	0.00	6.1	0.4	0.92	8.31	3.67	58.3	3.0	9.5	13.6	6.1
4.7	1.93	10.1	0.33	2.2	0.1	0.16	2.07	2.81	87.7	3.3	43.3	18.9	2.4
4.6	1.80	8.3	-1.43	6.5	4.7	1.75	17.34	3.48	79.0	5.3	38.0	7.4	4.9
7.6	0.02	0.2	0.02	3.6	0.3	0.70	7.64	4.35	87.3	3.6	33.7	14.7	5.1
7.3	0.61	2.6	0.27	4.8	2.5	1.22	12.48	3.23	62.7	5.9	48.8	6.8	6.5
8.4	0.00	0.0	-0.01	7.9	1.1	2.11	11.56	3.83	46.9	3.5	33.7	15.2	6.3
6.4	0.49	3.0	0.03	5.1	2.5	1.01	9.15	3.28	60.9	4.0	17.4	8.9	6.8
8.8	0.00	0.0	-0.01	3.2	0.7	0.68	8.54	2.76	74.8	4.0	17.7	8.5	4.6
8.5	0.20	0.9	0.00	4.1	0.6	0.95	9.07	2.84	70.9	4.6	37.7	11.1	5.9
7.2	0.00	0.0	-0.02	7.7	3.7	1.99	16.96	3.79	49.6	1.9	14.0	8.0	8.9
8.7	0.29	0.8	0.00	5.9	0.9	1.34	7.72	4.50	64.2	5.2	26.0	2.6	8.6
9.3	0.13	0.5	0.02	4.7	2.0	0.96	8.42	3.23	57.0	3.3	33.5	16.2	6.6
6.1	1.76	7.9	0.96	1.7	0.1	0.11	0.92	3.25	83.5	5.1	30.1	5.1	6.2
5.9	2.76	13.3	-0.01	4.4	6.7	0.78	5.91	3.33	76.2	3.3	9.7	4.3	10.0
7.4	0.73	3.7	0.35	5.2	4.8	1.31	10.06	3.33	66.0	4.1	21.8	9.2	8.0
8.1	1.66	4.1	0.21	7.5	2.6	1.73	10.90	3.50	47.1	5.1	59.9	14.4	9.7
7.5	2.19	6.7	0.05	2.5	0.1	0.37	2.46	3.00	88.7	5.3	44.0	6.3	6.9
5.7	2.27	11.0	0.03	3.6	0.4	0.48	3.97	3.66	84.2	5.1	37.2	8.2	6.1
6.2	3.81	13.8	0.06	2.0	0.3	0.16	1.41	2.98	94.9	4.3	37.8	12.6	6.8
7.6	0.22	1.1	-0.24	2.9	0.2	0.44	4.55	3.37	87.9	4.7	40.5	11.7	5.3
8.1	0.07	0.5	-0.16	6.8	1.4	1.96	22.08	3.70	58.7	2.5	23.4	17.2	5.0
5.2	1.45	8.1	0.00	6.3	2.2	1.46	13.50	4.36	68.3	4.2	23.7	8.5	6.6
5.2	0.99	5.8	0.22	7.2	6.6	1.77	16.87	3.88	58.1	3.4	29.8	14.4	7.6
8.1	0.29	1.3	0.02	4.7	2.0	0.94	8.31	3.19	58.9	4.1	28.4	10.8	7.0
7.2	1.63	5.8	0.00	2.8	0.5	0.56	4.11	3.11	82.9	5.9	57.0	9.8	6.2
7.6	1.24	3.9	0.11	2.5	0.3	0.29	2.62	3.28	84.3	7.4	74.2	2.8	4.8
7.5	0.59	2.5	0.40	7.8	7.8	2.00	16.06	3.86	39.6	2.7	42.2	25.3	9.6
5.0	1.42	8.5	0.36	4.5	1.1	0.72	6.65	3.61	63.4	2.5	15.4	16.4	6.4
9.8	0.23	0.3	0.04	4.1	0.9	0.98	6.72	2.45	67.6	5.3	73.5	15.1	7.7
2.3	3.85	33.0	0.12	10.0	16.6	2.41	24.08	6.89	43.3	0.5	7.0	14.8	8.1
6.5	0.61	3.0	0.03	4.5	0.9	0.73	7.00	3.72	67.6	2.5	35.9	23.5	5.8
6.9	0.70	3.9	0.13	2.9	0.2	0.37	4.06	4.42	91.7	4.4	20.9	6.5	4.7
5.0	0.90	6.1	0.04	4.8	0.7	1.17	12.76	3.53	67.3	4.0	20.6	9.6	5.5
9.8	0.10	0.1	0.22	4.8	0.6	1.28	7.07	2.64	55.1	3.1	75.5	36.1	8.4
8.4	1.11	3.3	-0.09	3.1	0.1	0.64	6.47	3.06	77.9	6.1	60.7	5.3	4.2
5.0	2.51	10.9	0.40	7.8	0.7	1.53	10.54	4.97	56.8	3.6	32.5	14.3	8.2
5.5	0.53	3.9	-0.03	3.9	0.5	0.85	10.23	4.16	77.4	4.3	17.3	7.2	4.5
8.3	0.06	0.4	0.02	4.8	1.3	1.13	10.77	4.34	71.1	1.7	15.7	21.4	6.6
4.9	4.38	11.6	0.02	9.8	4.1	2.35	10.30	3.87	25.4	5.9	37.3	3.0	8.9

Name	City	State	2015 Rating	2014 Rating	2014 Rating	Total Assets ($Mil)	One Year Asset Growth	Commercial Loans	Consumer Loans	Mortgage Loans	Securities	Capitalization Index	Leverage Ratio	Risk-Based Capital Ratio
First National Bank of Barry	Barry	IL	C-	B-	C+	103.8	-3.75	8.1	3.6	11.4	16.6	10.0	16.3	21.9
First National Bank of Bastrop	Bastrop	TX	B+	B+	B+	497.5	1.51	2.2	2.1	18.1	32.4	9.7	10.8	18.8
First National Bank of Battle Lake	Battle Lake	MN	A-	A-	A	78.7	1.85	2.8	3.9	13.9	48.2	10.0	11.4	20.7
First National Bank of Beardstown	Beardstown	IL	B+	B	B	110.4	-0.68	6.8	7.9	15.5	7.2	10.0	12.2	18.3
▲ First National Bank of Beeville	Beeville	TX	B+	B	C+	306.4	-2.53	8.7	0.6	11.7	16.4	8.1	9.8	13.8
First National Bank of Bellevue	Bellevue	OH	B-	B-	B-	212.7	9.89	14.1	1.2	7.5	14.3	6.1	9.2	11.8
First National Bank of Bellville	Bellville	TX	A-	A-	A-	661.6	10.56	1.8	1.7	9.3	68.7	9.1	10.4	26.9
First National Bank of Beloit	Beloit	KS	C-	B-	C+	74.9	-4.85	7.1	1.7	11.6	31.0	10.0	11.0	19.6
First National Bank of Bemidji	Bemidji	MN	A	A	A	659.8	3.03	10.9	11.9	13.3	38.7	10.0	14.0	20.2
First National Bank of Benton	Benton	LA	B	B	B	55.8	-1.29	2.6	1.9	35.0	23.8	10.0	17.2	41.2
First National Bank of Berlin	Berlin	WI	B-	B-	B-	383.7	6.95	11.9	1.6	16.6	13.8	7.9	9.6	13.4
First National Bank of Blanchester	Blanchester	OH	B+	B+	B+	59.1	1.35	1.7	6.7	47.0	23.4	10.0	11.9	20.6
First National Bank of Bosque County	Valley Mills	TX	C+	C+	B-	115.4	0.61	10.1	6.3	22.9	8.7	8.3	9.8	19.6
First National Bank of Brookfield	Brookfield	IL	D+	D	E-	158.6	4.26	0.6	0.2	28.9	12.2	7.6	9.4	17.0
First National Bank of Brooksville	Brooksville	KY	C	C	C	62.5	-1.50	1.1	3.1	40.4	33.5	9.9	11.0	23.5
First National Bank of Brownstown	Brownstown	IL	C	C	C	36.3	1.61	5.2	7.6	15.0	34.9	9.8	10.9	20.1
First National Bank of Brundidge	Brundidge	AL	B-	B-	B-	92.5	0.61	5.1	4.0	14.5	26.5	10.0	14.0	24.7
First National Bank of Buhl	Mountain Iron	MN	E	E-	E-	23.8	3.17	8.1	10.8	41.4	0.0	5.5	7.5	12.0
First National Bank of Burleson	Burleson	TX	B+	B+	A-	191.7	4.75	10.2	2.1	2.8	56.9	6.9	8.9	24.4
First National Bank of Carmi	Carmi	IL	B-	B-	C+	394.0	-1.29	14.1	1.6	6.5	16.3	6.3	8.7	12.0
First National Bank of Carrollton	Carrollton	KY	A-	A-	B	103.9	4.16	2.4	2.4	34.9	22.2	10.0	12.3	21.4
First National Bank of Catlin	Catlin	IL	C+	C	C	52.9	10.48	11.7	1.7	28.8	17.1	8.3	9.9	14.9
First National Bank of Central Texas	Waco	TX	B+	B+	B+	767.8	-3.09	16.0	1.6	12.1	9.9	5.7	8.7	11.6
First National Bank of Chadron	Chadron	NE	A-	A-	B+	120.3	-2.70	5.9	1.6	0.4	22.9	10.0	11.6	15.8
First National Bank of Chisholm	Chisholm	MN	D+	C-	C	83.5	2.83	1.8	1.6	4.9	76.8	6.1	8.1	19.9
First National Bank of Clarksdale	Clarksdale	MS	A-	B+	B+	366.7	-1.35	8.4	3.1	7.4	26.1	10.0	11.9	16.6
First National Bank of Clinton	Clinton	MO	B-	B-	B-	70.7	6.99	8.5	7.6	17.4	26.6	10.0	12.8	23.2
First National Bank of Coffee County	Douglas	GA	B	B+	B+	149.3	5.61	7.1	1.3	12.7	10.1	9.6	10.7	17.1
First National Bank of Cokato	Cokato	MN	C+	C+	C	51.5	1.76	10.6	3.2	8.7	26.9	5.8	7.8	15.1
First National Bank of Coleraine	Coleraine	MN	C	C	C	84.0	2.39	4.4	2.8	17.1	49.7	5.7	7.7	16.1
First National Bank of Coweta	Coweta	OK	C	C-	C-	75.1	2.85	5.9	3.0	12.0	47.7	6.4	8.4	21.4
First National Bank of Crossett	Crossett	AR	B+	B	C-	152.8	12.21	19.6	9.0	8.6	26.7	10.0	11.2	17.3
First National Bank of Crystal Falls	Crystal Falls	MI	C-	C-	C-	72.2	-0.64	5.2	2.3	20.1	4.7	10.0	12.3	24.6
First National Bank of Cunningham	Cunningham	KS	B	B-	B-	33.3	-1.38	2.1	2.5	6.3	53.5	9.8	10.9	21.0
First National Bank of Decatur County	Bainbridge	GA	B+	B	B-	114.5	4.37	16.2	4.4	18.6	17.7	10.0	12.1	17.4
First National Bank of Dennison	Dennison	OH	B-	C+	C+	223.0	3.18	4.5	21.3	16.1	26.9	7.8	9.6	16.1
First National Bank of Dighton	Dighton	KS	C+	C+	C+	58.3	-4.29	8.4	2.8	1.2	47.4	10.0	21.1	34.3
First National Bank of Dozier	Dozier	AL	B-	B-	B-	37.6	-2.22	2.7	3.0	3.6	64.0	10.0	13.2	39.5
First National Bank of Dryden	Dryden	NY	B+	B+	B+	146.6	3.95	4.0	5.1	16.3	46.9	10.0	11.5	31.8
First National Bank of Dublin	Dublin	TX	B+	B+	B	83.4	-3.85	12.1	8.2	5.7	2.2	9.0	10.4	14.2
First National Bank of Durango	Durango	CO	B-	B-	B-	470.4	-2.96	3.7	0.6	6.2	56.0	6.2	8.2	14.0
First National Bank of Dwight	Dwight	IL	B-	B-	C+	127.9	8.14	1.6	0.5	7.8	40.2	10.0	12.0	33.2
▲ First National Bank of Eagle Lake	Eagle Lake	TX	B-	B	B-	111.4	1.07	8.8	0.7	3.3	16.5	9.1	10.4	14.4
▲ First National Bank of Eastern Arkansas	Forrest City	AR	C+	C+	C+	383.3	2.82	7.0	2.2	6.1	39.6	9.0	10.3	20.5
First National Bank of Edgewood	Edgewood	TX	D+	D+	C-	24.7	3.58	3.1	5.3	11.0	25.8	6.2	8.2	21.1
First National Bank of Eldorado	Eldorado	TX	B	C+	B+	59.7	-7.95	8.2	3.7	13.3	44.6	10.0	12.7	26.3
▲ First National Bank of Elk River	Elk River	MN	C	C-	C-	259.4	-4.61	13.6	0.5	4.9	36.0	9.6	10.7	17.2
First National Bank of Elkhart	Elkhart	KS	B	B	B	78.6	-4.24	4.5	3.6	5.2	23.2	10.0	11.3	18.5
First National Bank of Elmer	Elmer	NJ	C+	C+	B-	239.6	-0.79	7.4	0.8	24.6	9.2	8.0	9.7	13.7
First National Bank of Ely	Ely	NV	B+	B+	A	93.6	4.49	2.6	0.4	2.7	82.0	10.0	12.4	38.2
▲ First National Bank of Evant	Evant	TX	B	C+	C+	74.8	0.37	6.6	7.1	36.6	13.6	8.0	9.6	16.8
First National Bank of Fairbury	Fairbury	NE	B	B	B+	148.2	2.37	2.4	2.3	2.0	47.7	10.0	17.0	27.3
▲ First National Bank of Fairfax	Fairfax	MN	B-	D+	B-	28.5	2.96	10.9	0.7	1.3	0.9	10.0	37.4	38.2
First National Bank of Fleming	Fleming	CO	C	C	D+	23.5	4.44	6.9	4.0	5.5	7.7	10.0	11.9	19.0
First National Bank of Fletcher	Fletcher	OK	B-	B-	B+	17.8	-5.91	6.8	5.8	3.9	52.7	10.0	12.0	22.5
First National Bank of Floydada	Floydada	TX	A-	A-	A-	101.1	-1.18	5.4	2.0	1.1	22.3	10.0	11.8	16.6
First National Bank of Fort Smith	Fort Smith	AR	B+	A-	B+	1259.1	4.26	12.0	1.1	8.8	21.7	10.0	11.8	16.2
First National Bank of Fort Stockton	Fort Stockton	TX	C+	C+	C+	102.7	-1.44	10.5	3.9	13.3	44.5	6.7	8.8	18.2
First National Bank of Frederick	Frederick	SD	B-	B-	C	21.7	9.59	3.7	0.7	0.0	20.6	10.0	13.3	23.5
First National Bank of Germantown	Germantown	OH	D+	D+	C-	55.7	5.60	7.2	3.7	29.0	16.9	6.1	8.1	13.8

Asset Quality Index	Adjusted Non-Performing Loans		Net Charge-Offs Avg Loans	Profitability Index	Net Income ($Mil)	Return on Assets (R.O.A.)	Return on Equity (R.O.E.)	Net Interest Spread	Overhead Efficiency Ratio	Liquidity Index	Liquidity Ratio	Hot Money Ratio	Stability Index
	as a % of Total Loans	as a % of Capital											
1.5	7.83	32.6	0.18	3.3	0.5	0.64	3.71	3.70	72.4	3.6	21.8	11.9	6.9
5.8	1.01	5.2	0.03	7.3	6.7	1.81	16.38	4.18	59.8	3.2	30.2	15.8	8.7
7.8	1.32	5.2	0.09	6.4	0.9	1.58	11.67	3.46	56.1	4.9	46.8	11.5	7.8
6.7	0.72	3.9	0.17	4.5	0.8	0.96	7.79	4.23	74.4	3.2	24.2	10.2	7.3
8.7	0.00	0.0	0.00	5.9	2.7	1.13	12.10	4.08	58.0	3.9	23.0	10.4	5.4
4.9	0.90	6.7	0.02	4.7	1.3	0.90	9.91	4.34	71.3	4.5	17.2	5.4	5.9
8.4	0.21	0.4	0.01	6.7	6.9	1.43	9.95	3.51	50.9	2.6	52.3	38.8	8.9
8.4	0.52	2.2	-0.03	1.7	0.1	0.10	0.85	3.31	87.4	3.6	13.5	10.9	6.3
6.1	1.10	4.5	0.11	7.7	10.4	2.17	14.33	3.85	51.9	2.6	31.1	19.2	10.0
8.8	0.64	2.1	0.00	4.4	0.3	0.77	4.46	3.66	70.9	3.6	26.3	12.4	7.4
5.7	0.51	3.6	0.24	3.4	1.4	0.50	5.17	3.95	78.4	2.8	16.9	10.7	4.9
7.9	0.75	4.1	0.10	4.6	0.4	0.79	6.71	3.89	73.0	4.0	21.5	9.4	6.6
6.5	0.41	2.3	0.13	3.6	0.7	0.80	8.21	3.25	75.3	4.5	30.9	9.6	5.9
4.8	1.58	10.1	0.19	4.3	1.2	1.03	11.15	3.89	68.2	4.3	27.4	8.9	1.3
6.9	0.74	3.8	0.11	2.9	0.3	0.50	4.70	3.28	83.9	4.0	13.4	8.4	5.9
4.8	1.46	6.8	0.32	2.9	0.1	0.49	4.49	3.40	80.8	4.6	33.6	9.8	4.7
7.9	0.53	2.1	-0.18	3.5	0.4	0.57	3.93	3.72	81.7	2.5	34.2	22.3	7.0
3.7	0.97	9.7	0.21	0.8	-0.1	-0.43	-4.61	4.55	106.5	1.5	12.8	23.9	0.7
9.9	0.00	0.0	0.01	5.1	1.7	1.19	13.53	3.45	61.8	6.3	59.5	7.6	6.4
5.6	0.70	5.4	0.04	4.3	2.1	0.71	7.82	3.51	72.0	4.0	19.7	9.1	5.0
6.8	1.02	5.2	0.08	6.1	1.1	1.44	11.96	3.89	66.9	1.6	23.8	25.0	7.8
5.6	1.18	8.3	-0.02	4.8	0.4	0.98	10.26	4.51	76.4	1.7	13.3	21.0	4.7
7.0	0.29	2.4	-0.01	8.0	11.2	1.96	21.81	3.92	49.7	2.6	7.7	15.3	7.7
7.8	0.28	1.3	0.02	6.1	1.4	1.47	11.22	3.87	61.9	4.1	16.6	8.3	8.0
9.9	0.34	0.6	0.21	1.6	0.2	0.28	2.96	2.42	103.4	6.4	56.1	4.5	5.0
8.3	0.25	1.3	-0.27	6.2	3.5	1.31	11.03	3.79	56.8	2.6	20.3	16.7	7.3
8.4	0.42	1.7	0.00	2.9	0.3	0.58	4.34	3.66	87.2	5.0	44.1	10.8	6.7
5.0	1.09	6.6	0.74	5.7	1.3	1.26	11.85	3.96	61.4	3.7	34.4	14.6	7.3
8.5	0.25	1.5	0.02	4.2	0.4	0.97	11.92	3.73	73.0	6.3	46.7	3.0	4.0
9.3	0.01	0.1	-0.02	3.3	0.4	0.64	7.89	3.21	74.3	4.6	38.5	11.6	3.8
7.0	0.72	3.1	-0.02	2.9	0.4	0.65	7.33	3.33	84.7	4.8	52.3	13.0	4.2
5.6	1.46	7.2	-0.14	6.2	1.3	1.16	10.39	4.48	68.8	1.9	19.7	20.4	5.4
5.7	2.71	9.4	0.61	1.3	0.0	-0.01	-0.09	2.82	90.1	6.1	54.6	6.0	5.9
8.9	0.27	0.9	0.00	5.1	0.3	1.26	11.29	4.10	66.4	5.6	40.8	6.2	6.5
6.2	0.91	5.1	0.27	5.3	0.9	1.03	8.85	3.81	62.5	1.8	16.2	21.0	5.9
7.2	0.18	1.1	0.10	4.0	1.1	0.66	7.31	3.64	74.1	4.8	27.5	6.1	5.6
8.7	0.21	0.4	-0.01	2.8	0.2	0.37	1.75	2.71	77.6	6.2	51.1	4.7	7.1
9.6	0.00	0.0	0.00	3.3	0.2	0.61	4.29	3.07	77.0	4.0	73.2	21.3	5.9
8.0	1.63	4.2	0.12	4.9	1.2	1.10	9.26	3.56	62.1	6.5	47.5	2.7	7.7
7.5	0.22	1.5	0.06	5.9	0.8	1.35	13.22	4.72	72.9	4.5	23.4	6.8	6.9
8.9	0.46	1.8	-0.09	3.3	2.1	0.59	6.65	3.23	86.1	6.6	57.6	5.5	6.1
9.1	1.65	3.9	-0.01	2.9	0.5	0.54	4.30	2.19	78.8	4.9	54.8	14.4	5.9
4.8	1.30	7.8	0.44	4.9	0.8	1.06	9.74	4.96	75.8	4.7	23.5	5.1	5.7
7.1	0.47	2.0	0.10	3.6	2.5	0.88	8.39	3.05	71.4	3.9	42.8	16.2	6.6
9.4	0.00	0.0	0.00	1.8	0.0	0.15	1.85	2.72	94.1	5.7	49.1	5.3	3.1
9.1	0.04	0.1	-0.03	4.3	0.4	0.92	7.53	4.40	77.9	4.3	27.9	9.6	6.7
6.4	0.66	2.8	0.39	2.9	1.1	0.56	5.27	2.86	86.0	4.0	17.5	7.1	4.8
5.2	1.29	7.0	0.00	4.9	0.6	0.96	8.02	4.15	69.8	1.3	7.2	25.1	6.7
3.2	1.53	11.9	0.07	3.7	0.8	0.44	4.54	4.22	77.3	3.9	14.1	9.2	6.1
8.8	1.79	1.5	0.49	4.5	0.8	1.09	9.24	2.72	64.1	7.6	75.5	0.0	7.1
4.8	1.09	7.6	0.06	8.4	1.2	2.12	23.22	4.47	56.9	3.3	21.6	13.1	6.3
9.0	0.45	1.0	0.65	3.5	0.8	0.69	3.98	3.05	77.7	5.1	49.2	11.9	8.3
6.7	0.97	1.6	-1.48	4.0	0.3	1.19	3.17	3.54	67.5	6.7	51.4	1.4	4.9
5.3	0.74	4.8	0.08	6.6	0.2	1.29	11.34	4.86	59.5	0.6	4.9	37.9	4.3
8.9	0.13	0.2	0.37	2.9	0.1	0.48	4.01	3.81	88.5	6.1	68.4	6.7	5.6
7.3	0.00	0.0	0.00	7.1	1.4	1.75	15.93	3.29	45.5	1.8	21.3	21.3	8.5
4.4	2.29	11.8	-0.16	8.5	13.4	1.44	11.05	3.82	52.5	4.7	25.6	9.0	9.4
8.0	0.16	0.7	0.26	3.5	0.5	0.67	6.53	3.92	80.9	2.8	34.9	19.2	6.3
8.9	0.00	0.0	0.00	3.2	0.1	0.55	3.93	3.24	78.7	5.5	55.9	8.0	5.9
1.9	3.21	25.2	0.01	2.0	0.1	0.16	1.79	3.81	93.5	4.7	25.9	5.9	3.7

Name	City	State	2015 Rating	2014 Rating	Rating	Total Assets ($Mil)	One Year Asset Growth	Commercial Loans	Consumer Loans	Mortgage Loans	Securities	Capitalization Index	Leverage Ratio	Risk-Based Capital Ratio
▲ First National Bank of Giddings	Giddings	TX	B	B	B	187.9	0.22	5.9	2.4	16.1	44.4	9.5	10.7	20.1
First National Bank of Gilbert	Gilbert	MN	C	C	C+	35.9	4.20	2.3	4.5	32.3	20.3	6.2	8.2	19.0
First National Bank of Gillette	Gillette	WY	B-	B	B	571.1	-3.97	5.6	1.9	3.0	69.9	9.5	10.7	31.8
First National Bank of Gilmer	Gilmer	TX	B-	C	C+	310.0	-5.92	10.5	6.7	26.7	16.0	10.0	12.6	19.7
First National Bank of Girard	Girard	KS	B	B	B	75.7	-2.28	9.8	2.9	23.8	31.4	10.0	11.2	19.6
First National Bank of Gordon	Gordon	NE	B+	B+	B+	197.8	9.05	5.3	3.1	0.3	41.0	10.0	12.4	20.1
First National Bank of Granbury	Granbury	TX	A-	B+	B-	543.4	12.14	3.1	3.1	22.4	33.9	10.0	11.1	20.2
First National Bank of Grayson	Grayson	KY	B+	B	B	238.0	-0.76	4.1	10.2	28.9	25.1	9.5	10.7	20.1
First National Bank of Griffin	Griffin	GA	D-	D	E-	257.3	5.67	2.7	2.7	6.6	34.3	3.1	5.1	10.6
First National Bank of Groton	Groton	NY	A-	A	A	173.0	10.34	7.6	9.0	20.0	43.7	10.0	13.1	26.1
First National Bank of Hartford	Hartford	AL	B-	B-	C+	122.8	5.44	5.4	4.9	18.2	37.7	10.0	13.5	24.0
First National Bank of Hartford	Hartford	WI	B-	B-	B-	191.9	4.11	10.8	0.6	16.6	17.0	10.0	11.4	16.6
First National Bank of Harveyville	Harveyville	KS	C	C-	C-	14.0	3.08	5.1	4.2	27.5	0.4	8.8	10.2	23.3
First National Bank of Hebbronville	Hebbronville	TX	A	A	A-	121.8	-10.13	2.3	9.2	9.3	56.5	10.0	12.8	39.4
First National Bank of Henning	Ottertail	MN	A-	A-	A	115.6	8.10	9.1	5.8	14.7	25.8	10.0	11.6	18.5
First National Bank of Hereford	Hereford	TX	C	C	C	159.0	2.44	17.0	1.3	8.7	10.9	8.6	10.1	13.8
First National Bank of Hooker	Hooker	OK	A-	A-	A-	69.7	3.07	8.8	2.9	9.6	38.6	10.0	13.9	22.6
▼ First National Bank of Hope	Hope	KS	D	D+	B-	81.6	12.05	6.7	1.9	2.5	18.7	9.6	12.1	14.7
First National Bank of Hughes Springs	Hughes Springs	TX	A+	A+	A+	245.6	2.02	14.9	6.3	19.2	18.7	10.0	13.2	20.6
First National Bank of Hugo	Hugo	CO	B+	B+	A-	111.9	2.27	1.7	1.9	5.6	25.4	10.0	12.3	24.1
First National Bank of Huntsville	Huntsville	TX	B-	B-	B-	448.3	-2.13	7.4	5.7	20.1	42.1	9.4	10.6	22.0
▲ First National Bank of Hutchinson	Hutchinson	KS	B	B-	B-	654.8	2.43	9.4	1.6	7.7	30.2	10.0	11.2	15.8
First National Bank of Izard County	Calico Rock	AR	A	A+	A+	159.8	0.45	1.9	4.7	18.0	31.2	10.0	34.3	63.8
First National Bank of Jackson	Jackson	KY	C	C+	C-	108.7	-3.12	3.9	5.5	17.0	48.9	10.0	13.8	35.8
First National Bank of Jasper	Jasper	TX	B	B-	B-	247.3	-1.98	2.7	4.2	8.6	68.0	10.0	12.1	40.0
First National Bank of Jeanerette	Jeanerette	LA	B	B	B-	218.3	-1.32	6.1	3.5	29.4	15.9	7.4	10.9	12.8
First National Bank of Johnson	Johnson	NE	C-	C-	C	71.3	-0.80	1.2	4.0	4.3	45.5	10.0	19.1	42.2
First National Bank of Kansas	Burlington	KS	B-	C-	D+	77.3	5.35	5.3	1.5	9.2	61.3	7.6	9.4	23.6
First National Bank of Kemp	Kemp	TX	C-	C-	C	68.4	8.32	11.0	2.8	13.0	24.3	8.9	10.3	20.6
▲ First National Bank of Lacon	Lacon	IL	C-	D	C-	67.0	6.94	5.7	3.9	12.8	7.5	6.3	8.3	12.6
First National Bank of Lake Jackson	Lake Jackson	TX	B	B	B	238.2	3.05	2.1	1.0	0.7	77.4	8.9	10.3	43.2
First National Bank of Las Animas	Las Animas	CO	A	A	A	324.8	0.87	6.0	1.4	12.6	15.0	9.4	10.9	14.5
First National Bank of Lawrence County	Walnut Ridge	AR	B	B+	A-	203.4	7.07	8.1	2.9	15.5	25.3	9.3	10.5	16.9
▲ First National Bank of Layton	Layton	UT	A-	B-	B-	319.0	6.82	12.8	0.7	4.1	21.1	10.0	12.9	17.9
First National Bank of Le Center	Le Center	MN	A-	B+	B+	92.9	4.80	8.6	4.8	17.5	7.4	10.0	13.3	20.7
First National Bank of Liberal	Liberal	KS	B	B	B-	300.5	1.23	8.4	1.4	2.4	37.9	7.9	9.6	15.6
First National Bank of Lilly	Lilly	PA	D+	D+	C	21.4	0.86	4.7	5.7	15.1	51.3	10.0	16.6	40.0
First National Bank of Lindsay	Lindsay	OK	B-	C+	C+	53.2	-3.01	13.4	2.8	9.8	29.7	9.4	10.6	18.0
First National Bank of Lipan	Lipan	TX	D-	D-	D-	22.2	8.78	3.8	12.4	12.6	22.7	6.4	8.5	21.6
First National Bank of Litchfield	Litchfield	IL	B	B	B	110.5	8.78	6.6	2.7	11.4	14.8	8.4	9.9	14.0
First National Bank of Livingston	Livingston	TX	A-	A-	A-	360.4	4.90	3.3	4.7	16.2	39.1	10.0	13.6	42.7
First National Bank of Long Island	Glen Head	NY	B	B	B	3434.4	14.74	3.4	0.2	34.4	24.8	6.9	8.9	16.0
First National Bank of Louisburg	Louisburg	KS	B-	B-	B-	101.1	2.10	2.2	0.6	23.6	48.4	10.0	13.8	29.3
First National Bank of Louisiana	Crowley	LA	A-	A-	A-	356.3	0.68	12.6	1.8	15.9	11.1	9.6	10.9	14.7
First National Bank of Manchester	Manchester	KY	C+	C+	B-	143.0	-5.64	2.6	3.0	12.5	49.9	10.0	12.0	23.5
First National Bank of Manchester	Manchester	TN	A-	B+	B+	246.2	2.86	12.0	7.2	23.6	13.5	10.0	12.9	27.0
First National Bank of Manning	Manning	IA	B	B	B	78.5	7.17	5.1	1.2	6.7	19.5	10.0	15.4	26.4
First National Bank of McConnelsville	McConnelsville	OH	C-	C+	C	140.7	2.40	1.1	4.3	36.7	23.3	5.6	7.6	17.9
First National Bank of McGregor	McGregor	TX	B	B	B	243.6	25.24	10.3	7.0	37.0	0.0	7.0	9.2	12.5
First National Bank of McHenry	McHenry	IL	C-	C-	C-	170.8	3.29	0.9	0.7	13.1	55.8	7.6	9.4	21.8
First National Bank of McIntosh	McIntosh	MN	C+	C+	C+	27.5	2.83	1.7	4.2	7.6	25.5	10.0	24.0	73.8
First National Bank of Menahga & Sebeka	Menahga	MN	A-	A-	A-	91.1	5.26	7.7	4.4	17.3	26.4	10.0	13.6	25.2
First National Bank of Mertzon	Mertzon	TX	C-	C-	D+	317.7	7.07	4.1	1.3	3.1	55.5	5.6	7.6	24.3
First National Bank of Michigan	Kalamazoo	MI	B+	B+	B+	432.6	6.52	16.3	0.9	6.4	16.6	6.8	9.6	12.4
First National Bank of Middle Tennessee	McMinnville	TN	B+	B	B	484.7	0.97	7.6	0.7	24.5	29.5	10.0	13.2	24.9
First National Bank of Mifflintown	Mifflintown	PA	B-	B	B	476.2	2.49	5.1	0.4	27.3	25.6	8.1	9.7	18.2
▼ First National Bank of Milaca	Milaca	MN	B+	A-	A-	195.5	1.18	11.9	5.2	17.4	23.5	10.0	11.6	21.5
First National Bank of Monterey	Monterey	IN	B	B-	B-	307.6	-0.39	3.6	1.4	11.2	33.6	10.0	12.1	18.2
First National Bank of Moody	Moody	TX	B	B	B	48.8	1.70	3.0	4.9	17.6	34.9	10.0	19.0	35.1
First National Bank of Moose Lake	Moose Lake	MN	B+	A-	B+	88.8	4.26	8.1	3.3	26.2	8.7	10.0	13.0	18.1

Asset Quality Index	Adjusted Non-Performing Loans as a % of Total Loans	as a % of Capital	Net Charge-Offs Avg Loans	Profitability Index	Net Income ($Mil)	Return on Assets (R.O.A.)	Return on Equity (R.O.E.)	Net Interest Spread	Overhead Efficiency Ratio	Liquidity Index	Liquidity Ratio	Hot Money Ratio	Stability Index
7.2	0.51	2.2	-0.02	5.6	1.7	1.21	11.34	3.97	62.2	2.9	32.7	17.8	6.6
9.2	0.08	0.5	-0.03	3.5	0.2	0.76	8.61	3.43	76.3	4.6	33.9	9.9	4.6
7.0	3.02	5.9	-0.01	3.8	3.2	0.72	6.54	2.30	64.6	4.0	71.2	24.9	6.5
3.6	2.97	15.1	0.13	5.6	3.1	1.30	9.53	4.34	72.3	2.3	16.1	17.5	7.9
8.1	0.37	1.9	0.01	4.9	0.7	1.12	10.24	3.68	68.6	2.1	8.0	18.0	7.0
3.6	4.61	18.3	0.94	6.3	2.0	1.43	10.88	3.92	47.8	1.5	5.5	21.9	8.3
7.7	0.85	4.0	0.03	5.9	4.5	1.16	10.53	3.83	58.4	4.6	42.8	12.5	6.6
5.6	0.60	3.3	0.11	6.1	1.9	1.08	10.50	3.78	64.3	3.0	18.6	14.5	6.7
5.3	1.34	9.4	0.16	2.3	0.6	0.34	6.72	3.21	94.5	6.0	48.3	6.3	0.7
6.4	1.56	5.8	0.63	6.5	1.5	1.21	8.99	4.59	57.4	4.0	22.7	9.5	6.9
6.6	1.95	6.6	0.20	3.7	0.8	0.87	6.20	3.89	80.1	2.5	31.1	19.8	6.3
8.7	0.48	2.7	0.00	4.0	1.0	0.70	5.90	3.73	74.3	4.9	26.6	4.6	6.5
8.8	0.00	0.0	-0.02	2.8	0.0	0.32	3.24	3.75	89.6	2.9	44.7	19.3	4.7
7.9	2.13	4.4	0.14	5.9	1.3	1.39	10.26	3.28	53.8	2.6	52.4	39.3	7.9
4.6	2.40	13.2	0.06	6.5	1.3	1.56	12.59	3.93	62.5	3.3	23.6	13.6	7.9
2.5	3.24	20.0	0.13	5.9	1.6	1.40	13.81	4.06	62.7	1.9	30.7	26.7	5.7
8.4	0.48	1.8	0.01	7.1	0.7	1.39	9.53	4.70	61.2	3.5	39.9	17.6	8.7
0.6	4.51	23.5	0.36	4.2	0.6	0.92	7.43	3.82	69.1	2.5	21.3	16.9	6.7
8.0	0.52	2.5	0.06	8.9	3.7	1.98	13.65	5.53	58.2	3.3	8.8	11.9	9.8
6.0	2.41	9.8	-0.02	5.0	1.1	1.27	9.90	4.33	68.6	4.6	28.9	7.9	8.1
8.4	0.04	0.2	0.00	4.0	2.4	0.71	6.14	3.02	72.2	4.1	31.9	11.8	7.1
8.5	0.44	2.2	0.03	4.0	4.3	0.83	7.22	3.44	74.7	4.4	14.8	5.8	7.7
8.3	2.14	2.8	-0.02	7.8	2.0	1.63	4.86	4.37	54.2	4.5	61.6	17.9	8.8
6.0	3.30	8.3	0.00	1.9	0.1	0.09	0.64	2.80	95.9	3.3	61.8	31.8	6.0
6.8	3.80	7.6	-0.05	3.4	1.2	0.61	5.03	2.66	73.2	3.1	36.5	18.6	6.7
4.2	2.40	14.7	0.31	6.2	2.3	1.38	13.05	4.70	62.9	2.4	8.9	16.3	7.3
9.0	0.17	0.3	0.67	1.9	0.2	0.31	1.57	2.11	84.7	6.9	75.6	5.0	5.9
9.6	0.01	0.0	-0.06	4.2	0.7	1.18	11.57	2.85	68.9	4.8	38.2	10.6	5.7
7.7	0.22	0.9	-0.07	1.9	0.1	0.18	1.36	3.59	91.6	5.0	40.4	9.9	5.8
5.3	0.00	0.0	0.01	3.9	0.4	0.77	9.34	3.80	75.4	3.2	25.1	13.9	3.0
10.0	0.00	0.0	0.07	4.6	2.1	1.12	10.00	2.25	49.8	3.1	33.6	17.4	7.6
8.3	0.16	1.0	0.06	9.6	5.8	2.31	19.85	4.53	51.2	2.9	10.2	13.7	9.3
6.6	0.52	2.9	0.29	4.1	1.3	0.87	8.26	3.85	75.3	0.9	9.8	31.6	6.8
6.1	1.49	7.0	-0.01	5.7	3.3	1.46	11.12	4.49	69.3	5.1	32.5	6.2	7.7
3.7	4.44	23.9	0.01	7.9	1.6	2.48	19.01	4.03	47.8	3.4	20.9	12.8	6.9
8.7	0.00	0.0	0.00	5.4	2.7	1.17	12.28	3.53	62.1	1.4	12.5	25.4	6.1
7.4	2.39	4.0	-0.02	1.4	0.0	0.17	0.96	3.05	95.6	5.9	85.0	11.2	5.4
5.4	1.63	6.8	-0.09	6.1	0.5	1.29	13.36	3.68	59.5	4.7	32.4	8.4	5.2
7.1	0.00	0.0	0.00	2.2	0.0	0.20	2.31	2.75	91.7	4.9	68.0	13.6	2.6
8.0	0.17	1.2	0.00	5.1	1.0	1.24	11.99	3.68	64.2	2.2	22.6	18.8	6.7
8.8	0.18	0.4	0.14	5.4	3.6	1.33	9.05	3.07	67.8	6.6	63.9	6.5	9.0
9.2	0.09	0.7	0.00	4.6	24.0	0.98	11.36	2.88	54.4	4.3	14.9	7.2	7.9
9.8	0.00	0.0	-0.18	3.7	0.7	0.85	5.76	3.11	73.0	6.7	58.4	4.8	8.0
8.1	0.25	1.7	-0.01	7.1	4.3	1.66	15.45	4.11	56.9	4.3	14.3	6.3	8.2
6.3	3.06	8.8	0.02	2.8	0.5	0.49	3.96	2.99	85.9	2.9	51.0	29.2	7.0
5.9	1.09	5.3	0.20	7.5	2.5	1.33	10.50	4.12	53.2	1.8	18.3	20.7	7.7
8.8	0.00	0.0	0.00	4.3	0.5	0.90	5.92	3.26	58.2	5.7	52.7	7.9	7.9
3.8	1.44	9.8	0.27	2.1	0.6	0.58	4.89	3.49	85.2	4.4	22.2	6.7	6.4
7.7	0.14	1.3	0.08	7.2	2.0	1.24	14.02	4.90	63.5	0.5	7.9	39.8	5.4
6.1	2.81	8.0	0.26	2.5	0.5	0.42	4.15	2.87	85.0	6.0	55.2	8.4	4.9
9.1	0.24	0.3	0.03	2.4	0.1	0.33	1.37	1.90	84.3	5.4	75.8	13.6	6.8
8.0	0.76	2.9	0.15	6.6	1.0	1.54	10.59	3.82	62.9	3.7	43.5	13.5	8.6
9.2	0.48	1.3	0.01	3.6	1.7	0.70	9.57	2.08	53.8	6.4	59.7	7.2	2.3
7.4	0.07	0.5	0.00	6.1	3.5	1.09	11.44	3.60	57.8	2.7	19.0	11.5	6.7
8.8	0.12	0.5	0.07	5.2	4.1	1.15	8.68	3.14	67.8	1.5	20.4	26.1	7.6
4.1	2.15	14.0	0.00	4.1	2.9	0.83	8.37	3.47	70.4	2.9	13.5	14.6	6.3
4.1	3.96	19.5	0.17	7.4	2.5	1.73	14.59	3.85	56.1	5.3	34.3	5.4	7.6
6.8	1.41	6.3	0.19	3.9	1.8	0.77	6.52	3.15	63.2	5.5	39.7	6.3	6.9
5.7	3.02	7.1	-0.41	4.8	0.4	1.12	5.72	4.03	70.0	4.0	51.7	12.1	7.4
5.0	2.21	11.9	-0.01	7.7	1.1	1.74	13.28	4.22	61.3	3.0	22.3	11.4	8.8

Name	City	State	Rating	2015 Rating	2014 Rating	Total Assets ($Mil)	One Year Asset Growth	Comm-ercial Loans	Cons-umer Loans	Mort-gage Loans	Secur-ities	Capital-ization Index	Lever-age Ratio	Risk-Based Capital Ratio
▲ First National Bank of Mount Dora	Mount Dora	FL	A-	B	B-	222.7	6.56	1.2	1.2	17.6	43.4	10.0	14.1	23.0
First National Bank of Mount Vernon	Mount Vernon	TX	B	B+	B+	208.9	3.05	0.8	2.2	25.3	60.4	9.0	10.3	29.6
First National Bank of Muscatine	Muscatine	IA	B+	B+	B	309.3	2.60	12.6	5.1	30.1	4.3	10.0	11.5	16.3
First National Bank of Nevada	Nevada	MO	B	B	B	103.3	-8.35	5.6	1.5	17.2	39.4	10.0	13.2	24.9
First National Bank of Nokomis	Nokomis	IL	B+	B+	A-	149.5	-2.76	5.4	2.8	15.6	21.9	10.0	11.3	17.6
▲ First National Bank of North Arkansas	Berryville	AR	B	B-	B-	186.9	1.15	7.4	8.6	33.5	4.6	10.0	11.2	17.1
First National Bank of Northern California	South San Francisco	CA	B	B	B-	1172.7	5.68	4.3	0.1	12.1	30.6	7.5	9.4	13.1
First National Bank of Northfield	Northfield	MN	B+	B+	B	172.3	7.31	8.0	0.8	19.7	7.0	7.8	9.5	13.3
First National Bank of Norway	Norway	MI	B+	B+	B+	96.6	1.07	8.8	2.5	31.3	21.8	10.0	11.5	20.6
First National Bank of Odon	Odon	IN	C+	C+	C+	94.4	6.31	4.4	3.1	15.5	43.0	6.1	8.2	17.9
First National Bank of Okawville	Okawville	IL	B-	B-	C+	60.0	3.01	1.4	2.0	9.1	43.4	10.0	11.8	18.9
First National Bank of Oklahoma	Oklahoma City	OK	B+	B	B	383.9	10.39	7.9	2.3	16.1	5.0	5.9	8.9	11.7
First National Bank of Omaha	Omaha	NE	B-	B-	C+	18592.3	5.44	10.0	32.0	4.1	16.4	6.9	9.8	12.4
First National Bank of Oneida	Oneida	TN	B	B	B-	209.2	2.33	3.2	2.1	24.4	25.2	9.8	10.9	19.3
First National Bank of Orwell	Orwell	VT	D+	D+	D+	64.3	14.60	5.5	2.4	66.5	0.0	5.9	7.9	13.0
First National Bank of Osakis	Osakis	MN	B+	B+	B+	62.2	0.78	3.7	2.9	29.1	27.2	10.0	12.8	22.5
First National Bank of Ottawa	Ottawa	IL	B	B-	C	281.0	-3.94	13.3	6.2	25.6	14.5	8.0	9.6	15.6
First National Bank of Paducah	Paducah	TX	D+	D	D	39.7	-10.30	6.3	7.9	3.3	36.5	9.0	10.3	17.5
First National Bank of Pana	Pana	IL	B+	A-	A-	173.2	20.85	6.1	2.3	17.9	21.3	8.7	10.1	16.4
First National Bank of Pandora	Pandora	OH	C+	C	C	157.9	4.45	5.4	2.2	20.3	20.4	6.8	8.8	13.0
First National Bank of Park Falls	Park Falls	WI	B	B	B	135.7	2.41	10.1	1.5	24.1	33.6	8.6	10.1	17.6
First National Bank of Pasco	Dade City	FL	C+	B-	C	139.6	7.77	1.1	8.1	20.2	35.8	9.8	10.9	20.7
First National Bank of Pawnee	Pawnee	OK	B	B-	B-	63.9	-4.36	4.0	2.9	6.7	48.8	10.0	13.0	25.8
First National Bank of Pennsylvania	Pittsburgh	PA	B-	B-	B-	21395.9	28.45	13.4	6.1	17.1	20.4	5.1	7.9	11.1
First National Bank of Peterstown	Peterstown	WV	B-	B-	B-	61.3	-0.89	1.5	4.0	34.9	36.5	10.0	12.1	27.7
▲ First National Bank of Picayune	Picayune	MS	B	B-	B-	208.9	1.71	1.8	4.4	26.8	21.9	10.0	12.8	21.5
First National Bank of Powhatan Point	Powhatan Point	OH	C+	C+	C+	50.6	6.14	4.2	2.9	6.3	46.0	6.5	8.5	26.9
First National Bank of Primghar	Primghar	IA	B-	B-	B-	33.8	0.34	7.3	1.9	4.8	23.6	10.0	15.9	21.0
First National Bank of Proctor	Proctor	MN	C-	C-	C-	24.2	9.47	2.2	5.0	36.1	7.4	8.9	10.2	25.9
First National Bank of Pulaski	Pulaski	TN	B	B	B	753.9	2.86	5.3	3.3	12.9	30.0	9.3	10.5	16.0
First National Bank of Quitaque	Quitaque	TX	B-	B	B-	49.5	-3.42	4.6	4.6	0.0	15.9	10.0	16.3	24.2
First National Bank of Raymond	Raymond	IL	B	B	B-	139.8	-1.38	3.4	3.1	10.9	30.9	10.0	11.4	17.5
First National Bank of Rembrandt	Rembrandt	IA	B+	B+	B	57.5	4.56	7.2	4.7	9.2	15.2	10.0	17.7	29.9
First National Bank of River Falls	River Falls	WI	B	B	C+	289.7	5.90	4.8	2.6	12.8	32.9	9.5	10.6	19.7
First National Bank of Russell Springs	Russell Springs	KY	B	B-	C+	207.7	0.85	6.4	2.0	7.2	45.2	10.0	12.8	23.6
First National Bank of Sandoval	Sandoval	IL	B-	B-	C+	45.0	-0.71	2.7	9.2	27.6	37.3	10.0	11.4	20.6
First National Bank of Santa Fe	Albuquerque	NM	C	D+	D+	1771.9	5.23	8.7	0.1	5.9	21.3	9.8	11.2	14.8
First National Bank of Scotia	Scotia	NY	C+	C+	C+	467.4	0.94	9.6	32.0	16.8	5.9	5.3	8.2	11.2
First National Bank of Scott City	Scott City	KS	B-	B+	B	116.5	-3.59	12.9	8.2	4.3	21.5	10.0	11.7	15.4
▲ First National Bank of Sedan	Sedan	KS	C	C	C	49.4	-14.10	7.9	1.5	6.9	43.5	10.0	12.3	24.3
First National Bank of Shiner	Shiner	TX	B+	B+	B+	656.0	15.83	1.6	0.9	3.0	82.1	6.7	8.7	24.3
First National Bank of Sonora	Sonora	TX	B-	B-	B-	334.7	0.51	6.3	5.2	22.0	8.7	8.6	10.1	16.6
First National Bank of South Carolina	Holly Hill	SC	B-	B-	B-	192.2	7.57	3.2	2.4	10.8	25.6	10.0	12.8	25.6
First National Bank of South Miami	South Miami	FL	C+	C	C	647.5	5.74	3.5	0.1	9.1	24.5	6.3	8.3	15.0
First National Bank of South Padre Island	South Padre Island	TX	C+	C+	C+	63.0	0.73	2.1	0.8	33.6	18.9	7.7	9.5	22.4
▲ First National Bank of Southern California	Riverside	CA	B	C+	D	232.5	40.89	3.8	0.1	5.9	6.6	10.0	15.1	19.3
▲ First National Bank of Sparta	Sparta	IL	B	B	B	82.9	0.97	6.4	7.3	22.1	39.7	10.0	11.6	26.1
First National Bank of Spearville	Spearville	KS	B-	B	B	31.9	3.53	8.5	3.0	0.0	12.5	10.0	14.8	21.5
First National Bank of St. Ignace	Saint Ignace	MI	C+	C+	C+	280.6	4.48	3.7	1.3	9.0	50.7	7.9	9.6	20.3
First National Bank of Stanton	Stanton	TX	B-	B-	B	154.5	2.47	8.9	3.2	2.1	57.3	10.0	11.1	24.0
First National Bank of Steeleville	Steeleville	IL	B+	B+	A-	223.3	14.04	4.1	3.6	17.6	42.9	10.0	12.5	26.9
First National Bank of Sterling City	Sterling City	TX	C+	B-	B-	158.3	-1.47	2.7	3.4	6.1	62.5	6.7	8.7	26.4
First National Bank of Stigler	Stigler	OK	B	B	B	108.4	2.40	6.0	2.2	5.6	44.5	6.0	8.0	19.4
▲ First National Bank of Suffield	Suffield	CT	B	B-	B	254.8	4.40	14.9	0.7	42.0	11.1	9.2	10.5	20.1
First National Bank of Sullivan	Sullivan	IL	C	C-	D+	61.3	-3.14	6.6	5.6	32.9	10.1	8.5	10.0	16.7
First National Bank of Sycamore	Sycamore	OH	B-	B-	B-	133.3	8.92	3.5	1.9	14.6	54.1	10.0	11.6	24.7
First National Bank of Syracuse	Syracuse	KS	B+	B+	B+	296.9	21.06	9.6	1.4	8.2	17.0	6.7	9.6	12.3
First National Bank of Tahoka	Tahoka	TX	C+	C	C	52.1	4.91	4.9	3.8	2.6	33.3	10.0	11.1	27.3
First National Bank of Tennessee	Livingston	TN	B-	B-	B-	783.9	5.08	8.2	3.7	14.6	22.1	7.6	9.4	16.2
First National Bank of Thomas	Thomas	OK	B+	B+	B+	43.5	2.70	1.2	1.2	9.4	29.1	10.0	16.0	29.7

Asset Quality Index	Adjusted Non-Performing Loans		Net Charge-Offs	Profitability Index	Net Income ($Mil)	Return on Assets (R.O.A.)	Return on Equity (R.O.E.)	Net Interest Spread	Overhead Efficiency Ratio	Liquidity Index	Liquidity Ratio	Hot Money Ratio	Stability Index
	as a % of Total Loans	as a % of Capital	Avg Loans										
5.7	4.56	13.6	0.21	5.3	1.7	1.07	7.03	3.73	73.8	6.1	51.3	6.1	6.6
9.8	0.26	0.9	0.08	4.0	1.4	0.89	7.87	2.88	69.8	4.1	53.7	17.7	7.9
6.9	0.91	5.9	0.27	5.6	2.3	0.97	8.52	3.25	61.1	3.9	13.9	9.0	6.8
8.9	0.45	1.7	0.14	4.4	0.8	1.01	7.71	3.69	69.5	5.4	50.1	10.3	7.3
5.6	1.48	8.0	0.07	6.3	1.7	1.52	13.20	3.72	57.8	3.5	26.4	13.2	8.2
4.7	1.76	11.4	0.03	5.0	1.6	1.11	10.12	4.95	79.8	3.0	17.4	13.7	6.8
5.4	1.38	8.9	0.01	5.5	7.7	0.90	9.09	4.03	65.8	4.9	25.7	8.1	8.4
8.1	0.30	2.2	0.04	5.2	1.6	1.22	12.79	3.87	70.8	4.2	17.5	7.5	6.2
5.9	1.30	6.8	0.12	4.5	0.6	0.86	7.48	4.03	73.2	4.0	34.3	12.9	6.9
6.9	0.57	2.5	0.00	3.6	0.5	0.65	7.91	3.20	75.9	7.1	63.0	1.0	4.4
9.7	0.00	0.0	-0.01	3.6	0.3	0.73	6.13	3.64	79.7	6.5	61.1	5.0	6.1
6.7	0.66	5.3	0.00	7.2	4.7	1.68	18.70	4.14	57.2	0.8	12.9	34.9	7.1
4.5	0.94	6.0	1.55	7.9	177.0	1.28	12.58	5.93	57.5	3.9	8.6	6.1	8.2
5.0	1.41	6.9	0.30	5.1	2.0	1.26	11.20	3.71	66.5	2.0	27.6	22.8	6.6
2.0	3.14	33.8	0.02	5.0	0.4	0.93	11.77	4.44	66.3	1.3	3.7	24.1	3.9
5.6	2.24	10.9	0.18	6.2	0.7	1.44	10.83	4.39	64.8	4.6	26.3	6.7	7.9
4.9	0.87	6.0	-0.11	5.9	2.4	1.11	10.69	4.04	65.6	4.4	6.3	5.0	6.1
4.5	1.35	6.6	-0.09	1.3	0.1	0.24	2.47	3.34	93.3	1.6	28.4	29.0	2.1
5.2	1.44	8.6	0.01	5.6	1.5	1.16	11.28	3.79	65.2	4.4	27.4	8.6	7.3
4.3	1.21	8.6	0.06	3.5	0.6	0.55	6.25	3.90	82.6	1.8	12.9	19.7	4.9
6.1	0.74	3.9	0.26	4.9	1.2	1.17	11.18	3.75	66.0	2.4	34.2	23.8	7.3
4.7	2.03	8.5	0.33	3.0	0.4	0.35	2.96	3.82	89.9	5.1	40.5	9.5	5.3
7.2	1.25	3.3	0.07	4.7	0.5	1.08	8.49	3.68	73.6	5.2	40.6	8.9	6.3
4.4	0.88	7.4	0.22	4.4	114.1	0.78	6.53	3.23	63.4	4.1	8.8	5.6	9.5
6.6	2.33	8.9	0.02	3.0	0.2	0.41	3.44	3.47	83.9	4.2	50.5	15.9	6.3
4.4	2.11	9.6	0.20	10.0	4.6	2.95	22.15	4.67	45.9	2.6	34.1	20.1	8.9
9.7	0.10	0.2	0.03	3.1	0.2	0.65	7.17	2.26	67.3	7.2	87.8	5.0	4.3
7.5	0.00	0.0	0.00	4.4	0.2	0.81	5.29	3.90	69.2	2.3	30.4	20.7	7.0
9.0	0.21	1.1	-0.05	1.9	0.1	0.28	2.67	3.45	91.7	5.3	48.1	7.1	3.9
5.0	1.38	7.5	0.02	5.6	5.7	1.01	9.69	3.65	64.4	2.0	24.5	19.9	6.7
5.4	1.56	6.2	0.50	4.5	0.3	0.87	5.63	4.58	65.9	2.4	25.6	18.2	7.2
7.2	0.48	2.6	0.12	4.0	1.0	0.92	8.11	3.46	75.1	3.4	33.6	15.6	6.9
7.7	0.99	3.2	0.19	5.4	0.5	1.05	6.07	2.98	38.0	5.5	41.9	7.4	7.6
5.7	1.04	5.1	-0.03	4.5	2.4	1.13	9.94	3.31	69.1	5.3	30.3	3.9	7.1
5.2	3.08	10.1	0.59	3.3	0.9	0.59	4.57	3.94	82.9	3.0	40.4	20.5	6.2
6.2	1.36	5.1	-0.01	4.1	0.3	0.80	6.90	3.85	77.8	4.9	48.4	11.9	6.0
6.3	0.08	0.4	0.00	2.9	9.3	0.72	4.66	3.58	87.8	2.7	21.1	17.3	7.4
4.3	0.52	4.9	0.18	3.2	1.4	0.42	5.58	3.40	77.7	4.8	10.9	2.7	4.4
3.6	4.89	26.3	0.21	5.2	0.9	0.94	8.31	3.93	57.6	3.7	13.6	10.2	6.5
9.4	0.21	0.6	0.01	2.6	0.4	0.86	7.82	3.05	87.5	4.2	40.2	14.2	5.3
9.9	0.32	0.5	0.21	5.4	5.8	1.22	11.36	3.46	46.6	3.2	61.9	32.8	7.2
4.7	0.90	6.5	0.14	4.5	2.3	0.93	8.94	4.56	76.8	1.9	9.3	19.2	6.4
5.6	2.80	8.8	0.38	2.9	0.5	0.34	2.60	3.29	84.6	6.5	57.2	5.8	7.2
6.2	0.85	5.7	-0.03	3.1	1.8	0.38	4.69	3.04	76.2	4.8	28.3	5.9	4.1
6.3	1.10	5.3	0.04	3.6	0.4	0.81	8.17	3.76	76.3	5.5	49.5	9.0	5.3
7.2	0.35	1.7	0.00	4.9	2.1	1.29	9.02	4.43	58.4	2.2	19.2	5.4	5.7
6.3	1.75	6.4	0.09	4.2	0.5	0.81	7.07	3.66	77.4	4.6	27.9	7.4	6.5
6.2	0.00	0.0	-0.09	6.0	0.3	1.03	6.19	3.48	52.5	2.3	27.6	19.6	7.6
5.0	2.80	8.2	0.06	2.9	0.9	0.49	4.85	2.80	82.3	4.8	70.9	17.2	5.5
7.0	2.60	7.2	0.45	3.4	0.7	0.55	5.12	3.21	69.2	5.6	48.0	8.7	5.5
7.5	1.31	4.1	0.17	4.1	1.6	1.03	7.39	3.19	71.8	4.7	40.7	11.8	7.3
9.3	0.27	0.6	0.53	3.4	0.9	0.71	8.63	2.47	70.8	5.5	48.1	9.2	4.8
7.6	1.21	4.8	0.05	4.8	1.0	1.23	14.44	3.14	62.2	5.4	52.9	11.1	5.9
8.4	0.24	1.7	0.00	4.9	1.7	0.92	8.76	3.37	62.4	3.8	20.1	10.2	6.4
4.2	1.76	11.1	0.13	3.3	0.3	0.60	6.02	3.67	82.0	4.7	25.4	5.4	4.2
7.1	1.64	5.2	0.01	3.0	0.7	0.68	5.36	3.21	83.0	5.3	49.4	10.7	7.4
6.7	0.24	1.8	0.00	8.5	3.2	1.56	14.63	4.87	50.9	0.9	18.3	32.9	7.1
8.9	0.59	1.8	0.01	3.4	0.3	0.68	6.35	3.03	74.2	3.8	65.4	21.3	4.7
5.6	0.72	4.6	0.00	4.5	5.9	1.03	11.29	3.04	68.1	3.4	34.9	16.0	6.8
9.1	0.00	0.0	-1.01	6.7	0.5	1.62	10.37	3.80	61.2	4.3	57.3	16.4	7.6

Name	City	State	2016 Rating	2015 Rating	2014 Rating	Total Assets ($Mil)	One Year Asset Growth	Commercial Loans	Consumer Loans	Mortgage Loans	Securities	Capitalization Index	Leverage Ratio	Risk-Based Capital Ratio
First National Bank of Tom Bean	Tom Bean	TX	C+	C+	C	80.6	14.10	20.3	10.3	23.6	16.1	6.6	8.7	16.2
▲ First National Bank of Trenton	Trenton	TX	C-	C	C-	211.3	23.38	0.6	0.6	35.1	38.5	6.5	8.5	17.3
First National Bank of Trinity	Trinity	TX	B-	B-	B-	58.2	1.17	3.2	13.0	12.5	45.9	8.0	9.7	19.7
First National Bank of Wakefield	Wakefield	MI	C	C	C	50.8	4.44	1.8	8.2	19.2	39.3	8.3	9.8	22.6
▼ First National Bank of Waseca	Waseca	MN	B	B+	B+	123.7	0.30	7.7	2.8	33.1	6.5	5.2	9.3	11.2
First National Bank of Washington	Washington	KS	B+	B+	B+	76.6	0.96	1.0	1.7	12.5	44.0	10.0	22.7	46.4
First National Bank of Waterloo	Waterloo	IL	C+	C+	C+	446.7	1.12	3.6	0.8	14.7	47.9	9.0	10.3	19.7
First National Bank of Wauchula	Wauchula	FL	C-	C-	D+	71.1	-1.80	6.0	3.1	29.9	23.6	10.0	11.6	20.2
First National Bank of Waverly	Waverly	OH	C-	D+	C+	164.1	-1.63	4.6	1.1	17.8	14.1	7.3	9.2	17.3
First National Bank of Waynesboro	Waynesboro	GA	A	A	A	125.1	9.63	6.9	9.0	25.6	14.8	10.0	16.8	30.6
First National Bank of Weatherford	Weatherford	TX	B-	B	B-	220.3	6.42	17.9	3.3	10.9	1.0	6.5	9.7	12.1
First National Bank of Williamson	Williamson	WV	C+	C-	A-	86.2	-1.70	4.8	5.9	32.5	30.6	10.0	13.5	29.6
▼ First National Bank of Winnsboro	Winnsboro	TX	B-	B-	B-	139.9	1.21	4.2	2.6	15.0	15.0	10.0	18.2	27.7
First National Bank of Woodsboro	Woodsboro	TX	C	C	C	65.2	7.14	2.9	5.0	15.1	48.0	6.6	8.6	21.5
First National Bank of Wynne	Wynne	AR	B+	B-	C+	284.6	2.74	6.2	1.3	5.9	27.9	10.0	11.4	16.8
First National Bank South	Alma	GA	A-	B+	B	340.7	3.18	8.0	5.5	16.4	5.2	10.0	15.8	23.7
First National Bank Texas	Killeen	TX	B-	B-	B	1528.5	12.93	0.2	13.5	12.7	39.0	6.6	8.6	24.7
▲ First National Bank USA	Boutte	LA	B-	C	C	132.3	1.04	5.4	1.2	24.0	2.5	10.0	12.5	19.7
First National Bank, Ames, Iowa	Ames	IA	A-	A-	A-	733.6	1.25	3.8	0.2	9.6	39.3	8.6	10.1	15.2
First National Bank, Cortez	Cortez	CO	C+	C+	C	104.3	0.44	4.8	2.1	9.7	47.6	7.6	9.4	19.9
First National Bankers Bank	Baton Rouge	LA	B	B	B-	870.1	-10.70	6.2	0.0	3.3	7.6	10.0	15.6	20.1
▲ First National Community Bank	Chatsworth	GA	B	C+	C-	147.3	7.46	7.2	1.4	14.4	11.1	9.6	10.7	16.8
First National Community Bank	New Richmond	WI	C+	C	C-	196.2	2.31	7.6	2.5	15.4	22.6	6.6	8.7	13.7
First National Trust Co.	Pittsburgh	PA	U	U	U	20.1	-5.80	0.0	0.0	0.0	0.0	10.0	100.	131.1
First Nations Bank	Chicago	IL	B+	B	B	321.0	3.43	4.3	1.1	6.7	7.7	10.0	11.7	16.1
First NaturalState Bank	McGehee	AR	C+	C+	C+	51.6	-4.27	7.1	5.3	11.4	42.2	10.0	11.9	23.8
▼ First NBC Bank	New Orleans	LA	E+	B-	B-	4922.2	14.54	27.8	0.6	8.4	7.1	2.0	7.3	9.0
First Nebraska Bank	Valley	NE	B	B	B-	276.9	4.55	9.5	1.8	8.9	22.2	6.4	9.7	12.0
First Neighbor Bank, N.A.	Toledo	IL	C	B-	B	326.0	0.43	17.6	5.3	15.9	11.7	10.0	12.2	15.2
First Neighborhood Bank	Spencer	WV	B-	C+	C+	140.8	-0.41	7.5	1.7	34.8	15.5	10.0	11.1	18.7
First Neodesha Bank	Neodesha	KS	B	B	B	93.5	2.04	9.9	5.5	23.8	11.9	6.4	8.8	12.0
First New Mexico Bank	Deming	NM	A	A-	A-	219.4	5.13	2.4	1.9	10.9	36.6	10.0	12.3	28.1
First New Mexico Bank of Silver City	Silver City	NM	A-	A-	A-	107.6	1.23	2.6	1.7	11.8	40.0	10.0	11.3	26.7
First New Mexico Bank, Las Cruces	Las Cruces	NM	A	A	A	122.1	3.53	4.8	5.1	13.3	24.6	10.0	12.5	23.5
First Northern Bank and Trust Co.	Palmerton	PA	C+	C+	C	722.5	2.38	4.0	0.6	29.1	24.3	10.0	14.1	22.4
First Northern Bank of Dixon	Dixon	CA	B-	C+	C+	1119.1	7.85	10.6	0.1	4.1	23.0	6.2	8.2	13.3
First Northern Bank of Wyoming	Buffalo	WY	B-	B	B	288.3	1.86	12.7	3.8	10.8	24.1	7.7	9.5	14.3
▲ First Oklahoma Bank	Jenks	OK	C	C	C	468.7	20.66	10.0	1.0	19.9	0.0	4.6	8.4	10.8
First Option Bank	Osawatomie	KS	B	B	B	289.4	4.67	3.5	2.1	24.0	51.7	6.6	8.6	21.3
First Palmetto Bank	Camden	SC	B	C+	C-	631.9	11.57	1.5	0.9	17.0	9.1	10.0	12.4	18.2
First Partners Bank	Birmingham	AL	B+	B+	A-	267.4	9.52	19.0	1.6	7.5	12.0	8.5	11.5	13.8
First Peoples Bank	Pine Mountain	GA	B	B	C+	107.1	46.24	7.4	3.1	21.8	18.2	10.0	13.9	22.3
First Peoples Bank of Tennessee	Jefferson City	TN	C-	D	C+	144.8	4.98	13.7	1.8	14.8	17.8	6.8	8.8	12.6
First Peoples Bank, Inc.	Mullens	WV	B-	C+	C+	130.8	6.16	0.7	3.7	21.4	37.0	10.0	15.4	54.7
First Personal Bank	Orland Park	IL	C-	C-	C-	151.9	-0.36	14.3	3.6	31.0	13.0	7.3	9.2	15.6
First Piedmont Federal S&L Assn. of Gaffn	Gaffney	SC	A+	A+	A+	361.4	6.72	2.4	1.2	33.9	3.0	10.0	24.6	37.9
First Pioneer National Bank	Wray	CO	B+	B+	B+	166.9	-1.75	2.4	3.3	3.2	27.2	10.0	13.3	19.5
First Port City Bank	Bainbridge	GA	A-	A-	A-	159.3	7.54	6.3	1.8	18.6	15.7	10.0	12.2	16.3
First Premier Bank	Sioux Falls	SD	A	A	A-	1486.9	-4.28	6.5	37.9	3.7	18.6	10.0	14.3	22.1
First Priority Bank	Malvern	PA	C+	C+	C+	571.6	12.45	9.9	2.1	30.1	8.0	6.2	8.2	12.0
First Progressive Bank	Brewton	AL	C-	C	C	31.1	0.11	7.6	3.2	10.7	60.9	10.0	26.0	70.9
First Pryority Bank	Pryor	OK	B	C+	C	141.3	17.34	18.2	9.7	2.2	7.2	10.0	12.5	17.0
First Reliance Bank	Florence	SC	C+	C+	C-	406.9	5.45	7.5	13.5	19.3	10.1	7.0	9.9	12.5
First Republic Bank	San Francisco	CA	B+	B+	B+	67993.6	22.79	7.2	2.5	37.2	19.8	7.4	9.3	14.3
First Resource Bank	Lino Lakes	MN	A-	A-	B+	67.0	-7.59	8.0	1.1	1.9	17.4	10.0	40.5	80.9
▲ First Resource Bank	Exton	PA	C-	C	C	221.7	11.15	7.6	0.2	20.3	5.2	5.8	7.8	12.5
First Robinson Savings Bank, N.A.	Robinson	IL	B-	B	B	292.6	1.21	6.4	4.2	23.4	25.3	6.9	8.9	15.4
First S&L Assn.	Mebane	NC	B-	B	B	50.3	-5.59	0.0	0.0	50.3	24.3	10.0	23.6	62.0
First Savanna Savings Bank	Savanna	IL	D	D	D	13.0	-9.74	0.0	10.4	55.9	17.8	9.8	10.9	20.3
▲ First Savings Bank	Danville	IL	B-	B-	C+	37.8	-2.40	0.0	0.4	26.8	58.7	10.0	24.7	61.3

Asset Quality Index	Adjusted Non-Performing Loans as a % of Total Loans	as a % of Capital	Net Charge-Offs Avg Loans	Profitability Index	Net Income ($Mil)	Return on Assets (R.O.A.)	Return on Equity (R.O.E.)	Net Interest Spread	Overhead Efficiency Ratio	Liquidity Index	Liquidity Ratio	Hot Money Ratio	Stability Index
5.0	0.68	4.8	0.25	5.2	0.8	1.29	14.92	4.06	70.4	1.0	25.2	41.0	5.4
6.5	0.86	5.4	0.10	2.1	0.3	0.25	2.64	3.12	94.1	4.3	22.9	8.1	4.7
8.3	0.22	1.0	0.31	4.5	0.4	1.02	10.89	3.75	76.7	5.4	43.5	8.4	5.0
6.5	0.78	3.1	0.23	3.6	0.3	0.74	7.60	3.88	80.6	4.1	58.3	17.7	4.8
5.3	0.62	5.0	0.01	7.0	1.5	1.61	15.72	4.72	66.7	3.9	3.5	6.8	8.1
8.6	2.64	4.4	0.02	5.1	0.6	1.02	4.48	2.90	51.3	4.0	32.1	12.2	8.2
6.7	0.86	3.4	0.16	3.2	1.9	0.57	4.99	3.18	81.3	5.4	46.5	9.6	6.2
1.9	6.58	30.0	0.18	2.6	0.2	0.35	3.07	4.33	92.1	1.6	27.4	28.7	4.6
2.5	4.39	22.5	0.19	4.2	0.9	0.71	7.42	3.98	75.0	5.1	35.6	7.4	5.1
8.2	0.55	1.9	0.09	6.8	1.2	1.33	8.00	4.45	62.5	3.3	29.7	14.9	8.1
8.0	0.02	0.1	0.07	6.3	2.0	1.21	13.98	4.75	68.0	2.0	12.4	18.9	6.0
7.1	1.03	4.1	0.26	2.0	0.1	0.21	1.39	4.21	91.9	2.7	39.2	24.0	6.7
2.9	6.65	22.2	0.19	4.9	1.0	0.92	5.19	4.38	72.3	1.9	21.8	20.1	7.3
7.6	0.80	3.1	0.00	2.5	0.2	0.49	5.43	2.90	89.6	6.2	55.2	5.4	3.8
6.6	0.60	3.0	0.12	5.5	2.2	1.05	8.21	3.77	64.0	2.9	24.3	15.3	7.2
6.0	1.05	4.5	0.90	9.9	6.4	2.52	16.34	5.39	43.2	3.4	16.3	11.9	7.6
8.5	0.44	1.9	3.24	4.3	11.6	1.03	11.61	2.96	88.6	7.5	58.8	1.7	6.0
3.7	2.65	13.5	-0.21	3.4	0.7	0.71	5.77	3.98	82.9	1.9	21.4	20.8	6.7
8.3	0.33	1.7	0.00	5.4	5.7	1.08	10.17	3.14	55.0	5.4	33.8	4.8	8.2
8.6	0.37	1.6	0.13	4.0	0.6	0.78	8.02	3.83	76.1	2.3	17.3	16.8	5.3
5.1	2.10	8.4	0.59	3.6	3.9	0.60	3.48	3.01	81.6	4.8	23.4	4.4	7.2
4.6	1.60	9.5	-0.11	4.9	0.9	0.83	6.00	3.98	69.6	3.7	20.7	10.8	5.2
3.5	2.19	15.4	0.11	4.1	1.3	0.90	10.02	3.86	78.3	4.3	18.5	6.9	5.6
6.5	na	0.0	na	10.0	3.8	25.82	29.69	0.00	77.8	4.0	164.7	0.0	5.7
6.5	0.44	2.5	0.19	6.3	2.6	1.05	9.09	3.28	49.1	0.7	10.0	37.9	7.2
5.9	2.07	7.8	0.09	2.7	0.2	0.44	3.73	3.20	86.6	5.0	43.1	10.5	5.2
1.7	4.36	39.5	0.37	1.3	38.1	1.05	11.13	3.18	108.3	1.1	4.3	27.8	1.0
5.6	1.69	10.5	0.05	5.0	2.5	1.23	12.39	3.53	67.2	4.7	18.8	4.8	6.1
2.5	3.69	21.8	0.43	5.1	2.6	1.05	8.34	3.97	69.9	1.7	10.0	20.0	7.0
8.8	0.37	2.2	0.01	3.5	0.6	0.54	4.90	3.90	79.3	4.3	24.4	7.8	6.1
8.1	0.02	0.2	0.00	7.5	1.2	1.73	18.68	3.96	58.8	1.9	7.1	18.7	6.3
9.6	1.01	2.8	0.04	6.1	2.0	1.22	10.21	3.83	57.1	6.8	56.7	3.7	7.7
10.0	0.26	0.8	0.01	5.7	1.0	1.21	10.90	4.25	64.8	6.9	66.7	5.1	7.5
9.3	0.19	0.6	0.00	7.1	1.1	1.22	10.02	4.70	59.9	5.6	52.9	10.2	8.2
5.1	2.66	12.5	0.16	3.0	3.0	0.59	4.04	3.49	74.8	3.5	20.4	11.8	7.5
6.5	0.99	6.5	0.06	4.2	5.9	0.73	9.00	3.38	65.0	6.1	38.6	5.3	6.1
4.4	1.83	12.0	0.51	6.0	2.8	1.32	13.55	4.60	70.2	1.8	10.3	19.4	6.8
5.3	0.23	2.1	0.11	3.2	1.6	0.47	5.53	3.87	80.4	0.6	10.0	49.8	4.3
7.3	0.57	2.7	0.27	5.5	2.9	1.34	14.52	3.22	66.5	4.4	21.1	6.8	6.2
4.1	2.34	12.8	-0.01	4.3	3.6	0.78	6.06	3.20	64.1	1.4	24.5	28.1	7.3
6.8	0.24	1.6	0.01	7.0	2.3	1.21	10.32	4.52	65.5	1.1	18.5	24.3	7.4
5.5	2.08	8.8	0.01	4.2	0.5	0.58	4.09	4.86	83.6	3.9	23.5	10.3	6.9
3.7	2.87	20.5	0.05	1.8	0.1	0.08	0.89	4.03	90.9	4.3	21.3	7.3	3.8
9.5	0.89	1.9	0.00	3.2	0.5	0.54	3.48	2.19	70.3	5.1	59.6	14.2	7.6
2.5	3.39	22.6	0.71	3.1	0.4	0.32	3.39	3.55	84.4	3.0	28.9	16.1	4.4
8.8	0.84	2.6	0.00	8.9	4.1	1.53	5.66	4.55	60.0	4.3	27.0	9.2	8.8
6.9	0.68	3.2	0.01	4.5	1.2	0.96	7.26	3.43	62.4	2.6	11.7	15.4	7.4
8.6	0.26	1.5	-0.01	7.7	1.7	1.40	11.55	4.40	53.8	2.4	13.5	16.8	7.9
6.8	0.25	1.0	0.13	6.6	18.7	1.52	10.88	3.41	64.1	2.4	15.8	4.6	10.0
5.7	0.43	4.6	0.06	2.8	1.6	0.43	4.72	3.37	81.8	0.6	5.2	10.5	4.6
9.2	0.50	0.5	0.00	1.7	0.0	0.07	0.26	2.85	97.3	4.8	97.7	19.3	6.3
7.8	0.18	0.9	0.04	4.1	0.9	0.87	6.76	4.50	61.7	1.2	24.8	32.3	5.9
4.0	0.98	7.3	0.00	5.5	2.9	1.00	8.32	4.61	77.0	3.8	12.3	7.4	5.3
9.0	0.12	1.0	0.00	4.9	494.3	1.03	10.77	3.19	60.7	4.3	13.7	6.9	8.6
8.4	0.52	0.5	-0.01	9.1	2.5	5.04	13.29	5.33	54.9	6.6	72.8	6.7	7.8
2.1	1.94	19.6	0.07	3.9	0.9	0.57	6.99	3.80	75.4	0.7	9.4	29.2	4.5
5.7	0.59	4.0	0.08	4.4	1.7	0.78	9.03	3.27	69.6	3.5	11.3	11.3	4.9
8.2	2.38	5.2	0.03	3.3	0.1	0.32	1.37	3.61	84.6	2.6	59.8	40.4	6.9
3.0	2.73	17.1	0.19	1.2	0.0	-0.02	-0.18	3.69	98.7	1.5	13.8	23.0	3.6
8.7	2.70	3.0	0.00	4.3	0.3	1.15	4.45	2.78	69.8	4.2	95.3	25.9	7.3

Name	City	State	2015 Rating	2014 Rating	Total Assets ($Mil)	One Year Asset Growth	Commercial Loans	Consumer Loans	Mortgage Loans	Securities	Capitalization Index	Leverage Ratio	Risk-Based Capital Ratio
First Savings Bank	Clarksville	IN	B-	B-	B-	794.1	6.85	4.1	0.9	22.5	22.4	5.4	8.1	11.3
First Savings Bank	Beresford	SD	A-	B+	B-	635.1	15.12	2.1	18.4	7.8	15.4	10.0	17.0	21.2
First Savings Bank of Hegewisch	Chicago	IL	B	B	B	675.8	12.05	0.0	0.1	53.3	18.7	10.0	14.6	43.8
▲ First Secure Bank and Trust Co.	Palos Hills	IL	D	D-	E-	72.1	28.51	5.3	0.0	23.0	0.8	10.0	12.2	17.5
First Secure Community Bank	Sugar Grove	IL	C+	C	D	185.1	22.86	14.1	1.2	9.6	3.9	6.4	10.0	12.1
First Security Bank	Searcy	AR	A+	A+	A+	5215.0	8.51	6.5	1.1	6.9	48.6	10.0	15.0	19.0
First Security Bank	Mackinaw	IL	C-	B-	B-	86.7	8.67	5.8	0.4	13.2	11.7	5.7	9.2	11.5
First Security Bank	Overbrook	KS	C+	C+	C+	57.6	3.99	12.5	1.1	19.3	7.9	6.4	8.4	13.4
First Security Bank	Byron	MN	C+	C+	C	60.8	2.27	5.4	2.8	18.1	24.2	6.6	8.6	12.8
First Security Bank	Union Star	MO	D+	D	D	28.6	4.01	8.2	4.7	23.7	38.9	5.2	7.2	16.4
First Security Bank	Batesville	MS	B+	B+	B+	534.1	5.64	3.5	3.8	19.0	28.4	10.0	11.6	18.5
First Security Bank	Bozeman	MT	B	B	B-	811.1	9.06	8.4	1.5	12.8	26.8	7.2	9.2	12.8
▲ First Security Bank	Beaver	OK	B	C+	C-	103.4	-4.52	11.1	2.7	10.7	4.3	9.5	10.7	14.6
First Security Bank & Trust Co.	Charles City	IA	D+	C+	B-	499.4	11.49	6.4	1.8	11.6	27.1	6.9	8.9	13.6
First Security Bank - Canby	Canby	MN	A-	A	A	69.9	3.38	26.1	1.8	2.5	12.4	10.0	12.8	17.9
First Security Bank - West	Beulah	ND	A-	A	A	66.3	-2.07	10.5	1.1	1.1	16.5	10.0	12.6	20.6
▲ First Security Bank and Trust Co.	Oklahoma City	OK	C-	D-	D+	51.8	6.53	19.0	1.9	33.1	2.7	6.3	8.8	12.0
▲ First Security Bank of Deer Lodge	Deer Lodge	MT	B-	C+	B-	33.1	4.42	9.4	4.9	35.8	0.6	8.5	10.0	17.9
First Security Bank of Helena	Helena	MT	C+	C	D+	45.2	14.03	10.2	3.2	31.3	12.6	10.0	14.2	21.1
First Security Bank of Malta	Malta	MT	B	B-	B-	34.0	2.31	7.5	8.9	1.2	18.2	10.0	11.0	20.4
First Security Bank of Nevada	Las Vegas	NV	A-	B	B-	155.8	-0.98	5.1	0.0	1.1	5.7	10.0	16.7	22.1
First Security Bank of Roundup	Roundup	MT	B+	B+	B-	47.4	-7.28	13.9	5.8	7.5	20.3	10.0	12.2	18.8
First Security Bank, Inc.	Owensboro	KY	B-	C+	C+	564.3	-2.66	6.0	1.3	33.8	10.4	6.8	8.9	13.9
First Security Bank-Hendricks	Hendricks	MN	B+	B	B	25.7	5.25	5.6	3.4	10.8	23.5	10.0	11.3	23.3
First Security Bank-Sleepy Eye	Sleepy Eye	MN	A-	A	A	200.3	1.86	8.3	1.9	9.5	15.8	10.0	12.8	17.6
First Security State Bank	Evansdale	IA	B-	B-	B-	91.2	-0.56	28.5	33.1	10.3	9.8	6.9	10.2	12.4
First Security State Bank	Cranfills Gap	TX	B-	B-	B	112.0	-1.26	2.4	4.3	15.5	53.8	5.2	7.2	18.8
▲ First Security Trust and Savings Bank	Elmwood Park	IL	C-	D+	D-	224.7	3.63	5.0	0.7	10.3	21.2	7.1	9.0	16.5
First Sentinel Bank	Richlands	VA	B	B	C+	195.3	4.38	3.1	20.4	31.0	0.4	8.4	10.0	15.2
First Sentry Bank, Inc.	Huntington	WV	B	B-	C+	540.2	6.00	13.8	2.3	15.9	14.8	7.8	9.5	15.6
First Service Bank	Greenbrier	AR	B	B	B	283.5	10.79	9.0	1.6	22.7	5.5	8.7	10.1	14.1
First Shore Federal S&L Assn.	Salisbury	MD	B-	B-	B-	305.1	1.26	1.6	5.0	57.6	5.2	10.0	14.0	24.1
First Sound Bank	Seattle	WA	C-	C-	D+	131.0	-0.96	42.5	0.3	0.8	0.6	5.7	9.1	11.5
First South Bank	Washington	NC	B-	C+	C+	984.7	7.87	4.0	0.7	15.1	19.6	6.9	8.9	13.1
First South Bank	Spartanburg	SC	E-	E-	E-	240.8	-3.32	11.5	0.2	11.6	12.2	0.4	4.5	6.7
First South Bank	Jackson	TN	B+	B	B-	461.9	4.37	7.6	1.6	12.4	33.4	8.7	10.1	15.9
First Southeast Bank	Harmony	MN	C-	C+	B-	101.6	1.61	9.6	3.1	9.5	3.4	4.9	8.4	11.0
First Southern Bank	Florence	AL	B-	B-	B-	217.3	4.81	11.3	2.7	28.8	12.6	6.8	8.8	14.3
First Southern Bank	Patterson	GA	E-	E-	E-	103.1	6.10	11.9	2.6	13.8	7.8	0.9	4.9	7.8
First Southern Bank	Marion	IL	B+	B+	B+	680.4	6.40	7.1	6.5	16.3	21.3	10.0	11.5	16.8
First Southern Bank	Columbia	MS	B-	B-	B-	195.6	1.20	5.4	5.6	17.4	21.5	8.3	9.8	16.1
First Southern National Bank	Lancaster	KY	B-	B-	B-	845.1	1.49	4.8	2.7	26.7	23.6	6.4	8.4	14.6
First Southern State Bank	Stevenson	AL	B	B	B	377.4	5.52	2.5	6.7	17.8	38.4	8.1	9.7	18.5
▲ First Southwest Bank	Alamosa	CO	C	C-	D+	280.1	8.48	8.4	0.8	10.7	13.1	7.0	9.0	13.6
First State B&T Co. of Larned	Larned	KS	A	A	A	141.5	8.91	7.2	0.7	3.7	27.1	10.0	12.9	21.4
First State Bank	Crossett	AR	B-	C+	C+	37.8	9.77	7.8	13.6	12.2	20.5	10.0	13.1	28.9
First State Bank	Lonoke	AR	D+	E+	D+	262.8	2.62	2.8	0.5	10.9	37.3	8.0	9.6	18.7
First State Bank	Russellville	AR	A-	A-	A-	234.2	5.22	12.5	1.2	19.5	11.8	10.0	11.4	15.2
First State Bank	Wrens	GA	C+	C-	D-	107.9	10.25	8.8	5.5	35.1	12.7	7.2	9.1	13.6
First State Bank	Belmond	IA	B	B	B	98.2	-0.91	8.5	3.0	8.9	49.8	10.0	11.2	24.3
First State Bank	Britt	IA	A	A	A	104.2	-0.16	2.8	1.3	11.1	41.5	10.0	11.7	20.6
First State Bank	Hawarden	IA	C+	C	C-	44.2	-3.23	9.3	2.4	9.4	2.7	7.5	9.6	12.9
First State Bank	Ida Grove	IA	A-	B+	B+	132.1	-3.57	6.7	4.7	11.0	21.6	10.0	12.0	15.9
First State Bank	Lynnville	IA	A-	B+	A-	172.4	7.03	6.5	2.2	11.1	16.4	10.0	11.7	15.3
First State Bank	Nashua	IA	B+	B+	B	46.8	4.34	9.2	2.6	23.1	12.4	10.0	12.0	17.4
First State Bank	Sioux Rapids	IA	B	B	B	39.3	9.71	5.6	1.3	2.4	39.0	10.0	14.1	40.0
First State Bank	Stuart	IA	B-	C+	C+	95.0	1.15	11.7	2.6	8.6	28.3	8.0	9.7	15.6
First State Bank	Sumner	IA	B-	B-	B-	102.1	-3.29	8.3	2.8	12.3	30.7	10.0	13.3	20.6
First State Bank	Webster City	IA	A-	A-	B+	456.0	23.78	8.5	0.7	6.9	8.5	9.3	12.1	14.4
First State Bank	Mendota	IL	C+	C+	C	949.1	11.98	8.6	1.1	25.1	10.4	4.1	7.6	10.5

Asset Quality Index	Adjusted Non-Performing Loans as a % of Total Loans	as a % of Capital	Net Charge-Offs Avg Loans	Profitability Index	Net Income ($Mil)	Return on Assets (R.O.A.)	Return on Equity (R.O.E.)	Net Interest Spread	Overhead Efficiency Ratio	Liquidity Index	Liquidity Ratio	Hot Money Ratio	Stability Index
4.4	1.44	11.0	0.04	3.9	6.1	1.07	10.20	3.90	83.0	2.1	28.2	7.0	7.7
5.2	1.66	6.3	4.57	10.0	8.7	1.99	11.92	10.33	45.8	2.7	12.0	15.2	8.5
10.0	0.33	1.2	0.15	3.4	2.1	0.45	3.37	2.52	71.2	3.4	48.6	20.7	7.7
1.7	3.73	23.1	-0.19	0.1	-0.2	-0.53	-4.73	4.04	112.1	0.8	18.5	41.2	0.1
3.2	1.62	12.6	-0.02	3.9	1.1	0.89	8.50	3.70	84.6	0.7	15.5	49.3	4.7
9.0	0.51	1.4	0.07	10.0	75.0	2.05	12.11	5.03	42.6	4.7	27.9	10.4	10.0
3.7	2.13	17.8	1.11	2.1	0.1	0.16	1.58	3.64	76.5	1.5	8.2	22.1	4.9
6.1	0.69	5.1	0.06	4.0	0.4	0.94	9.92	4.02	76.1	3.0	21.8	14.5	4.9
6.5	0.71	5.0	-0.01	4.2	0.4	0.96	11.18	3.96	76.2	3.7	28.9	12.8	4.5
8.9	0.00	0.0	-0.03	2.1	0.1	0.32	4.55	3.16	92.0	4.1	32.2	11.8	3.1
7.5	0.94	4.5	-0.17	5.1	4.0	0.97	8.21	4.12	70.1	4.1	15.8	8.0	7.1
6.0	0.49	3.0	-0.15	5.2	7.1	1.24	12.22	3.78	70.3	5.3	30.6	3.6	8.0
6.4	0.37	2.4	-0.09	6.3	1.3	1.64	16.93	3.51	53.5	0.8	18.4	39.8	5.4
1.4	6.07	38.2	0.44	3.8	2.2	0.58	5.45	3.69	71.6	4.1	29.7	8.5	6.2
7.8	0.09	0.4	0.00	8.9	1.0	1.94	12.86	4.20	49.8	5.4	23.8	0.8	8.5
8.8	0.16	0.6	0.00	6.5	0.8	1.53	11.43	3.49	50.7	6.6	45.1	0.8	8.5
5.7	0.00	0.0	0.51	4.6	0.5	1.34	15.64	5.12	75.4	0.9	5.7	30.5	3.9
8.6	0.00	0.0	-1.99	6.6	0.5	2.21	23.48	4.40	55.9	4.4	26.9	8.3	4.4
5.1	1.58	7.6	0.00	3.0	0.1	0.58	5.21	4.82	72.8	3.2	30.3	15.8	4.3
7.3	0.63	3.2	0.32	5.1	0.2	0.72	6.60	4.49	76.8	4.5	41.1	12.5	5.6
5.8	0.46	2.0	-0.11	6.6	1.4	1.11	5.62	4.46	63.4	3.1	19.2	13.9	7.9
5.1	1.19	5.7	-0.26	8.5	0.8	2.10	17.67	4.68	54.7	4.1	16.4	8.4	7.4
5.0	0.94	7.6	0.33	4.4	3.1	0.69	7.58	3.75	68.9	1.5	11.1	23.8	5.8
8.9	0.33	1.2	0.00	7.0	0.3	1.58	13.57	3.68	60.2	4.3	55.3	16.1	8.1
5.3	1.17	5.9	0.07	7.6	2.6	1.72	11.83	4.31	56.4	4.9	23.6	3.6	9.1
3.6	1.00	7.8	0.04	6.4	1.0	1.47	14.78	3.93	61.9	1.3	13.0	20.3	7.2
8.7	0.12	0.5	0.06	4.1	0.8	0.97	12.47	3.15	76.0	6.2	64.9	9.7	4.7
3.8	2.84	15.5	-0.04	2.2	0.9	0.46	4.14	3.15	84.6	5.2	44.9	10.1	5.3
5.0	0.47	3.5	0.36	6.2	1.5	1.07	10.77	5.12	64.3	1.7	13.9	21.1	5.9
5.3	0.71	4.7	0.01	5.5	3.9	1.00	9.92	3.54	56.7	1.3	23.5	15.1	5.9
4.8	1.16	8.6	0.01	5.0	2.3	1.13	11.05	4.59	78.5	1.5	12.1	13.2	5.6
5.5	1.69	9.1	0.07	3.4	1.2	0.52	3.76	3.33	75.4	1.6	15.7	23.0	7.3
6.6	0.14	1.2	0.21	1.8	0.1	0.07	0.74	3.62	101.0	1.4	14.8	22.8	3.1
6.2	0.46	3.4	0.03	4.2	5.3	0.75	7.47	3.89	77.0	2.6	24.2	14.4	5.2
0.3	6.39	82.3	0.03	1.6	0.5	0.25	5.82	3.10	103.2	1.0	19.9	32.8	0.6
6.7	0.36	2.0	0.19	6.4	5.0	1.46	11.71	3.80	68.8	3.1	23.5	14.2	8.2
1.6	2.41	22.4	0.03	5.4	0.9	1.23	14.57	4.22	65.2	1.6	4.1	18.6	6.6
5.2	0.94	7.0	-0.02	4.5	1.2	0.76	8.30	3.80	70.8	2.8	22.1	15.6	5.2
0.3	4.54	52.1	-0.12	1.3	-0.2	-0.22	-4.33	4.54	104.3	3.5	16.9	11.7	0.1
4.8	1.23	7.3	0.13	6.3	5.7	1.14	8.74	4.00	57.0	2.7	12.0	15.2	8.3
5.8	0.43	2.7	0.66	3.9	1.2	0.85	8.48	4.21	78.4	3.3	15.6	12.8	5.5
4.3	1.63	11.7	0.00	4.9	5.3	0.84	8.25	4.03	69.0	3.6	23.0	11.8	7.7
8.2	0.41	1.9	0.16	5.0	2.7	0.97	9.66	3.66	63.4	2.9	39.4	20.5	5.5
5.8	0.38	2.8	0.03	2.8	0.8	0.38	3.66	4.15	82.8	2.9	18.1	14.7	5.0
8.6	0.03	0.1	0.11	6.3	1.5	1.39	10.98	3.59	58.8	5.2	33.5	5.7	8.8
5.4	2.65	8.6	0.38	3.7	0.2	0.56	4.29	4.21	83.4	3.5	53.2	19.9	5.8
5.8	1.31	6.3	-0.02	1.1	0.4	0.20	1.98	2.88	100.1	1.9	33.4	30.3	4.4
8.6	0.08	0.5	0.01	6.3	2.0	1.14	10.31	3.85	60.2	1.9	14.4	18.7	7.1
5.0	0.64	5.1	0.08	7.4	1.0	1.24	13.87	5.85	66.8	1.4	15.1	26.3	3.8
9.1	0.02	0.1	-0.12	4.4	0.8	1.00	8.86	2.71	60.3	5.4	61.1	11.8	6.4
9.1	0.00	0.0	0.00	7.2	1.1	1.35	10.91	3.17	36.8	4.6	43.4	13.1	8.4
1.7	2.20	16.9	0.00	3.7	0.3	0.82	8.23	3.36	74.7	4.6	16.3	5.1	5.5
5.6	1.01	5.7	0.16	6.8	1.8	1.78	15.17	4.22	57.6	2.3	27.8	19.3	7.8
6.4	0.66	3.9	-0.02	8.0	2.4	1.88	15.42	4.38	50.6	2.3	15.8	15.5	8.4
8.5	0.00	0.0	0.02	7.5	0.4	1.24	10.70	3.35	49.8	0.9	19.3	34.3	7.0
9.9	0.61	1.0	-0.01	3.5	0.2	0.68	4.69	2.85	72.0	7.1	86.5	5.5	7.0
7.9	0.41	2.2	-0.17	3.8	0.5	0.69	7.35	3.26	74.9	5.0	32.3	6.9	5.3
8.4	0.01	0.0	0.05	4.0	0.6	0.73	5.11	3.68	71.3	4.1	41.6	14.7	6.6
7.4	0.42	2.5	0.00	7.2	3.5	1.22	9.76	3.39	60.0	3.8	30.2	12.9	8.1
4.5	0.88	8.5	0.12	4.3	5.5	0.82	9.37	3.57	74.6	2.5	7.0	15.3	5.3

Name	City	State	2015 Rating	2014 Rating	Total Assets ($Mil)	One Year Asset Growth	Comm-ercial Loans	Cons-umer Loans	Mort-gage Loans	Secur-ities	Capital-ization Index	Lever-age Ratio	Risk-Based Capital Ratio
First State Bank	Monticello	IL	B-	B-	C+	234.3	3.26	5.4	2.3	13.4	20.4	6.9	8.9	13.5
First State Bank	Ness City	KS	A-	A-	A-	58.3	-6.77	6.6	2.4	0.3	47.2	10.0	17.4	27.0
First State Bank	Norton	KS	B+	B+	B+	426.2	-1.15	9.8	2.4	2.2	38.9	8.7	10.1	16.1
First State Bank	Irvington	KY	A-	A-	B+	178.2	7.04	1.7	4.9	30.9	39.8	10.0	11.5	23.1
First State Bank	Saint Clair Shores	MI	B-	B-	B-	676.2	3.06	8.0	0.5	11.7	20.4	8.7	10.1	14.8
First State Bank	Holly Springs	MS	C+	C+	C-	115.6	6.77	10.4	2.2	16.9	30.7	8.5	10.0	18.2
First State Bank	Waynesboro	MS	A-	A-	B+	808.5	5.31	7.1	2.5	26.4	30.2	10.0	11.4	18.4
First State Bank	Buxton	ND	B+	B+	B	175.1	-0.04	15.9	0.8	12.0	5.4	8.4	11.8	13.7
▲ First State Bank	Farnam	NE	A	A-	C	125.2	111.02	8.5	3.3	5.2	22.2	10.0	12.0	17.0
First State Bank	Gothenburg	NE	B-	C+	C	447.1	25.81	6.8	1.5	3.7	19.7	7.9	10.2	13.2
First State Bank	Hordville	NE	B-	C+	C+	40.8	-4.51	12.0	1.1	5.0	1.3	8.5	11.0	13.7
First State Bank	Loomis	NE	B	B	B-	138.1	-1.83	6.1	3.8	6.1	13.2	6.0	9.3	11.7
First State Bank	Randolph	NE	B+	B+	A-	58.6	-4.28	1.8	1.4	2.3	3.9	10.0	13.3	18.1
First State Bank	Scottsbluff	NE	B+	B+	B+	244.7	-3.07	6.9	1.4	10.9	20.0	7.9	9.7	13.2
First State Bank	Socorro	NM	B	B+	B+	132.1	-5.01	0.3	0.6	3.7	87.6	9.4	10.6	50.2
First State Bank	Winchester	OH	B	B	B	435.2	20.16	1.9	7.4	21.6	28.1	7.1	9.1	14.4
First State Bank	Anadarko	OK	A-	A-	A-	92.4	-3.75	1.6	3.6	3.8	67.0	10.0	15.7	38.4
First State Bank	Boise City	OK	C+	C+	C+	72.7	6.74	5.8	7.2	1.7	12.0	5.4	10.0	11.3
First State Bank	Commerce	OK	C	C+	C+	11.1	2.67	12.0	11.6	14.5	31.9	10.0	11.8	19.3
▲ First State Bank	Elmore City	OK	C	D+	E+	11.8	5.83	25.0	8.1	19.6	0.5	8.3	11.7	13.6
First State Bank	Noble	OK	C+	C+	C	50.8	2.17	1.4	6.2	17.3	24.1	8.5	10.0	26.2
First State Bank	Oklahoma City	OK	C	C+	C+	282.6	23.04	16.4	0.6	11.8	4.0	6.2	9.5	11.9
First State Bank	Ryan	OK	C+	C+	C+	27.2	-6.85	11.1	5.0	13.6	0.0	10.0	12.4	19.5
First State Bank	Tahlequah	OK	B-	B	B-	64.5	0.75	8.3	2.0	13.9	20.6	10.0	14.2	20.4
▼ First State Bank	Valliant	OK	C-	B-	B-	54.4	19.33	6.1	6.0	9.9	19.8	7.1	9.1	12.8
First State Bank	Watonga	OK	B	B+	B	64.8	7.79	13.2	3.6	2.9	27.1	7.8	9.5	15.5
First State Bank	Waynoka	OK	D-	D-	D+	22.9	0.41	14.8	1.5	1.6	34.4	9.0	10.3	24.8
First State Bank	Wilmot	SD	B-	B	B-	45.8	6.73	15.2	3.2	1.9	19.8	9.2	10.9	14.3
First State Bank	Abernathy	TX	B-	B	B-	27.6	-9.46	2.7	8.3	0.7	16.6	10.0	13.6	20.5
▲ First State Bank	Abilene	TX	D+	D+	C-	41.6	4.34	8.7	2.1	5.7	3.2	4.6	6.6	18.9
First State Bank	Athens	TX	A	A	A-	422.5	9.10	6.8	4.0	24.6	29.8	9.7	10.8	21.0
▼ First State Bank	Chico	TX	D+	C+	C	189.8	-4.63	10.0	3.5	10.9	40.9	9.7	10.8	17.8
▲ First State Bank	Clute	TX	B-	C+	C+	169.8	2.54	11.4	8.4	9.5	31.3	6.7	8.7	16.6
First State Bank	Columbus	TX	B-	B	B	147.2	4.08	1.5	4.1	3.5	53.3	10.0	13.4	35.2
First State Bank	Gainesville	TX	B	B-	B-	1007.5	2.44	6.9	1.8	11.5	37.0	7.4	9.3	16.0
First State Bank	Graham	TX	A-	A-	B+	145.5	-0.07	14.8	3.1	15.1	10.2	7.5	9.4	16.3
First State Bank	Hemphill	TX	C	C+	B-	53.3	-0.14	1.7	2.3	7.5	65.4	10.0	15.9	46.0
First State Bank	Junction	TX	C+	C+	C+	46.7	-3.41	7.3	3.1	11.5	38.3	7.0	9.0	16.0
First State Bank	Louise	TX	B+	B+	B+	368.6	1.65	10.8	0.9	9.8	17.6	6.9	9.0	12.4
First State Bank	Mesquite	TX	D	D	D-	174.1	3.30	2.0	0.5	4.2	49.6	7.8	9.5	19.6
First State Bank	Rice	TX	B	C+	C+	128.9	-11.58	19.3	3.4	17.6	20.7	10.0	12.4	17.9
First State Bank	Shallowater	TX	A	A-	A-	106.2	26.67	13.9	2.0	3.9	10.5	10.0	12.1	16.2
First State Bank	Spearman	TX	B-	B-	B-	122.9	-8.08	9.2	0.8	1.7	23.4	7.6	9.4	19.8
First State Bank	Stratford	TX	B+	B+	B+	237.0	4.71	5.8	1.6	6.3	37.9	8.6	10.0	14.8
First State Bank	Three Rivers	TX	B-	C+	C+	157.2	-2.20	2.3	2.5	25.9	24.0	10.0	11.9	31.7
▲ First State Bank	Yoakum	TX	A	A-	A-	187.4	0.05	5.5	9.0	20.6	39.5	9.7	10.8	22.8
First State Bank	Danville	VA	E-	E-	E-	32.9	-15.12	6.7	7.7	16.2	17.3	0.0	2.7	4.8
First State Bank	New London	WI	B-	B-	C+	269.7	4.23	3.3	0.7	8.8	45.8	10.0	13.6	23.9
First State Bank	Barboursville	WV	E-	E-	D-	217.5	-9.83	12.2	1.7	32.3	7.0	2.7	6.1	9.7
First State Bank & Trust Co.	Fremont	NE	B-	B-	B-	216.3	4.71	18.7	2.7	14.6	13.3	6.1	8.8	11.8
First State Bank and Trust	Tonganoxie	KS	C+	C+	C-	253.8	4.98	2.9	2.1	20.1	14.6	6.3	8.3	12.9
First State Bank and Trust	Bayport	MN	B-	B-	B-	226.1	6.85	6.4	5.4	32.5	22.6	6.4	8.4	15.2
First State Bank and Trust Co.	Carthage	TX	A	A	A	484.5	-5.66	2.2	5.8	18.6	55.9	10.0	16.0	37.6
First State Bank and Trust Co., Inc.	Caruthersville	MO	A-	A-	A-	331.6	-5.37	6.2	4.5	19.9	15.5	10.0	12.3	16.4
First State Bank Central Texas	Austin	TX	A-	B+	B+	1354.0	-6.68	5.5	0.7	3.8	47.3	10.0	11.0	17.9
First State Bank in Temple	Temple	OK	B-	C+	C+	23.2	4.92	3.6	5.2	6.0	40.3	10.0	21.0	38.2
▼ First State Bank Minnesota	Le Roy	MN	C+	B-	C+	66.7	4.75	8.8	2.7	5.5	17.0	7.5	9.3	15.8
First State Bank Nebraska	Lincoln	NE	B	B	C+	471.8	6.73	9.8	1.8	16.0	11.8	7.0	9.0	13.2
▲ First State Bank of Arcadia	Arcadia	FL	B-	C	D+	136.9	-3.15	2.9	2.8	19.8	29.3	10.0	11.9	22.5
First State Bank of Ashby	Ashby	MN	C	C	C-	33.2	2.40	9.4	6.4	19.8	12.0	6.3	8.3	13.4

Asset Quality Index	Adjusted Non-Performing Loans as a % of Total Loans	as a % of Capital	Net Charge-Offs Avg Loans	Profitability Index	Net Income ($Mil)	Return on Assets (R.O.A.)	Return on Equity (R.O.E.)	Net Interest Spread	Overhead Efficiency Ratio	Liquidity Index	Liquidity Ratio	Hot Money Ratio	Stability Index
4.5	1.62	10.7	-0.01	5.2	2.2	1.27	13.02	3.68	69.7	4.0	19.5	9.5	5.4
8.9	0.00	0.0	-0.03	7.0	0.9	1.79	10.44	4.08	53.6	3.4	35.0	16.2	8.0
7.0	0.65	3.4	0.13	5.6	3.9	1.30	11.13	4.02	61.7	1.9	24.3	20.7	7.7
9.1	0.21	0.9	0.02	6.3	1.5	1.15	9.88	3.77	64.7	4.8	28.4	6.2	7.8
4.6	1.83	11.1	0.08	4.9	4.6	0.92	8.50	3.78	72.1	3.9	27.6	11.5	6.6
5.1	1.41	7.4	-0.05	3.6	0.6	0.74	7.55	3.74	80.4	2.0	20.4	19.5	4.5
8.1	0.63	3.3	0.07	6.2	6.7	1.13	8.96	3.85	56.2	1.8	18.1	20.6	7.7
5.6	0.44	3.1	0.00	6.5	2.0	1.56	13.40	3.71	60.2	0.8	2.4	21.8	7.8
7.9	0.39	1.9	-0.01	9.2	2.0	2.27	16.93	4.20	50.6	1.5	19.2	25.6	9.2
3.8	1.77	11.7	0.06	7.2	4.0	1.35	10.75	3.72	53.1	1.8	10.3	15.4	7.4
7.0	0.00	0.0	0.00	3.9	0.2	0.64	6.01	3.25	67.5	4.3	15.4	7.0	6.0
6.1	0.01	0.1	0.02	7.1	1.3	1.22	10.92	4.12	58.3	2.2	5.5	16.5	7.4
7.3	0.00	0.0	0.00	7.1	0.7	1.70	12.70	3.58	52.7	1.6	25.4	26.4	7.0
5.5	1.00	6.3	0.20	9.7	4.1	2.22	21.96	4.47	53.2	1.3	28.9	27.8	7.7
9.7	2.15	1.0	0.05	4.5	0.8	0.74	7.08	3.93	70.3	6.2	47.9	4.9	6.0
6.6	0.53	3.5	0.07	4.8	3.2	1.09	10.64	3.67	70.7	2.8	17.2	14.7	5.8
9.2	2.36	3.4	1.03	6.3	1.2	1.62	11.14	3.47	55.8	5.1	55.3	12.1	8.5
5.1	0.30	2.3	0.02	9.7	1.0	1.82	20.66	4.71	49.6	0.6	5.7	40.2	5.0
5.7	1.24	4.5	1.32	2.7	0.0	0.28	2.29	5.57	92.5	3.1	38.8	16.8	5.5
7.9	0.00	0.0	0.00	6.8	0.3	3.10	30.21	4.35	77.2	5.3	20.4	0.0	3.0
5.5	2.15	6.9	0.20	3.3	0.2	0.52	5.12	4.39	86.4	5.6	46.2	7.6	3.7
3.6	1.17	8.8	0.00	4.3	1.4	0.69	6.81	3.61	71.1	0.8	17.3	40.7	5.9
5.7	1.62	8.1	-0.08	3.0	0.1	0.47	3.86	4.11	89.4	2.4	31.2	20.9	5.7
5.3	2.63	10.3	0.59	2.8	0.2	0.38	2.67	3.23	81.8	3.0	40.1	20.2	6.3
6.4	0.63	4.5	-0.18	2.0	0.0	-0.03	-0.29	4.26	101.9	1.3	13.0	27.2	4.3
5.5	0.60	3.2	-0.44	8.0	1.0	2.11	21.06	4.65	60.0	3.9	35.6	13.9	7.3
6.7	1.78	3.9	-6.00	0.4	0.0	0.12	1.09	2.47	108.4	6.1	75.2	8.0	3.4
6.6	0.18	1.0	0.37	7.9	0.6	1.66	15.16	4.18	53.1	2.2	24.1	9.2	6.4
6.0	0.11	0.6	0.16	5.4	0.3	1.29	7.91	6.67	77.4	2.4	3.8	16.1	7.4
8.4	0.00	0.0	0.00	2.1	0.0	0.13	1.53	2.78	88.3	5.9	56.6	7.7	3.6
7.0	0.52	2.6	0.04	6.9	3.7	1.18	10.84	4.22	61.9	3.7	28.9	12.9	7.4
4.8	2.23	8.7	1.50	1.5	-0.1	-0.07	-0.63	3.36	91.2	2.8	27.8	16.9	5.2
6.7	0.21	1.1	0.30	4.1	1.2	0.92	10.49	3.47	76.7	5.2	44.9	10.3	4.2
9.6	0.18	0.2	0.03	3.4	1.0	0.93	6.83	2.28	74.0	2.7	53.7	35.0	7.9
8.4	0.03	0.2	0.03	4.9	9.6	1.28	12.92	3.68	68.7	5.5	36.7	9.2	6.8
7.4	0.65	3.8	0.13	6.3	1.6	1.45	15.31	3.90	63.3	2.6	38.6	24.7	6.8
10.0	0.00	0.0	0.00	2.3	0.2	0.37	2.35	2.40	83.2	3.6	71.6	26.1	6.8
8.9	0.00	0.0	0.04	3.8	0.3	0.88	9.54	4.00	79.7	3.8	15.1	9.7	5.1
8.4	0.08	0.6	0.09	7.4	4.8	1.72	19.33	4.78	62.6	3.8	14.8	10.0	7.1
5.7	3.17	8.9	-0.92	0.6	-0.4	-0.29	-3.24	2.40	110.6	7.0	67.1	4.4	3.3
4.2	2.32	12.1	0.01	4.2	0.9	0.92	7.16	4.36	74.3	2.4	8.4	16.5	5.8
7.4	0.03	0.2	0.01	9.6	1.8	2.46	16.48	5.23	44.8	0.7	8.1	35.4	9.5
6.2	1.53	6.6	0.36	3.4	0.6	0.66	8.78	2.80	76.4	3.1	51.5	26.9	4.5
6.0	1.32	6.4	0.00	5.8	2.6	1.45	13.99	3.39	60.0	4.5	42.8	13.4	7.4
6.4	2.04	8.3	0.01	3.7	1.0	0.86	7.72	3.00	71.8	5.1	49.0	11.5	5.5
8.3	0.32	1.4	0.07	7.4	2.5	1.76	15.86	3.94	56.4	4.5	49.5	14.7	8.2
0.3	3.90	67.9	-0.21	0.1	-0.2	-0.77	-24.41	4.42	121.6	0.7	19.5	53.3	0.0
7.3	1.86	5.4	-0.05	3.7	1.3	0.65	4.50	3.16	74.7	5.1	53.7	12.4	7.4
0.0	14.88	137.3	0.26	0.1	-0.6	-0.37	-5.64	3.68	106.0	0.7	12.8	33.8	1.2
5.1	0.55	4.0	0.01	5.1	1.8	1.10	12.47	4.15	68.9	2.8	10.9	14.5	6.2
7.8	0.10	0.8	-0.04	3.5	1.1	0.56	5.96	3.98	84.6	4.1	14.1	7.8	5.0
5.9	0.48	3.7	0.19	4.6	1.8	1.08	11.91	3.85	80.7	4.1	25.5	9.3	4.9
8.7	1.12	2.5	0.21	6.7	5.0	1.33	8.26	3.41	49.3	2.1	33.5	27.6	8.5
8.3	0.17	1.0	0.08	6.3	3.9	1.53	12.54	4.33	66.6	1.3	5.6	24.4	7.4
8.3	0.48	2.0	-0.07	6.6	13.1	1.28	11.27	3.56	57.2	3.4	35.2	19.2	9.3
8.2	0.50	1.2	0.01	5.6	0.3	1.63	7.94	4.31	65.3	1.5	29.1	27.1	5.0
3.8	1.95	12.2	0.17	4.1	0.4	0.90	9.35	3.78	62.0	6.0	32.5	0.2	5.5
5.6	0.29	2.3	0.15	5.0	3.9	1.12	10.41	3.69	66.1	3.7	8.2	9.4	7.2
3.5	4.56	18.3	0.79	5.0	1.4	1.29	10.92	4.01	71.1	4.4	41.8	13.5	7.2
8.4	0.00	0.0	0.00	4.6	0.3	1.12	13.39	4.21	72.3	3.7	24.3	11.3	4.1

Name	City	State	2015 Rating	2014 Rating	Total Assets ($Mil)	One Year Asset Growth	Commercial Loans	Consumer Loans	Mortgage Loans	Securities	Capitalization Index	Leverage Ratio	Risk-Based Capital Ratio
First State Bank of Bedias	Bedias	TX	A-	A-	A	160.8	-2.36	7.0	4.2	6.4	43.9	10.0	13.4	29.5
First State Bank of Beecher City	Beecher City	IL	B	B	B	68.4	-0.95	10.5	14.0	21.2	7.0	10.0	16.4	21.0
First State Bank of Ben Wheeler, Texas	Ben Wheeler	TX	A	A	A	137.1	-1.17	4.1	4.3	15.8	44.6	10.0	12.8	24.1
First State Bank of Bigfork	Bigfork	MN	D+	D+	D+	71.2	2.49	7.1	8.2	34.7	7.1	9.4	10.6	18.2
First State Bank of Blakely	Blakely	GA	A	A-	A-	466.7	6.06	5.8	2.7	12.2	7.6	10.0	12.4	17.3
First State Bank of Bloomington	Bloomington	IL	B-	B-	C+	109.4	-1.68	9.7	2.8	26.7	17.4	7.0	9.0	13.8
First State Bank of Brownsboro	Brownsboro	TX	B	B-	B-	98.3	0.05	4.7	11.2	19.7	38.6	8.7	10.2	18.1
First State Bank of Burnet	Burnet	TX	A-	A-	A-	259.2	3.31	3.3	1.9	6.4	68.6	10.0	12.0	30.3
First State Bank of Campbell Hill	Campbell Hill	IL	B-	C+	C+	108.9	-2.10	4.8	3.2	28.7	20.1	8.8	10.2	16.4
First State Bank of Cando	Cando	ND	C	C+	C	56.9	0.35	4.6	5.3	4.0	38.2	7.6	9.4	15.8
First State Bank of Claremont	Groton	SD	B+	B+	B+	58.1	2.90	9.6	2.4	0.0	21.8	10.0	12.6	15.7
First State Bank of Clearbrook	Clearbrook	MN	C+	B-	B-	48.8	1.16	4.3	6.0	7.5	30.6	6.4	8.4	16.3
First State Bank of Colfax	Colfax	IA	A	A	A	69.0	3.21	4.1	0.9	12.7	52.9	10.0	18.0	32.9
First State Bank of Colorado	Hotchkiss	CO	B-	B-	C	213.3	6.23	2.9	0.9	9.6	26.9	10.0	11.6	20.1
First State Bank of Decatur	Decatur	MI	B	B	B	56.0	-1.41	11.0	4.0	34.8	36.6	10.0	19.7	43.7
▲ First State Bank of DeKalb County	Fort Payne	AL	B	B-	B-	177.4	97.70	4.7	6.1	18.5	27.8	10.0	11.8	20.3
First State Bank of DeQueen	De Queen	AR	B+	B	B	216.4	1.92	7.8	4.6	15.2	18.0	7.7	9.5	14.2
First State Bank of Dongola	Dongola	IL	C-	C-	D	23.2	3.30	5.9	11.9	35.0	5.2	9.7	10.8	18.6
First State Bank of Forrest	Forrest	IL	B-	B	B	170.3	7.98	12.1	6.4	39.6	5.6	6.6	8.6	12.5
First State Bank of Forsyth	Forsyth	MT	B+	A-	B+	132.2	4.03	4.9	4.2	8.3	45.5	9.2	10.5	19.2
First State Bank of Fountain	Fountain	MN	D+	C-	C-	36.6	0.73	3.3	1.4	11.9	41.7	7.1	9.1	17.2
First State Bank of Golva	Golva	ND	B+	A-	B+	77.3	-2.67	4.9	1.9	4.8	43.6	8.3	9.9	16.1
First State Bank of Grove City	Grove City	MN	B-	B-	B	23.4	-6.01	7.9	4.1	25.7	7.0	10.0	22.0	40.0
First State Bank of Harvey	Harvey	ND	B-	B	B-	81.7	-3.96	3.3	2.2	4.8	51.4	8.2	9.8	20.5
First State Bank of Healy	Healy	KS	B+	A	A-	82.4	-3.17	11.3	1.3	1.6	35.1	10.0	17.8	23.6
▲ First State Bank of Illinois	Peoria	IL	C	C+	C+	343.6	3.52	11.0	1.6	14.2	10.6	7.9	9.6	13.9
First State Bank of Kiester	Kiester	MN	D+	D	E+	17.6	-3.33	8.5	1.2	5.2	2.2	7.8	9.5	17.6
First State Bank of Le Center	Le Center	MN	B+	B+	B+	75.6	1.73	14.7	7.2	16.6	17.7	9.3	10.5	17.0
First State Bank of Livingston	Livingston	TX	B	B	B	320.9	-0.14	2.0	4.3	5.2	50.0	10.0	15.0	37.0
First State Bank of Malta	Malta	MT	A-	A-	A-	143.2	7.03	3.9	1.8	0.2	31.3	10.0	14.5	20.2
▼ First State Bank of Middlebury	Middlebury	IN	B-	B	B-	498.2	9.44	12.3	1.9	23.4	19.1	8.6	10.0	13.9
First State Bank of Mobeetie	Mobeetie	TX	C+	C+	C	82.7	-4.81	4.0	2.8	0.8	72.5	9.8	10.9	38.2
First State Bank of Newcastle	Newcastle	WY	B	B	B+	145.9	-4.78	3.6	3.1	9.1	57.3	10.0	13.1	41.4
First State Bank of North Dakota	Arthur	ND	B+	B	B-	316.6	-7.97	8.4	1.9	4.7	1.8	7.1	11.1	12.6
First State Bank of Odem	Odem	TX	B	B-	C+	138.5	0.71	11.2	2.6	7.0	30.6	9.1	10.4	19.1
First State Bank of Okabena (Inc.)	Okabena	MN	D+	D	C+	18.5	2.63	3.8	1.0	4.4	25.9	7.8	9.6	25.3
First State Bank of Olmsted	Olmsted	IL	B-	B-	B-	47.7	-0.17	8.5	4.4	28.0	25.6	10.0	11.4	19.6
First State Bank of Paint Rock	Paint Rock	TX	B	B+	B+	94.8	1.05	6.9	4.1	4.1	31.9	10.0	11.5	19.3
First State Bank of Porter	Porter	IN	A-	B	C+	144.1	1.02	2.1	0.2	23.5	42.0	10.0	13.5	25.4
▼ First State Bank of Purdy	Monett	MO	C	C+	C	162.2	-5.14	11.3	1.1	4.9	27.9	6.2	8.2	13.9
First State Bank of Randolph County	Cuthbert	GA	C+	C	C	75.7	4.59	9.4	4.0	6.1	45.0	7.6	9.4	16.2
First State Bank of Ransom	Ransom	KS	B+	B+	B+	46.4	0.53	11.9	1.2	0.8	51.6	10.0	20.9	39.8
First State Bank of Red Wing	Red Wing	MN	D+	C-	C	76.9	4.10	5.7	4.4	11.3	44.2	6.5	8.5	23.6
First State Bank of Roscoe	Roscoe	SD	A-	A-	A-	101.4	-0.16	12.5	0.8	0.6	5.4	9.7	11.8	14.8
▼ First State Bank of Rosemount	Rosemount	MN	E	D-	D-	73.6	9.02	5.7	3.5	10.7	45.0	4.3	6.3	14.7
First State Bank of San Diego	San Diego	TX	C+	C+	B-	64.9	-7.40	14.0	5.9	5.5	36.8	6.7	8.7	19.8
First State Bank of Sauk Centre	Sauk Centre	MN	B	B+	B+	94.9	5.03	10.8	6.0	14.3	23.9	10.0	12.3	19.9
First State Bank of Shelby	Shelby	MT	A	A	A	128.9	-0.73	4.2	0.8	0.0	77.3	10.0	20.2	53.4
First State Bank of St. Charles, Missouri	Saint Charles	MO	A-	A-	B+	365.5	15.85	9.6	0.2	44.3	17.1	9.5	12.0	14.5
First State Bank of St. Peter	Saint Peter	IL	A-	A-	A-	27.6	-6.51	1.1	4.7	5.9	54.4	10.0	16.6	34.2
First State Bank of Swanville	Swanville	MN	C-	C-	C	25.3	-1.46	11.4	3.0	14.0	5.2	10.0	15.2	23.1
First State Bank of the Florida Keys	Key West	FL	B-	B-	C	868.0	6.52	3.8	0.7	21.6	33.7	7.1	9.1	15.5
First State Bank of the South, Inc.	Sulligent	AL	B+	B+	B+	100.1	3.16	4.9	7.5	11.4	51.0	10.0	15.6	27.5
First State Bank of Uvalde	Uvalde	TX	B	B	B	1502.1	6.75	2.6	0.8	6.4	49.5	5.1	7.1	29.0
First State Bank of Van Orin	Van Orin	IL	C-	C-	C-	41.7	1.73	3.1	1.6	3.6	32.9	6.9	8.9	21.6
First State Bank of Wabasha	Wabasha	MN	B-	B-	B-	126.8	-1.63	3.8	1.8	9.2	48.8	10.0	11.0	29.2
First State Bank of Warner, South Dakota	Warner	SD	B-	B-	C	65.0	-1.23	16.1	3.2	3.6	9.4	8.1	11.1	13.5
First State Bank of Warren	Warren	AR	C+	C+	B-	112.1	4.62	7.8	3.2	5.3	54.7	9.8	10.8	20.8
First State Bank of Wyoming	Wyoming	MN	A-	A-	B	174.2	5.08	3.9	1.5	12.8	56.9	10.0	15.9	34.7
First State Bank Shannon-Polo	Shannon	IL	B-	B-	B-	151.8	-2.80	6.0	2.4	9.9	27.7	8.5	10.1	13.8

Arrows denote recent upgrades ▲ or downgrades ▼

www.weissratings.com

Asset Quality Index	Adjusted Non-Performing Loans as a % of Total Loans	as a % of Capital	Net Charge-Offs Avg Loans	Profitability Index	Net Income ($Mil)	Return on Assets (R.O.A.)	Return on Equity (R.O.E.)	Net Interest Spread	Overhead Efficiency Ratio	Liquidity Index	Liquidity Ratio	Hot Money Ratio	Stability Index
6.6	1.28	3.6	0.10	7.8	2.2	1.82	13.52	3.65	50.0	3.5	62.4	29.1	9.0
3.4	3.26	15.6	0.69	9.3	1.1	2.10	13.14	4.51	48.5	3.1	10.8	13.3	8.9
8.5	0.82	3.0	-0.04	7.8	1.9	1.87	14.92	3.59	54.5	2.0	37.8	33.2	8.6
1.6	3.80	24.7	-0.02	4.2	0.3	0.64	6.03	4.13	71.1	4.0	19.7	9.1	5.7
7.5	0.72	4.1	0.05	7.8	4.5	1.28	10.07	4.07	51.3	0.7	14.2	23.8	7.8
3.5	2.20	16.7	0.02	4.8	0.8	1.00	10.53	3.75	74.7	3.8	9.4	9.5	5.5
5.5	0.81	4.2	0.04	5.5	1.0	1.32	13.40	3.84	68.3	3.0	28.1	15.9	5.7
8.9	0.07	0.1	-0.14	5.4	2.6	1.35	10.43	3.11	57.6	5.1	75.6	16.5	8.5
4.3	2.35	15.2	0.01	4.5	0.6	0.79	7.75	3.66	65.5	4.2	26.2	9.1	4.9
5.9	0.47	2.6	-0.02	3.3	0.3	0.69	7.06	3.47	78.1	2.3	25.3	18.8	5.7
4.1	2.72	14.5	0.00	5.8	0.6	1.28	10.83	4.34	67.4	4.3	19.5	7.3	6.4
8.1	0.00	0.0	0.00	4.7	0.5	1.22	14.14	3.49	65.0	5.7	39.9	5.1	5.6
7.7	2.07	4.8	-0.01	8.5	1.1	2.01	11.32	4.36	40.8	4.0	66.3	19.1	7.7
5.0	1.80	9.0	0.15	3.5	0.7	0.42	3.30	3.79	80.1	3.9	29.1	11.8	6.4
7.8	1.29	3.2	0.00	3.6	0.3	0.60	3.04	3.55	79.9	4.7	58.6	14.5	7.1
5.9	2.23	9.2	0.01	4.2	0.9	0.95	7.06	4.25	74.2	3.2	30.6	16.0	6.7
5.6	0.92	6.2	-0.01	7.1	2.7	1.67	18.19	4.40	62.0	0.7	12.1	28.6	7.2
1.9	3.88	22.9	0.06	3.0	0.1	0.56	5.34	3.94	84.0	3.2	27.7	13.6	4.7
3.5	1.57	14.7	0.13	6.8	2.1	1.69	19.70	3.42	50.4	1.6	6.1	20.6	7.0
4.6	3.78	15.1	0.06	6.2	1.2	1.19	10.84	3.51	51.1	3.4	50.4	22.3	7.1
9.3	0.00	0.0	0.00	1.7	0.1	0.26	2.83	3.15	94.8	5.7	51.6	7.8	4.5
6.7	0.69	3.4	0.00	7.4	1.1	1.85	17.04	4.14	50.2	4.6	30.9	8.8	7.6
5.4	2.62	7.4	1.02	6.0	0.3	1.42	6.63	3.84	65.8	5.0	40.2	6.7	5.0
8.2	0.02	0.1	0.02	3.8	0.6	1.01	9.50	2.86	74.0	5.8	62.2	9.3	6.2
3.7	9.68	28.7	-0.05	8.3	1.5	2.27	12.44	4.21	36.7	1.5	29.6	32.5	7.1
4.0	0.87	6.5	0.06	4.4	1.8	0.70	6.45	3.56	70.0	0.8	9.6	31.1	6.7
5.3	0.78	5.2	0.15	3.6	0.1	0.67	7.13	3.73	76.8	4.6	31.4	6.7	2.7
5.0	0.96	5.5	0.02	7.7	1.0	1.78	16.74	4.59	60.9	3.6	21.3	11.8	7.9
7.8	1.54	3.9	0.04	4.8	2.3	0.97	5.96	3.61	72.1	4.2	39.0	13.6	8.2
6.3	1.28	5.2	0.39	6.9	1.1	1.08	7.23	3.71	42.3	2.7	20.5	15.9	8.0
3.7	1.98	13.7	0.05	4.9	3.6	1.01	9.72	4.29	70.8	2.2	23.5	18.6	6.2
6.1	3.52	4.9	0.70	3.6	0.5	0.81	7.13	2.76	64.0	4.3	93.4	23.8	4.4
9.6	0.76	1.4	0.10	3.5	0.9	0.76	5.58	2.77	70.1	3.6	60.6	26.3	7.3
5.4	0.30	2.2	0.04	7.9	4.4	1.82	14.72	4.92	62.1	4.1	3.2	6.4	8.5
8.2	0.32	1.5	0.16	5.1	1.0	1.01	9.70	4.35	67.6	5.3	37.8	7.3	4.8
2.9	7.01	20.8	-0.02	1.3	0.0	0.00	0.00	2.47	99.4	6.2	73.6	7.3	6.2
7.2	0.43	2.3	0.00	5.0	0.4	0.96	8.42	3.92	66.8	2.1	11.3	18.2	6.3
5.3	3.16	12.8	1.71	4.7	0.8	1.03	9.36	3.86	58.4	3.6	42.0	17.5	7.1
6.5	1.56	5.5	0.54	5.6	1.3	1.23	8.62	3.88	63.3	2.9	47.8	26.6	7.5
2.6	3.73	22.5	0.00	5.0	1.8	1.41	17.60	3.58	71.2	3.3	36.7	8.6	3.8
5.2	1.48	6.5	0.21	3.1	0.4	0.69	7.43	3.30	82.4	5.0	40.0	9.9	4.8
9.0	0.21	0.4	-0.02	5.9	0.5	1.28	6.21	3.37	49.1	6.2	58.8	6.2	7.9
7.6	0.25	0.9	0.00	1.5	0.0	0.04	0.47	2.37	99.7	4.5	56.9	15.2	3.4
7.1	0.00	0.0	-0.01	7.9	1.4	1.81	14.94	4.07	47.5	2.9	5.7	13.4	8.5
2.7	4.65	24.6	0.28	1.6	0.1	0.17	2.50	2.75	89.7	6.0	48.4	5.3	0.7
6.7	1.50	5.9	0.09	4.5	0.5	1.02	12.22	3.10	70.1	3.6	36.5	16.1	4.6
7.9	0.36	1.8	-0.02	4.1	0.8	1.10	8.18	3.36	64.4	3.4	26.7	13.7	7.0
10.0	1.34	1.4	0.02	6.6	1.1	1.10	5.45	3.66	46.7	5.9	99.3	15.1	8.1
5.8	0.90	5.5	0.17	7.0	3.3	1.30	11.03	3.77	82.3	3.5	19.4	11.8	7.0
9.3	0.15	0.3	0.11	6.9	0.3	1.28	7.96	4.12	53.4	6.5	68.0	6.0	7.7
4.0	4.50	18.8	1.39	1.8	0.0	0.01	0.07	4.83	92.6	5.0	40.5	10.1	5.1
4.9	1.51	9.8	-0.18	5.3	9.3	1.45	15.64	3.30	67.7	4.7	26.0	5.5	5.5
8.9	0.49	1.0	0.07	4.5	0.6	0.86	5.26	3.98	71.5	3.9	59.8	20.6	8.0
9.8	0.13	0.4	0.01	4.7	12.3	1.10	13.94	2.23	42.5	3.2	61.5	42.1	6.2
4.0	4.76	15.5	0.03	2.9	0.2	0.50	5.16	2.50	78.8	6.1	60.7	7.4	4.6
7.8	1.41	3.7	-0.02	4.3	1.1	1.11	9.69	2.78	58.0	3.4	40.2	18.0	5.9
4.4	1.05	7.2	0.06	9.8	1.2	2.39	22.89	4.74	54.5	2.1	9.6	18.2	6.7
7.1	1.14	3.5	0.01	3.0	0.4	0.51	4.77	3.01	80.8	4.2	47.7	16.0	5.7
6.1	4.50	8.9	-0.01	5.7	1.4	1.06	6.42	3.39	57.7	6.2	62.2	9.4	7.6
7.2	0.17	1.0	0.00	4.4	1.2	1.09	9.72	3.22	71.7	3.9	15.9	9.4	6.3

Name	City	State	2015 Rating	2014 Rating	Rating	Total Assets ($Mil)	One Year Asset Growth	Asset Mix (As a % of Total Assets)				Capital-ization Index	Lever-age Ratio	Risk-Based Capital Ratio
								Comm-ercial Loans	Cons-umer Loans	Mort-gage Loans	Secur-ities			
First State Bank Southwest	Pipestone	MN	A	A	A	242.6	3.20	8.2	3.6	3.4	35.4	9.8	10.9	18.5
First State Bank, Inc.	Central City	KY	B-	B-	C+	122.2	15.66	10.2	3.5	42.5	9.1	6.1	8.1	13.2
First State Bank, Kiowa, Kansas	Kiowa	KS	B+	A-	A-	70.1	-8.07	9.2	3.1	9.6	17.5	10.0	16.2	23.7
First State Bank, Pond Creek, Oklahoma	Pond Creek	OK	C-	C-	B-	54.9	0.06	14.2	4.1	5.7	21.3	7.6	9.4	18.5
First State Community Bank	Farmington	MO	B	B	B	2037.8	17.08	5.6	2.4	26.6	12.9	6.9	9.5	12.5
▲ First State Financial, Inc.	Middlesboro	KY	C	D-	D	330.7	-2.39	6.9	3.8	28.3	13.1	7.0	9.0	13.2
First Tennessee Bank, N.A.	Memphis	TN	B-	C	B	28254.0	12.12	19.6	1.1	12.1	13.7	6.0	9.4	11.8
First Texas Bank	Georgetown	TX	C+	C+	C+	606.8	2.71	2.8	1.6	5.0	54.9	6.5	8.5	18.1
First Texas Bank	Killeen	TX	C	C+	C+	295.8	-0.32	1.2	0.4	11.3	53.4	9.9	11.0	26.3
First Texas Bank	Lampasas	TX	C	C+	B-	127.6	3.31	2.7	1.6	11.1	51.5	10.0	11.6	25.2
First Texoma National Bank	Durant	OK	B	B	C	169.8	5.37	6.5	7.2	27.9	10.4	10.0	11.9	18.2
First Tri-County Bank	Swanton	NE	C+	C+	C+	52.9	-2.23	9.1	5.8	19.0	8.4	8.4	10.4	13.7
▲ First Trust & Savings Bank	Marcus	IA	D	E+	C-	36.3	-5.23	5.4	8.1	4.9	45.0	9.2	10.4	16.7
First Trust & Savings Bank	Albany	IL	C	B	B	216.3	-7.56	8.1	3.3	31.2	6.4	8.2	9.8	14.0
▲ First Trust and Savings Bank	Coralville	IA	C+	C	C-	53.0	5.32	4.8	0.9	5.2	58.4	10.0	11.0	19.2
First Trust and Savings Bank	Wheatland	IA	C	B-	B-	150.5	5.06	11.2	3.3	6.9	4.8	7.3	10.8	12.8
First Trust and Savings Bank of Watseka	Watseka	IL	A	A	A	241.5	2.18	5.6	1.0	6.5	32.9	10.0	14.4	27.6
First Trust Bank of Illinois	Kankakee	IL	B+	B+	B+	235.6	1.96	14.9	1.9	6.9	52.9	8.6	10.0	15.2
▼ First United Bank	Park River	ND	B-	B	B	199.3	2.10	6.7	3.0	5.1	13.4	6.5	9.5	12.1
First United Bank	Dimmitt	TX	A-	A-	A-	1173.7	2.97	11.5	0.6	8.2	24.5	10.0	11.0	15.0
First United Bank & Trust	Oakland	MD	B-	B	B-	1318.7	0.45	5.4	1.8	24.3	18.1	10.0	11.0	16.7
First United Bank and Trust Co.	Madisonville	KY	A	A	A	271.8	35.04	6.8	3.5	26.4	28.0	10.0	13.4	21.8
First United Bank and Trust Co.	Durant	OK	B+	B	B	3372.7	8.26	11.1	4.3	19.0	21.1	6.7	8.7	12.9
First United National Bank	Fryburg	PA	B	B	B	267.0	3.53	3.3	7.2	42.9	21.8	6.7	8.7	18.5
First US Bank	Thomasville	AL	B	B	C	600.0	9.43	6.8	14.5	6.6	35.0	10.0	12.4	20.6
First Utah Bank	Salt Lake City	UT	C+	C	D+	326.7	-0.71	12.6	1.1	3.6	10.7	6.5	8.5	12.4
First Virginia Community Bank	Fairfax	VA	B-	B	B	837.0	22.71	9.7	2.5	10.4	11.8	9.4	12.4	14.5
First Vision Bank of Tennessee	Tullahoma	TN	A-	A-	A-	188.1	7.53	7.3	3.0	18.6	11.3	10.0	11.8	17.2
First Volunteer Bank	Chattanooga	TN	B-	B-	C+	926.3	3.96	7.7	2.3	18.3	5.9	9.1	10.4	14.9
First Western Bank	Booneville	AR	C+	C+	C+	365.1	10.02	2.5	1.6	38.1	3.0	5.4	8.1	11.3
First Western Bank & Trust	Minot	ND	B+	B+	B+	1003.0	4.17	12.8	2.2	3.7	33.2	8.4	9.9	14.0
First Western Federal Savings Bank	Rapid City	SD	A-	A-	A-	50.1	9.11	0.0	0.4	78.4	0.0	10.0	15.3	29.4
First Western Trust Bank	Denver	CO	D+	C-	D+	859.0	17.68	14.7	6.3	22.1	9.9	3.3	7.5	10.2
First Westroads Bank, Inc.	Omaha	NE	A-	A-	B+	252.5	-5.53	8.9	0.3	5.5	19.6	10.0	11.4	15.8
First Whitney Bank and Trust	Atlantic	IA	A-	A	A+	201.7	-1.61	11.6	1.4	5.6	29.1	7.4	10.8	12.9
First, A National Banking Assn.	Hattiesburg	MS	B-	B-	B-	1265.8	11.29	9.6	1.1	17.3	19.3	5.2	8.5	11.2
First-Citizens Bank & Trust Co.	Raleigh	NC	B-	B-	C+	32795.5	4.57	6.6	4.3	9.7	19.4	7.0	9.0	13.3
First-Lockhart National Bank	Lockhart	TX	B	B	B-	246.8	13.46	2.4	1.2	25.2	17.0	6.5	8.5	12.6
Firstar Bank, N.A.	Sallisaw	OK	B-	C+	B-	546.8	5.53	20.8	2.5	21.3	6.0	5.1	8.5	11.1
FirstAtlantic Bank	Jacksonville	FL	B+	B+	C	435.3	-2.30	5.5	0.5	14.9	18.6	10.0	13.0	17.9
FirstBank	Lakewood	CO	A-	A-	A-	16614.2	10.40	0.8	0.6	32.2	34.8	5.8	7.8	15.1
FirstBank	Antlers	OK	B	B	B	310.5	6.74	9.8	12.5	32.6	0.1	6.2	8.2	12.3
FirstBank	Nashville	TN	B	B	C+	3184.2	10.92	11.0	1.3	24.3	17.2	6.3	9.1	12.0
FirstBank of Nebraska	Wahoo	NE	B+	B	B	217.5	-2.92	3.6	1.4	8.7	29.6	7.6	10.8	13.0
FirstBank Puerto Rico	San Juan	PR	D	D	D	12059.1	-5.82	8.0	12.2	26.6	16.4	10.0	14.4	20.7
FirstBank Southwest	Amarillo	TX	B-	B-	B-	908.3	-3.49	11.9	3.1	7.6	33.8	7.9	9.6	15.5
FirstCapital Bank of Texas, N.A.	Midland	TX	B	B	B	970.3	1.92	18.5	0.8	14.2	15.4	8.8	10.2	14.4
▲ FirstCity Bank of Commerce	Palm Beach Gardens	FL	C-	D+	C-	83.0	14.44	13.3	0.2	34.8	11.8	8.2	9.8	14.7
▲ FirsTier Bank	Kimball	NE	A	B+	C	245.6	8.81	9.2	2.6	3.5	18.7	10.0	15.7	19.6
FirstOak Bank	Independence	KS	B+	B+	B+	116.4	13.74	10.1	2.2	16.4	5.4	6.3	9.4	12.0
▲ Firstrust Savings Bank	Conshohocken	PA	B+	B+	B+	3021.9	14.96	20.8	4.1	15.0	8.9	8.6	12.1	13.8
FirstState Bank	Lineville	AL	A-	A-	B	203.8	-4.69	5.0	5.3	11.8	32.0	10.0	12.7	19.5
Fisher National Bank	Fisher	IL	A-	A-	B+	114.6	2.61	5.4	3.4	36.8	15.8	10.0	11.0	17.4
Five Points Bank	Grand Island	NE	A-	A-	B+	948.9	2.23	17.1	1.9	7.9	22.2	8.7	11.0	13.9
Five Points Bank of Hastings	Hastings	NE	A-	A-	B+	277.4	0.39	8.0	0.7	4.9	33.8	10.0	11.6	17.9
Five Star Bank	Rocklin	CA	B+	B+	B	759.2	-4.71	8.8	0.5	3.4	9.0	4.4	8.5	10.7
Five Star Bank	Warsaw	NY	B	B	B	3652.7	9.49	7.4	20.5	12.3	30.1	6.0	8.0	12.3
Flagler Bank	West Palm Beach	FL	B	C+	D+	225.8	15.77	9.5	0.2	7.1	25.0	8.4	9.9	16.2
▼ Flagship Bank Minnesota	Wayzata	MN	D+	C	D+	102.1	2.98	9.7	0.3	25.0	3.1	6.3	9.1	11.9
Flagship Community Bank	Clearwater	FL	D+	D	D	105.7	-2.35	14.1	0.4	4.7	4.7	10.0	11.5	15.0

Arrows denote recent upgrades ▲ or downgrades ▼

Asset Quality Index	Adjusted Non-Performing Loans as a % of Total Loans	as a % of Capital	Net Charge-Offs Avg Loans	Profitability Index	Net Income ($Mil)	Return on Assets (R.O.A.)	Return on Equity (R.O.E.)	Net Interest Spread	Overhead Efficiency Ratio	Liquidity Index	Liquidity Ratio	Hot Money Ratio	Stability Index
8.5	0.08	0.4	0.00	8.0	3.4	1.88	16.76	3.67	57.6	4.3	26.1	8.9	8.7
4.6	1.09	10.0	0.00	4.9	0.8	0.89	11.14	4.51	75.3	1.3	12.2	26.4	5.0
6.2	1.42	5.8	0.07	7.7	1.0	1.81	12.05	4.20	47.5	3.6	21.6	11.7	6.7
2.2	4.92	22.7	-0.06	3.6	0.3	0.80	8.66	3.49	79.3	4.3	49.3	15.3	3.6
5.5	0.88	6.6	0.03	6.9	19.0	1.29	12.18	4.12	60.6	3.2	3.4	11.8	9.2
6.0	0.44	3.6	0.01	3.0	2.5	0.99	11.13	4.24	75.3	1.4	9.8	25.1	3.2
4.7	1.56	11.4	0.15	5.3	204.3	1.02	9.26	2.96	67.6	4.3	13.5	3.2	8.5
9.6	0.01	0.0	-0.04	3.8	3.1	0.70	8.10	2.51	65.4	6.3	63.1	8.6	5.3
8.9	1.15	3.1	-0.01	1.7	0.3	0.14	1.27	2.37	94.3	7.4	74.1	3.0	5.8
9.6	0.57	1.7	-0.03	2.4	0.3	0.27	2.31	2.68	77.1	6.7	68.1	6.4	6.7
8.0	0.13	0.8	0.06	4.2	0.9	0.75	6.20	4.23	79.0	2.9	17.2	12.2	6.0
6.1	0.02	0.1	-0.01	4.2	0.3	0.82	7.52	3.84	74.4	4.1	10.7	7.6	5.0
1.5	5.38	22.1	2.51	0.8	0.0	-0.08	-0.73	3.33	88.5	6.0	52.1	6.0	3.2
2.8	2.17	16.9	-0.01	5.0	1.8	1.06	9.64	3.57	67.2	1.3	9.8	11.5	7.1
5.0	3.35	9.2	0.09	3.2	0.4	0.99	8.74	3.56	82.3	2.2	46.2	40.3	5.5
2.5	1.63	12.2	-0.03	6.4	1.6	1.46	13.58	3.85	57.6	1.4	8.9	23.5	7.4
8.9	0.57	1.8	0.02	7.0	2.4	1.34	9.24	3.23	45.4	4.7	36.4	10.1	8.7
5.9	1.72	6.6	-0.01	4.7	1.8	1.00	9.49	3.36	58.0	3.3	33.5	16.6	6.8
3.2	1.21	9.0	0.00	6.8	2.4	1.68	17.34	4.28	54.6	2.6	8.2	12.7	6.8
5.9	1.54	9.0	0.01	7.1	14.5	1.72	14.37	3.97	58.8	1.2	8.9	27.6	10.0
4.7	2.47	14.2	0.31	3.9	6.8	0.70	6.67	3.35	72.0	3.5	14.0	11.9	8.4
8.8	0.28	1.2	-0.02	6.5	2.7	1.45	10.66	4.13	68.1	4.3	13.7	6.2	8.9
5.5	0.85	6.3	0.21	6.4	37.6	1.55	15.71	3.84	72.8	1.5	6.8	22.0	9.2
6.0	0.77	5.2	0.08	4.5	1.8	0.89	10.17	3.35	61.6	4.6	30.6	8.7	5.4
6.3	0.92	3.8	0.68	3.4	1.9	0.44	3.28	5.19	85.8	2.9	29.2	15.0	6.7
3.4	2.54	18.1	0.05	4.5	2.6	1.09	11.85	4.13	80.2	1.0	15.6	28.3	4.4
4.1	0.85	5.5	0.26	5.8	5.9	1.03	9.06	3.65	53.7	1.3	7.0	16.3	7.1
8.0	0.44	2.7	0.03	5.9	1.5	1.04	8.83	4.28	63.1	1.5	14.2	24.5	7.6
4.5	1.34	9.2	0.38	8.0	9.3	1.38	13.03	4.69	58.5	3.8	15.5	9.8	6.8
5.1	1.00	9.4	0.17	3.7	1.4	0.55	6.73	4.11	78.0	0.8	10.6	32.9	4.4
8.0	0.33	1.8	0.15	6.5	8.8	1.17	11.59	3.68	55.7	1.6	12.2	18.4	8.3
9.3	0.24	1.4	0.00	10.0	1.0	2.67	17.18	5.68	52.0	0.4	7.7	70.0	8.0
3.4	1.22	12.2	0.04	3.0	3.2	0.51	5.57	3.36	86.5	1.1	6.7	28.0	4.9
7.4	0.37	2.1	0.00	7.5	3.6	1.83	16.15	3.88	56.9	4.4	24.1	7.4	8.6
8.4	0.16	0.9	-0.01	9.1	3.3	2.12	19.27	3.74	34.9	3.7	24.4	11.6	8.7
5.6	0.89	6.9	-0.03	4.9	8.7	0.96	9.86	3.73	66.1	3.1	12.3	13.4	7.5
5.9	0.94	6.5	0.07	4.0	177.5	0.74	8.06	3.15	73.8	4.8	17.1	4.4	7.1
8.8	0.00	0.0	-0.03	4.8	2.0	1.18	13.35	3.85	73.7	1.8	16.2	20.6	5.8
3.8	1.07	9.3	0.09	6.5	6.1	1.50	13.56	4.52	68.7	1.6	8.6	20.4	8.7
6.7	0.43	2.3	0.04	5.3	2.8	0.86	6.57	4.07	67.8	3.2	24.8	14.0	6.1
9.4	0.33	2.3	0.07	7.5	156.0	1.31	15.89	3.55	52.8	6.2	34.1	3.7	7.9
4.5	0.57	5.3	0.65	7.3	3.7	1.58	18.76	6.40	69.9	0.6	10.5	47.1	6.8
5.2	0.71	5.6	0.03	7.9	32.4	1.48	14.87	4.22	76.7	4.2	8.9	6.9	9.1
6.8	0.74	3.5	0.01	5.8	1.9	1.17	10.38	3.67	57.5	4.8	24.5	3.7	6.7
0.5	9.06	41.7	1.32	4.2	70.4	0.75	4.85	4.22	63.0	0.8	13.1	16.6	7.2
6.1	0.89	4.9	0.03	4.3	7.2	1.03	10.53	3.03	68.9	3.4	23.8	13.1	6.4
6.4	1.03	6.4	0.01	5.2	7.0	0.96	9.72	4.22	63.1	0.9	19.9	33.6	6.5
3.0	1.99	16.2	0.69	2.1	0.2	0.29	3.02	3.57	86.6	1.2	16.7	29.8	4.1
8.2	0.01	0.0	-0.02	9.6	5.6	3.06	19.29	4.54	51.8	2.7	16.3	15.6	6.8
8.4	0.00	0.0	-0.20	7.6	1.6	1.86	20.16	5.60	64.7	2.2	18.8	18.4	5.8
6.3	0.60	3.9	0.03	5.7	29.8	1.40	11.51	4.18	74.9	3.5	7.0	8.4	9.9
6.8	1.04	4.6	0.13	6.3	2.1	1.36	10.84	4.45	64.6	1.6	21.9	25.2	6.7
6.0	0.88	5.9	0.74	7.8	1.6	1.86	16.54	4.17	59.5	2.7	10.7	14.9	8.1
8.5	0.05	0.3	-0.13	7.3	12.7	1.77	15.58	3.57	53.2	4.2	26.2	8.9	9.4
9.0	0.01	0.1	-0.20	5.1	2.2	1.08	9.64	3.02	56.7	5.8	40.6	5.2	8.1
6.8	0.27	2.2	-0.02	8.7	11.5	1.95	23.58	3.70	38.8	4.4	20.1	6.6	7.7
7.0	0.20	1.5	0.25	5.0	26.4	1.02	11.10	3.33	56.8	3.0	3.8	12.4	7.7
5.0	1.49	8.6	-0.22	8.5	3.7	2.24	23.58	4.05	46.0	1.6	34.2	41.1	5.2
5.2	0.74	6.3	0.15	1.1	-0.4	-0.56	-4.30	4.11	142.9	1.6	9.1	21.9	5.3
1.8	2.58	16.7	-0.02	3.1	0.3	0.39	3.18	3.90	84.3	2.1	19.1	9.6	5.9

Name	City	State	2017 Rating	2015 Rating	2014 Rating	Total Assets ($Mil)	One Year Asset Growth	Commercial Loans	Consumer Loans	Mortgage Loans	Securities	Capitalization Index	Leverage Ratio	Risk-Based Capital Ratio
Flagstar Bank, FSB	Troy	MI	B+	B-	D	14202.2	14.04	3.6	0.2	42.7	16.1	9.3	10.6	17.9
Flanagan State Bank	Flanagan	IL	B-	B	B	177.6	4.62	5.0	2.1	19.1	27.6	8.7	10.1	14.3
Flatirons Bank	Boulder	CO	A-	B+	B	132.9	-0.15	16.5	0.1	36.0	22.9	8.6	10.1	15.8
Fleetwood Bank	Fleetwood	PA	C+	C+	C	241.9	6.73	1.7	0.2	37.0	28.7	7.4	9.3	16.9
Flint Community Bank	Albany	GA	B-	B-	B-	195.1	8.47	7.4	0.9	33.2	1.5	6.4	8.4	12.2
▲ Flint Hills Bank	Eskridge	KS	A-	B	B	119.3	-2.44	6.5	3.6	12.0	35.9	10.0	11.5	21.4
Flora Bank & Trust	Flora	IL	B-	C+	C	66.3	-0.96	12.4	12.4	17.5	8.1	10.0	11.6	18.1
Flora Savings Bank	Flora	IL	C+	C	C-	29.5	4.49	5.0	6.4	41.6	24.1	10.0	11.0	20.0
Florence Bank	Florence	MA	B-	C+	C+	1275.5	10.81	3.3	0.0	46.2	16.4	8.6	10.1	15.2
Florida Business Bank	Melbourne	FL	B	B	B-	111.1	5.59	4.8	0.4	2.6	13.0	10.0	15.0	21.2
▲ Florida Capital Bank, N.A.	Jacksonville	FL	D+	D	E-	341.6	-0.84	5.3	0.2	24.8	7.8	6.7	8.7	13.5
Florida Community Bank, N.A.	Weston	FL	B-	C+	C+	8387.1	24.94	13.3	0.1	26.7	18.3	5.6	9.6	11.5
Florida Parishes Bank	Hammond	LA	B	B	B	268.4	14.63	4.3	2.5	17.4	26.7	9.6	10.7	17.4
▲ Floridian Community Bank, Inc.	Davie	FL	C-	D+	D	385.0	1.06	9.6	0.1	23.1	5.0	8.9	11.5	14.1
Flushing Bank	Uniondale	NY	B	B	B-	6006.8	9.05	6.1	0.0	11.7	15.2	6.9	8.9	13.0
▲ FMB Bank	Wright City	MO	C-	C-	C	35.7	3.74	5.7	4.0	22.4	26.9	8.4	9.9	15.4
FMS Bank	Fort Morgan	CO	B-	C+	C-	159.3	1.05	11.9	12.9	16.6	15.1	4.8	10.8	10.9
FNB Bank	Scottsboro	AL	A-	A-	B+	374.7	2.86	11.5	3.5	10.7	22.5	10.0	13.4	19.0
FNB Bank	Fontanelle	IA	A-	B+	B+	207.0	-1.49	5.5	1.0	8.1	15.4	10.0	11.6	15.3
FNB Bank, Inc.	Mayfield	KY	B	B	B	443.5	3.85	8.3	3.3	20.4	24.5	6.9	8.9	13.3
FNB Bank, Inc.	Romney	WV	C	C+	C	180.0	4.01	5.5	3.1	26.6	21.9	7.9	9.6	15.1
FNB Bank, N.A.	Danville	PA	B-	B-	B	350.0	1.75	3.4	3.5	25.1	16.7	9.6	10.7	16.9
FNB Community Bank	Midwest City	OK	C+	C+	C+	473.5	1.70	3.0	2.9	7.0	48.1	8.2	9.8	19.4
FNB New Mexico	Clayton	NM	B	B	B	220.2	8.97	5.0	2.4	8.3	22.1	7.0	9.0	13.7
FNB of Central Alabama	Tuscaloosa	AL	C	C+	C+	271.8	9.50	10.6	0.7	11.4	18.1	9.7	10.8	15.1
FNB Oxford	Oxford	MS	B+	B+	B+	285.4	8.62	4.4	1.7	22.2	34.9	10.0	11.8	20.2
FNBC Bank	Ash Flat	AR	B-	B-	B-	403.3	7.68	8.7	4.0	18.3	24.2	9.0	10.4	14.7
▲ FNBC Bank and Trust	La Grange	IL	B-	C-	C-	526.1	-1.16	2.2	0.8	22.3	33.3	7.3	9.2	16.6
▲ FNBT Bank	Fort Walton Beach	FL	B	B	B	403.0	7.46	1.9	0.8	9.1	1.6	10.0	12.0	27.1
FNCB Bank	Dunmore	PA	B-	B-	B-	1121.2	6.29	13.7	9.5	12.5	23.2	7.1	9.1	13.4
FNNB Bank	Newton	IA	C	C	C	80.7	1.63	14.3	0.8	11.5	25.9	6.7	8.7	14.2
Focus Bank	Charleston	MO	B-	C+	C+	741.7	4.81	7.2	2.1	24.9	3.5	8.5	10.2	13.7
Folsom Lake Bank	Folsom	CA	C+	C+	D+	194.1	16.17	7.6	0.4	5.3	32.1	6.8	8.8	14.2
Foothills Bank	Yuma	AZ	C	C-	D	315.6	7.56	6.2	0.2	2.7	8.5	8.8	11.5	14.0
Foothills Bank & Trust	Maryville	TN	B-	B-	C+	208.2	1.51	5.6	0.6	16.2	23.0	7.6	9.4	14.4
Foothills Community Bank	Dawsonville	GA	D-	E-	E-	82.2	14.89	2.1	2.9	9.0	13.3	9.7	10.8	15.7
Forcht Bank, N.A.	Lexington	KY	B	B	B-	1009.1	1.79	4.4	2.5	26.8	31.7	10.0	11.9	20.8
Ford County State Bank	Spearville	KS	B-	B-	B-	36.4	-12.70	18.7	1.7	5.5	12.5	10.0	13.8	19.0
▼ Foresight Bank	Plainview	MN	B-	B-	B-	192.0	3.60	5.4	2.2	37.2	9.9	7.2	9.6	12.7
Forest Park National Bank and Trust Co.	Forest Park	IL	C	C-	D+	235.9	3.91	4.2	0.4	19.8	7.5	6.0	8.1	12.0
Forrest City Bank, N.A.	Forrest City	AR	D-	D-	D-	47.0	-0.70	1.9	2.4	14.5	40.3	5.0	7.0	14.0
Forreston State Bank	Forreston	IL	B+	B+	B+	185.9	3.50	4.8	0.3	7.7	27.0	10.0	12.7	18.6
▲ Fort Davis State Bank	Fort Davis	TX	C+	D+	D-	76.2	7.97	12.5	4.0	8.1	23.5	8.8	10.2	17.6
Fort Gibson State Bank	Fort Gibson	OK	C-	C-	C-	61.4	-3.74	3.6	17.7	18.3	7.1	4.8	7.6	10.9
Fort Hood National Bank	Fort Hood	TX	C+	B-	B-	250.8	4.70	0.0	10.6	17.0	38.5	6.3	8.3	37.6
Fort Jennings State Bank	Fort Jennings	OH	B+	B+	B	175.8	2.78	9.8	3.8	25.0	5.4	8.5	10.0	14.0
Fortis Private Bank	Denver	CO	C-	C	C+	402.6	42.11	3.8	44.8	10.2	18.9	5.3	7.3	14.8
FortuneBank	Arnold	MO	C-	C	D	189.1	18.28	20.1	0.4	15.9	5.8	6.0	9.1	11.8
▲ Forward Financial Bank	Marshfield	WI	B-	C+	C+	388.4	6.01	10.1	1.6	15.2	3.3	6.2	9.1	11.9
Foundation Bank	Cincinnati	OH	B+	B+	B+	221.4	3.29	2.4	0.5	27.5	0.0	10.0	16.5	21.6
Foundation One Bank	Omaha	NE	C+	C+	C-	89.9	15.56	20.5	2.8	27.3	7.7	6.7	10.4	12.3
Founders Community Bank	San Luis Obispo	CA	B	B	B	198.5	6.74	10.1	0.1	1.7	1.1	7.2	9.1	16.0
Fountain Trust Co.	Covington	IN	A-	A-	B	289.9	5.58	4.6	1.9	22.7	30.6	10.0	14.5	24.5
Four Corners Community Bank	Farmington	NM	C	C	B	322.6	2.03	9.0	1.1	6.2	14.5	9.5	11.2	14.6
Four County Bank	Allentown	GA	B	B	B-	64.9	6.80	8.9	12.0	17.1	17.1	10.0	13.2	20.3
▲ Four Oaks Bank & Trust Co.	Four Oaks	NC	C+	C-	D-	721.3	1.11	2.7	1.2	13.4	16.4	9.7	10.8	15.7
Fowler State Bank	Fowler	CO	B	B	B	73.4	2.51	2.4	1.5	7.7	33.5	10.0	14.9	29.4
Fowler State Bank	Fowler	IN	A-	A-	A-	155.9	8.07	8.2	4.2	8.7	48.9	10.0	14.0	20.4
Fowler State Bank	Fowler	KS	C+	B-	C+	70.9	7.33	20.2	5.5	4.6	23.3	9.0	11.2	14.2
▲ Fox River State Bank	Burlington	WI	C+	C-	D	85.2	3.67	7.9	1.3	14.2	10.0	7.1	9.1	13.8

Asset Quality Index	Adjusted Non-Performing Loans as a % of Total Loans	as a % of Capital	Net Charge-Offs Avg Loans	Profitability Index	Net Income ($Mil)	Return on Assets (R.O.A.)	Return on Equity (R.O.E.)	Net Interest Spread	Overhead Efficiency Ratio	Liquidity Index	Liquidity Ratio	Hot Money Ratio	Stability Index
5.7	0.88	5.5	0.51	7.4	155.4	1.52	11.86	2.75	64.6	3.6	12.5	11.1	8.0
4.6	1.65	9.6	0.30	6.5	2.2	1.69	16.59	3.70	79.5	4.1	31.7	11.0	6.3
8.3	0.25	1.6	0.00	6.9	1.5	1.52	14.21	4.12	63.2	4.1	24.1	9.4	8.2
6.2	1.01	6.1	0.14	3.1	0.9	0.49	5.20	3.38	82.4	4.9	33.6	8.0	5.1
5.1	0.68	6.2	0.05	6.0	2.1	1.44	17.32	3.84	62.3	1.3	8.7	19.2	4.4
8.7	0.05	0.2	0.02	5.3	1.3	1.35	11.59	3.20	57.4	2.1	20.7	19.0	7.9
5.8	0.92	5.2	-0.01	3.7	0.3	0.55	4.74	3.60	77.6	4.9	22.5	3.5	5.3
3.9	3.23	18.4	0.00	2.8	0.1	0.38	3.42	3.64	85.8	1.6	29.7	30.9	4.6
8.1	0.47	3.5	0.03	4.1	6.5	0.70	7.22	3.30	69.2	3.4	20.0	12.9	7.1
7.0	0.75	3.3	0.21	4.8	0.7	0.87	5.70	4.02	67.1	5.0	32.1	6.7	7.5
4.4	1.35	10.7	-0.02	2.1	1.0	0.40	4.72	3.25	95.7	0.8	10.5	33.2	1.3
7.1	0.40	3.1	-0.03	6.5	73.9	1.27	12.01	3.52	44.6	1.5	15.7	24.9	6.7
5.0	1.74	8.7	-0.04	7.1	2.3	1.24	11.36	5.01	68.7	4.1	34.1	12.5	6.5
3.4	0.90	6.4	1.06	2.4	0.7	0.23	2.08	3.86	71.5	2.2	11.4	17.4	4.2
5.4	0.56	4.9	-0.01	6.6	51.0	1.16	12.96	3.06	49.3	1.4	14.0	15.3	7.4
2.4	5.44	25.1	0.01	2.0	0.0	0.13	1.35	3.44	96.8	4.5	18.8	6.1	4.6
5.4	0.53	3.3	0.04	6.8	2.0	1.68	16.02	4.88	69.1	2.8	14.9	13.3	6.7
5.8	1.41	6.8	0.08	6.5	3.5	1.27	9.58	4.54	65.5	2.8	23.5	15.7	7.4
6.7	0.12	0.7	-0.17	6.0	2.2	1.41	10.63	3.85	61.4	1.9	6.9	18.8	8.3
5.8	0.55	3.8	0.01	5.7	3.4	1.05	9.31	3.91	62.1	2.8	19.8	6.5	7.4
3.2	3.22	20.6	-0.61	5.0	1.5	1.16	11.32	3.75	67.1	1.6	15.8	23.9	5.5
4.9	1.02	6.9	0.19	3.4	1.6	0.59	5.15	3.30	78.8	3.8	6.4	8.8	6.7
9.0	0.13	0.5	0.05	3.4	2.7	0.76	7.53	3.12	79.1	5.0	35.5	7.9	6.2
6.5	0.31	2.1	0.26	4.5	1.6	1.01	10.49	4.58	76.8	3.2	11.1	12.5	6.0
5.0	1.35	7.7	-0.03	3.0	1.0	0.50	4.64	3.38	84.8	3.7	20.8	11.2	6.2
8.9	0.24	1.1	0.02	4.9	2.1	1.01	7.94	3.83	66.9	3.7	30.8	13.5	7.9
4.8	1.16	7.2	0.13	3.9	2.4	0.83	9.37	3.96	81.2	4.3	20.2	7.3	5.3
4.6	1.85	10.7	0.04	4.0	3.7	0.91	9.56	3.22	76.6	5.4	35.0	4.9	4.4
8.2	1.59	3.6	0.00	4.2	2.9	1.01	8.53	2.86	77.6	7.1	71.8	4.4	6.8
6.4	0.51	3.5	0.21	3.6	5.7	0.69	6.28	3.22	73.5	3.4	6.2	7.8	9.4
6.3	1.09	6.7	0.26	2.8	0.2	0.37	4.20	3.70	88.0	5.5	37.3	5.3	5.0
4.4	1.14	8.5	0.18	4.7	7.5	1.36	13.37	3.45	65.2	0.7	9.7	33.2	7.1
7.5	0.00	0.0	0.00	3.3	0.7	0.49	5.21	3.35	78.5	3.7	35.3	14.9	4.9
3.0	1.35	8.8	-0.20	6.5	3.0	1.27	9.83	4.57	63.8	5.0	14.1	2.1	7.0
8.6	0.21	1.4	0.02	4.4	1.3	0.83	8.66	3.37	63.7	3.5	15.9	11.4	5.7
3.5	2.20	10.5	0.96	0.0	-1.6	-2.71	-36.78	4.23	172.9	2.5	29.9	19.1	0.0
6.9	1.00	4.8	0.08	4.1	7.4	0.98	6.72	4.15	84.2	5.1	27.0	7.2	9.1
4.3	3.01	14.2	0.04	4.9	0.2	0.85	6.22	3.83	65.8	3.3	21.5	13.0	6.7
3.0	2.57	21.1	-0.02	6.7	2.4	1.67	17.36	3.85	59.8	1.2	12.1	28.7	7.0
3.0	1.82	15.2	-0.03	4.9	1.8	1.03	12.68	4.51	76.6	4.1	15.9	8.0	5.3
7.0	0.87	4.7	0.14	0.2	-0.2	-0.41	-4.18	2.89	120.7	4.2	36.0	12.8	3.2
5.8	1.40	7.0	-0.18	5.2	1.9	1.38	10.81	3.35	58.1	2.2	28.8	20.9	7.2
5.8	1.16	5.6	0.26	3.5	0.5	0.82	7.89	4.06	82.0	4.8	36.0	9.9	4.4
7.5	0.12	1.1	0.07	4.3	0.4	0.72	9.86	5.00	82.2	1.2	15.3	29.4	3.4
9.2	0.00	0.0	0.39	3.2	1.1	0.63	7.09	2.29	88.6	7.1	64.3	3.3	5.3
8.2	0.17	1.3	0.03	6.2	1.4	1.10	10.93	4.48	58.7	1.7	13.0	20.4	6.0
6.6	0.20	2.0	0.05	2.2	1.4	0.51	6.37	2.98	95.6	2.5	11.6	15.9	3.4
1.8	3.52	27.2	0.14	3.8	0.8	0.62	6.43	3.50	78.5	0.8	15.1	28.9	4.0
5.5	0.31	2.5	0.12	4.8	2.2	0.78	7.80	3.74	70.3	3.6	15.2	11.2	5.3
5.6	0.70	3.3	0.02	6.0	2.4	1.48	8.29	3.72	57.3	1.2	17.8	30.3	8.5
6.9	0.42	3.3	0.00	3.7	0.4	0.59	5.68	3.39	80.6	0.8	14.1	37.6	5.8
8.9	0.00	0.0	-0.01	4.6	0.9	0.62	6.75	3.89	73.7	5.5	47.1	9.3	5.3
6.2	2.08	8.2	0.07	5.7	2.3	1.08	7.31	4.14	64.2	5.5	38.3	5.6	7.8
2.2	2.59	16.2	0.23	8.3	4.4	1.90	16.80	4.43	53.9	1.5	11.7	23.3	8.3
5.5	1.30	6.5	0.87	7.0	0.8	1.69	13.27	4.40	58.4	1.5	27.5	30.7	6.9
5.5	0.83	4.7	-0.02	3.5	3.2	0.61	5.12	3.88	78.6	1.6	22.8	20.6	4.6
5.6	4.49	12.3	0.11	5.4	0.6	1.07	7.40	3.19	48.2	2.7	52.4	31.4	6.7
7.3	1.54	4.9	0.22	5.7	1.6	1.43	9.77	4.08	67.5	5.8	47.0	7.1	8.5
4.2	1.73	10.4	0.09	4.8	0.6	1.14	10.29	4.24	69.6	1.6	3.8	19.9	5.8
4.3	0.98	6.6	-0.38	3.6	0.3	0.51	3.80	3.89	79.0	2.9	22.2	15.2	5.4

Name	City	State	2015 Rating	2014 Rating	Rating	Total Assets ($Mil)	One Year Asset Growth	Commercial Loans	Consumer Loans	Mortgage Loans	Securities	Capitalization Index	Leverage Ratio	Risk-Based Capital Ratio
Fox Valley Savings Bank	Fond du Lac	WI	B-	B-	B-	320.6	4.70	1.9	0.6	29.4	39.3	10.0	14.0	21.7
Foxboro Federal Savings	Foxboro	MA	C+	B-	B-	162.9	1.77	0.0	0.4	58.1	15.7	10.0	15.3	35.1
Frandsen Bank & Trust	Lonsdale	MN	B-	B-	C+	1586.1	3.16	8.3	1.7	14.8	32.3	6.5	8.5	13.0
Franklin Bank	Pilesgrove	NJ	D+	D+	C-	261.0	5.51	1.4	2.7	42.7	17.9	6.5	8.5	17.6
▼ Franklin Bank & Trust Co.	Franklin	KY	B	B+	A-	449.6	9.59	24.3	1.4	17.0	2.5	9.1	10.9	14.3
Franklin Savings Bank	Farmington	ME	A-	A-	A-	360.7	4.20	6.6	3.3	42.7	2.1	10.0	27.6	36.5
Franklin Savings Bank	Franklin	NH	C	C+	C+	436.2	6.45	2.8	0.5	33.3	16.5	9.3	10.5	15.9
Franklin State Bank	Franklin	MN	B	B	B	28.8	-0.46	3.2	3.5	12.1	12.0	10.0	14.4	23.0
Franklin State Bank	Franklin	NE	B	B+	B+	46.5	-3.06	2.5	3.2	1.5	41.6	10.0	18.0	29.0
▼ Franklin State Bank & Trust Co.	Winnsboro	LA	C-	B+	B+	165.6	1.47	3.3	5.8	15.6	12.5	7.4	9.3	14.0
Franklin Synergy Bank	Franklin	TN	B+	B	B	2704.7	35.07	13.8	0.1	9.5	33.8	7.0	9.3	12.5
Frazer Bank	Altus	OK	B	B+	B+	314.5	1.29	13.7	0.8	7.1	40.7	7.5	9.3	16.2
Frederick County Bank	Frederick	MD	C-	C+	C+	381.7	6.67	12.8	0.6	12.7	4.7	6.8	10.4	12.4
Fredonia Valley Bank	Fredonia	KY	B+	B+	B+	79.3	5.01	2.8	3.2	43.0	17.6	10.0	15.0	24.3
Freedom Bank	Saint Petersburg	FL	C	E+	C-	179.3	6.36	15.9	1.6	3.2	3.4	4.7	8.5	10.9
Freedom Bank	Huntingburg	IN	A-	B+	A-	373.5	4.18	6.9	4.6	40.4	1.5	9.1	10.6	14.3
Freedom Bank	Overland Park	KS	B+	B+	B+	176.3	8.96	15.1	0.0	4.7	41.6	8.7	10.1	15.1
Freedom Bank	Columbia Falls	MT	B-	C+	C-	64.8	5.63	19.2	2.4	17.8	0.1	9.5	10.6	15.2
Freedom Bank	Maywood	NJ	B	B	B-	337.6	11.99	5.1	0.0	7.0	0.6	6.1	9.3	11.8
▲ Freedom Bank of Southern Missouri	Cassville	MO	B+	B	B-	249.7	5.13	9.0	3.1	19.6	10.0	8.0	9.7	14.7
Freedom Bank of Virginia	Fairfax	VA	C+	C	C+	494.0	26.63	10.9	3.2	17.6	9.4	8.1	10.7	13.4
Freedom Bank, Inc.	Belington	WV	D+	D+	D+	156.2	0.64	7.2	6.3	42.2	5.5	8.2	9.8	15.4
Freedom Financial Bank	West Des Moines	IA	B+	B+	B+	174.0	3.37	11.3	0.7	9.7	0.0	7.7	10.3	13.1
▲ Freedom National Bank	Greenville	RI	C	C-	D+	110.0	0.16	15.4	0.1	12.7	11.5	9.3	10.6	15.6
▲ FreedomBank	Elkader	IA	C+	B	B	255.7	-3.83	6.8	1.9	19.0	19.8	10.0	11.1	16.3
Freehold Savings Bank	Freehold	NJ	C	C	B-	306.4	6.88	0.0	0.0	14.8	66.5	10.0	11.9	26.1
Freeland State Bank	Freeland	MI	C-	D+	C-	52.8	-4.50	0.1	1.3	16.4	60.2	10.0	17.4	65.5
▲ Freeport State Bank	Harper	KS	D	E+	E+	23.4	-3.75	2.7	1.4	10.7	24.9	5.1	7.1	13.4
Freeport State Bank	Freeport	MN	B	B	B-	109.9	7.83	10.8	3.1	10.3	12.4	6.6	9.4	12.2
Fremont Bank	Fremont	CA	B+	A-	A-	3591.8	11.10	5.4	0.1	29.9	10.2	5.8	7.8	11.9
Fresno First Bank	Fresno	CA	B	B	C+	333.5	14.35	21.6	0.0	3.8	20.0	7.1	9.0	15.4
Friend Bank	Slocomb	AL	B	B	B	130.4	4.60	5.0	3.9	22.7	14.2	7.5	9.3	16.0
Friendly Hills Bank	Whittier	CA	C+	C	B-	142.6	10.03	4.6	0.1	13.0	21.5	9.3	10.5	16.5
▲ Friends Bank	New Smyrna Beach	FL	D+	D-	E-	103.8	9.46	0.2	0.7	22.7	2.3	5.9	7.9	13.9
Friendship State Bank	Friendship	IN	B+	B+	B	347.3	4.98	2.0	3.0	43.1	17.0	7.8	9.5	17.4
Frontier Bank	Lamar	CO	A	A	A	277.9	3.72	1.4	0.7	10.1	38.2	9.6	10.8	17.5
Frontier Bank	Omaha	NE	B	B	B-	739.6	116.14	11.2	2.5	10.8	13.9	5.0	8.9	11.0
Frontier Bank	Sioux Falls	SD	C+	C+	C+	200.8	3.34	4.9	1.4	11.7	21.3	5.3	8.5	11.2
Frontier Bank of Texas	Elgin	TX	B	B	B-	153.8	7.95	7.5	5.7	26.1	20.0	10.0	18.2	28.3
▲ Frontier Community Bank	Waynesboro	VA	C+	C	C	103.5	2.42	9.6	1.5	27.4	3.4	10.0	11.0	16.6
Frontier Savings Bank	Council Bluffs	IA	C-	C-	C-	41.2	13.21	2.6	0.2	11.3	0.0	9.8	10.8	33.7
Frontier State Bank	Oklahoma City	OK	D	C-	C	650.4	-3.23	15.2	0.7	15.9	10.5	8.9	10.7	14.0
Frost Bank	San Antonio	TX	B	B+	B+	29633.4	4.37	15.5	1.6	2.6	42.0	6.0	8.0	13.9
▼ Frost State Bank	Frost	MN	C	C	D+	47.7	4.07	11.8	4.7	4.3	2.1	9.0	11.7	14.2
FSNB, N.A.	Lawton	OK	A	A	A	390.0	10.97	0.0	3.5	11.7	37.8	10.0	14.0	29.4
Fullerton National Bank	Fullerton	NE	B	B	B	46.8	4.74	11.6	3.0	5.1	6.1	9.9	11.3	14.9
Fulton Bank of New Jersey	Mount Laurel	NJ	B-	B-	B-	3830.4	5.79	11.1	1.9	9.2	15.7	7.4	9.5	12.8
Fulton Bank, N.A.	Lancaster	PA	B	B-	B-	10556.2	5.27	13.5	1.5	10.0	10.1	7.0	10.1	12.5
Fulton Savings Bank	Fulton	NY	B+	B+	A-	378.9	1.19	0.4	0.9	23.4	35.8	10.0	26.8	57.6
G.W. Jones Exchange Bank	Marcellus	MI	C-	C	C	60.4	4.38	3.0	1.0	21.7	31.7	9.7	10.8	27.0
Galion Building and Loan Bank	Galion	OH	C	C	C-	63.9	0.30	1.0	1.8	59.8	14.5	10.0	11.2	26.7
Garden Plain State Bank	Wichita	KS	B+	A-	A-	86.8	-1.94	11.1	2.3	15.0	25.7	10.0	14.4	17.4
Garfield County Bank	Jordan	MT	D-	D	C	77.5	3.75	4.6	2.7	3.9	7.5	8.2	11.5	13.5
Garrett State Bank	Garrett	IN	B+	B	B	216.1	3.91	5.8	3.0	52.0	13.5	8.2	9.8	18.8
Garrison State Bank and Trust	Garrison	ND	B+	B	B	121.9	-0.78	5.7	6.0	3.2	14.5	10.0	11.5	15.5
Gary State Bank	Gary	MN	B-	B-	B-	13.4	5.56	13.2	7.1	1.8	0.0	10.0	14.1	18.1
Gate City Bank	Fargo	ND	B	B	B	1923.2	6.58	1.1	26.9	55.2	6.2	10.0	11.5	17.2
▲ Gates Banking and Trust Co.	Gates	TN	B+	B	B-	42.8	-4.41	2.5	1.1	4.4	65.3	10.0	11.9	26.5
▼ Gateway Bank	Rison	AR	C-	B-	C	58.2	36.94	28.3	6.1	3.9	8.6	7.2	9.5	12.7
Gateway Bank	Mendota Heights	MN	A-	A-	A-	155.6	13.02	27.6	3.0	11.9	0.9	7.3	9.2	13.5

Asset Quality Index	Adjusted Non-Performing Loans as a % of Total Loans	as a % of Capital	Net Charge-Offs Avg Loans	Profitability Index	Net Income ($Mil)	Return on Assets (R.O.A.)	Return on Equity (R.O.E.)	Net Interest Spread	Overhead Efficiency Ratio	Liquidity Index	Liquidity Ratio	Hot Money Ratio	Stability Index
8.0	1.09	3.9	0.17	3.7	1.6	0.69	4.77	2.74	68.6	4.6	39.4	11.7	6.7
10.0	0.01	0.1	0.00	3.3	0.6	0.53	3.39	2.78	76.9	4.5	39.3	12.4	7.8
4.4	1.35	8.5	0.13	5.9	16.3	1.39	10.90	3.85	68.5	5.0	18.9	3.0	9.9
5.7	1.24	7.9	0.20	1.5	0.3	0.16	1.80	2.89	89.4	4.3	31.4	10.7	3.9
5.6	0.79	5.6	0.52	4.5	2.5	0.78	7.12	3.73	62.0	4.2	13.7	7.0	6.6
7.1	1.27	4.1	0.16	5.9	2.7	1.00	3.89	4.89	68.8	3.9	3.1	7.6	7.8
6.3	0.65	4.4	0.05	2.6	1.1	0.33	3.13	3.21	86.4	3.1	15.7	13.5	5.7
8.6	0.06	0.3	0.00	4.5	0.2	0.71	5.01	3.26	62.5	3.7	37.7	15.7	7.2
8.5	0.13	0.4	-0.07	6.5	0.5	1.40	7.99	3.93	46.8	4.9	35.8	8.9	5.9
7.3	0.22	1.6	4.49	2.2	-1.9	-1.57	-18.06	4.38	64.3	1.5	16.0	25.5	6.3
8.7	0.10	0.6	0.01	6.5	22.1	1.20	12.33	3.53	50.8	0.7	9.0	30.7	7.3
5.5	1.41	7.3	0.23	5.1	2.9	1.23	11.86	3.62	66.1	1.3	14.5	27.4	6.9
2.3	2.18	15.6	0.08	3.4	1.3	0.47	4.58	3.72	80.1	2.1	16.3	13.2	5.7
5.2	2.82	11.8	0.91	6.5	0.7	1.22	8.27	4.60	60.8	4.8	28.2	6.2	8.0
5.4	0.12	0.9	-0.58	4.6	1.2	0.89	10.25	4.05	71.6	2.6	12.1	15.5	4.4
5.6	0.60	4.6	0.18	9.8	6.9	2.48	23.90	3.55	37.8	3.2	7.6	12.3	8.6
6.3	1.23	6.1	0.54	4.2	0.9	0.68	6.56	3.42	65.3	5.0	30.7	6.2	6.1
4.4	0.97	6.7	-0.61	7.3	0.7	1.56	14.61	5.23	73.4	1.2	17.2	30.3	6.1
7.3	0.10	0.9	-0.01	4.9	2.0	0.82	8.61	3.62	61.1	0.7	15.2	45.5	5.0
6.8	0.28	2.2	0.02	6.9	3.1	1.69	18.01	4.25	60.0	1.0	6.1	28.7	6.0
6.7	0.28	2.1	-0.02	3.5	1.8	0.54	4.87	3.87	77.8	0.7	13.6	37.5	5.7
1.6	3.89	28.0	0.75	3.3	0.6	0.54	5.45	3.71	79.5	3.9	12.0	8.9	4.9
6.1	0.40	3.1	0.00	6.0	1.8	1.43	13.56	3.42	53.4	0.6	11.1	35.4	7.4
4.9	0.49	3.4	0.08	3.2	0.4	0.43	4.03	3.63	82.5	2.9	14.4	14.6	4.3
3.9	2.54	15.5	0.02	5.0	2.2	1.13	9.29	3.18	63.6	1.9	17.1	20.0	8.9
10.0	0.73	1.4	-0.11	1.8	0.4	0.16	1.35	1.47	86.7	1.9	25.2	21.7	6.4
7.9	4.32	4.9	-0.24	1.4	0.1	0.13	0.73	1.93	93.0	7.2	94.7	6.0	6.4
8.7	0.00	0.0	0.00	2.2	0.1	0.42	5.88	4.13	95.1	4.4	19.8	6.4	2.0
7.9	0.22	1.8	-0.02	5.4	0.7	0.93	9.93	5.00	71.4	2.6	15.2	16.1	5.9
6.2	0.82	6.9	-0.09	7.2	42.2	1.69	21.26	3.71	70.8	4.9	20.3	4.0	8.9
6.8	0.14	1.0	1.30	5.8	2.2	0.96	10.29	4.23	55.6	3.9	33.4	13.1	4.2
4.2	1.98	12.7	0.35	4.8	1.1	1.15	12.09	4.17	69.2	4.1	26.8	10.0	4.9
7.3	0.93	4.5	0.13	3.0	0.3	0.33	2.80	3.37	86.0	6.3	45.3	3.4	6.7
2.7	3.57	24.9	-0.26	2.7	0.3	0.41	5.34	3.76	88.7	3.2	28.9	15.1	1.8
7.3	0.30	2.1	0.13	5.7	2.5	0.99	9.50	4.14	69.6	3.1	26.0	14.8	6.0
8.9	0.10	0.5	-0.07	7.3	3.8	1.80	15.96	3.77	53.5	3.2	25.0	13.9	8.8
4.6	0.91	7.8	0.12	8.3	8.8	1.68	15.18	3.68	48.4	1.3	12.8	17.4	8.7
4.0	1.61	12.4	0.00	3.8	1.2	0.83	9.16	3.48	75.1	1.1	19.4	17.4	5.8
8.5	0.15	0.6	0.04	4.0	0.7	0.66	3.62	4.33	75.9	3.2	34.9	17.2	7.9
8.7	0.00	0.0	0.00	3.2	0.4	0.52	4.77	3.26	75.8	1.0	16.0	32.6	5.9
8.0	0.00	0.0	0.12	1.0	-0.1	-0.16	-1.38	2.84	105.1	7.1	68.1	2.4	5.2
0.7	8.95	48.0	1.31	1.4	-0.3	-0.06	-0.57	2.38	78.6	1.1	28.7	47.8	5.1
6.6	1.02	4.9	0.33	4.7	224.3	1.06	9.75	3.39	65.1	7.2	49.6	1.9	9.1
2.5	1.80	12.5	0.07	9.7	0.6	1.59	14.27	3.78	32.6	0.5	9.5	59.8	7.1
9.5	0.87	2.3	3.39	10.0	10.9	3.86	26.54	4.03	71.7	6.9	59.5	3.8	8.0
7.1	0.05	0.3	0.21	6.7	0.5	1.48	13.23	3.65	58.8	2.5	22.9	17.1	6.3
3.6	1.41	10.0	0.21	4.0	19.1	0.68	5.01	3.37	72.3	4.3	12.3	6.6	7.1
4.6	1.16	8.7	0.10	5.4	81.0	1.07	9.08	3.15	64.7	4.1	7.1	7.3	8.3
8.5	2.27	3.0	0.16	4.9	3.8	1.36	5.13	4.14	78.3	6.9	80.9	7.6	8.1
7.8	0.73	2.7	0.47	2.2	0.2	0.32	3.02	3.37	90.8	6.5	60.2	4.5	4.9
7.5	1.16	6.6	0.10	1.8	0.1	0.13	1.13	3.05	95.0	4.0	33.4	13.0	5.2
5.2	3.77	11.1	0.07	5.1	0.7	1.02	7.17	3.22	60.5	4.9	56.9	13.2	7.1
0.0	7.97	50.9	0.46	6.0	0.5	0.82	7.14	4.24	58.1	0.7	8.5	37.0	7.4
5.4	1.26	8.9	0.20	6.9	2.7	1.66	16.69	3.71	54.4	1.5	24.2	21.1	7.1
5.8	0.78	4.8	0.15	8.1	1.2	1.31	12.08	4.23	53.7	3.3	13.1	12.2	6.6
6.8	0.03	0.1	-0.01	6.0	0.1	1.44	10.65	4.71	71.5	5.2	20.2	1.0	5.7
7.1	0.10	0.8	0.04	4.3	9.9	0.70	6.17	3.05	75.5	4.1	8.9	7.6	8.7
8.9	0.36	0.8	0.02	5.0	0.3	1.08	8.51	3.69	62.1	1.8	39.5	50.4	7.0
2.3	3.03	21.2	0.34	3.7	0.3	0.63	6.22	4.50	74.2	0.9	22.2	42.3	4.4
8.3	0.00	0.0	-0.02	6.8	1.8	1.62	17.33	3.58	56.1	3.2	28.7	13.2	7.1

Name	City	State	2015 Rating	2014 Rating	Rating	Total Assets ($Mil)	One Year Asset Growth	Comm- ercial Loans	Cons- umer Loans	Mort- gage Loans	Secur- ities	Capital- ization Index	Lever- age Ratio	Risk- Based Capital Ratio
Gateway Bank of Central Florida	Ocala	FL	B-	B-	C+	276.5	17.85	8.0	0.6	11.5	17.7	6.6	8.6	12.4
Gateway Bank of Florida	Daytona Beach	FL	C+	C+	C+	301.3	32.43	2.6	0.3	5.7	37.8	7.7	9.5	16.7
Gateway Bank of Southwest Florida	Sarasota	FL	B-	B-	C+	298.2	18.12	4.6	0.3	18.5	19.2	7.1	9.0	12.9
Gateway Bank, F.S.B.	Oakland	CA	E-	E-	E-	135.4	-4.76	0.1	0.0	47.1	1.7	3.8	5.8	15.3
Gateway Commercial Bank	Mesa	AZ	B+	B+	B	110.3	6.77	11.4	0.1	4.7	28.9	10.0	13.5	19.1
Gateway Community Bank	Roscoe	IL	C	C-	C-	86.2	-2.35	13.7	1.6	17.9	21.0	9.7	10.8	16.1
Gateway State Bank	Clinton	IA	B	B	B	152.2	5.94	8.6	2.0	12.6	25.0	6.7	8.7	14.5
▲ GBC International Bank	Los Angeles	CA	C+	B+	B-	485.3	-1.27	17.0	0.0	0.3	9.1	10.0	11.2	16.2
Geauga Savings Bank	Newbury	OH	C+	C	C-	356.6	-1.54	7.6	0.1	20.2	53.9	10.0	13.4	26.6
Geddes Federal S&L Assn.	Syracuse	NY	B+	B+	B+	534.8	0.39	0.0	0.1	87.8	2.3	10.0	15.0	27.7
Generations Bank	Camden	AR	B-	B-	C+	391.3	6.74	7.9	3.4	23.6	20.0	7.6	9.4	13.4
Generations Bank	Exeter	NE	C-	C-	C	39.2	-0.54	11.2	1.3	10.7	17.9	6.7	9.5	12.3
▼ Generations Bank	Seneca Falls	NY	C-	C	B-	277.9	-2.68	4.8	12.9	37.0	10.1	8.4	9.9	14.1
Genesee Regional Bank	Rochester	NY	B-	B-	B-	490.0	8.11	23.9	0.9	9.2	15.0	8.8	10.2	14.1
Genoa Banking Co.	Genoa	OH	C+	C+	C+	323.4	7.42	3.7	5.7	25.2	19.0	6.5	8.6	13.4
Genoa Community Bank	Genoa	NE	B	B-	D	57.3	-3.25	2.9	1.4	5.2	17.6	10.0	12.8	16.9
Geo. D. Warthen Bank	Sandersville	GA	C-	C	C-	164.4	-3.75	11.3	8.6	24.4	20.6	7.2	9.1	14.2
▼ Georgetown Bank	Georgetown	MA	C	C+	B-	315.1	9.51	6.4	0.1	33.2	6.9	8.2	9.8	13.6
Georgia Bank & Trust Co. of Augusta	Augusta	GA	B+	B+	B	1870.6	3.18	6.1	1.1	14.0	35.2	8.7	10.1	15.8
Georgia Banking Co.	Atlanta	GA	C	C	C+	467.4	38.90	3.8	7.8	70.9	4.2	5.2	7.2	12.3
▲ Georgia Heritage Bank	Dallas	GA	D+	D-	E-	78.4	5.73	4.9	0.7	11.4	13.8	6.6	8.6	12.2
Georgia Primary Bank	Atlanta	GA	D-	D	D-	163.0	6.06	13.6	0.2	5.9	21.5	10.0	11.1	15.0
Gerber State Bank	Argenta	IL	C+	C+	C+	79.4	0.17	3.8	1.4	9.9	57.6	9.4	10.6	28.7
German American Bancorp	Jasper	IN	A-	A-	B+	2972.6	28.91	13.0	1.0	9.4	24.6	6.4	9.2	12.1
German-American State Bank	German Valley	IL	B-	B-	B-	226.2	6.08	9.7	2.3	8.2	21.0	7.0	9.5	12.5
Germantown Trust & Savings Bank	Breese	IL	A	A	A	356.0	2.48	1.9	1.0	15.0	44.5	10.0	13.1	24.2
Gibraltar Bank	Parsippany	NJ	D-	C-	C	107.1	5.95	0.0	0.0	67.6	7.3	9.0	10.4	20.6
Gibraltar Private Bank & Trust Co.	Coral Gables	FL	D+	C-	D+	1624.2	4.12	2.8	1.2	58.8	1.8	6.5	8.6	13.2
Gibsland Bank & Trust Co.	Gibsland	LA	C-	C	C+	375.3	3.98	13.7	4.0	16.9	13.4	8.0	10.5	13.4
Gifford State Bank	Gifford	IL	B-	B	B	165.6	6.03	7.2	4.7	21.8	2.8	5.3	9.4	11.2
Gilmer National Bank	Gilmer	TX	B+	B+	B+	232.6	-2.16	5.9	10.3	16.7	23.9	10.0	12.7	22.3
Girard National Bank	Girard	KS	B-	B-	B-	645.2	15.94	14.6	2.1	9.4	25.9	8.6	10.5	13.8
Glacier Bank	Kalispell	MT	A-	A-	B+	9297.5	6.34	7.5	1.7	10.2	32.3	10.0	11.8	16.3
Gladewater National Bank	Gladewater	TX	B	B-	B-	40.8	-5.36	19.2	4.8	33.5	22.6	10.0	18.4	30.9
Glasford State Bank	Glasford	IL	C+	C+	C	37.9	4.48	0.9	10.5	29.5	29.2	5.8	7.8	16.8
Glen Burnie Mutual Savings Bank	Glen Burnie	MD	C-	C-	D+	89.8	4.61	0.0	0.0	72.7	1.9	5.8	7.8	17.4
Glen Rock Savings Bank	Glen Rock	NJ	D+	D	C	249.2	77.66	0.4	0.0	45.0	35.0	10.0	13.7	31.5
Glenmede Trust Co., N.A.	Philadelphia	PA	U	U	U	84.5	6.01	0.0	0.0	0.0	8.8	10.0	54.0	80.6
Glennville Bank	Glennville	GA	A-	A-	B	225.5	7.49	4.4	3.6	18.6	21.8	10.0	11.4	17.8
Glens Falls National Bank and Trust Co.	Glens Falls	NY	B+	B+	B+	2150.8	5.81	2.2	19.5	19.1	28.9	7.0	9.0	14.9
Glenview State Bank	Glenview	IL	C+	C+	C+	1252.6	2.48	7.7	19.0	8.0	52.6	8.9	10.5	14.1
Glenwood State Bank	Glenwood	IA	C-	C-	C-	180.9	4.43	1.3	2.3	7.4	57.6	7.8	9.5	26.1
▲ Glenwood State Bank	Glenwood	MN	C	C	C	253.6	7.61	21.2	1.8	17.0	0.4	5.4	9.5	11.3
▼ Global Bank	New York	NY	C	B-	B-	140.6	-0.12	1.1	0.0	15.0	7.9	10.0	11.9	17.2
GNB Bank	Grundy Center	IA	B	B	B	524.7	47.15	15.6	1.2	6.3	17.6	6.6	10.9	12.2
Gogebic Range Bank	Ironwood	MI	B	B	B	71.1	6.07	26.6	7.0	9.7	14.7	10.0	12.6	16.2
Gold Coast Bank	Chicago	IL	A	A	A-	370.5	6.90	3.6	0.1	28.1	0.0	10.0	11.4	16.1
▲ Gold Coast Bank	Islandia	NY	C+	C	C-	400.4	16.80	5.2	0.4	13.6	13.1	8.5	10.0	14.9
▲ Golden Bank, N.A.	Houston	TX	A-	B	B	693.7	10.59	2.8	0.1	9.7	11.8	10.0	13.8	17.1
▲ Golden Belt Bank, FSA	Ellis	KS	B	C+	C+	144.2	-3.12	8.5	4.8	35.3	12.6	10.0	14.0	15.2
▲ Golden Eagle Community Bank	Woodstock	IL	C	D	D+	147.3	6.65	9.5	0.4	12.3	12.8	9.7	11.1	14.7
▲ Golden Pacific Bank, N.A.	Sacramento	CA	C	D	D-	128.8	1.86	25.8	0.2	13.3	3.5	6.7	8.7	14.4
Golden State Bank	Glendale	CA	D	D-	E	149.0	26.12	7.3	0.1	3.4	0.0	6.1	9.9	11.8
Golden Valley Bank	Chico	CA	A-	A-	A-	187.9	2.71	8.9	0.1	8.4	17.5	10.0	11.4	16.6
Goldman Sachs Bank USA	New York	NY	A-	A-	A	158429.0	24.16	9.2	1.3	4.1	0.0	8.3	15.0	13.6
Goldman Sachs Trust Co., N.A.	New York	NY	U	U	U	57.9	-13.45	0.0	0.0	0.0	59.1	10.0	54.2	245.2
Goldwater Bank, N.A.	Phoenix	AZ	D-	E+	E	171.6	81.30	1.1	2.6	77.7	2.0	5.6	7.6	18.8
Goodfield State Bank	Goodfield	IL	A	A	A-	107.4	8.37	11.4	2.3	25.8	13.9	10.0	12.2	16.5
Goose River Bank	Mayville	ND	B	B	C+	123.5	-3.90	18.8	6.0	2.0	19.7	7.2	9.2	12.7
Goppert Financial Banks	Lathrop	MO	C+	C	C	81.9	-3.78	12.1	1.2	7.3	12.7	9.2	10.4	14.3

Asset Quality Index	Adjusted Non-Performing Loans as a % of Total Loans	as a % of Capital	Net Charge-Offs Avg Loans	Profitability Index	Net Income ($Mil)	Return on Assets (R.O.A.)	Return on Equity (R.O.E.)	Net Interest Spread	Overhead Efficiency Ratio	Liquidity Index	Liquidity Ratio	Hot Money Ratio	Stability Index
6.0	0.36	2.7	0.10	4.4	1.7	0.84	9.79	3.71	65.3	4.7	20.6	4.8	4.9
8.1	0.12	0.6	-1.17	2.8	1.4	0.66	6.43	3.15	73.9	4.4	40.0	12.1	5.2
9.0	0.00	0.0	0.00	4.4	1.8	0.86	9.32	3.57	67.8	2.8	22.8	13.7	5.7
0.3	7.88	67.7	0.41	0.0	-1.2	-1.16	-19.48	3.24	139.1	2.3	36.7	27.4	0.8
7.6	0.94	4.0	-0.01	4.7	0.8	0.91	6.81	3.45	59.3	4.4	31.1	10.3	7.9
4.3	1.72	10.4	0.06	2.9	0.3	0.41	3.91	3.56	88.0	1.7	26.1	25.7	4.9
4.0	2.34	16.3	0.05	3.5	0.7	0.61	6.29	3.06	69.3	1.7	16.7	22.2	6.6
3.8	1.86	12.8	-0.14	4.6	2.5	0.69	6.15	3.64	72.6	0.6	11.3	50.5	6.3
3.1	8.07	23.7	0.12	3.9	2.4	0.86	6.86	2.48	60.5	1.4	32.4	46.9	5.6
9.1	0.60	3.6	-0.02	4.2	2.7	0.67	4.56	2.40	55.8	0.7	9.2	37.3	8.7
4.2	1.67	11.6	0.45	4.5	2.1	0.72	7.68	3.89	74.4	1.2	15.6	29.4	6.2
3.7	1.39	10.1	0.00	5.3	0.3	1.06	10.00	4.18	64.9	1.6	10.1	15.1	5.9
4.3	1.28	8.8	0.72	1.9	0.1	0.05	0.57	3.63	94.9	2.1	16.4	18.8	4.9
4.1	1.73	12.5	0.01	6.9	4.3	1.21	12.06	3.96	61.7	3.9	21.8	10.0	5.7
7.8	0.11	0.8	0.14	3.6	1.5	0.61	7.15	3.81	78.8	1.4	14.3	20.0	4.7
7.1	0.15	0.8	0.00	6.2	0.5	1.23	10.15	3.90	66.4	3.2	4.7	11.9	6.7
4.6	1.47	9.6	0.37	2.5	0.4	0.34	3.82	4.46	85.3	3.9	19.2	9.7	4.3
6.0	0.60	5.0	0.00	2.6	0.5	0.20	2.03	3.51	89.7	0.9	4.2	29.6	5.5
6.1	1.60	8.0	0.07	6.1	15.6	1.12	11.01	3.28	60.0	4.0	31.0	6.5	8.1
4.6	0.85	10.5	0.00	4.8	2.9	0.98	12.77	3.57	72.2	0.4	3.2	41.0	3.0
3.5	1.39	10.1	0.86	6.2	0.8	1.43	17.65	5.00	64.2	1.7	14.5	20.8	1.4
0.3	6.72	36.1	-0.16	2.6	0.7	0.55	4.85	3.78	88.1	1.7	29.8	29.0	4.6
5.4	2.78	8.6	0.01	3.0	0.3	0.52	4.85	2.78	78.3	6.0	51.5	5.9	5.6
8.1	0.25	1.8	0.03	7.1	26.2	1.26	11.47	3.79	60.0	4.3	22.2	9.3	8.7
4.8	1.15	8.1	0.09	6.4	1.9	1.16	11.95	3.61	55.6	2.4	10.3	16.6	6.6
9.2	0.00	0.0	0.06	7.6	5.1	1.95	13.81	3.02	35.6	4.2	41.3	14.4	9.4
6.3	1.28	9.3	0.00	0.0	-1.1	-1.33	-10.97	2.52	177.3	1.6	21.5	25.5	6.2
5.0	1.68	15.2	-0.12	1.7	1.4	0.11	1.33	3.41	97.0	1.7	10.1	20.4	6.9
2.1	3.23	22.5	0.14	7.1	3.2	1.15	11.86	4.77	60.4	0.7	11.2	36.9	5.6
3.7	3.34	26.9	0.15	5.2	1.5	1.25	13.68	4.47	56.9	2.5	10.0	16.1	6.1
5.1	2.41	10.0	0.25	5.1	1.6	0.94	7.55	3.62	60.5	2.7	47.8	30.1	6.8
4.1	1.38	8.4	0.08	5.8	5.1	1.05	8.62	4.08	60.9	3.0	11.2	11.1	7.2
5.7	1.40	6.7	-0.04	7.8	94.9	1.40	10.61	4.11	59.0	4.3	18.5	7.5	9.4
4.2	5.07	17.9	0.17	3.0	0.0	0.10	0.54	4.14	90.3	3.3	34.4	16.7	6.0
7.7	0.25	1.7	0.17	3.1	0.2	0.58	6.92	3.28	80.7	5.1	30.6	4.2	4.6
3.7	2.83	26.2	0.00	1.8	0.1	0.20	2.62	0.96	80.6	5.6	26.3	0.0	4.0
7.4	1.06	4.2	0.03	0.9	-0.3	-0.16	-1.17	2.94	102.5	3.3	30.3	15.2	4.7
10.0	na	0.0	na	10.0	18.1	30.71	90.13	0.69	79.2	4.0	62.4	0.0	7.0
5.9	1.73	8.6	0.08	7.0	2.2	1.35	11.52	4.50	62.1	1.7	23.8	24.7	6.9
6.7	0.44	3.0	0.04	5.9	17.0	1.09	11.58	3.17	60.8	4.8	7.8	2.8	8.3
7.8	0.02	0.1	-0.02	3.3	7.0	0.75	7.00	2.13	72.3	6.9	51.6	4.0	8.5
9.5	0.37	1.0	0.09	2.1	0.3	0.20	2.16	2.20	89.0	7.0	67.8	4.4	4.7
3.5	1.56	13.9	0.00	7.0	3.1	1.64	17.42	4.06	59.8	3.7	4.3	9.6	7.2
6.6	0.00	0.0	-0.06	2.0	0.0	-0.01	-0.07	3.57	99.7	0.6	10.9	44.9	6.8
5.5	0.50	3.3	0.01	5.8	5.3	1.37	11.71	3.89	67.7	1.6	19.6	23.7	8.0
4.9	1.41	7.9	0.28	7.1	0.7	1.27	10.43	5.01	58.5	3.1	20.0	13.9	6.3
6.8	0.75	4.8	-0.18	8.3	3.1	1.15	10.30	4.07	43.0	0.6	13.5	39.9	7.7
7.5	0.20	1.4	0.00	3.4	1.6	0.55	5.87	3.22	71.0	3.2	14.6	12.6	5.5
5.8	0.63	3.3	0.00	6.8	5.8	1.16	8.26	4.01	52.4	1.5	23.9	27.0	8.8
4.8	1.67	8.9	0.00	8.0	2.0	1.83	12.32	3.68	58.0	4.4	12.7	6.1	9.4
4.1	0.71	4.4	-0.20	3.5	0.7	0.67	5.80	3.76	81.4	0.9	19.2	37.5	4.9
3.1	1.48	11.6	0.27	2.7	0.6	0.63	6.91	4.49	85.8	3.7	22.0	11.0	3.7
3.0	0.70	5.3	-0.42	1.2	0.2	0.19	1.79	4.02	102.0	1.0	20.4	34.3	2.8
8.8	0.10	0.5	0.00	5.3	1.3	0.94	8.23	3.96	66.4	5.1	36.2	8.0	7.2
9.2	0.48	1.0	0.05	5.6	1091.0	0.93	6.15	1.05	33.7	3.5	74.5	4.5	10.0
10.0	na	0.0	na	10.0	16.6	31.40	43.65	0.29	52.0	4.0	209.5	0.0	7.0
4.0	0.63	7.7	-0.06	7.1	3.1	3.25	43.51	4.25	94.5	0.5	7.6	60.9	0.6
6.0	1.31	7.9	0.00	9.7	1.9	2.43	19.93	4.08	52.3	2.3	14.6	17.4	9.2
6.6	0.53	3.7	0.00	6.0	1.4	1.54	15.99	4.11	64.7	3.2	7.3	12.0	6.3
6.0	0.81	5.5	0.13	3.8	0.4	0.59	5.73	3.83	75.2	3.6	12.9	11.0	5.2

Name	City	State	Rating	2015 Rating	2014 Rating	Total Assets ($Mil)	One Year Asset Growth	Commercial Loans	Consumer Loans	Mortgage Loans	Securities	Capitalization Index	Leverage Ratio	Risk-Based Capital Ratio
▲ Goppert State Service Bank	Garnett	KS	C+	C	C	156.9	1.06	14.9	4.5	14.4	21.3	10.0	11.0	17.0
Gorham Savings Bank	Gorham	ME	C+	C	C-	1018.2	1.93	8.0	0.5	23.7	13.8	8.3	10.1	13.6
▲ Gorham State Bank	Gorham	KS	C+	C	C	29.1	-8.84	11.0	4.4	9.5	2.4	8.0	9.7	17.6
Gothenburg State Bank	Gothenburg	NE	A-	B+	B+	139.0	-2.75	11.1	3.2	3.2	17.6	10.0	13.1	15.5
Gouverneur S&L Assn.	Gouverneur	NY	B+	A-	A-	140.9	1.05	1.7	2.3	59.2	13.6	10.0	20.4	36.0
Graham S&L, SSB	Graham	TX	A-	B+	B+	120.2	-2.62	1.5	1.0	48.0	7.6	10.0	12.4	25.1
Grand Bank	Tulsa	OK	B+	A-	A-	275.8	0.33	20.3	0.7	11.2	10.3	8.6	10.7	13.8
Grand Bank for Savings, FSB	Hattiesburg	MS	B	C+	C	77.7	-15.11	0.0	0.6	71.0	0.0	10.0	15.2	29.6
Grand Bank of Texas	Dallas	TX	B-	C+	C+	284.9	13.73	11.7	1.0	21.6	0.7	5.8	8.0	11.6
▲ Grand Bank, N.A.	Hamilton Square	NJ	D+	D	D-	219.1	11.78	8.6	0.3	14.7	1.3	8.5	10.0	15.3
Grand Marais State Bank	Grand Marais	MN	B	B	B	92.9	6.81	6.3	1.2	26.3	41.4	4.8	6.8	15.1
Grand Marsh State Bank	Grand Marsh	WI	B+	B+	A-	126.6	-10.08	0.8	2.2	17.5	45.5	10.0	14.6	32.8
Grand Mountain Bank, FSB	Granby	CO	C	C-	E+	101.3	7.92	2.3	0.4	36.3	10.3	5.8	7.8	16.6
Grand Rapids State Bank	Grand Rapids	MN	B-	B-	B	221.2	-1.97	12.6	4.4	12.5	26.8	8.1	9.7	14.3
Grand Ridge National Bank	Grand Ridge	IL	A-	A-	A-	137.9	0.76	7.2	0.0	13.0	2.9	10.0	12.9	16.7
▲ Grand River Bank	Grandville	MI	C+	C-	D	193.7	28.44	12.4	0.0	16.1	2.8	6.8	10.1	12.4
Grand Rivers Community Bank	Grand Chain	IL	E-	E	D-	67.9	-9.65	24.7	2.9	11.4	3.6	0.0	3.4	5.8
Grand Savings Bank	Grove	OK	B	B	B	366.3	16.68	7.1	10.0	22.8	9.3	7.8	9.6	13.6
Grand Timber Bank	McGregor	MN	C+	C+	C	42.5	-0.88	5.7	5.0	24.0	20.1	10.0	14.6	24.9
Grand Valley Bank	Heber City	UT	B-	B-	B-	360.8	1.94	1.8	0.4	9.1	53.0	7.5	9.4	18.8
Grandpoint Bank	Los Angeles	CA	B+	B	B-	3292.5	4.88	6.9	0.2	6.8	18.9	7.9	9.6	13.3
GrandSouth Bank	Greenville	SC	A-	B+	B	481.6	13.65	22.9	7.4	10.5	5.9	10.0	12.4	16.1
Grandview Bank	Grandview	TX	A-	A-	A-	182.1	18.31	10.4	6.7	18.7	26.9	7.7	9.4	17.4
Granger National Bank	Granger	TX	B-	B-	B-	32.6	1.26	1.3	2.4	5.1	52.3	10.0	15.5	38.9
▼ Granite Bank	Colebrook	NH	C	C+	C+	269.0	2.14	14.7	0.3	14.7	7.4	7.4	9.3	12.9
Granite Community Bank	Cold Spring	MN	C-	D	C	105.2	-0.07	8.5	1.7	10.5	4.6	4.7	8.3	10.9
Granite Falls Bank	Granite Falls	MN	B-	B-	B-	179.8	-33.50	4.6	0.6	1.5	58.5	6.5	8.5	17.4
Granite Mountain Bank, Inc.	Philipsburg	MT	C+	C+	C	73.7	6.91	12.2	2.4	12.9	11.6	6.8	8.8	17.8
▼ Grant County Bank	Ulysses	KS	B-	A-	B+	227.0	-1.12	3.9	2.6	21.1	32.2	10.0	13.2	22.2
Grant County Bank	Medford	OK	B-	B-	B	68.9	-7.98	5.3	5.3	2.4	48.0	10.0	13.3	26.8
Grant County Bank	Petersburg	WV	B-	B-	C+	246.7	0.53	5.1	3.6	31.1	7.6	10.0	13.4	18.1
Grant County State Bank	Swayzee	IN	B	B	B+	141.9	7.21	7.7	6.5	41.4	2.9	9.5	10.6	15.4
Grant County State Bank	Carson	ND	A-	A-	B+	34.5	-1.07	3.1	0.5	0.0	0.0	10.0	12.2	16.7
▲ Granville National Bank	Granville	IL	C	C	C	83.9	66.08	3.9	4.4	24.7	32.8	8.4	9.9	22.8
Grapeland State Bank	Grapeland	TX	C+	C+	C	33.0	0.68	12.0	8.4	15.6	25.3	10.0	12.0	19.1
Gratz Bank	Gratz	PA	B	B+	A	308.6	3.73	6.3	0.7	32.9	18.3	6.0	8.0	14.2
Grayson National Bank	Independence	VA	C+	C	D+	558.6	68.18	7.8	1.0	25.0	10.6	7.0	9.0	12.9
▲ Great American Bank	Lawrence	KS	B+	B+	C	176.0	5.08	7.4	0.5	22.0	1.1	8.2	9.8	13.8
Great Midwest Bank, S.S.B.	Brookfield	WI	B	B-	B-	657.4	9.53	0.0	0.1	69.4	8.5	10.0	17.2	23.2
▲ Great Nations Bank	Norman	OK	B-	C	D+	55.3	2.24	14.5	1.8	8.4	3.9	10.0	14.2	17.4
Great Plains Bank	Eureka	SD	D	B-	B	94.8	1.84	10.1	1.1	3.0	7.3	8.3	12.4	13.6
Great Plains National Bank	Hollis	OK	B+	B+	B	538.1	-2.62	12.1	5.5	18.3	4.3	8.4	10.8	13.7
▼ Great Plains State Bank	Petersburg	NE	D+	D+	D	97.0	146.26	7.2	1.8	0.5	4.8	4.9	10.1	11.0
Great Southern Bank	Springfield	MO	B-	B-	B	4444.9	9.17	6.4	12.9	11.9	4.6	7.3	10.7	12.7
Great Southern Bank	Meridian	MS	B	B	B+	294.3	5.87	3.9	8.6	11.5	54.8	7.3	9.2	24.6
Great State Bank	Wilkesboro	NC	C+	B-	B	112.1	8.96	10.6	1.1	14.3	9.5	8.8	10.2	16.1
Great Western Bank	Sioux Falls	SD	B-	B-	C+	11525.5	17.72	11.0	0.7	4.6	11.4	6.3	9.7	12.0
Greater Community Bank	Rome	GA	B-	C	C-	137.8	10.52	13.3	1.3	16.4	4.6	7.9	10.5	13.3
Greater Hudson Bank	Bardonia	NY	B-	B-	B-	459.9	11.14	13.3	0.0	0.4	30.1	10.0	12.2	16.5
Greater State Bank	Falfurrias	TX	D+	D-	D+	68.8	3.42	16.4	2.5	15.3	9.6	6.9	8.9	12.6
Green Bank, N.A.	Houston	TX	D-	C+	B+	3912.2	62.38	21.3	0.3	6.4	8.1	4.4	9.0	10.7
Green Belt Bank & Trust	Iowa Falls	IA	C+	C+	B-	439.0	9.69	9.7	2.6	8.3	9.4	4.5	8.6	10.7
Green Dot Bank	Provo	UT	B+	B+	B+	839.7	8.36	0.2	0.1	0.2	20.4	10.0	17.6	56.2
Greene County Commercial Bank	Catskill	NY	U	U	U	284.6	18.20	0.0	0.0	0.0	100.6	6.6	8.6	40.0
Greeneville Federal Bank, FSB	Greeneville	TN	B+	B	C-	148.1	2.30	10.1	1.4	31.9	2.3	10.0	13.7	20.7
Greenfield Banking Co.	Greenfield	IN	B-	B-	B-	533.6	10.41	4.3	2.0	4.6	36.3	7.5	9.3	20.9
Greenfield Banking Co.	Greenfield	TN	B-	B-	C+	53.7	4.48	9.3	12.5	22.3	9.0	9.7	12.1	14.8
Greenfield Co-operative Bank	Greenfield	MA	C+	C	C+	567.9	5.08	4.7	0.6	37.2	25.9	10.0	11.6	21.3
Greenfield Savings Bank	Greenfield	MA	B-	B-	C+	769.5	4.94	3.5	0.1	51.3	13.8	10.0	11.3	19.3
Greenleaf Wayside Bank	Greenleaf	WI	C+	C+	C+	85.0	5.12	4.8	0.9	18.6	29.3	7.6	9.4	17.6

Asset Quality Index	Adjusted Non-Performing Loans		Net Charge-Offs / Avg Loans	Profitability Index	Net Income ($Mil)	Return on Assets (R.O.A.)	Return on Equity (R.O.E.)	Net Interest Spread	Overhead Efficiency Ratio	Liquidity Index	Liquidity Ratio	Hot Money Ratio	Stability Index
	as a % of Total Loans	as a % of Capital											
8.0	0.20	1.2	-0.03	3.9	0.8	0.69	6.32	3.49	71.0	3.2	9.5	12.5	5.8
5.6	1.15	8.4	0.04	3.5	5.3	0.71	7.37	3.46	75.2	2.6	3.8	5.0	7.1
8.5	0.00	0.0	0.00	4.9	0.2	1.03	11.56	3.35	61.6	5.5	39.4	6.1	3.9
7.7	0.32	1.7	0.52	6.6	1.6	1.55	11.75	4.48	63.4	1.1	14.1	16.5	8.5
6.4	2.01	7.2	0.34	4.9	0.9	0.81	3.87	4.62	75.5	4.3	16.1	7.0	8.1
8.9	0.65	3.4	0.01	5.2	1.1	1.24	10.02	3.68	66.8	1.6	31.4	33.0	7.6
6.0	0.59	3.9	0.02	6.7	2.5	1.21	10.58	4.83	61.9	0.6	5.2	35.1	8.3
4.7	1.93	10.1	0.28	7.9	1.6	2.77	18.64	7.51	69.3	0.9	16.1	33.2	6.5
6.7	0.13	1.1	0.26	4.0	1.5	0.75	9.34	4.68	75.3	4.4	20.1	6.7	4.1
1.6	1.99	15.2	0.36	2.6	0.8	0.54	5.52	4.03	86.4	1.4	18.5	26.7	3.7
9.4	0.00	0.0	-0.02	4.5	0.8	1.13	15.76	3.32	67.6	4.6	25.2	6.4	5.2
6.7	3.24	9.2	0.16	4.0	0.8	0.79	5.87	2.47	55.2	5.7	62.9	11.6	7.0
4.6	1.83	12.4	-0.77	3.7	0.6	0.77	9.96	3.90	100.9	5.5	36.2	5.0	3.0
6.5	0.56	3.5	0.09	4.7	1.9	1.11	10.85	4.20	75.8	4.3	25.1	7.9	6.0
7.1	0.05	0.3	0.00	9.7	1.6	1.59	11.59	5.68	55.4	1.3	16.6	27.3	8.4
7.3	0.00	0.0	0.00	3.3	1.7	1.30	13.14	3.31	81.1	1.1	7.7	22.4	5.3
0.3	5.83	58.8	0.05	0.0	-2.0	-3.62	-62.50	2.82	106.0	0.6	16.6	60.6	1.7
4.7	0.82	6.4	0.12	7.9	5.7	2.16	22.22	4.68	59.0	1.8	13.0	20.0	5.3
3.1	6.56	23.1	0.16	5.7	0.4	1.22	8.16	4.11	75.9	5.5	33.8	3.8	7.5
8.7	0.23	1.0	-0.04	4.4	2.4	0.88	9.49	3.67	67.6	5.8	51.1	8.4	5.4
4.9	0.71	5.0	-0.02	6.5	25.7	1.07	9.54	3.70	51.5	4.3	28.7	12.0	9.2
6.0	1.14	7.1	0.67	6.6	2.9	0.87	6.91	6.60	69.1	1.5	17.3	20.9	6.5
8.2	0.19	1.1	0.04	7.1	1.7	1.31	13.37	4.00	57.8	3.7	37.3	15.4	6.4
9.6	1.48	1.9	0.06	3.4	0.2	0.76	4.62	3.44	75.8	5.3	82.3	14.8	7.3
5.4	0.68	5.2	0.08	2.5	0.8	0.39	3.85	3.40	88.7	3.2	18.1	13.3	5.3
2.9	1.12	10.0	0.00	5.0	0.9	1.17	14.05	4.11	72.5	1.2	11.7	28.4	5.4
6.2	1.30	5.1	-0.01	7.0	2.5	1.73	16.13	3.99	45.4	4.1	42.7	15.2	5.7
6.1	0.69	4.3	-0.05	3.5	0.3	0.51	5.75	4.32	77.3	5.7	35.5	3.4	4.6
3.0	6.79	29.4	0.41	5.2	2.1	1.23	8.82	3.57	59.5	1.6	12.1	21.4	7.9
5.6	4.72	9.6	0.01	3.3	0.5	0.85	6.54	2.55	78.0	2.4	44.4	31.7	5.2
4.1	2.61	15.2	0.05	5.9	1.9	1.03	8.11	4.48	65.4	2.2	9.3	17.5	6.3
4.6	1.15	8.6	0.08	8.8	2.3	2.20	21.03	4.11	39.9	1.2	8.9	27.0	7.8
6.9	0.00	0.0	0.00	9.9	0.6	2.37	20.59	4.51	47.1	3.4	10.9	11.7	8.3
6.0	1.03	4.8	0.07	2.8	0.3	0.42	4.20	2.85	80.7	5.9	47.2	5.8	4.8
7.0	0.62	3.0	0.21	3.1	0.1	0.50	4.14	4.67	83.8	1.7	33.3	32.3	5.4
6.6	0.46	3.5	-0.05	4.6	2.0	0.90	10.57	3.27	61.0	3.8	24.5	11.0	6.4
4.3	1.36	10.5	-0.02	3.6	1.9	0.64	7.30	4.01	80.4	2.9	18.6	14.7	3.7
6.1	0.00	0.0	-0.02	7.1	2.2	1.70	12.00	4.34	62.8	0.7	12.0	34.8	7.9
5.8	2.27	11.2	0.00	4.4	3.9	0.83	4.70	2.92	63.2	1.4	12.8	18.2	8.2
7.2	0.00	0.0	0.00	4.5	1.3	3.16	22.63	3.65	77.5	0.6	14.9	58.8	5.8
1.0	3.97	25.5	0.00	9.6	2.0	2.94	23.86	4.28	39.9	2.2	3.0	17.0	8.9
5.0	0.49	3.5	0.25	9.6	8.3	2.03	18.89	6.14	72.9	2.4	3.1	15.7	8.9
2.5	1.16	10.3	0.11	3.3	-0.1	-0.12	-1.11	3.67	85.8	0.6	7.7	47.7	6.0
3.7	0.84	6.1	0.30	5.7	33.0	1.02	10.35	4.20	63.6	1.3	7.8	25.3	8.3
6.9	0.78	2.7	0.40	4.3	1.5	0.71	7.49	4.44	78.3	5.8	63.7	11.4	5.4
6.9	0.55	3.7	0.01	3.8	0.5	0.59	5.76	3.34	66.5	1.5	26.3	28.8	6.1
3.4	1.65	13.1	0.16	7.0	97.3	1.23	7.86	3.98	50.2	3.9	8.9	6.9	9.3
5.4	0.85	5.9	-0.05	4.5	1.0	0.96	9.33	5.09	80.7	3.2	18.0	13.1	4.1
4.0	2.50	12.5	0.00	4.2	2.8	0.84	7.25	3.45	66.9	2.9	19.3	12.2	6.8
4.3	1.27	10.3	0.05	2.7	0.3	0.61	6.95	5.11	85.6	0.8	17.3	37.6	3.5
0.0	3.70	30.3	2.21	2.2	-1.7	-0.06	-0.53	3.85	54.2	1.1	15.2	32.2	7.9
4.8	0.33	2.8	0.08	5.6	4.0	1.25	13.71	3.52	49.7	1.4	13.3	25.3	6.9
9.8	11.61	0.5	0.04	8.4	9.4	1.44	7.61	0.78	23.4	8.5	109.1	1.0	7.0
10.0	na	0.0	na	6.4	2.5	1.22	14.19	2.49	12.6	5.0	0.0	0.2	7.0
5.8	1.31	7.1	0.11	5.1	0.7	0.66	4.80	4.45	79.3	2.4	14.0	17.0	6.4
5.4	2.27	8.4	0.10	4.1	3.2	0.84	8.81	3.38	69.8	7.3	64.6	1.9	5.8
3.7	1.78	10.5	0.06	4.0	0.3	0.68	5.78	3.93	75.3	1.3	23.5	30.4	5.9
6.0	1.54	8.3	0.01	2.9	1.7	0.40	3.40	2.71	76.2	3.3	28.5	14.9	6.6
8.7	0.48	3.2	0.02	3.7	3.9	0.69	6.18	3.42	74.8	2.2	17.8	18.4	7.1
9.1	0.17	0.9	-0.08	3.4	0.5	0.83	8.70	3.23	76.8	6.4	51.7	3.1	5.6

Name	City	State	Rating	2015 Rating	2014 Rating	Total Assets ($Mil)	One Year Asset Growth	Commercial Loans	Consumer Loans	Mortgage Loans	Securities	Capitalization Index	Leverage Ratio	Risk-Based Capital Ratio
Greensburg State Bank	Greensburg	KS	B	B+	B+	56.8	-3.70	1.1	3.8	1.1	75.2	10.0	20.1	61.5
Greenville Federal	Greenville	OH	B-	B-	B	159.1	6.44	19.1	0.6	56.9	2.1	10.0	12.5	17.3
▲ Greenville National Bank	Greenville	OH	B+	B	B	401.0	2.57	3.3	9.0	24.1	21.9	10.0	11.2	17.5
Greenville Savings Bank	Greenville	PA	B	B	B	241.0	4.52	3.5	0.9	52.0	18.7	10.0	12.5	20.4
Greenwood's State Bank	Lake Mills	WI	C+	C+	C+	167.9	3.73	12.6	2.7	22.0	8.2	7.1	9.2	12.6
Greer State Bank	Greer	SC	B-	B-	B-	379.9	2.48	6.8	1.2	15.2	34.5	9.0	10.3	15.9
▲ Grinnell State Bank	Grinnell	IA	A-	A-	A-	305.1	2.88	4.2	0.5	4.9	19.0	10.0	12.1	15.6
▲ Grundy Bank	Morris	IL	B	B-	B-	294.7	-5.48	5.4	0.4	16.4	17.4	7.4	9.3	17.6
Grundy National Bank	Grundy	VA	C	C+	B+	317.5	-2.27	8.3	5.7	7.7	42.2	10.0	21.6	41.0
Gruver State Bank	Gruver	TX	B+	B+	B+	67.1	-1.32	9.7	2.8	5.8	30.6	10.0	11.5	18.8
GSL Savings Bank	Guttenberg	NJ	C-	D+	D+	89.9	1.49	0.0	0.0	76.4	3.1	10.0	12.5	26.0
Guadalupe National Bank	Kerrville	TX	B	B-	B-	135.4	5.71	10.8	2.1	30.9	3.4	8.1	9.8	16.0
▼ Guaranty Bank	Springfield	MO	C	B-	C	680.9	5.71	11.8	0.6	16.4	14.2	9.7	12.2	14.7
Guaranty Bank	Milwaukee	WI	E-	E-	E-	999.8	-0.16	0.1	2.8	42.6	1.1	0.0	2.3	4.5
Guaranty Bank & Trust Co. of Delhi	Delhi	LA	A-	A-	A-	212.6	7.13	7.2	4.0	29.9	10.1	6.8	8.9	12.6
Guaranty Bank & Trust, N.A.	Mount Pleasant	TX	B	B+	B+	1791.8	11.61	8.7	3.0	19.6	19.1	6.9	8.9	12.7
Guaranty Bank and Trust Co.	Denver	CO	B	B	B	3343.0	46.41	10.1	0.3	11.9	16.5	8.3	13.5	13.6
Guaranty Bank and Trust Co.	Cedar Rapids	IA	B	B	B	258.1	-1.56	11.2	0.7	17.8	28.5	10.0	11.8	17.1
Guaranty Bank and Trust Co.	New Roads	LA	B+	A-	A-	196.9	1.30	3.0	3.3	28.7	12.5	10.0	11.2	20.2
Guaranty Bank and Trust Co.	Belzoni	MS	B	B	B	702.7	10.52	12.0	1.7	12.5	18.1	10.0	11.3	15.0
Guaranty State Bank and Trust Co.	Beloit	KS	B+	B+	A-	279.8	11.05	6.5	1.0	7.8	2.8	6.5	10.7	12.1
Guardian Bank	Valdosta	GA	B+	A-	B+	304.7	6.67	9.4	1.3	18.4	15.7	8.8	10.2	15.5
Guardian Savings Bank	Granite City	IL	C	C	C	39.9	4.25	0.0	0.4	22.6	56.0	10.0	19.7	92.1
▲ Guardian Savings Bank, F.S.B.	West Chester	OH	C+	C	C-	947.5	14.08	0.0	0.0	65.8	0.8	8.8	10.2	20.7
Guilford Savings Bank	Guilford	CT	B-	B	B	652.0	4.89	1.7	0.1	41.8	19.9	10.0	13.2	18.5
Gulf Coast Bank	Abbeville	LA	B+	B+	A-	379.0	-0.55	5.4	7.2	17.9	19.7	10.0	12.8	22.4
Gulf Coast Bank and Trust Co.	New Orleans	LA	C+	C+	C	1483.2	9.00	19.0	2.4	20.7	12.7	5.2	8.3	11.2
Gulf Coast Community Bank	Pensacola	FL	E-	E-	E-	135.4	-1.69	6.1	1.9	13.2	10.6	0.1	4.2	6.2
GulfShore Bank	Tampa	FL	C+	C+	C	331.2	15.06	9.2	1.1	13.4	4.8	8.9	10.8	14.1
Gunnison Bank and Trust Co.	Gunnison	CO	B	B	B-	85.1	1.44	3.0	0.6	20.3	14.2	7.4	9.3	14.7
Gunnison S&L Assn.	Gunnison	CO	C-	C	D+	106.7	1.68	0.0	0.5	46.0	0.3	9.3	10.5	27.5
Gunnison Valley Bank	Gunnison	UT	D-	D-	D-	87.8	7.03	23.6	28.7	3.5	2.6	7.4	10.5	12.8
Guthrie County State Bank	Panora	IA	B	B	B	120.5	3.79	6.9	3.8	20.3	22.2	8.9	10.3	15.4
Gwinnett Community Bank	Duluth	GA	E-	E-	E-	323.3	-5.63	5.2	0.5	9.0	25.5	0.0	3.0	5.7
H. F. Gehant Banking Co.	West Brooklyn	IL	B	B	B	58.4	1.15	5.1	2.9	17.0	14.0	10.0	13.8	21.2
Habib American Bank	New York	NY	B+	B	B	1131.8	12.50	5.3	0.5	5.7	4.4	7.1	9.1	16.0
▲ Haddon Savings Bank	Haddon Heights	NJ	C	D+	D+	313.2	-1.65	3.4	0.0	27.1	59.5	8.6	10.1	25.3
Halstead Bank	Halstead	KS	C+	C+	C+	111.3	7.85	9.1	7.7	17.6	7.5	4.6	9.2	10.8
Hamilton Bank	Towson	MD	D	D+	D	510.2	42.57	3.7	0.5	35.3	18.8	5.7	7.7	12.3
Hamilton Bank	Hamilton	MO	C+	C	C-	72.0	-0.21	3.5	3.8	15.1	31.1	8.2	9.8	15.9
▲ Hamilton State Bank	Hoschton	GA	A-	A-	B+	1816.2	-0.14	12.0	0.4	6.8	21.0	10.0	11.9	16.8
Hamler State Bank	Hamler	OH	B+	B+	B+	76.6	3.97	4.9	1.1	14.1	35.1	10.0	16.2	26.0
Hamlin Bank and Trust Co.	Smethport	PA	A	A	A	446.8	2.16	1.7	4.9	38.2	39.1	10.0	16.6	25.1
▼ Hamlin National Bank	Hamlin	TX	C	B	B+	86.5	-7.05	11.3	3.7	3.4	20.2	10.0	16.7	32.5
▲ Hancock Bank and Trust Co.	Hawesville	KY	C	C-	D	280.1	3.80	7.2	1.8	27.0	4.9	9.4	10.6	15.2
Hancock County Savings Bank, FSB	Chester	WV	B	B	B	340.0	-3.57	0.2	1.7	73.9	12.1	10.0	17.7	36.2
Hanmi Bank	Los Angeles	CA	A-	B+	B+	4396.4	4.45	7.3	0.1	7.5	12.5	9.5	11.4	14.6
Hanover Community Bank	Garden City Park	NY	B-	B-	C	362.2	62.02	1.9	0.1	45.6	0.4	9.8	10.9	19.0
Hantz Bank	Southfield	MI	B+	B+	B	211.8	11.64	10.5	0.4	31.7	2.1	10.0	11.0	16.2
▲ Happy State Bank	Happy	TX	B+	B	B-	3076.5	11.52	14.7	1.4	10.8	13.4	8.7	11.2	13.9
Harbor Bank of Maryland	Baltimore	MD	D-	D	D-	248.5	3.40	13.3	0.8	27.9	11.9	6.2	8.2	12.1
Harbor Community Bank	Fort Pierce	FL	B-	B-	B	1785.5	21.85	5.3	2.5	16.1	31.6	9.4	10.6	16.7
HarborOne Bank	Brockton	MA	C-	D+	U	2348.0	7.29	3.1	24.0	35.0	7.1	7.7	10.1	13.1
▲ Hardin County Bank	Savannah	TN	C	D+	D	449.6	2.45	23.7	4.0	21.2	12.0	6.6	8.8	12.2
Hardin County Savings Bank	Eldora	IA	C+	C+	C+	194.9	4.96	4.6	0.9	5.3	43.9	7.2	9.2	14.8
Hardware State Bank	Lovington	IL	D+	D+	D+	23.7	4.82	5.7	4.2	13.1	9.8	7.4	9.3	22.9
Harford Bank	Aberdeen	MD	C+	C	C	328.9	7.47	4.3	3.7	18.6	10.2	9.0	10.6	14.2
Harleysville Savings Bank	Harleysville	PA	B-	C+	C+	748.2	-3.02	1.2	0.1	44.4	20.1	6.7	8.7	13.7
Harrison Building and Loan Assn.	Harrison	OH	C	C	C	220.3	-0.12	2.1	0.3	37.2	35.3	10.0	14.2	30.7
Harrison County Bank	Lost Creek	WV	B	B-	B-	106.1	4.20	1.3	6.2	29.5	44.4	8.8	10.2	22.4

Asset Quality Index	Adjusted Non-Performing Loans as a % of Total Loans	as a % of Capital	Net Charge-Offs Avg Loans	Profitability Index	Net Income ($Mil)	Return on Assets (R.O.A.)	Return on Equity (R.O.E.)	Net Interest Spread	Overhead Efficiency Ratio	Liquidity Index	Liquidity Ratio	Hot Money Ratio	Stability Index
9.7	1.88	1.4	0.15	3.9	0.5	1.10	5.62	3.23	73.6	6.2	61.4	6.9	6.9
7.2	0.64	4.4	0.12	3.1	0.5	0.43	3.55	3.27	80.6	0.9	11.4	31.8	6.6
5.0	1.49	8.8	0.07	5.3	3.0	1.01	9.11	3.71	61.2	3.7	17.0	10.7	6.7
7.6	1.24	6.5	0.17	4.1	1.2	0.69	5.53	2.88	62.5	3.2	30.8	15.7	6.9
2.7	2.56	21.1	0.02	4.3	1.0	0.78	7.49	4.00	75.4	3.2	10.7	11.1	5.3
4.2	2.67	13.5	0.01	4.3	2.6	0.90	8.24	3.29	72.2	3.7	25.7	11.6	6.4
7.4	0.27	1.6	0.26	5.6	2.1	0.94	7.82	4.04	63.4	4.1	21.5	8.8	7.1
4.7	1.11	6.8	0.13	6.6	3.3	1.65	15.06	3.34	60.4	4.4	24.2	6.9	5.8
2.9	10.19	17.7	4.11	1.8	-0.1	-0.05	-0.24	3.24	79.9	4.2	60.8	19.1	8.0
5.8	2.43	11.8	0.00	4.8	0.6	1.11	9.89	3.44	60.2	2.1	29.4	22.7	7.6
10.0	0.00	0.0	0.00	1.6	0.2	0.23	1.68	2.71	103.2	1.5	17.5	24.9	7.1
8.9	0.00	0.0	0.01	5.3	1.2	1.27	13.39	4.10	71.6	5.0	28.0	4.7	6.2
2.6	2.19	13.1	0.10	5.0	4.9	0.97	7.99	3.46	61.7	3.3	8.8	11.7	6.9
0.3	6.86	161.2	0.71	1.1	-1.0	-0.13	-5.63	3.64	98.4	5.1	7.9	0.5	0.8
7.5	0.04	0.3	0.06	9.9	3.7	2.42	27.56	5.20	54.9	1.6	9.9	20.9	6.9
7.4	0.55	4.0	0.15	4.2	9.9	0.75	7.48	3.45	65.8	2.8	12.1	14.8	7.7
5.0	0.73	4.8	-0.02	5.8	18.9	1.03	9.22	3.80	62.7	4.1	16.4	6.3	8.5
6.4	1.15	6.3	0.02	3.9	1.7	0.87	7.23	3.64	78.9	5.0	27.4	4.3	6.6
5.6	1.66	9.8	0.02	6.5	1.6	1.07	9.98	4.23	63.2	4.0	18.8	9.5	7.4
4.7	2.29	13.5	-0.09	6.9	7.9	1.59	14.09	4.15	67.2	1.7	16.4	22.1	8.4
3.4	1.64	12.7	0.13	5.6	1.9	0.93	8.32	3.94	54.4	1.2	1.4	23.4	6.9
6.8	0.68	4.5	0.01	6.0	3.0	1.38	13.18	3.70	62.2	1.5	15.7	25.1	7.8
9.9	0.58	0.7	0.00	1.7	0.0	0.10	0.51	2.23	95.2	4.5	89.6	20.3	7.4
3.7	1.91	13.4	-0.13	8.7	15.7	2.33	22.15	2.43	47.6	1.8	22.9	22.4	8.9
7.4	0.86	4.6	0.05	3.2	3.1	0.66	4.90	3.38	81.2	3.3	22.0	13.3	8.2
5.3	2.13	9.6	0.24	4.5	2.2	0.78	6.27	4.30	75.2	5.2	36.6	7.2	6.7
3.8	2.12	18.6	0.22	7.9	17.0	1.63	18.79	5.92	74.3	1.2	18.2	23.4	8.2
3.4	1.60	16.8	0.01	0.9	-0.1	-0.10	-2.24	4.44	103.7	2.6	15.1	16.2	0.5
5.9	0.82	5.4	0.01	3.1	1.1	0.47	4.17	3.39	72.7	4.1	23.4	9.0	4.8
8.9	0.12	0.8	0.02	5.8	0.6	0.99	10.69	4.46	69.8	4.6	27.7	7.0	5.4
9.7	0.00	0.0	-0.02	2.2	0.2	0.22	2.11	2.49	86.4	3.4	51.7	22.7	5.5
0.2	7.21	48.7	2.43	3.2	0.3	0.40	4.09	6.25	43.2	1.5	11.4	22.6	4.3
5.0	1.39	8.1	0.08	4.2	0.8	0.93	8.63	4.00	77.5	3.5	18.8	11.9	6.6
0.3	7.13	91.2	0.02	1.4	0.8	0.31	10.53	2.55	93.5	1.3	29.1	36.8	0.3
6.5	1.27	5.7	-0.03	5.9	0.6	1.39	9.98	4.17	58.1	2.7	35.5	20.1	7.7
6.4	0.28	1.7	0.00	5.2	7.2	0.87	9.41	2.33	59.4	2.3	37.9	42.2	7.8
8.8	0.74	2.4	0.08	2.5	0.9	0.38	3.95	1.73	73.2	3.9	56.2	12.3	4.7
7.2	0.16	1.3	0.03	4.6	0.9	1.12	12.37	4.21	71.5	3.1	8.3	12.6	5.6
3.9	1.74	14.2	0.28	1.3	0.4	0.13	1.13	2.94	91.6	1.8	30.0	26.8	5.5
5.3	1.00	5.9	0.00	5.6	0.7	1.35	14.07	4.20	67.5	2.4	19.2	17.2	5.9
6.3	0.88	4.9	0.14	5.9	14.3	1.08	8.83	4.47	57.3	3.4	23.4	14.7	8.5
9.0	0.00	0.0	-0.09	5.2	0.7	1.30	8.04	3.20	56.4	3.8	38.1	15.2	8.4
6.2	3.00	8.9	0.33	7.2	4.7	1.44	7.86	3.87	52.0	5.2	50.0	11.6	9.3
5.2	7.14	15.5	0.16	1.7	0.3	0.46	2.56	3.35	82.6	4.2	51.0	15.9	7.0
4.4	1.54	10.6	0.07	2.9	1.3	0.65	5.83	3.95	84.7	1.5	10.3	22.8	4.7
7.5	1.23	5.2	0.19	4.1	1.9	0.72	4.18	3.43	69.4	3.6	16.7	11.4	7.5
6.3	0.44	2.9	-0.02	8.6	44.8	1.39	11.60	3.97	54.6	1.7	14.8	22.0	10.0
8.8	0.17	1.3	-0.01	3.8	1.5	0.65	6.22	3.49	61.1	0.9	9.1	32.3	5.0
6.1	0.80	5.5	0.69	6.2	1.8	1.18	10.48	4.45	63.5	3.2	17.8	9.3	6.7
5.7	0.88	5.6	0.15	5.4	24.9	1.16	9.22	4.22	66.3	2.0	11.6	9.4	8.4
2.1	3.60	30.2	-0.01	0.4	-0.5	-0.24	-2.52	3.66	111.0	1.5	7.1	21.7	4.5
4.6	2.68	14.4	0.14	3.6	6.1	0.46	3.74	3.75	78.3	3.6	25.0	14.1	5.7
2.5	1.73	14.2	0.04	2.5	5.9	0.35	3.62	2.84	87.4	2.8	2.2	12.6	7.3
3.8	1.61	12.8	0.07	5.0	4.0	1.19	14.04	4.21	61.4	0.7	10.9	25.8	3.3
6.4	1.36	6.8	0.03	3.5	1.2	0.84	11.56	2.72	75.1	2.5	34.3	22.1	4.7
8.9	0.00	0.0	0.11	1.8	0.1	0.27	2.83	2.30	89.4	4.2	57.5	15.1	3.7
2.7	2.01	14.3	0.15	4.0	1.3	0.53	4.95	3.72	74.3	2.7	11.1	14.8	5.9
5.1	1.63	12.9	0.07	4.2	4.6	0.80	9.42	2.87	58.0	4.5	14.1	4.9	5.2
4.8	5.08	18.3	0.09	2.4	0.5	0.32	2.20	2.78	80.6	4.8	48.7	12.9	6.6
9.1	0.01	0.1	0.02	4.4	0.6	0.72	7.14	3.64	71.2	5.1	48.9	11.9	5.5

Name	City	State	2015 Rating	2014 Rating	Rating	Total Assets ($Mil)	One Year Asset Growth	Asset Mix (As a % of Total Assets)				Capital-ization Index	Lever-age Ratio	Risk-Based Capital Ratio
								Comm-ercial Loans	Cons-umer Loans	Mort-gage Loans	Secur-ities			
Hart County Bank and Trust Co.	Munfordville	KY	B	B-	B	27.7	0.16	7.0	1.4	0.2	34.1	10.0	20.4	28.5
Hartsburg State Bank	Hartsburg	IL	C-	D+	E+	16.9	-3.50	10.3	1.4	5.9	28.5	10.0	11.2	16.1
Hartwick State Bank	Hartwick	IA	C-	D	C-	23.9	-4.32	2.5	2.3	13.3	38.1	6.8	8.8	18.8
▲ Harvard State Bank	Harvard	IL	B-	C	C-	218.5	2.36	4.4	2.0	21.8	33.7	8.5	10.0	19.0
Harvest Bank	Kimball	MN	B	B	B	129.1	0.99	8.7	3.0	18.0	14.7	7.8	9.5	14.3
Harvest Community Bank	Pennsville	NJ	E-	E-	D-	126.4	-17.17	14.8	0.8	23.6	12.4	0.0	1.7	3.5
Harwood State Bank	Harwood	ND	C-	C	C-	39.5	1.35	14.4	4.1	1.4	4.9	5.8	8.2	11.6
Haskell National Bank	Haskell	TX	B-	C+	C	73.4	-3.42	4.8	4.7	7.7	43.2	10.0	11.5	24.1
Hastings City Bank	Hastings	MI	C+	C	C	311.9	4.13	3.6	3.1	22.4	24.7	6.6	8.6	17.0
Hatboro Federal Savings, FA	Hatboro	PA	B-	B-	B	500.1	1.72	0.0	0.0	53.8	19.3	10.0	21.3	43.0
Havana National Bank	Havana	IL	B	B-	B-	230.0	1.58	6.5	2.5	10.3	21.5	6.7	9.6	12.3
Haven Savings Bank	Hoboken	NJ	C	C	C+	911.3	2.93	0.4	0.1	63.3	9.1	9.5	10.7	18.8
Haverford Trust Co.	Radnor	PA	A-	A-	A	125.1	12.18	7.8	44.3	0.2	22.0	10.0	17.1	16.2
Haverhill Bank	Haverhill	MA	C	C	C	373.6	6.56	6.2	0.4	45.6	15.2	8.9	10.3	17.6
Haviland State Bank	Haviland	KS	B	B-	B-	40.4	-0.09	4.7	1.0	2.4	29.3	10.0	12.3	19.9
Hawaii National Bank	Honolulu	HI	D	D	D	687.1	6.46	18.0	0.8	13.0	20.7	6.2	8.2	13.3
Hawthorn Bank	Jefferson City	MO	B	B	B-	1271.4	4.17	10.4	2.3	17.9	17.5	8.4	10.8	13.6
Headwaters State Bank	Land O'Lakes	WI	B+	B+	B+	66.0	-3.15	1.6	3.0	32.3	23.8	10.0	14.8	27.3
Heartland Bank	Little Rock	AR	D-	E+	B+	219.0	-12.01	50.1	0.5	4.6	5.4	8.4	11.5	13.6
Heartland Bank	Somers	IA	A-	A-	A	130.6	5.64	12.7	3.0	7.7	21.6	10.0	13.7	17.2
Heartland Bank	Geneva	NE	B-	B-	B-	407.2	4.82	5.9	1.0	2.4	12.8	5.2	9.0	11.2
Heartland Bank	Gahanna	OH	B	B	B-	790.2	12.84	8.6	1.2	16.7	14.7	7.8	9.5	13.2
Heartland Bank and Trust Co.	Bloomington	IL	A-	A-	B+	2976.7	20.06	11.5	1.0	10.5	22.8	8.1	9.7	13.4
Heartland National Bank	Sebring	FL	C+	B-	C	334.4	5.11	3.4	2.3	10.3	20.9	8.1	9.7	20.3
Heartland State Bank	Edgeley	ND	B-	B-	B-	60.1	-5.49	7.8	2.7	1.0	18.6	10.0	11.5	15.3
▲ Heartland State Bank	Redfield	SD	A-	B+	A-	77.3	-0.68	9.7	2.3	0.4	8.1	10.0	12.4	15.3
Hebron Savings Bank	Hebron	MD	D-	E+	C-	568.1	2.73	7.5	0.5	27.8	8.4	5.8	8.7	11.6
Helena National Bank	Helena	AR	C	B-	B-	179.5	-5.50	3.6	1.4	4.1	44.8	10.0	15.3	29.0
Helm Bank USA	Miami	FL	C+	C+	C+	764.2	6.11	1.2	1.8	53.3	35.9	10.0	12.4	31.4
Henderson Federal Savings Bank	Henderson	TX	B+	B+	A-	113.5	-0.99	2.0	3.3	47.6	20.1	10.0	18.6	41.1
Henderson State Bank	Henderson	NE	B	B	B-	266.4	11.03	17.6	0.7	0.1	12.8	5.7	9.8	11.5
Hendricks County Bank and Trust Co.	Brownsburg	IN	C+	C+	D+	148.3	1.34	5.8	1.4	18.1	25.5	10.0	12.1	20.1
Henry County Bank	Napoleon	OH	C-	D	C	282.6	4.71	4.6	2.9	11.0	49.6	8.0	9.7	20.6
▼ Henry State Bank	Henry	IL	C	B	B-	97.0	-5.25	5.6	8.6	10.5	32.3	10.0	14.0	21.8
▲ Heritage Bank	Hinesville	GA	D-	E-	E-	526.1	2.66	5.5	2.1	11.0	26.7	6.2	8.2	14.3
▲ Heritage Bank	Jonesboro	GA	C-	D	E	425.2	7.59	5.7	0.6	8.0	12.3	6.1	8.1	12.0
Heritage Bank	Marion	IA	D+	D+	D+	36.2	-0.31	6.8	2.1	20.6	41.7	8.6	10.1	20.0
▲ Heritage Bank	Topeka	KS	D+	E-	E-	53.6	6.64	13.9	0.8	24.5	4.6	10.0	11.5	18.5
Heritage Bank	Wood River	NE	A	A	A	577.7	-1.90	4.2	1.0	3.5	53.9	10.0	15.7	25.6
Heritage Bank	Pearland	TX	B-	B-	B-	243.9	15.12	9.4	1.1	16.0	3.8	5.9	9.1	11.7
Heritage Bank	Olympia	WA	B	B	B	3843.5	6.94	8.8	5.7	4.8	21.3	7.2	10.2	12.7
Heritage Bank	Spencer	WI	B	B	B	104.6	2.12	14.1	1.5	24.5	13.8	10.0	12.3	17.6
Heritage Bank & Trust	Columbia	TN	C+	C-	D	113.8	12.57	7.3	2.4	19.5	13.5	8.4	9.9	14.2
Heritage Bank of Commerce	San Jose	CA	B+	B+	B+	2527.4	11.87	21.4	0.7	2.2	22.8	6.7	8.7	12.6
Heritage Bank of Nevada	Reno	NV	B+	B	C+	695.8	15.71	4.9	0.1	2.8	15.7	10.0	11.7	15.1
Heritage Bank of Schaumburg	Schaumburg	IL	D+	C	C-	139.0	2.54	2.6	0.1	11.8	8.6	6.1	8.1	19.5
Heritage Bank of St. Tammany	Covington	LA	C-	D+	D	97.2	5.58	0.0	0.3	56.5	7.8	8.1	9.7	19.2
Heritage Bank of the Ozarks	Lebanon	MO	B-	B-	C	117.9	19.32	6.2	3.0	23.7	14.7	7.0	9.0	14.1
Heritage Bank USA, Inc.	Hopkinsville	KY	C	C	C	870.4	-1.11	7.1	1.0	17.2	24.5	9.6	10.8	16.8
Heritage Bank, Inc.	Erlanger	KY	C+	C	C	658.0	18.28	7.6	0.8	12.9	20.1	6.9	10.1	12.5
Heritage Bank, N.A.	Spicer	MN	B-	B-	B-	383.8	-2.25	13.8	3.4	8.0	8.5	8.7	10.9	13.9
Heritage Community Bank	Chamois	MO	B	B	B-	123.4	21.38	11.1	2.3	22.7	3.9	7.1	9.7	12.5
Heritage Community Bank	Hartsville	SC	C+	B-	B-	113.1	9.72	8.1	1.9	12.9	5.6	7.5	9.6	12.9
▲ Heritage Community Bank	Greeneville	TN	C-	D+	E	89.6	-1.12	6.9	7.9	37.7	4.5	6.8	8.8	13.9
Heritage First Bank	Rome	GA	C+	B+	B	116.7	13.14	11.1	7.3	19.2	5.2	8.2	10.9	13.5
Heritage Oaks Bank	Paso Robles	CA	B+	B+	B-	1986.6	6.13	9.3	0.2	10.2	23.0	7.5	9.4	13.5
Heritage State Bank	Lawrenceville	IL	B+	B+	B+	98.4	21.10	2.6	0.0	0.9	0.0	4.8	9.5	10.9
Heritage State Bank	Nevada	MO	B	B	B	134.6	-0.39	7.4	4.2	27.2	11.9	7.4	9.3	13.7
▼ Herring Bank	Amarillo	TX	B	B+	B	424.9	-3.08	11.7	3.7	7.6	12.7	10.0	11.9	15.7
Hershey State Bank	Hershey	NE	B+	B+	B+	73.7	-2.39	14.6	11.1	12.2	6.4	10.0	16.7	19.4

Asset Quality Index	Adjusted Non-Performing Loans as a % of Total Loans	as a % of Capital	Net Charge-Offs Avg Loans	Profitability Index	Net Income ($Mil)	Return on Assets (R.O.A.)	Return on Equity (R.O.E.)	Net Interest Spread	Overhead Efficiency Ratio	Liquidity Index	Liquidity Ratio	Hot Money Ratio	Stability Index
9.6	0.00	0.0	0.00	4.6	0.2	0.99	5.04	4.24	72.1	6.7	59.7	3.2	6.9
8.6	0.00	0.0	0.46	3.5	0.1	0.91	8.31	3.15	70.6	2.8	27.0	15.7	2.2
9.2	0.00	0.0	0.00	2.7	0.1	0.50	5.72	2.79	82.1	6.0	64.8	6.8	3.4
5.4	1.03	5.5	0.28	4.2	1.7	1.04	9.09	3.89	72.8	3.0	21.4	14.6	5.1
4.4	1.41	9.6	0.00	6.3	1.5	1.56	16.27	4.02	60.7	4.6	17.4	4.9	6.4
0.0	18.98	329.3	0.25	0.0	-1.4	-1.34	-61.41	2.96	145.3	2.6	7.6	15.0	0.5
7.9	0.08	0.7	0.00	3.8	0.2	0.56	6.73	3.63	74.4	3.9	26.5	11.1	4.1
8.7	0.55	2.0	0.23	3.6	0.4	0.79	6.93	3.37	79.7	5.2	42.7	9.0	5.8
5.3	1.14	7.2	0.07	3.2	1.3	0.58	6.17	3.33	82.9	6.1	39.4	2.4	5.1
6.5	4.18	11.7	0.03	3.5	2.4	0.64	3.01	2.53	61.2	2.4	38.4	27.5	7.8
3.9	0.96	6.7	0.09	6.2	2.0	1.16	11.47	3.65	56.1	3.2	8.9	12.3	6.4
6.0	0.71	5.4	0.00	2.9	2.4	0.35	3.14	2.79	81.5	0.9	9.5	31.6	7.1
6.7	0.00	0.0	0.00	9.5	4.7	5.39	31.38	2.14	82.0	2.1	49.5	89.2	9.7
7.0	0.43	2.9	-0.01	2.8	1.1	0.40	3.86	2.99	82.4	2.0	25.6	21.3	6.2
5.9	0.00	0.0	-0.08	7.9	0.4	1.48	11.59	5.04	52.6	3.4	22.3	12.7	7.3
8.7	0.12	0.8	0.01	1.2	0.2	0.05	0.55	3.46	97.8	2.3	25.1	18.6	4.9
6.7	0.66	4.3	0.02	4.5	6.9	0.75	6.94	3.60	70.5	2.7	6.8	14.9	8.2
4.8	2.98	11.8	0.00	6.5	0.7	1.45	9.63	4.82	62.0	3.9	43.1	15.9	8.9
0.2	18.28	105.5	5.05	3.1	0.1	0.04	0.34	4.86	70.0	3.9	15.9	9.4	8.2
6.7	0.70	3.6	0.03	9.1	1.9	1.95	12.91	4.73	54.6	1.7	11.4	20.8	9.9
4.2	0.59	4.8	-0.02	6.7	3.6	1.24	11.57	4.20	55.6	2.8	11.5	14.3	6.2
5.3	0.67	5.1	0.08	5.9	6.1	1.07	11.02	3.90	62.2	1.6	10.6	21.2	6.1
5.9	0.94	6.3	0.16	8.2	38.6	1.85	17.74	4.45	59.3	4.7	20.9	5.9	9.4
5.1	2.53	10.9	-0.15	4.0	1.7	0.65	6.90	3.22	64.8	5.4	53.1	11.2	5.2
4.1	2.07	12.1	0.00	4.3	0.4	0.94	7.39	3.98	75.0	2.8	16.1	15.2	6.6
6.7	0.37	2.4	-0.05	10.0	1.4	2.34	19.45	5.38	52.9	2.3	6.7	16.7	8.7
0.3	6.08	50.9	0.31	4.2	3.0	0.70	8.28	3.59	61.4	1.6	7.6	20.8	4.5
8.9	0.69	1.9	1.18	2.4	0.6	0.41	2.74	3.46	82.0	2.5	35.5	23.0	7.1
6.1	2.58	11.0	-0.06	3.1	2.7	0.47	3.79	3.62	88.1	5.7	47.5	8.0	6.8
5.7	3.41	11.2	0.29	4.3	0.6	0.71	3.86	3.34	65.3	0.8	17.9	42.9	7.7
5.0	0.39	3.0	-0.01	8.5	2.5	1.33	13.54	3.87	40.8	0.5	6.3	46.0	6.3
6.8	1.04	5.0	0.32	2.8	0.4	0.37	3.05	3.79	81.9	4.9	37.4	9.8	5.5
2.5	5.67	22.4	0.77	2.5	1.3	0.63	6.30	3.29	78.2	0.9	22.2	30.1	5.0
5.2	2.80	10.7	0.65	1.8	-0.1	-0.13	-0.91	3.32	70.2	3.0	26.5	15.6	7.0
1.5	8.73	46.7	5.11	0.0	-4.3	-1.09	-16.64	3.05	87.0	4.1	36.9	12.5	0.9
4.4	0.19	1.5	-0.04	4.4	6.7	2.22	25.58	3.89	80.8	3.3	18.4	13.0	2.1
8.4	0.35	1.7	0.00	1.6	0.0	0.04	0.39	3.63	97.8	5.6	51.4	8.6	4.4
7.1	0.51	3.1	-0.38	1.9	0.1	0.34	4.26	3.76	90.9	1.3	18.7	28.8	1.9
8.6	0.17	0.4	-0.09	7.2	7.5	1.69	10.66	2.69	45.3	5.0	32.7	4.3	9.7
5.0	0.19	1.6	0.42	5.1	1.6	0.92	8.82	4.76	61.3	1.5	8.3	22.4	7.5
5.2	0.73	4.7	0.18	5.8	31.3	1.13	8.40	4.12	63.0	4.7	20.4	5.5	9.1
7.0	0.76	4.2	0.13	4.5	0.6	0.80	6.62	3.55	66.3	3.2	17.7	13.5	7.0
4.1	0.86	5.8	0.24	3.8	0.7	0.84	9.02	4.03	80.8	1.9	23.9	21.8	4.5
7.6	0.31	2.0	-0.01	6.9	21.3	1.20	11.25	4.21	54.4	5.3	34.4	9.4	8.9
5.2	0.98	5.6	-0.03	9.8	9.0	1.86	15.80	4.44	42.0	3.8	24.7	10.9	7.9
1.4	3.09	20.7	0.04	3.9	0.9	0.87	6.47	3.18	71.1	5.4	43.9	8.4	7.8
5.5	0.97	7.0	0.15	2.3	0.2	0.32	3.33	3.49	85.2	0.9	20.3	38.8	4.5
6.8	0.00	0.0	0.00	5.3	0.8	0.98	10.76	4.31	68.5	1.6	20.4	24.3	5.4
4.3	2.54	15.1	0.01	2.3	2.1	0.33	2.92	3.40	87.4	1.5	10.3	22.9	6.4
3.5	2.35	15.4	0.06	5.3	4.4	0.95	9.14	4.05	65.1	2.5	11.5	13.7	6.3
6.2	0.60	4.3	0.17	4.6	2.9	1.03	9.64	4.40	76.2	3.1	13.7	12.2	5.9
6.4	0.28	2.3	-0.08	5.5	1.2	1.39	14.25	4.20	65.3	1.5	7.8	22.5	6.0
5.8	0.38	2.8	0.03	3.4	0.4	0.41	4.27	4.30	84.8	2.6	14.4	7.7	5.9
5.5	0.51	4.0	-0.11	3.2	0.4	0.65	7.79	4.24	84.9	1.5	10.6	23.4	2.5
6.5	0.29	2.2	0.14	3.1	0.3	0.34	3.03	5.19	89.0	2.7	10.2	15.0	5.1
6.0	0.76	5.1	-0.12	5.1	13.0	0.90	8.26	3.68	66.2	4.0	21.1	10.4	8.9
7.3	0.00	0.0	-0.03	9.9	1.7	2.44	24.67	5.31	53.1	1.3	6.7	24.8	7.4
5.3	0.75	5.7	0.02	4.2	0.9	0.92	9.84	4.19	80.2	3.2	10.3	12.6	6.6
4.4	2.20	12.9	0.10	3.7	2.2	0.71	5.68	4.44	83.9	3.1	18.3	13.7	6.9
5.1	0.86	4.2	0.16	9.8	0.9	1.66	10.65	4.87	49.9	0.6	10.1	41.2	9.1

| Name | City | State | 2016 Rating | 2015 Rating | 2014 Rating | Total Assets ($Mil) | One Year Asset Growth | Asset Mix (As a % of Total Assets) | | | | Capital-ization Index | Lever-age Ratio | Risk-Based Capital Ratio |
								Comm-ercial Loans	Cons-umer Loans	Mort-gage Loans	Secur-ities			
Hertford Savings Bank, SSB	Hertford	NC	C-	C	C	12.2	-6.68	0.0	2.9	50.1	2.3	10.0	16.5	32.1
Hiawatha Bank and Trust Co.	Hiawatha	IA	B-	B-	B-	52.1	10.06	10.2	1.6	18.4	0.7	7.1	10.3	12.6
Hiawatha National Bank	Hager City	WI	C+	C+	C	184.3	19.41	11.1	0.9	13.9	18.8	9.5	10.7	15.7
Hibernia Bank	New Orleans	LA	C	C	C	122.2	7.17	3.0	0.0	51.3	6.0	10.0	16.5	26.0
Hickory Point Bank and Trust	Decatur	IL	C	C	C+	640.7	-1.09	11.7	8.2	6.6	21.0	6.5	9.3	12.2
Hicksville Bank	Hicksville	OH	B-	B-	C+	112.3	0.06	3.3	2.0	16.6	33.9	10.0	12.2	19.6
High Country Bank	Salida	CO	B+	A-	B+	243.3	9.21	9.0	1.3	22.3	15.9	7.5	9.3	14.8
▼ High Desert Bank	Bend	OR	E-	E-	E-	26.6	-5.85	3.5	0.1	11.0	22.7	1.7	4.5	11.0
High Plains Bank	Flagler	CO	B+	B+	B+	141.1	3.63	6.4	1.5	14.7	10.5	6.9	9.2	12.4
▲ High Plains Bank	Keyes	OK	B+	B-	D+	83.2	5.52	7.3	3.8	7.9	7.0	6.9	10.2	12.4
Highland Bank	Saint Michael	MN	B-	C+	C+	497.8	2.19	11.5	0.4	8.6	39.7	8.2	9.8	16.0
Highland Federal S&L Assn.	Crossville	TN	C-	C-	C-	63.0	-0.78	0.0	0.2	34.1	4.9	10.0	21.6	51.4
Highland State Bank	Highland	WI	C+	C+	C	32.5	4.85	10.2	6.5	25.5	8.9	7.6	9.4	19.9
Highlands Bank	Jackson	LA	B+	B+	A-	147.8	6.91	13.1	1.3	13.6	18.4	10.0	12.7	19.2
▼ Highlands Community Bank	Covington	VA	B+	A-	B	140.3	6.28	3.4	11.6	20.5	35.7	10.0	11.8	20.1
Highlands State Bank	Vernon	NJ	C	C	D+	385.2	27.00	10.4	0.0	13.6	1.0	3.5	8.1	10.2
Highlands Union Bank	Abingdon	VA	D+	D+	D+	612.9	-0.49	5.1	3.0	32.7	15.8	5.6	7.6	13.1
Hill Bank & Trust Co.	Weimar	TX	B	B	B	133.3	1.35	0.7	0.9	3.3	85.6	10.0	16.8	32.1
Hill-Dodge Banking Co.	Warsaw	IL	B+	B+	B+	40.9	4.88	20.0	4.0	5.9	9.3	10.0	15.7	26.2
Hills Bank and Trust Co.	Hills	IA	A	A	A	2594.0	7.01	7.3	0.9	32.2	9.7	10.0	12.8	16.3
▲ Hillsboro Bank	Plant City	FL	A-	B+	B	131.4	15.29	5.3	1.2	14.4	27.2	10.0	12.5	23.7
▲ Hillsboro State Bank	Hillsboro	KS	D+	D+	D	19.4	6.08	3.8	2.9	16.1	9.7	6.5	8.5	19.8
Hillsdale County National Bank	Hillsdale	MI	C+	C+	C	564.2	12.62	14.6	3.7	26.7	4.7	6.5	8.5	12.3
Hilltop National Bank	Casper	WY	B+	B+	A-	838.8	11.79	3.5	2.9	11.1	44.4	6.3	8.3	28.3
Hingham Institution for Savings	Hingham	MA	B+	B+	B+	1960.4	15.93	0.0	0.0	43.0	1.3	5.9	7.9	13.1
Hinsdale Bank & Trust Co.	Hinsdale	IL	B-	B-	B-	2071.6	-0.71	32.1	12.3	3.6	9.7	5.5	10.0	11.4
HNB First Bank	Headland	AL	B	C+	C+	119.9	13.59	9.6	3.6	15.7	11.7	10.0	11.5	17.6
HNB National Bank	Hannibal	MO	A-	A-	B+	463.5	18.52	6.7	1.9	19.7	5.4	10.0	12.8	16.1
Hocking Valley Bank	Athens	OH	B-	B-	B	253.9	3.80	20.3	1.3	26.9	19.6	9.7	10.8	18.3
▼ Hodge Bank & Trust Co.	Hodge	LA	B+	A-	A-	65.1	-2.44	16.6	10.1	28.6	15.4	10.0	17.8	29.2
Holbrook Co-operative Bank	Holbrook	MA	C	C-	C	99.5	4.73	6.0	2.7	28.2	8.3	6.9	8.9	13.5
Holcomb State Bank	Holcomb	IL	C-	B-	C+	177.2	-0.92	12.6	1.9	13.3	14.3	7.9	9.7	13.3
Holladay Bank & Trust	Salt Lake City	UT	B	B	B-	52.1	2.64	6.9	3.2	16.4	1.5	10.0	14.0	22.2
Holmes County Bank & Trust Co.	Lexington	MS	C-	C	C-	106.7	-2.39	21.9	4.8	8.7	33.0	10.0	12.7	23.8
Home Bank and Trust Co.	Eureka	KS	C+	C+	C+	95.4	6.74	13.2	3.0	26.8	5.8	4.8	8.0	10.9
Home Bank of California	San Diego	CA	A	A	A	143.6	15.81	0.4	0.0	39.4	0.1	10.0	17.0	23.5
Home Bank SB	Martinsville	IN	C+	C+	C	252.1	7.35	2.5	1.3	36.4	24.8	10.0	13.7	20.6
▼ Home Bank, N.A.	Lafayette	LA	B	B+	B	1549.5	-0.42	8.9	2.8	24.6	11.9	8.1	9.7	13.6
Home Banking Co.	Selmer	TN	C+	C+	C+	87.3	0.91	5.8	7.2	16.0	38.6	8.5	10.0	18.7
Home City FSB of Springfield	Springfield	OH	B+	B	B	156.0	4.01	5.9	1.0	53.9	3.7	10.0	11.0	17.2
Home Exchange Bank	Jamesport	MO	A	A	A-	157.8	19.91	3.5	0.3	2.9	59.3	8.8	10.2	21.0
Home Federal Bank	Shreveport	LA	A-	A	A	389.9	6.44	7.0	0.1	35.2	14.4	10.0	11.5	18.4
Home Federal Bank Corp.	Middlesboro	KY	B	B-	C+	343.4	2.24	2.5	1.5	40.6	18.0	10.0	11.3	18.1
▲ Home Federal Bank of Hollywood	Hallandale Beach	FL	D	E-	E	40.9	4.75	1.0	0.1	38.9	0.0	10.0	14.8	27.9
Home Federal Bank of Tennessee	Knoxville	TN	B	B-	B-	2194.4	2.63	1.6	0.4	18.0	52.1	10.0	17.4	32.8
Home Federal S&L Assn.	Bamberg	SC	B-	C+	C+	41.4	1.23	0.0	3.0	68.9	3.9	10.0	11.6	21.9
▲ Home Federal S&L Assn. of Grand Island	Grand Island	NE	C	C+	C	273.9	21.15	9.3	4.3	14.9	26.3	10.0	11.1	16.9
Home Federal S&L Assn. of Niles Ohio	Niles	OH	C-	C-	C-	94.4	-6.33	0.2	0.3	22.6	51.0	10.0	12.9	28.4
Home Federal Savings Bank	Rochester	MN	B+	B+	B-	684.4	10.84	10.3	2.1	18.3	11.7	8.6	11.0	13.9
Home Loan Investment Bank, F.S.B.	Warwick	RI	D	D	D-	248.3	17.44	0.2	20.5	54.7	1.1	9.0	10.3	14.3
Home Loan Savings Bank	Coshocton	OH	A	A	A-	201.4	4.32	12.5	3.2	43.8	1.7	10.0	11.5	16.0
▲ Home Loan State Bank	Grand Junction	CO	C	C-	C	97.6	13.21	17.5	2.7	3.5	38.2	6.3	8.3	12.6
▼ Home National Bank	Racine	OH	C-	C-	D+	59.4	0.98	7.0	10.6	38.4	17.1	10.0	14.9	23.0
Home National Bank of Thorntown	Thorntown	IN	C	C	C	102.3	1.05	12.3	2.6	16.4	38.6	7.1	9.1	16.3
▲ Home S&L Assn. of Norborne, F.A.	Norborne	MO	C	C	D+	75.9	-3.63	1.8	4.0	47.1	10.1	10.0	18.3	36.6
Home S&L Co. of Kenton, Ohio	Kenton	OH	C+	B-	C	111.1	-1.42	1.7	1.4	32.8	34.5	10.0	29.2	55.4
Home S&L Co. of Youngstown	Youngstown	OH	B	B	C+	2157.8	9.45	4.9	2.0	40.2	21.3	10.0	11.3	17.2
Home Savings Bank	Chanute	KS	C	C-	C-	70.4	6.05	1.1	3.8	23.7	47.0	10.0	17.9	38.3
Home Savings Bank	Salt Lake City	UT	B+	B+	B	120.5	-0.06	0.3	0.1	31.0	17.6	10.0	12.1	16.2
▲ Home Savings Bank	Madison	WI	D	D-	D-	140.5	5.22	0.8	1.2	40.4	2.5	6.2	8.2	12.8

Arrows denote recent upgrades ▲ or downgrades ▼

Asset Quality Index	Adjusted Non-Performing Loans as a % of Total Loans	as a % of Capital	Net Charge-Offs Avg Loans	Profitability Index	Net Income ($Mil)	Return on Assets (R.O.A.)	Return on Equity (R.O.E.)	Net Interest Spread	Overhead Efficiency Ratio	Liquidity Index	Liquidity Ratio	Hot Money Ratio	Stability Index
3.4	6.90	26.1	0.00	2.3	0.0	0.30	1.86	3.82	90.7	4.3	39.5	11.0	5.6
5.7	0.10	0.9	0.43	7.9	0.5	1.36	13.25	4.15	50.5	1.5	4.1	20.6	5.7
4.3	1.47	9.5	0.00	4.1	1.3	0.94	8.56	3.97	72.2	1.6	19.1	5.8	6.4
9.3	0.32	1.5	0.00	2.2	0.2	0.21	1.27	3.21	86.8	0.8	15.9	41.7	7.4
4.6	0.71	5.1	0.20	3.0	2.3	0.48	5.28	3.01	80.3	4.1	15.2	7.9	5.5
5.0	2.89	12.6	-0.01	3.6	0.5	0.59	4.63	3.77	80.7	3.6	29.8	13.4	6.3
6.8	0.30	1.9	0.04	7.4	2.3	1.30	13.47	4.85	63.6	4.1	25.0	9.2	5.8
4.3	0.82	5.2	1.56	0.0	-1.1	-5.16	-81.34	2.99	196.0	4.2	40.9	14.4	1.6
8.5	0.00	0.0	0.14	7.0	1.7	1.63	17.65	5.03	69.8	2.4	11.6	16.5	6.4
7.7	0.00	0.0	0.00	9.2	1.5	2.37	21.22	4.25	45.3	0.6	14.4	52.5	8.2
7.6	0.18	1.0	-0.16	4.1	2.6	0.70	6.57	3.83	74.5	4.5	35.4	6.6	5.7
9.8	0.80	1.7	0.00	1.7	0.1	0.15	0.71	3.01	93.2	4.2	55.6	16.5	7.2
5.3	1.34	7.4	0.02	3.4	0.2	0.69	7.39	3.27	74.7	5.4	42.9	7.9	4.5
6.6	0.99	5.4	0.03	6.2	1.6	1.46	11.39	4.00	65.0	1.4	18.9	27.5	6.6
4.3	3.24	14.9	0.25	5.9	1.2	1.18	9.37	4.35	61.0	2.9	47.3	26.8	7.1
3.7	0.69	7.1	0.16	4.1	1.8	0.70	7.77	3.85	73.0	1.4	12.6	24.6	4.8
2.5	2.68	21.9	0.67	1.5	-0.1	-0.03	-0.29	3.64	94.0	4.0	19.9	9.5	3.9
10.0	1.50	0.7	-0.02	3.8	0.8	0.81	4.83	2.71	57.5	4.9	99.3	20.5	8.2
7.8	0.75	2.7	0.20	8.3	0.6	1.87	12.22	4.22	46.9	5.3	39.9	8.3	8.6
7.5	0.57	3.6	-0.10	7.0	24.9	1.31	10.55	3.38	54.4	4.0	10.5	7.2	10.0
9.3	0.25	0.9	0.00	5.4	1.0	1.08	7.90	3.72	57.5	4.8	56.7	15.3	7.0
8.4	0.21	1.2	0.23	3.0	0.1	0.49	5.81	3.68	80.4	4.1	46.9	13.7	3.0
3.9	1.27	11.5	0.07	5.1	3.9	0.96	11.03	4.21	69.9	2.0	11.7	6.6	5.6
9.2	0.32	1.0	0.09	4.8	8.1	1.16	13.36	2.33	62.1	6.6	71.1	7.9	7.2
9.0	0.28	2.7	0.00	7.9	17.1	1.21	15.66	3.09	32.9	1.2	18.7	31.6	7.3
3.3	1.48	11.5	0.05	6.3	16.6	1.12	8.19	3.64	53.1	2.4	10.2	15.9	7.7
6.7	0.82	4.3	0.08	4.2	0.8	0.95	8.13	3.60	78.2	2.4	31.5	20.2	5.9
6.1	0.97	5.8	0.10	9.7	7.2	2.35	18.03	4.25	52.9	4.4	16.0	6.2	8.5
6.9	0.60	3.5	0.09	4.6	1.6	0.84	7.94	3.52	69.9	3.9	11.0	8.7	6.6
4.8	2.79	10.3	0.21	10.0	1.4	2.83	16.67	5.00	46.8	2.2	28.9	20.5	9.4
4.9	0.82	6.6	0.08	2.4	0.1	0.17	1.90	3.63	91.1	3.8	18.2	10.4	4.5
2.1	3.10	22.3	0.62	2.2	0.1	0.08	0.76	4.25	73.2	1.4	9.7	23.8	5.1
8.0	0.69	3.0	-0.30	6.4	0.6	1.48	10.61	5.24	67.4	3.0	31.0	17.0	6.1
1.9	9.13	31.1	0.12	2.4	0.3	0.35	2.74	3.07	94.7	2.1	27.8	21.6	6.3
8.4	0.00	0.0	-0.01	5.3	0.9	1.29	16.24	4.16	72.3	1.5	7.5	22.9	4.3
7.7	0.00	0.0	0.00	10.0	2.5	2.50	14.88	5.09	44.6	0.5	8.1	57.1	9.2
6.9	1.37	6.1	0.14	3.2	1.0	0.55	4.04	3.50	86.6	3.9	31.5	12.5	6.8
4.1	1.72	13.3	0.01	5.7	11.8	1.02	10.18	4.40	63.1	3.8	8.7	9.6	9.0
8.0	0.38	1.5	-0.03	3.5	0.4	0.56	5.54	4.04	82.5	2.9	43.4	22.5	5.3
5.9	0.86	5.8	0.07	5.4	1.2	0.99	9.17	3.53	59.9	1.0	9.8	30.6	6.6
8.8	0.55	1.7	-0.13	8.8	2.5	2.29	20.18	3.15	34.8	1.1	22.2	17.6	9.4
8.9	0.33	2.2	0.00	6.0	2.9	1.06	9.01	3.84	62.4	1.1	17.8	26.4	8.2
7.0	0.88	5.2	0.01	4.2	2.0	0.80	7.25	4.07	76.4	2.3	19.5	17.8	6.1
8.2	0.25	1.0	0.00	0.0	-0.8	-2.72	-19.31	3.95	176.8	1.1	27.9	48.7	3.6
9.5	0.93	2.3	0.01	3.7	9.1	0.56	3.27	2.58	69.5	4.9	53.6	15.7	9.0
6.5	1.21	8.6	0.22	3.4	0.1	0.38	3.34	4.00	80.6	0.7	14.4	51.9	5.5
8.5	0.12	0.7	-0.01	2.1	0.3	0.15	1.42	3.64	95.3	4.6	28.2	7.8	6.2
7.5	2.47	6.4	0.09	1.2	0.1	0.18	1.43	1.87	106.4	2.3	49.3	37.6	6.6
5.3	0.76	5.1	-0.22	6.8	5.4	1.10	9.29	4.16	66.6	4.6	13.9	4.9	7.4
0.5	5.25	40.3	0.38	4.3	1.5	0.88	8.42	5.13	81.9	0.7	10.1	36.0	4.3
6.3	0.86	6.2	0.06	9.8	2.4	1.66	14.49	4.57	50.5	2.6	9.3	15.4	8.4
3.5	2.17	12.7	0.10	4.2	0.5	0.77	8.85	3.74	76.6	3.7	19.7	11.0	3.2
1.1	6.97	30.7	0.72	5.8	0.6	1.32	9.00	5.37	69.1	1.7	15.7	21.8	7.5
3.1	3.24	17.3	0.11	4.1	0.5	0.68	7.64	3.96	73.7	4.2	35.2	12.2	4.7
6.9	2.14	7.2	-0.24	2.8	0.3	0.51	2.85	2.70	71.3	2.9	35.8	19.2	6.2
7.4	2.55	4.5	0.19	2.6	0.3	0.33	1.16	2.93	80.3	5.4	58.1	12.5	7.3
5.4	1.92	11.8	0.31	4.6	14.1	0.92	8.05	3.17	60.5	3.6	18.2	9.9	8.0
9.4	0.24	0.6	0.00	2.6	0.2	0.42	2.08	2.95	83.4	2.1	27.1	20.5	6.1
7.5	0.10	0.6	0.30	4.4	0.6	0.68	5.65	4.14	65.3	0.9	25.0	43.4	6.9
6.2	0.56	5.3	0.00	0.9	0.2	0.14	1.76	3.28	96.7	2.6	9.3	15.1	2.7

Name	City	State	2016 Rating	2015 Rating	2014 Rating	Total Assets ($Mil)	One Year Asset Growth	Comm-ercial Loans	Cons-umer Loans	Mort-gage Loans	Secur-ities	Capital-ization Index	Lever-age Ratio	Risk-Based Capital Ratio
Home Savings Bank of Wapakoneta	Wapakoneta	OH	B-	B-	C+	35.8	-0.95	0.0	0.4	62.3	15.4	10.0	12.7	23.6
▼ Home Savings Bank, FSB	Ludlow	KY	D	C-	C-	26.5	-2.53	0.0	0.0	37.1	16.8	10.0	14.6	38.6
Home State Bank	Jefferson	IA	B	B	B-	218.7	6.15	17.1	1.9	5.2	9.9	4.8	8.4	10.9
Home State Bank	Royal	IA	A-	A-	A-	45.4	-2.23	1.6	0.6	3.1	37.1	10.0	28.7	41.8
▲ Home State Bank	Litchfield	MN	A-	B+	A-	145.7	4.79	14.2	2.6	10.6	28.6	10.0	12.0	16.1
Home State Bank, N.A.	Crystal Lake	IL	C+	C+	C+	589.1	-1.53	7.5	2.0	19.5	17.6	10.0	12.2	17.9
Home Trust & Savings Bank	Osage	IA	B+	B+	B+	219.8	3.56	6.2	1.7	14.1	30.2	8.5	10.0	15.6
▲ HomeBanc N.A.	Tampa	FL	B-	C+	C+	1006.2	2.27	0.9	0.2	40.8	21.0	6.7	8.7	14.4
▼ HOMEBANK	Palmyra	MO	B-	B+	B+	335.2	85.82	12.7	2.6	13.9	6.2	7.2	10.3	12.6
HomeBank of Arkansas	Portland	AR	B-	B-	C	72.3	-0.04	10.0	4.4	29.2	9.3	10.0	11.4	17.7
▲ HomeBank Texas	Seagoville	TX	C	C+	C	140.8	9.09	11.8	1.2	17.8	15.6	7.7	9.5	14.5
Homeland Community Bank	McMinnville	TN	C-	C	D	142.7	1.16	4.1	2.6	20.2	32.3	7.8	9.5	17.8
Homeland Federal Savings Bank	Columbia	LA	B-	B	B	206.7	22.42	9.2	12.7	27.5	5.1	8.3	10.2	13.6
HomePride Bank	Mansfield	MO	D-	E+	B	99.3	3.07	7.4	3.4	47.0	8.8	9.0	10.4	15.2
▲ HomeStar Bank and Financial Services	Manteno	IL	D-	E-	E-	347.2	2.91	2.3	2.4	19.9	29.0	3.9	5.9	11.2
Homestead Bank	Cozad	NE	A-	A-	A-	243.6	0.97	7.7	1.3	2.0	21.1	10.0	13.2	19.0
Homestead Savings Bank	Albion	MI	E-	E-	E+	67.3	-4.97	1.6	1.3	61.7	4.3	4.0	6.0	11.9
HomeStreet Bank	Seattle	WA	B-	C+	C-	6191.0	24.91	3.1	0.5	32.7	15.8	8.4	9.9	14.4
Hometown Bank	Oxford	MA	B-	B-	C	457.4	15.10	4.5	0.3	42.6	5.0	9.6	11.3	14.7
HomeTown Bank	Redwood Falls	MN	A-	A-	A-	261.3	6.89	14.6	3.1	17.4	13.3	9.0	10.7	14.1
Hometown Bank	Kent	OH	D+	D+	D	183.8	10.66	6.7	1.1	29.0	5.4	6.9	8.9	12.9
HomeTown Bank	Roanoke	VA	B	B	B-	507.7	7.35	9.7	1.5	19.4	10.7	7.5	10.6	12.9
Hometown Bank	Fond du Lac	WI	A-	B	B	272.5	29.75	20.5	0.9	9.1	6.9	10.0	12.9	17.6
HomeTown Bank of Alabama	Oneonta	AL	A	A-	A-	333.7	3.73	5.9	10.2	31.1	25.3	10.0	14.2	22.9
Hometown Bank of Corbin, Inc.	Corbin	KY	C+	C+	C	155.4	6.82	4.2	3.2	24.1	24.3	7.1	9.1	14.1
Hometown Bank of Pennsylvania	Bedford	PA	B	B	B	144.7	6.38	7.9	1.1	37.7	5.8	9.8	10.8	15.6
Hometown Bank of the Hudson Valley	Walden	NY	E-	E-	E-	123.0	1.20	2.4	0.2	56.6	2.9	2.1	5.7	9.1
Hometown Bank, N.A.	Carthage	MO	D-	D-	D	168.9	9.10	9.4	2.4	20.6	5.3	8.2	10.0	13.5
HomeTown Bank, N.A.	Galveston	TX	B+	A-	B+	583.6	9.44	4.3	2.2	16.4	37.3	8.4	9.9	17.7
Hometown Community Bank	Cyrus	MN	D+	D+	D	29.8	16.15	6.2	4.3	27.4	7.2	6.2	8.2	12.5
Hometown National Bank	LaSalle	IL	B	B	B	211.6	4.87	13.1	0.6	7.7	26.1	9.8	10.8	16.8
HomeTrust Bank	Asheville	NC	C	C	C+	2739.8	1.32	2.6	4.7	22.7	15.1	9.2	10.6	14.3
Homewood Federal Savings Bank	Baltimore	MD	B	B	B	58.1	-4.03	0.0	5.7	57.4	7.5	10.0	25.6	44.3
Hondo National Bank	Hondo	TX	B+	B+	B+	244.6	3.92	10.7	4.0	11.2	30.0	7.5	9.3	16.2
Honesdale National Bank	Honesdale	PA	A	A	A	609.2	1.24	11.5	4.2	26.8	18.2	10.0	15.1	19.8
Honor Bank	Honor	MI	C	D	C-	207.5	6.06	10.4	5.6	16.1	8.9	6.6	9.0	12.2
Hoosier Heartland State Bank	Crawfordsville	IN	B-	B-	B-	165.6	7.90	4.6	4.0	12.6	28.3	8.1	9.7	15.6
Hopeton State Bank	Hopeton	OK	C-	C-	C+	26.9	-3.56	7.9	5.3	0.0	47.0	9.5	10.7	17.1
Horatio State Bank	Horatio	AR	B+	A-	A-	178.0	12.93	4.6	19.5	32.4	11.4	9.8	10.8	17.9
Horicon Bank	Horicon	WI	B-	B-	B-	615.9	1.07	14.5	0.9	15.9	3.2	7.1	10.7	12.6
Horizon Bank	Fyffe	AL	B	B	B-	96.2	5.67	2.4	4.6	14.6	18.7	10.0	16.1	34.8
Horizon Bank	Waverly	NE	A	A	A	257.5	6.94	15.4	2.2	10.9	12.3	10.0	14.1	15.7
Horizon Bank, N.A.	Michigan City	IN	B	B	B	3308.8	27.18	5.3	5.3	17.3	22.7	8.0	9.7	13.3
▼ Horizon Bank, SSB	Austin	TX	B+	A-	B+	722.5	16.66	15.8	0.3	11.6	13.4	5.5	8.1	11.3
Horizon Community Bank	Lake Havasu City	AZ	C+	C	C	234.2	17.77	12.1	0.4	13.7	8.4	6.6	8.6	12.7
Horizon Financial Bank	Munich	ND	B+	B+	A-	136.8	-4.27	4.3	1.7	4.6	11.6	10.0	12.1	15.0
Horizon State Bank	Cameron	MO	E	E-	E+	20.4	1.98	9.7	2.6	25.5	2.2	5.5	7.5	13.5
▲ Horry County State Bank	Loris	SC	D-	E-	E-	381.3	0.76	6.1	1.3	15.5	29.3	7.6	9.4	16.3
Houghton State Bank	Red Oak	IA	B+	B+	B+	168.0	-1.47	21.5	1.0	5.0	12.7	7.1	9.1	13.9
Howard Bank	Ellicott City	MD	C+	C+	C+	1014.6	9.64	15.2	0.5	24.4	3.7	5.1	9.1	11.1
Howard State Bank	Howard	KS	C+	C+	C+	50.0	-7.78	3.0	3.6	6.5	29.4	8.6	10.1	23.8
Hoyne Savings Bank	Chicago	IL	D	D	D	265.9	-1.58	0.0	0.0	43.8	35.3	10.0	18.7	60.5
HSBC Bank USA, N.A.	McLean	VA	C-	C+	D+	203705.5	2.74	16.2	0.6	8.9	26.8	9.9	11.0	20.8
HSBC Trust Co. (Delaware), N.A.	Wilmington	DE	U	U	U	54.6	0.28	0.0	0.0	0.0	0.0	0.0	98.5	0.0
Huntingdon Savings Bank	Huntingdon	PA	B-	B-	C+	18.0	9.62	0.0	0.0	65.7	0.0	10.0	18.3	24.2
▲ Huntingdon Valley Bank	Huntingdon Valley	PA	C	D+	D	179.0	7.72	0.3	0.0	57.0	18.9	5.4	7.4	12.9
Huntington Federal Savings Bank	Huntington	WV	B	B	B	546.7	0.97	0.0	0.2	31.7	57.6	10.0	15.3	47.4
Huntington National Bank	Columbus	OH	B-	B-	B-	100416.3	43.42	19.7	15.4	10.4	21.3	7.3	10.3	12.8
Huntington State Bank	Huntington	TX	C	D+	C+	221.3	-4.82	11.7	3.1	15.1	9.3	9.6	10.7	17.5
Huron Community Bank	East Tawas	MI	B	B-	C+	206.2	0.16	11.5	0.8	13.0	13.5	10.0	11.8	16.6

Asset Quality Index	Adjusted Non-Performing Loans as a % of Total Loans	as a % of Capital	Net Charge-Offs Avg Loans	Profitability Index	Net Income ($Mil)	Return on Assets (R.O.A.)	Return on Equity (R.O.E.)	Net Interest Spread	Overhead Efficiency Ratio	Liquidity Index	Liquidity Ratio	Hot Money Ratio	Stability Index
9.9	0.00	0.0	0.00	3.1	0.1	0.46	3.61	3.80	84.4	3.2	22.8	13.7	6.8
7.9	1.95	6.6	0.70	0.0	-0.2	-1.06	-7.07	3.00	101.9	2.7	50.4	30.0	6.4
6.3	0.42	3.9	0.00	6.2	2.3	1.42	17.33	3.60	56.4	1.4	9.3	24.2	6.1
7.6	0.07	0.2	0.00	8.6	0.8	2.13	7.50	3.82	40.9	5.5	49.9	8.6	9.0
8.7	0.23	1.0	-0.01	5.4	1.4	1.34	10.93	3.95	70.9	2.7	20.2	16.2	8.2
4.7	2.62	13.5	0.23	2.9	2.3	0.51	4.22	3.75	87.4	4.1	20.0	8.8	6.4
8.0	0.36	2.1	0.00	5.7	2.3	1.42	14.03	2.79	43.5	3.4	30.3	14.8	6.0
8.8	0.38	3.0	0.01	4.1	5.3	0.70	8.62	2.63	61.9	2.0	21.8	11.8	5.5
3.7	1.71	12.9	0.01	5.9	3.4	1.36	13.24	4.04	67.3	3.0	9.2	13.2	7.2
3.5	3.06	18.2	0.21	3.3	0.2	0.41	3.71	4.44	85.1	0.8	19.3	47.5	5.4
3.7	1.86	12.0	0.00	5.5	1.4	1.32	13.61	4.14	66.4	4.7	30.7	7.6	5.5
4.4	2.34	10.7	-0.12	1.8	0.3	0.26	2.71	3.22	88.4	3.0	43.3	23.1	4.8
3.6	1.46	10.5	0.25	8.9	2.6	1.87	17.95	5.56	66.1	0.7	10.1	39.2	7.6
0.2	10.70	74.5	0.06	4.2	0.7	0.86	8.52	3.93	78.6	1.0	5.2	28.7	6.3
2.3	2.65	21.8	0.36	3.2	2.3	0.88	15.66	3.35	88.6	4.9	27.5	5.3	1.0
5.0	1.58	7.6	-0.23	7.4	3.4	1.82	13.68	4.14	60.0	4.5	15.9	5.8	8.0
1.7	4.17	46.6	0.24	0.0	-0.6	-1.21	-18.71	3.58	127.4	4.6	17.9	4.8	1.0
4.4	1.29	9.5	-0.03	7.5	57.6	1.37	13.00	3.55	76.6	2.2	15.9	13.3	8.1
4.4	0.99	7.3	0.00	3.7	1.6	0.70	6.33	3.69	66.5	1.5	10.3	23.4	6.6
6.8	0.05	0.3	-0.04	8.9	2.7	1.44	11.66	4.76	58.6	4.7	13.2	3.7	7.9
1.2	4.06	32.4	0.06	3.4	0.7	0.51	5.55	3.97	82.4	1.7	13.4	20.5	3.9
5.6	0.72	5.0	0.25	4.1	2.3	0.64	5.96	3.66	68.5	1.5	15.4	24.3	6.6
5.9	0.92	5.0	0.03	7.5	2.5	1.20	9.62	3.73	56.1	4.2	18.1	4.7	8.0
5.9	1.45	6.4	0.16	9.3	3.8	1.53	11.60	4.72	59.7	1.8	15.4	20.3	7.9
4.9	1.33	9.0	0.07	3.3	0.6	0.57	6.05	4.03	84.4	4.1	23.2	8.8	4.4
5.6	0.91	6.5	0.03	4.4	0.7	0.71	6.53	3.64	67.4	2.1	16.2	18.7	6.6
0.3	5.39	65.0	0.19	0.4	-0.3	-0.37	-5.87	3.90	106.9	2.9	7.8	13.7	2.4
5.6	1.00	7.0	0.11	0.4	-0.3	-0.21	-2.09	3.67	104.9	2.0	8.4	18.3	5.1
5.2	2.28	12.4	0.02	6.0	4.6	1.09	10.58	3.82	61.3	3.0	36.5	18.9	7.6
5.8	0.38	3.4	0.00	4.1	0.2	0.66	8.07	3.97	73.9	2.0	11.0	18.8	2.9
4.9	1.33	6.7	-0.07	5.0	1.5	0.97	8.69	3.71	69.6	5.5	35.7	4.9	6.7
5.0	1.75	10.7	0.09	3.2	10.3	0.50	4.21	3.39	79.0	4.1	20.1	9.1	7.8
7.3	1.40	3.7	0.15	3.8	0.2	0.47	1.87	3.50	72.2	2.5	38.1	26.1	6.6
8.6	0.00	0.0	0.06	5.2	2.2	1.22	12.32	3.77	65.7	3.2	40.7	19.3	6.1
7.7	0.59	2.7	0.08	6.4	5.6	1.24	8.12	4.00	59.6	3.3	16.2	12.8	9.5
4.0	1.17	9.2	0.15	3.1	0.6	0.40	4.21	4.58	87.8	4.7	19.2	4.8	3.6
4.9	1.70	9.8	0.07	4.3	0.9	0.75	7.71	4.06	74.5	4.8	31.4	7.7	5.8
8.6	0.02	0.1	-0.04	2.2	0.1	0.57	4.66	3.63	96.2	2.7	60.8	34.6	6.7
4.9	0.79	5.0	0.28	9.0	1.9	1.47	13.52	4.49	42.3	0.7	17.7	46.0	6.8
4.5	0.96	7.4	0.10	6.1	6.3	1.39	12.63	4.05	68.7	3.6	5.2	8.5	8.5
7.4	1.47	3.8	0.01	3.8	0.5	0.68	4.25	3.90	72.9	4.5	49.1	14.2	6.9
8.4	0.00	0.0	0.00	9.5	3.8	2.06	17.36	4.52	45.4	2.1	22.9	19.4	8.8
5.4	0.78	5.4	0.09	5.0	19.7	0.93	8.49	3.50	70.7	3.9	18.0	9.8	8.4
4.8	0.75	6.6	0.04	9.1	8.8	1.72	20.59	4.55	56.2	4.1	18.8	5.2	7.5
4.8	1.11	8.3	0.03	3.6	1.2	0.69	8.00	4.06	81.3	1.8	19.9	21.1	4.1
6.5	0.44	2.7	0.00	5.4	1.0	0.96	8.16	4.01	62.9	3.3	5.1	7.7	7.1
2.9	2.17	17.9	0.09	2.5	0.1	0.45	6.01	4.29	91.2	4.8	30.5	5.1	0.7
2.3	5.42	27.6	3.22	0.1	-9.1	-3.20	-52.06	2.91	433.5	1.3	28.5	34.3	0.4
6.8	0.35	2.4	0.00	5.2	1.2	0.90	7.79	3.48	59.3	4.5	21.7	6.0	7.2
5.5	0.82	7.5	0.09	5.0	4.8	0.67	7.36	3.83	76.8	1.6	8.9	21.3	5.0
7.7	0.28	1.0	0.00	3.5	0.3	0.77	7.79	3.30	76.8	5.8	38.3	4.1	5.3
7.9	1.96	4.8	-0.05	0.4	-0.3	-0.13	-0.70	2.34	118.4	4.2	60.4	19.2	5.1
5.9	2.96	9.5	0.35	2.0	222.4	0.15	1.23	1.37	78.5	3.8	60.5	19.6	7.7
10.0	na	0.0	na	4.3	0.3	0.76	0.77	0.66	59.9	4.0	na	0.0	5.4
7.5	1.61	6.1	0.00	3.7	0.1	0.59	3.14	3.00	70.9	1.6	35.4	30.8	7.9
5.8	1.09	9.4	0.04	3.7	0.9	0.71	9.70	2.90	81.2	3.4	21.6	12.5	2.6
8.1	2.41	5.8	0.01	4.0	2.6	0.63	4.30	2.57	59.9	4.1	72.5	22.9	7.9
3.7	1.23	9.2	0.20	5.1	554.4	0.97	10.75	3.17	64.7	5.2	19.1	1.7	8.1
5.3	0.90	4.7	-0.15	3.2	0.7	0.39	3.75	4.08	92.9	4.0	24.9	10.0	5.0
6.4	0.93	5.3	-0.12	4.5	1.2	0.84	6.98	3.87	71.8	4.6	20.3	5.7	6.2

Name	City	State	2015 Rating	2014 Rating	Rating	Total Assets ($Mil)	One Year Asset Growth	Commercial Loans	Consumer Loans	Mortgage Loans	Securities	Capitalization Index	Leverage Ratio	Risk-Based Capital Ratio
Huron National Bank	Rogers City	MI	B-	B-	B	65.1	4.99	6.1	8.1	37.2	5.9	10.0	14.9	16.8
Huron Valley State Bank	Milford	MI	B-	B-	B-	125.5	11.46	14.2	0.7	3.6	2.1	6.3	9.8	12.0
Hustisford State Bank	Hustisford	WI	B+	B+	B+	53.6	-2.34	3.5	2.3	56.7	11.5	10.0	18.2	29.2
Hyden Citizens Bank	Hyden	KY	B-	B-	B-	128.1	-1.25	5.8	4.0	26.3	34.2	7.1	9.1	15.8
▲ Hyperion Bank	Philadelphia	PA	D+	D	E+	84.0	9.84	8.8	0.0	27.2	4.2	4.2	7.3	10.6
iAB Financial Bank	Fort Wayne	IN	B-	B-	B	1081.4	4.43	9.7	0.5	10.8	20.3	9.3	10.5	14.6
▼ IBERIABANK	Lafayette	LA	C+	B-	B-	20717.8	6.52	17.4	3.2	12.2	14.4	5.6	9.4	11.4
Iberville Bank	Plaquemine	LA	C	C	C-	257.8	3.90	1.3	1.3	13.3	32.0	8.0	9.7	15.3
▲ Icon Bank of Texas, N.A.	Houston	TX	C	B-	B	782.4	8.43	17.0	1.8	11.0	0.2	5.2	8.6	11.1
Idabel National Bank	Idabel	OK	B+	B+	B+	122.0	-2.19	6.0	5.1	19.3	42.7	7.3	9.2	18.9
Idaho First Bank	McCall	ID	D+	C+	D	141.0	12.33	18.5	3.6	18.5	5.5	6.9	9.3	12.5
Idaho Independent Bank	Coeur D'Alene	ID	C+	C+	C	616.9	10.24	6.4	1.9	4.6	12.1	9.2	10.4	15.9
▲ Idaho Trust Bank	Boise	ID	B+	B	B+	84.3	0.52	20.0	1.1	1.6	1.1	10.0	18.3	27.4
Illini Bank	Springfield	IL	C-	C	C-	284.3	1.99	6.4	0.5	7.6	30.1	6.8	8.8	13.5
Illini State Bank	Oglesby	IL	B-	B-	B-	118.6	9.99	3.7	1.0	9.3	48.9	10.0	13.1	24.8
Illinois Bank & Trust	Rockford	IL	B-	B-	C+	748.8	-2.65	16.2	1.4	8.4	32.2	6.7	8.9	12.3
Illinois National Bank	Springfield	IL	C+	C+	C+	860.9	21.06	11.6	0.3	8.0	14.0	5.6	7.9	11.5
▲ Illinois-Service Federal S&L Assn.	Chicago	IL	D-	E-	E-	105.4	1.50	0.0	1.3	24.4	19.4	7.1	9.1	24.9
▼ Impact Bank	Wellington	KS	B	B+	B-	129.7	3.09	11.1	3.3	5.9	24.7	9.9	10.9	16.5
▼ Incommons Bank, N.A.	Mexia	TX	B	B+	B+	150.7	30.14	7.5	5.1	30.1	16.6	7.1	9.1	14.7
Independence Bank	Havre	MT	A	A	A	625.5	6.83	7.2	2.4	7.0	9.8	10.0	13.2	16.3
Independence Bank	Independence	OH	B	B	B	194.1	10.02	18.1	1.1	4.7	18.8	10.0	11.5	22.8
▼ Independence Bank	East Greenwich	RI	C+	B-	B	36.4	-3.40	54.4	0.6	11.2	0.0	10.0	21.0	31.9
Independence Bank of Kentucky	Owensboro	KY	A-	A-	A-	1934.5	11.71	5.1	0.6	15.6	41.9	5.5	7.5	12.2
Independence National Bank	Greenville	SC	D	D-	D+	93.3	-5.13	17.6	1.9	9.6	11.0	8.1	10.0	13.4
▼ Independence State Bank	Independence	WI	D	D+	D+	63.8	-6.10	9.0	1.3	9.4	12.3	6.8	8.8	13.2
Independence Trust Co.	Franklin	TN	U	U	U	4.2	-5.15	0.0	0.0	0.0	62.8	10.0	85.1	225.8
Independent Bank	Grand Rapids	MI	C+	C	C-	2526.8	6.01	7.8	10.6	20.4	23.9	8.6	10.1	15.4
▲ Independent Bank	Memphis	TN	C+	C	C	1018.1	8.28	8.6	53.6	2.0	0.9	4.7	9.8	10.9
Independent Bank	McKinney	TX	B+	B+	B+	5664.7	26.59	9.5	0.5	11.1	4.7	5.1	9.4	11.1
Independent Farmers Bank	Maysville	MO	B	B	B	116.6	7.90	4.6	3.0	9.3	48.4	6.9	8.9	17.3
Indiana First Savings Bank	Indiana	PA	B-	B-	B-	354.1	7.37	6.8	0.8	59.6	3.7	8.5	10.0	15.0
Indus American Bank	Edison	NJ	D	E+	D+	235.1	-6.21	9.2	0.2	7.8	12.2	5.8	8.0	11.6
▲ Industrial & Commerc. Bank of China (USA	New York	NY	C+	C-	D+	2136.7	35.31	22.0	0.0	5.0	1.0	10.0	12.7	15.1
Industrial Bank	Washington	DC	C-	D+	D+	388.5	4.23	6.4	0.3	26.1	17.6	7.7	9.5	14.9
Industrial State Bank	Kansas City	KS	B+	B+	B	139.1	-2.43	11.0	1.6	2.3	25.0	10.0	26.7	32.4
Industry State Bank	Industry	TX	A	A	A-	723.0	8.83	3.8	1.3	4.8	72.8	9.6	10.8	27.2
Inez Deposit Bank	Inez	KY	C	C	C	152.5	0.15	1.0	4.0	22.9	49.4	10.0	12.1	33.0
Inland Bank and Trust	Oak Brook	IL	B-	C+	C-	1039.7	-4.11	17.9	0.2	9.6	23.0	10.0	12.3	16.8
Inland Northwest Bank	Spokane	WA	B-	B-	C+	647.0	38.34	10.8	1.2	7.7	4.6	7.6	11.0	13.0
InsBank	Nashville	TN	B-	B	B	361.5	14.74	23.2	1.4	10.4	6.0	7.1	11.0	12.6
Insignia Bank	Sarasota	FL	C+	C+	B-	257.2	24.72	0.6	0.5	30.6	13.0	7.1	9.0	13.5
▲ INSOUTH Bank	Brownsville	TN	B-	C	C-	288.1	3.66	11.7	4.0	21.1	11.7	7.6	9.4	13.1
Institution for Savings	Newburyport	MA	C+	B-	B	2745.7	15.98	0.5	0.1	57.0	16.0	8.1	9.7	13.4
Integrity Bank & Trust	Monument	CO	B-	B-	B-	169.6	11.72	5.5	0.7	13.6	9.4	6.2	8.3	12.1
▲ Integrity Bank Plus	Wabasso	MN	C+	E+	B-	55.5	-5.75	3.3	1.1	6.1	10.7	10.0	11.5	16.7
Integrity Bank, SSB	Houston	TX	A-	A-	B+	726.5	16.44	18.6	0.9	9.5	3.4	7.4	10.0	12.8
▲ Integrity First Bank	Wausau	WI	B+	B	C+	82.6	5.17	21.3	0.3	24.6	4.6	10.0	12.0	15.5
Integrity First Bank, N.A.	Mountain Home	AR	B	B+	B+	432.4	1.46	3.4	2.0	32.3	14.5	9.1	10.4	14.6
▲ Inter National Bank	McAllen	TX	B+	B	B-	1708.3	-4.38	4.9	0.4	6.6	20.6	10.0	16.2	24.3
Interamerican Bank, A FSB	Miami	FL	D	D	D-	206.8	-5.88	0.7	0.4	31.2	0.0	10.0	12.6	19.3
Interaudi Bank	New York	NY	C+	C+	C+	1728.3	4.55	6.9	0.3	19.7	23.1	5.1	7.1	16.6
▼ InterBank	Oklahoma City	OK	C	C+	C+	2889.4	0.56	15.7	1.1	8.5	1.3	6.4	11.9	12.1
Intercity State Bank	Schofield	WI	A-	A-	A-	168.0	4.69	6.4	1.3	17.9	17.2	10.0	20.4	28.3
Intercontinental Bank	West Miami	FL	C+	C+	C+	143.3	-13.10	2.4	0.8	11.6	44.2	10.0	13.3	24.0
Intercredit Bank, NA	Miami	FL	C	C-	D-	348.6	0.07	9.7	2.5	23.4	15.3	9.1	10.4	15.0
International Bank	Raton	NM	B	B	C+	301.8	1.32	6.5	0.5	8.8	38.7	10.0	14.2	23.5
International Bank of Amherst	Amherst	WI	A-	A-	A-	60.6	6.68	8.0	1.4	15.7	34.5	10.0	14.2	27.1
International Bank of Chicago	Chicago	IL	B	B-	C-	517.1	-4.43	8.5	1.4	11.6	29.9	10.0	13.8	23.4
International Bank of Commerce	Brownsville	TX	A	A	A	975.0	-4.54	8.5	0.6	4.3	40.2	10.0	15.8	27.0

Asset Quality Index	Adjusted Non-Performing Loans as a % of Total Loans	as a % of Capital	Net Charge-Offs Avg Loans	Profitability Index	Net Income ($Mil)	Return on Assets (R.O.A.)	Return on Equity (R.O.E.)	Net Interest Spread	Overhead Efficiency Ratio	Liquidity Index	Liquidity Ratio	Hot Money Ratio	Stability Index
3.6	4.63	20.7	0.25	7.3	0.6	1.28	8.95	4.86	48.0	3.7	32.4	13.8	7.3
4.5	0.42	3.5	0.09	5.3	0.8	0.90	9.11	4.23	66.1	1.7	9.3	20.0	5.8
6.4	1.73	7.1	-0.01	7.2	0.5	1.16	6.55	4.75	58.4	3.3	16.8	12.4	7.6
5.5	1.42	8.6	0.20	4.2	1.0	0.99	10.11	4.10	76.2	2.2	14.5	17.9	5.4
3.6	1.68	16.6	0.01	3.9	0.5	0.71	9.85	4.51	86.4	0.7	15.1	43.5	3.1
6.3	0.78	4.8	0.00	4.3	7.2	0.90	7.53	3.41	68.4	4.4	24.0	10.0	9.0
3.2	1.94	14.8	0.24	5.3	145.0	0.97	7.71	3.64	60.9	3.8	15.8	6.8	9.5
4.5	2.27	12.7	0.02	3.1	1.1	0.58	5.86	3.87	86.6	4.9	27.4	5.2	4.9
3.2	1.29	11.1	0.80	4.4	3.1	0.54	6.07	4.99	70.6	1.2	13.9	28.2	5.6
8.8	0.06	0.3	0.16	6.5	1.5	1.57	16.46	3.55	60.0	2.2	35.7	27.9	8.2
4.2	1.36	11.2	0.17	1.2	-0.2	-0.22	-1.79	3.91	99.8	0.6	12.1	45.8	6.1
8.5	0.14	0.6	-0.09	3.3	3.0	0.69	6.14	3.45	81.9	6.4	41.8	1.2	5.9
6.6	1.56	5.1	0.00	5.3	0.9	1.47	6.56	2.91	85.0	4.0	37.8	14.1	7.0
3.6	2.84	15.9	2.41	1.5	0.1	0.05	0.56	3.32	77.4	5.2	28.8	3.9	4.2
5.6	2.61	8.0	0.01	3.4	0.6	0.75	4.46	2.89	70.6	4.1	49.4	6.8	7.8
5.6	0.74	4.8	-0.10	5.4	6.6	1.18	13.79	3.65	68.2	4.9	21.6	3.5	5.1
4.9	0.90	6.9	-0.02	3.8	6.1	0.95	11.94	3.04	77.1	4.3	18.7	6.6	5.1
1.7	11.83	45.1	1.74	0.0	-2.3	-2.94	-48.88	2.81	222.4	5.9	51.2	7.4	2.5
5.8	0.66	3.5	0.00	3.9	0.9	0.89	8.20	3.56	74.6	1.5	17.0	24.8	7.0
7.1	0.55	4.0	0.10	3.7	0.6	0.56	5.50	4.91	85.1	3.7	17.4	10.5	5.8
6.5	0.58	3.6	0.05	9.9	7.8	1.69	12.89	4.58	37.4	0.9	4.3	29.7	10.0
5.2	2.77	11.1	0.75	3.6	1.0	0.71	6.13	3.17	59.7	2.0	36.0	31.1	6.0
2.0	8.62	23.7	0.63	9.7	1.2	4.17	19.86	6.08	55.0	2.4	22.4	17.8	6.3
9.0	0.21	1.4	0.12	7.2	22.7	1.61	21.52	4.12	57.1	3.4	8.0	6.1	7.9
5.1	0.52	3.3	0.45	0.4	-0.4	-0.61	-5.87	4.01	118.1	1.6	24.8	26.1	3.3
0.8	5.90	43.4	0.03	2.7	0.3	0.53	5.99	3.81	87.9	3.0	19.3	14.3	3.8
10.0	na	0.0	na	9.5	0.1	3.12	3.60	1.99	87.7	5.0	480.1	100.0	5.5
3.6	2.86	17.4	-0.08	5.2	17.6	0.96	9.19	3.63	73.1	4.6	31.9	12.2	8.3
3.5	0.66	5.4	0.77	5.9	7.1	0.95	8.77	4.68	62.0	1.1	4.8	27.5	9.3
6.0	0.21	1.7	0.15	6.5	46.2	1.14	8.47	4.12	50.9	2.4	14.0	17.2	9.7
5.5	1.08	5.4	-0.03	5.5	1.0	1.12	11.35	4.27	61.6	3.7	34.1	14.4	6.0
5.4	1.06	8.7	0.01	3.9	1.4	0.54	5.34	3.67	74.1	1.8	3.7	18.9	6.2
0.6	4.26	33.6	-0.01	0.6	-0.2	-0.12	-1.50	3.44	101.1	0.9	21.9	40.9	2.3
6.3	0.28	1.8	0.00	2.7	5.2	0.36	2.17	2.87	77.6	0.9	19.6	48.5	8.2
2.0	3.88	26.8	0.13	3.1	1.0	0.32	3.19	4.39	88.5	1.2	11.9	26.6	5.5
6.4	2.42	5.4	0.01	5.8	1.1	1.03	3.93	4.29	67.1	5.9	49.3	7.1	8.5
9.7	0.03	0.1	-0.01	7.9	8.9	1.72	13.94	3.49	47.4	3.3	72.5	37.8	8.1
5.9	4.29	11.2	0.32	2.0	0.2	0.17	1.41	2.85	93.7	3.9	49.2	17.8	6.0
4.0	2.31	11.8	1.27	3.2	3.2	0.41	3.28	3.35	72.4	2.7	22.5	17.8	6.4
5.1	0.63	4.1	0.02	5.4	4.1	0.89	7.48	4.76	73.0	3.0	23.0	14.6	6.3
6.1	0.28	2.1	0.07	4.9	2.0	0.81	7.86	3.39	65.6	0.5	4.4	45.0	6.2
8.9	0.00	0.0	-0.02	3.5	1.0	0.56	5.92	3.44	76.4	3.4	22.9	12.9	5.9
4.4	1.19	9.1	0.56	4.3	1.6	0.73	7.08	4.40	76.6	2.5	10.6	15.8	4.9
9.2	0.28	2.1	0.00	3.3	18.9	0.95	9.53	2.20	72.7	1.0	20.2	40.3	8.6
5.2	1.08	8.1	0.12	6.0	1.5	1.16	14.24	4.22	71.8	3.5	22.0	11.6	4.9
3.3	0.63	3.6	-0.33	5.4	0.5	1.15	9.78	5.90	67.5	4.0	10.3	8.1	7.6
8.2	0.00	0.0	0.00	6.4	5.0	0.99	9.64	4.06	52.8	2.9	16.2	12.4	6.8
8.1	0.00	0.0	-0.02	5.1	0.6	0.93	6.18	4.46	67.6	1.8	10.1	15.3	6.9
8.0	0.11	0.7	0.04	4.6	2.7	0.84	6.60	3.85	72.8	4.1	4.2	6.7	7.7
5.1	0.65	2.5	0.03	5.1	13.0	0.97	3.79	3.68	65.4	1.2	13.5	29.4	8.9
0.3	10.19	51.9	-0.19	3.1	0.6	0.40	3.24	3.77	93.9	4.3	22.4	7.6	5.5
6.0	2.18	13.2	0.12	4.2	9.1	0.69	10.16	2.19	52.4	3.7	57.8	25.8	5.1
2.6	1.46	10.8	0.12	9.9	51.0	2.37	16.33	4.53	46.4	2.7	3.7	14.4	10.0
7.0	1.07	3.8	-0.01	7.4	1.6	1.26	6.46	3.34	46.0	3.7	26.8	12.3	7.7
9.5	0.00	0.0	0.03	2.7	0.5	0.45	3.53	2.27	74.1	2.9	61.8	48.5	5.6
3.7	0.85	5.9	0.01	3.1	1.6	0.62	6.00	3.55	85.6	1.1	15.9	28.6	4.5
5.5	2.53	8.5	0.53	4.8	1.9	0.86	6.18	3.92	69.5	3.1	24.9	14.4	6.7
9.3	0.47	1.8	0.00	5.8	0.6	1.37	9.77	4.17	65.4	5.8	44.4	5.8	8.2
4.5	2.85	12.3	0.10	8.8	9.6	2.54	18.22	4.38	42.1	1.9	36.1	24.5	8.0
6.8	2.59	7.3	0.14	8.9	11.0	1.47	8.92	3.51	49.9	2.6	43.4	28.9	9.2

Name	City	State	2015 Rating	2014 Rating	Total Assets ($Mil)	One Year Asset Growth	Commercial Loans	Consumer Loans	Mortgage Loans	Securities	Capitalization Index	Leverage Ratio	Risk-Based Capital Ratio
International Bank of Commerce	Laredo	TX	A	A	A-	9855.9	-0.04	8.6	0.6	8.5	34.3	10.0	12.4	17.4
International Bank of Commerce	Zapata	TX	A	A	A-	495.5	-7.13	3.8	1.4	13.5	62.8	10.0	13.4	34.5
International City Bank, N.A.	Long Beach	CA	A-	A-	A-	181.5	28.94	6.3	0.0	6.2	25.9	10.0	11.0	16.9
▲ International Finance Bank	Miami	FL	D+	D	D	354.5	14.26	20.9	1.0	35.2	8.0	8.0	9.7	15.6
Interstate Bank, SSB	Perryton	TX	B-	B-	B-	172.4	-3.55	14.8	6.2	13.1	25.1	8.6	10.0	14.3
Interstate Federal S&L Assn. of McGregor	McGregor	IA	C	C-	D+	7.9	-1.96	0.0	0.3	76.0	0.1	10.0	20.3	47.4
Intracoastal Bank	Palm Coast	FL	B+	B+	B+	294.0	11.31	4.7	0.2	2.2	31.9	6.5	8.6	12.1
INTRUST Bank, N.A.	Wichita	KS	B	B-	B-	4803.0	6.39	20.5	4.9	3.4	25.4	6.6	8.6	12.4
Investar Bank	Baton Rouge	LA	B	B	C+	1152.5	23.12	6.7	11.0	13.6	14.8	6.2	9.9	11.9
Investment Savings Bank	Altoona	PA	C+	B-	B-	107.9	-2.78	1.1	1.0	44.0	41.0	10.0	18.7	39.6
Investors Bank	Short Hills	NJ	B+	B+	B	22534.9	10.88	4.9	0.8	22.2	15.0	10.0	12.3	16.3
Investors Community Bank	Chillicothe	MO	B+	B+	A-	68.5	0.70	1.3	2.9	21.3	57.5	10.0	12.8	30.7
Investors Community Bank	Manitowoc	WI	C	B-	B	1209.8	43.30	6.0	0.0	2.2	10.3	8.0	11.2	13.3
InvesTrust, N.A.	Oklahoma City	OK	U	U	U	4.5	3.30	0.0	0.0	0.0	81.3	10.0	85.0	100.2
Inwood National Bank	Dallas	TX	A-	A	A+	2361.8	10.02	5.0	0.4	13.7	20.7	7.1	9.1	13.3
▲ Ion Bank	Naugatuck	CT	C+	C-	C	1183.5	7.78	5.7	11.0	32.9	7.4	7.4	9.3	13.0
Iowa Falls State Bank	Iowa Falls	IA	B	B+	B	139.0	11.48	11.7	2.3	9.3	31.8	8.9	10.2	14.7
▼ Iowa Prairie Bank	Brunsville	IA	C-	C	D+	68.5	0.00	9.6	2.8	2.3	41.0	5.9	7.9	13.6
Iowa Savings Bank	Carroll	IA	B	B	B-	195.9	6.15	15.5	0.9	4.2	30.9	6.4	8.4	13.0
▲ Iowa State Bank	Algona	IA	A-	B+	B+	290.0	1.41	7.8	2.0	10.6	19.4	10.0	11.1	15.2
Iowa State Bank	Clarksville	IA	C	B-	C+	340.1	5.92	11.5	0.7	3.2	18.7	5.7	8.6	11.5
Iowa State Bank	Des Moines	IA	A+	A+	A	373.8	1.66	3.9	0.4	11.0	53.2	10.0	16.1	27.0
Iowa State Bank	Hull	IA	A-	A-	A-	551.5	5.26	10.8	1.3	5.4	19.5	10.0	12.8	15.0
Iowa State Bank	Sac City	IA	B	B	B-	119.5	-1.28	9.2	4.2	20.1	13.8	9.7	10.8	16.3
▼ Iowa State Bank	Wapello	IA	C	C+	B	78.7	11.17	7.4	10.4	19.4	0.9	10.0	14.2	16.7
Iowa State Bank and Trust Co.	Fairfield	IA	B-	C	C+	116.9	-2.51	9.0	2.0	21.6	8.4	9.8	10.9	15.2
Iowa State Savings Bank	Creston	IA	D	C+	C+	234.1	2.72	5.0	2.7	13.3	16.4	4.2	7.1	10.6
Iowa State Savings Bank	Knoxville	IA	B-	B-	B-	152.3	10.61	9.6	5.2	4.6	27.0	6.4	8.4	13.8
Iowa Trust & Savings Bank	Emmetsburg	IA	A-	A-	B+	185.8	5.16	6.5	0.8	9.6	20.6	9.1	10.7	14.2
Iowa Trust and Savings Bank	Centerville	IA	A-	A-	A-	175.0	3.13	4.1	2.0	7.4	44.1	9.1	10.4	15.1
▲ Iowa-Nebraska State Bank	South Sioux City	NE	C+	C-	C	200.2	-5.63	6.5	3.7	14.1	20.9	8.8	10.4	14.0
Ipava State Bank	Ipava	IL	B+	B+	B+	110.8	5.41	9.2	3.3	10.6	12.8	7.9	9.6	13.8
Ipswich State Bank	Ipswich	SD	B	B	B	52.3	0.19	7.3	1.3	0.0	22.3	10.0	14.9	21.2
Ireland Bank	Malad City	ID	B-	B-	C	215.4	1.75	15.7	1.1	4.9	22.4	9.0	10.3	15.0
Iron Workers Savings Bank	Aston	PA	C	C	C	179.2	-0.52	0.2	0.0	47.3	6.9	7.1	9.1	13.8
▲ Iroquois Farmers State Bank	Iroquois	IL	B-	C+	C+	84.1	-1.36	5.3	3.6	12.4	18.1	10.0	11.9	17.8
Iroquois Federal S&L Assn.	Watseka	IL	B	B	B	588.5	5.54	7.4	1.6	24.9	19.3	10.0	11.4	16.7
Isabella Bank	Mount Pleasant	MI	B	B-	B-	1654.8	5.67	6.8	2.5	15.5	34.1	6.0	8.0	12.3
Islanders Bank	Friday Harbor	WA	A-	A-	A-	280.4	4.70	3.6	1.4	16.5	15.7	10.0	13.0	20.4
Israel Discount Bank of New York	New York	NY	C+	C+	C	9361.2	-5.12	27.7	1.2	0.2	29.2	7.6	9.4	13.7
Itasca Bank & Trust Co.	Itasca	IL	B-	B-	C+	483.8	6.17	20.1	0.3	11.1	21.5	7.6	9.5	13.0
ITS Bank	Johnston	IA	U	U	U	6.9	4.92	0.0	0.0	0.0	7.3	10.0	92.8	443.8
Iuka State Bank	Salem	IL	C-	D+	C-	88.1	14.28	12.9	6.9	16.3	1.6	5.2	8.2	11.1
▲ Ixonia Bank	Ixonia	WI	B-	D+	D+	303.4	8.78	12.2	0.2	5.1	29.7	10.0	11.9	18.0
Jacksboro National Bank	Jacksboro	TX	B	B	B	242.1	-6.80	6.0	2.4	13.4	44.1	8.7	10.1	19.1
Jackson County Bank	Seymour	IN	B-	B-	B-	500.1	2.60	2.9	0.8	19.1	20.2	7.8	9.6	14.9
Jackson County Bank	McKee	KY	A	A	A	129.0	0.08	2.2	10.8	21.0	38.3	10.0	26.7	50.1
Jackson County Bank	Black River Falls	WI	A-	A	A-	235.7	8.14	1.5	3.0	15.8	13.8	8.4	10.6	13.7
Jackson Federal S&L Assn.	Jackson	MN	B	B	B	38.6	-1.42	5.6	3.4	27.6	40.8	10.0	22.0	42.1
Jackson Parish Bank	Jonesboro	LA	C+	C+	B-	67.7	-1.40	4.6	5.6	11.4	59.8	10.0	13.0	46.8
Jackson Savings Bank, SSB	Sylva	NC	C+	C+	C+	34.3	2.48	0.0	0.9	59.8	0.0	10.0	19.1	35.9
Jacksonville Savings Bank	Jacksonville	IL	A-	A-	A-	330.7	8.00	6.9	4.2	15.8	28.2	10.0	13.2	20.2
James Polk Stone Community Bank	Portales	NM	B	B	B	209.2	3.83	5.0	5.6	22.2	25.2	9.3	10.5	19.8
▲ Jamestown State Bank	Jamestown	KS	C-	C-	C-	18.4	0.91	0.6	1.8	1.3	67.1	10.0	15.9	41.2
Janesville State Bank	Janesville	MN	A-	A-	A-	73.2	9.49	1.1	1.9	17.7	18.6	10.0	11.8	18.4
Jarrettsville Federal S&L Assn.	Jarrettsville	MD	C	C+	B-	118.4	5.39	0.0	0.1	63.3	11.3	10.0	13.5	28.7
JD Bank	Jennings	LA	B-	B	B	833.3	3.33	10.3	5.0	20.0	13.3	6.7	8.8	12.3
Jeff Bank	Jeffersonville	NY	B	B	B	481.5	3.43	5.6	0.7	21.0	24.9	9.8	10.9	18.3
Jefferson Bank	Greenville	MS	A-	A-	A-	121.3	0.59	18.0	0.5	0.9	21.7	10.0	15.2	19.9
Jefferson Bank	San Antonio	TX	B+	B+	B+	1636.0	8.12	6.8	1.2	19.7	29.4	6.9	8.9	13.5

Asset Quality Index	Adjusted Non-Performing Loans		Net Charge-Offs Avg Loans	Profitability Index	Net Income ($Mil)	Return on Assets (R.O.A.)	Return on Equity (R.O.E.)	Net Interest Spread	Overhead Efficiency Ratio	Liquidity Index	Liquidity Ratio	Hot Money Ratio	Stability Index
	as a % of Total Loans	as a % of Capital											
7.0	0.59	2.5	0.50	6.2	77.4	1.07	7.12	3.48	58.2	3.4	25.9	15.9	9.3
8.5	2.20	4.3	0.51	5.8	3.3	0.85	5.79	2.79	63.1	2.4	37.2	26.2	8.4
7.8	0.00	0.0	-0.27	5.6	1.2	0.93	8.21	4.35	74.4	1.9	26.1	23.0	7.9
2.6	2.54	18.6	0.03	1.7	0.6	0.25	2.03	4.06	92.6	2.0	18.5	19.3	5.0
4.3	1.55	9.5	0.21	5.8	2.0	1.47	14.29	3.79	66.6	2.5	27.9	18.5	5.3
9.9	0.39	1.4	0.00	2.9	0.0	0.45	2.21	3.45	80.4	3.6	23.7	9.7	7.3
7.9	0.00	0.0	0.00	6.1	3.2	1.50	16.48	3.66	56.2	3.3	38.8	18.0	6.3
5.3	0.89	5.4	0.09	5.9	55.2	1.57	18.99	2.80	60.3	5.0	22.2	4.6	6.8
5.0	1.04	7.8	0.07	4.3	6.4	0.79	7.57	3.38	64.8	2.0	15.1	19.3	7.7
10.0	0.20	0.5	0.00	2.8	0.4	0.45	2.37	2.99	80.3	3.9	48.0	17.6	7.6
6.2	0.56	3.5	0.08	4.9	132.1	0.81	6.53	3.03	53.8	3.2	15.1	9.2	9.1
7.0	2.39	6.7	0.30	4.7	0.6	1.10	8.32	3.76	67.2	4.3	66.4	16.9	7.6
3.1	1.70	11.8	0.18	6.5	8.0	0.99	8.89	3.32	52.8	0.6	10.1	28.5	9.5
10.0	na	0.0	na	9.5	0.1	3.47	4.00	1.84	92.2	4.0	443.5	0.0	5.7
7.3	0.01	0.1	-0.02	8.1	33.5	1.94	18.67	3.46	45.0	3.8	25.7	14.0	10.0
4.0	1.89	15.3	0.05	3.5	5.0	0.58	7.12	3.11	77.3	2.8	10.0	13.7	6.7
6.0	0.40	2.2	0.01	5.2	1.1	1.14	10.10	3.67	63.2	4.5	43.2	13.4	7.3
5.0	1.53	8.8	0.96	1.8	0.0	0.07	0.83	3.47	82.2	4.0	14.0	8.8	4.2
8.4	0.08	0.5	0.00	5.3	1.9	1.32	14.82	3.18	61.8	5.0	30.5	5.8	6.3
6.8	0.51	3.1	0.01	6.1	2.6	1.20	9.98	4.05	62.0	3.9	16.4	9.8	7.9
2.2	2.07	16.5	0.88	4.9	2.7	1.07	12.66	3.45	42.1	1.9	21.9	20.4	5.9
9.5	0.63	1.5	-0.10	8.4	5.3	1.92	11.32	3.48	59.9	6.6	65.7	6.7	9.8
5.3	0.76	4.2	0.02	7.5	6.0	1.45	10.99	3.82	51.6	3.8	21.0	10.7	8.8
5.0	0.81	5.1	0.10	6.9	1.5	1.62	14.55	3.49	52.9	3.8	23.0	10.9	8.3
1.9	3.98	23.4	0.04	2.8	0.2	0.38	2.57	3.74	91.5	2.6	5.2	14.9	5.9
5.8	0.66	4.4	0.00	4.6	0.7	0.79	7.79	3.81	63.8	3.4	16.7	12.2	5.5
0.7	3.89	35.0	1.30	1.7	-0.2	-0.08	-1.01	3.68	80.9	2.9	15.5	14.5	4.8
5.0	1.22	6.6	0.13	5.4	1.4	1.27	14.75	3.75	67.0	6.1	43.6	4.2	4.4
8.2	0.09	0.6	0.02	7.4	2.1	1.51	13.16	4.05	50.3	2.1	11.9	14.9	7.0
8.3	0.45	2.1	0.00	5.6	1.9	1.39	13.10	3.04	57.1	4.1	34.1	12.5	7.9
3.5	2.06	11.3	0.14	4.8	2.1	1.31	13.92	3.28	74.7	4.8	27.4	5.6	4.8
7.7	0.31	2.1	0.05	5.6	1.1	1.31	13.36	4.31	72.4	1.6	17.4	24.2	7.0
7.3	0.01	0.1	0.00	5.9	0.6	1.42	9.58	3.91	57.3	1.7	23.7	23.6	7.4
5.3	0.92	5.9	0.10	3.4	0.7	0.46	4.41	4.73	86.8	4.8	19.4	3.8	5.1
6.3	0.75	6.2	-0.01	2.7	0.5	0.33	3.64	3.12	83.3	2.0	14.6	18.9	4.8
6.1	1.55	7.7	0.15	3.4	0.5	0.70	6.97	3.13	76.0	3.7	24.5	11.5	5.8
6.5	0.80	4.9	0.05	4.2	3.3	0.76	6.56	3.09	66.0	1.0	11.8	21.9	7.6
5.9	1.10	7.9	-0.03	4.4	11.2	0.92	10.60	2.98	65.9	1.6	21.5	22.2	7.4
4.8	2.81	13.4	-0.01	7.8	2.8	1.35	10.16	3.88	52.1	5.1	32.8	5.9	8.3
6.3	0.80	5.0	0.52	3.5	42.4	0.62	6.57	2.34	57.5	1.5	25.5	25.1	6.1
4.1	1.84	12.8	0.02	5.3	3.5	0.97	10.24	3.89	65.1	1.8	17.2	20.1	4.9
10.0	na	0.0	na	9.5	0.2	4.79	5.20	2.43	21.2	4.0	na	100.0	5.7
3.6	1.31	11.9	0.04	4.0	0.3	0.47	5.95	3.50	75.2	0.8	14.1	29.9	4.1
7.2	0.20	0.8	0.90	4.2	13.9	6.39	45.54	3.21	81.9	5.1	42.9	10.3	4.5
5.4	1.24	5.9	0.37	4.8	2.2	1.16	10.94	3.94	73.4	4.2	33.0	11.6	7.0
4.1	2.08	13.2	0.08	3.4	2.0	0.52	5.63	2.83	80.2	4.2	25.2	7.6	6.4
8.0	1.33	2.5	0.42	6.0	1.1	1.14	4.39	3.90	62.7	3.3	45.9	20.0	7.8
6.2	0.18	1.2	-0.03	8.1	3.2	1.87	17.32	3.87	55.0	1.4	5.7	23.6	8.5
6.4	3.88	8.1	0.00	3.6	0.2	0.56	2.49	3.82	76.6	4.4	41.8	13.5	6.8
5.8	5.31	11.0	0.22	3.1	0.3	0.64	4.89	2.97	82.4	5.3	41.2	8.6	5.4
9.2	0.72	2.8	0.00	2.1	0.0	0.15	0.82	2.86	90.6	1.3	25.6	31.2	6.5
6.0	1.33	5.6	0.02	5.5	2.5	1.09	7.57	3.86	69.7	3.5	21.3	12.1	8.0
5.0	1.98	8.7	0.54	6.1	2.2	1.39	13.60	5.05	71.4	5.7	35.2	3.2	6.5
9.4	0.53	0.8	0.20	1.5	0.0	0.09	0.53	2.63	95.6	7.1	82.3	3.0	5.9
8.9	0.02	0.1	0.00	5.9	0.8	1.48	12.68	3.34	55.1	3.7	16.2	10.6	7.8
7.3	1.68	8.3	0.00	2.2	0.3	0.32	2.34	2.66	80.4	2.9	31.1	17.3	6.8
4.6	1.12	8.9	0.13	4.1	4.5	0.75	7.95	4.54	79.2	3.7	21.5	11.1	6.1
4.4	3.04	15.1	0.05	6.0	4.2	1.16	11.02	4.16	65.9	4.6	31.8	8.9	7.0
7.3	0.15	0.7	0.05	9.1	1.8	2.25	13.42	5.42	44.4	0.5	5.6	32.1	8.2
8.2	0.39	2.6	0.01	5.8	17.1	1.42	16.97	3.58	67.3	6.3	36.1	3.4	7.7

Name	City	State	2015 Rating	2014 Rating	Total Assets ($Mil)	One Year Asset Growth	Comm-ercial Loans	Cons-umer Loans	Mort-gage Loans	Secur-ities	Capital-ization Index	Lever-age Ratio	Risk-Based Capital Ratio
Jefferson Bank and Trust Co.	Saint Louis	MO	B-	B	C+	564.8	-1.04	13.6	0.5	4.5	22.6	8.9	11.8	14.1
Jefferson Bank of Florida	Oldsmar	FL	B-	B-	C+	279.2	12.33	6.6	0.6	6.7	18.2	8.9	10.3	14.1
Jefferson Bank of Missouri	Jefferson City	MO	B-	B-	B-	539.0	6.29	9.0	29.3	14.7	11.6	5.9	9.0	11.6
Jefferson County Bank	Daykin	NE	B+	B+	B+	44.5	0.13	1.1	2.0	1.2	20.1	10.0	14.2	21.9
Jefferson Security Bank	Shepherdstown	WV	C-	D+	C-	292.8	1.86	0.7	1.0	24.8	37.8	6.5	8.5	16.8
Jersey Shore State Bank	Williamsport	PA	B-	B-	B-	968.9	1.61	4.2	2.7	30.4	10.8	6.1	8.9	11.8
▼ Jersey State Bank	Jerseyville	IL	B+	A-	A-	145.5	-1.38	5.6	0.8	9.7	46.0	10.0	12.6	26.5
Jewett City Savings Bank	Jewett City	CT	C+	C+	C+	265.8	2.82	6.0	1.0	38.9	15.0	10.0	15.9	25.8
Jim Thorpe Neighborhood Bank	Jim Thorpe	PA	C+	C+	C+	192.3	4.85	1.2	0.5	27.4	43.6	7.5	9.3	22.0
John Deere Financial, F.S.B.	Madison	WI	A-	A-	A-	3017.5	12.79	4.9	13.4	0.0	0.0	9.9	15.7	14.9
John Marshall Bank	Reston	VA	B+	A-	A-	1017.5	15.03	7.7	0.2	7.6	9.3	7.0	11.7	12.5
Johnson Bank	Racine	WI	B-	B-	B-	4542.3	11.01	15.9	2.2	19.1	10.2	9.1	11.0	14.2
Johnson City Bank	Johnson City	TX	A-	A-	A-	114.9	0.70	8.4	9.8	24.6	3.7	10.0	12.2	21.5
Johnson County Bank	Mountain City	TN	C+	C	C-	119.6	-1.19	1.5	4.5	34.3	23.5	10.0	14.1	31.6
▲ Johnson State Bank	Johnson	KS	B	B-	B-	75.5	-0.37	4.2	2.3	3.8	38.5	10.0	15.1	26.5
Jonah Bank of Wyoming	Casper	WY	B+	B+	B+	316.7	5.31	13.7	0.3	8.2	16.5	8.1	9.8	15.2
Jones National Bank and Trust Co.	Seward	NE	B	B	B-	239.6	4.63	17.8	1.8	6.3	30.0	7.6	9.4	14.0
Jonesboro State Bank	Jonesboro	LA	A	A	A-	234.0	22.00	2.0	1.9	5.5	82.8	10.0	12.8	34.1
Jonesburg State Bank	Jonesburg	MO	B-	B-	B-	76.3	4.79	5.5	1.9	24.0	2.3	6.6	8.6	14.4
Jonestown Bank and Trust Co.	Jonestown	PA	C	C-	C-	494.6	6.25	3.9	13.5	23.9	8.6	7.5	9.4	13.2
Joy State Bank	Joy	IL	C-	C-	D+	43.3	-2.28	1.9	5.2	23.9	18.5	8.1	9.7	16.6
JPMorgan Chase Bank, Dearborn	Dearborn	MI	U	C+	C	60.1	-3.77	0.0	0.0	0.0	0.0	10.0	71.4	473.9
▲ JPMorgan Chase Bank, N.A.	Columbus	OH	B	C	C-	2118497.0	8.41	7.4	4.7	10.3	12.7	6.6	8.6	14.1
Junction National Bank	Junction	TX	B	B	B+	60.6	6.10	4.9	3.4	6.1	58.4	9.7	10.8	32.4
Juniata Valley Bank	Mifflintown	PA	B-	B-	B-	570.9	18.18	6.5	1.7	26.0	26.0	6.8	8.8	14.0
Justin State Bank	Justin	TX	A-	A-	A-	67.1	0.21	4.6	0.9	34.2	1.5	10.0	14.9	25.2
Kahoka State Bank	Kahoka	MO	C	C	C	48.8	1.62	4.0	4.1	21.9	33.7	8.3	9.9	19.5
▲ Kalamazoo County State Bank	Schoolcraft	MI	C	C-	C	100.4	7.24	2.5	8.5	12.0	46.3	10.0	11.2	21.6
▲ Kansas State Bank	Ottawa	KS	B-	C+	C+	119.4	0.04	4.7	1.9	12.3	55.8	7.6	9.4	20.8
Kansas State Bank Overbrook Kansas	Overbrook	KS	B+	B+	B	54.4	-1.62	9.5	4.9	7.7	38.5	10.0	13.0	20.5
KansasLand Bank	Quinter	KS	C+	C+	C	54.3	2.04	4.4	1.9	13.6	22.6	7.8	9.6	16.1
Kanza Bank	Kingman	KS	B-	B-	B-	202.8	-5.29	7.2	1.0	19.6	19.1	9.2	10.4	15.4
Kaplan State Bank	Kaplan	LA	A-	A-	A	87.9	-4.69	12.7	2.8	10.8	50.2	10.0	13.5	30.6
Karnes County National Bank	Karnes City	TX	B-	C+	C+	357.4	-4.33	3.2	1.7	5.9	62.6	8.0	9.7	23.6
Katahdin Trust Co.	Patten	ME	B-	B-	B-	743.7	8.22	21.1	2.0	19.9	11.2	7.4	9.3	13.0
Kaw Valley Bank	Topeka	KS	C	C	D	406.0	15.38	15.3	2.2	16.5	23.8	9.0	10.3	15.7
Kaw Valley State Bank	Eudora	KS	C	C+	C-	46.7	8.34	7.6	5.9	20.2	38.1	6.7	8.7	17.2
Kaw Valley State Bank and Trust Co.	Wamego	KS	A	A	A-	160.4	6.54	9.9	2.2	17.8	25.2	10.0	11.5	19.6
KCB Bank	Kearney	MO	B+	A-	B+	225.2	9.37	10.8	0.4	9.3	27.1	10.0	13.5	19.4
Kearney Trust Co.	Kearney	MO	A-	A-	A-	179.2	9.32	4.8	3.9	16.9	17.0	8.6	10.1	17.1
Kearny Bank	Fairfield	NJ	C+	C-	C-	4520.2	5.16	1.9	0.5	14.5	27.5	10.0	16.0	24.8
Kearny County Bank	Lakin	KS	A	A	A	196.4	3.70	14.1	2.2	11.3	21.5	10.0	16.0	22.5
KEB Hana Bank USA, N.A.	Fort Lee	NJ	D	D	D	232.4	-2.50	0.4	0.0	0.7	25.7	10.0	21.2	32.5
Kendall State Bank	Valley Falls	KS	C	C	E+	35.7	-2.52	5.8	2.3	10.9	1.1	7.3	9.2	16.1
Kennebec Federal S&L Assn. of Waterville	Waterville	ME	D+	D+	C-	91.2	8.34	0.3	0.2	72.5	2.5	6.5	8.5	13.7
Kennebec Savings Bank	Augusta	ME	B	B-	B-	854.3	6.80	3.4	0.4	57.4	12.8	10.0	13.6	18.7
Kennebunk Savings Bank	Kennebunk	ME	B	B	B+	1110.3	10.50	2.7	0.1	25.6	11.4	10.0	11.4	15.0
Kennett National Bank	Kennett	MO	C+	C+	B-	97.7	5.29	16.0	4.3	20.3	28.4	10.0	12.3	20.1
Kensington Bank	Kensington	MN	B	B	B-	151.8	4.75	14.4	2.0	13.0	10.0	6.9	10.5	12.5
Kentland Bank	Kentland	IN	A-	A-	A-	296.6	1.51	9.1	2.3	10.0	26.9	10.0	13.8	19.7
Kentland Federal S&L Assn.	Kentland	IN	D-	D-	D	4.8	-1.91	0.6	0.0	82.0	2.7	10.0	12.2	24.7
Kentucky Bank	Paris	KY	B-	B-	B-	988.7	6.19	3.5	1.9	19.2	25.9	6.9	8.9	13.9
Kentucky Farmers Bank Corp.	Ashland	KY	A	A-	A-	183.0	5.16	5.9	4.9	17.0	46.3	10.0	23.3	31.6
Kentucky Federal S&L Assn.	Covington	KY	D-	D	D	35.6	0.62	0.0	0.8	45.6	12.4	6.3	8.3	22.3
▲ Kentucky Neighborhood Bank	Elizabethtown	KY	B-	C	C	134.0	-1.95	4.4	1.1	30.7	13.7	8.3	11.0	13.6
Kerndt Brothers Savings Bank	Lansing	IA	B	B	B+	272.7	14.38	8.7	0.6	5.9	19.3	6.8	9.9	12.4
Key Community Bank	Inver Grove Heights	MN	C-	D+	D	47.2	5.51	9.0	4.0	7.8	1.0	8.4	9.9	18.6
Key National Trust Co. of Delaware	Wilmington	DE	U	U	U	3.6	4.32	0.0	0.0	0.0	0.0	10.0	99.6	490.8
▼ KeyBank N.A.	Cleveland	OH	B	B+	B	101264.9	8.72	26.2	4.5	6.3	23.7	7.3	9.5	12.7
▲ KeySavings Bank	Wisconsin Rapids	WI	C-	D+	D+	76.2	0.55	0.0	0.7	42.9	36.4	10.0	14.6	39.6

Asset Quality Index	Adjusted Non-Performing Loans as a % of Total Loans	as a % of Capital	Net Charge-Offs Avg Loans	Profitability Index	Net Income ($Mil)	Return on Assets (R.O.A.)	Return on Equity (R.O.E.)	Net Interest Spread	Overhead Efficiency Ratio	Liquidity Index	Liquidity Ratio	Hot Money Ratio	Stability Index
7.5	0.14	0.8	-0.02	4.4	3.7	0.87	7.27	2.90	56.3	3.0	9.2	13.3	7.1
7.2	0.17	1.2	0.00	4.1	1.3	0.66	6.64	3.51	70.3	3.7	19.3	10.6	5.3
4.1	0.50	3.9	0.29	9.4	6.1	1.54	17.61	4.12	51.5	3.9	12.8	9.2	7.2
8.8	0.00	0.0	0.00	6.5	0.5	1.58	11.27	3.84	51.7	4.8	51.9	13.0	8.5
3.0	3.67	21.4	-0.03	2.5	0.9	0.43	5.63	3.19	86.3	3.7	20.8	10.8	2.8
5.0	1.19	9.9	0.01	5.1	7.8	1.07	12.30	3.40	65.2	3.5	4.4	10.5	6.9
6.3	2.57	7.9	-0.01	4.9	1.0	0.95	6.94	3.45	67.0	5.4	44.2	8.9	7.3
6.5	1.76	7.5	0.01	3.0	0.9	0.43	2.62	3.55	85.0	4.6	26.4	6.8	7.2
9.0	0.52	2.2	0.02	3.0	0.8	0.52	5.42	3.02	82.9	5.5	39.8	6.6	5.0
5.8	0.12	0.7	1.88	10.0	53.2	2.77	14.68	7.06	37.5	0.0	0.0	99.4	10.0
7.0	0.07	0.5	0.44	4.9	5.6	0.78	6.67	3.78	57.0	0.6	6.0	40.7	8.5
6.0	0.75	4.9	-0.08	4.0	21.7	0.67	5.47	3.34	76.7	4.4	13.6	6.0	7.4
6.0	0.96	5.0	0.18	5.9	1.1	1.32	10.99	4.05	65.7	2.1	35.2	28.6	8.0
3.0	6.46	22.9	-0.06	5.2	1.0	1.09	7.64	3.71	68.2	2.2	38.2	30.4	7.2
8.4	1.05	2.7	-0.21	4.1	0.5	0.95	6.29	3.79	73.7	5.0	36.3	8.3	7.7
4.9	1.22	7.2	0.06	5.2	1.9	0.89	8.67	3.93	72.6	5.1	37.0	8.0	6.7
8.2	0.21	1.4	-0.05	4.6	1.8	1.05	10.97	3.53	68.5	3.1	7.8	12.6	5.7
8.4	3.95	4.0	0.10	7.7	3.2	2.12	14.35	4.11	46.0	2.9	61.3	46.6	8.8
7.3	0.37	2.9	0.10	7.2	1.0	1.71	20.90	4.19	62.3	3.0	25.5	15.2	5.7
3.0	1.94	15.5	0.16	4.9	3.5	0.96	10.58	3.57	64.6	2.0	11.4	18.0	5.9
3.6	2.33	13.2	0.42	3.3	0.2	0.54	5.28	3.76	81.0	2.9	25.8	15.6	4.6
10.0	na	0.0	0.00	2.4	0.2	0.29	0.35	0.53	0.9	4.0	na	78.4	8.4
5.8	1.72	7.3	0.27	4.6	13774.0	0.92	9.23	2.03	62.0	6.9	55.0	4.3	7.3
9.5	0.02	0.1	-0.04	4.6	0.5	1.13	10.46	2.92	69.4	6.2	75.5	9.8	6.5
4.5	1.51	11.0	0.06	4.3	3.8	0.88	9.06	3.60	73.2	4.4	23.1	6.9	6.1
6.7	1.55	7.1	-0.04	8.6	1.0	1.97	13.83	5.10	64.4	5.1	27.4	3.8	9.3
7.8	0.37	1.7	-0.01	2.9	0.1	0.35	3.54	2.86	80.2	2.8	42.5	23.5	4.8
8.1	0.50	1.9	0.33	2.3	0.3	0.41	3.49	3.23	88.5	6.2	60.3	8.7	6.2
9.5	0.27	1.0	0.04	4.0	0.9	0.97	10.41	2.86	68.5	4.0	16.9	8.9	5.6
7.9	0.23	0.9	0.02	5.5	0.5	1.13	8.78	4.21	61.7	3.9	40.1	15.6	6.9
7.5	0.24	1.5	0.01	3.6	0.3	0.80	7.54	3.83	80.1	0.9	18.1	34.7	5.1
7.6	0.37	2.3	0.01	3.7	1.1	0.72	6.53	3.98	81.9	2.4	12.5	16.4	6.3
8.8	1.00	2.8	0.16	5.6	0.9	1.26	8.06	3.71	68.4	3.6	44.9	17.8	8.6
6.6	3.99	10.3	0.79	4.4	2.3	0.82	8.74	3.03	47.0	6.8	68.3	6.0	4.0
4.2	1.10	9.3	0.10	4.3	3.7	0.70	7.11	3.89	71.6	1.6	10.0	20.1	6.6
2.8	2.94	16.7	-0.04	3.6	1.8	0.64	5.56	3.37	75.7	1.0	25.5	38.6	4.7
3.4	3.59	17.8	0.24	4.0	0.3	0.93	9.74	3.93	82.7	5.2	35.3	6.8	6.0
8.6	0.48	2.4	-0.04	6.9	1.9	1.63	13.66	3.55	59.2	3.7	30.8	13.7	8.6
8.7	0.14	0.7	0.30	5.0	2.0	1.23	8.94	4.21	68.8	3.9	21.5	10.0	8.0
8.7	0.06	0.3	-0.04	5.4	1.7	1.35	13.10	3.49	64.7	4.9	37.5	9.6	7.7
6.4	0.81	3.2	0.06	3.0	13.5	0.40	2.28	2.38	67.6	2.7	29.3	22.3	8.6
7.6	0.63	2.6	-0.04	10.0	3.3	2.27	13.00	4.84	49.6	2.2	16.0	18.3	9.2
4.8	1.61	4.4	0.02	0.0	-4.5	-2.46	-12.37	2.73	180.0	3.7	32.1	13.8	5.1
3.7	3.75	23.1	0.21	4.1	0.2	0.62	6.14	3.94	82.3	5.8	36.9	3.5	3.7
7.3	0.30	3.1	0.05	1.9	0.2	0.24	2.78	3.47	89.6	2.7	5.4	14.4	4.4
7.1	0.96	5.7	0.03	4.0	5.3	0.86	6.33	3.31	72.1	3.0	11.7	12.1	7.9
6.8	0.85	5.4	0.01	4.4	5.7	0.74	6.76	3.95	76.5	4.9	12.7	3.1	8.3
7.0	0.29	1.3	0.16	2.5	0.5	0.67	5.28	3.47	90.6	1.9	29.4	26.1	6.2
4.8	1.05	7.9	0.01	5.5	1.1	0.98	8.94	3.97	79.3	3.9	9.8	8.7	6.2
6.7	1.08	4.3	0.03	6.3	2.7	1.22	8.71	4.14	59.2	3.0	34.5	18.3	7.9
1.7	5.82	38.0	0.00	0.5	0.0	-0.31	-2.51	3.60	108.9	0.9	17.7	33.4	6.0
4.6	1.05	7.4	-0.02	4.0	6.0	0.81	7.82	3.67	78.3	2.4	8.0	16.0	6.9
7.7	1.32	2.1	-0.41	10.0	4.2	3.16	13.14	5.56	56.9	6.2	69.2	10.0	9.1
6.2	2.19	12.4	0.35	0.1	-0.1	-0.46	-5.52	2.79	114.3	2.7	44.1	26.8	2.9
3.9	2.02	13.2	0.10	4.5	0.9	0.88	7.92	3.92	73.3	1.8	16.1	20.0	6.6
6.7	0.52	3.5	-0.03	4.2	1.7	0.84	7.48	3.70	75.1	3.4	27.2	13.8	6.9
5.8	0.28	1.4	0.98	2.0	0.1	0.28	2.87	3.37	92.5	6.6	51.6	1.9	2.7
10.0	na	0.0	na	6.0	0.2	5.60	5.68	6.35	57.2	4.0	na	0.0	7.0
5.7	1.08	6.9	0.30	4.6	624.9	0.85	8.10	2.79	66.8	5.3	25.5	3.4	9.5
7.9	1.43	5.0	0.22	1.5	0.1	0.18	1.21	2.59	93.4	4.9	52.9	12.9	6.4

Name	City	State	2015 Rating	2014 Rating	Rating	Total Assets ($Mil)	One Year Asset Growth	Commercial Loans	Consumer Loans	Mortgage Loans	Securities	Capitalization Index	Leverage Ratio	Risk-Based Capital Ratio
Keystone Savings Bank	Keystone	IA	B+	B+	B	99.7	6.73	4.8	2.9	24.0	30.4	10.0	11.8	16.4
Killbuck Savings Bank Co.	Killbuck	OH	B	B-	B-	493.7	2.39	9.7	1.2	21.1	29.0	9.0	10.4	15.8
▲ Kindred State Bank	Kindred	ND	C	C-	D	25.6	-1.73	5.9	7.0	6.0	10.0	7.3	9.2	16.5
King Southern Bank	Chaplin	KY	A-	A-	B	170.7	-4.61	6.3	0.9	26.3	12.3	10.0	11.6	15.6
▲ Kingsley State Bank	Kingsley	IA	A-	A-	B+	180.2	1.59	7.3	2.3	9.5	22.5	10.0	13.1	17.6
Kingston National Bank	Kingston	OH	B	B	B	282.5	8.23	8.0	1.9	20.4	28.8	7.5	9.3	15.1
Kingstree Federal S&L Assn.	Kingstree	SC	C-	C+	C+	34.2	0.32	0.8	0.7	38.4	17.6	10.0	14.8	37.7
Kinmundy Bank	Kinmundy	IL	B+	B+	B	45.4	7.64	6.0	20.2	26.7	15.4	7.9	9.6	14.5
Kirkpatrick Bank	Edmond	OK	B-	B-	B-	762.6	6.20	6.0	0.4	5.6	21.2	6.3	8.9	12.0
Kirkwood Bank and Trust Co.	Bismarck	ND	B-	B-	C+	219.0	-0.53	10.0	3.3	10.2	15.7	6.9	8.9	13.1
Kirkwood Bank of Nevada	Las Vegas	NV	B-	B-	C+	74.9	3.46	8.5	0.0	1.7	0.0	10.0	13.7	18.1
Kish Bank	Belleville	PA	C+	C+	C+	726.5	5.05	10.2	1.7	21.1	24.2	6.9	9.1	12.4
▲ Kitsap Bank	Port Orchard	WA	B	C+	C+	1150.1	3.44	4.4	0.6	7.1	35.8	6.4	8.4	14.3
Kleberg Bank, N.A.	Kingsville	TX	B-	B-	B-	513.4	6.74	6.1	14.1	11.4	31.5	7.2	9.1	15.3
KleinBank	Chaska	MN	B-	C+	C+	1917.2	2.35	7.8	2.3	5.9	37.3	7.0	9.0	13.6
▲ KodaBank	Drayton	ND	B	B+	A-	148.1	2.18	12.7	8.0	8.6	11.9	10.0	11.1	15.2
Kopernik Bank	Baltimore	MD	C+	C	C+	89.1	47.30	0.0	0.2	78.2	0.0	10.0	17.3	32.6
Kress National Bank	Kress	TX	B-	B-	B-	40.8	-3.75	10.9	4.5	0.9	27.5	10.0	11.3	18.5
▲ KS Bank, Inc.	Smithfield	NC	B-	C	C-	352.0	6.55	4.0	0.7	25.2	18.9	7.9	9.6	14.2
KS StateBank	Manhattan	KS	A-	A-	A-	1600.8	12.04	14.8	0.5	17.7	17.6	6.9	8.9	13.5
La Monte Community Bank	La Monte	MO	B+	B+	B	27.0	1.02	5.2	3.6	19.0	16.7	10.0	11.6	18.0
Labette Bank	Altamont	KS	B	B	B	399.2	7.80	2.4	3.0	22.9	25.0	9.0	10.4	15.9
Ladysmith Federal S&L Assn.	Ladysmith	WI	D	C	D+	48.1	5.51	11.6	3.8	45.0	16.8	9.7	10.8	19.6
Lafayette Ambassador Bank	Bethlehem	PA	B	B	B-	1545.4	3.02	7.7	1.0	14.0	16.9	9.4	10.9	14.5
Lafayette Community Bank	Lafayette	IN	C+	C+	C+	172.6	0.65	7.9	0.2	18.2	12.3	9.7	10.9	14.8
Lafayette State Bank	Mayo	FL	E-	E-	D-	76.7	-8.10	5.0	2.8	15.5	11.2	0.0	3.8	6.0
▲ Lake Area Bank	Lindstrom	MN	C+	C-	D	308.1	4.51	7.8	0.4	17.7	27.5	7.4	9.3	13.8
▼ Lake Bank	Two Harbors	MN	D	D+	D-	122.6	7.50	8.4	1.2	35.5	17.2	7.1	9.0	12.9
Lake City Bank	Warsaw	IN	A-	A-	B+	4185.6	14.52	29.9	1.4	4.2	12.0	7.7	10.4	13.1
Lake City Federal Bank	Lake City	MN	C-	C-	C-	70.8	2.75	2.2	2.9	43.8	12.3	9.8	10.9	18.3
Lake Community Bank	Long Lake	MN	B+	B+	B-	119.7	3.60	6.0	1.1	7.0	14.7	10.0	13.4	18.4
Lake Country Community Bank	Morristown	MN	C-	D	D-	26.7	-1.08	11.7	2.7	27.5	1.2	6.8	8.8	13.7
▲ Lake Elmo Bank	Lake Elmo	MN	B	C+	C+	338.9	6.47	4.2	2.0	19.3	27.9	7.5	9.4	15.7
Lake Forest Bank & Trust Co.	Lake Forest	IL	B+	B	B	3423.8	23.38	47.8	1.9	2.7	9.6	6.2	10.3	11.9
Lake Region Bank	New London	MN	C+	C+	C	104.1	0.06	20.5	4.4	7.0	27.6	7.0	9.0	13.9
Lake Shore Savings Bank	Dunkirk	NY	B	B	B	479.0	1.28	4.0	0.3	34.3	19.0	10.0	14.8	24.0
Lake Sunapee Bank, FSB	Newport	NH	B-	B-	B-	1583.4	6.31	4.2	0.3	44.1	9.8	6.7	8.7	13.5
Lake-Osceola State Bank	Baldwin	MI	C+	C	C	232.2	11.72	4.1	14.4	27.7	8.2	6.9	8.9	13.0
Lakeland Bank	Oak Ridge	NJ	B-	B-	B	4893.9	30.94	6.7	0.4	12.6	12.6	6.3	9.5	12.0
Lakeside Bank	Chicago	IL	A-	B	C	1382.1	10.22	4.6	0.1	8.5	3.2	10.0	13.1	16.0
Lakeside Bank	Lake Charles	LA	B-	C+	C	166.9	13.46	7.1	2.4	14.1	26.6	10.0	13.3	20.4
Lakeside Bank of Salina	Salina	OK	B	C+	C	34.5	8.76	9.0	25.4	33.5	11.0	10.0	12.1	19.5
▼ Lakeside National Bank	Rockwall	TX	C	B-	B	64.2	4.73	4.2	4.7	15.5	17.0	7.1	9.1	21.6
Lakeside State Bank	Oologah	OK	B-	B-	B-	67.3	3.91	5.5	10.7	14.6	48.8	6.8	8.8	19.4
Lakeview Bank	Lakeville	MN	C-	C-	C	68.5	6.98	16.2	1.8	33.4	9.2	7.7	9.6	13.1
Lamar Bank and Trust Co.	Lamar	MO	A-	A-	A-	145.5	8.94	5.0	2.0	21.1	21.4	8.1	9.7	15.0
Lamar National Bank	Paris	TX	A-	A-	A-	138.2	2.07	13.6	6.2	30.1	13.2	10.0	11.7	20.7
Lamesa National Bank	Lamesa	TX	B-	B-	B-	281.2	-2.66	7.5	0.2	0.0	44.2	9.2	10.5	18.9
Lamont Bank of St. John	Saint John	WA	B-	C+	C	42.9	-2.10	3.0	4.6	0.1	55.7	10.0	12.5	28.7
Landmands Bank	Audubon	IA	B-	B-	B-	61.0	1.57	5.4	2.7	3.9	6.0	5.7	9.0	11.5
▼ Landmark Bank	Clinton	LA	D+	D+	C+	115.5	6.59	7.2	2.2	25.9	24.1	8.6	10.1	15.7
▲ Landmark Bank, N.A.	Fort Lauderdale	FL	C	D	D	463.0	18.32	7.4	0.1	9.3	0.4	10.0	12.9	17.5
Landmark Bank, N.A.	Columbia	MO	B+	B+	B+	2583.9	10.66	6.6	2.7	16.0	33.7	6.7	8.7	14.1
Landmark Community Bank	Pittston	PA	D+	C-	C-	306.5	12.55	9.1	5.8	12.5	18.5	7.0	9.5	12.5
Landmark Community Bank	Collierville	TN	B	B	B-	898.0	14.66	5.7	1.3	61.4	11.4	6.3	8.3	15.1
▲ Landmark National Bank	Manhattan	KS	B+	B	C+	905.1	4.67	6.8	0.3	15.6	40.2	8.2	9.8	17.1
▲ Laona State Bank	Laona	WI	B	C	C-	179.5	3.66	5.7	3.3	32.0	26.7	10.0	11.1	20.1
▼ Lapeer County Bank & Trust Co.	Lapeer	MI	B+	A-	B+	339.2	6.67	6.4	1.1	12.5	37.8	10.0	11.4	20.9
LaSalle State Bank	La Salle	IL	C+	C+	C	137.4	7.68	9.4	1.3	9.7	45.4	6.7	8.7	17.1
Latimer State Bank	Wilburton	OK	B-	B-	B	72.4	-7.98	9.2	2.4	6.3	14.9	10.0	17.5	33.4

Asset Quality Index	Adjusted Non-Performing Loans as a % of Total Loans	as a % of Capital	Net Charge-Offs Avg Loans	Profitability Index	Net Income ($Mil)	Return on Assets (R.O.A.)	Return on Equity (R.O.E.)	Net Interest Spread	Overhead Efficiency Ratio	Liquidity Index	Liquidity Ratio	Hot Money Ratio	Stability Index
7.9	0.87	4.1	0.00	4.7	0.7	1.04	8.72	3.79	74.9	4.7	39.0	11.0	7.1
8.1	0.02	0.1	0.00	5.4	3.9	1.07	10.20	3.46	57.7	3.6	26.6	12.4	6.3
8.2	0.11	0.7	-0.04	3.4	0.2	0.72	8.69	3.21	81.1	5.5	34.3	4.1	3.3
8.2	0.22	1.4	0.18	7.9	2.4	1.86	16.25	4.60	60.2	0.8	13.2	36.4	7.7
8.5	0.01	0.1	-0.11	5.9	2.0	1.45	11.07	3.50	57.2	2.5	33.9	21.0	8.4
7.6	0.38	2.4	0.03	4.4	1.6	0.79	8.26	3.56	68.7	2.0	21.3	19.5	6.1
6.1	2.60	10.0	1.07	1.1	0.0	-0.05	-0.33	2.95	82.6	2.3	41.6	30.9	6.8
4.3	0.90	7.1	0.53	9.9	0.6	1.69	13.09	5.12	44.7	3.5	13.7	11.3	8.7
6.1	0.34	2.4	0.00	3.9	5.4	0.99	11.34	3.29	64.1	3.9	13.0	9.3	6.2
6.0	0.37	2.4	0.70	4.5	1.3	0.78	8.95	3.50	72.4	4.7	26.3	6.0	5.4
3.7	2.23	11.9	0.00	4.9	0.5	0.87	6.34	4.26	65.4	0.9	22.1	44.3	5.9
5.4	0.89	6.1	0.00	3.5	3.8	0.72	7.53	3.41	79.0	2.3	21.4	16.5	6.7
8.4	0.05	0.3	0.00	4.6	9.1	1.09	10.06	3.76	74.0	6.4	40.3	4.3	8.9
4.6	0.94	5.7	0.27	4.3	4.3	1.16	8.99	3.88	78.5	3.7	22.8	11.3	7.1
6.1	0.96	5.3	0.00	4.3	16.1	1.13	10.24	3.48	73.4	6.0	32.8	4.1	8.5
4.3	1.77	11.8	0.04	9.3	2.8	2.61	22.83	4.34	41.6	1.5	5.9	21.3	7.9
2.6	5.61	27.3	0.32	4.1	0.6	0.92	5.45	3.68	77.7	1.2	7.6	26.3	6.4
5.7	2.64	12.4	0.00	5.2	0.4	1.25	11.04	3.93	64.4	1.2	16.0	29.5	6.2
4.5	1.21	8.6	-0.07	4.1	1.7	0.64	6.54	3.56	76.0	1.3	9.5	25.3	5.5
6.8	0.80	6.3	-0.12	9.2	25.7	2.20	24.88	3.49	51.3	0.8	18.3	43.6	9.3
7.5	0.12	0.7	-0.01	3.5	0.1	0.43	3.84	3.53	82.0	3.7	6.8	9.7	6.0
7.2	0.37	2.0	-0.01	4.8	2.7	0.93	8.57	3.67	71.6	2.5	21.8	17.0	6.6
2.1	4.87	29.9	0.25	1.1	0.0	0.03	0.29	3.35	88.7	1.1	19.8	31.5	4.8
6.5	0.57	3.9	0.28	5.0	10.7	0.93	7.94	3.33	65.3	4.0	5.5	7.6	7.7
5.1	1.17	7.4	-0.02	3.2	0.7	0.53	4.80	3.24	80.8	4.0	23.5	9.8	6.4
0.0	27.61	404.6	5.19	0.0	-0.5	-0.93	-24.15	3.45	110.2	2.1	15.9	15.7	1.2
3.5	2.67	16.3	-0.03	5.0	2.8	1.26	12.25	3.78	82.9	3.7	31.1	13.4	5.1
1.1	5.62	44.5	0.27	3.4	0.3	0.37	4.00	3.73	67.0	1.4	14.8	19.3	3.9
7.4	0.38	2.6	0.03	8.0	40.5	1.36	12.61	3.22	45.9	1.3	15.8	28.1	9.6
1.9	5.70	34.2	-0.01	3.0	0.2	0.41	3.69	3.32	81.9	2.1	20.3	19.1	5.3
6.7	0.56	2.8	0.00	6.4	1.0	1.14	8.67	3.74	58.1	4.6	29.7	8.1	6.1
5.2	1.54	10.1	0.16	3.4	0.1	0.50	5.19	4.35	88.4	5.3	36.6	6.7	3.4
5.8	0.77	4.5	-0.05	5.1	2.1	0.86	9.21	3.32	70.3	4.9	28.8	6.0	5.4
7.0	0.48	3.4	0.23	9.7	40.2	1.75	16.68	3.20	44.6	2.6	17.3	4.7	7.8
3.9	2.29	13.8	0.03	3.0	0.5	0.57	6.17	3.62	89.3	6.0	40.9	3.7	5.3
6.5	1.85	8.3	0.07	4.0	3.5	0.98	6.46	3.62	77.2	3.1	27.9	15.4	7.9
5.6	0.65	5.7	0.04	4.2	9.7	0.83	7.46	3.20	72.1	2.9	5.3	9.0	8.7
3.7	1.24	10.4	0.10	5.5	1.7	1.00	10.92	4.23	66.7	3.7	15.7	10.7	4.5
4.2	0.73	5.9	0.13	5.2	30.3	0.90	8.53	3.51	60.3	4.0	10.9	8.2	8.3
6.5	0.39	2.2	0.03	10.0	25.2	2.58	19.84	3.89	40.4	0.9	17.2	17.9	10.0
8.8	0.11	0.5	0.00	3.4	0.6	0.47	3.38	3.52	74.5	2.0	30.2	25.1	6.7
4.5	1.70	8.8	0.00	9.5	0.4	1.54	12.99	6.02	60.8	3.4	17.2	12.4	6.8
7.1	0.43	1.8	0.72	2.6	0.2	0.32	3.53	3.07	80.7	5.8	62.4	9.5	4.6
6.7	0.80	3.4	0.42	4.6	0.6	1.17	12.05	4.10	74.8	3.8	32.1	13.2	5.7
2.4	2.41	19.2	0.01	6.2	0.5	1.00	10.07	4.90	64.7	4.4	12.5	5.7	5.3
6.4	0.48	3.3	0.27	8.1	1.9	1.76	18.24	3.80	52.5	2.4	13.2	15.4	8.0
8.6	0.01	0.1	0.04	5.4	1.4	1.31	10.98	4.28	72.4	4.3	34.3	11.5	8.1
4.3	4.57	15.5	-0.21	4.3	2.3	1.02	10.19	2.05	48.1	1.4	22.6	28.5	5.4
9.0	0.00	0.0	0.05	5.0	0.4	1.15	9.88	3.34	46.8	7.5	69.1	0.0	3.9
5.2	0.26	2.3	0.01	5.7	0.6	1.24	13.31	3.91	72.5	2.7	8.7	14.9	6.6
1.3	5.68	34.3	0.12	3.7	0.6	0.75	7.11	4.07	80.5	4.1	25.9	9.7	6.4
2.2	2.50	14.2	0.39	5.6	1.5	0.51	3.86	4.00	61.3	2.0	27.0	22.0	7.5
6.2	0.93	5.9	0.10	5.6	22.2	1.19	12.66	3.95	67.8	1.7	17.0	20.7	8.0
0.7	4.05	30.3	0.02	4.1	1.7	0.75	7.81	3.91	74.3	3.1	8.0	13.0	4.8
6.7	0.39	3.6	0.09	5.4	5.9	0.91	10.90	3.13	51.5	0.5	5.6	41.6	5.3
5.6	0.87	4.2	0.28	5.5	6.9	1.04	8.76	3.56	68.8	4.3	23.4	7.6	7.9
4.6	2.63	14.0	0.03	4.5	1.1	0.83	7.16	3.65	63.0	2.9	35.9	19.1	6.4
7.9	0.09	0.4	0.10	4.6	2.2	0.90	7.90	3.47	73.8	5.1	32.1	6.0	5.9
5.7	1.20	5.8	0.14	3.5	0.9	0.90	9.35	3.22	76.0	4.0	27.2	10.6	5.1
6.3	9.23	9.8	0.27	3.3	0.4	0.73	4.19	2.02	64.4	3.4	81.1	33.5	6.4

Name	City	State	2016 Rating	2015 Rating	2014 Rating	Total Assets ($Mil)	One Year Asset Growth	Asset Mix (As a % of Total Assets) Commercial Loans	Consumer Loans	Mortgage Loans	Securities	Capitalization Index	Leverage Ratio	Risk-Based Capital Ratio
Lauderdale County Bank	Halls	TN	C	C	C	50.5	-2.09	17.7	6.2	13.2	32.8	8.2	9.8	20.0
▲ Laura State Bank	Williamsfield	IL	D+	D	D+	18.0	9.33	3.5	8.4	7.1	5.5	8.8	10.2	29.4
Laurens State Bank	Laurens	IA	B	B	B	64.7	0.69	4.1	2.7	8.7	25.2	10.0	11.6	23.5
Lawrenceburg Federal Bank	Lawrenceburg	TN	B+	B+	B+	58.6	2.22	0.0	3.0	85.1	0.0	10.0	24.2	41.1
Lawson Bank	Lawson	MO	C+	C+	C+	128.6	4.30	3.3	1.3	10.7	34.4	8.8	10.2	19.5
LCA Bank Corp.	Park City	UT	A	A	A	161.3	16.44	2.1	0.0	0.0	0.8	8.1	11.9	13.4
LCNB National Bank	Lebanon	OH	B	B	B-	1332.6	4.61	3.0	1.4	17.7	29.1	6.5	8.5	13.2
Lea County State Bank	Hobbs	NM	B-	B-	C+	289.1	-7.47	9.0	4.4	0.9	71.6	9.2	10.5	24.6
Lead Bank	Garden City	MO	E	D-	D	168.9	19.51	11.5	0.8	16.6	3.3	2.1	7.7	9.1
Leader Bank, N.A.	Arlington	MA	A	A	A	1179.3	22.17	2.3	0.1	39.9	1.1	7.1	9.5	12.6
Leaders Bank	Oak Brook	IL	D-	D-	E+	334.7	-3.10	15.3	0.0	6.5	8.5	9.5	11.6	14.6
Ledyard National Bank	Norwich	VT	B	B	B-	470.5	7.77	5.2	3.4	21.9	27.7	6.7	8.7	13.7
▲ Lee Bank	Lee	MA	C	C-	D+	323.3	4.82	5.8	0.2	35.8	9.1	7.9	9.6	13.4
Lee Bank and Trust Co.	Pennington Gap	VA	B-	C+	C-	156.1	2.09	13.7	5.8	22.4	13.3	10.0	15.1	24.7
Lee County Bank	Fort Madison	IA	A-	B	B	149.2	5.01	8.3	2.9	38.2	0.0	10.0	12.3	17.9
Legacy Bank	Wiley	CO	B+	B+	B	305.3	8.39	11.1	0.6	8.9	19.7	10.0	13.0	17.6
Legacy Bank	Altoona	IA	D	D-	D-	97.5	5.48	14.4	3.0	26.7	11.8	5.2	7.2	11.3
Legacy Bank	Colwich	KS	B-	C+	C-	328.0	10.31	7.5	0.8	20.3	12.1	8.2	9.8	13.7
▲ Legacy Bank	Hinton	OK	C	D	D+	418.2	-5.58	15.1	0.9	11.6	4.3	5.7	8.8	11.5
Legacy Bank & Trust Co.	Rogersville	MO	B-	B-	C+	153.7	11.32	9.2	2.0	27.2	1.7	5.0	8.4	11.0
Legacy Bank of Florida	Boca Raton	FL	C+	C	D	322.4	13.95	10.0	0.1	8.1	14.2	6.4	9.3	12.1
▲ Legacy National Bank	Springdale	AR	B+	B	B-	400.5	18.90	7.4	1.2	15.5	7.0	10.0	11.7	15.4
Legacy State Bank	Loganville	GA	E-	E-	E-	78.9	9.93	2.1	0.1	9.3	13.4	1.2	5.7	8.2
Legacy Trust Co., N.A.	Houston	TX	U	U	U	23.4	7.37	0.0	0.0	0.0	83.0	10.0	94.9	213.3
LegacyTexas Bank	Plano	TX	B	B+	A-	8442.8	22.71	20.6	0.5	12.3	7.9	4.7	9.7	10.8
Legence Bank	Eldorado	IL	B	B-	C+	305.7	1.18	12.2	3.4	5.3	28.3	7.9	9.6	15.7
Legend Bank, N.A.	Bowie	TX	A-	A-	A-	610.7	0.17	12.0	1.4	12.1	23.9	9.3	10.5	15.4
Legends Bank	Linn	MO	A-	A-	B+	334.4	12.94	5.0	7.4	22.6	18.4	10.0	16.1	23.9
Legends Bank	Clarksville	TN	B	B-	B-	408.5	1.45	6.1	0.3	7.5	18.5	8.3	10.3	13.6
Leighton State Bank	Pella	IA	A-	A-	A-	175.4	9.81	8.8	1.4	15.1	16.3	9.3	10.5	14.8
▲ Lemont National Bank	Lemont	IL	D+	D	C-	57.8	0.74	0.0	0.0	8.9	40.8	3.6	5.6	23.2
Lena State Bank	Lena	IL	B-	C+	C+	92.3	4.52	21.9	0.4	3.2	27.5	8.4	9.9	13.8
▼ Level One Bank	Farmington Hills	MI	B	B	B-	1103.3	21.59	26.2	0.1	10.0	7.3	5.1	9.3	11.1
Lewis & Clark Bank	Oregon City	OR	B	B	B	169.7	14.01	4.9	0.2	11.3	0.0	8.4	11.5	13.6
Lewisburg Banking Co.	Lewisburg	KY	A-	A-	A-	112.1	2.24	15.2	5.0	24.9	26.5	9.3	10.5	17.1
Liberty Bank	Geraldine	AL	B	B+	B+	128.4	14.70	2.4	9.2	13.5	35.1	10.0	12.2	17.7
Liberty Bank	South San Francisco	CA	C+	C+	C	268.3	6.20	7.3	0.3	2.4	28.3	7.7	12.0	13.1
Liberty Bank	Middletown	CT	B	B	B	4471.7	12.85	9.7	0.4	20.0	16.5	10.0	13.9	16.7
▲ Liberty Bank	Alton	IL	B	C+	C+	320.4	3.48	14.0	1.0	8.2	36.3	10.0	11.1	17.8
Liberty Bank	Ironton	OH	B-	B-	C+	54.3	-1.84	4.7	3.5	40.7	17.4	10.0	14.4	28.9
Liberty Bank	Hurst	TX	B-	B-	B-	441.2	11.32	13.8	1.1	13.8	13.9	7.4	9.3	13.2
Liberty Bank and Trust Co.	New Orleans	LA	C+	C+	C+	611.6	-4.14	2.9	2.7	21.2	41.8	6.3	8.3	17.4
Liberty Bank for Savings	Chicago	IL	C+	C+	C+	830.3	1.22	0.0	0.0	48.1	42.8	10.0	22.3	54.6
Liberty Bank Minnesota	Saint Cloud	MN	A	A+	A+	202.5	4.53	0.0	2.3	38.1	18.7	9.6	10.7	23.0
Liberty Bank, Inc.	Salt Lake City	UT	E-	E-	E+	12.0	9.69	23.6	2.3	33.0	7.7	6.7	8.7	18.9
Liberty Bank, N.A.	Beachwood	OH	B	B	B-	221.5	6.23	17.7	10.0	7.9	0.0	10.0	14.4	16.4
▲ Liberty Bay Bank	Poulsbo	WA	C	C-	D+	92.4	19.41	4.9	0.7	6.3	26.2	7.4	9.3	15.0
Liberty Bell Bank	Marlton	NJ	E+	E-	E-	145.1	0.39	7.3	0.1	15.9	7.9	4.3	6.7	10.7
Liberty Capital Bank	Addison	TX	B+	B+	B	201.2	7.53	13.4	0.3	12.6	0.0	8.1	9.8	13.4
Liberty Federal Savings Bank	Enid	OK	E-	E-	E-	86.3	-7.04	1.2	0.6	45.9	19.4	0.8	4.1	9.2
Liberty First Bank	Monroe	GA	B+	B-	C-	117.0	1.28	3.2	1.2	21.7	26.4	10.0	11.9	18.1
Liberty National Bank	Sioux City	IA	B	B	B-	344.8	5.63	14.3	1.1	12.9	15.5	6.9	9.5	12.4
Liberty National Bank	Ada	OH	B-	B-	C+	282.7	8.60	7.3	0.4	15.5	16.0	6.9	8.9	13.7
Liberty National Bank	Lawton	OK	B	B	B-	432.4	-2.59	10.5	1.9	13.7	17.2	10.0	11.5	16.4
Liberty National Bank in Paris	Paris	TX	B+	B+	B+	279.7	6.81	2.8	4.1	20.4	46.9	10.0	16.7	40.8
Liberty Savings Assn., FSA	Fort Scott	KS	C-	C-	C-	34.9	-4.18	0.5	3.2	19.3	62.8	10.0	18.3	82.9
Liberty Savings Bank, F.S.B.	Wilmington	OH	B	B	C	673.6	4.16	0.2	0.0	79.6	4.4	7.8	9.5	17.4
Liberty State Bank	Powers Lake	ND	A-	A-	A-	81.7	-8.58	2.9	3.6	8.4	38.0	10.0	11.4	19.5
Liberty Trust & Savings Bank	Durant	IA	A	A	A	151.4	1.74	6.7	2.3	8.2	43.7	10.0	18.3	31.7
Libertyville Bank & Trust Co.	Libertyville	IL	B-	B-	B-	1313.4	5.58	26.2	12.9	3.2	16.9	5.5	9.6	11.4

Asset Quality Index	Adjusted Non-Performing Loans as a % of Total Loans	as a % of Capital	Net Charge-Offs Avg Loans	Profitability Index	Net Income ($Mil)	Return on Assets (R.O.A.)	Return on Equity (R.O.E.)	Net Interest Spread	Overhead Efficiency Ratio	Liquidity Index	Liquidity Ratio	Hot Money Ratio	Stability Index
4.5	2.97	13.3	0.04	3.5	0.2	0.54	5.51	3.62	80.3	2.6	47.0	30.2	5.1
6.0	1.22	4.0	0.00	1.3	0.0	0.14	1.35	2.34	94.3	6.9	71.9	2.5	3.9
8.9	0.26	1.0	0.04	4.9	0.6	1.21	10.44	3.01	61.2	5.5	55.1	9.8	7.0
8.0	1.45	5.5	0.01	4.3	0.3	0.79	3.32	2.71	74.7	1.2	6.3	26.0	7.7
9.3	0.00	0.0	0.00	3.4	0.7	0.78	7.94	3.49	81.9	5.6	45.1	7.8	5.4
8.2	0.22	1.5	1.41	10.0	2.1	1.78	15.23	6.36	34.7	0.2	7.2	0.0	8.0
5.0	1.41	10.1	0.03	4.8	9.3	0.96	8.71	3.48	66.2	4.5	19.0	6.8	8.1
8.2	1.39	2.8	-0.03	4.5	3.3	1.49	12.65	3.32	71.8	5.5	67.7	10.1	6.5
0.9	2.04	20.4	0.92	2.1	0.1	0.10	1.21	4.75	90.8	1.5	5.7	21.2	0.3
8.3	0.17	1.5	0.01	9.4	12.9	1.62	15.97	3.25	50.8	1.2	6.2	14.6	9.5
0.0	8.90	55.2	0.07	3.8	2.2	0.86	7.18	3.56	71.6	0.8	19.7	43.7	4.2
5.5	0.93	5.7	0.00	4.5	3.2	0.97	10.20	3.29	79.0	4.8	28.4	6.4	6.1
3.5	2.38	18.9	0.03	2.3	0.8	0.35	3.75	3.49	90.7	3.8	12.0	9.5	4.9
4.7	2.67	11.6	0.05	3.6	0.6	0.51	3.64	4.28	73.9	0.8	15.4	36.0	5.8
6.9	0.94	5.2	-0.01	6.2	1.7	1.48	12.27	3.64	62.1	5.4	26.0	1.3	6.4
4.1	2.85	14.3	0.07	6.8	3.7	1.67	11.36	4.09	53.1	1.6	21.4	24.4	7.5
2.4	2.08	18.3	0.06	2.0	0.1	0.19	2.70	3.75	95.0	4.5	19.2	6.0	2.6
5.1	1.09	7.6	0.21	4.1	1.7	0.69	6.93	3.72	64.8	1.2	12.7	24.1	5.1
4.4	0.50	4.0	-0.25	3.0	2.1	0.63	7.29	4.97	91.1	4.4	7.4	4.9	3.9
6.4	0.25	2.3	0.15	5.9	1.2	1.01	10.29	4.57	62.5	2.6	2.4	14.7	6.4
5.0	0.33	2.7	0.11	3.6	1.3	0.56	4.94	3.53	75.7	3.7	19.0	11.0	4.2
5.2	1.40	8.7	0.11	5.1	2.5	0.90	7.71	3.80	60.0	3.0	16.0	13.9	7.1
5.6	0.54	5.1	0.37	1.6	0.1	0.25	4.27	3.35	95.3	3.2	17.3	13.3	0.7
10.0	na	0.0	na	9.5	1.6	9.42	10.06	1.82	75.3	4.0	na	0.0	6.7
5.6	0.58	5.0	0.16	7.8	76.6	1.33	11.58	4.00	45.9	1.6	9.6	21.4	9.1
4.9	1.14	6.9	0.10	7.8	4.5	1.98	17.48	5.38	67.7	3.3	18.7	13.0	7.4
7.4	0.36	2.1	0.10	7.0	7.4	1.61	13.13	4.73	65.6	2.9	17.4	14.8	8.5
6.0	1.49	6.8	0.08	6.4	2.5	1.10	6.70	3.77	58.2	3.1	10.7	13.3	7.7
6.9	0.16	1.0	0.03	4.5	2.5	0.82	8.17	4.03	71.4	3.2	12.8	5.6	5.4
5.9	0.51	3.3	0.01	7.0	1.9	1.52	12.20	3.90	63.5	2.4	22.5	17.5	8.4
10.0	0.00	0.0	0.00	1.9	0.2	0.39	5.06	2.49	87.8	7.4	81.2	2.3	3.4
6.5	0.30	1.6	0.00	6.2	0.9	1.26	12.38	3.49	45.5	1.7	18.8	23.3	5.7
4.1	1.21	10.5	0.10	7.0	9.1	1.18	11.89	4.95	60.1	1.4	10.9	20.2	8.1
4.7	0.68	4.6	0.00	5.8	1.1	0.93	8.00	4.41	66.5	0.7	12.6	45.9	7.2
6.3	1.04	5.9	0.01	6.5	1.4	1.60	14.97	3.96	62.0	3.4	19.4	12.5	7.9
5.6	1.58	6.3	0.42	4.0	0.6	0.61	4.78	5.06	82.7	2.9	42.5	23.8	7.2
6.4	0.24	1.3	-0.03	3.5	1.5	0.73	6.12	3.69	80.9	5.3	33.0	4.6	7.5
7.3	0.65	3.4	0.06	3.8	27.7	0.84	5.92	3.20	75.1	4.2	22.9	10.4	8.8
5.1	1.89	9.0	0.01	4.8	2.3	0.94	7.71	3.54	64.1	3.7	20.9	11.1	5.5
6.3	1.96	8.0	0.17	3.2	0.2	0.48	3.31	4.10	84.7	4.4	32.1	10.3	6.7
7.1	0.19	1.4	-0.06	4.4	2.3	0.72	6.22	3.83	70.1	1.0	24.5	34.1	7.0
4.5	2.63	12.9	0.39	3.2	3.0	0.65	7.68	4.03	87.0	1.8	12.9	19.6	4.5
9.7	0.69	1.6	0.04	3.0	2.6	0.42	1.84	2.69	77.9	5.0	57.5	14.6	7.6
8.3	0.03	0.1	0.07	9.0	3.5	2.41	20.63	3.09	63.6	6.3	44.0	2.5	8.5
1.7	8.74	49.3	-0.04	0.0	-0.2	-2.34	-30.14	8.07	130.2	0.7	28.9	75.3	2.5
4.9	0.49	2.8	-0.47	5.9	1.7	0.98	7.19	4.12	67.8	3.8	12.0	9.9	6.7
8.7	0.04	0.2	0.00	3.3	1.1	1.65	15.98	3.77	96.0	4.8	32.9	8.4	6.1
1.4	2.19	22.6	-0.09	1.5	0.1	0.12	1.85	3.68	96.6	1.6	11.6	21.6	1.0
6.5	0.00	0.0	0.00	6.6	2.4	1.62	17.14	3.52	51.4	4.5	23.0	6.6	6.6
0.3	9.26	104.0	-0.59	0.6	0.0	-0.03	-1.57	2.71	113.3	2.4	33.3	23.0	0.5
5.4	1.99	10.7	0.00	5.2	1.1	1.25	10.88	3.86	67.7	2.3	32.5	23.5	6.9
5.0	0.69	5.1	0.16	5.2	2.4	0.93	7.71	3.83	64.4	1.8	13.8	19.9	7.4
4.5	1.21	8.9	0.03	4.5	1.6	0.79	8.28	4.01	68.7	2.1	13.1	12.9	5.5
4.9	1.31	7.8	0.18	6.7	5.0	1.51	12.02	4.70	68.8	3.5	13.0	11.5	8.0
9.5	0.32	0.7	0.09	4.5	1.9	0.95	5.61	2.89	61.2	5.9	51.8	7.8	7.8
9.6	1.71	2.5	0.00	1.8	0.1	0.25	1.41	2.37	88.0	4.6	87.6	19.1	6.5
4.4	1.76	15.5	-0.53	5.5	7.7	1.66	13.91	2.65	72.3	1.0	6.6	29.7	6.8
8.6	0.01	0.0	0.01	8.9	1.4	2.17	18.14	4.32	39.8	3.6	26.7	12.8	7.6
8.8	0.14	0.4	-0.05	6.6	1.4	1.28	6.77	3.85	52.7	6.2	58.1	7.8	8.8
6.0	0.53	4.1	0.03	5.3	9.2	0.97	9.78	2.99	52.4	2.7	12.4	12.4	7.0

I. Index of Banks

Name	City	State	2016 Rating	2015 Rating	2014 Rating	Total Assets ($Mil)	One Year Asset Growth	Commercial Loans	Consumer Loans	Mortgage Loans	Securities	Capitalization Index	Leverage Ratio	Risk-Based Capital Ratio
Libertyville Savings Bank	Fairfield	IA	B	B+	B+	339.2	4.96	9.1	1.3	9.9	24.1	7.8	10.0	13.2
Lifestore Bank	West Jefferson	NC	C	C	C-	264.6	3.19	3.5	1.1	32.9	18.9	9.3	10.5	18.0
Lighthouse Bank	Santa Cruz	CA	A	A	A	209.2	18.77	3.4	0.0	10.0	5.8	10.0	14.1	15.6
▼ Lincoln 1st Bank	Lincoln Park	NJ	D+	C-	C	332.7	32.96	4.2	0.2	24.2	64.6	4.9	6.9	15.4
Lincoln Community Bank	Merrill	WI	B+	B	B-	57.7	0.18	5.1	5.8	22.7	10.4	10.0	12.5	18.7
Lincoln FSB of Nebraska	Lincoln	NE	C+	B-	C+	312.5	9.70	0.2	0.0	45.7	28.5	9.2	10.5	25.0
Lincoln National Bank	Hodgenville	KY	B+	B+	A-	280.3	1.08	2.7	5.4	37.0	8.5	10.0	12.8	20.8
Lincoln Savings Bank	Reinbeck	IA	C+	B-	C+	930.2	11.14	9.5	1.0	12.2	13.8	5.8	9.4	11.6
Lincoln State Bank	Hankinson	ND	C	C	C	67.7	1.79	7.1	6.4	4.5	30.5	6.2	8.2	12.5
LincolnWay Community Bank	New Lenox	IL	D+	D	D+	187.3	11.32	8.1	0.0	16.0	3.1	8.4	10.7	13.7
Lindell Bank & Trust Co.	Saint Louis	MO	A	A	A	541.0	15.82	8.3	0.4	15.9	42.1	10.0	13.1	26.1
Lisle Savings Bank	Lisle	IL	B	B	B-	539.6	-0.09	0.8	0.0	35.1	45.0	10.0	20.5	48.3
Litchfield Bancorp	Litchfield	CT	C-	C-	C-	233.0	4.96	3.5	2.5	36.0	20.0	6.3	8.3	14.4
Litchfield National Bank	Litchfield	IL	C+	B-	C+	94.0	15.74	2.6	5.6	20.0	15.4	6.9	8.9	13.2
Little Bank, Inc.	Kinston	NC	B	B	B	366.5	0.38	5.8	0.5	15.9	21.6	8.6	10.0	15.1
Little Horn State Bank	Hardin	MT	C+	B-	C	87.0	9.49	6.3	2.9	14.4	3.4	4.5	8.6	10.7
Little River Bank	Lepanto	AR	D	D+	D+	31.5	-9.54	4.0	4.0	12.7	39.2	10.0	13.6	30.9
Live Oak Banking Co.	Wilmington	NC	B+	B-	C	1602.7	69.33	18.6	0.0	0.2	4.4	5.7	8.2	11.5
Liverpool Community Bank	Liverpool	PA	A-	A	B-	45.1	0.69	3.1	2.8	56.5	12.0	10.0	20.6	38.2
Livingston State Bank	Livingston	WI	B+	A-	A-	163.6	-0.42	4.8	1.5	16.9	8.4	8.6	10.0	13.8
Llano National Bank	Llano	TX	B	B	B-	158.0	-0.40	2.8	5.0	17.7	37.7	10.0	11.7	22.3
▲ LNB Community Bank	Lynnville	IN	B-	C+	C+	108.0	-4.29	4.0	3.9	47.0	19.0	8.6	10.1	19.3
Logan Bank & Trust Co.	Logan	WV	C+	C+	C+	263.2	-0.54	8.1	3.4	21.0	41.9	7.4	9.3	24.4
Logan County Bank	Scranton	AR	B	B+	B+	83.1	3.56	3.3	5.9	18.8	60.8	10.0	18.6	48.6
▼ Logan State Bank	Logan	IA	B	B+	B+	44.2	40.47	2.3	2.5	7.8	4.8	8.6	10.1	14.8
Logansport Savings Bank	Logansport	IN	A-	A-	A-	170.0	1.94	10.8	0.9	20.7	23.4	10.0	12.8	19.5
Lone Star Bank	Houston	TX	C	D+	D	111.4	7.42	5.0	0.2	25.2	0.2	8.9	10.3	14.3
Lone Star Capital Bank, N.A.	San Antonio	TX	C	C	C	243.8	5.15	9.2	1.2	14.2	16.9	8.3	9.8	14.6
Lone Star National Bank	McAllen	TX	B-	B-	B	2151.5	0.57	5.4	1.4	10.9	33.7	10.0	11.7	19.0
▼ Lone Star State Bank of West Texas	Lubbock	TX	C+	B+	B+	787.6	1.40	25.7	1.3	4.2	3.1	7.3	11.3	12.7
Longview Bank	Ogden	IL	B-	B-	C+	179.7	2.46	6.5	1.4	14.4	16.1	7.8	9.6	14.7
Loomis Federal S&L Assn.	Chicago	IL	B-	B-	B	75.9	-4.59	2.0	0.0	32.0	24.8	10.0	23.9	85.0
Lorraine State Bank	Lorraine	KS	C+	C+	B	23.2	-2.71	2.3	8.3	9.7	20.4	10.0	14.4	18.3
Los Alamos National Bank	Los Alamos	NM	C-	D+	D	1405.1	-1.54	6.1	1.2	14.7	29.1	8.2	9.8	16.6
▼ Louisa Community Bank	Louisa	KY	D+	C+	C+	34.8	4.45	10.6	5.4	20.4	1.5	10.0	13.6	17.7
Lovelady State Bank	Lovelady	TX	C-	C-	C	46.3	-7.64	8.2	11.8	13.4	22.8	7.6	9.4	17.7
Lowell Five Cent Savings Bank	Lowell	MA	B-	C+	C+	1035.4	4.50	5.4	0.2	26.1	12.6	9.4	11.9	14.5
Lowry State Bank	Lowry	MN	C-	C	D+	46.3	-1.14	15.3	6.2	21.4	0.8	7.4	9.7	12.9
Luana Savings Bank	Luana	IA	B+	B+	B+	838.7	11.95	1.1	2.3	23.9	15.5	5.1	8.9	11.1
Lubbock National Bank	Lubbock	TX	B-	B-	B-	989.7	5.50	12.8	0.9	4.3	38.0	8.1	9.7	16.8
Lumbee Guaranty Bank	Pembroke	NC	B-	B-	C	335.2	8.24	2.6	2.0	13.9	33.0	9.7	10.8	18.4
Lusitania Savings Bank	Newark	NJ	B+	B+	B+	299.7	6.99	0.1	0.9	36.7	18.0	10.0	14.4	38.5
Lusk State Bank	Lusk	WY	A-	A-	B+	55.5	-1.15	3.1	4.1	1.3	14.4	10.0	11.8	16.4
Luther Burbank Savings	Manhattan Beach	CA	B+	B+	A-	4824.1	15.72	0.0	0.0	35.5	8.8	10.0	11.3	22.6
Luzerne Bank	Luzerne	PA	C+	B-	B-	382.2	10.73	12.6	1.5	14.1	6.5	5.0	8.6	11.0
Lyndon State Bank	Lyndon	KS	D+	C-	C+	71.5	0.17	5.9	3.0	29.6	24.4	8.5	10.0	15.8
▲ Lyon County State Bank	Emporia	KS	B-	C	C	149.7	-1.48	5.6	1.8	14.1	48.5	5.7	7.7	19.0
Lyons Federal Bank	Lyons	KS	B	B	C+	81.6	-2.87	5.1	4.1	18.4	1.2	10.0	12.2	17.2
Lyons National Bank	Lyons	NY	B	B	B	926.5	7.48	9.7	3.0	23.9	21.7	5.9	7.9	11.9
Lyons State Bank	Lyons	KS	B	B	B-	97.8	-1.07	7.7	4.5	9.4	28.4	10.0	11.1	16.1
Lytle State Bank of Lytle, Texas	Lytle	TX	B+	B+	B+	80.9	1.00	4.1	16.5	4.8	54.9	10.0	17.6	42.9
M C Bank & Trust Co.	Morgan City	LA	B+	B+	A-	332.4	-4.47	7.1	2.7	8.4	42.6	10.0	18.4	33.5
M.Y. Safra Bank, FSB	New York	NY	D	D	U	238.5	7.52	0.9	0.0	17.9	55.8	10.0	15.7	28.3
Mabrey Bank	Bixby	OK	B-	B-	B-	880.0	9.72	22.5	1.7	15.5	18.9	5.3	7.9	11.2
Macatawa Bank	Holland	MI	B	B-	B-	1651.9	-0.35	23.6	0.5	14.9	14.8	9.9	11.6	14.9
▲ Machias Savings Bank	Machias	ME	B	B-	B-	1234.2	8.21	13.9	0.9	21.2	2.8	10.0	12.6	15.1
▲ Mackinac Savings Bank, FSB	Boynton Beach	FL	C	D+	D	109.5	0.92	0.2	0.0	62.2	0.0	6.8	8.8	26.5
Macon Bank and Trust Co.	Lafayette	TN	B	B-	B-	382.5	5.94	2.1	4.7	12.5	49.3	10.0	12.5	28.5
▼ Macon-Atlanta State Bank	Macon	MO	C	C+	B	278.4	0.10	3.7	2.2	7.6	34.1	6.7	8.7	14.0
Madison Bank of Maryland	Forest Hill	MD	D+	D	D	132.6	-1.34	0.0	0.0	55.6	16.5	10.0	18.1	37.8

Asset Quality Index	Adjusted Non-Performing Loans as a % of Total Loans	as a % of Capital	Net Charge-Offs Avg Loans	Profitability Index	Net Income ($Mil)	Return on Assets (R.O.A.)	Return on Equity (R.O.E.)	Net Interest Spread	Overhead Efficiency Ratio	Liquidity Index	Liquidity Ratio	Hot Money Ratio	Stability Index
5.0	0.90	5.4	0.08	4.7	3.1	1.24	10.79	3.98	65.1	4.7	31.4	8.5	7.0
3.3	2.87	16.0	0.07	3.5	1.4	0.70	6.47	3.35	79.2	3.2	31.7	16.3	5.5
7.6	0.01	0.0	0.00	7.9	1.5	1.06	7.15	4.94	53.0	2.6	12.1	15.8	8.6
4.0	4.26	19.0	0.00	3.0	0.8	0.39	5.57	2.33	73.2	1.7	37.7	20.4	2.4
5.6	1.02	5.5	0.15	6.0	0.5	1.14	9.20	4.25	63.0	4.4	22.0	6.7	6.6
4.3	2.95	14.4	-0.01	3.1	1.3	0.50	4.26	2.41	89.8	2.2	33.3	25.5	7.3
8.2	0.38	2.1	0.04	4.8	1.8	0.84	6.45	4.07	69.2	2.5	19.9	17.0	8.0
3.9	1.62	12.7	0.07	5.0	6.3	0.95	8.47	4.00	68.7	1.6	5.9	19.2	6.4
5.4	0.51	3.6	0.67	4.1	0.5	0.97	12.26	3.47	67.8	3.5	21.8	12.1	4.4
2.0	1.85	12.9	0.02	8.4	1.8	1.37	13.14	5.10	59.8	0.9	15.4	33.4	5.8
7.7	1.15	3.7	-0.17	7.1	6.4	1.66	10.42	3.88	60.5	4.9	33.7	7.8	8.3
5.3	7.48	15.2	0.07	4.5	4.7	1.15	5.69	2.75	62.1	4.0	61.7	20.6	8.0
5.0	1.14	9.3	0.07	1.8	0.3	0.20	2.24	3.20	91.7	2.9	27.0	11.6	4.7
4.5	1.12	8.8	0.07	4.3	0.5	0.72	8.27	3.76	74.1	1.6	16.0	23.4	4.4
7.0	0.42	2.6	-0.01	5.2	2.5	0.90	9.11	3.52	64.9	2.0	26.4	13.7	6.3
5.4	1.00	8.7	-0.01	4.6	0.5	0.78	8.28	4.98	75.1	3.4	10.3	11.6	4.3
3.7	7.93	23.4	0.26	0.0	-0.2	-0.64	-4.95	3.06	116.3	4.6	51.8	14.0	4.0
7.1	0.34	2.9	0.13	9.4	14.7	1.54	16.01	3.62	66.0	1.5	27.3	45.9	8.7
7.8	1.97	7.0	0.00	7.5	0.4	1.24	6.04	4.38	59.2	3.4	22.0	12.6	7.0
3.7	1.39	10.8	-0.04	5.1	0.5	0.36	2.78	4.03	60.5	1.9	13.5	19.0	6.4
5.0	2.91	11.0	0.06	5.0	1.0	0.89	7.39	4.15	63.1	4.2	52.7	17.3	7.3
4.8	1.63	9.7	0.15	4.0	0.8	0.91	9.37	3.41	79.6	4.6	12.4	4.5	6.5
5.7	2.05	7.7	0.18	3.4	1.1	0.56	6.09	2.74	73.7	4.5	48.0	14.4	5.2
6.6	3.94	7.2	0.02	4.7	0.6	1.01	5.44	3.09	57.8	4.4	58.5	16.3	7.6
7.2	0.07	0.6	0.00	4.1	0.2	0.74	6.65	4.43	81.9	3.2	14.8	4.4	6.0
6.3	1.37	7.0	0.02	6.5	1.6	1.20	9.18	3.83	58.6	4.1	22.6	9.0	7.5
6.0	0.00	0.0	0.27	3.2	0.6	0.72	6.95	3.84	79.7	0.8	14.6	37.5	5.0
7.6	0.08	0.5	0.09	3.1	0.7	0.39	2.94	3.77	86.7	2.6	25.3	16.8	6.4
3.4	4.93	21.3	0.09	3.4	9.6	0.60	4.97	3.45	83.2	1.2	12.9	27.0	8.6
3.0	1.85	13.2	0.35	4.0	3.6	0.63	5.12	3.77	51.7	0.6	5.8	42.7	8.4
5.2	1.28	8.9	0.02	6.2	1.5	1.07	11.50	3.67	54.2	2.1	12.9	18.0	5.3
7.4	4.13	6.2	-0.09	3.2	0.3	0.43	1.84	2.88	80.5	6.4	81.9	9.1	7.3
6.5	0.62	3.2	-0.05	5.2	0.2	0.98	7.05	3.77	60.0	2.0	22.4	19.4	5.0
2.1	5.87	30.4	-0.07	2.5	6.9	0.65	6.83	3.45	88.7	5.3	37.8	10.6	6.3
1.8	4.71	26.4	0.29	0.9	-0.3	-1.31	-8.56	4.21	119.9	0.6	12.3	48.1	6.0
4.5	1.30	6.3	-0.11	4.7	0.4	1.07	11.92	4.19	71.3	3.2	49.1	20.9	4.0
7.6	0.77	4.8	0.03	3.4	4.5	0.58	5.03	3.42	76.1	4.2	19.1	8.7	8.7
1.4	4.04	32.5	0.02	9.1	0.7	1.93	18.55	4.82	58.1	4.2	11.0	6.8	7.4
6.9	0.28	2.3	0.01	9.3	13.4	2.22	23.90	3.48	34.6	0.6	18.6	10.3	8.3
5.0	1.78	8.8	0.43	4.6	6.6	0.92	8.98	3.53	64.7	2.5	43.5	26.6	6.6
3.6	3.59	16.8	0.07	3.9	1.7	0.68	6.50	4.13	81.1	3.5	25.0	12.7	5.9
7.5	1.33	4.4	0.07	4.4	1.5	0.69	4.78	2.74	55.8	4.5	51.8	15.7	7.7
7.8	0.22	1.1	0.00	7.4	0.7	1.77	15.27	3.87	59.6	4.9	30.2	6.1	8.3
7.7	0.16	1.2	-0.02	5.2	44.4	1.29	11.21	2.26	54.5	0.7	11.5	40.1	9.7
3.0	1.24	10.2	0.06	3.8	1.9	0.68	5.50	3.49	70.1	4.0	16.1	8.7	6.7
5.8	0.62	3.5	0.28	1.2	-0.2	-0.31	-2.74	4.82	103.9	3.2	25.4	14.2	5.2
9.5	0.04	0.2	0.02	4.1	1.3	1.16	13.22	3.00	75.8	6.1	51.0	6.5	5.2
7.1	0.75	4.4	0.00	4.6	0.5	0.79	6.46	3.80	69.6	2.3	13.9	17.5	6.7
5.8	0.62	4.9	0.02	4.7	6.4	0.93	12.11	3.36	66.7	3.0	9.3	11.4	5.8
7.6	0.50	2.7	0.31	4.3	0.7	0.92	8.16	4.05	75.9	1.8	15.9	20.4	7.2
7.6	1.53	2.5	0.36	4.3	0.6	0.99	5.49	3.64	76.6	4.5	60.7	16.0	7.2
5.1	4.28	10.3	0.54	4.9	2.3	0.90	4.83	3.72	63.6	4.2	54.9	17.8	7.9
9.9	0.00	0.0	0.00	0.0	-1.9	-1.02	-6.31	1.46	164.7	3.2	70.9	23.8	6.5
6.2	0.43	3.6	0.04	5.0	7.8	1.23	15.77	3.89	73.6	1.6	13.3	20.2	5.7
5.8	1.26	7.4	-0.10	5.0	12.9	1.03	8.96	3.20	66.7	5.2	20.6	2.2	9.7
4.2	2.27	13.9	0.14	4.9	6.7	0.77	6.01	4.43	74.1	2.3	12.6	14.2	9.2
9.3	0.03	0.2	-0.32	3.1	0.6	0.72	8.56	2.78	89.6	5.0	36.3	8.5	3.7
8.9	0.54	1.6	-0.04	3.8	2.3	0.81	6.33	3.35	74.3	3.1	55.1	30.5	7.2
2.5	3.59	21.2	0.01	3.8	0.9	0.44	4.81	3.06	66.3	2.1	17.1	18.9	5.1
5.6	4.61	16.2	0.12	0.2	-0.4	-0.39	-2.13	2.52	126.2	1.9	32.9	30.1	5.7

151

Name	City	State	2015 Rating	2014 Rating	Rating	Total Assets ($Mil)	One Year Asset Growth	Comm-ercial Loans	Cons-umer Loans	Mort-gage Loans	Secur-ities	Capital-ization Index	Lever-age Ratio	Risk-Based Capital Ratio
Madison County Bank	Madison	NE	A	A	A	352.0	8.48	1.5	1.3	12.8	17.6	10.0	18.2	17.8
Madison County Community Bank	Madison	FL	C+	C+	C	117.4	8.05	5.5	2.3	9.4	32.4	6.8	8.8	18.0
Magnolia Bank	Hodgenville	KY	B+	B+	B	198.6	19.25	10.0	1.0	24.2	9.7	7.8	9.6	15.4
Magnolia State Bank	Bay Springs	MS	B	B+	B+	311.2	0.03	7.1	6.2	23.4	17.4	8.9	10.3	14.6
Magyar Bank	New Brunswick	NJ	C-	D+	D+	584.4	6.14	6.7	1.6	29.6	10.1	6.3	8.3	12.2
Mahopac Bank	Brewster	NY	B	B	B-	1279.3	13.83	9.6	1.4	16.2	26.4	6.5	8.6	13.0
▼ Main Bank	Albuquerque	NM	B+	A-	A-	122.6	9.82	5.9	0.1	12.6	14.9	8.3	9.8	15.4
Main Street Bank	Bingham Farms	MI	B	B	B-	215.6	9.89	16.1	0.5	30.3	3.9	6.7	9.0	12.3
Main Street Bank Corp.	Wheeling	WV	C+	C+	C+	400.2	14.45	13.3	3.2	40.3	8.1	6.5	8.5	13.1
Mainland Bank	Texas City	TX	B+	B+	B+	137.3	6.79	31.9	1.0	8.2	12.1	7.4	10.0	12.8
MainSource Bank	Greensburg	IN	A-	A-	B+	4014.2	20.20	8.2	1.5	18.3	25.5	8.2	9.8	15.0
Mainstreet Bank	Ashland	MO	C	C-	D	42.1	-4.60	9.2	1.1	25.0	30.5	10.0	12.7	21.0
MainStreet Bank	Fairfax	VA	C+	C+	C	535.9	11.42	7.1	14.9	11.4	9.9	3.9	8.7	10.5
Mainstreet Community Bank of Florida	Deland	FL	B	B	B-	317.0	17.86	12.0	1.5	9.3	21.2	6.3	8.7	12.0
Malaga Bank F.S.B.	Palos Verdes Estates	CA	A	A	A	998.5	1.95	0.1	0.0	14.3	0.0	10.0	13.6	25.7
▲ Malvern Federal Savings Bank	Paoli	PA	C+	C	D	820.9	26.40	4.7	0.2	30.6	13.1	9.7	10.8	15.2
Malvern National Bank	Malvern	AR	C-	C	C+	511.2	6.64	6.7	1.1	8.6	38.1	8.5	10.0	16.4
Malvern Trust & Savings Bank	Malvern	IA	C+	C+	C	135.8	19.47	20.8	18.1	19.5	1.4	6.2	9.2	11.9
Manasquan Bank	Manasquan	NJ	B	B-	B-	1048.0	12.87	8.6	0.1	38.2	6.6	7.9	10.5	13.3
Manhattan Bank	Manhattan	MT	B	B-	C+	159.6	3.38	4.2	2.1	11.2	34.2	7.0	9.0	15.0
Manor Bank	Manor	PA	D-	D-	D	40.4	27.81	0.7	0.2	36.7	15.3	6.1	8.1	15.2
Mansfield Co-operative Bank	Mansfield	MA	C+	C+	C	482.6	4.84	2.1	0.0	29.6	11.4	8.4	10.0	15.9
▲ Manson State Bank	Manson	IA	B-	C+	C+	35.8	-6.82	5.5	0.8	7.5	47.1	10.0	11.1	20.6
Manufacturers and Traders Trust Co.	Buffalo	NY	C+	C+	C	126239.2	30.00	13.9	5.0	18.7	11.3	6.8	8.8	12.8
Manufacturers Bank	Los Angeles	CA	C+	C+	C+	2726.5	8.67	39.2	0.0	0.1	23.5	8.0	12.2	13.3
Manufacturers Bank & Trust Co.	Forest City	IA	A-	A-	A-	325.9	7.32	9.1	2.4	11.9	24.8	10.0	11.9	15.1
▲ Maple Bank	Champlin	MN	C-	D+	D	48.8	7.11	20.6	0.3	7.9	0.0	10.0	11.8	16.8
Maple City Savings Bank, FSB	Hornell	NY	C-	C-	C-	69.6	6.90	5.6	1.1	62.4	0.1	9.0	10.3	18.6
Maquoketa State Bank	Maquoketa	IA	B+	B+	B+	329.1	-0.36	7.2	2.7	5.8	33.7	10.0	15.6	20.6
Marathon Savings Bank	Wausau	WI	C	C+	D-	145.0	-0.51	2.1	0.4	33.3	29.4	10.0	12.1	22.4
Marblehead Bank	Marblehead	MA	C-	C-	C-	194.0	6.44	1.2	0.4	53.5	4.7	8.5	10.0	16.1
Marblehead Bank	Marblehead	OH	C	C	C	48.3	2.79	2.6	4.9	24.4	59.1	8.8	10.2	27.6
Maries County Bank	Vienna	MO	B	B	B	449.4	0.32	2.9	5.8	15.7	35.1	10.0	13.9	21.8
Marine Bank	Springfield	IL	C	C-	C-	602.1	-1.61	8.8	0.6	8.3	15.5	8.7	11.1	13.9
Marine Bank & Trust Co.	Vero Beach	FL	C+	C+	D	203.0	9.94	9.4	0.3	36.9	8.3	6.7	8.8	14.6
Mariner's Bank	Edgewater	NJ	C	C-	D+	310.7	3.62	7.6	4.1	21.0	2.3	7.4	9.3	12.9
Marion Bank and Trust Co.	Marion	AL	A-	A-	B+	254.0	1.65	1.4	4.3	10.2	27.2	10.0	12.2	18.3
Marion Center Bank	Indiana	PA	C	C-	D+	272.6	-0.23	11.4	1.5	24.9	21.7	5.8	7.8	11.8
Marion County Savings Bank	Salem	IL	C	C-	C+	174.7	2.47	3.3	28.6	31.3	13.7	8.0	9.7	14.8
Marion County State Bank	Pella	IA	A	A	A	283.1	0.82	10.7	1.1	13.7	24.7	10.0	11.0	15.3
Marion National Bank	Marion	KS	C-	C	C	21.8	-4.25	3.9	2.3	8.9	43.4	10.0	11.7	23.4
Marion State Bank	Marion	LA	B	B	B	174.4	4.19	8.0	4.6	18.0	26.2	8.2	9.8	16.6
Marion State Bank	Marion	TX	A-	A-	A-	102.9	8.20	8.1	7.9	0.5	46.9	10.0	12.7	20.7
Markesan State Bank	Markesan	WI	D-	E+	C-	168.2	2.78	6.2	2.2	12.6	9.4	9.1	10.8	14.3
Marlborough Savings Bank	Marlborough	MA	C+	B-	B-	521.2	2.42	5.2	0.6	27.0	18.9	10.0	11.3	15.0
Marlin Business Bank	Salt Lake City	UT	A	A	A	844.2	15.07	22.1	0.0	0.0	4.2	10.0	16.1	18.0
Marquette Bank	Orland Park	IL	C+	C+	C	1546.6	2.57	1.9	0.0	16.2	15.1	6.5	8.5	13.2
Marquette Farmers State Bank	Marquette	KS	B-	B-	C+	32.6	-4.14	4.1	4.8	16.1	27.6	10.0	14.4	25.7
Marquette Savings Bank	Erie	PA	B+	B+	B+	839.0	3.76	4.1	0.4	44.8	31.0	10.0	16.9	32.2
▼ Marquis Bank	Coral Gables	FL	B-	B	B-	408.2	24.51	9.1	0.4	5.7	3.9	5.6	9.0	11.5
Mars National Bank	Mars	PA	C-	C-	C-	370.6	1.86	3.4	0.7	30.5	29.3	7.7	9.5	15.9
Marseilles Bank	Marseilles	IL	B	B	B-	59.3	5.50	0.4	7.2	29.7	49.4	8.6	10.1	20.0
Marshall County State Bank	Newfolden	MN	B	B	B	33.1	0.39	3.1	4.2	13.3	21.2	10.0	17.0	56.8
Martha's Vineyard Savings Bank	Edgartown	MA	B+	B+	B+	752.7	13.10	1.9	0.3	44.9	7.9	10.0	11.4	18.4
Martinsburg Bank and Trust	Mexico	MO	A-	B+	B+	193.0	-2.51	5.9	0.8	13.5	17.6	10.0	13.4	19.9
Martinsville First Savings Bank	Martinsville	VA	C+	C-	C-	43.6	3.62	0.0	0.2	49.5	17.0	10.0	14.4	36.5
Maryland Financial Bank	Towson	MD	D-	D	D	60.2	11.07	8.5	4.9	15.3	11.1	6.5	8.5	13.4
Mascoma Savings Bank	Lebanon	NH	C+	C	C	1476.1	5.07	7.7	0.4	39.2	9.4	7.7	9.5	13.5
Mason Bank	Mason	TX	A-	A-	A	111.0	1.66	5.3	4.0	10.1	57.4	10.0	16.7	39.8
Mason City National Bank	Mason City	IL	B	B	B	70.4	-4.00	0.8	1.5	10.4	52.8	10.0	16.2	38.0

Asset Quality Index	Adjusted Non-Performing Loans as a % of Total Loans	as a % of Capital	Net Charge-Offs Avg Loans	Profitability Index	Net Income ($Mil)	Return on Assets (R.O.A.)	Return on Equity (R.O.E.)	Net Interest Spread	Overhead Efficiency Ratio	Liquidity Index	Liquidity Ratio	Hot Money Ratio	Stability Index
7.3	0.42	1.6	0.00	6.7	3.5	1.32	7.29	3.78	52.9	4.8	18.6	3.6	8.6
5.1	1.57	7.8	0.20	3.4	0.4	0.52	5.96	3.11	77.7	3.4	49.4	21.6	3.8
6.3	0.20	1.5	0.03	8.5	3.1	2.13	20.01	3.42	81.2	1.3	9.5	25.2	8.2
5.5	0.48	3.3	0.04	4.0	1.8	0.78	7.75	4.11	78.3	2.2	10.7	17.7	6.8
3.7	1.49	13.5	0.38	2.1	0.9	0.21	2.47	3.27	82.3	2.0	8.1	15.7	4.2
5.7	0.85	6.1	0.01	5.0	7.4	0.84	7.89	3.44	62.5	3.8	8.8	7.8	7.0
5.0	1.32	8.5	0.00	7.4	1.5	1.69	16.98	4.06	54.7	3.4	30.2	14.5	7.7
6.3	0.19	1.8	0.34	8.9	2.3	1.45	16.74	4.05	75.9	0.6	9.8	34.3	6.2
3.6	1.85	16.5	0.01	7.1	3.4	1.19	14.08	4.08	50.6	1.2	5.8	16.1	5.3
5.8	0.38	2.5	0.48	8.7	2.4	2.51	24.46	4.69	52.6	4.2	22.7	8.4	6.8
6.4	0.70	4.5	0.06	6.2	31.5	1.14	9.29	3.65	65.3	4.7	23.4	7.8	9.0
4.9	1.57	6.5	-0.07	3.4	0.2	0.67	4.75	4.86	67.6	1.5	33.5	40.2	5.2
6.3	0.04	0.4	0.10	4.2	2.8	0.75	8.55	3.79	71.1	0.6	10.3	42.1	4.6
5.3	0.99	7.2	-0.01	3.9	1.5	0.68	7.42	3.82	81.7	4.3	26.3	8.0	4.8
7.4	0.00	0.0	0.00	8.2	9.1	1.21	8.99	3.18	35.2	1.3	11.7	26.5	9.3
7.7	0.45	2.9	0.02	4.2	10.8	1.85	18.18	2.57	66.2	1.2	27.7	27.5	4.7
5.2	1.61	7.6	0.01	1.7	0.6	0.17	1.66	3.20	93.9	2.3	27.3	19.0	5.9
4.7	0.52	4.6	0.21	4.5	1.0	1.03	11.38	3.65	58.2	0.6	10.5	50.0	4.7
6.8	0.61	4.6	0.01	4.4	5.3	0.70	6.67	3.21	62.5	1.6	11.7	22.7	7.8
4.2	1.94	11.5	-0.03	4.7	1.3	1.10	11.90	4.08	73.9	5.4	38.0	6.7	6.1
7.7	0.74	5.3	0.00	0.0	-0.3	-1.47	-15.74	3.47	155.4	5.7	42.2	5.6	3.4
5.8	0.83	6.0	-0.02	3.4	1.8	0.52	5.16	3.34	80.6	1.8	20.6	21.9	6.2
8.9	0.00	0.0	0.00	3.7	0.3	0.91	7.76	3.05	70.7	6.3	66.8	7.1	5.3
3.4	1.61	12.6	0.16	6.3	998.2	1.08	8.72	3.12	55.4	4.6	18.6	4.9	10.0
8.2	0.24	1.3	-0.02	3.5	9.9	0.50	4.17	2.59	64.2	2.2	23.0	13.3	8.9
8.5	0.24	1.3	-0.09	6.8	3.8	1.58	12.98	3.95	61.8	3.1	27.5	15.2	8.2
3.5	3.37	18.7	0.00	1.4	0.1	0.20	1.42	4.17	92.9	0.9	24.6	23.3	5.6
5.4	1.01	8.4	0.00	2.4	0.2	0.33	3.19	3.96	85.8	4.0	7.0	7.7	4.7
6.1	1.51	5.3	-0.02	6.2	3.0	1.23	7.77	3.50	58.6	4.3	35.3	11.8	8.6
3.7	4.57	20.3	1.84	2.2	0.3	0.23	1.87	3.69	93.6	4.1	38.8	13.9	5.3
6.1	0.76	6.1	0.01	1.5	0.0	0.03	0.29	3.31	100.9	4.6	13.2	4.7	4.8
9.3	0.00	0.0	0.00	3.1	0.3	0.71	6.78	3.08	80.4	5.4	50.0	9.4	5.4
8.2	0.56	2.1	0.22	4.7	3.1	0.92	6.50	4.16	70.1	3.3	23.2	13.2	7.9
3.2	1.17	7.3	-0.03	5.9	6.9	1.50	13.69	3.21	69.0	4.2	18.0	8.0	7.3
7.1	0.23	1.9	0.24	3.6	0.7	0.47	5.13	3.66	81.1	1.8	20.2	15.6	4.8
3.1	1.23	10.6	0.01	3.2	1.6	0.69	7.65	3.48	78.6	1.3	12.1	26.0	4.7
5.0	2.80	14.1	0.21	5.5	2.5	1.31	10.48	3.83	57.0	1.4	19.1	27.8	7.2
3.1	1.96	16.7	0.36	3.6	1.4	0.68	8.64	3.64	73.5	3.3	24.5	13.6	3.2
2.7	1.83	14.1	0.33	2.9	0.5	0.39	4.01	3.71	80.3	3.3	5.3	11.8	5.5
8.6	0.23	1.5	0.00	9.1	4.7	2.18	18.95	3.92	44.1	4.4	24.6	7.0	8.7
7.8	0.00	0.0	0.10	1.6	0.0	0.19	1.22	3.43	98.0	4.8	53.4	11.5	6.4
7.2	0.45	2.5	0.08	4.0	0.8	0.59	6.14	3.77	79.7	2.4	19.5	17.7	6.0
7.6	0.07	0.2	0.05	7.2	1.4	1.87	14.41	3.71	49.3	1.7	32.0	30.9	7.9
0.0	7.90	54.2	1.00	3.2	0.6	0.45	4.07	4.00	60.7	2.4	16.4	17.0	5.6
6.7	0.77	4.3	0.00	3.0	1.7	0.44	3.86	3.14	83.3	3.6	29.8	13.6	7.4
8.7	0.21	1.2	1.37	10.0	11.3	1.90	11.77	10.07	57.3	0.3	11.2	38.2	8.7
3.3	1.52	12.0	0.21	3.3	4.9	0.42	3.85	3.55	82.0	4.4	16.3	6.5	7.6
5.0	3.14	10.7	0.00	4.5	0.2	0.90	6.24	3.73	68.4	2.8	50.7	28.5	7.2
8.9	0.72	2.6	0.02	4.2	5.1	0.82	4.79	3.38	66.3	3.8	36.9	15.0	8.7
5.6	0.34	2.9	0.00	4.8	2.4	0.80	8.51	3.55	60.1	1.0	15.0	31.7	6.1
7.9	0.08	0.5	0.00	2.3	1.0	0.36	3.70	2.80	88.4	5.2	28.0	3.6	5.7
6.4	1.46	6.4	0.10	6.1	0.6	1.39	13.11	3.73	62.2	3.2	52.1	23.4	6.7
8.9	1.61	2.8	0.00	4.3	0.3	1.02	5.90	2.33	56.3	6.8	65.1	3.6	7.7
7.9	0.36	2.5	0.00	4.6	3.9	0.71	6.09	3.59	66.1	4.7	15.5	3.9	8.2
7.8	0.68	3.1	0.00	6.9	2.5	1.72	12.66	3.60	59.0	4.3	13.9	6.4	8.8
2.8	7.94	27.5	0.04	3.5	0.2	0.58	4.02	2.83	75.2	2.6	53.0	33.0	7.1
2.7	1.82	14.6	1.46	0.0	-0.8	-1.75	-18.00	2.63	126.8	0.5	25.0	94.6	2.6
5.8	0.78	6.4	0.18	3.5	5.9	0.55	5.56	3.54	79.2	3.5	10.3	9.4	7.7
9.1	0.17	0.4	0.03	5.8	1.1	1.37	8.13	3.69	62.4	5.8	68.1	12.2	9.3
9.3	0.73	1.6	0.02	4.4	0.6	1.20	7.08	2.97	62.2	5.1	67.9	14.0	7.9

Name	City	State	2017 Rating	2015 Rating	2014 Rating	Total Assets ($Mil)	One Year Asset Growth	Commercial Loans	Consumer Loans	Mortgage Loans	Securities	Capitalization Index	Leverage Ratio	Risk-Based Capital Ratio
Mason State Bank	Mason	MI	B-	B-	C+	114.6	-8.30	7.0	0.3	38.6	19.4	10.0	11.6	21.1
Maspeth Federal S&L Assn.	Maspeth	NY	B	B	B	1758.9	0.60	0.0	0.0	52.6	0.9	10.0	32.5	40.5
Massena S&L	Massena	NY	B	B	B	151.7	2.92	0.9	7.2	74.0	0.0	10.0	12.4	19.6
MassMutual Trust Co., FSB	Enfield	CT	U	U	U	74.8	4.51	0.0	0.0	0.0	87.8	10.0	25.2	41.0
Mauch Chunk Trust Co.	Jim Thorpe	PA	C+	B-	B	394.7	5.64	1.7	0.7	16.5	52.0	7.9	9.6	17.7
Maxwell State Bank	Maxwell	IA	A	A	A	28.7	0.51	1.5	0.7	3.8	68.2	10.0	14.6	30.6
Maynard Savings Bank	Maynard	IA	B+	B+	B+	59.6	3.19	7.2	8.3	24.0	18.2	10.0	13.9	19.2
Mayville Savings Bank	Mayville	WI	C+	C	C+	57.9	6.16	8.5	2.1	51.6	9.5	9.5	10.7	18.2
Mayville State Bank	Mayville	MI	C+	C+	C+	90.8	1.65	1.0	2.3	30.7	38.1	8.9	10.3	26.6
MB Financial Bank, N.A.	Chicago	IL	B-	C+	C+	19260.1	29.00	28.4	3.1	11.4	15.8	5.3	10.3	11.2
mBank	Manistique	MI	C+	C	C+	955.8	28.06	14.2	2.2	19.9	9.3	5.8	9.3	11.6
MBank	Gresham	OR	C+	C-	D	157.6	-3.80	6.5	0.7	17.5	1.9	6.4	9.7	12.1
MBL Bank	Minden	LA	A	A	A	319.4	5.45	9.7	2.2	20.2	32.6	10.0	16.2	27.5
McClain Bank	Purcell	OK	B+	B	B	199.7	-2.58	7.9	2.6	22.9	11.1	9.6	10.7	15.9
McClave State Bank	McClave	CO	B-	B	B-	38.0	21.42	10.5	1.7	3.9	12.9	7.8	10.7	13.1
McCook National Bank	McCook	NE	A-	A-	A-	332.4	2.99	6.8	0.9	6.9	18.2	10.0	14.8	18.7
▲ McCurtain County National Bank	Broken Bow	OK	A-	B+	B+	223.6	3.15	3.6	8.4	16.3	20.3	10.0	11.2	21.7
McFarland State Bank	McFarland	WI	B	B-	C	439.2	5.78	6.9	0.1	8.1	6.0	8.1	10.9	13.4
McGehee Bank	McGehee	AR	A-	A-	B+	140.9	7.34	20.2	1.1	2.3	12.3	10.0	14.7	16.1
McHenry Savings Bank	McHenry	IL	E-	E-	E-	254.7	3.52	7.1	6.9	33.7	20.5	0.5	3.6	7.7
▲ McIntosh County Bank	Ashley	ND	C+	C+	C-	91.2	-1.40	3.8	2.4	0.4	22.6	10.0	11.1	15.0
McKenzie Banking Co.	McKenzie	TN	B	B+	A-	128.2	5.04	8.8	5.3	19.3	15.9	10.0	16.2	33.6
MCNB Bank and Trust Co.	Welch	WV	D+	C-	C-	294.0	-0.30	7.3	2.6	11.4	23.9	8.9	10.3	14.6
Meade County Bank	Brandenburg	KY	B+	B+	B+	175.6	-9.20	1.6	3.3	37.0	37.8	8.4	9.9	19.3
Meadows Bank	Las Vegas	NV	B+	A	A	650.4	22.29	25.3	0.1	3.9	3.9	6.7	10.5	12.3
▼ Mechanics and Farmers Bank	Durham	NC	D	C	D	310.0	2.90	3.2	0.3	2.1	24.5	10.0	11.1	19.2
Mechanics Bank	Walnut Creek	CA	B	B-	B-	3758.1	5.82	3.3	3.7	7.9	18.0	10.0	11.8	20.4
Mechanics Bank	Water Valley	MS	D+	D+	C+	217.9	0.80	11.7	3.1	28.7	22.3	9.2	10.5	16.6
Mechanics Bank	Mansfield	OH	C+	C+	C+	475.0	9.08	1.7	0.8	62.5	8.0	6.8	8.8	16.4
Mechanics Cooperative Bank	Taunton	MA	B-	B-	B-	502.6	4.22	5.0	1.2	30.4	14.2	7.0	9.0	13.6
Mechanics Savings Bank	Auburn	ME	B	B-	C+	381.5	3.06	8.9	1.2	49.3	8.8	10.0	12.0	18.3
▼ Medallion Bank	Salt Lake City	UT	D	C+	B+	1116.4	3.89	29.6	62.3	0.0	3.3	10.0	15.6	17.3
▲ Mediapolis Savings Bank	Mediapolis	IA	B-	B-	B	156.2	5.90	6.1	2.4	18.3	13.7	7.5	10.4	12.9
Medina S&L Assn.	Medina	NY	D	D	D	51.2	4.52	0.6	2.0	40.2	10.4	6.9	8.9	21.8
Meetinghouse Bank	Dorchester	MA	C-	C-	D+	119.9	-0.03	2.3	0.7	52.9	11.3	5.9	7.9	14.4
Mega Bank	San Gabriel	CA	B	B-	C+	325.8	5.96	1.4	0.0	15.3	6.6	10.0	12.1	18.1
Melrose Co-operative Bank	Melrose	MA	C+	C+	C+	262.3	19.70	0.0	0.1	62.0	11.0	10.0	13.6	22.1
▲ Melvin Savings Bank	Melvin	IA	B+	B	B-	66.7	0.98	6.3	2.2	4.8	39.9	10.0	18.3	35.0
MEMBERS Trust Co.	Tampa	FL	U	U	U	33.8	4.59	0.0	0.0	0.0	76.6	10.0	94.4	359.7
Menard Bank	Menard	TX	B-	B-	B-	33.3	-2.18	5.9	0.6	10.2	39.4	10.0	14.1	24.5
Menno State Bank	Menno	SD	C+	B-	C+	35.9	-2.68	5.7	1.3	1.1	25.3	9.7	10.8	15.9
Mer Rouge State Bank	Mer Rouge	LA	C+	C+	C+	43.7	2.37	15.6	1.1	3.9	17.0	10.0	11.7	17.7
▲ Meramec Valley Bank	Ellisville	MO	C-	D+	C-	101.3	8.55	10.3	1.0	17.8	12.6	5.8	8.7	11.6
Mercantil Commercebank Trust Co., N.A.	Coral Gables	FL	U	U	U	9.8	8.77	0.0	0.0	0.0	70.7	10.0	92.0	183.6
Mercantil Commercebank, N.A.	Coral Gables	FL	C	C	C	8457.6	5.38	20.6	1.5	2.9	25.9	6.9	9.2	12.4
▲ Mercantile Bank	Quincy	IL	B	B	C-	444.9	6.11	9.0	17.9	17.2	13.7	7.6	9.4	13.8
Mercantile Bank of Louisiana, Missouri	Louisiana	MO	A-	A-	B	107.0	0.18	1.5	1.1	21.4	24.3	10.0	21.1	37.1
Mercantile Bank of Michigan	Grand Rapids	MI	B+	B	B	3043.8	6.36	21.6	1.5	8.3	10.7	7.7	11.3	13.1
Mercer County State Bank	Sandy Lake	PA	B	B	B	394.3	7.15	4.8	1.1	18.9	36.7	8.2	9.8	15.6
Mercer Savings Bank	Celina	OH	D+	D+	D+	114.2	2.06	1.3	1.9	55.8	15.4	8.1	9.8	19.6
Merchants & Citizens Bank	McRae	GA	B	B-	B	105.7	3.27	2.8	4.1	12.7	51.9	10.0	14.5	33.5
Merchants & Farmers Bank	Eutaw	AL	C-	D-	C	62.6	1.72	8.8	7.7	12.1	35.1	7.6	9.4	18.6
Merchants & Farmers Bank	Holly Springs	MS	C	C	C+	96.3	4.94	6.6	5.1	12.0	38.0	9.8	10.8	20.9
▲ Merchants & Farmers Bank & Trust Co.	Leesville	LA	B-	C+	B-	379.2	1.24	3.1	1.7	24.1	32.4	8.7	10.1	18.3
Merchants & Marine Bank	Pascagoula	MS	B	B	B	558.3	1.89	6.9	4.8	13.1	36.4	10.0	12.5	22.6
Merchants & Planters Bank	Clarendon	AR	C+	C	C+	45.7	-0.92	5.3	1.9	3.1	54.8	10.0	11.7	30.8
Merchants & Planters Bank	Newport	AR	B-	B-	C+	250.4	1.07	15.2	5.4	10.8	20.4	8.6	10.0	14.0
Merchants & Planters Bank	Bolivar	TN	B+	B	B	88.0	4.54	5.9	3.7	17.2	21.6	10.0	12.3	18.9
Merchants and Farmers Bank	Dumas	AR	B-	B-	C+	135.3	13.84	13.4	3.3	7.3	11.0	6.6	10.6	12.2
Merchants and Farmers Bank of Salisbury	Salisbury	MO	C+	C+	C+	97.1	-3.62	4.2	2.3	17.1	27.6	7.1	9.0	14.5

Arrows denote recent upgrades ▲ or downgrades ▼

Asset Quality Index	Adjusted Non-Performing Loans as a % of Total Loans	as a % of Capital	Net Charge-Offs Avg Loans	Profitability Index	Net Income ($Mil)	Return on Assets (R.O.A.)	Return on Equity (R.O.E.)	Net Interest Spread	Overhead Efficiency Ratio	Liquidity Index	Liquidity Ratio	Hot Money Ratio	Stability Index
6.7	0.77	4.3	-0.01	3.8	0.8	0.92	8.08	3.44	74.9	2.0	25.1	10.7	6.0
4.5	4.98	13.9	0.02	8.8	14.7	1.11	3.48	4.11	44.2	3.7	7.2	10.1	10.0
4.0	2.48	17.6	0.36	4.2	0.8	0.73	5.96	3.51	65.1	0.8	2.6	31.9	6.5
10.0	na	0.0	na	10.0	2.0	3.56	14.73	1.31	84.0	3.8	128.4	100.0	7.8
8.4	0.66	2.7	0.09	3.5	2.4	0.85	8.34	3.15	75.9	3.3	28.0	4.3	5.3
9.6	0.00	0.0	0.00	5.7	0.3	1.23	8.02	3.57	51.0	5.5	78.7	13.0	8.4
4.9	2.33	12.1	0.27	8.5	0.8	1.89	13.02	4.47	46.4	2.6	24.8	17.1	7.9
5.8	0.80	5.8	0.00	3.6	0.2	0.48	4.48	3.58	74.3	1.7	20.8	22.6	4.7
6.6	1.29	4.9	0.33	3.7	0.5	0.71	6.90	3.20	73.8	6.3	61.4	6.0	5.2
4.2	0.73	5.5	0.07	6.1	133.1	1.11	7.83	3.77	69.8	3.4	14.1	5.0	8.9
4.5	1.07	9.0	0.10	4.1	4.0	0.63	5.77	4.30	77.2	1.7	14.7	4.6	5.9
5.5	0.23	1.6	-0.03	2.7	0.2	0.16	1.27	4.65	97.4	1.7	16.9	22.2	5.8
6.8	1.95	7.1	0.00	8.8	3.6	1.52	9.62	3.65	38.7	1.7	20.1	22.3	8.9
5.6	0.61	3.9	-0.04	6.5	1.7	1.15	11.04	4.39	64.0	4.1	13.0	7.7	6.5
3.8	2.11	14.8	0.24	9.1	0.4	1.66	15.27	5.02	47.2	0.5	8.6	53.1	6.7
6.5	0.73	3.3	0.00	6.5	2.7	1.09	7.35	3.86	54.2	1.6	9.7	19.7	8.7
6.5	1.11	4.9	0.02	5.9	1.8	1.06	9.82	3.22	51.2	4.0	46.6	16.6	6.8
4.8	0.50	3.5	-0.21	8.3	5.7	1.81	16.50	4.04	66.6	1.4	6.1	22.8	7.7
6.3	0.64	3.8	0.19	6.8	1.6	1.70	11.72	4.11	52.8	2.5	7.4	15.5	9.3
1.7	3.44	48.3	0.33	1.3	0.1	0.04	1.13	3.43	98.8	0.9	19.5	39.3	0.3
3.5	2.73	14.7	0.00	6.7	1.1	1.53	14.47	3.97	53.3	3.6	10.5	10.4	8.3
4.6	4.60	12.7	0.35	9.9	3.9	4.08	27.60	5.08	42.9	5.2	56.9	13.1	7.9
4.0	2.09	11.9	0.29	1.7	0.5	0.21	2.09	3.36	93.3	3.1	22.8	14.2	5.2
9.2	0.12	0.7	0.00	5.3	1.4	0.98	10.08	3.47	61.5	5.5	42.9	7.9	5.9
5.1	0.32	2.6	0.04	9.4	6.5	1.45	13.05	5.02	56.7	3.1	11.1	13.1	8.6
2.2	8.19	33.7	4.66	0.3	-3.6	-1.60	-13.60	3.19	109.5	1.8	38.5	40.8	6.2
7.3	0.44	2.1	-0.01	4.7	21.9	0.82	5.33	3.59	67.5	5.6	35.6	7.6	8.5
1.5	6.03	34.5	1.24	3.6	1.1	0.69	6.61	3.99	72.1	1.4	22.5	27.9	5.6
5.5	1.14	10.0	0.12	3.5	2.0	0.59	6.58	3.49	74.2	3.9	8.3	8.5	5.1
5.3	0.73	6.1	0.05	4.9	3.1	0.83	9.62	3.81	65.2	1.3	16.8	27.5	4.7
4.6	2.21	14.6	0.12	4.5	2.1	0.74	6.46	3.83	71.5	0.8	9.3	15.5	6.3
0.2	5.04	23.4	1.11	9.8	13.9	1.67	10.86	8.24	24.2	0.3	10.8	0.1	9.7
4.6	1.20	8.5	-0.02	4.8	1.3	1.10	10.73	3.52	62.4	1.6	14.7	23.7	6.8
6.1	1.17	6.1	0.02	0.9	0.1	0.19	2.64	2.77	105.9	5.4	52.6	9.6	2.8
6.6	0.42	3.8	0.01	2.4	0.2	0.26	3.30	2.80	91.8	1.0	24.5	38.7	4.0
4.9	2.32	12.9	0.17	3.3	1.0	0.45	3.61	2.95	77.0	0.8	24.3	62.9	7.3
9.8	0.00	0.0	0.00	2.7	0.9	0.48	3.35	2.47	76.0	1.0	20.9	33.3	6.6
8.9	0.08	0.2	0.00	5.3	0.7	1.38	7.71	3.49	54.5	6.3	66.0	7.1	7.5
8.7	na	0.0	na	9.5	1.4	5.60	5.84	1.89	88.0	4.0	na	0.0	8.0
9.7	0.00	0.0	0.00	3.5	0.2	0.82	5.96	3.73	84.2	3.0	47.8	24.4	6.8
4.5	1.14	5.9	0.00	5.4	0.3	0.96	9.36	3.50	54.0	5.9	36.4	2.2	5.4
6.9	0.63	2.8	-0.05	2.7	0.1	0.39	3.29	3.48	86.8	2.5	35.9	23.4	5.8
8.5	0.01	0.1	-0.01	2.1	0.3	0.36	4.11	3.34	94.8	3.3	15.5	11.4	4.2
10.0	na	0.0	na	9.5	0.4	5.23	5.76	1.91	71.4	4.0	na	0.0	4.3
5.3	1.25	8.6	0.37	2.7	22.9	0.38	3.97	2.59	76.7	1.8	20.6	13.4	6.9
5.1	0.45	3.1	0.20	5.6	4.4	1.32	12.58	3.60	63.3	1.9	17.4	9.2	7.0
7.7	1.49	3.6	-0.07	5.6	1.1	1.31	5.87	3.36	60.8	4.8	47.6	13.0	8.9
6.3	0.56	3.8	0.03	6.0	24.3	1.10	8.77	3.95	60.1	1.8	10.3	16.3	9.5
5.3	1.53	8.2	0.05	4.0	2.4	0.83	7.86	3.43	73.7	4.1	36.6	13.3	6.5
6.3	0.81	5.7	0.34	1.7	0.2	0.18	1.79	3.24	93.0	4.5	25.1	7.1	4.7
5.6	3.35	7.2	0.78	4.0	0.7	0.87	5.28	3.37	69.3	2.6	41.0	27.0	7.4
4.1	2.63	12.9	0.14	2.9	0.3	0.64	6.43	4.08	81.8	4.5	28.7	8.3	3.5
3.2	4.62	17.9	0.25	2.4	0.3	0.46	4.18	3.41	91.5	2.6	36.5	21.8	5.4
6.1	0.52	2.8	0.12	4.3	2.4	0.84	7.43	3.71	70.6	4.0	29.8	11.4	6.6
7.1	1.30	4.7	0.10	4.1	3.4	0.77	6.74	3.19	70.8	3.3	30.0	15.0	6.8
9.4	0.75	1.5	0.56	2.9	0.2	0.57	4.99	3.02	81.7	3.2	52.1	23.0	5.1
4.6	1.25	8.0	0.10	4.4	1.6	0.87	8.92	3.99	74.6	1.8	9.0	18.9	5.0
8.3	0.17	0.8	-1.49	5.7	0.7	1.10	8.48	4.49	81.3	3.1	33.1	17.2	6.1
6.2	0.46	3.4	0.16	4.3	0.7	0.81	7.49	4.50	73.1	1.4	9.9	24.0	5.4
8.8	0.15	1.0	0.02	3.3	0.5	0.73	8.19	3.32	83.1	3.0	24.0	15.1	4.6

Name	City	State	2015 Rating	2014 Rating	Rating	Total Assets ($Mil)	One Year Asset Growth	Commercial Loans	Consumer Loans	Mortgage Loans	Securities	Capitalization Index	Leverage Ratio	Risk-Based Capital Ratio
Merchants and Manufacturers Bank	Joliet	IL	C+	C+	C+	227.7	3.90	29.7	31.6	5.6	2.9	4.7	8.1	10.8
Merchants and Planters Bank	Raymond	MS	C-	D+	C-	88.5	-5.29	5.0	1.4	11.7	36.9	6.1	8.2	15.8
▲ Merchants Bank	Jackson	AL	B	C+	C	207.9	2.21	6.2	3.6	15.6	27.6	10.0	11.4	17.1
Merchants Bank	Rugby	ND	B	B	B	108.2	-0.74	10.0	2.3	4.1	24.9	7.1	9.1	13.1
Merchants Bank	South Burlington	VT	B-	B	B	1999.3	9.71	12.7	0.3	23.7	19.6	6.7	8.7	15.3
▲ Merchants Bank of Alabama	Cullman	AL	B-	C+	C	271.2	4.30	5.9	3.9	19.6	24.3	7.9	9.6	15.9
Merchants Bank of Bangor	Bangor	PA	C+	C+	C+	370.9	5.41	3.1	1.0	21.3	35.0	6.6	8.6	14.5
▼ Merchants Bank of California, N.A.	Carson	CA	D+	B+	B+	64.8	-14.68	5.9	0.0	0.3	0.0	10.0	25.5	88.5
Merchants Bank of Indiana	Carmel	IN	A-	A-	B+	3072.1	25.67	3.0	0.3	2.7	10.5	5.9	8.5	11.7
Merchants Bank, N.A.	Winona	MN	B+	B+	B+	1651.9	6.51	18.9	2.6	11.5	9.3	7.0	10.4	12.5
▼ Merchants Commercial Bank	Saint Thomas	VI	D-	D-	D	157.1	13.23	9.3	0.7	19.9	19.5	6.5	8.5	14.7
Merchants National Bank	Hillsboro	OH	B	B-	C+	671.6	1.25	4.7	2.7	25.5	6.4	8.0	9.7	13.5
Merchants National Bank of Sacramento	Sacramento	CA	B-	B-	B-	217.1	8.92	0.9	0.1	12.8	57.1	8.7	10.1	26.1
▲ Merchants State Bank	Freeman	SD	B-	C+	B-	151.1	0.86	6.5	1.9	2.2	20.4	10.0	11.4	15.3
Meredith Village Savings Bank	Meredith	NH	B-	B-	B-	823.3	7.71	3.4	3.4	44.5	6.5	9.8	10.9	17.5
Meridian Bank	Malvern	PA	B-	B-	C	747.7	15.45	22.1	0.0	24.4	6.1	7.8	9.6	13.5
▲ Merit Bank	Overland Park	KS	B-	C+	C+	102.1	7.74	19.2	2.7	25.2	3.8	5.4	8.8	11.3
Merrick Bank Corp.	South Jordan	UT	C	C	C	2843.2	18.31	0.0	96.6	0.0	1.8	10.0	21.0	23.6
Merrimack County Savings Bank	Concord	NH	B-	B-	B-	763.2	6.17	6.9	3.9	32.4	9.9	8.2	9.8	13.7
▲ MetaBank	Sioux Falls	SD	B+	B-	B-	3995.7	57.99	4.8	0.4	3.9	52.6	9.0	10.4	22.4
Metairie Bank & Trust Co.	Metairie	LA	B-	B-	B-	375.4	4.08	4.0	2.5	32.6	18.6	8.7	10.2	16.1
Metamora State Bank	Metamora	OH	C+	C+	C	71.9	10.66	5.2	0.8	21.2	17.7	6.7	8.7	15.3
Methuen Co-operative Bank	Methuen	MA	D+	C-	C-	89.9	1.16	0.5	1.9	48.5	21.9	9.0	10.3	22.8
Metro Bank	Pell City	AL	A-	A-	A-	684.7	-0.52	5.3	2.5	13.6	25.7	10.0	14.1	23.1
Metro Bank	Louisville	KY	D+	C-	C-	31.5	-1.58	10.6	0.2	4.7	21.9	10.0	16.9	30.9
▲ Metro City Bank	Doraville	GA	A	B+	B-	960.6	44.34	4.5	2.3	36.9	3.0	10.0	11.6	15.3
Metro Phoenix Bank	Phoenix	AZ	B	B	C+	141.8	10.42	18.5	0.1	6.3	0.0	9.4	10.6	15.7
Metropolitan Bank	Oakland	CA	B	B-	D+	146.0	3.56	2.7	0.1	24.3	8.7	10.0	11.5	18.1
Metropolitan Bank	Ridgeland	MS	C+	C+	C+	1118.0	17.55	16.9	2.0	16.3	11.2	5.4	9.2	11.3
▼ Metropolitan Capital Bank & Trust	Chicago	IL	C-	C+	C	226.8	11.88	61.0	0.3	4.3	10.1	5.2	8.9	11.1
▲ Metropolitan Commercial Bank	New York	NY	B-	C+	C-	1090.6	19.91	27.9	1.4	9.0	4.3	8.7	10.7	13.9
Metuchen Savings Bank	Metuchen	NJ	D	D	D+	263.4	-3.97	3.7	0.0	34.8	27.7	9.6	10.7	23.0
Metz Banking Co.	Nevada	MO	A-	A-	B	73.3	2.75	8.0	1.6	11.5	16.2	10.0	11.6	16.1
Miami Savings Bank	Miamitown	OH	B	B	B	123.4	4.86	4.2	0.4	37.2	1.7	10.0	14.2	25.8
Mid America Bank	Linn	MO	B+	A-	B-	388.2	10.37	9.8	2.0	25.5	14.7	9.2	10.5	15.9
Mid America Bank & Trust Co.	Dixon	MO	B+	A-	A	153.4	3.73	7.8	5.5	18.1	12.8	10.0	18.8	27.9
Mid Penn Bank	Millersburg	PA	C+	C+	C+	1042.1	13.93	12.8	0.2	16.6	16.6	5.1	7.4	11.1
Mid-America Bank	Baldwin City	KS	C+	C+	B+	134.8	18.96	4.2	3.2	48.9	0.0	3.1	11.1	10.1
Mid-Central Federal Savings Bank	Wadena	MN	B-	C+	C+	103.3	7.72	3.1	16.1	54.5	1.0	7.2	9.2	14.9
Mid-Missouri Bank	Springfield	MO	B-	B-	B-	591.8	1.66	7.0	1.2	20.5	2.2	7.7	9.4	13.1
Mid-Southern Savings Bank, FSB	Salem	IN	B-	C+	D+	181.2	-1.39	1.4	1.1	37.9	25.8	10.0	12.9	22.3
MidAmerica National Bank	Canton	IL	B	B	B	344.2	0.96	5.9	3.6	11.7	39.6	10.0	12.4	20.9
MidCoast Community Bank	Wilmington	DE	D+	D-	D-	195.4	3.09	6.9	0.0	20.6	5.7	5.7	8.7	11.5
MidCountry Bank	Bloomington	MN	C	C+	C+	787.8	7.50	8.7	2.0	16.1	8.9	10.0	13.3	16.3
Middleburg Bank	Middleburg	VA	C+	C+	C+	1329.2	5.87	13.6	1.5	19.7	27.3	7.3	9.2	17.2
Middlefield Banking Co.	Middlefield	OH	B-	B-	B-	760.6	7.33	7.0	0.6	23.8	16.0	7.0	9.0	13.0
Middlesex Federal Savings, F.A.	Somerville	MA	C-	C-	C	375.9	3.43	1.1	0.1	37.0	13.1	9.4	10.6	15.6
Middlesex Savings Bank	Natick	MA	B	B	B	4439.7	5.62	7.7	0.3	26.2	30.1	10.0	11.9	16.8
Middleton Community Bank	Middleton	WI	A-	A-	A-	291.6	2.81	16.8	0.8	4.0	24.3	10.0	13.2	17.7
Middletown State Bank	Middletown	IL	B+	B+	B+	33.6	-4.79	3.0	1.5	26.6	13.3	9.2	10.4	30.3
▲ Middletown Valley Bank	Middletown	MD	C	D+	C+	277.0	28.72	11.3	0.3	26.4	16.8	7.6	9.4	15.0
MidFirst Bank	Oklahoma City	OK	B	B	B	12903.9	10.31	7.3	0.8	36.1	9.0	7.6	9.4	14.5
Midland Community Bank	Kincaid	IL	B-	C+	C+	53.6	3.26	10.6	2.8	42.2	22.7	8.3	9.9	16.2
Midland Federal S&L Assn.	Bridgeview	IL	D+	D+	D+	119.7	0.58	0.0	0.3	39.9	31.0	6.8	8.8	30.1
▲ Midland National Bank	Newton	KS	C	C	C-	139.0	-1.10	5.6	3.8	11.4	47.8	8.8	10.2	14.5
Midland States Bank	Effingham	IL	B-	C+	B-	3248.5	14.55	11.2	6.7	7.5	10.5	6.0	10.0	11.7
MidSouth Bank	Dothan	AL	C	C	C-	406.4	4.97	11.2	1.0	10.3	20.0	9.6	10.8	15.6
MidSouth Bank, N.A.	Lafayette	LA	D+	C-	B+	1953.6	-1.00	23.1	4.5	7.0	21.6	7.8	9.5	13.4
Midstate Community Bank	Baltimore	MD	B-	B-	B-	169.1	-1.70	0.0	0.2	51.6	24.7	10.0	14.4	34.2
▼ Midstates Bank, N.A.	Council Bluffs	IA	B	A-	A-	388.7	0.35	1.8	0.5	9.2	32.0	9.3	10.5	15.1

Asset Quality Index	Adjusted Non-Performing Loans as a % of Total Loans	as a % of Capital	Net Charge-Offs Avg Loans	Profitability Index	Net Income ($Mil)	Return on Assets (R.O.A.)	Return on Equity (R.O.E.)	Net Interest Spread	Overhead Efficiency Ratio	Liquidity Index	Liquidity Ratio	Hot Money Ratio	Stability Index
6.8	0.00	0.0	-0.03	4.1	1.1	0.66	8.04	4.12	75.5	1.5	4.4	21.5	4.6
7.3	0.88	4.1	-0.47	1.8	0.1	0.20	2.27	2.96	94.0	5.2	35.8	6.6	3.8
4.5	2.57	13.0	-0.30	4.5	1.6	1.03	9.16	3.99	78.8	1.9	23.3	21.4	5.5
7.2	0.09	0.6	0.04	7.0	1.1	1.29	13.79	4.48	50.1	3.9	13.5	9.1	5.2
8.3	0.29	2.4	0.03	4.3	13.0	0.88	10.04	3.07	64.8	4.3	5.7	5.8	7.5
4.9	1.46	8.4	0.17	4.3	1.4	0.73	7.58	3.73	76.1	3.4	33.3	15.7	4.7
5.4	1.48	9.2	0.00	3.0	1.4	0.51	6.00	3.28	82.2	4.6	21.1	5.7	4.3
9.9	1.43	0.9	-2.85	0.7	-2.3	-3.92	-16.10	2.57	160.1	4.4	105.6	27.7	7.5
7.9	0.17	1.4	0.00	9.1	27.8	1.44	16.79	2.37	29.1	3.2	24.3	0.9	8.2
4.3	1.40	10.2	0.04	5.6	10.8	0.89	7.89	4.09	66.1	4.0	2.2	6.7	9.6
0.3	12.82	78.9	0.19	3.7	0.6	0.54	6.24	4.16	73.9	5.6	37.8	5.0	3.9
4.7	1.20	9.1	0.09	6.4	5.8	1.15	12.03	3.76	55.9	2.7	11.1	8.2	6.8
9.7	0.23	0.8	0.00	3.5	1.0	0.64	6.26	2.55	67.3	4.0	64.2	21.5	6.1
3.9	1.81	10.4	0.00	7.7	2.0	1.75	15.35	4.25	53.9	4.2	10.0	6.6	6.9
5.4	0.95	7.1	0.08	4.2	4.4	0.74	6.78	3.78	70.8	2.7	4.5	11.1	6.7
4.7	1.08	9.5	0.11	5.0	4.3	0.84	8.66	3.86	85.8	0.5	3.7	20.9	5.5
8.1	0.13	1.2	-0.44	7.3	1.0	1.46	15.33	4.60	73.4	0.5	6.6	54.2	4.3
2.0	4.10	12.2	8.68	10.0	105.8	5.14	24.50	22.00	25.9	0.4	7.1	18.3	9.3
4.6	0.70	5.7	0.03	3.4	3.0	0.54	5.23	3.60	78.4	3.6	2.2	7.6	6.6
8.6	0.15	0.4	0.77	5.5	29.9	1.29	12.10	3.31	72.3	2.8	49.8	3.8	6.6
8.3	0.21	1.4	0.05	4.0	1.9	0.67	6.69	3.81	75.7	5.0	25.0	3.7	6.1
5.0	1.52	10.9	0.02	4.3	0.4	0.74	7.76	3.88	75.4	2.4	29.8	19.4	4.0
4.9	2.77	15.4	0.00	1.3	0.0	-0.04	-0.41	2.73	102.4	3.7	41.6	16.6	5.4
6.6	1.67	6.3	0.70	6.6	5.9	1.14	8.43	4.20	56.3	2.9	38.8	20.6	7.9
6.0	3.36	8.4	-0.06	0.1	-0.2	-0.77	-4.45	2.39	119.7	2.1	54.8	81.9	6.8
7.6	0.23	1.8	0.00	10.0	14.9	2.57	21.21	4.89	44.3	0.6	10.1	43.6	8.0
4.6	1.21	8.2	0.35	5.6	0.8	0.74	6.23	5.13	65.3	3.9	21.9	10.0	7.3
4.0	2.03	11.5	0.01	6.1	1.5	1.38	12.30	4.06	65.7	2.6	17.7	16.4	6.6
8.1	0.17	1.4	0.14	3.8	5.3	0.65	7.66	3.16	70.6	1.6	5.8	19.8	6.8
2.1	3.55	27.7	-0.01	4.6	1.1	0.64	7.21	5.92	80.1	0.7	16.9	38.2	5.1
4.5	0.70	5.2	0.07	4.3	5.2	0.64	6.71	3.55	66.4	3.9	10.0	8.8	8.4
7.5	0.57	2.8	0.00	1.2	0.1	0.04	0.43	2.31	96.5	4.9	47.9	12.4	5.2
6.2	1.57	9.1	0.02	7.4	0.9	1.75	15.02	4.20	54.9	2.3	24.8	18.5	7.5
8.2	0.39	1.9	0.00	4.5	0.8	0.83	5.90	3.25	63.7	1.1	24.7	33.0	7.4
5.9	0.84	5.5	0.13	7.5	5.1	1.78	16.98	3.83	53.3	2.9	16.4	14.4	6.7
4.4	3.02	10.2	0.12	10.0	4.2	3.67	19.16	3.80	39.0	5.2	37.5	7.5	9.4
6.0	0.71	6.7	0.00	4.3	6.0	0.82	10.13	3.88	70.4	3.7	5.2	8.7	6.0
8.4	0.13	0.9	0.13	6.2	1.1	1.16	10.36	4.32	66.0	0.9	13.4	32.3	7.7
4.2	0.98	9.1	0.08	4.9	0.9	1.21	13.41	4.22	73.9	3.3	4.7	11.7	5.2
5.7	0.69	5.4	0.06	5.2	3.9	0.89	9.58	3.86	69.6	1.7	15.6	14.3	5.9
4.9	3.50	15.7	0.05	3.8	1.0	0.74	5.72	3.43	79.3	4.2	38.1	13.1	6.5
6.3	1.17	4.8	0.23	4.3	2.1	0.85	5.90	3.53	69.4	5.0	29.3	5.6	7.4
4.5	0.58	5.1	-0.16	1.3	0.7	0.46	5.22	3.16	103.7	0.9	14.4	28.0	2.7
3.9	2.92	16.1	0.15	2.5	1.2	0.22	1.49	3.71	95.6	3.1	17.7	13.5	7.1
5.4	1.55	9.9	-0.02	3.8	7.6	0.77	8.25	3.23	71.0	2.7	24.8	16.5	7.1
4.4	1.27	10.0	0.09	5.3	5.8	1.03	10.25	3.86	66.4	2.7	11.7	15.1	6.8
6.7	0.70	4.6	-0.01	2.5	0.7	0.24	2.39	2.73	88.3	0.9	20.5	32.0	6.3
7.6	0.64	3.3	0.02	4.0	22.7	0.69	5.55	2.79	64.2	4.1	35.5	15.8	8.8
6.3	1.08	5.2	0.08	7.2	2.6	1.17	9.02	3.31	56.8	1.9	31.9	9.3	7.7
8.2	0.00	0.0	0.00	8.2	0.5	1.91	18.17	3.56	42.2	4.2	27.0	9.8	7.0
5.3	1.13	8.2	0.06	2.7	0.7	0.35	3.63	3.45	80.7	3.7	14.6	10.6	4.7
5.1	0.69	5.5	-0.01	7.8	159.5	1.71	19.08	4.01	61.3	2.8	11.5	13.0	9.4
5.3	1.19	8.4	-0.04	6.4	0.4	1.11	11.44	3.37	54.0	2.7	22.4	16.1	5.1
4.7	3.75	18.0	0.01	1.1	0.0	-0.02	-0.22	2.72	101.9	5.7	55.8	10.4	4.3
4.9	2.17	8.8	0.01	3.1	0.5	0.48	4.35	3.51	86.7	6.3	54.1	6.3	5.7
3.9	1.15	8.6	0.22	5.6	22.9	1.01	8.69	4.23	68.9	2.8	9.4	7.9	8.1
7.7	0.44	2.2	0.00	3.3	2.2	0.72	6.70	3.04	76.4	2.8	29.9	17.8	5.8
1.0	4.72	29.7	0.40	4.1	8.0	0.56	4.81	4.29	72.1	4.6	13.7	5.0	8.0
5.6	3.87	15.9	0.06	3.3	0.6	0.44	3.14	2.79	69.6	2.1	42.7	42.3	6.5
3.3	3.27	16.9	0.35	7.0	4.9	1.64	14.60	3.71	55.3	4.1	28.3	3.8	8.7

Name	City	State	2015 Rating	2014 Rating	Rating	Total Assets ($Mil)	One Year Asset Growth	Comm-ercial Loans	Cons-umer Loans	Mort-gage Loans	Secur-ities	Capital-ization Index	Lever-age Ratio	Risk-Based Capital Ratio
Midwest Bank	Monmouth	IL	B-	B-	B	451.5	3.20	6.6	2.5	7.7	30.9	7.7	9.5	16.3
Midwest Bank	Detroit Lakes	MN	A-	A-	A-	375.6	3.88	18.8	2.8	16.9	5.7	5.9	9.2	11.6
▲ Midwest Bank N.A.	Pierce	NE	A-	B+	A-	666.0	3.07	7.3	2.7	3.6	14.0	9.7	10.9	14.7
Midwest BankCentre	Saint Louis	MO	B-	B-	B-	1838.8	14.14	9.4	1.0	17.6	22.5	7.3	9.2	12.7
▲ Midwest Community Bank	Freeport	IL	B-	C	D	235.6	11.74	3.9	0.1	24.8	0.8	8.1	9.8	13.5
Midwest Community Bank	Plainville	KS	B	B-	C-	61.4	-0.31	12.9	0.3	8.0	53.5	10.0	13.9	34.0
Midwest Heritage Bank, FSB	West Des Moines	IA	A	A	A	237.4	16.94	4.5	17.1	24.9	14.8	10.0	11.5	16.4
▲ Midwest Independent Bank	Jefferson City	MO	B	C+	C	272.6	7.92	1.6	0.0	2.5	17.4	10.0	13.3	22.9
▼ Midwest Regional Bank	Festus	MO	C	C	C	457.9	13.41	18.1	0.5	9.4	7.7	3.1	9.1	10.0
MidWestOne Bank	Iowa City	IA	B+	B+	A-	2995.5	73.53	11.7	1.2	13.4	19.7	6.5	9.0	12.2
Mifflin County Savings Bank	Lewistown	PA	C	C	B-	142.8	4.30	6.5	8.6	35.1	19.2	10.0	12.6	20.7
Mifflinburg Bank & Trust Co.	Mifflinburg	PA	B+	B+	B+	411.9	8.74	10.7	4.3	20.9	17.2	8.8	10.2	15.6
Milford Bank	Milford	CT	C	C	C	421.3	7.67	7.8	4.6	41.2	6.7	10.0	11.2	16.5
▲ Milford Building and Loan Assn., SB	Milford	IL	C-	D+	D	27.4	0.34	0.0	0.0	67.5	0.1	6.4	8.4	17.0
Milford Federal S&L Assn.	Milford	MA	C+	C+	C	374.7	3.96	0.0	0.2	75.9	3.9	10.0	12.1	20.7
Milford National Bank and Trust Co.	Milford	MA	C+	C	C-	317.5	7.42	8.2	1.9	25.1	8.4	6.9	8.9	12.7
Millbury National Bank	Millbury	MA	B-	B-	B-	88.5	5.95	9.9	1.3	26.4	17.9	9.3	10.6	16.6
Millbury Savings Bank	Millbury	MA	B-	C+	C+	224.5	8.43	6.1	0.8	30.2	17.7	10.0	11.7	16.6
Milledgeville State Bank	Milledgeville	IL	A	A	A	122.2	3.44	15.8	2.1	7.3	27.0	9.5	10.7	15.4
▲ Millennium Bank	Des Plaines	IL	B	C+	C-	82.1	7.95	6.7	0.4	24.0	0.0	9.7	10.8	14.9
Millennium Bank	Junction City	KS	C+	C+	C+	36.1	0.00	9.4	1.5	23.2	0.5	10.0	13.2	18.8
Millennium Bank	Ooltewah	TN	B	B	C	159.1	13.17	13.2	0.3	12.5	10.7	9.0	10.3	15.9
Millington Bank	Millington	NJ	C	C	C-	433.6	16.92	3.6	0.1	38.3	9.9	10.0	13.5	18.9
Mills County State Bank	Goldthwaite	TX	B-	B	B	293.4	0.06	4.9	4.7	15.0	46.9	8.2	9.8	18.6
Millville S&L Assn.	Millville	NJ	C	C	C	136.0	-1.07	0.0	0.0	18.3	48.8	10.0	12.9	34.7
Milton Savings Bank	Milton	PA	B	B+	B+	65.3	-0.76	0.0	1.0	60.3	17.0	10.0	21.4	57.7
Minden Exchange Bank & Trust Co.	Minden	NE	A-	B+	B+	147.6	-1.88	5.3	3.4	1.8	36.6	10.0	16.1	24.0
Mineola Community Bank, SSB	Mineola	TX	B-	B-	B	200.8	0.78	1.7	1.7	53.1	20.5	10.0	14.4	25.2
▲ Miner County Bank	Howard	SD	C+	C+	B-	44.2	3.96	5.3	1.8	0.3	15.9	8.5	10.0	16.4
Miners and Merchants Bank	Thomas	WV	B-	B-	B-	55.0	5.03	0.1	1.9	24.6	50.1	10.0	15.7	49.2
Miners Exchange Bank	Coeburn	VA	C+	C+	C+	111.2	-3.91	1.1	6.0	25.5	22.9	8.3	9.9	19.1
Miners National Bank of Eveleth	Eveleth	MN	D+	D+	D+	64.8	7.42	2.5	3.3	14.5	35.5	6.2	8.2	21.1
▲ Miners State Bank	Iron River	MI	C-	D	D+	126.9	2.43	14.6	0.3	5.8	22.2	9.0	10.3	14.4
Minnesota Bank & Trust	Edina	MN	B-	B-	C+	238.8	26.16	18.0	3.0	5.3	30.7	5.4	8.4	11.3
Minnesota First Credit and Savings, Inc.	Rochester	MN	B-	B-	B-	27.9	-0.20	1.6	35.6	52.5	0.0	10.0	14.4	21.5
Minnesota Lakes Bank	Delano	MN	C+	C+	C+	92.6	5.14	6.9	2.6	7.6	24.5	8.9	10.3	18.2
Minnesota National Bank	Sauk Centre	MN	B	B	B	198.2	-2.51	14.7	3.1	17.1	15.0	7.8	9.5	13.4
▼ MinnStar Bank N.A.	Lake Crystal	MN	C-	C+	C+	127.0	4.25	6.0	0.8	21.1	3.8	6.3	8.6	12.0
Minnwest Bank	Redwood Falls	MN	B	B	B-	1600.4	3.27	6.9	0.9	4.5	7.4	7.2	10.1	12.7
Minster Bank	Minster	OH	B+	B+	B+	455.8	9.78	5.9	0.6	10.9	25.5	6.6	8.6	15.8
MINT National Bank	Kingwood	TX	B+	B	B-	128.3	41.42	4.3	0.1	15.9	2.7	9.8	10.8	16.3
Mission Bank	Kingman	AZ	C	C	C-	96.9	9.52	5.0	0.6	6.6	19.1	8.4	9.9	14.8
Mission Bank	Bakersfield	CA	B	B	B	521.6	20.11	6.4	0.0	6.5	10.8	6.5	8.6	12.2
Mission Bank	Mission	KS	B+	B+	B	552.5	0.96	7.2	0.3	0.3	31.1	10.0	16.5	23.6
▼ Mission National Bank	San Francisco	CA	B-	B-	B-	267.1	50.77	2.7	0.9	27.9	0.0	8.5	10.0	14.6
Mission Valley Bank	Sun Valley	CA	A-	A-	B-	309.9	10.68	21.3	0.1	1.6	5.9	10.0	13.5	17.6
Mississippi County S&L Assn.	Charleston	MO	D	D+	D+	8.8	-8.41	0.0	0.1	32.2	9.0	10.0	27.1	37.6
Mississippi River Bank	Belle Chasse	LA	A	A	A-	117.6	-7.47	25.1	1.5	10.1	22.1	10.0	13.2	22.4
Missouri Bank	Warrenton	MO	A-	A-	B+	215.5	11.70	6.1	1.0	16.4	25.0	9.7	10.8	16.5
Missouri Bank and Trust Co.	Kansas City	MO	B-	B-	C+	636.0	8.82	31.7	1.4	7.6	2.3	4.0	7.5	10.5
Missouri Bank II	Sedalia	MO	A-	A-	B+	84.1	-0.69	3.1	1.2	30.5	23.5	10.0	11.8	19.3
Mitchell Bank	Milwaukee	WI	C+	C-	C	51.0	-2.01	7.5	0.2	16.7	0.0	10.0	15.7	38.4
▼ Mizuho Bank (USA)	New York	NY	C+	B-	B-	6815.0	21.84	44.4	0.0	0.1	0.4	10.0	16.4	16.0
Mizuho Trust & Banking Co. (USA)	New York	NY	U	U	U	783.3	-5.03	0.0	0.0	0.0	0.0	6.2	8.2	60.0
Modern Bank, N.A.	New York	NY	C+	C+	C	754.9	11.73	40.8	0.0	3.9	25.7	9.4	10.6	14.6
Mohave State Bank	Lake Havasu City	AZ	C-	D+	D	600.0	84.58	3.0	0.2	5.3	22.6	8.4	10.6	13.7
Monitor Bank	Big Prairie	OH	B-	C+	C+	41.9	-4.34	16.7	2.9	9.2	7.3	10.0	13.6	22.5
Monona State Bank	Monona	WI	B	B	C	465.8	9.75	11.7	0.5	15.6	6.0	8.3	11.3	13.6
▲ Monroe Bank & Trust	Monroe	MI	B	B-	C	1341.7	1.97	7.1	3.1	10.8	38.0	9.3	10.5	18.2
Monroe Federal S&L Assn.	Tipp City	OH	C+	C	B-	91.8	2.69	6.7	0.4	28.4	15.8	10.0	12.3	21.0

Asset Quality Index	Adjusted Non-Performing Loans		Net Charge-Offs	Profitability Index	Net Income ($Mil)	Return on Assets (R.O.A.)	Return on Equity (R.O.E.)	Net Interest Spread	Overhead Efficiency Ratio	Liquidity Index	Liquidity Ratio	Hot Money Ratio	Stability Index
	as a % of Total Loans	as a % of Capital	Avg Loans										
3.2	2.60	14.9	0.49	4.5	2.7	0.82	6.44	3.38	63.9	2.2	15.1	12.1	6.8
5.1	0.78	6.8	0.01	9.2	5.9	2.12	22.47	3.98	51.2	4.1	12.4	7.8	7.8
5.9	0.33	2.1	0.01	6.5	5.9	1.19	10.72	3.77	55.7	1.2	11.3	27.9	8.2
6.6	0.68	4.6	-0.01	4.0	10.6	0.83	8.25	3.13	69.6	3.8	12.3	9.3	8.2
4.2	0.94	7.4	0.60	5.4	1.9	1.35	13.00	3.57	81.1	1.5	6.6	10.3	5.3
8.2	0.50	1.3	-0.01	4.5	0.6	1.27	9.10	3.11	63.6	2.7	39.0	23.8	6.8
7.2	0.05	0.3	0.03	7.6	2.2	1.25	10.59	3.76	73.3	5.3	25.3	1.2	7.2
8.9	0.00	0.0	-0.07	4.1	1.5	0.69	5.35	2.22	74.9	5.6	51.1	9.5	6.3
4.4	1.01	8.4	0.15	4.7	2.7	0.83	9.06	3.38	67.3	1.6	10.9	22.5	5.6
6.0	0.97	7.3	0.09	5.3	17.9	0.93	9.55	4.50	69.8	3.4	17.9	12.7	8.6
5.8	1.13	6.1	0.22	2.4	0.3	0.30	2.33	2.88	86.6	1.8	22.5	21.3	6.6
5.8	0.66	4.2	0.10	5.4	3.2	1.10	10.64	3.34	56.2	2.8	12.1	14.8	7.0
7.2	0.45	3.2	0.07	2.6	0.9	0.31	2.87	3.51	87.7	4.4	12.1	5.5	5.9
8.9	0.00	0.0	0.27	2.9	0.1	0.33	4.04	2.89	68.9	1.2	21.4	30.6	4.2
6.2	1.19	8.3	0.01	2.7	1.1	0.39	3.23	2.90	82.0	3.2	9.7	12.4	6.5
3.9	0.79	6.8	0.02	3.9	1.3	0.59	6.59	3.62	74.9	3.7	6.3	9.1	5.2
5.6	0.71	4.7	0.51	3.5	0.3	0.41	4.12	4.19	79.2	0.6	10.4	45.9	5.4
7.4	0.69	4.0	0.00	3.2	0.9	0.56	4.71	3.43	76.1	2.4	22.1	17.8	6.4
8.4	0.00	0.0	0.02	7.9	1.6	1.80	15.72	3.79	44.9	1.3	30.5	38.7	8.5
5.4	0.67	4.8	0.05	9.2	1.7	2.75	28.26	4.79	55.6	0.6	10.2	49.9	5.7
7.3	0.31	1.7	0.59	3.0	0.2	0.57	4.37	4.09	80.5	1.5	18.6	25.1	6.4
4.8	1.21	7.2	-0.04	5.8	1.6	1.41	12.87	4.21	69.0	2.5	28.4	18.6	6.0
4.7	2.91	16.4	0.03	2.3	0.8	0.28	2.01	3.14	81.8	3.2	19.9	13.4	5.2
3.8	3.47	15.5	0.14	4.5	2.3	1.02	9.33	3.74	70.6	3.2	36.4	17.6	7.2
9.7	0.93	1.8	0.55	2.6	0.4	0.37	2.80	2.55	84.3	7.2	74.1	4.3	6.4
7.7	2.55	7.3	0.00	4.5	0.4	0.77	3.63	3.51	65.6	5.6	44.3	7.0	7.3
8.4	0.00	0.0	-0.02	5.5	1.5	1.27	8.21	3.41	57.6	4.7	15.9	4.0	8.5
7.2	1.27	6.1	-0.04	3.1	0.6	0.42	2.97	3.52	85.1	1.5	27.6	30.2	7.5
6.5	0.00	0.0	0.01	4.2	0.3	0.94	7.07	3.61	61.6	4.1	25.3	9.2	5.9
7.4	3.68	7.1	-0.02	3.1	0.2	0.51	3.28	2.86	78.5	6.1	80.1	10.6	7.3
4.0	3.28	15.5	0.39	3.3	0.3	0.34	3.48	4.51	87.6	5.2	43.7	9.9	4.6
9.4	0.00	0.0	0.01	1.6	0.1	0.11	1.27	3.07	96.6	4.9	51.3	12.6	3.8
2.2	3.88	23.3	0.01	3.8	0.6	0.68	6.40	4.11	76.2	3.8	32.8	13.0	5.6
8.6	0.00	0.0	0.00	4.7	1.8	1.07	12.87	3.77	74.7	5.9	40.4	2.8	5.9
6.8	0.07	0.4	0.01	4.6	0.1	0.63	4.46	6.81	82.5	3.8	8.6	6.6	6.3
5.1	0.66	3.1	0.42	2.5	0.3	0.38	2.75	3.96	85.2	5.6	32.0	2.6	6.0
4.1	1.48	10.0	-0.01	4.3	1.4	0.94	8.23	3.55	68.7	2.9	12.3	14.4	7.4
1.8	2.97	24.5	-0.01	3.6	0.7	0.69	8.05	3.94	74.1	2.9	9.6	14.2	5.2
5.1	1.19	8.7	0.00	5.5	11.2	0.92	8.99	3.90	61.9	2.3	10.2	12.3	8.8
7.1	0.67	3.7	0.07	5.8	3.7	1.12	13.17	3.20	58.3	5.5	33.4	4.1	5.9
5.8	0.67	4.2	0.00	6.8	1.1	1.25	11.17	3.90	65.7	1.0	28.0	57.0	7.9
6.1	0.78	4.7	0.37	2.4	0.2	0.23	2.26	4.02	88.8	5.0	37.0	8.6	5.0
6.8	0.41	3.0	-0.06	6.1	3.8	1.02	11.64	3.96	58.6	4.9	25.2	4.1	5.7
5.4	3.24	9.6	-0.01	5.2	4.1	1.01	5.71	3.45	55.2	6.0	47.8	6.0	7.8
3.6	1.21	9.3	-0.03	5.2	1.3	0.72	6.94	3.83	68.2	0.8	17.1	39.9	5.7
6.5	0.59	3.2	0.27	6.5	2.3	1.03	7.65	4.07	65.8	3.7	21.8	10.9	7.5
10.0	1.64	2.0	0.00	0.0	-0.1	-0.72	-2.68	2.75	128.2	5.9	89.7	11.5	6.8
8.5	0.04	0.2	-0.14	9.0	2.2	2.51	19.66	5.16	57.7	4.9	32.5	7.2	8.2
6.4	0.81	4.1	0.07	6.5	2.4	1.50	13.18	4.10	60.2	4.1	15.4	7.8	7.6
8.2	0.00	0.0	0.00	5.9	7.8	1.68	23.29	3.46	61.6	4.8	22.5	4.2	4.7
8.6	0.38	1.8	0.02	6.7	0.9	1.43	12.09	3.87	64.4	2.3	15.1	17.5	7.3
4.1	6.59	15.8	1.45	2.5	0.2	0.46	2.84	3.25	90.4	6.6	63.0	4.3	6.0
8.0	0.00	0.0	0.00	2.2	6.2	0.12	0.67	1.24	94.0	0.6	13.5	6.8	8.0
10.0	na	0.0	na	3.7	3.5	0.57	7.11	0.64	84.7	8.6	106.8	0.1	4.3
4.3	1.64	10.2	-0.04	2.9	1.6	0.30	2.68	2.67	76.0	0.3	6.3	72.8	7.3
2.5	3.36	19.6	0.02	5.9	3.1	1.02	9.68	4.07	62.7	5.1	38.8	8.5	4.9
7.3	1.22	4.8	-0.02	3.9	0.2	0.67	5.00	3.25	66.7	4.7	42.3	12.0	6.0
6.2	0.28	2.0	0.03	5.2	3.1	0.89	7.85	3.78	65.6	1.6	6.7	20.8	7.1
5.7	2.07	9.1	0.06	5.0	11.1	1.11	10.32	3.11	68.3	6.3	41.5	4.7	7.4
6.4	1.60	8.4	0.00	2.5	0.2	0.34	2.75	3.38	88.3	4.5	30.4	9.0	5.8

Name	City	State	2015 Rating	2014 Rating	Rating	Total Assets ($Mil)	One Year Asset Growth	Asset Mix (As a % of Total Assets)				Capital-ization Index	Lever-age Ratio	Risk-Based Capital Ratio
								Comm-ercial Loans	Cons-umer Loans	Mort-gage Loans	Secur-ities			
Monroe Savings Bank	Williamstown	NJ	C+	C+	C+	95.5	1.60	0.5	7.3	46.4	13.3	10.0	12.1	24.7
Monson Savings Bank	Monson	MA	C+	B-	C+	338.5	12.63	7.5	0.7	27.8	12.3	7.7	9.5	15.1
Montana State Bank	Plentywood	MT	B-	B-	B-	74.6	-4.96	6.0	2.4	0.4	4.8	6.9	8.9	18.3
Montecito Bank & Trust	Santa Barbara	CA	B+	B+	B	1300.6	6.81	11.0	1.8	4.5	34.1	7.6	10.1	13.0
Monterey County Bank	Monterey	CA	C-	D+	E	189.3	2.98	14.9	0.3	11.8	16.5	6.7	8.7	13.7
▲ Montezuma State Bank	Montezuma	IA	C+	C-	D+	35.7	-0.14	11.4	4.4	11.3	27.7	9.9	10.9	19.8
Montgomery Bank, N.A.	Sikeston	MO	C+	C+	C+	896.0	5.50	17.0	0.9	24.2	8.8	6.3	8.7	12.0
Monticello Banking Co.	Monticello	KY	B	B	B-	554.6	-0.10	6.0	5.9	17.8	22.4	9.6	10.8	15.9
Montrose Savings Bank	Montrose	MO	B	B	B	43.8	-3.59	5.4	3.7	16.3	27.0	10.0	14.1	23.1
Monument Bank	Doylestown	PA	C	C	C	285.9	9.64	0.3	0.2	27.8	23.9	6.1	8.1	14.3
Moody National Bank	Galveston	TX	B	B	B	965.9	-13.51	8.3	0.8	7.5	32.9	10.0	12.8	19.1
Morgan Federal Bank	Fort Morgan	CO	C+	C+	B-	116.0	1.74	4.1	0.4	28.2	43.1	9.4	10.6	18.3
Morgan Stanley Bank, N.A.	Salt Lake City	UT	A-	A-	B+	126826.0	-2.95	9.0	8.9	0.0	42.5	8.7	10.1	17.5
Morgan Stanley Private Bank, N.A.	New York	NY	B+	B	B-	52063.0	41.63	2.7	6.5	45.1	20.9	9.3	10.5	26.7
Morganton Savings Bank, S.S.B.	Morganton	NC	C+	C+	B-	77.7	-3.58	0.0	0.1	18.3	18.2	10.0	32.1	41.4
Morgantown Bank & Trust Co., Inc.	Morgantown	KY	B-	B-	B-	173.0	7.80	4.1	4.1	40.0	18.6	6.9	8.9	15.0
Morrill and Janes Bank and Trust Co.	Merriam	KS	B-	B-	B-	862.8	2.09	21.5	0.6	3.2	34.7	6.2	8.9	11.9
Morris Bank	Dublin	GA	C	C-	C	571.9	4.00	10.0	5.2	15.1	10.3	8.4	10.5	13.7
Morris County National Bank	Naples	TX	B-	B	B	96.8	2.58	10.5	7.0	13.9	23.8	7.5	9.3	14.8
Morris Plan Co. of Terre Haute, Inc.	Terre Haute	IN	A-	A-	B	75.9	3.78	0.5	85.9	5.9	4.0	10.0	27.2	30.6
Morris State Bank	Morris	OK	B-	B-	B-	77.6	3.14	4.3	10.4	35.2	14.2	6.5	8.5	15.1
Morton Community Bank	Morton	IL	B+	A-	B+	3332.7	11.02	12.9	1.4	10.6	22.4	9.3	10.8	14.4
Mound City Bank	Platteville	WI	B	B	B	330.4	10.29	2.7	0.7	20.0	11.5	7.9	9.6	13.2
Mount Vernon Bank	Vidalia	GA	B	B	B	138.9	4.94	3.8	3.0	12.8	31.2	8.1	9.7	16.6
Mount Vernon Bank and Trust Co.	Mount Vernon	IA	A	A	A	114.3	2.68	7.1	3.3	32.1	20.7	10.0	14.2	24.0
Mountain Commerce Bank	Knoxville	TN	B-	B-	C	577.0	17.84	9.3	1.6	19.7	5.7	4.8	8.8	10.9
Mountain Pacific Bank	Everett	WA	C+	C+	C	217.6	21.48	13.2	0.5	8.3	4.9	6.7	11.2	12.3
Mountain Valley Bank	Walden	CO	B-	B-	B-	166.1	8.68	15.3	0.8	10.6	12.0	7.8	11.0	13.2
Mountain Valley Bank	Dunlap	TN	C-	D+	D+	93.4	-1.00	1.5	6.9	39.7	22.2	7.7	9.5	16.7
Mountain Valley Bank, N.A.	Elkins	WV	B	B	B	135.2	1.79	7.4	1.9	28.3	27.0	10.0	13.5	23.6
Mountain Valley Community Bank	Cleveland	GA	B	B	C+	182.8	7.41	5.4	1.4	10.9	21.7	8.6	10.0	16.0
Mountain View Bank of Commerce	Westminster	CO	C-	B-	C+	94.0	23.07	7.2	0.0	7.0	0.0	6.1	9.1	11.9
MountainOne Bank	North Adams	MA	C+	C+	C	861.0	3.22	9.1	0.1	34.4	10.2	8.2	10.3	13.5
▼ MRV Banks	Sainte Genevieve	MO	B	B+	B	199.8	22.87	33.9	0.6	11.2	4.0	5.5	8.8	11.4
Mt. McKinley Bank	Fairbanks	AK	B+	B+	A-	423.6	13.20	5.9	0.1	3.8	51.2	10.0	18.8	38.6
Mt. Victory State Bank	Mount Victory	OH	C-	C-	C	18.0	7.49	2.1	11.9	9.5	18.5	9.6	10.7	17.8
Muenster State Bank	Muenster	TX	A	A+	A+	175.1	3.70	2.3	1.7	7.5	71.0	10.0	14.2	39.1
▲ MUFG Union Bank, N.A.	New York	NY	C+	C+	C+	116911.8	2.23	17.3	1.0	25.1	20.7	10.0	11.3	15.6
Muleshoe State Bank	Muleshoe	TX	C+	C+	C	109.0	-3.92	10.0	4.8	5.1	40.1	5.9	7.9	13.7
Muncy Bank and Trust Co.	Muncy	PA	A-	A-	A-	394.3	5.37	3.8	2.8	46.5	14.3	10.0	11.0	17.2
Municipal Trust and Savings Bank	Bourbonnais	IL	A	A-	B+	305.3	8.80	0.5	0.5	21.9	10.2	10.0	19.6	40.2
Murphy Bank	Fresno	CA	B	B+	B	235.6	8.50	26.7	21.7	16.5	0.0	9.8	11.2	14.8
Murphy-Wall State Bank and Trust Co.	Pinckneyville	IL	B	B	B	116.8	-2.22	8.4	1.8	17.4	32.7	10.0	11.4	21.6
Murray Bank	Murray	KY	B	B-	B-	286.5	8.95	7.6	3.4	22.8	21.6	7.4	9.3	15.1
Murray State Bank	Murray	NE	C+	C	C	52.4	4.07	8.9	3.0	13.9	18.9	9.8	10.9	15.9
Mutual Bank	Whitman	MA	C+	C	C-	474.4	6.75	2.2	5.6	41.6	16.7	7.1	9.0	14.8
▲ Mutual Federal Bank	Chicago	IL	C+	C-	D	79.1	2.08	0.1	0.0	38.2	6.3	10.0	17.1	24.2
Mutual of Omaha Bank	Omaha	NE	C+	C+	C+	7623.4	10.56	13.4	1.4	23.7	17.5	4.8	8.6	10.9
Mutual S&L Assn.	Metairie	LA	B	B	B	45.6	13.82	0.0	0.3	83.4	0.0	10.0	28.0	48.8
Mutual Savings Assn., FSA	Leavenworth	KS	B	B	B	194.6	-0.17	4.9	1.1	36.2	17.2	10.0	31.1	50.4
Mutual Savings Bank	Franklin	IN	B-	C+	C+	133.7	6.26	3.1	1.9	32.8	7.0	10.0	11.0	15.2
Mutual Savings Bank	Hartsville	SC	D	D	D	38.6	-0.68	2.7	1.9	25.3	6.3	10.0	34.9	66.8
MutualBank	Muncie	IN	B-	B-	C+	1531.5	5.17	7.1	11.2	32.0	16.8	7.3	9.2	13.4
MutualOne Bank	Framingham	MA	B+	B+	A-	696.9	13.82	17.2	1.0	18.2	4.6	10.0	18.2	23.3
MVB Bank, Inc.	Fairmont	WV	C+	C+	C+	1465.9	12.36	12.4	1.0	15.5	10.3	6.7	9.6	12.3
MWABank	Rock Island	IL	D+	D+	D+	278.4	6.35	0.3	2.3	67.1	16.2	7.5	9.3	20.6
▲ MyBank	Belen	NM	B	C+	C+	166.6	-0.48	1.8	1.0	8.8	41.5	10.0	11.4	23.0
Nantahala Bank & Trust Co.	Franklin	NC	E-	E-	E-	155.7	6.20	4.8	0.7	18.0	16.4	1.4	5.3	8.4
Napoleon State Bank	Napoleon	IN	A-	B+	B	201.9	2.72	8.9	8.1	24.4	7.6	10.0	11.5	15.6
Nashville Savings Bank	Nashville	IL	B	B	B-	58.1	5.40	7.4	3.5	24.0	13.2	10.0	11.1	16.7

Asset Quality Index	Adjusted Non-Performing Loans as a % of Total Loans	as a % of Capital	Net Charge-Offs Avg Loans	Profitability Index	Net Income ($Mil)	Return on Assets (R.O.A.)	Return on Equity (R.O.E.)	Net Interest Spread	Overhead Efficiency Ratio	Liquidity Index	Liquidity Ratio	Hot Money Ratio	Stability Index
5.8	1.63	8.8	0.20	2.8	0.2	0.27	2.23	3.07	83.6	1.8	32.2	29.8	6.2
5.2	0.82	6.2	0.25	3.4	1.3	0.55	5.78	3.37	77.3	1.8	20.4	15.7	5.2
8.2	0.32	1.7	-0.02	2.1	0.1	0.16	1.86	2.87	94.4	6.0	50.7	6.0	5.1
7.1	0.54	3.1	-0.01	4.9	11.0	1.15	10.59	3.90	74.8	6.2	35.2	3.7	9.8
8.9	0.15	0.8	0.43	2.1	0.2	0.15	1.72	3.81	97.9	2.7	31.8	18.9	2.5
3.6	3.37	14.9	0.02	3.4	0.1	0.44	3.80	3.53	74.6	5.7	40.9	5.7	5.4
4.4	1.39	11.5	0.04	3.7	6.0	0.91	10.30	3.44	74.0	4.1	7.2	6.7	5.3
5.0	1.10	6.3	0.16	5.1	4.5	1.07	9.94	3.98	69.0	1.7	19.4	23.2	6.6
5.9	1.91	7.9	0.01	5.6	0.5	1.38	10.16	3.76	60.4	4.1	36.6	13.4	8.1
4.7	1.33	10.7	0.08	2.6	0.9	0.40	4.75	3.03	82.7	1.0	24.3	35.6	4.4
3.9	4.28	18.4	0.20	5.1	8.4	1.08	8.90	3.51	67.5	3.5	26.7	13.0	8.0
9.7	0.14	0.6	0.00	3.4	0.6	0.72	6.66	2.94	80.7	3.4	41.7	18.6	6.5
8.0	0.65	2.6	0.13	8.6	1522.0	1.52	14.62	1.84	14.8	7.6	55.4	0.0	8.9
9.0	0.07	0.5	0.00	4.9	312.0	0.91	8.59	2.08	33.6	6.5	31.4	0.0	7.6
4.2	10.15	15.6	0.28	2.2	0.1	0.16	0.51	3.72	86.1	3.1	47.2	21.5	6.9
8.6	0.14	1.1	0.08	3.8	0.8	0.63	7.20	3.88	80.4	2.3	13.1	17.3	5.6
7.9	0.04	0.3	0.00	4.7	6.4	0.97	10.14	3.43	63.3	4.8	19.9	4.1	6.8
2.2	1.20	8.3	0.21	9.1	8.1	1.94	17.98	5.00	55.8	1.2	9.4	24.5	8.8
7.1	0.18	1.1	0.25	5.4	1.0	1.43	14.50	4.46	69.8	1.7	14.4	21.0	6.1
3.9	1.71	5.1	2.49	10.0	2.4	4.31	16.28	14.10	30.4	0.5	2.5	36.4	8.7
6.3	0.26	2.1	0.02	9.4	1.3	2.21	26.42	4.78	59.0	1.0	25.1	34.5	5.7
5.0	1.94	12.2	0.10	6.5	37.4	1.57	14.22	3.23	49.6	1.8	11.8	14.6	9.7
6.1	0.70	5.4	0.00	6.0	2.5	1.04	10.93	3.61	59.3	1.6	12.0	21.0	5.4
7.8	0.42	2.1	-0.08	5.0	1.4	1.34	12.62	3.75	70.9	3.5	41.3	17.9	5.9
8.8	0.00	0.0	0.00	5.9	0.9	1.10	7.81	3.36	55.5	4.4	33.0	8.5	8.5
5.3	0.38	3.4	-0.01	5.0	3.5	0.87	9.83	3.78	61.3	2.4	6.4	16.1	4.8
3.4	1.27	9.2	0.00	3.3	0.6	0.42	3.32	4.16	80.7	2.5	9.8	16.1	6.9
3.1	2.46	16.9	0.11	4.2	0.9	0.80	6.82	4.94	67.3	1.5	13.3	23.2	6.1
2.6	3.08	20.5	0.26	2.1	0.2	0.22	2.37	4.42	90.1	2.7	13.6	15.6	3.7
8.0	0.89	4.2	0.65	3.8	0.5	0.53	4.15	3.77	76.5	4.4	22.2	7.2	6.9
6.3	0.63	3.4	-0.06	4.6	1.1	0.81	7.96	3.92	71.2	2.7	25.9	16.7	5.8
2.7	2.66	21.4	0.23	1.5	-0.1	-0.14	-1.43	3.67	85.6	0.8	17.3	36.4	4.8
4.9	1.18	8.6	0.28	3.1	2.9	0.46	4.37	3.03	81.2	1.0	8.9	22.8	5.8
8.2	0.00	0.0	0.27	4.7	1.1	0.80	8.83	3.41	57.8	1.5	8.9	22.2	5.2
10.0	0.59	1.1	0.37	4.5	3.1	1.00	5.19	3.76	71.3	6.7	62.8	5.7	8.3
7.2	0.67	1.7	0.07	2.2	0.0	0.30	2.89	2.63	88.9	5.4	62.6	9.9	4.6
9.1	2.06	3.2	0.01	6.8	2.3	1.83	12.29	3.02	43.7	5.9	76.9	12.5	9.8
5.5	1.24	7.2	0.37	3.7	575.4	0.59	4.35	2.69	73.8	5.2	29.1	3.6	9.5
7.6	0.02	0.1	-0.16	3.4	0.4	0.53	6.84	3.62	79.5	4.3	38.1	12.8	3.8
7.4	0.91	6.1	0.39	5.7	2.9	1.03	9.23	3.94	64.7	1.5	4.1	21.1	7.5
7.5	1.38	4.0	0.00	8.3	4.4	2.04	10.40	3.16	39.5	4.2	48.9	11.2	9.0
4.8	0.42	3.1	0.20	10.0	4.1	2.37	21.35	5.12	46.2	0.5	13.5	68.6	9.0
6.2	1.05	4.9	0.13	4.1	0.7	0.83	6.54	4.14	74.3	4.7	27.0	6.5	7.0
5.7	0.93	6.0	0.15	4.4	1.8	0.83	8.97	3.16	61.6	2.8	22.8	15.9	5.8
8.6	0.00	0.0	0.00	3.3	0.2	0.50	4.53	3.17	79.8	4.6	31.2	8.8	5.3
6.2	0.43	3.4	0.00	3.7	2.5	0.73	8.33	3.12	75.0	1.8	17.7	15.8	4.8
2.9	5.35	24.0	0.11	2.7	0.2	0.41	2.44	3.94	90.4	1.3	21.0	29.5	6.0
4.3	1.36	11.2	0.01	3.3	27.1	0.48	4.62	3.22	74.1	4.1	17.3	8.5	8.0
9.8	0.00	0.0	0.00	4.1	0.2	0.60	2.14	3.89	75.9	0.5	2.6	47.0	7.8
4.8	7.43	13.6	-0.04	4.4	1.3	0.86	2.81	3.43	68.1	3.5	29.6	14.1	7.1
5.8	0.77	5.2	-0.01	3.5	0.5	0.51	4.58	3.66	81.4	3.8	16.2	9.9	6.4
9.3	0.24	0.3	0.33	0.2	-0.1	-0.21	-0.59	2.90	107.0	4.0	76.8	22.5	5.0
6.1	0.62	4.7	0.08	4.4	9.8	0.87	8.88	3.29	72.0	3.1	20.5	14.5	8.1
5.2	1.88	7.8	0.03	5.5	5.0	0.97	5.21	3.76	58.5	0.9	19.1	38.3	8.3
3.8	1.10	9.1	0.21	4.4	9.9	0.92	8.94	3.48	74.5	3.1	7.1	12.4	7.5
5.6	0.96	7.3	0.22	1.3	0.0	0.02	0.18	2.89	98.1	4.1	22.3	8.7	5.5
7.2	1.25	4.6	0.04	4.3	1.0	0.78	6.90	3.97	75.5	5.6	52.4	10.2	6.0
0.3	6.10	63.9	0.24	1.3	0.2	0.13	2.42	3.23	98.7	2.0	23.7	19.9	0.8
6.7	0.49	3.3	0.02	7.6	1.9	1.27	11.36	4.37	52.8	2.7	13.8	15.5	6.5
4.8	1.52	10.0	0.00	5.5	0.4	0.97	8.86	3.22	53.0	1.2	10.7	28.5	6.0

Data as of September 30, 2016

Name	City	State	2015 Rating	2015 Rating	2014 Rating	Total Assets ($Mil)	One Year Asset Growth	Comm-ercial Loans	Cons-umer Loans	Mort-gage Loans	Secur-ities	Capital-ization Index	Lever-age Ratio	Risk-Based Capital Ratio
Natbank, N.A.	Hollywood	FL	B-	C+	C	175.0	12.03	1.4	2.0	75.2	2.9	10.0	15.6	30.7
National Advisors Trust Co., FSB	Kansas City	MO	U	U	U	8.0	7.50	0.0	0.0	0.0	48.8	10.0	87.0	260.0
National Bank	Hillsboro	IL	B-	B-	B-	334.4	-1.36	7.7	0.5	12.9	20.2	8.7	10.1	14.2
National Bank	Gatesville	TX	B	B+	B+	622.3	7.30	5.1	7.0	11.8	22.8	8.9	10.3	16.3
National Bank & Trust	La Grange	TX	B-	B-	B	217.1	-3.86	1.2	4.5	15.3	63.7	9.6	10.8	29.5
National Bank of Adams County	West Union	OH	C	C	C	84.2	2.01	1.4	2.6	26.2	13.9	9.9	10.9	26.8
National Bank of Andrews	Andrews	TX	A-	A-	A-	174.9	-6.93	26.1	3.2	10.4	19.6	9.9	11.0	16.0
National Bank of Blacksburg	Blacksburg	VA	A	A	A	1201.0	5.17	3.3	2.7	11.2	36.3	10.0	15.2	25.6
National Bank of Commerce	Birmingham	AL	B	B	B-	1776.9	31.73	12.3	1.1	11.4	5.8	6.5	9.4	12.1
National Bank of Commerce	Superior	WI	A-	A-	B+	576.7	2.90	10.5	3.9	12.8	17.5	10.0	12.3	16.2
National Bank of Coxsackie	Coxsackie	NY	C	C+	C+	298.4	1.04	2.8	3.0	23.2	42.1	6.8	8.9	20.1
▲ National Bank of Georgia	Athens	GA	B+	B	B	415.3	11.74	5.5	0.6	18.0	1.6	7.8	10.4	13.2
National Bank of Indianapolis	Indianapolis	IN	B-	B-	C+	1916.0	9.55	15.4	2.0	13.3	17.8	5.6	7.7	11.5
National Bank of Malvern	Malvern	PA	B+	A-	A-	152.3	2.47	0.4	0.0	25.9	22.5	10.0	16.5	25.3
National Bank of Middlebury	Middlebury	VT	C+	C+	C+	336.6	3.63	4.4	0.4	38.2	22.8	6.7	8.7	14.6
National Bank of New York City	Flushing	NY	B+	B	C+	221.9	15.28	1.2	0.0	5.8	2.1	10.0	19.0	22.8
▲ National Bank of Petersburg	Petersburg	IL	B-	B-	B-	139.9	-4.86	2.2	5.2	16.8	37.6	10.0	11.5	21.6
National Bank of St. Anne	Saint Anne	IL	C+	C+	C+	50.2	4.39	3.8	7.8	18.9	6.0	7.4	9.2	14.0
National Bank of Texas at Fort Worth	Fort Worth	TX	C	C	C	234.5	12.95	12.4	5.3	13.5	39.6	6.3	8.3	16.8
National Bank of Waupun	Waupun	WI	B+	B	B-	143.8	2.36	14.3	3.9	11.5	19.7	10.0	11.5	15.4
▲ National Capital Bank of Washington	Washington	DC	B+	C	B-	406.5	-1.87	5.9	0.4	29.8	39.0	9.6	10.7	26.1
National Cooperative Bank, N.A.	Hillsboro	OH	B-	B-	B	2201.8	6.87	21.0	0.9	17.6	4.5	9.2	12.2	14.3
National Exchange Bank and Trust	Fond du Lac	WI	A	A	A	2025.1	49.87	8.7	1.2	6.4	23.0	10.0	17.4	23.7
National Grand Bank of Marblehead	Marblehead	MA	B+	B+	A-	312.6	6.11	1.4	1.2	59.3	18.6	10.0	11.2	20.5
National Iron Bank	Salisbury	CT	C	C-	C-	122.5	4.49	0.6	1.4	47.4	30.1	6.0	8.0	18.6
National Union Bank of Kinderhook	Kinderhook	NY	B-	B	B	448.4	11.63	7.2	0.7	17.2	17.5	8.5	10.0	13.9
▼ Nationwide Bank	Columbus	OH	C-	C+	B	6852.2	7.13	1.4	20.0	30.6	29.0	5.9	8.2	11.7
Native American Bank, N.A.	Denver	CO	C-	D	D	89.6	15.71	58.3	1.2	1.7	7.7	7.2	9.1	27.4
Nature Coast Bank	Hernando	FL	C+	C+	C-	57.3	0.21	5.7	1.6	5.2	11.2	10.0	11.7	15.9
NBC Oklahoma	Oklahoma City	OK	C+	B-	C+	583.9	1.59	25.4	1.1	13.5	6.6	5.0	8.4	11.0
▲ NBH Bank	Greenwood Village	CO	C	C	C+	4592.6	-3.72	15.3	0.6	15.5	28.9	6.6	8.6	12.8
▲ NBKC Bank	Overland Park	KS	A	A-	B	603.9	5.83	2.6	3.6	33.9	24.1	10.0	13.2	18.9
NBT Bank, N.A.	Norwich	NY	B	B-	B-	8699.8	7.49	9.4	18.7	16.9	20.3	5.7	8.4	11.5
Nebraska Bank of Commerce	Lincoln	NE	C	B-	C+	123.1	9.10	10.2	1.2	15.4	0.0	6.4	9.3	12.1
Nebraska State Bank	Bristow	NE	C+	C+	C+	16.6	-2.22	9.9	3.7	1.8	0.0	10.0	15.8	26.0
▲ Nebraska State Bank	Lynch	NE	C	C	C	14.0	-5.71	6.0	1.5	3.3	0.0	10.0	15.5	28.7
Nebraska State Bank	Oshkosh	NE	A-	A-	B+	49.1	-6.16	0.5	0.1	0.0	0.1	10.0	14.7	19.4
Nebraska State Bank and Trust Co.	Broken Bow	NE	B+	B+	B+	215.5	3.56	10.7	2.8	10.8	6.8	7.8	10.9	13.2
NebraskaLand National Bank	North Platte	NE	B+	B+	A-	673.7	1.43	21.5	0.8	3.9	15.0	7.2	10.7	12.6
▲ Necedah Bank	Necedah	WI	C+	C	C	35.7	5.40	6.3	1.4	14.8	12.4	9.2	11.9	14.3
Needham Bank	Needham	MA	B	B+	B+	1997.9	7.97	1.3	0.1	50.5	10.4	10.0	12.5	17.8
Neffs National Bank	Neffs	PA	A	A	A	330.7	0.99	1.5	1.6	22.4	48.2	10.0	18.3	35.1
Nehawka Bank	Nehawka	NE	C	C	C-	15.9	-2.11	1.0	3.5	40.8	1.3	10.0	16.5	22.4
▲ Neighborhood National Bank	San Diego	CA	C-	D-	E	56.4	-14.46	7.8	0.1	5.5	4.0	6.8	8.8	18.4
▲ Neighborhood National Bank	Mora	MN	B-	C+	B-	217.6	-0.53	8.0	2.8	17.5	34.2	10.0	11.2	18.4
Nekoma State Bank	La Crosse	KS	C	C-	C-	43.2	-6.60	2.4	1.3	2.0	54.9	6.9	8.9	20.0
Nekoosa Port Edwards State Bank	Nekoosa	WI	B+	B+	B+	212.9	4.44	3.6	1.6	30.2	23.2	10.0	13.4	26.5
Nelsonville Home & Savings Bank	Nelsonville	OH	B-	B-	B-	27.3	0.24	0.0	3.2	59.1	5.5	10.0	11.1	24.8
Neuberger Berman Trust Co. of Delaware	Wilmington	DE	U	U	U	9.5	5.87	0.0	0.0	0.0	0.0	10.0	90.6	337.5
Neuberger Berman Trust Co., N.A.	New York	NY	U	U	U	36.3	8.42	0.0	0.0	0.0	0.0	10.0	82.0	280.3
Nevada Bank and Trust Co.	Caliente	NV	C+	C+	C+	113.7	2.82	4.1	4.8	8.8	45.7	9.8	10.8	25.2
New Albin Savings Bank	New Albin	IA	A+	A+	A+	220.4	3.33	2.4	1.2	10.3	68.8	10.0	17.1	53.1
New Buffalo Savings Bank	New Buffalo	MI	D	D	D	100.7	10.24	0.4	0.5	37.8	0.0	10.0	12.7	18.5
New Carlisle Federal Savings Bank	New Carlisle	OH	C+	C+	C	96.3	12.96	11.2	1.7	35.4	2.1	10.0	11.2	15.9
New Century Bank	Belleville	KS	B	B	B	42.6	27.66	3.8	4.0	32.6	0.6	8.7	10.2	14.0
New Covenant Trust Co., N.A.	Jeffersonville	IN	U	U	U	6.3	6.38	0.0	0.0	0.0	45.9	10.0	94.7	328.7
New Era Bank	Fredericktown	MO	A-	A-	A	334.8	3.92	3.8	1.4	29.7	21.8	7.6	9.4	14.7
New Foundation Savings Bank	Cincinnati	OH	C-	C	C	21.5	5.45	0.0	0.0	68.8	0.9	7.7	9.4	17.3
▼ New Frontier Bank	Saint Charles	MO	C	C+	C-	95.5	1.86	8.0	0.4	7.3	20.7	8.4	9.9	14.9
New Horizon Bank, N.A.	Powhatan	VA	C	B-	C+	70.0	17.03	13.3	2.3	15.7	13.8	8.9	11.2	14.1

Asset Quality Index	Adjusted Non-Performing Loans as a % of Total Loans	as a % of Capital	Net Charge-Offs Avg Loans	Profitability Index	Net Income ($Mil)	Return on Assets (R.O.A.)	Return on Equity (R.O.E.)	Net Interest Spread	Overhead Efficiency Ratio	Liquidity Index	Liquidity Ratio	Hot Money Ratio	Stability Index
6.8	1.38	7.2	0.00	3.1	0.4	0.34	2.16	3.64	86.7	1.6	19.1	23.9	6.6
8.4	na	0.0	na	9.5	0.2	3.67	4.18	1.06	97.2	5.0	402.8	100.0	5.7
4.1	1.90	12.4	0.35	4.2	1.9	0.76	7.57	3.38	63.7	4.3	14.0	6.6	5.5
5.9	0.81	3.9	0.12	4.9	4.2	0.95	9.20	3.58	68.6	5.1	40.7	9.4	6.9
9.4	0.32	0.9	0.10	3.7	1.4	0.84	7.40	2.46	69.8	3.6	54.1	21.7	6.4
4.3	4.20	17.4	0.06	3.2	0.5	0.71	6.56	2.78	74.1	4.9	44.1	11.0	6.3
5.3	1.24	6.0	0.39	10.0	3.3	2.52	21.83	4.66	56.5	4.8	33.9	8.8	7.3
6.9	1.26	4.3	0.25	7.1	11.6	1.30	8.72	3.53	53.3	5.7	33.3	6.4	10.0
7.4	0.24	2.0	0.07	6.1	13.3	1.10	9.22	4.25	59.9	2.6	9.5	14.0	9.1
5.6	1.07	6.2	0.07	7.7	7.8	1.85	14.10	4.38	61.3	1.6	12.8	10.7	9.1
4.1	3.58	17.7	0.43	2.5	1.0	0.44	5.10	2.88	82.6	4.1	18.7	8.3	4.7
5.9	0.28	2.1	-0.02	7.5	3.7	1.21	11.73	3.70	50.2	3.2	12.8	13.0	6.2
5.3	1.27	10.3	0.00	4.1	10.6	0.74	9.80	2.94	68.6	5.0	24.4	6.3	6.0
5.1	4.07	15.9	0.00	4.6	0.9	0.79	4.86	3.52	68.2	4.1	28.3	10.7	8.3
5.8	0.79	5.7	-0.01	3.2	1.5	0.61	6.79	3.33	80.9	4.9	23.0	3.8	5.2
7.3	0.00	0.0	-0.09	4.5	1.5	0.94	4.95	3.06	65.2	0.6	17.1	48.6	7.9
8.7	0.12	0.5	0.14	3.6	0.9	0.83	8.01	2.71	73.5	5.3	43.2	8.9	5.9
6.6	0.11	0.8	0.00	4.9	0.3	0.69	5.33	4.27	68.1	1.7	22.8	23.9	5.7
8.6	0.11	0.6	0.04	3.2	1.1	0.67	8.00	3.26	79.3	5.0	53.4	13.2	4.9
5.7	1.39	8.1	0.05	6.3	1.3	1.16	9.96	4.40	59.5	2.5	22.9	17.4	6.9
5.6	2.00	8.8	-1.72	6.5	3.8	1.22	12.07	2.80	70.4	5.4	39.6	7.2	5.6
4.3	1.99	12.7	0.01	4.2	14.6	0.91	7.66	3.49	75.3	2.7	19.7	13.7	8.5
7.8	1.26	3.9	0.09	9.6	18.9	1.64	8.85	4.61	53.7	6.0	37.8	5.0	10.0
7.6	0.69	4.5	-0.01	4.8	2.0	0.87	7.61	3.41	64.0	4.5	23.8	6.5	7.0
9.9	0.00	0.0	0.00	2.6	0.4	0.48	5.80	2.83	85.9	3.4	37.4	17.1	4.7
5.1	0.96	6.6	-0.04	4.5	2.5	0.78	7.88	3.70	68.2	3.3	12.7	12.0	5.9
7.5	0.23	1.9	0.54	2.2	5.5	0.11	1.34	2.04	90.0	1.6	26.7	37.4	5.0
3.7	1.42	12.2	-0.01	2.9	0.3	0.48	5.05	4.50	90.8	0.4	5.4	66.6	3.7
6.0	0.96	5.2	-0.02	2.8	0.1	0.26	2.02	3.78	88.3	3.4	24.6	13.2	6.6
5.6	0.57	5.2	0.04	4.3	4.1	0.96	11.50	4.10	73.4	2.3	13.1	17.1	5.9
4.2	2.07	14.1	1.08	3.2	17.0	0.49	4.70	3.55	69.9	4.1	24.7	11.6	7.6
8.3	0.44	2.0	-0.10	8.3	14.7	3.18	25.52	2.31	80.4	1.3	22.4	30.3	9.7
4.6	0.77	6.2	0.33	5.0	56.4	0.89	8.13	3.46	61.0	4.2	5.0	3.5	8.6
6.3	0.24	1.9	0.00	3.1	0.5	0.53	5.69	2.97	81.2	1.8	14.6	20.0	4.3
8.4	0.00	0.0	0.00	4.6	0.1	1.01	6.50	4.06	73.9	2.7	55.6	27.6	6.5
7.3	2.14	5.9	-0.15	2.6	0.1	0.41	2.81	3.44	74.1	4.1	62.6	16.5	5.6
7.7	0.30	1.4	0.03	10.0	1.3	3.48	25.73	4.85	41.7	1.5	22.1	26.2	7.0
7.0	0.01	0.1	0.01	5.6	2.0	1.29	11.63	3.76	63.6	1.0	6.0	9.9	7.7
8.3	0.06	0.4	0.00	4.7	4.4	0.87	8.20	3.65	66.4	1.0	3.9	16.3	7.4
6.8	0.70	4.1	0.00	3.5	0.2	0.59	4.92	3.34	76.2	3.4	19.1	12.6	5.3
7.6	0.85	5.5	0.04	4.2	9.8	0.66	5.32	3.20	64.7	0.8	13.3	37.2	8.2
8.1	1.49	4.1	0.03	7.1	3.4	1.39	7.73	3.60	45.2	3.9	53.0	18.9	8.9
4.2	2.82	14.3	0.05	2.5	0.0	0.28	1.67	3.97	93.2	3.8	10.9	9.3	5.9
4.6	2.34	10.6	-0.74	4.4	0.6	1.37	16.69	4.14	109.8	3.8	42.5	16.2	3.7
7.7	0.33	1.6	-0.25	4.0	1.1	0.66	5.73	3.97	78.1	4.5	28.7	8.6	6.4
8.8	0.00	0.0	0.32	3.1	0.3	0.86	9.33	3.13	82.3	6.6	52.3	2.2	4.6
8.6	0.79	3.2	0.05	5.1	2.0	1.27	9.47	2.80	47.7	2.4	46.2	34.0	8.2
9.1	0.51	3.1	-0.03	4.6	0.2	0.79	7.30	3.45	58.9	1.9	26.5	23.6	5.8
10.0	na	0.0	na	10.0	0.2	2.78	3.08	9.30	95.1	4.0	na	0.0	5.3
10.0	na	0.0	na	10.0	0.5	2.06	2.57	8.21	96.2	4.0	289.3	0.0	6.7
6.6	1.90	6.1	0.19	3.1	0.4	0.44	4.01	3.36	83.8	7.0	56.8	2.4	6.7
9.7	0.00	0.0	-0.02	7.0	2.5	1.52	8.33	3.01	28.4	4.2	74.5	21.7	9.7
4.7	2.61	15.0	0.13	0.3	-0.3	-0.34	-2.60	2.91	108.9	1.1	14.1	27.8	5.3
7.5	0.51	3.6	0.10	3.1	0.2	0.35	3.07	3.75	87.3	1.8	13.7	20.2	5.3
8.4	0.07	0.5	0.05	10.0	0.9	3.04	30.28	6.59	58.4	0.6	10.5	47.1	7.0
10.0	na	0.0	na	9.3	0.2	5.10	5.41	0.50	82.6	4.0	na	0.0	5.6
7.3	0.06	0.5	0.02	6.8	4.2	1.70	16.41	3.22	54.1	4.5	15.9	5.5	8.7
8.3	0.48	3.9	0.00	4.5	0.0	1.09	11.87	3.20	88.0	1.6	16.2	23.2	4.3
7.4	0.71	3.8	-0.09	2.5	0.1	0.19	1.90	3.43	95.2	3.4	27.8	9.3	4.1
3.3	2.57	18.1	0.01	3.8	0.3	0.53	4.49	4.55	81.0	1.4	18.1	26.6	6.1

Name	City	State	2015 Rating	2014 Rating	2014 Rating	Total Assets ($Mil)	One Year Asset Growth	Asset Mix (As a % of Total Assets)				Capital-ization Index	Lever-age Ratio	Risk-Based Capital Ratio
								Comm-ercial Loans	Cons-umer Loans	Mort-gage Loans	Secur-ities			
New Jersey Community Bank	Freehold	NJ	D-	D-	D+	101.9	-19.29	0.2	0.0	10.5	11.3	8.7	10.2	15.0
New Market Bank	Elko New Market	MN	C-	C-	C-	105.9	7.30	7.6	1.4	7.4	24.4	6.0	8.0	14.4
New Mexico Bank & Trust	Albuquerque	NM	B	B	B	1318.2	2.76	15.4	0.4	7.9	23.6	5.0	8.1	11.0
New Millennium Bank	New Brunswick	NJ	D	D	E-	274.4	29.16	16.1	0.0	4.1	3.5	5.6	7.6	11.7
New OMNI Bank, N.A.	Alhambra	CA	A-	B+	B-	416.5	21.24	3.0	0.3	36.4	0.0	10.0	11.3	19.1
New Peoples Bank, Inc.	Honaker	VA	C-	D+	D+	633.7	0.02	4.1	3.6	37.5	11.8	8.5	10.0	17.0
New Republic Savings Bank	Roanoke Rapids	NC	B-	B-	B-	62.5	2.04	0.7	1.4	57.4	0.0	8.8	10.2	15.6
New Resource Bank	San Francisco	CA	C+	B	B-	320.4	14.40	22.7	0.0	0.5	9.9	8.9	11.4	14.1
New Tripoli Bank	New Tripoli	PA	B+	B+	B+	401.0	3.50	3.0	0.5	49.8	23.8	10.0	12.4	20.7
New Washington State Bank	New Washington	IN	B	B+	B	293.8	13.67	9.8	15.0	20.8	9.8	8.5	10.1	13.7
New Windsor State Bank	Taneytown	MD	B-	B-	C+	312.0	5.97	3.0	1.1	19.7	7.8	6.3	9.4	12.0
New York Commercial Bank	Westbury	NY	B	B	B	3799.7	-10.96	13.3	0.0	0.3	10.5	8.9	10.3	14.2
New York Community Bank	Westbury	NY	B-	B-	B	45898.6	2.16	1.7	0.0	5.9	8.0	5.4	8.4	11.3
NewBank	Flushing	NY	A	A	A-	284.2	12.08	31.7	0.0	0.4	0.2	10.0	12.8	19.7
Newburyport Five Cents Savings Bank	Newburyport	MA	B	B+	B+	768.4	4.87	2.4	0.1	38.3	14.7	10.0	15.4	18.8
NewDominion Bank	Charlotte	NC	D	D-	E-	328.4	9.11	4.9	0.2	18.1	5.7	8.8	10.2	14.4
Newfield National Bank	Newfield	NJ	C	C+	C+	641.4	7.03	5.5	0.6	17.5	38.5	6.8	8.8	17.5
NewFirst National Bank	El Campo	TX	A-	B+	B	623.1	3.71	11.2	1.1	9.6	6.3	8.9	10.2	15.0
Newport Federal Bank	Newport	TN	B	B	B	201.7	3.66	0.2	1.3	39.4	43.6	9.2	10.4	25.4
Newton Federal Bank	Covington	GA	B	B	C+	233.5	2.92	7.0	1.0	56.8	3.2	10.0	19.3	32.1
Newtown Savings Bank	Newtown	CT	C	C	C-	1131.8	6.21	7.2	1.4	47.9	7.8	6.0	8.0	12.6
NexBank SSB	Dallas	TX	A-	A-	B+	4004.7	77.84	14.4	0.4	37.0	10.5	7.3	9.7	12.7
NexTier Bank, N.A.	Butler	PA	B	B-	B-	1151.6	17.00	9.2	1.8	26.4	10.1	9.8	10.8	14.9
Nicolet National Bank	Green Bay	WI	B+	B+	B	2265.9	96.80	16.9	0.6	13.8	16.0	6.9	9.6	12.4
Nicollet County Bank of Saint Peter	Saint Peter	MN	C+	C+	C+	174.6	5.86	7.9	2.6	7.0	22.7	5.6	7.6	17.0
NOA Bank	Duluth	GA	A	A	A	271.4	19.80	3.8	0.0	0.8	10.6	10.0	12.3	15.1
Noah Bank	Elkins Park	PA	B-	B-	D-	319.7	3.44	14.9	0.1	0.0	1.0	10.0	12.0	18.8
▲ NobleBank & Trust	Anniston	AL	B-	C	C+	222.8	12.36	10.0	2.1	11.4	28.8	6.9	8.9	13.8
Nodaway Valley Bank	Maryville	MO	A	B+	B-	840.2	1.47	6.0	1.1	7.4	19.8	10.0	11.9	17.1
Nokomis Savings Bank	Nokomis	IL	B-	B-	B-	26.2	-4.05	22.5	1.8	6.5	29.9	10.0	17.6	93.9
▼ Nordstrom FSB	Scottsdale	AZ	A-	A	A-	237.3	-30.32	0.0	20.5	0.0	0.0	9.3	10.5	24.0
Normangee State Bank	Normangee	TX	B+	B+	A-	122.1	2.31	4.4	17.2	24.3	26.4	10.0	14.3	25.0
NorStates Bank	Waukegan	IL	C-	C-	D	506.7	9.75	2.4	0.2	9.4	16.8	9.4	10.6	17.6
North Adams State Bank	Ursa	IL	B-	B-	B-	35.0	1.04	14.8	4.7	12.9	14.4	10.0	13.6	21.9
North Alabama Bank	Hazel Green	AL	C+	C-	C	95.1	2.25	3.4	1.5	10.8	8.2	9.0	10.3	14.4
North American Banking Co.	Roseville	MN	B+	B	C+	383.6	0.43	14.7	0.4	8.0	14.5	7.3	9.7	12.8
North American Savings Bank, F.S.B.	Grandview	MO	A-	A-	B	1932.0	27.79	1.4	0.1	59.1	12.4	8.7	11.2	13.9
North American State Bank	Belgrade	MN	B-	C+	C-	97.7	-0.17	5.3	2.3	12.6	10.4	10.0	11.8	16.9
North Arundel Savings Bank	Pasadena	MD	C	B-	B-	44.2	2.59	0.0	9.6	58.7	1.9	10.0	11.7	21.7
North Brookfield Savings Bank	North Brookfield	MA	B-	B-	B-	282.2	4.78	0.9	1.9	46.3	22.7	10.0	12.2	23.1
North Cambridge Co-operative Bank	Cambridge	MA	C+	B-	B-	88.8	-0.59	0.0	0.2	50.2	12.3	10.0	21.2	59.6
North Central Bank	Hennepin	IL	B	B-	B	132.7	0.47	7.5	3.5	11.6	35.8	10.0	11.3	19.6
North Country Savings Bank	Canton	NY	B-	B-	B-	246.9	0.53	0.2	2.3	70.1	1.3	10.0	14.6	24.7
North County Savings Bank	Red Bud	IL	C	C	C	49.3	5.58	0.0	3.7	48.1	21.1	6.6	8.6	19.3
North Dallas Bank & Trust Co.	Dallas	TX	C+	C+	C+	1385.7	-2.85	4.4	0.6	15.9	33.9	9.2	10.5	26.7
North Easton Savings Bank	South Easton	MA	C-	C-	C-	524.6	3.42	0.8	1.0	52.4	17.7	6.9	8.9	15.5
▲ North Georgia National Bank	Calhoun	GA	B-	C-	C-	116.9	-0.15	5.9	1.1	16.6	19.5	10.0	11.9	21.5
North Middlesex Savings Bank	Ayer	MA	C	C	C-	427.4	9.05	5.7	1.8	34.5	14.5	7.1	9.1	12.9
North Salem State Bank	North Salem	IN	B-	B-	C+	278.2	15.26	5.6	4.3	18.8	8.2	6.3	8.3	13.2
North Shore Bank of Commerce	Duluth	MN	C+	C+	C+	261.7	6.18	4.0	0.6	34.9	7.7	4.6	6.6	12.0
North Shore Bank, a Co-operative Bank	Peabody	MA	C+	C+	C	789.0	18.66	9.4	0.3	21.2	13.1	9.4	10.6	14.6
North Shore Bank, FSB	Brookfield	WI	C+	C	C	1757.3	-2.74	1.3	16.1	23.5	11.6	10.0	12.3	18.4
North Shore Trust and Savings	Waukegan	IL	C-	C-	C-	233.9	-2.50	0.1	0.0	35.5	35.6	10.0	18.5	58.6
North Side Bank and Trust Co.	Cincinnati	OH	B+	B+	B+	545.1	5.18	22.5	1.3	10.4	17.9	10.0	13.8	15.8
North Side Federal S&L Assn. of Chicago	Chicago	IL	D	D+	D+	44.5	-1.57	0.1	0.1	39.6	3.2	9.5	10.7	27.8
North Star Bank	Roseville	MN	C+	C+	C+	257.1	5.02	11.5	0.7	4.5	30.6	8.3	9.8	16.1
North State Bank	Raleigh	NC	B-	B-	B-	794.7	7.20	6.2	0.4	27.3	2.6	6.0	8.4	11.7
North Valley Bank	Thornton	CO	A	A-	B+	150.0	2.54	2.8	0.2	31.8	4.7	10.0	11.9	19.1
North Valley Bank	Zanesville	OH	C+	C+	C+	207.1	11.87	7.0	3.7	18.7	28.8	6.8	8.8	14.6
Northbrook Bank & Trust Co.	Northbrook	IL	B-	B-	B-	1907.7	26.22	30.5	9.5	4.1	9.9	5.5	8.9	11.4

| Asset Quality Index | Adjusted Non-Performing Loans | | Net Charge-Offs | Profitability Index | Net Income ($Mil) | Return on Assets (R.O.A.) | Return on Equity (R.O.E.) | Net Interest Spread | Overhead Efficiency Ratio | Liquidity Index | Liquidity Ratio | Hot Money Ratio | Stability Index |
	as a % of Total Loans	as a % of Capital	Avg Loans										
4.2	1.34	7.9	-0.07	0.0	-1.3	-1.61	-14.98	3.20	149.1	0.9	25.1	44.6	4.2
4.2	2.22	13.7	0.46	2.6	0.4	0.46	5.60	3.18	85.1	6.4	47.0	3.1	4.1
5.2	1.41	11.3	-0.13	6.7	13.6	1.38	15.85	4.15	57.3	3.9	7.2	8.2	6.8
2.7	1.21	9.8	0.03	3.5	1.9	0.93	12.36	3.06	75.3	1.1	27.3	43.6	1.1
9.0	0.00	0.0	0.00	5.5	2.7	0.90	7.81	3.65	58.4	0.7	24.7	66.8	7.4
2.2	3.61	24.1	0.19	2.9	2.5	0.52	5.23	4.01	92.2	2.3	16.7	16.9	4.8
5.4	0.75	5.9	0.00	4.4	0.3	0.65	6.01	4.69	80.8	0.4	6.7	65.4	6.1
6.9	0.21	1.3	0.00	3.4	0.7	0.32	2.40	4.14	81.0	4.0	22.7	9.4	7.3
6.2	1.19	6.4	0.08	5.8	4.1	1.39	10.75	4.02	55.8	1.7	9.3	20.1	7.9
5.3	0.35	2.6	0.02	6.6	3.3	1.55	15.07	4.36	67.1	4.4	15.9	5.8	7.4
4.3	0.88	7.4	0.08	3.9	1.4	0.61	6.49	3.86	79.1	2.0	5.2	18.2	5.0
4.5	0.69	5.0	-0.02	4.6	21.4	0.74	4.65	3.20	52.8	4.2	20.1	9.0	8.3
6.0	0.14	1.4	0.00	5.0	382.5	1.12	8.95	2.92	40.8	1.6	6.1	14.5	8.6
5.8	1.65	8.1	0.40	9.8	4.3	2.11	16.40	3.58	45.1	1.9	38.2	35.6	8.0
8.4	0.44	2.2	-0.01	4.1	4.4	0.80	5.08	3.39	66.6	1.8	20.1	17.8	8.6
6.8	0.06	0.4	0.14	1.1	0.6	0.25	2.43	3.42	92.9	1.6	19.1	24.9	1.8
5.5	1.45	8.3	0.11	2.8	2.6	0.55	6.15	3.22	81.2	5.5	39.9	6.3	5.5
6.3	0.42	2.7	-0.14	9.9	12.6	2.70	25.11	4.87	52.6	4.9	25.6	4.5	8.7
7.6	0.85	3.6	0.26	4.4	1.1	0.70	6.78	3.13	65.2	1.9	34.9	31.9	5.6
5.5	3.11	12.3	1.11	4.1	0.9	0.51	2.64	4.27	82.4	2.0	16.5	19.1	6.1
5.7	0.91	8.7	0.11	3.3	4.9	0.59	7.72	3.33	76.8	3.9	8.6	8.6	5.4
8.7	0.03	0.2	-0.01	8.9	55.3	2.43	26.55	2.98	34.6	4.8	26.9	8.0	7.4
4.7	1.65	11.0	0.08	5.7	8.3	0.98	9.20	3.77	66.3	4.5	14.8	5.9	8.3
5.2	1.33	9.5	0.02	5.6	13.0	0.96	8.23	4.26	68.6	4.7	22.5	5.7	7.9
4.9	1.57	8.8	0.03	3.5	1.1	0.84	10.92	2.63	69.1	5.3	37.9	7.0	3.9
6.8	0.33	2.0	0.04	9.8	6.6	3.47	26.46	4.48	51.3	0.7	17.8	56.1	9.2
5.3	0.95	6.2	1.00	2.9	-1.3	-0.58	-4.47	4.01	100.7	0.6	13.8	56.0	6.1
6.3	0.68	4.1	0.08	4.1	1.3	0.81	8.89	3.90	74.4	3.7	32.4	14.0	4.5
6.9	0.43	2.3	0.14	9.1	13.7	2.18	16.56	3.94	52.5	4.0	24.8	9.9	9.9
8.5	0.01	0.0	0.00	2.7	0.1	0.30	1.75	3.24	82.0	4.4	44.3	13.9	7.2
6.0	1.49	2.6	1.44	9.8	101.6	50.95	500.30	4.35	37.6	2.9	57.6	35.1	8.2
4.3	2.27	9.8	0.52	8.4	1.5	1.60	11.13	5.24	45.3	1.2	19.2	30.4	8.7
4.7	2.38	11.5	0.09	2.5	1.4	0.37	2.76	3.07	85.9	4.1	33.3	12.2	5.7
4.9	2.20	11.0	0.00	4.4	0.2	0.80	5.73	4.15	71.5	4.5	27.8	8.0	6.9
2.6	4.46	26.1	-0.35	4.7	0.6	0.84	6.95	4.72	76.8	1.6	21.7	25.2	4.4
8.5	0.06	0.4	0.00	8.0	5.8	1.93	20.47	3.77	53.0	1.7	22.6	24.0	6.0
5.6	1.40	9.9	-0.11	8.9	17.5	1.35	11.16	3.78	70.8	1.1	14.7	30.0	9.5
6.4	1.11	5.6	0.07	3.7	0.5	0.62	5.22	3.78	83.2	2.9	25.0	15.6	6.4
2.1	4.22	27.8	0.00	2.4	0.1	0.15	1.31	3.87	85.4	1.0	17.4	33.5	5.8
7.1	1.29	7.0	0.02	3.8	1.2	0.58	4.64	3.53	77.5	3.8	28.7	12.4	7.1
9.3	1.15	2.9	0.00	2.7	0.2	0.32	1.48	2.65	80.3	3.2	56.8	24.8	7.7
6.3	0.89	3.8	-0.37	4.5	1.1	1.12	8.54	3.44	68.9	4.4	36.9	11.8	8.0
8.3	0.70	3.8	0.07	2.5	0.3	0.16	1.29	3.69	92.9	4.7	10.7	3.3	6.7
9.6	0.00	0.0	0.00	2.9	0.2	0.44	5.18	2.64	79.5	2.9	44.2	23.6	3.8
9.4	0.31	1.2	-0.10	3.3	5.2	0.52	4.94	2.25	67.5	6.3	56.9	9.4	8.0
7.4	0.50	3.8	0.04	2.4	1.3	0.32	3.80	2.71	85.4	4.3	27.0	9.1	5.1
7.6	0.54	2.3	-0.17	4.2	0.7	0.78	6.65	3.52	81.4	4.4	25.9	7.4	5.6
4.5	1.60	12.6	0.03	3.2	1.9	0.60	6.67	3.40	80.5	1.6	14.9	22.3	4.9
5.6	0.38	3.3	0.12	5.9	2.1	1.13	13.36	4.43	58.5	1.4	14.8	24.3	5.2
5.4	1.12	11.1	0.14	7.3	3.8	2.03	30.94	3.74	68.1	5.1	23.2	2.7	3.7
6.4	0.61	4.3	0.00	2.9	2.5	0.43	3.93	3.47	80.2	3.3	18.6	12.9	6.9
4.4	1.24	7.6	-0.04	2.1	4.1	0.31	2.42	3.17	94.2	4.3	16.5	7.2	7.7
7.8	2.44	5.2	0.14	1.7	0.3	0.16	0.87	2.49	93.0	4.6	66.0	17.5	6.3
7.7	0.86	4.2	0.01	5.0	3.8	0.96	6.90	3.25	57.2	3.8	20.7	10.6	7.8
3.4	4.43	21.9	-0.11	0.8	-0.1	-0.14	-1.39	3.31	106.0	4.5	42.7	13.0	5.1
5.2	1.46	7.2	-0.33	3.2	1.0	0.55	5.60	3.14	88.4	5.8	46.1	6.8	4.9
5.1	0.43	4.0	0.01	6.3	9.1	1.53	18.37	3.61	75.0	4.7	12.9	3.4	4.6
8.4	0.27	1.6	0.00	9.5	2.4	2.18	18.81	5.03	56.7	4.5	17.3	5.5	7.3
5.5	0.61	3.9	0.35	3.3	0.8	0.50	5.41	3.72	81.7	3.7	16.4	8.8	4.3
6.0	0.43	3.5	-0.09	5.1	11.0	0.84	9.47	2.87	50.6	2.7	18.7	14.2	6.9

Name	City	State	Rating	2015 Rating	2014 Rating	Total Assets ($Mil)	One Year Asset Growth	Asset Mix (As a % of Total Assets)				Capital-ization Index	Lever-age Ratio	Risk-Based Capital Ratio
								Comm-ercial Loans	Cons-umer Loans	Mort-gage Loans	Secur-ities			
Northeast Bank	Lewiston	ME	B+	B+	B	985.1	14.86	10.4	0.6	10.7	9.6	10.0	12.1	16.7
Northeast Bank	Minneapolis	MN	A	A	B+	406.8	3.60	18.6	0.4	5.5	14.4	10.0	12.0	15.1
NorthEast Community Bank	White Plains	NY	B	C+	C	677.7	23.41	7.5	0.0	2.4	1.0	10.0	13.4	15.2
Northeast Georgia Bank	Lavonia	GA	B	B-	C+	449.4	5.94	3.7	5.3	7.6	23.3	9.2	10.5	19.2
Northeast Missouri State Bank	Kirksville	MO	A-	A-	A-	108.0	2.42	1.0	3.2	9.1	46.9	10.0	11.3	22.4
Northeast Security Bank	Sumner	IA	A-	A-	A-	140.4	10.73	8.3	0.9	9.0	20.7	10.0	11.6	16.5
Northern Bank & Trust Co.	Woburn	MA	B+	B+	B+	1654.3	19.63	30.8	0.1	10.8	2.7	6.5	11.4	12.1
Northern California National Bank	Chico	CA	C+	B-	B-	202.0	6.49	7.9	0.9	9.6	14.6	7.1	9.1	23.6
▼ Northern Hancock Bank & Trust Co.	Newell	WV	D+	C	C	25.7	-3.64	5.4	10.2	46.0	2.4	10.0	13.3	22.2
Northern Michigan Bank & Trust	Escanaba	MI	D+	D+	D-	251.1	3.13	11.2	5.1	13.7	18.5	5.6	9.2	11.5
Northern State Bank	Ashland	WI	B-	B-	B-	242.4	2.00	6.2	1.5	29.8	32.2	6.3	8.3	16.2
Northern State Bank of Gonvick	Gonvick	MN	C-	D+	C-	39.9	12.90	2.3	4.7	3.6	21.8	10.0	17.5	82.6
▲ Northern State Bank of Thief River Falls	Thief River Falls	MN	B-	C+	C+	275.0	-4.73	7.3	4.8	12.9	18.9	9.9	10.9	25.6
▲ Northern State Bank of Virginia	Virginia	MN	D+	D	D+	61.9	0.67	7.0	4.2	36.7	8.0	5.4	7.4	13.1
Northern Trust Co.	Chicago	IL	B	B	B-	119702.5	0.05	4.9	0.3	5.7	36.7	5.0	7.0	12.9
Northfield Bank	Staten Island	NY	B	B	B	3785.7	19.00	1.8	0.1	12.8	14.8	10.0	14.5	18.4
Northfield Savings Bank	Berlin	VT	B-	B	B	883.3	6.14	5.0	0.2	41.6	18.6	10.0	12.3	18.8
Northmark Bank	North Andover	MA	B+	B+	B+	346.4	0.79	7.9	0.6	37.5	8.4	10.0	12.4	18.7
▲ Northpointe Bank	Grand Rapids	MI	C-	D+	D+	616.7	41.25	0.2	0.1	41.5	1.4	4.7	8.7	10.9
Northrim Bank	Anchorage	AK	B+	A-	A	1531.1	-0.25	15.6	0.6	7.8	19.4	8.9	11.2	14.1
Northside Bank	Adairsville	GA	E-	E-	E-	122.8	-5.98	4.7	0.9	8.5	20.1	1.6	4.7	8.6
Northside Community Bank	Gurnee	IL	B-	B-	C	229.2	-2.58	16.1	0.1	7.0	2.7	10.0	20.9	25.6
NorthStar Bank	Tampa	FL	C-	C-	D+	217.2	7.83	16.1	1.6	7.5	32.5	7.7	9.4	13.8
NorthStar Bank	Estherville	IA	A-	B	B	176.0	-3.17	5.3	1.5	19.5	8.3	9.3	10.5	14.9
Northstar Bank	Bad Axe	MI	C-	C-	C-	591.1	11.88	11.2	1.6	13.6	6.6	5.9	9.3	11.7
Northstar Bank	Denton	TX	B+	B+	B	1698.6	0.58	8.3	1.0	9.3	18.7	7.6	9.9	13.0
Northumberland National Bank	Northumberland	PA	C+	C+	B-	498.2	3.73	10.7	0.9	36.9	30.9	8.9	10.2	19.5
Northview Bank	Sandstone	MN	B	B-	B-	322.9	0.56	8.3	3.3	20.2	18.7	8.2	9.8	14.0
Northway Bank	Berlin	NH	C+	C+	C+	884.6	-5.89	6.3	0.9	18.7	26.3	8.1	9.7	16.0
Northwest Bank	Spencer	IA	B	B-	B-	1416.7	0.39	14.5	2.1	15.7	8.6	6.2	9.4	11.9
Northwest Bank	Boise	ID	A-	A-	B+	498.4	8.81	33.4	0.3	0.9	4.8	8.5	13.2	13.8
▼ Northwest Bank	Warren	PA	B-	B	B	9758.9	8.83	5.8	6.5	37.7	9.3	8.5	10.6	13.7
Northwest Bank & Trust Co.	Davenport	IA	B	C+	C-	179.4	-1.44	12.6	1.3	13.0	7.2	8.0	9.6	15.6
Northwest Bank of Rockford	Rockford	IL	C+	C	C+	264.9	8.24	18.9	0.5	14.2	15.2	7.1	9.5	12.5
Northwest Community Bank	Winsted	CT	C	C-	C-	343.2	0.04	3.9	2.5	44.7	18.9	10.0	12.0	20.2
Northwestern Bank	Orange City	IA	A-	B+	A-	220.0	2.92	5.9	0.8	7.2	8.5	10.0	13.2	15.6
Northwestern Bank	Chippewa Falls	WI	A-	A-	A-	418.2	3.26	14.6	1.1	9.8	21.7	8.8	10.2	14.3
Northwestern Bank, N.A.	Dilworth	MN	B-	B-	C+	136.0	-1.97	16.8	3.0	9.6	12.4	8.6	10.0	13.8
Northwestern Mutual Wealth Mgmt Co.	Milwaukee	WI	U	U	U	207.1	5.35	0.0	0.0	0.0	96.8	10.0	64.1	250.3
Northwoods Bank of Minnesota	Park Rapids	MN	B-	B	B-	109.1	2.81	3.7	3.4	26.1	29.0	9.6	10.7	16.7
Norway Savings Bank	Norway	ME	B-	B-	B	1095.9	5.92	4.0	4.9	28.0	8.4	9.2	13.4	14.3
Norwood Co-operative Bank	Norwood	MA	B-	C+	C+	441.9	5.77	1.3	0.1	34.8	12.9	10.0	14.8	21.0
NSB Bank	Mason City	IA	B+	B+	B+	197.3	3.18	17.0	1.2	6.7	17.5	7.2	9.6	12.7
NVE Bank	Englewood	NJ	B-	B-	B-	676.3	2.30	0.1	0.1	37.5	19.7	10.0	14.0	22.7
NXT Bank	Central City	IA	C+	C	C	261.6	2.97	9.4	0.4	15.1	12.3	8.4	10.2	13.7
O'Bannon Banking Co.	Buffalo	MO	B-	B-	B-	173.5	5.01	7.6	2.9	24.4	12.1	7.0	9.4	12.5
Oak Bank	Chicago	IL	B	B-	C+	199.7	-0.10	5.7	0.2	9.2	0.0	10.0	16.0	21.2
Oak Bank	Fitchburg	WI	A-	A-	A-	269.4	7.71	14.1	0.6	17.8	12.6	10.0	11.0	15.2
▼ Oak Creek Valley Bank	Valparaiso	NE	B	B+	A	84.4	2.62	3.8	0.6	7.5	29.4	9.3	11.0	14.4
Oak Valley Community Bank	Oakdale	CA	B	B	B+	946.9	19.31	7.0	0.1	2.8	16.9	5.2	8.2	11.2
Oak View National Bank	Warrenton	VA	C+	C+	C	196.0	13.43	7.6	1.2	37.1	1.0	8.4	10.0	15.3
Oakdale State Bank	Oakdale	IL	C	C	C	19.3	0.95	8.4	4.3	27.9	6.2	9.9	11.0	16.2
OakStar Bank	Springfield	MO	B	B	B	466.9	19.65	14.2	0.9	23.4	0.0	6.6	8.8	12.2
Oakwood State Bank	Oakwood	TX	B-	B	B	6.4	-1.50	5.5	9.9	0.0	26.1	10.0	21.3	73.0
Oakworth Capital Bank	Birmingham	AL	A-	A	A	438.1	15.59	26.1	1.6	1.9	9.5	9.8	13.3	14.8
Ocean Bank	Miami	FL	B-	C-	D	3417.5	4.94	9.1	0.7	7.8	9.4	8.2	10.7	13.5
Ocean City Home Bank	Ocean City	NJ	B-	C+	C+	1094.3	2.79	0.7	0.0	59.3	9.2	7.7	9.5	19.2
OceanFirst Bank	Toms River	NJ	B-	B	B-	4156.1	62.24	3.9	0.2	31.9	11.6	6.5	8.5	12.5
Oconee Federal S&L Assn.	Seneca	SC	A-	A-	A	485.6	3.58	0.0	1.0	51.7	25.7	10.0	15.7	31.4
Oconee State Bank	Watkinsville	GA	B-	C+	C	322.8	11.16	3.4	1.3	7.0	39.3	7.0	9.0	18.0

Asset Quality Index	Adjusted Non-Performing Loans as a % of Total Loans	as a % of Capital	Net Charge-Offs Avg Loans	Profitability Index	Net Income ($Mil)	Return on Assets (R.O.A.)	Return on Equity (R.O.E.)	Net Interest Spread	Overhead Efficiency Ratio	Liquidity Index	Liquidity Ratio	Hot Money Ratio	Stability Index
4.4	1.54	9.2	0.08	6.0	7.1	1.00	8.29	4.45	69.6	1.4	25.5	30.2	7.5
6.4	0.63	3.9	-0.02	6.5	4.5	1.49	12.16	4.50	65.4	4.9	14.5	2.5	7.8
5.3	0.78	4.9	0.07	4.3	3.3	0.68	4.69	3.67	69.6	0.7	6.8	34.7	7.0
4.8	2.13	8.9	0.03	4.5	3.8	1.11	11.61	2.99	67.3	4.2	33.8	11.7	4.8
8.3	0.07	0.2	-0.14	5.2	1.0	1.31	9.79	3.35	60.0	3.8	50.2	18.6	8.8
8.0	0.17	0.9	0.04	6.8	1.2	1.20	9.45	3.71	52.7	4.1	20.4	9.0	7.7
8.1	0.28	2.0	-0.11	9.1	15.0	1.36	13.03	4.44	44.1	0.8	7.2	22.6	9.1
9.4	0.00	0.0	0.03	3.6	0.9	0.58	6.56	2.33	57.7	5.4	58.7	12.6	4.9
1.7	5.33	28.6	0.29	2.4	0.0	0.19	1.44	7.79	96.0	1.5	20.6	26.9	5.4
0.2	6.25	46.9	0.33	4.4	1.8	1.22	9.69	4.71	70.2	2.5	21.2	17.0	4.6
5.7	1.03	7.3	-0.04	4.1	1.7	0.94	11.28	3.05	70.4	4.7	24.9	5.6	5.2
9.4	0.84	0.9	0.99	1.5	0.1	0.20	1.19	1.58	87.3	7.2	89.1	5.4	6.0
5.4	2.52	9.5	0.13	4.1	2.2	1.02	9.54	2.23	58.1	6.3	50.6	4.9	7.2
5.6	0.03	0.2	0.58	1.7	0.0	0.05	0.64	4.12	86.6	3.6	19.5	11.3	3.1
9.0	0.62	2.5	0.02	4.8	741.9	0.86	11.96	1.16	69.4	6.8	45.9	3.4	5.7
5.5	0.98	5.1	0.04	4.0	18.1	0.65	4.25	2.96	67.0	3.3	8.2	8.3	8.6
8.9	0.42	2.4	0.03	3.3	3.8	0.59	4.70	3.27	78.1	1.9	13.1	19.2	8.0
8.9	0.09	0.6	0.00	5.0	1.9	0.77	6.26	3.68	64.4	1.1	12.4	30.1	7.3
2.2	1.72	17.2	0.02	10.0	12.4	3.33	35.83	4.26	62.8	0.3	5.6	44.1	6.2
5.4	1.56	9.1	0.03	6.6	11.6	1.08	8.83	4.39	74.3	4.7	21.5	6.4	10.0
3.3	1.44	12.3	2.59	0.0	-3.5	-3.76	-79.54	3.36	195.9	3.0	33.6	18.1	0.0
5.3	2.51	7.7	-0.19	3.7	0.9	0.53	2.35	3.65	83.5	4.1	22.1	8.8	6.5
6.2	0.49	3.1	0.02	2.6	0.5	0.30	3.00	3.91	87.0	1.7	16.2	21.5	5.2
7.6	0.15	1.0	0.00	6.3	2.1	1.50	11.93	3.62	56.4	3.3	11.4	12.3	7.6
1.9	2.86	22.8	0.07	5.4	5.5	1.33	13.48	4.10	69.5	3.5	15.5	11.2	6.8
4.8	0.98	6.8	0.06	6.6	15.2	1.25	8.35	4.01	62.9	4.3	20.7	8.7	9.7
6.5	0.78	4.5	0.04	3.1	2.0	0.56	5.60	3.11	80.8	3.5	22.6	12.0	5.4
4.0	1.73	11.7	0.03	7.4	3.9	1.62	15.35	4.78	63.2	2.8	16.9	10.4	6.6
5.3	0.84	4.9	0.15	3.2	4.5	0.66	6.44	3.15	83.1	4.1	18.8	8.9	6.3
8.0	0.20	1.6	-0.01	4.8	13.1	1.24	12.73	3.48	69.7	3.3	11.9	12.4	7.8
7.0	0.06	0.4	0.02	7.2	4.3	1.19	8.63	4.91	59.8	1.8	15.8	10.2	7.9
4.3	1.31	10.4	0.20	3.2	27.3	0.41	3.04	3.88	83.5	4.4	12.8	6.1	8.9
4.7	1.84	9.9	0.51	5.2	1.6	1.18	12.37	3.38	73.5	5.0	34.5	7.3	5.5
1.9	2.81	19.8	0.05	4.6	1.8	0.92	9.49	3.80	69.6	1.7	14.9	21.4	5.9
7.1	1.04	5.9	0.00	3.0	1.2	0.48	3.94	3.04	78.5	3.3	20.7	11.8	5.9
7.0	0.33	1.8	-0.04	9.6	2.7	1.69	12.66	3.77	37.9	3.4	20.0	9.3	9.1
6.0	0.68	4.3	0.05	9.1	7.0	2.30	20.28	3.95	45.6	4.3	20.1	3.6	6.8
4.7	0.77	5.3	0.11	3.4	0.6	0.60	5.41	4.06	81.1	3.1	14.2	9.4	6.8
10.0	na	0.0	na	9.5	17.7	11.30	18.54	1.21	92.5	5.0	276.7	100.0	9.5
4.7	2.05	10.6	0.15	4.4	0.9	1.08	9.49	4.19	74.3	4.3	29.1	9.7	6.5
7.9	0.37	2.1	0.04	4.4	7.0	0.89	6.47	4.08	76.3	4.1	12.9	8.4	9.7
7.4	0.84	4.3	0.00	3.5	1.8	0.56	3.72	3.01	72.5	1.5	11.1	24.0	6.8
6.4	0.39	2.9	-0.03	8.6	3.0	2.07	21.55	3.92	46.4	4.4	9.2	5.3	7.6
8.4	0.75	3.6	0.00	3.4	2.3	0.46	3.31	2.97	77.1	4.5	20.0	5.8	7.7
7.3	0.00	0.0	0.01	3.3	1.2	0.58	5.52	3.16	74.2	1.1	11.5	28.8	6.0
4.8	0.77	6.0	0.33	4.6	1.0	0.78	8.44	4.43	68.3	3.5	5.4	10.3	5.5
4.6	1.79	7.8	-0.01	3.9	0.9	0.62	3.78	3.35	69.5	1.7	22.4	24.2	7.4
8.6	0.17	1.0	0.01	6.8	2.3	1.17	10.47	3.77	53.8	3.8	22.7	7.6	6.8
3.4	0.90	5.3	0.00	6.3	0.8	1.36	8.67	4.37	56.8	3.0	25.2	15.0	7.6
5.7	0.48	3.4	0.00	5.0	5.6	0.82	9.31	3.87	66.7	4.9	25.9	4.3	5.7
8.9	0.04	0.3	0.00	3.6	0.8	0.59	5.90	3.71	75.1	1.7	14.6	22.0	5.5
5.1	0.95	6.2	0.02	6.3	0.2	1.22	11.29	4.45	61.0	3.0	18.0	14.2	5.0
7.0	0.29	2.6	0.00	5.7	3.2	0.99	11.11	3.32	67.0	1.1	7.7	28.7	5.6
8.8	1.03	1.1	-0.21	4.8	0.0	0.71	3.42	2.89	77.6	7.4	77.1	0.0	7.8
8.2	0.00	0.0	0.00	5.5	2.8	0.92	6.77	3.63	67.7	4.1	22.9	8.8	7.9
4.3	1.17	8.0	-0.06	4.5	18.4	0.73	5.81	3.97	74.1	1.8	16.2	21.8	9.2
7.0	0.86	6.6	0.06	3.9	5.2	0.66	6.68	2.94	66.9	4.0	14.8	9.1	7.6
5.4	1.03	8.7	0.16	4.5	17.9	0.69	7.26	3.54	71.4	4.5	14.2	6.0	7.4
6.9	1.67	6.5	0.12	6.6	4.5	1.25	7.76	3.88	56.0	2.9	36.9	19.2	8.3
7.2	0.59	2.8	-0.02	4.5	2.0	0.87	9.08	3.65	68.7	4.9	41.5	11.1	4.1

Name	City	State	2015 Rating	2014 Rating	Rating	Total Assets ($Mil)	One Year Asset Growth	Comm-ercial Loans	Cons-umer Loans	Mort-gage Loans	Secur-ities	Capital-ization Index	Lever-age Ratio	Risk-Based Capital Ratio
Oculina Bank	Vero Beach	FL	B-	C	C	283.0	26.01	2.4	0.3	69.3	1.3	7.7	9.5	16.6
▼ Odin State Bank	Odin	MN	D-	D+	B	44.1	5.75	9.2	6.2	7.9	16.0	9.8	10.8	15.0
Ohana Pacific Bank	Honolulu	HI	B-	B-	B-	123.7	4.01	6.0	0.4	11.7	0.0	10.0	12.5	17.8
Ohio Valley Bank Co.	Gallipolis	OH	C+	C	C+	954.8	20.41	7.3	11.3	28.2	13.2	10.0	11.0	15.4
Ohnward Bank & Trust	Cascade	IA	B+	B+	B+	242.3	7.84	7.4	2.2	7.7	16.7	9.1	11.6	14.3
Ojai Community Bank	Ojai	CA	B-	B-	C+	260.6	31.89	10.5	0.3	20.7	2.7	6.8	9.1	12.4
Oklahoma Bank and Trust Co.	Clinton	OK	B+	B+	B	152.7	-3.73	3.6	1.3	10.6	46.7	10.0	14.5	27.7
Oklahoma Capital Bank	Tulsa	OK	D	D-	D-	123.4	148.40	18.1	2.7	16.1	8.0	10.0	23.7	29.4
Oklahoma Heritage Bank	Stratford	OK	C	C	C	100.8	6.82	8.3	15.3	30.2	12.2	6.5	8.5	14.1
Oklahoma State Bank	Buffalo	OK	B	B-	B-	51.8	-10.52	5.4	10.5	3.6	31.5	8.1	9.7	15.7
Oklahoma State Bank	Guthrie	OK	C-	C-	C-	123.9	33.07	31.6	1.0	15.3	1.6	3.9	8.6	10.4
Oklahoma State Bank	Vinita	OK	D+	D+	B+	140.8	7.04	8.4	3.3	17.6	6.5	8.4	9.9	13.8
▲ Old Dominion National Bank	North Garden	VA	D-	D-	E	69.1	39.98	12.8	0.6	14.5	4.7	10.0	35.3	57.4
Old Exchange National Bank of Okawville	Okawville	IL	B-	B-	C+	62.2	0.45	2.5	0.8	6.9	36.3	9.2	10.4	19.6
Old Fort Banking Co.	Old Fort	OH	B	B	B	496.2	5.30	8.9	0.9	10.4	34.3	6.4	8.4	13.6
Old Line Bank	Bowie	MD	C+	B-	B-	1646.0	24.28	8.2	0.3	12.3	12.3	6.2	10.1	11.9
Old Mission Bank	Sault Sainte Marie	MI	B-	B-	C+	107.7	0.36	8.5	3.5	14.3	28.5	10.0	11.3	18.6
Old Missouri Bank	Springfield	MO	C+	B-	B	331.0	19.93	11.2	1.9	15.1	8.8	5.4	8.6	11.3
Old National Bank	Evansville	IN	C+	C+	C+	14610.6	24.16	9.3	8.8	16.9	25.2	6.6	8.6	12.7
Old Plank Trail Community Bank, N.A.	Mokena	IL	B-	B-	B-	1318.0	11.08	34.2	9.7	2.9	15.1	5.5	9.6	11.3
Old Point National Bank of Phoebus	Hampton	VA	C	C	C	900.2	2.99	5.3	5.5	12.7	17.5	8.3	10.0	13.6
Old Point Trust & Financial Services, N.A.	Newport News	VA	U	U	U	5.8	0.16	0.0	0.0	0.0	82.2	10.0	98.2	137.1
Old Second National Bank	Aurora	IL	B+	B+	B-	2092.0	3.24	8.1	0.3	8.4	25.4	9.5	10.7	16.2
▲ Olmsted National Bank	Rochester	MN	B-	C	D+	70.5	21.88	14.1	0.9	20.3	4.2	8.3	10.3	13.6
Olpe State Bank	Olpe	KS	B	B	B	36.5	1.65	5.3	2.4	16.1	25.1	10.0	15.9	27.7
Olympia Federal S&L Assn.	Olympia	WA	B-	B-	B-	587.0	1.07	0.0	0.2	60.1	11.4	10.0	15.8	26.5
OmniBank	Bay Springs	MS	C-	D+	D-	48.4	2.80	13.1	9.8	18.1	15.0	10.0	11.7	20.6
▲ One American Bank	Sioux Falls	SD	C+	B-	C+	82.8	3.56	12.6	19.8	2.3	3.3	10.0	16.4	19.4
One Bank & Trust, N.A.	Little Rock	AR	E-	E	E-	310.7	-5.68	11.3	4.1	23.0	15.8	1.3	4.4	8.3
One South Bank	Chipley	FL	C+	C+	B-	48.0	1.40	9.3	2.8	20.6	1.1	10.0	12.9	17.6
▲ One World Bank	Dallas	TX	C-	D	D+	83.7	1.39	5.3	0.1	0.3	13.0	10.0	12.1	18.1
OneUnited Bank	Boston	MA	D	D	D	646.1	1.67	0.0	0.3	5.1	17.1	4.4	6.4	11.4
Oostburg State Bank	Oostburg	WI	B	B	C+	195.0	6.28	14.2	2.3	19.1	19.8	10.0	13.9	18.0
Open Bank	Los Angeles	CA	A-	A-	B+	721.6	19.03	11.8	0.6	14.2	5.3	8.7	11.3	13.9
▲ Opportunity Bank of Montana	Helena	MT	B-	C	C	669.2	10.49	8.6	2.2	21.1	19.5	7.3	9.2	14.0
Optima Bank & Trust Co.	Portsmouth	NH	C-	C	C	409.9	15.94	4.1	0.2	39.1	2.8	5.0	7.0	11.5
▲ OptimumBank	Plantation	FL	D+	D	E	121.5	1.78	11.1	1.7	23.6	18.0	5.8	7.8	12.4
Optum Bank, Inc.	Salt Lake City	UT	A+	A+	A+	5672.3	42.37	3.9	0.0	0.0	75.1	9.0	10.3	17.1
Opus Bank	Irvine	CA	B-	B+	B+	7709.4	24.68	23.9	0.0	1.6	2.0	6.1	8.1	12.2
Orange Bank & Trust Co.	Middletown	NY	C-	D+	B	951.1	21.25	10.7	0.0	6.5	31.1	8.6	10.0	17.1
Oregon Coast Bank	Newport	OR	A-	A	A	222.8	11.72	2.9	0.9	11.4	42.9	10.0	11.2	17.1
Oregon Community Bank	Oregon	WI	A-	A-	B-	260.3	17.45	3.5	0.4	16.0	4.6	10.0	13.2	15.5
Oregon Pacific Banking Co.	Florence	OR	C	C-	D	229.2	12.95	14.4	0.4	10.0	8.7	7.4	9.3	14.9
Oregon Trail Bank	Guernsey	WY	C+	C+	D	39.3	3.41	7.3	4.8	12.2	13.7	9.2	10.5	14.9
Oriental Bank	San Juan	PR	D	D-	D-	6549.8	-8.47	5.3	18.5	21.9	19.8	10.0	12.1	18.3
▲ Origin Bank	Choudrant	LA	C	B-	B-	3920.6	0.89	28.2	0.6	9.3	9.8	5.5	9.7	11.4
Oritani Bank	Township of Washing	NJ	A	A	A-	3793.8	14.33	0.6	0.0	5.8	9.4	10.0	12.9	15.3
Ormsby State Bank	Ormsby	MN	B+	B+	B+	27.0	3.03	3.2	2.7	2.8	28.0	7.7	9.4	17.4
Orrstown Bank	Shippensburg	PA	C+	C+	C+	1353.4	6.28	5.1	0.5	15.5	27.7	6.5	8.5	13.4
OSB Community Bank	Brooklyn	MI	E-	E-	D-	65.5	-10.71	17.1	0.3	17.8	2.4	0.7	4.5	7.4
Osgood State Bank	Osgood	OH	B-	B-	B-	189.8	5.95	16.8	2.6	12.3	32.2	7.4	9.3	13.9
Ossian State Bank	Ossian	IN	C+	C+	C+	94.4	-1.92	5.7	0.8	9.8	19.0	8.2	9.8	17.0
▲ Ottawa Savings Bank	Ottawa	IL	B	C+	C	276.1	26.48	4.7	5.3	32.4	16.0	10.0	13.0	19.7
Ottoville Bank Co.	Ottoville	OH	A-	A-	A-	84.9	6.96	4.6	0.9	14.1	35.6	10.0	18.6	31.8
Ouachita Independent Bank	Monroe	LA	A-	A	A	688.8	1.99	9.9	0.8	10.8	18.4	8.5	10.4	13.8
Our Community Bank	Spencer	IN	B-	B-	B-	66.9	1.30	0.0	1.4	56.6	16.0	10.0	12.2	24.4
Owen County State Bank	Spencer	IN	B-	C+	C+	191.8	1.89	6.9	3.6	30.7	13.6	8.4	9.9	16.3
Owingsville Banking Co.	Owingsville	KY	C	C	C-	65.1	8.58	1.8	5.9	41.9	14.7	9.8	10.9	18.1
Oxford Bank	Oxford	MI	C	C-	D-	359.2	11.33	10.7	0.6	11.1	6.4	6.8	8.8	13.0
Oxford Bank & Trust	Oak Brook	IL	D+	D+	D	490.8	5.96	1.7	10.6	4.9	28.3	6.7	8.7	13.1

Asset Quality Index	Adjusted Non-Performing Loans		Net Charge-Offs Avg Loans	Profitability Index	Net Income ($Mil)	Return on Assets (R.O.A.)	Return on Equity (R.O.E.)	Net Interest Spread	Overhead Efficiency Ratio	Liquidity Index	Liquidity Ratio	Hot Money Ratio	Stability Index
	as a % of Total Loans	as a % of Capital											
8.2	0.06	0.6	0.00	4.6	1.6	0.84	9.11	3.34	64.9	1.0	7.3	29.4	3.9
0.0	6.62	39.7	0.52	5.0	0.4	1.10	9.85	3.94	64.5	2.0	26.2	20.9	5.7
7.7	0.26	1.7	0.00	3.2	0.4	0.47	3.57	3.44	77.6	1.5	16.1	24.4	7.7
3.1	2.30	15.6	0.29	3.9	4.2	0.64	6.07	4.02	74.8	3.5	12.4	8.6	6.2
7.6	0.33	2.0	0.00	5.2	1.6	0.89	7.28	3.54	62.3	1.8	17.2	19.9	7.8
8.7	0.00	0.0	-0.11	4.0	1.1	0.61	6.92	4.11	70.9	4.1	18.4	6.0	4.5
9.0	0.37	1.2	0.03	5.1	1.6	1.27	9.16	3.07	57.4	1.8	25.1	22.6	8.3
6.8	1.02	3.3	-0.08	0.4	-0.2	-0.21	-0.78	4.08	88.2	0.7	18.1	51.5	5.2
4.2	0.79	6.1	0.51	5.1	0.7	0.88	10.35	4.39	65.4	0.8	17.4	42.5	3.8
8.0	0.11	0.6	0.08	9.4	1.0	2.30	25.65	4.55	54.0	3.7	16.6	10.4	5.9
4.6	0.44	4.3	0.00	2.7	0.4	0.50	4.68	3.88	88.5	0.5	5.2	44.9	4.9
1.5	3.32	24.3	-0.12	7.7	1.8	1.73	17.30	4.54	64.0	0.7	8.7	34.2	7.2
5.2	1.96	3.1	0.03	0.0	-1.5	-3.91	-20.10	3.67	217.4	3.4	66.5	26.6	3.9
7.4	0.93	4.8	-0.02	4.5	0.5	1.14	10.49	3.28	61.1	3.1	40.7	19.7	6.1
6.5	0.38	2.5	0.43	4.9	3.8	1.03	12.05	3.19	64.0	4.5	31.0	9.1	5.3
5.2	0.68	5.4	-0.01	4.6	9.6	0.82	8.33	3.74	68.0	1.6	13.2	23.4	7.7
5.6	1.63	8.0	-0.01	3.7	0.6	0.73	6.29	4.35	81.8	4.2	39.4	13.7	6.8
3.9	0.99	9.0	-0.06	6.0	2.5	1.07	11.27	4.07	55.9	0.6	7.3	42.5	5.4
3.4	1.53	11.2	0.06	5.0	90.8	0.92	7.04	3.65	70.4	4.5	19.0	5.2	9.1
5.6	0.51	3.9	0.13	3.9	4.6	0.49	4.99	3.24	71.7	3.9	9.7	8.7	6.8
4.8	1.64	10.0	0.29	2.9	3.0	0.47	4.66	3.68	84.9	2.9	19.5	15.0	5.5
10.0	na	0.0	na	9.5	0.4	9.39	9.54	1.19	81.9	4.0	na	0.0	4.3
6.3	1.41	7.2	0.14	5.3	13.9	0.88	8.69	3.47	66.3	4.5	24.1	9.4	9.0
8.2	0.00	0.0	-0.31	5.0	0.6	1.21	10.85	4.51	75.0	1.3	15.6	27.9	4.5
8.3	0.13	0.4	0.38	4.0	0.2	0.86	5.32	3.47	67.4	4.5	36.3	11.5	6.9
9.4	0.25	1.2	-0.02	3.0	1.9	0.43	2.79	3.45	81.5	2.3	20.0	17.9	8.3
5.0	2.10	10.4	-0.50	1.6	0.1	0.17	1.40	4.33	108.9	4.2	27.7	10.1	3.9
5.6	1.23	4.9	4.12	2.7	0.2	0.37	2.03	9.79	61.9	1.3	12.8	24.5	7.7
2.0	2.29	27.4	1.21	0.6	-4.7	-1.97	-39.94	2.93	142.9	1.4	22.5	14.1	0.3
4.0	2.58	16.1	0.04	3.7	0.2	0.70	5.24	4.57	78.3	0.7	12.5	41.9	5.6
1.6	3.92	18.1	-0.07	1.4	0.1	0.16	1.30	3.18	101.1	1.7	25.3	25.6	5.5
1.1	2.19	24.9	0.06	1.3	1.0	0.20	2.64	2.72	95.3	0.7	13.6	39.8	4.2
4.0	3.93	18.7	0.00	4.3	1.3	0.89	6.52	4.07	70.1	3.9	22.7	10.3	7.4
7.0	0.08	0.6	0.03	6.9	5.3	1.05	9.28	4.30	62.4	1.3	8.6	20.9	8.0
6.0	0.36	2.7	0.08	4.4	4.3	0.88	8.50	3.70	73.4	2.4	20.9	17.7	6.5
5.5	0.64	6.8	0.14	3.2	1.4	0.47	6.75	3.08	74.1	0.8	15.9	34.6	3.3
2.8	2.34	14.7	-2.97	2.6	0.3	0.29	3.83	3.32	92.7	1.0	24.5	36.2	3.0
8.5	0.37	0.3	0.11	9.2	60.4	1.52	12.26	2.16	46.4	8.6	100.0	0.0	10.0
4.0	0.72	7.0	0.90	4.5	30.4	0.56	4.44	3.78	51.4	4.4	11.5	6.0	9.9
3.8	3.05	16.5	0.30	2.6	2.6	0.39	3.84	3.27	83.4	2.9	16.5	14.2	5.1
8.3	0.57	2.2	0.00	5.8	2.2	1.43	12.57	3.93	66.4	5.4	42.7	8.0	7.6
7.1	0.32	2.0	-0.06	9.5	2.9	1.62	12.26	4.26	45.7	1.6	10.4	11.3	7.6
3.8	1.96	13.0	-0.05	3.4	0.9	0.56	5.80	3.82	82.0	4.7	23.4	5.2	4.1
5.8	0.72	4.6	0.00	0.0	-0.3	-1.10	-9.42	3.90	116.5	2.8	17.5	15.3	5.0
0.4	6.85	33.6	2.58	4.1	43.5	0.86	6.39	4.88	62.2	1.5	16.9	13.7	7.2
3.7	1.85	14.0	0.94	2.9	14.9	0.51	5.07	3.31	67.3	2.6	8.5	14.6	7.6
7.1	0.33	2.1	0.03	6.8	31.0	1.14	9.12	2.92	44.3	1.3	3.7	23.4	10.0
6.7	1.01	4.3	0.00	5.5	0.3	1.37	8.96	3.19	57.0	3.4	60.9	25.1	8.3
5.1	1.65	11.1	-0.01	3.5	6.6	0.67	7.14	3.11	82.8	2.8	10.8	9.7	6.0
1.8	2.54	29.0	1.66	0.0	-0.8	-1.70	-31.98	4.36	115.7	3.1	22.9	14.4	0.6
6.5	0.43	2.6	-0.04	4.1	1.1	0.81	8.18	3.88	77.7	4.3	25.3	8.5	5.8
8.2	0.08	0.4	0.16	3.5	0.5	0.76	7.84	3.11	77.9	5.2	36.7	7.2	6.1
4.3	3.06	15.1	0.20	4.2	1.1	0.67	4.72	3.95	71.5	4.2	42.3	14.4	5.3
9.0	0.47	1.3	0.09	5.7	0.8	1.21	6.34	3.99	56.9	1.5	23.5	26.8	8.6
7.5	0.19	1.3	0.01	7.6	8.8	1.73	16.50	3.98	61.2	3.8	11.0	9.5	9.5
5.9	2.11	10.8	0.51	3.1	0.3	0.59	4.81	4.43	86.7	2.1	33.4	27.0	5.4
5.5	0.92	6.1	0.02	4.5	1.1	0.75	7.50	3.90	71.2	3.1	24.7	14.4	5.7
4.0	2.11	12.6	0.38	3.3	0.3	0.53	6.22	5.13	80.5	1.7	16.8	21.5	3.0
3.2	2.26	16.8	-0.06	3.6	1.4	0.57	5.73	3.84	79.1	5.2	29.6	4.2	4.5
1.9	2.76	19.1	0.05	3.5	2.8	0.76	8.28	4.06	80.4	4.9	25.2	4.3	4.0

Name	City	State	2015 Rating	2014 Rating	Total Assets ($Mil)	One Year Asset Growth	Comm-ercial Loans	Cons-umer Loans	Mort-gage Loans	Secur-ities	Capital-ization Index	Lever-age Ratio	Risk-Based Capital Ratio
Oxford University Bank	Oxford	MS	B-	B-	C+	128.2	6.14	9.3	5.4	28.3	13.1	8.1	9.7	14.6
Ozark Bank	Ozark	MO	B-	B-	B-	205.3	4.32	6.8	0.6	17.2	23.9	10.0	11.8	18.0
▲ Ozarks Federal S&L Assn.	Farmington	MO	B-	C+	C+	220.1	4.81	0.0	0.4	61.6	7.7	10.0	15.2	20.9
Ozona National Bank	Ozona	TX	B-	B	B	232.6	1.73	7.1	1.5	10.4	18.8	9.1	10.4	15.8
Pacific Alliance Bank	Rosemead	CA	B	B-	C-	275.7	6.75	7.2	0.0	15.7	2.6	9.2	11.1	14.4
Pacific City Bank	Los Angeles	CA	B+	B	C	1177.2	14.42	11.4	2.8	12.2	7.5	8.1	10.6	13.4
Pacific Coast Bankers' Bank	Walnut Creek	CA	B	B-	B	869.3	9.61	5.0	0.0	0.6	18.1	5.7	7.7	16.4
Pacific Commerce Bank	Los Angeles	CA	B-	C+	B	551.8	57.87	12.5	0.0	4.3	0.0	6.5	9.7	12.1
Pacific Continental Bank	Eugene	OR	B+	A-	A	2533.1	34.93	24.5	0.1	2.0	19.0	6.2	11.3	11.9
Pacific Crest Savings Bank	Lynnwood	WA	B-	B-	C	201.3	2.44	0.0	0.2	20.9	8.9	9.0	10.4	16.0
Pacific Enterprise Bank	Irvine	CA	B+	A-	A	468.0	6.54	39.5	0.0	5.4	0.8	9.2	10.4	17.6
Pacific Global Bank	Chicago	IL	A-	B+	B-	178.6	6.72	0.4	0.0	60.3	10.4	10.0	11.0	22.3
▼ Pacific Mercantile Bank	Costa Mesa	CA	D-	C-	D+	1060.8	-1.00	26.5	3.9	6.3	4.4	6.4	8.9	12.0
▲ Pacific National Bank	Miami	FL	B-	C-	C-	462.6	9.97	2.9	0.1	6.7	14.6	10.0	12.1	23.3
Pacific Premier Bank	Irvine	CA	A-	A-	A-	3752.4	38.58	20.7	0.1	2.2	8.6	7.3	11.0	12.8
Pacific Valley Bank	Salinas	CA	C+	C	C-	249.0	0.22	15.9	1.0	5.6	0.1	9.4	10.8	14.5
Pacific West Bank	West Linn	OR	C	C-	E-	61.5	8.05	7.5	0.8	11.7	0.0	9.1	10.5	14.2
Pacific Western Bank	Beverly Hills	CA	B-	B-	B-	21266.7	27.29	28.7	1.2	0.8	15.7	7.8	11.5	13.2
Paducah Bank and Trust Co.	Paducah	KY	A	A	A	595.5	5.95	9.5	2.4	22.3	20.8	10.0	11.7	16.7
Palm Beach Community Bank	West Palm Beach	FL	A-	A-	A-	332.9	2.69	10.7	0.2	24.9	10.2	10.0	11.7	16.8
Palmetto Heritage Bank & Trust	Pawleys Island	SC	B-	C+	C	154.2	6.28	4.4	2.5	34.5	4.5	8.4	9.9	14.3
Palmetto State Bank	Hampton	SC	A	A	A-	537.0	6.21	5.0	2.4	8.1	54.4	10.0	14.9	28.0
Palo Savings Bank	Palo	IA	A-	A-	A-	32.3	2.30	1.6	2.6	30.0	36.5	10.0	13.2	41.4
Pan American Bank & Trust	Melrose Park	IL	C-	C-	C-	298.3	-0.27	10.0	0.7	25.8	13.1	6.9	8.9	12.4
Panola National Bank	Carthage	TX	C+	C+	B-	123.7	-4.83	4.6	7.1	24.4	42.3	7.9	9.6	27.8
Panora State Bank	Panora	IA	A	A	A	72.0	1.36	1.7	0.9	18.2	58.1	10.0	16.1	34.9
Paper City Savings Assn.	Wisconsin Rapids	WI	B	B	B	161.1	0.59	0.0	2.1	53.4	1.6	10.0	12.2	22.8
Paradise Bank	Boca Raton	FL	A	A-	B-	306.1	6.44	8.4	0.6	12.3	9.1	10.0	11.3	17.1
▲ Paragon Bank	Memphis	TN	C+	D+	C-	330.2	13.22	19.0	4.6	20.7	9.2	9.3	10.6	14.5
▲ Paragon Commercial Bank	Raleigh	NC	B+	B-	B-	1479.3	8.67	11.2	0.3	13.2	12.1	7.5	10.4	12.9
Paris National Bank	Paris	MO	B+	B	B	82.7	5.17	2.9	1.9	9.9	37.8	10.0	13.1	23.4
Park Bank	Holmen	WI	B-	B-	C+	54.1	6.41	10.1	2.7	19.2	26.9	10.0	14.7	24.1
Park Bank	Madison	WI	C	D+	D	776.5	1.96	11.0	1.0	18.0	10.2	8.1	11.1	13.4
Park Bank	Milwaukee	WI	B	B-	C+	908.4	1.51	25.6	1.6	1.2	29.1	9.8	10.8	15.2
Park National Bank	Newark	OH	C+	C+	C	7300.6	1.00	8.4	14.3	20.8	19.5	5.3	7.3	11.5
Park Ridge Community Bank	Park Ridge	IL	A-	B+	A-	302.6	2.25	2.7	0.1	17.0	37.2	10.0	12.7	21.7
▲ Park State Bank	Duluth	MN	C-	D+	E-	44.7	39.56	7.1	4.0	36.3	0.2	10.0	16.0	25.7
Park State Bank & Trust	Woodland Park	CO	C-	D+	D	98.9	6.93	1.8	1.1	25.2	16.4	6.1	8.1	15.8
Park Sterling Bank	Charlotte	NC	B-	B	B-	3219.7	30.07	10.6	0.6	12.4	15.5	8.0	11.0	13.4
Parke Bank	Sewell	NJ	C+	C-	D	954.2	10.41	2.0	1.7	28.7	4.2	10.0	15.0	18.0
Parkside Financial Bank & Trust	Clayton	MO	B	B	B	440.3	22.86	35.1	0.3	2.5	6.1	4.2	9.3	10.6
Parkway Bank and Trust Co.	Harwood Heights	IL	C	D+	D	2494.9	10.85	6.9	0.1	2.0	5.4	7.7	9.7	13.1
Partners Bank of California	Mission Viejo	CA	B-	B-	C	177.7	19.64	15.0	0.6	7.0	9.4	9.2	12.0	14.3
▲ Partnership Bank	Cedarburg	WI	C+	C	C+	255.5	10.45	9.3	1.3	19.3	10.5	6.3	9.0	12.0
Passumpsic Savings Bank	Saint Johnsbury	VT	C-	C-	D+	662.8	10.58	5.0	9.2	39.3	9.0	7.2	9.1	13.7
Pataskala Banking Co.	Pataskala	OH	D-	D	D	31.0	2.76	5.5	3.1	27.7	23.1	5.7	7.7	21.2
Pathfinder Bank	Oswego	NY	C+	C+	C+	716.4	18.13	8.8	0.8	28.0	25.5	8.0	9.7	15.1
Pathway Bank	Cairo	NE	B-	B-	B-	146.9	7.13	10.8	2.2	3.0	9.5	8.4	11.5	13.7
▲ Patriot Bank	Trinity	FL	B-	C	C-	144.6	5.06	11.1	2.1	5.2	3.4	7.6	10.8	13.0
Patriot Bank	Tulsa	OK	B+	B+	B	294.9	35.91	23.6	0.1	18.3	0.0	5.4	10.3	11.3
Patriot Bank	Millington	TN	B	B	B-	309.9	11.51	5.8	2.4	13.4	49.2	6.9	8.9	16.6
▼ Patriot Bank, N.A.	Stamford	CT	C	C	C-	682.7	6.58	9.8	4.5	18.8	4.1	5.8	9.7	11.6
Patriot Community Bank	Woburn	MA	A-	A-	A-	172.8	14.04	8.6	0.1	19.1	0.0	10.0	11.1	16.8
▲ Patriot Federal Bank	Canajoharie	NY	C	D+	D+	139.7	9.60	8.4	6.5	40.3	16.3	6.8	8.8	14.7
Patriots Bank	Garnett	KS	B-	C+	C	97.4	3.83	4.8	2.7	18.3	22.4	8.9	10.3	16.0
Patterson State Bank	Patterson	LA	B+	B+	B+	218.5	-3.17	5.6	2.7	46.0	29.4	9.1	10.4	19.3
Pauls Valley National Bank	Pauls Valley	OK	B-	B	B	234.9	-2.21	16.9	10.9	5.6	33.9	8.8	10.2	15.5
Pavillion Bank	Richardson	TX	B	B-	B-	76.8	-6.50	7.5	1.0	20.0	8.9	10.0	13.4	22.4
Payne County Bank	Perkins	OK	A+	A+	A+	158.8	1.12	4.8	8.2	18.7	34.9	10.0	17.3	29.4
PBI Bank, Inc.	Louisville	KY	D-	E+	D-	914.6	-3.74	9.3	1.1	18.5	20.5	5.0	7.0	11.2

Arrows denote recent upgrades ▲ or downgrades ▼

Asset Quality Index	Adjusted Non-Performing Loans as a % of Total Loans	as a % of Capital	Net Charge-Offs Avg Loans	Profitability Index	Net Income ($Mil)	Return on Assets (R.O.A.)	Return on Equity (R.O.E.)	Net Interest Spread	Overhead Efficiency Ratio	Liquidity Index	Liquidity Ratio	Hot Money Ratio	Stability Index
6.5	0.23	1.7	0.05	4.4	0.7	0.76	7.70	3.97	71.5	0.8	16.1	36.4	5.3
8.8	0.25	1.4	0.00	3.8	1.3	0.84	7.09	3.39	76.6	2.2	12.0	17.5	6.6
5.9	2.13	10.6	0.00	3.4	0.9	0.56	3.98	3.19	76.8	2.6	15.4	16.0	7.0
7.8	0.42	2.6	0.49	3.4	1.2	0.70	6.73	4.38	82.6	4.5	29.2	8.4	6.8
6.0	0.09	0.5	0.00	5.0	1.7	0.86	7.80	2.96	48.3	1.2	28.1	39.4	6.6
6.4	0.31	2.4	0.00	8.5	9.9	1.20	12.55	4.15	56.2	0.6	5.3	33.4	8.7
9.3	0.24	0.9	-0.13	5.1	5.7	0.89	10.93	2.27	69.3	4.0	34.8	6.3	6.3
6.4	0.21	1.7	-0.04	5.0	2.3	0.69	5.93	4.61	73.8	1.6	17.8	23.8	7.1
6.2	0.75	5.3	0.03	5.6	13.9	0.91	7.61	4.21	62.5	4.9	25.2	4.0	9.0
4.1	1.27	8.4	0.04	5.8	2.1	1.38	13.03	3.65	59.4	1.7	26.1	20.4	6.7
5.6	0.53	3.6	0.04	8.0	3.7	1.04	10.26	5.10	68.5	0.9	22.1	38.2	7.1
7.3	0.71	4.3	0.16	6.0	1.1	0.86	7.51	4.19	63.5	2.3	23.1	18.0	6.0
4.2	1.80	13.2	2.54	0.1	-33.7	-4.13	-35.48	3.39	89.5	1.7	18.7	24.5	8.9
7.0	0.92	5.0	0.02	3.8	3.2	0.95	7.70	3.53	68.4	1.4	25.8	29.2	5.9
6.4	0.18	1.4	0.10	7.4	31.6	1.20	8.98	4.62	55.2	2.9	10.7	8.5	9.5
3.2	1.91	11.6	-0.14	3.5	0.8	0.45	3.99	3.79	81.4	4.1	26.7	9.9	6.2
6.6	0.26	1.7	-0.03	3.4	0.3	0.59	5.37	4.28	86.1	1.6	22.8	25.6	3.3
3.9	1.44	9.2	0.08	9.9	266.7	1.70	8.16	5.41	41.1	3.4	21.0	8.5	10.0
6.3	0.88	5.0	0.12	7.7	7.8	1.77	13.61	4.26	62.4	3.9	12.2	3.2	9.7
8.7	0.26	1.8	0.00	7.1	4.1	1.67	14.05	4.26	58.0	1.0	15.5	31.5	8.3
6.0	0.54	3.9	-0.13	4.6	0.9	0.78	7.92	3.90	69.0	0.6	11.6	45.3	4.8
7.9	1.37	3.0	-0.29	6.8	4.7	1.18	7.96	3.31	55.0	5.0	52.4	13.0	8.2
8.8	0.64	2.5	0.02	8.3	0.4	1.81	12.68	4.16	49.9	3.9	45.2	16.2	8.0
2.4	2.72	22.6	0.22	3.2	1.2	0.55	6.08	4.19	86.8	1.1	18.5	31.8	4.3
8.1	0.51	2.2	0.01	3.1	0.7	0.69	6.98	3.15	86.5	4.8	50.5	13.5	6.1
8.7	0.00	0.0	0.00	9.3	1.1	2.04	10.65	4.43	32.0	4.3	62.7	17.3	8.9
5.6	1.76	11.0	0.02	4.1	0.8	0.64	5.36	2.91	70.2	2.7	23.2	16.2	6.4
8.4	0.12	0.8	-0.10	8.5	4.2	1.79	16.06	4.12	66.0	4.1	21.2	8.9	8.4
7.6	0.26	2.0	-0.17	3.7	1.6	0.66	6.05	4.09	76.2	2.8	5.5	3.9	5.2
7.6	0.08	0.6	0.01	5.5	10.4	1.00	10.27	3.57	55.4	2.0	15.2	10.9	8.1
8.3	0.18	0.7	0.00	5.4	0.6	1.04	7.63	3.80	57.7	3.8	35.1	14.2	6.7
4.7	4.64	16.1	0.41	3.5	0.3	0.62	4.20	4.92	86.0	4.6	14.7	4.7	6.1
2.7	1.35	9.5	0.00	6.5	6.3	1.10	9.85	3.85	77.1	4.5	13.0	4.7	6.9
8.5	0.05	0.3	-0.28	5.2	9.0	1.35	12.61	3.24	62.5	5.7	41.1	5.9	6.5
3.3	1.79	15.8	0.06	6.6	68.3	1.24	15.53	3.37	56.1	3.4	7.5	8.2	7.3
6.4	1.59	6.8	0.00	8.4	4.4	2.03	15.56	4.01	46.3	3.9	14.2	9.3	8.8
8.3	0.00	0.0	0.00	2.4	0.2	0.63	3.78	4.89	94.3	2.2	31.1	22.6	2.2
3.4	2.95	18.5	0.27	3.1	0.5	0.69	8.30	3.90	89.2	5.2	36.9	7.1	3.5
7.5	0.43	2.9	-0.03	4.5	18.1	0.77	6.27	3.83	70.6	2.3	14.3	14.1	8.2
3.0	2.97	15.9	0.33	10.0	15.6	2.34	16.34	3.92	35.0	1.3	8.2	25.1	8.1
8.1	0.00	0.0	0.03	6.3	3.1	1.06	11.28	3.66	58.9	2.0	23.5	9.2	5.2
2.9	2.00	14.4	0.20	4.3	13.2	0.74	7.18	3.01	53.6	0.9	14.6	23.0	7.2
4.5	0.56	3.6	0.22	3.7	0.6	0.48	3.63	3.94	74.4	3.4	13.1	4.0	7.1
3.5	1.69	14.5	0.08	3.7	1.2	0.62	6.81	3.47	75.8	3.8	12.6	6.4	3.9
3.5	1.31	11.0	0.15	2.1	2.4	0.51	4.53	3.40	86.3	3.9	10.8	8.4	5.8
4.6	2.28	15.7	0.07	0.5	-0.1	-0.43	-5.66	4.79	110.5	6.3	41.1	1.3	2.0
5.2	0.96	6.4	0.08	3.3	2.9	0.58	5.87	3.41	76.0	2.6	20.6	16.5	5.9
3.4	2.54	15.8	-0.24	4.3	0.8	0.74	6.19	3.66	74.7	1.7	16.6	21.2	6.8
5.1	0.28	2.0	0.03	4.2	0.8	0.72	6.04	3.77	67.9	1.8	9.5	19.6	6.0
6.9	0.04	0.3	0.03	8.5	4.2	2.14	19.25	4.11	39.8	0.5	5.1	42.7	8.2
5.7	2.12	9.7	0.16	5.7	2.6	1.19	12.25	3.47	64.9	1.1	19.8	31.9	5.2
5.0	1.11	9.2	0.06	2.7	1.3	0.27	2.39	3.79	76.9	1.0	11.2	19.5	5.6
6.4	1.35	8.9	0.00	5.2	1.1	0.83	6.84	3.06	65.4	0.9	22.4	42.9	7.0
5.0	0.89	7.1	0.03	2.6	0.4	0.35	3.78	3.67	79.7	1.4	11.6	24.0	4.9
4.2	2.16	12.9	-0.28	5.5	0.9	1.31	12.45	4.47	70.7	3.0	16.3	14.3	5.7
6.0	1.90	11.2	0.13	4.6	1.4	0.82	7.94	4.18	75.2	3.5	12.1	11.0	6.1
4.9	1.01	5.0	0.27	4.1	1.2	0.67	6.29	4.24	77.2	3.2	42.8	19.5	6.0
8.2	0.65	2.9	-0.36	6.2	0.7	1.21	9.14	4.10	64.2	3.9	38.6	14.9	6.0
8.1	0.80	2.4	0.15	8.5	2.5	2.09	11.43	4.45	51.3	4.0	46.4	16.8	9.7
3.0	2.01	17.0	0.14	2.7	5.3	0.77	12.24	3.52	87.3	1.7	23.0	24.2	2.2

Name	City	State	2015 Rating	2014 Rating	Rating	Total Assets ($Mil)	One Year Asset Growth	Commercial Loans	Consumer Loans	Mortgage Loans	Securities	Capitalization Index	Leverage Ratio	Risk-Based Capital Ratio
PBK Bank, Inc.	Stanford	KY	B	B	C+	111.5	5.04	3.8	3.4	23.3	7.1	10.0	11.9	20.6
PCSB Bank	Clarinda	IA	C+	C+	B+	215.3	3.76	10.4	4.6	9.2	22.7	9.9	10.9	15.1
PCSB Bank	Yorktown Heights	NY	C-	C-	C	1255.3	4.02	3.1	0.0	17.8	30.4	6.8	8.9	14.4
PCSB Commercial Bank	Brewster	NY	U	U	U	52.6	15.07	0.0	0.0	0.0	92.4	10.0	14.2	96.3
▲ Peach State Bank & Trust	Gainesville	GA	B-	C	D+	177.9	13.15	9.1	3.0	13.5	23.9	6.5	8.5	14.0
Peapack-Gladstone Bank	Bedminster	NJ	B-	C+	C+	3773.5	15.45	5.1	1.5	14.3	6.6	7.3	9.4	12.8
Pearland State Bank	Pearland	TX	B+	B+	A-	188.2	7.09	3.0	0.9	5.2	71.9	10.0	11.3	32.1
Pecos County State Bank	Fort Stockton	TX	B-	B	B	210.2	-1.82	6.5	5.6	11.6	44.6	6.4	8.4	18.0
Pee Dee Federal Savings Bank	Marion	SC	D	D	D	37.6	1.17	10.1	8.7	9.9	18.0	10.0	18.9	41.2
Pegasus Bank	Dallas	TX	B-	B-	B-	474.9	24.99	13.8	6.6	15.6	16.6	5.3	7.3	11.7
Pelham Banking Co.	Pelham	GA	A-	B+	B+	74.1	3.74	3.4	3.7	6.6	46.5	10.0	14.9	27.0
Pendleton Community Bank, Inc.	Franklin	WV	B	B-	C+	283.2	4.45	4.3	4.0	27.7	11.6	10.0	12.5	18.1
Penn Community Bank	Perkasie	PA	C+	C	C+	1862.2	1.17	3.0	0.3	35.4	24.4	10.0	13.1	20.3
PennCrest BANK	Altoona	PA	B	C+	C+	174.6	42.97	0.4	5.5	52.1	20.7	10.0	15.3	26.3
Pennsville National Bank	Pennsville	NJ	C	C+	C+	198.1	6.73	1.3	1.2	19.1	58.4	6.6	8.6	14.7
Pentucket Bank	Haverhill	MA	C+	C+	C+	662.8	3.39	9.9	0.2	34.6	18.0	10.0	12.6	16.5
▲ People's B&T Co. of Pickett County	Byrdstown	TN	C	D+	D	115.8	3.51	15.1	10.8	20.7	10.0	10.0	11.7	18.5
People's Bank of Commerce	Medford	OR	B-	B-	B-	264.6	13.60	7.7	1.3	11.1	14.2	7.8	9.5	13.2
People's Bank of Seneca	Seneca	MO	B	B	B	165.0	13.43	12.8	3.0	32.6	14.2	5.0	8.6	11.0
People's Intermountain Bank	American Fork	UT	A	A	B	1617.2	6.53	9.4	0.9	5.0	21.7	10.0	11.9	17.0
People's United Bank, N.A.	Bridgeport	CT	B-	B-	C+	40279.0	8.77	16.1	0.1	16.6	16.5	6.6	8.6	12.8
▲ PeopleFirst Bank	Joliet	IL	C	D	D+	110.4	-2.94	2.4	0.2	12.8	14.5	10.0	12.6	18.7
▲ Peoples B&T Co. of Clinton County	Albany	KY	C	D+	D	33.0	-0.10	5.1	23.2	29.0	4.4	7.7	9.5	14.6
Peoples B&T Co. of Madison County	Berea	KY	C	D+	D	395.4	1.31	1.9	2.4	19.8	32.4	10.0	11.4	20.6
Peoples B&T Co. of Pointe Coupee Parish	New Roads	LA	A	A-	B-	223.5	4.56	5.7	2.0	33.8	2.3	10.0	13.1	19.3
Peoples Bank	Magnolia	AR	B+	B	B	160.6	6.33	1.5	13.6	43.8	16.3	10.0	11.2	20.3
Peoples Bank	Sheridan	AR	A	A	A	136.5	2.42	8.7	3.8	9.7	34.1	10.0	14.3	25.5
▼ Peoples Bank	Eatonton	GA	E-	D-	D-	127.1	-6.24	1.5	3.5	27.6	11.0	2.8	4.9	10.1
Peoples Bank	Lyons	GA	C+	C-	D+	80.5	20.76	8.6	2.6	15.1	3.1	6.1	8.1	12.4
Peoples Bank	Willacoochee	GA	B	B	B	72.4	1.16	2.2	5.4	14.0	21.2	10.0	12.4	24.6
Peoples Bank	Rock Valley	IA	B+	A-	B+	462.9	3.08	10.6	1.4	4.4	5.5	8.4	11.6	13.7
Peoples Bank	Brownstown	IN	C+	C+	B-	203.7	5.99	1.8	5.6	17.2	53.0	7.9	9.6	20.3
Peoples Bank	Coldwater	KS	B	B+	B+	51.1	-0.24	4.9	1.4	8.1	48.2	10.0	11.2	20.0
Peoples Bank	Lawrence	KS	B	B	B	521.1	12.75	8.0	0.4	43.2	6.7	8.9	10.3	14.8
Peoples Bank	Pratt	KS	B-	B-	B	360.4	1.33	12.0	1.5	9.1	35.6	9.9	10.9	19.5
Peoples Bank	Lebanon	KY	B-	B-	C+	54.4	6.13	11.7	3.0	7.2	36.6	7.8	9.5	13.9
Peoples Bank	Marion	KY	D+	D+	C-	41.9	11.60	33.7	5.3	18.4	4.9	9.2	11.1	14.3
Peoples Bank	Taylorsville	KY	B+	B	B+	107.7	-0.10	2.6	3.0	22.5	31.4	10.0	11.8	22.4
Peoples Bank	Chatham	LA	C	C	C+	63.6	26.82	5.3	12.8	24.8	0.8	7.2	10.0	12.6
▼ Peoples Bank	Chestertown	MD	C-	C-	D+	252.6	8.86	3.4	0.4	28.3	11.1	8.5	10.0	18.1
Peoples Bank	Cuba	MO	B+	B+	B+	193.5	2.89	4.1	3.3	37.9	15.4	8.5	10.0	15.4
▲ Peoples Bank	Mendenhall	MS	C	C	C+	283.8	14.06	9.7	4.8	17.1	10.9	7.9	9.6	14.0
▲ Peoples Bank	Ripley	MS	A-	B+	B	388.5	0.06	14.4	9.2	15.0	49.6	9.0	10.3	22.2
Peoples Bank	Newton	NC	B+	B	B	1095.4	5.83	8.3	0.9	15.9	23.8	10.0	11.0	15.7
Peoples Bank	Gambier	OH	C	C	C	57.1	2.97	1.3	6.2	42.1	22.7	7.7	9.4	18.1
Peoples Bank	Marietta	OH	B-	B-	B	3355.3	4.18	11.1	9.0	16.4	23.8	7.2	9.1	13.4
Peoples Bank	Tulsa	OK	C+	C+	C	108.8	11.30	27.3	5.1	12.6	1.5	6.5	8.7	12.2
Peoples Bank	Westville	OK	A-	A-	B+	50.7	13.22	6.1	3.0	8.6	29.7	10.0	14.2	20.0
Peoples Bank	Iva	SC	B-	C	C-	297.5	1.23	1.9	2.3	17.7	34.2	9.1	10.4	17.2
Peoples Bank	Clifton	TN	C-	D+	D+	163.8	9.05	19.6	11.5	16.2	7.7	7.0	9.0	12.5
Peoples Bank	Sardis	TN	B	B-	B-	76.3	6.15	6.1	5.6	29.9	15.1	8.8	10.2	15.6
Peoples Bank	Lubbock	TX	B	B	B	445.0	11.55	7.6	2.7	6.5	11.4	6.0	9.4	11.7
▼ Peoples Bank	Paris	TX	B	B+	B+	146.3	4.40	8.8	1.1	26.1	41.1	6.2	8.2	17.6
Peoples Bank	Rose Hill	VA	B-	B-	C+	129.2	11.30	12.4	1.2	36.3	6.3	7.4	9.3	13.4
Peoples Bank	Bellingham	WA	B+	B+	B+	1554.0	6.00	5.1	8.6	10.2	1.2	8.4	10.7	13.6
Peoples Bank	Elkhorn	WI	B-	C	C-	232.8	6.15	2.0	0.2	15.6	3.9	9.6	10.7	16.9
Peoples Bank & Trust	Buford	GA	C	D+	E	279.6	3.76	2.5	1.6	14.0	29.4	7.0	9.0	16.6
▼ Peoples Bank & Trust	Pana	IL	B	B+	B	406.5	5.75	14.7	0.3	5.6	14.8	5.1	8.2	11.1
Peoples Bank & Trust Co.	Owenton	KY	B+	B+	B	53.9	1.10	1.7	3.9	28.4	16.8	10.0	13.8	20.8
Peoples Bank & Trust Co.	Troy	MO	C	C	C-	447.7	3.69	8.3	0.6	7.9	39.5	7.0	9.0	14.0

Asset Quality Index	Adjusted Non-Performing Loans as a % of Total Loans	as a % of Capital	Net Charge-Offs Avg Loans	Profitability Index	Net Income ($Mil)	Return on Assets (R.O.A.)	Return on Equity (R.O.E.)	Net Interest Spread	Overhead Efficiency Ratio	Liquidity Index	Liquidity Ratio	Hot Money Ratio	Stability Index
4.2	2.85	15.6	0.05	6.0	0.9	1.11	9.42	4.39	68.0	4.4	25.6	7.8	6.9
5.9	0.68	4.0	0.68	2.8	0.6	0.38	3.35	3.87	80.4	5.4	33.7	4.7	5.5
4.6	1.97	12.9	0.25	2.2	2.4	0.26	2.86	2.92	83.1	4.5	31.4	12.9	6.2
10.0	na	0.0	na	2.7	0.2	0.40	2.70	0.79	21.8	5.2	8.7	0.0	4.4
7.1	0.07	0.5	0.09	4.3	0.9	0.70	7.40	3.62	71.0	3.0	32.4	17.4	4.6
5.4	0.53	4.6	0.05	4.2	20.2	0.75	8.73	2.81	59.2	2.7	7.0	11.9	6.1
9.8	0.00	0.0	0.11	4.9	1.7	1.24	9.99	2.51	56.0	3.9	74.4	26.3	7.8
5.1	1.13	5.7	0.76	5.2	2.1	1.24	14.35	4.03	63.6	2.8	10.6	14.8	5.9
5.4	3.54	6.6	0.15	0.4	-0.1	-0.22	-1.16	3.24	102.8	5.7	70.4	11.7	4.5
8.3	0.00	0.0	0.00	4.4	2.7	0.82	11.17	3.01	61.7	6.1	40.3	2.8	3.7
9.0	0.18	0.4	0.01	5.6	0.8	1.43	9.34	3.59	63.7	3.9	46.5	16.5	7.8
4.8	1.78	10.4	0.40	6.7	2.4	1.18	9.15	4.67	61.2	2.7	13.7	15.1	6.7
6.6	0.99	4.8	0.15	3.1	6.1	0.44	3.23	3.00	77.9	3.4	23.3	12.4	7.6
6.5	1.58	6.3	-0.01	3.8	1.0	0.83	5.34	3.42	78.2	4.8	34.8	9.1	7.0
7.1	1.35	5.2	0.03	3.0	0.7	0.44	4.95	2.40	78.4	6.3	45.4	3.4	5.1
7.0	0.79	4.5	0.04	2.6	3.1	0.65	5.09	3.24	86.0	2.3	19.5	17.8	7.2
2.4	4.10	21.9	0.37	5.7	0.9	1.04	8.68	4.76	67.5	0.9	23.1	37.7	5.2
5.2	0.58	4.1	-0.01	4.0	1.4	0.69	7.30	4.13	73.8	4.5	21.2	4.6	5.4
5.0	0.73	6.0	0.35	8.0	1.6	1.36	16.04	4.16	49.4	3.0	7.1	12.9	5.0
5.9	0.71	3.9	0.01	9.5	17.6	1.53	13.03	4.67	55.2	5.5	28.7	5.5	9.2
4.7	0.78	6.6	0.06	4.2	215.3	0.73	5.85	2.90	66.5	3.5	15.3	7.1	9.6
2.8	2.88	15.1	0.73	3.4	1.9	2.25	17.99	3.60	82.2	1.0	21.0	33.3	6.0
1.9	2.08	15.5	0.25	4.1	0.2	0.62	6.80	5.19	81.9	0.8	19.3	50.5	3.5
2.2	4.89	23.4	0.08	4.0	2.3	0.75	5.68	3.69	74.7	3.5	26.7	13.1	6.7
5.8	1.78	11.5	-0.02	10.0	2.8	1.74	13.70	4.70	45.3	1.3	11.3	26.5	7.8
5.4	1.65	9.8	0.17	6.9	1.9	1.67	14.53	4.15	59.7	1.0	26.6	14.1	7.5
8.7	0.11	0.4	0.07	8.0	1.3	1.30	9.15	3.62	48.2	4.0	32.5	12.4	9.0
0.3	7.95	81.6	0.52	0.0	-2.7	-2.84	-45.28	3.66	163.6	4.5	26.0	7.1	1.1
8.5	0.10	0.8	-0.04	4.0	0.4	0.68	8.32	4.32	77.0	3.6	27.5	13.0	3.1
8.9	0.26	0.9	0.00	4.1	0.5	0.88	7.27	3.52	77.0	2.6	39.3	25.7	6.7
4.8	0.81	5.7	-0.02	9.6	7.6	2.21	18.09	4.27	48.0	1.6	6.7	13.9	9.2
4.5	3.00	11.7	1.75	3.1	0.8	0.51	5.24	3.14	65.8	6.6	66.1	6.7	4.8
6.9	0.42	1.6	-0.01	3.7	0.3	0.77	5.95	3.95	78.3	1.3	23.7	29.6	6.5
5.3	0.53	4.0	-0.15	9.6	9.3	2.59	24.64	4.48	82.9	4.9	8.5	1.9	6.5
3.7	2.43	11.2	1.05	6.9	4.4	1.44	11.28	3.84	54.7	1.5	18.7	26.2	7.6
8.9	0.00	0.0	-0.02	3.8	0.3	0.65	6.88	3.60	84.5	3.8	39.9	16.1	5.1
1.4	3.70	25.5	0.77	5.0	0.3	1.03	9.11	5.05	74.8	3.2	12.8	12.8	4.7
5.0	3.32	14.6	-0.07	4.9	0.9	1.12	9.04	3.90	72.5	4.8	35.8	9.2	6.7
4.7	0.50	4.1	0.02	4.3	0.2	0.56	5.55	4.82	77.4	0.5	12.0	64.1	5.1
1.8	5.14	27.9	0.04	3.3	1.0	0.57	5.59	3.06	87.1	5.1	37.5	8.3	4.7
5.3	1.00	7.1	0.15	7.3	2.6	1.71	16.65	4.37	61.7	2.8	8.9	14.5	8.0
2.9	1.97	15.2	0.37	9.2	4.3	2.10	22.17	5.77	65.5	1.1	5.5	27.8	7.2
8.8	0.10	0.4	0.31	6.8	4.2	1.42	13.85	3.26	53.2	3.4	49.6	21.3	6.1
7.1	0.67	3.7	0.08	5.2	8.4	1.05	9.06	4.03	74.0	4.8	26.7	9.0	8.5
6.1	0.53	3.5	0.10	2.6	0.2	0.38	4.01	3.46	86.8	2.9	27.7	16.4	4.9
4.3	1.10	7.8	0.09	5.5	25.4	1.03	8.54	3.54	66.5	4.2	9.9	6.6	7.7
5.1	0.41	3.6	0.23	4.7	0.8	1.06	11.86	4.69	75.1	1.1	14.2	29.7	4.2
5.5	2.45	10.7	-0.06	9.8	0.9	2.40	18.18	5.06	60.1	2.7	38.4	23.2	7.9
4.6	2.56	12.5	0.18	4.6	2.4	1.08	9.77	3.73	73.1	3.4	38.5	17.2	5.7
2.7	1.08	8.2	0.36	4.2	0.8	0.66	7.49	4.89	74.6	0.9	13.6	32.9	4.3
6.0	0.61	4.2	0.02	5.0	0.6	0.98	9.77	4.71	71.2	1.3	14.7	26.7	5.4
7.8	0.07	0.6	0.03	5.8	3.2	1.03	10.48	4.31	67.1	1.8	15.3	20.0	5.7
8.0	0.38	2.2	0.00	4.4	1.0	0.98	11.39	3.55	79.4	2.8	3.8	8.2	6.7
8.2	0.15	1.4	-0.04	7.0	1.1	1.17	12.42	4.26	57.2	1.1	10.8	20.8	4.4
6.2	0.57	4.1	-0.01	5.8	11.4	1.01	9.59	3.89	70.0	2.2	15.8	18.6	9.0
4.4	2.03	12.3	-0.04	4.7	1.5	0.85	8.04	3.19	77.3	3.9	27.3	9.1	6.5
3.9	2.51	12.5	0.29	4.7	1.7	0.81	8.45	3.57	67.1	2.6	41.1	27.2	3.2
6.5	0.33	2.8	0.00	7.2	5.4	1.84	19.14	4.25	58.0	1.9	14.4	19.3	6.5
5.6	2.06	8.9	0.02	6.7	0.6	1.36	9.89	4.70	72.7	3.5	18.3	11.7	8.8
2.5	4.18	22.7	-0.11	4.3	3.6	1.06	11.35	3.39	74.9	4.1	19.5	8.6	4.7

Name	City	State	2015 Rating	2014 Rating	Rating	Total Assets ($Mil)	One Year Asset Growth	Comm-ercial Loans	Cons-umer Loans	Mort-gage Loans	Secur-ities	Capital-ization Index	Lever-age Ratio	Risk-Based Capital Ratio
Peoples Bank & Trust Co.	North Carrollton	MS	B+	B+	B+	69.7	5.72	0.3	5.6	15.4	45.1	10.0	14.0	40.4
Peoples Bank & Trust Co.	Ryan	OK	C+	B	B	30.8	5.96	3.6	0.8	27.5	0.1	10.0	15.7	21.2
Peoples Bank & Trust Co.	Manchester	TN	B-	B	C-	94.9	8.46	6.4	4.2	15.7	17.1	10.0	11.0	19.7
▼ Peoples Bank & Trust Co. of Hazard	Hazard	KY	D-	D-	C-	261.7	-3.66	17.6	3.9	24.1	7.1	6.6	8.6	12.6
Peoples Bank and Trust Co.	McPherson	KS	B+	B+	A-	448.0	-0.10	15.8	2.5	4.7	33.7	10.0	13.2	17.4
Peoples Bank Co.	Coldwater	OH	A-	A-	A-	476.4	1.31	4.0	2.2	15.0	40.8	9.1	10.4	20.9
Peoples Bank Midwest	Hayward	WI	A	A	A-	321.9	-0.15	9.3	0.4	11.6	16.7	10.0	19.8	26.1
Peoples Bank MT. Washington	Mount Washington	KY	B	C+	C-	85.5	6.15	1.7	0.6	9.4	14.6	10.0	12.2	17.5
Peoples Bank of Alabama	Cullman	AL	B	B-	C	662.5	4.42	18.8	3.4	12.5	10.3	7.0	10.1	12.5
Peoples Bank of Altenburg	Altenburg	MO	C	C	C-	58.9	1.27	5.6	2.5	29.7	21.9	8.4	9.9	14.8
Peoples Bank of Commerce	Cambridge	MN	B+	B+	C+	299.7	4.32	15.3	0.4	10.2	35.0	10.0	11.2	17.1
Peoples Bank of Deer Lodge	Deer Lodge	MT	C+	C+	C+	32.8	17.72	6.6	4.4	16.1	29.5	7.9	9.6	15.1
▲ Peoples Bank of East Tennessee	Madisonville	TN	C+	D+	D+	201.6	-1.99	4.1	3.7	30.7	20.1	10.0	11.4	17.8
Peoples Bank of Graceville	Graceville	FL	A-	A-	A-	91.4	6.56	1.3	1.8	17.0	46.3	10.0	13.0	38.5
▲ Peoples Bank of Greensboro	Greensboro	AL	B	B-	B-	97.2	5.86	5.9	6.8	13.6	47.0	6.8	8.8	17.1
▲ Peoples Bank of Kankakee County	Bourbonnais	IL	B-	C+	C+	191.1	1.13	4.1	1.4	16.0	40.1	6.6	8.6	16.9
Peoples Bank of Kentucky, Inc.	Flemingsburg	KY	B	B-	C+	284.9	8.75	5.0	7.5	17.6	11.8	10.0	11.3	15.4
Peoples Bank of Macon	Macon	IL	C+	C+	C+	20.1	-12.34	10.9	6.1	10.4	49.2	10.0	14.3	33.4
Peoples Bank of Middle Tennessee	Shelbyville	TN	B+	B+	B	142.2	32.39	5.4	6.5	17.3	12.9	8.7	11.4	13.9
Peoples Bank of Moniteau County	Jamestown	MO	C-	C-	C-	62.0	4.00	5.7	4.7	20.7	30.1	6.3	8.3	13.1
Peoples Bank of Red Level	Red Level	AL	C+	B-	B-	16.1	-2.34	2.5	20.2	13.5	37.9	10.0	12.5	26.2
Peoples Bank of Talbotton	Talbotton	GA	C+	C	C-	61.9	22.85	7.3	9.3	29.8	17.4	8.3	9.8	14.9
Peoples Bank of the South	LaFollette	TN	C-	D+	D+	144.5	2.27	2.3	1.9	30.2	0.2	10.0	14.2	20.9
Peoples Bank of Wyaconda	Kahoka	MO	B	B	B	89.0	3.03	4.0	3.9	16.9	27.5	8.0	9.6	16.1
▲ Peoples Bank, Biloxi, Mississippi	Biloxi	MS	D+	D	D	679.4	4.01	7.3	0.8	9.0	36.0	10.0	12.7	21.9
Peoples Bank, Savings Bank	Munster	IN	B	B	B-	899.6	6.80	8.4	0.1	20.2	26.7	6.9	8.9	13.8
Peoples Community Bank	Greenville	MO	A+	A+	A+	425.5	25.00	2.7	7.3	32.9	19.7	10.0	14.5	20.7
Peoples Community Bank	Montross	VA	C+	C	C	170.5	4.59	4.1	0.9	41.2	9.9	6.8	8.8	14.0
Peoples Community Bank	Mazomanie	WI	A-	A-	A-	270.0	5.41	5.8	1.7	10.1	18.1	10.0	12.3	17.4
Peoples Exchange Bank	Winchester	KY	B-	B-	B-	355.6	6.16	5.4	1.7	28.7	3.4	7.2	9.1	13.1
Peoples Exchange Bank of Monroe County	Monroeville	AL	C+	B-	B-	62.5	0.72	12.7	4.8	17.0	19.4	10.0	14.9	21.0
Peoples Federal S&L Assn.	Sidney	OH	C+	C+	C-	111.3	0.62	2.6	1.9	49.1	9.0	10.0	13.5	25.9
Peoples First Savings Bank	Mason	OH	C-	C	C	70.7	4.23	0.0	0.0	51.1	3.1	8.0	9.7	19.8
Peoples Independent Bank	Boaz	AL	B+	B	B	206.8	4.08	4.9	1.2	7.1	36.2	7.0	9.0	14.4
Peoples National Bank	Colorado Springs	CO	B	B	B	410.3	14.20	2.8	0.1	42.5	12.7	8.9	10.3	15.9
Peoples National Bank	Niceville	FL	D+	D	C-	105.4	-1.84	3.8	1.1	20.0	32.4	8.9	10.3	22.3
Peoples National Bank of Checotah	Checotah	OK	B+	B+	B+	134.3	1.22	0.8	11.5	10.6	50.0	10.0	15.3	39.6
Peoples National Bank of Kewanee	Kewanee	IL	A-	A-	A-	251.0	-0.82	3.0	2.1	7.6	45.0	10.0	17.6	28.1
Peoples National Bank of Mount Pleasant	Mount Pleasant	OH	B-	B-	B-	59.4	-1.45	0.7	29.8	30.5	3.1	10.0	12.4	22.7
Peoples National Bank of New Lexington	New Lexington	OH	C+	C+	C+	122.7	5.11	4.1	9.7	39.2	11.5	6.7	8.7	14.3
Peoples National Bank, N.A.	Mount Vernon	IL	B-	B-	B-	1087.9	4.78	17.8	0.4	5.2	5.9	5.1	9.1	11.0
Peoples S&L Assn. of Monticello Indiana	Monticello	IN	C	C-	C-	32.4	-4.63	0.0	0.4	58.6	15.5	10.0	39.1	93.8
Peoples S&L Co.	Bucyrus	OH	B-	B-	B-	141.3	0.12	0.0	0.5	36.5	37.6	10.0	19.4	58.0
Peoples S&L Co.	West Liberty	OH	B-	C+	C+	49.7	-1.57	1.5	1.7	56.0	11.5	10.0	13.7	25.6
Peoples Savings Bank	Crawfordsville	IA	B-	B-	B-	37.9	9.56	8.4	1.3	7.6	48.9	6.6	8.6	13.2
Peoples Savings Bank	Elma	IA	B-	C+	C+	65.1	1.34	9.5	1.1	7.4	0.2	6.6	10.8	12.2
Peoples Savings Bank	Indianola	IA	B-	B-	C+	235.1	5.48	9.9	1.3	8.5	42.1	8.0	9.7	17.5
▲ Peoples Savings Bank	Montezuma	IA	C+	C	C-	35.4	0.69	8.8	7.3	5.8	49.0	10.0	11.2	18.6
Peoples Savings Bank	Wellsburg	IA	C+	C+	C+	89.3	-10.90	12.5	2.0	5.8	22.0	7.7	9.5	13.5
Peoples Savings Bank	New Matamoras	OH	B	B	B	59.8	-4.24	5.4	3.8	29.8	44.6	10.0	11.9	32.0
Peoples Savings Bank	Urbana	OH	C-	D+	D	114.1	7.21	1.0	2.3	56.4	2.1	8.6	10.1	16.4
Peoples Savings Bank of Rhineland	Rhineland	MO	B-	B-	B-	226.8	4.24	8.3	1.7	28.1	11.7	7.2	9.2	12.9
Peoples Security Bank and Trust Co.	Scranton	PA	B	B	B-	1965.2	11.52	10.5	6.8	16.8	13.3	7.7	10.0	13.1
Peoples Southern Bank	Clanton	AL	B	B+	B+	172.1	3.43	2.1	4.0	9.7	54.6	10.0	13.0	29.1
Peoples State Bank	Lake City	FL	C-	D+	D	79.7	6.11	4.2	1.9	16.4	6.9	6.6	8.6	12.4
Peoples State Bank	Albia	IA	B-	B+	B+	122.6	31.34	9.8	1.9	19.9	33.8	9.2	10.4	18.9
Peoples State Bank	Ellettsville	IN	B+	B+	A-	243.8	6.99	6.9	0.8	5.1	42.2	9.8	10.9	17.1
Peoples State Bank	Cherryvale	KS	B-	B-	B-	18.9	1.48	9.8	5.3	20.7	1.1	10.0	25.7	30.6
Peoples State Bank	Manhattan	KS	B	B-	C	64.0	39.01	14.9	1.4	12.2	1.3	7.3	9.4	12.7
Peoples State Bank	McDonald	KS	B	B-	C	123.8	-8.06	14.7	2.0	8.9	6.1	7.5	9.6	12.9

Asset Quality Index	Adjusted Non-Performing Loans as a % of Total Loans	as a % of Capital	Net Charge-Offs Avg Loans	Profitability Index	Net Income ($Mil)	Return on Assets (R.O.A.)	Return on Equity (R.O.E.)	Net Interest Spread	Overhead Efficiency Ratio	Liquidity Index	Liquidity Ratio	Hot Money Ratio	Stability Index
9.4	0.00	0.0	0.00	4.5	0.5	0.86	6.30	2.46	52.1	2.8	63.8	36.9	7.6
4.3	3.41	14.6	5.70	10.0	0.8	3.37	20.73	4.68	92.5	0.9	20.3	38.6	8.1
8.7	0.03	0.1	-0.14	4.0	0.4	0.63	5.62	4.21	78.6	4.2	33.9	12.0	6.5
0.2	9.26	74.9	0.44	2.1	0.5	0.23	2.60	3.64	84.6	1.3	17.1	27.7	4.4
7.3	0.90	3.6	0.07	4.9	3.0	0.91	6.77	3.82	69.2	4.3	27.5	8.9	7.9
9.1	0.01	0.0	0.00	6.2	4.2	1.19	11.30	2.92	47.6	5.6	43.7	7.3	7.1
7.6	0.28	1.0	0.00	7.6	4.3	1.78	8.89	4.14	54.9	4.0	17.1	8.8	8.6
4.9	2.75	14.2	-0.01	6.1	0.9	1.49	11.88	4.43	69.9	5.2	33.5	6.1	5.3
4.2	1.56	10.9	-0.08	6.0	7.3	1.49	14.59	4.43	73.2	4.1	7.8	7.3	6.5
4.6	1.79	11.8	0.00	4.1	0.4	0.87	8.45	3.75	76.9	4.6	23.7	5.8	6.0
5.6	1.72	8.3	0.24	4.9	2.6	1.16	9.56	3.78	74.0	5.0	29.2	5.1	7.4
4.2	2.93	14.4	-0.01	3.3	0.1	0.36	3.62	4.13	83.8	6.3	41.7	1.6	4.8
3.3	3.46	19.7	0.04	3.9	1.2	0.75	6.74	4.32	82.0	3.3	25.1	13.6	4.8
7.9	1.70	4.7	0.10	5.6	0.9	1.39	9.71	2.95	57.7	5.0	71.6	15.3	8.9
6.0	0.71	3.5	0.03	6.1	1.2	1.70	18.05	3.56	63.4	3.1	47.9	22.4	5.6
4.6	2.31	12.0	0.19	4.5	1.8	1.21	14.08	3.06	72.2	5.5	38.3	5.7	5.0
4.1	1.85	11.3	0.09	5.7	2.2	1.07	8.93	4.09	64.1	1.6	8.4	21.5	7.6
9.1	0.00	0.0	0.05	2.7	0.1	0.40	2.92	2.66	82.8	5.0	42.9	7.9	5.8
4.4	1.46	9.4	0.07	6.8	1.0	1.07	8.77	4.96	57.4	0.7	13.6	25.3	6.7
5.1	0.91	6.5	0.17	1.8	0.2	0.36	4.22	3.32	94.1	2.4	28.5	19.0	4.0
4.2	5.34	16.3	-0.20	5.4	0.1	1.00	8.38	5.22	74.3	6.9	66.2	0.8	5.4
4.7	1.07	7.5	-0.07	4.4	0.3	0.74	7.45	5.24	79.2	0.7	11.1	24.0	4.5
2.0	2.54	13.7	-0.01	8.9	2.4	2.25	15.64	5.41	59.1	1.5	16.6	25.0	8.3
7.8	0.38	2.3	0.05	5.0	0.7	0.99	10.60	3.34	54.8	2.6	21.5	16.8	6.0
4.5	4.40	15.2	0.51	0.9	0.7	0.13	0.98	3.02	95.9	4.1	21.4	8.8	5.6
5.1	1.08	7.4	0.07	4.8	6.6	1.00	10.47	3.83	68.1	3.7	27.7	12.6	6.5
6.3	1.60	7.6	0.17	10.0	9.7	3.05	20.25	5.44	43.9	2.1	16.1	18.8	9.2
4.6	1.98	15.2	0.04	3.8	0.8	0.67	7.62	4.00	76.9	1.8	12.9	19.7	5.4
5.8	1.20	6.4	0.01	6.1	2.0	1.00	7.77	3.69	64.8	3.9	10.4	8.6	7.4
6.1	0.43	3.5	0.10	4.3	1.8	0.71	7.59	3.90	76.8	2.6	10.7	15.5	5.2
8.0	0.89	3.5	0.02	3.1	0.2	0.43	2.98	3.92	90.4	4.7	33.7	9.1	7.0
4.7	2.94	15.3	-0.07	3.0	0.4	0.44	3.29	3.71	83.0	4.6	25.9	6.2	6.5
9.6	0.00	0.0	0.00	2.4	0.1	0.21	2.12	3.28	86.6	2.1	19.1	18.8	5.4
7.7	0.20	1.1	0.10	5.5	2.1	1.37	13.34	4.30	67.1	4.6	43.9	12.9	6.3
5.1	0.67	5.3	-0.01	9.7	6.7	2.48	25.14	3.80	74.3	4.5	5.9	4.2	7.4
4.7	2.97	13.1	-0.30	1.8	0.2	0.25	2.32	3.73	97.1	5.5	51.8	10.6	3.9
8.5	0.73	1.5	-0.04	4.1	1.0	0.95	6.09	3.01	73.9	5.0	62.8	15.3	8.1
8.4	1.29	2.8	0.07	5.3	1.7	0.91	4.94	4.54	67.5	6.3	56.3	6.6	7.4
5.6	0.82	4.5	0.26	3.4	0.2	0.46	3.74	4.10	78.3	3.9	34.4	13.5	5.5
4.7	0.68	5.5	0.22	3.0	0.4	0.45	4.82	4.13	85.5	3.3	11.3	12.3	5.2
4.6	1.31	11.4	0.07	5.3	9.5	1.20	12.99	4.21	71.4	1.5	1.8	20.4	8.2
8.1	2.39	3.7	0.52	1.9	0.0	0.17	0.45	2.80	91.9	5.9	59.7	8.3	6.7
9.1	1.47	3.0	0.16	3.2	0.7	0.68	3.57	3.28	79.2	4.7	68.1	17.6	7.8
9.4	0.18	0.9	0.00	3.4	0.2	0.52	3.82	3.95	80.4	3.2	24.3	14.0	6.9
6.1	1.77	6.4	-2.50	7.6	0.7	2.44	25.72	3.20	41.6	6.5	63.0	5.0	4.8
5.3	0.04	0.3	0.39	8.7	1.0	1.99	19.38	4.49	51.5	2.5	6.3	15.1	7.8
7.9	0.33	1.5	-0.02	4.6	2.0	1.25	11.57	3.39	63.6	5.7	46.2	7.7	5.9
4.9	3.65	11.9	0.00	3.3	0.2	0.79	6.83	3.62	77.7	6.1	68.0	8.9	4.9
3.2	1.81	11.6	1.23	2.8	0.1	0.08	0.91	3.42	74.6	1.2	15.4	28.9	4.1
6.9	2.27	7.5	0.06	4.5	0.4	0.84	6.93	3.88	72.3	6.2	53.5	5.1	6.6
2.2	3.10	26.2	0.23	2.4	0.2	0.28	3.10	4.31	86.2	1.5	8.8	21.9	4.0
5.7	0.61	5.0	0.23	3.7	1.1	0.65	7.04	4.00	79.2	4.1	5.9	6.8	5.2
4.7	0.87	6.6	0.08	5.1	15.0	1.06	8.08	3.78	62.0	3.8	8.2	9.0	9.5
9.2	0.23	0.6	-0.09	4.4	1.4	1.05	7.73	2.97	70.8	5.4	55.3	11.7	8.2
1.7	5.00	35.5	-0.04	3.2	0.2	0.40	4.42	3.92	89.7	4.6	24.8	5.7	3.8
6.5	0.65	3.4	0.00	4.3	0.9	0.93	8.01	3.75	74.1	3.0	41.6	21.5	6.9
6.7	0.70	3.0	-0.01	4.8	2.3	1.30	11.52	3.51	77.8	5.2	41.4	9.5	7.3
4.8	3.18	10.8	0.24	10.0	0.4	2.44	9.78	6.10	54.5	1.6	8.5	21.3	7.9
6.0	0.31	2.6	0.00	3.6	0.3	0.62	5.89	5.07	74.6	0.6	7.2	46.8	5.2
5.9	0.41	3.0	0.00	10.0	3.1	3.23	30.84	5.32	44.7	1.1	9.7	28.7	6.7

Name	City	State	2015 Rating	2014 Rating	Rating	Total Assets ($Mil)	One Year Asset Growth	Comm-ercial Loans	Cons-umer Loans	Mort-gage Loans	Secur-ities	Capital-ization Index	Lever-age Ratio	Risk-Based Capital Ratio
▲ Peoples State Bank	Fairmount	ND	D+	D-	D	25.6	4.12	9.1	7.3	2.4	27.2	5.4	7.4	12.7
Peoples State Bank	Westhope	ND	B	B	B	67.4	-10.85	3.7	2.6	1.1	34.4	10.0	12.5	18.9
Peoples State Bank	Blair	OK	B-	B-	B-	16.3	5.58	31.9	11.3	3.8	15.9	8.3	10.0	13.6
Peoples State Bank	Summit	SD	B	B-	B-	66.1	4.09	14.0	4.3	3.2	16.3	6.4	11.3	12.1
Peoples State Bank	Rocksprings	TX	A-	A	A	77.1	2.04	1.9	2.1	8.4	49.0	10.0	12.2	27.4
Peoples State Bank	Shepherd	TX	B-	B-	B-	105.9	-0.36	1.8	3.8	11.1	48.0	7.0	9.0	22.0
Peoples State Bank	Prairie Du Chien	WI	B	B	B	714.5	10.68	11.1	0.7	9.4	26.7	7.3	9.2	14.1
Peoples State Bank	Wausau	WI	B	B	B	808.1	6.54	11.3	0.4	19.6	20.2	7.7	9.5	13.8
Peoples State Bank of Colfax	Colfax	IL	B	B	B	35.5	3.40	4.9	8.3	20.7	19.0	10.0	11.4	20.8
Peoples State Bank of Commerce	Nolensville	TN	D	D-	E-	155.7	4.48	9.2	5.9	14.5	15.3	9.6	10.7	17.1
Peoples State Bank of Hallettsville	Hallettsville	TX	C+	C+	C+	275.1	-0.40	1.3	1.4	7.8	45.3	9.6	10.7	39.2
Peoples State Bank of Munising	Munising	MI	B+	B-	B-	133.4	0.42	7.3	5.4	17.9	31.4	10.0	12.6	19.4
Peoples State Bank of Newton, Illinois	Newton	IL	B	B	B	377.2	4.94	12.6	3.3	11.2	21.7	8.2	10.5	13.5
Peoples State Bank of Plainview	Plainview	MN	B	B	B-	250.0	25.59	8.7	3.2	15.6	20.8	6.4	8.4	12.3
Peoples State Bank of Velva	Velva	ND	C	C+	C+	111.7	-8.84	11.5	3.0	9.2	7.6	5.8	8.7	11.6
▼ Peoples State Bank of Wells	Wells	MN	B	B+	B+	56.3	91.51	6.7	2.6	12.5	7.6	10.0	17.2	15.7
Peoples Trust & Savings Bank	Clive	IA	B-	B-	C+	315.6	7.56	7.2	2.5	18.0	17.0	7.1	9.1	12.6
▼ Peoples Trust & Savings Bank	Boonville	IN	B	B+	B	173.9	3.14	3.3	0.8	34.2	31.4	10.0	16.0	27.1
Peoples Trust and Savings Bank	Riverside	IA	B-	B-	B-	29.7	-0.04	14.0	2.6	21.5	36.2	5.6	7.6	12.7
Peoples Trust Co. of St. Albans	Saint Albans	VT	C+	C+	C+	258.8	1.04	2.1	1.0	22.6	28.6	10.0	11.9	20.9
PeoplesBank	Holyoke	MA	C+	C+	C+	2061.5	1.26	5.6	0.1	29.0	16.6	8.5	10.0	14.2
PeoplesBank, A Codorus Valley Co.	York	PA	B	B	B	1519.6	9.06	10.2	0.6	12.3	13.2	8.7	10.3	13.9
▼ PeoplesSouth Bank	Colquitt	GA	B	B+	B+	713.4	42.01	3.8	4.7	13.0	28.1	7.5	9.3	15.6
PeoplesTrust Bank	Hamilton	AL	B-	C+	C+	92.1	6.22	18.7	5.3	9.2	27.7	9.0	10.4	14.6
Perennial Bank	Darwin	MN	B-	B-	B-	97.1	142.37	4.6	4.3	8.3	42.5	6.7	8.7	23.9
Perpetual Federal Savings Bank	Urbana	OH	A-	B	B	386.9	9.71	1.3	1.3	46.9	0.3	10.0	17.2	28.9
Perryton National Bank	Perryton	TX	B	B	B	174.1	-2.18	7.7	5.5	5.7	50.8	10.0	11.8	28.1
▲ Persons Banking Co.	Forsyth	GA	E+	E-	D-	329.2	0.24	6.7	2.7	16.4	16.4	4.4	6.4	10.8
Peru Federal Savings Bank	Peru	IL	B-	B-	B-	141.8	2.44	3.2	2.0	31.5	40.7	10.0	13.0	27.7
Peshtigo National Bank	Peshtigo	WI	A-	A-	A-	198.3	1.57	4.7	2.7	20.7	20.4	10.0	12.1	21.0
Petefish, Skiles & Co.	Virginia	IL	A-	A-	A-	170.6	-0.27	2.8	9.0	11.9	27.6	10.0	11.9	16.8
Petit Jean State Bank	Morrilton	AR	A-	A-	A-	184.1	-0.97	12.4	2.6	15.0	32.1	10.0	12.4	24.5
Phelps County Bank	Rolla	MO	B	B	B	367.4	7.07	3.5	2.3	32.4	36.9	5.1	7.1	15.5
Phenix-Girard Bank	Phenix City	AL	B	B+	B+	181.2	6.30	1.3	0.6	9.3	40.7	10.0	14.9	28.8
Philadelphia Trust Co.	Philadelphia	PA	B+	A-	A-	20.0	8.06	1.8	7.4	4.8	10.0	10.0	68.1	156.0
Philo Exchange Bank	Philo	IL	C+	C+	C+	89.0	3.28	1.3	1.3	7.8	29.2	8.7	10.1	14.9
Phoenixville Federal Bank and Trust	Phoenixville	PA	C+	C+	C+	415.2	7.75	3.2	0.1	37.8	25.9	10.0	12.0	20.2
Pickens S&L Assn., FA	Pickens	SC	C+	C+	C-	91.9	-0.44	1.4	1.0	37.3	25.5	9.4	10.6	20.3
Piedmont Bank	Norcross	GA	C	C	D-	513.1	18.66	15.5	1.0	3.7	4.2	5.2	9.3	11.1
Piedmont Federal Savings Bank	Winston-Salem	NC	C+	C+	C+	898.7	-1.11	0.0	0.0	55.5	32.6	10.0	25.2	65.6
Pigeon Falls State Bank	Pigeon Falls	WI	B-	B	B	76.2	2.89	6.2	0.7	11.0	5.0	9.6	11.1	14.7
Piggott State Bank	Piggott	AR	B+	B+	B+	80.4	3.19	5.9	3.8	14.6	50.5	7.1	9.1	19.5
Pike National Bank	McComb	MS	B	B	B	226.2	8.24	6.3	6.0	18.8	21.3	10.0	13.6	21.7
Pikes Peak National Bank	Colorado Springs	CO	C+	C	C-	88.2	-0.88	5.4	1.6	4.4	0.0	9.5	10.7	29.6
Pilgrim Bank	Cohasset	MA	C	C	C-	250.9	26.96	0.6	0.9	52.9	7.1	7.7	9.5	14.4
Pilgrim Bank	Pittsburg	TX	B-	B-	B-	559.6	-6.20	2.7	1.3	11.3	32.5	9.1	10.4	16.8
Pilot Bank	Tampa	FL	C-	D+	E	237.7	4.79	23.2	19.8	5.3	12.8	6.7	9.1	12.3
Pilot Grove Savings Bank	Pilot Grove	IA	B+	B+	B+	575.1	1.69	7.0	3.6	26.5	14.0	5.1	8.0	11.1
Pine Country Bank	Little Falls	MN	B	B	B-	161.2	-1.89	8.3	1.2	6.7	23.1	8.0	9.6	14.2
Pine Island Bank	Pine Island	MN	B-	C+	B-	89.3	9.47	5.1	1.2	25.1	14.0	8.3	9.9	14.5
Pine River State Bank	Pine River	MN	C+	C+	C	116.9	5.57	4.9	1.9	14.6	22.7	5.9	7.9	15.5
Pineland Bank	Alma	GA	C+	C-	D+	286.5	232.28	5.0	2.5	9.3	7.7	7.8	9.5	14.7
Pineries Bank	Stevens Point	WI	B	B	B	82.8	9.55	2.6	2.2	34.5	6.0	8.2	9.8	17.9
Pinnacle Bank	Jasper	AL	B	B	B	225.5	-1.27	8.9	1.8	6.1	47.6	10.0	11.7	19.9
Pinnacle Bank	Rogers	AR	C-	C	C	89.4	2.20	1.3	0.1	10.7	28.1	10.0	11.2	20.5
Pinnacle Bank	Scottsdale	AZ	B	B+	B+	185.6	15.60	7.3	0.0	31.3	0.0	10.0	12.1	16.3
Pinnacle Bank	Gilroy	CA	B-	C+	C+	281.7	15.94	12.0	0.4	3.9	1.3	5.2	9.3	11.2
Pinnacle Bank	Orange City	FL	E-	E-	E-	107.5	-29.59	17.9	2.8	3.4	31.7	0.0	2.3	5.7
Pinnacle Bank	Elberton	GA	B	B-	C+	668.7	2.99	7.4	2.6	7.9	20.2	7.3	10.5	12.8
Pinnacle Bank	Marshalltown	IA	A-	B+	B	191.8	3.86	11.7	2.7	5.4	52.4	10.0	11.6	26.6

| Asset Quality Index | Adjusted Non-Performing Loans | | Net Charge-Offs | Profitability Index | Net Income ($Mil) | Return on Assets (R.O.A.) | Return on Equity (R.O.E.) | Net Interest Spread | Overhead Efficiency Ratio | Liquidity Index | Liquidity Ratio | Hot Money Ratio | Stability Index |
	as a % of Total Loans	as a % of Capital	Avg Loans										
8.3	0.00	0.0	-0.09	3.0	0.1	0.40	5.45	3.65	84.4	4.8	18.3	3.5	2.5
7.5	0.00	0.0	-0.01	5.6	0.7	1.36	10.72	3.77	59.7	3.3	32.4	15.8	7.3
7.4	0.00	0.0	-0.01	7.8	0.2	1.92	19.49	5.16	68.4	4.3	28.0	8.1	5.7
4.5	0.83	5.0	0.01	10.0	1.3	2.73	24.08	4.97	40.0	0.9	12.9	32.5	7.6
9.4	0.00	0.0	0.00	6.4	0.9	1.62	13.14	3.15	43.4	3.7	62.2	20.1	8.6
9.1	0.00	0.0	-0.51	4.2	0.7	0.85	9.50	3.35	77.7	3.4	36.8	17.0	5.2
4.6	1.18	7.6	0.00	6.4	7.4	1.47	13.84	3.53	58.2	2.1	24.8	18.9	8.6
5.1	0.90	6.5	0.06	6.1	6.4	1.09	11.42	3.58	59.9	2.5	18.7	9.0	6.7
8.4	0.00	0.0	-0.09	6.1	0.3	1.17	10.13	3.82	57.4	3.8	31.6	13.2	6.2
1.9	3.85	21.0	0.35	5.4	3.0	2.68	26.85	4.12	75.4	1.9	19.4	20.4	1.2
7.2	3.44	7.0	0.00	3.4	1.4	0.69	6.20	2.38	62.4	3.4	69.3	32.1	6.6
5.0	1.83	7.7	-0.01	5.3	0.9	0.93	6.70	4.28	68.6	3.4	36.8	16.8	7.6
5.2	0.69	4.6	0.00	6.2	3.1	1.13	10.51	3.48	49.1	2.0	10.1	13.0	6.3
4.6	1.15	9.1	0.07	5.0	1.9	1.20	12.30	3.74	68.6	3.0	20.5	14.5	5.9
3.5	1.29	10.6	0.00	4.9	0.9	1.05	12.09	4.30	61.7	1.3	8.8	25.1	5.2
7.1	0.16	1.1	0.01	5.8	0.3	1.36	10.13	4.17	67.6	1.7	16.1	21.7	7.1
5.7	0.51	4.1	0.03	5.0	2.3	1.02	10.72	3.91	67.5	2.0	14.0	19.0	5.3
8.6	1.05	3.9	-0.02	3.3	0.7	0.55	3.26	3.64	82.9	3.5	43.1	18.1	8.2
2.8	4.28	24.3	3.17	1.7	-0.3	-1.32	-18.22	2.59	93.8	4.9	50.6	12.5	4.9
4.6	3.12	14.2	0.17	3.2	1.1	0.54	4.37	3.81	84.2	4.8	35.3	8.9	6.0
8.9	0.18	1.3	0.04	3.3	9.0	0.59	6.22	2.83	72.8	3.5	7.7	9.2	7.3
7.8	0.37	2.7	0.10	5.0	9.7	0.88	8.19	3.90	65.3	2.7	6.2	14.5	8.8
3.9	2.13	13.3	0.21	4.8	4.5	0.84	9.02	3.60	65.2	2.8	26.6	16.7	6.2
5.1	0.90	4.9	-0.18	4.5	0.6	0.84	7.69	3.86	70.0	3.1	35.0	17.6	5.2
8.4	0.42	1.3	-0.21	3.9	0.6	0.83	9.48	3.36	73.8	6.9	65.8	3.0	4.6
5.4	1.77	8.4	-0.21	7.5	3.8	1.33	7.61	3.01	33.4	0.8	16.1	40.8	7.7
6.5	3.23	8.6	0.04	5.0	1.7	1.26	10.73	2.79	52.4	4.2	62.9	19.6	7.5
1.4	5.37	49.0	0.77	2.3	1.1	0.46	7.24	3.99	82.4	3.4	26.5	13.3	0.9
7.0	2.34	8.5	-0.12	3.3	0.6	0.59	4.54	2.86	76.4	4.2	44.3	15.1	6.9
7.8	0.68	3.6	0.03	5.8	2.0	1.36	11.28	4.08	64.6	3.5	25.5	12.3	8.4
7.2	0.54	2.7	0.19	5.3	1.6	1.24	8.70	3.99	70.8	3.7	18.5	10.8	8.4
7.3	1.02	3.5	0.14	6.3	1.6	1.15	9.83	3.49	47.3	2.7	36.7	20.6	6.6
8.4	0.27	2.0	0.10	5.4	3.8	1.43	19.47	3.46	65.6	4.8	19.0	3.9	5.0
8.0	1.39	3.3	0.71	4.3	1.5	1.07	7.29	3.14	68.8	4.7	28.9	6.7	7.9
8.9	0.00	0.0	0.00	9.5	0.9	5.71	8.62	1.74	78.5	5.3	205.1	65.8	7.0
5.7	0.66	3.7	0.13	3.8	0.6	0.92	8.23	3.01	68.4	4.8	27.3	5.5	6.7
7.2	1.10	5.6	0.00	3.1	1.5	0.48	4.00	3.11	80.5	3.7	29.4	12.8	6.2
4.8	2.56	13.3	-0.32	3.2	0.3	0.49	4.48	3.59	84.4	2.9	40.3	21.1	5.1
3.3	0.71	5.9	0.05	5.4	3.2	0.85	7.12	3.99	61.1	0.7	11.1	37.7	5.5
10.0	0.10	0.2	0.02	2.6	1.8	0.26	1.05	2.55	82.4	2.7	53.5	34.1	8.2
3.7	3.06	21.1	-0.01	4.4	0.4	0.63	5.67	4.14	75.2	0.8	13.0	34.5	6.5
9.1	0.16	0.7	0.02	5.3	0.8	1.30	12.86	3.59	62.5	3.6	44.3	17.9	7.2
4.8	2.45	10.6	0.05	5.2	1.4	0.85	6.33	4.32	70.7	2.4	16.7	17.1	7.2
3.7	4.75	16.4	-0.04	3.6	0.4	0.57	5.44	3.29	84.0	6.3	67.2	7.4	5.3
5.2	0.85	7.4	0.01	2.8	0.7	0.38	3.84	2.97	77.0	0.9	13.4	30.2	4.1
6.2	0.47	2.5	0.04	4.1	4.3	1.01	8.71	3.40	72.5	2.3	21.7	18.2	7.4
3.5	1.03	7.6	-0.02	2.4	0.5	0.30	2.71	3.59	87.5	3.0	15.5	9.1	4.5
6.5	0.28	2.6	0.12	7.1	7.4	1.71	17.98	3.74	52.8	4.0	12.4	8.3	7.4
3.2	2.99	19.3	0.00	4.2	0.9	0.74	7.74	4.21	70.6	4.1	18.6	8.3	5.2
4.5	0.85	6.3	0.00	5.6	0.9	1.42	12.51	3.90	60.8	1.0	9.0	23.6	6.5
4.9	1.90	11.5	0.07	3.5	0.7	0.76	9.40	3.66	78.2	5.5	39.0	6.0	3.9
4.2	1.80	10.9	0.14	4.5	1.0	0.84	11.18	7.92	84.1	2.8	30.1	17.5	4.0
5.1	1.49	9.5	0.00	5.4	0.8	1.34	13.38	3.35	60.3	2.5	34.6	21.3	7.3
9.1	0.17	0.6	-0.05	5.0	1.8	1.09	8.65	3.74	67.5	4.6	45.4	13.5	6.8
5.0	3.77	14.6	0.00	1.1	0.1	0.14	1.26	2.34	108.8	0.6	21.1	71.7	5.3
4.8	1.96	12.1	0.57	6.4	1.2	0.95	7.55	3.89	66.0	0.9	21.0	31.7	8.1
6.4	0.20	1.6	-0.37	5.1	1.7	0.85	8.48	4.12	75.3	3.9	18.6	9.6	5.4
0.3	4.58	54.6	0.26	0.0	-0.6	-0.69	-32.49	2.63	127.0	0.8	18.1	47.3	0.0
4.6	1.14	6.9	0.11	6.1	7.8	1.55	13.28	4.37	71.0	4.2	11.7	7.1	7.3
6.7	1.10	3.3	0.00	6.7	1.8	1.31	9.76	3.58	51.7	7.3	61.4	1.9	7.2

Name	City	State	Rating	2015 Rating	2014 Rating	Total Assets ($Mil)	One Year Asset Growth	Asset Mix (As a % of Total Assets)				Capital-ization Index	Lever-age Ratio	Risk-Based Capital Ratio
								Comm-ercial Loans	Cons-umer Loans	Mort-gage Loans	Secur-ities			
Pinnacle Bank	Lincoln	NE	A-	A-	B+	4363.2	2.20	7.0	1.3	10.2	20.4	7.1	9.6	12.6
Pinnacle Bank	Nashville	TN	B	B+	B+	10910.7	27.91	26.4	2.2	6.2	11.5	4.1	8.6	10.6
Pinnacle Bank	Keene	TX	B+	B+	B	729.0	9.87	6.1	2.4	13.4	28.3	6.7	8.7	13.8
Pinnacle Bank - Wyoming	Torrington	WY	B+	B+	B	722.9	0.41	6.7	2.7	16.5	15.3	6.8	9.2	12.4
Pinnacle Bank Sioux City	Sioux City	IA	B-	C+	B	70.2	-6.71	4.1	1.7	23.4	30.5	10.0	14.7	27.1
Pinnacle Bank, Inc.	Vanceburg	KY	B-	B-	B-	49.7	-1.37	6.2	8.1	40.1	6.8	10.0	12.6	17.6
Pioneer Bank	Sioux City	IA	B	B	B	152.9	1.07	8.6	0.9	22.4	16.5	7.7	9.5	13.1
Pioneer Bank	Mapleton	MN	B	B	B-	403.3	3.49	15.0	1.5	12.7	3.4	6.6	9.1	12.2
▲ Pioneer Bank	Roswell	NM	B-	C+	C+	815.5	15.80	2.4	0.4	24.9	48.2	7.7	9.5	22.4
Pioneer Bank	Stanley	VA	D	D	D+	191.3	9.49	5.6	9.4	32.2	3.5	9.4	10.6	14.7
Pioneer Bank	Auburndale	WI	C	C-	C	134.7	7.91	5.9	0.9	12.2	6.4	7.2	10.4	12.7
Pioneer Bank & Trust	Belle Fourche	SD	A-	A-	A-	630.8	1.99	9.0	1.7	5.1	43.7	8.1	9.7	17.2
Pioneer Bank of Wisconsin	Ladysmith	WI	B	B	B	70.3	3.72	5.6	1.0	5.3	44.3	7.7	9.5	17.6
Pioneer Bank, SSB	Austin	TX	B-	B	B	1181.3	178.06	6.3	2.6	26.7	7.1	5.1	8.6	11.1
Pioneer Commercial Bank	Albany	NY	U	U	U	190.8	32.35	0.0	0.0	0.0	17.5	4.8	6.8	28.7
Pioneer Community Bank, Inc.	Iaeger	WV	B	B	B	112.6	-3.45	2.2	4.8	66.6	4.8	10.0	13.9	21.3
Pioneer Federal S&L Assn.	Dillon	MT	B	B	B	97.7	0.65	2.6	1.6	53.4	27.5	10.0	16.2	34.5
Pioneer National Bank of Duluth	Duluth	MN	B	B	B-	80.7	1.35	14.3	3.1	18.0	3.6	10.0	11.0	17.6
Pioneer Savings Bank	Troy	NY	C+	C+	B-	1082.1	13.72	13.3	0.4	24.2	9.9	7.5	10.2	12.9
Pioneer Savings Bank	Cleveland	OH	B-	B-	B-	35.2	7.66	0.0	0.2	41.8	35.0	10.0	19.4	50.3
Pioneer State Bank	Earlville	IL	D+	C-	D	102.7	48.90	4.6	1.0	12.9	17.5	10.0	11.5	17.6
Pioneer Trust Bank, N.A.	Salem	OR	A+	A+	A	452.1	12.07	11.7	0.5	7.6	20.3	10.0	11.3	16.1
Piqua State Bank	Piqua	KS	C	C-	D+	24.9	-5.72	6.8	3.5	11.1	26.5	9.4	10.6	18.5
Piscataqua Savings Bank	Portsmouth	NH	B-	B-	B-	248.7	3.52	0.0	0.4	47.7	27.9	10.0	17.3	30.8
Pitney Bowes Bank, Inc.	Salt Lake City	UT	B+	B	B	724.6	-0.16	41.4	0.0	0.0	54.4	8.1	9.7	16.9
Pittsfield Co-operative Bank	Pittsfield	MA	C+	C+	C+	288.7	7.84	4.1	0.5	43.6	14.1	10.0	15.4	22.0
Plains Commerce Bank	Hoven	SD	D+	D+	B+	628.1	6.80	8.1	0.9	8.3	9.2	8.4	12.4	13.7
▲ Plains State Bank	Plains	KS	C	C	C+	107.7	-11.64	5.1	0.8	2.6	60.4	10.0	12.3	25.8
▼ Plains State Bank	Humble	TX	C+	B	B+	374.3	9.37	10.6	0.5	7.3	9.8	8.7	10.3	13.9
PlainsCapital Bank	Dallas	TX	A	A	A-	9204.5	10.26	11.4	0.4	25.3	8.7	10.0	12.7	15.9
Planters and Citizens Bank	Camilla	GA	C	C+	C-	109.1	-3.93	3.0	1.8	2.7	32.9	8.0	9.7	23.8
Planters Bank & Trust Co.	Indianola	MS	B	B	B	1026.6	26.29	9.4	3.4	16.8	32.3	7.5	9.4	15.4
Planters Bank, Inc.	Hopkinsville	KY	B+	B+	B+	930.0	3.70	6.0	1.1	14.8	21.5	6.5	9.2	12.1
Planters First Bank	Hawkinsville	GA	D+	D+	E	277.7	3.88	4.6	2.4	15.8	15.0	8.4	9.9	14.7
Plaquemine Bank and Trust Co.	Plaquemine	LA	B-	B-	B-	140.4	6.76	10.2	3.8	12.7	30.5	10.0	11.6	19.7
Platinum Bank	Brandon	FL	B-	B-	B-	583.9	5.41	16.7	0.6	6.7	5.7	7.0	9.4	12.5
▼ Platinum Bank	Oakdale	MN	C+	B+	A-	176.1	-1.25	25.4	4.6	13.3	8.7	9.2	11.0	14.4
Platinum Bank	Lubbock	TX	C-	D	B-	253.5	5.96	11.1	0.8	14.9	10.6	8.8	10.4	14.0
Platte Valley Bank	North Bend	NE	B	B	B	72.6	4.18	13.2	3.6	3.2	20.5	10.0	14.0	19.6
Platte Valley Bank	Scottsbluff	NE	B	B	B	530.7	13.40	15.8	3.2	23.1	7.2	6.3	9.2	12.0
Platte Valley Bank	Torrington	WY	B+	B+	B+	346.0	1.61	26.8	2.9	16.9	5.5	8.0	11.0	13.3
Platte Valley Bank of Missouri	Platte City	MO	A-	A-	B+	510.2	10.13	4.5	1.2	15.1	23.2	7.7	9.5	13.5
Plattsmouth State Bank	Plattsmouth	NE	C	C	C	89.6	-7.60	11.3	1.2	6.7	40.1	6.9	9.8	12.5
Plaza Bank	Irvine	CA	B+	B	C-	1191.9	15.65	15.3	5.5	7.9	2.2	7.4	10.9	12.8
▲ Plaza Bank	Seattle	WA	C-	D-	D	65.4	-12.16	21.7	0.0	1.4	11.7	9.8	11.7	14.8
Plaza Park State Bank	Waite Park	MN	B-	B-	C	201.2	7.30	7.2	2.9	15.8	14.9	8.4	9.9	14.2
▲ Pleasant Hill Bank	Pleasant Hill	MO	C+	C	C	78.7	3.37	5.7	2.3	18.7	27.2	9.5	10.7	20.1
Pleasants County Bank	Saint Marys	WV	B-	B-	B	62.8	-8.03	12.0	7.1	20.8	24.7	10.0	11.1	21.8
Plumas Bank	Quincy	CA	B-	C+	C+	656.6	8.28	6.5	8.8	3.4	15.3	7.5	9.3	13.4
▼ Plus International Bank	Miami	FL	D+	C	B	88.4	-17.90	12.7	0.0	23.7	23.9	10.0	16.1	24.9
PNC Bank, N.A.	Wilmington	DE	C+	C+	C	357858.7	1.81	19.6	7.3	8.0	22.1	6.7	8.7	12.5
Poca Valley Bank, Inc.	Walton	WV	B	B-	B-	336.8	4.04	14.0	8.3	29.3	12.3	9.2	10.5	16.3
Pocahontas State Bank	Pocahontas	IA	A	A	A	98.9	-0.30	5.7	0.3	4.7	52.4	10.0	21.9	36.0
Pointbank	Pilot Point	TX	B	B	B-	456.7	6.51	7.0	0.9	7.1	31.7	8.5	10.0	17.9
▲ Points West Community Bank	Julesburg	CO	B+	B+	B+	224.8	1.94	9.2	0.7	9.4	25.8	7.7	9.4	15.1
▲ Points West Community Bank	Sidney	NE	B+	B+	B+	357.4	-0.42	3.4	2.3	7.1	38.6	8.1	9.7	19.2
▲ POINTWEST Bank	West	TX	B-	C+	C	104.0	-2.32	1.4	7.8	16.6	33.0	6.6	8.7	21.0
Polonia Bank	Huntingdon Valley	PA	D	C-	C-	275.7	-4.05	0.0	0.6	53.9	24.7	10.0	11.4	25.1
Ponce De Leon Federal Bank	Bronx	NY	B-	C+	C-	736.3	2.32	2.1	0.1	42.4	8.5	10.0	13.5	19.7
▼ Pony Express Bank	Liberty	MO	B-	B+	B	152.3	1.83	18.0	1.7	19.6	6.7	9.7	10.9	14.8

Arrows denote recent upgrades ▲ or downgrades ▼

www.weissratings.com

Asset Quality Index	Adjusted Non-Performing Loans as a % of Total Loans	Adjusted Non-Performing Loans as a % of Capital	Net Charge-Offs Avg Loans	Profitability Index	Net Income ($Mil)	Return on Assets (R.O.A.)	Return on Equity (R.O.E.)	Net Interest Spread	Overhead Efficiency Ratio	Liquidity Index	Liquidity Ratio	Hot Money Ratio	Stability Index
7.3	0.51	3.6	0.03	7.5	58.7	1.83	17.91	3.49	52.7	3.7	6.5	9.9	7.0
5.5	0.42	3.7	0.37	8.1	94.1	1.31	9.79	3.71	50.9	4.0	6.8	7.4	9.6
4.4	0.98	6.6	0.04	7.9	10.3	1.91	14.75	3.95	57.4	3.9	26.6	11.0	8.8
6.0	0.28	2.1	0.14	8.7	11.6	2.18	23.14	4.22	55.0	2.4	3.7	15.7	8.5
5.8	2.40	9.0	0.18	2.8	0.3	0.46	3.15	3.04	82.5	4.3	45.1	14.1	5.7
6.3	0.86	5.2	0.07	4.4	0.2	0.49	3.35	4.72	71.2	0.7	5.5	27.6	6.7
7.5	0.28	2.0	0.01	6.0	1.5	1.34	13.70	3.74	62.4	1.7	14.6	20.9	6.5
3.9	1.10	9.2	0.31	5.0	3.3	1.11	10.81	4.16	56.9	1.4	9.4	23.9	7.1
9.3	0.11	0.4	0.10	4.1	5.9	1.02	11.21	2.95	73.6	5.1	47.6	11.2	5.4
1.4	3.45	25.0	0.40	5.3	1.3	0.92	8.51	4.98	71.9	2.5	12.8	16.2	7.0
6.0	0.30	2.2	0.01	2.6	0.3	0.29	2.68	4.49	89.1	3.7	15.9	10.8	5.8
9.0	0.03	0.2	0.00	7.3	6.4	1.38	14.37	3.17	46.4	4.6	33.5	9.7	8.0
6.8	0.46	2.0	0.04	4.6	0.4	0.84	7.40	3.55	67.5	5.6	49.8	8.1	6.4
7.6	0.32	2.6	0.10	3.7	11.9	1.52	13.41	4.10	96.1	1.3	16.7	29.5	8.3
10.0	na	0.0	na	3.3	0.6	0.56	8.92	1.15	21.9	8.2	86.6	0.0	4.1
4.2	3.40	17.8	0.07	4.4	0.5	0.58	4.23	4.91	77.2	3.8	12.2	9.8	7.1
9.8	0.00	0.0	-0.01	3.8	0.4	0.50	3.08	3.62	79.0	2.9	41.9	22.7	7.3
8.0	0.38	2.3	0.00	4.4	0.6	0.93	8.44	4.18	76.8	5.1	28.5	4.3	6.3
6.6	0.73	5.3	0.04	3.5	3.7	0.49	5.11	3.52	79.4	4.5	9.5	4.8	6.3
7.0	2.46	6.4	0.57	2.7	0.1	0.36	1.83	3.26	79.9	1.9	39.1	35.2	6.7
5.6	2.48	12.0	-0.05	1.7	0.1	0.10	0.78	3.65	96.9	4.0	26.9	10.7	5.1
8.7	0.03	0.2	-0.12	9.8	6.4	1.97	17.33	3.81	36.2	5.6	36.3	4.2	8.5
7.0	0.22	1.0	-0.01	3.4	0.1	0.71	6.67	4.37	83.7	5.8	45.3	3.3	4.5
10.0	0.28	0.9	0.00	3.1	0.8	0.43	2.57	2.48	80.4	3.4	46.7	19.6	7.8
5.6	1.22	5.0	1.40	10.0	51.7	9.60	91.50	13.63	2.8	7.6	63.1	0.0	7.2
7.2	1.12	5.3	0.09	2.7	1.2	0.55	3.49	3.27	82.4	2.4	20.8	17.7	7.4
1.4	3.85	24.5	0.28	9.9	10.3	2.27	16.77	4.84	62.3	0.7	9.3	28.1	10.0
7.6	1.34	3.2	-0.01	2.2	0.2	0.24	1.91	3.10	91.1	2.7	42.5	26.5	5.5
2.9	1.59	11.5	0.42	5.9	2.8	1.02	9.68	4.12	57.1	0.8	15.3	34.0	6.6
6.3	0.73	4.5	0.61	9.7	106.7	1.67	11.15	4.69	75.3	2.6	8.2	13.7	10.0
8.6	0.52	1.3	0.04	2.6	0.4	0.40	4.30	2.52	79.5	7.1	66.3	3.9	5.1
5.3	1.43	8.4	0.66	5.5	8.2	1.08	11.31	3.67	60.3	2.5	21.4	18.4	7.3
6.3	0.60	4.3	0.08	6.9	10.9	1.60	17.08	3.81	56.5	1.2	7.2	18.2	8.3
1.6	5.14	33.2	0.02	5.4	2.6	1.24	12.92	4.34	77.4	3.4	21.6	12.5	5.3
6.3	1.32	6.2	0.20	3.5	0.6	0.52	4.57	3.50	75.8	1.9	23.7	21.3	6.0
5.4	0.29	2.2	0.02	4.8	5.0	1.19	12.57	3.79	66.1	1.4	21.6	21.5	6.5
2.9	2.57	17.8	0.09	5.8	1.6	1.26	11.30	4.08	59.8	2.8	13.3	14.9	7.0
2.4	1.75	11.6	0.07	2.9	0.8	0.42	3.36	4.03	81.3	0.8	19.1	42.9	5.0
8.1	0.13	0.6	0.00	4.2	0.4	0.71	5.03	3.67	73.9	4.8	21.6	3.9	7.2
4.5	0.92	7.6	0.09	6.3	4.2	1.13	11.85	4.09	59.7	1.6	7.4	20.2	6.9
4.8	0.79	5.4	0.60	8.1	3.1	1.21	10.80	5.27	58.8	0.9	9.7	30.9	7.7
8.8	0.10	0.7	0.03	6.9	5.9	1.61	17.29	3.99	69.0	3.6	11.0	10.4	6.3
8.9	0.09	0.4	-0.09	3.0	0.3	0.42	4.73	3.60	86.9	2.8	33.7	18.7	3.7
6.6	0.16	1.2	0.01	7.0	8.3	1.03	8.85	4.92	62.4	1.8	15.1	21.2	8.8
3.5	0.82	4.4	0.27	2.3	0.4	0.70	5.95	3.79	94.0	1.4	8.8	24.8	4.2
4.6	1.43	9.5	0.10	6.1	2.2	1.49	14.63	4.09	65.3	4.3	27.9	9.2	7.1
5.7	1.14	5.3	0.00	2.3	0.2	0.30	2.78	3.02	84.8	5.4	33.7	4.9	5.1
8.2	0.69	2.9	0.01	3.8	0.3	0.57	5.32	3.50	79.0	5.2	46.6	10.1	5.8
4.4	1.00	6.9	0.06	7.8	5.7	1.25	12.97	4.38	58.2	4.9	19.0	3.5	5.9
8.1	0.00	0.0	0.28	0.7	-0.1	-0.17	-1.13	3.99	114.4	1.8	45.6	79.6	7.1
4.0	1.52	10.0	0.28	5.0	2403.4	0.96	8.78	2.71	64.9	6.2	32.9	2.6	9.8
4.7	1.12	7.3	0.03	4.4	1.9	0.77	7.07	4.15	75.8	3.7	23.2	11.0	5.3
8.3	0.00	0.0	0.00	10.0	1.9	2.57	10.91	4.57	22.5	4.0	70.5	20.3	9.3
7.7	0.69	3.5	0.06	4.7	3.6	1.03	10.20	3.85	75.0	4.3	25.1	7.7	6.8
5.7	0.49	3.1	0.01	9.7	3.7	2.19	21.74	4.57	48.8	2.0	16.4	18.9	7.7
7.0	0.36	1.7	0.01	5.2	3.4	1.28	11.95	3.43	62.5	2.2	15.7	17.9	7.4
9.0	0.03	0.1	0.22	4.0	0.8	1.09	12.81	3.09	73.9	5.8	50.8	8.1	4.5
6.8	1.76	8.9	0.21	0.0	-0.5	-0.21	-1.84	2.26	129.6	2.6	38.6	24.0	5.6
4.1	3.19	18.3	-0.15	2.9	1.2	0.22	1.71	4.02	91.9	0.7	13.0	36.3	7.2
3.6	0.72	5.3	0.67	6.8	1.5	1.38	10.34	4.62	56.9	3.9	8.7	8.4	8.9

Name	City	State	2015 Rating	2014 Rating	Rating	Total Assets ($Mil)	One Year Asset Growth	Commercial Loans	Consumer Loans	Mortgage Loans	Securities	Capitalization Index	Leverage Ratio	Risk-Based Capital Ratio
Pony Express Community Bank	Saint Joseph	MO	C+	B-	C+	72.9	-15.17	4.6	2.1	14.5	41.6	9.5	10.7	20.3
Poplar Grove State Bank	Poplar Grove	IL	A	A	A	81.5	0.95	8.4	0.8	9.0	60.7	10.0	24.2	53.4
Port Austin State Bank	Port Austin	MI	B+	B+	B+	51.9	3.56	3.3	4.6	42.1	7.8	10.0	17.9	28.5
Port Richmond Savings	Philadelphia	PA	B	B	B	68.4	1.60	0.0	0.0	63.1	0.0	10.0	18.3	32.5
Port Washington State Bank	Port Washington	WI	C+	C+	C	512.7	6.26	8.6	3.1	18.7	23.3	6.7	8.7	13.0
Portage Community Bank	Ravenna	OH	B	B	B-	315.2	7.37	7.4	0.7	26.6	19.4	9.9	10.9	16.6
▼ Portage County Bank	Almond	WI	C+	B-	B-	100.5	0.96	6.0	0.3	13.4	17.6	8.8	10.2	15.6
Post Oak Bank, N.A.	Houston	TX	B+	B+	B+	1140.7	12.67	11.7	1.1	17.0	3.7	8.5	10.4	13.7
Potter State Bank of Potter	Potter	NE	B-	B-	B-	38.6	-1.80	12.2	3.4	1.8	25.0	10.0	12.7	18.8
Powell State Bank	Powell	TX	C	C-	D+	29.1	0.82	13.8	14.6	7.1	26.8	10.0	11.4	20.6
Powell Valley National Bank	Jonesville	VA	A-	A-	A-	265.3	-0.55	4.1	5.0	26.3	23.3	10.0	16.8	26.3
Prairie Bank of Kansas	Stafford	KS	D+	D+	C-	107.5	1.00	4.5	1.4	5.7	37.0	6.5	8.5	15.2
▲ Prairie Community Bank	Marengo	IL	D+	D-	D-	111.1	6.09	11.9	1.8	22.3	10.6	6.8	8.8	14.2
▲ Prairie Mountain Bank	Great Falls	MT	C+	C-	B-	88.5	2.84	10.7	3.8	11.6	0.4	6.9	8.9	14.1
Prairie State Bank & Trust	Springfield	IL	A-	A-	A-	703.1	-0.01	8.1	1.0	19.2	20.7	9.9	10.9	16.2
Prairie Sun Bank	Milan	MN	D+	D	D	32.1	-4.82	4.8	5.1	3.4	26.9	5.8	7.9	11.6
Preferred Bank	Los Angeles	CA	A-	A-	B	3112.2	36.34	21.0	0.0	10.7	6.7	7.7	9.5	14.4
Preferred Bank	Casey	IL	C-	C-	C	51.7	3.69	23.5	4.4	21.8	19.4	8.8	10.2	15.8
Preferred Bank	Rothville	MO	B	B+	B+	107.9	-2.69	3.4	3.7	9.6	57.0	5.9	7.9	19.6
Preferred Bank	Houston	TX	A-	B+	B+	244.1	2.12	4.8	0.3	24.5	15.7	10.0	16.2	26.9
▲ Preferred Community Bank	Fort Myers	FL	A-	B-	C	107.1	14.19	1.0	0.1	39.3	14.0	10.0	11.1	19.5
Premier Bank	Dubuque	IA	B	B-	C+	288.2	8.11	16.1	1.5	15.6	12.4	7.5	9.7	12.9
▼ Premier Bank	Rock Valley	IA	B	B+	B+	365.6	11.58	11.3	2.1	5.0	2.9	9.0	11.7	14.2
Premier Bank	Maplewood	MN	C-	D+	D	676.0	6.74	10.0	0.4	6.0	10.6	7.7	10.4	13.1
▲ Premier Bank	Omaha	NE	B	B-	B	223.7	12.99	17.8	0.3	8.1	7.9	6.2	11.2	11.9
Premier Bank & Trust	North Canton	OH	C+	C+	C+	344.9	9.70	19.8	2.2	20.0	5.8	6.7	9.5	12.3
Premier Bank Minnesota	Hastings	MN	B-	B-	C+	202.4	7.94	12.9	0.2	4.9	10.9	7.2	9.8	12.7
Premier Bank of the South	Cullman	AL	B	B	B	164.6	6.77	10.8	4.6	18.8	16.8	7.7	9.5	24.0
Premier Bank Rochester	Rochester	MN	C+	C+	B-	176.2	14.11	7.2	0.3	7.3	9.0	7.1	9.9	12.6
Premier Bank, Inc.	Huntington	WV	B	B-	C+	1093.7	24.62	6.2	2.0	19.9	17.8	8.9	10.3	15.0
Premier Business Bank	Los Angeles	CA	B	B	C+	484.2	82.49	5.6	0.2	21.1	2.5	7.4	9.3	12.8
Premier Community Bank	Hillsboro	OR	C+	C+	C-	374.3	7.15	22.6	0.5	2.9	5.8	7.7	11.6	13.1
Premier Community Bank	Marion	WI	C+	C+	C+	272.4	-1.71	4.7	1.1	12.0	18.1	8.0	9.7	13.3
Premier Valley Bank	Fresno	CA	C+	C+	C	635.6	-6.90	9.2	0.2	8.0	27.4	9.3	10.6	14.5
PremierBank	Fort Atkinson	WI	B	B	B	303.4	4.26	10.0	1.3	13.8	22.6	10.0	12.2	17.0
Prescott State Bank	Prescott	KS	B-	C+	C+	13.6	-3.44	7.5	3.5	14.1	19.9	10.0	14.1	25.6
Presidential Bank, FSB	Bethesda	MD	C-	C-	D+	594.9	9.01	3.9	0.9	41.1	12.6	8.2	9.8	16.5
Presidio Bank	San Francisco	CA	B-	B-	B-	737.9	20.08	17.3	4.3	1.0	1.3	7.5	9.5	12.9
Primary Bank	Bedford	NH	D	D		71.0	110.04	12.7	0.0	2.4	5.9	10.0	41.4	45.4
▼ Prime Alliance Bank	Woods Cross	UT	C-	B-	B	235.8	26.84	29.2	0.1	1.4	9.4	7.3	11.8	12.7
Prime Bank	Orange	CT	C	C	C	78.9	4.28	21.5	3.3	1.6	46.7	10.0	12.0	26.9
Prime Bank	Edmond	OK	A-	A-	A-	262.6	16.88	18.8	0.6	23.7	0.0	6.7	10.2	12.3
Prime Meridian Bank	Tallahassee	FL	B	B	C	290.1	18.61	16.3	1.6	21.2	11.3	7.0	9.0	12.8
▲ Prime Security Bank	Karlstad	MN	C-	D	D-	63.3	10.55	4.8	0.6	16.0	1.5	7.2	9.1	12.6
Primebank	Le Mars	IA	A-	B	B-	386.8	12.44	11.8	1.3	17.0	13.6	10.0	11.6	15.6
PrimeSouth Bank	Tallassee	AL	B	B	B-	211.7	5.19	6.9	2.5	18.1	15.8	7.9	10.0	13.2
PrimeSouth Bank	Blackshear	GA	B-	C	D	360.4	5.00	5.7	3.2	18.1	15.0	8.9	10.3	16.5
Princeville State Bank	Princeville	IL	C+	C+	C+	73.6	-0.26	9.1	5.2	5.9	41.2	8.0	9.6	16.9
Principal Bank	Des Moines	IA	B+	B+	B	2367.0	7.28	0.0	0.4	23.6	68.3	6.2	8.2	13.9
PrinsBank	Prinsburg	MN	A-	B+	C	127.2	2.26	3.8	0.9	4.1	3.8	10.0	13.9	18.3
Priority Bank	Fayetteville	AR	C	C	B-	81.5	3.42	1.5	0.8	81.3	0.0	6.1	8.1	16.6
▲ PriorityOne Bank	Magee	MS	A-	B-	B-	590.6	0.03	7.5	4.4	18.6	15.5	10.0	11.3	15.9
Private Bank of Buckhead	Atlanta	GA	C+	C-	D+	329.4	25.72	9.8	0.8	18.8	3.1	4.2	8.3	10.6
Private Trust Co., N.A.	Cleveland	OH	U	U	U	19.5	2.62	0.0	0.0	0.0	80.6	10.0	94.4	246.8
PrivateBank and Trust Co.	Chicago	IL	B+	B+	B+	19090.5	13.18	31.7	0.7	3.5	19.0	6.5	10.8	12.1
Produce State Bank	Hollandale	MN	C+	C+	C+	61.9	4.07	12.6	4.6	4.6	8.9	7.4	9.3	17.0
Professional Bank	Coral Gables	FL	C	C	C-	371.6	21.40	9.4	0.2	31.3	8.8	6.8	8.8	12.7
Proficio Bank	Cottonwood Heights	UT	E-	E-	C	80.3	-29.06	12.5	0.0	5.2	14.8	0.5	4.1	7.0
Profile Bank	Rochester	NH	C	C+	C+	210.3	10.92	2.1	1.7	32.3	14.1	10.0	12.2	21.3
▲ Profinium, Inc.	Truman	MN	B-	C+	C	358.3	8.27	9.8	1.4	11.4	16.7	7.0	9.2	12.5

Asset Quality Index	Adjusted Non-Performing Loans as a % of Total Loans	as a % of Capital	Net Charge-Offs Avg Loans	Profitability Index	Net Income ($Mil)	Return on Assets (R.O.A.)	Return on Equity (R.O.E.)	Net Interest Spread	Overhead Efficiency Ratio	Liquidity Index	Liquidity Ratio	Hot Money Ratio	Stability Index
4.1	3.51	15.0	0.18	3.1	0.3	0.46	4.03	3.05	80.2	5.4	42.1	7.7	5.0
8.1	3.42	4.1	0.00	7.1	1.0	1.59	6.34	3.62	50.2	6.4	70.8	7.8	8.6
8.7	0.57	2.4	0.07	5.5	0.5	1.36	7.70	3.68	59.6	3.4	27.4	14.0	8.6
4.7	2.89	12.8	0.05	6.6	0.8	1.55	8.71	4.34	52.8	2.4	13.3	17.1	7.3
4.2	1.84	13.1	0.23	3.8	2.8	0.73	8.54	3.24	69.9	4.0	12.8	8.2	4.8
5.8	0.94	5.7	0.02	4.9	2.1	0.93	8.50	3.52	67.1	4.3	21.8	7.1	6.0
6.2	0.74	4.2	0.02	2.0	0.0	0.06	0.53	3.85	98.4	2.2	39.0	30.5	5.6
6.1	0.77	5.5	0.05	6.1	8.6	1.03	9.84	4.24	57.7	1.8	19.4	22.6	8.5
7.1	0.00	0.0	-0.02	4.1	0.2	0.79	6.32	4.27	73.6	3.1	40.8	19.6	6.5
3.3	3.91	17.6	0.16	4.7	0.2	0.97	8.60	4.51	74.3	2.3	32.4	23.3	5.1
6.6	1.30	4.6	0.16	5.4	2.0	0.98	5.69	4.21	67.0	1.9	21.3	20.8	7.9
4.3	2.28	11.8	0.18	1.6	0.3	0.33	3.52	3.30	87.1	3.9	26.5	10.8	3.7
1.4	6.85	44.4	0.48	4.6	0.9	1.10	12.41	3.63	73.2	2.3	25.5	18.5	4.0
8.2	0.00	0.0	0.02	4.4	0.6	0.91	10.55	4.46	68.5	4.1	29.8	11.0	3.4
6.8	0.31	2.0	0.05	6.3	7.7	1.46	13.44	3.43	63.0	3.8	11.1	9.4	9.0
4.4	1.04	7.6	0.55	3.5	0.2	0.66	8.62	4.34	78.8	4.6	12.9	4.2	3.0
7.3	0.07	0.5	0.16	8.6	26.3	1.26	12.62	3.79	40.3	0.8	14.0	34.8	7.8
2.5	3.04	18.5	0.17	3.2	0.2	0.61	6.02	3.62	76.5	4.6	27.0	6.1	5.4
5.8	2.14	9.5	0.47	4.1	0.9	1.01	11.83	3.22	69.3	6.3	50.4	5.0	6.0
6.4	2.07	7.7	-0.37	5.7	1.6	0.93	5.81	3.91	70.7	3.6	44.8	18.3	7.3
9.4	0.00	0.0	-0.01	6.9	1.1	1.33	11.55	4.00	58.2	1.7	19.2	23.0	5.7
8.4	0.13	1.0	0.00	5.0	2.9	1.37	14.32	3.27	63.7	2.6	12.5	12.5	5.6
3.5	1.24	8.4	0.04	9.8	6.9	2.65	21.89	4.06	31.0	0.7	12.0	38.0	8.7
2.7	1.70	11.6	-0.16	7.8	5.5	1.14	11.06	3.82	54.1	4.3	14.1	6.7	6.2
8.1	0.03	0.2	0.01	4.8	1.2	0.80	6.62	3.93	70.0	3.9	19.7	9.8	7.1
4.8	0.81	6.8	-0.01	3.6	1.4	0.57	5.68	3.09	73.6	1.4	9.9	24.7	4.9
3.8	0.78	5.8	-0.27	6.3	2.3	1.56	15.89	4.04	66.5	3.9	13.2	9.4	5.7
5.6	0.76	4.9	0.18	4.6	1.4	1.09	11.67	4.32	78.6	2.1	12.6	14.5	5.7
3.9	0.73	5.4	-0.11	5.7	1.6	1.28	12.56	4.01	69.7	3.8	22.3	10.5	5.5
4.2	2.18	13.9	0.02	5.6	6.9	0.86	7.04	4.08	65.1	3.3	17.3	13.0	8.4
7.6	0.06	0.5	0.00	7.2	4.6	1.43	15.30	4.02	57.4	1.2	17.7	24.0	6.0
3.5	1.15	7.5	-0.01	5.4	2.8	1.02	8.79	4.41	63.1	2.4	12.3	15.3	6.6
5.9	0.73	4.7	-0.05	3.5	1.2	0.56	5.52	3.75	84.6	4.2	25.5	8.6	6.3
3.4	1.16	6.6	0.00	5.0	5.5	1.08	6.94	4.40	65.5	5.0	37.2	8.4	7.7
4.0	2.70	12.9	0.05	4.4	1.6	0.73	5.00	3.55	69.1	4.5	18.6	5.9	7.5
8.7	0.16	0.7	0.00	2.9	0.1	0.46	3.44	3.36	85.3	1.4	27.7	28.1	5.6
2.3	3.94	28.5	0.35	7.1	5.5	1.27	13.53	3.95	77.8	3.6	14.3	10.8	6.0
7.4	0.20	1.5	0.00	4.3	3.3	0.66	7.06	3.69	68.6	4.3	27.5	9.1	5.4
8.0	0.00	0.0	0.00	0.0	-1.7	-4.58	-8.54	2.39	227.2	2.7	35.0	19.6	1.0
2.3	3.19	21.3	0.81	6.4	2.0	1.21	10.25	4.56	36.5	0.5	13.3	74.4	8.3
5.0	2.95	7.9	-0.08	2.0	0.4	0.68	5.66	2.65	89.2	2.9	51.9	26.9	5.3
7.3	0.00	0.0	0.00	10.0	5.1	2.72	26.66	4.58	39.0	1.2	6.4	18.7	8.0
7.2	0.51	4.1	0.01	4.8	1.8	0.89	9.67	3.84	63.1	4.3	17.5	7.2	5.0
5.6	0.00	0.0	-0.03	4.3	0.5	1.08	12.11	4.58	78.7	3.6	12.6	10.8	3.3
6.1	0.81	5.3	-0.05	8.7	6.7	2.47	20.69	4.03	48.1	1.9	18.3	20.0	6.6
5.8	0.56	3.5	0.26	5.3	1.6	0.99	9.93	3.78	59.3	1.4	18.5	19.6	5.2
4.3	2.05	11.6	0.26	8.4	7.1	2.65	25.05	4.78	59.2	2.4	21.9	17.9	4.8
5.6	1.12	5.0	0.32	3.7	0.4	0.69	6.55	3.60	77.0	2.1	36.2	19.3	5.2
6.9	2.41	8.0	0.10	8.4	24.2	1.41	17.60	2.32	25.3	6.1	77.0	12.9	6.5
5.7	1.44	6.8	-0.16	10.0	4.1	4.32	32.40	4.81	39.1	3.4	27.5	13.8	7.7
2.9	2.67	23.5	0.07	7.7	1.2	1.90	23.25	4.20	74.5	0.9	8.9	22.6	7.3
6.6	0.65	3.9	0.13	7.5	7.8	1.73	16.12	4.11	65.5	2.6	21.1	16.4	8.5
3.4	0.88	8.5	0.07	6.4	3.2	1.42	17.22	5.23	78.0	4.0	10.3	5.9	5.2
6.8	na	0.0	na	10.0	1.6	11.52	12.29	0.66	60.6	4.0	na	0.0	6.0
6.4	0.81	5.5	0.08	7.5	166.6	1.24	11.00	3.38	47.5	1.4	21.6	11.4	8.6
5.6	1.68	8.3	0.10	4.4	0.5	1.06	11.83	2.90	60.9	5.9	51.2	6.2	5.5
8.8	0.08	0.7	0.00	3.0	1.0	0.39	4.37	3.60	77.4	1.4	18.4	27.6	5.0
2.2	1.79	23.4	-0.31	0.0	-3.0	-4.10	-131.90	3.16	173.2	0.4	19.9	98.4	2.2
8.0	1.00	4.9	0.00	2.1	0.4	0.24	2.02	3.15	91.7	4.8	38.2	10.6	6.4
4.1	1.30	9.8	-0.04	4.7	2.1	0.77	7.43	3.54	68.4	3.7	10.6	5.4	5.7

Name	City	State	2015 Rating	2014 Rating	Rating	Total Assets ($Mil)	One Year Asset Growth	Comm-ercial Loans	Cons-umer Loans	Mort-gage Loans	Secur-ities	Capital-ization Index	Lever-age Ratio	Risk-Based Capital Ratio
Progress Bank and Trust	Huntsville	AL	B-	B-	C+	708.6	12.89	13.5	1.8	12.8	10.2	5.3	9.9	11.3
Progressive Bank	Monroe	LA	B	B	B	538.6	0.09	12.1	0.8	15.5	7.7	8.1	10.8	13.4
Progressive Bank, N.A.	Wheeling	WV	C-	C	C+	340.9	-1.68	3.7	0.8	6.9	59.8	8.1	9.7	24.1
Progressive National Bank	Mansfield	LA	C	C	C	43.9	5.97	2.6	3.7	27.4	22.3	6.7	8.7	18.7
Progressive Ozark Bank	Salem	MO	A-	B+	A-	114.9	-0.59	3.5	7.4	53.2	8.5	9.1	10.4	17.9
Progressive Savings Bank	Jamestown	TN	C+	C	C	283.2	11.38	4.6	2.8	29.2	7.9	5.7	9.0	11.6
▼ Progressive-Home Federal S&L Assn.	Pittsburgh	PA	C-	C	C	51.8	-1.88	0.0	0.3	51.4	29.9	10.0	12.4	26.5
ProGrowth Bank	Nicollet	MN	C	C-	C-	122.4	-5.38	6.3	1.3	12.1	33.6	7.5	9.3	15.9
Prospect Federal Savings Bank	Worth	IL	D	D	D	238.4	-0.90	0.0	0.0	13.2	49.2	10.0	13.1	42.2
Prosperity Bank	El Campo	TX	B+	B+	B+	21390.3	-0.76	6.0	0.6	12.4	42.8	6.0	8.0	14.3
Providence Bank	Alpharetta	GA	D-	E+	E	109.7	-2.54	2.1	0.9	4.7	2.4	3.1	7.5	10.0
Providence Bank	Columbia	MO	C	C	C-	929.4	1.72	19.5	0.2	12.3	15.9	10.0	12.8	16.5
Providence Bank	Rocky Mount	NC	B+	A-	B	268.1	9.90	6.9	0.4	12.2	1.5	8.6	10.6	13.8
Providence Bank & Trust	South Holland	IL	B-	B-	B	521.4	4.99	15.8	0.1	7.9	16.9	7.8	10.4	13.2
Providence Bank of Texas	Southlake	TX	B-	C+	C-	126.0	8.94	4.1	0.7	19.0	0.0	10.0	13.5	17.4
Provident Bank	Amesbury	MA	B	B-	B-	768.4	9.86	17.7	0.2	12.4	15.1	10.0	13.2	17.2
Provident Bank	Iselin	NJ	B-	B-	C+	9389.7	5.99	7.3	0.4	16.2	16.3	5.8	8.4	11.6
Provident Savings Bank, F.S.B.	Riverside	CA	C	C	C	1242.4	5.54	0.1	0.0	46.5	3.8	7.5	9.3	15.6
Provident State Bank, Inc.	Preston	MD	C+	C+	C+	362.4	16.67	5.1	1.3	26.2	11.8	6.6	9.0	12.2
Prudential Bank & Trust, FSB	Hartford	CT	U	U	U	19.9	12.19	0.0	0.0	0.0	91.4	10.0	88.5	185.6
Prudential Savings Bank	Philadelphia	PA	B-	B-	C+	558.7	14.75	0.0	0.1	40.8	32.1	10.0	18.2	35.5
PS Bank	Wyalusing	PA	B	B	B-	328.1	10.50	6.9	0.9	22.5	28.4	6.7	8.7	14.2
Pueblo Bank and Trust Co.	Pueblo	CO	B+	B-	C	382.1	8.86	4.1	0.3	6.0	33.7	10.0	11.2	18.6
Puget Sound Bank	Bellevue	WA	B+	B+	B	525.4	15.15	29.0	0.8	2.1	13.7	8.5	10.8	13.8
Pulaski Savings Bank	Chicago	IL	D-	D	D	43.3	1.71	0.0	1.1	47.2	16.2	9.6	10.7	27.2
Putnam 1st Mercantile Bank	Cookeville	TN	B+	B	B	117.6	-0.02	18.6	4.0	21.2	13.9	10.0	12.1	17.7
▲ Putnam Bank	Putnam	CT	C	D+	C	495.8	6.06	1.8	0.1	38.6	39.2	10.0	12.2	21.7
Putnam County Bank	Hurricane	WV	B+	A-	B+	657.9	1.84	7.5	1.3	34.1	17.5	10.0	14.0	23.4
Putnam County National Bank of Carmel	Carmel	NY	C-	D	D	170.1	5.74	2.3	0.2	19.5	10.1	10.0	19.9	49.6
▲ Putnam County State Bank	Unionville	MO	A-	B+	B+	189.2	8.81	11.5	3.3	8.0	3.9	10.0	12.1	15.0
PyraMax Bank, FSB	Greenfield	WI	C-	D+	D+	438.8	4.32	3.1	0.3	27.6	18.7	6.7	8.7	12.6
QNB Bank	Quakertown	PA	B-	B-	C+	1063.6	3.05	11.1	0.5	12.5	33.9	6.4	8.4	12.4
Quad City Bank and Trust Co.	Bettendorf	IA	B	B-	B-	1432.1	6.00	15.1	0.6	8.0	17.2	5.9	8.9	11.7
Quail Creek Bank, N.A.	Oklahoma City	OK	B-	B-	C+	596.8	5.85	6.1	1.2	16.4	15.9	8.6	10.0	14.0
Quaint Oak Bank	Southampton	PA	B-	B-	B	208.1	20.11	2.8	0.0	31.2	4.8	6.9	8.9	14.2
Quality Bank	Page	ND	D+	D	D+	30.4	5.09	7.6	3.3	1.7	5.8	5.4	9.1	11.3
▲ Quantum National Bank	Suwanee	GA	A-	B-	D+	391.2	7.02	15.6	0.1	8.0	1.1	9.4	11.2	14.5
Quarry City S&L Assn.	Warrensburg	MO	B-	B-	B-	51.5	0.52	0.6	1.6	41.2	0.0	10.0	16.4	26.8
▼ Queensborough National Bank & Trust Co.	Louisville	GA	C-	C-	D+	943.5	17.69	4.5	1.4	13.1	18.8	8.1	9.7	14.7
▲ Queenstown Bank of Maryland	Queenstown	MD	B+	B	C-	469.5	3.97	3.1	1.6	37.4	1.9	10.0	11.9	17.3
▲ Quoin Financial Bank	Miller	SD	A-	B	B-	146.5	-0.53	8.3	2.8	2.5	19.8	10.0	11.9	16.2
Quontic Bank	Astoria	NY	B+	B+	B	226.8	37.66	0.3	0.1	70.3	0.9	7.9	9.6	19.1
R Bank	Round Rock	TX	C+	C+	C+	410.7	25.75	11.3	0.6	14.5	18.9	6.8	8.8	12.4
▲ Rabobank, N.A.	Roseville	CA	C	D-	C-	14159.0	-4.71	3.3	0.1	10.1	21.3	10.0	11.0	15.6
Rabun County Bank	Clayton	GA	C-	C-	D+	163.2	2.44	1.3	3.5	30.2	3.0	9.8	10.8	19.9
Raccoon Valley Bank	Perry	IA	B-	B-	C+	241.9	3.69	12.3	1.5	10.7	24.3	5.9	7.9	12.0
▲ Radius Bank	Boston	MA	C-	C	C-	850.1	8.83	9.1	22.1	23.3	8.2	5.4	8.5	11.3
Ramsey National Bank	Devils Lake	ND	A	A	A-	260.3	-0.61	13.1	0.7	7.9	21.3	10.0	12.1	17.6
Rancho Santa Fe Thrift & Loan Assn.	San Marcos	CA	B+	B+	A-	66.8	29.28	0.0	79.6	5.7	0.0	10.0	43.2	48.2
Randall State Bank	Randall	MN	B	B	B	39.1	4.84	6.1	1.9	22.4	10.5	10.0	12.5	17.0
▲ Randolph Savings Bank	Stoughton	MA	C	D-	D+	489.9	26.95	0.4	0.6	45.5	14.5	10.0	14.5	26.0
Range Bank, N.A.	Marquette	MI	B-	B-	B-	369.3	9.73	10.0	0.9	10.6	30.0	7.4	9.3	14.2
Raritan State Bank	Raritan	IL	B-	C	B-	161.2	2.14	10.8	5.7	25.1	16.4	10.0	11.4	16.5
▲ Rawlins National Bank	Rawlins	WY	C	D+	D	177.1	0.12	6.2	1.5	4.1	27.0	6.9	8.9	17.5
Raymond Federal Bank	Raymond	WA	C-	C-	C-	60.2	9.03	0.0	0.6	67.3	12.8	8.6	10.1	24.5
Raymond James Bank, N.A.	Saint Petersburg	FL	A-	A-	B	17012.7	16.01	43.6	9.7	14.3	4.3	8.4	9.9	14.0
Raymond James Trust, N.A.	Saint Petersburg	FL	U	U	U	25.0	2.50	0.0	0.0	0.0	4.6	10.0	89.5	139.1
Rayne Building and Loan Assn.	Rayne	LA	B+	B+	A-	63.6	-2.95	0.9	1.1	20.4	56.9	10.0	21.6	71.3
Rayne State Bank & Trust Co.	Rayne	LA	A-	A-	A-	361.7	-3.55	8.3	0.5	19.1	20.8	10.0	11.0	17.5
RBC Bank (Georgia), N.A.	Raleigh	NC	C+	C+	C-	3673.4	22.26	0.0	2.4	18.7	66.3	5.5	7.5	30.0

Asset Quality Index	Adjusted Non-Performing Loans as a % of Total Loans	as a % of Capital	Net Charge-Offs Avg Loans	Profitability Index	Net Income ($Mil)	Return on Assets (R.O.A.)	Return on Equity (R.O.E.)	Net Interest Spread	Overhead Efficiency Ratio	Liquidity Index	Liquidity Ratio	Hot Money Ratio	Stability Index
8.5	0.02	0.2	0.05	4.0	4.0	0.81	8.11	3.38	71.0	1.7	13.2	21.6	6.0
8.3	0.21	1.4	0.04	4.4	2.8	0.70	6.50	4.04	77.0	3.2	14.2	12.9	7.6
5.5	2.76	7.9	0.01	2.2	1.4	0.55	5.09	2.72	92.4	6.0	51.2	7.2	6.6
9.4	0.11	0.6	0.02	3.3	0.2	0.50	5.76	3.49	82.9	1.9	30.1	26.3	4.2
6.5	0.29	2.1	0.26	7.5	1.5	1.69	16.01	4.43	68.2	4.5	7.0	4.0	8.1
5.2	1.27	9.7	0.00	3.4	1.3	0.65	7.13	4.03	86.9	1.3	11.9	26.7	5.0
7.2	1.71	8.0	0.00	1.4	0.0	0.11	0.76	2.81	100.8	3.3	43.2	19.1	7.1
5.5	1.15	6.7	0.00	3.2	0.3	0.32	3.50	3.55	83.1	5.0	26.3	4.0	3.0
7.5	4.05	6.5	0.01	0.2	-0.7	-0.38	-2.92	1.72	126.3	4.3	85.3	24.3	5.5
6.5	0.46	2.6	0.25	7.8	210.7	1.28	8.20	3.36	40.6	4.5	23.3	8.6	10.0
2.5	3.59	26.6	-0.03	2.9	0.2	0.29	2.81	3.82	85.1	0.8	15.7	34.6	1.7
5.2	1.31	7.1	0.04	2.7	3.8	0.55	3.72	3.42	85.6	1.6	8.4	20.1	6.4
5.8	0.45	3.2	0.03	5.6	1.8	0.91	8.61	3.67	60.1	0.8	16.1	28.0	7.0
4.5	0.71	4.5	-0.07	6.3	4.0	1.06	10.02	4.40	66.0	3.6	21.2	11.4	6.7
4.2	2.05	10.1	0.01	3.5	0.4	0.45	3.31	4.00	82.6	1.1	26.4	39.3	7.6
7.6	0.50	2.8	0.00	4.7	4.6	0.82	6.08	3.71	69.2	3.3	11.2	4.8	8.1
3.9	0.72	6.1	0.09	5.0	64.7	0.95	7.50	3.16	58.7	4.5	8.5	4.5	9.4
2.7	2.73	25.3	-0.19	4.6	6.0	0.68	6.81	3.06	83.4	2.4	3.6	15.7	7.6
4.6	1.29	10.9	0.22	3.2	1.0	0.41	4.98	3.83	75.7	2.9	13.2	14.3	3.9
8.4	na	0.0	na	10.0	2.4	18.03	20.45	1.78	27.9	4.0	na	100.0	7.0
4.9	4.77	16.0	-0.05	3.2	2.4	0.59	3.24	2.71	71.3	2.3	42.2	31.8	7.2
6.2	0.59	4.0	0.12	5.2	2.3	0.95	10.72	3.72	67.2	3.4	32.9	15.6	5.0
6.2	1.22	5.0	-0.41	5.5	3.5	1.29	11.41	3.50	74.4	6.0	40.6	3.4	5.5
7.9	0.25	1.6	0.26	5.2	3.1	0.85	7.52	3.70	59.2	4.3	19.4	7.0	6.7
6.3	1.97	9.1	0.00	0.0	-0.2	-0.59	-5.51	2.54	120.9	4.4	52.3	15.0	3.2
7.1	0.77	4.3	0.14	5.3	0.7	0.80	6.91	3.83	58.9	0.9	18.8	30.9	6.8
6.3	1.69	7.0	0.08	2.1	0.9	0.24	1.86	2.34	84.1	3.0	22.3	14.9	5.4
3.2	5.60	25.7	0.16	4.6	3.3	0.69	5.12	3.13	40.8	0.8	22.3	47.3	8.3
2.6	10.17	24.0	-0.01	1.3	0.4	0.35	1.56	2.64	86.6	5.9	51.7	7.8	5.4
5.8	0.64	4.2	0.09	9.3	2.0	1.43	12.28	3.89	35.2	0.5	7.8	50.4	8.4
4.7	1.19	9.0	0.06	1.9	1.3	0.42	4.68	2.87	89.9	1.9	26.9	13.0	3.9
5.5	1.43	9.1	0.02	4.2	6.4	0.84	9.73	3.03	66.1	4.2	22.5	10.4	7.2
6.3	0.84	6.1	0.31	4.7	11.3	1.08	11.54	3.61	66.9	4.4	23.8	8.5	6.5
4.0	0.83	6.0	0.03	9.2	9.7	2.19	21.24	4.39	49.8	3.4	20.9	12.6	8.8
5.1	1.13	9.7	0.00	4.7	1.1	0.75	7.98	3.47	71.4	0.8	17.8	38.6	5.3
3.6	1.63	13.7	-0.09	4.4	0.2	1.00	11.12	3.26	70.8	1.1	10.6	28.7	3.0
7.2	0.12	0.8	-0.02	9.7	6.0	2.12	19.46	4.79	42.6	2.3	12.1	17.1	6.3
8.4	0.13	0.6	0.05	3.4	0.2	0.39	2.45	3.51	84.3	2.6	24.2	17.0	7.1
1.9	3.74	23.6	0.14	4.4	5.4	0.78	7.72	4.03	77.1	2.6	21.8	15.5	5.7
5.0	1.75	11.0	0.25	6.8	3.9	1.13	9.62	4.05	50.3	1.3	15.6	27.3	6.0
6.3	0.90	4.8	0.01	6.8	1.4	1.24	10.70	4.42	58.4	2.2	18.7	18.5	6.4
8.3	0.18	1.7	-0.24	5.8	1.9	1.27	11.43	4.76	86.1	0.5	9.3	65.3	6.3
5.9	0.53	3.9	0.12	3.1	1.3	0.44	4.20	3.70	84.0	1.9	23.5	20.8	5.3
4.8	1.51	8.8	-0.11	2.7	55.0	0.51	4.10	2.75	72.8	4.3	16.1	5.7	7.6
2.3	4.81	23.9	0.07	3.3	0.8	0.71	6.57	3.40	81.0	5.2	35.8	6.5	4.5
6.4	0.36	2.8	0.03	4.5	1.8	0.99	12.58	3.36	67.3	2.4	14.8	17.0	5.4
3.2	1.09	10.7	0.00	2.6	1.2	0.45	5.50	3.70	76.6	2.8	6.8	8.6	4.5
8.2	0.01	0.1	0.36	6.5	2.9	1.46	12.02	3.64	58.0	4.0	9.1	7.7	9.1
5.5	0.09	0.2	0.14	7.3	0.9	1.85	4.34	5.36	56.4	0.5	24.0	100.0	9.0
4.4	2.55	15.4	0.01	8.8	0.6	2.01	16.11	5.06	60.3	2.9	20.7	15.1	8.8
5.9	1.34	6.6	0.02	3.3	3.3	1.04	11.06	3.06	84.5	3.5	23.8	12.3	4.5
4.9	1.29	7.6	0.31	3.8	1.7	0.68	6.74	3.69	77.9	5.1	45.4	10.5	5.5
4.2	1.86	12.3	0.12	7.1	1.4	1.19	10.62	3.91	50.9	2.6	14.7	16.1	6.2
6.4	0.84	3.9	-0.11	2.8	0.7	0.53	5.78	3.54	85.6	3.9	32.7	13.1	4.5
7.9	0.40	2.7	0.00	2.2	0.1	0.27	2.64	3.48	84.3	1.9	29.2	26.3	4.6
6.0	0.57	4.7	0.02	8.4	181.1	1.48	15.05	3.12	25.9	4.9	9.0	1.4	9.1
10.0	0.00	0.0	0.00	10.0	2.3	15.50	18.44	0.44	86.4	4.0	190.9	0.0	7.0
9.8	1.41	1.8	0.06	4.2	0.4	0.85	3.73	3.17	66.5	3.2	86.9	58.2	8.0
5.6	2.93	17.4	0.96	5.2	3.1	1.14	10.21	4.19	57.4	4.6	26.0	6.3	8.3
9.8	0.56	1.7	0.11	3.8	17.6	0.66	8.99	1.75	61.6	8.1	82.1	1.7	5.2

Name	City	State	2015 Rating	2014 Rating	Rating	Total Assets ($Mil)	One Year Asset Growth	Asset Mix (As a % of Total Assets)				Capital-ization Index	Lever-age Ratio	Risk-Based Capital Ratio
								Comm-ercial Loans	Cons-umer Loans	Mort-gage Loans	Secur-ities			
RCB Bank	Claremore	OK	B	B+	B+	2859.5	16.54	4.8	5.3	8.6	28.3	5.7	7.7	12.2
▼ RCSBank	New London	MO	D	C-	C-	58.5	1.97	16.4	1.4	8.9	13.4	8.5	10.2	13.7
Reading Cooperative Bank	Reading	MA	B-	B-	C+	504.1	2.02	4.5	0.4	45.4	11.5	6.7	8.7	14.4
Readlyn Savings Bank	Readlyn	IA	A-	A-	A	71.4	-0.97	8.1	1.2	14.7	29.3	10.0	13.3	17.5
ReconTrust Co., N.A.	Simi Valley	CA	U	U	U	358.7	0.06	0.0	0.0	0.0	0.0	10.0	99.6	458.4
Red River Bank	Alexandria	LA	B	B+	B+	1649.0	12.22	13.1	1.8	19.6	18.9	8.2	9.8	14.0
Red River State Bank	Halstad	MN	B	B	B	75.2	78.84	28.5	14.0	5.0	8.5	10.0	11.1	19.8
Red Rock Bank	Sanborn	MN	B	B	C	23.3	19.10	8.3	5.0	18.0	0.0	10.0	12.0	15.2
Redding Bank of Commerce	Redding	CA	C+	C+	C	1111.7	12.20	12.0	4.7	6.2	17.1	8.6	11.0	13.9
Redstone Bank	Centennial	CO	A-	A-	B+	104.5	12.51	11.7	0.3	19.5	1.7	10.0	11.5	16.3
Redwood Capital Bank	Eureka	CA	B	B	B	334.9	3.93	5.4	0.8	7.5	8.3	6.1	8.1	11.9
Reelfoot Bank	Union City	TN	C+	C+	C+	158.8	6.62	10.5	5.5	15.7	25.5	9.8	10.9	18.6
Regal Bank	Livingston	NJ	C+	C+	C+	474.6	23.43	1.6	0.1	4.6	8.8	7.8	9.5	15.5
Regent Bank	Tulsa	OK	C	C+	C-	321.9	38.86	18.6	1.3	14.5	3.0	3.2	8.6	10.1
Regional Missouri Bank	Marceline	MO	B	B	C+	205.1	7.84	6.9	2.1	19.7	12.5	6.9	9.5	12.4
Regions Bank	Birmingham	AL	C+	C+	C	124196.2	0.27	18.2	5.7	13.7	20.4	8.7	10.3	13.9
Reliabank Dakota	Estelline	SD	B	B+	B+	323.7	10.01	11.8	2.5	4.7	17.8	5.7	9.5	11.5
Reliance Bank	Athens	AL	B-	B	B-	210.1	27.25	7.6	0.2	10.7	24.7	7.9	9.6	13.5
Reliance Bank	Faribault	MN	B-	B	B-	116.2	23.79	24.0	1.7	11.0	12.2	5.6	10.2	11.4
Reliance Bank	Frontenac	MO	B-	C+	C+	1264.8	8.31	5.8	0.1	4.8	23.9	8.1	11.0	13.4
Reliance Savings Bank	Altoona	PA	B-	C+	C+	434.8	3.72	3.1	2.1	30.8	14.6	10.0	11.4	15.4
Reliance State Bank	Story City	IA	A-	A-	A-	217.3	0.67	4.5	1.0	8.7	31.9	9.5	11.4	14.6
Reliant Bank	Brentwood	TN	B+	B+	B+	919.9	7.73	12.6	1.9	13.7	16.5	9.0	10.9	14.2
Relyance Bank, N.A.	Pine Bluff	AR	B+	B+	A-	702.8	22.77	6.1	1.6	9.0	10.7	9.8	11.9	14.8
Renasant Bank	Tupelo	MS	B	B-	B-	8520.3	7.82	7.9	1.3	18.2	12.4	6.3	9.1	12.0
▲ Republic Bank	Bountiful	UT	C	C+	B+	83.5	-45.36	18.0	0.0	0.0	0.0	10.0	24.9	29.2
Republic Bank & Trust	Norman	OK	C	B-	B+	512.8	4.52	15.3	1.7	14.4	19.3	6.6	9.9	12.2
Republic Bank & Trust Co.	Louisville	KY	A-	B+	A-	4819.4	19.52	4.1	1.9	27.9	10.8	8.8	11.5	14.0
Republic Bank of Chicago	Oak Brook	IL	C+	C	C-	1753.7	5.42	17.4	0.1	9.6	13.0	9.6	11.9	14.7
Republic Bank, Inc.	Duluth	MN	C+	C+	C	368.7	7.92	19.5	1.1	14.9	1.6	7.6	10.6	13.0
Republic Banking Co.	Republic	OH	B-	B-	B-	45.0	1.38	4.2	6.8	42.1	7.1	10.0	14.8	33.2
Republic First Bank	Philadelphia	PA	C-	D+	C-	1728.8	25.66	7.7	0.1	5.7	30.2	5.7	7.8	11.5
RepublicBankAz, N.A.	Phoenix	AZ	B	B-	C	90.0	0.66	6.5	0.9	7.0	23.2	10.0	15.0	24.1
Resolute Bank	Maumee	OH	D-	D+	D-	38.0	-1.90	20.2	2.2	20.3	0.0	7.5	9.4	18.8
Resource Bank	Covington	LA	B-	B	B	605.3	2.05	5.7	1.5	19.4	5.7	8.6	11.7	13.8
Resource Bank, N.A.	DeKalb	IL	C-	C-	C-	428.3	6.98	5.0	0.7	14.3	32.2	7.4	9.3	14.6
Resurgens Bank	Tucker	GA	A-	A-	B+	158.2	16.47	11.2	0.3	14.4	3.2	9.5	11.8	14.6
Revere Bank	Laurel	MD	B-	B	C+	1327.3	66.99	10.8	0.1	14.8	5.9	5.8	7.8	12.5
Reynolds State Bank	Reynolds	IL	A+	A+	A+	105.5	2.48	2.7	0.2	0.2	81.2	10.0	22.8	59.9
Rhinebeck Bank	Poughkeepsie	NY	C-	D+	D	721.6	6.79	7.4	26.6	8.0	22.1	5.9	8.0	11.6
Richland County Bank	Richland Center	WI	B-	B-	B	101.3	4.56	3.0	4.4	11.4	42.5	10.0	17.5	35.4
Richland State Bank	Rayville	LA	B+	B+	A-	298.6	-2.56	16.0	1.9	12.5	24.4	9.2	10.5	14.7
Richland State Bank	Bruce	SD	A-	A-	A-	46.1	2.34	2.7	6.5	2.2	42.8	10.0	26.3	54.8
Richton Bank & Trust Co.	Richton	MS	B-	B	B-	61.4	2.28	7.0	3.4	13.2	32.4	10.0	14.4	25.8
Richwood Banking Co.	Richwood	OH	B	B-	B-	475.3	1.67	4.3	0.8	11.0	38.8	8.0	9.6	15.2
Riddell National Bank	Brazil	IN	C	C-	D+	197.1	1.84	10.8	6.1	36.5	12.5	7.4	9.3	12.8
Ridgewood Savings Bank	Ridgewood	NY	C	C	C	5300.6	3.65	0.0	0.1	34.4	33.0	10.0	11.8	21.7
Riley State Bank of Riley, Kansas	Riley	KS	B	B	B	85.8	4.27	11.7	5.1	6.6	27.6	8.4	9.9	15.2
Rio Bank	McAllen	TX	B	B-	B-	287.5	6.02	18.1	1.2	5.6	21.7	6.9	8.9	13.2
Rio Grande S&L Assn.	Monte Vista	CO	C+	C+	C+	99.8	4.19	1.4	2.8	59.7	14.1	10.0	11.5	22.7
▼ Ripley Federal Savings Bank	Ripley	OH	D-	D	D+	67.7	2.10	0.4	1.0	47.0	0.8	8.6	10.1	15.3
River Bank	La Crosse	WI	B+	B+	B	455.0	3.77	6.7	0.5	12.1	9.1	10.0	12.3	15.4
River Bank & Trust	Prattville	AL	B	B	B-	766.5	66.18	10.3	2.7	15.7	22.4	8.6	10.0	14.0
River Cities Bank	Wisconsin Rapids	WI	A-	A-	A-	227.1	1.30	14.1	0.2	10.9	15.4	10.0	13.7	20.2
River City Bank	Sacramento	CA	B+	A-	A-	1671.8	17.59	5.5	0.0	7.7	27.0	8.6	10.1	14.3
River City Bank	Rome	GA	C-	C	C-	147.9	-3.77	10.3	1.8	13.1	18.3	6.4	8.5	12.1
River City Bank, Inc.	Louisville	KY	A	A	A-	256.8	-7.02	1.3	0.6	36.6	33.9	10.0	14.6	27.2
River Community Bank, N.A.	Martinsville	VA	B-	C+	C+	115.7	1.52	18.3	0.8	27.2	4.4	8.3	9.9	13.5
River Falls State Bank	River Falls	WI	B-	B-	B-	84.9	0.35	1.7	2.5	30.8	20.8	10.0	15.6	30.3
River Town Bank	Dardanelle	AR	C	C-	D+	140.7	-2.92	4.1	2.3	29.1	20.8	10.0	11.5	19.9

Asset Quality Index	Adjusted Non-Performing Loans as a % of Total Loans	as a % of Capital	Net Charge-Offs Avg Loans	Profitability Index	Net Income ($Mil)	Return on Assets (R.O.A.)	Return on Equity (R.O.E.)	Net Interest Spread	Overhead Efficiency Ratio	Liquidity Index	Liquidity Ratio	Hot Money Ratio	Stability Index
7.1	0.64	4.4	0.04	4.7	22.4	1.14	11.40	3.35	68.7	4.0	20.3	10.2	8.5
5.8	0.48	3.0	0.03	0.6	-0.9	-2.06	-22.12	3.73	99.8	4.8	10.0	2.9	4.6
8.0	0.16	1.4	-0.01	3.6	2.0	0.55	6.39	3.58	78.6	2.3	14.8	11.9	4.9
8.6	0.16	0.8	0.00	7.1	0.9	1.69	12.46	3.62	45.4	2.8	36.0	19.7	9.0
10.0	na	0.0	na	1.1	-0.3	-0.12	-0.12	0.07	101.3	4.0	na	0.0	7.0
7.6	0.37	2.5	0.06	4.8	11.4	0.98	9.91	3.36	64.9	3.1	21.2	15.3	8.1
4.6	1.33	7.9	0.08	8.0	1.1	1.93	17.72	4.50	56.9	2.4	31.0	20.2	7.8
3.7	3.83	26.5	0.04	4.2	0.2	0.95	7.81	3.70	67.5	2.9	14.3	14.4	5.3
4.6	1.75	10.4	-0.12	3.6	4.5	0.56	4.94	3.89	81.4	2.8	23.3	17.3	8.5
8.3	0.47	2.9	-0.01	6.3	0.7	0.93	8.04	5.47	61.9	1.2	19.9	30.0	7.4
5.8	0.31	2.5	-0.04	5.8	2.4	0.97	12.03	3.99	59.8	4.3	21.7	7.5	5.1
4.2	2.80	11.9	-0.21	3.9	0.7	0.58	5.42	3.88	79.0	4.9	46.6	12.4	5.8
4.3	1.45	11.4	0.00	3.0	1.2	0.36	3.82	3.47	82.0	1.0	16.1	28.0	5.7
4.2	0.98	9.2	0.17	4.5	1.6	0.76	7.43	4.46	67.6	0.6	7.8	38.5	4.8
5.1	0.68	5.3	0.01	7.7	2.8	1.83	18.49	4.20	53.0	1.5	5.8	21.6	7.6
3.6	2.11	12.7	0.32	5.3	950.4	1.02	7.66	3.18	61.4	4.7	17.6	3.0	9.5
6.7	0.52	3.7	0.12	8.1	4.3	1.88	19.19	4.25	60.3	3.4	15.4	12.1	6.4
7.5	0.35	2.1	0.10	3.5	0.8	0.56	5.26	3.39	81.9	3.4	28.3	14.0	5.7
7.3	0.08	0.6	-0.26	6.9	1.3	1.62	15.75	4.09	60.0	2.9	23.8	13.7	5.4
7.7	0.00	0.0	-0.07	4.2	7.8	0.84	6.63	2.84	63.0	1.8	16.6	21.4	7.8
8.1	0.49	3.1	0.03	3.5	2.1	0.64	5.46	3.28	76.4	2.2	9.2	14.9	6.7
7.8	0.11	0.6	0.00	6.9	2.1	1.28	9.45	3.70	46.6	4.8	30.1	6.8	8.4
4.7	1.08	7.0	-0.04	5.3	7.6	1.07	9.13	4.09	69.6	1.1	18.6	22.3	6.8
5.8	0.40	2.5	-0.02	5.4	4.2	0.89	7.07	4.12	69.5	1.4	8.6	17.0	7.7
4.6	0.71	5.8	0.05	6.3	69.8	1.12	8.05	4.25	66.6	3.1	7.8	12.8	9.2
2.3	9.60	22.1	2.70	2.8	-0.4	-0.41	-1.83	3.00	110.0	0.5	10.2	11.6	8.1
2.5	3.25	21.9	0.01	7.4	6.2	1.66	15.50	4.66	68.0	3.2	26.7	14.7	7.3
6.1	0.86	6.1	0.25	6.1	36.0	1.08	9.36	3.66	60.7	4.7	14.4	3.8	9.9
4.0	2.73	15.2	-0.10	6.9	19.5	1.51	13.09	3.85	61.3	1.7	21.5	25.9	9.4
4.0	0.77	6.0	0.06	5.9	3.7	1.38	12.89	4.10	65.3	1.1	12.4	18.5	7.1
4.8	2.59	14.0	0.18	6.7	0.5	1.32	9.32	3.96	55.7	1.8	16.8	20.3	6.4
4.6	2.32	16.4	0.12	2.3	4.3	0.37	4.36	3.36	87.6	4.7	17.2	4.6	4.2
5.4	1.19	4.7	0.26	5.1	0.6	0.87	5.88	4.44	82.7	1.7	36.1	38.2	8.2
4.2	1.51	9.6	-0.40	0.4	-0.2	-0.65	-8.11	3.09	103.0	2.2	28.8	20.9	3.2
4.2	1.11	7.7	0.00	6.4	4.7	1.07	9.47	4.63	65.9	4.1	10.0	7.5	7.8
2.4	3.80	22.7	-0.01	3.5	2.0	0.65	6.50	3.85	85.5	4.2	28.5	10.1	5.7
7.5	0.12	0.8	0.00	6.5	1.8	1.58	13.52	4.25	66.2	1.0	14.9	28.3	8.4
7.5	0.13	1.3	0.02	5.0	6.2	0.73	8.76	3.76	58.9	0.7	11.9	35.2	6.6
10.0	1.51	0.7	0.20	7.6	1.3	1.70	6.96	3.34	29.3	5.8	106.8	16.6	10.0
2.9	1.39	11.1	0.11	3.0	2.1	0.41	5.05	3.58	81.8	3.6	25.6	12.0	4.2
8.9	0.55	1.3	0.00	3.3	0.5	0.69	3.91	2.98	76.9	6.2	61.3	8.9	7.7
8.0	0.39	2.3	0.58	4.9	2.5	1.15	10.88	4.49	69.0	2.8	20.2	15.4	7.5
8.7	0.04	0.1	0.03	8.4	0.7	2.19	8.31	3.04	52.0	4.2	83.4	21.9	8.0
9.1	0.02	0.1	0.25	3.0	0.2	0.45	2.94	3.50	88.8	5.7	50.1	7.9	7.7
8.3	0.41	2.1	0.22	4.3	3.0	0.86	8.43	3.72	74.3	2.8	15.9	15.0	5.7
3.2	1.99	15.8	0.19	4.3	1.1	0.75	8.88	3.87	68.8	2.7	15.2	15.7	4.6
6.9	0.94	4.7	-0.02	2.1	13.4	0.34	2.62	2.14	86.9	4.2	40.3	16.7	8.6
8.1	0.00	0.0	0.09	4.8	0.8	1.21	12.26	3.51	64.5	2.0	14.5	18.8	6.5
4.9	0.91	6.1	0.28	6.0	2.3	1.08	12.05	5.09	71.3	3.9	29.5	11.9	5.7
6.8	1.42	8.4	0.03	2.9	0.2	0.29	2.55	4.25	89.3	1.8	25.4	24.0	5.6
1.7	5.06	35.2	1.23	0.0	-0.6	-1.26	-12.45	3.26	104.0	1.6	12.2	21.7	4.7
5.2	0.88	5.8	0.01	7.7	6.1	1.82	14.13	3.56	44.1	1.3	9.5	26.4	8.6
5.1	0.77	4.9	0.05	5.9	6.1	1.11	9.57	4.27	60.6	3.4	24.4	12.9	6.0
7.0	0.86	3.9	0.05	7.0	2.2	1.29	9.31	3.84	49.1	4.4	21.4	6.0	8.4
7.7	0.17	1.0	-0.04	5.4	10.2	0.86	8.30	3.01	53.8	3.3	6.2	11.9	9.4
4.5	1.67	12.7	0.41	2.1	0.3	0.30	2.83	3.69	84.8	3.0	18.5	14.5	4.7
8.7	0.81	3.0	0.45	8.0	2.9	1.42	9.95	4.08	69.2	5.9	44.2	5.3	8.0
4.5	0.76	6.1	1.35	6.1	0.8	0.94	9.50	4.96	83.4	0.7	7.7	33.7	6.0
9.2	0.51	1.8	-0.03	3.4	0.5	0.77	5.01	3.04	77.3	5.7	41.9	6.0	7.8
4.8	2.99	15.9	0.38	2.5	0.3	0.25	2.06	3.93	88.0	3.7	26.7	12.2	5.2

Name	City	State	Rating	2015 Rating	2014 Rating	Total Assets ($Mil)	One Year Asset Growth	Asset Mix (As a % of Total Assets) Commercial Loans	Consumer Loans	Mortgage Loans	Securities	Capitalization Index	Leverage Ratio	Risk-Based Capital Ratio
River Valley Bank	Wausau	WI	B-	B-	C+	1133.4	8.09	16.1	1.9	12.4	12.4	6.1	8.8	11.8
▲ River Valley Community Bank	Yuba City	CA	B-	B-	B-	278.2	27.82	5.3	0.3	2.6	38.9	8.2	9.8	16.5
RiverBank	Pocahontas	AR	B-	B-	C+	78.6	44.32	10.3	1.0	10.8	2.9	7.7	9.5	14.3
▲ RiverBank	Spokane	WA	D+	D	D-	127.2	2.56	8.4	1.2	9.5	0.2	8.5	10.0	14.0
▲ RiverBend Bank	Fort Worth	TX	B	B+	B+	54.5	7.72	14.9	1.5	5.5	4.1	9.2	10.5	15.6
RiverHills Bank	Port Gibson	MS	B	B-	B-	323.0	12.05	7.4	1.8	12.8	23.2	7.5	9.3	16.5
▲ RiverHills Bank	Milford	OH	C	D	D	138.4	6.93	8.8	0.3	11.0	12.3	7.6	10.4	13.0
▲ Riverland Bank	Jordan	MN	C+	D+	D	104.4	37.85	13.4	0.8	20.1	2.9	10.0	14.0	17.6
Riverside Bank	Sparkman	AR	B	B	B	61.1	-0.43	16.5	7.1	55.5	1.7	6.6	8.6	12.5
▲ Riverview Bank	Marysville	PA	C	D	C+	526.9	16.61	6.4	0.8	24.8	13.7	5.1	7.7	11.1
▼ Riverview Community Bank	Vancouver	WA	C+	C+	D+	982.4	9.91	4.0	3.2	9.4	15.5	9.9	11.0	16.1
Riverwind Bank	Augusta	AR	B-	B-	B	91.9	-0.16	11.6	3.0	14.5	26.4	9.0	10.3	16.4
RiverWood Bank	Bemidji	MN	C+	C+	C	346.3	5.25	6.7	5.6	19.1	7.5	7.2	9.2	12.7
Roanoke Rapids Savings Bank, SSB	Roanoke Rapids	NC	C	B-	C	50.7	-4.29	1.3	2.8	29.2	10.7	10.0	17.3	32.2
Roanoke Valley Savings Bank, SSB	Roanoke Rapids	NC	C-	D+	C-	37.1	-2.13	0.0	0.5	32.6	4.3	10.0	25.9	58.6
Robert Lee State Bank	Robert Lee	TX	C+	C+	C+	42.1	-4.19	4.2	6.4	15.9	41.5	10.0	13.0	29.4
Roberts County National Bank of Sisseton	Sisseton	SD	B+	B+	B+	58.8	-1.16	2.2	0.6	1.6	61.1	10.0	14.3	33.0
Robertson Banking Co.	Demopolis	AL	A-	A-	A-	276.2	3.72	10.5	2.1	24.8	10.7	10.0	11.1	16.2
▲ Rochelle State Bank	Rochelle	GA	B-	C	C+	29.2	1.95	5.5	4.3	1.5	51.3	10.0	15.4	32.2
▲ Rochester State Bank	Rochester	IL	B-	C	C	92.4	5.39	2.1	2.3	7.2	71.2	9.9	10.9	20.4
▼ Rock Canyon Bank	Provo	UT	B-	B-	B	288.4	3.62	12.2	0.4	8.1	0.0	6.5	10.4	12.1
Rockefeller Trust Co., N.A.	New York	NY	U	U	U	10.4	1.26	0.0	0.0	0.0	85.7	10.0	91.1	415.9
Rockford Bank and Trust Co.	Rockford	IL	B-	C+	C+	393.2	9.13	21.7	1.0	14.5	12.7	6.3	9.5	12.0
▲ Rockhold, Brown & Co. Bank	Bainbridge	OH	C	D+	D	33.9	-1.77	2.9	1.4	41.3	0.8	8.6	10.1	16.0
▲ Rockland Savings Bank, FSB	Rockland	ME	C	E+	C-	75.9	-5.21	3.6	4.0	50.9	0.3	10.0	11.8	19.3
Rockland Trust Co.	Rockland	MA	B+	B	B	7499.6	5.18	11.2	0.2	17.9	11.1	7.5	9.5	12.9
Rockwood Bank	Eureka	MO	B	B	B-	255.7	3.98	2.9	1.1	22.5	1.0	10.0	12.8	17.5
Rocky Mountain Bank	Billings	MT	B	B	B-	481.4	-3.94	11.7	2.7	13.8	16.5	7.5	9.8	12.9
Rocky Mountain Bank	Jackson	WY	B-	C+	D+	287.1	10.89	4.5	0.9	27.5	3.3	8.4	10.0	16.9
Rocky Mountain Bank & Trust	Florence	CO	D-	D-	D-	64.0	2.22	22.1	4.0	20.5	23.4	6.4	8.5	12.1
Rolette State Bank	Rolette	ND	D	D+	D	41.0	5.28	20.2	3.6	3.6	9.3	6.8	8.8	12.3
Rolfe State Bank	Rolfe	IA	A-	A-	A-	44.3	-3.25	8.4	2.2	5.9	27.1	10.0	12.0	17.7
Rolling Hills Bank & Trust	Atlantic	IA	B-	C	C	241.6	6.68	6.1	0.8	3.1	0.4	6.4	10.5	12.1
Rollstone Bank & Trust	Fitchburg	MA	C+	C+	C	585.6	2.58	4.8	0.2	29.6	18.2	9.7	10.8	15.8
▼ Rondout Savings Bank	Kingston	NY	C+	B-	B-	326.6	3.02	5.2	0.4	42.0	16.4	9.9	10.9	18.8
Root River State Bank	Chatfield	MN	C+	C+	C+	68.1	0.87	5.0	1.3	9.9	39.5	10.0	11.5	20.0
Roscoe State Bank	Roscoe	TX	B	B	B	148.3	-4.45	6.8	2.8	13.7	42.9	9.1	10.4	18.5
Rose Hill Bank	Rose Hill	KS	C+	B-	B-	314.5	-4.27	10.5	3.5	10.7	31.4	7.3	9.2	13.6
Rosedale Federal S&L Assn.	Baltimore	MD	A-	A-	A	822.1	2.87	0.0	0.0	36.7	16.3	10.0	24.9	45.3
Roselle Savings Bank	Roselle	NJ	C	C	C+	401.9	-1.70	0.7	0.0	21.8	67.1	10.0	17.1	60.4
Round Top State Bank	Round Top	TX	B	B+	B+	492.2	4.03	3.2	2.2	23.2	32.2	9.2	10.5	17.8
Roundbank	Waseca	MN	B-	C+	C	301.3	3.52	10.8	1.4	21.4	20.5	10.0	11.9	15.2
Rowley Savings Bank	Rowley	IA	D-	D-	D	16.5	0.48	8.6	5.0	11.9	0.0	5.2	7.2	29.6
Roxboro Savings Bank, SSB	Roxboro	NC	A-	B+	B+	215.0	0.66	1.2	0.5	28.8	40.0	10.0	19.5	46.3
Roxbury Bank	Roxbury	KS	C	C	C-	15.7	2.92	8.9	1.2	14.4	2.4	9.9	10.9	20.5
Royal Bank	Elroy	WI	B-	B-	B-	354.5	5.03	8.9	4.3	17.2	20.7	8.7	10.2	15.9
Royal Bank America	Bala Cynwyd	PA	C+	C	C	807.0	6.46	3.5	0.3	10.5	21.0	9.3	10.6	15.0
Royal Banks of Missouri	Saint Louis	MO	D+	D	D	638.1	54.46	7.3	1.9	8.3	8.1	10.0	13.7	15.6
Royal Business Bank	Los Angeles	CA	A-	A	A-	1445.7	37.42	8.5	0.0	18.9	2.6	10.0	12.3	16.1
▼ Royal Savings Bank	Chicago	IL	B+	B+	C+	301.6	47.06	2.1	0.2	27.4	22.8	6.5	8.5	15.7
RSI Bank	Rahway	NJ	B-	C+	C+	508.7	1.57	1.0	0.1	45.0	31.3	10.0	16.0	33.0
RSNB Bank	Rock Springs	WY	B-	B	B+	373.6	2.62	2.8	1.0	3.6	63.7	9.9	11.0	25.0
▲ Ruby Valley Bank	Twin Bridges	MT	C+	C-	D+	94.7	3.53	8.8	1.8	4.4	35.8	10.0	14.4	22.8
Rushford State Bank (Inc.)	Rushford	MN	C-	D+	D+	55.8	2.69	5.3	4.4	16.2	11.3	5.3	7.8	11.2
Rushville State Bank	Rushville	IL	B+	B+	B+	96.3	-1.58	4.2	2.3	4.1	46.3	10.0	14.5	26.7
▲ S Bank	Glennville	GA	C-	D+	D	110.4	11.76	9.0	2.5	15.8	12.8	6.1	8.4	11.9
S&T Bank	Indiana	PA	B-	B	B	6697.0	8.10	15.0	0.9	12.5	9.9	5.3	8.5	11.2
Sabadell United Bank, N.A.	Miami	FL	B	B-	B-	5550.1	10.50	15.0	0.2	27.1	18.0	8.0	9.7	15.7
Sabal Palm Bank	Sarasota	FL	C	C-	C-	137.6	6.01	2.7	0.4	22.5	12.5	8.2	9.8	14.8
Sabine State Bank and Trust Co.	Many	LA	B+	A-	A-	839.8	4.56	14.1	1.8	10.0	13.2	6.3	10.0	11.9

Asset Quality Index	Adjusted Non-Performing Loans		Net Charge-Offs	Profitability Index	Net Income ($Mil)	Return on Assets (R.O.A.)	Return on Equity (R.O.E.)	Net Interest Spread	Overhead Efficiency Ratio	Liquidity Index	Liquidity Ratio	Hot Money Ratio	Stability Index
	as a % of Total Loans	as a % of Capital	Avg Loans										
3.9	1.94	15.9	0.18	6.4	12.9	1.57	15.25	4.18	66.3	4.2	14.0	7.5	8.1
9.2	0.05	0.3	0.56	4.0	1.3	0.72	7.28	3.12	56.8	6.2	45.1	3.8	5.7
6.2	0.24	2.3	0.00	7.0	0.8	1.67	15.68	4.25	57.3	0.5	4.7	43.0	5.7
3.5	1.07	7.2	-0.01	1.6	0.2	0.20	1.95	3.68	94.6	1.6	25.6	26.9	4.4
5.2	1.07	6.0	-0.01	5.3	0.5	1.23	11.95	3.84	78.8	5.5	34.9	4.5	7.7
4.8	2.18	12.1	0.05	5.1	3.0	1.31	14.24	3.13	58.0	1.7	22.3	23.0	6.0
2.6	1.56	9.0	-0.01	3.7	0.8	0.82	8.24	3.59	82.2	2.1	19.8	9.3	6.1
5.6	1.31	7.0	-0.01	3.1	0.4	0.57	4.05	3.93	75.2	0.7	17.2	46.3	4.4
7.9	0.12	1.1	0.06	10.0	1.2	2.62	29.20	4.90	50.2	0.9	4.8	30.3	6.3
5.4	0.40	3.7	0.33	3.3	2.7	0.67	7.56	3.89	78.7	3.4	6.9	11.0	4.6
3.0	1.26	7.4	-0.05	4.4	5.1	0.73	5.29	3.86	76.4	4.7	29.1	7.2	7.2
4.7	1.35	7.7	0.33	4.3	0.5	0.72	7.10	4.31	74.3	1.4	23.2	27.7	5.7
5.2	0.71	5.6	0.00	3.6	1.3	0.52	5.25	3.71	78.9	1.7	10.6	15.8	5.0
8.4	0.81	3.0	0.00	1.8	0.1	0.13	0.76	3.68	96.5	4.1	30.8	11.6	6.8
7.8	3.64	5.6	0.09	1.2	0.0	0.06	0.23	2.28	100.0	2.7	62.9	43.9	6.4
8.9	0.25	0.7	0.22	2.3	0.1	0.38	2.95	3.30	91.8	2.5	33.2	20.3	6.5
9.5	0.00	0.0	0.03	4.7	0.5	1.17	7.71	3.37	58.4	6.5	66.5	5.7	8.3
8.6	0.11	0.7	0.08	6.4	3.0	1.48	13.41	4.10	62.4	1.7	14.8	20.6	7.6
8.9	0.77	1.6	0.20	3.4	0.2	0.74	4.81	3.55	82.2	2.3	42.3	31.9	6.8
7.7	2.92	4.4	0.00	4.1	0.7	1.06	8.95	2.89	66.0	7.0	83.8	6.0	6.0
3.6	1.17	9.0	0.00	8.1	2.9	1.34	13.41	5.76	70.0	1.5	10.5	23.6	6.7
10.0	na	0.0	na	3.7	0.0	-0.13	-0.14	0.40	100.3	4.0	na	0.0	5.3
6.5	0.50	3.7	0.06	4.4	2.3	0.81	8.90	3.52	65.5	1.2	13.7	16.3	6.2
4.3	1.95	14.2	-0.06	5.0	0.3	1.26	13.15	5.43	77.7	3.0	14.8	13.7	3.2
4.0	2.33	14.5	1.70	2.5	0.2	0.42	3.18	3.78	80.7	1.2	15.2	28.3	4.6
5.8	0.64	4.9	-0.01	6.2	60.7	1.11	9.33	3.52	60.6	4.7	11.6	4.1	9.1
7.7	0.18	0.9	-0.10	4.1	1.3	0.68	5.29	3.91	65.4	4.4	18.8	6.2	6.1
5.3	0.70	5.1	0.07	6.1	4.0	1.11	10.79	4.44	74.2	4.0	12.9	8.7	6.7
6.8	0.15	0.9	0.03	4.9	2.3	1.16	10.50	3.74	66.0	3.1	28.8	8.0	4.1
2.9	1.77	11.8	0.27	1.5	0.0	-0.01	-0.15	4.10	99.0	4.1	20.2	8.9	0.6
1.7	2.71	22.9	0.22	5.1	0.4	1.22	14.22	4.54	73.7	1.6	7.8	15.0	4.5
4.8	2.51	12.4	-0.05	5.4	0.4	1.16	9.91	4.36	69.6	5.5	39.3	6.2	7.2
4.8	0.00	0.0	0.01	5.4	1.7	0.93	7.30	3.83	59.4	4.5	7.1	4.2	7.5
5.5	1.08	6.8	0.03	3.4	3.1	0.69	6.34	3.03	73.8	0.9	9.9	15.5	7.1
5.4	1.47	8.7	0.21	3.1	1.1	0.42	4.05	3.59	81.5	1.7	10.9	20.5	6.2
7.3	1.06	4.6	-0.02	2.9	0.2	0.46	3.95	3.25	82.6	5.3	39.3	7.8	5.7
8.9	0.00	0.0	0.01	5.2	1.5	1.31	11.81	4.13	67.4	2.8	33.0	18.8	6.6
4.3	0.83	5.0	0.33	3.2	1.2	0.48	4.56	3.44	79.3	3.4	30.2	14.7	6.6
5.8	3.54	9.3	-0.50	6.3	5.8	0.96	3.85	3.50	59.5	4.0	39.9	15.2	9.2
10.0	0.79	1.1	0.00	1.4	0.0	0.01	0.04	1.69	103.4	4.0	75.0	25.8	6.5
8.9	0.00	0.0	0.01	5.0	4.0	1.09	10.65	3.26	55.0	1.8	29.3	27.1	6.8
3.8	2.95	16.4	0.08	6.7	3.3	1.50	12.13	4.25	73.8	2.5	15.2	16.3	7.9
6.9	1.69	6.0	-1.44	2.3	0.0	0.28	3.99	2.47	87.2	6.9	75.1	2.8	1.7
6.7	3.28	8.1	0.09	5.1	2.0	1.23	6.48	3.22	58.7	3.5	56.8	24.4	8.3
5.2	1.23	6.0	-0.03	4.3	0.1	0.93	8.71	4.31	78.0	5.8	40.5	1.6	4.6
4.5	1.15	7.2	0.11	6.2	2.8	1.08	10.11	4.24	64.7	4.0	23.9	9.8	7.3
4.5	0.93	5.7	0.10	3.9	6.0	1.06	12.74	3.45	68.9	2.4	16.4	17.1	4.2
1.2	3.36	18.3	0.32	5.9	3.6	0.98	7.29	3.87	58.3	1.5	8.9	22.8	7.4
7.0	0.07	0.5	0.03	9.3	14.3	1.39	10.12	4.51	44.3	0.6	11.3	55.0	10.0
7.8	0.29	2.2	0.02	5.1	1.0	0.50	3.90	4.01	73.9	3.5	29.4	14.0	8.8
8.0	1.40	4.9	-0.04	3.3	1.9	0.50	3.19	2.63	71.2	4.2	41.9	14.5	7.4
8.7	0.42	1.0	0.79	4.2	3.0	1.06	9.16	3.14	61.0	5.2	45.5	10.5	7.6
3.5	3.41	12.4	-0.12	9.1	1.4	2.02	13.93	4.58	57.4	4.5	45.3	13.3	9.0
5.2	0.58	5.3	0.22	3.2	0.2	0.53	6.74	4.23	82.7	4.4	13.5	5.5	3.5
8.9	0.39	1.1	0.03	5.1	1.0	1.30	8.81	3.25	57.8	4.2	45.4	14.9	8.3
2.8	2.97	22.3	-0.01	3.2	0.5	0.61	6.31	4.90	83.8	1.5	7.7	20.7	4.1
4.3	0.86	8.0	0.17	6.1	56.2	1.16	9.36	3.48	54.9	2.3	8.3	13.6	9.5
5.8	0.76	5.2	0.00	4.8	34.6	0.85	7.75	3.10	59.1	3.9	22.4	11.5	8.8
8.9	0.00	0.0	-0.03	3.2	0.4	0.40	3.39	3.65	82.8	2.4	18.4	17.4	5.4
5.2	0.68	4.9	0.11	6.3	9.1	1.44	14.56	4.27	69.2	3.8	6.6	9.1	8.4

Name	City	State	2015 Rating	2014 Rating	Total Assets ($Mil)	One Year Asset Growth	Comm-ercial Loans	Cons-umer Loans	Mort-gage Loans	Secur-ities	Capital-ization Index	Lever-age Ratio	Risk-Based Capital Ratio
▲ Saco & Biddeford Savings Institution	Saco	ME	B	C+	C+	879.9	2.44	1.7	0.9	50.6	11.9	10.0	11.1	16.7
Sacramento Deposit Bank	Sacramento	KY	A-	A-	A-	68.1	-2.17	6.1	6.5	19.8	31.2	10.0	13.4	21.1
Safra National Bank of New York	New York	NY	C-	C+	C+	7853.4	22.13	12.1	0.0	0.4	41.7	4.7	6.7	14.2
▲ Sage Bank	Lowell	MA	D	E+	D	155.7	-5.63	1.5	0.1	51.8	0.2	6.5	8.5	15.2
Sage Capital Bank, N.A.	Gonzales	TX	B	B	B-	343.1	1.66	4.5	1.0	9.9	19.8	9.4	10.6	15.5
Saint Casimir's Savings Bank	Baltimore	MD	D	D	C-	88.4	-5.58	0.0	0.1	17.7	57.7	10.0	21.7	76.5
Sainte Marie State Bank	Sainte Marie	IL	C	D+	D+	20.6	5.75	6.7	1.3	1.3	10.0	10.0	21.5	24.6
Salem Co-operative Bank	Salem	NH	C+	C+	C+	408.3	2.50	1.6	0.1	60.0	18.6	10.0	16.0	29.4
▲ Salem Five Cents Savings Bank	Salem	MA	B	B	B	4079.8	8.97	9.9	2.1	29.2	21.7	9.3	10.6	15.4
Salin Bank and Trust Co.	Indianapolis	IN	B	B	B+	835.2	9.57	9.8	1.4	16.1	22.6	9.9	11.0	14.9
▲ Salisbury Bank and Trust Co.	Lakeville	CT	C	C	C	928.5	2.69	13.8	0.6	31.7	8.3	7.5	9.3	12.9
Sallie Mae Bank	Salt Lake City	UT	C	B+	A-	17508.5	22.76	0.0	85.3	0.0	1.2	8.1	11.6	13.5
Salyersville National Bank	Salyersville	KY	B+	B+	B+	113.8	-4.34	3.5	3.0	16.6	58.2	10.0	13.7	32.7
Samson Banking Co., Inc.	Samson	AL	B-	B-	B	75.1	4.15	3.5	4.9	18.8	44.2	10.0	13.0	26.6
San Diego Private Bank	Coronado	CA	A-	A-	B+	498.0	13.63	13.2	0.1	8.7	5.8	9.6	12.0	14.6
San Luis Valley Federal Bank	Alamosa	CO	B	B	B	265.7	3.83	0.7	0.9	37.8	29.3	10.0	15.9	25.8
Sanborn Savings Bank	Sanborn	IA	B	B	B	63.2	3.38	5.0	3.4	13.7	13.5	9.3	10.5	14.4
Sandhills Bank	North Myrtle Beach	SC	D+	C-	C+	161.0	12.83	2.9	3.1	40.2	10.1	6.6	8.6	13.7
Sandhills State Bank	Bassett	NE	C+	C	C	178.1	7.11	10.8	1.1	0.1	9.4	5.5	8.8	11.4
Sandy Spring Bank	Olney	MD	B+	B+	B	4799.0	4.20	8.3	0.5	20.0	13.4	7.3	9.2	12.8
Sanford Institution for Savings	Sanford	ME	B-	B-	B-	522.4	4.01	4.7	0.9	37.8	5.8	9.8	11.4	14.8
Sanger Bank	Sanger	TX	A	A	A	127.2	-2.50	7.2	3.1	18.1	27.3	10.0	13.7	26.4
Sanibel Captiva Community Bank	Sanibel	FL	B-	B-	D+	328.3	21.98	1.9	1.4	46.7	3.0	5.5	7.5	11.9
Santa Anna National Bank	Santa Anna	TX	A-	A-	A-	45.6	-3.09	14.6	7.2	3.9	40.1	10.0	12.5	21.4
Santa Cruz County Bank	Santa Cruz	CA	B+	B+	B	578.2	10.42	9.0	0.6	3.6	9.2	6.5	8.6	13.2
Santander Bank, N.A.	Boston	MA	C	C+	C+	85473.9	-4.43	20.2	1.7	8.5	18.6	10.0	12.3	17.0
Saratoga National Bank and Trust Co.	Saratoga Springs	NY	B+	B	B	430.3	12.39	4.3	24.1	20.1	14.7	7.2	9.3	12.6
Sargent County Bank	Forman	ND	A+	A+	A+	112.1	-7.04	2.4	1.6	0.1	47.9	10.0	15.8	24.9
Sauk Valley Bank & Trust Co.	Sterling	IL	B-	B-	B-	355.6	9.86	9.7	0.6	12.1	22.7	6.4	8.4	12.3
Savanna-Thomson State Bank	Savanna	IL	B	B	B	95.0	-1.01	22.0	0.7	9.9	29.5	10.0	11.3	18.5
Savannah Bank, N.A.	Savannah	NY	B-	C+	C+	141.0	1.29	8.0	1.1	17.1	42.8	6.2	8.2	16.0
Savers Co-operative Bank	Southbridge	MA	B-	C+	C+	492.0	6.21	2.9	5.6	41.9	11.2	10.0	11.0	17.2
SaviBank	Burlington	WA	D+	C-	E	174.7	27.12	10.4	3.9	16.1	4.6	4.0	9.2	10.5
▼ Savings Bank	Primghar	IA	B	B+	B+	185.0	1.35	13.0	2.8	9.1	19.9	7.7	10.4	13.1
Savings Bank	Wakefield	MA	C+	C+	C+	539.1	3.31	2.3	0.1	52.0	12.5	10.0	11.5	20.9
Savings Bank	Circleville	OH	B-	B-	B	356.0	6.21	2.5	4.1	32.9	35.3	9.4	10.6	21.6
▲ Savings Bank of Danbury	Danbury	CT	B	B-	C+	957.0	5.37	4.0	0.1	46.8	8.1	9.4	10.6	15.2
Savings Bank of Mendocino County	Ukiah	CA	A-	A-	B+	1058.5	5.19	3.7	0.6	7.3	49.3	10.0	15.7	26.8
Savings Bank of Walpole	Walpole	NH	C-	C-	C-	374.7	7.58	4.2	0.3	37.5	27.0	5.8	7.8	15.6
Savings Institute Bank and Trust Co.	Willimantic	CT	C	C-	C-	1530.6	5.82	14.1	0.2	28.2	10.8	7.5	9.4	15.5
Savoy Bank	New York	NY	D	D	D	261.0	50.45	7.9	0.0	12.8	1.3	6.2	8.9	11.9
Sawyer Savings Bank	Saugerties	NY	C-	C+	C+	240.7	9.70	2.0	0.1	39.0	33.6	9.3	10.5	22.8
Schaumburg Bank & Trust Co., N.A.	Schaumburg	IL	B-	B-	C+	1014.9	20.54	27.2	9.5	2.3	16.1	6.0	10.1	11.7
▼ Schertz Bank & Trust	Schertz	TX	B	B+	B	307.7	23.26	4.6	0.4	3.0	8.1	5.6	10.1	11.5
Schuyler Savings Bank	Kearny	NJ	C	C	C	116.9	2.12	0.0	0.1	52.0	18.4	10.0	15.9	39.4
Scotiabank de Puerto Rico	San Juan	PR	D	D	D	4488.0	-2.70	8.3	9.4	42.2	9.5	10.0	18.7	32.2
Scott State Bank	Bethany	IL	B-	B-	B-	166.5	3.00	8.5	2.7	15.3	38.3	10.0	14.6	26.7
Scott Valley Bank	Yreka	CA	B-	B-	B-	629.1	3.89	11.7	0.3	1.6	26.2	8.7	10.9	13.9
▼ Scottdale Bank & Trust Co.	Scottdale	PA	C-	C+	B	266.6	1.09	0.9	0.6	11.5	66.4	10.0	16.9	32.8
Scottrade Bank	Saint Louis	MO	B-	B-	B-	16606.4	5.10	1.9	0.3	15.2	76.0	5.8	7.8	24.4
Scottsburg Building and Loan Assn.	Scottsburg	IN	C+	C	C	94.7	1.58	2.2	0.3	43.4	39.3	10.0	12.9	28.7
Scribner Bank	Scribner	NE	A-	A-	A-	63.2	-2.14	10.1	1.9	4.7	19.4	10.0	12.6	18.7
Seacoast Commerce Bank	San Diego	CA	B+	B	C+	578.8	11.47	0.5	0.0	0.0	0.6	6.4	8.5	20.9
Seacoast National Bank	Stuart	FL	B-	B-	C	4513.8	33.55	7.2	3.2	15.5	28.0	6.7	8.8	12.9
▼ Seamen's Bank	Provincetown	MA	D+	C-	C-	370.0	2.47	1.9	0.2	34.5	23.1	9.7	10.8	16.6
Seaside National Bank & Trust	Orlando	FL	C+	C+	C-	1483.3	20.47	32.7	1.2	10.0	22.4	5.7	7.9	11.5
▲ Seattle Bank	Seattle	WA	C+	C	D+	256.6	36.19	28.6	0.2	13.4	4.0	10.0	26.2	27.7
Seaway Bank and Trust Co.	Chicago	IL	E-	E-	D-	361.0	-6.41	5.7	0.6	22.5	4.2	0.0	1.9	4.5
Sebree Deposit Bank	Sebree	KY	D-	D	D	23.3	1.80	9.6	5.9	35.5	13.3	9.8	10.8	21.0
▼ Second Federal S&L Assn. of Philadelphia	Philadelphia	PA	C-	B-	B	14.6	13.60	0.0	0.0	29.4	64.2	10.0	44.2	56.1

Arrows denote recent upgrades ▲ or downgrades ▼

www.weissratings.com

Asset Quality Index	Adjusted Non-Performing Loans		Net Charge-Offs Avg Loans	Profitability Index	Net Income ($Mil)	Return on Assets (R.O.A.)	Return on Equity (R.O.E.)	Net Interest Spread	Overhead Efficiency Ratio	Liquidity Index	Liquidity Ratio	Hot Money Ratio	Stability Index
	as a % of Total Loans	as a % of Capital											
6.5	0.92	6.4	0.00	4.0	5.3	0.80	7.35	3.18	72.7	1.0	11.3	28.4	6.8
8.5	0.40	1.8	0.41	7.9	0.9	1.83	14.15	4.73	58.5	2.5	41.4	28.7	8.3
9.3	0.16	0.8	0.00	2.0	30.4	0.53	6.13	1.44	94.1	1.6	28.1	11.7	6.5
5.7	0.82	7.8	-0.01	1.3	0.3	0.29	3.58	3.14	98.4	0.9	13.1	33.0	3.1
8.4	0.00	0.0	0.04	5.1	2.4	0.93	8.22	4.20	68.4	3.2	20.6	13.4	6.9
10.0	0.08	0.1	0.00	0.0	-0.5	-0.65	-3.07	2.13	130.0	6.9	98.8	9.1	6.2
7.3	0.00	0.0	0.00	2.4	0.1	0.41	1.87	2.77	84.5	1.6	15.6	22.3	5.8
8.9	0.57	2.6	0.00	2.6	1.1	0.38	2.38	2.99	80.9	2.5	24.5	17.4	7.5
7.4	0.50	3.4	0.07	4.8	24.2	0.84	7.78	2.84	63.3	2.9	21.3	16.2	8.3
6.6	0.50	3.0	-0.10	4.2	5.3	0.87	7.56	3.57	80.2	4.8	19.8	3.7	7.4
2.7	1.94	15.9	0.21	4.4	5.9	0.86	7.89	3.70	68.5	3.9	6.5	8.2	7.1
2.3	1.77	12.6	0.64	9.7	183.7	1.56	13.58	5.78	36.7	0.6	9.4	6.2	9.2
9.4	0.88	2.1	0.19	4.1	0.7	0.79	5.83	3.51	75.8	2.7	41.8	25.4	7.7
5.8	2.96	9.9	0.04	3.1	0.3	0.53	4.13	3.28	77.6	5.1	48.7	11.1	7.5
7.4	0.05	0.3	-0.01	6.0	3.2	0.92	7.20	4.27	60.6	2.5	21.4	11.8	8.0
5.8	3.01	10.8	0.02	3.9	1.3	0.67	4.26	3.44	75.0	4.8	44.4	12.1	7.6
7.4	0.29	2.0	0.00	5.4	0.6	1.28	11.79	3.57	58.5	4.5	22.0	6.5	6.0
4.7	1.23	9.9	0.01	1.9	0.1	0.07	0.59	3.72	94.5	1.3	15.0	27.3	6.0
6.8	0.03	0.2	0.03	3.9	1.1	0.89	9.19	3.79	71.3	0.8	4.7	31.6	5.3
5.7	0.80	6.4	0.07	5.4	34.5	0.98	9.08	3.42	62.8	3.8	6.2	9.0	9.3
7.9	0.36	2.3	-0.03	3.7	2.3	0.59	5.26	3.56	81.0	2.6	16.5	14.3	6.9
9.2	0.23	0.9	0.00	5.8	1.1	1.09	8.22	3.97	64.2	2.9	39.4	21.5	8.3
6.7	0.29	3.0	-0.04	8.6	3.2	1.41	17.08	4.39	52.1	2.3	13.5	17.4	4.2
8.2	0.00	0.0	0.02	9.3	0.6	1.76	14.06	4.71	51.4	3.1	34.1	17.3	8.0
8.6	0.00	0.0	-0.02	7.0	4.7	1.14	13.29	4.13	56.0	3.7	25.3	11.7	6.1
4.8	1.48	7.4	0.19	2.3	166.6	0.25	1.65	2.22	86.5	3.9	21.4	3.1	7.6
6.0	0.20	1.7	0.08	5.6	3.1	1.02	11.11	3.18	54.2	4.0	8.0	7.7	6.8
8.8	0.00	0.0	0.00	8.8	1.8	2.03	12.87	4.02	40.7	4.5	41.0	12.8	9.7
5.4	0.63	4.9	0.32	4.7	2.2	0.86	10.00	3.85	68.5	2.3	12.4	12.7	5.2
5.7	0.97	4.8	-0.02	4.4	0.7	1.04	7.00	3.44	68.4	5.7	32.7	2.4	7.2
7.9	0.89	5.2	0.01	4.0	1.2	1.08	12.75	3.43	72.3	1.6	16.4	23.5	4.8
5.1	1.42	9.7	0.01	3.3	2.0	0.56	5.07	3.42	77.5	2.9	16.2	14.4	6.9
3.5	0.86	7.7	0.04	3.1	0.7	0.62	6.38	4.40	83.0	3.0	12.2	13.7	2.9
3.0	2.66	18.6	0.05	7.7	2.4	1.74	17.16	3.49	41.7	2.1	11.7	17.7	6.9
8.8	0.42	2.8	-0.02	2.6	2.2	0.55	4.26	3.10	90.0	2.7	19.1	16.0	7.7
5.3	1.75	8.7	0.04	3.7	1.9	0.74	6.84	3.32	74.3	3.4	20.0	12.8	6.4
5.1	1.29	10.0	0.16	4.7	6.3	0.90	8.63	3.43	64.2	1.4	1.4	22.1	6.3
8.2	1.02	2.7	0.03	5.1	7.2	0.93	5.85	3.23	57.7	6.5	52.3	7.2	9.6
5.6	1.27	9.3	0.05	2.4	1.0	0.36	4.53	2.67	87.7	5.1	34.6	6.7	4.4
5.8	0.90	7.3	0.02	2.9	5.1	0.45	4.42	2.89	75.7	1.9	15.8	17.6	7.0
1.2	2.74	22.0	0.00	8.4	2.6	1.57	14.56	4.60	54.8	1.2	29.7	47.8	5.0
5.6	1.83	10.2	-0.05	2.0	0.5	0.31	2.72	3.08	94.1	1.7	37.1	27.5	6.2
5.2	0.68	4.9	0.07	4.5	5.7	0.80	7.50	3.07	64.6	1.6	16.7	24.8	7.2
6.2	0.29	2.2	0.00	7.3	2.9	1.34	13.14	4.30	53.1	0.8	8.8	33.4	5.6
6.8	2.20	8.0	0.00	2.0	0.2	0.17	1.07	2.89	93.8	2.3	36.3	26.5	7.1
0.2	13.80	44.7	0.73	2.5	5.5	0.16	0.75	4.59	74.5	2.0	22.0	23.1	9.2
7.8	1.57	4.9	0.20	3.3	0.8	0.70	4.60	3.38	75.5	5.7	45.4	6.9	7.2
6.6	0.50	2.7	-0.04	4.5	3.5	0.78	7.14	3.98	71.6	4.7	34.0	9.5	7.1
9.2	3.13	4.4	0.00	1.5	0.0	0.01	0.07	2.94	97.9	7.9	85.7	1.5	7.4
10.0	0.52	1.4	0.11	4.2	127.0	1.05	13.35	1.52	29.5	5.5	51.8	0.0	6.5
9.4	0.08	0.3	0.00	3.2	0.4	0.56	4.43	2.77	70.9	1.5	34.2	49.4	6.5
8.2	0.07	0.3	0.01	7.6	0.7	1.35	10.98	3.73	65.2	5.0	25.2	3.3	7.0
5.8	0.26	2.0	0.00	8.3	5.2	1.29	14.97	4.48	70.5	5.2	24.8	2.0	6.4
5.6	0.99	6.9	-0.11	4.0	19.5	0.64	5.64	3.83	76.6	5.2	25.7	5.6	7.4
1.7	6.44	35.0	0.00	1.9	0.6	0.24	2.14	3.08	96.3	5.3	40.5	8.1	6.5
5.3	0.85	7.4	0.13	3.9	6.8	0.65	7.71	3.15	67.1	2.2	18.5	12.9	6.0
5.2	2.21	7.9	-0.13	3.6	17.1	10.30	46.59	3.59	91.6	1.4	13.4	25.8	5.7
0.3	9.52	175.0	1.32	0.0	-12.5	-4.49	-71.36	3.01	196.4	1.3	24.4	29.8	2.1
8.7	0.11	0.6	0.12	0.3	-0.1	-0.32	-2.76	3.39	109.9	2.0	30.9	20.9	4.6
10.0	0.00	0.0	0.00	1.7	0.0	-0.05	-0.10	3.59	101.8	4.6	125.8	28.0	7.0

Name	City	State	Rating	2015 Rating	2014 Rating	Total Assets ($Mil)	One Year Asset Growth	Asset Mix (As a % of Total Assets) Commercial Loans	Consumer Loans	Mortgage Loans	Securities	Capitalization Index	Leverage Ratio	Risk-Based Capital Ratio
▲ Securant Bank & Trust	Milwaukee	WI	C-	D	E-	188.3	5.49	17.2	0.2	28.2	10.2	7.8	9.5	13.6
Securian Trust Co., N.A.	Saint Paul	MN	U	U	U	14.4	3.80	0.0	0.0	0.0	87.1	10.0	99.3	99.0
Security Bank	Stephens	AR	B-	B-	B-	62.4	3.76	7.3	6.3	48.9	9.0	6.4	8.4	14.6
Security Bank	Rich Hill	MO	C+	C+	C	47.0	-1.45	12.1	4.6	30.7	3.2	6.2	8.7	11.9
▲ Security Bank	Laurel	NE	B+	B-	B-	198.2	4.69	8.6	2.7	2.6	16.0	10.0	11.7	17.2
Security Bank	Tulsa	OK	A	A	B+	490.3	1.56	28.4	1.4	8.4	4.7	9.2	12.1	14.4
Security Bank	Dyersburg	TN	B	B	B	182.8	3.47	1.6	1.9	4.9	57.7	10.0	11.4	22.6
Security Bank	Midland	TX	D	B	B+	789.7	-11.70	22.1	0.8	4.6	21.9	7.3	9.2	14.3
Security Bank	New Auburn	WI	C+	C-	C+	96.3	6.96	8.4	1.5	18.6	15.8	10.0	12.5	17.0
Security Bank & Trust Co.	Glencoe	MN	B+	B+	B+	516.5	5.00	6.1	0.6	6.4	38.3	7.1	9.1	16.6
Security Bank and Trust Co.	Maysville	KY	B+	A-	B+	51.2	1.28	4.4	2.3	21.4	34.3	10.0	20.8	21.2
Security Bank and Trust Co.	Miami	OK	B	B-	B-	81.6	2.29	9.7	4.4	15.0	38.2	9.9	10.9	19.3
Security Bank and Trust Co.	Paris	TN	A-	A-	A	212.9	13.96	15.4	1.6	18.8	14.1	5.7	9.1	11.5
Security Bank Minnesota	Albert Lea	MN	A-	A-	A-	122.5	15.33	45.3	5.0	5.3	12.8	7.5	9.5	12.9
Security Bank of Crawford	Crawford	TX	D	D	D	31.9	41.11	3.0	5.3	37.8	3.9	10.0	12.2	18.6
Security Bank of Kansas City	Kansas City	KS	B	B	C+	831.4	-0.40	8.1	0.3	2.0	22.8	10.0	12.2	16.0
Security Bank of Pulaski County	Waynesville	MO	C	C-	C-	101.1	5.08	9.5	4.5	21.8	15.5	6.6	8.9	12.2
▲ Security Bank of Southwest Missouri	Cassville	MO	C+	C-	C+	81.4	-0.03	6.2	5.1	26.4	19.4	10.0	11.1	19.0
▲ Security Bank of the Ozarks	Eminence	MO	C-	C-	C-	99.4	112.39	9.1	10.2	9.5	9.2	7.0	9.0	13.1
▲ Security Bank USA	Bemidji	MN	A-	B+	B	140.4	7.31	16.3	5.4	21.2	5.5	7.7	9.5	13.1
Security Bank, s.b.	Springfield	IL	D	D	D-	126.6	-0.18	5.1	7.2	44.4	16.9	8.1	9.8	17.1
Security Federal Bank	Aiken	SC	B-	B-	C+	823.6	2.88	2.0	2.0	12.3	49.6	9.9	11.0	22.1
Security Federal Bank	Elizabethton	TN	B+	B+	B+	63.7	4.84	2.2	2.1	35.9	20.4	10.0	19.3	36.4
Security Federal Savings Bank	Jasper	AL	C	C+	C+	40.4	5.00	0.8	10.4	26.2	26.8	10.0	11.2	19.8
Security Federal Savings Bank	Logansport	IN	C+	C	B-	234.6	9.17	5.2	0.8	35.6	16.1	10.0	12.2	20.1
Security Financial Bank	Durand	WI	B	B	B	412.8	1.59	9.5	0.4	8.7	23.4	9.2	10.5	16.2
Security First Bank	Fresno	CA	C	C	C+	104.0	-3.80	14.3	0.1	7.8	9.7	10.0	13.6	15.8
Security First Bank	Lincoln	NE	C+	C+	C+	950.5	7.60	7.4	2.4	8.8	22.7	6.3	8.8	12.0
Security First Bank	Cheyenne	WY	B+	B+	B+	70.8	1.37	4.8	2.3	7.6	20.7	7.9	9.6	14.2
Security First Bank of North Dakota	Center	ND	A	A	A	182.8	1.45	15.0	3.0	10.1	3.5	9.2	12.6	14.3
Security First National Bank of Hugo	Hugo	OK	B+	B+	B+	103.3	1.17	2.0	3.8	20.7	9.4	6.7	8.9	12.3
Security FSB of McMinnville	McMinnville	TN	B-	B-	B-	185.8	1.14	15.5	5.6	25.8	18.7	8.5	10.0	15.2
▲ Security Home Bank	Malmo	NE	B-	C+	C+	39.4	1.05	6.2	2.7	20.1	4.3	9.7	10.8	15.1
Security National Bank	Witt	IL	B-	B-	B-	81.5	4.44	4.5	4.4	23.8	27.6	8.9	10.3	16.4
▲ Security National Bank of Enid	Enid	OK	B+	A-	A-	318.0	-2.87	4.5	1.7	21.1	33.7	6.4	8.4	13.4
Security National Bank of Omaha	Omaha	NE	B+	B+	A-	877.8	10.11	16.4	2.8	5.9	26.8	8.6	10.0	15.1
Security National Bank of Sioux City, Iowa	Sioux City	IA	A-	A-	A-	990.5	1.84	5.3	1.2	13.6	30.2	8.0	9.7	17.0
Security National Bank of South Dakota	Dakota Dunes	SD	A-	A-	B+	182.3	2.38	7.7	1.6	8.9	36.0	9.3	10.5	18.9
Security National Trust Co.	Wheeling	WV	U	U	U	5.4	3.67	0.0	0.0	0.0	77.8	10.0	119.	126.9
Security Savings Bank	Gowrie	IA	B+	B	B	126.5	2.79	4.4	2.1	12.4	37.1	7.6	9.4	15.6
Security Savings Bank	Monmouth	IL	C	C	C+	184.6	2.03	3.7	5.4	12.0	13.8	9.1	10.4	15.7
Security Savings Bank	Canton	SD	B	B	B	204.6	5.47	5.3	2.0	8.4	3.9	6.1	9.3	11.8
Security State Bank	McRae	GA	B+	B+	B+	42.3	0.96	17.0	3.4	6.6	35.2	10.0	14.8	25.8
Security State Bank	Algona	IA	A-	A-	A-	110.7	7.29	10.7	2.1	3.2	12.5	10.0	13.2	15.3
Security State Bank	Independence	IA	A-	A-	A-	103.5	0.63	5.3	0.9	10.3	46.3	10.0	12.4	21.7
▲ Security State Bank	Radcliffe	IA	C	C	C	92.9	-3.47	9.7	1.9	12.9	22.8	9.4	10.6	20.0
Security State Bank	Sutherland	IA	B	B-	B-	120.4	7.72	10.3	3.6	4.8	0.0	5.1	9.2	11.1
Security State Bank	Waverly	IA	B+	B+	B+	78.8	-5.45	1.3	3.7	15.8	40.8	9.5	10.7	16.4
Security State Bank	Scott City	KS	A-	A-	A-	224.4	10.56	14.2	1.7	1.7	14.2	10.0	15.0	18.1
▼ Security State Bank	Wellington	KS	C-	D+	C	59.6	-1.83	2.6	1.1	10.2	58.7	10.0	11.4	26.7
Security State Bank	Ansley	NE	C+	C+	C+	220.0	20.73	13.1	0.8	17.5	4.6	5.6	8.7	11.4
Security State Bank	Cheyenne	OK	A	A	A-	175.3	-6.46	7.4	3.3	13.0	38.1	10.0	14.0	21.8
Security State Bank	Alexandria	SD	B	B	B-	76.2	-2.90	7.1	3.4	3.3	28.4	9.4	10.6	16.1
Security State Bank	Emery	SD	B-	B-	B-	42.3	3.51	15.5	3.9	0.4	29.8	10.0	14.0	20.3
Security State Bank	Tyndall	SD	C+	B-	C+	162.4	18.92	9.0	1.5	1.6	12.0	5.5	8.1	11.4
Security State Bank	Farwell	TX	A-	A-	A-	132.1	11.09	10.6	0.5	11.3	16.7	10.0	13.0	20.7
Security State Bank	Pearsall	TX	A-	A-	B+	534.4	7.36	3.2	1.8	1.1	38.8	9.0	10.3	14.9
Security State Bank	Winters	TX	C+	C+	C+	53.5	-1.78	7.5	8.3	7.6	37.6	6.7	8.7	18.2
Security State Bank	Centralia	WA	B+	B+	B	416.7	8.07	9.5	1.8	6.5	2.4	10.0	11.4	21.5
Security State Bank	Iron River	WI	C-	C-	C	85.6	4.39	12.2	1.7	11.2	21.5	10.0	18.5	24.6

Asset Quality Index	Adjusted Non-Performing Loans as a % of Total Loans	as a % of Capital	Net Charge-Offs Avg Loans	Profitability Index	Net Income ($Mil)	Return on Assets (R.O.A.)	Return on Equity (R.O.E.)	Net Interest Spread	Overhead Efficiency Ratio	Liquidity Index	Liquidity Ratio	Hot Money Ratio	Stability Index
2.0	3.79	26.5	-0.05	3.1	0.7	0.52	4.94	3.52	88.7	0.6	7.9	39.2	3.6
10.0	na	0.0	na	9.8	0.2	2.02	2.11	3.55	91.3	4.0	na	0.0	6.7
6.7	0.51	4.3	0.34	4.5	0.4	0.85	10.07	4.14	67.1	0.6	12.7	39.9	4.7
8.4	0.13	1.1	0.00	5.1	0.4	1.06	12.19	5.11	77.8	3.6	14.2	10.7	4.5
5.7	0.27	1.6	0.02	6.1	2.0	1.38	11.48	4.59	67.7	3.8	18.3	10.6	8.1
6.9	0.20	1.2	0.04	9.8	10.2	2.73	22.58	4.49	34.5	0.7	11.1	38.0	8.8
5.9	3.65	9.7	0.04	4.8	1.4	1.02	8.35	3.62	72.6	2.9	40.8	22.1	7.1
0.8	5.56	31.8	1.05	4.8	4.8	0.81	6.80	4.87	71.2	4.8	30.7	7.5	8.3
3.5	2.16	12.6	-0.15	6.2	0.7	1.04	8.56	3.79	59.4	1.4	21.5	21.5	6.2
5.2	2.11	10.7	0.04	6.7	6.2	1.65	17.51	3.08	54.0	4.9	33.5	8.0	7.3
8.9	0.17	0.5	-0.10	4.6	0.4	1.14	5.57	3.29	66.3	5.0	45.7	11.1	8.2
8.7	0.00	0.0	0.01	5.1	0.9	1.39	12.32	4.13	70.0	3.3	31.2	15.7	6.4
8.5	0.17	1.4	0.00	8.8	3.0	1.97	21.01	4.13	48.7	1.3	10.2	26.7	7.0
7.7	0.03	0.2	-0.09	6.9	1.5	1.61	15.09	4.21	59.0	1.6	16.1	22.6	7.8
6.9	1.03	6.4	-0.02	0.0	-0.2	-0.95	-6.84	3.62	125.4	0.7	17.5	54.9	4.7
5.4	1.21	5.2	-0.16	5.0	6.3	0.99	6.30	3.64	65.3	4.8	28.8	6.1	7.8
4.3	1.52	11.2	0.07	3.2	0.4	0.58	6.35	4.39	82.9	1.4	11.1	23.9	4.2
4.0	2.89	16.8	0.15	8.6	1.3	2.05	18.89	4.34	55.2	2.4	25.5	18.2	8.0
7.1	0.30	2.0	-0.03	2.5	0.1	0.14	1.66	4.50	96.6	2.3	23.8	18.6	4.1
7.7	0.20	1.6	0.09	9.0	2.2	2.19	23.36	4.54	57.2	3.9	14.2	9.6	7.5
1.4	4.61	33.1	0.28	1.1	0.0	-0.03	-0.33	3.53	98.4	4.8	24.1	4.8	3.6
5.3	2.36	8.8	0.06	4.3	5.4	0.89	7.47	3.47	73.1	3.6	44.5	12.2	6.5
6.5	2.19	7.3	0.03	5.9	0.6	1.25	6.12	4.18	68.3	0.9	20.5	40.5	8.1
8.9	0.04	0.1	-0.06	2.2	0.1	0.29	2.78	3.22	94.0	1.9	38.2	35.1	4.4
5.5	2.13	11.1	0.14	2.9	0.8	0.46	3.76	4.13	84.4	4.5	27.8	8.1	6.2
6.9	0.48	2.9	0.00	5.2	3.7	1.21	10.09	3.63	64.1	4.6	21.0	5.7	7.3
2.3	4.07	21.2	-0.21	3.0	0.4	0.47	3.45	4.26	85.9	4.6	12.6	4.7	6.5
6.9	0.31	2.2	-0.05	3.9	5.0	0.74	7.41	3.44	71.4	3.5	19.2	11.8	6.7
6.5	1.15	5.4	-0.25	4.4	0.5	1.01	10.42	4.03	73.1	2.7	48.2	20.2	6.4
6.3	0.88	5.7	0.06	9.5	2.9	2.19	17.48	4.80	58.5	3.1	3.6	12.2	9.1
5.3	0.75	6.1	0.00	9.8	1.3	1.67	20.64	5.28	55.4	2.0	6.9	18.1	6.7
6.7	0.21	1.4	-0.12	4.3	1.0	0.71	7.22	3.31	71.1	1.7	19.1	23.1	5.7
7.2	0.00	0.0	0.00	5.0	0.3	0.85	8.13	3.65	61.3	1.5	16.0	24.4	5.9
5.0	1.77	9.8	0.06	4.3	0.5	0.74	6.94	3.67	70.8	2.5	34.5	21.5	6.1
6.4	0.60	3.9	0.11	7.7	4.6	1.82	20.50	3.40	50.1	4.3	19.4	7.2	7.6
8.5	0.16	0.8	0.03	5.3	8.5	1.32	12.46	3.14	68.0	5.8	37.1	3.6	8.2
7.3	0.69	3.4	-0.03	6.2	8.6	1.16	11.94	2.88	59.6	5.1	33.3	5.8	8.3
8.9	0.06	0.3	-0.01	7.2	1.6	1.19	11.54	2.48	54.4	3.4	41.7	15.6	7.7
10.0	na	0.0	na	9.5	0.6	20.22	16.67	1.77	83.2	4.0	na	0.0	5.7
7.7	0.43	2.3	0.01	5.1	1.2	1.27	12.96	3.44	59.1	3.1	31.4	16.6	6.6
6.3	0.31	2.1	0.19	3.1	0.6	0.47	4.51	2.90	76.5	1.8	22.0	21.8	5.7
3.8	1.42	11.5	0.00	5.7	2.1	1.36	13.04	3.70	59.8	1.0	11.0	30.2	6.9
8.7	0.00	0.0	0.00	5.8	0.4	1.35	9.00	4.55	70.3	5.1	48.4	10.7	7.2
7.7	0.58	3.2	0.00	6.6	0.9	1.21	9.27	4.13	50.2	1.9	25.1	21.7	7.8
8.9	0.07	0.2	-0.01	5.0	0.8	0.98	7.56	3.43	66.5	5.9	52.4	8.3	7.9
3.8	2.89	13.6	0.07	4.2	0.7	1.01	9.04	3.09	60.9	6.0	50.2	5.8	5.9
6.7	0.00	0.0	0.00	9.8	2.4	2.63	28.85	4.38	32.7	1.0	4.2	28.4	7.8
8.9	0.09	0.5	0.05	5.2	0.8	1.26	11.68	3.32	57.3	4.4	23.8	7.4	6.4
7.0	0.07	0.4	-0.08	7.9	2.2	1.32	8.78	3.75	48.9	0.6	11.2	46.6	8.0
2.9	10.18	25.2	0.90	1.5	0.2	0.35	2.91	3.01	90.0	6.1	56.6	6.3	4.4
3.1	1.99	18.2	0.16	4.9	1.9	1.06	12.18	4.11	66.7	0.4	4.0	53.6	5.2
6.1	2.13	8.1	0.17	9.0	3.5	2.58	17.77	4.15	42.6	1.3	13.0	26.9	8.8
5.9	0.43	2.4	-0.01	4.7	0.6	1.04	9.64	3.58	67.1	2.1	27.0	20.0	6.6
8.5	0.00	0.0	0.00	3.9	0.2	0.66	4.72	3.08	66.8	5.3	46.1	9.1	6.9
4.1	0.69	5.7	0.01	4.5	1.2	1.03	12.13	3.79	69.7	3.0	24.8	12.7	4.8
8.7	0.33	1.5	0.00	7.1	1.8	1.80	14.58	3.72	40.1	1.9	29.9	26.1	7.5
7.3	0.82	4.2	0.00	6.5	4.6	1.21	11.04	3.62	56.3	1.9	20.4	20.7	7.8
8.4	0.20	0.8	0.20	4.3	0.4	1.04	11.87	3.32	71.8	4.6	37.5	11.3	4.7
5.2	2.35	9.2	0.15	5.1	3.8	1.25	10.66	3.75	67.3	6.1	50.4	6.2	6.9
1.0	9.22	32.8	0.40	6.1	0.7	1.07	5.65	4.19	64.7	2.2	30.4	20.9	6.1

Name	City	State	2015 Rating	2014 Rating	Total Assets ($Mil)	One Year Asset Growth	Commercial Loans	Consumer Loans	Mortgage Loans	Securities	Capitalization Index	Leverage Ratio	Risk-Based Capital Ratio
Security State Bank	Basin	WY	B+	B+	A-	320.9	-1.88	7.0	3.3	9.7	24.6	10.0	11.4	19.9
Security State Bank & Trust	Fredericksburg	TX	A-	A-	B	931.7	8.70	10.3	2.9	12.0	33.4	10.0	13.3	32.6
▲ Security State Bank of Aitkin	Aitkin	MN	B+	B-	B-	95.3	-1.37	13.9	2.6	11.4	23.9	10.0	11.5	17.8
Security State Bank of Fergus Falls	Fergus Falls	MN	C+	C+	C+	125.0	-4.78	9.4	0.4	7.9	19.3	7.4	9.9	12.8
Security State Bank of Hibbing	Hibbing	MN	B	B-	C+	130.1	3.11	18.6	1.3	12.3	23.2	9.3	10.5	20.2
Security State Bank of Kenyon	Kenyon	MN	D-	D	D	52.8	-3.47	8.2	1.1	12.7	3.0	9.8	11.0	14.9
Security State Bank of Lewiston	Lewiston	MN	D+	D+	D+	63.6	0.15	7.9	2.9	7.6	22.0	6.8	8.8	13.0
Security State Bank of Marine	Marine On Saint Croi	MN	B+	B+	B	125.4	3.26	4.1	2.1	38.5	5.1	8.9	10.3	15.6
Security State Bank of Oklee	Oklee	MN	B-	B-	C+	29.5	-4.86	2.1	6.5	12.4	28.0	10.0	17.4	47.4
Security State Bank of Wanamingo	Wanamingo	MN	B	B	B	65.8	3.40	5.2	1.3	5.6	20.2	9.9	11.0	17.3
▼ Security State Bank of Warroad	Warroad	MN	C-	C	B-	93.4	3.62	13.0	12.8	3.8	33.3	10.0	18.9	26.3
Security State Bank of Wewoka, Oklahoma	Wewoka	OK	C+	C+	B-	203.7	3.14	9.7	9.6	16.3	15.8	6.1	8.7	11.9
Security State Bank, Wishek, North Dakota	Wishek	ND	B-	B-	B-	71.0	0.38	6.1	3.3	2.0	43.1	10.0	12.0	19.3
Security Trust & Savings Bank	Storm Lake	IA	C+	B-	B-	205.0	1.11	3.0	0.7	6.9	53.9	9.4	10.6	25.1
SEI Private Trust Co.	Oaks	PA	U	U	U	145.2	7.67	0.0	0.0	0.0	73.2	10.0	87.9	278.2
Seiling State Bank	Seiling	OK	C+	C+	C+	95.6	3.08	11.2	3.5	8.1	27.9	8.0	9.7	14.0
Select Bank	Forest	VA	B-	B-	C+	188.7	26.18	26.8	2.1	23.9	0.7	7.5	9.3	15.4
Select Bank & Trust Co.	Dunn	NC	B-	B	B-	844.2	7.41	7.1	0.6	11.1	7.8	9.6	12.6	14.7
Senath State Bank	Senath	MO	A-	A	A	67.0	-0.53	6.0	11.0	36.9	8.1	10.0	16.0	28.8
▲ Seneca Federal S&L Assn.	Baldwinsville	NY	C	C-	D+	154.4	13.72	7.9	0.8	59.4	12.1	7.0	9.0	16.9
▼ Sentry Bank	Saint Joseph	MN	B	B+	B+	212.8	8.88	13.8	2.1	9.9	22.6	5.8	7.8	12.9
ServisFirst Bank	Birmingham	AL	B+	B+	B+	6002.2	25.80	30.5	0.9	5.9	6.3	6.3	9.1	12.0
Settlers Bank	Marietta	OH	B+	B	B	120.1	-2.66	4.9	4.3	46.3	4.5	10.0	11.8	17.6
▲ Settlers bank	Windsor	WI	B-	C+	B-	210.0	8.57	18.8	1.6	16.0	1.6	7.3	9.9	12.8
▲ Severn Savings Bank, FSB	Annapolis	MD	B	C+	C	774.0	0.43	2.8	0.2	37.8	8.9	10.0	12.7	17.5
Sevier County Bank	Sevierville	TN	E+	E+	E-	321.8	4.52	2.3	0.6	8.8	10.9	2.4	6.0	9.5
Sewickley Savings Bank	Sewickley	PA	B-	B-	B-	311.5	0.29	2.8	0.1	3.9	67.9	10.0	27.2	67.3
Seymour Bank	Seymour	MO	B	B	B	125.1	-7.25	2.0	5.6	21.1	26.3	10.0	14.3	22.3
Shamrock Bank, N.A.	Coalgate	OK	B+	A-	B	289.9	0.86	6.3	6.0	15.6	31.2	10.0	12.0	19.6
Sharon Savings Bank	Darby	PA	D	D	D	170.4	-9.95	0.2	0.1	24.8	52.4	9.5	10.7	16.1
Shelby County State Bank	Harlan	IA	B-	B-	B	253.6	1.74	3.2	2.2	6.0	19.2	8.2	9.8	14.5
Shelby County State Bank	Shelbyville	IL	B	B	B	218.2	-0.56	5.8	3.0	16.1	23.0	9.4	10.6	14.8
Shelby Savings Bank, SSB	Center	TX	B+	B+	A-	301.7	12.62	12.0	4.9	16.8	14.4	10.0	11.8	16.0
Shelby State Bank	Shelby	MI	B-	B-	C+	236.0	3.48	4.8	1.8	13.2	26.6	6.6	8.6	13.1
Shell Lake State Bank	Shell Lake	WI	A-	A-	A	183.1	4.16	4.7	2.5	21.9	48.8	10.0	16.9	35.8
Sherburne State Bank	Becker	MN	B	B+	B+	102.4	10.05	8.7	1.8	12.3	16.3	6.8	8.8	14.4
Sherwood Community Bank	Creighton	MO	C-	C-	C-	46.7	2.27	2.0	1.7	28.5	14.1	7.0	9.0	16.5
▲ Sherwood State Bank	Sherwood	OH	B-	D+	C+	61.4	8.17	7.0	9.1	24.5	26.3	10.0	11.8	20.7
Shinhan Bank America	New York	NY	B+	B	B+	1133.5	11.51	20.4	0.3	15.6	5.8	10.0	13.5	18.2
Shore Community Bank	Toms River	NJ	C+	C+	C	263.7	10.17	3.6	0.1	19.7	16.9	8.2	9.8	15.6
▲ Shore United Bank	Easton	MD	B	C+	C	1130.0	133.19	5.5	0.6	23.6	14.7	9.4	10.6	14.6
▼ Sibley State Bank	Sibley	IA	C	B-	B-	77.8	-0.38	2.8	2.0	5.4	8.0	7.3	10.1	12.8
Sicily Island State Bank	Sicily Island	LA	B	B	B+	55.0	12.15	8.2	9.0	34.3	5.3	10.0	12.0	16.3
Sidney Federal S&L Assn.	Sidney	NE	E+	E+	D-	18.3	-18.29	0.0	1.6	59.7	27.6	5.4	7.4	19.7
Sidney State Bank	Sidney	MI	B-	B-	C+	55.2	4.26	2.2	4.7	56.0	9.4	10.0	11.7	20.5
Signature Bank	Rosemont	IL	B-	B-	C	609.2	16.05	35.4	0.3	5.2	4.8	5.2	8.4	11.1
Signature Bank	Minnetonka	MN	B-	B-	C+	370.0	12.70	29.9	2.7	11.2	7.7	5.4	8.8	11.3
Signature Bank	New York	NY	A-	A-	A-	37792.3	18.40	11.2	0.5	1.5	22.0	7.8	9.5	13.6
Signature Bank of Arkansas	Fayetteville	AR	B	B-	D	509.4	0.18	13.4	1.4	19.5	9.4	9.8	12.4	14.9
▼ Signature Bank of Georgia	Sandy Springs	GA	D-	D	D-	99.9	14.72	12.5	0.5	2.6	25.9	8.0	9.7	16.7
Signature Bank, N.A.	Toledo	OH	B	B	B	782.5	9.16	20.3	1.2	10.9	2.2	6.2	9.7	11.9
Silex Banking Co.	Silex	MO	B	B+	B+	71.9	0.82	3.5	0.7	9.1	51.2	10.0	15.0	29.5
Silicon Valley Bank	Santa Clara	CA	B	B+	B+	42664.5	3.84	22.2	0.2	4.1	48.1	5.7	7.7	13.8
▲ Silver Lake Bank	Topeka	KS	B	C+	C	250.8	0.19	9.5	1.0	19.0	29.8	10.0	11.3	20.0
Silvergate Bank	La Jolla	CA	B	B+	B+	986.2	10.85	3.8	0.0	44.3	8.5	7.2	9.1	14.5
Simmesport State Bank	Simmesport	LA	B	B+	B+	75.4	6.48	6.9	17.0	38.4	4.6	10.0	15.1	23.2
Simmons Bank	Pine Bluff	AR	B-	B-	C+	7660.8	1.92	8.9	6.5	14.8	18.6	8.6	10.1	14.2
Simsbury Bank & Trust Co.	Simsbury	CT	C	C	C-	504.8	21.61	14.7	7.4	30.0	12.6	5.6	7.6	11.8
Siouxland National Bank	South Sioux City	NE	C	C	C	52.4	-0.90	9.1	3.0	21.3	0.2	7.6	9.4	20.0
SJN Bank of Kansas	Saint John	KS	A-	A-	A-	99.8	5.22	14.6	2.9	6.4	19.3	10.0	12.6	17.6

Asset Quality Index	Adjusted Non-Performing Loans as a % of Total Loans	as a % of Capital	Net Charge-Offs Avg Loans	Profitability Index	Net Income ($Mil)	Return on Assets (R.O.A.)	Return on Equity (R.O.E.)	Net Interest Spread	Overhead Efficiency Ratio	Liquidity Index	Liquidity Ratio	Hot Money Ratio	Stability Index
7.0	1.10	5.5	0.08	4.8	1.9	0.79	7.02	3.75	69.0	1.7	18.7	22.6	7.1
5.7	2.40	10.1	0.02	6.7	10.1	1.51	11.23	4.04	61.4	4.4	23.2	6.9	8.3
8.8	0.33	1.5	0.00	5.1	0.9	1.26	11.15	4.07	67.4	5.1	27.3	4.0	5.9
0.9	4.22	30.1	0.00	4.0	0.9	0.90	8.92	3.47	73.0	3.6	5.6	8.4	4.9
4.2	2.88	13.0	0.02	5.2	0.8	0.89	8.90	3.66	64.4	3.8	42.3	16.7	5.2
0.0	8.17	51.0	0.21	3.2	0.2	0.49	4.52	4.27	82.5	2.5	10.7	16.1	5.7
4.1	2.43	15.8	-0.04	2.3	0.1	0.22	2.59	3.86	93.2	5.3	29.5	2.9	3.0
5.3	1.31	8.8	-0.01	7.2	1.6	1.79	17.45	4.27	60.7	3.5	23.8	12.3	6.3
8.7	1.09	2.3	-0.01	3.8	0.2	0.90	5.48	1.87	66.4	6.0	55.6	6.9	7.3
6.0	1.04	5.3	0.00	4.3	0.5	1.05	9.25	3.33	70.6	4.5	39.2	12.2	6.7
1.6	10.87	26.9	1.52	3.0	0.2	0.30	1.55	3.83	80.8	5.4	42.6	8.3	6.6
3.6	1.56	12.7	0.43	6.9	2.3	1.56	17.51	5.02	57.9	0.8	7.5	32.4	4.1
8.4	0.82	2.5	0.07	3.9	0.5	0.91	7.70	2.96	67.9	5.7	53.7	8.5	6.7
9.0	0.39	1.1	0.57	3.0	1.2	0.75	6.49	2.72	64.2	6.4	69.7	8.9	6.3
10.0	na	0.0	na	9.5	33.6	30.96	34.72	2.14	71.0	4.0	na	100.0	10.0
7.9	0.17	1.1	0.01	3.7	0.6	0.83	8.26	4.10	77.1	0.6	8.0	37.8	5.7
5.7	0.36	3.3	0.08	4.3	0.9	0.72	7.62	3.52	67.9	0.5	8.0	56.1	4.5
3.8	1.02	6.0	0.00	5.0	5.7	0.92	6.91	4.20	63.2	1.1	14.3	30.0	7.6
7.5	1.10	4.3	0.15	7.5	1.0	1.87	12.34	3.99	59.4	5.1	30.8	5.0	9.1
5.2	1.19	10.2	0.16	2.6	0.4	0.33	4.16	3.50	84.9	1.3	9.5	25.2	3.9
5.0	0.58	4.3	0.01	7.0	2.6	1.65	14.60	3.57	47.9	2.2	29.3	20.9	7.9
8.1	0.14	1.1	0.11	8.2	61.4	1.47	16.08	3.52	38.2	4.1	16.9	8.8	8.2
5.1	1.43	9.5	-0.05	6.4	1.1	1.16	10.04	3.82	55.1	1.6	6.8	20.1	7.4
8.2	0.00	0.0	0.00	4.2	1.0	0.68	7.03	3.53	68.6	0.8	17.2	40.6	5.3
4.6	3.02	17.7	-0.02	4.6	14.8	2.56	17.36	3.17	78.3	1.1	16.8	29.2	6.7
3.8	0.89	8.0	0.00	1.3	0.1	0.06	0.93	3.21	98.3	1.2	16.6	29.5	1.0
10.0	0.02	0.0	0.00	3.6	1.5	0.63	2.34	1.90	53.0	4.6	107.1	27.8	7.6
8.6	0.06	0.3	0.00	4.3	0.9	0.91	6.59	4.22	75.3	3.6	27.1	12.7	7.3
7.8	0.57	2.7	0.12	5.1	2.8	1.25	10.36	4.23	71.2	3.4	37.7	17.2	7.5
6.6	2.34	6.5	0.11	1.0	-0.2	-0.11	-0.98	2.70	95.9	5.3	62.6	14.0	5.1
4.1	0.62	4.0	0.00	5.2	1.8	0.96	8.95	3.48	59.5	4.7	25.4	5.4	6.6
8.1	0.21	1.4	-0.01	4.8	1.7	1.06	9.93	3.51	69.5	4.2	15.1	7.4	6.7
8.0	0.43	2.5	0.11	5.2	2.7	1.26	10.44	3.81	66.9	1.2	13.5	27.9	7.5
4.4	1.95	12.7	0.03	4.1	1.2	0.70	7.63	3.78	81.9	4.6	27.7	7.1	5.0
8.8	1.42	3.5	0.17	5.8	1.9	1.37	7.40	3.93	58.0	5.6	45.4	8.2	8.5
4.0	2.18	14.4	0.00	7.8	1.4	1.89	20.59	4.22	58.8	4.8	29.3	7.0	6.1
4.5	1.29	8.8	0.20	3.4	0.2	0.70	7.70	4.29	84.4	4.2	23.1	8.7	4.6
4.3	2.10	10.5	0.17	3.3	0.2	0.39	3.42	4.74	85.8	4.4	28.1	8.6	5.5
6.5	0.38	2.5	-0.39	5.3	7.3	0.91	6.34	3.34	71.5	0.8	10.6	29.7	8.1
6.3	0.74	4.6	-0.04	3.9	1.2	0.66	6.54	3.67	69.8	1.8	19.7	21.6	5.4
5.0	1.92	13.0	0.29	6.9	6.5	1.24	13.50	5.61	64.7	3.2	8.6	12.4	5.9
2.7	3.17	24.2	0.01	5.8	0.6	0.96	9.67	3.66	61.8	0.9	5.3	30.2	5.8
5.6	0.98	6.5	-0.28	8.0	0.7	1.75	14.66	5.74	71.2	0.5	9.6	58.9	8.1
7.1	0.42	3.3	0.00	0.0	-0.1	-0.70	-7.38	2.81	144.9	3.5	34.8	13.7	2.5
4.4	2.67	16.8	0.15	4.0	0.3	0.76	6.56	4.34	77.4	4.2	21.4	8.0	5.8
4.4	1.21	9.8	0.06	7.2	5.3	1.20	14.47	3.69	49.8	4.1	27.2	5.4	5.5
5.1	0.50	4.3	-0.01	6.5	4.3	1.55	17.36	4.23	62.0	3.6	14.6	7.2	6.0
5.3	0.79	6.0	0.63	7.1	282.4	1.05	11.19	3.23	32.4	4.8	15.7	4.1	8.4
6.8	0.63	3.8	0.48	4.9	3.1	0.81	6.59	4.10	71.6	0.7	11.9	33.1	6.4
7.4	0.00	0.0	0.05	0.3	-0.4	-0.47	-4.41	4.29	112.3	4.9	22.4	3.9	2.1
8.1	0.08	0.6	-0.04	5.7	6.1	1.07	11.01	3.39	54.1	3.2	21.1	9.9	6.9
9.6	0.00	0.0	0.00	4.7	0.6	1.05	7.14	3.30	60.7	5.5	60.3	10.7	7.7
8.0	0.59	3.2	0.47	4.9	274.4	0.85	11.16	2.78	51.8	7.5	52.1	0.1	5.8
5.4	2.60	12.5	0.08	4.3	1.7	0.85	7.44	2.91	73.7	2.9	13.3	14.6	5.8
6.5	0.38	3.4	0.00	5.3	5.7	0.83	8.98	3.77	63.0	1.1	14.7	20.0	5.8
3.3	2.98	16.0	0.40	9.2	1.0	1.72	11.87	5.24	48.4	0.7	14.5	45.2	7.9
3.6	1.66	11.1	0.35	7.8	77.4	1.37	9.77	4.25	59.0	4.1	13.9	8.4	9.1
4.5	0.78	7.8	0.00	2.5	1.3	0.36	4.57	3.19	83.6	4.1	14.9	7.8	3.5
6.1	1.17	6.4	0.11	2.7	0.2	0.42	4.56	2.67	82.4	2.9	41.4	21.8	4.5
8.1	0.23	1.1	0.20	9.7	1.3	1.81	14.48	4.82	45.2	1.5	15.9	24.9	8.0

www.weissratings.com
193
Data as of September 30, 2016

Name	City	State	2015 Rating	2014 Rating	Total Assets ($Mil)	One Year Asset Growth	Comm-ercial Loans	Cons-umer Loans	Mort-gage Loans	Secur-ities	Capital-ization Index	Lever-age Ratio	Risk-Based Capital Ratio
			Rating										
Skagit Bank	Burlington	WA	B-	B-	B-	891.3	6.64	6.0	4.4	7.3	34.7	6.9	8.9	14.2
Skowhegan Savings Bank	Skowhegan	ME	B-	B-	B-	609.6	8.72	3.6	9.3	34.3	15.1	10.0	12.7	19.6
Sloan State Bank	Sloan	IA	A-	A-	B+	52.7	-0.32	5.2	4.1	14.6	45.6	10.0	11.0	21.9
Slovenian S&L Assn. of Canonsburg	Strabane	PA	A-	A-	A-	358.9	5.37	0.0	0.3	37.6	51.0	10.0	14.1	25.1
Slovenian S&L Assn. of Franklin-Conemau	Conemaugh	PA	C+	C+	C+	130.5	-0.21	0.0	1.2	50.2	26.8	10.0	11.9	26.1
Smackover State Bank	Smackover	AR	B	B	B	183.0	-3.31	1.6	4.4	15.4	55.2	10.0	12.0	28.3
Small Business Bank	Lenexa	KS	D+	D-	C+	88.1	-12.12	16.6	13.4	9.9	28.3	8.5	10.0	16.0
Small Town Bank	Wedowee	AL	A	A	A	211.5	-1.49	4.4	2.6	8.2	35.4	10.0	16.0	28.1
SmartBank	Pigeon Forge	TN	C+	C+	B	1037.6	83.89	8.0	0.7	13.5	13.4	6.1	9.6	11.8
SNB Bank, N.A.	Shattuck	OK	C-	C	C	116.2	23.61	17.1	6.9	1.4	15.1	6.5	8.6	12.4
Solera National Bank	Lakewood	CO	B-	C+	D+	149.3	7.08	4.4	9.7	15.2	27.2	10.0	13.2	20.4
Solomon State Bank	Solomon	KS	A	A	A	201.1	-1.27	3.2	1.9	51.7	4.8	10.0	13.8	22.9
Solon State Bank	Solon	IA	B	B	B	91.8	1.82	19.6	1.8	9.6	34.1	10.0	22.6	25.1
▲ Solutions North Bank	Stockton	KS	B	B-	B-	229.7	277.80	6.5	1.9	4.8	18.8	8.5	10.2	13.8
Solvay Bank	Solvay	NY	B	B	B	866.2	5.25	8.9	8.7	27.2	34.2	7.0	9.0	17.2
Somerset Savings Bank, SLA	Bound Brook	NJ	C+	B-	B-	572.0	2.21	0.0	0.0	41.4	32.3	10.0	19.7	50.0
Somerset Trust Co.	Somerset	PA	B-	B-	B	1038.9	4.83	16.1	3.4	10.9	29.9	6.7	9.3	12.3
Somerville National Bank	Somerville	OH	C+	B-	B-	163.7	-1.18	2.0	1.3	23.5	30.5	10.0	11.4	22.7
Sonabank	McLean	VA	B+	B+	A-	1135.0	11.55	10.2	0.1	18.9	8.1	8.1	10.5	13.4
Sooner State Bank	Tuttle	OK	A	A	A	190.6	2.35	12.9	2.8	19.5	23.4	10.0	11.4	18.0
▲ Sound Banking Co.	Morehead City	NC	C+	C	C+	190.6	16.07	4.8	1.5	26.3	8.2	6.5	8.5	12.5
Sound Banking Co.	Lakewood	WA	B-	B-	C+	56.3	15.53	17.9	1.7	18.8	0.0	6.4	8.4	14.6
Sound Community Bank	Seattle	WA	B	B-	B-	565.6	12.78	3.8	7.2	29.4	1.2	8.0	10.1	13.4
South Atlantic Bank	Myrtle Beach	SC	C+	C+	C+	436.2	13.29	4.6	1.0	25.0	10.4	5.2	7.8	11.2
South Carolina Community Bank	Columbia	SC	E	E-	E-	51.3	-6.26	4.5	0.6	14.7	14.0	5.8	8.2	11.6
South Central Bank, Inc.	Glasgow	KY	B	B	B	932.4	8.13	5.2	2.5	17.0	20.7	10.0	11.9	17.1
South Central Bank, N.A.	Chicago	IL	C-	C-	C-	296.8	12.94	13.7	1.5	10.7	50.7	5.9	7.9	15.9
South Central State Bank	Campbell	NE	B+	B	B	118.4	-1.23	6.8	1.3	1.4	23.2	7.4	10.9	12.8
South Coast Bank & Trust	Brunswick	GA	B-	B-	D	100.6	16.27	5.2	1.1	18.2	7.4	7.9	10.0	13.3
▲ South County Bank, N.A.	Irvine	CA	C-	D	E	157.1	13.93	9.2	0.2	4.8	23.9	8.6	10.1	16.0
▲ South Georgia Bank	Glennville	GA	A-	B	B-	143.2	8.65	3.1	4.2	19.2	17.2	10.0	11.2	18.8
South Georgia Banking Co.	Tifton	GA	B+	B-	B-	433.7	-1.07	4.5	2.6	10.7	21.6	10.0	11.3	19.4
South Lafourche Bank & Trust Co.	Larose	LA	D-	E+	C	164.8	2.02	18.7	4.2	41.9	4.9	9.4	10.6	15.7
South Louisiana Bank	Houma	LA	A	A	A	449.1	-4.89	17.0	2.3	9.4	15.7	10.0	13.8	20.3
South Ottumwa Savings Bank	Ottumwa	IA	B	B	C+	400.5	4.91	3.3	1.0	14.4	45.5	10.0	11.4	21.7
South Porte Bank	Marion	IL	C-	D+	D	69.4	22.74	4.6	2.4	28.3	8.5	6.4	8.4	13.3
South Shore Bank	South Weymouth	MA	C	C-	C-	1058.7	3.19	3.5	0.5	29.7	20.2	9.4	10.6	16.7
South Side Trust & Savings Bank of Peoria	Peoria	IL	B+	B+	B+	663.1	0.64	5.2	2.0	26.2	33.1	10.0	11.9	19.3
South Sound Bank	Olympia	WA	B	B	C	162.6	-1.16	14.8	0.6	7.3	14.4	10.0	13.3	18.1
▲ South State Bank	Columbia	SC	B+	B-	C+	8794.0	3.44	5.6	5.9	22.8	10.6	7.0	9.4	12.5
South Story Bank & Trust	Huxley	IA	B-	B	B	162.5	13.16	14.5	1.1	18.2	9.4	6.0	8.0	11.7
Southbridge Savings Bank	Southbridge	MA	C	C-	C	543.8	9.58	3.7	2.2	53.9	3.2	5.2	8.1	11.2
▲ SouthCrest Bank NA	Tyrone	GA	C+	D+	D	541.5	0.68	3.9	1.4	16.5	33.3	7.5	9.3	15.0
▲ SouthEast Bank	Farragut	TN	C+	C	C-	1140.4	38.20	4.6	55.1	6.4	0.0	7.2	9.1	17.9
Southeast First National Bank	Summerville	GA	C	C+	C	60.3	8.69	0.6	2.5	10.0	57.6	10.0	11.3	39.1
Southeast National Bank	Moline	IL	B-	B-	C+	203.6	8.94	9.0	1.1	14.6	38.3	8.6	10.1	18.8
▲ Southeastern Bank	Darien	GA	B-	C	C-	407.2	4.33	4.2	1.7	9.5	28.0	9.7	10.8	19.0
Southern Bancorp Bank	Arkadelphia	AR	B	B	B-	1193.5	0.74	9.2	3.1	17.6	16.3	8.3	9.9	14.2
Southern Bank	Sardis	GA	B	B-	C	78.3	0.71	1.0	14.0	30.0	19.2	10.0	11.7	18.9
Southern Bank	Poplar Bluff	MO	B+	A-	A-	1465.9	11.66	7.5	1.3	19.6	8.5	5.6	9.2	11.5
Southern Bank & Trust	Clarkesville	GA	B	B	B	141.9	13.22	3.8	3.4	21.5	14.7	9.3	10.5	14.5
Southern Bank and Trust Co.	Mount Olive	NC	C+	C	C+	2440.5	10.26	6.5	1.1	10.9	26.5	7.1	9.1	13.9
▼ Southern Bank Co.	Gadsden	AL	D	D	D	95.2	-2.97	12.0	1.6	5.9	35.1	10.0	11.3	19.3
Southern Bank of Tennessee	Mount Juliet	TN	C+	C-	D	237.5	13.08	8.0	1.3	23.1	10.3	8.6	10.3	13.8
Southern Community Bank	Tullahoma	TN	C+	C+	C	235.1	30.40	8.7	1.6	20.5	13.7	3.5	8.2	10.2
Southern First Bank	Greenville	SC	B-	B-	C+	1287.3	9.93	12.4	1.4	22.9	5.3	6.0	9.1	11.8
Southern Heritage Bank	Jonesville	LA	A-	A-	A-	281.3	-0.20	9.7	5.9	28.0	21.4	10.0	11.9	20.5
Southern Hills Community Bank	Leesburg	OH	C+	C+	C+	87.6	5.52	2.5	4.3	40.8	0.0	10.0	15.3	31.6
Southern Illinois Bank	Johnston City	IL	B+	B	B	108.7	4.31	7.9	2.2	17.7	30.9	9.4	10.6	16.5
Southern Independent Bank	Opp	AL	B	B-	B-	214.7	-5.09	17.4	2.4	16.5	31.7	9.9	11.0	18.8

Asset Quality Index	Adjusted Non-Performing Loans as a % of Total Loans	as a % of Capital	Net Charge-Offs Avg Loans	Profitability Index	Net Income ($Mil)	Return on Assets (R.O.A.)	Return on Equity (R.O.E.)	Net Interest Spread	Overhead Efficiency Ratio	Liquidity Index	Liquidity Ratio	Hot Money Ratio	Stability Index
7.2	0.38	2.2	-0.10	4.0	5.1	0.80	8.99	3.21	71.2	4.6	35.9	10.7	5.8
5.0	1.57	9.0	0.07	3.7	2.8	0.66	4.87	3.66	76.5	4.5	21.3	6.2	8.2
8.8	0.14	0.5	-0.02	7.4	0.7	1.74	14.76	3.79	46.2	6.1	51.6	5.3	8.0
6.1	4.72	14.8	0.01	5.9	2.5	0.92	6.69	2.66	36.0	3.0	62.7	47.0	7.8
9.1	0.78	3.5	0.06	2.9	0.4	0.41	3.61	2.97	80.9	4.3	47.1	15.4	6.0
8.3	1.25	3.2	0.10	4.4	1.2	0.88	7.20	3.09	60.0	3.2	57.4	30.2	7.2
4.6	1.12	6.0	0.18	1.6	0.3	0.39	3.98	3.10	93.0	5.1	26.3	3.1	3.8
6.0	2.41	6.8	-0.01	6.5	1.9	1.16	6.83	4.18	60.9	4.4	46.6	14.5	7.4
6.1	0.36	2.8	0.00	4.1	4.7	0.62	6.89	3.98	74.9	1.5	11.2	19.9	6.3
3.7	2.00	15.6	0.22	2.9	0.4	0.57	7.02	3.27	72.5	0.7	15.4	44.9	4.2
8.7	0.09	0.4	-0.10	3.7	1.2	1.09	8.09	3.15	69.9	0.7	19.2	53.9	7.2
7.2	0.82	4.2	0.40	8.6	2.6	1.74	12.50	3.78	37.1	1.5	12.2	23.6	8.4
4.8	3.35	8.5	0.88	10.0	1.8	2.61	10.62	5.61	46.0	5.9	50.1	6.0	8.4
5.7	1.72	10.5	-0.16	8.0	1.8	2.02	25.38	7.05	67.2	3.7	11.8	10.3	5.7
5.5	0.75	4.8	0.06	4.4	5.2	0.83	9.32	2.92	64.2	2.5	19.7	17.1	6.1
10.0	0.28	0.6	0.02	2.8	1.4	0.34	1.75	2.17	78.5	6.2	65.4	9.4	8.2
4.6	2.03	12.5	0.23	4.1	8.1	1.05	11.78	4.45	80.5	3.3	27.9	10.4	7.9
5.7	2.48	11.9	0.28	2.5	0.4	0.33	2.89	2.84	87.7	3.9	46.1	16.9	5.9
7.2	0.29	2.2	0.61	5.7	8.2	1.02	9.07	4.03	51.1	0.5	6.5	49.0	8.7
8.6	0.15	0.8	0.01	6.6	2.2	1.53	13.01	4.22	63.2	2.8	29.9	17.9	8.5
4.5	1.28	10.6	0.05	3.8	0.8	0.57	6.35	4.15	76.2	1.9	19.4	18.9	4.2
5.7	0.53	3.9	0.00	8.5	0.8	2.02	22.43	4.64	52.4	3.9	26.2	11.0	5.4
4.3	1.16	9.2	0.01	5.8	3.9	0.96	9.52	4.38	67.9	1.5	12.2	23.1	5.8
5.9	0.59	5.5	-0.03	3.7	2.0	0.62	7.72	3.84	78.1	3.2	13.6	9.8	4.4
0.0	22.42	145.1	0.44	0.0	-0.9	-2.31	-26.98	3.69	151.5	0.8	16.1	35.4	1.1
6.4	1.17	6.1	0.07	4.4	5.3	0.77	6.47	3.59	73.8	3.0	21.3	14.7	6.3
4.7	3.26	12.5	0.20	2.0	0.5	0.23	2.76	3.07	93.0	5.0	53.0	13.0	3.5
8.3	0.05	0.3	0.02	5.8	1.0	1.15	11.13	3.60	59.4	3.1	30.5	16.5	6.7
7.2	0.22	1.6	0.07	3.3	0.6	0.78	7.71	3.91	78.2	0.8	18.2	35.6	5.2
8.2	0.21	1.1	-0.62	2.4	0.6	0.55	5.15	3.32	96.8	2.3	26.5	15.7	3.3
8.5	0.31	1.6	-0.07	9.7	2.6	2.44	21.77	6.14	59.3	1.6	29.3	29.7	6.0
5.7	1.38	5.8	-0.06	6.1	3.7	1.11	8.36	3.69	62.8	3.8	41.3	16.5	7.7
0.1	13.18	91.7	0.39	1.9	0.1	0.08	0.73	3.46	76.7	1.0	12.8	30.7	6.4
5.8	1.66	7.0	0.02	7.0	4.1	1.19	9.00	4.12	61.5	1.9	22.3	20.0	8.5
8.1	0.66	2.7	-0.18	4.9	3.9	1.30	10.02	3.26	59.9	2.7	41.5	26.4	7.0
6.3	0.38	3.1	0.02	2.4	0.2	0.46	5.55	2.83	82.9	1.0	24.8	36.4	3.9
5.7	1.41	9.0	0.08	2.7	3.1	0.40	3.56	2.87	82.1	3.9	22.6	12.0	8.1
6.9	1.28	5.6	0.19	4.7	4.0	0.80	6.53	3.01	66.4	3.8	29.8	12.7	7.8
8.4	0.15	0.7	0.15	4.1	1.0	0.78	5.46	3.89	72.4	4.5	23.5	6.1	6.2
5.5	0.48	3.8	0.05	7.3	81.4	1.25	9.68	4.25	62.7	4.6	12.3	4.6	9.0
2.9	1.77	15.5	0.02	5.5	1.5	1.28	12.68	4.32	69.1	1.9	13.4	19.3	5.9
4.3	1.17	12.8	0.06	2.7	1.4	0.37	4.54	3.10	85.0	1.7	7.3	19.6	5.0
5.1	1.45	7.7	0.18	4.2	10.3	2.50	24.69	3.56	84.0	4.3	25.9	8.3	4.4
3.6	0.64	6.5	0.03	5.9	5.7	0.79	8.94	3.96	69.8	0.7	10.1	16.7	5.1
6.2	4.33	7.6	0.57	2.3	0.1	0.23	2.04	2.67	89.3	6.2	57.4	5.8	5.2
7.2	0.40	2.1	0.00	3.7	1.1	0.75	6.94	3.78	82.1	5.6	37.5	4.9	6.5
5.3	1.62	6.8	-0.12	4.2	2.6	0.86	7.71	3.59	73.1	5.2	37.6	7.8	5.3
4.2	1.75	11.8	0.28	4.8	7.9	0.91	7.20	4.26	70.2	3.4	8.7	11.5	9.0
5.6	1.56	8.4	0.43	3.9	0.4	0.73	6.33	5.22	79.7	1.7	14.9	22.0	5.5
6.3	0.69	5.7	0.12	6.3	11.3	1.09	11.50	3.86	58.3	1.4	3.7	23.4	8.8
4.4	1.53	10.3	0.03	4.6	0.9	0.89	8.41	4.45	71.3	3.2	22.6	13.6	6.7
7.5	0.50	3.3	0.14	3.7	10.6	0.59	5.93	3.90	78.5	5.0	23.4	5.4	6.5
2.9	6.04	29.1	3.54	0.0	-1.3	-1.69	-12.69	3.57	114.2	1.2	17.0	29.0	6.3
8.4	0.00	0.0	-0.11	4.0	1.6	0.97	8.73	3.57	76.5	1.2	22.1	30.5	6.1
5.4	0.47	4.3	0.11	4.7	1.3	0.80	8.78	3.81	64.7	0.6	6.4	41.2	5.1
5.7	0.89	7.7	0.15	5.8	10.1	1.09	12.25	3.70	57.1	1.5	6.2	15.0	7.5
7.0	0.97	5.4	0.05	6.4	3.1	1.47	11.97	4.42	69.8	2.7	13.2	15.4	8.3
9.1	0.39	1.5	0.23	2.4	0.1	0.20	1.28	3.59	90.1	5.6	40.8	6.1	6.4
7.8	0.02	0.1	0.15	5.3	0.7	0.93	8.73	3.76	60.4	4.9	11.6	2.0	6.2
7.9	0.47	2.2	0.06	5.2	1.7	1.04	9.66	3.37	57.8	2.0	37.3	31.8	5.2

Name	City	State	2016 Rating	2015 Rating	2014 Rating	Total Assets ($Mil)	One Year Asset Growth	Commercial Loans	Consumer Loans	Mortgage Loans	Securities	Capitalization Index	Leverage Ratio	Risk-Based Capital Ratio
Southern Michigan Bank & Trust	Coldwater	MI	B	B-	B-	619.5	6.34	8.7	1.2	10.5	17.8	7.5	9.9	12.9
▼ Southern Missouri Bank of Marshfield	Marshfield	MO	B	B+	B-	91.7	-1.02	3.6	3.1	29.1	7.6	9.9	11.0	24.5
Southern States Bank	Anniston	AL	B-	B-	B-	608.0	70.68	7.1	0.8	11.5	5.7	6.3	9.5	11.9
SouthernTrust Bank	Goreville	IL	D	D+	D	49.7	2.65	5.8	2.3	24.0	27.0	7.5	9.4	17.8
SouthFirst Bank	Sylacauga	AL	C-	C-	C-	89.8	-0.21	1.8	0.8	35.4	10.2	10.0	11.0	19.2
SouthPoint Bank	Birmingham	AL	B-	C+	C	269.4	15.70	19.1	1.4	11.6	16.5	6.0	9.0	11.7
▲ Southport Bank	Kenosha	WI	C+	D+	D	272.7	3.39	8.3	0.3	11.1	4.4	6.4	9.7	12.0
Southside Bank	Tyler	TX	B	B	B	5458.8	12.97	3.0	2.3	11.8	44.6	8.4	9.9	16.9
SouthStar Bank, S.S.B.	Moulton	TX	B+	B+	B+	783.7	11.48	2.8	0.9	19.3	8.7	6.1	10.5	11.8
SouthTrust Bank, N.A.	George West	TX	D+	B+	B+	352.0	-2.95	6.4	1.9	8.8	18.1	9.0	10.3	14.3
Southwest Bank	Fort Worth	TX	B+	B+	B	2013.8	21.41	13.3	0.8	11.3	3.2	6.7	11.4	12.3
Southwest Bank	Odessa	TX	B	B	B	324.4	-3.00	40.8	1.6	9.4	15.3	5.7	8.3	11.5
Southwest Capital Bank	Albuquerque	NM	B+	B+	A-	342.9	2.35	13.1	0.4	10.6	9.1	6.9	10.1	12.4
Southwest Georgia Bank	Moultrie	GA	B-	B-	C+	441.8	12.88	7.2	0.8	18.3	23.4	6.6	8.6	13.5
Southwest Missouri Bank	Carthage	MO	B	B	B	663.6	3.75	7.4	8.1	24.7	27.0	8.2	9.8	17.7
Southwest National Bank	Wichita	KS	B+	B+	B+	439.7	-0.65	7.1	40.8	5.8	10.8	6.3	9.7	12.0
Southwest National Bank	Weatherford	OK	A-	B+	B+	70.4	-4.10	3.3	3.5	15.3	26.4	10.0	11.8	19.2
Southwestern National Bank	Houston	TX	B	B	B	368.0	5.40	1.3	0.0	0.5	25.1	10.0	12.6	20.9
▲ Southwind Bank	Natoma	KS	B	B-	C+	116.2	-2.21	5.9	3.8	11.3	53.6	7.8	9.5	17.0
Sovereign Bank	Dallas	TX	B-	B-	C+	1097.8	-2.74	25.7	0.2	1.1	17.5	8.2	11.6	13.5
Soy Capital Bank and Trust Co.	Decatur	IL	A	A	A	410.0	4.85	7.7	7.3	2.5	24.3	10.0	15.1	23.2
Spencer County Bank	Santa Claus	IN	C+	C+	C+	119.1	8.80	3.6	3.6	26.4	31.3	9.3	10.6	21.8
Spencer Savings Bank	Spencer	MA	C+	B-	B-	564.2	16.08	3.1	0.6	48.7	4.6	9.3	10.5	15.6
Spencer Savings Bank, SLA	Elmwood Park	NJ	B-	B	B	2585.2	2.10	0.8	0.0	27.8	20.2	10.0	11.7	16.7
Spirit of Texas Bank, SSB	College Station	TX	B	B	B	940.5	12.28	12.2	0.6	21.0	0.9	6.9	9.4	12.4
SpiritBank	Tulsa	OK	C-	D+	D+	746.6	4.93	10.1	1.1	24.7	5.2	7.1	11.0	12.6
Spiro State Bank	Spiro	OK	C-	C-	C-	50.3	-6.18	3.3	5.0	11.2	49.4	10.0	12.4	23.9
Spratt S&L Assn.	Chester	SC	C+	C+	C+	108.4	1.93	2.3	0.3	11.3	52.1	10.0	25.9	70.3
Spring Bank	Bronx	NY	A-	A	B-	157.2	20.64	16.6	0.3	12.5	6.4	10.0	12.0	17.1
▲ Spring Bank	Brookfield	WI	C	D+	C-	240.7	12.56	12.5	0.1	12.9	7.4	8.7	11.0	13.9
Spring Hill State Bank	Longview	TX	B	B-	B-	189.3	1.53	6.3	4.9	50.4	8.2	8.5	10.0	18.6
Spring Valley Bank	Wyoming	OH	B+	B+	B-	71.1	8.45	1.6	0.1	26.4	0.7	10.0	41.7	48.3
Spring Valley City Bank	Spring Valley	IL	B+	B+	B+	187.2	-2.86	2.6	3.1	17.1	47.8	10.0	14.4	31.5
Springfield First Community Bank	Springfield	MO	B-	B-	B	480.8	22.83	13.5	0.9	14.4	0.3	6.7	8.8	12.2
▲ Springfield State Bank	Springfield	KY	A-	B+	A-	299.5	2.26	3.1	2.2	23.9	43.8	10.0	14.5	24.4
Springfield State Bank	Springfield	NE	B	B	B	42.2	-1.35	5.7	4.2	8.2	20.9	10.0	12.3	20.0
Springs Valley Bank & Trust Co.	Jasper	IN	B-	B-	B-	344.9	11.99	5.8	2.8	24.7	14.6	7.9	9.6	13.9
▲ Spur Security Bank	Spur	TX	C+	C-	C	42.4	-4.69	1.9	4.7	2.5	66.4	10.0	11.5	29.6
SSB Bank	Pittsburgh	PA	C	C	D+	138.9	9.11	5.3	0.9	54.3	2.6	6.2	8.2	14.2
SSB Community Bank	Strasburg	OH	C+	C+	B-	72.7	15.58	9.8	1.0	42.7	0.0	7.4	9.3	14.2
▲ SSBBank	Stockbridge	MI	D	D	D	66.3	4.79	5.8	5.3	28.8	28.5	6.3	8.3	15.4
St. Ansgar State Bank	Saint Ansgar	IA	B+	A-	A-	100.7	-0.06	7.7	1.9	9.7	15.8	10.0	13.1	18.2
St. Charles Bank & Trust Co.	Saint Charles	IL	B-	B-	C+	863.6	8.98	28.3	15.9	4.5	8.1	5.3	9.5	11.2
St. Clair County State Bank	Osceola	MO	A-	A-	A-	131.2	2.35	7.3	4.8	22.8	10.6	10.0	12.8	16.9
St. Clair State Bank (Inc.)	Saint Clair	MN	A-	A-	A-	88.6	8.10	7.8	7.4	13.3	3.2	10.0	12.0	16.2
St. Henry Bank	Saint Henry	OH	A+	A+	A+	317.6	5.35	4.0	1.0	13.4	36.3	10.0	13.2	21.7
St. Johns Bank and Trust Co.	Saint Louis	MO	D	D-	D	293.3	-3.09	4.7	0.5	7.3	22.0	7.5	9.3	13.9
St. Landry Bank and Trust Co.	Opelousas	LA	C	C	C+	292.6	3.90	2.3	1.1	3.1	52.2	10.0	11.1	31.6
St. Landry Homestead FSB	Opelousas	LA	B-	B-	C	227.3	0.69	0.9	3.0	52.8	12.5	10.0	20.2	36.4
St. Louis Bank	Town And Country	MO	C	C-	D+	408.6	6.86	13.1	0.2	10.4	10.3	6.4	8.4	12.2
St. Martin Bank and Trust Co.	Saint Martinville	LA	B-	B-	B-	569.5	7.42	5.9	4.6	25.6	10.1	6.2	9.7	11.9
St. Martin National Bank	Saint Martin	MN	B	B	B	21.6	5.11	6.5	4.0	23.8	14.8	10.0	14.4	28.0
St. Marys State Bank	Saint Marys	KS	B-	B	B-	95.4	4.40	8.1	3.0	19.1	26.6	10.0	11.1	15.6
Stafford Savings Bank	Stafford Springs	CT	B-	B	B	266.7	7.22	0.0	0.3	24.2	50.5	10.0	28.6	33.3
Standard Bank and Trust Co.	Hickory Hills	IL	B-	C+	C-	2417.0	0.34	20.7	0.1	7.0	9.1	7.6	10.4	13.0
Standard Bank, PaSB	Monroeville	PA	B	B	B	493.3	5.51	2.6	0.1	53.6	12.7	10.0	12.8	21.4
Standing Stone Bank	Lancaster	OH	D+	D+	C	106.8	3.67	8.0	8.4	19.3	24.8	5.0	7.0	12.0
▲ Stanley Bank	Overland Park	KS	C+	D+	C-	105.2	2.92	36.4	2.3	4.8	0.0	10.0	16.9	24.5
Stanton State Bank	Stanton	NE	C-	C-	C-	45.8	0.23	10.3	4.5	17.1	27.0	6.8	8.8	15.2
Star Bank	Maple Lake	MN	B+	B	B-	239.6	1.74	8.4	2.7	13.0	1.9	6.0	9.6	11.7

Asset Quality Index	Adjusted Non-Performing Loans as a % of Total Loans	as a % of Capital	Net Charge-Offs Avg Loans	Profitability Index	Net Income ($Mil)	Return on Assets (R.O.A.)	Return on Equity (R.O.E.)	Net Interest Spread	Overhead Efficiency Ratio	Liquidity Index	Liquidity Ratio	Hot Money Ratio	Stability Index
5.2	0.46	3.1	0.15	5.4	4.6	1.01	8.41	3.83	68.6	4.2	22.6	8.2	7.6
7.3	0.38	2.4	-0.09	4.0	0.6	0.82	7.60	4.11	80.2	1.4	11.5	24.9	6.7
4.0	0.52	4.2	-0.06	6.2	4.5	1.08	9.99	4.63	63.1	0.7	12.4	31.8	6.5
2.3	4.40	24.7	1.45	0.7	0.0	-0.10	-1.04	3.48	90.9	2.1	27.6	21.3	4.0
5.0	1.81	10.0	-0.04	2.6	0.3	0.41	3.74	3.66	90.8	2.7	29.7	17.8	4.8
6.7	0.12	1.0	0.00	6.0	2.3	1.23	12.87	3.99	72.7	1.0	3.9	26.9	4.5
3.3	1.08	8.2	-0.08	5.0	2.5	1.20	12.07	3.72	58.3	3.9	10.7	8.8	5.1
7.5	0.41	2.0	0.63	4.5	40.6	1.06	10.34	3.33	60.3	2.4	24.5	19.2	7.7
6.5	0.24	2.0	0.18	6.3	5.5	1.06	10.03	4.96	68.5	1.7	8.3	19.9	6.3
1.6	3.41	20.8	0.39	3.4	1.4	0.52	5.05	4.10	76.7	1.8	13.9	20.2	7.4
6.6	0.04	0.3	0.00	6.1	14.4	1.07	8.13	3.96	60.9	3.6	6.6	10.3	9.5
6.1	0.49	3.9	-0.03	5.8	3.5	1.43	16.48	4.41	71.4	4.3	19.7	7.6	5.7
6.3	0.18	1.2	0.25	8.6	4.8	1.88	18.52	5.05	54.0	2.0	11.5	18.7	8.1
6.8	0.28	2.0	0.03	4.7	3.1	0.97	11.63	4.18	73.5	3.5	18.8	11.9	4.6
4.5	1.67	10.2	0.62	4.0	3.8	0.75	7.83	4.06	76.7	4.2	19.4	7.9	6.2
6.7	0.15	1.2	0.35	6.4	4.3	1.34	13.77	3.95	62.4	1.2	11.8	13.0	7.2
8.4	0.70	3.0	-0.39	7.0	0.7	1.33	10.90	4.14	60.6	3.3	48.6	20.0	7.0
8.1	0.00	0.0	-0.28	4.1	2.7	1.01	7.64	2.94	73.8	3.7	55.0	21.1	7.1
5.8	1.10	4.7	0.19	4.7	1.0	1.08	10.88	3.57	60.0	5.3	45.2	9.6	6.0
3.5	1.89	11.7	-0.01	4.1	6.5	0.79	6.99	3.66	62.9	1.1	22.1	43.6	8.4
6.9	0.89	3.0	0.00	5.9	3.1	1.00	6.16	2.68	79.7	4.5	17.1	5.7	8.7
6.4	1.03	4.8	0.23	2.9	0.3	0.41	3.82	3.05	83.1	3.0	41.7	20.9	5.7
5.6	0.86	6.7	0.02	3.3	2.2	0.54	5.07	3.25	73.7	1.8	8.4	19.4	5.8
6.3	1.19	7.1	0.01	3.6	11.6	0.60	5.38	2.68	67.5	2.4	21.0	18.7	8.9
5.9	0.53	4.3	0.06	4.4	4.9	0.74	7.11	4.27	74.6	0.8	19.2	41.0	6.0
1.7	3.57	27.2	0.19	4.0	2.1	0.41	3.34	4.61	93.9	0.4	5.3	55.5	5.5
9.5	0.68	1.4	0.10	1.9	0.1	0.19	1.51	3.52	94.2	6.1	59.2	7.3	5.7
10.0	0.24	0.3	0.00	2.2	0.2	0.26	0.99	2.36	89.5	5.0	93.6	19.2	7.6
5.9	0.81	5.7	0.01	8.1	1.3	1.24	10.21	4.75	60.7	0.6	15.4	45.1	8.4
2.8	1.37	9.3	0.01	7.1	2.0	1.16	10.52	3.54	46.9	0.8	17.8	39.7	6.7
5.0	1.10	7.6	0.17	5.0	1.2	0.87	8.87	3.87	68.4	1.8	17.1	19.8	6.1
5.8	1.77	3.3	0.21	10.0	2.1	3.99	9.55	6.12	31.9	2.0	29.9	25.3	8.7
6.4	2.07	6.1	0.03	4.8	1.4	0.97	6.64	3.17	58.7	4.4	51.1	15.8	7.6
7.2	0.12	1.1	0.00	6.0	5.2	1.60	19.15	3.38	51.9	1.4	13.0	26.1	5.0
9.9	0.40	1.3	0.25	5.5	2.6	1.15	8.43	3.60	57.7	2.9	42.0	23.5	7.7
7.7	0.01	0.0	-0.19	4.9	0.4	1.19	10.25	3.62	66.5	5.6	32.4	2.4	6.8
4.7	1.17	8.5	0.00	5.2	2.3	0.93	9.37	3.77	68.0	1.3	15.9	19.7	5.3
9.3	0.14	0.3	-0.06	2.7	0.2	0.51	4.48	2.80	80.5	2.6	59.2	41.2	5.3
3.3	1.81	17.2	0.04	3.5	0.6	0.55	6.60	2.54	66.2	0.6	12.0	53.5	4.9
4.8	1.43	12.9	-0.01	4.5	0.5	1.05	11.19	3.57	69.8	2.3	11.4	17.0	5.2
2.7	2.82	18.6	0.36	1.9	0.1	0.18	2.14	3.98	94.1	5.2	35.0	6.2	2.4
8.5	0.30	1.5	1.28	3.7	0.5	0.63	4.87	3.42	62.4	4.8	29.4	6.9	7.7
4.3	0.61	5.0	0.03	5.4	5.5	0.87	8.15	3.22	58.2	1.7	12.4	15.6	6.9
6.3	0.85	5.1	0.00	7.0	1.3	1.26	10.00	3.76	53.9	2.6	5.2	14.9	7.9
7.8	0.42	2.5	-0.05	9.2	1.5	2.36	19.55	3.67	33.9	2.1	26.3	20.5	8.5
9.1	0.00	0.0	0.00	9.1	5.0	2.15	15.44	3.55	38.1	3.9	39.1	11.4	10.0
0.9	3.29	22.3	0.63	2.7	0.8	0.37	3.81	3.76	83.7	4.7	19.2	4.5	4.7
5.8	5.28	12.5	0.06	2.6	0.8	0.38	3.47	1.76	81.4	6.6	59.6	6.0	6.1
3.7	6.17	22.2	0.39	3.9	0.9	0.53	2.66	3.71	69.8	0.9	19.6	39.1	7.3
3.9	1.13	8.7	-0.07	3.0	1.6	0.51	5.42	2.85	72.0	0.8	20.4	44.2	4.2
3.6	1.83	13.6	0.04	10.0	11.2	2.70	26.87	5.31	48.4	3.5	18.6	11.6	8.8
8.8	0.00	0.0	0.00	7.8	0.3	1.96	13.94	3.59	58.5	5.4	46.7	6.5	6.3
8.7	0.32	1.6	0.02	3.9	0.5	0.69	5.97	3.63	80.6	4.3	31.1	10.6	6.2
10.0	1.05	1.1	-0.01	3.1	0.9	0.55	1.44	2.91	79.2	6.9	105.5	11.0	8.6
4.4	1.88	12.6	0.61	5.0	15.1	0.82	7.97	3.53	64.2	3.5	13.5	8.8	7.7
8.7	0.18	1.1	0.05	3.8	2.4	0.67	4.60	2.93	70.8	2.8	13.0	14.7	7.6
8.5	0.04	0.3	-0.09	1.5	0.3	0.33	4.59	3.41	97.9	4.0	31.9	12.3	3.3
3.5	1.55	5.9	3.23	3.9	0.6	0.82	4.82	3.56	55.4	4.9	31.4	6.7	6.7
8.4	0.25	1.4	0.00	2.5	0.2	0.43	5.03	2.85	85.1	4.4	24.4	7.4	4.5
7.0	0.30	2.6	0.00	7.8	3.2	1.82	18.22	5.14	63.5	4.4	3.6	4.4	6.8

Name	City	State	2015 Rating	2014 Rating	Total Assets ($Mil)	One Year Asset Growth	Asset Mix (As a % of Total Assets)				Capital-ization Index	Lever-age Ratio	Risk-Based Capital Ratio
				Rating			Comm-ercial Loans	Cons-umer Loans	Mort-gage Loans	Secur-ities			
STAR Financial Bank	Fort Wayne	IN	B	B	B	1847.0	7.39	18.8	2.8	13.0	20.3	7.8	10.4	13.1
Starion Bank	Bismarck	ND	A-	B+	B+	1220.8	3.20	9.0	1.6	12.5	26.0	8.2	9.8	14.1
Start Community Bank	New Haven	CT	D-	D	D	117.4	23.26	8.4	1.8	36.4	9.3	9.1	10.4	15.6
State Bank	La Junta	CO	B-	B-	C+	102.8	0.62	2.0	2.5	8.3	12.1	10.0	12.7	20.8
State Bank	New Hampton	IA	B	B+	B+	379.2	1.23	3.5	2.1	10.5	38.2	7.0	9.0	13.4
State Bank	Spencer	IA	D+	C	C	68.5	-0.42	7.0	3.6	19.5	11.2	5.9	7.9	12.4
State Bank	Spirit Lake	IA	B-	B-	C+	70.6	-0.56	7.5	1.1	14.3	23.8	10.0	11.7	17.7
State Bank	Freeport	IL	B-	B-	B-	234.6	5.26	22.7	0.3	6.5	22.6	7.6	10.1	13.0
▼ State Bank	Wonder Lake	IL	B-	B	B	301.9	78.12	4.0	1.5	27.8	12.0	6.6	8.7	14.8
▲ State Bank	Hoxie	KS	B-	C+	C+	148.3	1.13	9.3	1.4	0.1	3.0	10.0	13.5	15.0
State Bank	Fenton	MI	B	B	C+	499.9	15.24	10.3	0.4	25.4	4.3	6.7	9.5	12.3
State Bank	Richmond	MO	B	B	B	32.4	-5.57	2.7	4.7	25.7	38.4	6.1	8.2	19.0
State Bank	Gresham	WI	B	B	B	21.8	-10.76	8.7	3.9	9.1	4.6	10.0	13.1	17.6
State Bank	Green River	WY	C+	C+	C+	36.9	-8.09	7.0	2.9	9.5	14.0	10.0	13.3	22.3
▲ State Bank & Trust	Winfield	AL	B	C+	B+	230.8	2.56	1.9	6.8	11.4	56.9	10.0	12.1	28.4
State Bank & Trust Co.	Nevada	IA	A-	A-	A-	154.8	-3.27	11.2	0.6	14.3	28.8	10.0	12.2	17.0
State Bank & Trust Co.	Golden Meadow	LA	D-	E+	B-	127.9	-8.81	25.1	4.1	15.7	10.3	9.8	10.9	14.9
State Bank & Trust Co.	Ridgeland	MS	B-	C+	C+	1068.0	6.86	5.3	1.8	18.2	9.9	5.8	8.9	11.6
State Bank & Trust of Kenmare	Kenmare	ND	B-	B+	B	111.4	-8.48	11.0	2.8	11.3	25.5	8.7	10.1	14.5
State Bank and Trust Co.	Macon	GA	A-	A-	A-	3600.6	6.29	7.4	1.2	6.4	24.4	10.0	12.9	15.6
State Bank and Trust Co.	Defiance	OH	B-	B-	C+	800.3	11.47	11.7	1.0	18.6	11.6	5.5	9.3	11.4
State Bank Financial	La Crosse	WI	C+	C+	B-	317.6	-5.01	7.2	0.4	7.2	34.8	8.6	10.1	18.1
▼ State Bank Northwest	Spokane Valley	WA	C+	B	B-	141.5	10.39	16.7	0.7	8.0	10.9	8.7	10.1	15.7
State Bank of Alcester	Alcester	SD	C+	C	B-	117.0	0.52	5.9	5.3	9.7	22.1	7.0	9.0	14.2
State Bank of Arcadia	Arcadia	WI	C+	C+	B-	170.1	3.50	3.8	2.0	18.8	24.3	9.4	10.6	22.1
State Bank of Arthur	Arthur	IL	A-	A-	B+	129.5	0.12	14.5	6.9	11.8	28.3	10.0	14.1	25.8
State Bank of Belle Plaine	Belle Plaine	MN	B-	B	B	109.8	7.47	3.0	1.0	12.6	41.8	9.4	10.6	21.1
State Bank of Bellingham	Bellingham	MN	B-	C+	C+	49.3	6.93	1.9	0.6	0.2	3.4	7.6	10.3	13.0
State Bank of Bement	Bement	IL	B-	B-	B-	85.6	4.16	14.1	3.7	8.3	28.0	10.0	14.2	20.1
State Bank of Bern	Bern	KS	A-	A-	A-	92.4	3.02	4.8	2.2	3.3	46.2	10.0	14.5	23.0
State Bank of Blue Rapids	Blue Rapids	KS	C+	C	C	46.0	0.32	8.0	10.0	19.7	41.5	9.8	10.9	21.6
State Bank of Bottineau	Bottineau	ND	C+	C+	C	78.3	3.46	8.9	3.3	21.2	6.2	5.5	8.6	11.3
State Bank of Brooks	Corning	IA	C	C-	C	16.1	-6.07	2.8	5.8	10.6	42.7	10.0	12.6	36.0
▼ State Bank of Burnettsville	Burnettsville	IN	D-	D-	C	40.2	-1.31	5.7	9.1	26.3	25.3	9.2	10.5	17.7
▲ State Bank of Burrton	Burrton	KS	C-	C-	D+	9.6	-3.76	4.2	3.1	20.4	12.3	10.0	11.5	31.4
State Bank of Bussey	Bussey	IA	C-	D+	D+	47.8	2.86	7.2	2.5	25.4	2.1	6.1	8.1	13.1
State Bank of Canton	Canton	KS	C	C+	C+	29.6	-6.92	10.2	1.5	4.3	45.6	10.0	18.5	42.0
State Bank of Cazenovia	Cazenovia	WI	C+	C+	C+	36.1	0.88	1.4	3.6	13.4	24.7	10.0	17.3	37.7
State Bank of Cerro Gordo	Cerro Gordo	IL	B-	B-	B-	27.7	-3.00	13.2	4.5	11.0	41.1	10.0	13.2	22.0
State Bank of Ceylon	Ceylon	MN	D-	E-	D	13.0	-4.28	2.8	4.0	1.2	23.4	7.5	9.3	28.5
State Bank of Chandler	Chandler	MN	B	B	B-	43.2	-0.69	5.2	3.8	2.8	12.8	10.0	12.2	17.0
State Bank of Cherry	Cherry	IL	B	B	B	85.7	1.31	1.2	2.7	13.4	31.2	10.0	12.7	28.9
▼ State Bank of Chilton	Chilton	WI	C+	B-	B-	252.6	48.03	11.1	1.1	13.2	6.8	10.0	11.2	16.2
State Bank of Chrisman	Chrisman	IL	C+	C+	C+	86.3	3.17	5.6	1.6	7.8	19.8	6.2	8.2	12.4
State Bank of Cochran	Cochran	GA	B	B	B	209.6	1.19	5.3	7.8	18.6	8.7	10.0	15.0	27.3
State Bank of Cold Spring	Cold Spring	MN	C+	C+	C-	57.5	3.66	2.8	5.2	21.6	20.5	7.3	9.2	17.9
▼ State Bank of Colon	Colon	NE	D	D+	D-	17.1	2.65	5.5	0.6	1.6	9.9	7.7	9.4	13.7
▼ State Bank of Cross Plains	Cross Plains	WI	D+	C-	C-	834.4	6.86	8.2	1.6	15.1	17.5	9.1	11.3	14.2
State Bank of Danvers	Benson	MN	B-	B	B	47.4	-1.54	3.8	1.0	1.1	38.6	10.0	11.0	19.3
State Bank of Davis	Davis	IL	C+	C+	C+	160.6	-6.53	21.7	0.7	7.1	20.5	7.1	9.6	12.6
State Bank of De Kalb	De Kalb	TX	A	A	A	187.4	3.42	17.4	2.1	15.2	0.6	10.0	12.6	17.3
State Bank of Delano	Delano	MN	D+	D-	E+	84.9	-4.08	6.4	1.6	5.9	21.5	6.3	8.3	16.0
State Bank of Downs	Downs	KS	B	B	B-	94.8	0.00	14.3	1.8	22.8	5.8	9.7	10.8	16.5
▼ State Bank of Eagle Butte	Eagle Butte	SD	D+	C+	C+	64.5	-3.15	6.9	28.5	3.3	32.1	6.6	8.6	14.2
State Bank of Easton	Easton	MN	C-	C	C-	21.3	-11.39	16.7	3.9	6.9	12.4	10.0	13.5	19.2
State Bank of Ewen	Ewen	MI	B+	B+	B+	65.4	8.32	4.1	7.5	17.6	42.8	10.0	14.8	34.6
▲ State Bank of Fairmont	Fairmont	MN	C-	D	C+	105.5	2.78	20.7	5.4	5.1	16.3	10.0	11.0	16.2
State Bank of Faribault	Faribault	MN	B-	B	B-	186.0	3.93	7.2	3.2	14.6	23.3	9.0	11.1	14.2
▲ State Bank of Florence	Florence	WI	C	C-	D+	96.4	5.85	8.0	6.6	22.4	21.8	7.6	9.4	16.3
State Bank of Geneva	Geneva	IL	D-	D	D+	87.0	4.33	4.4	1.6	10.1	30.0	6.9	8.9	17.1

Asset Quality Index	Adjusted Non-Performing Loans as a % of Total Loans	as a % of Capital	Net Charge-Offs Avg Loans	Profitability Index	Net Income ($Mil)	Return on Assets (R.O.A.)	Return on Equity (R.O.E.)	Net Interest Spread	Overhead Efficiency Ratio	Liquidity Index	Liquidity Ratio	Hot Money Ratio	Stability Index
5.9	1.29	8.1	0.02	4.5	11.7	0.85	8.23	3.40	72.3	5.3	23.6	3.5	8.7
6.0	0.89	5.9	-0.02	6.8	13.9	1.53	14.98	3.69	60.9	2.1	14.5	17.7	10.0
8.6	0.00	0.0	0.01	0.6	0.1	0.09	0.80	2.96	92.8	0.6	11.4	53.1	5.6
6.4	1.46	5.7	0.07	3.4	0.4	0.58	4.44	3.74	83.6	4.2	33.9	12.1	6.6
7.8	0.27	1.5	-0.16	4.7	3.1	1.10	9.61	3.55	65.8	5.5	44.0	7.8	7.0
4.6	0.85	6.7	0.68	1.6	-0.1	-0.28	-3.66	3.47	79.5	1.8	17.7	20.0	4.2
5.8	1.03	5.5	0.36	4.6	0.6	1.10	9.47	3.53	63.0	1.8	24.0	22.0	5.3
4.6	1.42	9.1	0.28	8.1	2.3	1.37	13.21	3.54	44.1	2.5	12.2	16.2	6.9
3.0	2.63	18.8	0.26	3.5	0.9	0.57	5.42	3.49	79.4	3.5	20.6	12.2	4.2
4.5	0.93	5.7	0.00	10.0	3.0	2.68	21.19	4.59	38.2	2.1	6.4	17.9	9.3
7.6	0.14	1.2	-0.05	6.2	3.7	1.05	10.99	3.92	67.9	3.0	13.2	11.2	5.1
5.9	0.65	3.7	0.03	4.0	0.3	0.99	11.54	3.25	71.4	5.6	39.9	6.2	4.8
5.6	1.18	6.3	0.00	4.1	0.1	0.58	3.25	3.60	72.7	1.9	32.0	22.8	7.1
5.0	4.10	14.9	-0.01	2.6	0.1	0.32	2.39	3.81	91.0	5.1	45.5	10.2	5.4
4.9	4.05	10.4	0.38	4.0	1.8	1.07	8.55	2.99	61.1	3.2	71.1	48.7	6.1
7.4	1.13	5.6	-0.04	8.8	1.8	1.53	12.28	3.69	42.5	4.0	24.1	9.9	8.8
0.0	11.82	74.3	0.06	4.8	1.2	1.22	11.60	3.81	67.8	1.8	15.2	20.2	4.5
4.8	0.95	7.8	-0.08	4.3	5.3	0.70	6.25	4.01	72.1	2.9	9.7	14.2	8.1
4.1	1.65	10.9	-0.02	5.3	1.1	1.25	12.37	3.33	57.7	3.5	19.2	12.2	5.5
5.6	0.74	3.8	0.10	8.9	38.2	1.46	10.52	4.63	59.7	4.6	22.6	7.1	9.2
4.4	0.59	4.6	-0.02	6.6	7.1	1.22	11.01	3.66	66.6	2.3	6.0	14.3	7.3
7.2	0.59	2.5	0.31	3.1	1.4	0.57	5.06	3.01	83.8	5.1	36.5	7.5	7.0
3.1	3.53	21.0	0.00	4.2	0.9	0.89	8.78	4.49	79.8	4.3	36.5	12.2	5.6
6.9	0.18	1.4	0.00	3.3	0.6	0.66	7.36	3.30	80.5	2.0	23.1	19.5	5.3
6.4	0.64	3.1	0.05	3.4	1.0	0.76	6.51	2.81	70.0	5.3	41.6	8.7	6.4
7.5	0.91	3.0	0.62	5.3	0.8	0.89	6.27	3.93	58.8	6.2	54.9	7.1	7.7
8.3	0.69	2.9	-0.01	3.9	0.6	0.81	6.99	3.83	77.3	5.3	40.1	8.2	6.9
7.1	0.00	0.0	0.00	10.0	0.8	2.29	23.63	4.29	31.1	1.0	2.1	27.5	5.5
8.3	0.33	1.4	0.09	3.8	0.4	0.69	4.76	4.25	77.3	4.0	26.3	10.5	6.6
7.7	1.43	4.5	0.02	7.5	1.0	1.37	9.20	3.90	42.7	3.3	48.9	20.3	8.9
3.9	2.41	11.0	0.00	2.9	0.2	0.46	4.15	2.89	80.1	5.2	47.1	10.1	4.9
8.1	0.00	0.0	-0.01	5.4	0.7	1.27	14.74	4.39	67.1	2.5	5.0	15.2	4.5
6.1	5.26	10.3	-0.23	3.1	0.1	0.62	5.30	2.52	72.8	6.8	80.1	4.9	4.7
1.2	5.07	29.3	2.22	0.0	-0.4	-1.22	-10.48	4.09	110.7	2.7	22.3	16.2	5.0
9.4	0.00	0.0	0.07	1.3	0.0	0.01	0.12	3.09	101.2	4.1	48.3	14.0	5.4
6.5	0.30	2.6	-0.10	3.4	0.2	0.57	6.93	3.83	82.5	3.5	20.9	12.0	3.0
9.1	0.27	0.5	-0.01	2.4	0.1	0.31	1.67	2.75	79.9	7.1	75.9	3.7	6.3
9.0	0.00	0.0	0.02	2.3	0.1	0.31	1.87	3.46	89.3	6.2	59.3	6.4	6.7
8.5	0.10	0.3	0.01	1.9	0.1	0.34	2.27	3.39	93.3	5.2	47.2	10.1	6.1
2.0	13.35	32.4	2.44	0.7	0.0	-0.08	-0.84	2.02	104.3	4.0	81.5	20.4	4.0
7.0	0.04	0.2	0.03	5.3	0.3	0.95	7.83	4.09	63.7	4.1	20.8	8.7	6.7
9.2	0.00	0.0	0.06	4.4	0.8	1.19	8.92	2.99	59.1	4.6	63.5	16.0	7.3
2.3	2.81	17.6	-0.05	4.4	1.7	0.94	7.67	3.55	66.7	3.4	16.7	11.9	7.2
4.2	0.85	6.3	0.02	3.7	0.3	0.49	6.07	3.10	75.7	3.7	29.4	13.2	4.0
4.6	3.38	11.7	-0.07	7.0	2.7	1.67	11.62	4.03	61.2	3.4	37.2	17.2	7.8
5.6	1.18	6.2	0.49	3.2	0.3	0.64	6.76	3.24	81.7	6.0	40.0	3.4	4.8
3.8	1.07	6.5	-0.01	1.8	0.0	0.22	2.24	2.95	93.3	1.7	32.6	26.8	4.2
1.2	2.86	17.9	0.06	4.5	5.0	0.84	7.01	3.47	70.3	4.2	15.4	7.4	6.5
4.9	2.37	8.8	0.37	3.8	0.3	0.87	7.45	3.40	69.7	4.5	31.1	9.3	7.0
4.0	1.89	12.1	0.16	6.4	1.6	1.32	13.63	3.41	44.0	1.4	14.7	25.5	6.4
8.2	0.29	1.8	-0.01	9.6	3.5	2.51	20.20	4.40	52.5	2.5	14.7	16.5	9.5
6.8	0.75	3.8	0.00	6.5	1.1	1.76	22.80	3.40	68.9	6.6	50.4	1.4	1.6
4.6	2.99	18.6	0.18	5.4	1.0	1.28	12.61	3.84	57.4	4.8	27.3	6.1	6.1
2.4	2.43	14.9	1.54	3.3	0.2	0.35	3.92	5.72	77.2	1.5	5.8	21.5	3.8
4.1	3.71	16.6	-0.07	4.4	0.2	0.98	7.55	3.55	67.1	3.1	31.3	15.1	5.7
7.3	1.80	3.8	0.68	5.1	0.6	1.25	7.83	3.65	67.1	4.0	75.8	22.2	7.2
1.8	4.62	26.8	-0.01	6.0	1.2	1.47	13.60	3.65	55.2	3.3	30.2	15.1	6.1
8.6	0.15	0.8	-0.01	4.4	1.4	1.01	8.76	4.32	77.6	4.7	17.9	4.1	6.4
3.4	2.92	17.1	-0.01	3.1	0.3	0.48	5.58	4.17	82.4	1.5	32.4	36.2	4.7
4.1	2.25	10.6	0.15	0.2	-0.2	-0.37	-4.02	2.83	112.5	2.6	32.9	19.5	2.4

Name	City	State	2015 Rating	2014 Rating	Total Assets ($Mil)	One Year Asset Growth	Commercial Loans	Consumer Loans	Mortgage Loans	Securities	Capitalization Index	Leverage Ratio	Risk-Based Capital Ratio
▲ State Bank of Georgia	Fayetteville	GA	B	C+	C+	91.7	43.33	1.9	2.8	10.1	9.2	10.0	13.7	19.8
State Bank of Graymont	Graymont	IL	B-	B-	B	209.6	0.53	7.0	1.9	6.7	30.1	8.8	10.2	14.6
▲ State Bank of Hamburg	Hamburg	MN	E	E-	D-	23.8	2.52	6.2	2.3	7.9	25.6	5.9	7.9	16.9
State Bank of Herscher	Herscher	IL	C	C-	E-	143.4	-1.62	12.0	0.6	13.8	36.5	10.0	12.2	19.8
▲ State Bank of India (California)	Los Angeles	CA	D+	D+	C	602.3	-18.35	18.1	0.0	0.0	13.9	10.0	19.1	25.9
State Bank of Industry	Industry	IL	B	B	B	51.1	6.50	7.8	5.5	22.7	24.4	10.0	14.4	20.0
State Bank of Jeffers	Jeffers	MN	C+	C+	C+	27.1	2.20	9.4	4.0	4.1	0.7	10.0	11.5	16.9
▼ State Bank of Kansas	Fredonia	KS	B+	A-	A-	64.6	-0.47	4.0	1.1	10.0	11.3	10.0	13.4	27.9
State Bank of Lake Park	Lake Park	MN	C	C	C	36.9	4.97	9.2	7.3	20.8	18.1	7.6	9.4	17.3
State Bank of Lakota	Lakota	ND	C+	C+	C	44.8	-7.48	8.9	6.7	9.9	16.0	9.4	10.6	15.5
State Bank of Lincoln	Lincoln	IL	B+	B+	B	337.9	0.51	12.9	0.4	4.5	49.8	7.7	9.5	21.2
▲ State Bank of Lismore	Lismore	MN	C+	C-	C-	53.0	3.02	9.2	3.1	0.0	1.0	6.5	10.4	12.1
State Bank of Lizton	Lizton	IN	B	B	B	396.4	9.62	7.3	0.6	7.1	16.0	10.0	11.8	15.9
▼ State Bank of Marietta	Marietta	MN	D	D+	C-	13.5	-2.17	13.0	3.3	1.7	24.4	6.3	8.3	14.4
State Bank of Medora	Medora	IN	B+	B+	B+	82.6	10.78	1.2	5.0	20.2	57.1	10.0	14.8	34.5
State Bank of Missouri	Concordia	MO	B-	B-	B-	86.9	5.99	2.3	2.0	25.9	39.6	6.2	8.2	19.1
State Bank of Nauvoo	Nauvoo	IL	D	E-	D-	30.4	-6.24	5.2	9.4	36.5	1.1	5.5	7.5	13.3
State Bank of New Prague	New Prague	MN	A-	A-	B	111.7	2.78	2.1	1.1	18.5	52.1	10.0	12.1	22.5
State Bank of New Richland	New Richland	MN	C-	C+	C+	99.2	-0.32	5.8	1.8	17.4	13.0	7.5	9.6	12.9
State Bank of Newburg	Newburg	WI	B	B	B	167.8	1.68	0.6	0.8	32.0	16.1	10.0	18.6	26.5
State Bank of Odell	Odell	NE	C	C	C	27.3	4.98	0.4	20.3	4.4	7.3	7.4	9.2	15.1
State Bank of Pearl City	Pearl City	IL	B-	C+	C	51.3	3.70	3.1	39.4	7.2	25.1	10.0	11.3	15.7
State Bank of Reeseville	Reeseville	WI	B	B	B-	68.7	6.26	9.3	2.2	14.8	36.6	10.0	11.6	19.6
State Bank of Richmond	Richmond	MN	B	B	B	89.4	4.01	5.1	1.7	14.9	23.3	10.0	11.1	16.6
State Bank of Saunemin	Saunemin	IL	B-	B-	C	35.7	2.37	11.3	2.8	8.1	26.0	8.2	9.8	15.8
State Bank of Schaller	Schaller	IA	B+	B+	B+	36.5	2.54	2.8	0.8	0.9	59.0	9.8	10.9	32.0
State Bank of Scotia	Scotia	NE	B-	C	D+	38.3	2.91	6.8	2.7	8.7	15.8	10.0	24.1	30.5
State Bank of Southern Utah	Cedar City	UT	A	A	A-	942.9	9.04	5.4	2.1	2.4	31.7	10.0	13.2	19.0
State Bank of Southwest Missouri	Springfield	MO	C+	C+	C	112.2	10.10	3.2	4.8	45.9	8.1	3.1	6.9	10.1
▼ State Bank of Speer	Speer	IL	C+	B-	C+	182.5	2.74	6.5	0.8	10.5	46.3	7.5	9.4	16.8
State Bank of Spring Hill	Spring Hill	KS	C	C	C-	38.3	-1.36	5.5	1.4	9.9	55.0	8.4	9.9	23.4
State Bank of St. Jacob	Saint Jacob	IL	B-	B+	B+	60.6	2.31	5.0	6.1	15.5	29.8	10.0	15.7	30.9
State Bank of Table Rock	Table Rock	NE	C-	C	C-	71.7	6.81	10.0	4.6	9.1	2.5	6.2	8.6	11.9
▲ State Bank of Taunton	Taunton	MN	D	D	E+	47.9	-10.71	8.9	1.6	8.1	12.9	7.3	9.2	14.2
State Bank of Texas	Dallas	TX	A-	B+	B+	688.3	3.55	1.8	0.1	2.0	14.9	10.0	18.5	22.1
State Bank of Texas	Houston	TX	C	C	C-	186.6	6.89	16.6	11.4	4.5	15.4	6.9	8.9	22.6
State Bank of the Lakes	Antioch	IL	B-	C+	C+	1049.9	9.84	25.7	19.8	3.4	11.5	5.3	8.5	11.2
State Bank of Toledo	Toledo	IA	C	C	C	114.4	5.02	5.2	4.6	29.3	5.6	6.4	9.3	12.0
State Bank of Toulon	Toulon	IL	B+	B+	B	209.4	3.03	8.9	1.6	5.7	26.6	8.7	10.1	14.4
▲ State Bank of Townsend	Townsend	MT	C+	C+	B-	56.6	3.72	4.2	1.6	6.9	22.2	9.2	10.5	24.4
State Bank of Wapello	Wapello	IA	C+	C+	C+	46.3	25.19	1.2	4.0	10.0	24.5	9.2	10.5	22.3
State Bank of Waterloo	Waterloo	IL	D	C-	D	151.9	1.05	2.1	0.8	23.3	16.2	7.8	9.6	15.2
State Bank of Wheaton	Wheaton	MN	A-	A-	B+	76.2	-2.71	6.8	1.2	2.1	5.6	10.0	21.5	25.5
State Bank of Whittington	Benton	IL	B-	B-	B-	127.8	1.66	2.7	13.9	16.4	36.0	8.0	9.7	16.9
State Bank of Wynnewood	Wynnewood	OK	A	A	A	80.0	1.00	3.2	1.9	5.5	46.9	10.0	15.7	24.5
State Central Bank	Bonaparte	IA	D-	E+	E-	39.6	-24.58	25.8	1.6	15.5	2.1	7.7	9.5	16.3
State Exchange Bank	Mankato	KS	C+	C+	C	34.7	-4.91	4.0	6.1	4.7	43.4	10.0	11.8	21.2
State Exchange Bank	Lamont	OK	B-	B+	B+	57.0	6.45	21.8	1.5	4.5	6.3	10.0	11.6	15.3
State Farm Bank, FSB	Bloomington	IL	C	C	C	16821.2	0.35	0.8	41.5	18.5	34.6	9.3	10.5	17.7
State Guaranty Bank	Okeene	OK	B	B	B	46.1	1.72	13.0	1.0	1.2	15.5	10.0	12.2	15.4
▲ State National Bank in West	West	TX	C	C-	C-	69.1	-1.99	5.8	3.0	3.1	63.8	6.9	8.9	24.2
State National Bank of Big Spring	Big Spring	TX	C	C	C	309.9	2.72	4.7	1.4	0.3	59.4	8.7	10.2	32.7
▼ State National Bank of Groom	Groom	TX	D	D+	D	36.4	5.15	12.6	1.6	0.5	9.1	6.9	9.7	12.4
State Nebraska Bank & Trust	Wayne	NE	A-	B+	B	146.7	0.06	11.0	1.6	9.2	36.1	10.0	12.0	17.0
State Savings Bank	Creston	IA	B-	B+	B+	113.2	9.44	10.6	4.8	18.5	0.4	5.9	9.3	11.7
▼ State Savings Bank	Rake	IA	D	C	C-	69.6	4.79	8.6	1.0	1.1	5.1	7.3	11.0	12.7
State Savings Bank	West Des Moines	IA	A-	A-	A-	116.2	5.04	9.1	1.2	24.8	0.7	7.9	10.0	13.2
State Savings Bank	Frankfort	MI	C-	C-	C+	118.8	11.01	4.7	0.7	35.0	3.2	10.0	11.7	16.2
State Savings Bank of Manistique	Manistique	MI	B-	C+	C+	124.4	5.68	9.5	4.0	14.7	44.0	10.0	11.6	17.8
State Street B&T Co. of California, N.A.	Los Angeles	CA	U	U	U	15.4	3.33	0.0	0.0	0.0	0.0	10.0	95.6	351.7

Arrows denote recent upgrades ▲ or downgrades ▼

www.weissratings.com

Asset Quality Index	Adjusted Non-Performing Loans as a % of Total Loans	as a % of Capital	Net Charge-Offs Avg Loans	Profitability Index	Net Income ($Mil)	Return on Assets (R.O.A.)	Return on Equity (R.O.E.)	Net Interest Spread	Overhead Efficiency Ratio	Liquidity Index	Liquidity Ratio	Hot Money Ratio	Stability Index
4.8	2.15	9.8	0.09	4.7	0.5	0.79	5.17	4.47	71.7	3.6	40.7	17.3	5.7
6.3	0.69	4.0	0.02	4.3	1.3	0.86	8.07	3.03	63.3	4.9	34.6	8.4	6.2
4.7	0.95	4.8	0.10	0.5	0.0	-0.24	-3.09	2.69	109.0	5.6	58.0	7.9	1.9
1.2	9.65	35.2	0.02	2.1	0.4	0.33	2.47	5.62	58.1	4.8	32.8	8.4	4.4
4.0	2.85	10.8	0.63	1.0	0.7	0.14	0.79	3.17	90.0	1.6	27.8	28.8	5.4
5.6	1.64	7.9	0.13	7.4	0.7	1.76	12.35	3.88	53.4	0.9	20.0	32.6	8.1
8.2	0.00	0.0	-0.02	3.3	0.1	0.44	3.96	3.83	76.3	5.5	39.5	6.7	5.9
5.9	3.16	10.8	-0.10	4.0	0.4	0.91	6.26	3.01	68.8	5.5	45.8	7.9	9.0
4.3	2.57	13.8	0.21	4.9	0.3	1.19	12.63	4.38	67.1	4.4	36.9	11.9	4.7
4.9	0.73	4.7	0.16	5.3	0.5	1.37	13.34	4.15	60.2	3.1	12.8	13.3	4.8
6.9	0.60	2.3	0.02	8.1	5.0	1.97	20.18	3.10	61.4	5.3	44.5	9.3	7.2
6.5	0.14	1.1	0.00	6.1	0.6	1.50	14.97	4.34	63.9	1.1	4.2	27.4	5.0
7.7	0.38	2.2	0.20	4.4	2.3	0.80	6.74	3.77	73.0	3.0	15.5	13.8	6.4
2.8	3.58	16.1	-0.09	4.9	0.1	1.20	11.61	3.82	61.3	6.2	57.1	3.4	2.3
8.1	1.48	3.4	0.12	4.3	0.5	0.79	5.28	2.95	61.2	3.8	70.5	23.0	7.2
6.7	0.73	4.0	0.08	3.9	0.6	0.89	10.52	3.29	74.3	5.2	34.7	6.6	5.2
4.6	1.26	10.6	-0.01	3.1	0.2	0.84	11.23	3.99	78.5	4.3	27.8	9.1	1.1
9.7	0.60	1.8	-0.03	7.7	1.6	1.89	12.96	4.03	57.9	3.7	34.6	14.9	8.1
2.4	2.04	16.0	0.12	9.2	1.8	2.35	23.25	3.95	37.8	0.8	7.8	21.2	7.8
4.5	4.33	17.0	-0.02	9.2	1.7	1.39	7.50	3.80	40.4	1.6	24.2	26.2	8.8
3.6	0.86	5.0	-0.11	3.3	0.1	0.66	7.12	3.73	76.5	5.9	45.0	5.4	4.8
6.3	0.30	1.6	0.00	4.4	0.4	0.99	8.31	4.46	73.4	2.7	32.6	19.1	6.1
8.7	0.10	0.5	-0.17	4.6	0.5	1.00	8.49	3.77	66.2	3.3	44.3	19.1	6.3
8.8	0.27	1.5	0.00	3.8	0.5	0.83	7.17	3.29	69.8	4.8	32.0	8.1	6.7
8.2	0.13	0.8	0.01	5.0	0.4	1.31	13.13	3.34	59.4	4.7	30.6	7.7	5.6
7.9	0.90	1.6	0.16	4.9	0.3	1.07	10.04	2.74	61.7	6.0	76.2	10.8	8.1
4.2	1.27	3.8	-0.04	9.2	0.5	1.69	7.16	4.90	41.6	4.0	21.1	9.5	6.7
8.3	0.41	1.8	-0.01	9.2	10.7	1.60	12.23	3.98	48.2	4.1	33.7	12.2	8.3
5.7	0.47	5.5	0.27	4.9	1.0	1.21	18.22	3.71	74.2	3.6	8.8	10.2	4.0
5.7	0.86	4.1	0.37	3.2	0.8	0.57	5.52	2.94	66.0	2.3	25.8	19.0	5.0
7.9	1.58	4.5	0.00	2.4	0.1	0.36	3.45	2.99	86.6	5.3	40.5	8.1	5.6
6.4	2.24	5.4	0.67	3.9	0.4	0.89	5.78	2.82	57.2	5.9	60.9	8.8	6.9
4.6	0.47	4.1	-0.01	3.7	0.4	0.74	8.95	3.80	78.1	3.2	13.7	12.8	4.2
6.1	0.10	0.6	-0.06	1.5	0.1	0.14	1.56	3.87	99.1	2.1	26.7	20.3	2.5
6.4	0.41	1.5	0.22	10.0	32.4	6.41	34.72	6.90	18.2	1.0	25.4	40.2	9.5
7.2	0.23	1.3	0.00	2.6	0.4	0.30	3.29	2.74	83.6	2.5	51.6	50.7	4.8
3.9	0.70	6.1	0.05	4.1	5.3	0.70	5.20	3.07	62.4	1.7	11.2	16.7	8.1
3.0	1.91	15.9	0.02	6.7	1.2	1.52	16.89	4.24	63.5	3.1	11.2	12.7	6.1
7.1	0.29	1.8	0.07	5.4	2.1	1.36	11.97	3.69	59.7	3.5	18.2	11.7	6.8
4.0	3.04	14.2	0.02	3.6	0.3	0.66	6.31	3.89	84.4	3.9	46.4	16.5	6.2
9.2	0.13	0.4	0.01	2.8	0.2	0.54	4.85	2.37	78.1	7.1	60.8	0.3	4.2
4.2	1.30	8.2	0.47	1.1	0.3	0.22	2.25	3.19	96.3	3.0	25.7	15.4	5.0
6.3	1.12	4.2	-0.02	9.7	1.6	2.71	13.05	4.29	36.9	1.9	10.8	19.1	9.8
4.9	1.13	5.5	0.25	4.3	1.0	1.04	11.06	4.11	75.5	5.0	35.7	8.0	5.2
8.9	0.14	0.4	-0.03	5.9	0.9	1.51	9.22	4.11	68.2	3.2	48.1	20.9	9.6
0.0	30.12	135.0	-0.15	3.6	0.5	1.42	13.85	3.17	138.1	4.4	28.7	8.8	3.4
5.7	2.24	8.1	0.23	3.9	0.3	0.92	7.79	3.42	69.3	5.2	33.5	5.6	4.6
3.3	1.97	11.0	0.03	7.4	0.6	1.34	11.89	4.42	58.9	0.7	14.4	38.1	7.8
3.6	1.76	9.5	0.75	2.3	20.1	0.16	1.46	2.63	81.4	1.2	24.0	27.5	7.3
8.3	0.00	0.0	-0.03	7.1	0.6	1.82	14.54	3.75	50.8	1.3	18.1	28.1	5.7
6.7	1.91	5.1	-0.25	2.7	0.2	0.31	3.53	2.51	81.6	6.9	74.2	4.8	3.2
9.6	0.35	0.7	-0.02	2.8	1.1	0.47	4.66	1.86	76.8	6.5	74.9	9.4	5.3
2.9	1.50	10.7	-0.14	1.7	0.0	0.01	0.11	4.27	94.2	2.2	9.9	17.6	4.1
6.0	1.64	7.6	0.04	5.7	1.2	1.14	9.52	3.38	52.8	3.3	14.6	12.2	7.2
3.8	1.15	10.4	0.02	8.4	1.6	1.94	21.38	4.05	51.3	2.6	8.1	15.2	6.7
0.9	3.83	28.0	0.20	7.2	0.7	1.29	12.14	3.47	35.9	0.6	11.7	47.4	5.5
6.2	0.57	4.3	-0.04	6.8	1.3	1.50	15.18	4.03	63.3	3.8	9.9	9.7	8.1
5.9	1.13	7.5	0.03	0.3	-0.5	-0.65	-5.13	3.87	117.6	4.7	17.3	4.6	4.7
5.6	2.49	10.0	-0.05	3.8	0.7	0.72	5.91	3.83	75.5	5.5	49.7	10.1	6.0
10.0	na	0.0	na	3.5	-0.2	-1.27	-1.29	0.21	112.9	4.0	na	0.0	7.0

Name	City	State	2015 Rating	2014 Rating	Total Assets ($Mil)	One Year Asset Growth	Comm-ercial Loans	Cons-umer Loans	Mort-gage Loans	Secur-ities	Capital-ization Index	Lever-age Ratio	Risk-Based Capital Ratio
State Street Bank and Trust Co.	Quincy	IL	C+	C+	C+	204.1	8.17	5.1	25.6	20.2	20.5	6.2	8.2	12.4
State Street Bank and Trust Co.	Boston	MA	B-	B-	B-	251545.4	3.77	1.4	0.1	0.0	39.7	5.1	7.1	18.0
State Street Bank and Trust Co., N.A.	New York	NY	U	U	U	32.5	-2.81	0.0	0.0	0.0	0.0	10.0	91.0	222.1
▲ STC Capital Bank	Saint Charles	IL	B-	B-	C+	236.8	17.98	8.0	0.5	15.7	11.1	7.7	11.0	13.1
Stearns Bank Holdingford N.A.	Holdingford	MN	A-	A-	A	74.8	-15.59	71.8	0.4	3.1	3.2	10.0	18.7	21.0
Stearns Bank N.A.	Saint Cloud	MN	A-	A-	A	1829.3	2.73	55.6	0.3	2.3	4.2	10.0	17.7	19.3
Stearns Bank Upsala N.A.	Upsala	MN	A-	A-	A	66.9	-11.21	72.9	0.2	2.8	3.9	10.0	15.9	17.6
Stephenson National Bank and Trust	Marinette	WI	B-	B-	B-	495.1	8.42	14.1	1.2	15.3	18.7	7.7	9.4	14.6
Sterling Bank	Poplar Bluff	MO	A-	B	B+	1406.0	70.16	32.5	0.3	4.9	2.2	6.4	9.1	12.1
Sterling Bank	Barron	WI	B+	B+	B+	222.1	1.33	6.0	0.6	13.7	26.1	7.1	9.1	13.0
Sterling Bank and Trust, FSB	Southfield	MI	A-	A-	A-	2030.6	32.99	0.4	0.0	74.5	3.5	7.4	9.3	16.1
Sterling Federal Bank, F.S.B.	Sterling	IL	C-	C-	C-	451.1	2.89	1.8	0.6	28.9	43.4	8.6	10.0	17.6
Sterling National Bank	Montebello	NY	B-	B-	C+	13581.6	17.46	23.6	0.1	5.5	20.8	6.7	8.7	12.6
Sterling State Bank	Austin	MN	C	C+	C	340.5	7.88	9.2	1.0	7.6	38.1	6.6	8.6	16.4
Steuben Trust Co.	Hornell	NY	A-	B+	B+	527.9	6.45	4.4	3.5	14.9	35.2	9.0	10.3	17.1
Stifel Bank and Trust	Saint Louis	MO	B+	B+	B+	11208.5	142.70	17.5	10.4	17.3	48.5	5.5	7.5	14.5
Stifel Trust Co. Delaware, N.A.	Wilmington	DE	U	U	U	11.8	-7.60	0.0	0.0	0.0	90.0	10.0	86.6	266.9
Stifel Trust Co., N.A.	Saint Louis	MO	U	U	U	17.6	-76.91	0.0	0.0	0.0	84.3	10.0	92.1	311.8
Stillman BancCorp, N.A.	Stillman Valley	IL	C+	C	C-	424.0	2.80	4.5	1.2	9.5	46.9	7.3	9.2	20.3
Stock Exchange Bank	Caldwell	KS	C-	C-	D+	50.6	0.51	4.3	3.9	35.3	17.5	5.4	7.4	12.1
Stock Exchange Bank	Woodward	OK	A-	A-	B+	253.7	-9.03	5.5	3.2	8.1	53.1	10.0	12.8	25.0
Stock Growers Bank	Napoleon	ND	A-	A-	A-	62.9	1.37	1.1	1.7	3.9	38.0	10.0	13.2	18.8
Stock Yards Bank & Trust Co.	Louisville	KY	A	A	A-	2936.2	12.00	21.3	1.2	9.1	18.5	7.2	10.3	12.6
Stockgrowers State Bank	Ashland	KS	B	B	B+	125.2	2.54	8.2	1.2	2.1	39.8	10.0	13.8	21.0
Stockgrowers State Bank	Maple Hill	KS	A-	A-	A-	73.1	0.59	5.2	1.1	8.7	55.2	10.0	11.5	23.0
Stockman Bank of Montana	Miles City	MT	A-	A-	A-	3166.1	2.58	4.5	0.9	6.7	18.6	7.8	9.5	13.1
▼ Stockmans Bank	Altus	OK	D-	D+	D+	204.3	17.19	6.8	1.4	11.9	1.1	5.4	8.6	11.3
Stockmens Bank	Colorado Springs	CO	B+	B	B-	103.3	10.25	16.2	0.6	10.3	0.2	6.6	8.6	16.6
Stockmens Bank	Cascade	MT	B-	B-	B-	33.8	-3.00	4.7	2.7	4.9	17.1	10.0	12.0	30.6
▲ Stockmens National Bank in Cotulla	Cotulla	TX	B-	C+	C+	86.0	-18.05	5.0	3.5	4.1	36.0	9.9	10.9	40.0
Stone Bank	Mountain View	AR	B	B	B-	134.8	39.88	13.7	1.9	11.6	5.3	10.0	12.6	17.0
Stonebridge Bank	West Chester	PA	E-	E-	E-	92.8	-23.81	6.8	0.2	31.5	10.3	4.7	6.7	11.1
Stonegate Bank	Pompano Beach	FL	B+	B	B	2937.2	26.98	9.9	0.3	10.4	4.0	5.9	10.0	11.7
StonehamBank	Stoneham	MA	C+	C+	C+	577.8	14.91	12.8	0.2	33.5	9.5	6.0	9.0	11.7
Stoughton Co-operative Bank	Stoughton	MA	D+	D+	C-	111.7	3.71	0.1	0.4	57.3	28.6	6.4	8.5	15.7
Strasburg State Bank	Strasburg	ND	B-	C+	B-	64.0	4.52	3.3	0.9	0.0	22.3	6.7	8.7	15.1
Stratford State Bank	Stratford	WI	B	B-	B	109.0	1.99	7.9	2.5	7.9	38.5	10.0	12.5	20.9
Streator Home Savings Bank	Streator	IL	B-	B	B	167.2	-0.29	0.0	1.0	24.8	67.1	10.0	23.3	84.8
Stroud National Bank	Stroud	OK	C+	C+	C+	82.4	-1.07	10.2	4.8	21.6	27.3	9.8	10.9	19.2
Sturdy Savings Bank	Cape May Court Hou	NJ	C	C	C	832.1	9.57	2.1	0.1	24.4	33.9	6.6	8.6	13.6
▲ Sturgis Bank & Trust Co.	Sturgis	MI	C	C-	D+	407.4	12.46	8.4	1.2	25.4	15.3	6.3	8.3	14.1
▼ Success Bank	Bloomfield	IA	B	B+	B+	167.9	13.26	7.8	2.6	10.6	3.4	8.0	11.4	13.3
Suffolk County National Bank of Riverhead	Riverhead	NY	B	B	B-	2196.1	6.27	9.5	0.2	8.3	9.7	8.4	9.9	13.8
▲ Sugar River Bank	Newport	NH	C	C-	C-	279.9	7.96	6.4	2.4	45.2	17.1	10.0	14.2	23.6
Sumitomo Mitsui Trust Bank (U.S.A.) Ltd.	Hoboken	NJ	C+	U	U	3001.1	22.82	0.0	0.0	0.0	0.0	6.8	8.8	27.9
Summit Bank	Oakland	CA	A-	A-	C	244.9	6.42	18.2	0.2	2.1	0.2	10.0	11.2	17.8
Summit Bank	Eugene	OR	B	B-	C	267.1	14.14	23.5	1.5	2.6	2.3	6.2	9.3	11.9
Summit Bank of Kansas City	Lee's Summit	MO	C+	C-	D	41.8	3.86	21.4	1.4	17.5	0.0	10.0	11.3	15.6
Summit Bank, N.A.	Panama City	FL	B+	B+	A-	362.1	-0.92	10.6	0.9	6.0	27.8	10.0	12.5	16.2
Summit Community Bank, Inc.	Moorefield	WV	B+	B+	B-	1650.3	12.88	6.0	1.2	17.3	15.9	8.1	10.5	13.4
Summit National Bank	Hulett	WY	D+	D+	D	74.7	15.87	5.7	4.4	8.6	11.5	6.6	8.6	12.8
Summit State Bank	Santa Rosa	CA	A-	A	A-	513.7	1.60	9.0	0.2	10.1	21.9	9.3	11.0	14.4
Sumner Bank & Trust	Gallatin	TN	C	C	D+	154.3	-2.28	6.2	1.0	15.3	23.3	6.7	8.7	12.8
Sun National Bank	Mount Laurel	NJ	C	C	D-	2186.0	-4.36	8.4	0.1	12.8	13.4	10.0	13.4	19.3
Suncrest Bank	Visalia	CA	B	B-	C	353.2	62.00	8.4	0.1	8.3	13.4	10.0	12.4	16.1
Sundance State Bank	Sundance	WY	B	B	B	179.4	0.22	13.7	5.3	8.6	34.1	8.5	10.0	15.6
▲ Sundown State Bank	Sundown	TX	B+	B	B-	135.4	-14.83	14.7	1.2	1.9	25.5	10.0	11.5	16.5
Sunflower Bank, N.A.	Salina	KS	C+	B	B	1858.5	11.89	11.6	1.2	23.2	17.5	8.1	9.7	13.9
SunMark Community Bank	Hawkinsville	GA	B	B-	B	219.5	-1.27	4.8	3.8	19.8	12.1	10.0	11.4	17.5
Sunnyside Federal S&L Assn. of Irvington	Irvington	NY	D+	D	D	91.8	0.52	1.1	6.4	29.7	37.4	10.0	12.2	26.1

Asset Quality Index	Adjusted Non-Performing Loans as a % of Total Loans	as a % of Capital	Net Charge-Offs Avg Loans	Profitability Index	Net Income ($Mil)	Return on Assets (R.O.A.)	Return on Equity (R.O.E.)	Net Interest Spread	Overhead Efficiency Ratio	Liquidity Index	Liquidity Ratio	Hot Money Ratio	Stability Index
4.6	0.17	1.4	0.13	4.4	1.5	0.98	11.74	3.62	73.3	4.5	26.8	7.4	5.5
8.8	0.01	0.0	0.02	4.2	1577.5	0.94	9.82	1.33	74.4	3.2	66.2	57.2	7.8
10.0	na	0.0	na	9.5	0.9	3.61	3.84	0.21	92.1	4.0	na	0.0	5.7
7.6	0.08	0.5	0.13	4.0	1.5	0.90	8.11	4.18	72.2	1.3	17.9	28.3	6.2
6.7	1.07	5.0	0.27	6.0	0.6	1.05	5.93	2.80	31.2	0.5	7.2	47.4	9.2
6.1	0.92	4.1	0.34	10.0	43.5	3.16	18.32	7.50	35.9	0.4	2.4	26.6	9.6
5.9	1.07	6.0	0.27	5.6	0.5	0.99	6.61	2.87	32.5	0.5	6.8	50.6	8.4
4.3	1.65	11.2	0.04	6.8	5.8	1.63	15.97	3.92	64.5	3.6	16.3	10.8	7.4
8.2	0.17	1.3	0.00	7.3	11.6	1.28	12.43	3.56	47.8	1.6	26.7	17.8	8.4
6.0	0.99	7.1	0.14	7.0	2.7	1.63	18.58	4.03	59.0	1.9	27.4	22.8	7.3
9.5	0.13	1.2	-0.17	10.0	27.4	1.96	23.19	4.13	30.1	1.6	5.1	14.8	8.2
5.2	2.18	9.5	0.05	2.0	0.0	0.01	0.11	2.86	91.8	3.4	50.6	21.3	5.4
4.4	0.93	7.5	0.08	6.0	105.9	1.12	8.07	3.63	53.0	4.5	12.0	5.0	8.1
5.8	1.01	5.5	-0.01	2.9	1.2	0.47	4.96	3.16	88.4	4.3	27.0	8.9	5.0
8.5	0.27	1.4	-0.02	5.7	4.1	1.06	10.13	3.64	63.5	1.6	15.0	18.7	7.5
7.5	0.52	3.6	0.01	8.2	82.5	1.26	19.00	2.42	14.2	0.8	16.3	0.0	5.7
10.0	na	0.0	na	0.0	0.0	-0.34	-0.39	0.18	101.3	4.0	na	0.0	7.0
10.0	na	0.0	na	8.0	0.4	3.47	3.15	0.60	88.9	4.0	na	100.0	6.3
8.4	0.51	2.0	0.12	3.6	2.8	0.88	9.50	2.32	72.3	3.6	41.6	17.2	4.8
8.0	0.20	1.8	-0.01	3.2	0.2	0.42	5.65	4.13	79.5	1.1	9.8	28.5	3.6
9.2	0.82	2.2	0.22	6.0	2.2	1.08	8.96	3.37	55.6	4.8	32.1	8.1	7.1
8.7	0.09	0.3	0.00	7.2	0.8	1.74	13.15	4.14	50.2	4.0	35.0	13.2	8.5
8.0	0.34	2.4	0.04	8.7	31.6	1.48	14.50	3.58	56.3	4.7	10.5	4.0	8.8
6.1	2.59	9.9	-0.01	4.1	1.0	1.04	7.42	3.48	72.8	2.9	38.2	19.7	7.5
9.1	0.00	0.0	-0.02	5.9	0.8	1.36	9.56	4.17	58.7	3.8	27.2	11.7	7.2
6.6	0.71	4.8	0.15	8.0	45.3	1.93	19.77	3.60	51.5	3.6	10.6	7.5	10.0
0.2	2.95	29.9	0.02	8.1	2.9	1.97	24.26	5.25	61.6	0.5	2.4	36.6	5.5
8.4	0.00	0.0	-0.01	7.0	1.3	1.72	18.80	4.10	56.7	2.2	25.8	19.5	6.0
8.1	1.03	3.1	0.00	3.3	0.2	0.70	5.70	3.32	78.2	4.2	68.9	18.9	6.6
9.5	0.00	0.0	0.24	4.1	0.7	1.01	10.07	2.23	59.1	5.0	56.0	12.7	4.0
3.3	3.13	19.9	0.38	9.9	1.5	1.68	11.90	4.94	60.7	0.4	5.9	48.5	7.0
0.3	13.20	107.7	-0.21	0.0	-0.8	-1.03	-15.68	2.67	140.6	1.1	14.0	29.8	0.1
5.1	0.60	4.6	-0.03	6.1	19.9	1.04	8.85	3.88	55.6	4.5	14.7	5.3	9.1
6.0	0.41	3.5	0.03	3.2	2.2	0.54	5.72	3.38	77.8	1.6	9.5	21.5	5.9
8.2	0.63	4.5	-0.17	1.8	0.3	0.32	3.84	2.61	92.2	2.2	34.4	26.8	4.5
7.5	0.00	0.0	0.00	4.7	0.4	0.82	9.68	3.91	64.2	4.2	22.9	8.5	4.9
6.2	2.00	7.9	0.19	3.9	0.5	0.66	4.92	3.25	69.6	2.0	39.0	32.8	7.2
10.0	1.26	1.4	0.18	3.4	0.7	0.55	2.37	2.46	68.9	4.5	88.4	23.6	7.6
3.3	2.74	13.5	0.11	2.8	0.2	0.39	3.50	4.39	92.6	4.9	33.0	7.8	5.9
5.8	0.79	5.2	0.00	3.0	3.1	0.52	5.55	3.39	77.9	5.5	29.9	1.9	5.7
2.7	2.29	17.3	0.11	4.1	2.1	0.74	7.92	3.80	77.4	4.5	24.3	4.2	4.5
4.4	0.81	5.7	0.07	9.0	2.3	1.90	16.84	4.58	54.4	2.5	3.9	15.1	8.6
6.9	0.38	2.8	0.01	5.0	16.1	0.98	10.59	3.77	64.7	4.0	10.8	8.5	7.6
7.8	0.95	4.4	0.05	2.0	0.9	0.43	3.12	3.39	87.5	3.4	25.8	13.2	7.1
10.0	0.00	0.0	0.00	3.1	8.6	0.39	4.33	0.28	80.1	8.8	108.3	0.0	6.6
8.7	0.09	0.4	-0.04	6.1	1.5	0.82	7.42	3.73	64.3	5.2	49.6	11.4	7.0
7.1	0.10	0.8	0.40	8.2	2.1	1.14	12.29	5.19	55.0	4.2	16.8	7.4	5.9
7.9	0.03	0.2	0.21	5.0	0.4	1.32	10.97	4.53	78.0	1.8	19.3	20.8	4.1
6.3	1.23	5.4	-0.03	5.1	2.5	0.92	7.75	3.59	66.2	5.4	37.8	6.4	6.8
5.5	1.18	8.3	0.04	5.8	13.2	1.14	10.75	3.44	54.1	0.9	11.1	18.6	7.8
1.5	2.59	21.2	0.29	3.7	0.3	0.57	5.93	4.30	74.0	3.4	4.8	11.0	3.9
6.0	0.89	5.5	-0.01	6.4	3.8	0.98	8.55	3.71	60.5	1.2	23.4	25.3	8.6
5.7	0.92	6.0	0.01	3.0	0.5	0.44	4.96	3.45	79.5	3.2	29.4	15.3	5.0
7.0	0.44	2.3	0.04	2.3	7.3	0.44	3.01	3.07	89.2	3.5	14.4	9.5	7.1
6.1	1.09	5.6	-0.01	4.8	1.6	0.70	5.35	4.51	71.5	2.7	37.5	21.9	6.8
5.2	1.57	8.5	0.03	5.6	1.5	1.06	10.74	3.92	54.5	2.9	25.4	15.7	5.6
8.8	0.38	2.0	0.35	5.1	1.2	1.13	10.63	4.39	69.3	2.6	17.4	16.2	5.3
6.8	0.58	4.2	0.08	3.3	8.4	0.62	5.74	3.44	80.6	4.4	6.6	4.9	9.1
4.9	1.94	10.2	0.51	5.3	2.2	1.30	11.83	4.34	71.1	3.7	22.5	11.3	7.0
8.0	1.20	4.8	0.00	0.6	0.0	0.03	0.23	2.87	105.6	3.5	35.2	12.1	5.4

Name	City	State	Rating	2015 Rating	2014 Rating	Total Assets ($Mil)	One Year Asset Growth	Asset Mix (As a % of Total Assets)				Capital-ization Index	Lever-age Ratio	Risk-Based Capital Ratio
								Comm-ercial Loans	Cons-umer Loans	Mort-gage Loans	Secur-ities			
Sunrise Bank	Cocoa Beach	FL	B+	B+	C+	154.3	28.73	5.6	0.7	7.5	14.9	10.0	18.6	26.5
Sunrise Bank Dakota	Onida	SD	B	B	B	61.9	0.05	5.9	2.5	4.5	19.2	10.0	11.3	18.8
Sunrise Banks, N.A.	Saint Paul	MN	B-	B+	B+	794.1	-2.25	8.7	0.3	9.9	13.7	9.1	10.4	14.7
▼ Sunset Bank & Savings	Waukesha	WI	C	C	C	128.6	-1.71	6.3	0.5	32.5	15.7	9.9	10.9	18.3
Sunshine Bank	Plant City	FL	D+	D	D	563.4	27.53	9.4	0.3	13.2	10.8	10.0	12.6	15.8
Sunshine Community Bank	Tallahassee	FL	C-	C-	C-	167.2	9.83	1.1	6.1	32.3	10.8	10.0	11.8	16.0
SunSouth Bank	Dothan	AL	E-	E-	E-	148.0	-7.55	25.2	0.5	11.7	27.7	0.9	4.1	9.3
Sunstate Bank	Miami	FL	C+	B-	C+	161.9	-3.25	1.1	0.1	31.8	3.8	10.0	13.3	17.2
SunTrust Bank	Atlanta	GA	C+	C+	C	200200.8	9.30	23.2	12.3	15.8	14.5	7.1	9.7	12.6
▲ Sunwest Bank	Irvine	CA	B-	D+	C-	1053.9	16.35	8.6	0.2	3.3	6.3	8.3	12.0	13.5
▲ Superior Bank	Hazelwood	MO	E+	E-	E-	26.9	-0.90	6.8	0.2	19.9	0.0	4.0	6.6	10.5
▲ Superior National Bank & Trust Co.	Hancock	MI	B+	B	B	595.0	2.10	4.0	6.8	20.5	46.2	10.0	11.9	23.6
Superior Savings Bank	Superior	WI	C+	C	C+	64.5	-2.39	4.0	1.3	49.9	5.5	10.0	17.9	33.5
Surety Bank	Deland	FL	C	D+	D	93.0	-3.75	3.3	0.8	5.2	31.8	10.0	13.3	22.0
Surrey Bank & Trust	Mount Airy	NC	A	A	A-	268.0	-3.00	20.5	1.3	9.2	2.0	10.0	14.9	19.6
Sussex Bank	Rockaway	NJ	C+	C+	C-	818.2	26.88	4.2	0.1	14.3	12.0	6.3	9.0	12.0
Sutton Bank	Attica	OH	B+	B+	B	452.3	9.19	10.6	0.9	5.7	23.2	7.7	9.4	14.0
▲ Swedish-American State Bank	Courtland	KS	C-	D-	D+	57.2	-0.70	11.5	4.6	9.1	21.5	5.8	8.0	11.6
▼ Sweet Water State Bank	Sweet Water	AL	C	B-	B-	96.0	2.70	15.1	4.2	9.1	14.2	9.4	10.6	16.5
Swineford National Bank	Hummels Wharf	PA	B-	B	B	317.6	4.60	11.3	1.3	11.1	21.5	9.5	10.6	16.6
Swisher Trust & Savings Bank	Swisher	IA	C+	C+	C+	49.8	4.90	3.0	4.9	18.6	48.0	9.6	10.7	28.7
Sycamore Bank	Senatobia	MS	B	B-	B-	211.4	4.66	5.0	4.0	21.1	17.3	7.8	9.5	14.7
Synchrony Bank	Draper	UT	C	C+	C+	69521.4	21.64	1.7	77.9	0.0	2.6	10.0	13.3	17.4
Synergy Bank	Houma	LA	C-	A-	B+	497.9	1.43	16.5	2.2	13.3	17.3	9.7	10.8	16.6
▲ Synergy Bank, S.S.B.	McKinney	TX	C-	D+	C-	151.9	13.77	8.6	6.1	12.2	4.8	7.7	9.5	13.4
Synovus Bank	Columbus	GA	B+	B	C+	29492.2	5.73	16.6	2.8	10.3	12.2	7.8	10.9	13.2
Synovus Trust Co., N.A.	Columbus	GA	U	U	U	80.6	3.40	0.0	0.0	0.0	23.3	10.0	97.2	145.5
Systematic Savings Bank	Springfield	MO	D	D	D	30.3	-7.63	0.1	0.9	58.9	0.0	10.0	22.3	47.2
T Bank, N.A.	Dallas	TX	A	A	A-	211.1	24.98	44.5	1.5	2.8	10.5	10.0	13.9	17.2
Table Grove State Bank	Table Grove	IL	B-	B-	C+	44.7	-5.82	1.3	8.4	2.6	27.8	10.0	11.3	17.9
▲ Table Rock Community Bank	Kimberling City	MO	C	C	C	81.8	16.25	7.7	5.3	29.0	1.1	4.9	8.0	11.0
▲ Talbot State Bank	Woodland	GA	D	D-	D-	69.4	-1.43	0.0	0.8	44.6	32.9	6.3	8.4	21.3
Tallahatchie County Bank	Charleston	MS	C	C	C+	57.3	-2.01	2.6	7.0	7.3	41.3	8.9	10.3	20.8
Tampa State Bank	Tampa	KS	B-	C+	C+	50.6	-0.01	10.5	3.0	18.1	27.1	9.5	10.7	15.8
Tarboro Savings Bank, SSB	Tarboro	NC	B	B	B	44.5	1.61	0.0	0.1	60.9	0.1	10.0	14.5	26.1
Taylor County Bank	Campbellsville	KY	A	A	A	182.7	3.08	6.9	6.0	22.9	17.4	10.0	12.9	18.3
Taylorsville Savings Bank, SSB	Taylorsville	NC	C	C-	D+	101.6	2.16	1.3	1.1	51.0	8.5	7.5	9.4	15.4
▼ TBK Bank, SSB	Dallas	TX	B-	B-	B-	2545.1	353.83	33.8	1.0	3.7	12.3	5.6	10.7	11.4
TCF National Bank	Sioux Falls	SD	C+	C+	C-	21095.4	4.75	22.5	13.7	11.6	7.7	8.3	10.3	13.6
TCM Bank, N.A.	Tampa	FL	B+	A-	B+	306.0	67.23	12.3	74.3	0.0	1.3	10.0	15.1	17.9
TD Bank USA, N.A.	Wilmington	DE	C+	C+	C	21117.3	10.57	0.0	34.3	0.0	19.2	6.4	8.5	23.4
TD Bank, N.A.	Wilmington	DE	C	C	C	264527.9	9.72	11.5	9.2	8.4	35.2	6.6	8.6	14.6
▼ Teche Bank & Trust Co.	Saint Martinville	LA	B+	A-	A-	103.3	-7.35	19.1	4.8	19.6	27.2	8.1	9.7	17.4
Tecumseh Federal Bank	Tecumseh	NE	B-	B	B	53.7	-6.29	2.3	0.8	45.3	20.5	10.0	17.6	40.0
Tejas Bank	Monahans	TX	B+	A-	A-	129.9	2.35	17.5	3.1	6.3	22.6	8.4	10.0	15.6
Templeton Savings Bank	Templeton	IA	A-	A-	A-	115.9	0.30	8.1	3.0	12.6	19.2	10.0	12.8	17.8
Tempo Bank	Trenton	IL	C	C+	C+	94.7	-2.52	0.0	1.9	79.2	0.0	10.0	11.7	23.9
Tennessee State Bank	Pigeon Forge	TN	C-	D	D-	642.5	3.06	1.4	1.0	17.1	18.3	8.8	10.2	15.0
Tensas State Bank	Newellton	LA	B+	A-	A-	153.6	6.34	22.4	1.3	10.9	33.3	10.0	12.1	18.9
▼ Terrabank, N.A.	Miami	FL	C	C+	C-	339.6	8.24	1.4	0.2	7.7	19.8	8.0	9.6	13.7
▲ Terre Haute Savings Bank	Terre Haute	IN	C	C-	C-	319.5	3.78	6.5	0.8	31.0	25.9	6.9	8.9	14.3
Territorial Savings Bank	Honolulu	HI	A-	B+	B+	1848.2	3.65	0.2	0.0	68.3	24.3	10.0	11.9	25.9
▲ Teutopolis State Bank	Teutopolis	IL	A	A-	A-	212.7	4.43	6.6	2.4	10.7	32.6	10.0	13.3	21.1
Texan Bank, N.A.	Houston	TX	D+	D+	C-	219.9	6.81	11.1	0.3	3.1	3.4	5.5	8.8	11.4
Texana Bank, N.A.	Linden	TX	D+	D+	B-	143.7	-1.37	28.0	5.7	32.1	3.9	6.9	9.0	12.4
Texas Advantage Community Bank, N.A.	Alvin	TX	C+	C-	C-	106.6	-5.65	25.4	3.3	6.4	19.0	7.2	9.1	17.9
Texas Bank	Henderson	TX	B	B-	C+	420.7	20.49	4.5	5.2	10.3	49.1	10.0	12.3	21.2
Texas Bank and Trust Co.	Longview	TX	B+	B+	B+	2279.3	3.77	16.4	3.9	28.3	7.6	7.4	9.6	12.8
Texas Bank Financial	Weatherford	TX	B+	B+	B-	200.6	23.72	2.3	0.4	64.3	2.0	8.2	9.8	19.9
▲ Texas Brand Bank	Garland	TX	B+	B-	C+	158.3	11.48	12.7	0.3	8.7	5.0	9.7	10.8	15.3

Asset Quality Index	Adjusted Non-Performing Loans as a % of Total Loans	as a % of Capital	Net Charge-Offs Avg Loans	Profitability Index	Net Income ($Mil)	Return on Assets (R.O.A.)	Return on Equity (R.O.E.)	Net Interest Spread	Overhead Efficiency Ratio	Liquidity Index	Liquidity Ratio	Hot Money Ratio	Stability Index
7.4	0.34	1.2	0.00	3.8	0.4	0.35	2.24	3.56	84.2	1.3	30.5	41.0	6.7
7.3	0.09	0.5	0.00	5.5	0.7	1.37	12.80	3.63	57.3	1.7	20.6	22.8	7.3
7.1	0.31	2.1	-0.01	3.7	4.8	0.80	7.90	3.76	89.8	1.2	22.5	4.7	6.0
3.3	3.63	20.6	0.34	2.5	0.3	0.33	2.56	3.48	89.6	2.2	29.8	21.4	6.0
8.0	0.37	2.2	0.01	1.2	0.9	0.22	1.65	3.65	90.3	2.2	21.0	18.4	6.0
4.2	2.46	15.9	0.16	1.5	0.0	0.03	0.26	4.11	96.9	4.7	21.6	4.8	5.9
0.3	5.16	50.4	1.29	0.0	-2.3	-2.06	-40.02	3.07	101.8	0.9	7.1	27.2	1.4
6.8	1.31	6.3	-0.66	2.0	0.2	0.19	1.31	3.48	103.9	4.5	32.0	10.0	6.1
3.5	1.51	10.9	0.32	5.4	1468.4	1.02	8.23	3.02	60.1	5.0	21.6	2.5	9.7
5.1	0.46	3.0	-0.22	7.8	9.8	1.36	11.23	5.21	56.0	3.5	13.2	3.9	9.8
8.8	0.00	0.0	-0.03	1.2	0.1	0.25	3.84	3.78	105.5	1.7	15.2	20.9	2.0
5.2	2.87	10.9	0.47	5.2	4.1	0.94	7.48	3.68	62.1	4.2	50.4	16.7	6.9
5.4	3.24	11.4	0.20	3.1	0.2	0.44	2.50	3.12	79.9	4.5	34.6	10.7	6.5
2.4	5.37	20.5	0.02	6.1	1.2	1.64	12.04	4.40	67.0	3.5	47.0	18.9	6.0
6.0	1.36	6.8	0.10	8.7	2.8	1.44	9.48	4.54	56.2	3.1	16.4	13.3	8.3
3.8	0.80	6.8	0.07	3.9	4.3	0.76	8.28	3.44	70.0	1.6	10.3	16.1	4.7
5.3	1.05	6.5	0.14	8.1	6.3	1.96	19.59	3.87	58.3	3.3	22.9	2.7	7.1
4.2	0.56	4.7	0.24	4.4	0.3	0.79	10.04	3.93	65.3	0.5	2.6	41.2	3.6
2.4	3.48	22.0	0.19	5.5	0.9	1.24	11.62	5.51	73.3	1.0	13.6	32.2	6.7
3.9	2.32	13.3	0.05	3.4	1.2	0.50	4.32	3.13	82.5	4.4	28.3	8.5	7.4
9.3	0.00	0.0	0.00	3.3	0.2	0.66	5.88	2.72	74.4	7.2	73.7	2.5	5.6
4.9	1.35	8.8	0.09	4.6	1.3	0.82	8.52	4.02	72.1	4.0	16.3	8.7	5.1
2.2	2.35	10.6	4.55	10.0	1261.3	2.63	19.22	12.99	35.3	1.3	24.1	27.4	10.0
2.0	5.43	30.5	0.02	6.3	3.7	0.98	9.37	3.83	56.9	2.3	25.9	18.6	8.3
2.2	1.50	12.0	0.06	2.2	0.2	0.19	1.50	6.00	90.3	1.5	15.6	25.2	6.3
5.6	1.05	7.2	0.12	5.5	209.8	0.97	8.39	3.42	59.2	3.1	11.6	8.3	9.9
6.5	na	0.0	na	9.5	3.2	5.39	5.47	0.35	83.2	4.0	na	0.0	7.0
7.1	1.40	4.5	-0.04	0.0	-0.4	-1.56	-6.99	4.02	136.7	4.0	27.4	11.0	4.8
7.8	0.03	0.2	0.26	10.0	3.0	2.02	14.43	4.63	70.3	0.7	12.9	47.8	8.8
6.7	0.19	1.1	0.01	4.0	0.3	0.88	7.94	3.82	78.8	4.6	30.9	8.9	5.8
4.2	0.73	7.0	0.09	5.6	0.5	0.93	11.80	4.72	77.7	2.8	14.7	15.1	3.8
3.3	4.30	23.2	0.15	1.5	0.3	0.56	7.11	3.09	101.4	2.1	47.4	50.5	2.8
4.8	2.88	9.1	1.18	2.5	0.2	0.41	4.11	3.38	86.0	4.4	36.4	11.6	4.6
5.3	1.15	6.2	-0.16	4.4	0.5	1.19	10.56	3.87	77.3	2.4	17.0	17.1	6.0
9.0	0.00	0.0	0.14	4.3	0.2	0.66	4.52	4.10	66.7	0.9	20.4	35.1	7.5
5.8	1.46	7.9	0.14	8.7	2.5	1.85	14.52	4.53	58.6	3.2	22.7	13.9	8.7
3.1	2.80	20.8	0.02	4.0	0.5	0.64	7.00	3.65	77.2	1.6	16.0	23.2	5.2
3.6	2.11	16.6	0.18	7.0	13.7	0.99	7.82	6.18	69.8	1.1	9.9	27.3	10.0
3.8	1.44	11.2	0.34	6.2	164.4	1.09	10.05	4.42	69.0	2.5	12.0	12.4	8.6
4.7	0.69	3.6	2.56	6.7	1.3	0.76	3.79	9.33	74.2	0.3	14.4	99.7	8.0
4.3	2.09	7.0	2.99	4.8	118.7	0.78	9.31	8.03	72.1	7.0	68.0	0.0	5.5
4.1	1.26	7.5	0.25	3.1	992.0	0.53	3.99	2.48	69.2	3.9	41.4	1.5	8.1
4.0	2.16	12.4	0.20	5.3	0.9	1.16	10.41	4.51	71.1	2.0	25.3	20.9	7.7
9.3	0.85	2.7	-0.07	3.6	0.2	0.55	3.25	3.06	78.2	3.3	41.6	18.7	6.6
5.1	1.66	9.6	2.19	6.4	1.2	1.31	11.08	4.17	57.1	1.3	26.7	32.6	8.5
7.8	0.33	1.8	-0.01	6.3	1.0	1.09	7.75	3.64	53.6	3.3	27.0	14.0	8.5
8.1	0.51	3.7	0.02	2.0	0.1	0.16	1.44	2.69	90.9	1.8	12.7	19.7	5.8
3.7	1.64	9.9	0.15	2.9	3.0	0.64	6.40	3.64	89.6	3.3	19.9	7.6	5.3
4.9	2.84	12.7	0.08	5.8	1.5	1.36	10.71	3.98	63.4	2.4	36.2	25.3	8.7
6.6	0.04	0.3	-0.01	2.6	0.9	0.36	3.69	3.68	91.6	1.4	24.9	27.7	6.0
5.1	1.48	9.9	0.08	2.6	1.0	0.42	4.56	3.39	85.2	3.2	31.5	16.2	4.9
9.6	0.42	2.5	0.00	5.2	12.4	0.90	7.89	3.29	56.0	3.7	15.2	11.1	9.4
8.9	0.45	1.9	0.00	6.5	1.9	1.23	9.28	3.20	44.7	5.8	38.9	4.1	7.7
1.1	3.83	29.3	0.83	1.0	-0.5	-0.29	-2.88	3.77	87.2	1.0	24.8	36.0	4.8
4.6	0.69	6.2	0.11	1.4	-0.3	-0.28	-3.06	4.84	102.1	1.1	5.9	16.0	3.9
8.1	0.07	0.5	0.02	4.1	0.8	0.92	10.50	3.57	69.6	1.2	26.7	29.9	3.8
6.8	1.47	5.8	0.41	6.1	3.8	1.46	13.73	5.44	73.0	3.2	48.6	23.2	5.0
5.9	0.73	5.7	0.11	6.1	18.8	1.12	11.08	3.56	58.0	3.1	9.9	13.3	8.7
6.8	0.45	3.5	0.09	9.9	4.1	2.90	31.37	5.17	69.8	0.7	14.3	41.1	7.1
7.4	0.00	0.0	-0.08	6.5	1.6	1.43	13.55	4.30	60.2	0.9	23.5	46.8	5.5

Name	City	State	2015 Rating	2014 Rating	Rating	Total Assets ($Mil)	One Year Asset Growth	Commercial Loans	Consumer Loans	Mortgage Loans	Securities	Capitalization Index	Leverage Ratio	Risk-Based Capital Ratio
Texas Capital Bank, N.A.	Dallas	TX	B-	B-	B-	22202.3	19.03	25.5	0.1	4.0	0.1	4.5	8.3	10.7
Texas Champion Bank	Corpus Christi	TX	D	D+	B-	346.2	-9.73	16.1	0.8	5.0	9.3	6.4	9.4	12.1
Texas Citizens Bank, N.A.	Pasadena	TX	C+	C+	C	402.6	8.24	23.9	3.0	7.9	2.5	5.4	9.2	11.3
Texas Community Bank	Laredo	TX	B	B	C+	1210.3	-1.18	11.4	1.3	13.5	17.6	7.9	9.6	17.8
▲ Texas Exchange Bank, SSB	Crowley	TX	A-	B-	C	404.8	214.58	25.1	0.0	1.6	15.6	10.0	11.9	16.2
▲ Texas Financial Bank	Eden	TX	B	B-	B-	100.8	0.11	1.9	1.0	1.3	33.9	10.0	11.1	21.2
Texas First Bank	Texas City	TX	B	B	B	969.5	2.50	9.5	1.1	2.5	41.2	8.4	9.9	16.7
Texas First State Bank	Riesel	TX	C+	C+	C+	392.6	6.11	7.4	1.1	9.9	50.5	6.3	8.3	16.7
Texas Gulf Bank, N.A.	Houston	TX	B+	B+	B+	553.9	2.30	9.4	0.9	13.8	29.2	9.4	10.6	15.0
Texas Heritage Bank	Boerne	TX	B	C+	B+	139.2	12.88	5.8	2.1	17.2	3.1	6.6	8.6	14.9
Texas Heritage National Bank	Daingerfield	TX	B	B+	B	129.8	3.05	8.5	4.9	16.1	6.5	9.3	10.8	14.4
▲ Texas Hill Country Bank	Bandera	TX	B-	C+	C	94.7	39.26	19.0	1.4	14.0	9.6	10.0	12.6	16.6
Texas National Bank	Mercedes	TX	B	B	B-	220.9	18.89	7.1	2.1	20.9	11.3	6.9	9.0	13.2
Texas National Bank	Sweetwater	TX	C+	C+	B-	133.9	5.80	5.1	1.5	3.6	59.5	7.3	9.2	23.5
Texas National Bank of Jacksonville	Jacksonville	TX	B+	B+	B	485.9	5.36	15.6	4.2	33.4	1.9	7.5	9.3	13.6
Texas Regional Bank	Harlingen	TX	C	C	C-	606.9	14.47	13.4	0.9	5.1	31.4	6.5	8.6	12.7
Texas Republic Bank, N.A.	Frisco	TX	A-	A-	B+	180.1	8.82	10.6	1.0	40.6	0.0	9.3	10.5	15.2
Texas Security Bank	Dallas	TX	B+	B+	B	324.6	8.80	19.1	0.5	20.4	7.3	7.4	10.1	12.9
Texas Star Bank	Van Alstyne	TX	B+	B+	B	352.1	2.14	17.0	6.4	9.6	4.5	9.0	10.3	14.4
▲ Texas State Bank	Lufkin	TX	C+	C	B-	121.2	1.62	16.1	7.1	18.0	4.6	6.8	8.9	12.4
Texas State Bank	San Angelo	TX	B+	B+	B+	246.7	-0.33	8.4	1.3	15.3	37.6	10.0	11.7	23.1
TexasBank	Brownwood	TX	A+	A+	A+	431.2	3.44	3.7	2.3	18.9	11.4	10.0	13.6	19.8
Texico State Bank	Texico	IL	D-	E+	D	7.7	-4.12	0.5	3.1	44.1	0.0	6.9	9.0	16.8
TexStar National Bank	Universal City	TX	B	B-	B-	231.6	9.31	10.8	0.8	9.8	10.1	9.5	10.7	15.2
Thayer County Bank	Hebron	NE	D+	D	C	56.3	1.65	13.5	2.7	16.2	22.2	9.6	10.8	14.7
The Bank	Oberlin	KS	B-	A-	A-	340.3	-0.75	3.7	0.6	0.8	12.4	8.1	9.9	13.4
The Bank	Jennings	LA	B+	A-	A-	222.8	9.19	19.5	13.5	23.3	15.8	9.2	10.5	15.9
▲ The Bankers Bank	Oklahoma City	OK	C-	C	B-	266.8	-0.28	4.8	0.4	2.9	0.6	10.0	11.1	17.8
Think Mutual Bank	Rochester	MN	B-	B-	C+	1579.1	4.27	0.8	13.2	42.7	27.0	10.0	15.0	27.4
Third Coast Bank, SSB	Humble	TX	C+	C+	C+	471.8	16.56	29.5	1.1	6.3	0.3	6.3	9.6	12.0
Third Federal S&L Assn. of Cleveland	Cleveland	OH	B-	B-	B-	12869.4	4.33	0.0	0.0	81.0	4.0	10.0	11.7	22.2
▲ Thomas County Federal S&L Assn.	Thomasville	GA	C-	D	C-	252.4	1.97	1.2	0.6	36.3	8.8	10.0	13.4	18.6
Thomaston Savings Bank	Thomaston	CT	C+	C+	C+	938.2	9.66	4.4	1.0	35.7	21.0	10.0	11.9	19.4
Thomasville National Bank	Thomasville	GA	B+	B+	B-	753.0	8.66	13.7	1.9	28.0	3.8	5.8	8.5	11.6
Three Rivers Bank of Montana	Kalispell	MT	A-	A-	A-	131.6	10.59	15.8	2.5	7.5	23.8	10.0	13.5	18.4
Thrivent Trust Co.	Appleton	WI	U	U	U	10.6	-0.09	0.0	0.0	0.0	64.5	10.0	78.5	393.9
Thumb National Bank and Trust Co.	Pigeon	MI	C+	C-	D+	236.6	8.48	6.7	1.3	9.7	24.8	7.6	9.4	14.4
TIAA-CREF Trust Co., FSB	Saint Louis	MO	D	D	C-	4303.9	29.25	6.3	0.0	57.0	16.5	10.0	13.0	22.1
TIB-The Independent BankersBank	Farmers Branch	TX	B-	B	B-	2687.3	8.53	4.5	3.0	1.9	16.8	6.8	8.9	17.3
Tilden Bank	Tilden	NE	B-	B-	B-	82.0	-3.73	6.6	2.6	1.8	13.6	9.5	10.7	15.9
Timberland Bank	Hoquiam	WA	C+	C-	D	890.4	9.24	4.7	0.5	15.3	1.1	8.9	10.3	15.6
Timberline Bank	Grand Junction	CO	B-	C+	C+	238.8	25.10	11.5	0.6	7.7	12.9	6.6	8.6	13.9
Timberwood Bank	Tomah	WI	A-	A-	B+	171.0	0.81	8.8	0.7	13.5	22.9	10.0	11.6	17.6
Time Federal Savings Bank	Medford	WI	B+	B+	B+	613.4	0.20	0.0	0.2	59.2	33.9	10.0	20.8	51.5
▲ Tioga Franklin Savings Bank	Philadelphia	PA	B-	C	C-	36.2	9.76	0.0	0.9	70.6	9.3	10.0	12.7	25.0
Tioga State Bank	Spencer	NY	A-	A-	A-	455.0	6.81	10.4	1.7	21.0	30.9	10.0	11.8	19.3
Tipton Latham Bank, N.A.	Tipton	MO	B+	B+	B-	117.9	4.83	10.8	3.4	23.2	23.9	10.0	11.5	17.9
Titan Bank, N.A.	Mineral Wells	TX	B+	B+	B+	96.5	21.57	3.1	8.9	12.1	22.5	9.4	10.6	22.8
Titonka Savings Bank	Titonka	IA	C	C	C	177.0	3.84	2.9	1.4	8.1	51.4	10.0	11.0	22.3
TNBANK	Oak Ridge	TN	C	C-	C-	205.1	8.98	5.1	1.1	17.4	16.8	4.3	8.4	10.7
▼ Today's Bank	Huntsville	AR	C-	C+	A-	184.4	66.86	6.8	1.5	12.7	15.1	8.4	13.5	13.7
Tolleson Private Bank	Dallas	TX	B	B	B	523.8	-3.61	15.1	4.2	36.9	19.2	5.9	7.9	13.8
Tomahawk Community Bank, SSB	Tomahawk	WI	B-	B-	B-	94.1	9.23	3.6	4.1	37.8	14.2	10.0	11.6	15.7
Tompkins State Bank	Avon	IL	B-	C	C	199.8	6.53	6.5	1.9	11.3	27.3	7.1	9.1	13.9
Tompkins Trust Co.	Ithaca	NY	B+	B+	B+	1842.6	3.98	5.5	1.5	24.9	34.4	5.9	7.9	13.2
Torrington Savings Bank	Torrington	CT	B-	B-	B-	813.0	0.39	0.1	0.2	48.2	31.8	10.0	18.4	44.8
▲ TotalBank	Miami	FL	B	B-	C	3006.1	8.19	5.7	0.2	24.8	18.5	10.0	11.6	17.7
Touchmark National Bank	Alpharetta	GA	B+	B+	B	236.6	19.94	7.0	0.2	5.2	8.4	10.0	13.0	15.0
Towanda State Bank	Towanda	KS	E-	D-	D-	10.4	3.55	0.4	8.7	51.4	11.7	6.3	8.3	16.5
Tower Community Bank	Jasper	TN	C+	C+	C+	148.2	7.99	22.2	4.6	22.2	13.3	6.6	8.6	12.3

Asset Quality Index	Adjusted Non-Performing Loans		Net Charge-Offs	Profitability Index	Net Income ($Mil)	Return on Assets (R.O.A.)	Return on Equity (R.O.E.)	Net Interest Spread	Overhead Efficiency Ratio	Liquidity Index	Liquidity Ratio	Hot Money Ratio	Stability Index
	as a % of Total Loans	as a % of Capital	Avg Loans										
4.6	0.96	8.9	0.21	4.7	111.9	0.74	8.58	3.14	53.0	5.1	17.9	2.3	7.6
0.4	6.60	44.7	1.38	2.7	0.7	0.26	2.71	4.19	80.7	2.2	14.3	17.6	4.8
5.9	0.39	3.1	0.08	4.1	1.8	0.60	6.55	5.10	79.2	2.7	11.2	9.0	4.8
8.3	0.53	3.1	0.01	4.4	7.3	0.81	8.50	3.08	64.8	2.1	25.5	26.3	7.7
8.6	0.00	0.0	0.00	7.4	4.2	2.31	16.54	4.04	34.3	2.7	62.9	52.5	5.7
9.4	0.03	0.1	0.02	4.2	0.6	0.81	7.91	3.32	69.8	4.3	32.6	11.2	5.9
5.4	1.31	6.1	0.07	5.6	9.8	1.35	13.52	4.02	68.6	4.3	36.8	12.3	6.8
8.5	0.50	2.3	0.10	2.9	1.2	0.41	5.09	2.72	81.7	3.0	41.3	21.0	3.8
5.7	0.83	4.8	0.02	5.0	4.5	1.11	10.02	3.95	71.1	2.6	26.9	17.8	8.0
5.7	0.10	0.7	0.00	6.2	1.5	1.51	17.00	4.16	66.9	4.5	30.0	8.6	6.4
4.9	0.84	5.4	0.03	6.0	1.2	1.27	11.89	4.20	68.1	1.6	19.7	24.7	7.8
8.4	0.07	0.4	0.00	3.4	0.4	0.65	5.05	3.70	78.8	0.9	21.1	36.0	6.4
6.1	0.51	3.6	0.04	5.4	1.4	0.90	9.90	5.15	71.9	1.4	17.2	26.2	5.5
9.2	0.00	0.0	0.66	3.5	0.8	0.75	7.19	2.91	78.1	5.6	47.3	8.6	7.2
5.3	0.95	8.1	-0.01	7.3	4.5	1.26	13.56	4.08	52.0	0.5	5.5	47.2	6.8
5.7	0.67	4.1	0.17	3.3	2.7	0.60	6.66	3.84	78.5	2.4	32.3	21.3	6.3
8.3	0.14	1.0	-0.01	7.3	1.6	1.25	11.29	5.34	62.6	2.2	13.5	18.0	6.9
7.4	0.26	2.0	0.00	6.1	2.7	1.14	11.05	3.91	61.0	1.3	9.0	25.3	7.0
6.6	0.29	1.9	0.01	6.8	3.3	1.23	12.35	4.24	58.0	2.0	19.6	19.4	6.1
5.1	0.41	3.5	0.13	3.9	0.7	0.73	7.67	4.53	84.5	3.0	15.3	13.9	4.6
9.2	0.00	0.0	0.02	5.0	2.2	1.16	9.76	3.60	68.6	5.6	39.9	6.0	7.8
8.3	0.29	1.5	0.05	9.7	7.5	2.43	17.79	4.48	53.4	3.7	20.2	10.9	9.5
6.8	1.47	8.5	0.00	2.6	0.0	0.49	5.69	4.28	88.6	6.4	47.2	0.0	1.7
7.3	0.09	0.6	0.00	4.5	1.7	1.03	9.25	4.09	73.1	1.7	19.4	22.1	7.2
1.8	4.94	28.3	-0.19	3.9	0.3	0.58	5.29	4.02	74.7	2.3	8.3	16.4	4.5
4.0	0.96	7.2	0.01	9.5	5.7	2.25	20.78	4.28	38.7	2.6	5.2	6.4	8.1
5.6	0.49	3.1	0.66	7.5	2.0	1.20	11.73	5.18	59.6	2.6	16.6	16.3	6.8
8.4	0.00	0.0	0.08	1.9	0.2	0.08	0.69	2.85	98.2	1.9	36.8	6.1	6.7
8.3	0.18	0.7	0.08	3.6	7.5	0.64	4.31	2.99	72.9	6.4	39.0	3.8	8.7
3.9	0.57	4.7	-0.01	4.9	2.7	0.81	8.65	4.96	73.8	1.2	11.8	28.1	4.5
6.6	1.20	9.1	0.01	3.9	63.0	0.67	5.83	2.19	58.0	0.9	6.5	25.1	8.3
5.4	1.38	7.2	-0.06	1.9	0.9	0.46	3.78	3.39	83.5	2.6	22.8	16.6	5.0
5.9	1.78	9.9	0.03	2.5	3.5	0.51	4.39	3.11	86.8	1.9	26.4	21.1	7.5
5.9	0.47	4.2	0.01	9.6	8.7	1.58	17.86	3.64	47.0	3.5	5.5	10.7	7.0
5.8	1.22	5.7	0.02	6.0	1.0	1.01	7.26	4.86	71.4	3.1	29.6	16.1	7.2
10.0	na	0.0	na	4.2	0.0	0.45	0.57	1.72	98.9	5.0	369.4	100.0	6.5
3.3	2.71	17.1	0.01	4.1	1.5	0.83	8.40	4.04	80.9	3.5	32.7	15.1	5.9
9.6	0.04	0.2	0.00	0.0	-6.1	-0.21	-1.66	1.99	99.7	3.7	14.1	4.3	7.1
8.5	0.05	0.2	0.24	3.8	13.8	0.68	7.58	1.68	81.1	4.8	45.0	13.6	7.4
3.8	1.40	7.8	-0.04	4.8	0.6	0.98	9.38	3.72	67.3	4.6	20.3	5.5	5.9
3.7	1.01	6.8	0.01	6.7	7.7	1.20	11.31	3.84	63.0	4.0	20.4	9.0	7.4
5.9	0.58	4.3	-0.02	5.0	2.0	1.23	13.51	4.19	73.2	4.5	31.2	9.2	3.9
7.5	0.66	3.5	-0.13	6.7	1.6	1.25	9.34	3.91	59.0	1.4	19.7	18.5	8.1
10.0	0.50	1.5	0.04	4.1	3.3	0.72	3.49	2.54	54.5	3.1	45.9	23.4	8.6
5.1	3.20	18.4	0.00	6.4	0.3	1.29	10.01	3.71	56.0	0.8	17.9	43.4	5.6
8.4	0.65	3.2	0.04	5.3	3.4	1.01	8.48	3.98	68.8	3.8	12.2	9.7	7.6
6.2	1.67	8.6	0.02	6.2	1.6	1.79	16.22	3.44	53.4	1.4	31.7	35.4	6.8
6.2	0.41	1.9	0.59	6.0	0.8	1.20	10.54	4.32	69.8	2.7	46.3	22.8	7.1
9.0	0.33	1.2	0.01	2.7	0.6	0.50	4.37	3.16	85.7	4.4	60.4	18.1	6.6
3.9	1.48	11.6	0.09	3.1	0.7	0.47	4.92	3.84	80.9	1.1	12.6	29.8	4.8
1.8	5.27	34.2	0.16	7.6	1.5	1.69	11.81	5.12	74.1	0.9	21.4	34.8	6.7
7.5	0.43	3.7	0.00	5.9	6.2	1.51	20.34	2.63	56.2	5.0	27.4	4.1	6.5
5.9	1.70	8.7	-0.02	3.3	0.3	0.46	3.90	4.04	86.1	5.5	32.3	3.0	5.9
7.5	0.23	1.6	0.05	4.6	1.5	1.04	9.61	3.51	69.3	3.3	14.3	12.0	6.3
9.1	0.27	1.9	-0.02	7.7	17.7	1.30	18.33	3.10	67.3	4.3	9.0	5.2	6.6
10.0	0.68	2.0	0.01	3.1	3.1	0.51	2.75	2.24	69.8	3.9	49.1	17.6	8.2
5.2	0.94	5.7	-0.01	4.2	17.0	0.78	4.87	2.94	61.6	1.9	18.8	16.3	8.8
7.2	0.00	0.0	-0.01	5.1	1.5	0.90	6.51	3.78	64.3	0.8	14.8	37.9	7.4
2.7	2.81	21.3	-0.03	1.1	0.0	-0.06	-0.76	4.39	100.5	4.1	18.5	7.9	0.3
5.0	0.96	7.0	0.21	3.2	0.6	0.53	6.42	4.91	87.5	2.7	11.3	14.8	4.0

Name	City	State	Rating	2015 Rating	2014 Rating	Total Assets ($Mil)	One Year Asset Growth	Asset Mix (As a % of Total Assets)				Capital- ization Index	Lever- age Ratio	Risk- Based Capital Ratio
								Comm- ercial Loans	Cons- umer Loans	Mort- gage Loans	Secur- ities			
Town & Country Bank	Salem	MO	A-	A-	B+	513.2	1.93	1.9	3.3	36.9	16.7	10.0	11.2	17.0
Town & Country Bank	Ravenna	NE	A-	B+	B	157.0	-8.84	6.2	2.2	2.2	23.7	9.4	11.5	14.5
▲ Town & Country Bank	Las Vegas	NV	B	C+	C+	141.8	8.52	3.0	0.0	3.5	0.6	10.0	11.7	15.9
▲ Town & Country Bank and Trust Co.	Bardstown	KY	A-	B	C	284.4	7.80	5.2	1.1	20.6	23.5	10.0	11.7	18.9
Town & Country Bank, Inc.	Saint George	UT	B-	B	C+	120.2	13.33	12.2	4.8	2.6	4.6	10.0	11.5	15.0
Town and Country Bank	Springfield	IL	B-	B-	B-	735.4	46.42	8.7	1.4	16.1	26.1	6.2	8.2	12.0
Town and Country Bank Midwest	Quincy	IL	A-	A-	A-	179.0	5.01	18.6	2.1	14.8	9.2	8.8	10.2	14.2
Town Bank	Hartland	WI	B	B	B-	1859.1	21.83	20.4	16.5	5.7	6.7	5.5	9.5	11.3
▲ Town Center Bank	New Lenox	IL	C-	D+	D+	101.4	-2.68	8.3	3.3	1.9	31.3	7.8	9.5	15.5
Town Square Bank	Ashland	KY	B	B	B	448.7	5.47	8.2	4.1	41.0	12.9	10.0	13.9	21.4
Town-Country National Bank	Camden	AL	A	A	A	104.9	3.91	11.5	12.8	15.4	27.5	10.0	16.5	26.6
TowneBank	Portsmouth	VA	B+	B+	B	7830.1	26.83	9.4	2.5	15.8	9.9	6.9	10.2	12.4
Toyota Financial Savings Bank	Henderson	NV	B+	A	B	857.6	-5.67	0.0	0.1	69.9	5.4	10.0	19.1	52.2
Traders & Farmers Bank	Haleyville	AL	B	B	B	377.9	4.11	2.3	5.0	19.3	48.5	10.0	14.9	27.8
Tradition Capital Bank	Edina	MN	B-	B-	C+	525.2	37.97	9.8	1.1	11.5	12.4	4.8	8.5	10.9
Traditional Bank, Inc.	Mount Sterling	KY	B+	B+	B	1325.1	10.80	4.3	0.6	26.1	24.7	8.9	10.2	14.7
Traditions Bank	Cullman	AL	B	B	B	315.8	6.22	11.3	9.6	35.1	6.0	8.5	10.0	14.0
Traditions First Bank	Erin	TN	B	B	B	119.6	1.96	8.2	2.8	22.7	19.9	9.0	10.4	16.3
TrailWest Bank	Lolo	MT	B+	B	B-	440.7	11.39	11.7	3.0	27.8	6.7	7.9	9.7	13.2
▼ Trans Pacific National Bank	San Francisco	CA	B-	B-	C	139.3	19.04	14.2	0.0	6.6	6.1	10.0	11.3	16.6
TransCapital Bank	Sunrise	FL	C+	D+	E+	182.5	1.53	0.0	0.0	27.8	2.1	10.0	16.4	23.5
TransPecos Banks, SSB	Pecos	TX	B-	C+	C	148.7	5.75	15.4	2.7	15.5	12.7	10.0	11.4	15.3
▲ Transportation Alliance Bank, Inc.	Ogden	UT	B	B-	C-	698.9	6.15	67.5	3.8	0.1	7.0	10.0	13.2	15.9
Traverse City State Bank	Traverse City	MI	C	D+	D+	310.4	5.56	17.2	0.9	14.5	2.2	8.1	9.7	14.3
Treynor State Bank	Treynor	IA	C-	C+	B-	419.6	29.84	3.3	0.5	2.4	52.7	7.3	9.2	12.7
Tri City National Bank	Oak Creek	WI	B-	B-	C+	1380.2	7.79	3.2	0.6	13.0	33.2	8.6	10.0	17.5
Tri Counties Bank	Chico	CA	B+	B-	C+	4465.4	11.08	3.9	0.7	8.2	26.3	9.3	10.5	14.6
Tri Valley Bank	Talmage	NE	C	C	C	43.3	2.40	11.8	0.7	12.6	2.5	5.1	8.2	11.1
Tri-County Bank	Brown City	MI	B+	B+	B	265.9	8.58	5.8	1.3	10.3	28.0	9.0	10.3	16.9
Tri-County Bank	Stuart	NE	B-	B-	C	103.8	-2.18	9.1	3.1	13.5	19.5	6.6	8.9	12.2
Tri-County Bank & Trust Co.	Roachdale	IN	B	B	B	188.1	-0.81	4.9	2.6	11.6	42.3	10.0	12.4	24.9
Tri-County Trust Co.	Glasgow	MO	B+	B+	B	55.7	3.48	7.3	6.7	26.8	20.3	9.6	11.5	14.6
Tri-Parish Bank	Eunice	LA	B+	A-	B+	222.7	11.68	18.6	2.0	8.5	38.2	10.0	11.2	19.9
Tri-State Bank of Memphis	Memphis	TN	D+	D	D-	102.4	-14.69	9.5	5.9	10.0	16.7	10.0	12.0	17.4
Tri-Valley Bank	San Ramon	CA	C-	D+	D-	134.1	30.16	9.0	0.0	10.4	4.8	8.4	10.2	13.7
Tri-Valley Bank	Randolph	IA	C	C-	C-	62.3	-2.55	7.2	1.3	10.2	40.1	10.0	12.4	19.3
Triad Bank	Frontenac	MO	C+	B-	B-	283.1	9.10	15.8	0.3	14.1	6.2	6.1	9.5	11.8
Triad Bank, N.A.	Tulsa	OK	B	B	B-	180.1	0.93	10.2	1.9	34.6	0.0	8.3	9.8	17.7
▲ TriCentury Bank	De Soto	KS	B-	D+	D	70.4	36.30	10.8	0.1	15.1	0.0	10.0	13.3	15.4
Trinity Bank	Dothan	AL	B-	B-	B-	140.8	13.48	14.6	1.5	19.7	8.4	7.3	9.2	14.8
Trinity Bank, N.A.	Fort Worth	TX	A	A	A	226.8	6.79	29.7	0.6	7.4	35.7	10.0	12.7	21.1
TriStar Bank	Dickson	TN	C+	C+	C+	250.7	5.70	4.5	4.2	22.5	24.5	6.5	8.5	14.1
TriState Capital Bank	Pittsburgh	PA	B-	B-	C	3635.3	18.68	31.8	23.4	2.2	6.3	6.3	8.3	12.9
TriSummit Bank	Kingsport	TN	C	C	D+	350.9	5.76	7.2	0.6	22.0	17.8	6.5	8.7	12.2
Triumph Bank	Memphis	TN	B-	B-	C+	556.8	8.13	23.9	1.8	10.9	16.8	6.6	10.2	12.2
Triumph State Bank	Trimont	MN	C	C	C-	61.1	-3.65	10.7	4.5	2.2	21.0	8.2	9.8	13.6
Troy Bank & Trust Co.	Troy	AL	C	C-	C-	878.0	6.68	8.9	3.3	12.5	33.7	7.8	9.5	14.1
TruBank	Oskaloosa	IA	B+	B+	B+	134.0	10.31	5.8	4.3	10.5	5.8	8.3	10.6	13.6
TruPoint Bank	Grundy	VA	D+	D+	C-	434.1	1.11	2.0	3.0	17.5	37.7	6.2	8.2	17.5
▼ Trust Bank	Lenox	GA	C-	C	C-	39.4	16.24	5.4	7.1	16.6	6.3	7.5	9.3	16.2
Trust Co. of America	Centennial	CO	U	U	U	700.3	-13.26	0.0	0.0	0.0	86.0	3.9	5.9	22.8
Trust Co. of Toledo, N.A.	Holland	OH	U	U	U	5.7	6.46	0.0	0.0	0.0	79.7	10.0	90.1	296.3
Trust Co. of Virginia	Richmond	VA	U	U	U	8.3	-0.89	0.0	0.0	0.0	66.6	10.0	90.5	206.4
▲ TrustBank	Olney	IL	A-	B	B	184.7	9.89	6.5	3.9	21.0	12.7	10.0	11.9	15.6
TrustCo Bank	Glenville	NY	B	B	B	4811.6	1.76	0.5	0.2	59.4	14.7	6.7	8.7	18.4
Trustmark National Bank	Jackson	MS	B	B	B-	13160.3	6.23	11.1	1.3	11.6	27.2	8.2	9.8	13.6
TrustTexas Bank, SSB	Cuero	TX	B-	C+	B-	308.3	1.28	4.1	1.4	19.8	32.2	10.0	11.8	22.3
Truxton Trust Co.	Nashville	TN	A-	A-	A-	396.6	-18.44	6.1	6.9	14.9	18.8	9.3	10.6	15.1
TSB Bank	Lomira	WI	B	B	B-	114.7	-4.30	10.0	1.7	15.1	18.0	9.6	10.9	14.7
Tucumcari Federal S&L Assn.	Tucumcari	NM	B-	C+	B-	37.2	-5.44	0.0	0.7	52.8	28.0	10.0	13.4	35.3

Arrows denote recent upgrades ▲ or downgrades ▼

www.weissratings.com

Asset Quality Index	Adjusted Non-Performing Loans as a % of Total Loans	as a % of Capital	Net Charge-Offs Avg Loans	Profitability Index	Net Income ($Mil)	Return on Assets (R.O.A.)	Return on Equity (R.O.E.)	Net Interest Spread	Overhead Efficiency Ratio	Liquidity Index	Liquidity Ratio	Hot Money Ratio	Stability Index
7.0	0.59	3.5	0.03	6.2	5.6	1.47	11.98	3.90	66.2	2.9	14.2	14.4	8.9
7.2	0.00	0.0	0.01	7.0	1.6	1.34	11.97	3.81	51.6	3.0	17.1	14.3	7.0
4.8	0.98	5.0	-0.30	6.6	1.7	1.66	14.17	4.39	66.6	2.0	25.8	20.6	6.4
8.2	0.68	3.1	-0.12	5.6	6.1	2.86	21.63	3.20	84.3	5.7	37.2	4.1	5.3
4.2	1.65	9.6	-0.10	4.6	0.5	0.60	5.11	4.18	83.3	0.9	23.7	38.8	6.8
4.9	0.78	5.8	0.02	3.5	2.9	0.56	5.85	3.33	77.6	3.5	23.5	11.2	6.2
6.7	0.34	2.2	0.63	9.1	2.9	2.07	20.12	4.15	51.4	3.7	23.2	11.5	8.4
5.9	0.56	4.5	0.07	4.0	8.3	0.63	4.72	3.25	62.5	3.9	11.9	6.5	7.8
6.4	1.06	5.5	-0.06	3.1	0.6	0.79	8.42	3.15	97.2	1.9	35.6	32.2	4.4
5.8	1.58	8.4	0.14	3.9	2.0	0.62	4.03	4.15	74.8	1.3	12.7	26.4	7.7
7.5	0.73	2.4	0.18	8.6	1.5	1.91	11.71	5.05	58.6	1.7	35.4	33.9	9.3
6.5	0.44	3.2	0.03	5.4	48.3	1.01	7.44	3.45	76.4	2.8	9.4	12.1	9.1
9.6	0.69	2.4	-0.23	3.7	-1.6	-0.24	-1.28	1.00	190.0	1.4	34.8	30.1	8.8
7.9	1.30	3.7	0.42	4.1	2.3	0.81	5.37	3.86	72.9	3.2	49.4	24.4	7.2
4.7	0.47	4.2	-0.02	6.2	5.4	1.48	17.37	3.53	52.5	2.0	17.3	8.1	6.1
6.0	1.28	8.2	0.03	7.8	18.3	1.91	17.79	3.72	51.6	2.9	16.6	13.5	9.2
5.2	0.70	5.2	0.53	6.4	2.4	1.06	10.71	5.79	70.3	1.5	9.6	16.1	5.7
8.8	0.10	0.6	0.00	4.4	0.7	0.80	7.28	4.22	73.0	1.6	21.6	24.5	6.7
6.0	0.50	3.8	-0.23	7.3	5.5	1.73	17.83	4.50	64.3	4.0	14.0	8.4	6.5
5.9	0.70	4.1	-0.02	3.1	0.5	0.53	4.12	4.31	85.8	1.5	29.5	31.7	7.2
3.3	5.53	22.7	0.04	6.7	2.2	1.67	10.19	3.49	61.3	0.9	21.9	43.6	6.6
7.9	0.09	0.6	0.29	3.9	0.8	0.75	6.53	4.76	87.0	3.4	13.8	11.5	6.5
4.5	1.89	10.2	-2.39	9.9	19.2	3.72	30.54	6.16	71.7	0.6	19.2	35.0	6.6
2.7	2.10	15.7	-0.05	5.4	2.1	0.94	9.14	3.65	69.6	3.4	22.6	5.8	5.7
7.5	1.10	4.0	2.74	1.9	3.8	1.50	16.56	4.45	92.1	1.7	36.2	30.5	5.2
5.3	2.16	11.3	0.19	4.1	7.2	0.72	7.05	3.45	72.5	6.3	36.1	3.4	7.5
5.6	1.02	5.7	-0.10	6.5	33.6	1.03	8.59	4.30	68.7	5.8	30.6	5.1	8.7
8.2	0.00	0.0	0.00	7.9	0.7	2.04	24.23	3.66	46.7	1.4	7.5	23.8	5.0
6.5	0.49	2.9	0.05	7.0	2.8	1.43	13.38	4.34	61.1	4.9	34.4	8.2	5.7
7.4	0.06	0.5	-0.03	4.3	0.7	0.90	10.45	4.55	76.4	4.2	23.3	7.9	5.1
8.2	0.97	3.2	-0.01	3.9	1.0	0.73	5.77	3.13	68.1	5.9	65.1	11.0	7.1
4.3	1.89	11.2	0.17	7.3	0.7	1.71	14.76	4.53	61.8	0.8	13.5	32.9	7.8
6.5	2.36	9.7	0.19	3.2	0.8	0.50	4.23	3.24	87.1	4.5	40.2	12.4	7.9
0.3	10.87	55.4	1.65	0.6	-0.7	-0.83	-6.05	4.22	85.9	1.4	19.3	26.1	5.0
7.5	0.00	0.0	-0.13	1.5	0.2	0.19	1.82	3.48	94.7	1.5	20.2	26.5	3.6
5.2	2.10	8.6	-0.13	2.3	0.1	0.27	2.28	3.66	92.8	5.8	48.6	6.4	4.2
4.4	0.47	3.8	0.00	4.6	1.5	0.74	7.75	3.63	64.0	1.4	12.9	7.5	5.7
5.1	0.83	6.0	0.34	5.6	1.6	1.31	12.98	4.27	61.0	4.2	23.0	8.7	6.8
7.5	0.19	1.3	0.01	4.4	0.5	1.06	7.90	4.15	57.1	1.5	10.4	22.6	5.3
7.3	0.08	0.6	-0.01	5.7	1.1	1.06	11.68	3.92	58.4	1.4	19.3	27.3	4.0
6.1	2.56	10.7	-0.03	9.3	2.9	1.78	13.41	3.76	41.8	5.4	50.7	10.8	8.6
5.9	0.40	2.8	0.05	3.9	1.3	0.69	7.81	3.98	75.9	1.8	20.3	22.1	4.6
4.6	0.66	6.7	-0.12	3.8	17.8	0.70	8.13	2.31	60.4	1.0	10.2	25.9	6.1
6.2	0.58	4.5	0.01	2.5	1.0	0.39	3.97	3.53	89.2	1.2	18.2	30.4	5.3
4.8	0.77	5.7	0.12	5.7	4.0	1.00	9.77	3.70	65.3	0.9	19.5	21.3	6.2
3.6	2.07	12.5	0.08	3.9	0.3	0.55	5.66	4.14	75.3	4.9	36.0	8.6	3.8
2.6	3.63	19.2	-0.20	4.0	5.7	0.89	8.54	3.66	68.8	3.0	27.3	16.0	5.7
7.9	0.05	0.3	0.00	4.3	0.4	1.04	8.92	4.65	59.6	1.9	21.7	20.1	6.1
5.2	1.16	6.6	0.68	1.7	0.5	0.14	1.54	3.21	88.1	3.5	6.0	10.6	3.5
2.4	3.37	20.6	0.00	5.1	0.4	1.21	13.20	5.63	78.3	1.2	24.8	31.4	4.1
10.0	na	0.0	na	5.4	6.8	1.40	20.32	1.79	77.9	6.2	35.6	0.0	5.6
10.0	na	0.0	na	10.0	1.7	46.02	53.26	1.64	66.5	4.0	na	0.0	5.8
10.0	na	0.0	na	9.5	0.9	14.82	17.31	2.36	79.5	4.0	na	0.0	6.3
7.9	0.27	1.8	0.03	5.5	1.8	1.39	10.71	4.02	73.9	3.6	13.8	10.8	7.7
7.4	0.94	6.9	0.13	5.3	32.5	0.91	10.48	3.10	57.9	4.0	25.6	12.8	7.3
5.8	0.71	4.3	0.15	4.5	81.3	0.84	6.96	3.48	72.2	4.3	18.2	7.3	9.7
8.7	0.99	4.0	0.01	3.8	2.6	1.12	9.43	3.81	80.9	5.1	46.1	10.8	6.5
8.4	0.17	1.0	0.00	6.5	3.6	1.16	11.56	3.14	65.1	3.7	27.0	6.2	6.7
6.8	0.48	3.2	0.00	4.8	0.8	0.92	8.97	3.85	65.1	3.2	7.3	12.1	5.7
8.5	1.32	5.5	-0.01	2.9	0.1	0.38	2.91	3.08	87.6	0.7	13.4	47.5	5.2

Name	City	State	2015 Rating	2014 Rating	Total Assets ($Mil)	One Year Asset Growth	Asset Mix (As a % of Total Assets)				Capital-ization Index	Lever-age Ratio	Risk-Based Capital Ratio
							Comm-ercial Loans	Cons-umer Loans	Mort-gage Loans	Secur-ities			
Turbotville National Bank	Turbotville	PA	A	A	A	136.1	5.78	3.3	2.5	22.9	31.6	10.0	15.8	26.0
▼ Turtle Mountain State Bank	Belcourt	ND	D-	C	C-	32.2	-9.75	21.8	8.2	6.2	9.5	6.4	8.4	22.8
Tuscola National Bank	Tuscola	IL	C-	C	C	83.8	5.83	2.9	1.1	7.2	38.2	10.0	13.5	31.5
Tustin Community Bank	Tustin	CA	B+	A-	A-	78.2	3.59	4.2	46.2	2.6	0.0	10.0	13.2	16.0
▲ Twin City Bank	Longview	WA	C-	D+	D+	52.4	6.72	12.1	0.5	13.4	0.0	7.3	9.2	14.3
Twin Lakes Community Bank	Flippin	AR	B-	C+	C	125.0	10.80	7.5	12.2	29.4	1.9	7.5	10.0	12.9
Twin River National Bank	Clarkston	WA	C+	C+	C+	101.9	10.95	8.7	2.8	13.7	3.4	5.2	7.2	16.2
Twin Valley Bank	West Alexandria	OH	B	B	B-	59.3	8.44	10.9	2.7	22.0	18.3	10.0	12.3	17.3
Two River Community Bank	Tinton Falls	NJ	C+	C-	D+	908.7	7.90	5.8	0.1	9.3	8.7	6.9	10.2	12.5
Two Rivers Bank	Blair	NE	B	B-	C+	150.1	2.03	6.5	2.1	13.6	33.5	10.0	11.4	16.8
▼ Two Rivers Bank & Trust	Burlington	IA	C+	B-	C+	747.5	2.71	17.2	1.3	17.9	14.3	6.0	9.1	11.8
U.S. Bank N.A.	Minneapolis	MN	B-	C+	C+	448401.2	9.13	15.5	11.6	14.7	24.6	6.6	8.7	12.7
U.S. Bank Trust Co., N.A.	Portland	OR	U	U	U	16.4	3.70	0.0	0.0	0.0	0.0	10.0	101.	499.7
U.S. Bank Trust N.A.	Wilmington	DE	U	U	U	596.4	1.58	0.0	0.0	0.0	0.0	10.0	98.0	496.7
U.S. Bank Trust N.A. SD	Sioux Falls	SD	U	U	U	79.5	7.54	0.0	0.0	0.0	0.0	10.0	98.9	352.6
▲ U.S. Century Bank	Doral	FL	D	D-	E-	896.5	-1.37	5.0	0.2	13.6	14.2	6.9	8.9	13.7
UBank	Jellico	TN	B	B	B	66.3	0.94	5.3	7.7	20.2	27.9	10.0	13.1	23.8
UBS Bank USA	Salt Lake City	UT	A-	B+	B+	55346.8	10.73	11.3	41.6	17.6	11.1	6.9	9.0	32.7
Uinta Bank	Mountain View	WY	B-	B-	B-	145.9	9.56	8.2	0.9	3.9	59.7	6.9	9.0	25.2
Ulster Savings Bank	Kingston	NY	D+	D+	C-	814.9	6.61	1.4	0.1	44.4	11.3	10.0	11.1	18.1
Ultima Bank Minnesota	Winger	MN	C+	C	C	169.6	-1.91	13.5	1.7	6.0	0.0	6.6	9.7	12.2
UMB Bank & Trust, N.A.	Saint Louis	MO	U	U	U	3.0	0.17	0.0	0.0	0.0	0.0	10.0	99.9	103.0
UMB Bank, N.A.	Kansas City	MO	C+	C+	C+	19452.0	6.26	23.3	1.9	2.7	38.0	5.5	8.2	11.4
Umpqua Bank	Roseburg	OR	B+	B+	B	24730.5	6.78	10.2	2.5	13.5	10.2	8.3	10.4	13.6
▼ UNB Bank	Mount Carmel	PA	D+	D+	C-	132.0	6.45	2.8	0.9	46.8	26.6	9.4	10.6	24.4
UniBank	Lynnwood	WA	B-	C	B-	254.1	-6.71	6.5	0.0	0.0	6.2	10.0	14.4	18.5
UniBank for Savings	Whitinsville	MA	B-	C+	C+	1597.6	6.14	7.1	19.7	20.6	22.9	6.3	8.3	13.1
UNICO Bank	Mineral Point	MO	B+	B+	B	240.5	1.78	5.6	3.2	29.4	20.2	10.0	11.3	16.0
Unified Trust Co., N.A.	Lexington	KY	U	U	U	13.7	10.16	0.0	0.0	0.0	37.8	10.0	96.0	81.4
Union Bank	Marksville	LA	C+	C-	D+	251.2	4.91	1.5	10.9	27.8	15.0	8.3	9.9	16.1
Union Bank	Lake Odessa	MI	C	D+	D+	169.7	4.55	5.1	0.6	11.4	13.5	7.2	9.8	12.7
Union Bank	Halliday	ND	B-	C+	B	151.7	1.28	8.2	7.1	12.8	13.8	6.1	9.0	11.8
▲ Union Bank	Jamestown	TN	B-	C+	C-	211.1	-1.47	8.6	8.7	19.1	29.5	10.0	11.1	19.8
Union Bank	Morrisville	VT	B	B	B	671.7	8.48	4.9	0.6	24.8	9.1	6.6	8.6	13.4
Union Bank & Trust	Richmond	VA	B	B	B	8242.2	8.86	6.2	6.6	12.7	14.0	5.6	9.8	11.5
Union Bank & Trust Co.	Monticello	AR	C	B-	C-	207.3	5.89	10.5	5.8	15.7	18.2	7.8	9.6	13.4
Union Bank & Trust Co.	Oxford	NC	B	B+	B+	299.5	13.16	9.5	1.1	21.6	9.9	8.4	10.3	13.7
Union Bank & Trust Co.	Livingston	TN	C+	C+	B-	83.0	-1.49	6.1	5.6	28.2	16.3	10.0	12.8	21.3
Union Bank & Trust Co.	Evansville	WI	B	B-	B-	235.0	11.23	6.8	0.6	15.4	21.1	6.9	8.9	12.5
Union Bank and Trust Co.	Minneapolis	MN	C+	C+	C+	132.6	-7.33	7.1	0.1	0.8	16.3	6.3	8.3	22.2
Union Bank and Trust Co.	Lincoln	NE	B+	B+	B	3556.8	6.85	11.6	19.2	3.7	15.1	6.9	9.4	12.5
Union Bank Co.	Columbus Grove	OH	B+	B+	B	615.2	0.04	7.2	0.7	12.8	31.2	10.0	12.0	16.9
Union Bank of Blair	Blair	WI	C+	B-	C+	108.4	6.91	18.1	3.9	14.3	9.8	10.0	12.0	16.0
Union Bank of Mena	Mena	AR	A-	A-	A-	229.8	8.42	5.1	13.4	37.9	12.1	9.6	10.8	18.7
Union Bank, Inc.	Middlebourne	WV	B	B	B-	233.6	-0.72	4.5	3.1	15.2	44.7	6.2	8.2	19.2
Union Banking Co.	West Mansfield	OH	B+	B+	B+	57.5	1.31	0.6	0.5	7.5	78.9	10.0	11.2	36.4
Union Building and Loan Savings Bank	West Bridgewater	PA	B-	B-	B-	33.5	0.39	0.0	0.0	84.1	0.0	10.0	23.3	42.6
Union Community Bank	Mount Joy	PA	B-	B+	A-	522.8	2.66	5.7	0.4	16.0	19.5	10.0	16.6	23.5
Union County Savings Bank	Elizabeth	NJ	B-	B-	B-	1765.4	5.05	0.0	0.1	5.2	75.7	10.0	12.5	47.3
▲ Union Federal S&L Assn.	Kewanee	IL	C+	C	B-	154.5	49.53	0.9	0.1	48.3	15.6	10.0	12.4	25.2
Union National Bank	Elgin	IL	B	B-	C	283.4	-5.45	10.0	0.1	3.0	1.1	10.0	13.2	19.1
Union National Bank & Trust Co.	Sparta	WI	A-	A-	A-	118.3	0.36	11.3	2.3	9.7	19.5	10.0	16.6	20.0
Union S&L Assn.	Connersville	IN	C	C	C	138.6	4.95	1.4	9.7	44.9	0.9	8.8	10.2	16.5
Union S&L Assn.	New Orleans	LA	C	C+	C+	77.9	1.36	0.0	0.2	34.5	50.0	10.0	40.9	126.4
Union Savings Bank	Danbury	CT	C+	C	C	2248.4	0.99	2.9	0.2	35.4	14.8	8.3	9.9	14.7
UNION Savings BANK	Freeport	IL	D+	D	D	154.8	2.70	2.4	4.3	35.9	21.9	6.8	9.2	12.4
Union Savings Bank	Cincinnati	OH	B	B-	B-	2848.4	16.47	0.2	0.2	63.5	1.6	6.6	8.6	14.7
Union State Bank	Pell City	AL	D-	D-	D-	226.1	0.62	4.5	2.9	6.1	30.1	4.4	6.4	11.7
Union State Bank	Greenfield	IA	B-	B-	B-	76.3	-0.66	3.9	4.2	22.5	10.9	7.2	9.3	12.7
Union State Bank	Winterset	IA	C+	C+	C+	88.0	4.01	3.6	2.1	25.3	26.4	6.3	8.3	12.2

Asset Quality Index	Adjusted Non-Performing Loans as a % of Total Loans	as a % of Capital	Net Charge-Offs Avg Loans	Profitability Index	Net Income ($Mil)	Return on Assets (R.O.A.)	Return on Equity (R.O.E.)	Net Interest Spread	Overhead Efficiency Ratio	Liquidity Index	Liquidity Ratio	Hot Money Ratio	Stability Index
8.1	0.20	0.7	0.02	5.9	1.2	1.20	7.48	3.32	53.7	3.7	44.9	17.6	8.7
2.7	6.73	34.5	4.06	0.7	-0.4	-1.52	-15.95	2.64	86.3	2.4	53.2	43.8	2.5
9.3	0.39	1.0	-0.02	0.9	-0.1	-0.10	-0.67	2.94	106.5	6.0	69.2	9.5	7.2
5.7	0.06	0.3	1.28	8.2	1.1	1.91	14.17	8.12	63.2	0.8	18.4	38.5	8.5
4.7	0.54	3.9	-0.01	3.4	0.1	0.38	4.14	4.72	89.4	2.2	28.6	20.3	3.8
3.7	0.87	7.3	0.05	5.9	1.4	1.47	11.30	5.68	56.1	0.6	6.4	36.7	6.2
6.7	0.56	3.6	0.00	3.2	0.5	0.67	9.25	3.07	78.2	6.2	51.3	5.5	3.7
8.7	0.16	0.9	0.00	3.6	0.3	0.62	5.17	4.16	80.3	4.0	15.8	8.9	6.2
3.5	0.75	5.7	0.02	5.5	6.6	0.98	8.33	3.71	60.6	2.6	9.6	10.5	7.9
7.9	0.45	2.1	0.03	4.1	1.3	1.15	9.89	3.74	72.5	2.0	27.1	10.0	5.7
3.0	2.14	17.2	-0.01	4.7	4.0	0.74	7.80	3.67	71.7	3.1	5.5	12.4	6.2
4.1	1.24	8.4	0.47	7.8	4228.9	1.35	12.97	3.08	55.1	5.1	31.1	2.3	9.5
10.0	na	0.0	na	10.0	0.5	4.18	4.16	4.44	20.8	4.0	na	0.0	5.7
9.1	na	0.0	na	7.1	5.9	1.31	1.34	0.55	42.5	4.0	na	0.0	6.3
10.0	na	0.0	na	9.5	3.9	6.75	6.87	0.44	32.1	4.0	na	0.0	5.7
1.1	2.36	18.7	-0.24	0.9	1.0	0.15	1.59	3.43	96.2	1.7	19.8	23.2	2.6
5.8	1.66	6.8	0.10	5.4	0.6	1.19	8.72	4.87	71.0	1.8	32.3	30.5	7.1
6.8	0.00	0.0	0.00	6.5	475.3	1.15	12.31	2.15	18.4	6.0	26.0	0.0	8.3
3.5	7.20	24.7	-0.01	4.1	0.8	0.75	8.27	2.70	66.7	2.3	42.9	22.9	5.2
4.8	2.13	13.0	0.24	1.3	0.7	0.12	0.98	3.57	93.6	3.5	16.8	11.7	5.6
3.2	0.86	7.5	-0.02	10.0	3.1	2.49	26.37	5.39	50.0	1.0	3.4	27.8	7.2
10.0	na	0.0	na	2.3	0.0	0.13	0.13	5.93	99.9	4.0	0.0	0.0	6.5
6.5	0.92	5.6	0.21	3.9	107.7	0.75	8.53	3.00	72.9	4.8	18.4	4.4	5.8
6.1	0.43	3.1	0.19	5.8	173.9	0.97	5.56	4.23	64.3	3.2	10.9	8.7	9.5
9.4	0.04	0.2	0.00	1.5	0.1	0.11	1.05	2.65	99.8	2.5	20.1	17.1	6.0
3.9	1.67	8.0	0.00	7.7	2.6	1.31	9.90	3.82	58.9	2.5	24.0	17.6	7.3
6.5	0.37	2.9	0.06	3.8	7.5	0.62	7.70	2.78	71.4	5.5	31.3	7.0	6.4
6.0	1.52	9.4	0.15	5.4	2.4	1.32	12.12	3.98	68.3	1.3	14.2	27.4	6.9
10.0	na	0.0	na	9.5	3.5	44.66	50.85	0.10	82.4	4.0	193.9	0.0	6.4
3.9	1.11	7.4	0.57	4.8	2.1	1.13	11.58	4.17	66.0	1.3	11.8	27.0	4.8
2.3	2.96	20.2	-0.02	2.9	0.5	0.39	3.37	4.07	89.2	4.9	19.4	3.3	5.5
5.8	0.26	2.1	0.01	4.7	0.9	0.81	7.98	4.48	64.7	4.2	10.2	6.8	4.5
4.5	3.41	15.2	0.23	3.7	0.9	0.53	4.82	3.89	77.8	1.3	30.5	40.4	5.0
4.9	0.77	6.8	0.03	6.7	6.4	1.32	15.47	4.19	67.9	4.1	15.3	7.4	6.5
6.3	0.38	3.0	0.11	5.3	61.0	1.03	7.64	3.80	64.8	4.0	11.0	8.5	8.9
2.4	3.80	26.8	0.28	5.9	2.2	1.49	15.58	3.88	67.0	1.5	13.2	24.0	5.9
5.3	0.94	6.7	0.12	4.5	1.4	0.64	6.08	4.72	75.3	1.3	14.8	19.2	6.1
3.0	3.62	18.3	0.66	9.7	1.3	2.06	16.43	5.24	53.1	2.4	24.0	17.7	8.4
8.7	0.00	0.0	0.00	4.8	1.4	0.84	8.94	4.04	71.2	1.7	8.7	19.6	4.3
9.4	0.00	0.0	-0.02	3.6	0.5	0.53	5.92	2.90	79.3	7.0	70.0	5.2	3.7
5.8	0.44	3.4	0.04	5.3	24.5	0.94	10.08	3.21	65.4	2.6	15.0	13.6	8.9
5.8	1.95	9.3	-0.09	5.0	4.6	1.00	7.18	3.72	71.0	4.6	34.6	9.6	7.8
1.4	6.12	38.1	0.01	6.8	0.9	1.14	9.10	3.88	53.6	0.9	18.5	36.4	4.5
5.6	0.80	4.9	0.09	8.4	3.1	1.84	17.18	4.37	62.9	3.1	15.6	13.8	8.2
6.4	0.86	4.0	0.00	4.7	2.1	1.19	9.91	3.44	65.0	5.3	36.7	6.3	7.6
8.2	4.17	4.7	0.00	6.0	0.6	1.41	9.85	3.97	49.3	2.1	34.5	28.5	8.1
5.7	2.43	9.4	0.00	3.5	0.1	0.45	1.96	4.13	78.7	1.0	3.7	28.4	7.7
8.1	0.82	3.2	0.05	3.3	1.8	0.47	2.79	3.76	82.2	4.4	27.6	8.8	8.0
10.0	0.67	0.3	0.18	3.5	9.4	0.71	5.68	1.26	40.3	4.0	106.4	58.1	8.8
7.4	1.61	8.0	0.16	3.8	0.8	0.68	6.13	3.59	75.1	4.5	30.5	9.1	4.9
5.1	0.71	4.0	0.12	5.1	2.8	1.31	9.91	3.25	65.6	0.7	17.1	50.0	5.0
5.6	2.09	8.9	0.06	5.5	0.9	1.06	6.47	3.77	60.7	1.5	24.4	20.7	7.5
4.5	1.07	8.0	0.19	3.1	0.4	0.40	3.96	3.33	81.7	2.4	15.9	17.1	5.1
9.9	2.52	2.2	0.00	2.0	0.1	0.19	0.45	2.66	92.1	4.4	94.2	22.6	7.6
4.7	2.04	14.3	0.07	3.4	9.5	0.57	5.66	3.17	75.2	4.2	5.0	6.4	6.7
4.9	1.42	9.5	0.40	1.7	0.2	0.19	2.03	3.27	93.2	4.7	32.5	8.8	3.6
4.6	1.49	13.5	0.01	9.0	45.2	2.25	23.30	2.85	51.6	1.6	12.5	22.6	9.6
2.1	6.42	32.9	0.05	1.3	0.2	0.13	2.12	3.39	98.2	4.8	38.0	10.3	1.2
4.4	0.32	2.6	0.04	8.2	1.0	1.75	11.75	4.53	52.4	0.8	6.0	32.1	9.2
7.8	0.48	3.4	-0.19	3.4	0.4	0.59	6.70	3.67	85.6	4.0	17.1	8.6	4.5

Name	City	State	2015 Rating	2014 Rating	Rating	Total Assets ($Mil)	One Year Asset Growth	Commercial Loans	Consumer Loans	Mortgage Loans	Securities	Capitalization Index	Leverage Ratio	Risk-Based Capital Ratio
Union State Bank	Arkansas City	KS	B	B	B	291.5	-0.31	10.0	1.7	16.9	22.1	6.9	8.9	13.2
Union State Bank	Clay Center	KS	C+	C+	C+	144.6	4.59	2.2	0.8	9.5	54.1	9.5	10.7	20.9
Union State Bank	Olsburg	KS	B	B+	B+	28.7	-2.19	15.6	4.6	7.9	20.6	10.0	15.8	29.5
▲ Union State Bank	Uniontown	KS	C-	C-	D	48.4	3.97	7.7	5.0	22.8	15.2	5.6	7.7	11.4
Union State Bank	Florence	TX	C+	C+	C+	474.4	1.03	4.1	0.8	8.3	47.6	7.9	9.6	18.4
Union State Bank of Browns Valley	Browns Valley	MN	B-	B-	C+	21.2	-7.14	6.4	2.4	0.8	22.6	10.0	11.3	29.0
▲ Union State Bank of Everest	Everest	KS	C+	C-	C-	312.4	4.96	9.6	2.7	16.8	23.5	6.9	8.9	13.0
Union State Bank of Fargo	Fargo	ND	C+	C	D+	93.6	2.87	13.4	4.4	25.6	6.1	6.6	9.1	12.2
▲ Union State Bank of Hazen	Hazen	ND	B+	B	C+	130.6	-2.03	5.5	6.6	14.0	32.2	8.7	10.1	16.1
Union State Bank of West Salem	West Salem	WI	B	B+	B+	76.4	9.96	7.9	5.0	28.3	17.3	10.0	12.0	17.5
▲ Unison Bank	Jamestown	ND	B-	C	C-	273.3	6.29	4.6	10.4	22.6	18.4	8.5	10.0	14.2
United American Bank	San Mateo	CA	C+	C+	C	311.5	2.92	9.5	0.2	7.4	23.6	6.2	8.2	13.0
United Bank	Atmore	AL	C+	C+	C	571.0	13.09	6.7	3.0	12.4	28.3	7.9	9.6	16.7
United Bank	Springdale	AR	B+	B+	B	167.8	14.78	6.8	1.0	33.6	4.9	10.0	13.5	18.1
United Bank	Glastonbury	CT	B-	B-	C+	6533.1	11.89	8.3	2.5	23.3	16.4	6.7	8.9	12.3
United Bank	Zebulon	GA	A-	B+	B+	1246.9	9.97	4.7	2.5	13.1	32.0	9.0	10.3	18.1
United Bank	Vienna	VA	B	B-	B-	8868.9	21.38	4.0	0.6	9.8	10.2	7.9	10.3	13.3
United Bank	Osseo	WI	B	B-	B-	254.4	7.21	6.9	0.9	13.4	12.5	7.7	10.9	13.1
United Bank & Trust	Marysville	KS	A-	A-	B+	581.6	-3.41	7.0	2.0	8.0	17.3	9.4	10.7	14.5
United Bank & Trust Co.	Versailles	KY	B-	B	C+	466.6	-8.24	1.7	0.4	15.4	20.8	10.0	12.5	18.5
United Bank & Trust N.A.	Marshalltown	IA	A-	A-	A-	110.4	-0.95	6.7	3.0	12.9	40.3	10.0	12.7	20.0
▲ United Bank and Trust Co.	Hampton	IA	A-	B+	B+	154.1	2.43	3.6	3.7	14.2	32.0	10.0	13.7	22.0
▲ United Bank of El Paso del Norte	El Paso	TX	B-	C+	C+	214.7	1.76	13.2	0.8	2.5	11.2	7.0	10.0	12.5
▼ United Bank of Iowa	Ida Grove	IA	B+	A-	A-	1396.1	5.50	4.8	3.3	8.0	13.6	9.0	10.8	14.2
United Bank of Michigan	Grand Rapids	MI	C-	D+	D	592.6	15.40	6.8	1.5	12.0	0.6	5.6	9.8	11.5
United Bank of Philadelphia	Philadelphia	PA	E-	E-	E-	56.0	-5.37	7.1	1.9	13.6	11.2	1.5	4.7	8.5
United Bank of Union	Union	MO	D+	D	C-	301.2	0.31	15.0	1.0	20.5	18.6	9.6	11.3	14.7
United Bank, Inc.	Parkersburg	WV	B	B-	B-	6060.0	12.13	14.6	8.5	16.7	7.2	6.1	9.6	11.8
▲ United Bankers' Bank	Bloomington	MN	B	B	B	923.5	24.71	9.5	0.5	0.6	21.6	8.6	10.1	15.3
United Business Bank, F.S.B.	Oakland	CA	C+	C+	C	450.7	16.87	5.2	0.0	10.3	6.6	6.8	8.8	14.2
United Citizens Bank & Trust Co.	Campbellsburg	KY	B	B	B+	106.4	-1.04	2.5	1.6	19.4	16.7	10.0	11.8	20.2
United Citizens Bank of Southern Kentucky	Columbia	KY	C+	C	C-	136.9	3.85	6.4	4.6	31.2	12.4	10.0	12.3	17.5
United Community Bank	Blairsville	GA	B+	B+	B	10278.9	9.62	9.2	5.8	11.0	25.0	7.6	9.4	13.3
United Community Bank	Milford	IA	B-	B-	B-	202.8	1.16	9.2	1.1	13.9	0.9	4.3	9.1	10.7
United Community Bank	Chatham	IL	B+	B+	B+	1064.1	7.56	10.8	1.1	12.9	28.2	6.8	8.8	12.6
United Community Bank	Lawrenceburg	IN	B-	B-	C+	525.5	1.48	0.9	0.9	27.7	36.3	10.0	11.4	22.4
▼ United Community Bank	Raceland	LA	C	C+	B	550.2	0.53	24.0	1.1	12.8	3.9	9.1	12.8	14.3
United Community Bank	Perham	MN	B-	B-	B-	274.6	2.05	11.6	2.9	11.6	30.4	7.6	9.4	16.0
United Community Bank	Poynette	WI	B+	B	B-	165.6	64.07	4.1	0.6	19.7	7.8	10.0	12.0	15.6
United Community Bank of North Dakota	Leeds	ND	B+	B+	A-	339.0	4.03	19.1	1.6	6.9	13.1	7.5	10.0	12.9
United Community Bank of W Kentucky	Morganfield	KY	A	A	A	240.2	6.09	12.1	6.1	16.5	27.7	10.0	12.6	18.8
United Cumberland Bank	Whitley City	KY	B-	B-	C	289.3	4.24	5.7	10.8	27.9	26.9	10.0	12.1	21.0
United Farmers State Bank	Adams	MN	A-	A-	A	145.0	1.95	4.6	1.1	2.7	9.5	9.6	11.7	14.7
United Fidelity Bank, FSB	Evansville	IN	A-	B+	B-	394.3	13.69	1.7	0.2	9.7	57.2	7.3	9.2	27.1
United Midwest Savings Bank	De Graff	OH	D-	D-	E+	201.5	13.45	10.3	16.4	21.1	0.2	7.0	9.0	14.2
United Minnesota Bank	New London	MN	C-	C-	D+	30.6	5.71	14.9	11.1	23.5	4.6	5.9	7.9	13.0
United Mississippi Bank	Natchez	MS	B-	B-	B-	356.6	1.95	7.8	3.9	14.9	17.4	7.1	9.7	12.6
United National Bank	Cairo	GA	B	B-	B-	194.0	2.91	11.4	4.6	14.9	2.2	10.0	13.4	18.1
United Orient Bank	New York	NY	B-	B-	C+	93.5	-8.64	1.8	0.0	27.3	3.3	10.0	12.8	17.0
▼ United Pacific Bank	City of Industry	CA	B	B+	B	118.8	11.01	0.1	0.0	1.9	1.6	10.0	18.2	24.7
United Prairie Bank	Mountain Lake	MN	B-	B-	B-	552.1	-3.79	13.0	0.9	6.4	13.9	7.4	9.9	12.8
United Republic Bank	Elkhorn	NE	B-	B	B-	120.1	-9.70	14.3	1.3	17.2	3.0	9.0	11.6	14.2
United Roosevelt Savings Bank	Carteret	NJ	D	D	D+	97.2	8.65	4.8	0.0	56.2	12.7	10.0	15.5	27.5
United Savings Bank	Philadelphia	PA	B-	B-	B-	339.9	-0.33	0.3	0.1	29.0	27.3	10.0	15.8	36.6
United Security Bank	Fresno	CA	B	B	B	783.2	8.69	7.8	4.7	13.0	7.7	10.0	13.3	17.3
United Security Bank	Auxvasse	MO	A-	A-	A-	59.5	7.28	3.4	7.7	32.2	23.6	10.0	15.0	25.2
United Southern Bank	Umatilla	FL	C+	C	C-	492.7	12.56	2.4	0.8	15.5	26.2	7.0	9.0	15.3
▲ United Southern Bank	Hopkinsville	KY	C-	C-	B-	245.4	-9.53	4.1	2.4	23.5	20.4	8.3	9.9	14.8
United Southwest Bank	Cottonwood	MN	C-	C-	D+	52.1	18.59	2.4	1.9	0.6	33.2	5.3	7.3	13.9
United State Bank	Lewistown	MO	C	B-	B	169.3	4.14	5.8	2.1	6.1	10.6	4.1	8.1	10.5

Asset Quality Index	Adjusted Non-Performing Loans as a % of Total Loans	as a % of Capital	Net Charge-Offs Avg Loans	Profitability Index	Net Income ($Mil)	Return on Assets (R.O.A.)	Return on Equity (R.O.E.)	Net Interest Spread	Overhead Efficiency Ratio	Liquidity Index	Liquidity Ratio	Hot Money Ratio	Stability Index
7.5	0.16	1.0	0.01	4.2	2.1	0.96	7.79	3.72	76.5	2.0	16.4	18.9	7.6
7.0	0.92	3.3	0.19	3.0	0.5	0.49	4.27	2.56	80.0	1.7	16.4	22.2	6.2
4.7	3.99	12.1	-0.50	5.6	0.3	1.38	8.74	4.05	58.3	5.5	48.6	8.3	7.1
3.6	1.55	12.9	0.15	4.6	0.4	0.98	12.51	4.64	76.4	2.8	19.3	15.6	4.0
7.0	0.78	3.4	0.04	3.3	2.6	0.75	7.67	2.99	81.4	2.6	36.3	21.2	5.6
8.9	0.08	0.3	0.00	4.4	0.2	1.04	9.49	2.73	59.6	4.7	53.0	12.1	6.3
3.4	1.47	10.5	0.14	6.4	3.3	1.41	13.73	4.24	63.2	3.7	11.0	10.0	7.7
4.8	0.49	4.0	0.42	5.1	0.6	0.89	9.98	4.12	69.0	3.4	12.9	11.9	5.3
6.0	0.61	3.0	0.15	5.4	1.4	1.35	13.06	4.19	66.2	4.4	31.8	10.0	6.3
4.0	3.11	18.8	-0.04	4.5	0.5	0.83	6.78	3.84	67.6	3.1	16.2	13.4	6.6
4.3	0.80	5.2	-0.05	7.3	2.8	1.41	12.68	4.31	55.6	1.7	12.8	10.4	6.4
5.9	0.68	4.7	-0.19	2.8	0.7	0.30	3.57	3.22	87.2	4.9	35.1	8.3	5.2
5.9	0.92	4.9	-0.02	3.8	2.8	0.68	6.99	3.54	76.4	4.9	39.6	10.4	5.2
5.0	1.96	10.9	-0.07	4.6	1.3	1.06	7.34	4.08	78.7	0.9	14.4	33.5	8.1
5.1	1.00	8.0	0.08	3.7	39.9	0.84	8.15	3.05	64.8	1.3	13.0	20.1	9.0
6.3	1.33	6.4	-0.22	7.7	16.9	1.92	17.89	3.80	63.1	5.7	38.4	8.3	9.4
5.4	0.48	3.1	0.22	6.9	69.6	1.18	6.24	3.64	46.6	3.1	19.3	14.0	8.3
5.3	0.74	5.1	0.02	5.6	1.8	1.02	9.83	3.51	67.0	4.7	16.9	3.9	6.9
7.7	0.20	1.3	-0.01	6.8	5.5	1.25	10.83	3.70	52.0	3.0	4.4	12.7	8.2
5.4	2.49	11.5	0.03	2.5	1.7	0.45	3.47	3.34	95.8	4.3	25.8	8.6	6.4
8.9	0.50	2.0	-0.01	5.7	1.0	1.23	9.32	3.25	54.7	4.2	43.9	12.4	8.5
8.7	0.23	0.9	0.00	5.5	1.6	1.38	9.92	3.40	55.3	5.8	46.2	6.6	8.5
4.7	0.47	3.3	0.28	5.0	1.4	0.89	9.03	4.86	67.4	1.7	16.7	22.1	5.6
4.6	1.24	8.0	0.08	7.2	17.0	1.65	14.65	3.32	52.0	1.4	16.7	27.5	10.0
2.4	1.77	14.9	0.03	4.5	3.2	0.78	8.01	4.02	74.7	3.3	8.7	6.9	5.9
0.0	8.43	111.6	0.17	1.1	0.0	0.00	0.00	4.84	101.5	3.5	21.3	11.9	0.0
1.4	4.76	28.5	0.79	5.8	3.2	1.42	12.74	3.64	60.9	3.1	6.9	12.9	7.6
3.7	1.53	12.3	0.37	5.8	43.0	1.02	9.35	3.41	53.0	4.1	7.1	7.1	7.5
7.0	0.43	2.3	-0.01	5.3	3.4	1.95	21.55	9.49	79.9	2.0	39.5	1.9	5.7
6.6	0.00	0.0	-0.20	4.8	2.7	0.86	9.52	3.96	69.8	5.4	29.5	2.7	3.9
7.2	0.94	4.4	0.00	3.8	0.6	0.71	6.11	3.48	74.1	5.1	36.0	7.7	6.8
2.6	3.59	21.4	0.06	5.6	1.1	1.02	8.45	4.27	64.0	1.5	15.0	24.7	6.5
5.6	0.82	5.5	0.11	6.5	78.0	1.05	9.16	3.57	58.3	4.1	16.0	7.2	8.1
7.7	0.00	0.0	0.00	6.8	2.5	1.61	15.53	4.21	59.5	2.9	1.9	13.2	7.8
6.1	0.85	6.0	0.20	5.0	10.1	1.31	13.15	3.12	69.0	4.5	14.8	3.1	8.5
6.3	1.51	6.6	0.21	3.4	2.6	0.68	5.53	2.99	77.0	3.7	38.8	16.0	6.8
2.5	3.57	19.4	0.09	3.7	2.5	0.63	4.84	4.39	67.6	3.4	13.6	11.6	7.4
5.0	1.74	9.8	-0.02	4.9	2.5	1.23	12.43	3.63	67.0	2.5	33.9	19.6	6.2
5.2	0.99	5.9	-0.05	7.1	1.4	1.13	9.37	3.82	59.3	4.3	16.1	7.0	6.9
8.1	0.00	0.0	-0.03	10.0	4.7	1.91	19.12	4.96	38.9	2.4	7.1	16.4	6.3
8.3	0.22	1.1	0.04	8.7	2.7	1.53	12.20	4.33	53.3	4.2	20.7	8.1	8.5
3.6	3.67	17.7	0.42	6.1	3.0	1.40	11.49	4.27	67.2	1.7	23.6	23.9	7.4
6.7	0.24	1.5	0.06	8.9	2.3	2.05	17.43	4.37	46.6	3.4	13.5	11.3	8.8
7.2	0.80	2.4	0.13	8.4	4.5	1.54	11.78	3.42	64.8	3.1	42.8	18.7	7.4
0.5	3.31	23.8	0.81	4.6	1.4	0.96	9.19	4.89	74.2	1.0	21.3	34.6	3.5
4.5	0.76	6.4	-0.26	4.5	0.2	0.97	12.57	4.06	77.0	4.6	25.5	6.4	3.7
4.6	1.20	8.8	0.08	4.5	2.7	1.00	9.93	4.24	79.1	2.3	21.3	18.1	6.0
4.4	1.79	10.9	0.61	6.6	1.6	1.03	7.89	4.40	59.8	0.8	1.8	31.2	7.6
7.1	0.16	1.1	0.00	3.7	0.3	0.43	3.46	5.05	85.6	2.2	8.0	17.4	5.9
5.2	1.61	6.1	0.00	3.4	0.6	0.64	3.51	3.19	83.5	1.2	28.4	41.9	7.7
5.2	0.61	4.4	0.03	4.4	4.2	1.01	8.82	4.28	75.5	4.1	12.3	7.5	7.4
7.5	0.02	0.1	0.09	4.4	0.7	0.77	7.14	3.83	70.3	0.7	15.4	44.8	6.4
9.7	0.19	0.9	0.00	0.0	-0.1	-0.11	-0.75	2.64	116.8	2.1	19.0	18.8	6.8
10.0	0.03	0.1	0.00	3.1	1.1	0.43	2.64	2.13	72.2	4.4	48.9	15.1	7.9
4.8	1.72	9.0	0.20	6.6	6.0	1.08	8.01	4.13	60.0	4.1	22.4	8.9	7.5
8.0	0.80	3.4	0.00	6.4	0.7	1.57	10.36	4.32	64.0	3.2	23.3	13.7	8.3
3.5	3.15	17.2	-0.10	3.9	2.2	0.61	6.53	3.36	75.8	6.1	43.0	3.5	4.6
2.8	3.19	19.3	0.79	2.2	0.2	0.12	1.26	3.74	71.6	1.5	21.8	26.8	4.8
8.9	0.14	0.7	0.07	2.3	0.1	0.19	2.32	4.15	90.7	6.8	59.0	1.9	3.5
3.5	1.35	11.6	0.02	5.8	1.6	1.30	15.96	3.74	60.5	2.4	9.3	16.1	5.9

Name	City	State	2015 Rating	2014 Rating	Total Assets ($Mil)	One Year Asset Growth	Comm-ercial Loans	Cons-umer Loans	Mort-gage Loans	Secur-ities	Capital-ization Index	Lever-age Ratio	Risk-Based Capital Ratio
United Texas Bank	Dallas	TX	B-	B	B	333.8	6.58	21.9	0.4	6.3	14.6	10.0	12.1	17.7
United Trust Bank	Palos Heights	IL	E-	E-	E-	38.9	4.26	0.1	0.4	19.0	0.7	3.1	5.4	10.1
United Valley Bank	Cavalier	ND	B-	B-	C+	249.0	-2.07	12.1	2.4	7.3	17.5	5.8	8.5	11.6
Uniti Bank	Buena Park	CA	A-	A-	B	235.8	0.55	13.1	0.1	1.5	3.1	10.0	13.9	19.0
Unity Bank	Rush City	MN	C-	C-	C	204.7	9.11	6.5	2.2	15.4	2.5	6.0	8.0	12.0
Unity Bank	Clinton	NJ	C+	C+	C	1150.3	9.34	3.1	0.1	27.2	6.3	5.4	8.3	11.3
▼ Unity Bank	Augusta	WI	C+	B-	B	144.6	8.48	5.2	1.7	11.1	9.2	4.0	7.8	10.5
Unity Bank North	Red Lake Falls	MN	B+	B+	B+	85.9	13.54	19.9	7.9	22.7	9.5	6.5	8.5	13.0
Unity National Bank of Houston	Houston	TX	D+	D	D	84.2	-0.12	5.5	3.7	22.5	17.9	7.9	9.6	14.7
▲ Universal Bank	West Covina	CA	B	B	C	355.8	6.31	0.0	0.1	7.1	1.1	10.0	14.8	23.5
University Bank	Ann Arbor	MI	C+	C+	B-	247.6	53.70	1.4	0.1	36.2	0.9	6.9	8.9	15.4
University National Bank of Lawrence	Lawrence	KS	D+	D	D	73.5	-2.36	3.5	1.5	36.4	7.1	6.8	8.8	14.2
Univest Bank and Trust Co.	Souderton	PA	B	B	B-	4107.1	45.13	16.0	0.8	13.1	11.8	6.1	10.4	11.8
Upper Peninsula State Bank	Escanaba	MI	A-	A-	B	182.1	3.50	4.5	5.2	18.3	25.0	10.0	18.1	26.5
Upstate National Bank	Ogdensburg	NY	C-	C+	C+	107.5	8.65	8.0	0.1	14.3	15.8	10.0	12.1	17.4
Urban Partnership Bank	Chicago	IL	E-	E-	D-	574.0	-14.58	15.5	0.0	8.3	16.0	1.8	5.5	8.8
US Metro Bank	Garden Grove	CA	B+	B	D+	170.2	32.69	12.9	0.0	0.6	0.0	10.0	15.1	20.2
USAA Federal Savings Bank	San Antonio	TX	C	C	C	76188.8	8.78	0.0	51.0	5.3	24.0	7.0	9.0	15.0
USAA Savings Bank	Las Vegas	NV	U	U	U	1686.2	1.17	0.0	0.0	0.0	11.2	10.0	12.0	81.1
USAmeriBank	Clearwater	FL	B-	B-	B-	4037.7	14.62	15.2	0.4	8.8	12.4	5.5	9.0	11.4
USNY Bank	Geneva	NY	B+	B+	B+	298.7	17.61	13.1	0.4	11.0	4.2	6.6	10.0	12.2
Utah Independent Bank	Salina	UT	A-	A-	B+	70.8	7.27	17.6	5.2	13.1	11.1	10.0	14.9	19.5
Uwharrie Bank	Albemarle	NC	C+	C+	C+	550.4	4.80	6.0	1.8	16.0	20.5	8.2	9.8	14.5
Valley Bank & Trust	Brighton	CO	B-	C	C-	314.1	0.77	7.1	0.6	6.1	39.9	8.0	9.7	16.4
Valley Bank & Trust	Mapleton	IA	B+	A	A	70.8	-1.83	2.8	1.9	2.3	12.6	10.0	13.4	17.5
Valley Bank of Commerce	Roswell	NM	B	B	B+	175.7	5.36	10.2	0.9	3.0	0.3	7.1	9.1	28.0
Valley Bank of Glasgow	Glasgow	MT	B	B-	B-	36.9	-2.56	5.6	6.4	12.7	10.6	9.2	10.4	15.8
Valley Bank of Kalispell	Kalispell	MT	B	B+	B	121.9	2.41	10.7	3.9	13.1	44.6	10.0	11.4	18.7
Valley Bank of Nevada	North Las Vegas	NV	D-	D-	E-	95.1	1.20	18.8	0.2	1.7	2.6	5.2	8.9	11.2
Valley Bank of Ronan	Ronan	MT	B-	B-	B-	96.7	2.55	6.4	5.3	13.7	7.2	8.0	9.7	20.2
Valley Business Bank	Visalia	CA	A-	B+	B	429.4	6.97	7.9	0.7	2.2	11.4	10.0	11.5	16.1
Valley Central Bank	Liberty Township	OH	C+	B-	B	110.1	2.67	0.9	0.0	51.8	2.0	10.0	25.0	40.8
▼ Valley Exchange Bank	Lennox	SD	C-	C	C	68.4	2.10	6.1	2.4	1.6	4.0	9.3	10.6	26.8
Valley National Bank	Wayne	NJ	C+	C+	C+	22312.3	14.10	10.0	7.2	13.7	14.2	5.4	7.9	11.3
Valley National Bank	Tulsa	OK	D+	C	C+	504.5	13.20	20.2	1.5	9.0	8.0	3.7	9.0	10.4
Valley Premier Bank	Hawley	MN	B	B	B	105.3	-1.52	12.8	3.5	15.7	30.6	8.2	9.8	16.8
Valley Republic Bank	Bakersfield	CA	B-	B-	C+	548.2	13.42	10.0	0.4	7.1	12.7	6.7	9.2	12.3
Valley State Bank	Russellville	AL	B-	B-	B-	124.4	3.70	6.5	1.8	17.8	51.1	10.0	15.7	53.2
Valley State Bank	Belle Plaine	KS	B	B-	B-	124.9	-1.06	9.3	7.6	15.4	36.8	10.0	12.8	23.4
Valley State Bank	Syracuse	KS	C+	C+	C+	114.0	7.84	12.4	3.6	9.1	17.2	5.1	8.5	11.1
Valley View State Bank	Overland Park	KS	B+	B-	B-	860.2	0.26	3.8	0.3	1.8	54.5	10.0	13.8	27.0
Valliance Bank	Oklahoma City	OK	C	B-	C+	373.5	13.02	23.3	0.4	12.0	8.4	7.0	9.7	12.5
Valor Bank	Grandfield	OK	C	D+	D	46.4	37.66	8.5	1.0	35.5	4.0	7.5	9.3	13.3
ValueBank Texas	Corpus Christi	TX	B+	B	B	217.5	5.48	4.2	0.8	19.0	12.4	8.2	9.8	17.6
Van Wert Federal Savings Bank	Van Wert	OH	C+	B-	B-	115.4	1.96	0.0	0.6	47.3	31.0	10.0	20.5	53.9
Vanguard National Trust Co., N.A.	Malvern	PA	U	U	U	69.1	-28.73	0.0	0.0	0.0	72.1	10.0	87.9	478.1
Vantage Bank	Alexandria	MN	D	D+	D	22.2	15.33	9.2	5.4	23.1	0.0	6.7	8.7	12.5
Vantage Bank of Alabama	Albertville	AL	B	B	B-	113.0	0.76	9.7	6.2	14.9	19.4	10.0	12.5	20.5
Vantage Bank Texas	San Antonio	TX	B-	C+	C	497.0	7.60	22.1	1.6	5.1	9.5	6.4	9.5	12.0
Venture Bank	Bloomington	MN	B+	B+	B-	611.8	11.42	32.6	0.7	4.7	9.5	5.5	9.8	11.4
Vergas State Bank	Vergas	MN	B-	B	B	49.2	-2.11	4.5	3.0	10.1	32.9	10.0	14.3	35.1
Veritex Community Bank	Dallas	TX	B+	B+	B-	1268.7	25.73	21.6	0.3	10.7	6.8	7.5	9.9	12.9
Vermilion Bank & Trust Co.	Kaplan	LA	B	B	B	112.0	0.86	13.3	6.4	22.0	24.1	9.0	10.3	15.9
Vermilion Valley Bank	Piper City	IL	A	A	A	125.6	2.39	2.8	1.7	11.8	20.0	10.0	14.0	20.0
Vermillion State Bank	Vermillion	MN	A+	A+	A	521.8	-1.48	15.6	1.3	10.6	39.0	10.0	14.0	24.1
▲ Vermont State Bank	Vermont	IL	E+	E-	D-	26.4	10.25	8.6	27.6	33.9	9.0	6.5	8.5	12.9
▼ Versailles S&L Co.	Versailles	OH	D+	B-	C+	57.5	8.38	1.7	2.0	52.5	0.4	10.0	18.1	32.6
Verus Bank	Derby	KS	B	B-	B	136.4	4.37	3.5	2.9	24.4	27.4	7.5	9.3	14.1
Verus Bank of Commerce	Fort Collins	CO	A	A	A	252.3	-8.95	3.4	0.0	9.4	0.0	10.0	13.8	16.5
Victor State Bank	Victor	IA	A	A	A	50.5	4.14	19.2	1.3	7.3	50.2	10.0	27.0	43.9

Asset Quality Index	Adjusted Non-Performing Loans as a % of Total Loans	as a % of Capital	Net Charge-Offs Avg Loans	Profitability Index	Net Income ($Mil)	Return on Assets (R.O.A.)	Return on Equity (R.O.E.)	Net Interest Spread	Overhead Efficiency Ratio	Liquidity Index	Liquidity Ratio	Hot Money Ratio	Stability Index
8.7	0.12	0.6	0.00	3.8	1.9	0.77	6.86	3.27	68.5	2.5	45.0	31.4	6.5
2.4	3.03	27.6	0.10	0.0	-0.7	-2.54	-40.20	3.20	171.3	1.2	29.7	46.3	1.7
6.3	0.22	1.8	0.11	5.5	2.6	1.44	14.86	4.11	67.9	2.7	15.2	10.6	6.4
7.1	0.12	0.6	-0.15	6.1	1.6	0.91	6.14	3.79	71.3	2.0	26.8	22.0	8.4
2.2	2.31	20.7	0.00	3.8	1.2	0.77	9.32	4.47	80.9	1.9	12.2	16.0	5.4
4.7	0.65	5.8	0.16	6.0	9.3	1.11	14.49	3.62	57.5	2.1	13.2	12.6	7.2
6.5	0.11	1.0	0.21	3.6	0.7	0.61	7.10	4.30	80.3	1.6	11.8	22.1	5.0
7.5	0.18	1.5	0.00	5.3	0.7	1.10	12.16	4.59	82.1	2.6	11.3	15.3	6.0
1.5	4.67	29.9	-0.16	4.1	0.8	1.21	13.82	4.06	81.6	1.6	35.5	50.0	5.1
6.0	0.71	3.4	-0.11	4.8	7.2	2.76	20.42	3.25	85.3	1.1	21.3	33.1	6.6
4.7	0.73	6.3	-0.01	8.9	2.3	1.87	20.64	3.70	87.2	6.3	38.5	1.0	3.5
8.6	0.00	0.0	-0.04	1.5	0.1	0.10	1.03	3.68	97.7	3.0	17.2	14.2	2.8
4.7	0.98	7.4	0.17	4.2	17.3	0.71	5.39	3.94	80.6	3.3	5.0	9.7	8.7
5.9	2.22	7.5	0.15	6.6	1.6	1.21	6.96	4.37	59.1	4.0	33.4	13.0	8.0
5.3	0.96	5.8	-0.02	1.8	0.1	0.18	1.46	3.46	95.1	0.9	19.8	39.6	7.9
0.0	8.82	72.7	0.65	0.0	-12.5	-2.69	-45.45	4.80	149.0	1.2	28.6	36.1	4.3
7.1	0.00	0.0	-0.47	7.8	2.1	1.81	13.72	3.52	69.7	1.3	31.6	46.6	5.2
3.1	1.13	7.2	1.32	6.7	587.4	1.08	11.99	4.62	64.5	5.0	41.2	7.5	7.9
10.0	na	0.0	0.00	10.0	129.2	10.69	101.91	0.43	67.1	3.6	97.0	60.5	10.0
4.5	0.94	7.7	-0.01	6.4	33.0	1.15	12.59	3.58	52.1	1.6	10.3	16.4	7.8
5.8	0.44	3.5	0.11	7.9	2.7	1.25	12.45	4.07	44.8	0.6	9.4	32.8	7.1
8.3	0.55	2.2	0.13	7.5	0.9	1.76	12.41	4.60	65.9	5.0	37.8	8.8	7.9
5.9	0.87	5.4	0.04	3.5	2.4	0.60	5.96	3.66	84.9	4.5	19.3	5.8	5.4
3.9	3.70	16.5	-0.19	4.5	2.4	1.05	10.48	4.19	76.7	6.1	48.6	5.8	5.2
3.4	2.49	12.1	1.17	4.7	0.3	0.57	3.10	3.53	58.9	4.7	33.6	9.4	8.4
9.4	0.23	0.7	0.00	4.4	1.3	1.02	11.47	2.42	56.3	7.4	75.8	3.6	5.5
8.0	0.00	0.0	0.03	5.8	0.2	0.89	8.79	5.09	70.7	2.3	18.7	17.8	5.1
4.0	4.34	18.5	0.12	4.0	0.6	0.70	5.68	3.89	76.2	6.4	53.3	5.3	6.2
0.6	6.88	49.1	0.00	2.1	0.1	0.14	1.60	4.19	91.7	2.7	17.3	15.7	3.6
5.1	1.23	6.2	-0.19	4.5	0.4	0.61	6.23	4.12	77.1	6.0	49.5	5.3	5.3
5.4	0.76	4.6	-0.37	6.3	3.6	1.14	9.95	4.23	68.3	3.6	17.9	11.1	7.5
9.1	0.38	1.3	0.00	2.2	0.1	0.11	0.45	3.35	90.4	0.8	9.2	33.3	7.5
8.4	0.53	1.8	0.55	2.1	0.1	0.17	1.59	2.55	86.2	6.5	66.8	6.2	5.8
4.3	0.81	7.7	0.03	4.1	121.7	0.74	6.93	3.12	64.3	3.6	11.4	10.0	8.2
2.9	1.40	11.8	0.17	4.1	2.6	0.74	8.02	3.73	68.7	0.7	16.5	46.9	4.0
6.6	0.86	5.0	0.00	4.7	0.9	1.15	11.61	3.73	70.1	5.3	37.2	7.0	6.9
8.7	0.00	0.0	0.00	4.4	3.4	0.88	9.36	3.29	57.5	5.3	24.4	1.1	6.0
8.7	0.18	0.4	0.03	3.6	0.6	0.61	3.82	2.83	68.6	3.9	48.8	17.7	7.6
7.3	0.64	2.8	0.19	4.2	0.7	0.73	5.61	3.56	71.0	1.6	18.4	19.8	6.6
8.1	0.12	1.0	0.03	4.9	1.0	1.15	12.88	4.21	71.7	0.6	9.9	43.5	5.7
6.8	3.35	7.6	-0.07	4.4	5.8	0.89	6.36	2.75	55.9	6.6	66.8	7.2	7.4
3.3	1.91	14.4	0.21	3.9	2.1	0.77	7.78	3.95	74.3	0.8	14.8	39.2	6.0
7.2	0.06	0.5	0.00	6.7	0.7	1.94	20.09	4.92	70.0	0.6	6.6	29.2	3.9
8.9	0.00	0.0	0.07	4.8	1.5	0.91	8.93	4.33	80.5	4.5	31.9	10.0	6.3
9.9	0.52	1.3	0.00	2.9	0.4	0.45	2.23	2.42	79.1	3.5	51.6	20.6	7.6
10.0	na	0.0	na	10.0	9.4	16.03	21.99	0.30	53.8	4.0	na	0.0	6.3
7.7	0.00	0.0	0.00	3.2	0.1	0.69	6.68	4.01	84.6	1.5	5.7	21.9	3.0
4.3	2.62	12.7	0.05	5.8	1.0	1.15	8.65	4.39	64.3	3.0	33.4	18.0	7.5
5.3	0.14	1.1	-0.13	4.6	4.3	1.21	11.82	4.04	74.6	3.2	19.5	13.3	6.0
7.8	0.05	0.4	-0.02	9.8	9.7	2.21	22.62	4.55	53.5	2.3	11.8	12.7	7.7
8.4	1.72	4.2	-0.08	3.2	0.2	0.54	3.75	2.58	77.0	4.5	69.0	17.1	6.8
7.7	0.19	1.4	0.04	6.3	10.0	1.16	9.78	3.85	52.8	3.5	23.5	10.5	9.1
4.6	1.31	8.1	0.27	6.2	1.2	1.48	14.58	4.40	67.9	2.4	12.4	16.8	6.6
6.4	0.80	4.1	0.05	7.2	1.6	1.70	11.60	3.82	46.2	3.8	9.2	9.0	8.9
7.6	1.46	5.2	-0.05	9.8	10.2	2.58	18.08	3.55	27.3	5.8	50.0	7.6	9.6
0.8	3.46	29.2	-0.06	4.5	0.2	1.19	13.92	3.93	63.7	0.6	14.5	54.3	3.3
9.4	0.00	0.0	0.00	1.0	-0.2	-0.50	-2.75	3.17	126.0	3.8	28.0	12.0	7.3
8.8	0.00	0.0	0.05	4.5	1.0	1.00	10.55	3.67	76.0	4.5	24.4	6.9	6.2
7.2	0.06	0.4	0.00	9.8	3.9	1.99	14.64	4.50	37.5	2.8	10.0	1.3	8.9
9.6	0.00	0.0	0.00	10.0	1.0	2.62	10.31	4.55	21.9	5.3	70.3	13.4	8.9

Name	City	State	2015 Rating	2014 Rating	Total Assets ($Mil)	One Year Asset Growth	Comm-ercial Loans	Cons-umer Loans	Mort-gage Loans	Secur-ities	Capital-ization Index	Lever-age Ratio	Risk-Based Capital Ratio
Victory Bank	Limerick	PA	C	C	C	193.0	15.76	19.5	3.0	15.7	0.5	3.4	8.5	10.2
Victory Community Bank	Fort Mitchell	KY	A-	A-	A	168.9	3.85	0.0	0.3	60.4	1.6	10.0	13.7	23.9
▲ Victory State Bank	Staten Island	NY	B-	C+	C+	332.6	3.74	5.7	0.2	2.5	50.3	6.9	8.9	19.0
Vidalia Federal Savings Bank	Vidalia	GA	C+	C+	C+	227.0	-0.28	0.0	0.9	24.8	47.6	10.0	13.0	47.1
▼ Viking Savings Bank	Alexandria	MN	B-	B-	C+	177.4	0.85	9.8	1.5	25.1	4.4	9.6	11.3	14.7
Villa Grove State Bank	Villa Grove	IL	B	B-	C+	72.7	-1.61	5.4	2.3	47.7	12.1	8.6	10.0	17.7
Village Bank	Saint Libory	IL	C+	C+	C+	81.5	-4.53	4.4	7.1	21.8	18.9	8.4	9.9	19.6
Village Bank	Auburndale	MA	B	B	B-	990.4	15.52	3.4	0.3	45.0	13.6	10.0	11.1	17.7
▲ Village Bank	Saint Francis	MN	D+	D	D-	229.7	19.50	14.8	1.3	14.6	11.6	6.8	9.3	12.3
Village Bank	Midlothian	VA	C-	D+	D-	443.1	5.42	8.5	12.1	17.1	6.0	9.4	10.6	15.3
Village Bank & Trust	Arlington Heights	IL	B-	B-	B-	1396.4	15.89	36.0	11.5	3.1	13.6	5.2	9.1	11.2
Vinings Bank	Smyrna	GA	B+	B+	A-	284.8	9.00	6.7	0.2	1.9	52.5	7.3	9.2	15.5
Vintage Bank Kansas	Leon	KS	B	B	C	60.3	5.94	6.0	3.7	22.0	21.3	10.0	11.4	18.4
Vinton County National Bank	McArthur	OH	B	B	B+	891.4	3.10	2.7	11.4	34.3	21.8	10.0	11.1	18.0
▲ Virginia Bank and Trust Co.	Danville	VA	A-	B+	A-	187.6	3.94	11.4	9.6	22.0	15.9	10.0	13.7	19.8
Virginia Commonwealth Bank	Petersburg	VA	C+	C+	C+	323.6	7.18	9.4	11.1	11.8	7.4	8.6	10.4	13.8
Virginia Community Bank	Louisa	VA	B-	C+	D+	233.4	8.68	10.7	1.8	20.3	19.2	8.3	10.3	13.6
Virginia National Bank	Charlottesville	VA	B	B-	B	569.1	3.80	10.6	10.4	9.8	12.4	7.3	10.0	12.7
Virginia Partners Bank	Fredericksburg	VA	C	C	C	322.6	10.66	8.3	0.8	19.8	16.6	6.1	8.6	11.8
Vision Bank, N.A.	Ada	OK	B-	B-	B-	624.8	-1.86	6.6	5.3	23.8	24.8	8.4	9.9	15.5
VisionBank	Topeka	KS	B-	B-	C+	134.0	8.87	15.9	2.5	17.3	1.4	6.6	8.6	12.9
VisionBank	Saint Louis Park	MN	B	B	B-	70.8	40.88	23.0	1.7	15.9	0.0	9.6	10.7	15.7
VISIONBank	Fargo	ND	D	D+	D+	165.1	4.99	23.6	3.4	20.5	0.1	7.7	10.6	13.1
VisionBank of Iowa	Ames	IA	B-	C+	C+	446.7	9.95	4.6	0.2	8.3	3.1	7.3	10.6	12.7
VIST Bank	Wyomissing	PA	B	B	B-	1563.6	9.39	8.9	0.1	16.0	14.9	6.0	8.9	11.8
Vista Bank	Ralls	TX	B+	B+	C+	398.9	24.49	16.2	2.1	13.3	9.0	10.0	11.3	15.1
VNBTrust, N.A.	Charlottesville	VA	U	U	U	9.6	-3.33	0.0	0.0	0.0	0.0	0.0	92.3	0.0
Volunteer Federal Savings Bank	Madisonville	TN	B-	B	B	174.4	0.30	1.1	5.3	48.7	0.9	10.0	14.6	25.8
Volunteer State Bank	Portland	TN	B	B-	B-	613.5	16.64	9.7	0.8	31.9	4.6	5.2	9.6	11.2
Wabash Savings Bank	Mount Carmel	IL	D	D-	D+	10.1	-9.73	2.8	6.7	29.4	12.2	10.0	13.1	30.8
▲ Wadena State Bank	Wadena	MN	A	A	A-	123.4	-3.11	9.8	3.0	14.0	27.8	10.0	11.4	19.6
Waggoner National Bank of Vernon	Vernon	TX	A+	A+	A+	273.6	0.74	5.8	6.3	8.4	29.9	10.0	13.8	19.0
Wahoo State Bank	Wahoo	NE	C+	C+	C	71.9	1.99	4.4	3.0	28.4	21.5	5.0	7.0	11.3
▲ Wake Forest Federal S&L Assn.	Wake Forest	NC	B+	B	B	106.0	-0.54	0.0	0.2	24.4	2.1	10.0	22.0	41.6
Wakefield Co-operative Bank	Wakefield	MA	C	C	C	201.8	5.69	0.0	0.0	55.6	24.6	6.1	8.1	16.1
Walcott Trust and Savings Bank	Walcott	IA	B	B+	A-	123.4	10.65	7.1	0.4	15.1	29.5	10.0	16.3	28.4
Walden Savings Bank	Montgomery	NY	C	C	C-	516.2	5.79	6.8	0.3	29.5	21.2	6.9	8.9	15.7
Waldo State Bank	Waldo	WI	B	B	B	68.7	4.20	9.9	2.2	36.0	24.0	10.0	12.7	20.6
Walker State Bank	Walker	IA	B-	B-	B-	41.0	-3.33	5.0	2.7	13.2	24.1	7.4	9.9	12.8
Wallis State Bank	Wallis	TX	B+	B+	B	502.0	7.49	7.0	0.5	2.8	2.6	6.7	10.3	12.3
Wallkill Valley Federal S&L Assn.	Wallkill	NY	C	C	C	193.7	3.12	2.6	1.2	49.6	6.1	10.0	15.4	19.8
Walpole Co-operative Bank	Walpole	MA	B	B	B	465.7	7.11	2.9	0.0	18.4	14.3	10.0	19.0	23.1
Walters Bank and Trust Co.	Walters	OK	B	B+	B+	57.5	3.76	2.8	5.2	20.0	37.0	10.0	20.8	60.1
Walton State Bank	Walton	KS	D-	E	E	8.3	-5.80	3.1	4.3	18.1	30.6	5.9	7.9	20.2
Wanda State Bank	Wanda	MN	B	B	B	127.4	0.32	1.3	0.8	3.0	23.0	10.0	15.9	22.5
Warehouse Trust Co. LLC	New York	NY	U	U	U	7.4	-27.91	0.0	0.0	0.0	0.0	10.0	76.4	194.5
Warren Bank and Trust Co.	Warren	AR	B	B+	A-	136.9	-0.45	2.4	3.4	16.1	63.9	10.0	16.3	44.5
Warren-Boynton State Bank	New Berlin	IL	A	A	A	130.3	2.33	5.3	2.2	14.9	24.6	10.0	15.8	21.6
Warrington Bank	Pensacola	FL	C-	C-	C-	85.8	1.15	0.0	0.5	2.0	59.9	10.0	17.8	50.3
Warsaw Federal S&L Assn.	Cincinnati	OH	C-	D+	D+	72.1	15.93	0.0	0.1	74.5	1.3	10.0	12.1	18.7
Washington Business Bank	Olympia	WA	B	B-	B-	68.7	1.44	33.1	0.0	7.0	0.3	10.0	12.6	16.3
Washington County Bank	Blair	NE	B+	B+	B	362.4	6.03	7.0	1.6	7.4	14.2	7.0	9.5	12.5
Washington Federal Bank for Savings	Chicago	IL	A	A	A	152.8	10.45	0.0	0.0	73.5	0.0	10.0	12.2	25.0
Washington Federal, N.A.	Seattle	WA	A-	B+	B	14885.4	2.14	4.2	0.9	38.0	22.6	10.0	11.5	18.5
Washington Financial Bank	Washington	PA	B	B	C+	1088.7	2.75	5.4	4.9	33.6	19.1	10.0	11.7	18.3
Washington Savings Bank	Effingham	IL	C+	C+	C+	349.3	33.36	7.4	2.6	30.9	21.3	10.0	16.5	26.6
Washington Savings Bank	Lowell	MA	C-	C-	C-	213.7	4.35	0.9	0.1	51.2	13.2	6.9	8.9	14.0
Washington Savings Bank	Philadelphia	PA	D	D	D	158.4	1.23	0.7	2.0	61.0	4.9	6.3	8.4	13.3
Washington State Bank	Washington	IA	A-	A-	A-	298.6	25.78	5.5	1.3	26.7	26.6	10.0	12.4	19.6
▼ Washington State Bank	Washington	IL	C	B-	B-	59.5	4.42	3.1	6.6	32.4	36.5	8.5	10.0	23.0

Asset Quality Index	Adjusted Non-Performing Loans as a % of Total Loans	as a % of Capital	Net Charge-Offs Avg Loans	Profitability Index	Net Income ($Mil)	Return on Assets (R.O.A.)	Return on Equity (R.O.E.)	Net Interest Spread	Overhead Efficiency Ratio	Liquidity Index	Liquidity Ratio	Hot Money Ratio	Stability Index
4.2	1.08	11.0	0.06	4.0	0.9	0.65	7.68	4.24	72.4	2.5	1.9	13.5	4.6
5.5	1.78	10.5	0.15	9.4	3.0	2.44	17.89	3.06	51.9	1.5	16.5	25.5	9.2
5.8	2.09	8.3	0.22	4.0	1.8	0.73	8.12	3.12	68.1	4.0	47.7	17.1	4.6
7.0	3.61	7.6	0.05	2.4	0.5	0.31	2.38	2.12	80.3	3.5	78.6	34.3	6.7
3.4	1.46	9.8	-0.05	7.5	2.3	1.81	10.86	3.43	47.7	2.9	15.2	14.7	9.9
7.6	0.30	2.1	0.10	6.9	0.9	1.70	17.28	3.93	55.1	3.6	11.3	10.8	5.8
7.2	0.52	2.8	0.05	3.6	0.5	0.79	8.36	3.07	72.9	5.5	37.2	5.2	5.5
6.6	0.66	4.6	0.00	4.5	5.7	0.80	7.17	3.35	61.4	1.5	16.3	24.3	7.1
1.5	3.89	29.3	-0.39	9.8	3.6	2.18	22.52	4.55	62.3	3.6	19.7	11.4	5.5
2.5	2.37	17.2	0.06	4.3	10.5	3.31	33.63	3.54	89.9	1.7	13.0	20.7	3.4
5.2	0.51	4.2	0.17	5.4	9.5	0.97	8.54	3.11	49.6	1.2	13.9	23.1	7.8
7.4	0.65	2.4	0.34	5.2	2.8	1.37	12.91	4.01	69.5	4.9	35.6	8.8	6.3
8.1	0.04	0.2	-0.03	4.8	0.5	1.14	9.18	3.95	68.3	3.4	17.6	12.1	6.3
5.7	0.98	6.0	0.14	4.6	5.4	0.82	6.96	3.70	70.1	3.1	14.4	13.7	7.3
6.4	0.13	0.6	0.03	5.4	1.3	0.91	6.97	4.10	73.7	4.9	27.6	5.4	7.8
4.4	0.78	5.5	0.27	3.7	1.5	0.63	5.84	3.40	70.0	1.7	14.9	20.7	5.4
4.4	1.51	9.9	-0.02	4.8	1.5	0.94	8.91	4.38	77.6	4.1	20.0	8.8	5.1
6.6	0.39	2.8	0.00	5.1	4.5	1.06	10.57	3.46	65.0	2.3	14.8	17.3	6.9
7.3	0.12	1.0	0.00	2.9	0.9	0.39	4.48	3.33	83.5	0.9	19.8	39.2	4.5
5.0	1.19	7.4	0.11	4.3	4.5	0.96	9.32	4.09	77.8	1.6	8.5	20.2	6.7
4.4	0.87	7.8	-0.04	5.2	0.8	0.84	9.30	3.87	67.8	1.5	12.2	23.0	5.3
7.8	0.24	1.8	0.01	6.1	0.7	1.55	13.90	4.05	56.3	0.7	18.8	54.1	6.4
0.5	4.09	32.3	0.33	4.3	0.8	0.69	6.40	4.26	73.8	2.4	7.7	16.4	6.3
4.2	0.66	4.8	-0.03	4.7	3.5	1.08	9.86	3.56	69.4	1.7	12.3	9.1	6.7
5.5	0.66	5.7	0.06	4.3	7.7	0.69	5.90	3.50	69.4	2.8	5.1	11.8	7.5
6.0	0.79	5.1	0.19	5.5	2.6	0.99	7.69	4.94	67.8	0.8	15.3	32.1	6.2
8.2	na	0.0	na	0.5	-0.2	-2.17	-2.34	0.54	116.2	4.0	na	0.0	6.7
7.5	0.48	2.3	0.05	3.4	0.5	0.41	2.83	3.75	83.0	3.0	23.7	15.0	7.2
5.6	0.31	2.8	0.00	9.6	10.9	2.75	25.51	4.23	67.4	2.3	5.7	16.4	7.7
5.6	3.13	10.9	-0.03	0.0	0.0	-0.55	-4.23	3.15	121.0	4.5	60.2	14.1	4.2
8.6	0.12	0.5	-0.08	6.3	1.4	1.50	12.02	4.43	62.7	5.8	48.0	7.3	8.1
8.3	0.05	0.2	0.11	10.0	6.3	3.05	22.09	4.41	44.2	2.5	14.6	16.3	9.4
8.0	0.09	0.7	0.00	3.3	0.3	0.59	8.10	3.67	82.7	4.6	23.5	6.0	3.8
9.3	0.80	1.8	-0.13	5.5	0.8	0.98	4.52	2.95	48.4	3.1	57.5	31.4	7.5
5.4	1.37	11.7	0.00	2.7	0.8	0.53	6.52	2.79	80.7	1.9	27.9	25.1	4.7
7.6	0.97	3.5	0.33	3.5	0.5	0.51	2.97	3.32	81.0	5.4	44.5	9.0	6.4
3.0	2.79	19.6	0.07	3.1	1.7	0.44	4.86	3.27	80.6	5.1	27.3	3.8	5.5
5.8	1.38	6.5	0.00	5.7	0.5	0.98	7.65	4.05	55.4	3.5	31.3	13.8	6.8
6.2	0.57	3.6	0.00	8.1	0.5	1.52	14.78	3.82	48.9	3.7	31.2	13.5	5.0
7.1	0.11	0.8	0.08	9.7	8.5	2.33	23.05	4.82	59.2	1.6	14.3	22.9	8.6
4.2	3.44	17.8	0.07	2.6	0.4	0.30	1.75	3.79	86.3	2.2	7.4	17.2	6.2
6.3	0.91	3.7	-0.01	4.5	2.3	0.69	3.62	3.37	64.7	1.2	18.6	30.0	7.8
8.9	0.00	0.0	-0.03	4.2	0.4	0.99	4.71	3.16	72.4	4.7	48.2	12.8	7.1
8.8	0.00	0.0	0.04	1.7	0.0	0.14	1.92	3.15	97.1	4.5	39.6	10.0	1.0
7.1	0.81	2.9	0.04	3.9	0.7	0.74	4.54	3.27	64.5	3.9	41.7	16.1	8.0
10.0	na	0.0	na	10.0	5.8	108.74	124.00	na	51.7	4.0	148.7	0.0	5.5
9.4	1.25	2.4	0.05	4.1	1.0	0.99	5.74	3.03	71.8	4.0	66.3	21.8	7.5
6.8	1.12	4.8	-0.01	6.8	1.2	1.21	7.76	3.91	56.7	2.3	18.0	17.8	8.6
10.0	0.00	0.0	0.00	1.9	0.1	0.12	0.68	2.17	91.2	7.0	86.9	5.8	5.5
5.7	2.17	14.2	0.12	1.2	0.0	-0.04	-0.31	5.42	100.6	1.2	12.8	27.8	5.7
8.1	0.00	0.0	0.09	4.8	0.3	0.66	5.13	4.59	78.2	0.7	12.9	40.3	6.4
8.1	0.14	1.1	-0.01	6.0	2.8	1.10	11.66	3.48	58.0	3.4	9.9	11.1	6.2
9.8	0.00	0.0	0.00	9.7	1.7	1.52	12.54	4.58	46.5	0.7	15.3	47.4	7.8
6.1	1.01	5.7	-0.16	6.3	129.2	1.17	8.80	3.06	47.4	2.7	27.2	20.1	10.0
8.2	0.28	1.7	0.06	4.0	5.9	0.74	6.38	3.19	68.1	4.5	13.1	5.7	8.6
7.2	1.03	4.1	0.03	2.9	1.1	0.41	2.46	2.78	78.8	3.8	31.4	13.4	7.0
5.5	1.17	9.5	-0.01	2.5	0.6	0.36	4.03	3.06	84.6	1.9	20.4	16.9	4.5
6.8	0.39	3.5	0.03	1.2	0.1	0.07	0.81	3.04	94.4	1.8	9.2	19.7	3.9
6.5	1.00	5.1	0.31	7.5	3.2	1.46	11.97	3.94	50.0	3.6	28.9	13.2	7.4
5.2	2.39	11.0	0.81	2.6	0.1	0.15	1.47	3.23	59.9	3.6	28.3	13.2	5.4

Name	City	State	2015 Rating	2014 Rating	Rating	Total Assets ($Mil)	One Year Asset Growth	Comm-ercial Loans	Cons-umer Loans	Mort-gage Loans	Secur-ities	Capital-ization Index	Lever-age Ratio	Risk-Based Capital Ratio
Washington State Bank	Washington	LA	B-	B	B-	168.7	6.02	12.7	2.2	12.1	18.0	9.9	11.0	16.0
Washington Trust Bank	Spokane	WA	B+	B	B	5368.8	6.00	17.9	1.9	8.0	22.3	7.8	9.7	13.1
Washington Trust Co. of Westerly	Westerly	RI	B+	B+	B	4203.5	14.44	4.2	0.9	27.0	13.9	6.7	8.9	12.3
▲ WashingtonFirst Bank	Reston	VA	B+	B-	C+	1912.2	19.91	8.7	0.2	13.6	12.5	8.5	10.9	13.8
Washita State Bank	Burns Flat	OK	B	B-	B-	123.2	-7.60	9.3	0.2	2.4	22.3	10.0	13.3	30.2
Washita Valley Bank	Fort Cobb	OK	B+	B+	B+	40.6	3.09	3.7	11.1	1.3	34.8	10.0	17.9	23.6
Watch Hill Bank	Cincinnati	OH	C	C-	D	124.3	7.72	2.1	0.3	52.0	3.1	10.0	12.1	18.2
Waterford Bank, N.A.	Toledo	OH	B+	B+	B+	629.6	14.22	20.3	0.4	3.8	5.9	6.5	10.1	12.1
Waterford Commercial and Savings Bank	Waterford	OH	B	B	B-	43.1	-1.04	0.7	8.5	26.9	32.7	10.0	13.2	28.8
▲ Waterman State Bank	Waterman	IL	D-	D-	D-	40.1	-8.40	6.3	0.6	5.8	47.7	6.5	8.5	15.1
▲ WaterStone Bank, SSB	Wauwatosa	WI	A-	A-	B	1790.7	2.85	1.6	0.0	34.9	14.0	10.0	20.7	29.6
Watertown Savings Bank	Watertown	MA	C	C+	C+	1143.8	3.07	0.2	0.2	35.4	39.1	8.7	10.1	23.1
Watertown Savings Bank	Watertown	NY	A-	A-	B-	627.8	5.35	5.5	1.2	15.1	19.6	10.0	12.5	17.7
Watkins Savings Bank	Watkins	IA	A-	A-	A-	70.2	-0.58	0.8	1.0	6.9	59.6	10.0	15.6	33.1
Wauchula State Bank	Wauchula	FL	B-	C+	C-	647.1	6.68	2.3	1.2	18.3	22.3	10.0	11.7	17.8
▲ Waukesha State Bank	Waukesha	WI	A-	B+	B-	931.2	4.31	9.0	1.4	11.3	30.3	10.0	13.0	18.6
Waukon State Bank	Waukon	IA	A+	A+	A+	270.0	-0.55	8.9	2.0	15.4	17.6	10.0	13.4	17.5
Waumandee State Bank	Waumandee	WI	C+	C+	C+	174.1	5.06	7.4	3.5	20.4	13.2	7.6	9.4	13.7
Wawel Bank	Garfield	NJ	D-	D-	D	73.1	-0.02	1.6	0.1	43.2	0.0	8.2	9.8	17.6
Waycross Bank & Trust	Waycross	GA	B-	B-	B-	155.1	4.66	8.2	0.3	13.6	30.3	7.9	9.6	17.2
Wayland State Bank	Mount Pleasant	IA	A	A	A	87.5	2.75	9.5	2.6	12.8	26.6	10.0	19.5	30.1
Wayne Bank	Honesdale	PA	B+	B+	B+	1123.6	50.22	3.4	4.3	20.6	27.6	7.9	9.6	13.3
Wayne Bank and Trust Co.	Cambridge City	IN	B	B	C+	136.5	2.16	2.6	3.6	21.7	24.2	10.0	13.1	19.5
Wayne County Bank	Waynesboro	TN	C+	C	C-	307.0	0.01	13.0	9.6	18.8	9.1	10.0	13.2	17.3
Wayne Savings Community Bank	Wooster	OH	C+	C	C+	446.0	5.07	4.8	0.3	38.0	20.1	6.7	8.7	14.3
WCF Financial Bank	Webster City	IA	C+	C+	C+	121.9	12.62	0.0	4.9	41.0	36.0	10.0	15.2	37.6
WebBank	Salt Lake City	UT	A	A	A	378.2	35.67	21.8	28.7	0.0	2.5	10.0	23.1	28.3
Webster Bank, N.A.	Waterbury	CT	B	B	B-	25621.9	6.51	18.9	1.1	19.7	27.9	5.8	7.8	11.7
Webster Five Cents Savings Bank	Webster	MA	B	B	B	745.9	7.08	4.5	2.9	31.6	16.0	10.0	12.1	16.6
Welch State Bank of Welch, Oklahoma	Welch	OK	A	A	A	253.0	10.50	4.0	3.2	16.3	17.4	10.0	13.3	15.8
▼ Welcome State Bank	Welcome	MN	C	B+	B+	28.4	11.55	13.0	7.5	5.4	5.7	9.3	10.5	14.9
Wellesley Bank	Wellesley	MA	B-	B-	B-	664.5	13.02	5.7	0.0	40.5	10.2	7.4	9.3	13.3
Wellington State Bank	Wellington	TX	B	B-	B-	333.4	40.24	6.6	3.0	6.8	22.5	8.7	10.1	14.3
Wellington Trust Co., N.A.	Boston	MA	U	U	U	86.6	0.07	0.0	0.0	0.0	0.0	10.0	36.6	37.0
Wells Bank	Platte City	MO	A-	A-	A-	196.0	51.22	5.2	0.8	27.7	15.7	7.8	9.5	14.0
Wells Fargo Bank Northwest, N.A.	Salt Lake City	UT	B	B	C+	8651.4	12.38	0.0	0.0	59.2	9.3	10.0	14.5	35.6
Wells Fargo Bank South Central, N.A.	Houston	TX	C-	C-	D+	8955.2	10.28	0.0	0.1	84.3	0.0	10.0	14.2	27.0
Wells Fargo Bank, Ltd.	Los Angeles	CA	U	U	U	698.2	-1.57	0.0	0.0	0.0	0.0	10.0	77.0	34.9
Wells Fargo Bank, N.A.	Sioux Falls	SD	C+	C+	C-	1740819.0	10.24	10.7	6.9	15.8	21.6	5.8	7.8	12.5
Wells Fargo Delaware Trust Co., N.A.	Wilmington	DE	U	U	U	383.9	1.56	0.0	0.0	0.0	0.0	10.0	94.6	461.3
Wells Fargo Financial National Bank	Las Vegas	NV	B-	C+	C	8860.0	19.82	0.0	80.0	0.0	3.4	10.0	13.6	17.2
Wells Federal Bank	Wells	MN	B	B	C+	265.0	-1.27	4.4	3.1	24.9	13.2	8.4	9.9	14.7
Wells River Savings Bank	Wells River	VT	C-	C-	C+	167.5	-2.86	4.6	3.2	32.6	33.0	10.0	11.8	21.4
Wenona State Bank	Wenona	IL	C	C	C+	33.2	0.11	5.2	3.1	5.7	40.7	10.0	13.8	23.2
WesBanco Bank, Inc.	Wheeling	WV	B	B-	B-	9799.4	16.20	7.1	3.6	17.6	24.4	7.6	10.1	13.0
West Alabama Bank & Trust	Reform	AL	A-	A-	B+	581.5	4.33	7.5	1.8	9.7	34.7	10.0	12.5	19.8
West Bank	West Des Moines	IA	B+	B+	A-	1807.7	4.94	18.2	0.1	2.9	18.2	5.1	9.2	11.1
West Central Bank	Ashland	IL	C	C	C	192.9	-4.54	9.7	6.8	22.5	9.1	5.6	8.3	11.4
West Central Georgia Bank	Thomaston	GA	A	A	A	118.2	0.64	2.6	5.4	18.9	45.5	10.0	24.9	50.1
West End Bank, S.B.	Richmond	IN	C	C	C	285.6	4.09	5.1	33.0	21.2	8.5	8.0	9.9	13.3
West Gate Bank	Lincoln	NE	B+	B+	B	470.2	11.74	12.1	0.5	16.3	11.5	7.7	10.1	13.0
West Iowa Bank	West Bend	IA	A-	A-	B+	117.0	-1.12	7.3	1.9	10.1	28.7	10.0	12.0	17.8
West Michigan Community Bank	Hudsonville	MI	C	C	D+	380.7	21.97	23.2	0.8	9.3	8.4	7.9	10.6	13.3
West Milton State Bank	West Milton	PA	A-	A-	A-	394.2	6.32	4.2	3.4	9.7	40.2	7.8	9.5	15.3
West Plains Bank	Ainsworth	NE	A-	B+	B+	103.4	-3.23	17.0	1.8	0.3	16.9	9.4	12.6	14.5
West Plains Bank and Trust Co.	West Plains	MO	A	A	A	360.3	4.78	11.3	2.5	14.8	21.8	10.0	11.1	15.7
West Plains S&L Assn.	West Plains	MO	B	B	B	78.7	-2.57	0.0	0.6	60.5	19.0	10.0	20.4	45.5
West Point Bank	Radcliff	KY	A-	A-	B+	241.5	40.26	0.0	1.9	20.6	54.2	6.1	8.1	15.6
▲ West Pointe Bank	Oshkosh	WI	C	C-	D+	266.8	0.42	14.8	0.2	20.3	13.3	10.0	18.5	23.6
West Shore Bank	Ludington	MI	B-	C+	C+	429.1	11.04	8.2	4.3	19.6	25.2	6.3	8.3	13.0

Asset Quality Index	Adjusted Non-Performing Loans as a % of Total Loans	as a % of Capital	Net Charge-Offs Avg Loans	Profitability Index	Net Income ($Mil)	Return on Assets (R.O.A.)	Return on Equity (R.O.E.)	Net Interest Spread	Overhead Efficiency Ratio	Liquidity Index	Liquidity Ratio	Hot Money Ratio	Stability Index
7.9	0.07	0.4	0.00	4.3	1.2	0.98	8.83	3.92	77.8	1.7	10.0	19.9	7.0
7.4	0.44	2.8	0.01	5.8	39.8	1.03	11.08	3.58	63.6	5.5	24.9	3.3	8.1
5.6	0.83	7.0	0.18	6.7	34.2	1.17	11.20	3.06	59.0	1.5	4.6	9.2	8.6
5.7	0.50	3.6	0.19	6.0	14.8	1.12	9.81	3.62	62.5	1.4	13.0	26.1	7.8
5.7	6.25	13.4	0.02	4.8	1.2	1.23	9.60	2.09	45.3	2.8	57.8	32.5	7.0
6.7	0.37	1.1	0.21	8.7	0.5	1.57	9.02	5.39	54.3	3.5	44.4	18.2	8.1
6.1	1.32	9.1	-0.02	2.5	0.9	1.01	8.12	2.58	90.9	1.6	6.0	20.7	5.4
8.3	0.00	0.0	-0.02	6.1	4.5	1.09	10.66	3.77	60.8	3.6	23.8	11.1	6.7
8.8	0.22	0.8	0.02	4.1	0.2	0.73	5.57	4.03	78.3	5.6	40.5	6.2	5.8
3.2	4.67	20.6	3.61	0.0	-0.8	-2.57	-29.31	3.05	94.2	1.8	32.4	29.8	2.5
7.2	1.01	3.6	0.09	7.7	19.7	1.50	7.16	2.75	74.8	1.6	14.4	24.0	8.9
9.5	0.53	2.5	0.00	2.7	2.6	0.30	3.08	2.69	83.4	6.1	50.3	9.6	7.2
5.4	1.34	6.5	0.06	5.5	4.7	1.01	7.26	3.29	58.7	4.8	20.4	4.1	8.7
9.3	0.00	0.0	0.00	5.1	0.6	1.14	6.85	3.35	53.2	4.8	70.0	15.9	8.3
3.8	3.56	19.6	0.13	8.7	10.3	2.16	19.15	4.44	50.9	1.7	25.6	24.7	7.6
8.6	0.74	3.0	0.09	6.8	12.2	1.76	13.88	3.52	62.5	5.9	36.3	2.6	7.8
7.9	0.72	3.7	-0.04	9.0	4.0	1.97	14.33	3.90	45.3	4.7	31.3	8.5	9.0
3.9	1.24	9.2	0.04	5.3	1.2	0.94	8.99	4.07	65.5	2.3	20.0	17.5	6.7
5.3	0.58	3.7	-0.23	0.1	-0.3	-0.59	-5.78	3.85	145.0	2.9	19.4	14.9	4.2
5.0	1.80	9.7	0.00	3.6	1.1	0.91	9.23	3.19	71.4	3.9	33.2	13.4	6.3
8.8	0.39	1.0	0.04	5.9	0.7	1.06	5.50	3.27	49.9	5.8	52.0	7.6	8.6
6.5	0.39	2.8	0.61	4.5	5.4	0.86	7.19	3.66	65.3	3.3	12.3	12.3	7.2
6.8	1.12	5.4	0.18	3.7	0.8	0.79	5.96	4.31	85.8	5.5	29.9	2.4	6.2
3.2	3.43	17.4	0.32	5.8	2.4	1.04	7.97	4.79	57.8	0.7	15.6	43.3	6.3
5.5	0.90	7.0	0.04	3.6	2.1	0.62	6.86	3.31	74.7	2.7	11.8	13.1	5.1
7.8	1.20	3.7	0.12	2.3	0.3	0.32	2.65	2.99	90.2	4.6	54.5	15.6	6.8
6.8	0.18	0.4	-0.04	10.0	22.0	8.45	38.70	16.53	27.3	2.4	55.0	11.0	9.0
4.9	1.22	9.7	0.26	5.0	170.3	0.91	9.52	3.14	61.0	4.3	20.1	4.0	8.5
6.4	0.89	5.4	0.06	4.0	3.5	0.63	5.16	3.59	77.1	2.9	14.0	5.5	7.5
7.1	1.19	6.1	0.22	7.9	3.1	1.74	12.65	5.19	64.7	0.7	15.2	42.7	9.1
2.4	3.54	21.8	-0.27	9.2	0.5	2.34	22.71	4.34	49.2	4.7	25.2	5.5	7.0
8.4	0.11	0.9	0.03	3.8	3.0	0.64	6.85	3.29	68.4	1.1	15.3	30.4	5.6
4.5	2.72	15.6	0.08	5.1	3.3	1.27	12.35	4.42	63.5	2.8	13.5	14.9	5.0
10.0	na	0.0	na	9.8	1.7	2.62	7.41	na	98.7	4.0	9.1	0.0	7.0
8.8	0.00	0.0	0.00	9.7	3.5	2.39	25.73	4.49	47.8	3.2	8.2	12.5	7.5
10.0	0.02	0.1	0.00	10.0	154.9	2.43	16.32	2.96	11.3	6.5	39.2	0.0	7.0
0.3	10.41	56.3	-0.02	10.0	212.9	3.21	22.67	3.94	13.7	5.4	16.5	0.0	8.1
6.5	na	0.0	na	9.5	18.4	3.42	4.54	0.38	88.0	9.3	315.2	4.4	6.3
4.0	1.82	12.0	0.35	7.0	15071.0	1.20	12.90	2.92	55.6	5.8	37.4	5.0	8.4
10.0	na	0.0	na	9.3	4.6	1.60	1.70	0.52	23.9	4.0	na	0.0	6.3
3.2	1.22	6.0	2.77	10.0	221.8	3.51	26.58	10.07	20.5	6.1	25.8	0.0	8.1
4.4	1.61	11.2	-0.05	6.1	1.9	0.96	9.74	3.86	69.1	4.5	15.5	5.2	6.2
6.3	1.83	7.8	0.96	1.7	0.5	0.40	3.18	3.85	97.8	6.3	49.5	4.3	6.2
3.3	4.24	13.7	1.07	2.4	0.1	0.58	4.20	3.28	85.9	6.1	44.7	3.5	5.4
5.2	0.56	4.1	0.14	5.4	66.9	1.04	7.27	3.36	59.6	3.8	14.4	10.1	9.1
7.6	0.72	3.1	0.04	6.4	5.3	1.24	9.17	3.61	58.1	2.2	34.8	27.3	7.8
7.3	0.07	0.6	-0.01	7.6	17.4	1.30	14.08	3.57	47.6	4.6	14.8	4.3	9.1
5.8	0.28	2.5	0.14	3.1	0.8	0.52	5.79	3.71	87.2	1.4	15.9	26.3	5.1
9.1	0.27	0.4	0.17	5.8	0.9	1.06	4.27	4.46	64.8	5.1	57.1	13.8	8.5
2.6	1.51	11.8	0.65	4.5	1.6	0.77	7.70	4.44	64.2	1.1	13.0	30.0	4.9
7.0	0.02	0.2	-0.01	6.9	6.0	1.74	16.35	4.45	72.4	3.3	15.3	12.1	8.1
8.0	0.63	2.9	-0.01	5.5	1.0	1.11	9.00	3.46	60.0	5.4	41.1	8.0	7.8
6.7	0.42	3.0	-0.03	3.4	1.3	0.50	4.58	3.71	76.8	4.1	17.5	7.0	5.0
8.9	0.20	1.0	0.66	5.2	3.4	1.23	11.42	3.52	61.3	4.1	29.9	10.9	7.2
7.1	0.00	0.0	-0.01	7.0	1.1	1.32	10.75	4.05	50.9	3.7	8.3	9.7	7.5
8.5	0.18	1.0	-0.04	7.9	4.9	1.84	16.13	3.91	55.9	3.4	9.0	11.6	8.4
8.9	1.12	3.6	0.02	4.5	0.5	0.84	4.23	3.27	59.1	2.0	37.9	33.3	7.7
7.4	0.50	2.1	-0.01	4.6	1.4	0.86	9.70	2.85	57.4	4.7	16.3	4.5	6.3
2.1	5.67	22.6	-0.25	7.0	2.3	1.15	6.28	3.81	55.1	0.7	17.6	48.0	8.1
4.4	1.57	11.5	0.06	3.2	1.5	0.50	5.44	3.82	83.7	3.2	26.1	14.6	4.2

Name	City	State	Rating	2015 Rating	2014 Rating	Total Assets ($Mil)	One Year Asset Growth	Commercial Loans	Consumer Loans	Mortgage Loans	Securities	Capitalization Index	Leverage Ratio	Risk-Based Capital Ratio
West Suburban Bank	Lombard	IL	C+	C+	C+	2213.4	3.54	14.8	0.3	5.8	46.3	7.2	9.2	15.4
West Texas National Bank	Midland	TX	B+	A-	A-	1128.1	6.19	14.1	1.9	4.8	44.3	7.1	9.1	16.9
▼ West Texas State Bank	Odessa	TX	D+	B-	B	392.6	-8.17	34.4	2.2	3.8	18.3	9.2	10.8	14.4
▼ West Texas State Bank	Snyder	TX	D	A	B	129.2	-9.66	13.1	5.7	7.6	31.0	10.0	11.9	17.2
West Town Bank & Trust	North Riverside	IL	C	C-	C-	259.7	27.65	15.7	0.4	18.1	2.0	8.7	10.4	13.9
West Union Bank	West Union	WV	C+	C+	C+	165.0	3.49	4.7	11.7	12.4	36.9	6.7	8.7	16.5
West Valley National Bank	Goodyear	AZ	D-	D	D	54.0	5.05	18.9	0.3	2.8	8.4	8.6	10.1	17.3
West View Savings Bank	Pittsburgh	PA	C+	C+	C+	335.0	0.59	0.3	0.1	16.1	72.6	7.3	9.2	17.8
WestAmerica Bank	San Rafael	CA	B	B+	B+	5267.5	6.16	4.7	6.2	1.8	60.8	4.8	6.8	12.6
▼ Westbound Bank	Katy	TX	B-	B+	B+	184.5	12.04	14.3	0.9	4.2	13.2	9.5	12.6	14.6
Westbury Bank	West Bend	WI	C	C-	D	702.8	10.36	5.8	0.5	22.8	13.7	8.3	10.2	13.5
Westchester Bank	White Plains	NY	B	B	B	686.0	20.29	32.5	0.5	3.2	9.4	7.0	9.4	12.5
▲ Western Alliance Bank	Phoenix	AZ	A-	B+	B	16943.3	22.50	19.5	0.1	1.0	15.8	7.0	9.9	12.5
Western Bank	Alamogordo	NM	B	B	B	66.3	2.16	1.7	1.4	13.4	26.2	10.0	15.2	28.4
▲ Western Bank	Lordsburg	NM	B+	B	B	168.1	4.54	3.6	2.6	7.3	47.0	10.0	12.0	27.5
Western Bank	Lubbock	TX	B	B-	C+	208.9	10.48	7.7	1.0	13.1	27.7	8.3	9.9	14.6
Western Bank of Clovis	Clovis	NM	B+	B+	B+	59.3	-0.04	8.0	1.5	3.4	18.0	10.0	13.1	18.5
Western Bank of Wolf Point	Wolf Point	MT	B+	B+	B	95.3	4.70	4.8	1.9	3.4	39.1	8.4	9.9	18.3
Western Bank, Artesia, New Mexico	Artesia	NM	A-	A-	A-	193.5	-1.91	28.4	1.6	0.8	28.0	8.0	9.7	17.8
Western Commerce Bank	Carlsbad	NM	B+	A-	A-	411.7	-7.29	9.8	0.5	12.4	28.1	6.5	8.5	20.8
Western Dakota Bank	Timber Lake	SD	D+	D+	C-	35.1	4.47	1.8	2.7	0.1	8.9	5.7	7.7	24.7
▼ Western Heritage Bank	Las Cruces	NM	C-	B	B-	88.5	21.26	2.4	4.4	12.0	15.2	9.2	10.5	18.1
Western National Bank	Duluth	MN	B-	B-	B-	119.4	-2.39	8.9	1.7	15.7	5.2	7.4	9.3	15.9
Western National Bank	Chester	NE	B	B	C+	80.7	4.17	4.6	1.6	17.8	1.4	7.3	9.2	13.1
Western National Bank of Cass Lake	Cass Lake	MN	B-	B-	B-	35.1	10.86	5.2	6.7	23.5	10.1	6.2	8.2	15.9
Western Nebraska Bank	Curtis	NE	C	C+	C	100.5	21.97	17.2	1.8	1.9	12.8	5.7	9.2	11.6
Western State Bank	Garden City	KS	A-	A-	A-	424.3	-6.63	8.5	0.3	6.9	20.5	10.0	11.6	15.9
Western State Bank	Devils Lake	ND	B	B	B	913.8	16.24	36.7	1.9	10.0	5.2	7.6	11.0	13.0
Western States Bank	Laramie	WY	C+	B	B	475.5	190.56	7.8	2.6	11.2	9.6	8.4	10.1	13.6
Westfield Bank	Westfield	MA	C+	C+	C+	1375.9	1.49	10.9	0.1	29.0	21.4	9.7	10.8	15.2
Westfield Bank, FSB	Westfield Center	OH	B	B	C+	1219.2	13.07	16.3	14.4	12.2	11.8	6.6	9.5	12.2
Westmoreland Federal S&L Assn.	Latrobe	PA	C+	C+	B-	168.3	0.59	0.0	0.0	40.0	27.9	10.0	24.4	89.8
WestSide Bank	Hiram	GA	D-	E-	E-	117.3	0.37	3.2	0.6	7.6	8.5	6.7	8.7	12.6
Westside State Bank	Westside	IA	C+	B-	B-	98.7	4.02	9.4	2.0	25.0	7.7	5.6	7.6	11.9
WestStar Bank	El Paso	TX	A-	A-	B+	1480.2	33.36	12.3	0.2	3.9	20.0	5.5	9.6	11.4
WEX Bank	Midvale	UT	A-	A	A	2113.4	4.09	67.5	0.2	0.0	1.2	9.2	12.1	14.3
▲ Wheatland Bank	Spokane	WA	B-	C+	C	369.0	7.08	3.9	0.5	2.6	10.0	6.1	9.0	11.8
Wheaton Bank & Trust Co.	Wheaton	IL	B-	B-	B-	1333.4	10.50	28.1	12.0	3.3	11.7	5.7	8.6	11.6
Wheaton College Trust Co., N.A.	Wheaton	IL	U	U	U	3.4	0.33	0.0	0.0	0.0	93.2	0.0	95.5	0.0
Wheeler County State Bank	Alamo	GA	B+	B	B	98.0	9.77	8.2	4.6	15.2	9.6	10.0	14.1	22.3
▲ Whitaker Bank, Inc.	Lexington	KY	C+	C-	D+	1336.5	-1.15	3.0	2.8	16.7	42.5	10.0	11.5	22.2
White State Bank	South English	IA	B-	B-	B-	36.6	4.26	9.0	2.4	14.6	26.2	10.0	14.0	19.5
Whitesville State Bank	Whitesville	WV	C	C+	C+	105.8	3.12	2.3	20.7	25.3	22.7	6.9	8.9	16.4
Whitney Bank	Gulfport	MS	C+	B-	B	23022.8	7.03	22.5	4.7	10.7	21.0	6.1	8.8	11.8
Wilcox County State Bank	Abbeville	GA	B	B-	B-	79.9	0.86	4.3	7.0	40.5	12.3	10.0	11.4	18.5
Wilkinson County Bank	Irwinton	GA	B	B	B	44.6	-1.45	6.0	5.8	36.0	35.8	10.0	15.9	32.8
Willamette Community Bank	Albany	OR	C+	C+	C-	98.3	1.47	16.2	0.4	3.5	13.0	7.7	11.0	13.0
▲ Willamette Valley Bank	Salem	OR	A-	B-	B	179.1	19.91	3.4	0.1	35.3	0.0	10.0	11.7	15.6
William Penn Bank,	Levittown	PA	B+	B+	B+	315.5	1.49	0.0	0.3	52.6	2.9	10.0	18.5	31.2
Williamstown Bank, Inc.	Williamstown	WV	B	B	B-	154.8	5.41	7.9	12.6	39.9	7.4	10.0	11.7	17.3
Williamsville State Bank & Trust	Williamsville	IL	C	C	C	103.4	-6.82	3.3	3.7	26.5	50.5	10.0	13.0	34.1
▲ Wilmington Savings Bank	Wilmington	OH	C	C-	D+	132.6	12.85	1.2	0.9	59.6	12.4	10.0	21.4	36.3
▼ Wilmington Savings Fund Society, FSB	Wilmington	DE	B+	A-	B+	6603.1	30.45	12.3	1.0	11.4	14.4	6.2	10.1	11.9
Wilmington Trust, N.A.	Wilmington	DE	B	B	C+	4294.5	132.55	0.0	0.0	1.9	0.1	10.0	15.6	49.3
Wilson & Muir Bank & Trust Co.	Bardstown	KY	B	B	B	453.9	0.58	10.0	2.8	16.8	28.6	6.2	8.2	14.4
Wilson Bank and Trust	Lebanon	TN	A-	A-	A-	2162.2	11.17	1.6	1.6	18.0	18.4	8.1	10.9	13.4
Wilson State Bank	Wilson	KS	B-	B	B	94.9	11.16	17.6	2.8	23.2	16.3	6.1	8.8	11.9
Winchester Co-operative Bank	Winchester	MA	B	B	B	603.5	2.57	0.0	0.4	56.7	22.8	10.0	12.3	26.4
Winchester Federal Bank	Winchester	KY	A-	A-	B+	142.0	-8.00	0.5	0.2	59.8	5.7	10.0	12.9	24.1
Winchester Savings Bank	Winchester	MA	C+	C+	C+	543.1	3.64	0.9	0.1	48.9	18.7	10.0	12.0	18.9

Arrows denote recent upgrades ▲ or downgrades ▼

www.weissratings.com

Asset Quality Index	Adjusted Non-Performing Loans		Net Charge-Offs Avg Loans	Profitability Index	Net Income ($Mil)	Return on Assets (R.O.A.)	Return on Equity (R.O.E.)	Net Interest Spread	Overhead Efficiency Ratio	Liquidity Index	Liquidity Ratio	Hot Money Ratio	Stability Index
	as a % of Total Loans	as a % of Capital											
4.5	2.72	13.0	0.16	3.8	10.5	0.63	6.81	2.93	71.1	6.9	48.6	3.3	6.6
4.2	3.52	15.5	1.46	3.9	6.2	0.75	7.17	3.26	56.3	6.8	61.3	6.4	8.9
1.7	9.28	41.8	1.08	2.7	0.6	0.20	1.86	3.55	56.6	4.6	37.9	11.1	6.3
0.3	13.63	57.3	-0.02	2.3	-0.7	-0.66	-5.43	3.75	64.5	3.7	27.1	12.3	8.4
2.9	1.66	12.7	0.29	9.3	2.5	1.42	13.09	4.33	74.0	0.6	10.4	36.2	7.0
6.2	1.08	5.7	0.13	3.1	0.7	0.59	6.68	3.10	78.6	5.7	37.1	3.8	5.3
8.6	0.00	0.0	-0.03	0.0	-0.7	-1.81	-16.28	3.79	143.9	5.0	36.5	8.6	6.0
10.0	0.37	0.8	0.00	3.1	1.1	0.45	4.93	1.68	60.6	5.8	37.6	3.7	5.1
7.0	0.74	2.7	0.02	6.0	45.1	1.16	12.43	3.05	57.2	7.4	60.4	2.7	8.3
7.2	0.00	0.0	-0.02	3.6	0.6	0.49	3.70	4.12	85.0	1.6	25.5	27.1	7.4
6.0	0.36	2.6	0.03	2.6	2.7	0.52	4.91	3.34	79.1	2.8	16.1	15.0	5.6
5.5	0.34	2.7	0.02	4.9	4.2	0.86	8.91	3.68	58.1	4.6	12.3	4.4	6.9
6.3	0.45	3.4	0.07	9.4	192.4	1.64	14.67	4.55	45.3	3.5	14.7	9.9	9.6
5.9	3.10	9.8	0.24	3.7	0.3	0.51	3.38	4.32	81.6	2.5	38.2	25.4	7.1
5.5	3.08	9.1	-0.02	5.5	1.7	1.37	10.67	4.03	65.6	6.1	55.8	7.6	7.1
7.8	0.01	0.1	0.13	5.1	1.9	1.26	12.60	3.95	62.3	1.5	19.4	25.7	6.1
8.6	0.17	0.8	0.00	4.7	0.3	0.74	5.77	4.44	72.4	1.6	14.6	22.3	7.3
7.4	1.04	4.6	0.83	5.2	1.0	1.39	13.29	3.94	60.9	3.8	44.5	12.5	7.3
5.6	2.44	10.3	0.16	7.8	2.7	1.86	19.47	3.42	45.2	5.2	52.8	12.1	7.6
7.7	0.06	0.3	0.12	5.9	4.4	1.37	16.72	3.46	61.4	4.9	46.8	12.0	6.7
9.4	0.00	0.0	0.02	1.5	0.0	0.10	1.39	2.48	97.7	7.0	72.5	3.8	2.8
6.8	1.03	4.1	0.24	2.3	-0.2	-0.35	-3.10	2.84	108.2	2.4	52.9	44.1	5.6
3.2	2.15	13.6	0.22	4.1	0.8	0.85	7.50	3.79	75.8	1.6	34.2	34.8	6.3
5.9	0.30	2.5	-0.09	4.9	0.7	1.17	10.74	3.44	62.6	0.8	13.2	35.8	6.9
5.1	1.26	8.2	0.73	3.5	0.1	0.50	5.11	4.93	84.3	1.6	31.6	31.4	4.5
4.3	0.79	6.0	-0.01	3.8	0.4	0.54	5.22	4.17	77.9	1.3	9.4	16.6	5.4
5.3	1.52	8.1	-0.13	7.2	5.8	1.77	15.21	3.91	57.3	3.1	13.2	13.4	8.2
4.1	1.51	10.8	0.29	9.7	9.9	1.53	14.15	5.59	52.5	1.9	9.8	10.0	7.8
5.7	0.62	4.1	0.13	3.2	1.5	0.55	5.77	2.93	78.5	2.0	18.3	19.4	6.9
6.9	0.81	5.0	-0.10	2.9	3.7	0.37	3.64	2.61	81.5	1.8	10.7	19.3	8.0
5.1	0.63	4.8	0.11	4.2	6.5	0.75	6.79	3.45	69.1	3.8	16.9	10.3	8.4
9.6	1.91	3.1	0.00	2.3	0.2	0.19	0.78	1.64	84.2	6.4	77.5	10.1	7.7
0.0	13.51	78.4	0.51	1.0	-0.2	-0.18	-2.11	4.02	97.4	1.7	21.7	23.4	0.7
5.9	0.59	5.9	0.44	3.5	0.4	0.54	6.19	3.93	72.9	1.2	11.6	20.1	5.8
6.2	0.83	6.3	0.00	8.8	18.1	1.97	19.17	4.18	58.9	3.1	21.1	14.8	9.5
5.5	1.62	9.5	1.64	10.0	113.9	8.49	76.93	20.04	52.1	1.2	25.2	0.0	9.9
5.9	0.35	2.4	0.00	4.2	1.9	0.72	7.87	3.99	76.5	5.4	27.3	1.8	5.2
5.4	0.53	4.6	0.03	5.4	9.4	0.97	7.93	3.44	53.0	3.3	10.4	12.2	7.1
10.0	na	0.0	na	1.3	0.0	-0.39	-0.41	0.42	101.7	4.0	na	0.0	0.0
7.8	0.80	3.1	-0.04	5.3	0.9	1.33	9.16	4.16	70.4	2.3	39.6	29.8	7.1
3.6	4.04	16.5	0.25	3.3	6.1	0.60	4.84	3.48	81.2	4.1	32.3	14.9	7.2
7.2	0.85	3.5	0.01	9.3	0.4	1.60	9.62	3.60	40.5	4.3	41.0	13.5	5.7
4.2	1.17	6.9	0.45	2.9	0.3	0.41	4.55	3.51	86.5	2.5	34.8	22.7	4.8
3.2	1.96	14.3	0.32	3.8	105.5	0.61	5.52	3.27	66.6	3.7	7.6	5.7	8.4
5.4	1.21	7.2	0.03	5.4	0.6	0.94	8.49	4.62	72.0	2.3	8.1	16.6	6.0
7.5	1.33	4.3	0.03	4.7	0.3	0.71	5.08	4.28	72.6	3.4	21.7	12.6	6.4
3.8	1.32	8.5	-0.01	3.8	0.4	0.55	4.99	4.66	82.8	4.8	16.5	3.6	6.0
7.6	0.34	2.4	-0.01	9.1	3.3	2.67	23.30	4.16	75.6	1.1	11.4	24.0	7.7
6.5	2.17	8.4	-0.03	4.6	1.9	0.80	4.39	3.22	57.9	1.6	25.8	27.2	8.0
4.5	1.58	10.4	0.12	6.2	1.2	1.03	8.72	4.49	61.8	3.8	14.8	10.1	7.3
8.6	1.59	4.6	0.10	1.7	0.1	0.12	0.92	2.90	96.4	6.0	60.9	10.3	5.9
2.1	9.44	28.8	0.16	2.4	0.2	0.19	0.84	3.45	89.5	1.6	10.2	20.9	5.6
5.8	0.68	4.7	0.20	6.3	47.3	1.08	9.08	3.85	63.3	4.3	19.8	5.9	7.9
9.9	2.54	1.6	0.40	4.6	9.0	0.45	2.49	2.88	89.4	8.7	103.5	0.2	7.7
6.6	0.46	2.9	0.02	7.0	6.0	1.70	19.77	3.76	60.5	5.1	29.7	4.6	6.0
7.0	0.40	2.5	-0.01	7.5	19.1	1.21	10.98	3.80	58.1	3.1	12.7	13.6	8.9
5.4	1.27	10.2	-0.01	5.3	0.8	1.19	12.13	3.92	66.5	1.6	8.8	20.7	5.0
6.7	1.63	8.9	0.00	3.9	2.9	0.64	5.31	2.34	56.5	1.9	35.5	32.1	7.5
7.2	1.05	6.3	0.05	5.3	1.7	1.52	12.02	3.15	65.1	0.8	14.4	37.7	7.6
8.7	0.56	3.2	0.03	2.4	1.3	0.33	2.78	2.61	83.7	2.9	28.4	16.5	7.1

Name	City	State	2015 Rating	2014 Rating	Total Assets ($Mil)	One Year Asset Growth	Asset Mix (As a % of Total Assets) Commercial Loans	Consumer Loans	Mortgage Loans	Securities	Capitalization Index	Leverage Ratio	Risk-Based Capital Ratio
Windsor Federal S&L Assn.	Windsor	CT	B-	B-	B-	441.9	7.03	6.2	0.1	31.5	19.6	10.0	12.1	17.4
Winnsboro State Bank & Trust Co.	Winnsboro	LA	B	B+	B+	152.2	13.51	7.7	3.9	11.2	21.2	8.3	10.3	13.6
Winona National Bank	Winona	MN	B+	B+	B+	287.0	7.56	9.7	1.0	12.5	40.0	10.0	12.5	19.5
Winter Hill Bank, FSB	Somerville	MA	C	C	C	307.1	0.58	0.0	0.4	40.8	9.8	8.1	9.8	16.1
Wintrust Bank	Chicago	IL	B-	B-	B-	4070.3	18.13	39.4	6.9	5.0	4.9	5.4	8.9	11.3
Wisconsin Bank & Trust	Madison	WI	B	B	B-	1068.3	-2.74	15.6	0.9	6.9	20.9	8.1	9.7	14.1
Wisconsin River Bank	Sauk City	WI	B+	B+	B	107.4	9.25	5.8	0.3	21.6	6.7	8.9	10.3	14.6
Wolf River Community Bank	Hortonville	WI	A-	B+	B+	147.9	8.77	10.8	1.7	25.9	15.7	10.0	13.1	19.0
Wolverine Bank, Federal Savings Bank	Midland	MI	B-	B-	B-	370.2	7.76	5.5	0.3	17.8	0.1	10.0	17.0	23.8
Wood & Huston Bank	Marshall	MO	A-	A-	A-	659.8	10.77	11.7	2.4	19.5	12.0	8.7	11.1	13.9
Woodford State Bank	Monroe	WI	B	B	B	193.2	3.39	4.4	1.0	14.6	18.0	7.3	9.2	13.5
Woodforest National Bank	The Woodlands	TX	A-	A-	A-	4808.9	7.16	14.2	1.1	17.2	18.6	6.5	8.5	14.6
Woodhaven Bank	Fort Worth	TX	B+	B+	B+	559.6	12.77	11.6	1.0	14.2	16.6	7.5	10.3	13.0
Woodland Bank	Deer River	MN	B-	B-	C+	87.5	9.83	14.5	4.8	22.3	8.1	10.0	12.3	17.1
Woodlands Bank	Williamsport	PA	B-	B-	B-	388.2	4.93	9.6	0.4	29.9	18.1	6.9	8.9	13.2
Woodlands National Bank	Hinckley	MN	A-	B+	B	195.4	19.96	14.3	4.4	7.1	21.7	10.0	11.0	20.4
Woodruff Federal S&L Assn.	Woodruff	SC	C+	C+	C	86.2	-2.72	0.0	0.0	46.0	5.6	10.0	35.7	73.7
Woodsboro Bank	Woodsboro	MD	C	C-	C-	237.9	3.50	5.4	0.7	20.1	18.9	6.4	8.4	14.6
Woodsfield Savings Bank	Woodsfield	OH	C	C-	D+	54.6	0.44	0.1	5.9	27.1	28.4	8.3	9.9	26.2
▼ Woodsville Guaranty Savings Bank	Woodsville	NH	C	C+	C+	453.5	5.73	9.7	1.5	41.1	13.1	6.9	8.9	14.4
▼ WoodTrust Bank	Wisconsin Rapids	WI	B-	B	B	374.9	3.12	8.8	1.2	6.5	28.8	7.5	9.6	12.9
Woori America Bank	New York	NY	B+	A-	B-	1519.7	11.93	9.0	0.3	16.7	7.1	9.7	11.1	14.8
World's Foremost Bank	Lincoln	NE	C+	C+	C	5731.8	19.46	0.0	93.0	0.0	0.1	6.5	10.4	12.1
Worthington Federal Savings Bank, FSB	Worthington	MN	B	B	B	73.9	-2.47	0.2	1.4	59.2	15.9	10.0	14.6	38.7
Worthington National Bank	Arlington	TX	B	B-	C+	209.6	11.66	12.3	1.6	24.3	4.4	10.0	11.5	16.2
Wray State Bank	Wray	CO	C-	C-	C	146.0	18.68	9.0	4.3	8.3	11.4	4.1	8.0	10.5
Wrentham Co-operative Bank	Wrentham	MA	C+	C+	C+	114.9	1.73	0.1	1.7	57.4	7.6	10.0	13.4	28.1
WSB Municipal Bank	Watertown	NY	U	U	U	102.2	3.31	0.0	0.0	0.0	76.0	9.0	10.3	67.8
Wyoming Bank & Trust	Cheyenne	WY	A-	B+	B	176.1	-0.04	6.9	0.6	8.0	27.0	9.9	11.0	17.8
Wyoming Community Bank	Riverton	WY	B	B	B	140.8	4.75	9.0	3.4	8.4	33.3	7.1	9.0	15.7
Xenith Bank	Richmond	VA	B-	C+	C	3326.3	108.26	15.5	8.5	10.4	9.8	6.8	11.6	12.4
Yadkin Bank	Statesville	NC	B-	B	B-	7348.2	68.65	9.8	0.9	9.6	13.7	6.2	10.1	11.9
Yakima Federal S&L Assn.	Yakima	WA	B+	B+	A-	1794.6	0.85	0.0	0.0	33.5	39.5	10.0	22.7	59.2
Yampa Valley Bank	Steamboat Springs	CO	B	B	C+	240.3	12.42	10.1	2.3	17.3	19.0	6.7	9.0	12.3
Yellowstone Bank	Laurel	MT	A	A	A	695.8	3.42	11.8	1.5	12.0	6.7	10.0	15.6	20.0
▼ YNB	Yukon	OK	C-	C	C-	190.6	0.92	5.4	3.3	19.2	26.3	6.3	8.3	13.3
Yoakum National Bank	Yoakum	TX	A-	A-	A-	221.9	-4.46	4.4	5.0	16.6	52.1	10.0	12.7	30.9
York State Bank	York	NE	B-	B-	B-	148.4	3.21	9.3	1.9	5.5	8.5	5.5	9.0	11.4
York Traditions Bank	York	PA	B-	B-	B-	397.6	16.13	16.7	0.2	22.6	13.5	6.3	8.3	12.9
Yorktown Bank	Pryor	OK	C	C	C	84.0	6.49	19.0	2.9	22.0	0.2	10.0	12.9	16.8
Young Americans Bank	Denver	CO	D-	D-	D-	18.3	7.11	0.0	0.3	0.0	0.7	5.3	7.3	223.2
Zapata National Bank	Zapata	TX	B+	A-	A-	84.1	-0.35	4.0	5.2	22.2	31.8	10.0	12.3	31.6
Zavala County Bank	Crystal City	TX	B+	B+	B+	70.3	6.45	1.5	5.4	0.8	61.8	10.0	12.3	41.4
ZB, N.A.	Salt Lake City	UT	B+	B+	B	60878.0	230.88	19.8	1.1	10.1	18.1	9.5	11.2	14.6

Asset Quality Index	Adjusted Non-Performing Loans as a % of Total Loans	Adjusted Non-Performing Loans as a % of Capital	Net Charge-Offs Avg Loans	Profitability Index	Net Income ($Mil)	Return on Assets (R.O.A.)	Return on Equity (R.O.E.)	Net Interest Spread	Overhead Efficiency Ratio	Liquidity Index	Liquidity Ratio	Hot Money Ratio	Stability Index
5.4	1.64	9.4	-0.01	3.6	2.1	0.65	5.30	3.38	76.1	4.0	16.6	8.8	6.8
5.0	1.25	8.0	0.16	4.2	0.9	0.82	7.95	4.65	77.7	1.5	19.9	26.3	5.4
8.4	0.45	1.9	-0.04	4.4	1.9	0.90	6.59	3.81	79.2	5.8	36.0	3.1	7.6
8.0	0.27	2.0	0.00	2.6	0.8	0.32	3.39	3.18	85.5	2.6	22.1	16.7	5.5
5.6	0.55	4.6	0.08	6.0	29.7	1.01	11.16	3.08	59.7	3.1	11.1	11.2	6.7
5.3	0.90	5.9	0.17	6.9	10.2	1.24	10.14	4.63	61.9	4.4	19.7	5.5	7.8
2.8	3.27	23.7	0.09	4.8	0.6	0.78	7.45	3.58	61.2	1.0	8.2	29.4	6.9
5.8	1.31	6.6	0.10	6.0	1.1	1.06	8.02	4.10	65.9	3.7	20.5	10.8	8.0
3.7	2.23	10.0	-0.01	7.3	3.7	1.30	8.02	3.60	52.4	0.7	14.5	48.2	8.2
7.0	0.32	2.1	0.07	7.4	8.4	1.81	15.77	3.79	58.0	2.2	15.9	18.3	8.0
5.2	0.92	5.8	0.03	6.2	2.1	1.49	15.98	3.98	63.5	4.5	28.6	8.1	6.9
7.4	0.77	4.7	0.16	7.1	62.8	1.80	20.66	2.91	85.6	6.6	36.6	1.4	8.9
3.8	1.11	7.8	-0.01	4.6	4.4	1.05	6.39	4.15	67.6	2.0	16.8	19.3	8.2
4.2	2.76	15.5	0.06	3.9	0.3	0.53	4.22	4.67	83.4	1.4	14.1	23.7	6.5
4.9	1.22	9.2	0.01	4.7	2.5	0.89	9.86	3.61	68.6	3.8	6.5	8.4	5.2
5.7	1.31	6.1	0.27	5.5	1.3	0.94	7.33	3.93	65.4	6.2	48.1	4.8	7.2
7.1	5.48	8.9	0.00	2.6	0.3	0.39	1.09	2.97	79.6	2.3	48.5	36.7	7.8
5.4	1.40	9.2	0.00	2.4	0.6	0.31	3.51	3.28	91.2	5.0	37.6	9.1	4.3
4.9	2.59	10.6	0.02	2.8	0.2	0.51	5.15	3.07	79.8	5.8	60.4	9.0	3.6
6.4	0.45	3.7	0.32	2.7	1.9	0.57	6.13	3.42	83.2	3.4	15.3	11.7	5.1
3.6	2.80	16.0	1.55	9.5	6.4	2.34	23.09	3.12	48.3	5.1	31.0	5.0	7.5
5.5	0.64	4.6	0.07	4.5	8.9	0.81	7.32	3.36	66.4	2.5	9.8	16.1	8.9
3.5	0.70	5.3	1.92	10.0	100.5	2.48	24.27	9.42	62.2	0.2	8.7	99.2	8.9
10.0	0.43	1.8	0.00	4.0	0.4	0.65	4.59	3.02	63.1	5.0	41.5	10.1	7.4
8.6	0.17	1.1	-0.02	3.9	0.8	0.55	4.83	4.26	80.5	1.6	18.1	23.1	5.7
3.3	1.09	9.8	0.01	3.7	0.6	0.59	6.34	3.89	74.5	1.4	6.8	24.2	5.1
9.8	0.23	1.1	0.00	2.6	0.3	0.31	2.35	2.73	85.6	3.7	33.7	14.2	7.1
10.0	na	0.0	na	3.9	0.5	0.69	6.97	1.16	9.6	5.5	38.9	5.9	4.7
7.1	0.41	1.9	0.00	8.9	2.7	2.18	19.63	3.47	83.1	5.3	42.4	8.7	8.3
4.5	2.14	12.1	0.05	4.7	1.1	1.02	10.60	4.00	74.9	2.3	32.0	22.7	6.5
3.4	2.25	16.4	0.01	2.9	53.7	3.18	21.52	3.53	93.8	1.8	12.8	19.4	7.8
4.8	0.70	5.2	0.13	5.4	45.0	0.89	5.95	4.05	65.8	2.1	12.8	11.7	8.1
10.0	0.33	0.5	0.00	4.5	9.4	0.70	3.12	2.40	48.3	4.0	76.3	29.6	10.0
5.1	0.97	7.0	-0.07	8.5	3.4	1.98	21.13	4.68	61.0	4.1	21.1	8.9	6.7
7.1	0.66	3.1	0.00	9.8	13.8	2.67	16.71	4.24	40.8	4.5	16.9	5.8	9.8
5.5	0.70	4.5	0.08	2.2	0.6	0.39	4.39	3.60	96.1	3.5	28.0	13.3	4.8
8.7	0.86	2.4	-0.12	5.6	2.4	1.37	10.62	3.09	53.0	3.5	51.0	20.8	7.9
4.7	0.37	3.1	0.01	5.0	0.9	0.85	7.06	3.50	65.4	2.9	10.7	13.7	7.3
4.5	1.16	10.8	0.14	4.4	2.4	0.86	10.22	3.32	69.8	2.8	1.6	12.1	4.9
5.3	0.24	1.5	0.34	2.4	0.2	0.24	1.42	3.99	85.7	3.3	19.7	12.7	6.9
10.0	0.00	0.0	0.00	0.0	-0.9	-6.34	-86.66	0.99	694.4	8.1	106.4	0.6	1.4
9.0	0.44	1.4	4.20	3.0	-0.1	-0.13	-1.04	3.36	57.2	1.2	29.0	46.1	8.6
9.4	0.00	0.0	0.09	4.0	0.5	0.92	7.36	3.12	74.8	2.5	49.1	31.4	7.3
5.1	1.57	9.3	0.33	5.8	350.2	0.79	6.22	3.44	65.0	5.6	25.4	3.1	9.8

Section II

Weiss
Recommended Banks by State

A compilation of those

U.S. Commercial Banks and Savings Banks

receiving a Weiss Safety Rating
of A+, A, A-, or B+.

Institutions are ranked by Safety Rating
in each state where they have a branch location.

Section II Contents

This section provides a list of Weiss Recommended Banks by State and contains all financial institutions receiving a Safety Rating of A+, A, A-, or B+. Recommended institutions are listed in each state in which they currently operate one or more branches. If a company is not on this list, it should not be automatically assumed that the firm is weak. Indeed, there are many firms that have not achieved a B+ or better rating but are in good condition with adequate resources to weather an average recession. Not being included in this list should not be construed as a recommendation to immediately withdraw deposits or cancel existing financial arrangements.

Institutions are ranked within each state by their Weiss Safety Rating, and then listed alphabetically by city. Institutions with the same rating should be viewed as having the same relative safety regardless of their ranking in this table.

1. Institution Name	The name under which the institution was chartered. A bank's name can be very similar to, or the same as, the name of other banks which may not be on our Recommended List, so make sure you note the exact name, city, and state of the main branch listed here before acting on this recommendation.
2. City	The city in which the institution's headquarters or main office is located. With the adoption of intrastate and interstate branching laws, many institutions operating in your area may actually be headquartered elsewhere. So, don't be surprised if the location cited is not in your particular city.
3. State	The state in which the institution's headquarters or main office is located. With the adoption of interstate branching laws, some institutions operating in your area may actually be headquartered in another state. Even so, there are no restrictions on your ability to do business with an out-of-state institution.
4. Telephone	The telephone number for the institution's headquarters, or main office. If the number listed is not in your area, or a local phone call, consult your local phone directory for the number of a location near you.
5. Safety Rating	Weiss rating assigned to the institution at the time of publication. Our ratings are designed to distinguish levels of insolvency risk and are measured on a scale from A to F based upon a wide range of factors. Highly rated companies are, in our opinion, less likely to experience financial difficulties than lower rated firms. See *About Weiss Safety Ratings* for more information and a description of what each rating means.

Weiss Safety Ratings are not deemed to be a recommendation concerning the purchase or sale of the securities of any bank that is publicly owned.

Alabama

City	Name	Telephone	City	Name	Telephone

Rating: A+

City	Name	Telephone
Boaz	First Bank of Boaz	(256) 593-8670

Rating: A

City	Name	Telephone
Oxford	Cheaha Bank	(256) 835-8855
Winfield	Citizens Bank of Winfield	(205) 487-4277
Waterloo	Farmers & Merchants Bank	(256) 766-2579
Muscle Shoals	First Metro Bank	(256) 386-0600
Hamilton	First National Bank	(205) 921-7435
Oneonta	HomeTown Bank of Alabama	(205) 625-4434
Wedowee	Small Town Bank	(256) 357-4936
Camden	Town-Country National Bank	(334) 682-4155

Rating: A-

City	Name	Telephone
Dothan	BankSouth	(334) 677-2265
Calera	Central State Bank	(205) 668-0711
Camden	Community Neighbor Bank	(334) 682-4215
Cullman	Cullman Savings Bank	(256) 734-1740
Talladega	First Bank of Alabama	(256) 362-2334
Luverne	First Citizens Bank	(334) 335-3346
Lineville	FirstState Bank	(256) 396-2187
Scottsboro	FNB Bank	(256) 259-6000
Marion	Marion Bank and Trust Co.	(334) 683-6131
Pell City	Metro Bank	(205) 884-2265
Birmingham	Oakworth Capital Bank	(205) 263-4700
Demopolis	Robertson Banking Co.	(334) 289-3564
Reform	West Alabama Bank & Trust	(205) 375-6261

Rating: B+

City	Name	Telephone
Auburn	AuburnBank	(334) 821-9200
Vernon	Bank of Vernon	(205) 695-7141
Brantley	Brantley Bank and Trust Co.	(334) 527-3206
Greensboro	Citizens Bank	(334) 624-8888
Altoona	Exchange Bank of Alabama	(205) 589-6334
LaFayette	Farmers and Merchants Bank	(334) 864-9941
Wadley	First Bank	(256) 395-2255
Linden	First Bank of Linden	(334) 295-8741
Wetumpka	First Community Bank of Central Alabama	(334) 567-0081
Birmingham	First Partners Bank	(205) 822-5500
Sulligent	First State Bank of the South, Inc.	(205) 698-8116
Boaz	Peoples Independent Bank	(256) 593-8844
Birmingham	ServisFirst Bank	(205) 949-0302

Alaska

City	Name	Telephone	City	Name	Telephone

Rating:		**A**			
Anchorage	First National Bank Alaska	(907) 777-4362			

Rating:		**B+**			
Fairbanks	Mt. McKinley Bank	(907) 452-1751			
Anchorage	Northrim Bank	(907) 562-0062			

Arizona

City	Name	Telephone	City	Name	Telephone

Rating: A-

City	Name	Telephone
Scottsdale	Nordstrom FSB	(480) 596-3459
Phoenix	Western Alliance Bank	(602) 389-3500

Rating: B+

City	Name	Telephone
Glendale	BNC National Bank	(602) 508-3760
Mesa	Gateway Commercial Bank	(480) 358-1000

Arkansas

City	Name	Telephone	City	Name	Telephone

Rating: A+

City	Name	Telephone
Searcy	First Security Bank	(501) 279-3400

Rating: A

City	Name	Telephone
Calico Rock	First National Bank of Izard County	(870) 297-3711
Sheridan	Peoples Bank	(870) 942-5707

Rating: A-

City	Name	Telephone
Delight	Bank of Delight	(870) 379-2293
England	Bank of England	(501) 842-2555
Lake Village	Bank of Lake Village	(870) 265-2241
Van Buren	Citizens Bank & Trust Co.	(479) 474-1201
Wynne	Cross County Bank	(870) 238-8171
Fordyce	FBT Bank & Mortgage	(870) 352-3107
Paragould	First National Bank	(870) 215-4000
Paris	First National Bank at Paris	(479) 963-2121
Russellville	First State Bank	(479) 498-2400
McGehee	McGehee Bank	(870) 222-3151
Morrilton	Petit Jean State Bank	(501) 354-4988
Mena	Union Bank of Mena	(479) 394-2211

Rating: B+

City	Name	Telephone
Star City	Bank of Star City	(870) 628-4286
Little Rock	Bank of the Ozarks	(501) 978-2265
Stamps	Bodcaw Bank	(870) 533-4486
Little Rock	Central Bank	(501) 221-6400
De Witt	DeWitt Bank and Trust Co.	(870) 946-3531
Murfreesboro	Diamond Bank	(870) 285-2172
Marion	First Community Bank of Eastern Arkansas	(870) 739-7300
El Dorado	First Financial Bank	(870) 863-7000
Crossett	First National Bank of Crossett	(870) 364-1300
Fort Smith	First National Bank of Fort Smith	(479) 782-2041
Wynne	First National Bank of Wynne	(870) 238-2361
De Queen	First State Bank of DeQueen	(870) 642-4423
Horatio	Horatio State Bank	(870) 832-2501
Springdale	Legacy National Bank	(479) 717-1900
Magnolia	Peoples Bank	(870) 234-5777
Piggott	Piggott State Bank	(870) 598-3802
Pine Bluff	Relyance Bank, N.A.	(870) 535-7222
Springdale	United Bank	(479) 756-8811

California

Rating: A

City	Name	Telephone
Santa Rosa	AltaPacific Bank	(707) 236-1500
Riverside	Bank of Hemet	(951) 248-2000
San Francisco	California Pacific Bank	(415) 399-8000
Ontario	Citizens Business Bank	(909) 980-4030
Long Beach	Farmers & Merchants Bank of Long Beach	(562) 437-0011
San Diego	Home Bank of California	(858) 270-5881
Santa Cruz	Lighthouse Bank	(831) 600-4000
Palos Verdes Estate	Malaga Bank F.S.B.	(310) 375-9000

Rating: A-

City	Name	Telephone
City of Industry	American Continental Bank	(626) 363-8988
Arcadia	American Plus Bank, N.A.	(626) 821-9188
Yuba City	Bank of Feather River	(530) 755-3700
Stockton	Bank of Stockton	(209) 929-1600
Porterville	Bank of the Sierra	(559) 782-4900
Walnut Creek	Bay Commercial Bank	(925) 476-1800
San Diego	Bofl Federal Bank	(858) 350-6200
Irvine	California First National Bank	(949) 255-5300
Irvine	CommerceWest Bank	(949) 251-6959
West Sacramento	Community Business Bank	(916) 830-3597
Lodi	Farmers & Merchants Bank	(209) 367-2300
Chico	Golden Valley Bank	(530) 894-1000
Los Angeles	Hanmi Bank	(213) 382-2200
Long Beach	International City Bank, N.A.	(562) 436-9800
Sun Valley	Mission Valley Bank	(818) 394-2300
Alhambra	New OMNI Bank, N.A.	(626) 284-5555
Los Angeles	Open Bank	(213) 892-9999
Irvine	Pacific Premier Bank	(949) 864-8000
Los Angeles	Preferred Bank	(213) 891-1188
Los Angeles	Royal Business Bank	(213) 627-9888
Coronado	San Diego Private Bank	(619) 437-1000
Ukiah	Savings Bank of Mendocino County	(707) 462-6613
Oakland	Summit Bank	(510) 839-8800
Santa Rosa	Summit State Bank	(707) 568-6000
Buena Park	Uniti Bank	(714) 736-5700
Visalia	Valley Business Bank	(559) 622-9000

Rating: B+

City	Name	Telephone
Santa Barbara	American Riviera Bank	(805) 965-5942
Chula Vista	Balboa Thrift and Loan Assn.	(619) 397-7700
Irvine	Banc of California, N.A.	(949) 236-5436
Novato	Bank of Marin	(415) 763-4520
San Juan Capistran	Capital Bank	(949) 489-4200
Los Angeles	Cathay Bank	(213) 625-4791
Fresno	Central Valley Community Bank	(559) 298-1775
Chino	Chino Commercial Bank, N.A.	(909) 393-8880
Pasadena	CIT Bank, N.A.	(626) 535-4870
El Centro	Community Valley Bank	(760) 352-7777
Pasadena	East West Bank	(626) 768-6000
Pasadena	EverTrust Bank	(626) 993-3800
Santa Rosa	Exchange Bank	(707) 524-3301
Cerritos	First Choice Bank	(562) 345-9092
San Francisco	First Republic Bank	(415) 392-1400
Rocklin	Five Star Bank	(916) 626-5000
Fremont	Fremont Bank	(510) 505-5226
Los Angeles	Grandpoint Bank	(213) 542-2700
San Jose	Heritage Bank of Commerce	(408) 947-6900
Paso Robles	Heritage Oaks Bank	(805) 369-5200
Manhattan Beach	Luther Burbank Savings	(310) 220-2041
Santa Barbara	Montecito Bank & Trust	(805) 564-0256
Los Angeles	Pacific City Bank	(213) 210-2000
Irvine	Pacific Enterprise Bank	(949) 623-7600
Irvine	Plaza Bank	(949) 502-4300
San Marcos	Rancho Santa Fe Thrift & Loan Assn.	(760) 736-2000
Sacramento	River City Bank	(916) 567-2600
Santa Cruz	Santa Cruz County Bank	(831) 457-5000
San Diego	Seacoast Commerce Bank	(858) 432-7000
Chico	Tri Counties Bank	(530) 898-0300
Tustin	Tustin Community Bank	(714) 730-5662
Garden Grove	US Metro Bank	(714) 620-8888

Colorado

City	Name	Telephone	City	Name	Telephone

Rating: A

City	Name	Telephone
Colorado Springs	Academy Bank, N.A.	(719) 265-6756
Ault	Farmers Bank	(970) 834-2121
Las Animas	First National Bank of Las Animas	(719) 456-1512
Lamar	Frontier Bank	(719) 336-4351
Thornton	North Valley Bank	(303) 452-5500
Fort Collins	Verus Bank of Commerce	(970) 204-1010

Rating: A-

City	Name	Telephone
Alamosa	Alamosa State Bank	(719) 589-2564
Greenwood Village	AMG National Trust Bank	(303) 694-2190
Fort Collins	Bank of Colorado	(970) 206-1160
Buena Vista	Collegiate Peaks Bank	(719) 395-2472
Lamar	Community State Bank	(719) 336-3272
Dolores	Dolores State Bank	(970) 882-7600
Brush	Farmers State Bank of Brush	(970) 842-5101
Lakewood	FirstBank	(303) 232-2000
Boulder	Flatirons Bank	(303) 530-4999
Centennial	Redstone Bank	(720) 880-5000

Rating: B+

City	Name	Telephone
Glenwood Springs	Alpine Bank	(970) 945-2424
Denver	Bankers' Bank of the West	(303) 291-3700
Castle Rock	Castle Rock Bank	(303) 688-5191
Denver	CoBiz Bank	(303) 293-2265
Cheyenne Wells	Eastern Colorado Bank	(719) 767-5652
Hugo	First National Bank of Hugo	(719) 743-2415
Wray	First Pioneer National Bank	(970) 332-4824
Salida	High Country Bank	(719) 539-2516
Flagler	High Plains Bank	(719) 765-4000
Wiley	Legacy Bank	(719) 829-4811
Julesburg	Points West Community Bank	(970) 474-3341
Pueblo	Pueblo Bank and Trust Co.	(719) 545-1834
Colorado Springs	Stockmens Bank	(719) 955-2800

Delaware

City	Name	Telephone	City	Name	Telephone
Rating:	**A-**				
Wilmington	Applied Bank	(888) 839-7952			
Rating:	**B+**				
Wilmington	Deutsche Bank Trust Co. Delaware	(302) 636-3301			
Wilmington	Wilmington Savings Fund Society, FSB	(302) 792-6000			

District of Columbia

City	Name	Telephone	City	Name	Telephone

Rating: **B+**

City	Name	Telephone
Washington	National Capital Bank of Washington	(202) 546-8000

Federated States of Micronesia

City	Name	Telephone	City	Name	Telephone

Rating: **B+**

| Pohnpei | Bank of the Federated States of Micronesia | | | | |

Florida

City	Name	Telephone	City	Name	Telephone

Rating: A

City	Name	Telephone
Boca Raton	Paradise Bank	(561) 392-5444

Rating: A-

City	Name	Telephone
Oakland Park	American National Bank	(954) 491-7788
Miami Lakes	BankUnited, N.A.	(786) 313-1010
Chiefland	Drummond Community Bank	(352) 493-2277
Maitland	First Colony Bank of Florida	(407) 740-0401
Destin	First Florida Bank	(850) 269-1201
Mount Dora	First National Bank of Mount Dora	(352) 383-2111
Plant City	Hillsboro Bank	(813) 707-6506
West Palm Beach	Palm Beach Community Bank	(561) 681-7200
Graceville	Peoples Bank of Graceville	(850) 263-3267
Fort Myers	Preferred Community Bank	(239) 728-2265
Saint Petersburg	Raymond James Bank, N.A.	(727) 567-8000

Rating: B+

City	Name	Telephone
Coconut Grove	Biscayne Bank	(305) 447-5050
Fernandina Beach	CBC National Bank	(904) 321-0400
The Villages	Citizens First Bank	(352) 753-9515
Jacksonville	FirstAtlantic Bank	(904) 348-3100
Palm Coast	Intracoastal Bank	(386) 447-1662
Pompano Beach	Stonegate Bank	(954) 315-5500
Panama City	Summit Bank, N.A.	(850) 785-3669
Cocoa Beach	Sunrise Bank	(321) 784-8333
Tampa	TCM Bank, N.A.	(813) 287-4880

Georgia

City	Name	Telephone	City	Name	Telephone
			Thomasville	Thomasville National Bank	(229) 226-3300
			Alpharetta	Touchmark National Bank	(770) 407-6700
			Blairsville	United Community Bank	(706) 745-2151
			Smyrna	Vinings Bank	(770) 437-0004
			Alamo	Wheeler County State Bank	(912) 568-7191

Rating: A

City	Name	Telephone
Douglas	Douglas National Bank	(912) 384-2233
Doraville	First Intercontinental Bank	(770) 451-7200
Athens	First Madison Bank & Trust	(706) 389-7979
Waynesboro	First National Bank of Waynesboro	(706) 554-8100
Blakely	First State Bank of Blakely	(229) 723-3711
Doraville	Metro City Bank	(770) 455-4989
Duluth	NOA Bank	(678) 385-0800
Thomaston	West Central Georgia Bank	(706) 647-8951

Rating: A-

City	Name	Telephone
Macon	American Pride Bank	(478) 784-1448
Dawson	Bank of Dawson	(229) 995-2141
Greensboro	BankSouth	(706) 453-2943
West Point	CharterBank	(706) 645-1391
Hahira	Citizens Community Bank	(229) 794-2111
Fitzgerald	Community Banking Co. of Fitzgerald	(229) 423-4321
Twin City	Durden Banking Co., Inc.	(478) 763-2121
Milledgeville	Exchange Bank	(478) 452-4531
Alma	First National Bank South	(912) 632-7262
Bainbridge	First Port City Bank	(229) 246-6200
Glennville	Glennville Bank	(912) 654-3471
Hoschton	Hamilton State Bank	(770) 868-2660
Pelham	Pelham Banking Co.	(229) 294-2341
Suwanee	Quantum National Bank	(770) 945-8300
Tucker	Resurgens Bank	(404) 297-2200
Glennville	South Georgia Bank	(912) 654-1051
Macon	State Bank and Trust Co.	(478) 796-6200
Zebulon	United Bank	(770) 567-7211

Rating: B+

City	Name	Telephone
Camilla	Bank of Camilla	(229) 336-5225
Trenton	Bank of Dade	(706) 657-6842
Sparta	Bank of Hancock County	(706) 444-5781
Cartersville	Century Bank of Georgia	(770) 387-1922
Trenton	Citizens Bank & Trust, Inc.	(706) 657-5678
Crawford	Commercial Bank	(706) 743-8184
Lawrenceville	Embassy National Bank	(770) 822-9111
Washington	F&M Bank	(706) 678-2187
Lincolnton	Farmers State Bank	(706) 359-3131
Dublin	Farmers State Bank	(478) 275-3223
Bainbridge	First National Bank of Decatur County	(229) 246-3131
Augusta	Georgia Bank & Trust Co. of Augusta	(706) 738-6990
Valdosta	Guardian Bank	(229) 241-9444
Monroe	Liberty First Bank	(770) 207-3000
Athens	National Bank of Georgia	(706) 355-3122
McRae	Security State Bank	(229) 868-6431
Tifton	South Georgia Banking Co.	(229) 382-4211
Columbus	Synovus Bank	(706) 649-2106

Hawaii

City	Name	Telephone	City	Name	Telephone

Rating: A-

City	Name	Telephone
Honolulu	Central Pacific Bank	(808) 544-0500
Honolulu	Territorial Savings Bank	(808) 946-1400

Rating: B+

City	Name	Telephone
Honolulu	American Savings Bank, F.S.B.	(808) 627-6900
Honolulu	First Hawaiian Bank	(808) 525-6340

Idaho

City	Name	Telephone	City	Name	Telephone

Rating: A

City	Name	Telephone
Ammon	Bank of Commerce	(208) 525-9108

Rating: A-

City	Name	Telephone
Boise	Northwest Bank	(208) 332-0700

Rating: B+

City	Name	Telephone
Idaho Falls	Bank of Idaho	(208) 524-5500
Burley	D.L. Evans Bank	(208) 678-8615
Buhl	Farmers Bank	(208) 543-4351
Boise	Idaho Trust Bank	(208) 373-6500

Illinois

City	Name	Telephone

Rating: A+

City	Name	Telephone
Taylorville	First National Bank in Taylorville	(217) 824-2241
Reynolds	Reynolds State Bank	(309) 372-4242

Rating: A

City	Name	Telephone
Prophetstown	Farmers National Bank	(815) 537-2348
Chicago	Federal Savings Bank	(312) 738-6000
Chicago	First Eagle Bank	(312) 850-2900
East Saint Louis	First Illinois Bank	(618) 271-8700
Watseka	First Trust and Savings Bank of Watseka	(815) 432-2494
Breese	Germantown Trust & Savings Bank	(618) 526-4202
Chicago	Gold Coast Bank	(312) 587-3200
Goodfield	Goodfield State Bank	(309) 965-2221
Milledgeville	Milledgeville State Bank	(815) 225-7171
Bourbonnais	Municipal Trust and Savings Bank	(815) 935-8000
Poplar Grove	Poplar Grove State Bank	(815) 765-3333
Decatur	Soy Capital Bank and Trust Co.	(217) 428-7781
Teutopolis	Teutopolis State Bank	(217) 857-3166
Piper City	Vermilion Valley Bank	(815) 686-2258
New Berlin	Warren-Boynton State Bank	(217) 488-6091
Chicago	Washington Federal Bank for Savings	(773) 254-3422

Rating: A-

City	Name	Telephone
Carbondale	Bank of Carbondale	(618) 549-2181
Farmington	Bank of Farmington	(309) 245-2441
Pontiac	Bank of Pontiac	(815) 844-6155
Rantoul	Bank of Rantoul	(217) 892-2143
Geneseo	Central Bank Illinois	(309) 944-5601
Mascoutah	Citizens Community Bank	(618) 566-8800
Albion	Citizens National Bank of Albion	(618) 445-2344
Easton	Community Bank of Easton	(309) 562-7420
Palatine	Cornerstone National Bank & Trust Co.	(847) 654-3000
Effingham	Crossroads Bank	(217) 347-7751
Pinckneyville	First National Bank in Pinckneyville	(618) 357-9393
Staunton	First National Bank in Staunton	(618) 635-2234
Ava	First National Bank of Ava	(618) 426-3303
Saint Peter	First State Bank of St. Peter	(618) 349-8343
Fisher	Fisher National Bank	(217) 897-1136
Grand Ridge	Grand Ridge National Bank	(815) 249-6414
Bloomington	Heartland Bank and Trust Co.	(309) 662-4444
Jacksonville	Jacksonville Savings Bank	(217) 245-4111
Chicago	Lakeside Bank	(312) 435-5100
Chicago	Pacific Global Bank	(312) 225-2323
Park Ridge	Park Ridge Community Bank	(847) 384-9200
Kewanee	Peoples National Bank of Kewanee	(309) 853-3333
Virginia	Petefish, Skiles & Co.	(217) 452-3041
Springfield	Prairie State Bank & Trust	(217) 993-6260
Arthur	State Bank of Arthur	(217) 543-2111
Quincy	Town and Country Bank Midwest	(217) 222-0015

City	Name	Telephone
Olney	TrustBank	(618) 395-4311

Rating: B+

City	Name	Telephone
Anna	Anna State Bank	(618) 833-2151
Bourbonnais	Bank of Bourbonnais	(815) 933-0570
O'Fallon	Bank of O'Fallon	(618) 632-3595
Milan	Blackhawk Bank & Trust	(309) 787-4451
Chester	Buena Vista National Bank	(618) 826-2331
Champaign	Busey Bank	(217) 351-6500
Casey	Casey State Bank	(217) 932-2136
Mount Vernon	Community First Bank of the Heartland	(618) 244-3000
Du Quoin	Du Quoin State Bank	(618) 542-2111
Fairfield	Fairfield National Bank	(618) 842-2107
Galesburg	Farmers & Mechanics Bank	(309) 343-7141
Elgin	First Community Bank	(847) 622-8800
Xenia	First Community Bank, Xenia-Flora	(618) 678-2202
Plainfield	First Community Financial Bank	(815) 436-6300
Minier	First Farmers State Bank	(309) 392-2623
Mattoon	First Mid-Illinois Bank & Trust, N.A.	(217) 258-0434
Vandalia	First National Bank	(618) 283-1141
Allendale	First National Bank of Allendale	(618) 299-4411
Beardstown	First National Bank of Beardstown	(217) 323-4105
Nokomis	First National Bank of Nokomis	(217) 563-8311
Pana	First National Bank of Pana	(217) 562-3961
Steeleville	First National Bank of Steeleville	(618) 965-3441
Chicago	First Nations Bank	(773) 594-5900
Marion	First Southern Bank	(618) 997-4341
Kankakee	First Trust Bank of Illinois	(815) 929-4000
Forreston	Forreston State Bank	(815) 938-3121
Lawrenceville	Heritage State Bank	(618) 943-1038
Warsaw	Hill-Dodge Banking Co.	(217) 256-4224
Ipava	Ipava State Bank	(309) 753-8202
Jerseyville	Jersey State Bank	(618) 498-6466
Kinmundy	Kinmundy Bank	(618) 547-3533
Lake Forest	Lake Forest Bank & Trust Co.	(847) 234-2882
Middletown	Middletown State Bank	(217) 445-2616
Morton	Morton Community Bank	(309) 266-5337
Aurora	Old Second National Bank	(630) 892-0202
Chicago	PrivateBank and Trust Co.	(312) 564-2000
Chicago	Royal Savings Bank	(773) 768-4800
Rushville	Rushville State Bank	(217) 322-3323
Peoria	South Side Trust & Savings Bank of Peoria	(309) 676-0521
Johnston City	Southern Illinois Bank	(618) 983-8433
Spring Valley	Spring Valley City Bank	(815) 663-2211
Lincoln	State Bank of Lincoln	(217) 735-5551
Toulon	State Bank of Toulon	(309) 286-2861
Chatham	United Community Bank	(217) 483-2491

Indiana

City	Name	Telephone	City	Name	Telephone

Rating: A

City	Name	Telephone
Geneva	Bank of Geneva	(260) 368-7288

Rating: A-

City	Name	Telephone
South Bend	1st Source Bank	(574) 235-2000
Terre Haute	First Financial Bank, N.A.	(812) 238-6000
Porter	First State Bank of Porter	(219) 926-2136
Covington	Fountain Trust Co.	(765) 793-2237
Fowler	Fowler State Bank	(765) 884-1200
Huntingburg	Freedom Bank	(812) 683-8998
Jasper	German American Bancorp	(812) 482-1314
Kentland	Kentland Bank	(219) 474-5155
Warsaw	Lake City Bank	(574) 267-6144
Logansport	Logansport Savings Bank	(574) 722-3855
Greensburg	MainSource Bank	(812) 663-0133
Carmel	Merchants Bank of Indiana	(317) 569-7420
Terre Haute	Morris Plan Co. of Terre Haute, Inc.	(812) 238-6063
Napoleon	Napoleon State Bank	(812) 852-4002
Evansville	United Fidelity Bank, FSB	(812) 424-0921

Rating: B+

City	Name	Telephone
Francesville	Alliance Bank	(219) 567-9151
Bath	Bath State Bank	(765) 732-3022
Merrillville	Centier Bank	(219) 756-2265
Avilla	Community State Bank	(260) 897-3361
Corydon	First Harrison Bank	(812) 738-2198
Muncie	First Merchants Bank	(765) 747-1500
Friendship	Friendship State Bank	(812) 667-5101
Garrett	Garrett State Bank	(260) 357-3133
Ellettsville	Peoples State Bank	(812) 876-2228
Medora	State Bank of Medora	(812) 966-2601

Iowa

City	Name	Telephone	City	Name	Telephone
			Webster City	First State Bank	(515) 832-2520
Rating:	**A+**		Atlantic	First Whitney Bank and Trust	(712) 243-3195
			Fontanelle	FNB Bank	(641) 745-2141
Williamsburg	Farmers Trust & Savings Bank	(319) 668-2525	Grinnell	Grinnell State Bank	(641) 236-3174
Des Moines	Iowa State Bank	(515) 288-0111	Somers	Heartland Bank	(515) 467-5561
New Albin	New Albin Savings Bank	(563) 544-4214	Royal	Home State Bank	(712) 933-5511
Waukon	Waukon State Bank	(563) 568-3451	Algona	Iowa State Bank	(515) 295-3595
			Hull	Iowa State Bank	(712) 439-1025
Rating:	**A**		Emmetsburg	Iowa Trust & Savings Bank	(712) 852-3451
			Centerville	Iowa Trust and Savings Bank	(641) 437-4500
Breda	Breda Savings Bank	(712) 673-2321	Kingsley	Kingsley State Bank	(712) 378-2341
Belle Plaine	Chelsea Savings Bank	(319) 444-3144	Fort Madison	Lee County Bank	(319) 372-2243
Cherokee	Cherokee State Bank	(712) 225-3000	Pella	Leighton State Bank	(641) 628-1566
Spillville	Citizens Savings Bank	(563) 562-3674	Forest City	Manufacturers Bank & Trust Co.	(641) 585-2825
Wyoming	Citizens State Bank	(563) 488-2211	Sumner	Northeast Security Bank	(563) 578-3251
Corydon	Corydon State Bank	(641) 872-2212	Estherville	NorthStar Bank	(712) 362-3322
Decorah	Decorah Bank & Trust Co.	(563) 382-9661	Orange City	Northwestern Bank	(712) 737-4911
Waukon	Farmers & Merchants Savings Bank	(563) 568-3417	Palo	Palo Savings Bank	(319) 851-2241
Marion	Farmers State Bank	(319) 377-4891	Marshalltown	Pinnacle Bank	(641) 752-2393
Hampton	First Bank Hampton	(641) 456-4793	Le Mars	Primebank	(712) 546-4175
Albia	First Iowa State Bank	(641) 932-2144	Readlyn	Readlyn Savings Bank	(319) 279-3321
Keosauqua	First Iowa State Bank	(319) 293-3794	Story City	Reliance State Bank	(515) 733-4396
Britt	First State Bank	(641) 843-4411	Rolfe	Rolfe State Bank	(712) 848-3480
Colfax	First State Bank of Colfax	(515) 674-3533	Sioux City	Security National Bank of Sioux City, Iowa	(712) 277-6500
Hills	Hills Bank and Trust Co.	(319) 679-2291	Algona	Security State Bank	(515) 295-9501
Durant	Liberty Trust & Savings Bank	(563) 785-4441	Independence	Security State Bank	(319) 334-7035
Pella	Marion County State Bank	(641) 628-2191	Sloan	Sloan State Bank	(712) 428-3344
Maxwell	Maxwell State Bank	(515) 387-1175	Nevada	State Bank & Trust Co.	(515) 382-2191
West Des Moines	Midwest Heritage Bank, FSB	(515) 278-6541	West Des Moines	State Savings Bank	(515) 457-9533
Mount Vernon	Mount Vernon Bank and Trust Co.	(319) 895-8835	Templeton	Templeton Savings Bank	(712) 669-3322
Panora	Panora State Bank	(641) 755-2141	Marshalltown	United Bank & Trust N.A.	(641) 753-5900
Pocahontas	Pocahontas State Bank	(712) 335-3567	Hampton	United Bank and Trust Co.	(641) 456-5587
Victor	Victor State Bank	(319) 647-2231	Washington	Washington State Bank	(319) 653-2151
Mount Pleasant	Wayland State Bank	(319) 385-8189	Watkins	Watkins Savings Bank	(319) 227-7773
			West Bend	West Iowa Bank	(515) 887-7811
Rating:	**A-**				
			Rating:	**B+**	
Tripoli	American Savings Bank	(319) 882-4279			
Atkins	Atkins Savings Bank & Trust	(319) 446-7700	Osceola	American State Bank	(641) 342-2175
Boone	Boone Bank & Trust Co.	(515) 432-6200	Ashton	Ashton State Bank	(712) 724-6326
Carroll	Carroll County State Bank	(712) 792-3567	West Union	Bank 1st	(563) 422-3883
Storm Lake	Citizens First National Bank	(712) 732-5440	Cedar Rapids	BankIowa of Cedar Rapids	(319) 395-9100
Sheldon	Citizens State Bank	(712) 324-2519	Blairstown	Benton County State Bank	(319) 454-6230
Nevada	Community Bank	(515) 382-3050	Mount Vernon	Bridge Community Bank	(319) 895-8200
Spencer	Community State Bank	(712) 262-3030	Muscatine	CBI Bank & Trust	(563) 263-3131
Winterset	Farmers & Merchants State Bank	(515) 462-4242	Cedar Rapids	Cedar Rapids Bank and Trust Co.	(319) 862-2728
Colesburg	Farmers Savings Bank	(563) 856-2525	Elkader	Central State Bank	(563) 245-2110
Marcus	Farmers State Bank	(712) 376-4154	Shenandoah	Century Bank	(712) 246-2205
Buffalo Center	Farmers Trust and Savings Bank	(641) 562-2696	Johnston	Charter Bank	(515) 331-2265
Mason City	First Citizens Bank	(641) 423-1600	Hawkeye	Citizens Savings Bank	(563) 427-3255
Ames	First National Bank, Ames, Iowa	(515) 232-5561	Anamosa	Citizens Savings Bank	(319) 462-3561
Ida Grove	First State Bank	(712) 364-3181			
Lynnville	First State Bank	(641) 527-2535			

Iowa

City	Name	Telephone	City	Name	Telephone
Monticello	Citizens State Bank	(319) 465-5921			
Clear Lake	Clear Lake Bank and Trust Co.	(641) 357-7121			
Ankeny	Community State Bank	(515) 331-3100			
Paton	Community State Bank	(515) 968-4131			
Danville	Danville State Savings Bank	(319) 392-4261			
De Witt	De Witt Bank & Trust Co.	(563) 659-3211			
Dubuque	Dubuque Bank and Trust Co.	(563) 589-2000			
Fostoria	Farmers Savings Bank	(712) 262-2708			
Victor	Farmers Savings Bank	(319) 647-3141			
Mason City	Farmers State Bank	(641) 424-3053			
Creston	First National Bank in Creston	(641) 782-2195			
Muscatine	First National Bank of Muscatine	(563) 263-4221			
Rembrandt	First National Bank of Rembrandt	(712) 286-5491			
Nashua	First State Bank	(641) 435-4943			
West Des Moines	Freedom Financial Bank	(515) 223-1113			
Osage	Home Trust & Savings Bank	(641) 732-3763			
Red Oak	Houghton State Bank	(712) 623-4823			
Keystone	Keystone Savings Bank	(319) 442-3218			
Luana	Luana Savings Bank	(563) 539-2166			
Maquoketa	Maquoketa State Bank	(563) 652-2491			
Maynard	Maynard Savings Bank	(563) 637-2289			
Melvin	Melvin Savings Bank	(712) 736-2420			
Iowa City	MidWestOne Bank	(319) 356-5800			
Mason City	NSB Bank	(641) 423-7638			
Cascade	Ohnward Bank & Trust	(563) 852-7696			
Rock Valley	Peoples Bank	(712) 476-2746			
Pilot Grove	Pilot Grove Savings Bank	(319) 469-3951			
Des Moines	Principal Bank	(800) 672-3343			
Gowrie	Security Savings Bank	(515) 352-3333			
Waverly	Security State Bank	(319) 352-3500			
Saint Ansgar	St. Ansgar State Bank	(641) 713-4501			
Schaller	State Bank of Schaller	(712) 275-4261			
Oskaloosa	TruBank	(641) 673-8405			
Ida Grove	United Bank of Iowa	(712) 364-3393			
Mapleton	Valley Bank & Trust	(712) 881-1131			
West Des Moines	West Bank	(515) 222-2300			

Kansas

City	Name	Telephone	City	Name	Telephone
			Syracuse	First National Bank of Syracuse	(620) 384-7441
Rating:	**A**		Washington	First National Bank of Washington	(785) 325-2221
			Norton	First State Bank	(785) 877-3341
Fort Leavenworth	Armed Forces Bank, N.A.	(913) 682-9090	Healy	First State Bank of Healy	(620) 398-2215
Tescott	Bank of Tescott	(785) 283-4217	Ransom	First State Bank of Ransom	(785) 731-2261
Colby	Farmers & Merchants Bank of Colby	(785) 460-3321	Kiowa	First State Bank, Kiowa, Kansas	(620) 825-4147
Great Bend	Farmers Bank & Trust	(620) 792-2411	Independence	FirstOak Bank	(620) 331-2265
Phillipsburg	Farmers National Bank	(785) 543-6541	Overland Park	Freedom Bank	(913) 563-5600
Westphalia	Farmers State Bank of Aliceville, Kansas	(785) 489-2468	Wichita	Garden Plain State Bank	(316) 721-1500
Larned	First State B&T Co. of Larned	(620) 285-6931	Lawrence	Great American Bank	(785) 838-9704
Wamego	Kaw Valley State Bank and Trust Co.	(785) 456-2021	Beloit	Guaranty State Bank and Trust Co.	(785) 738-3501
Lakin	Kearny County Bank	(620) 355-6222	Kansas City	Industrial State Bank	(913) 831-2000
Overland Park	NBKC Bank	(913) 905-2100	Overbrook	Kansas State Bank Overbrook Kansas	(785) 665-7121
Solomon	Solomon State Bank	(785) 655-2941	Manhattan	Landmark National Bank	(785) 565-2000
			Mission	Mission Bank	(913) 831-2400
Rating:	**A-**		McPherson	Peoples Bank and Trust Co.	(620) 241-2100
			Wichita	Southwest National Bank	(316) 291-5221
Weir	CBW Bank	(620) 396-8221	Fredonia	State Bank of Kansas	(620) 378-2114
Hutchinson	Central Bank and Trust Co.	(620) 663-0666	Overland Park	Valley View State Bank	(913) 381-3311
Marysville	Citizens State Bank	(785) 562-2186			
Hugoton	Citizens State Bank	(620) 544-4331			
Seneca	Community National Bank	(785) 336-6143			
Holton	Denison State Bank	(785) 364-3131			
Council Grove	Farmers and Drovers Bank	(620) 767-5138			
McPherson	Farmers State Bank	(620) 241-3090			
Westmoreland	Farmers State Bank	(785) 457-3316			
Oakley	Farmers State Bank of Oakley, Kansas	(785) 672-3251			
Phillipsburg	First National Bank and Trust	(785) 543-6511			
Fredonia	First National Bank in Fredonia	(620) 378-2151			
Ness City	First State Bank	(785) 798-3347			
Eskridge	Flint Hills Bank	(785) 449-2266			
Manhattan	KS StateBank	(785) 587-4000			
Scott City	Security State Bank	(620) 872-7224			
Saint John	SJN Bank of Kansas	(620) 549-3225			
Bern	State Bank of Bern	(785) 336-6121			
Maple Hill	Stockgrowers State Bank	(785) 256-4241			
Marysville	United Bank & Trust	(785) 562-2333			
Garden City	Western State Bank	(620) 275-4128			
Rating:	**B+**				
Greeley	Bank of Greeley	(785) 867-2010			
Holyrood	Bank of Holyrood	(785) 252-3239			
Salina	BANK VI	(785) 825-4321			
Salina	Bennington State Bank	(785) 827-5522			
Cheney	Citizens State Bank of Cheney, Kansas	(316) 542-3142			
Parsons	Commercial Bank	(620) 421-1000			
Coffeyville	Community State Bank	(620) 251-1313			
Wichita	Emprise Bank	(316) 383-4301			
Atchison	Exchange National Bank & Trust Co.	(913) 367-6000			
Osborne	Farmers Bank of Osborne, Kansas	(785) 346-2147			
Sterling	First Bank	(620) 278-2161			
Marysville	First Commerce Bank	(785) 562-5558			

Kentucky

City	Name	Telephone	City	Name	Telephone
			Hopkinsville	Planters Bank, Inc.	(270) 886-9030
			Salyersville	Salyersville National Bank	(606) 349-3131
			Maysville	Security Bank and Trust Co.	(606) 564-3304
			Mount Sterling	Traditional Bank, Inc.	(859) 498-0414

Rating: A

City	Name	Telephone
Arlington	Citizens Deposit Bank of Arlington, Inc.	(270) 655-6921
Somerset	Cumberland Security Bank, Inc.	(606) 679-9361
Edmonton	Edmonton State Bank	(270) 432-3231
Marion	Farmers Bank and Trust Co.	(270) 965-3106
Princeton	Farmers Bank and Trust Co.	(270) 365-5526
Madisonville	First United Bank and Trust Co.	(270) 821-5555
McKee	Jackson County Bank	(606) 287-8484
Ashland	Kentucky Farmers Bank Corp.	(606) 929-5000
Paducah	Paducah Bank and Trust Co.	(270) 575-5700
Louisville	River City Bank, Inc.	(502) 585-4600
Louisville	Stock Yards Bank & Trust Co.	(502) 582-2571
Campbellsville	Taylor County Bank	(270) 465-4196
Morganfield	United Community Bank of W Kentucky	(270) 389-3232

Rating: A-

City	Name	Telephone
Clarkson	Bank of Clarkson	(270) 242-2111
Lexington	Bank of the Bluegrass & Trust Co.	(859) 233-4500
West Liberty	Commercial Bank	(606) 743-3195
Hartford	Commonwealth Community Bank, Inc.	(270) 298-3261
Carrollton	First National Bank of Carrollton	(502) 732-4406
Irvington	First State Bank	(270) 547-2271
Owensboro	Independence Bank of Kentucky	(270) 686-1776
Chaplin	King Southern Bank	(502) 673-3154
Lewisburg	Lewisburg Banking Co.	(270) 755-4818
Louisville	Republic Bank & Trust Co.	(502) 584-3600
Sacramento	Sacramento Deposit Bank	(270) 736-2212
Springfield	Springfield State Bank	(859) 336-3939
Bardstown	Town & Country Bank and Trust Co.	(502) 348-3911
Fort Mitchell	Victory Community Bank	(859) 341-2265
Radcliff	West Point Bank	(270) 351-1414
Winchester	Winchester Federal Bank	(859) 744-1900

Rating: B+

City	Name	Telephone
Bowling Green	American Bank & Trust Co., Inc.	(270) 796-8444
Brownsville	Bank of Edmonson County	(270) 597-2175
Hickman	Citizens Bank	(270) 236-2525
Covington	Citizens Federal S&L Assn.	(859) 431-0087
Somerset	Citizens National Bank of Somerset	(606) 679-6341
Danville	Farmers National Bank of Danville	(859) 236-2926
Scottsville	Farmers National Bank of Scottsville	(270) 237-3141
Prestonsburg	First Commonwealth Bank of Prestonsburg, In	(606) 886-2321
Grayson	First National Bank of Grayson	(606) 474-2000
Fredonia	Fredonia Valley Bank	(270) 545-3301
Hodgenville	Lincoln National Bank	(270) 358-4116
Hodgenville	Magnolia Bank	(270) 358-3111
Brandenburg	Meade County Bank	(270) 422-4141
Taylorsville	Peoples Bank	(502) 477-2244
Owenton	Peoples Bank & Trust Co.	(502) 484-3466

Louisiana

City	Name	Telephone	City	Name	Telephone

Rating: A

City	Name	Telephone
Jonesboro	Jonesboro State Bank	(318) 259-4411
Minden	MBL Bank	(318) 377-0523
Belle Chasse	Mississippi River Bank	(504) 392-1111
New Roads	Peoples B&T Co. of Pointe Coupee Parish	(225) 638-3713
Houma	South Louisiana Bank	(985) 851-3434

Rating: A-

City	Name	Telephone
DeRidder	Beauregard Federal Savings Bank	(337) 463-4493
Bossier City	Citizens National Bank, N.A.	(318) 747-6000
Houma	Coastal Commerce Bank	(985) 580-2265
New Iberia	Community First Bank	(337) 365-6677
Natchitoches	Exchange Bank and Trust Co.	(318) 352-8141
Vacherie	First American Bank and Trust	(225) 265-2265
Crowley	First National Bank of Louisiana	(337) 783-4014
Delhi	Guaranty Bank & Trust Co. of Delhi	(318) 878-3703
Shreveport	Home Federal Bank	(318) 841-1170
Kaplan	Kaplan State Bank	(337) 643-7110
Monroe	Ouachita Independent Bank	(318) 338-3014
Rayne	Rayne State Bank & Trust Co.	(337) 334-3191
Jonesville	Southern Heritage Bank	(318) 339-8505

Rating: B+

City	Name	Telephone
Opelousas	American Bank & Trust Co.	(337) 948-3056
Montgomery	BOM	(318) 646-3386
DeRidder	City Savings Bank & Trust Co.	(337) 463-8661
Delhi	Commercial Capital Bank	(318) 878-2274
Saint Joseph	Cross Keys Bank	(318) 766-3246
Church Point	Farmers State Bank & Trust Co.	(337) 684-3301
Clinton	Feliciana Bank & Trust Co.	(225) 683-8565
DeRidder	First National Bank in DeRidder	(337) 463-6231
New Roads	Guaranty Bank and Trust Co.	(225) 638-8621
Abbeville	Gulf Coast Bank	(337) 893-7733
Jackson	Highlands Bank	(225) 634-7741
Hodge	Hodge Bank & Trust Co.	(318) 259-7362
Morgan City	M C Bank & Trust Co.	(985) 384-2100
Patterson	Patterson State Bank	(985) 395-6131
Rayne	Rayne Building and Loan Assn.	(337) 334-7535
Rayville	Richland State Bank	(318) 728-2024
Many	Sabine State Bank and Trust Co.	(318) 256-7000
Saint Martinville	Teche Bank & Trust Co.	(337) 394-9726
Newellton	Tensas State Bank	(318) 467-5401
Jennings	The Bank	(337) 824-0033
Eunice	Tri-Parish Bank	(337) 457-7341

Maine

City	Name	Telephone	City	Name	Telephone
Rating:	**A-**				
Farmington	Franklin Savings Bank	(207) 778-3339			
Rating:	**B+**				
Bar Harbor	Bar Harbor Bank & Trust	(207) 288-3314			
Lewiston	Northeast Bank	(207) 786-3245			

Maryland

City	Name	Telephone	City	Name	Telephone

Rating: A-

City	Name	Telephone
Berlin	Calvin B. Taylor Banking Co.	(410) 641-1700
Bethesda	EagleBank	(240) 497-2075
Baltimore	Rosedale Federal S&L Assn.	(410) 668-4400

Rating: B+

City	Name	Telephone
Ocean City	Bank of Ocean City	(410) 213-0173
Queenstown	Queenstown Bank of Maryland	(410) 827-8881
Olney	Sandy Spring Bank	(301) 774-6400

Massachusetts

City	Name	Telephone	City	Name	Telephone

Rating:	**A**	
Arlington	Leader Bank, N.A.	(781) 646-3900

Rating:	**A-**	
Boston	Boston Trust & Investment Mgmt Co.	(617) 726-7250
Woburn	Patriot Community Bank	(781) 935-3318

Rating:	**B+**	
Cambridge	Cambridge Trust Co.	(617) 876-5500
Everett	Everett Co-operative Bank	(617) 387-1110
Hingham	Hingham Institution for Savings	(781) 749-2200
Edgartown	Martha's Vineyard Savings Bank	(774) 310-2001
Framingham	MutualOne Bank	(508) 820-4000
Marblehead	National Grand Bank of Marblehead	(781) 631-6000
Woburn	Northern Bank & Trust Co.	(781) 937-5400
North Andover	Northmark Bank	(978) 686-9100
Rockland	Rockland Trust Co.	(781) 878-6100

Michigan

City	Name	Telephone	City	Name	Telephone

Rating: A-

City	Name	Telephone
Ann Arbor	Ann Arbor State Bank	(734) 761-1475
Southfield	Sterling Bank and Trust, FSB	(248) 355-2400
Escanaba	Upper Peninsula State Bank	(906) 789-7000

Rating: B+

City	Name	Telephone
Ann Arbor	Bank of Ann Arbor	(734) 662-1600
Chelsea	Chelsea State Bank	(734) 475-1355
Carsonville	Exchange State Bank	(810) 657-9333
Kalamazoo	First National Bank of Michigan	(269) 349-0100
Norway	First National Bank of Norway	(906) 563-9233
Troy	Flagstar Bank, FSB	(248) 312-2000
Southfield	Hantz Bank	(248) 304-3500
Lapeer	Lapeer County Bank & Trust Co.	(810) 664-2977
Grand Rapids	Mercantile Bank of Michigan	(616) 242-7760
Munising	Peoples State Bank of Munising	(906) 387-2006
Port Austin	Port Austin State Bank	(989) 738-5235
Ewen	State Bank of Ewen	(906) 988-2821
Hancock	Superior National Bank & Trust Co.	(906) 482-0404
Brown City	Tri-County Bank	(810) 346-2745

Minnesota

City	Name	Telephone	City	Name	Telephone
			Litchfield	Center National Bank	(320) 693-3255
Rating:	**A+**		Park Rapids	Citizens National Bank of Park Rapids	(218) 732-3393
			Isanti	Community Pride Bank	(763) 444-8800
Vermillion	Vermillion State Bank	(651) 437-4433	Saint Paul	Drake Bank	(651) 224-5000
			Glenwood	Eagle Bank	(320) 634-4545
Rating:	**A**		Caledonia	Eitzen State Bank	(507) 725-3329
			Foley	Falcon National Bank	(320) 968-6300
Long Prairie	American Heritage National Bank	(320) 732-6131	Appleton	Farmers and Merchants State Bank	(320) 289-1454
Edina	Fidelity Bank	(952) 831-6600	Hoffman	Farmers State Bank of Hoffman	(320) 986-2026
Bemidji	First National Bank of Bemidji	(218) 751-2430	Watkins	Farmers State Bank of Watkins	(320) 764-2600
Pipestone	First State Bank Southwest	(507) 825-0055	Cannon Falls	First Farmers & Merchants Bank	(507) 263-3030
Saint Cloud	Liberty Bank Minnesota	(320) 252-2841	Fairmont	First Farmers & Merchants National Bank	(507) 235-5556
Minneapolis	Northeast Bank	(612) 379-8811	Brownsdale	First Farmers & Merchants State Bank	(507) 567-2219
Wadena	Wadena State Bank	(218) 631-1860	Grand Meadow	First Farmers & Merchants State Bank	(507) 754-5123
			Minnetonka	First Minnesota Bank	(952) 933-9550
Rating:	**A-**		Minnetonka	First Minnetonka City Bank	(952) 465-0323
			Walker	First National Bank North	(218) 547-1160
Castle Rock	Castle Rock Bank	(651) 463-7590	Milaca	First National Bank of Milaca	(320) 983-3101
Roseau	Citizens State Bank of Roseau	(218) 463-2135	Moose Lake	First National Bank of Moose Lake	(218) 485-4441
Blue Earth	First Bank Blue Earth	(507) 526-3241	Northfield	First National Bank of Northfield	(507) 645-5656
Battle Lake	First National Bank of Battle Lake	(218) 864-5275	Osakis	First National Bank of Osakis	(320) 859-2101
Ottertail	First National Bank of Henning	(218) 367-2735	Hendricks	First Security Bank-Hendricks	(507) 275-3141
Le Center	First National Bank of Le Center	(507) 357-2273	Le Center	First State Bank of Le Center	(507) 357-2225
Menahga	First National Bank of Menahga & Sebeka	(218) 564-4171	Rochester	Home Federal Savings Bank	(507) 535-1309
Lino Lakes	First Resource Bank	(651) 785-9320	Long Lake	Lake Community Bank	(952) 473-7347
Canby	First Security Bank - Canby	(507) 223-7231	Winona	Merchants Bank, N.A.	(507) 457-1100
Sleepy Eye	First Security Bank-Sleepy Eye	(507) 794-3911	Roseville	North American Banking Co.	(651) 636-9654
Wyoming	First State Bank of Wyoming	(651) 462-7611	Ormsby	Ormsby State Bank	(507) 736-2941
Mendota Heights	Gateway Bank	(651) 209-4800	Cambridge	Peoples Bank of Commerce	(763) 689-1212
Litchfield	Home State Bank	(320) 593-2001	Glencoe	Security Bank & Trust Co.	(320) 864-3171
Redwood Falls	HomeTown Bank	(507) 637-1000	Aitkin	Security State Bank of Aitkin	(218) 927-3765
Janesville	Janesville State Bank	(507) 234-5108	Marine On Saint Cr	Security State Bank of Marine	(651) 433-2424
Detroit Lakes	Midwest Bank	(218) 847-4771	Maple Lake	Star Bank	(320) 963-3161
Prinsburg	PrinsBank	(320) 978-6351	Red Lake Falls	Unity Bank North	(218) 253-2143
Albert Lea	Security Bank Minnesota	(507) 373-1481	Bloomington	Venture Bank	(952) 830-9999
Bemidji	Security Bank USA	(218) 751-1510	Winona	Winona National Bank	(507) 454-8800
Saint Clair	St. Clair State Bank (Inc.)	(507) 245-3636			
New Prague	State Bank of New Prague	(952) 758-4491			
Wheaton	State Bank of Wheaton	(320) 563-8142			
Holdingford	Stearns Bank Holdingford N.A.	(320) 746-2261			
Saint Cloud	Stearns Bank N.A.	(320) 253-6607			
Upsala	Stearns Bank Upsala N.A.	(320) 573-2111			
Adams	United Farmers State Bank	(507) 582-3448			
Hinckley	Woodlands National Bank	(320) 384-6191			
Rating:	**B+**				
Faribault	1st United Bank	(507) 334-2201			
Loretto	21st Century Bank	(763) 479-2178			
Saint Paul	Anchor Bank, N.A.	(651) 747-2900			
Avon	Avon State Bank	(320) 356-7334			
Maple Plain	Bank of Maple Plain	(763) 479-1931			
Saint Paul	Bremer Bank, N.A.	(651) 288-3751			
Bloomington	Bridgewater Bank	(952) 893-6868			

Mississippi

City	Name	Telephone	City	Name	Telephone

Rating: A

City	Name	Telephone
Corinth	Commerce Bank	(662) 286-5577

Rating: A-

City	Name	Telephone
Morton	Bank of Morton	(601) 732-8944
New Albany	BNA Bank	(662) 534-8171
Baldwyn	Farmers and Merchants Bank	(662) 365-1200
Clarksdale	First National Bank of Clarksdale	(662) 627-3261
Waynesboro	First State Bank	(601) 735-3124
Greenville	Jefferson Bank	(662) 332-7545
Ripley	Peoples Bank	(662) 837-8191
Magee	PriorityOne Bank	(601) 849-3311

Rating: B+

City	Name	Telephone
Tupelo	BancorpSouth Bank	(662) 680-2000
Greenwood	Bank of Commerce	(662) 453-4142
Walnut Grove	Bank of Walnut Grove	(601) 253-2411
Wiggins	Bank of Wiggins	(601) 928-5233
Lucedale	Century Bank	(601) 947-7511
Meridian	Citizens National Bank of Meridian	(601) 484-5269
Batesville	First Security Bank	(662) 563-9311
Oxford	FNB Oxford	(662) 234-2821
North Carrollton	Peoples Bank & Trust Co.	(662) 237-9272

Missouri

City	Name	Telephone

Rating: A+

City	Name	Telephone
Greenville	Peoples Community Bank	(573) 224-3267

Rating: A

City	Name	Telephone
Old Monroe	Bank of Old Monroe	(636) 665-5601
Saint Louis	Cass Commercial Bank	(314) 506-5500
Cole Camp	Citizens-Farmers Bank of Cole Camp	(660) 668-4416
El Dorado Springs	Community Bank of El Dorado Springs	(417) 876-6811
West Plains	Community First Banking Co.	(417) 255-2265
Jamesport	Home Exchange Bank	(660) 684-6114
Saint Louis	Lindell Bank & Trust Co.	(314) 645-7700
Maryville	Nodaway Valley Bank	(660) 562-3232
West Plains	West Plains Bank and Trust Co.	(417) 256-2147

Rating: A-

City	Name	Telephone
Cape Girardeau	Alliance Bank	(573) 334-1010
Advance	Bank of Advance	(573) 722-3517
Kansas City	Bank of Grain Valley	(816) 373-1905
Saint Elizabeth	Bank of St. Elizabeth	(573) 493-2313
Kansas City	BankLiberty	(816) 407-9200
Bloomsdale	Bloomsdale Bank	(573) 483-2514
Charleston	Citizens Bank of Charleston	(573) 683-3373
Edina	Citizens Bank of Edina	(660) 397-2266
Kansas City	Commerce Bank	(816) 234-2000
Lincoln	Farmers Bank of Lincoln	(660) 547-3311
Unionville	Farmers Bank of Northern Missouri	(660) 947-2474
Caruthersville	First State Bank and Trust Co., Inc.	(573) 333-1700
Saint Charles	First State Bank of St. Charles, Missouri	(636) 940-5555
Hannibal	HNB National Bank	(573) 221-0050
Kearney	Kearney Trust Co.	(816) 628-6666
Lamar	Lamar Bank and Trust Co.	(417) 682-3348
Linn	Legends Bank	(573) 897-2204
Mexico	Martinsburg Bank and Trust	(573) 581-6566
Louisiana	Mercantile Bank of Louisiana, Missouri	(573) 754-6221
Nevada	Metz Banking Co.	(417) 667-4550
Warrenton	Missouri Bank	(636) 456-3441
Sedalia	Missouri Bank II	(660) 827-5520
Fredericktown	New Era Bank	(573) 783-3336
Grandview	North American Savings Bank, F.S.B.	(816) 765-2200
Kirksville	Northeast Missouri State Bank	(660) 665-6161
Platte City	Platte Valley Bank of Missouri	(816) 858-5400
Salem	Progressive Ozark Bank	(573) 729-4146
Unionville	Putnam County State Bank	(660) 947-2477
Senath	Senath State Bank	(573) 738-2646
Osceola	St. Clair County State Bank	(417) 646-8128
Poplar Bluff	Sterling Bank	(573) 778-3333
Salem	Town & Country Bank	(573) 729-3155
Auxvasse	United Security Bank	(573) 386-2233
Platte City	Wells Bank	(816) 858-2121

City	Name	Telephone
Marshall	Wood & Huston Bank	(660) 886-6825

Rating: B+

City	Name	Telephone
Alton	Alton Bank	(417) 778-7211
Moberly	Bank of Cairo and Moberly	(660) 263-2280
Perryville	Bank of Missouri	(573) 547-6541
New Madrid	Bank of New Madrid	(573) 748-5551
Odessa	Bank of Odessa	(816) 230-4512
Versailles	Bank of Versailles	(573) 378-4626
Bethany	BTC Bank	(660) 425-7285
Clayton	Business Bank of Saint Louis	(314) 721-8003
Gainesville	Century Bank of the Ozarks	(417) 679-3321
Oak Grove	Commercial Bank of Oak Grove	(816) 690-4416
Monett	Community National Bank	(417) 235-2265
Bowling Green	Community State Bank of Missouri	(573) 324-2233
Concordia	Concordia Bank	(660) 463-7911
Kansas City	Country Club Bank	(816) 931-4060
Saint Louis	Enterprise Bank & Trust	(314) 725-5500
Holden	F & C Bank	(816) 850-5516
Gladstone	First Bank of Missouri	(816) 436-1900
Cassville	Freedom Bank of Southern Missouri	(417) 846-1719
Chillicothe	Investors Community Bank	(660) 646-3733
Kearney	KCB Bank	(816) 628-6050
La Monte	La Monte Community Bank	(660) 347-5656
Columbia	Landmark Bank, N.A.	(573) 499-7333
Linn	Mid America Bank	(573) 897-2211
Dixon	Mid America Bank & Trust Co.	(573) 759-2121
Paris	Paris National Bank	(660) 327-4181
Cuba	Peoples Bank	(573) 885-2511
Poplar Bluff	Southern Bank	(573) 778-1800
Saint Louis	Stifel Bank and Trust	(314) 317-6900
Tipton	Tipton Latham Bank, N.A.	(660) 433-2004
Glasgow	Tri-County Trust Co.	(660) 338-2234
Mineral Point	UNICO Bank	(573) 438-5421

Montana

City	Name	Telephone	City	Name	Telephone

Rating: A

City	Name	Telephone
Shelby	First State Bank of Shelby	(406) 434-5567
Havre	Independence Bank	(406) 265-1241
Laurel	Yellowstone Bank	(406) 628-7951

Rating: A-

City	Name	Telephone
Broadus	1st Bank	(406) 436-2611
Missoula	Bank of Montana	(406) 829-2662
Malta	First State Bank of Malta	(406) 654-2340
Kalispell	Glacier Bank	(406) 756-4200
Miles City	Stockman Bank of Montana	(406) 234-8420
Kalispell	Three Rivers Bank of Montana	(406) 755-4271

Rating: B+

City	Name	Telephone
Roundup	First Security Bank of Roundup	(406) 323-1100
Forsyth	First State Bank of Forsyth	(406) 346-2112
Lolo	TrailWest Bank	(406) 273-2400
Wolf Point	Western Bank of Wolf Point	(406) 653-5500

Nebraska

City	Name	Telephone	City	Name	Telephone
			Sidney	Points West Community Bank	(308) 254-7110
			Laurel	Security Bank	(402) 256-3247
			Omaha	Security National Bank of Omaha	(402) 344-7300
			Campbell	South Central State Bank	(402) 756-8601
			Lincoln	Union Bank and Trust Co.	(402) 323-1828
			Blair	Washington County Bank	(402) 426-2111
			Lincoln	West Gate Bank	(402) 434-3456

Rating: A

City	Name	Telephone
Elkhorn	American Interstate Bank	(402) 289-2551
Republican City	Commercial State Bank	(308) 799-3995
Farnam	First State Bank	(308) 569-2311
Kimball	FirsTier Bank	(308) 235-4633
Wood River	Heritage Bank	(308) 583-2262
Waverly	Horizon Bank	(402) 786-2555
Madison	Madison County Bank	(402) 454-6511

Rating: A-

City	Name	Telephone
Ogallala	Adams Bank & Trust	(308) 284-4071
Adams	Adams State Bank	(402) 988-2255
Auburn	Auburn State Bank	(402) 274-4342
Norfolk	BankFirst	(402) 371-8005
Seward	Cattle National Bank & Trust Co.	(402) 643-3636
Chadron	First National Bank of Chadron	(308) 432-5552
Omaha	First Westroads Bank, Inc.	(402) 330-7200
Grand Island	Five Points Bank	(308) 384-5350
Hastings	Five Points Bank of Hastings	(402) 462-2228
Gothenburg	Gothenburg State Bank	(308) 537-7181
Cozad	Homestead Bank	(308) 784-2000
McCook	McCook National Bank	(308) 345-4240
Pierce	Midwest Bank N.A.	(402) 329-6221
Minden	Minden Exchange Bank & Trust Co.	(308) 832-1600
Oshkosh	Nebraska State Bank	(308) 772-3234
Lincoln	Pinnacle Bank	(402) 434-3127
Scribner	Scribner Bank	(402) 664-2561
Wayne	State Nebraska Bank & Trust	(402) 375-1130
Ravenna	Town & Country Bank	(308) 452-3225
Ainsworth	West Plains Bank	(402) 387-2381

Rating: B+

City	Name	Telephone
Elgin	Bank of Elgin	(402) 843-2228
Brunswick	Brunswick State Bank	(402) 842-2435
Ceresco	CerescoBank	(402) 665-3431
Chambers	Chambers State Bank	(402) 482-5222
Saint Paul	Citizens Bank & Trust Co.	(308) 754-4426
Clarkson	Clarkson Bank	(402) 892-3411
Norfolk	Elkhorn Valley Bank & Trust	(402) 371-0722
Gibbon	Exchange Bank	(308) 468-5741
Cozad	First Bank and Trust Co.	(308) 784-2515
Gordon	First National Bank of Gordon	(308) 282-0050
Randolph	First State Bank	(402) 337-0323
Scottsbluff	First State Bank	(308) 632-4158
Wahoo	FirstBank of Nebraska	(402) 443-4117
Hershey	Hershey State Bank	(308) 368-5555
Daykin	Jefferson County Bank	(402) 446-7233
Broken Bow	Nebraska State Bank and Trust Co.	(308) 872-2466
North Platte	NebraskaLand National Bank	(308) 534-2100

Nevada

City	Name	Telephone	City	Name	Telephone

Rating: A-

City	Name	Telephone
Las Vegas	Bank of George	(702) 851-4200
Carson City	Eaglemark Savings Bank	(775) 886-3000
Las Vegas	First Security Bank of Nevada	(702) 853-0900

Rating: B+

City	Name	Telephone
Reno	Charles Schwab Bank	(775) 689-6800
Ely	First National Bank of Ely	(775) 289-4441
Reno	Heritage Bank of Nevada	(775) 348-1000
Las Vegas	Meadows Bank	(702) 471-2265
Henderson	Toyota Financial Savings Bank	(702) 477-2100

New Jersey

City	Name	Telephone	City	Name	Telephone

Rating: A

City	Name	Telephone
Teaneck	Cross River Bank	(201) 808-7000
Township of Washin	Oritani Bank	(201) 664-5400

Rating: A-

City	Name	Telephone
Vineland	Capital Bank of New Jersey	(856) 690-1234
Ewing	Cenlar FSB	(609) 883-3900
Kenilworth	Enterprise Bank N.J.	(877) 604-5705

Rating: B+

City	Name	Telephone
Woodbridge	Bessemer Trust Co.	(212) 708-9386
Short Hills	Investors Bank	(855) 422-6548
Newark	Lusitania Savings Bank	(973) 344-5125

New Mexico

City	Name	Telephone	City	Name	Telephone

Rating: A

City	Name	Telephone
Alamogordo	First National Bank	(575) 437-4880
Deming	First New Mexico Bank	(575) 546-2691
Las Cruces	First New Mexico Bank, Las Cruces	(575) 556-3000

Rating: A-

City	Name	Telephone
Taos	Centinel Bank of Taos	(575) 758-6700
Farmington	Citizens Bank	(505) 599-0100
Las Cruces	Citizens Bank of Las Cruces	(575) 647-4100
Artesia	First American Bank	(575) 746-8000
Silver City	First New Mexico Bank of Silver City	(575) 388-3121
Artesia	Western Bank, Artesia, New Mexico	(575) 748-1345

Rating: B+

City	Name	Telephone
Carlsbad	Carlsbad National Bank	(575) 234-2500
Clayton	Farmers & Stockmens Bank	(575) 374-8301
Albuquerque	Main Bank	(505) 880-1700
Albuquerque	Southwest Capital Bank	(505) 243-1890
Lordsburg	Western Bank	(575) 542-3521
Clovis	Western Bank of Clovis	(575) 769-1975
Carlsbad	Western Commerce Bank	(575) 887-6686

New York

City	Name	Telephone	City	Name	Telephone

Rating: A

City	Name	Telephone
Flushing	NewBank	(718) 353-9100

Rating: A-

City	Name	Telephone
Groton	First National Bank of Groton	(607) 898-5871
New York	Goldman Sachs Bank USA	(212) 902-1000
New York	Signature Bank	(646) 822-1500
Bronx	Spring Bank	(718) 879-5000
Hornell	Steuben Trust Co.	(607) 324-5010
Spencer	Tioga State Bank	(607) 589-7000
Watertown	Watertown Savings Bank	(315) 788-7100

Rating: B+

City	Name	Telephone
New York	Alpine Capital Bank	(212) 328-2555
Flushing	Amerasia Bank	(718) 463-3600
Glen Cove	American Community Bank	(516) 609-2900
Catskill	Bank of Greene County	(518) 943-2600
Utica	Bank of Utica	(315) 797-2700
New York	Bessemer Trust Co., N.A.	(212) 708-9100
Bridgehampton	Bridgehampton National Bank	(631) 537-1000
New York	Chinatown Federal Savings Bank	(212) 334-9191
De Witt	Community Bank, N.A.	(315) 445-2282
Brooklyn	Dime Community Bank	(718) 343-1801
New York	Eastbank, N.A.	(212) 219-9000
Dryden	First National Bank of Dryden	(607) 844-8141
Fulton	Fulton Savings Bank	(315) 592-4201
Syracuse	Geddes Federal S&L Assn.	(315) 468-6281
Glens Falls	Glens Falls National Bank and Trust Co.	(518) 793-4121
Gouverneur	Gouverneur S&L Assn.	(315) 287-2600
New York	Habib American Bank	(212) 532-4444
New York	Morgan Stanley Private Bank, N.A.	(212) 762-1803
Flushing	National Bank of New York City	(718) 358-4400
Astoria	Quontic Bank	(718) 215-4000
Saratoga Springs	Saratoga National Bank and Trust Co.	(518) 583-3114
New York	Shinhan Bank America	(646) 843-7300
Ithaca	Tompkins Trust Co.	(607) 273-3210
Geneva	USNY Bank	(315) 789-1500
New York	Woori America Bank	(212) 244-1500

North Carolina

City	Name	Telephone	City	Name	Telephone

Rating: A

Mount Airy	Surrey Bank & Trust	(336) 783-3900

Rating: A-

Roxboro	Roxboro Savings Bank, SSB	(336) 599-2137

Rating: B+

Wilmington	Live Oak Banking Co.	(910) 790-5867
Raleigh	Paragon Commercial Bank	(919) 788-7770
Newton	Peoples Bank	(828) 464-5620
Rocky Mount	Providence Bank	(252) 443-9477
Wake Forest	Wake Forest Federal S&L Assn.	(919) 556-5146

North Dakota

City	Name	Telephone	City	Name	Telephone

Rating: A+

City	Name	Telephone
Forman	Sargent County Bank	(701) 724-3216

Rating: A

City	Name	Telephone
Mott	Commercial Bank of Mott	(701) 824-2593
Devils Lake	Ramsey National Bank	(701) 662-4024
Center	Security First Bank of North Dakota	(701) 794-8758

Rating: A-

City	Name	Telephone
Williston	American State Bank & Trust Co	(701) 774-4100
Bowman	Dakota Western Bank	(701) 523-5803
Beulah	First Security Bank - West	(701) 873-4301
Carson	Grant County State Bank	(701) 622-3491
Powers Lake	Liberty State Bank	(701) 464-5421
Bismarck	Starion Bank	(701) 223-6050
Napoleon	Stock Growers Bank	(701) 754-2226

Rating: B+

City	Name	Telephone
Grand Forks	Alerus Financial, N.A.	(701) 795-3200
Dickinson	American Bank Center	(701) 483-6811
Fargo	American Federal Bank	(701) 461-5900
Fargo	Bell Bank	(701) 298-1500
Fargo	Choice Financial Group	(701) 356-9700
Hebron	Dakota Community Bank & Trust, N.A.	(701) 878-4416
Hunter	Dakota Heritage Bank of North Dakota	(701) 874-2161
Langdon	Farmers and Merchants State Bank	(701) 256-5431
Williston	First National B&T Co. of Williston	(701) 577-2113
Buxton	First State Bank	(701) 847-2600
Golva	First State Bank of Golva	(701) 872-3656
Arthur	First State Bank of North Dakota	(701) 967-8914
Minot	First Western Bank & Trust	(701) 852-3711
Garrison	Garrison State Bank and Trust	(701) 463-2262
Munich	Horizon Financial Bank	(701) 682-5331
Hazen	Union State Bank of Hazen	(701) 748-2233
Leeds	United Community Bank of North Dakota	(701) 466-2000

Ohio

City	Name	Telephone	City	Name	Telephone

Rating: A+

City	Name	Telephone
Mason	FDS Bank	(513) 573-2265
Saint Henry	St. Henry Bank	(419) 678-2358

Rating: A

City	Name	Telephone
Beverly	Citizens Bank Co.	(740) 984-2381
Coshocton	Home Loan Savings Bank	(740) 622-0444

Rating: A-

City	Name	Telephone
Upper Arlington	Arlington Bank	(614) 486-9000
Spencer	Farmers Savings Bank	(330) 648-2441
Tiffin	First Bank of Ohio	(419) 448-9740
Ottoville	Ottoville Bank Co.	(419) 453-3313
Coldwater	Peoples Bank Co.	(419) 678-2385
Urbana	Perpetual Federal Savings Bank	(937) 653-1700

Rating: B+

City	Name	Telephone
Lorain	Buckeye Community Bank	(440) 233-8800
Martins Ferry	Citizens Savings Bank	(740) 633-0445
Bethel	Community Savings Bank	(513) 734-4445
Deshler	Corn City State Bank	(419) 278-0015
Cincinnati	Eagle Savings Bank	(513) 574-0700
Archbold	Farmers & Merchants State Bank	(419) 446-2501
Blanchester	First National Bank of Blanchester	(937) 783-2451
Fort Jennings	Fort Jennings State Bank	(419) 286-2527
Cincinnati	Foundation Bank	(513) 721-0120
Greenville	Greenville National Bank	(937) 548-1114
Hamler	Hamler State Bank	(419) 274-3955
Springfield	Home City FSB of Springfield	(937) 390-0470
Minster	Minster Bank	(419) 628-2351
Cincinnati	North Side Bank and Trust Co.	(513) 542-7800
Marietta	Settlers Bank	(740) 373-9200
Wyoming	Spring Valley Bank	(513) 761-6688
Attica	Sutton Bank	(419) 426-3641
Columbus Grove	Union Bank Co.	(419) 659-2141
West Mansfield	Union Banking Co.	(937) 355-6511
Toledo	Waterford Bank, N.A.	(419) 720-3900

Oklahoma

City	Name	Telephone	City	Name	Telephone
			Lawton	City National B&T Co. of Lawton, Oklahoma	(580) 355-3580
			Alva	Community Bank	(580) 327-5500
			Bristow	Community Bank	(918) 367-3343
			Fairview	Fairview S&L Assn.	(580) 227-3735

Rating: A+

City	Name	Telephone
Perkins	Payne County Bank	(405) 547-2436

Rating: A

City	Name	Telephone
Guymon	Bank of the Panhandle	(580) 338-2593
Cleo Springs	Cleo State Bank	(580) 438-2223
Okarche	Community National Bank of Okarche	(405) 263-7491
Fairview	Farmers and Merchants National Bank	(580) 227-3773
Perry	First Bank & Trust Co.	(580) 336-5562
Okarche	First Bank of Okarche	(405) 263-7215
Owasso	First Bank of Owasso	(918) 272-5301
Lawton	FSNB, N.A.	(580) 357-9880
Tulsa	Security Bank	(918) 664-6100
Cheyenne	Security State Bank	(580) 497-3354
Tuttle	Sooner State Bank	(405) 381-2326
Wynnewood	State Bank of Wynnewood	(405) 665-2001
Welch	Welch State Bank of Welch, Oklahoma	(918) 788-3373

Rating: A-

City	Name	Telephone
Broken Bow	1st Bank & Trust	(580) 584-9123
Ardmore	American Nation Bank	(580) 226-6222
Stilwell	Bank of Commerce	(918) 696-7745
Cushing	Bank of Cushing	(918) 225-2010
Hydro	Bank of Hydro	(405) 663-2214
Oklahoma City	Bank2	(405) 946-2265
Poteau	Central National Bank of Poteau	(918) 647-2233
Newkirk	Eastman National Bank of Newkirk	(580) 362-2511
Wagoner	First Bank & Trust Co.	(918) 485-2173
Duncan	First Bank & Trust Co.	(580) 255-1810
Chandler	First Bank of Chandler	(405) 258-1210
Hooker	First National Bank of Hooker	(580) 652-2448
Anadarko	First State Bank	(405) 247-2471
Broken Bow	McCurtain County National Bank	(580) 584-6262
Westville	Peoples Bank	(918) 723-5453
Edmond	Prime Bank	(405) 340-2775
Weatherford	Southwest National Bank	(580) 774-0900
Woodward	Stock Exchange Bank	(580) 256-3314

Rating: B+

City	Name	Telephone
Alva	Alva State Bank & Trust Co.	(580) 327-3300
Atoka	AmeriState Bank	(580) 889-3375
Oklahoma City	BancFirst	(405) 270-1086
Chelsea	Bank of Commerce	(918) 789-2567
Laverne	Bank of Laverne	(580) 921-3321
Thomas	Bank of the West	(580) 661-3541
McAlester	Bank, N.A.	(918) 423-2265
Edmond	Citizens Bank of Edmond	(405) 341-6650
Okemah	Citizens State Bank	(918) 623-1551
Guymon	City Bank and Trust Co.	(580) 338-6561

City	Name	Telephone
Lawton	City National B&T Co. of Lawton, Oklahoma	(580) 355-3580
Alva	Community Bank	(580) 327-5500
Bristow	Community Bank	(918) 367-3343
Fairview	Fairview S&L Assn.	(580) 227-3735
Erick	First Bank	(580) 526-3332
Waurika	First Farmers National Bank of Waurika	(580) 228-2326
Oklahoma City	First Liberty Bank	(405) 608-4500
Okmulgee	First National B&T Co. of Okmulgee	(918) 756-8440
Heavener	First National Bank	(918) 653-3200
Elk City	First National Bank & Trust of Elk City	(580) 225-2580
Okeene	First National Bank in Okeene	(580) 822-3300
Oklahoma City	First National Bank of Oklahoma	(405) 848-2001
Thomas	First National Bank of Thomas	(580) 661-3515
Durant	First United Bank and Trust Co.	(580) 924-2211
Tulsa	Grand Bank	(918) 491-9700
Hollis	Great Plains National Bank	(580) 688-3323
Keyes	High Plains Bank	(580) 546-7511
Idabel	Idabel National Bank	(580) 286-7656
Purcell	McClain Bank	(405) 527-6503
Clinton	Oklahoma Bank and Trust Co.	(580) 323-2345
Tulsa	Patriot Bank	(918) 209-5200
Checotah	Peoples National Bank of Checotah	(918) 473-2237
Hugo	Security First National Bank of Hugo	(580) 326-9641
Enid	Security National Bank of Enid	(580) 234-5151
Coalgate	Shamrock Bank, N.A.	(580) 927-2311
Fort Cobb	Washita Valley Bank	(405) 643-2305

Oregon

City	Name	Telephone	City	Name	Telephone

Rating: **A+**

City	Name	Telephone
Salem	Pioneer Trust Bank, N.A.	(503) 363-3136

Rating: **A**

City	Name	Telephone
Sandy	Clackamas County Bank	(503) 668-5501

Rating: **A-**

City	Name	Telephone
Newport	Oregon Coast Bank	(541) 265-9000
Salem	Willamette Valley Bank	(503) 485-2222

Rating: **B+**

City	Name	Telephone
Eugene	Pacific Continental Bank	(541) 686-8685
Roseburg	Umpqua Bank	(541) 440-3961

Pennsylvania

City	Name	Telephone	City	Name	Telephone
Rating:	**A**				
Smethport	Hamlin Bank and Trust Co.	(814) 887-5555			
Honesdale	Honesdale National Bank	(570) 253-3355			
Neffs	Neffs National Bank	(610) 767-3875			
Turbotville	Turbotville National Bank	(570) 649-5118			
Rating:	**A-**				
Wellsboro	Citizens & Northern Bank	(570) 724-3411			
Bloomsburg	First Columbia Bank & Trust Co.	(570) 784-1660			
Radnor	Haverford Trust Co.	(610) 995-8700			
Liverpool	Liverpool Community Bank	(717) 444-3714			
Muncy	Muncy Bank and Trust Co.	(570) 546-2211			
Strabane	Slovenian S&L Assn. of Canonsburg	(724) 745-5000			
West Milton	West Milton State Bank	(570) 568-6851			
Rating:	**B+**				
Landisburg	Bank of Landisburg	(717) 789-3213			
Bryn Mawr	Bryn Mawr Trust Co.	(610) 525-1700			
Latrobe	Commercial Bank & Trust of PA	(724) 539-3501			
Elderton	Elderton State Bank	(724) 354-2111			
Rochester	Farmers Building and Savings Bank	(724) 774-4970			
Mansfield	First Citizens Community Bank	(570) 662-2121			
Conshohocken	Firstrust Savings Bank	(610) 238-5001			
Erie	Marquette Savings Bank	(814) 455-4481			
Mifflinburg	Mifflinburg Bank & Trust Co.	(570) 966-1041			
Malvern	National Bank of Malvern	(610) 647-0100			
New Tripoli	New Tripoli Bank	(610) 298-8811			
Philadelphia	Philadelphia Trust Co.	(215) 979-3434			
Honesdale	Wayne Bank	(570) 253-1455			
Levittown	William Penn Bank,	(215) 269-1200			

Rhode Island

City	Name	Telephone	City	Name	Telephone

Rating: **B+**

City	Name	Telephone
Westerly	Washington Trust Co. of Westerly	(401) 348-1200

South Carolina

City	Name	Telephone	City	Name	Telephone
Rating:	**A+**				
Gaffney	First Piedmont Federal S&L Assn. of Gaffney	(864) 489-6046			
Rating:	**A**				
Hampton	Palmetto State Bank	(803) 943-2671			
Rating:	**A-**				
Manning	Bank of Clarendon	(803) 433-4451			
Charleston	CresCom Bank	(855) 273-7266			
Greenville	GrandSouth Bank	(864) 770-1000			
Seneca	Oconee Federal S&L Assn.	(864) 882-2765			
Rating:	**B+**				
Charleston	Bank of South Carolina	(843) 724-1500			
Greer	Citizens Building and Loan, SSB	(864) 877-2054			
Clover	Clover Community Bank	(803) 222-6754			
Honea Path	Commercial Bank	(864) 369-7326			
Columbia	South State Bank	(803) 771-2265			

South Dakota

City	Name	Telephone	City	Name	Telephone

Rating: A

City	Name	Telephone
Herreid	Campbell County Bank, Inc.	(605) 437-2294
Fort Pierre	First National Bank	(605) 223-2521
Philip	First National Bank in Philip	(605) 859-2525
Sioux Falls	First Premier Bank	(605) 357-3000

Rating: A-

City	Name	Telephone
Wessington Springs	American Bank & Trust	(605) 539-1222
Brookings	First Bank & Trust	(605) 696-2265
Sioux Falls	First Bank & Trust	(605) 978-9300
Burke	First Fidelity Bank	(605) 775-2641
Beresford	First Savings Bank	(605) 763-2009
Roscoe	First State Bank of Roscoe	(605) 287-4451
Rapid City	First Western Federal Savings Bank	(605) 341-1203
Redfield	Heartland State Bank	(605) 475-5500
Belle Fourche	Pioneer Bank & Trust	(605) 892-2536
Miller	Quoin Financial Bank	(605) 853-2473
Bruce	Richland State Bank	(605) 627-5671
Dakota Dunes	Security National Bank of South Dakota	(605) 232-6060

Rating: B+

City	Name	Telephone
Wagner	Commercial State Bank of Wagner	(605) 384-3646
Fort Pierre	Dakota Prairie Bank	(605) 223-2337
Sioux Falls	Department Stores National Bank	
Plankinton	Farmers and Merchants State Bank	(605) 942-7781
Stickney	Farmers State Bank	(605) 732-4264
Sioux Falls	First National Bank in Sioux Falls	(605) 335-5200
Groton	First State Bank of Claremont	(605) 397-2711
Sioux Falls	MetaBank	(605) 361-4347
Sisseton	Roberts County National Bank of Sisseton	(605) 698-7621

Tennessee

City	Name	Telephone	City	Name	Telephone

Rating: A+

City	Name	Telephone
Carthage	Citizens Bank	(615) 735-1490

Rating: A

City	Name	Telephone
Memphis	Financial Federal Bank	(901) 756-2848
Shelbyville	First Community Bank of Tennessee	(931) 684-5800

Rating: A-

City	Name	Telephone
Athens	Athens Federal Community Bank, N.A.	(423) 745-1111
Bells	Bank of Crockett	(731) 663-2031
Gleason	Bank of Gleason	(731) 648-5506
Fayetteville	Bank of Lincoln County	(931) 433-1708
Waynesboro	Bank of Waynesboro	(931) 722-2265
Elizabethton	Citizens Bank	(423) 543-2265
Paris	Commercial Bank & Trust Co.	(731) 642-3341
Elizabethton	Elizabethton Federal Savings Bank	(423) 543-5050
Portland	Farmers Bank	(615) 325-2265
Lewisburg	First Commerce Bank	(931) 359-4322
Dickson	First Federal Bank	(615) 446-2822
Manchester	First National Bank of Manchester	(931) 728-3518
Tullahoma	First Vision Bank of Tennessee	(931) 454-0500
Paris	Security Bank and Trust Co.	(731) 642-6644
Nashville	Truxton Trust Co.	(615) 515-1700
Lebanon	Wilson Bank and Trust	(615) 444-2265

Rating: B+

City	Name	Telephone
Greeneville	Andrew Johnson Bank	(423) 783-1000
Frankewing	Bank of Frankewing	(931) 363-1796
Halls	Bank of Halls	(731) 836-7515
Rutledge	Citizens B&T Co. of Grainger County	(865) 828-5237
Dyersburg	First Citizens National Bank	(731) 285-4410
McMinnville	First National Bank of Middle Tennessee	(931) 473-4402
Jackson	First South Bank	(731) 668-2265
Franklin	Franklin Synergy Bank	(615) 236-8310
Gates	Gates Banking and Trust Co.	(731) 836-7741
Greeneville	Greeneville Federal Bank, FSB	(423) 638-4154
Lawrenceburg	Lawrenceburg Federal Bank	(931) 762-7571
Bolivar	Merchants & Planters Bank	(731) 658-7788
Shelbyville	Peoples Bank of Middle Tennessee	(931) 684-7222
Cookeville	Putnam 1st Mercantile Bank	(931) 528-6372
Brentwood	Reliant Bank	(615) 221-2020
Elizabethton	Security Federal Bank	(423) 543-1000

Texas

City	Name	Telephone	City	Name	Telephone
			Granbury	First National Bank of Granbury	(817) 573-2655
			Livingston	First National Bank of Livingston	(936) 327-1234

Rating: A+

City	Name	Telephone
Tyler	Citizens 1st Bank	(903) 581-1900
Brady	Commercial National Bank of Brady	(325) 597-2961
Hughes Springs	First National Bank of Hughes Springs	(903) 639-2521
Brownwood	TexasBank	(325) 649-9200
Vernon	Waggoner National Bank of Vernon	(940) 552-2511

Rating: A

City	Name	Telephone
Laredo	Commerce Bank	(956) 724-1616
Albany	First National Bank of Albany	(325) 762-2222
Hebbronville	First National Bank of Hebbronville	(361) 527-3221
Athens	First State Bank	(903) 676-1900
Shallowater	First State Bank	(806) 832-4525
Yoakum	First State Bank	(361) 293-3572
Carthage	First State Bank and Trust Co.	(903) 693-6606
Ben Wheeler	First State Bank of Ben Wheeler, Texas	(903) 833-5861
Industry	Industry State Bank	(979) 357-4437
Brownsville	International Bank of Commerce	(956) 547-1000
Zapata	International Bank of Commerce	(956) 765-8361
Laredo	International Bank of Commerce	(956) 722-7611
Muenster	Muenster State Bank	(940) 759-2257
Dallas	PlainsCapital Bank	(214) 525-9100
Sanger	Sanger Bank	(940) 458-4600
De Kalb	State Bank of De Kalb	(903) 667-2553
Dallas	T Bank, N.A.	(972) 720-9000
Fort Worth	Trinity Bank, N.A.	(817) 763-9966

Rating: A-

City	Name	Telephone
Houston	American First National Bank	(713) 596-2888
College Station	American Momentum Bank	(979) 774-1111
Wichita Falls	American National Bank & Trust	(940) 397-2300
Mount Pleasant	American National Bank of Mount Pleasant	(903) 572-1776
Anahuac	Anahuac National Bank	(409) 267-3106
Bryan	Bank and Trust of Bryan/College Station	(979) 260-2100
Midland	Bank of Texas	(432) 221-6100
Marfa	Big Bend Banks, N.A.	(432) 729-4344
Buckholts	Buckholts State Bank	(254) 593-3661
Buffalo	Citizens State Bank	(903) 322-4256
Miles	Citizens State Bank	(325) 468-3311
Corrigan	Citizens State Bank	(936) 398-2566
Sealy	Citizens State Bank	(979) 885-3571
Kingwood	Commercial State Bank	(281) 318-4600
Longview	Community Bank	(903) 236-4422
San Antonio	Crockett National Bank	(210) 384-9300
Laredo	Falcon International Bank	(956) 723-2265
Fayetteville	Fayetteville Bank	(979) 378-4261
Abilene	First Financial Bank, N.A.	(325) 627-7200
Bellville	First National Bank of Bellville	(979) 865-3181
Floydada	First National Bank of Floydada	(806) 983-3717

City	Name	Telephone
Graham	First State Bank	(940) 549-8880
Austin	First State Bank Central Texas	(512) 231-8821
Bedias	First State Bank of Bedias	(936) 395-2141
Burnet	First State Bank of Burnet	(512) 756-2191
Dimmitt	First United Bank	(806) 647-4151
Houston	Golden Bank, N.A.	(713) 777-3838
Graham	Graham S&L, SSB	(940) 549-2066
Grandview	Grandview Bank	(817) 866-3316
Houston	Integrity Bank, SSB	(713) 335-8700
Dallas	Inwood National Bank	(214) 358-5281
Johnson City	Johnson City Bank	(830) 868-7131
Justin	Justin State Bank	(940) 648-2753
Paris	Lamar National Bank	(903) 785-0701
Bowie	Legend Bank, N.A.	(940) 872-2221
Marion	Marion State Bank	(830) 420-2331
Mason	Mason Bank	(325) 347-5911
Andrews	National Bank of Andrews	(432) 523-6800
El Campo	NewFirst National Bank	(979) 543-3349
Dallas	NexBank SSB	(972) 934-4700
Rocksprings	Peoples State Bank	(830) 683-2119
Houston	Preferred Bank	(281) 556-6443
Santa Anna	Santa Anna National Bank	(325) 348-3108
Pearsall	Security State Bank	(830) 334-3606
Farwell	Security State Bank	(806) 481-3327
Fredericksburg	Security State Bank & Trust	(830) 997-7575
Dallas	State Bank of Texas	(972) 252-6000
Crowley	Texas Exchange Bank, SSB	(817) 297-4331
Frisco	Texas Republic Bank, N.A.	(972) 334-0700
El Paso	WestStar Bank	(915) 532-1000
The Woodlands	Woodforest National Bank	(832) 375-2505
Yoakum	Yoakum National Bank	(361) 293-5225

Rating: B+

City	Name	Telephone
Jacksonville	Austin Bank, Texas N.A.	(903) 586-1526
Austin	Austin Capital Bank SSB	(512) 693-3600
Bellville	Austin County State Bank	(979) 865-4200
Del Rio	Bank and Trust, SSB	(830) 774-2555
Brenham	Bank of Brenham, N.A.	(979) 836-3332
McLean	Bank of Commerce	(806) 779-2461
Desoto	Bank of DeSoto, N.A.	(972) 780-7777
Richwood	Brazos National Bank	(979) 265-1911
Lubbock	Centennial Bank	(806) 775-8044
Houston	Central Bank	(832) 485-2300
Waco	Central National Bank	(254) 776-3800
Graham	Ciera Bank	(940) 549-2040
Abilene	Citizens Bank, N.A.	(325) 695-3000
Brownwood	Citizens National Bank at Brownwood	(325) 643-3545
Somerville	Citizens State Bank	(979) 596-1421

Texas

City	Name	Telephone	City	Name	Telephone
Colorado City	City National Bank of Colorado City	(325) 728-5221	Fort Worth	Southwest Bank	(817) 292-4820
Comanche	Comanche National Bank	(325) 356-2577	Sundown	Sundown State Bank	(806) 229-2111
Nacogdoches	Commercial Bank of Texas, N.A.	(936) 715-4100	Monahans	Tejas Bank	(432) 943-4230
Andrews	Commercial State Bank	(432) 523-3440	Longview	Texas Bank and Trust Co.	(903) 237-5500
Waco	Community Bank & Trust	(254) 753-1521	Weatherford	Texas Bank Financial	(817) 596-9998
Corsicana	Community National B&T of Texas	(903) 654-4500	Garland	Texas Brand Bank	(972) 494-9800
Maypearl	Cowboy Bank of Texas	(972) 435-2131	Houston	Texas Gulf Bank, N.A.	(713) 595-7400
Dilley	Dilley State Bank	(830) 965-1511	Jacksonville	Texas National Bank of Jacksonville	(903) 586-0931
Groesbeck	Farmers State Bank	(254) 729-3272	Dallas	Texas Security Bank	(469) 398-4800
Wichita Falls	Fidelity Bank	(940) 763-2100	Van Alstyne	Texas Star Bank	(903) 482-5234
Waco	Fidelity Bank of Texas	(254) 755-6555	San Angelo	Texas State Bank	(325) 949-3721
Burkburnett	First Bank	(940) 569-2221	Mineral Wells	Titan Bank, N.A.	(940) 325-9821
Lubbock	First Bank & Trust	(806) 788-0800	Corpus Christi	ValueBank Texas	(361) 888-4451
Diboll	First Bank & Trust East Texas	(936) 829-4721	Dallas	Veritex Community Bank	(972) 349-6200
Spearman	First National Bank	(806) 659-5544	Ralls	Vista Bank	(806) 253-2511
Wichita Falls	First National Bank	(940) 696-3000	Wallis	Wallis State Bank	(979) 478-6151
Rotan	First National Bank	(325) 735-2224	Midland	West Texas National Bank	(432) 685-6500
Alvin	First National Bank of Alvin	(281) 331-3151	Fort Worth	Woodhaven Bank	(817) 496-6700
Aspermont	First National Bank of Aspermont	(940) 989-3505	Zapata	Zapata National Bank	(956) 765-4302
Bastrop	First National Bank of Bastrop	(512) 321-2561	Crystal City	Zavala County Bank	(830) 374-5866
Beeville	First National Bank of Beeville	(361) 358-1530			
Burleson	First National Bank of Burleson	(817) 295-0461			
Waco	First National Bank of Central Texas	(254) 772-9330			
Dublin	First National Bank of Dublin	(254) 445-4400			
Shiner	First National Bank of Shiner	(361) 594-3317			
Stratford	First State Bank	(806) 396-5521			
Louise	First State Bank	(979) 648-2691			
Gilmer	Gilmer National Bank	(903) 843-5653			
Gruver	Gruver State Bank	(806) 733-5061			
Happy	Happy State Bank	(806) 558-2265			
Henderson	Henderson Federal Savings Bank	(903) 657-2577			
Galveston	HomeTown Bank, N.A.	(409) 763-1271			
Hondo	Hondo National Bank	(830) 426-3355			
Austin	Horizon Bank, SSB	(512) 637-5730			
McKinney	Independent Bank	(972) 562-9004			
McAllen	Inter National Bank	(956) 664-8400			
San Antonio	Jefferson Bank	(210) 734-4311			
Addison	Liberty Capital Bank	(469) 375-6600			
Paris	Liberty National Bank in Paris	(903) 785-5555			
Lytle	Lytle State Bank of Lytle, Texas	(830) 709-3601			
Texas City	Mainland Bank	(409) 948-1625			
Kingwood	MINT National Bank	(281) 359-6468			
Normangee	Normangee State Bank	(936) 396-3611			
Denton	Northstar Bank	(940) 591-1200			
Pearland	Pearland State Bank	(281) 485-3211			
Keene	Pinnacle Bank	(817) 645-8861			
Houston	Post Oak Bank, N.A.	(713) 439-3900			
El Campo	Prosperity Bank	(979) 543-2200			
Center	Shelby Savings Bank, SSB	(936) 598-5688			
Moulton	SouthStar Bank, S.S.B.	(361) 596-4611			

Utah

City	Name	Telephone	City	Name	Telephone

Rating: A+

City	Name	Telephone
Salt Lake City	Optum Bank, Inc.	(866) 234-8913

Rating: A

City	Name	Telephone
Ogden	Bank of Utah	(801) 409-5000
Park City	LCA Bank Corp.	(435) 658-4824
Salt Lake City	Marlin Business Bank	(888) 479-9111
American Fork	People's Intermountain Bank	(801) 756-7681
Cedar City	State Bank of Southern Utah	(435) 865-2300
Salt Lake City	WebBank	(801) 456-8350

Rating: A-

City	Name	Telephone
Midvale	Ally Bank	(801) 790-5000
Salt Lake City	BMW Bank of North America	(801) 461-6500
Salt Lake City	Brighton Bank	(801) 943-6500
Provo	Central Bank	(801) 375-1000
Salt Lake City	Continental Bank	(801) 595-7000
Layton	First National Bank of Layton	(801) 813-1600
Salt Lake City	Morgan Stanley Bank, N.A.	(801) 236-3600
Salt Lake City	UBS Bank USA	(801) 741-0310
Salina	Utah Independent Bank	(435) 529-7459
Midvale	WEX Bank	(801) 568-4345

Rating: B+

City	Name	Telephone
Salt Lake City	American Express Bank, FSB	(801) 945-5000
Salt Lake City	American Express Centurion Bank	(801) 945-5000
Salt Lake City	EnerBank USA	(801) 832-0700
Provo	Green Dot Bank	(801) 344-7020
Salt Lake City	Home Savings Bank	(801) 487-0811
Salt Lake City	Pitney Bowes Bank, Inc.	(801) 832-4440
Salt Lake City	ZB, N.A.	(801) 844-7171

Virginia

City	Name	Telephone	City	Name	Telephone
Rating:	**A**				
Carson	Bank of Southside Virginia	(434) 246-5211			
Kenbridge	Benchmark Community Bank	(434) 676-9054			
Lebanon	First Bank and Trust Co.	(276) 889-4622			
Blacksburg	National Bank of Blacksburg	(540) 951-6205			
Rating:	**A-**				
Danville	American National Bank and Trust Co.	(434) 792-5111			
Phenix	Bank of Charlotte County	(434) 542-5111			
Alexandria	Burke & Herbert Bank & Trust Co.	(703) 549-6600			
Blackstone	Citizens Bank and Trust Co.	(434) 292-8100			
New Castle	Farmers & Merchants Bank	(540) 864-5156			
Appomattox	Farmers Bank of Appomattox	(434) 352-7171			
Jonesville	Powell Valley National Bank	(276) 346-1414			
Danville	Virginia Bank and Trust Co.	(434) 793-6411			
Rating:	**B+**				
Reston	Access National Bank	(703) 871-2100			
Berryville	Bank of Clarke County	(540) 955-2510			
Luray	Blue Ridge Bank	(540) 743-6521			
McLean	Cardinal Bank	(703) 584-3400			
West Point	Citizens and Farmers Bank	(804) 843-2360			
Pennington Gap	Farmers and Miners Bank	(276) 546-4692			
Covington	Highlands Community Bank	(540) 962-2265			
Reston	John Marshall Bank	(703) 584-0840			
McLean	Sonabank	(703) 893-7400			
Portsmouth	TowneBank	(757) 638-7500			
Reston	WashingtonFirst Bank	(703) 840-2410			

Washington

City	Name	Telephone	City	Name	Telephone

Rating: A-

City	Name	Telephone
Mountlake Terrace	1st Security Bank of Washington	(800) 683-0973
Walla Walla	Banner Bank	(509) 527-3636
Cashmere	Cashmere Valley Bank	(509) 782-2624
Renton	First Financial Northwest Bank	(425) 255-4400
Friday Harbor	Islanders Bank	(360) 378-3658
Seattle	Washington Federal, N.A.	(206) 204-3446

Rating: B+

City	Name	Telephone
Tacoma	Columbia State Bank	(253) 305-1900
Bellingham	Peoples Bank	(360) 715-4200
Bellevue	Puget Sound Bank	(425) 455-2400
Centralia	Security State Bank	(360) 736-0763
Spokane	Washington Trust Bank	(509) 353-4204
Yakima	Yakima Federal S&L Assn.	(509) 248-2634

West Virginia

City	Name	Telephone	City	Name	Telephone
Rating:	**A-**				
Clay	Clay County Bank, Inc.	(304) 587-4221			
Parkersburg	Community Bank of Parkersburg	(304) 485-7991			
Rating:	**B+**				
Union	Bank of Monroe	(304) 772-3034			
Charleston	City National Bank of West Virginia	(304) 769-1100			
Bruceton Mills	Clear Mountain Bank	(304) 379-2265			
Hurricane	Putnam County Bank	(304) 562-9931			
Moorefield	Summit Community Bank, Inc.	(304) 530-1000			

Wisconsin

City	Name	Telephone
Rating: A+		
Prairie Du Sac	Bank of Prairie Du Sac	(608) 643-3393
Rating: A		
Alma	Bank of Alma	(608) 685-4461
Deerfield	Bank of Deerfield	(608) 764-5411
Eau Claire	Charter Bank	(715) 832-4254
Waupaca	Farmers State Bank of Waupaca	(715) 258-1400
Fond du Lac	National Exchange Bank and Trust	(920) 921-7700
Hayward	Peoples Bank Midwest	(715) 634-2674
Rating: A-		
Brodhead	Bank of Brodhead	(608) 897-2121
Galesville	Bank of Galesville	(608) 582-2233
Sun Prairie	Bank of Sun Prairie	(608) 837-4511
Little Chute	BLC Community Bank	(920) 788-4141
De Forest	DMB Community Bank	(608) 846-3711
Kendall	Farmers and Merchants Bank of Kendall	(608) 463-7101
Hillsboro	Farmers State Bank Hillsboro	(608) 489-2621
Whitewater	First Citizens State Bank	(262) 473-2112
Bangor	First National Bank of Bangor	(608) 486-2386
Fond du Lac	Hometown Bank	(920) 907-0788
Schofield	Intercity State Bank	(715) 359-4231
Amherst	International Bank of Amherst	(715) 824-3325
Black River Falls	Jackson County Bank	(715) 284-5341
Madison	John Deere Financial, F.S.B.	(608) 821-2000
Middleton	Middleton Community Bank	(608) 824-3200
Superior	National Bank of Commerce	(715) 394-5531
Chippewa Falls	Northwestern Bank	(715) 723-4461
Fitchburg	Oak Bank	(608) 441-6000
Oregon	Oregon Community Bank	(608) 835-3168
Mazomanie	Peoples Community Bank	(608) 795-2120
Peshtigo	Peshtigo National Bank	(715) 582-4512
Wisconsin Rapids	River Cities Bank	(715) 422-1100
Shell Lake	Shell Lake State Bank	(715) 468-7858
Tomah	Timberwood Bank	(608) 372-2265
Sparta	Union National Bank & Trust Co.	(608) 269-6737
Wauwatosa	WaterStone Bank, SSB	(414) 761-1000
Waukesha	Waukesha State Bank	(262) 549-8500
Hortonville	Wolf River Community Bank	(920) 779-7000
Rating: B+		
Dorchester	Advantage Community Bank	(715) 654-5100
Fort Atkinson	Badger Bank	(920) 563-2478
Manitowoc	Bank First National	(920) 684-6611
Bonduel	Bonduel State Bank	(715) 758-2141
La Crosse	Citizens State Bank of La Crosse	(608) 785-2265
Loyal	Citizens State Bank of Loyal	(715) 255-8526
Platteville	Clare Bank, N.A.	(608) 348-2727
Denmark	Denmark State Bank	(920) 863-2161
Milton	First Community Bank	(608) 868-7644
Darlington	First National Bank at Darlington	(608) 776-4071
Grand Marsh	Grand Marsh State Bank	(608) 339-3351
Land O'Lakes	Headwaters State Bank	(715) 547-3383
Hustisford	Hustisford State Bank	(920) 349-3241
Wausau	Integrity First Bank	(715) 845-0900
Merrill	Lincoln Community Bank	(715) 536-8301
Livingston	Livingston State Bank	(608) 943-6351
Waupun	National Bank of Waupun	(920) 324-5551
Nekoosa	Nekoosa Port Edwards State Bank	(715) 886-3104
Green Bay	Nicolet National Bank	(920) 430-1400
La Crosse	River Bank	(608) 457-2100
Barron	Sterling Bank	(715) 537-3141
Medford	Time Federal Savings Bank	(715) 748-2231
Poynette	United Community Bank	(608) 635-4351
Sauk City	Wisconsin River Bank	(608) 643-6300

Wyoming

City	Name	Telephone	City	Name	Telephone

Rating: A-

City	Name	Telephone
Jackson	Bank of Jackson Hole	(307) 733-8064
Lusk	Lusk State Bank	(307) 334-2500
Cheyenne	Wyoming Bank & Trust	(307) 632-7733

Rating: B+

City	Name	Telephone
Rawlins	Bank of Commerce	(307) 324-2265
Afton	Bank of Star Valley	(307) 885-0000
Casper	Hilltop National Bank	(307) 265-2740
Casper	Jonah Bank of Wyoming	(307) 237-4555
Torrington	Pinnacle Bank - Wyoming	(307) 532-2181
Torrington	Platte Valley Bank	(307) 532-2111
Cheyenne	Security First Bank	(307) 775-6500
Basin	Security State Bank	(307) 568-2483

Section III

Rating Upgrades
and Downgrades

A list of all

U.S. Commercial Banks and Savings Banks

receiving a rating upgrade or downgrade
during the current quarter.

Section III Contents

This section identifies those institutions receiving a rating change since the previous edition of this publication, whether it be a rating upgrade, rating downgrade, newly-rated company or the withdrawal of a rating. A rating upgrade or downgrade may entail a change from one letter grade to another, or it may mean the addition or deletion of a plus or minus sign within the same letter grade previously assigned to the company. Ratings are normally updated once each quarter of the year. In some instances, however, an institution's rating may be downgraded outside of the normal updates due to overriding circumstances.

1. **Institution Name**   The name under which the institution was chartered. A company's name can be very similar to, or the same as, that of another, so verify the company's exact name, city, and state to make sure you are looking at the correct company.

2. **New Safety Rating**   Weiss rating assigned to the institution at the time of publication. Our ratings are designed to distinguish levels of insolvency risk and are measured on a scale from A to F based upon a wide range of factors. Highly rated companies are, in our opinion, less likely to experience financial difficulties than lower rated firms. See *About Weiss Safety Ratings* for more information and a description of what each rating means.

3. **State**   The state in which the institution's headquarters or main office is located.

4. **Date of Change**   Date that rating was finalized.

Rating Upgrades

Name	State	Date of Change

Rating: A

Name	State	Date of Change
California Pacific Bank	CA	11/30/16
Clackamas County Bank	OR	11/30/16
First National Bank Alaska	AK	11/30/16
First State Bank	NE	11/30/16
First State Bank	TX	11/30/16
FirsTier Bank	NE	11/30/16
Metro City Bank	GA	11/30/16
NBKC Bank	KS	11/30/16
Teutopolis State Bank	IL	11/30/16
Wadena State Bank	MN	11/30/16

Rating: A-

Name	State	Date of Change
American Continental Bank	CA	11/30/16
American National Bank	FL	11/30/16
Applied Bank	DE	11/30/16
Bank of Crockett	TN	11/30/16
BankSouth	AL	11/30/16
Central Bank	UT	11/30/16
Citizens Bank of Edina	MO	11/30/16
Community Bank of Parkersburg	WV	11/30/16
Continental Bank	UT	11/30/16
Cornerstone National Bank & Trust Co.	IL	11/30/16
EagleBank	MD	11/30/16
Farmers Bank	TN	11/30/16
Farmers Bank of Appomattox	VA	11/30/16
Farmers Bank of Northern Missouri	MO	11/30/16
First American Bank	NM	11/30/16
First National Bank of Layton	UT	11/30/16
First National Bank of Mount Dora	FL	11/30/16
Flint Hills Bank	KS	11/30/16
Golden Bank, N.A.	TX	11/30/16
Grinnell State Bank	IA	11/30/16
Hamilton State Bank	GA	11/30/16
Heartland State Bank	SD	11/30/16
Hillsboro Bank	FL	11/30/16
Home State Bank	MN	11/30/16
Iowa State Bank	IA	11/30/16
Kingsley State Bank	IA	11/30/16
McCurtain County National Bank	OK	11/30/16
Midwest Bank N.A.	NE	11/30/16
Peoples Bank	MS	11/30/16
Preferred Community Bank	FL	11/30/16
PriorityOne Bank	MS	11/30/16
Putnam County State Bank	MO	11/30/16
Quantum National Bank	GA	11/30/16
Quoin Financial Bank	SD	11/30/16
Security Bank USA	MN	11/30/16
South Georgia Bank	GA	11/30/16

Name	State	Date of Change
Springfield State Bank	KY	11/30/16
Texas Exchange Bank, SSB	TX	11/30/16
Town & Country Bank and Trust Co.	KY	11/30/16
TrustBank	IL	11/30/16
United Bank and Trust Co.	IA	11/30/16
Virginia Bank and Trust Co.	VA	11/30/16
WaterStone Bank, SSB	WI	11/30/16
Waukesha State Bank	WI	11/30/16
Western Alliance Bank	AZ	11/30/16
Willamette Valley Bank	OR	11/30/16

Rating: B+

Name	State	Date of Change
Alton Bank	MO	11/30/16
American Bank & Trust Co.	LA	11/30/16
American Riviera Bank	CA	11/30/16
Bank 1st	IA	11/30/16
Bank of Frankewing	TN	11/30/16
Bank of Halls	TN	11/30/16
Bank of Idaho	ID	11/30/16
Bank of Marin	CA	11/30/16
Bank of Vernon	AL	11/30/16
Bank, N.A.	OK	11/30/16
Bridgewater Bank	MN	11/30/16
Buckeye Community Bank	OH	11/30/16
Central State Bank	IA	11/30/16
Central Valley Community Bank	CA	11/30/16
Century Bank of Georgia	GA	11/30/16
Citizens Bank & Trust, Inc.	GA	11/30/16
Citizens Federal S&L Assn.	KY	11/30/16
Citizens Savings Bank	IA	11/30/16
Citizens State Bank	TX	11/30/16
Commercial Bank	GA	11/30/16
Community Pride Bank	MN	11/30/16
Community State Bank	KS	11/30/16
Country Club Bank	MO	11/30/16
Danville State Savings Bank	IA	11/30/16
Farmers State Bank	IA	11/30/16
First Bank and Trust Co.	NE	11/30/16
First Choice Bank	CA	11/30/16
First Community Bank	WI	11/30/16
First National Bank in Creston	IA	11/30/16
First National Bank of Beeville	TX	11/30/16
Firstrust Savings Bank	PA	11/30/16
Freedom Bank of Southern Missouri	MO	11/30/16
Gates Banking and Trust Co.	TN	11/30/16
Great American Bank	KS	11/30/16
Greenville National Bank	OH	11/30/16
Happy State Bank	TX	11/30/16
High Plains Bank	OK	11/30/16
Idaho Trust Bank	ID	11/30/16

Rating Upgrades

Name	State	Date of Change	Name	State	Date of Change
Integrity First Bank	WI	11/30/16	Cottonport Bank	LA	11/30/16
Inter National Bank	TX	11/30/16	Country Bank for Savings	MA	11/30/16
Landmark National Bank	KS	11/30/16	County Bank	IA	11/30/16
Legacy National Bank	AR	11/30/16	E*TRADE Bank	VA	11/30/16
Melvin Savings Bank	IA	11/30/16	ESB Financial	KS	11/30/16
MetaBank	SD	11/30/16	Farmers Bank	KY	11/30/16
National Bank of Georgia	GA	11/30/16	Farmers Bank	GA	11/30/16
National Capital Bank of Washington	DC	11/30/16	FCN Bank, N.A.	IN	11/30/16
Paragon Commercial Bank	NC	11/30/16	Fidelity Bank	IA	11/30/16
Points West Community Bank	NE	11/30/16	Fidelity Bank	LA	11/30/16
Points West Community Bank	CO	11/30/16	First Commercial Bank	MS	11/30/16
Queenstown Bank of Maryland	MD	11/30/16	First Electronic Bank	UT	11/30/16
Security Bank	NE	11/30/16	First National Bank in Port Lavaca	TX	11/30/16
Security National Bank of Enid	OK	11/30/16	First National Bank Minnesota	MN	11/30/16
Security State Bank of Aitkin	MN	11/30/16	First National Bank of Evant	TX	11/30/16
South State Bank	SC	11/30/16	First National Bank of Giddings	TX	11/30/16
Sundown State Bank	TX	11/30/16	First National Bank of Hutchinson	KS	11/30/16
Superior National Bank & Trust Co.	MI	11/30/16	First National Bank of North Arkansas	AR	11/30/16
Texas Brand Bank	TX	11/30/16	First National Bank of Picayune	MS	11/30/16
Union State Bank of Hazen	ND	11/30/16	First National Bank of Southern California	CA	11/30/16
Wake Forest Federal S&L Assn.	NC	11/30/16	First National Bank of Sparta	IL	11/30/16
WashingtonFirst Bank	VA	11/30/16	First National Bank of Suffield	CT	11/30/16
Western Bank	NM	11/30/16	First National Community Bank	GA	11/30/16
			First Security Bank	OK	11/30/16

Rating: B

Name	State	Date of Change	Name	State	Date of Change
			First State Bank of DeKalb County	AL	11/30/16
Albany Bank and Trust Co., N.A.	IL	11/30/16	FNBT Bank	FL	11/30/16
American Bank	MT	11/30/16	Golden Belt Bank, FSA	KS	11/30/16
American Savings Bank, FSB	OH	11/30/16	Grundy Bank	IL	11/30/16
Amistad Bank	TX	11/30/16	Johnson State Bank	KS	11/30/16
Bank of Bennington	NE	11/30/16	JPMorgan Chase Bank, N.A.	OH	11/30/16
Bank of Cashton	WI	11/30/16	Kitsap Bank	WA	11/30/16
Bank of Commerce	LA	11/30/16	KodaBank	ND	11/30/16
Bank of Okolona	MS	11/30/16	Lake Elmo Bank	MN	11/30/16
Bank of Orchard	NE	11/30/16	Laona State Bank	WI	11/30/16
Bank of Tampa	FL	11/30/16	Liberty Bank	IL	11/30/16
Bank of the Prairie	KS	11/30/16	Machias Savings Bank	ME	11/30/16
Bank of York	AL	11/30/16	Mercantile Bank	IL	11/30/16
BTH Bank, N.A.	TX	11/30/16	Merchants Bank	AL	11/30/16
Byron State Bank	NE	11/30/16	Midwest Independent Bank	MO	11/30/16
Capital Bank, N.A.	MD	11/30/16	Millennium Bank	IL	11/30/16
CBank	OH	11/30/16	Monroe Bank & Trust	MI	11/30/16
Central Bank of Boone County	MO	11/30/16	MyBank	NM	11/30/16
Central Bank of Kansas City	MO	11/30/16	Ottawa Savings Bank	IL	11/30/16
Citizens Bank	MO	11/30/16	Peoples Bank of Greensboro	AL	11/30/16
Citizens Bank of Clovis	NM	11/30/16	Premier Bank	NE	11/30/16
Citizens Community Bank	MO	11/30/16	RiverBend Bank	TX	11/30/16
Citizens State Bank and Trust Co.	KS	11/30/16	Saco & Biddeford Savings Institution	ME	11/30/16
Cleveland State Bank	WI	11/30/16	Salem Five Cents Savings Bank	MA	11/30/16
Coconut Grove Bank	FL	11/30/16	Savings Bank of Danbury	CT	11/30/16
Commerce Bank of Temecula Valley	CA	11/30/16	Severn Savings Bank, FSB	MD	11/30/16

Rating Upgrades

Name	State	Date of Change	Name	State	Date of Change
Shore United Bank	MD	11/30/16	F & M Bank Minnesota	MN	11/30/16
Silver Lake Bank	KS	11/30/16	Farmers & Merchants Bank	GA	11/30/16
Solutions North Bank	KS	11/30/16	Farmers & Traders Savings Bank	IA	11/30/16
Southwind Bank	KS	11/30/16	First American Bank	OK	11/30/16
State Bank & Trust	AL	11/30/16	First American Bank and Trust Co.	GA	11/30/16
State Bank of Georgia	GA	11/30/16	First Bank	MO	11/30/16
Texas Financial Bank	TX	11/30/16	First Bank	AK	11/30/16
TotalBank	FL	11/30/16	First Bank Kansas	KS	11/30/16
Town & Country Bank	NV	11/30/16	First Commons Bank, N.A.	MA	11/30/16
Transportation Alliance Bank, Inc.	UT	11/30/16	First Federal Bank Littlefield, Texas	TX	11/30/16
United Bankers' Bank	MN	11/30/16	First FSB of Twin Falls	ID	11/30/16
Universal Bank	CA	11/30/16	First General Bank	CA	11/30/16

Rating: B-

Name	State	Date of Change	Name	State	Date of Change
			First National Bank Mahnomen Twin Valley	MN	11/30/16
			First National Bank of Arenzville	IL	11/30/16
1st National Bank	OH	11/30/16	First National Bank of Eagle Lake	TX	11/30/16
Abacus Federal Savings Bank	NY	11/30/16	First National Bank of Fairfax	MN	11/30/16
BAC Community Bank	CA	11/30/16	First National Bank USA	LA	11/30/16
Bank of Bennington	VT	11/30/16	First Savings Bank	IL	11/30/16
Bank of Brookfield-Purdin, N.A.	MO	11/30/16	First Security Bank of Deer Lodge	MT	11/30/16
Bank of Estes Park	CO	11/30/16	First State Bank	TX	11/30/16
Bank of Gravett	AR	11/30/16	First State Bank of Arcadia	FL	11/30/16
Bank of Hope	CA	11/30/16	FNBC Bank and Trust	IL	11/30/16
Bank of Lake Mills	WI	11/30/16	Forward Financial Bank	WI	11/30/16
Bank of New York Mellon	NY	11/30/16	Great Nations Bank	OK	11/30/16
Bank of Perry County	TN	11/30/16	Harvard State Bank	IL	11/30/16
Bank of the West	TX	11/30/16	HomeBanc N.A.	FL	11/30/16
Bank of Wedowee	AL	11/30/16	INSOUTH Bank	TN	11/30/16
Bank of Zumbrota	MN	11/30/16	Iroquois Farmers State Bank	IL	11/30/16
Bankers' Bank of Kansas	KS	11/30/16	Ixonia Bank	WI	11/30/16
Baraboo National Bank	WI	11/30/16	Kansas State Bank	KS	11/30/16
Benchmark Bank	TX	11/30/16	Kentucky Neighborhood Bank	KY	11/30/16
BNY Mellon, N.A.	PA	11/30/16	KS Bank, Inc.	NC	11/30/16
Broadway Federal Bank, F.S.B.	CA	11/30/16	LNB Community Bank	IN	11/30/16
Burton State Bank	TX	11/30/16	Lyon County State Bank	KS	11/30/16
Central Bank	FL	11/30/16	Manson State Bank	IA	11/30/16
Centrue Bank	IL	11/30/16	Mediapolis Savings Bank	IA	11/30/16
Charlotte State Bank & Trust	FL	11/30/16	Merchants & Farmers Bank & Trust Co.	LA	11/30/16
Chesapeake Bank & Trust Co.	MD	11/30/16	Merchants Bank of Alabama	AL	11/30/16
Citizens Bank of Kentucky	KY	11/30/16	Merchants State Bank	SD	11/30/16
Citizens Bank of Rogersville	MO	11/30/16	Merit Bank	KS	11/30/16
Citizens Bank of Swainsboro	GA	11/30/16	Metropolitan Commercial Bank	NY	11/30/16
Civic Bank & Trust	TN	11/30/16	Midwest Community Bank	IL	11/30/16
Commonwealth Bank and Trust Co.	KY	11/30/16	National Bank of Petersburg	IL	11/30/16
Community Bank of Oklahoma	OK	11/30/16	Neighborhood National Bank	MN	11/30/16
Community First Bank	MO	11/30/16	NobleBank & Trust	AL	11/30/16
Community State Bank Of Southwestern Indiana	IN	11/30/16	North Georgia National Bank	GA	11/30/16
Connection Bank	IA	11/30/16	Northern State Bank of Thief River Falls	MN	11/30/16
Cooperative Bank	MA	11/30/16	Olmsted National Bank	MN	11/30/16
Cornerstone Bank	KS	11/30/16	Opportunity Bank of Montana	MT	11/30/16
Exchange Bank and Trust Co.	OK	11/30/16	Ozarks Federal S&L Assn.	MO	11/30/16

Rating Upgrades

Name	State	Date of Change	Name	State	Date of Change
Pacific National Bank	FL	11/30/16	Brunswick Bank and Trust Co.	NJ	11/30/16
Patriot Bank	FL	11/30/16	Burling Bank	IL	11/30/16
Peach State Bank & Trust	GA	11/30/16	Central Bank	IA	11/30/16
Peoples Bank of Kankakee County	IL	11/30/16	Central Savings Bank	MI	11/30/16
Pioneer Bank	NM	11/30/16	CFBank	OH	11/30/16
POINTWEST Bank	TX	11/30/16	Citizens Bank	MO	11/30/16
Profinium, Inc.	MN	11/30/16	Citizens Bank of Florida	FL	11/30/16
River Valley Community Bank	CA	11/30/16	Coastway Community Bank	RI	11/30/16
Rochelle State Bank	GA	11/30/16	Community Bank of Bergen County, NJ	NJ	11/30/16
Rochester State Bank	IL	11/30/16	Culbertson Bank	NE	11/30/16
Security Home Bank	NE	11/30/16	Dutton State Bank	MT	11/30/16
Settlers bank	WI	11/30/16	Eclipse Bank, Inc.	KY	11/30/16
Sherwood State Bank	OH	11/30/16	Essex Bank	VA	11/30/16
Southeastern Bank	GA	11/30/16	Essex Savings Bank	CT	11/30/16
State Bank	KS	11/30/16	Evans Bank, N.A.	NY	11/30/16
STC Capital Bank	IL	11/30/16	Fairview State Banking Co.	IL	11/30/16
Stockmens National Bank in Cotulla	TX	11/30/16	Farmers Bank of Willards	MD	11/30/16
Sunwest Bank	CA	11/30/16	Farmers State Bank	SD	11/30/16
Texas Hill Country Bank	TX	11/30/16	Farmers State Bank	KS	11/30/16
Tioga Franklin Savings Bank	PA	11/30/16	First Bank and Trust Co. of Illinois	IL	11/30/16
TriCentury Bank	KS	11/30/16	First Bank Richmond, N.A.	IN	11/30/16
Union Bank	TN	11/30/16	First Federal Bank, A FSB	AL	11/30/16
Unison Bank	ND	11/30/16	First Federal S&L Assn. of Pascagoula-Moss Point	MS	11/30/16
United Bank of El Paso del Norte	TX	11/30/16	First National Bank and Trust	KY	11/30/16
Victory State Bank	NY	11/30/16	First Trust and Savings Bank	IA	11/30/16
Wheatland Bank	WA	11/30/16	Fort Davis State Bank	TX	11/30/16
			Four Oaks Bank & Trust Co.	NC	11/30/16
			Fox River State Bank	WI	11/30/16

Rating: C+

Name	State	Date of Change	Name	State	Date of Change
1880 Bank	MD	11/30/16	FreedomBank	IA	11/30/16
1st Bank Yuma	AZ	11/30/16	Frontier Community Bank	VA	11/30/16
AB&T National Bank	GA	11/30/16	GBC International Bank	CA	11/30/16
Abington Bank	MA	11/30/16	Gold Coast Bank	NY	11/30/16
Albina Community Bank	OR	11/30/16	Goppert State Service Bank	KS	11/30/16
Alliance Bank Central Texas	TX	11/30/16	Gorham State Bank	KS	11/30/16
American Bank of Baxter Springs	KS	11/30/16	Grand River Bank	MI	11/30/16
American Eagle Bank	IL	11/30/16	Guardian Savings Bank, F.S.B.	OH	11/30/16
American National Bank of Beaver Dam	WI	11/30/16	Independent Bank	TN	11/30/16
American State Bank	TX	11/30/16	Industrial & Commerc. Bank of China (USA), N.A.	NY	11/30/16
Amory Federal S&L Assn.	MS	11/30/16	Integrity Bank Plus	MN	11/30/16
Andalusia Community Bank	IL	11/30/16	Ion Bank	CT	11/30/16
Banesco USA	FL	11/30/16	Iowa-Nebraska State Bank	NE	11/30/16
Bank of Evergreen	AL	11/30/16	Lake Area Bank	MN	11/30/16
Bank of Hamilton	ND	11/30/16	Malvern Federal Savings Bank	PA	11/30/16
Bank of Hazlehurst	GA	11/30/16	McIntosh County Bank	ND	11/30/16
Bank of Santa Clarita	CA	11/30/16	Miner County Bank	SD	11/30/16
Bank of Washington	WA	11/30/16	Montezuma State Bank	IA	11/30/16
Bank of Whittier, N.A.	CA	11/30/16	MUFG Union Bank, N.A.	NY	11/30/16
BankFirst Financial Services	MS	11/30/16	Mutual Federal Bank	IL	11/30/16
Bay Bank	WI	11/30/16	Necedah Bank	WI	11/30/16
Benchmark Bank	OH	11/30/16	One American Bank	SD	11/30/16

Rating Upgrades

Name	State	Date of Change	Name	State	Date of Change
Paragon Bank	TN	11/30/16	Equitable Bank	MA	11/30/16
Partnership Bank	WI	11/30/16	Farmers State Bank	TX	11/30/16
Peoples Bank of East Tennessee	TN	11/30/16	Farmers State Bank of Canton	SD	11/30/16
Peoples Savings Bank	IA	11/30/16	First American National Bank	MS	11/30/16
Pleasant Hill Bank	MO	11/30/16	First Bank of Highland Park	IL	11/30/16
Prairie Mountain Bank	MT	11/30/16	First Bank of Utica	NE	11/30/16
Riverland Bank	MN	11/30/16	First Federal S&L Assn. of Lorain	OH	11/30/16
Ruby Valley Bank	MT	11/30/16	First National Bank	MO	11/30/16
Seattle Bank	WA	11/30/16	First National Bank in Wadena	MN	11/30/16
Security Bank of Southwest Missouri	MO	11/30/16	First National Bank of Elk River	MN	11/30/16
Sound Banking Co.	NC	11/30/16	First National Bank of Sedan	KS	11/30/16
SouthCrest Bank NA	GA	11/30/16	First Oklahoma Bank	OK	11/30/16
SouthEast Bank	TN	11/30/16	First Southwest Bank	CO	11/30/16
Southport Bank	WI	11/30/16	First State Bank	OK	11/30/16
Spur Security Bank	TX	11/30/16	First State Bank of Illinois	IL	11/30/16
Stanley Bank	KS	11/30/16	First State Financial, Inc.	KY	11/30/16
State Bank of Lismore	MN	11/30/16	Freedom National Bank	RI	11/30/16
State Bank of Townsend	MT	11/30/16	Glenwood State Bank	MN	11/30/16
Texas State Bank	TX	11/30/16	Golden Eagle Community Bank	IL	11/30/16
Union Federal S&L Assn.	IL	11/30/16	Golden Pacific Bank, N.A.	CA	11/30/16
Union State Bank of Everest	KS	11/30/16	Granville National Bank	IL	11/30/16
Whitaker Bank, Inc.	KY	11/30/16	Haddon Savings Bank	NJ	11/30/16
			Hancock Bank and Trust Co.	KY	11/30/16

Rating: C

Name	State	Date of Change	Name	State	Date of Change
			Hardin County Bank	TN	11/30/16
Adams County Building and Loan Co.	OH	11/30/16	Home Federal S&L Assn. of Grand Island	NE	11/30/16
Anchor Commercial Bank	FL	11/30/16	Home Loan State Bank	CO	11/30/16
Arthur State Bank	SC	11/30/16	Home S&L Assn. of Norborne, F.A.	MO	11/30/16
Atlantic Capital Bank, N.A.	TN	11/30/16	HomeBank Texas	TX	11/30/16
Atlantic Coast Bank	FL	11/30/16	Huntingdon Valley Bank	PA	11/30/16
Banco Santander Puerto Rico	PR	11/30/16	Icon Bank of Texas, N.A.	TX	11/30/16
Bank of Greeleyville	SC	11/30/16	Kalamazoo County State Bank	MI	11/30/16
Bank of Harlan	KY	11/30/16	Kindred State Bank	ND	11/30/16
Bank of Newington	GA	11/30/16	Landmark Bank, N.A.	FL	11/30/16
Bank of Palmer	KS	11/30/16	Lee Bank	MA	11/30/16
Bank of Steinauer	NE	11/30/16	Legacy Bank	OK	11/30/16
Baybank	MI	11/30/16	Liberty Bay Bank	WA	11/30/16
BayCoast Bank	MA	11/30/16	Mackinac Savings Bank, FSB	FL	11/30/16
BCBank, Inc.	WV	11/30/16	Middletown Valley Bank	MD	11/30/16
Brush Country Bank	TX	11/30/16	Midland National Bank	KS	11/30/16
Capital Bank	AR	11/30/16	NBH Bank	CO	11/30/16
Catahoula-LaSalle Bank	LA	11/30/16	Nebraska State Bank	NE	11/30/16
Century Bank of Kentucky, Inc.	KY	11/30/16	Origin Bank	LA	11/30/16
CIBM Bank	IL	11/30/16	Park Bank	WI	11/30/16
Cincinnati Federal	OH	11/30/16	Patriot Federal Bank	NY	11/30/16
Citizens Bank	TN	11/30/16	PeopleFirst Bank	IL	11/30/16
Clay County Savings Bank	MO	11/30/16	Peoples B&T Co. of Clinton County	KY	11/30/16
Community Bank of the South	FL	11/30/16	People's B&T Co. of Pickett County	TN	11/30/16
Decatur County Bank	TN	11/30/16	Peoples Bank	MS	11/30/16
Eagle State Bank	NE	11/30/16	Plains State Bank	KS	11/30/16
Encore Bank	FL	11/30/16	Putnam Bank	CT	11/30/16

Rating Upgrades

Name	State	Date of Change
Rabobank, N.A.	CA	11/30/16
Randolph Savings Bank	MA	11/30/16
Rawlins National Bank	WY	11/30/16
Republic Bank	UT	11/30/16
RiverHills Bank	OH	11/30/16
Riverview Bank	PA	11/30/16
Rockhold, Brown & Co. Bank	OH	11/30/16
Rockland Savings Bank, FSB	ME	11/30/16
Salisbury Bank and Trust Co.	CT	11/30/16
Security State Bank	IA	11/30/16
Seneca Federal S&L Assn.	NY	11/30/16
Spring Bank	WI	11/30/16
State Bank of Florence	WI	11/30/16
State National Bank in West	TX	11/30/16
Sturgis Bank & Trust Co.	MI	11/30/16
Sugar River Bank	NH	11/30/16
Table Rock Community Bank	MO	11/30/16
Terre Haute Savings Bank	IN	11/30/16
West Pointe Bank	WI	11/30/16
Wilmington Savings Bank	OH	11/30/16

Rating: C-

Name	State	Date of Change
1st Equity Bank Northwest	IL	11/30/16
American Investors Bank and Mortgage	MN	11/30/16
Artisans' Bank	DE	11/30/16
Auburn Savings Bank, FSB	ME	11/30/16
Bank of Bird-in-Hand	PA	11/30/16
Bank of Crocker	MO	11/30/16
Bank of Wrightsville	GA	11/30/16
Beal Bank USA	NV	11/30/16
Catskill Hudson Bank	NY	11/30/16
Chappell Hill Bank	TX	11/30/16
City First Bank of D.C., N.A.	DC	11/30/16
Commercial Bank of Ozark	AL	11/30/16
Community Bank Mankato	MN	11/30/16
Empire State Bank	NY	11/30/16
First Bank and Trust of Childress	TX	11/30/16
First Bank of the Lake	MO	11/30/16
First Community Bank	IA	11/30/16
First Federal Community Bank of Bucyrus	OH	11/30/16
First Financial Bank	AL	11/30/16
First National Bank in Pratt	KS	11/30/16
First National Bank of America	MI	11/30/16
First National Bank of Lacon	IL	11/30/16
First National Bank of Trenton	TX	11/30/16
First Resource Bank	PA	11/30/16
First Security Bank and Trust Co.	OK	11/30/16
First Security Trust and Savings Bank	IL	11/30/16
FirstCity Bank of Commerce	FL	11/30/16
Floridian Community Bank, Inc.	FL	11/30/16
FMB Bank	MO	11/30/16
Heritage Bank	GA	11/30/16
Heritage Community Bank	TN	11/30/16
Jamestown State Bank	KS	11/30/16
KeySavings Bank	WI	11/30/16
Maple Bank	MN	11/30/16
Meramec Valley Bank	MO	11/30/16
Milford Building and Loan Assn., SB	IL	11/30/16
Miners State Bank	MI	11/30/16
Neighborhood National Bank	CA	11/30/16
Northpointe Bank	MI	11/30/16
One World Bank	TX	11/30/16
Park State Bank	MN	11/30/16
Plaza Bank	WA	11/30/16
Prime Security Bank	MN	11/30/16
Radius Bank	MA	11/30/16
S Bank	GA	11/30/16
Securant Bank & Trust	WI	11/30/16
Security Bank of the Ozarks	MO	11/30/16
South County Bank, N.A.	CA	11/30/16
State Bank of Burrton	KS	11/30/16
State Bank of Fairmont	MN	11/30/16
Swedish-American State Bank	KS	11/30/16
Synergy Bank, S.S.B.	TX	11/30/16
The Bankers Bank	OK	11/30/16
Thomas County Federal S&L Assn.	GA	11/30/16
Town Center Bank	IL	11/30/16
Twin City Bank	WA	11/30/16
Union State Bank	KS	11/30/16
United Southern Bank	KY	11/30/16

Rating: D+

Name	State	Date of Change
American Metro Bank	IL	11/30/16
Bank of Iberia	MO	11/30/16
Byline Bank	IL	11/30/16
Central Bank	TN	11/30/16
Citizens State Bank of Tyler, Inc.	MN	11/30/16
CoastalStates Bank	SC	11/30/16
Community State Bank	IN	11/30/16
Community State Bank of Rock Falls	IL	11/30/16
Conway Bank, N.A.	KS	11/30/16
County Bank	DE	11/30/16
Covenant Bank	PA	11/30/16
First Community Bank and Trust	IL	11/30/16
First Federal of South Carolina, FSB	SC	11/30/16
First State Bank	TX	11/30/16
Florida Capital Bank, N.A.	FL	11/30/16
Friends Bank	FL	11/30/16
Georgia Heritage Bank	GA	11/30/16
Grand Bank, N.A.	NJ	11/30/16

Rating Upgrades

Name	State	Date of Change
Heritage Bank	KS	11/30/16
Hillsboro State Bank	KS	11/30/16
Hyperion Bank	PA	11/30/16
International Finance Bank	FL	11/30/16
Laura State Bank	IL	11/30/16
Lemont National Bank	IL	11/30/16
Northern State Bank of Virginia	MN	11/30/16
OptimumBank	FL	11/30/16
Peoples Bank, Biloxi, Mississippi	MS	11/30/16
Peoples State Bank	ND	11/30/16
Prairie Community Bank	IL	11/30/16
RiverBank	WA	11/30/16
State Bank of India (California)	CA	11/30/16
Village Bank	MN	11/30/16

Rating: D

Name	State	Date of Change
Allied First Bank,sb	IL	11/30/16
Bank of Eastman	GA	11/30/16
Brainerd S&L Assn., A Federal Assn.	MN	11/30/16
Farmers and Merchants Bank	NE	11/30/16
Farmers State Bank	IL	11/30/16
First Secure Bank and Trust Co.	IL	11/30/16
First Trust & Savings Bank	IA	11/30/16
Freeport State Bank	KS	11/30/16
Home Federal Bank of Hollywood	FL	11/30/16
Home Savings Bank	WI	11/30/16
Sage Bank	MA	11/30/16
SSBBank	MI	11/30/16
State Bank of Taunton	MN	11/30/16
Talbot State Bank	GA	11/30/16
U.S. Century Bank	FL	11/30/16

Rating: D-

Name	State	Date of Change
1st Advantage Bank	MO	11/30/16
Citizens First State Bank of Walnut	IL	11/30/16
Cornerstone Bank	NJ	11/30/16
Heritage Bank	GA	11/30/16
HomeStar Bank and Financial Services	IL	11/30/16
Horry County State Bank	SC	11/30/16
Illinois-Service Federal S&L Assn.	IL	11/30/16
Old Dominion National Bank	VA	11/30/16
Waterman State Bank	IL	11/30/16

Rating: E+

Name	State	Date of Change
Commonwealth National Bank	AL	11/30/16
Corn Growers State Bank	NE	11/30/16
Persons Banking Co.	GA	11/30/16
Superior Bank	MO	11/30/16
Vermont State Bank	IL	11/30/16

Rating: E

Name	State	Date of Change
Citizens Commerce National Bank	KY	11/30/16
Commercial State Bank	NE	11/30/16
State Bank of Hamburg	MN	11/30/16

Rating Downgrades

Name	State	Date of Change

Rating: A-

Name	State	Date of Change
American Bank & Trust	SD	11/30/16
Dakota Western Bank	ND	11/30/16
Nordstrom FSB	AZ	11/30/16

Rating: B+

Name	State	Date of Change
Austin Bank, Texas N.A.	TX	11/30/16
Bank of the West	OK	11/30/16
BTC Bank	MO	11/30/16
Ciera Bank	TX	11/30/16
Citizens Bank	AL	11/30/16
Citizens State Bank	OK	11/30/16
City National B&T Co. of Lawton, Oklahoma	OK	11/30/16
City Savings Bank & Trust Co.	LA	11/30/16
Clare Bank, N.A.	WI	11/30/16
Farmers and Merchants State Bank	ND	11/30/16
Farmers Savings Bank	IA	11/30/16
First Mid-Illinois Bank & Trust, N.A.	IL	11/30/16
First National Bank & Trust of Elk City	OK	11/30/16
First National Bank of Milaca	MN	11/30/16
Highlands Community Bank	VA	11/30/16
Hodge Bank & Trust Co.	LA	11/30/16
Horizon Bank, SSB	TX	11/30/16
Jersey State Bank	IL	11/30/16
Lapeer County Bank & Trust Co.	MI	11/30/16
Main Bank	NM	11/30/16
Royal Savings Bank	IL	11/30/16
State Bank of Kansas	KS	11/30/16
Teche Bank & Trust Co.	LA	11/30/16
United Bank of Iowa	IA	11/30/16
Wilmington Savings Fund Society, FSB	DE	11/30/16

Rating: B

Name	State	Date of Change
Americas United Bank	CA	11/30/16
Bank of Prescott	AR	11/30/16
Brookline Bank	MA	11/30/16
Coleman County State Bank	TX	11/30/16
Community Bank	IL	11/30/16
CUSB Bank	IA	11/30/16
Exchange Bank of Missouri	MO	11/30/16
Farmers and Merchants Bank	MD	11/30/16
First Community Bank	TX	11/30/16
First Community Bank of the Heartland, Inc.	KY	11/30/16
First Farmers & Merchants National Bank	MN	11/30/16
First Foundation Bank	CA	11/30/16
First International Bank & Trust	ND	11/30/16
First National Bank of Waseca	MN	11/30/16
Franklin Bank & Trust Co.	KY	11/30/16
Herring Bank	TX	11/30/16

Name	State	Date of Change
Home Bank, N.A.	LA	11/30/16
Impact Bank	KS	11/30/16
Incommons Bank, N.A.	TX	11/30/16
KeyBank N.A.	OH	11/30/16
Level One Bank	MI	11/30/16
Logan State Bank	IA	11/30/16
Midstates Bank, N.A.	IA	11/30/16
MRV Banks	MO	11/30/16
Oak Creek Valley Bank	NE	11/30/16
Peoples Bank	TX	11/30/16
Peoples Bank & Trust	IL	11/30/16
Peoples State Bank of Wells	MN	11/30/16
Peoples Trust & Savings Bank	IN	11/30/16
PeoplesSouth Bank	GA	11/30/16
Premier Bank	IA	11/30/16
Savings Bank	IA	11/30/16
Schertz Bank & Trust	TX	11/30/16
Sentry Bank	MN	11/30/16
Southern Missouri Bank of Marshfield	MO	11/30/16
Success Bank	IA	11/30/16
United Pacific Bank	CA	11/30/16

Rating: B-

Name	State	Date of Change
Affiliated Bank	TX	11/30/16
American Bank & Trust Wisconsin	WI	11/30/16
American Exchange Bank	OK	11/30/16
American State Bank	IA	11/30/16
American Trust and Savings Bank	IA	11/30/16
America's Community Bank	MO	11/30/16
Astra Bank	KS	11/30/16
Bank of Beaver City	OK	11/30/16
Bank of Commerce and Trust Co.	KS	11/30/16
Commencement Bank	WA	11/30/16
Community Bank of Mississippi	MS	11/30/16
Cornerstone Bank	NE	11/30/16
Farmers and Merchants Bank	SC	11/30/16
Farmers Bank and Trust Co.	AR	11/30/16
Field & Main Bank	KY	11/30/16
First Federal Community Bank, SSB	TX	11/30/16
First Financial Bank	ND	11/30/16
First Liberty National Bank	TX	11/30/16
First National Bank in Carlyle	IL	11/30/16
First National Bank of Winnsboro	TX	11/30/16
First State Bank of Middlebury	IN	11/30/16
First United Bank	ND	11/30/16
Foresight Bank	MN	11/30/16
Grant County Bank	KS	11/30/16
HOMEBANK	MO	11/30/16
Marquis Bank	FL	11/30/16
Mission National Bank	CA	11/30/16

Rating Downgrades

Name	State	Date of Change
Northwest Bank	PA	11/30/16
Pony Express Bank	MO	11/30/16
Rock Canyon Bank	UT	11/30/16
State Bank	IL	11/30/16
TBK Bank, SSB	TX	11/30/16
Trans Pacific National Bank	CA	11/30/16
Viking Savings Bank	MN	11/30/16
Westbound Bank	TX	11/30/16
WoodTrust Bank	WI	11/30/16

Rating: C+

Name	State	Date of Change
American Commerce Bank, N.A.	GA	11/30/16
Bank of Abbeville & Trust Co.	LA	11/30/16
Bank of Baker	MT	11/30/16
Bank of Little Rock	AR	11/30/16
Banner Capital Bank	NE	11/30/16
Border State Bank	MN	11/30/16
Corner Stone Bank	MO	11/30/16
First County Bank	IL	11/30/16
First State Bank Minnesota	MN	11/30/16
IBERIABANK	LA	11/30/16
Independence Bank	RI	11/30/16
Lone Star State Bank of West Texas	TX	11/30/16
Mizuho Bank (USA)	NY	11/30/16
Plains State Bank	TX	11/30/16
Platinum Bank	MN	11/30/16
Portage County Bank	WI	11/30/16
Riverview Community Bank	WA	11/30/16
Rondout Savings Bank	NY	11/30/16
State Bank Northwest	WA	11/30/16
State Bank of Chilton	WI	11/30/16
State Bank of Speer	IL	11/30/16
Two Rivers Bank & Trust	IA	11/30/16
Unity Bank	WI	11/30/16

Rating: C

Name	State	Date of Change
BancCentral, N.A.	OK	11/30/16
Banco Do Brasil Americas	FL	11/30/16
Bank of Kremlin	OK	11/30/16
Bay Bank, FSB	MD	11/30/16
Beardstown Savings s.b.	IL	11/30/16
Citizens Bank	IA	11/30/16
Community State Bank	IL	11/30/16
Congressional Bank	MD	11/30/16
First Federal Bank of Wisconsin	WI	11/30/16
First Federal of Northern Michigan	MI	11/30/16
First State Bank of Purdy	MO	11/30/16
Frost State Bank	MN	11/30/16
Georgetown Bank	MA	11/30/16
Global Bank	NY	11/30/16
Granite Bank	NH	11/30/16
Guaranty Bank	MO	11/30/16
Hamlin National Bank	TX	11/30/16
Henry State Bank	IL	11/30/16
InterBank	OK	11/30/16
Iowa State Bank	IA	11/30/16
Lakeside National Bank	TX	11/30/16
Macon-Atlanta State Bank	MO	11/30/16
Midwest Regional Bank	MO	11/30/16
New Frontier Bank	MO	11/30/16
Patriot Bank, N.A.	CT	11/30/16
Sibley State Bank	IA	11/30/16
Sunset Bank & Savings	WI	11/30/16
Sweet Water State Bank	AL	11/30/16
Terrabank, N.A.	FL	11/30/16
United Community Bank	LA	11/30/16
Washington State Bank	IL	11/30/16
Welcome State Bank	MN	11/30/16
Woodsville Guaranty Savings Bank	NH	11/30/16

Rating: C-

Name	State	Date of Change
Bank of Nebraska	NE	11/30/16
Bank of Oak Ridge	LA	11/30/16
Basile State Bank	LA	11/30/16
CFG Community Bank	MD	11/30/16
Citizens State Bank	FL	11/30/16
Community National Bank	TX	11/30/16
Community State Bank	AR	11/30/16
Currie State Bank	MN	11/30/16
Farmers State Bank, Allen, Oklahoma	OK	11/30/16
First Commercial Bank	MO	11/30/16
First State Bank	OK	11/30/16
Franklin State Bank & Trust Co.	LA	11/30/16
Gateway Bank	AR	11/30/16
Generations Bank	NY	11/30/16
Home National Bank	OH	11/30/16
Iowa Prairie Bank	IA	11/30/16
Metropolitan Capital Bank & Trust	IL	11/30/16
MinnStar Bank N.A.	MN	11/30/16
Nationwide Bank	OH	11/30/16
Peoples Bank	MD	11/30/16
Prime Alliance Bank	UT	11/30/16
Progressive-Home Federal S&L Assn.	PA	11/30/16
Queensborough National Bank & Trust Co.	GA	11/30/16
Scottdale Bank & Trust Co.	PA	11/30/16
Second Federal S&L Assn. of Philadelphia	PA	11/30/16
Security State Bank	KS	11/30/16
Security State Bank of Warroad	MN	11/30/16
Today's Bank	AR	11/30/16
Trust Bank	GA	11/30/16

Rating Downgrades

Name	State	Date of Change	Name	State	Date of Change
Valley Exchange Bank	SD	11/30/16	State Bank of Marietta	MN	11/30/16
Western Heritage Bank	NM	11/30/16	State National Bank of Groom	TX	11/30/16
YNB	OK	11/30/16	State Savings Bank	IA	11/30/16
			West Texas State Bank	TX	11/30/16

Rating: D+

Name	State	Date of Change
Bank of Akron	NY	11/30/16
Bank of Commerce	OK	11/30/16
Bank of Kaukauna	WI	11/30/16
Chelten Hills Savings Bank	PA	11/30/16
Citizens Bank & Trust Co.	MS	11/30/16
Citizens State Bank of Ouray	CO	11/30/16
Clay City Banking Co.	IL	11/30/16
Community First Bank	NE	11/30/16
Equitable S&L Co.	OH	11/30/16
Farmers & Merchants Bank	ND	11/30/16
First Bank, Upper Michigan	MI	11/30/16
First Citrus Bank	FL	11/30/16
First State Bank	TX	11/30/16
Flagship Bank Minnesota	MN	11/30/16
Great Plains State Bank	NE	11/30/16
Landmark Bank	LA	11/30/16
Lincoln 1st Bank	NJ	11/30/16
Louisa Community Bank	KY	11/30/16
Merchants Bank of California, N.A.	CA	11/30/16
Northern Hancock Bank & Trust Co.	WV	11/30/16
Plus International Bank	FL	11/30/16
Seamen's Bank	MA	11/30/16
State Bank of Cross Plains	WI	11/30/16
State Bank of Eagle Butte	SD	11/30/16
UNB Bank	PA	11/30/16
Versailles S&L Co.	OH	11/30/16
West Texas State Bank	TX	11/30/16

Rating: D

Name	State	Date of Change
Alma Bank	NY	11/30/16
American Bank and Trust Co., N.A.	IA	11/30/16
Bank of Pine Hill	AL	11/30/16
Bluegrass Community Bank	KY	11/30/16
Citizens State Bank of Hayfield	MN	11/30/16
Farmers and Merchants State Bank	MN	11/30/16
First Bank of Pike	GA	11/30/16
First National Bank of Hope	KS	11/30/16
Home Savings Bank, FSB	KY	11/30/16
Independence State Bank	WI	11/30/16
Lake Bank	MN	11/30/16
Mechanics and Farmers Bank	NC	11/30/16
Medallion Bank	UT	11/30/16
RCSBank	MO	11/30/16
Southern Bank Co.	AL	11/30/16
State Bank of Colon	NE	11/30/16

Rating: D-

Name	State	Date of Change
AllNations Bank	OK	11/30/16
Audubon Savings Bank	NJ	11/30/16
Bank of Fincastle	VA	11/30/16
Bank of Glen Ullin	ND	11/30/16
Business Bank of Texas, N.A.	TX	11/30/16
Chesterfield State Bank	IL	11/30/16
Citizens State Bank	TX	11/30/16
F&M Bank and Trust Co.	MO	11/30/16
Fidelity Bank of Florida, N.A.	FL	11/30/16
Merchants Commercial Bank	VI	11/30/16
Odin State Bank	MN	11/30/16
Pacific Mercantile Bank	CA	11/30/16
Peoples Bank & Trust Co. of Hazard	KY	11/30/16
Ripley Federal Savings Bank	OH	11/30/16
Signature Bank of Georgia	GA	11/30/16
State Bank of Burnettsville	IN	11/30/16
Stockmans Bank	OK	11/30/16
Turtle Mountain State Bank	ND	11/30/16

Rating: E+

Name	State	Date of Change
First NBC Bank	LA	11/30/16

Rating: E

Name	State	Date of Change
First State Bank of Rosemount	MN	11/30/16

Rating: E-

Name	State	Date of Change
Columbia S&L Assn.	WI	11/30/16
Equitable Bank, S.S.B.	WI	11/30/16
First Chatham Bank	GA	11/30/16
High Desert Bank	OR	11/30/16
Peoples Bank	GA	11/30/16

Appendix

RECENT BANK FAILURES
2016

Institution	Headquarters	Date of Failure	At Date of Failure	
			Total Assets ($Mil)	Safety Rating
Allied Bank	Mulberry, AR	09/23/16	66.3	E- (Very Weak)
Woodbury Banking Company	Woodbury, GA	08/19/16	22.5	E- (Very Weak)
First Cornerstone Bank	King of Prussia, PA	05/06/16	107.0	E- (Very Weak)
Trust Co Bank	Memphis, TN	04/29/16	20.7	E- (Very Weak)
North Milwaukee State Bank	Milwaukee, WI	03/11/16	67.1	E- (Very Weak)

2015

Institution	Headquarters	Date of Failure	At Date of Failure	
			Total Assets ($Mil)	Safety Rating
Bramble Savings Bank	Milford, OH	12/17/15	47.5	E- (Very Weak)
Bank of Georgia	Peachtree City, GA	10/02/15	294.2	E- (Very Weak)
Hometown National Bank	Longview, WA	10/02/15	4.9	E+ (Very Weak)
Premier Bank	Denever, CO	07/10/15	31.7	E- (Very Weak)
Edgebrook Bank	Chicago, IL	05/08/15	90.0	E- (Very Weak)
Doral Bank	San Juan, PR	02/27/15	5,900.0	E+ (Very Weak)
Capitol City Bank & Trust Co	Atlanta, GA	02/13/15	272.3	E- (Very Weak)
Highland Community Bank	Chicago, IL	01/23/15	54.7	E- (Very Weak)
First National Bank of Crestview	Crestview, FL	01/16/15	79.7	E- (Very Weak)

2014

Institution	Headquarters	Date of Failure	At Date of Failure Total Assets ($Mil)	Safety Rating
Northern Star Bank	Makato, MN	12/19/14	18.8	E- (Very Weak)
Frontier Bank, FSB	Palm Desert, CA	11/07/14	86.4	E- (Very Weak)
National Republic Bk of Chicago	Chicago, IL	10/24/14	954.4	E- (Very Weak)
NBRS Financial	Rising Sun, MD	10/17/14	188.2	E- (Very Weak)
Greenchoice Bank FSB	Chicago, IL	07/25/14	72.9	E- (Very Weak)
Eastside Commercial Bank	Conyers, GA	07/18/14	169.0	E- (Very Weak)
Freedom State Bank	Freedom, OK	06/27/14	22.8	D (Weak)
Valley Bank	Moline, IL	06/20/14	456.4	E+ (Very Weak)
Valley Bank	Fort Lauderdale, FL	06/20/14	81.8	E- (Very Weak)
Slavie Federal Savings Bank	Bel Air, MD	05/30/14	140.1	E- (Very Weak)
Columbia Savings Bank	Cincinnati, OH	05/23/14	36.5	E- (Very Weak)
AztecAmerica Bank	Berwyn, IL	05/16/14	66.3	E- (Very Weak)
Allendale County Bank	Fairfax, SC	04/25/14	54.5	E- (Very Weak)
Millennium Bank NA	Sterling, VA	02/28/14	130.3	E- (Very Weak)
Vantage Point Bank	Horsham, PA	02/28/14	63.5	E- (Very Weak)
Syringa Bank	Boise, ID	01/31/14	153.4	E- (Very Weak)
Bank of Union	El Reno, OK	01/24/14	331.4	D- (Weak)
DuPage National Bank	West Chicago, IL	01/17/14	61.7	E- (Very Weak)

2013

Institution	Headquarters	Date of Failure	At Date of Failure	
			Total Assets ($Mil)	Safety Rating
Texas Community Bank	The Woodlands, TX	12/13/13	160.1	E- (Very Weak)
Bank of Jackson County	Graceville, FL	10/30/13	25.5	E- (Very Weak)
Communitys Bank	Bridgeport, CT	09/13/13	26.3	E- (Very Weak)
First National Bank	Edinburg, TX	09/13/13	3100.0	E- (Very Weak)
Community South Bank	Parsons, TN	08/24/13	386.9	E- (Very Weak)
Sunrise Bank of Arizona	Phoenix, AZ	08/24/13	202.2	E- (Very Weak)
Bank of Wausau	Wausau, WI	08/09/13	43.6	E- (Very Weak)
First Community Bank of SW FL	Fort Meyers, FL	08/02/13	265.7	E- (Very Weak)
Mountain National Bank	Sevierville, TN	06/07/13	437.3	E- (Very Weak)
1st Commerce Bank	N. Las Vegas, NV	06/06/13	20.2	E- (Very Weak)
Banks of Wisconsin	Kenosha, WI	05/31/13	134.0	E- (Very Weak)
Central Arizona Bank	Scottsdale, AZ	05/14/13	31.6	E- (Very Weak)
Pisgah Community Bank	Asheville, NC	05/10/13	21.9	E- (Very Weak)
Sunrise Bank	Valdosta, GA	05/10/13	60.8	E- (Very Weak)
Douglas County Bank	Douglasville, GA	04/26/13	316.5	E- (Very Weak)
Parkway Bank	Lenoir, NC	04/26/13	108.6	E- (Very Weak)
Chipola Community Bank	Marianna, FL	04/19/13	39.2	E- (Very Weak)
First Federal Bank	Lexington, KY	04/19/13	100.1	E- (Very Weak)
Heritage Bank of North Florida	Orange Park, FL	04/19/13	110.9	E- (Very Weak)
Gold Canyon Bank	Gold Canyon, AZ	04/05/13	44.2	E- (Very Weak)
Frontier Bank	LaGrange, GA	03/08//13	258.8	E- (Very Weak)
Covenant Bank	Chicago, IL	02/15/13	58.4	E- (Very Weak)
1st Regents Bank	Andover, MN	01/18/13	50.2	E- (Very Weak)
Westside Community Bank	University Place, WA	01/11/13	97.7	E- (Very Weak)

2012

Institution	Headquarters	Date of Failure	At Date of Failure	
			Total Assets ($Mil)	Safety Rating
Community Bank of the Ozarks	Sunrise Beach, MO	12/14/12	42.8	E- (Very Weak)
Hometown Community Bank	Braselton, GA	11/16/12	124.6	E- (Very Weak)
Citizens First National Bank	Princeton, IL	11/02/12	924.0	E- (Very Weak)
Heritage Bank of Florida	Lutz, FL	11/02/12	225.5	E- (Very Weak)
NOVA Bank	Berwyn, PA	10/26/12	483.0	E- (Very Weak)
Excel Bank	Sedalia, MO	10/19/12	200.6	E- (Very Weak)
First East Side Savings Bank	Tamarac, FL	10/19/12	67.2	E- (Very Weak)
Gulfsouth Private Bank	Destin, FL	10/19/12	159.1	E- (Very Weak)
First United Bank	Crete, IL	09/28/12	328.4	E- (Very Weak)
Truman Bank	St Louis, MO	09/14/12	282.3	E- (Very Weak)
First Commercial Bank	Bloomington, MN	09/07/12	215.9	E- (Very Weak)
Waukegan Savings Bank	Waukegan, IL	08/03/12	88.9	E- (Very Weak)
Jasper Banking Co	Jasper, GA	07/27/12	216.7	E- (Very Weak)
First Cherokee State Bank	Woodstock, GA	07/20/12	222.7	E- (Very Weak)
Georgia Trust Bank	Buford, GA	07/20/12	119.8	E- (Very Weak)
Heartland Bank	Leawood, KS	07/20/12	110.0	E- (Very Weak)
Royal Palm Bank of Florida	Naples, FL	07/20/12	87.0	E- (Very Weak)
Second Federal Savings & Loan Assn of Chicago	Chicago, IL	07/20/12	199.1	E- (Very Weak)
Glasgow Savings Bank	Glasgow, MO	07/13/12	24.8	E- (Very Weak)
Montgomery Bank & Trust	Ailey, GA	07/06/12	173.6	E- (Very Weak)
Farmers Bank of Lynchburg	Lynchburg, TN	06/15/12	163.9	E- (Very Weak)
Putnam State Bank	Palatka, FL	06/15/12	169.5	E- (Very Weak)
Security Exchange Bank	Marietta, GA	06/15/12	151.0	E- (Very Weak)
Carolina Federal Savings Bank	Charleston, SC	06/08/12	54.4	E- (Very Weak)
Farmers & Traders State Bank	Shabbana, IL	06/08/12	43.1	E- (Very Weak)
First Capital Bank	Kingfisher, OK	06/08/12	46.1	E- (Very Weak)
Waccamaw Bank	Whiteville, NC	06/08/12	533.1	E- (Very Weak)

Alabama Trust Bank, NA	Sylcauga, AL	05/18/12	51.5	E- (Very Weak)
Security Bank NA	North Lauderdale, FL	05/04/12	101.0	E- (Very Weak)
Bank of the Eastern Shore	Cambridge, MD	04/27/12	166.7	E- (Very Weak)
HarVest Bank of Maryland	Gaithersburg,MD	04/27/12	164.3	E- (Very Weak)
InterSavings Bank FSB	Maple Grove, MN	04/27/12	481.6	E- (Very Weak)
Palm Desert National Bank	Palm Desert, CA	04/27/12	125.8	E- (Very Weak)
Plantation Federal Bank	Pawleys Island, SC	04/27/12	486.4	E- (Very Weak)
Fort Lee Federal Savings Bank FSB	Fort Lee, NJ	04/20/12	51.9	E- (Very Weak)
Fidelity Bank	Dearborn, MI	03/30/12	747.6	E- (Very Weak)
Covenant Bank & Trust	Rock Springs, GA	03/23/12	95.7	E- (Very Weak)
Premier Bank	Wilmette, IL	03/23/12	268.7	E- (Very Weak)
New City Bank	Chicago, IL	03/09/12	71.2	E- (Very Weak)
Global Commerce Bank	Doraville, GA	03/02/12	143.7	E- (Very Weak)
Central Bank of Georgia	Ellaville, GA	02/24/12	278.9	E- (Very Weak)
Home Savings of America	Little Falls, MN	02/24/12	434.1	E- (Very Weak)
Charter National Bank & Trust	Hoffman Estates, IL	02/10/12	93.9	E- (Very Weak)
SCB Bank	Shellbyville, IN	02/10/12	182.6	E- (Very Weak)
BankEast	Knoxville, TN	01/27/12	272.6	E- (Very Weak)
First Guaranty Bank & Trust of Jacksonville	Jacksonville, FL	01/27/12	377.9	E- (Very Weak)
Patriot Bank Minnesota	Forest Lake, MN	01/27/12	111.3	E- (Very Weak)
Tennessee Commerce Bank	Franklin, TN	01/27/12	1185.0	E- (Very Weak)
American Eagle Savings Bank	Boothwyn, PA	01/20/12	19.6	E- (Very Weak)
Central Florida State Bank	Belleview, FL	01/20/12	79.1	E- (Very Weak)
First State Bank, The	Stockbridge, GA	01/20/12	536.9	E- (Very Weak)

2011

Institution	Headquarters	Date of Failure	At Date of Failure	
			Total Assets ($Mil)	Safety Rating
Central Progressive Bank	Lacombe, LA	11/18/11	383.1	E- (Very Weak)
Polk County Bank	Johnston, LA	11/18/11	91.6	E- (Very Weak)
Community Bank of Rockmart	Rockmart, GA	11/10/11	62.4	E- (Very Weak)
Mid City Bank Inc	Omaha, NE	11/04/11	106.1	E- (Very Weak)
SunFirst Bank	St. George, UT	11/04/11	198.1	E- (Very Weak)
All American Bank	Des Plaines, IL	10/28/11	37.8	E- (Very Weak)
Community Banks of Colorado	Greenwood, CO	10/21/11	13800.0	E- (Very Weak)
Community Capital Bank	Jonesboro, GA	10/21/11	181.2	E- (Very Weak)
Decatur First Bank	Decatur, GA	10/21/11	191.5	E- (Very Weak)
Old Harbor Bank	Clearwater, FL	10/21/11	215.9	E- (Very Weak)
Blue Ridge Savings Bank	Asheville, NC	10/14/11	161.0	E- (Very Weak)
County Bank	Aledo, IL	10/14/11	190.6	E- (Very Weak)
First State Bank	Cranford, NJ	10/14/11	204.4	E- (Very Weak)
Piedmont Community Bank	Gray, GA	10/14/11	201.7	E- (Very Weak)
RiverBank	Wyoming, MN	10/07/11	417.4	E- (Very Weak)
Sun Security Bank	Ellington, MO	10/07/11	355.9	E- (Very Weak)
First International Bank	Plano, TX	09/30/11	239.9	E- (Very Weak)
Bank of the Commonwealth	Norfolk, VA	09/23/11	985.1	E- (Very Weak)
Citizens Bank of Northern California	Nevada City, CA	09/23/11	288.8	E- (Very Weak)
First National Bank of Florida	Milton, FL	09/09/11	296.8	E- (Very Weak)
CreekSide Bank	Woodstock, GA	09/02/11	102.3	E- (Very Weak)
Patriot Bank of Georgia	Cumming, GA	09/02/11	150.8	E- (Very Weak)
First Choice Bank	Geneva, IL	08/19/11	141.0	E- (Very Weak)
First Southern National Bank	Statesboro, GA	08/19/11	164.6	E- (Very Weak)
Lydian Private Bank	Palm Beach, FL	08/19/11	1700.0	E- (Very Weak)
Public Savings Bank	Huntingdon Valley, PA	08/18/11	46.8	E- (Very Weak)
First National Bank of Olathe	Olathe, KS	08/12/11	538.1	E- (Very Weak)
Bank of Shorewood	Shorwood, IL	08/05/11	110.7	E- (Very Weak)

Bank of Whitman	Colfax, WA	08/05/11	548.6	E- (Very Weak)
BankMeridian NA	Columbia, SC	07/29/11	239.8	E- (Very Weak)
Integra Bank NA	Evansville, IN	07/29/11	2200.0	E- (Very Weak)
Virginia Business Bank	Richmond, VA	07/29/11	95.8	E- (Very Weak)
Bank of Choice	Greeley, CO	07/22/11	10700.0	E- (Very Weak)
Landmark Bank of Florida	Sarasota, FL	07/22/11	275.0	E- (Very Weak)
Southshore Community Bank	Apollo, FL	07/22/11	46.3	E- (Very Weak)
First Peoples Bank	Port St. Lucie, FL	07/15/11	228.3	E- (Very Weak)
High Trust Bank	Stockbridge, GA	07/15/11	192.5	E- (Very Weak)
One Georgia Bank	Atlanta, GA	07/15/11	186.3	E- (Very Weak)
Summit Bank	Prescott, AZ	07/15/11	72.0	E- (Very Weak)
Colorado Capital Bank	Castle Rock, CO	07/08/11	717.5	E- (Very Weak)
First Chicago Bank & Trust	Chicago, IL	07/08/11	959.3	E- (Very Weak)
Signature Bank	Windsor, CO	07/08/11	66.7	E- (Very Weak)
Mountain Heritage Bank	Clayton, GA	06/24/11	103.7	E- (Very Weak)
First Comm. Bank of Tampa Bay	Tampa, FL	06/17/11	98.6	E- (Very Weak)
McIntosh State Bank	Jackson, GA	06/17/11	339.9	E- (Very Weak)
Atlantic Bank & Trust	Charleston, SC	06/03/11	208.2	E- (Very Weak)
First Heritage Bank	Snohomish, WA	05/27/11	173.5	E- (Very Weak)
Atlantic Southern Bank	Macon, GA	05/20/11	741.9	E- (Very Weak)
First Heritage Bank	Snohomish, WA	05/27/11	173.5	E- (Very Weak)
Atlantic Southern Bank	Macon, GA	05/20/11	741.9	E- (Very Weak)
First Georgia Banking Company	Franklin, GA	05/20/11	731.0	E- (Very Weak)
Summit Bank	Burlington, WA	05/20/11	142.7	E- (Very Weak)
Coastal Bank	Cocoa Beach, FL	05/06/11	129.4	E- (Very Weak)
Community Central Bank	Mount Clemens, MI	04/29/11	476.3	E- (Very Weak)
Cortez Community Bank	Brooksville, FL	04/29/11	70.9	E- (Very Weak)
First Choice Community Bank	Dallas, GA	04/29/11	308.5	E- (Very Weak)

First Nat. Bank of Central Florida	Winter Park, FL	04/29/11	352.0	E- (Very Weak)
Park Avenue Bank	Valdosta, GA	04/29/11	827.7	E- (Very Weak)
Bartow Conty Bank	Cartersville, GA	04/15/11	330.2	E- (Very Weak)
Heritage Banking Group	Cartahge, MS	04/15/11	224.0	E- (Very Weak)
New Horizons Bank	East Ellijay, GA	04/15/11	110.7	E- (Very Weak)
Nexity Bank	Birmingham, AL	04/15/11	793.7	E- (Very Weak)
Rosemount National Bank	Rosemount, MN	04/15/11	37.6	E- (Very Weak)
Superior Bank	Birmingham, AL	04/15/11	3000.0	E- (Very Weak)
Nevada Commerce Bank	Las Vegas, NV	04/08/11	144.9	E- (Very Weak)
WesternSprings Nat. Bank&Trust	Western Springs, IL	04/08/11	181.9	E- (Very Weak)
Bank of Commerce	Wood Dale, IL	03/25/11	163.1	E- (Very Weak)
First National Bank of Davis	Davis, OK	03/11/11	90.2	C (Fair)
Legacy Bank	Milwaukee, WI	03/11/11	190.4	E -(Very Weak)
Valley Community Bank	St. Charles, IL	02/25/11	123.8	E- (Very Weak)
Charter Oak Bank	Napa, CA	02/18/11	120.8	E- (Very Weak)
Citizens Bank of Effingham	Springfield, GA	02/18/11	214.3	E- (Very Weak)
Habersham Bank	Clarkesville, GA	02/18/11	387.6	E- (Very Weak)
San Luis Trust Bank FSB	San Luis Obispo, CA	02/18/11	332.6	E- (Very Weak)
Badger State Bank	Cassville, WI	02/11/11	83.8	E- (Very Weak)
Canyon National Bank	Palm Springs, CA	02/11/11	210.9	E- (Very Weak)
Peoples State Bank	Hamtramck, MI	02/11/11	390.5	E- (Very Weak)
Sunshine State Community Bank	Port Orange, FL	02/11/11	125.5	E- (Very Weak)
American Trust Bank	Roswell, GA	02/04/11	238.2	E- (Very Weak)
Community First Bank	Chicago, IL	02/04/11	51.1	E- (Very Weak)
North Georgia Bank	Watkinsville, GA	02/04/11	153.2	E- (Very Weak)
Evergreen State Bank	Stoughton, WI	01/28/11	246.5	E- (Very Weak)
First Community Bank	Taos, NM	01/28/11	2310.0	E- (Very Weak)
First State Bank	Camargo, OK	01/28/11	43.5	C- (Fair)

FirsTier Bank	Broomfield, CO	01/28/11	781.5	E- (Very Weak)
Bank of Asheville	Asheville, NC	01/21/11	195.1	E- (Very Weak)
CommunitySouth Bank & Trust	Easley, SC	01/21/11	440.6	E- (Very Weak)
Enterprise Banking Co	McDonough, GA	01/21/11	100.9	E- (Very Weak)
United Western bank	Denver, CO	01/21/11	1650.0	E- (Very Weak)
Oglethorpe Bank	Brunswick, GA	01/14/11	230.6	E- (Very Weak)
First Commercial Bank of Fl.	Orlando, FL	01/07/11	598.5	E- (Very Weak)
Legacy Bank	Scottsdale, AZ	01/07/11	150.6	E- (Very Weak)

How Do Banks and Credit Unions Differ?

Since credit unions first appeared in 1946, they have been touted as a low-cost, friendly alternative to banks. But with tightening margins, pressure to compete in technology, branch closures, and the introduction of a host of service fees — some even higher than those charged by banks — the distinction between banks and credit unions has been gradually narrowing. Following are the key differences between today's banks and credit unions.

	Banks	**Credit Unions**
Access	Practically anyone is free to open an account or request a loan from any bank. There are no membership requirements.	Credit unions are set up to serve the needs of a specific group who share a "common bond." In order to open an account or request a loan, you must demonstrate that you meet the credit union's common bond requirements.
Ownership	Banks are owned by one or more investors who determine the bank's policies and procedures. A bank's customers do not have direct input into how the bank is operated.	Although they may be sponsored by a corporation or other entity, credit unions are owned by their members through their funds on deposit. Therefore, each depositor has a voice in how the credit union is operated.
Dividends and Fees	Banks are for-profit organizations where the profits are used to pay dividends to the bank's investors or are reinvested in an effort to increase the bank's value to investors. In an effort to generate more profits, bank services and fees are typically more costly.	Credit unions are not-for-profit organizations. Any profits generated are returned to the credit union's members in the form of higher interest rates on deposits, lower loan rates, and free or low-cost services.
Management and Staffing	A bank's management and other staff are employees of the bank, hired directly or indirectly by its investors.	Credit unions are frequently run using elected members, volunteer staff, and staff provided by the credit union's sponsor. This helps to hold down costs.
Insurance	Banks are insured by the Federal Deposit Insurance Corporation, an agency of the federal government.	Credit unions are insured by the National Credit Union Share Insurance Fund, which is managed by the National Credit Union Administration, an agency of the federal government.

Glossary

This glossary contains the most important terms used in this publication.

ARM	Adjustable-Rate Mortgage. This is a loan whose interest rate is tied to an index and is adjusted at a predetermined frequency. An ARM is subject to credit risk if interest rates rise and the borrower is unable to make the mortgage payment.
Average Recession	A recession involving a decline in real GDP that is approximately equivalent to the average of the postwar recessions of 1957-58, 1960, 1970, 1974-75, 1980 and 1981-82. It is assumed, however, that in today's market, the financial losses suffered from a recession of that magnitude would be greater than those experienced in previous decades. (See also "Severe Recession.")
Bank Holding Company	A company that holds stock in one or more banks and possibly other companies.
Bank Insurance Fund (BIF)	A unit of Federal Deposit Insurance Corporation (FDIC) that provided deposit insurance for banks, other than thrifts. BIF was formed as part of the 1989 savings and loan association bailout bill to keep separate the administration of the bank and thrift insurance programs. There were thus two distinct insurance entities under the FDIC: BIF and savings association insurance fund (SAIF). (See also Federal Deposit Insurance Corporation.")
Brokered Deposits	Deposits that are brought into an institution through a broker. They are relatively costly, volatile funds that are more readily withdrawn from the institution if there is a loss of confidence or intense interest rate competition. Reliance on brokered deposits is usually a sign that the institution is having difficulty attracting deposits from its local geographic markets and could be a warning signal if other institutions in the same areas are not experiencing similar difficulties.
Capital	The cushion an institution has of its own resources to help withstand losses. The basic component of capital is stockholder's equity which consists of common and preferred stock and retained earnings. (See also "Core Capital")
Cash & Equivalents	Cash plus highly liquid assets which can be readily converted to cash.
Core (Tier 1) Capital	A measurement of capital defined by the federal regulatory agencies for evaluating an institution's degree of leverage. Core capital consists of the following: common stockholder's equity, preferred stockholder's equity up to certain limits, and retained earnings net of any intangible assets.
Critical Ranges	Guidelines developed to help you evaluate the levels of each index contributing to a company's Weiss Safety Rating. The sum or average of these grades does not necessarily have a one-to-one correspondence with the final rating for an institution because the rating is derived from a wider range of more complex calculations.

Deposit Insurance Fund (DIF)	In 2005 Congress passed legislation merging the SAIF and BIF into one insurance fund called the deposit insurance fund (DIF). The same law also raised the federal deposit insurance level from $100,000 to $250,000 on a temporary basis. (See also "Emergency Economic Stabilization Act.")
Emergency Stabilization Act	In 2008 Congress passed the Emergency Economic Stabilization Act that temporarily increased the basic limit on deposit insurance for all ownership categories from $100,000 to $250,000. This temporary increase is set to expire in 2013.
Equity	Total assets minus total liabilities. This is the "capital cushion" the institution has to fall back on in times of trouble. (See also "Capital.")
FDIC	Federal Deposit Insurance Corporation. The provider of insurance on deposits. This agency also plays an active role when banks are found to be insolvent or in need of federal assistance. It is the governing body of the Deposit Insurance Fund (DIF) that now incorporates both the Bank Insurance Fund (BIF) and the Savings Association Insurance Fund (SAIF). (See also "Deposit Insurance Fund.")
Federal Home Loan Bank (FHLB)	A quasi-governmental agency (reporting to the Federal Housing Finance Board) whose chartered purpose is to promote the issuance of mortgage loans by providing increased liquidity to lenders. This agency raises money by issuing notes and bonds and then lends the money to banks and other mortgage lenders.
Federal Reserve	America's central bank, regulating all banks that offer transaction accounts. It works hand-in-hand with the FDIC, providing examination and regulation of its member banks.
Safety Rating	Weiss Safety Ratings, which grade institutions on a scale from A (Excellent) to F (Failed). Ratings are based on many factors, emphasizing capitalization, asset quality, profitability, liquidity, and stability.
FSB	Federal Savings Bank. A thrift institution operating under a federal charter.
Goodwill	The value of an institution as a going concern, meaning the value which exceeds book value on a balance sheet. It generally represents the value of a well-respected business name, good customer relations, high employee morale and other intangible factors which would be expected to translate into greater than normal earning power. In a bank acquisition, goodwill is the value paid by a buyer of the institution in excess of the value of the institution's equity because of these intangible factors.
Hot Money	Individual deposits of $100,000 or more plus those deposits received through a broker. These types of deposits are considered "hot money" because they tend to chase whoever is offering the best interest rates at the time and are thus relatively costly and fairly volatile sources of funds.
Loan Loss Reserves	The amount of capital an institution sets aside to cover any potential losses due to the nonrepayment of loans.
N.A.	National Association. A commercial bank operating under a federal charter.

Net Charge-offs	The amount of foreclosed loans written off the institution's books since the beginning of the year, less any previous write-offs that were recovered during the year.
Net Interest Spread	The difference between the interest income earned on the institution's loans and investments and the interest expense paid on its interest-bearing deposits and borrowings. This "spread" is most commonly analyzed as a percentage of average earning assets to show the institution's net return on income-generating assets.
	Since the margin between interest earned and interest paid is generally where the company generates the majority of its income, this figure provides insight into the company's ability to effectively manage interest spreads. A low Net Interest Spread can be the result of poor loan and deposit pricing, high levels of nonaccruing loans, or poor asset/liability management.
Net Profit or Loss	The bottom line income or loss the institution has sustained in its most recent reporting period.
Nonaccruing Loans	Loans for which payments are past due and full repayment is doubtful. Interest income on these loans is no longer recorded on the income statement. (See also "Past Due Loans.")
Nonperforming Loans	The sum of loans past due 90 days or more and nonaccruing loans. These are loans the institution made where full repayment is now doubtful. (See also "Past Due Loans" and "Nonaccruing Loans.")
Past Due Loans	Loans for which payments are at least 90 days in arrears. The institution continues to record income on these loans, even though none is actually being received, because it is expected that the borrower will eventually repay the loan in full. It is likely, however, that at least a portion of these loans will move into nonaccruing status. (See also "Nonaccruing Loans.")
OCC	Office of the Comptroller of the Currency. This agency of the U.S. Treasury Department is the primary regulator of national banks.
Overhead Expense	Expenses of the institution other than interest expense, such as salaries and benefits of employees, rent and utility expenses, and data processing expenses. A certain amount of "fixed" overhead is required to operate a bank, so it is important that the institution leverage that overhead to the fullest extent in supporting its revenue-generating activities.
RBCR	See "Risk-Based Capital Ratio."
Resolution Trust Corp. (RTC)	The now-defunct federal agency that was formed to handle the liquidation of insolvent savings and loans.
Restructured Loans	Loans whose terms have been modified in order to enable the borrower to make payments which he otherwise would be unable to make. Modifications could include a reduction in the interest rate or a lengthening of the time to maturity.

Risk-Based Capital Ratio	A ratio originally developed by the International Committee on Banking as a means of assessing the adequacy of an institution's capital in relation to the amount of credit risk on and off its balance sheet. (See also "Risk-weighted Assets.")
Risk-Weighted Assets	The sum of assets and certain off-balance sheet items after they have been individually adjusted for the level of credit risk they pose to the institution. Assets with close to no risk are weighted 0%; those with minor risk are weighted 20%; those with low risk, 50%; and those with normal or high risk, 100%.
R.O.A	Return on Assets calculated as net profit or loss as a percentage of average assets. This is the most commonly used measure of bank profitability.
R.O.E.	Return on Equity calculated as net profit or loss as a percentage of average equity. This represents the rate of return on the shareholders' investment.
S.A.	Savings Association.
Savings and Loan (S&L)	A financial institution that traditionally offered primarily home mortgages to individuals and served small depositors. However, in 1980, savings and loans were given power to diversify into other areas of lending. Also known as a thrift.
Savings and Loan Holding Company	A company that holds stock in one or more savings and loans and possibly other companies.
Savings Association Insurance Fund (SAIF)	Fund created in 1989 by Congress to replace the FSLIC as the provider of deposit insurance to thrifts. This fund is administered by the Federal Deposit Insurance Corporation (FDIC). (See also "Bank Insurance Fund.")
Savings Bank	A financial institution created to serve primarily the small saver and to lend mortgage money to individuals. Though savings banks have expanded their services, they are still primarily engaged in providing consumer mortgages and accepting consumer deposits. Also known as a thrift.
Severe Recession	A drop in real GDP which is significantly greater than that of an average postwar recession. (See also "Average Recession.")
Stockholder's Equity	See "Equity."
Thrift	Generic term for an institution formed primarily as a depository for consumer savings and a lender for home mortgages, such as a savings and loan or a savings bank.
Total Assets	Total resources of an institution, primarily composed of cash, securities (such as municipal and treasury bonds), loans, and fixed assets (such as real estate, buildings, and equipment).
Total Equity	See "Equity."

Total Liabilities All debts owed by an institution. Normally, the largest liability of a bank is its deposits.

Trust Company A financial institution chartered to provide trust services (legal agreements to act for the benefit of another party), which may also be authorized to provide banking services.